SOCIAL FOUNDATIONS
OF THOUGHT
AND ACTION

SOCIAL FOUNDATIONS OF THOUGHT AND ACTION
A Social Cognitive Theory

Albert Bandura

Stanford University

Prentice-Hall, Inc., Englewood Cliffs, New Jersey 07632

Library of Congress Cataloging in Publication Data

Bandura, Albert (date)
  Social foundations of thought and action.

  (Prentice-Hall series in social learning theory)
  Bibliography: p.
  Includes index.
  1. Social psychology. 2. Cognition—Social aspects.
3. Social perception. I. Title. II. Series.
HM251.B433 1986   302   85-9310
ISBN 0-13-815614-X

Editorial/production supervision and
  interior design: Linda Benson
Cover design: Ben Santora
Manufacturing buyer: Barbara Kelly Kittle

PRENTICE-HALL SERIES IN SOCIAL LEARNING THEORY
ALBERT BANDURA, EDITOR

Printed in the United States of America

10 9 8 7 6 5 4

ISBN 0-13-815614-X 01

Prentice-Hall International, Inc., *London*
Prentice-Hall of Australia Pty. Limited, *Sydney*
Editora Prentice-Hall do Brasil, Ltda., *Rio de Janeiro*
Prentice-Hall Canada Inc., *Toronto*
Prentice-Hall Hispanoamericana, S.A., *Mexico*
Prentice-Hall of India Private Limited, *New Delhi*
Prentice-Hall of Japan, Inc., *Tokyo*
Prentice-Hall of Southeast Asia Pte. Ltd., *Singapore*
Whitehall Books Limited, *Wellington, New Zealand*

To Ginny, Mary, and Carol

CONTENTS

3
ENACTIVE LEARNING 106

4
SOCIAL DIFFUSION AND INNOVATION 142

5
PREDICTIVE KNOWLEDGE AND FORETHOUGHT 182

6
INCENTIVE MOTIVATORS 228

7
VICARIOUS MOTIVATORS 283

8
SELF-REGULATORY MECHANISMS 335

9
SELF-EFFICACY 390

10
COGNITIVE REGULATORS 454

REFERENCES 523

AUTHOR INDEX 583

SUBJECT INDEX 599

PREFACE

This volume presents a theoretical framework for analyzing human motivation, thought, and action from a social cognitive perspective. One of its organizing themes is the emphasis placed on reciprocal determinism. Social cognitive theory embraces an interactional model of causation in which environmental events, personal factors, and behavior all operate as interacting determinants of each other. Reciprocal causation provides people with opportunities to exercise some control over their destinies as well as sets limits of self-direction.

The conceptualization of personal determinants of psychosocial functioning accords a central role to cognitive, vicarious, self-regulatory, and self-reflective processes. Human thought is a powerful instrument for comprehending the environment and dealing with it. Hence, the diverse ways in which cognitive causation enters into human affect and action are analyzed extensively. However, in keeping with the interactional perspective, much attention is devoted to the social origins of thought. Widespread growth of interest in issues concerning the structure and operation of thought has led to serious neglect of the mechanisms of performance. This work broadens the scope of inquiry by also addressing itself to mechanisms by which knowledge is transformed into appropriate action.

People are not only knowers and performers. They are also self-reactors with a capacity for self-direction. The self-regulation of motivation and action operates partly through internal standards and evaluative reactions to one's own performances. The capability of forethought adds another dimension to the process of self-regulation. Most human behavior is directed toward goals and outcomes projected into the future. By being represented cognitively in the present, conceived futures can have causal impact on current behavior. The capability for self-reflection concerning one's own thinking and personal efficacy is another dimension of self-influence that receives prominent attention in this volume.

Psychological theories have traditionally emphasized learning through the effects of one's actions. Fortunately, humans have evolved an advanced capacity for observational learning that is better suited for expeditious acquisition of competencies and survival than is learning solely from the consequences of trial and error. Enormous advances in the technology of telecommunications have greatly increased the role played by vicarious learning from symbolic environments. By drawing on ideas portrayed symbolically, people can transcend the bounds of their immediate environment. Not only is modeling an important vehicle for diffusing ideas, values, and styles of conduct within societies, it is also wielding increasing influence in transcultural change. The mechanisms of observational learning and the process of social diffusion receive detailed consideration in this volume.

New technologies are transforming the nature and scope of human influence and the way in which people live their lives. In this book I have tried to analyze human functioning from a broad social perspective. This requires delving into multidisciplinary research bearing on a wide range of psychosocial phenomena. It is a formidable task to canvass the immense literature in the various subspecialties of one's own field, let alone to embark on excursions into other disciplinary domains. Such analytic venturesomeness is important to a broad understanding of human functioning because its determinants transcend the arbitrary boundaries of academic disciplines.

For convenience of communication, theories need to be given summary labels that reflect their underlying conceptual nature. The theoretical approach presented in this volume is usually designated as social learning theory. However, the scope of this approach has always been much broader than its descriptive label, which is becoming increasingly ill-fitting as various aspects of the theory are further developed. From the outset it encompassed psychosocial phenomena, such as motivational and self-regulatory mechanisms, that extend beyond issues of learning. Moreover, many readers construe learning theory as a conditioning model of response acquisition, whereas within this theoretical framework learning is conceptualized mainly as knowledge acquisition through cognitive processing of information. The labeling problem is further compounded because several theories with dissimilar postulates—Dollard and Miller's drive theory, Rotter's expectancy theory, and Patterson's conditioning theory—all bear the social learning label. In the interests of more fitting and separable labeling, the theoretical approach of this book is designated as *social cognitive theory*. The social portion of the terminology acknowledges the social origins of much human thought and action; the cognitive portion recognizes the influential causal contribution of thought processes to human motivation, affect, and action. The relabeling carries no claim of theoretical parentage.

Theories are interpreted in different ways depending on the stage of development of the field of study. In advanced disciplines, theories integrate laws; in less advanced fields, theories specify the determinants and mechanisms governing the phenomena of interest. It is in the latter sense that the term *theory* is used in this book. Meaningful propositions about human behavior have verifiable consequences. Like other approaches, social cognitive formulations are falsifiable in their particulars. Because theories are rarely free of imperfections, the research they stimulate delineates the range of conditions under which a given theory enjoys explanatory and predictive success.

Experimental analyses clarify determinants and the mechanisms through which they operate and suggest theoretical refinements that bring us closer to understanding the phenomena being studied. Rapid progress is best assured by applying the dual criteria of falsification and predictive generality, whereas reliance on falsification alone may waste immense effort that could be applied more profitably elsewhere. Weak theories are discarded not because they are falsified, but because they are withered by so many boundary conditions that their predictive generality is too limited to be of much use. When better theoretical alternatives exist, there is little value in pursuing the final truth or falsity of a theory that can, at best, explain behavior under only a very narrow range of conditions.

Some sections of this book include revised material from periodical articles and chapters I have written under the following titles: The self system in reciprocal determinism, *American Psychologist,* 1978; Self-efficacy mechanism in human agency, *American Psychologist,* 1978; The psychology of chance encounters and life paths, *American Psychologist,* 1982 (Copyright 1978, 1982 by the American Psychological Association and adapted by permission of the publisher); Self-referent thought: A developmental analysis of self-efficacy, in *Social cognitive development,* Cambridge University Press, 1981; The self and mechanisms of agency, in *Psychological perspectives on the self,* Erlbaum, 1982. This material has been substantially expanded, revised, and updated. An abbreviated version of some of the issues discussed here in much greater depth appeared in a concise overview, *Social learning theory,* published in 1977 by Prentice-Hall.

Many people have contributed to this venture in various ways, and I welcome this opportunity to express my gratitude to them. A work of this magnitude reflects the contributions of numerous scholars, as attested by citations that run into the thousands. I should like to pay tribute to them collectively. To my students, most of whom appear as coauthors in citations throughout this book, I have a special debt of gratitude for their friendship and scholarly collaboration. I remain ever grateful to my distinguished colleagues at Stanford and to a university ethos that is singularly conducive to scholarly pursuits. Over the years, my own research reported in this book was greatly aided by continuous grant support from the National Institute of Mental Health.

A number of people have lightened my labors in the arduous task of preparing the manuscript for publication. I thank Phyllis Robinson and Jena Sklinchar for their generous assistance in typing this manuscript through various revisions. I was most fortunate to have the invaluable help of Julia Baskett. I have benefited greatly from her patient and skillful editing of the manuscript.

It is with profound gratitude that I dedicate this volume to my family, who have put up with me during this extended venture. They are good companions to have on a long journey.

Albert Bandura

SOCIAL FOUNDATIONS
OF THOUGHT
AND ACTION

1

MODELS OF HUMAN NATURE AND CAUSALITY

Many theories have been proposed over the years to explain human behavior. The basic conceptions of human nature that they embrace and the causal processes that they posit require careful examination for several reasons. What theorists believe people to be influences which determinants and mechanisms of human functioning they explore most thoroughly and which they leave unexamined. Such beliefs affect not only what theorists study but also the analytic tools they devise to explore the factors they consider to be most relevant. If a guiding conception has some merit, then the results of scientific inquiry will clarify the aspects of human functioning singled out for close scrutiny.

Conceptions of human nature thus focus inquiry on selected processes and are, in turn, strengthened by findings of research paradigms embodying the particular point of view. For example, theorists who exclude the capacity for self-direction from their view of human potentialities confine their research to external influences. If investigatory efforts are restricted to how conduct is affected by reward and punishment, one will find ample evidence that human action is, indeed, often influenced by the effects it produces. But there is more to human regulatory functions than external feedback. Theorists who view humans as possessing capabilities for self-direction employ research paradigms that shed light on how people can affect their own motivation and actions by exercising self-influence.

The view of human nature embodied by psychological theories is more than just a philosophical issue. As psychological knowledge is put into practice, the conceptions on which social technologies rest have even greater implications. They can affect which

1

human potentialities will be cultivated and which will be left undeveloped. In this way, theoretical conceptions of human nature can influence what people actually become.

The present chapter is devoted mainly to the model of human nature and causality embodied by social cognitive theory. Other theoretical formulations are also briefly reviewed here. However, the scope of this comparative analysis is limited to the basic structure of contemporary theories that embrace distinctly different causal models, rather than aimed at providing an encyclopedic survey of psychological theories that have been proposed over the years. Additional lines of theorizing are, of course, considered in the subsequent chapters, which address the determinants and mechanisms of different facets of human functioning.

PSYCHODYNAMIC THEORY

Human behavior is commonly viewed as motivated from within by various needs, drives, impulses, and instincts. In psychodynamic theory, for example, human behavior is the manifestation of the dynamic interplay of inner forces, most of which operate below the level of consciousness (Freud, 1917, 1933). Since the proponents of this school of thought consider the principal causes of behavior to be drives within an individual, that is where they look for the explanations of why people behave as they do. Although this theory has gained widespread acceptance and is deeply entrenched in the public view of human behavior, it has not gone unchallenged.

Theories of this sort are criticized on both conceptual and empirical grounds. The inner determinants are often inferred from the very behavior they supposedly caused, creating interpretive circularities in which the description becomes the causal explanation. A hostile impulse, for example, is deduced from a person's irascible behavior, which is then attributed to the action of an underlying hostile impulse. Similarly,

the existence of achievement motives is deduced from achievement behavior; dependency motives from dependent behavior; curiosity motives from inquisitive behavior; power motives from domineering behavior, and so on. There is no limit to the number of drives one can find by inferring them from behavior. Indeed, different theories propose diverse lists of motivators, some containing a few all-purpose drives, others encompassing an assortment of specific drives. If causal propositions concerning drives are to be empirically testable, then drives must be specified by the antecedent conditions that activate them and govern their strength, rather than being inferred from the behavior they supposedly produce.

The conceptual structure of theories that invoke drives or impulses as the principal motivators of behavior has been further criticized for disregarding the complex and changeable patterning of human action. An internal motivator cannot adequately account for marked shifts in a given behavior under differing situational circumstances. When varying social conditions produce predictable changes in behavior, the postulated cause cannot reside mainly in a drive in the organism, nor can the cause be less complex than its diverse effects.

Psychodynamic theory assumes a thorough psychic determinism, but it does not, as a rule, postulate definite relationships between the unconscious inner life and human thought and action. In fact, the inner dynamics are said to produce any variety of effects, even opposite forms of behavior. Such formulations are, therefore, not easily testable nor refutable by empirical evidence. While the conceptual adequacy of psychodynamic drive theories could be debated at length, their empirical limitations cannot be ignored indefinitely. They provide ready interpretations of behavior that has already happened, but, as we shall see shortly, they are deficient in predicting future behavior. Almost any theory can explain things after the fact. Findings from research conducted from other perspectives have underscored the need to shift the focus of causal analysis from internal dynamics to reciprocal causation between personal and environmental factors. Behavior patterns commonly attributed to unconscious inner causes can be instated, eliminated, and reinstated by varying appropriate social influences and by altering people's ways of thinking. Such findings indicate that the major determinants of behavior arise from transactional dynamics, rather than flow unidirectionally from inner dynamics of unconscious mental functions.

The explanatory power of a psychological theory is gauged in several ways. First, theories must demonstrate predictive power. Second, the methods the theories yield must be capable of effecting significant changes in human affect, thought, and action. Weaknesses in theories become readily apparent when they are put to work and can be judged by the results they produce. One can predict and change events without knowing the basis for the successes. So third, theories must identify the determinants of human behavior and the intervening mechanisms by which they produce their effects. But explanations that have no predictive value will be pseudo-explanations. The adequacy of explanation is, therefore, judged largely in terms of predictive accuracy. Psychodynamic formulations have been found wanting on all these counts.

Predictive Efficacy

Theories that attribute behavior to unconscious inner determinants face the formidable task of assessing them. Because they are hidden by defensive functions, also operating unconsciously, individuals presumably are not privy to the factors governing their behavior. Access to unconscious motivators, therefore, requires surreptitious means that circumvent ever-vigilant defenses. In the projective techniques developed for this purpose, people are asked to tell what they see in inkblots, to make up sto-ries for ambiguous pictures, to complete sentence stems, to draw persons, and to give free associations to words. Responses to such ambiguous stimuli are believed to reveal the otherwise concealed strivings and conflicting mental functions. The hidden meanings of words, actions, and dreams are also probed for their revelations of unconscious mental life.

The predictive record of projective measures of psychodynamic determinants of behavior is a poor one—they are not of much help in predicting how people are likely to behave in different situations (Mischel, 1968; Zubin, Eron, & Schumer, 1965). Self-appraisal is a much better predictor of future behavior than are personality tests which supposedly measure determinants of people's behavior of which they are unaware (Shrauger & Osberg, 1982). Moreover, an actuarial prediction system combining a few predictor variables is at least as good and often superior to clinical judgment in predicting how people will behave (Dawes & Corrigan, 1974).

Nor have laboratory investigations for evidence of unconscious determination of affective reactions to threatening stimuli met with much success. The unconscious self presumably possesses sensitive discriminative capabilities for detecting threats and mobilizing defensive functions to keep these threats out of the realm of awareness. However, carefully designed experiments in which cognitive, autonomic, and motor reactions to threatening events are recorded concurrently have failed to unearth an unconscious agency of the type assumed by psychodynamic theory (Eriksen, 1958, 1960). And other predictive claims for the theory (Kline, 1972) have not stood up under close scrutiny (Erwin, 1980; Eysenck & Wilson, 1973). Psychodynamic theorists generally favor clinical verification of theory. In a scholarly analysis of the foundations of psychoanalytic theory, Grünbaum (1984) seriously questions the evidential value of clinical data produced in treatment sessions. Such data are too tainted by therapists' suggestive influence to inform on the validity of a theory.

Change Efficacy

The value of a theory is ultimately judged by its usefulness as evidenced by the power of the methods it yields to effect psychological changes. Other scientific enterprises are evaluated by their eventual contributions to prediction and technical innovations using that knowledge. Suppose, for example, that aeronautical scientists developed certain principles of aerodynamics in wind-tunnel tests. If in applying these principles they could never design an aircraft that could fly, the value of their theoretical formulations would be highly suspect. The same judgment would be applied to theorizing in the medical field if certain theories about physiological processes never led to any effective means of preventing or treating physical maladies.

Questionable theories can withstand tests of falsification by invoking new qualifying factors to reconcile conflicting findings. This is because even the more elaborately formalized theories do not always specify all the supplementary assumptions that are relevant to deriving predictions from the proposition in question. In the process of developing and testing a theory, additional factors are often uncovered that further specify the necessary and sufficient conditions for certain events to occur. Moreover, a theoretical proposition may be sound, but some of the auxiliary assumptions may be faulty. Refuting evidence is more likely to prompt the revision of the auxiliary assumptions than the abandonment of basic theory. The theory is modified accordingly, without fretting over whether the amended version is still essentially the same theory. Conceptual frameworks that provide poor explanations of behavior are eventually discarded, not because they are proven false, but because they begin to take on so many limiting conditions that their explanatory and predictive value is severely limited. In-

terest wanes in pursuing the final truth or falsity of an amended theory that can, at best, apply only to a narrow set of conditions. Weak theories can, therefore, more easily survive tests of falsifiability than tests of usefulness. They are eventually retired through replacement by a better theory than by exhaustive falsification.

Psychological approaches that attribute behavior to the operation of unconscious impulses consider the achievement of insight or self-awareness essential for producing enduring behavior changes. Through the process of labeling people's impulses, which may manifest themselves in many guises in what they say and do, the underlying determinants of their behavior are gradually made conscious. After these impulses are brought into awareness, they presumably cease to function as instigators, or they become more susceptible to conscious control.

Studies measuring actual changes in behavior have had difficulty demonstrating that the behavior of persons who receive psychodynamically-oriented treatment changes appreciably more than that of comparable people who have not undergone the treatment (Bandura, 1969a; Rachman & Wilson, 1980). Such treatments look somewhat better on the basis of clinical ratings rather than on the direct assessment of behavioral functioning (Luborsky, Singer, & Luborsky, 1975; Sloane, Staples, Cristol, Yorkston, & Whipple, 1975). Outcome measures relying extensively on verbal reports of change show that treated cases improve more than do controls (Smith & Glass, 1977). However, if one uses verbal reports, rather than actual measurements of how well people are functioning, then even control cases, who have received no therapeutic ministrations, look as though they have achieved notable improvements.

It is not entirely surprising that self-insights are often unaccompanied by changes in behavior. It is easier to alter people's beliefs about the causes of their behavior than to change how they behave. Alcoholics, for example, can be more easily persuaded that they drink because of a fixated oral dependency than they can be induced to foresake alcohol. Moreover, many insights appear arbitrary. As Marmor (1962), among others, has noted, each psychodynamic approach has its own favorite set of inner causes and its own preferred brand of insight. The presupposed determinants can be readily confirmed in self-validating interviews by the therapist making suggestive interpretations and reacting favorably whenever a client's accounts are consistent with the therapist's beliefs (Murray, 1956; Truax, 1966). Thus, advocates of differing theoretical orientations repeatedly discover their chosen motivators at work but rarely find evidence for the motivators emphasized by proponents of competing viewpoints. One can similarly predict from a therapist's conceptual orientation whether or not clients will find an unconscious mind and what will be in it. A Freudian unconscious differs from a Jungian one. Many theories do not even postulate one; yet they achieve success in prediction and psychological change without appealing to an unconscious inner life.

Gaining insight into one's underlying motives, it seems, is more like a belief conversion than a self-discovery process. Hence, one can predict better the types of insights and unconscious motivators that persons are apt to discover in themselves in the course of psychodynamic analyses from knowledge of the therapists' conceptual belief system than from the clients' actual psychological status. Questions about belief conversions in the name of self-awareness would apply equally to other theoretical approaches if they, too, mainly taught people to construe their actions in the parlance of the theory but failed to alleviate the behavioral problems for which aid was sought. For this reason, regardless of whatever other measures are used, psychological methods should be evaluated in terms of their effectiveness in changing actual psychosocial functioning.

That insight into dubious unconscious psychodynamics has little effect on behavior does not mean that actions are uninfluenced by awareness of authentic determinants. Evidence will be reviewed later showing that awareness of the factors that contribute to one's behavior and the effects it produces significantly influence emotional reactions and behavior. These conscious determinants of behavior are readily demonstrable and amenable to empirical verification. People benefit more from changing and developing their conscious cognitive functioning than from searching for an unconscious mental life. Indeed, the very notion of unconscious thought embodies a contradiction. Thought refers to acts of reasoning, reflection, imagining, and other ideational activities that one does consciously. To render thought unconscious abolishes its customary meaning. People do, of course, routinize cognitive operations by repeated use to the point where they execute them with little accompanying awareness. People often react with fixed ways of thinking unreflectively, and with habitual ways of behaving unthinkingly. However, the routinization of thought and action should be distinguished from an unconscious mental life that orchestrates behavior.

TRAIT THEORY

Trait theory is another line of theorizing that emphasizes the internal determination of behavior (Allport, 1961; Cattell, 1966). It posits that human actions are governed by traits, which are regarded as broad enduring dispositions to behave in certain ways. Trait theorists have been less concerned with how dispositions generate behavior and motivate and guide it than with assessing personality traits and testing their predictive utility. If behavior is largely the product of a disposition, then actions should be fairly consistent across situations and stable over time. The major controversies revolve around this basic assumption, as well as disagreements about the number and kinds of prime traits that personality embodies.

Predictive Utility of Trait Measures

Over the years numerous studies have been published showing that measures of personality traits usually correlate weakly with social behavior in different settings (Mischel, 1968; Peterson, 1968; Vernon, 1964). When they show significant relationships, such measures usually account for about 10 percent of the variance in performance. Past behavior predicts future behavior in similar situations with moderate success, but conduct varies across situations differing in properties that affect the functional value of a particular form of behavior. Thus, for example, a measure of an aggressive trait does not help much in predicting whether or not a person will behave aggressively in dissimilar situations.

The view that traits regulate behavior has many adherents despite substantial evidence to the contrary. In commenting on the tenaciousness of the belief in generalized dispositions, Mischel (1968) has identified a number of factors that may lead people to see behavioral uniformity where it does not exist. Physical sameness in appearance, speech, and expressive behavior can sway impressions of consistency although the person's actions are variable. In everyday life, people are often repeatedly observed only in a particular setting, such as work, social functions, or their home, rather than in all these different places, where they may vary widely in how they behave. That a limited sampling of situations fosters global dispositional inferences is suggested by studies comparing how performers and observers perceive causes of behavior (Jones & Nisbett, 1972; Ross, 1977). When observers judge others from only a single transaction, they tend to see their behavior as springing from a personal disposition. In contrast, performers, who know full well they alter their behavior to meet changing demands, are more inclined to see their own actions varying as a function of situational circumstances and constraints.

Reliance on verbal measures of overt behavior can be a further source of artifactual generality. In studying the cross-situational predictiveness of trait measures, people are often asked to rate their typical behavior in nondescript, rather than specific, settings. Variable responsiveness must, therefore, be glossed over or ignored in efforts to extract typicality from diversity. Perceptions of behavior are, of course, strongly colored by preconceptions of oneself and others. Actions tend to be selectively noticed, processed, and remembered in ways that are consistent with preconceptions. As a result of selective cognitive processing, people's ratings of their own behavior yield consistencies, although in actuality the behavior may vary considerably. Hence, behavior appears more consistent in verbal reports, on which trait theorists rely heavily, than would be the case in direct assessments of the behavior itself.

Search for Methodological Solutions

Efforts to strip traits and dispositions of their causal sovereignty have not gone uncontested. Proponents of these theories argue that seemingly different behaviors may be manifestations of the same underlying motive. This argument has not been especially persuasive because no reliable criteria have been provided for identifying the behaviors that are expressions of a particular root motive and those that are not. A more common response to the limited yield of trait predictors is to fault the methods used to study relationships between trait indices and behavior. The prescribed methodological rectifications take several forms, as do the critiques of them.

Classifying People and Individualizing Trait Dimensions. Bem and Allen (1974) have advanced the view that some people are highly consistent in some behaviors, but that evidence of cross-situational generality is obscured when data from consistent and variable responders are combined and researchers, rather than the respondents, select which traits are relevant and which types of behavior represent them. From this perspective, a psychological theory which seeks to predict actions from traits must settle for the modest goal of predicting only some of the actions of only consistent people, provided one can identify beforehand who is likely to be consistent in what realm of behavior. Bem and Allen use people's judgments of themselves as either consistent or changeable for the traits in question as the identifier. To demonstrate that self-reported consistency foretells uniformity, students were measured for their friendly and conscientious behavior and rated by their parents, by a peer, and by themselves for friendliness and conscientiousness on a questionnaire describing many different situations. The ratings for each of the two traits were summed for each judge across the situations described in a global score, and then the degree of agreement between judges was computed. Students who viewed themselves as consistent were rated by others with higher agreement than those who judged themselves highly variable in behavior.

Correlating verbal reports of behavior averaged across specific situations does little to illuminate the central issue of whether trait measures predict how people will actually behave under different conditions. Scores pooled across situations may embody high, moderate, or low behavioral variability. In testing for behavioral generality, one must measure directly how individuals vary in their behavior under different circumstances, rather than how, on the average, they stand in relation to others, or how well judges agree among themselves in their over-all impressions of the individuals selected to study. In the few behaviors that Bem and Allen actually measured, the self-described unchangeables were found to be more consistent for talkativeness but not for conscientious actions, thus revealing an inconsistency in the predictor of behavioral consistency. In a more comprehensive study examining different measures of self-reported consistency and many personality dimensions, Chaplin and Goldberg (1984)

found that self-reported consistency is uniformly unpredictive. Not only do different indices of consistency disagree but, however it is measured, the self-reported consistent types are no more uniform in their behavior than the changeable types on any personality dimension.

That sorting people into consistency types gains little predictive power, as far as behavior is concerned, has been further confirmed by Peake and Lutsky (1981). Others agree more closely in their over-all impression of persons who see themselves as unchangeable than for those who characterize themselves as variable, but both groups show little uniformity in their actual trait behavior in different settings. The different social impressions probably arise because others often cannot observe how those they are rating act in various milieus and must either guess how they are likely to behave or rely on what they tell them. Presenting oneself as a highly consistent person may thus foster social impressions of consistency, but it does not improve the predictability of trait measures.

The source of this erroneous impression about behavioral generality has itself become the subject of study. Mischel and Peake (1982) have found that people's perceptions of others' self-consistency is related to how uniform the latters' behavior is in key features of the trait over time in similar situations but is unrelated to how they actually behave in different situations. People thus misread cross-situational generality in behavior from temporal stability in similar situations. Observers, whose information is limited about how others conduct themselves in diverse situations, would be especially prone to mistake behaving similarly in the same setting over time as indicative of behaving similarly in different settings. If the eyes do not behold a wide range of transactional situations, then behavior will appear consistent in the eyes of those beholders.

Studies of situational generality of behavior devote much attention to what trait behaviors should be assessed but give little consideration to the kinds of environments that should be sampled. It is perhaps not entirely surprising that approaches attributing behavior to traits would neglect the properties of the social environment. The most informative methodology for studying cross-situational generality would be to record how much people vary their behavior across situations which differ measurably in the functional value of the behavior being examined in those settings. Situations chosen for study should be scaled and selected in terms of the incentives and sanctions they customarily provide for the particular behavior, rather than chosen arbitrarily. Such studies would undoubtedly reveal that all people behave discriminatively most of the time, being more prone to express a given form of behavior when it is advantageous to do so than when it serves no useful purpose or brings detrimental results. It is only by including a range of environmental dispositions that the transsituational fixedness, or nonfixedness, of behavior can be adequately evaluated.

Psychological knowledge is better advanced by exploring the sources of variability of behavior than by searching for subtypes of people who behave invariantly, regardless of circumstances. It would be a misleading and truncated theory that called on persons to choose which of their actions are predictable but viewed persons as unpredictable in areas of functioning in which they very sensibly vary their actions to suit the changing circumstances. Because aggressive youngsters bully their subordinate peers, while acting compliantly toward tougher peers, does not mean that their differential conduct renders them unpredictable. Nor is it the case that behavior under differing circumstances is predictable only from idiographic phenomenology (Lord, 1982). Knowing how situations are perceived aids prediction, but situational patterning of behavior is predictable from prevailing social conditions on which the perceptions are partly based (Bandura, 1969a; Bower & Hilgard, 1981).

Progress in gaining predictive knowledge requires research that systematically varies factors that contribute to behavioral variability as well as examines correlations among behaviors in naturally occurring settings. The number of persons who act invariantly would fluctuate depending upon the behavior selected for study, the extent to which the situations sampled differ in their likely consequences for the given conduct, how much variability is tolerated in the criterion of consistency, and whether one measures verbal reports of behavior or the behavior itself. Behaviors that are highly functional in diverse settings, as, for example, acting intelligently, would be more consistent than behaviors that have different effects under dissimilar circumstances. It would be difficult to find adolescents who are consistently aggressive toward parents, teachers, peers, and police officers, because the consequences for the same conduct vary markedly (Bandura & Walters, 1959). Even in the case of a widely acceptable behavior such as friendliness, the ranks of the consistent responders would shrink simply by including some situations in which friendliness is an unlikely response, as, for example, when individuals are being exploited or discriminated against. Only those who are grossly undiscerning or who have a poor sense of reality would remain steadfastly amiable.

Template or Profile Matching. A second methodological effort to increase the predictability of trait measures, proposed by Bem and Funder (1978), attempts to redress the neglect of environmental characteristics. They note that many situations which appear similar are, in fact, functionally dissimilar in that they require different personal attributes for success. Hence, one should not expect generality in conduct across functionally divergent situations. Presumably the predictive power of trait measures can be raised by determining how well personal attributes fit the ideal personality type for the behavior called for in the setting under consideration.

The matching procedure used for this

purpose relies on the Q-sort technique which contains a standard set of descriptive personality statements, sufficiently general to characterize the ideal personality correlates of performance in any domain of functioning (e.g., "Is aggressive"; "Is restless and fidgety"). Persons describe themselves and the type of person most likely to perform the selected behavior well in a particular situation. The closer the fit between a person's self-rated traits and those of the ideal trait set, the greater the probability the person will behave in the predicted way.

Bem and Funder (1978) report that seemingly similar situations, such as two tasks requiring delay of gratification, can have different trait correlates. The trait profiles are said to provide a basis for predicting how subsets of persons will behave. However, since in the supporting research neither the trait correlates nor the behavior of the same persons was measured in different situations, the predictive gains attributed to this approach rest on implication, rather than on empirical demonstration.

Research conducted by Lord (1982) comparing predictors of behavioral consistency shows that neither situational trait templating nor self-template matching is needed for this purpose. Having people simply rate how functional a given behavior would be for them in different situations predicts behavioral consistency as well as the unwieldy sorting and matching of numerous trait descriptions for self and situations. Persons behave more consistently in different situations if the behavior has similar functional value for them than if its functionality varies across settings. To cite facets of the conscientiousness trait used in this study, if careful note taking raises course grades, but compulsive room cleaning detracts from recreation and study time, one will find many good note takers with messy rooms. In fact, one can disregard the personality traits of performers and predict behavioral consistency from situational similarities in people's judgments of the trait behaviors called for in each situation. The latter measure of situational similarity is not as different from functionality judgments as it may appear. The behavior traits that best characterize a situation are likely to be the very behavior patterns most useful in that situation. Scaling situational similarities in terms of personal functionality has the advantage not only of handiness but of sensitivity, in that small changes in sanctions can produce big differences in conduct.

The claims of increased predictability through template matching have come under close scrutiny by Mischel and Peake (1982). They demonstrate that even subtle changes in situations produce different behavior though the trait correlates are the same, indicating the insensitivity of the template predictors. By introducing appropriate incentives, one could easily demonstrate that people will behave similarly in situations having dissimilar trait correlates and act differently in situations with similar trait correlates. Because the templates produced by a purely empirical approach are sensitive to different situational influences, one would have to construct a huge catalogue of templates to predict human adaptiveness to changing environmental circumstances. Moreover, unless contructed through cross-validation, some of the distinctive features of personality profiles files ideal for performance can be quite elusive, appearing in one study but disappearing in another. Personality typing in terms of Q-sort profiles does not seem to hold the answer to behavioral diversity any more than does self-typing as a consistent or a changeable character.

Averaging across Situations, Occasions, and Forms of Behavior. Another remedy for the weak predictability of trait indices, prescribed by Epstein (1983), is to average ratings of behavior across situations and occasions. Any single sample of behavior is said to reflect the influence of transient factors and "situational uniqueness," which are treated as sources of error in the measure. By averaging ratings of behavior taken at different times and places, errors are reduced, and, presumably, a truer index of the trait is obtained. As testimony for the benefits of such averaging, Epstein reports the common finding that trait measures based on many ratings of a behavior are more reliable than those based on only a few ratings. Evidence that past behavior correlates with future behavior in similar situations is presented as further testimony that generalized dispositions govern action.

As Mischel and Peake (1982) point out, the averaging approach addresses the wrong issue and provides an ineffectual remedy for the problems of predictability that are of major concern. Evidence that multiple measurement provides a more reliable estimate of a given behavior leaves unanswered the question of whether that form of behavior will be expressed uniformly or selectively in different social situations. To give a banal example, superiors may behave in consistently different ways toward subordinates and bosses, respectively. The matter of temporal stability of behavior in similar situations is not an issue much in dispute. If significant features of a given social milieu remain similar over time, people are likely to behave similarly on future occasions (Block, 1981; Mischel, 1983). It is cross-situational variability in behavior that bedevils trait theories. What little evidence Epstein (1983) provides on this issue either has little bearing on it or confirms the familiar findings that people vary in how they behave in dissimilar situations.

That the aggregation remedy fails to raise the transsituational predictability of trait measures appreciably is shown by Mischel and Peake (1982). Forms of behavior that are assumed to represent the same trait correlate poorly with each other, regardless of whether each form of behavior is measured only once or measured repeatedly and averaged over a number of occasions. Even when multiple assessments across occasions raise correlations, the gain is not all that much when the actual behavior, rather than self-reports of behavior in different situations, is measured (Rushton, Brainerd, & Pressley, 1983). Clearly, the fault does not lie in the unreliability of the measures nor does the solution lie in averaging of ratings. No amount of aggregation will resurrect high correlations between behaviors that differential social sanctions have disjoined. Aggressive acts by delinquents toward parish priests and rival gang members will correlate poorly, however much averaging one does.

Other efforts to boost correlates include averaging different forms of conduct. If a trait measure cannot predict a particular kind of aggression, one can opt for a vaguer criterion by lumping different kinds of physical aggression, verbal aggression, and oppositional behavior into an indefinite conglomerate. Mixing behaviors obscures the understanding of psychological functioning as does the mixing of situations. To be able to predict through aggregation that individuals will sometime, somewhere, do something within a wide assortment of acts is of no great interest. For example, people want to know whether adolescent offenders are likely to commit physical assaults, not whether some-time, somewhere, they may say or do something untoward. Aggregation inflates correlations but yields indeterminate or empty predictions.

Measures containing conglomerations of behavior under different circumstances may correlate higher than a particular form of behavior with a shapeless average of different behaviors in varied situation. But to compare correlations of conglomerate-to-average measure with particular-to-average measure is to lose sight of the fact that it is not formless averages that psychology is called upon to explain and predict; rather, it seeks to predict how individuals are likely to perform under given circumstances. Particular predictors serve this purpose better than do conglomerate predictors. Thus, the aggression of children toward their peers will be better predicted from a child's proneness to peer aggression under specifiable circumstances than from an average of the child's aggressive behavior toward parents, teachers, and peers.

To gain predictive power, a psychological theory must specify the sources of behavioral variability. This goal cannot be realized if situational influences, which operate as important determinants of behavior, are treated as troublesome sources of error to be decreased by lumping many situations together. Indeed, averaging behavior across social conditions not only obscures the analysis of causal processes, but it also reduces the predictability, because an average index is less indicative of how people are likely to behave in dissimilar situations than is the knowledge of how they typically behave in each different situation. Thus, for example, if a child is domineering toward subordinate peers but subservient toward peers of higher status in the power hierarchy (Polsky, 1962), one loses rather than gains predictive power by trying to predict social behavior toward peers from an averaged value, which typifies neither situation. Predictive power lies in reliable micromeasures rather than in mixed conglomerates. The situational averaging solution reminds one of the nonswimmer who drowned while crossing a river that averaged only four feet in depth.

It is unfortunate that the label "consistency" has been applied to the issue of behavioral variability, because the term carries the misleading connotation that perpetuates the search for behavioral fixedness. Consistency not only implies virtues of steadfastness, and principled conduct, but it sets up the contrast of "inconsistency" as implying instability and expediency. In fact, the opposite is usually the case. People would have to be grossly inattentive to the world around them, obtuse, or indifferent to the personal and social effects of their conduct to act the same irrespective of the circumstances. Nevertheless, the inversion of value implications in the term consistency serves to divert attention from the analysis of reciprocal determinants to an elusive search for ways in which variable conduct can flow from a general disposition.

Trait theory rouses protracted disputes under the banners of the *idiographic* view that people behave idiosyncratically, or the *nomothetic* view that people's behavior follows general principles, as though individuals have no processes in common and the search for general laws grants no individuality. People, obviously, differ somewhat in their make-up, but they are not entirely unique in how they react to social influences, in how they acquire skills and knowledge, and in how they regulate their actions. The study of uniquenesses, which happen to occur through the idiosyncratic combination of influences, can yield no generalizable information because novel admixtures of determinants do not reappear for others. In actuality, cultures provide numerous common experiences, thus creating many common determinants and processes of behavior across individuals. If individual behavior reflected no general principles, psychological knowledge would lack predictive value and would have little to say about the psychosocial conditions conducive to human development and change. A psychology solely of uniqueness would, indeed, be a feeble scientific enterprise.

Much ink has been spilt in fruitless debates about whether behavior is characterized by uniformity or specificity. In fact, all people both generalize and differentiate their responsiveness, depending on which is most advantageous under given circumstances. A theory of broad scope must explain both phenomena and the mechanisms that govern them. Whether people behave uniformly or variably depends heavily upon the functional equivalence of the environments. Thus, if acting intelligently in diverse settings has functional value, people will be consistently intelligent in situations that otherwise differ markedly. By contrast, if issuing orders to police officers brings punishment, while ordering store clerks about brings better service, then people will behave authoritatively with clerks but cautiously with the police. Nor is consistency across expressive modalities a blessing that might race the pulse of dispositionists. If people acted on every thought that entered their head, or if their affect ruled every act, they would get themselves repeatedly into very serious trouble.

Social cognitive theory is concerned with the conditions determining both generality and specificity of conduct, rather than championing only variability in behavior. Behavior patterns are not necessarily locked in temporally; otherwise, people would not alter their behavior during the course of their development to suit their age and the changing demands of life. Changes occurring throughout the life span often take diverse forms, rather than follow a consistent, unidirectional course (Baltes, 1982). Whether social behavior is invariant or changes over time depends, partly, on the degree of continuity of social conditions over the time span. A comprehensive theory must, therefore, also explain both temporal continuities and change.

RADICAL BEHAVIORISM

In a vigorous effort to avoid spurious inner causes, Skinner (1953, 1969) proposed a theory that depicts behavior as being controlled jointly by genetic endowment and environmental contingencies. This conceptual scheme relies on a three-element model $S^d \rightarrow R \rightarrow S^r$, in which situational cues (S^d) set the occasion for behavior (R), and its consequences (S^r) shape and control it. Thus, the answer to the source of causation is sought in control by contingent stimuli. Behavior is, presumably, cued by the stimuli that precede it and shaped and controlled by the reinforcing stimuli that follow it. In reducing the determinants of human behavior to contingency control, proponents of this approach place the agency of action in environmental forces, and they strip thought and other internal events of any causal efficacy.

Radical behaviorists do not deny that inner events are linked to behavior, but they express little interest in them because they are assumed to be caused by external stimuli. Through the presumption that inner events transmit but cannot create influences, internal determinants get dubbed

as a redundant link in the causal chain. Behavior thus becomes fully explainable by relating external stimuli to actions without regard to the intervening inner link.

Nature and Locus of Agency

External events may create the occasion for doing something, but, except in simple reflexive acts, they are not the originators of affect and action. External stimuli give rise to courses of action through personal agency. The manner in which human agency operates can be conceptualized in at least three different ways—as either *autonomous* agency, *mechanical* agency, or *interactive* agency. The notion that humans serve as autonomous agents of their own actions has few, if any, serious advocates. However, this notion is often brought up by radical behaviorists in arguments repudiating self-influence in causal processes. Thus, for example, Skinner (1971) invokes the metaphor of the "autonomous inner man" when dismissing theories contending that people can influence through thought what they will do.

A second approach to self processes is to treat them in terms of mechanical agency. In this view, people act automatically without thinking, or their thoughts are simply intervening events under remote control of environmental forces. Environmental stimuli trigger the inner events to produce predictable acts. Because the agency resides in environmental forces, and the self system is merely a conduit for them, one can bypass the internal link in the causal chain.

In the social cognitive model of interactive agency, persons are neither autonomous agents nor mechanical conveyers of animating environmental forces. Rather, they serve as a reciprocally contributing influence to their own motivation and behavior within a system of reciprocal causation involving personal determinants, action, and environmental factors. These sets of determinants affect each other bidirectionally rather than unidirectionally. This model of triadic reciprocality is analyzed in considerable detail in later sections of this chapter.

Control by Contingent Stimuli

The notion of mechanical agency rests on presuppositions that have not fared well empirically. An assumption that is crucial to the argument of external control is that environmental stimuli control behavior automatically. One can dispense with the so-called internal link in causal chains only if thought cannot affect action. The model of mechanical agency leans most heavily on the assumption of automaticity of reinforcement. In fact, as will be amply documented throughout this book, most external influences operate through cognitive processing. During transactions with their environment, people are not merely emitting responses and experiencing outcomes. They form beliefs from observed regularities about the outcomes likely to result from actions in given situations and regulate their behavior accordingly. Contrary to claims that behavior is controlled by its immediate consequences, behavior is related to its outcomes at the level of aggregate consequences, rather than immediate effects (Baum, 1973). Response consequences convey probabilistic information for forming expectancies about how outcomes relate to actions, rather than stamp in responses. People process and synthesize contextual and outcome information from sequences of events over long intervals about what behavior is needed to produce given outcomes.

The notion that consequences influence behavior fares better for anticipated than for actual consequences (Bandura, 1977a). In studies of the power of belief over consequents, the same environmental consequences have markedly different effects on behavior, depending on people's beliefs of how their actions are related to outcomes and the meaning of those outcomes (Dulany, 1968; Kaufman, Baron, & Kopp, 1966). When belief differs from actuality, which is not uncommon, behavior is weakly influenced by its actual consequences, until more realistic expectations are developed through repeated experiences. But it is not always expectations that change in the direction of social reality. When a person acts on an erroneous belief, it can alter how others behave, thus shaping the social reality in the direction of the initially mistaken belief (Snyder, 1980).

While undergoing reinforcing experiences, people are doing more than just learning the probabilistic relation between actions and outcomes. They observe the progress they are making and tend to set themselves goals for progressive improvement. External incentives thus influence behavior partly through their effects on the goals people have set for themselves. When variations in personal goals are partialled out, the effects of "reinforcers" on performance are reduced (Locke, Bryan, & Kendall, 1968). Performance attainments also provide an important source of efficacy information for judging one's capabilities. People's self-percepts of efficacy influence their thought patterns, behavior, and emotional arousal (Bandura, 1982a).

Because thought mediates the effects of outcomes, to trace behavior back to environmental "reinforcers" by no means completes an explanatory regress. To predict how outcomes will affect behavior, one must know how they are cognitively processed. To understand fully the mechanisms through which consequences change behavior requires analysis of the reciprocally contributing influence of cognitive factors.

The preceding comments speak to the explanatory and predictive deficiencies of conditioning theories that make "reinforcers" the mainspring of action. Antecedent stimuli are equally inadequate to the task of explaining the origin of human affect and action with disavowal of cognitive agency. Consider some examples. In studies of cognitive self-arousal, in which persons generate emotionally arousing or neutral thoughts in a sequence of their own choosing, it is self-produced thoughts that create autonomic reactivity (Schwartz, 1971). No differential external stimuli are present to serve as the causes or the predictors of the emotional reactions. In associative learning, merging paired elements into memorable constructed images produces considerably better learning than does repetitive, paired exposure to stimulus elements (Bower, 1972). In observational learning of complex novel actions, persons who simply observe the modeled patterns learn little, whereas those who cognitively transform actions to memorable symbolic codes achieve superior learning and retention of modeled activities (Bandura & Jeffery, 1973; Bandura, Jeffery, & Bachicha, 1974). Stimulus inputs are of little predictive value in contrast to constructed symbolic codes, which predict with high accuracy which modeled actions are mastered and how well they are retained over time. When an indefinite social prompt gives rise to novel cognitive constructions, as when a person creates a poem in response to an indeterminate suggestion to devise something new, the generative thought is not simply a conduit for the doings of external stimuli. These are but a few examples in which cognition functions as a generative, rather than as a redundant, link automatically cued by external stimuli.

Cognitive processes are not publicly observable, but they do have indicants through which they can become known indirectly. The indicants of thought are separate from the behavior to be explained. Verbal probes provide one indirect means of access. In exploring laws about how internal events govern behavior, persons are often asked to verbalize their prior thoughts. Such studies establish orderly functional relationships between indirectly gauged thought and subsequent action (Bandura, 1969a; Brewer, 1974; Ericsson & Simon, 1980). Thought probes, of course, are not confined to verbal indicants. Nonverbal probes also provide indirect ways of measuring what people know, as when physical symbols are used to convey understanding of the structure and meaning of events. Other sciences have made rapid strides in explaining and predicting events from the properties of postulated

mediators that are not directly observable but are known by indirect means. Atomic theory, for example, has done well in accounting for physical phenomena even though atoms, which serve as explanatory factors, are not given to direct public view.

By focusing on the verbal mode of the thought probe, rather than on what it reveals about content and structure of thought that can affect action, operant analysts dub thought as merely verbal response, thereby divesting it of any causal efficacy (Lacey & Rachlin, 1978). When persons describe the cognitive operations they go through as they generate a solution for action, it is not vocal sounds but the thought processes they reveal that are the subject of interest. Relabeling thought contents as verbal behavior does not erase their causal significance. The fidelity with which words represent ongoing thoughts is a separate issue to be addressed later.

In arguing for the causative irrelevance of cognitive events, operant analysts typically portray causal chains in such a way that both thought and actions spring from stimuli outside the organism. This rendering of causal linkage makes external stimuli causative and thoughts dispensable connectives. In fact, neither thought nor action covaries all that closely with external stimuli. It is often the case that cognitive events bear the lawful relationship to behavior, while external stimuli are only weakly related to both thought and action. Laws of cognitive events and their structural properties are, therefore, required to understand human behavior.

Because some of the inner causes invoked by theorists over the years have been ill-founded does not justify banishing cognitive determinants from scientific inquiry. A large body of research now exists in which cognitive events are instructionally activated, their presence is assessed indirectly, and their function al relationship to behavior is systematically examined. Results of such studies, which will be analyzed fully in later chapters, reveal that people acquire and retain behavioral capabilities much better by generating and using cognitive aids than by reinforced repetitive performances. With growing evidence that cognition has causal effects on behavior, the arguments against internal determinants as mentalistic fictions have lost their force. Thoughts are brain processes, not disembodied mental events.

A theory that denies that thoughts can regulate actions does not lend itself readily to the explanation of complex human behavior. Although cognitive determinants are disavowed by radical behaviorism, their causal contributions cannot be excised all that easily. Therefore, adherents of radical behaviorism translate cognitive determinants into stimulus operations, move them outside the organism, and then ascribe their effects to the direct action of the externally relocated events. The relabeling and externalization of cognitive determinants take many forms. When informative cues affect behavior through the intervening influence of thought, the process is portrayed as one of stimulus control; that is, stimuli are seen as prompting behavior directly, without reference to the judgmental link. When people act protectively in the presence of stimuli previously associated with painful experiences, the stimuli are said to have become aversive rather than that the individuals have learned to expect and avoid aversive events. In fact, it is people's knowledge of their environment, not the stimuli, that is changed by correlated experience. Thus, for example, if a given word foreshadows physically painful stimulation, the word assumes predictive significance for the individual, not the painful properties of the physical stimuli. We have already seen how cognitive factors governing the effects of response outcomes go unexamined in behavioristic analyses, with the result that control gets invested in external reinforcers.

It has always been the cardinal rule in operant conditioning theory that behavior is controlled by its immediate consequences. Indeed, the automaticity assumption demands immediacy of reinforcement. Unless action and outcome occur contiguously, any irrelevant response that happened to appear just before the reward, rather than the intended remote one, would become the main beneficiary of reinforcement. Proponents of operant conditioning continue to endorse the automaticity of reinforcement, but the principle of immediacy of reinforcement is being discarded. In the words of Lacey and Rachlin (1978), "The idea that factors which cause an event are immediately antecedent or temporally contiguous to it dies hard" (p. 185). However, the view that behavior is often unaffected by its immediate antecedents and consequences, which is in keeping with substantial evidence (Estes, 1971), contests the very assumption on which the notion of contingency control rests. Moreover, it leaves one with contradictory propositions that immediate outcomes affect prior actions automatically but immediate outcomes often do not affect prior actions.

There is ample reason, even within common findings of operant research, to question the notion that contingent stimuli are the driving forces of behavior. If momentary response effects determined performance, organisms should rapidly cease responding when only occasionally reinforced, whereas, in fact, their behavior is most persistent under such conditions. Thus, if only every 50th response is rewarded, 98 percent of the outcomes are extinctive, while only a paltry 2 percent are reinforcing. Because behavior continues to be performed despite abounding dissuading effects, one must look beyond immediate consequences for the determinants. Operant researchers eventually have come to view behavior as regulated by integrated feedback rather than by its immediate effects. In this broadened perspective (Baum, 1973, 1981), organisms integrate information on how often and when their responses are reinforced over a long period, and they regulate their actions according to the aggregate consequences. The integrating mechanism remains unspecified, however. This type of analysis comes close to linking the effect of consequences on action through the integrating influence of thought. People have to remember when, where, and how often their behavior is reinforced and to extract rules from sequences of events over time. Cognitive skills in extracting correlations between actions and outcomes from probabilistic information represent the integrating capability.

Control by Past Stimulus Inputs

With mounting evidence that antecedent stimuli do not account all that well for the form behavior takes and that immediate outcomes do not necessarily strengthen the behavior after it appears, proponents of the contingency model of causation now increasingly place the explanatory burden on the residuum of past contingencies—the "history of reinforcement." Personal determinants of behavior are thus reduced to past stimulus inputs. In this enlarged model of causation, behavior is under the dual control of current external stimuli and the past environmental inputs.

It is a truism that people are affected by their past experiences. The theoretical disputes center on whether transactions with the environment create internal determinants by unidirectional or bidirectional causation and whether human behavior is steered by implanted stimulus inputs or partly regulated by thought processes. Past experiences obviously contribute to the development of knowledge structures and self-functions that influence current perceptions, thoughts, and actions. But past events did not emanate as unidirectional environmental forces. Because personal and environmental factors affect each other reciprocally, persons are partial creators of their history. Self phenomena lie at the very heart of causal processes because, not only do they function as the proximal determinants of behavior, they give shape to the more distal external influences emerging from transactions with the environment.

Personal determinants arising from past experiences are not simply preserved replicas of previous environmental contingen-cies. Rather, the representation of the past involves constructive processes. Environmental events are filtered through personal meanings and biases and are cognitively transformed into propositional knowledge. When experiences are incongruent with belief, memory for those past experiences is distorted in the direction of belief (Cordua, McGraw, & Drabman, 1979; Signorella & Liben, 1984). For example, seeing a female doctor interacting with a male nurse produces stereotypically distorted recollections, in which the male becomes the doctor and the female the nurse. Most of the distortion of incongruent events occurs in recollection rather than during the encoding of them (Martin & Halverson, 1983). People serve as partial authors not only of their past experiences but of their memory of them as well. Radical behaviorists now assign a greater role to historical determinants of behavior, especially with the growing acknowledgment that contingency control is not all it was claimed to be. But, it is cognitively-oriented research that is contributing most to the understanding of how past events are perceived and how the personally edited information is coded for memory representation and acted on by cognitive operations to guide judgment and action.

The preceding discussion is not meant to imply that the external factors on which radical behaviorists center their attention do not play an important role in behavior. They obviously do. People partly guide their actions on the basis of predictive situational cues and the outcomes they expect their actions to produce. But external factors operate through generative self processes as guides for action, rather than as independent controllers of action. Indeed, as has already been noted, the view of behavior as regulated by the stimuli that precede and follow it in the model of contingency control fares poorly under empirical scrutiny. Nor does the notion of a mechanically imprinted "history of reinforcement" jibe with what is known about the reconstructive nature of memory systems and the creative and generative nature of human thought. The residuum of past stimuli cannot serve as the proxy for cognitive processes, which largely involve propositional knowledge and cognitive operations dealing with what one knows.

Psychophysical Functions and Epiphenomenalism

In behavioristic analyses, thoughts are merely by-products of bodily events that in no way affect how people behave. To treat thoughts as incidental residues of conditioned responses hardly captures the active, reflective, and creative aspects of human thought. People analyze their experiences to gain generic knowledge about themselves and their environment. They anticipate, plan, and reflect on their own thinking. Their thoughts have greater coherence, direction, continuity, and novelty than do their autonomic or motor responses to make these conditioned responses the oracle.

Any stance toward the mind-body issue, which has been heatedly debated for centuries, raises knotty philosophical problems. Dualistic doctrines that regard mind and body as separate entities do not provide much enlightenment on the nature of the disembodied mental state or on how an immaterial mind and bodily events act on each other. Were one to perform Bunge's (1982) hypothetical brain transplant, the donor's unique psychic life would undoubtedly accompany the brain to the new host, rather than remain behind with the donor as a separate mental entity. Nor does epiphenomenalism, which treats thoughts as psychic by-products of bodily events, solve the problem. It too fails to explain how bodily events generate psychic ones and how and where they maintain their separate existence. Monistic solutions have been sought by positioning a unidirectionally-wired bodily system in which thoughts occur as physical, rather than as psychic, accompaniments of bodily events without any capacity to affect how the body behaves. Actually, neural and other bodily structures contain too many reciprocal mechanisms to contend that the cortical processes representing thought cannot affect bodily systems.

Psychoneural Monism. To grant thought causal efficacy is not to invoke a disembodied mental state. Thoughts can be construed as higher brain processes that activate visceral, motoric, and other physical processes, which can, in turn, affect the brain activities representing thought processes. Ideational and neural terminology are different ways of representing the same brain processes, as identity theorists have argued for years. In this type of solution to the mind-body problem, thoughts are causative but not immaterial. Bunge (1980) presents a detailed analysis of cognitive processes as a set of brain activities in plastic neural systems of the cerebral cortex and interprets psychophysical relations as involving reciprocal actions between specialized subsystems of the organism.

The view that cognitive events are neural occurrences does not mean that psychological laws regarding cognitive and behavioral functioning are derivable from neurophysiological ones. It is important to distinguish between how cortical systems function and the personal and social means by which they can be orchestrated to produce different contents serving different purposes. Psychological knowledge of how best to structure influences to create belief systems and behavioral competencies is not derivable from knowledge of the neurophysiological mechanisms that subserve such changes. Thus, knowing how cortical neurons function in learning does not tell one much about how best to present and organize instructional contents, how to code them for memory representation, and how to motivate learners to attend to, process, and rehearse what they are learning. Nor does understanding of how the brain works furnish rules on how to create social conditions conducive to skills needed to become a successful parent, teacher, or politician. The optimal conditions are provided by psychological principles.

The influences needed to produce the

neural occurrences underlying complex human behavior include events , external to the organism, acting together with cognitively generated ones. The laws of psychology inform on how to structure environmental influences and to enlist cognitive activities to achieve given purposes. Although psychological laws cannot violate what is known about the physiological system that subserves them, they need to be pursued in their own right. Were one to embark on the road to reductionism, the journey would successively traverse biology, chemistry, and eventually end in atomic particles with neither the intermediate locales nor the final stop supplying the psychological laws of human behavior.

The construal of cognitions as cortical processes raises the intriguing question of how people come to be producers of thoughts that may be novel, inventive, or visionary, or that take complete leave of reality as in flights of fancy. One can originate fanciful but coherent thoughts, as, for example, visualizing hippopotami gracefully navigating hang gliders over lunar craters. Similarly, one can get oneself to cognize several novel acts and choose to execute one of them. Cognitive production, with its initiating and creative properties, defies explanation in terms of external cueing of preexisting cognitive packets. Neither situational cues, knowledge structures, conditioned responses, nor prior brainwaves are likely to be predictive of the specific forms fanciful thoughts will take.

If thought processes are conceived of as cortical processes, the relevant question is not how mind and body act on each other, but how people can bring into being cognitive or cortical productions. The concocted scenario of gliding hippopotami was brought into being by the intentional exercise of personal agency. Intentionality and agency raise the fundamental question of how people actuate the cortical processes that characterize the exercise of agency and lead to the realization of particular intentions. In addition to explaining how people bring about thoughts and actions is the intriguing question of how people occasion self-perceiving and self-reflecting activities.

SOCIAL COGNITIVE THEORY

In the social cognitive view people are neither driven by inner forces nor automatically shaped and controlled by external stimuli. Rather, human functioning is explained in terms of a model of triadic reciprocality in which behavior, cognitive and other personal factors, and environmental events all operate as interacting determinants of each other. The nature of persons is defined within this perspective in terms of a number of basic capabilities. These are discussed briefly below and analyzed fully in the chapters that follow.

Symbolizing Capability

The remarkable capacity to use symbols, which touches virtually every aspect of people's lives, provides them with a powerful means of altering and adapting to their environment. Through symbols people process and transform transient experiences into internal models that serve as guides for future action. Through symbols they similarly give meaning, form, and continuance to the experiences they have lived through.

By drawing on their knowledge and symbolizing powers, people can generate innovative courses of action. Rather than solving problems solely by enacting options and suffering the costs of missteps, people usually test possible solutions symbolically and discard or retain them on the basis of estimated outcomes before plunging into action. An advanced cognitive capability coupled with the remarkable flexibility of symbolization enables people to create ideas that transcend their sensory experiences. Through the medium of symbols, they can communicate with others at almost any distance in time and space. Other distinctive human characteristics to be discussed shortly are similarly founded on symbolic capability.

To say that people base many of their actions on thought does not necessarily mean they are always objectively rational. Rationality depends on reasoning skills which are not always well developed or used effectively. Even if people know how to reason logically, they make faulty judgments when they base their inferences on inadequate information or fail to consider the full consequences of different choices. Moreover, they often missample and misread events in ways that give rise to erroneous conceptions about themselves and the world around them. When they act on their misconceptions, which appear subjectively rational, given their errant basis, such persons are viewed by others as behaving in an unreasoning, if not downright foolish, manner. Thought can thus be a source of human failing and distress as well as human accomplishment.

Forethought Capability

People do not simply react to their immediate environment, nor are they steered by implants from their past. Most of their behavior, being purposive, is regulated by forethought. The future time perspective manifests itself in many ways. People anticipate the likely consequences of their prospective actions, they set goals for themselves, and they otherwise plan courses of action for cognized futures, for many of which established ways are not only ineffective but may also be detrimental. Through exercise of forethought, people motivate themselves and guide their actions anticipatorily. By reducing the impact of immediate influences, forethought can support foresightful behavior, even when the present conditions are not especially conducive to it.

The capability for intentional and purposive action is rooted in symbolic activity. Future events cannot serve as determinants of behavior, but their cognitive represent-

ation can have a strong causal impact on present action. Images of desirable future events tend to foster the behavior most likely to bring about their realization. By representing foreseeable outcomes symbolically, people can convert future consequences into current motivators and regulators of foresightful behavior. Forethought is translated into action through the aid of self-regulating mechanisms.

In analyses of telic or purposive mechanisms through goals and outcomes projected forward in time, the future acquires causal efficacy by being represented cognitively in the present. Cognized futures thus become temporally antecedent to actions. Some writers have misinterpreted the acknowledgment that experience influences thought to mean that thoughts are nothing more than etchings of environmental inputs in the host organism (Rychlak, 1979). When thought is miscast as mechanical mediationism, it is imprinted histories, rather than cognized futures, that impel and direct behavior. This is clearly not the view of cognition and personal agency to which social cognitive theory subscribes. Forethought is the product of generative and reflective ideation.

Vicarious Capability

Psychological theories have traditionally assumed that learning can occur only by performing responses and experiencing their effects. Learning through action has thus been given major, if not exclusive, priority. In actuality, virtually all learning phenomena, resulting from direct experience, can occur vicariously by observing other people's behavior and its consequences for them. The capacity to learn by observation enables people to acquire rules for generating and regulating behavioral patterns without having to form them gradually by tedious trial and error.

The abbreviation of the acquisition process through observational learning is vital for both development and survival. Because mistakes can produce costly, or even fatal consequences, the prospects for survival would be slim indeed if one could learn only from the consequences of trial and error. For this reason, one does not teach children to swim, adolescents to drive automobiles, and novice medical students to perform surgery by having them discover the requisite behavior from the consequences of their successes and failures. The more costly and hazardous the possible mistakes, the heavier must be the reliance on observational learning from competent examplars. The less the behavior patterns draw on inborn properties, the greater is the dependence on observational learning for the functional organization of behavior.

Humans come with few inborn patterns. This remarkable plasticity places high demand on learning. People must develop their basic capabilities over an extended period, and they must continue to master new competencies to fulfill changing demands throughout their life span. It therefore comes as no surprise that humans have evolved an advanced vicarious learning capability. Apart from the question of survival, it is difficult to imagine a social transmission system in which the language, life styles, and institutional practices of the culture are taught to each new member just by selective reinforcement of fortuitous behaviors, without the benefit of models to exemplify these cultural patterns.

Some complex skills can be mastered only through the aid of modeling. If children had no exposure to the utterances of models, it would be virtually impossible to teach them the linguistic skills that constitute a language. It is doubtful that one could ever shape intricate words, let alone grammatical rules, by selective reward of random vocalization. In other behavior patterns that are formed by unique combinations of elements selected from numerous possibilities, there is little, if any, chance of producing the novel patterns spontaneously, or something even resembling them. Where novel forms of behavior can be conveyed effectively only by social cues, modeling is an indispensable aspect of learning. Even when it is possible to establish new patterns of behavior through other means, the acquisition process can be considerably shortened through modeling.

Most psychological theories were cast long before the advent of enormous advances in the technology of communication. As a result, they give insufficient attention to the increasingly powerful role that the symbolic environment plays in present-day human lives. Indeed, in many aspects of living, televised vicarious influence has dethroned the primacy of direct experience. Whether it be thought patterns, values, attitudes, or styles of behavior, life increasingly models the media.

Self-Regulatory Capability

Another distinctive feature of social cognitive theory is the central role it assigns to self-regulatory functions. People do not behave just to suit the preferences of others. Much of their behavior is motivated and regulated by internal standards and self-evaluative reactions to their own actions. After personal standards have been adopted, discrepancies between a performance and the standard against which it is measured activate evaluative self-reactions, which serve to influence subsequent behavior. An act, therefore, includes among its determinants self-produced influences.

Self-directedness is exercised by wielding influence over the external environment as well as enlisting self-regulatory functions. Thus, by arranging facilitative environmental conditions, recruiting cognitive guides, and creating incentives for their own efforts, people make causal contribution to their own motivation and actions. To be sure, self-regulatory functions are fashioned from, and occasionally supported by, external influences. Having some external origins and supports, however, does not refute the fact that the exercise of self-influence partly determines the course of one's behavior.

Self-Reflective Capability

If there is any characteristic that is distinctively human, it is the capability for reflective self-consciousness. This enables people to analyze their experiences and to think about their own thought processes. By reflecting on their varied experiences and on what they know, they can derive generic knowledge about themselves and the world around them. People not only gain understanding through reflection, they evaluate and alter their own thinking. In verifying thought through self-reflective means, they monitor their ideas, act on them or predict occurrences from them, judge the adequacy of their thoughts from the results, and change them accordingly. While such metacognitive activities usually foster veridical thought (Flavell, 1978a), they can also produce faulty thought patterns through reciprocal causation. Forceful actions arising from erroneous beliefs often create social effects that confirm the misbeliefs (Snyder, 1980).

Among the types of thoughts that affect action, none is more central or pervasive than people's judgments of their capabilities to deal effectively with different realities. It is partly on the basis of self-percepts of efficacy that they choose what to do, how much effort to invest in activities, how long to persevere in the face of disappointing results, and whether tasks are approached anxiously or self-assuredly (Bandura, 1982a). In the self-appraisal of efficacy, there are many sources of information that must be processed and weighed through self-referent thought. Acting on one's self-percepts of efficacy brings successes or missteps requiring further self-reappraisals of operative competencies. The self-knowledge which underlies the exercise of many facets of personal agency is largely the product of such reflective self-appraisal.

Self-reflectivity entails shifting the perspective of the same agent, rather than reifying different internal agents or selves regulating each other. Thus, in their daily transactions, people act on their thoughts and later analyze how well their thoughts have served them in managing events. But it is the one and the same person who is doing the thinking and then later evaluating the adequacy of his or her knowledge, thinking skills, and action strategies. The shift in perspective does not transform one from an agent to an object. One is just as much an agent reflecting on one's experiences as in executing the original courses of action. The same self performing multiple functions does not require positing multiple selves pursuing different roles.

The Nature of Human Nature

Seen from the social cognitive perspective, human nature is characterized by a vast potentiality that can be fashioned by direct and observational experience into a variety of forms within biological limits. To say that a major distinguishing mark of humans is their endowed plasticity is not to say that they have no nature or that they come structureless (Midgley, 1978). The plasticity, which is intrinsic to the nature of humans, depends upon neurophysiological mechanisms and structures that have evolved over time. These advanced neural systems for processing, retaining, and using coded information provide the capacity for the very characteristics that are distinctly human—generative symbolization, forethought, evaluative self-regulation, reflective self-consciousness, and symbolic communication.

Plasticity does not mean that behavior is entirely the product of post-natal experience. Some innately organized patterns of behavior are present at birth; others appear after a period of maturation. One does not have to teach infants to cry or suck, toddlers to walk, or adolescents how to copulate. Nor does one have to teach somatic motivators arising from tissue deficits and aversive events or to create somatically-based rewards. Infants come equipped with some attentional selectivity and interpretive predilections as well (von Cranach, Foppa, Lepenies, & Ploog, 1979). This neural programming for basic physiological functions is the product of accumulated ancestral experiences that are stored in the genetic code.

Most patterns of human behavior are organized by individual experience and retained in neural codes, rather than being provided ready-made by inborn programming. While human thought and conduct may be fashioned largely through experience, innately determined factors enter into every form of behavior to some degree. Genetic factors affect behavioral potentialities. Both experiential and physiological factors interact, often in intricate ways, to determine behavior. Even in behavioral patterns that are formed almost entirely through experience, rudimentary elements are present as part of the natural endowment. For example, humans are endowed with basic phonetic elements which may appear trivial compared to complex acquired patterns of speech, but the elements are, nevertheless, essential. Similarly, even action patterns regarded as instinctual, because they draw heavily on inborn elements, require appropriate experience to be developed. The level of psychological and physiological development, of course, limits what can be acquired at any given time. Because behavior contains mixtures of inborn elements and learned patterns, dichotomous thinking, which separates activities neatly into innate and acquired categories, is seriously inaccurate.

RECIPROCAL DETERMINISM

One-Sided Determinism

Over the years the locus of the causes of human behavior has been debated vigorously in terms of dispositional and environmental determinants, which are often portrayed as operating in a unidirectional manner. Exponents of *environmental determinism* study and theorize about how behavior is controlled by situational influences. The view of unidirectional environmental determinism has been carried to its extreme in the more radical forms of behaviorism. In this one-sided determinism, acts are regulated by current external stimuli and the residuum of past environmental inputs (Day, 1977; Skinner, 1974).

It is not that the interdependence of personal and environmental influences is never acknowledged by advocates of this point of view. Indeed, Skinner (1971) has often commented on people's capacity for countercontrol. However, the notion of countercontrol portrays the environment as the instigator against which individuals can counteract. In fact, people create environments and set them in motion as well as rebut them. People are foreactive, not simply counteractive. A further conceptual problem is that, having been acknowledged, the reality of bidirectional causation gets negated, and the preeminent control of behavior by the environment is reasserted (e.g., "A person does not act upon the world, the world acts upon him," Skinner, 1971, p. 211). The environment thus reappears as an autonomous force that automatically shapes, orchestrates, and controls behavior. Whatever allusions are made to two-way processes, environmental rule clearly emerges as the reigning metaphor in this view of reality.

Theorists favoring *personal determinism* seek the causes of human behavior in dispositional sources in the form of instincts, drives, traits, and other motivational forces within the individual. Existentialists, who stress the human capacity for conscious judgment and intentional action, contend that people determine what they become by their own free choices. In extreme formulations of cognitivism, thought supplants actuality in the explanation of human affect and action. The words of the Stoic philosopher Epictetus are widely quoted (Ellis, 1973) as testimony for the power of thought over social reality: "Men are disturbed not by things but by the views which they take of them."

Conceptions of human behavior in terms of unidirectional personal determinism are just as unsatisfying as are those espousing unidirectional environmental determinism. To contend that the mind creates reality, or that people are distressed, not by what happens to them, but by their views of it, is to ignore that environmental factors partly determine what people perceive and think. There is a marked difference between acknowledging that cognition can alter the impact of happenings and denying that the happenings play any role in the human condition. One would be hard pressed to convince parents who had just lost their child in a fatal accident that they are deeply grieved not by the death but by how they view it. Nor could one convince older unemployed workers, who cannot find gainful employment to provide for their families and to fend off bill collectors and foreclosers, that it is their perceptions, not the social reality, that is the major source of their anguish. The human condition is better improved by altering detrimental circumstances and personal perspectives than by trying to alter personal outlooks, while ignoring the very circumstances that serve to nourish them.

One-Sided Interactionism

Most contemporary theorists subscribe to some form of interactional model of causality that portrays behavior as a product of personal and situational influences (Bowers, 1973; Endler & Magnusson, 1976; Pervin & Lewis, 1978). Hence, the major issues in contention center less on interactionism than on the type of interactional model espoused. Explanatory models regarding major classes of determinants as interactional in form have been conceptualized in at least three ways. Two of these formulations and their accompanying methodologies subscribe to a one-sided interactionism with respect to behavior.

In the unidirectional view of interaction, persons and situations are treated as independent entities that unite in unspecified ways to produce behavior. A basic problem with this conception is that personal and environmental factors do not function as inde-

pendent determinants; rather, they determine each other. People create, alter, and destroy environments. The changes they produce in environmental conditions, in turn, affect their behavior and the nature of future life.

The partially bidirectional conception of interaction acknowledges that persons and situations affect each other. But it treats influences relating to behavior as flowing in only one direction—the person-situation interchange unidirectionally produces the behavior, but the behavior itself does not affect the ongoing transaction between the person and the situation. A major limitation of this conception is that, except for their social stimulus value, persons cannot affect the environment other than through their actions. Their actions take the dominant role in how people influence the situations which, in turn, will affect their thoughts, emotional reactions, and behavior. It is difficult to conceive of behavior as the offspring of an intimate exchange between a behaviorless person and the environment. This would be analogous to an immaculate conception. Behavior is interacting and exerting influence at the meeting and is active throughout events, rather than being procreated by a union of a behaviorless person and a situation. In short, behavior is an interacting determinant, not a detached byproduct that plays no role in the production process.

Triadic Reciprocality

Social cognitive theory favors a conception of interaction based on triadic reciprocality (Bandura, 1977a, 1978a). In this model of reciprocal determinism, which is summarized schematically in Figure 1, behavior, cognitive and other personal factors, and environmental influences all operate interactively as determinants of each other. In this triadic reciprocal determinism, the term reciprocal refers to the mutual action between causal factors. The term determinism is used here to signify the production of effects by certain factors, rather

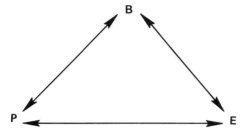

FIGURE 1. Schematization of the relations between the three classes of determinants in triadic reciprocal causation.

than in the doctrinal sense of actions being completely determined by a prior sequence of causes operating independently of the individual. Many factors are often needed to create a given effect. Because of the multiplicity of interacting influences, the same factor can be a part of different blends of conditions that have different effects. Particular factors are, therefore, associated with effects probabilistically rather than inevitably.

Differential Contributions of the Triadic Factors. Reciprocality does not mean symmetry in the strength of bidirectional influences. Nor is the patterning and strength of mutual influences fixed in reciprocal causation. The relative influence exerted by the three sets of interacting factors will vary for different activities, different individuals, and different circumstances. When environmental conditions exercise powerful constraints on behavior, they emerge as the overriding determinants. If people are dropped into deep water, they will all promptly swim, however uniquely varied they might be in their cognitive and behavioral repertoires. There are times when behavior and its intrinsic feedback are the central factors in the interacting system. One example of this would be persons who play the piano for their own enjoyment. Such behavior is self-regulated over a long period by its sensory effects, whereas the cognitive activities and situational influences are involved to a lesser extent in the process.

When situational constraints are weak, personal factors serve as the predominant influence in the regulatory system. In deciding what novel to check out from vast library holdings, people's preferences hold sway. The activation and maintenance of defensive behavior is another illustration in which cognition exerts the foremost influence. False beliefs activate avoidant behavior that keeps individuals out of touch with prevailing reality, thus creating a strong reciprocal interaction between beliefs and action, which is protected from corrective environmental influence. In extreme cases, behavior is so powerfully controlled by bizarre beliefs that neither the beliefs nor the accompanying actions are much affected by even extremely punishing social consequences (Bateson, 1961).

In most instances, the development and activation of the three sets of interacting factors are all highly interdependent. Television viewing provides a common example. Personal preferences influence when and which programs, from among the available alternatives, individuals choose to watch on television (Fenigstein, 1979). Although the potential televised environment is identical for all viewers, their actual televised environment depends on what they choose to watch. Through their viewing behavior, they partly shape the nature of the future televised environment. Because production costs and commercial requirements also determine what people are shown (Brown, 1971), the options provided in the televised environment partly shape the viewers' preferences. Here, all three factors—viewer preferences, viewing behavior, and televised offerings—reciprocally affect each other. What people watch exerts some influence on their preferences, thoughts, and actions (Bandura, 1973; Comstock et al., 1978). The analysis of reciprocal causation could, therefore, be extended to include the bidirectional links involving social behavior and the interpersonal environment.

It should be noted in passing that reciprocal processes also operate within each of the three constituent factors: Within the behavioral domain, many actions are mutually related so that their occurrences co-vary positively or negatively. Similarly, in the environmental domain situational happenings are often interactional, as when changes in a milieu set in motion other environmental changes. In the personal realm of affect and thought, there exist reciprocal escalating processes, as when frightening thoughts arouse internal turmoil that, in turn, breeds even more frightening thoughts.

Temporal Dynamics of Triadic Reciprocality. The triadic factors do not operate in the manner of a simultaneous wholistic interaction. Reciprocality does not mean simultaneity of influence (Bandura, 1983a; Phillips & Orton, 1983). Although each of the segments of reciprocality involve bidirectional influence processes, the mutual influences and their reciprocal effects do not spring forth all at the same instant. It takes time for a causal factor to exert its influence. Interacting factors work their mutual effects sequentially over variable time courses. Even when bidirectionality of influence is almost immediate, as in verbal interchanges in which a question by one person evokes a prompt reply from another, an influence is not altered before it has exerted itself. The production of a reciprocal effect takes time. In the example just cited, questions and replies do not occur simultaneously. To pursue the television example cited earlier, selecting a television program does not instantly change the viewer's preference or immediately cause the television industry to alter its programming; acquiring preferences and behavioral competencies through televised modeling does not, at that precise moment, trigger action effects; executing an act does not instantly transform the social milieu. The time lags between causal events will vary for different activities. For example, punching a reckless driver will produce a quicker reciprocal effect than filing a police complaint.

Because the triadic factors do not operate simultaneously as a wholistic entity, it is possible to gain some understanding of how different segments of two-way causation operate without having to mount a Herculean effort to study every possible interactant at the same time. This is true even in the case of physiological functioning where the subsystems are closely interrelated and the time course of reciprocal action is generally much shorter. The body contains numerous reciprocally activating systems, so that any gigantic attempt to study all these reciprocal actions at once would produce investigatory paralysis. It is the subsystems and their various interrelations, rather than the entirety, that are analyzed. Clarifying how the various subsystems function interactively advances understanding of how the superordinate system operates. James's (1884) critique of wholistic notions—"Either this Whole System, just as it stands or Nothing at all" (p. 283)—points to the constraints of such views. A doctrine of simultaneous wholistic causation has paralytic effects on efforts to study causal processes empirically.

Analytic Decomposition of Triadic Reciprocality. Different subspecialities of psychology center their inquiry on selected segments of reciprocality. Researchers who select the interactive relation between thought and action as their sector of interest examine how conceptions, beliefs, self-percepts, and intentions shape and direct behavior. What people think, believe, and feel affects how they behave. The natural and extrinsic effects of their actions, in turn, partly determine their thought patterns and affective reactions (Bandura, 1982a; Bower, 1975; Neisser, 1976).

Consider next the segment of reciprocality between the person and the environment in the triadic system. Environmental influences can affect persons apart from their behavior, as when thoughts and feelings are modified through modeling, tuition, or social persuasion (Bandura, 1977a; Rosenthal & Zimmerman, 1978; Zimbardo,

Ebbesen, & Maslach, 1977). Personal determinants are not disembodied from the person presiding over them and his or her physical characteristics. People also evoke different reactions from their social environment simply by their physical characteristics, such as their age, size, race, sex, and physical attractiveness (Lerner, 1982). People similarly activate different reactions depending on their socially conferred roles and status. For example, those who have high prestige and power in hierarchies elicit more deferential and accommodating reactions than do those of lowly status. Thus, by their observable characteristics people can affect their social environment before they say or do anything. The social reactions so elicited, in turn, affect the recipients' conceptions of themselves and others in ways that either strengthen or reduce the environmental bias.

Even erroneous information about a person's characteristics can set off social interchanges in directions that create behavioral validation for the initially erroneous conceptions (Snyder, Tanke, & Berscheid, 1977). Males led to believe they were conversing on the telephone with physically attractive females had more positive expectations about them, talked more animatedly and humorously with them, and found them to be more interesting and enthusiastic than if they thought their conversants were unattractive. The females, in turn, were more humorous, friendlier, and socially adept when they conversed with males who believed them to be attractive rather than unattractive. Erroneous beliefs thus prompted actions causing others to behave in ways that confirmed the original misbeliefs. The processes by which people's perceptions of each other influence the course of their interactions have been subjects of major concern to researchers working within the field of person perception (Schneider, Hastorf, & Ellsworth, 1979).

Of all the various segments in the triadic interacting system, the reciprocal relationship between behavior and environmental events has received the greatest attention. Indeed, some theories focus exclusively on this portion of reciprocity in the explanation of behavior (Skinner, 1974). In the transactions of everyday life, behavior alters environmental conditions, and it is, in turn, altered by the very conditions it creates (Cairns, 1979; Patterson, 1976; Raush, Barry, Hertel, & Swain, 1974; Thomas & Malone, 1979).

Viewed from the perspective of reciprocal determinism, the common practice of searching for the ultimate environmental cause of behavior is an idle exercise. This is because, in an interacting process, the one and the same event can be either an environmental stimulus, a response, or an environmental "reinforcer," depending arbitrarily on when and on which side of the ongoing exchange one happens to look first in the flow of events. Figure 2, which represents the sequence of actions of two persons (A and B), shows how the same events change their status from behavior to environments and from environments to behavior at different entry points in the flow of the two-way interaction. For example, event A_2 is an environmental stimulus in the third starting point of the analysis, a response in the second entry point, and an environmental reinforcer in the first entry point. One cannot speak of "behavior" and its "controlling environmental conditions" as though these two factors were fundamentally different events with inherent indicators of what they are supposed to be.

Confining analysis to a particular interactive segment sheds some light on causal processes. But it inevitably leaves unexplained some of the observed variance in events, when other determinants in the triadic system make causal contributions at various points in the transactions. For example, the interactive relationship between behavior and environmental events in social interchanges is not governed solely by the immediate behavioral reciprocities between actions and social counterreactions. While behaving, people entertain thoughts about where their actions are likely to lead and what they may eventually produce. Forethought can enhance, attenuate, or nullify the proximal effects of action.

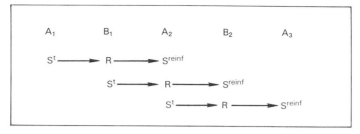

FIGURE 2. Illustration of how the same events change their status from behavior to environment and from environment to behavior at different entry points in the flow of interaction between two people. The As are successive responses by one person, and the Bs successive responses by the second person in the dual interaction: S^t represents "stimulus"; R represents "response"; S^{reinf} represents "reinforcer."

Consider investigations of reciprocal coercive behavior in an ongoing dyadic interaction. In discordant families, coercive behavior by one member tends to elicit coercive counteractions from recipients in mutually escalating aggression (Patterson, 1976). However, coercion often does not produce coercive counteractions. To understand fully the interactive relation between behavior and environment, the analysis must be extended temporally and broadened to include cognitive determinants operating in the triadic interlocking system. This requires tapping into what people are thinking as they perform responses and experience their effects. Counterresponses to antecedent acts are influenced not only by their immediate effects, but also by people's judgments of eventual outcomes should they pursue that course of action. Thus, aggressive children will continue, or even escalate, their coercive behavior, although immediately punished, when they expect persistence to gain them what they seek eventually (Bandura & Walters, 1959). But the same momentary punishment will serve as an inhibitor, rather than as an escalator, of coercion when they expect that the continuance of the aversive conduct will be ineffective. How actions are influenced by their momentary effects thus depends on people's thoughts about the rules governing outcomes (Baron, Kaufman, & Stauber, 1969; Estes, 1972; Kaufman et al., 1966;

Spielberger & DeNike, 1966), the meaning they attribute to the outcomes (Dulany, 1968), and their beliefs about how their actions are likely to change future outcomes over the course of sequential interchanges (Bandura & Barab, 1971).

In the preceding studies, thoughts were analyzed as influencers rather than as influenceable factors. But cognitions do not arise in a vacuum, nor do they function as autonomous causes of behavior. People's conceptions about themselves and the nature of things are developed and verified through four different processes: direct experience of the effects produced by their actions, vicarious experience of the effects produced by somebody else's actions, judgments voiced by others, and derivation of further knowledge from what they already know by using rules of inference. External influences play a role not only in the development and authentication of cognitions but in their activation as well. Different sights, smells, and sounds will elicit quite different trains of thought. Thus, while it is true that conceptions govern behavior, the conceptions themselves are partly fashioned from direct or socially mediated transactions with the environment. The relationship between thought and action involves two-way causation.

Empirical analyses of reciprocal processes have thus far rarely examined more than one interactive subsystem concurrently. Intricate analysis of triadic reciprocality still awaits the tools for gauging how multiple reciprocal links of influence operate together and the time courses in which they operate. This is a formidable task not only because the triadic systems are interactive, but because each subsystem itself contains multiple reciprocal processes.

Just as reciprocal determinism does not demand that all the interacting constituents be studied at once, nor does it prescribe only reciprocal investigatory methods. It is important to understand how certain determinants produce change in the first place, regardless of how the resultant changes, in turn, affect the subsequent operation of the determinants. To continue with the television example, to gain knowledge of how personal attributes and televised influences interactively foster learning aggression requires a separate analysis. Explaining how aggressive conduct is learned from televised models does not require that one simultaneously study how the acquired aggressiveness and the social milieu affect each other bidirectionally, or how acquired preferences for aggressive contents aggregately affect television offerings. The study of initial and reciprocal effects are separable and require different analytic methods. Both approaches are needed for a full understanding of psychological functioning.

Gauging Personal Determinants

Different causal models adopt different paradigms for elucidating how personal determinants contribute to human behavior. Personality theories traditionally approach the issue in terms of omnibus tests of personal attributes designed to serve varied purposes. Such personality tests consist of a fixed set of items, many of which may have limited bearing on the activities of interest in any particular instance. Moreover, in an effort to serve all purposes, the items are often cast in a general form requiring respondents to fill in the unspecified particulars concerning the nature of the actions, the settings in which they are performed, the persons toward whom the actions are directed, how often they are expressed, and their intensity. The more indefinite the items, the more contents the respondents have to fill in, and the less one can know exactly what is being measured.

It is unrealistic to expect such all-purpose tests to predict with high accuracy how people will perform diverse activities under diverse circumstances. We saw earlier that trait measures usually yield modest correlations. Tests of this sort have some practical value in that some predictive gain, however small, is better than sheer guesswork. But progress in understanding how personal factors affect actions and situations is best advanced through the microanalysis of interactive processes. This requires measures of personal determinants that are specifically tailored to the domain of functioning being analyzed. The study of individual differences by trait measures derived from omnibus tests is a method of convenience, which unfortunately sacrifices explanatory and predictive power.

Selective Activation of Potential Influences

The environment is not simply a fixed property that inevitably impinges upon individuals. For the most part, the environment is inoperative until it is actualized by appropriate action. Lecturers do not influence students unless they attend their classes, books do not affect people unless they select and read them, electric stove tops do not burn people unless they touch them, and rewarding and punishing influences remain quiescent until activated by performances. What part of the potential environment becomes the actual environment thus depends upon how people behave. Similarly, personal determinants are inoperative as influencers unless they are activated. People who can converse knowledgeably about certain issues can affect the course of social interaction if they speak but not if they remain silent or their areas of knowledgeability go otherwise untapped. Thus, behavior partly determines which of the many potential environmental influences will come into play and what forms they will take; environmental influences, in turn, partly determine which forms of behavior are developed and activated. In this two-way influence process, the environment is influenceable, as is the behavior it affects.

Social environments provide an especially wide latitude for creating conditions that can have a reciprocal effect on one's own behavior. People can converse on a number of topics, they can express different interests, and they can pursue a variety of activities. In social transactions, the behavior of each participant governs which of their potential qualities and interests will be actualized and which will remain unexpressed. We are all acquainted with problem-prone individuals who, through their irksome conduct, breed negative social climates wherever they go. Others are equally skilled at bringing out the best in those with whom they interact.

At the social level, people seek through collective action to alter the social conditions that affect the course and quality of their lives. Special-interest pressure groups exert influence over political and legislative matters. Labor unions negotiate to obtain the working conditions and pay schedules they favor. Other groups, similarly, use the power of collective pressure to change social practices in ways that improve their life situations.

Because personal and environmental influences function as interdependent determinants, rather than autonomously, research aimed at estimating the relative percentage of behavioral variation due to persons or to situations is ill suited for clarifying the transactional nature of human functioning. Nor is evidence that much of the variation is usually due to the joint effects of personal characteristics and situational conditions especially instructive. Rather, to elucidate the interdependencies between personal and environmental influences, one must analyze how each is conditional on the other. The methodology best suited for this purpose specifies the conditional probabilities that interacting factors will affect the likelihood of each other's oc-

currence in an ongoing sequence of events (Thomas & Malone, 1979). Interdependency does not mean that there is symmetry among the reciprocal influences. Disparities in social power, competencies, and self-regulatory skills create asymmetries in their mutual influences.

Analyses of sequential interchanges in social relationships provide numerous examples of reciprocal influence processes. Studies of dyadic exchanges document how one person's behavior activates particular responses from the partner which, in turn, prompt reciprocal actions that mutually shape the social milieu in a predictable direction (Bandura, Lipsher, & Miller, 1960; Snyder, 1980). For example, hostile acts generally draw aggressive counterresponses from others, whereas cordial antecedent acts seldom do (Raush, 1965; Raush et al., 1974). Aggressive persons thus create through their actions a hostile environment, while those who act in a more friendly manner generate an amicable social milieu. The growing recognition of reciprocal causation has ushered in new perspectives on socialization processes. One-sided developmental analyses of how parents influence their children have given way to transactional analyses of how parents and children mutually influence each other (Bell & Harper, 1977; Cairns, 1979; Lewis & Rosenblum, 1974).

The course of social transactions is not governed solely by people's actions. When personal characteristics predict how persons are likely to behave, those who possess those characteristics can set in motion certain reciprocal interaction sequences just by their presence alone. The mere appearance of some adults will elicit different amounts of cooperation, depending on whether or not they have previously rewarded children for such behavior (Redd, 1976). In addition, role prescriptions, specifying how people are supposed to behave in carrying out their assigned roles, structure the nature of reciprocal exchanges. For instance, behavior toward the same person in the same setting will differ when that person is in the role of a work supervisor or a confidante. Therefore, in analyzing how the behavior of one person affects the counterreactions of another, one must consider, in addition to the immediate effects of each action, the anticipated changes in mutual consequences over time, predictive cues, and the socially structured constraints of roles on behavior and its circumstances.

It might be argued that if individuals are producers of their own environments, then there is no one remaining to be influenced. One's behavior, of course, is not the sole determinant of subsequent events. As we have seen, situational constraints, the roles people occupy, and many other factors partly determine what one can or cannot do in response to how others behave. Moreover, reciprocal influences occur in alternating patterns rather than concurrently. It is precisely because influences are altered by their reciprocal effects that unidirectional control rarely exists. Rather, counterinfluences undergo reciprocal adjustments during ongoing sequences of interactions.

The inadvertent production of coercive conduct in children is a familiar illustration of how the interdependent influences change with successive feedback (Patterson, 1976). Children's mild requests often go unheeded, because the parent is uninterested or preoccupied with other matters. If their further bids for attention go unrewarded, children generally intensify their behavior until it becomes aversive to the parent. At this stage in the interaction, the child is exerting coercive control over the parent. Eventually the parent is forced to terminate the aversive behavior by attending to the child, which, in turn, rewards the behavior. Thus, the child exerts coercive influence over the parent, and the parent's reactions unintentionally teach the child to use coercive techniques. Since the child gains parental attention and the parent gains temporary peace, the behavior of both participants is reinforced, although the long-term effects benefit neither.

Detrimental reciprocal systems are readily created and mutually sustained when adverse social practices evoke coercive behavior, which, due to its aversive properties, gains periodic benefits likely to perpetuate it. Analyses of the sequential probabilities of behavior in family interactions by Patterson and his colleagues reveal how family members become, through interlocking contingencies, both developers and victims of coercive relationships (Patterson, 1982). Family members learn to control each other by behavior that inflicts pain in families lacking positive reciprocity. If positive behavior is not reciprocated in kind by other family members, each member begins to treat the others inconsiderately. Antagonistic behavior accelerates aggressive counteractions in an escalating power struggle. By escalating reciprocal aggression, each member provides the aversive instigation for the other, and each member is periodically reinforced for behaving coercively by overpowering the other through more painful counteractions. Aversive reciprocal systems can be converted to more wholesome ones by reducing the success of coercive conduct, developing constructive ways of securing consideration from others, and raising the level of positive reciprocity (Patterson & Reid, 1973; Weinrott, Bauske, & Patterson, 1979).

DETERMINISM AND FORTUITOUS DETERMINANTS OF LIFE PATHS

Analyzing determinism in terms of triadic reciprocality of influence clarifies how people are influenced by, and are influencers of, their environment. However, there is a fortuitous element in some of the events they may encounter in their daily lives. Yet, it is such fortuitous encounters that often play a prominent role in shaping the course of lives. A comprehensive theory must therefore include the fortuitous determinants of life paths if it is to provide a full explanation of human behavior.

Psychological theories of human development focus extensively on the growth of cognitive and behavioral competencies, especially during the early formative years. But the fundamental issue of what determines people's life paths has received little attention. Knowledge of cognitive and behavioral competencies does not, in itself, tell us much about what course personal lives will take. Several factors may account for the neglect of this crucial aspect of human development.

Developmental Determinism

Most developmental models of human behavior presuppose a developmental determinism, in which childhood experiences set the course of later development. According to psychoanalytic theory (Freud, 1933), personality patterns are firmly set in the first few years of life. Thereafter, the child's inner life becomes the major source of action and the definer of social reality. Socialization theories, while granting that discordant changes can occur, nevertheless tend to view life patterns as largely the product of childhood socialization (Goslin, 1969). Stage theorists portray development in terms of an invariant succession of distinct stages (Piaget & Inhelder, 1969). People may differ in the rate and final level of their development, but the path itself has been foreordained.

The appearance of continuities in the lives of many people adds credence to the primacy of early experience. The scholastically gifted are more likely than school truants to enter the ranks of eminent scientists. The metamorphoses of social isolates into vivacious personalities, or aggressors into passive personalities, are not all that common. There are two psychological processes by which the products of early development can foster continuity of behavioral patterns. One process operates through the selection of environments, the second through the production of environments. After people acquire certain preferences and standards of behavior, they tend to select activities and associates who share similar value systems, thereby mutually reinforcing preexisting bents (Bandura & Walters, 1959; Bullock & Merrill, 1980; Elkin & Westley, 1955). Through their actions, people create as well as select environments. By constructing their own circumstances, they achieve some regularity in

behavior (Bandura, 1977a; Raush et al., 1974).

Continuity has a distinct meaning when it is applied to particular forms of behavior, but it becomes quite indefinite where life paths are concerned. One can always find linkages between early and later endeavors, as, for example, between the pursuit of scholarship in childhood and professional careers in adulthood. However, at this level of generality, continuity can be achieved through a variety of life paths. Personal lives, whether marked by continuities or discontinuities, have their particular characters. A theory must, therefore, specify factors that set and alter particular life courses.

Theorists who approach human development from a life-span perspective call attention to the need for an expanded orientation to the study of lives (Baltes, Reese, & Lipsitt, 1980; Brim & Kagan, 1980). In this view, the environment is treated not as a situational entity but as a varied succession of life events that vary in their properties to affect the direction lives take (Brim & Ryff, 1980; Hultsch & Plemons, 1979). Some of these include biological events, many comprise customary social events, others involve unpredictable occurrences in the physical world, and still others involve irregular life events such as career changes, divorce, migration, accidents, and illness.

Social and technological changes alter, often considerably, the kinds of life events that become customary. Even life experiences of successive cohorts (generations), under the same social conditions, will differ because they are encountered at different points in the life span (Elder, 1981). Thus, for example, economic prosperity or depression will affect more profoundly career pursuits of those entering adulthood than those of cohorts who have passed through such conditions at a younger age. The impact of sociocultural change on life patterns—economic depressions, wars and cultural upheavals, technological revolutions, and other social events that make life markedly different—therefore receives attention within the life-span framework.

Whatever the social conditions might be,

there is still the task of explaining the varied directions that personal lives take at any given time and place. This requires a personal, as well as a social, analysis of life paths. Analysis of behavioral patterns across the life span reveals that fortuitous encounters often exert an important influence on the course of human lives (Bandura, 1982c). The power of most fortuitous influences lies not in the properties of the events themselves but in the interactive processes they initiate.

Chance Encounters as Contributing Determinants of Life Paths

A chance encounter is defined as an unintended meeting of persons unfamiliar to each other. Consider, by way of example, the following fortuitous encounter that profoundly altered this person's life. Paul Watkins was a talented teenager headed on a promising course of personal development—he enjoyed a close family life, was well liked by his peers, excelled in academic activities, and served as student-body president of his high school, hardly the omens of a disordered destiny (Watkins & Soledad, 1979). One day he decided to visit a friend who lived in a cabin in Topanga Canyon in Los Angeles. Unbeknownst to Watkins, the friend had since moved elsewhere, and the Manson "family" now lived there. This fortuitous visit led to a deep entanglement in the Manson gang, in the period before they embarked on their "helter, skelter" killings. To an impressionable youth, the free flow of communal love, group sex, drugs, spellbinding revelations of divine matters, and isolation from the outside world provided a heady counterforce that launched him on a divergent life path requiring years to turn his life around again.

In the preceding case, the initial meeting was entirely due to happenstance. Human encounters involve degrees of fortuitiveness. People often intentionally seek certain types of experiences, but the persons who, thereby, enter their lives are determined by a large element of chance. It is not uncommon for college students to decide to sample a given subject matter, only to leave the enrollment in a particular course to the vagaries of time allocation and course scheduling. Through this semifortuitous process, some meet inspiring teachers who have a decisive influence on the students' choice of career during this formative period.

Such a twist of events launched one of my colleagues into an academic career in psychology. Having to fulfill an area distribution requirement, he was faced with a choice between either two philosophy courses or an additional course in psychology, a subject which he had grown to dislike through contact with instructors unburdened by infectious enthusiasm. Choosing what he viewed to be the lesser of two woes, he opted for a psychology course that enjoyed some popularity. However, because of heavy overenrollment, an additional section had to be created, a gifted scholar was persuaded to teach it on short notice, and the disconsolate undergraduate had the good fortune to be cast into it. What he discovered was very much to his liking. This compounded fortuity of distribution requirements, overenrollment, faculty recruitment, and chance section assignment set a career path. Had any one of these factors been absent, his occupational pursuit would doubtless have taken an entirely different course. A striking finding in the analysis of life histories (Stagner, 1981) is that people often embark designedly on a particular vocational pursuit only to be redirected by fortuitous factors along an entirely different career path.

One can similarly document the influential role that initial chance encounters often play in the formation of marriage partnerships. People, whose paths would otherwise have never crossed, are brought together through a fortuitous constellation of events. While attending a speech devoted to this topic (Bandura, 1982c), a science editor quickly took the nearest seat available as the room filled up. The fortuitous meeting with the person in the adjoining seat eventually led to their marriage. With only a momentary change in the time of entry, seating constellations would have altered, and this particular social intersect would probably never have occurred. A marital partnership was thus fortuitously formed at a talk devoted to fortuitous determinants of life paths! A further variant of fortuity includes scenarios in which chance events give rise to arranged encounters that alter life paths. Nancy Davis met her future husband, Ronald Reagan, through such a turn of events (Reagan & Libby, 1980). While pursuing her acting career, she began to receive announcements of communist meetings in the mail intended for another person bearing the same name, which appeared on a Hollywood list of communist sympathizers. Fearing that her career might be jeopardized by mistaken identity, she voiced concern to her film director, who arranged a meeting with Ronald Reagan, then president of the Screen Actors Guild. Before long they were wed. In this instance, a coincidental likeness of names and a postal mix-up altered the course of lives.

The discussion thus far has focused on direct chance encounters that profoundly affect life paths. Sometimes the path-setting event involves a fortuitous symbolic encounter mediated through another's actions. In his Nobel lecture, Herbert Brown (1980) recounted how he happened to decide to pursue doctoral research in the exotic area of boron hydrides. As a baccalaureate gift, his girlfriend presented him with a copy of the book, *The Hydrides of Boron and Silicon*, which launched his interest in the subject. This was during the Depression when money was scarce. She happened to select this particular chemistry book undesignedly, because it was the least expensive one ($2.06) available in the university bookstore. Had his girlfriend been a bit more affluent, Brown's research career would in all likelihood have taken a different route.

As the preceding examples illustrate, some of the most important determinants of life paths often arise through the most trivial of circumstances. Although the separate chains of events in a chance encounter have their own causal determinants, their intersection occurs fortuitously rather than through deliberate plan (Nagel, 1961). The profusion of independent chains of events provides myriad opportunities for fortuitous intersects.

Predicting the Impact of Fortuitous Intersects

Some chance encounters touch people only lightly, others leave more lasting effects, and still others branch people into new trajectories of life. Psychology cannot foretell the occurrence of particular fortuitous intersects, however sophisticated its knowledge of human behavior. The unforeseeability and branching power of fortuitous influences makes the specific course of lives neither easily predictable nor easily socially engineerable. Fortuity of influence does not mean that behavior is undetermined. The unforeseeability of determinants and the determination of actions, by whatever events happen to occur, are separate matters. Fortuitous influences may be unforeseeable, but having occurred, they enter as evident factors in causal chains, in the same way as prearranged ones do. A science of psychology does not have much to say about the occurrence of fortuitous intersects, except that personal proclivities, the settings in which one moves, and the kinds of people who populate those settings make some types of intersects more probable than others. However, psychology can provide the basis for predicting the nature, scope, and strength of the impact these encounters will have on human lives.

Analyses of the power of chance encounters to inaugurate enduring change generally emphasize personal susceptibilities to social influence. These are usually treated as personal vulnerabilities in influences judged to be negative and as personal competencies in influences that lead toward beneficial futures. Personal attributes certainly play a significant role in determining what changes, if any, fortuitous influences may produce. However, the attributes of social environments into which persons are fortuitously inducted also operate as highly influential determiners of degree and direction of personal change. Indeed, closed social systems, wielding strong coercive and rewarding power, can work profound irreversible changes even in the seemingly invulnerable. As the Watkins case cited earlier illustrates, even the best laid personal foundations can be undermined by powerful group influences. Neither personal proclivities nor situational imperatives operate as independent shapers of life courses. Chance encounters affect life paths through the reciprocal influence of personal and social factors.

Personal Determinants of the Impact of Chance Encounters

Entry Skills. If persons are to affiliate with those whom they have had the good or bad fortune to meet, they must possess at least some of the personal resources needed to gain sufficient acceptance to sustain their continued involvement with them. Mismatches of attributes and interests cut short fortuitous encounters through lack of interest or rejection. Personal attributes mediate the effects of fortuitous encounters on life paths in another important way. The skills and interests people cultivate determine the circles in which they move and, hence, the kinds of social encounters they are most likely to experience. The contrasting everyday activities of students in Ivy League colleges and delinquent gangs will bring them into contact with quite different types of associates.

Different affiliations cultivate different interests and skills. Individuals contribute to their own destiny by developing potentialities that afford access to particular social milieus. The branching power of fortuitous encounters is most graphically revealed when a chance incident can permanently alter the course of people's lives by bringing them into an entirely new circle of associates. Induction into a markedly different group is unlikely to take hold without adequate preparedness of at least an entry level of attributes required by the group.

Groups vary in the types and level of entry skills they demand for rewarding affiliation. Chance encounters are more likely to produce converts to undemanding life styles than to those built by toil on complex competencies. Thus, for example, to gain entry into an enclave of molecular biologists would require substantial knowledge of science and academic skills achievable only by arduous effort over a long period. Other groups, such as quasi-religious cults and authoritarian collectives, initially require little beyond that of personal compliance (Richardson, 1978). The all-too-easy entry into semiclosed milieus arouses public fears about the hazards such groups pose for young people's futures. Groups relying on deceptive recruitment and heavy-handed constraints to bar defections are of the greatest concern to the public.

Emotional Ties. Chance meetings are most likely to affect life courses when individuals come to like the people they meet or gain other satisfactions from them. Interpersonal attraction seals chance encounters into lasting bonds. Once established, binding relationships serve as a vehicle for personal changes that can have long-range effects.

The way in which an encounter can set events in motion that alter the entire course of a person's life through a subsequent affectional involvement is vividly documented by the tragic case of Diana Oughton (Powers, 1971). She was a sensitive, gentle woman whose background and personal attributes contradicted the common correlates of political activism. While on a humanitarian mission abroad, she happened to meet a visiting scholar who, having grown cynical about the prospects for peaceful social change, argued persuasively that only revolutionary force could bring the needed social reforms. This encounter set her on the path of militant action. Upon her return to the United States, she became increasingly involved in the Students for a Democratic Society which, at the time, was splintering into opposing ideological camps. She was drawn into the violent Weatherman faction, not by studied design, but through affectional attachment to a leader of this faction. Her brief career as a revolutionary ended with tragic suddenness in a townhouse bomb factory, when a bomb intended to help destroy the society she had come to hate took her life instead.

Values and Personal Standards. Human behavior is partly governed by value preferences and self-evaluative standards (Bandura, 1977a). Through internal guidance, people give direction to their lives and derive satisfaction from what they do. Valuational mechanisms, therefore, partly govern the extent to which chance encounters may shape the course of personal development. Fortuitous influences are more likely to leave their marks if the persons involved share similar standards and value systems than if they clash.

Lives follow less predictable courses when personal standards have been inadequately developed, and there is much cultural confusion about what is valued. In the absence of internal guides and normative consensus, fortuitous influences hold sway more easily. The cultural upheaval of the recent past—when countercultures were springing up around mystical and religious cults, makeshift communes, drugs, and merchandised human potential movements —left many dislocated lives in its wake.

Personal vulnerability to recruitment into unusual life paths has aroused the greatest interest in relation to cultist influences (Bromley & Shupe, 1979; Singer, 1979). For the most part, the recruits to quasi-religious cults and regimented communes are teenagers and young adults who feel lonely and despondent, who find their lives devoid of meaning, and who lack career skills around which to organize their lives. Cults provide instant friendship, an ideology that gives purpose and meaning to one's existence, and a communal regimen that imposes order on one's everyday activities. For youths leading unhappy and empty lives, cultist offerings can hold considerable appeal.

Social Determinants of the Impact of Fortuitous Encounters

Milieu Rewards. The course that human behavior follows is substantially influenced by the effects it produces. Hence, the rewards a group provides play a crucial role in determining whether chance encounters will enduringly link individuals to groups that favor certain life paths over others. In studies in which the social rewards are systematically varied, individuals affiliate with groups when social rewards are high but withdraw from them when rewards are low (Baer & Wolf, 1970).

Groups can supply a variety of benefits. Because individuals differ in what they value and desire, they may become strongly attracted to a particular social milieu for quite varied reasons. Whatever the initial affiliative inducements might be, once individuals become attached to a primary group, they are socialized into its ideology and life style through a vast network of proximal rewards and social sanctions that members provide for each other in their daily transactions.

Symbolic Environment and Information Management. Constraints of time, resources, and physical separation impose severe limits on the amount of information that can be gained through direct personal experience. To a large extent people, therefore, must act on their images of reality. Fortuitous induction into a group not only brings one into contact with new incentive systems, it furnishes a distinctive symbolic environment as well. Symbolic systems help build affinity and solidarity and shape ideological perspectives on life. A libertine who, through an unusual turn of events, becomes converted to a born-again religion will come to experience a markedly different social and symbolic life. Through a similar inaugural process, individuals who choose paths that lead to medical schools, athletic fields, or to the theatrical world become deeply immersed in distinctive symbolic environments.

In a pluralistic society, groups embracing diverse ideologies must vie for attention and influence. As a result, the persuasiveness of any one group can be attenuated or nullified by the sway of others. In communal life where members are cut off from outside influences, the symbolic system becomes a powerful force that can shape even the most bizarre patterns of collective thought and action (Winfrey, 1979).

Milieu Reach and Closedness. The social contexts within which interpersonal influences operate vary in how extensively they touch personal lives and their degree of closedness. The least confining milieus involve loose alliances centered on a few activities that constrain neither personal ties nor beliefs nor latitude of action. At the opposite end of the continuum are the totalistic milieus structured around an insulated communal life, which prescribes beliefs and behavior patterns for virtually all aspects of living. If needed, heavy-handed methods are used to counteract dissent and defection. In the moderately constraining milieus, personal lives are extensively shaped by one's primary affiliations but active participation in mainstream societal activities creates opportunities for competing influences to exert their effects.

Chance encounters have the greatest potential for abruptly branching people into new trajectories of life when they induct them into a relatively closed milieu. A totalistic environment supplies a pervading new reality—new kinships, strongly held group beliefs and values, all-encompassing codes of conduct, few vestiges of individuality, and substantial rewarding and coercive power to alter the entire course of personal lives (Bromley & Shupe, 1979). Encapsulation is often further buttressed by curtailing personal ties and exposure to influences outside the group.

Psychological Closedness. People seek and hold firmly to beliefs because they serve valuable functions. Indeed, life would be most taxing and chaotic if people had no conceptions of themselves and the world around them. Their experiences would lack coherence. They would have to cede the substantial benefits of foresightfulness, something which requires a conceptual system for predicting conditional happenings in daily affairs. They would lack guides for action, and situational influences would pull them in all directions. And finally, they would be without basic goals for organizing their efforts over long time spans. Belief systems thus help to provide structure, direction, and purpose to life. Because personal identity and security become heavily invested in belief systems, they are not readily discardable once acquired.

Group affiliation instills and strengthens beliefs in accordance with its ideological commitments. Once initiates get caught up in the belief system, it can exert a selective influence on the course of their development for better or for worse, depending on the nature and imperativeness of the creed. Belief systems vary in their immutability, ranging from authoritarian prescriptions to be accepted unquestioningly to provisional conceptions that invite change through experience and critical analyses (Rokeach, 1960). Induction into a group that invests its own system of beliefs with infallability and treats those of others as mistaken, if not evil, erects a psychological closedness to outside influence.

While beliefs provide direction and meaning to experience, they distort it as well. Adherents see what they want to see, reinterpret incongruities to their liking, and even rewrite their memory of events they have experienced (Greenwald, 1980; Snyder, 1980). Moreover, by influencing actions anticipatorily, beliefs channel social interactions in ways that create their own self-validating realities (Snyder, 1981). Thus, through selective perception and processing of information and anticipatory construction of social realities, belief systems take on self-perpetuating properties. Control through indoctrination is much more profound than control through milieu constraints. Once a creed is fully adopted, behavioral adherence to it even in diverse settings no longer requires the presence and sanctions of advocates.

Nonsocial Fortuitous Events

The preceding discussion has centered mainly on fortuitous interpersonal encounters, because most of the influences that alter the course of lives are socially mediated. But nonsocial happenings can also profoundly affect life paths (Munn, 1983). Sometimes major industries spring from happenstance. The Kellogg brothers managed a health sanitarium designed to rid the body of what they saw to be the evils of meat and liquor (Sinclair, 1981). One day while boiling wheat dough to prepare a nutriment that might add variety to the sanitarium menu, they were called away. Upon returning hours later they decided to run the dough through steel rollers, even though it was no longer fresh. During the delay the wheat berries in the dough had absorbed the moisture so that, much to their surprise, the Kellogg brothers got flakes for their patrons, rather than the sheets of wheat they set out to make. The fortuitous delay gave prompt birth to the breakfast-food industry.

Fortuitous happenings often play an important role in scientific discoveries that have changed the course of exploration and scientific careers (Austin, 1978; Cannon, 1945; Merbaum & Lowe, 1982). In conducting their research, investigators try to minimize the operation of extraneous factors, but they can neither foresee nor completely control every event that might occur in an experiment. Imperfect experimental control permits unintended factors to combine in unexplained ways with those factors the investigators have designedly introduced to occasionally produce unexpected results of considerable import. Sometimes the unexpected occurrences arise from unplanned interactions between factors introduced adventitiously. Alexander Fleming, the Nobel laureate, discovered the bactericidal effect of penicillin because his tardiness in discarding old culture dishes gave the penicillin mold sufficient time to develop.

Serendipitous findings will not spawn new directions of research if their significance goes unnoticed. Pasteur put it well when he said that chance favors the prepared mind. Strong preconceptions and competing interests can, however, obscure the apperception of unexpected findings instead of launching a search for their determinants (Mahoney, 1976). More than one scientist may thus accidentally produce the same phenomenon, but one dismisses it, while another grasps its significance and branches out into new research directions (Barber & Fox, 1958). Austin (1978) documents how the combined effects of several personal attributes can contribute to serendipitous scientific discoveries. Ingenuity and individualized interests influence whether investigators introduce critical ingredients into the mixture of events; perseverence in exploratory activities increases the likelihood that events will be combined in new ways; specialized experience and knowledge affect whether the significance of anomalous findings will be recognized and pursued. Austin notes that fortuity favors those who pursue an active life with an inquiring attitude. This is because the pursuit of new experiences increases one's exposure to ideas and people who can branch one into new directions.

Further progress in illuminating the determinants of life paths awaits methodological advances for charting life events and the processes they set into motion to alter the course of lives. Such a procedure should center on the major facets of life, such as educational pursuits, occupational choices, and formation of significant partnerships. Within each of these domains of functioning, the mode of inquiry would ferret out the events that have played a key role in setting the direction of life paths. The primary data for life-path analysis should include the patterns of direction-setting choices and the set of factors that operate at each juncture. Through this technique the network of branching influences operating at different turning points in the life span can be reconstructed. However, the study of life courses need not be solely reconstructive. In a predictive analysis of life paths, the probabilities of a certain path can be estimated from the interactive effects of personal and situational determinants. Knowledge of particular combinations of personal attributes and milieu properties provides the basis for predicting the probability with which alternative directions are likely to be followed.

Fostering Valued Futures

Knowing what factors mediate the impact of chance encounters on life paths provides guides for how to foster and safeguard valued futures. At the personal level, one set of factors concerns the mastery of the means for shaping one's own destiny. A strong sense of personal agency requires the development of competencies, self-percepts of efficacy, and self-regulatory capabilities for exercising self-directedness (Bandura, 1982b). These personal resources expand one's freedom of action and enable people to serve as causal contributors to their own life course by selecting, influencing, and constructing their own circumstances. Mastering the tools of personal agency does not necessarily assure desired futures. But with such skills, people are better able to provide supports and direction for their actions, to capitalize on planned or fortuitous opportunities, to resist social traps that lead down detrimental paths, and to disengage themselves from such predicaments should they become enmeshed in them.

To exercise some measure of control over one's developmental course requires, in addition to effective tools of personal agency, a great deal of social support. Emotional resources are especially important during formative years when preferences and personal standards are in a state of flux, and there are many conflicting sources of influence with which to contend. Social ties contribute in several ways toward the achievement of a secure sense of self-direction. The internal standards through which people influence their own motivation and actions are acquired through modeling and evaluative reactions by significant others (Bandura, 1977a). Self-directed influences do not act as autonomous regulators of behavior. To surmount the obstacles and stresses encountered in the life paths people take, they also need social supports to give incentive, meaning, and worth to what they do. When social ties are weak or lacking, a person's vulnerability is increased to whatever fortuitous influences may offer friendship in exchange for conformity to prescribed life styles and ideologies.

Humans have an unparalleled capability to become many things. The life paths that realistically become open to them are also partly determined by the nature of the cultural agencies to which their development is entrusted. Social systems that cultivate generalizable competencies, provide aidful resources, and allow ample room for self-directedness increase the chances that people will realize what they wish to become.

FREEDOM AND DETERMINISM

The discussion of causal processes raises the fundamental issues of determinism and personal freedom. In examining these questions it is essential to distinguish between the metaphysical and the social aspects of freedom. Many of the disputes on this topic arise as much, if not more, from ambiguities about the dimensions of freedom being discussed as from disagreements over the doctrine of determinism.

Freedom as Exercise of Self-Influence

Freedom is often considered antithetical to determinism. When viewed from a social cognitive perspective, there is no incompatibility between freedom and determinism. Freedom is not conceived negatively as the absence of influences or simply the lack of external constraints. Rather, it is defined positively in terms of the exercise of self-influence. This is achieved through thought, using skills at one's command, and other tools of self-influence which choice of action requires. Self-generated influences operate deterministically on behavior the same way as external sources of influence do. Given the same environmental conditions, persons who have the capabilities for exercising many options and are adept at regulating their own behavior will have greater freedom than will those who have limited means of personal agency. It is because self-influence operates deterministically on action that some measure of freedom is possible.

Judgments regarding environmental factors enter into the choice of particular courses of action from among possible alternatives. Choices are not completely and involuntarily determined by environmental events. Rather, making choices is aided by reflective cognitive activity, through which self-influence is largely exercised. People exert some influence over what they do by the alternatives they consider, how they foresee and weigh the consequences, and how they appraise their capabilities to execute successfully the possibilities they are entertaining. Indeed, it is because thought can affect action that people can make causal contribution to their own behavior. The more novel the circumstances encountered and the more uncertain the environmental information, the more one has to rely on inferential thought for guidance.

Arguments against the causal efficacy of thought and other means of self-influence usually invoke a selective regression of causes. Such analyses emphasize how people's judgments and actions are determined by external events, but they neglect the prior cause in the chain of occurrences, showing that the environmental events themselves are partly determined by people's actions. In the regress of prior causes, for every chicken discovered by a unidirectional environmentalist, a social cognitive theorist can identify a prior egg. Psychological analyses of the mechanisms of personal agency show how people can contribute to the attainment of deserved futures by regulating their own behavior. They direct their efforts toward valued goals by enlisting cognitive guides and self-incentives and by arranging environmental conditions conducive to goal attainment. Individuals may be told how to go about this process and be given some initial external support for their efforts, but that does not negate the fact that self-produced influences also contribute to future goal attainment. Any account of the determinants of human action must, therefore, include self-generated influences as a contributing factor.

To say that people contribute to the nature of their situations does not mean that they are the sole authors of them. Numerous other influences—some social, some institutional, and some physical—also contribute to the shape situations take. Because people are only partially the authors of their situations, the analysis of interactive determinants does not invite an infinite regress in which behavior is determined solely by past behavior. Rather, behavior is determined by a multiauthored influence.

Nor is determinism incompatible with personal responsibility. The capability for self-influence carries the responsibilities as well as the benefits of self-directedness. Behavior always involves choices from among the various options one can pursue in a particular situation. In the face of situational inducements to behave in a particular way, persons can, and do, choose to behave otherwise by exerting counteracting self-influence. Obviously, they are not the sole source of the determinants, but they do contribute partly to their own actions, which shape the nature of their situations. Because persons can exercise some degree of control over how situations will influence them, they cannot be entirely absolved of the responsibility for their behavior. Partial personal causation of action involves at least partial responsibility for it. If, in fact, people's actions were exclusively dictated by external forces, it would be pointless to hold anyone accountable for whatever he or she might do. Transgressors would not be answerable for their crimes, judges for their sentencing practices (Frankl, 1971), jailers for their treatment of inmates, and the citizenry for the criminogenic social conditions their public policies breed.

The long-standing debate over the issue of freedom was enlivened by Skinner's (1971) contention that, apart from genetic contributions, human behavior is controlled solely by environmental contingencies. A major problem with this type of analysis is that it depicts the environment as autonomously and automatically shaping and controlling behavior. Environments have causes, as do behaviors. As was previously shown, behavior partly creates the environment, and the environment reciprocally influences the behavior.

To contend, as environmental determinists do, that people are controlled by external forces and then to advocate that they redesign society by applying the psychotechnologies created by the experts contradicts the basic premise of the argument. If humans were, in fact, incapable of influencing their own actions, they might describe and forecast environmental events, but they could not exercise any intentional control over them. When it comes to the advocacy of social change, however, thoroughgoing environmental determinists become ardent advocates of people's power to shape their future by altering their environment. Boring (1957) provided a thoughtful analysis of the "egocentric predicament" in which advocatory environmental determinists get themselves entangled by regarding themselves as self-directing but others as being externally determined. Advocates thus exempt themselves from the thoroughgoing environmental control that presumably shepherds the rest of the populace; otherwise, the advocate's own views simply become conditioned utterances that hold no special truth value. However, should members of the populace adopt the theory and techniques of the advocate, they are suddenly conferred freedom to improve their lives and to exercise some control over their own future.

In backward causal analyses, environmental events are usually portrayed as ruling people, whereas forward deterministic analyses of the goals that people set for themselves and their later attainments reveal how people can shape conditions to suit their own purposes. Some are better at it than others. The greater their foresight, proficiency, and their means of self-influence, all of which are acquirable skills, the greater the progress toward their goals. Because of the capacity for reciprocal influence, people are at least partial architects of their own destinies. It is not the principle of determinism that is in dispute but whether determinism should be treated as a one-sided or a two-way process. Because of the bidirectional causality in personal and environmental factors, determinism does not imply the fatalistic view that people are only pawns of external forces.

Psychological perspectives on determinism, like other aspects of theorizing, influence the nature and scope of research and social practice. Environmental determinists tend to apply one-sided paradigms to bidirectional processes. Environmental control is minutely analyzed, while personal control is relatively neglected. To cite one example, there exist countless demonstrations of how behavior varies under different schedules of reward, but one can look in vain for studies of how people succeed, either individually or by collective action, to negotiate reward schedules to their own liking. The scarcity of research on personal control is not because people exert no influence on their environment or because such efforts are without effect. Quite the contrary. Most of the systems of incentives, wage contracts, and social sanctions that affect important aspects of social living are instituted and altered by the exercise of collective influence. A theory of limited inclusiveness may receive support from findings generated by its own paradigm for the things it studies but may offer a deficient conception of human behavior because of the phenomena it chooses to disregard. Thus, a theory generating evidence that incentives can affect actions may have little to say about human memory if advocates of the theory rarely study it. The adequacy of a theory must, therefore, be measured by its power to explain, predict, and effect change in diverse aspects of psychosocial functioning (Lacey, 1979).

Environmental determinists are apt to use their methods primarily in the service of institutionally prescribed patterns of behavior. Personal determinists are more inclined to attempt to cultivate people's potential for self-direction. Social cognitive and humanistic approaches have much in common in emphasizing the development of human potential and self-direction. Social learning theory however, does not regard "self-actualization" as impelled by an inborn drive which, if externally unencumbered, will necessarily produce competencies and the best human qualities. Personal development profits more from guidance and support that cultivate interests and skills for realizing personal potentialities than from dwelling on how not to thwart an inborn drive. "Self-actualization" is by no means confined to human virtues alone. People have vast potentialities that can be actualized for good or ill. Over the years, many have suffered considerably, and will continue to do so, at the hands of self-actualized egotists and tyrants. A self-centered ethic of self-realization must, therefore, be tempered by concern for the social consequences of one's conduct.

When the environment is regarded as an autonomous rather than as an influenceable determinant of behavior, the valuation of human dignity and accomplishments is diminished. If inventiveness stems from external circumstances, environments should be honored for people's achievements and chastised for their failings or inhumanities. Contrary to the unidirectional view, human accomplishments result from the reciprocal influences of external circumstances, a host of personal determinants, including endowed potentialities, acquired competencies, reflective thought, and a high level of self-initiative. Composers and their interpreters, for example, help to shape musical tastes by their creative efforts, and the public, in turn, supports their activities, until advocates of new styles generate new public preferences. Each succeeding form of artistry results from a similar two-way influence process for which neither the artists nor the circumstances deserve sole credit.

Superior accomplishments, whatever the field, require considerable self-disciplined application. After individuals adopt standards of excellence, they spend large amounts of time, on their own, improving their performances to the point of self-satisfaction. At this level of functioning, persistence is an endeavor under self-evaluative control. Creative endeavors are pursued and skills are perfected as much, or more, to please oneself as to please the public.

Without self-generated influences, most innovative effort would be difficult to sustain. This is because the unconventional is initially resisted and is accepted gradually, only as it proves functionally valuable or wins prestigious advocates. As a result, the early efforts of innovators generally bring rebuffs rather than rewards or recognition. In the history of creative endeavors, it is not uncommon for artists, composers, and social reformers to be scorned when they depart markedly from conventional forms and styles. Some gain recognition later in their careers. Others are sufficiently convinced of the worth of their work that they labor tirelessly, even though their productions are ignored or devalued throughout their lifetimes. Ideological and, to a lesser extent, technological changes follow similar courses. While innovative endeavors may receive occasional social support in early phases, environmental conditions alone are not especially conducive to unconventional endeavors.

Freedom as Options and Rights

When viewed from a social perspective, freedom is defined by the number of options available to people and their right to exercise them. The more behavioral alternatives and prerogatives people have, the greater is their freedom of action. Freedom is thus a social reality of considerable import rather than an illusion or simply a philosophical notion, as some writers have maintained.

Personal freedom can be limited in many different ways. Deficiencies in knowledge and skills restrict possible choices and otherwise curtail opportunities to realize personal preferences. Freedom can, therefore, be fostered by cultivating competencies that serve varied pursuits. The use to which people put their knowledge and skills partly depends on their self-percepts of efficacy. Those who believe themselves to be inefficacious constrain their options and fearfully avoid activities, even though they are within their capabilities. In addition to personal encumbrances resulting from self-disbeliefs and accompanying fears, the restraints of stringent internal standards restrict the range of activities in which individuals can engage. When constraints are cognitively based, freedom is expanded by instilling affirmative self-beliefs and altering self-impeding internal standards.

In maximizing freedom, a society must place some limits on conduct because complete license for any individual will encroach on the freedom of others. Societal prohibitions against behavior that is socially injurious create additional curbs on conduct. There are few disagreements about placing limits on behavior that directly injures or seriously infringes on the rights of others. Conflict often arises, however, over be-havioral restrictions when many members of society question conventional customs and when legal sanctions are used more to enforce a particular brand of morality than to prohibit socially detrimental conduct.

The issue of whether individuals should be allowed to engage in activities that are self-injurious but not detrimental to society has been debated vigorously over the years. Prohibitionists argue that it is difficult for anyone, other than a recluse, to impair him- or herself without inflicting secondary harm on others. Should self-injury produce incapacities, society usually ends up bearing the costs of treatment and subsistence. Others argue from a moral, rather than an empirical, perspective that a society has an obligation to prohibit people from debasing themselves. Libertarians do not find such arguments sufficiently convincing to justify a specific prohibition, because some of the self-injurious activities that society allows may be as bad or worse than many it outlaws. Normative changes over time regarding private conduct generally favor an individualistic ethic. Consequently, many activities that at one time were prohibited by law have now been exempted from legal sanctions. Legal remedies for conduct that some segments of society regard as immoral, but many do not, receive low compliance at high costs of stigmatizing nonconformists and discrediting enforcement systems (Kaplan, 1971). In such instances, laws eventually accommodate to the prevailing social customs.

The freedom of disfavored groups is often curtailed by socially sanctioned discrimination. Here, the alternatives available to a person are prejudicially limited by skin color, sex, religion, ethnic background, or social class, regardless of capabilities. When self-determination is restricted by institutionalized prejudices, those who are affected strive to gain the freedom enjoyed by other segments of the society by removing inequitable social practices.

The exercise of freedom involves rights as well as options and the means to pursue them. Struggles for freedom are principally aimed at creating institutional safeguards that exempt certain forms of behavior from coercive control. At the collective level, the freedoms people enjoy are instituted in the social structure. The less social jurisdiction there is over certain activities, the greater is the causal contribution of self-influence to choice of action in those domains. After protective laws are built into the system, there are certain things that a society may not do to individuals who choose to challenge conventional values or vested interests, however much it might like to. Legal prohibitions against unauthorized societal control create personal freedoms that are realities, not illusory abstractions. Societies differ in their institutions of freedom and in the number and type of activities that are officially exempted from punitive control. Social systems that protect journalists from criminal sanctions for criticizing government officials, for example, are freer than those that allow authoritative power to be used to silence critics or their vehicles of expression. Societies that possess a judiciary independent of other government institutions ensure greater social freedom than those that do not.

Reciprocal Influence and the Limits of Social Control

The operation of reciprocal influence bears importantly on the public's concern that advances in psychological knowledge will heighten the calculated manipulation and control of people. A common rejoinder of environmental determinists to such fears is that all behavior is inevitably controlled. Social influence, therefore, does not entail imposing controls where none have existed before. This type of argument has some cogency in the sense that every act has a set of prior causes, although, as we have seen, not all of the contributing determinants reside in the environment. But it is not the principle of causality that worries people. At the societal level, their misgivings center on the distribution of controlling power, the means and purposes for which knowledge is used,

and the availability of mechanisms for exercising reciprocal influence over institutional practices. At the individual level, they are uneasy about the implications of psychotechnology for programming human relations. Enlarging the knowledge and the methods of social influence does not necessarily raise the level of social control. This is because the personal and social mechanisms of reciprocal influence place constraints on how much people can control each other.

Individual Safeguards

Possible remedies for exploitative use of psychological knowledge and methods of influence are usually discussed in terms of individual safeguards. Increasing people's knowledge about the means of social influence is prescribed as the best defense against such manipulation. When people are informed about how behavior can be swayed, they tend to resist evident attempts at influence, thus making manipulation more difficult. Awareness alone, however, is a weak countervalence. People are fully aware that advertisers attempt to influence their purchasing behavior by exaggerated claims, modeled testimonials, pseudo-experiments demonstrating the superiority of their products, paired association with emotion evokers, and portrayal of the benefits secured to product users. Such knowledge does not make people immune to advertising influences. The same is true of persuasion through response consequences. Coercion can extract compliance, and rewards can induce accommodating behavior, even though people recognize that the incentives are influencing their actions.

Exploitation was successfully thwarted long before the discipline of psychology existed to formulate principles and means of social influence. A reliable personal source of counterinfluence to manipulative control resides in the reciprocal consequences of human transactions. People resist being taken advantage of, and will continue to do so in the future, because compliant behavior often produces unfavorable consequences for them. Sophisticated efforts at influence in no way reduce the aversiveness of yielding to that which is personally disadvantageous. Because of reciprocal consequences, no one is able to manipulate others at will, and everyone experiences some feeling of powerlessness in getting what they want. This is true at all levels of functioning, both individual and collective. Parents cannot get their children to follow all their wishes, while children feel constrained by their parents in doing what they desire. At universities, the administrators, faculty, students, and alumni each feel that the other constituencies are unduly influential in promoting their self-interests but that they themselves have insufficient power to alter the institutional practices. In the political arena, Congress feels that the executive branch possesses excessive power, and, conversely, the executive branch feels thwarted in implementing its policies by congressional counteraction.

Social Safeguards

If protection against exploitation relied solely upon individual safeguards, people would be continually subjected to the most unscrupulous and coercive pressures. Accordingly, people create institutional sanctions which set limits on the control of human behavior. The integrity of individuals is largely secured by societal safeguards that place constraints on improper means of influence and foster reciprocity through the balancing of interests. This is achieved by establishing formal mechanisms for exercising reciprocal influence over organizational practices through legal systems, regulatory agencies, due process of law, and elective procedures. Institutional reciprocal mechanisms not only safeguard against arbitrary and coercive control, they provide the means for changing institutions and policies that affect the conditions of life. The limits set by law and social rules on the degree and form of control people can exercise over each other tend to be overlooked

in discussions of the social implications of psychological knowledge.

Because individuals are conversant with psychological means of influence does not grant them license to use them to control others. Industrialists, for example, know full well that productivity is higher when payment is made for amount of work completed rather than for the length of time at work. Nevertheless, they cannot use the incentive system that is most advantageous to them. When industrialists commanded exclusive power, they paid workers at a piece-rate basis and hired and fired them at will. Reductions in the disparity of power between employers and employees resulted in a gradual change in the nature of the contingency contracts. As workers gained coercive economic strength through collective action, they were able to negotiate guaranteed wages on a daily, weekly, monthly, and eventually on an annual basis. At periodic intervals new contractual contingencies are adopted that are mutually acceptable. Over the course of time, as better means of collective action are developed, other constituents use their influence to modify arrangements that benefit certain segments of labor and industry but may adversely affect the environment and quality of life for other sectors of society.

As the previous example illustrates, improved knowledge about how to influence behavior does not necessarily raise the level of social control. If anything, recent years have witnessed the diffusion of power, creating increased opportunities to further personal and shared purposes through reciprocal instruments of influence. This has enabled people to challenge social inequities, to effect changes in institutional practices, to counteract infringements on their rights, and to extend grievance procedures and due process of law to activities in social contexts that hitherto operated under unilateral control. The fact that more people can wield power does not, in and of itself, ensure a humane society. In the final analysis, the important consideration is the purposes that power serves, however it might be distributed. Nor does knowledge about means of psychological influence necessarily produce mechanical responsiveness in personal relations. Whatever their orientations in their efforts at mutual influence, people model, expound, and reward what they value. Behavior arising out of purpose and commitment is no less genuine than improvised action.

Novels depicting authoritarian systems and utopian societies based on behavioral principles generate public fear that a particular mode of life may be imposed on everyone. Advocates of utopian societies prescribe the life styles they like. Since personal preferences differ widely, most people question the values reflected either in the specific prescriptions of a particular utopia or in the value orientation of the whole design. Even those who regard the guiding values as acceptable, nevertheless express concern over the homogenization of life within a single social arrangement. Others fear that should the instruments of influence fall into the wrong hands, they could be used to engineer public consent for authoritarian rule or benevolent despotism. What is intended as a visionary process for an experimenting society thus becomes a frightening prospect.

When only a single form of utopian social living is presented as founded on psychological principles, as in *Walden Two* (Skinner, 1948), the means for developing better social systems get confounded with the particular brand of life style that is being promulgated. As a result, effective means of achieving human ideals are repudiated because the mode of life being advocated may be uninviting. Psychological principles can be separated from particular ideologies and social practices by exemplifying alternative types of social living founded on the same principles. Under a pluralistic framework, people have options as to which life styles they wish to pursue. Those who do not find a particular form of life to their liking can try other forms. Wholesale manipulation is difficult to achieve because the value preferences and networks of influences differ across groups. Given the appropriate value commitments, social cognitive principles can be used to cultivate diversity.

Literary futurists, conjuring up scary images of societies populated with human marionettes (Orwell, 1949), divert public attention from less sensational regulative influences that pose continual threats to human welfare. Most societies have instituted reciprocal systems protected by rules of law or social codes to prohibit imperious control of human behavior. Although abuses of institutional power arise from time to time, it is not totalitarian rule that constitutes the impending peril. The hazards lie more in the intentional pursuit of personal gain, whether material or otherwise, than in control by coercion. Detrimental social practices occur and resist change, even within an open society, when many people benefit from them. To take a prevalent example, inequitable treatment of disadvantaged groups for private gain can enjoy public support without requiring despotic rule.

People, of course, have more to contend with than inhumane treatment at the hands of others. When the harmful consequences of otherwise rewarding life styles are delayed and accumulate imperceptibly, people can become willful agents of their own self-destruction. Thus, if enough people derive benefits from activities that progressively degrade their environment, then, barring contravening influences, they will eventually devastate their environment. People are more likely to resist tyrannical authority than the immediate gratification of self-interest.

With growing populations and the spread of life styles emphasizing material consumption, both of which tax finite resources, people will have to learn to cope with new realities of existence. Widespread pursuit of activities that maximize personal rewards can produce harmful consequences that must be borne by all. These new realities will require a greater consideration of, and a heightened sense of responsibility for, the social consequences of one's behavior. Pressures will mount to subordinate individual choices to collective interests. The challenge ahead is the development of social practices which promote the common good in ways that still preserve the greatest possible individual freedom.

Changing widespread practices that are immediately rewarding, but detrimental in the long run, does not necessarily require curtailing freedom of choice. It is a well-established principle that behavior is altered far more effectively by providing better alternatives than by imposing prohibitions. Birth rates, for example, have been substantially reduced through economic development, public enlightenment about the perils of overpopulation, family planning, and the development of birth control devices—without resorting to the restriction of sexual activities or the imposition of breeding quotas. In this case, broader societal interests coincide with individual ones. In other instances, detrimental practices would also be rapidly discarded in favor of more beneficial alternatives if their development were not resisted by vested interests. Dependence on polluting automobiles, which also consume huge quantities of unreplenishable resources, could be diminished faster by providing convenient and economical rapid-transit systems than by continuing to produce millions of automobiles yearly, constructing more freeways, and then increasing the costs and aversiveness of driving cars. Because vast numbers of people benefit financially, either directly or indirectly, from the profusion of automobiles, the restriction of choice to means that produce detrimental effects secures wide public support.

These are but a few examples of how collective survival practices are best promoted by expanding rather than curtailing individual choice. Change is achieved most rapidly by applying a dual strategy that provides advantageous options and raises the costs of traditional practices that produce adverse delayed consequences. When alternative means of obtaining benefits are lacking, people are slow to abandon behavior that operates against their long-term welfare, even in the face of mounting negative consequences.

Psychology cannot tell people how they ought to live their lives. It can, however, provide them with the means for effecting personal and social change. And it can aid them in making value choices by assessing the effects of alternative life styles and institutional arrangements. As a science concerned with the social consequences of its applications, psychology must promote public understanding of psychological issues that bear on social policies to ensure that its findings are used in the service of human betterment.

2
OBSERVATIONAL LEARNING

If knowledge could be acquired only through the effects of one's own actions, the process of cognitive and social development would be greatly retarded, not to mention exceedingly tedious. The constraints of time, resources, and mobility impose severe limits on the situations and activities that can be directly explored. Without informative guidance, much of one's efforts would be expended on costly errors and needless toil. Fortunately, most human behavior is learned by observation through modeling. By observing others, one forms rules of behavior, and on future occasions this coded information serves as a guide for action. Because people can learn approximately what to do through modeling before they perform any behavior, they are spared the costs and pain of faulty effort. The capacity to learn by observation enables people to expand their knowledge and skills on the basis of information exhibited and authored by others. Much social learning is fostered by observing the actual performances of others and the consequences for them. However, a special virtue of modeling is that it can transmit simultaneously knowledge of wide applicability to vast numbers of people through the medium of symbolic models. By drawing on conceptions of behavior portrayed in words and images, observers can transcend the bounds of their immediate environment.

DIFFERENTIATION OF MODELING PHENOMENA

Through the years, modeling has always been acknowledged to be one of the most powerful means of transmitting values, attitudes, and patterns of thought and behavior. In psychological theorizing and research the modeling process, or at least certain aspects of it, is called by different names. Following conceptual traditions, many theorists have conceptualized modeling as *imitation*. They view it as a process by which one organism matches the actions of another, usually close in time. The conceptualization of modeling as simply response mimicry has left a legacy that minimizes the power of modeling and has limited the scope of research for many years. Studies conducted within this tradition have been largely confined to paradigms in which a model performs a few responses, and observers are tested for precise reproduction of the modeled behavior in similar situations. Such studies can yield only mimicry of specific acts. In actuality, in cultivating human competencies, modeling imparts conceptions and rules for generating variant forms of behavior to suit different purposes and circumstances. In skill acquisition, modeling is more accurately represented as rule learning than as response mimicry. Nevertheless, theorists, who accept the mimicry conception at face value, place arbitrary limitations on the psychological changes that can be achieved by modeling influences.

Drawing on the psychodynamic tradition, a number of personality theorists and developmentalists interpret modeling processes as *identification*. Except for the common assumption that identification involves wholesale incorporation of personality patterns, there has been little agreement among its proponents on how the construct should be conceptualized. Identification means different things to different writers. They variously ascribe identification with the adoption of either diverse patterns of behavior (Kohlberg, 1963; Parsons, 1955), symbolic representation of the model (Emmerich, 1959), similar meaning systems (Lazowick, 1955), or motives, values, ideals, and conscience (Gewirtz & Stingle, 1968).

Identification is also frequently distinguished from imitation in terms of the determinants assumed to apply to each. In Parsons's (1951) view, identification requires a "generalized cathectic attachment" to the model, but imitation does not. Kohlberg (1963) reserves the term identification for matching behavior that is presumably sustained by the intrinsic satisfactions derived from perceived similarity. He considers imitation to be matching behavior that is supported by extrinsic rewards. Others define matching behavior in the presence of the model as imitation, and matching behavior performed in the model's absence as identification (Kohlberg, 1963; Mowrer, 1950). Not only is there little consensus of how imitation should be distinguished from identification, but some theorists assume that imitation produces identification, while others contend, with equally strong conviction, that identification produces imitation!

The arbitrary distinctions noted above receive little support from empirical evidence (Bandura, 1971a). The same factors influence, in much the same way, observational learning of a specific behavior or a set of behaviors. All modeled information must be symbolically represented if it is to be retained as a guide for future action. Hence, there is little to be gained from seeking differentiation in terms of symbolic representation. Neither theory nor evidence can really support the view that modeled activities later performed in the model's presence were originally learned by different processes than those later performed in the model's absence. To define modeling by what sustains the resultant behavior is to confuse its source and structure with the function it serves. Powerful modeling influences can simultaneously change observers' behavior, thought patterns, emotional reactions, and evaluations (Rosenthal & Bandura, 1978). Arbitrary designations of some of these forms of changes as identification and others as imitation only becloud modeling phenomena.

In social cognitive theory, the generic term *modeling* is used to characterize psychological matching processes. This construct is adopted because modeling influences have much broader psychological effects than the simple response mimicry implied by the term imitation, and the defining criteria of identification are too diffuse, arbitrary, and empirically questionable to clarify issues or to aid scientific inquiry. Social cognitive theory distinguishes among several modeling phenomena, each governed by different determinants and underlying mechanisms. Differentiating phenomena in terms of effects reflecting different operative mechanisms provides a better basis for clarifying psychosocial modeling than does differentiation by arbitrary criteria, which only yield disputable taxonomies.

Observational Learning Effects

Observers can acquire cognitive skills and new patterns of behavior by observing the performance of others. The learning may take varied forms, including new behavior patterns, judgmental standards, cognitive competencies, and generative rules for creating behaviors. Observational learning is shown most clearly when models exhibit novel patterns of thought or behavior which observers did not already possess but which, following observation, they can produce in similar form (Bandura, 1971a; Bandura & Jeffery, 1973; Rosenthal & Zimmerman, 1978). Any behavior that, prior to modeling, had a zero probability of occurrence, even when observers are given appropriate inducements, qualifies as a novel form.

Modeling influences teach component skills and provide rules for organizing them into new structures of behavior. To take a simple example, children can produce a variety of phonemes as part of their natural endowment. By drawing on their stock of elemental sounds, they can acquire a novel modeled expression such as *supercalifragilisticexpialidocious*. Although they may already possess the components, the organization is new.

Some writers have questioned whether behavior formed by unique integrations of preexisting elements really represents learning, because individuals already possess the components (Aronfreed, 1969;

Kuhn, 1973). When viewed from that disputable stance, pianists who master a Beethoven concerto have learned nothing new insofar as they already possess the stock of fingering movements in their repertoires. By the same reasoning, Beethoven would not be credited with creating new symphonies because he merely arranged preexisting notes.

Inhibitory and Disinhibitory Effects

A second main function of modeling influences is to strengthen or to weaken inhibitions over behavior that has been previously learned. The effects of modeling on behavioral restraint rely heavily on the information conveyed about the performability and probable consequences of modeled courses of action. The direction and strength of the impact of such information on personal restraint largely depends on three factors: on observers' judgments of their ability to execute the modeled behavior, on their perception of the modeled actions as producing rewarding or punishing consequences, and on their inferences that similar or unlike consequences would result if they themselves were to engage in analogous activities.

Inhibitory effects are indicated when observers either reduce their performance of the kind of behavior being modeled or become generally more restrained in their actions as a result of seeing models experience negative consequences. Disinhibitory effects are evident when observers increase their performance of formerly inhibited behavior after having seen others engage in threatening or prohibited activities without experiencing adverse effects.

Response Facilitation Effects

The actions of others can also serve as social prompts for previously learned behavior that observers can perform but have not done so because of insufficient inducements, rather than because of inhibition. People's looking upward upon seeing others gaze skyward is a common example of the facilitation of responsiveness by modeling. Such response-cueing effects are distinguished from observational learning and disinhibition because no new responses have been acquired, and disinhibitory processes are not involved because the elicited behavior is socially acceptable and not encumbered by restraints.

The influence of models in activating, channeling, and supporting the behavior of others is abundantly documented in both laboratory and field studies (Bandura, 1969a). By exemplification one can get people to behave altruistically, to volunteer their services, to delay or seek gratification, to show affection, to select certain foods and apparel, to converse on particular topics, to be inquisitive or passive, to think creatively or conventionally, or to engage in other permissible courses of action. Thus, the types of models that prevail within a social milieu partly determine which qualities, from among many alternatives, are selectively activated.

Environmental Enhancement Effects

The behavior of models not only functions as prompts for similar actions, it also draws the observers' attention to the particular objects or environmental settings that others favored. As a result, the observers may subsequently use the same objects to a greater extent, although not necessarily in the same way or for the same purposes. In one study illustrating this effect, children who had observed a doll being pummeled with a mallet not only adopted this specific aggressive action, they also used the mallet more in other types of activities than children who had not observed this instrument used by others (Bandura, 1962).

Even similarities in performance may sometimes result from attention-directing, rather than behavior-cueing, functions of modeling. In such instances, a model's behavior channels the observers' attention to particular stimuli or draws observers into settings which elicit similar behavior

(Bindra, 1974; Bullock & Neuringer, 1977). For example, animals will consume more food when they are fed in pairs than when they are fed alone. Further, even satiated chickens will begin to eat at the sight of other birds feeding. It is entirely possible that the sociable chicks' eating was reinstated and maintained by the grain to which their attention has been redirected, not by the model's eating. Determinants of similar behavior can be clarified only by comparing how observers behave when their attention is directed to eliciting cues with nonsocial means or by modeling the behavior but concealing the stimuli prompting the model's behavior from the observers' view.

Arousal Effects

Social interactions commonly involve displays of emotion. Seeing models express emotional reactions tends to elicit emotional arousal in observers. Heightened arousal, depending on how it is perceived, can alter the intensity and form of ongoing behavior (Tannenbaum & Zillman, 1975). When emotions are vicariously aroused in conjunction with certain places, persons, or things, observers begin to develop anticipatory emotional reactions toward these associated events (Berger, 1962).

In sum, modeling influences can serve as instructors, inhibitors, disinhibitors, facilitators, stimulus enhancers, and emotion arousers. Although the different modeling functions can operate separately, in nature they often work concurrently. Thus, for example, in the spread of new aggressive styles, models serve as both teachers and disinhibitors. When novel modeled conduct is punished, observers are likely to learn the conduct that was punished as well as the restraints. A novel example can both teach and prompt similar acts.

Distinguishing between the different modeling phenomena is useful in avoiding conceptual confusions and in guiding research into the determinants and mechanisms governing the various effects. Some of the disputes about observational learning have resulted from failure to distinguish modeling studies designed to clarify learning effects from those devised to explain disinhibitory, social facilitation, or environmental enhancement effects (Aronfreed, 1969). This chapter is principally concerned with observational learning of rules of thought and behavior.

MULTIPROCESS ANALYSIS OF OBSERVATIONAL LEARNING

Learning is largely an information-processing activity in which information about the structure of behavior and about environmental events is transformed into symbolic representations that serve as guides for action. In the social cognitive analysis of observational learning (Bandura, 1977a), modeling influences operate principally through their informative function. Providing a model of thought and action is one of the most effective ways to convey information about the rules for producing new behavior.

In this formulation, which is summarized schematically in Figure 3, observational learning is governed by four constituent processes: *Attentional processes* regulate exploration and perception of modeled activities; through *retention processes*, transitory experiences are converted for memory representation into symbolic conceptions that serve as internal models for response production and standards for response correction; *production processes* govern the organization of constituent subskills into new response patterns; and *motivation processes* determine whether or not observationally acquired competencies will be put to use.

Attentional Processes

People cannot learn much by observation unless they attend to, and accurately perceive, the relevant aspects of modeled activities. Attentional processes determine what is selectively observed in the profusion of modeling influences and what information is extracted from ongoing modeled events. Selective attention is, therefore, one of the crucial subfunctions in observational learning.

A number of factors influence the exploration and perception of what is modeled in the social and symbolic environment. Some of these relate to the cognitive skills and other attributes of the observers. Others concern the properties of the modeled activities themselves. Still others pertain to the structural arrangements of human interactions, which largely determine the types of models available for observation.

Properties of Modeled Activities. The rate and level of observational learning will be affected by the salience, discriminability, and complexity of modeled activities. Simple acts that are highly conspicuous can be readily learned through observation. However, young children, who are easily distractable and have deficient attentional skills, have difficulty learning even simple modeled acts that fail to gain and hold their attention. Any attention attractants inherent in the modeled actions aid observational learning. Infants, for example, show more attentiveness to modeled actions that are accompanied by conspicuous objects and sounds, and they learn them better, than if the same response patterns are modeled silently or without objects (Abravanel, Levan-Goldschmidt, & Stevenson, 1976). Level of attentiveness is a reasonably good predictor of infant imitativeness. Parents often increase the salience of behavior they seek to foster in young children by modeling it in an expressive fashion designed to capture attention. Such vivid enactments facilitate adoption of modeled behavior (Waxler & Yarrow, 1975).

In the more complex forms of modeling, observers learn generative rules from examples rather than the specific examples themselves. This is an especially difficult task because the rules must be extracted from responses that otherwise differ in many irrelevant aspects. To help observers sift pertinent features from irrelevant ones, model-

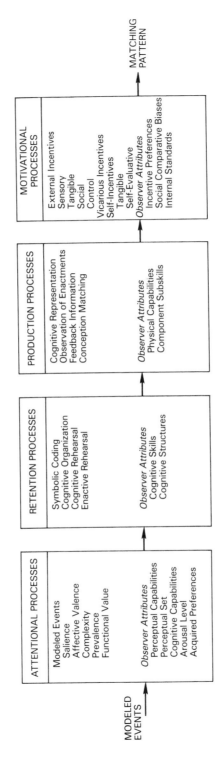

FIGURE 3. Subprocesses governing observational learning.

ing usually has to be supplemented with other attention-directing aids. Linguistic modeling is a good example of this process. The common properties that exemplify linguistic rules are made more easily distinguishable by simplifying the modeled utterances, exaggerating the essential aspects, providing concrete semantic referents for abstract concepts, and furnishing informative feedback (Bandura & Harris, 1966; Brown, 1976; Snow & Ferguson, 1977).

Observer Determinants. The process of attention is not simply a matter of absorbing sensory information that happens to impinge upon a person. Rather, it involves self-directed exploration of the environment and construction of meaningful perceptions from ongoing modeled events. Perceptions are guided by preconceptions. Observers' cognitive competencies and perceptual sets dispose them to look for some things but not others. Their expectations not only channel what they look for but partly affect what features they extract from observations and how they interpret what they see and hear. By giving coherence and meaning to available information, cognition is very much involved in perception.

Observational habits and perceptual selectivities partly reflect the level of psychological development. Observers' capabilities for processing modeled information sets limits on the amount of observational learning that can be achieved from brief exposures. If modeled events occur at a rate or level of complexity that overtaxes the observers' cognitive skills, observational learning will necessarily be fragmentary. For this reason, repeated exposures are often necessary to acquire an adequate conception of modeled activities. Modeling influences effect changes most rapidly and reliably when they are adjusted to the cognitive capabilities of observers (Bullock, 1983). We shall return later to detailed consideration of how developmental factors affect observational learning.

The greater the cognitive skills and prior knowledge, the more subtleties observers will perceive. As a result of familiarization and training, experienced people recognize fine differences in performance that are undistinguishable to the untutored. Regardless of whether the performances entail social, athletic, artistic, or academic activities, what appears proficient to the novice may be flawed to the discerning specialist.

Functional Value. Modeled strategies vary in their usefulness for dealing with the environment. Successful modes of behavior are, therefore, more worthy of attention than are less effective ones. Much selective attention is maintained by expectations that one will have to manage situations comparable to those handled by others. The anticipated benefits of modeled skills and strategies provide incentives for paying attention to how others behave. When events compete for attention, people who expect to perform similar tasks pay greater attention to modeled conduct and learn it better, than if they consider the modeled activities to be personally irrelevant (Kanfer, Duerfeldt, Martin, & Dorsey, 1971).

Attentional involvement in ongoing activities is affected by consequences experienced by others, as well as by the consequences one experiences directly. People pay close attention to modeled performances that produce rewarding outcomes but disregard those having no noticeable effects. That the experiences of others can operate through attentional mechanisms to enhance observational learning is clearly shown by Yussen (1974). Seeing models either rewarded or punished for their responses both raised children's attentiveness to what the models were doing. The more often and the longer children attended to the models' behavior, the higher was their level of observational learning. Observed punishment was just as effective as observed reward in promoting observational learning.

A model's efficacy is inferred partly from tangible evidence of the results of his or her actions and partly from symbols that signify competence and past success. When the value of alternative courses of action is not immediately evident, observers may deploy their attention to models who display symbols of skill and previous attainments. They pay attention to models reputed to be effective and ignore those who, by appearance or reputation, are presumed to be ineffectual.

As is true of most influences, the attention-enhancing effects of response consequences operate within certain limits. When modeled actions are sufficiently salient to command attention by themselves, observational learning can occur regardless of subsequent outcomes. Although observed punishment draws attention to the actions being censured and thereby facilitates learning, people generally avoid models who experience painful consequences that observers find aversive (Bandura & Rosenthal, 1966). And given the choice, people are more likely to select models who are proficient at producing good outcomes than those who repeatedly get punished.

Sway of Attraction. Attention to models is channeled not only by the functional value of their behavior but also by their attractiveness. Models who are interesting and otherwise rewarding tend to be sought out, whereas those who lack attractive qualities are ignored or actively rejected, even though they may excel in other ways. Control of attention through attraction is perhaps nowhere better illustrated than in televised modeling. Much televised modeling commands the attention of people of all ages for extended periods daily. Indeed, televised models can be so effective in holding attention that viewers learn the behavior they depict regardless of whether or not they are given extra incentives to do so (Bandura, Grusec, & Menlove, 1966).

In tests of developmental theories of modeling, children often have no choice but to observe the models presented to them. Such tests may yield misleading results when the factors being studied actually affect modeling through their influence on associational preferences. For example, children who are required to observe nurturant and nonnurturant models for an equivalent time may learn about as much from both. But given a choice, they are likely to seek nurturant models and ignore unresponsive ones. If nonnurturant models are largely avoided, their behavior will not be learned. Even when both types of models are simultaneously present, a nurturant model draws more attention from children than does a neutral one and also holds their attention better in the face of distraction (Yussen & Levy, 1975). Selectivity of attention predicts the level of observational learning. For similar reasons, gender and other factors that bias one's choice of association will have substantially different effects on observational learning under conditions of either forced or self-selected exposure to models.

Enhancing Modeling by Attentional Means. In applications of modeling principles, observational learning is often retarded by attentional deficits arising from deficient cognitive skills, prior faulty learning, distracting preoccupations, or insufficient incentives. In such instances, various procedures, some of which have already been discussed, can be used to heighten attentional involvement in the modeled activities. Observers' attention can be channeled by physically accentuating the essential features of the performances. Attention-directing narration also provides a convenient means of steering attention to what is important and for specifying the general strategy of action of which the modeled performances are simply examples (McGuire, 1961; Sheffield & Maccoby, 1961). Contrast modeling of good and poor performance is a further device to make important aspects of superior renditions more recognizable (Debus, 1970).

Subdividing complex activities into natural segments and separately highlighting the constituent skills result in better observational learning than massed exposure to entire performances (Sheffield & Maccoby, 1961). It is much easier to focus and hold attention by concentrating on mastering different parts. Unguided massive modeling often begets misperception. When people simply observe entire performances, they often fail to grasp crucial details. Indeed, burdening observers with too much modeled information can produce erroneous, rather than merely incomplete, observational learning. Observers confuse aspects of what they have seen and heard and develop mistaken conceptions of the modeled behavior (Bandura, Grusec, & Menlove, 1966).

Ordinarily, learners need opportunities between observations to practice what they have seen. Evident deficiencies in their enactments show them what to look for in subsequent observation of modeled performances. Feedback from behavioral enactment tends to direct attention to inadequately mastered aspects of the modeled activities (Kanfer et al., 1971). Such selective, concentrated enactments augment observational learning of modeled skills.

Structural Arrangements and Observability of Behavior Patterns.

Much of the discussion thus far has dealt with personal factors that influence perceptual selectivity. Among the various attentional determinants, associational networks are clearly of major importance. The people with whom one regularly associates, either through preference or imposition, delimit the behavioral patterns that will be repeatedly observed and, hence, learned most thoroughly. Opportunities for learning aggressive conduct, for example, differ markedly for children who happen to reside in communities in which aggressive models abound than in more pacific locales (Short, 1968; Wolfgang & Ferracuti, 1967).

The way in which a society is socially organized largely determines the types of models to which its members have easy access. Associational patterns that characterize different societies have been the subject of extensive study by anthropologists and sociologists. Ethnographic reports document how the social universe is very different for domestic groupings based on nuclear and extended families and for social groupings of people in a community based on kinship and age-grade units.

The degree of social differentiation in a society affects the observability of behavior patterns. Social systems that are sharply demarcated along age, sex, and class lines isolate groups of people from one another. In less structured systems, people can more readily observe each others' activities. Consider age divisions. In some cultures, children and adolescents are temporarily separated from adults. Where discontinuities in socialization exist, special modeling arrangements are used to transmit the cultural knowledge and skills needed to fulfill adult roles (Spindler & Spindler, 1982). In other societies, such as the Lesu, children are permitted to observe all aspects of adult life (Powdermaker, 1933). They not only accompany adults in their daily activities, but they are also present at all adult functions and observe activities, such as the sexual behavior of adults, that in other cultures are concealed from children.

The introduction of television technology has produced major changes in the models of behavior to which people now have access. It enables them to transcend the bounds of their immediate social life. From televised representations, they learn the values and styles of behavior of different segments of their own society, as well as those of other cultures. While modeling exerts its influence through cognitive processing of behavioral and contingency information, structural arrangements determine what can readily become known to members of a given social system.

Retention Processes

People cannot be greatly influenced by observation of modeled activities if they do not remember them. The second major subfunction governing observational learning concerns retention of knowledge about activities that have been modeled at one time or another. In order for observers to profit from the behavior of others, when they are no longer present to provide direction, the modeled information must be represented in memory in symbolic form. Through the medium of symbols, transitory modeling experiences can be maintained in permanent memory. The advanced capacity for symbolization enables humans to learn much of their behavior by observation.

Symbolic Transformations.
Retention involves the active transformation and restructuring of information about events. The full content of most modeled activities is too copious and contains too many irrelevancies to be retained exactly as portrayed. Learners must, therefore, transform what they observe into succinct symbols to capture the essential features and structures of the modeled activities.

Observational learning and retention are aided by symbolic transformations because they carry a great deal of information in an easily remembered form. After modeled activities have been converted into images and readily utilizable verbal symbols, these conceptions function as guides for subsequent action. Representational guides play an especially influential role in the early phases of response acquisition. After a given behavior pattern has been repeatedly performed, it eventually becomes so routinized that it can be enacted smoothly and automatically without requiring representational guidance.

Cognitive representations of experiences may differ on several dimensions such as modality, conciseness, and structure. With regard to modality, information may be coded in images or verbal symbols in the form of conceptions, rules, and propositions. Symbolic codes may be reductive ones, which distill events to concise form, or they may include elaborative linguistic and imaginal constructions. Moreover, they may be structurally isomorphic with the modeled behavior, or they may be rules that capture the underlying conceptual structure but bear little resemblance to the details of the exemplars.

Representational Systems.
Observational learning relies mainly upon two representational systems involving imaginal and verbal constructions. Information about some forms of behavior is largely represented in imaginal codes. There has been much recent theorizing and research on the nature of the imagery system and how it represents information (Kosslyn, 1980; Shepard, 1978; Shepard & Podgorny, 1978). To shed light on the structure of representational imagery, people are presented problems requiring them to construct and transform images of external events. For example, the time is recorded for how long it takes them to mentally rotate figures at varying angular discrepancies from a sample, until they match it, or to visualize objects at varying distances from each other on a map, that has been committed to memory. The findings indicate that imaginal representations have spatial properties analogous to the spatial relations of the corresponding physical events. The more a figure has to be turned to match a sample, the longer the mental rotation takes, just as would occur if it were rotated physically; the farther apart objects are on an imaginary map, the longer it takes to make the mental trip. Images seem to be functionally equivalent to percepts. If information were represented solely in verbal form, imaginary long and short distances should be traversed with equal speed because one could report distant places just as quickly as near ones. Moreover, reaction times differ when persons are instructed to extract relevant information from images, rather than from nonimaginal representation of the same events.

Imaginal representations are abstractions of events, rather than simply mental pictures of past observances. As a result of repeated exposure to modeled events, observers extract distinctive features and form composite, enduring images of the behavior patterns. Activities are, of course, rarely performed in exactly the same way on repeated occasions. No two tennis serves are identical; no two apples are the very same. Observers have to construct a general conception that encompasses essential aspects from specific instances that vary around a basic pattern. Studies of abstraction from particular instances show that, through repeated encounters with different examples of a common prototype, people develop a conception of the prototype, even though they have never seen it before (Posner, 1973). Moreover, they remember the prototype better than the individual examples from which it has been constructed. This is undoubtedly true of most observational learning in everyday life. People possess good visual memory for how a skill should be enacted, but they have difficulty recalling the examples they drew upon in learning it.

It is generally assumed that imaginal codes are generated from abstract knowledge about the events being visualized (Kosslyn, Pinker, Smith, & Schwartz, 1979). If images are constructed from propositional knowledge, the question arises as to whether imaginal codes provide any unique guidance for judgment and action, that is not directly furnished by the propositional codes themselves. According to Kosslyn and his colleagues, on many tasks, especially those involving spatial relations, people convert general information to imaginal representations, rather than encoding them directly. Relevant information is then obtained by scanning the image. How abstract representation produces images remains to be explained. Recalling relational features presumably activates neural patterns that have been experienced phenomenally as imagery. Some confusion arises about what an image is when theorists disavow the picture metaphor but continue to characterize imagery in pictorial terms. Neural patterns that are self-generated symbolically are no more like pictures in the head than are similar neural patterns generated by the external events themselves.

The question of whether images provide more information than is available in the propositional mode is the subject of active debate (Anderson, 1978). It may be that propositional information about configural features furnishes the skeletal image, but specific exemplars provide the detail. It would be exceedingly difficult to visualize an abstract house without recourse to a familiar dwelling to supply the needed details. However, as Antrobus (1979) has noted, if a proposition is defined broadly as any relational statement, then the structure of even the most elementary object can be characterized by propositions about the relations between its parts. Theorists who assume that all information can be represented propositionally would argue that an image may require an exhaustive set of propositions to convey the detailed structural information, but, nonetheless, the image is derivable from them. The convergent findings of Shepard, Kosslyn, and the others discussed earlier lend weight to the view that representational imagery is depictive rather than just verbally descriptive. But the issue of whether a common abstract representation produces both depictive and verbally descriptive codes is not easily resolvable.

Research on observational learning complements the study of the nature of imagery by exploring the functions it serves. In the concern over the nature of internal representation, it is all too easy to lose sight of the fact that the imagery system evolved because it aids effective transactions with the environment. The processes by which imagery functions as an internal model for the production and correction of response patterns command major interest in studies of psychological modeling.

After representational imagery has been developed, images (i.e., centrally aroused perceptions) can be readily summoned up of events that are physically absent. Indeed, when things are highly correlated, as in linking a name to a particular person, it is virtually impossible to hear the name without experiencing an image of that person. Similarly, mere reference to activities (e.g., surfing, typing), places (e.g., bank, hospital), and things (e.g., hippopotamus, ostrich) that have been repeatedly observed readily activate their imaginal analogs.

Visual memory plays a prominent role in observational learning during early periods of development when verbal competencies are lacking. Even after linguistic skills have been fully developed, visual imagery continues to serve as a significant retention aid for behavior patterns that are not easily represented in words. These usually include intricate actions conveying information about spatial and temporal coordinations that is more subtle than the words available to describe them. A golf swing, for example, is much better visualized than described. In such activities, modeled information is largely retained in nonverbal form.

The second representational system, which accounts for the notable efficacy of observational learning and retention in humans, involves coding modeled events in a verbal-conceptual form. Most of the cognitive processes that regulate behavior are primarily conceptual rather than imaginal. Because of the extraordinary flexibility of verbal symbols, the intricacies and complexities of behavior can be conveniently captured in words. To take a simple example, the details of a route traveled by a model can be acquired, retained, and later performed more accurately by converting the visual information into a verbal code describing a series of right and left turns (e.g., RLRRL) than by reliance on visual imagery of the circuitous route, with its many irrelevant details.

Although verbal symbols embody a major share of knowledge acquired by modeling, it is often difficult to separate representation modes. Representational activities usually involve both systems to some degree (Paivio, 1975). Words tend to evoke corresponding imagery, and images of events are often verbally cognized as well. When visual and verbal stimuli convey similar meanings, people integrate the information presented by these different modalities into a common conceptual representation (Rosenberg & Simon, 1977). The amenability of diverse sources of information to common abstract representation and the relative merits of imaginal and verbal modes of presentation will, of course, depend on the nature of the activity and on the learners' cognitive competencies.

The influential role of symbolic representation in observational learning is revealed by studies conducted with both children (Bandura, Grusec, & Menlove, 1966; Coates & Hartup, 1969) and adults (Bandura, 1971a; Gerst, 1971; Rosenthal & Zimmerman, 1978). Observers who transform modeled activities into either concise verbal codes or vivid imagery learn and retain behavior much better than those who simply observe or who are mentally preoccupied with other matters while watching.

Studies of observational learning generally include behaviors formed by novel combinations of familiar elements. The partial familiarity simplifies symbolization of behavior and enables observers to use memory aids they have found helpful in the past, regardless of whether or not they are encouraged by researchers to do so. The role of cognitive factors in observational learning is, therefore, best clarified with modeled activities involving highly complex, new information for which observers would have to develop entirely new symbolic coding and organizational schemes.

In one experiment using novel action patterns (Bandura & Jeffery, 1973), adults either simply observed a model perform the different patterns, or they coded them into concise verbal symbols from which they could later reproduce the activities. Symbolic codes are of little value if they are forgotten. Rehearsal was, therefore, examined as a further means of enhancing retention. After being tested for their observational learning after exposure to each action pattern, the observers practiced the modeled responses, or mentally rehearsed the codes symbolizing the actions, or they were prevented from rehearsing what they had seen. The results underscore the importance of cognitive factors in observational learning and retention of behavior over time. Observers who neither coded nor rehearsed the modeled action patterns retained virtually nothing of what they had seen. By contrast, those who coded the modeled events and cognitively rehearsed the symbolic codes, from which the behavior could be reconstructed, remembered the modeled events. Rehearsing the symbolic guides for action enhanced retention better than simply performing the action patterns themselves. People rarely reproduced modeled patterns when their cognitive codes were forgotten or faulty. Neither rehearsal without symbolic coding nor coding without rehearsal in immediate memory significantly improved retention of modeled behavior. Without the benefit of both memory aids, observers rapidly lost most of what they had seen.

Retention improves by transforming the meaningless into what is already well known. In the preceding experiment, action patterns were learned and maintained better by using familiar memory codes, rather than symbolic transformations devoid of meaning. The advantage of meaningful symbols became progressively greater when retention was measured over time. Improvement of memory through meaningful cognitive organization of modeled information is further revealed in a study in which reductive coding and verbal elaboration were combined into meaningful cognitive structures (Bandura, Jeffery, & Bachicha, 1974). As observers watched modeled performances, they first condensed the new information into concise symbols and then embedded the symbols in personally meaningful verbal codes that they could easily recall on later occasions. Observers who employed this dual coding scheme retained much more of the modeled activities than those who used only concise symbols, which were quickly forgotten due to their lack of inherent meaning. Even for the dual coders, the more meaningful the linguistic mnemonics they constructed, the better they retained the modeled patterns. Analyses of the availability of codes and the probability of accurate reproduction of the modeled patterns provide the most definitive evidence for the crucial role of symbolic guides in observational learning and retention. Regardless of whether tests were conducted immediately after observation, an hour later, or a week later, observers who retained the symbolic codes executed the action patterns without fail, whereas those who were unable to summon up the appropriate symbolic codes could not produce the behavior.

Results of the preceding experiments bear on a number of conceptual issues. They highlight the limitations of behavioristic theories that view observational learning solely as formation of stimulus-response associations (Gewirtz, 1971). Adults who have been rewarded on numerous past occasions for behaving like others achieve little or no observational learning unless they transform the observations into an enduring symbolic form. Simply performing responses does little to improve retention without meaningful cognitive transformation of the action patterns.

The findings also question the generality of theories that depict observational learning as essentially a template-matching process (Aronfreed, 1969). In this view, observed behavior is stored as a cognitive template for action. Some modeled activities are encoded as imaginal or verbal facsimiles. But symbolic representations need not be exact replicas or templates of external activities. Indeed, the changes that could be produced through modeling influences would be severely limited if representations were always structurally isomorphic to the response of others.

Symbolic transformation primarily involves a constructive rather than a template-matching process. Most modeled information is learned and retained in abstract symbols that bear little resemblance to the surface characteristics of observed events. The important consideration is the effectiveness of the symbolization in organizing modeled information into easily remembered forms. The symbolic codes must preserve the pertinent information and include the operations for translating symbols into actions. But the codes and the modeled events need not be alike. Indeed, it is the higher-order symbolic constructions that have the widest generality. Because remembrance requires observers to transform and organize modeled information, there is considerable selectivity about what they retain and what they forget, a process which is not without its benefit. If people completely retained everything they observed, they would be too overwhelmed with information, most of it useless, to manage to retrieve guides for action.

The role of meaningfulness in the comprehension and retention of novel behavior warrants some comment. Novel response patterns are acquired most easily if they are related to what is already known. Observational learning in everyday life is often accelerated by likening new performances to familiar and meaningful activities. A skiing example illustrates effective application of this principle. Members of a beginning ski class had considerable difficulty learning how to transfer their weight to the downhill ski, despite repeated demonstrations by the instructor, because of their natural inclination to lean into the hill. They promptly mastered the maneuver when asked to ski as though they were pointing a serving tray downhill throughout the turns and traverses.

What is known was, at some earlier point, itself new. To explain learning in terms of stored meanings fails to provide a mechanism for the initial acquisition of new information (Bransford & Franks, 1976). Unless one posits innate knowledge, people have to draw on their experiences to get to know things from the start. Moreover, if new activities could be learned only by being understood in terms of what is already known, then preexisting knowledge would restrict the ability to acquire new meanings and competencies. Were learning entirely driven by domain-specific preconceptions, people would be captive of whatever initial misconceptions they may have formed. They could never transcend them.

Learning involves the bidirectional influence of preconception and experience. New things can become familiar to people who have little prior knowledge by having them build up generalized conceptions of events through repeated experiences with them. During this initial phase, the events to be learned must be simplified, repeated often, and their significant aspects made highly salient. The rate of learning is relatively slow, and newly acquired information must be cognitively reinstated from time to time, if it is to remain available for future use. A growing body of knowledge, in turn, accelerates subsequent learning. Although acquisition of modeled information is expedited by drawing on existing knowledge, it is not reducible to it. In the process of mastering new modeled information, preexisting conceptions are themselves altered and expanded.

Rehearsal and Retention. As already alluded to, rehearsal serves as an important memory aid. People who cognitively rehearse or actually perform modeled patterns of behavior are less likely to forget them than those who neither think about them nor practice what they have seen. It is worth distinguishing here between the contribution of rehearsal to both acquisition and improvement of behavior patterns. If modeled events are not rehearsed when they are first observed, they are vulnerable to being lost from memory, and delayed rehearsal is of little value (Bandura & Jeffery, 1973). Ordinarily, modeled activities are cognitively reinstated from time to time, rather than only when first observed or after a long period has elapsed. Modeled patterns can be strengthened in memory through cumulative rehearsal (Bandura, Jeffery, & Bachicha, 1974).

Rehearsal probably augments learning and retention through more than one mechanism. While modeled events are reinstated cognitively, they can be semantically elaborated, transformed, and reorganized into meaningful memory codes that aid recall. In addition, retention can be improved by rehearsing coded information, even though it does not undergo additional cognitive processing. Repetition itself may contribute to retention by increasing the strength or number of memory traces. It would appear, however, that the facilitative effects of rehearsal on long-term retention derive more from applying memory strategies to modeled information than from sheer repetition (Bandura, Jeffery, & Bachicha, 1974; Bower, 1972; Rosenthal & Zimmerman, 1978). Similar processes undoubtedly contribute to the benefits of enactive rehearsal as well, especially when intermixed with modeling (Swanson, Henderson, & Williams, 1979). Enactments provide opportunities to organize and verify what one knows and to heighten attentiveness to problematic aspects in subsequent modeling. By enhancing and channeling attention, enactive rehearsal can refine the symbolic representation of the activity (Carroll & Bandura, 1985).

Cognitive Rehearsal. Much of what is observed cannot be easily practiced in action. In some instances the activities are socially prohibited. In others the necessary resources or tools are not available. In still others the constraints of time and circumstances limit what people can do. Of considerable interest is evidence that cognitive rehearsal, in which individuals visualize themselves executing the correct sequence of actions, and which may be readily realized when behavioral enactment is either impeded or impracticable, can increase proficiency in activities. Comparative studies show that cognitive rehearsal improves subsequent motor performances but usually not as well as repeated physical practice does. The benefits of cognitive rehearsal have been demonstrated with athletic skills, vocational activities, and conceptual tasks (Corbin, 1972; Feltz & Landers, 1983). Activities are mastered more rapidly through combined cognitive and physical rehearsal than by physical practice alone (Rawlings,

Rawlings, Chen, & Yilk, 1972). Daily cognitive rehearsal has also been demonstrated to aid retention of a psychomotor skill after it has already been learned (Sackett, 1935).

In addition to facilitating acquisition and retention of skills, preparatory cognitive rehearsal can enhance immediate performance of well-learned activities. Individuals who visualize themselves performing what they are about to do generally perform better than those who do not use this cognitive aid (Richardson, 1967). Further research is needed to determine whether such preparatory cognitive rehearsal benefits performance by creating the appropriate cognitive set for the activity, by diverting attention from stressful disruptive thoughts to more helpful ones, or by boosting perceived self-efficacy.

Considering that skeletal responding is centrally regulated, it is not at all surprising that cognitive rehearsal can improve psychomotor skills. Neural signals controlling particular action patterns can be elicited by imaginal enactment of behavior. When people visualize themselves performing an activity, they exhibit muscle electromyographic changes in the same muscle groups that would have been activated had they actually performed the responses. The greater the imagined responses, the stronger is the innervation of the appropriate muscles. Thus, imagining oneself lifting heavy weights produces greater muscle-action currents than imagining lifting light weights (Shaw, 1940). Ulich (1967) extended the research one step further by relating level of electromyographic activity during cognitive enactment of a manual dexterity task to subsequent actual performance. He found that individuals who displayed moderate levels of muscle-action potentials during imaginal rehearsal improved their actual performance on the task 72 percent, while those who showed low or excessively high levels of muscle potential improved 47 percent and 37 percent, respectively. The muscular innervation produced by cognitive enactment does not necessarily duplicate that produced by overt action. Therefore, to the extent that the symbolic innervation facilitates performance, it probably does so by fostering psychoneural organization of the action pattern, rather than by strengthening faint expressions of the action. Physical practice has the advantage, however, of providing informative feedback for identifying and correcting deficiencies in both conception and performance.

Not all the benefits of cognitive rehearsal necessarily derive from improvements in conceptualizing the skill and in psychoneuromuscular organization. Some of the gains may be due to heightening attention to aspects of the skill which might otherwise go unnoticed. Closer self-monitoring of performance details can, in itself, affect enactment of intricate action patterns. In addition, cognitive rehearsal can improve performance through motivational means. Having people visualize themselves executing activities skillfully raises their perceived efficacy that they will be able to perform better (Bandura & Adams, 1977; Clark, 1960; Kazdin, 1979). Such boosts of self-efficacy are likely to improve performance by reducing impeding self-doubts and by enlisting the effort needed to do well.

The extent to which cognitive rehearsal improves performance depends on a number of factors. The content and timing of such practices are especially influential. Achievement of skilled performance requires an adequate conception of the behavior. During initial phases of learning, therefore, efforts are best deployed by gaining a clear conception of the skilled performance for the purpose of later rehearsal and response production (Carroll & Bandura, 1982; Jeffery, 1976). Provisional enactments furnish information for refining action plans, but acting without an adequate notion to guide one is of limited value. The highest level of learning is best achieved by first organizing the modeled behavior cognitively and then alternating cognitive and motor performances (Richardson, 1967).

What people visualize during cognitive enactments affects later performance. Imagining accurate cognitive enactments improves subsequent performances, while imagining faulty ones impairs them (Powell, 1973). The greater the experience and aptitude in the type of activity being perfected, the more individiuals benefit from cognitive rehearsal (Corbin, 1972). A certain amount of prior experience undoubtedly helps to clarify the symbolic representation of the skill. Without a clear conception of what a good performance is like, one is at a loss to know what to rehearse cognitively or how to identify sources of error. Under these conditions, there is high likelihood that many faulty habits will be rehearsed.

The types of psychological functions called for in a given activity is another factor influencing the effects of cognitive rehearsal on skill acquisition and retention. As a rule, activities that rely extensively on cognitive processing, such as complex performances, benefit more and faster from cognitive rehearsal that those that involve simpler motor acts (Feltz & Landers, 1983; Perry, 1939). However, the extent to which symbolic rehearsal improves later performance, even on tasks with extensive manual components, will depend on how the activities are exemplified. Action patterns consist of sequences of movements coordinated in terms of positions and temporal order. In studies of how people partition the stream of behavior, Newtson (1976) finds that breakpoints, where one action component ends and the next one begins, carry much of the information about the behavior. During slow-motion presentations, observers not only produce finer segmentation but become more informed about the distinctive changes required at successive breakpoints. When an activity is performed rapidly in its entirety, learners do not fully observe all the constituent responses and how they are spatially and temporally integrated into skilled movement. If exemplifications are slowed down, and the component movements and transitional changes are accented, the manual aspects can be subdivided into perceptual units of position and sequential change. In this way, manual activities are made more ideational and thus should be even more amenable to improvement by cognitive enactment.

Cognitive enactment is being increasingly used both to perfect athletic skills and to ply them well by using cognitive rehearsal immediately prior to performing athletic events. Testimonials abound that cognitive rehearsal improves athletic performance. Although evidence from controlled studies is generally supportive of the beneficial effects, it is far from conclusive (Suinn, 1983). As Suinn points out, because cognitive rehearsal is only a tool, achieving consistent benefits with it requires understanding the processes governing skill acquisition and proficient execution of mastered skills. Such knowledge is needed to know what to rehearse cognitively. There are many facets to athletic skills that can be the focus of attention. They include the cognitive aspects of performance (strategies, self-efficacious ideation), the motor aspects (mechanisms of action patterns, sensations accompanying bodily movements), and the emotive aspects (stress, muscular tension). These constituent factors are likely to contribute differentially to athletic performance, depending on the nature of the skills, their phase of development, and competitive stressors.

No account of memory mechanisms would be complete without mentioning motivational determinants. Incentives exert selective influence on which observed response patterns are most likely to be rehearsed and thus fixed in memory. Modeled conduct that effectively secures beneficial results or forestalls punishing ones will be covertly practiced more than behavior having little or no functional value. However, incentives should be regarded as facilitative rather than necessary. Given repeated observation of modeled activities, people will learn and retain at least part of what they have seen, even though it may serve no evident purpose, and there was no intent to learn it. It is doubtful that viewers could keep from learning something about how basketball is played even from casual observation of such performances, however little interest such feats may hold for them.

Production Processes

The third component of modeling involves converting symbolic conceptions into appropriate actions. To understand representational guidance of enactments requires the analysis of the conceptual-motor mechanisms of performance. Most modeled activities are abstractly represented as conceptions and rules of action which specify what to do. Behavioral production is achieved by organizing responses spatially and temporally in accordance with the conception of the activity.

Locus of Response Integration. Theories differ on whether component activities are integrated into new forms mainly at central or peripheral levels. The early associational theories of imitation (Allport, 1924; Guthrie, 1952; Holt, 1931; Humphrey, 1921) did not address themselves to the issue of response acquisition. They were principally concerned with how existing responses come to be elicited by social cues. Presumably, if modeled acts and the observer's similar responses occur together repeatedly, modeled acts become cues for imitative responses. Modeling stimuli were believed to acquire this eliciting capacity most rapidly by initial reverse imitation. According to Holt's conceptualization, when a child's behavior is copied by an adult, the child tends to repeat the reiterated action. As this circular imitation continues, the adult's behavior becomes an increasingly effective stimulus for the child's responses. If, during this spontaneous mutual imitation, the adult performs a response that is new to the child, the child will copy it.

Association theories described how existing behavior may be cued by modeled acts. But they failed to explain how novel responses are initially acquired. With the advent of reinforcement principles, conceptualizations of imitation shifted attention to the consequences of imitative responses. Imitative learning was still conceptualized in terms of the formation of associational linkages between modeling cues and matching responses, but reinforcement was added as the selective factor, determining which of the many modeled responses will be imitated (Miller & Dollard, 1941; Skinner, 1953).

Reinforcement theories assume that people extract constituent responses from the observer's ongoing performances by reinforcing those portions that resemble the modeled forms. As the observer continues to emit responses, more and more of the matching elements are gradually singled out and additively chained by selective reinforcement. Because, in this view, behavior is shaped into new patterns during response execution, learning requires overt responding and immediate reinforcement.

In the social cognitive analysis, behavior is organized chiefly through central integrative mechanisms before it is executed. By observing modeled performances, one forms a conception of how constituent acts must be combined and temporally sequenced to produce new forms of behavior. In other words, the modeled behavior is largely learned as a whole in symbolic form before it is executed. Response production mainly involves a conception-matching process.

Conception-Matching Process. For purposes of analysis, behavioral enactment can be separated into several distinct processes. These include cognitive organization of response patterns, centrally guided initiation, monitoring of response enactments, and matching action to conception through corrective performance adjustments. Behavior is formed by combining component responses into new patterns which may, in themselves, represent intricate skills. In the initial phase of behavioral enactment, re-

sponses are selected and organized at the cognitive level. A conception of the action, derived from exemplars, enables learners to produce from the outset at least a rough approximation of the activity.

The conceptual representation provides the internal model for response production and the standard for response correction. Behavioral production primarily involves a conception-matching process in which the incoming sensory feedback from enactments is compared to the conception. The behavior is then modified on the basis of the comparative information to achieve progressively closer correspondence between conception and action.

It is sometimes claimed that controversy over the locus of learning cannot be satisfactorily resolved because learning must be inferred from performance. This view arose from experimentation with animals, which have limited ways of revealing what they know. To determine whether animals have mastered a maze, one must run them through it. With humans, there are other indices of learning that are independent of motor performance.

The degree of observational learning can be measured in several different ways. In *verbal production tests* observers describe what they have learned by observation (Bandura, Jeffery, & Bachicha, 1974; Bandura, Ross, & Ross, 1963b). Symbolic conceptions of modeled activities can also be measured by *recognition tests*. Here observers identify the modeled prototype from alternatives that differ from it in subtle ways, or they construct the modeled pattern by arranging photographs that depict in a scrambled order each of the various component acts (Carroll & Bandura, 1985). In rule-governed behavior, the conceptions embody a rule or principle for generating new instances of the behavior. Observational rule learning is assessed by having observers either specify the rule underlying the modeled responses or demonstrate their understanding in *comprehension tests* that depict occurrences embodying the rule (Brown,

1976; Rosenthal & Zimmerman, 1978). In *maximizing enactment tests,* observers are explicitly encouraged to perform, with positive incentives and minimal constraints, all they have learned from models (Bandura, 1965b; Bandura, Grusec, & Menlove, 1966). Studies in which observational learning is inferred from matching responses performed spontaneously probably underestimate the amount of observational learning, because people usually perform less than they have learned unless actively encouraged to do so. Experiments using multiple measures of acquisition show that people can learn by observing before they actually perform (Bandura & Jeffery, 1973; Bandura, Ross, & Ross, 1963a; Brown, 1976; Rosenthal & Zimmerman, 1978).

Faulty Conception and Response Production. In many instances, of course, observational learning alone is not sufficient to produce faultless performance. Errors may arise from a variety of causes. When people observe modeled activities only briefly or sporadically, they generally acquire, at best, a fragmentary sketch of the activities. Behavioral production is flawed because the guiding internal conception is inadequate. Overt practice helps to identify those aspects that were missed entirely or only partially learned. Given further opportunities to observe the same modeled activities, observers are apt to concentrate their attention on troublesome segments to fill in the missing guides for achieving accurate performance.

Conception Matching and Motor Deficits. Even when the conceptual representation is accurate, errors may arise from mismatches of motor subskills. The rate and level of observational learning will be partly dependent, at the response-production stage, on the availability of component skills. Learners who possess the constituent skills can easily integrate them to produce new behavior patterns. But if some of the subskills are lacking, behavioral production will be faulty. When deficits exist, the subskills required for complex performances must first be developed by modeling and guided practice. Then, in a stepwise fashion, increasingly complex forms of behavior can be created. In language learning, for example, mute, autistic children, who failed to adopt modeled utterances, succeeded after the speech components were established through rewarded modeling (Lovaas, 1966). Most skills are developed by hierarchically organizing components of activities. Hence, simpler components must be mastered first. As will be shown later, graduated modeling has proven highly effective in building competencies out of simpler ingredients.

Even though symbolic representations of modeled activities are acquired and retained, and the subskills exist, a person may be unable to coordinate various actions in the required pattern and sequence because of physical limitations. Young children can learn through observation the repertoire for driving an automobile and be adept at executing the component acts, but if they are too short to operate the controls, they cannot maneuver the vehicle successfully. Biological structure can affect behavioral potentialities. Therefore, among observers who differ in physique, height, weight, and agility, some will learn modeled manual skills faster and better than others.

Accurate behavioral enactment of modeled activities is also difficult to achieve when the model's performance is governed by subtle adjustments of internal responses, which are not observable or easily described. An aspiring operatic singer may benefit considerably from observing an accomplished vocal coach; but the aspiring singer's vocal production is hampered because the model's laryngeal and respiratory responses are, at best, only partially observable.

Conception Matching and Feedback Information. The preceding discussion has focused on discrepancies between conception and action arising from deficits in motor subskills. Conceptions are rarely transformed into corresponding actions without error on the first attempt, even if the physical capabilities exist. Skilled performances are regulated by both conceptions of action and perception of information from the ongoing enactments. Accurate matches are usually achieved by corrective adjustments of preliminary efforts on the basis of informative response feedback. Disparities between conception and action indicate the amount and direction in which behavior must be altered to approximate the desired performance.

During initial enactments of observationally learned behavior, people closely monitor ongoing feedback from their behavior and compare it to the conceptual representation for error correction. Some of the feedback is intrinsic to the behavior in the form of visual, auditory, and kinesthetic information arising naturally from actions. People improve and perfect their performances by seeing, hearing, and feeling what they are doing. These sources of response information are often augmented by extrinsic feedback, such as knowledge about the results of one's actions or social evaluation, which indicates proficiencies and errors in performance. However, as action patterns become well organized through practice, they can be executed rapidly and skillfully without requiring much conscious monitoring. The automatization of skills will be discussed in more detail later.

Making the Unobservable Observable.
A common problem in learning is that people cannot fully observe their own behavior. It is difficult to enact accurately what cannot be visually monitored. In coordinated skills, such as tennis or swimming, performers cannot see much of what they are doing and must, therefore, rely greatly on kinesthetic feedback and an onlooker's verbal reports to inform them. As a result, during early phases of execution, learners may practice a number of incorrect responses, while as-

suming all along that they are following the required pattern. This is equally true of social behavior. People are often surprised at what they say and do in interpersonal interactions during replays of their performances.

It is difficult to guide actions that are only partially observable or to identify the corrective adjustments needed to make behavior congruent with symbolic conceptions. When performers have a clear representation of a given behavior and can observe their responses completely, they are able to improve their performances by matching them against their conception in the absence of information about response outcomes (Newell, 1976). However, when responses are only partially observable, performers infer what they are doing wrong from the evident results of their actions. Golfers, for example, try to diagnose and correct the faults of their swing from seeing the golf ball slice to the left or hook to the right. Their knowledge of what specific faulty movements produce such outcomes indicates what needs to be corrected. The less observable the responses are to performers, the more dependent they are on response-correlated outcomes to try to match action and contion.

That behavioral production is greatly aided by conception acquisition and optimal timing of observation of enactments is revealed in studies of performances that normally lie outside the performer's field of vision (Carroll & Bandura, 1982). Learners do not reproduce modeled patterns very accurately if they cannot see what they were doing, or if they observe their enactments on a video monitor but before they have formed an adequate conceptual representation of the activity. Without a conception to serve as a standard, they cannot use the visual feedback correctively. However, after learners have conceptualized the action pattern, their ability to observe their own enactments markedly facilitates accurate performance. The more accurate the conception, the better is the performance (Carroll & Bandura, 1985).

Simultaneous performance feedback would be of little value if performers remained dependent on it, because eventually the activities must be performed under conditions where such feedback is not provided. Ballet dancers can practice with mirrors, but they must later perform without them. Subsequent enactments must be monitored by the feel and the observable correlated outcomes of the actions. Such a transfer does indeed occur (Carroll & Bandura, 1982, 1985). After conceptions are translated into visually guided enactments, the activities continue to be performed accurately even though the concurrent, visual feedback has been discontinued.

The benefits of performance feedback will depend on its timing, specificity, and informativeness. Delayed self-observation makes it difficult to detect and correct mismatches between conception and action, because it is easy to get absorbed in the replay of a past performance without constantly comparing it to a memory of how it should be done. Moreover, in early phases of memory, the conception of the activity may be too sketchy to provide an adequate internal model for correcting the erroneous features of enactments. Consequently, even brief delays in observing replays of prior performances reduces the instructive value of the self-observation (Carroll & Bandura, 1985). If people visualize the modeled activity just as they are about to observe their earlier performances, then mismatches between their conception and action become more salient for error correction. Visualization may serve as one way of compensating for the limitations of delayed self-observation.

Self-observation through recordings and videotape replays is increasingly used to aid acquisition of skills. Providing delayed, unguided feedback, as is commonly done, usually produces poor results (Hung & Rosenthal, 1981; Rothstein & Arnold, 1976). Simply being shown replays of one's behavior or being told that one's performances were either faulty or successful has unpredictable effects. Such uninstructed replays do not necessarily ensure that observers will notice what they are doing wrong or that they will glean from their behavior the necessary corrective changes. Summary evaluations identify whether or not one is on the right track, but they convey little information about the specifics of one's performances. Without informative feedback and progressive subgoals to place current attainments in the proper perspective, self-observation of flawed performances can diminish observers' perceptions of their capabilities (Brown, 1980). Performance feedback should be structured in ways that build self-percepts of efficacy as well as skill. This dual goal is promoted by highlighting successes and gains, while correcting the deficiencies in subskills (Dowrick, 1983).

Feedback augmented by information provided visually, auditorily, or verbally is most likely to facilitate learning when one's performances are only partially observable or the natural feedback is difficult to monitor and perceive. Corrective feedback that directs attention to relevant aspects of subskills can aid the development of proficiency (Del Rey, 1971). Comparative studies show that people master modeled activities more rapidly with videotape feedback than if they have only limited knowledge of their performances (Neufeld & Neufeld, 1972). Once a skill has been mastered, the artificial feedback can be discontinued without any loss of proficiency.

The feedback that is most informative and achieves the greatest gains relies on corrective modeling (Vasta, 1976). In this approach—which typifies guided skill acquisition, be it tennis, dramatics, violin virtuosity, or social skills—troublesome segments of a performance are identified, and adept ways of performing them are modeled by those who are proficient at it. Learners then rehearse those subskills until they master them. For ongoing tasks, periodic feedback about how one is doing fosters goal setting and heightens attentional involvement in related activities. As a result, informative feedback not only improves the behavior singled out for attention, it also facilitates the observational learning of new activities in the same setting, even though no feedback is provided (Vasta, 1976).

Motivational Processes

Social cognitive theory distinguishes between acquisition and performance. This distinction is emphasized because people do not enact everything they learn. They may acquire and retain the capabilities to execute modeled activities adeptly but rarely or never perform them. Discrepancies between learning and performance are most likely to arise when acquired behavior has little functional value or carries high risk of punishment. When positive incentives are provided, observational learning, which has previously remained unexpressed, is promptly translated into action (Bandura, 1965b; Dubanoski & Parton, 1971; Madsen, 1968).

Performance of observationally learned behavior is influenced by three sources of incentives—direct, vicarious, and self-produced. People are more likely to exhibit modeled behavior if it results in valued outcomes than if it has unrewarding or punishing effects. The way in which external incentives selectively influence performance of modeled behavior is revealed in a study by Bandura and Barab (1971). When exposed to different models exhibiting different patterns of behavior, children selectively imitate the behavior that produces rewarding effects but decline imitating unrewarded behavior. In everyday situations, the external incentives for modeling may take the form of material benefits, enjoyable or unpleasant sensory stimulation, positive or negative social reactions, or the rewards of efficacy in exercising control over events by using the modeled skills.

Observed outcomes influence the performance of modeled behavior in much the same way. Among the countless behaviors acquired through observation, those that seem to be effective for others are favored over those behaviors that have been observed to produce negative consequences (Bandura, 1965b). Personal standards of conduct provide a further source of motivation. The evaluative reactions people generate to their own behavior regulate which observationally learned activities they are most likely to pursue. They express what they find self-satisfying but reject what they personally disapprove (Hicks, 1971; Slife & Rychlak, 1982). The processes by which observed and self-evaluative incentives operate as motivators are examined in later chapters.

Mowrer (1960) proposed a sensory-feedback theory that emphasized classically conditioned positive and negative emotions as the motivators of imitative behavior. The formulation goes as follows: While performing, models often reward and punish observers, or they intuit the model's own satisfaction and discomforts. Through such repeated associations between modeled behavior and affective experiences, positive and negative emotions eventually become conditioned to the imitative responses themselves. As a result, observers are disposed to perform positively conditioned responses and to refrain from imitative responses that have been endowed with negative affect.

There exist substantial data that imitation in children can be increased by noncontingent nurturance from models or by seeing modeled behavior rewarded. However, the results of these studies raise more reservations than support for the affective conditioning theory. Even though the models' nurturance is uniformly associated with the different behaviors they exhibit, it increases imitation of some responses but not of others (Bandura & Huston, 1961; Madsen, 1968; Mischel & Grusec, 1966; Rosenhan & White, 1967); it may even diminish adoption of self-stringent conduct (Bandura,

Grusec, & Menlove, 1967; Grusec, 1971). Moreover, the effects of model nurturance on imitativeness vary in different situations and times and for different behavior (Yarrow & Scott, 1972). Level of model nurturance is, therefore, of limited value in predicting when, where, and what type of modeled behavior will be performed.

Studies in which models exhibit specific responses while simultaneously rewarding observers, thereby creating the necessary conditioning requirements, raise even more serious doubts about the affective conditioning theory. Observers imitate modeled responses to the same extent, regardless of whether the responses are displayed alone or in conjunction with rewards (Dubanoski, 1972; Foss, 1964). When observed consequences influence imitativeness, as they often do, there are strong indications that such changes are cognitively mediated through self-efficacy judgments and outcome expectations, rather than conditioning of emotion to the behavior itself.

In an elaboration of the affective-feedback theory of imitation, Aronfreed (1969) has advanced the view that pleasurable and aversive affective states become conditioned to cognitive templates of modeled actions, as well as to somatic cues arising from actions. This conceptualization of imitation is difficult to test empirically, because it does not specify in sufficient detail the characteristics of templates, the process by which templates are acquired, the manner in which emotions become coupled to templates, and how the emotionally arousing properties of templates are transferred to intentions and to somatic cues, which are intrinsic to actions.

Rapid selection of responses from available alternatives cannot be governed by affective feedback, because few responses can be activated, even incipiently, during the instant when people must decide how to respond to rapidly changing events. Recognizing this problem, Mowrer (1960) speculated that the initial scanning and selection of responses occurs primarily at the cognitive,

rather than the action, level. This is consistent with the view that human behavior is largely regulated by the anticipated consequences of prospective actions.

Actions cannot be regulated by affective qualities implanted in the behavior itself, because its expression varies widely with circumstances. Aggressive behavior is a good example. The act of hitting, whether it is directed toward parents, peers, or inanimate objects, differs little, if at all. Nevertheless, children inhibit hitting parents, whereas they more readily aggress toward peers (Bandura & Walters, 1959, 1963). In certain well-defined contexts, as in competitive boxing, otherwise nonassaultive people will pummel each other freely. Aggression is better predicted from information about the social context (church or gymnasium), the target (parent, teacher, police officer, or peer), perceived physical efficacy, and other factors signifying potential consequences, than from assessments of the emotions infused in aggressive acts or their cognitive templates. The same subskills must serve diverse purposes. If the regulators were built into the behavior itself, the flexibility and adaptiveness of human functioning would be seriously impaired. It is because the mechanism of control operates mainly at the cognitive level that the same behavior can be freely expressed, remain unutilized, or be actively self-restrained, depending on circumstances.

Multiprocess Analysis of Modeling Deficits. Because of numerous factors governing observational learning, exposure to models, even highly effective ones, will not automatically create similar competencies. One can, of course, produce some imitative behavior without considering the underlying processes. A model who demonstrates desired activities over and over, who instructs observers to follow the behavior, who prompts them verbally and physically when they fail, and who then rewards them when they succeed, will eventually evoke matching performances. If, on the other hand, one seeks to explain how modeling occurs and how to achieve its effects predictably, one must consider the subprocesses governing this mode of influence.

A theory of observational learning must account for the failures of modeling as well as its successes. In any given instance, faulty modeling may result from deficiencies in any of the four subfunctions. Many failures in observational learning undoubtedly come from attentional deficits. In other instances, observers may attend to modeled activities but fail to profit from such experiences because they lack the cognitive skills for symbolizing and rehearsing what they have observed. In still other instances, observational learning may create poor performances because of deficiencies in motor production or motivation. Thus, a multiprocess analysis of observational learning specifies the possible sources of dysfunction and the psychological aspects requiring change.

Modeling Process and the Medium of Information Transmission

A major function of modeling is to transmit information to observers about how subskills can be synthesized into new patterns. Such information can be conveyed through physical demonstration, pictorial representation, or verbal description. Much social learning occurs on the basis of casual or directed observation of other people in everyday situations. Learning in young children depends extensively on the behavioral modeling that pervades their daily lives. Indeed, in many languages the word for "teach" is the same as the word for "show" (Reichard, 1938).

As linguistic competence is developed, verbal modeling often substitutes for or supplements behavioral modeling as the preferred mode of guidance. By following written descriptions of how to behave, people are aided in mastering social, occupational, and recreational skills, in assembling and operating complicated equipment, and

in learning the appropriate conduct for different situations. Verbal modeling is used extensively, because one can convey with words an almost infinite variety of behaviors that may be too inconvenient or time-consuming to portray behaviorally. Because verbal description is effective in focusing attention on relevant aspects of ongoing activities, verbal modeling often accompanies behavioral exemplifications.

Another influential source of social learning at any age is the abundant and varied symbolic modeling provided by television, films , and other visual media. The advent of television has greatly expanded the range of the models available to people. Whereas previously modeling influences were largely confined to the behavior exhibited in one's immediate community, nowadays diverse styles of conduct are brought to people within the comfort of their homes through the vehicle of television. Both children and adults acquire attitudes, thought patterns, emotional bents, and new styles of conduct through symbolic modeling (Bandura, 1973; Comstock et al., 1978; Liebert, Sprafkin, & Davidson, 1982). In view of the efficacy of, and extensive public exposure to, televised modeling, the mass media play an influential role in shaping human thought and action. Further developments in communication technology will enable people to observe on request almost any desired activity at any time on computer-linked television consoles. Videodisc systems with random access to a huge amount of auditory and visual information provide a further medium for effective modeling of valued skills. Symbolic modeling can convey most of the knowledge about skills, so that personal instruction can be devoted to perfecting and applying the new competencies.

A major significance of symbolic modeling lies in its tremendous multiplicative power. Unlike learning by doing, which requires shaping the actions through repeated trial-and-error experiences, in observational learning a single model can transmit new ways of thinking and behaving simultaneously to many people in widely dispersed locales. There is another aspect of symbolic modeling that magnifies its psychological and social effects. During the course of their daily lives, people have direct contact with only a small sector of the environment. Consequently, their conceptions of social reality are greatly influenced by vicarious experiences—what they see, hear, and read in the mass media—without direct experimental correctives. The more people's images of reality depend upon the media's symbolic environment, the greater is its social impact.

New technologies alter the mode of modeling to boost its instructive power. One promising development is the use of computer graphics to model and improve physical skills. Some skills are difficult to grasp and perfect because the constituent actions may occur in a split second. Learners have difficulty not only seeing what is being modeled but also in monitoring their own enactments, because much of the activity occurs outside their visual field. Ultra-highspeed cameras are used to capture what the eye cannot easily see in modeled performances (Gustkey, 1979). The picture frames are then translated into moving figures of the performance on a computer screen, enabling observers to discover what best to do at any given point in the action. The instructiveness of performance feedback can be augmented by this means. Electronic analysis of filmed enactments graphically pinpoints mistakes in the execution of skills.

Computerized self-modeling of optimal performances is also increasingly used to perfect skills (Grayson, 1980). In this application, a person's performances are captured on film and electronically analyzed for correctness. The film is then edited so that only a perfectly executed performance remains. Learners watch themselves performing skillfully over and over again to master the ideal conception of the activity. Self-modeling of successes by videotape replay has been shown to improve performance (Dowrick, 1983). However, anecdotal reports that computerized self-modeling

produces superior performances await empirical confirmation.

Response information can be transmitted, although less precisely, through modalities other than auditory or visual ones. In learning to speak, persons who are deaf and blind rely on kinesthetic modeling by matching through touch the mouth and laryngeal muscular responses of verbalizing models (Keller, 1927; Young & Hawk, 1955). Blind and visually impaired individuals have benefitted substantially from tactile modeling coupled with verbal descriptions (Burleson, 1973). Laryngographic visual displays of larynx vibrations corresponding to speech patterns are replacing tactile modeling for hearing impaired persons who have the benefit of sight (Fourcin & Abberton, 1972). Speakers develop their speech by matching their speech to those waveforms of the utterances that have been modeled for them.

Social cognitive theory is more concerned with the process involved in the representational guidance of action than with the particular medium by which response information is conveyed. The basic conception-matching process is the same, regardless of whether the conception of the behavior has been constructed from words, pictures, or actions. Analysis of the common processes governing learning from different modeling modalities provides better understanding of learning mechanisms than creating separate theories to explain each modeling modality.

This is not to say that different forms of modeling are equally effective. They may differ in the amount of information they convey and in their power to command attention. How information is communicated can also affect how it is cognitively processed. Verbal and pictorial modeling call upon different cognitive skills and ways of coding for extracting the most pertinent information (Salomon, 1979). To benefit from verbal modeling requires more in the way of linguistic and conceptual proficiencies than does pictorial modeling, which lends itself easily to simpler imaginal representation. Observers can, of course, extract more from pictorial modeling if the information it conveys is coded into generic verbal rules for memory representation. Different modes of modeling may enlist different levels of cognitive processing. Salomon (1984, 1983) finds that the more cognitive effort people invest in extracting relevant information and elaborating its meaning, the better they learn and remember what is presented by a particular medium. Because children generally view pictorial media as easy and print media as difficult, they tend to invest less cognitive effort in learning from pictures than from the printed word. Media that provide equivalent information but differ in perceived level of demand may produce dissimilar observational learning because they do not mobilize the same amount of cognitive processing.

How well different forms of modeled information are cognitively processed will depend on observers' developmental level. In the earliest years of life, infants and young children at the preverbal level of development must rely on physical examples for information about effective ways of behaving. As they gain linguistic competence and cognitive skills, they can acquire ways of thinking and behaving from verbal modeling. Words can be easily used to symbolize not only specific actions but also the rules for generating new instances of the modeled behavior.

The flexibility of verbal symbols greatly extends the range and utility of modeling, but the verbal modality has limitations. It is often difficult to convey through words the same amount of information contained in pictorial or live demonstrations. Moreover, actions are usually more effective than words in commanding attention. Televised displays are generally more compelling to both children and adults than oral or written reports of the same subject. Furthermore, verbal modes rely more heavily upon cognitive prerequisites for their effects. Observers whose conceptual and verbal skills are underdeveloped are likely to benefit more from behavioral demonstrations than from verbal modeling (Rosenthal & Zimmerman, 1978). In everyday life, of course, observational learning is rarely restricted to a single modality. People pattern their behavior on information conveyed by both the overt actions and the words of others.

Comparison of Modes of Modeling. As already alluded to, the relative effectiveness of the different modalities of modeling will depend on the developmental competence of observers and the complexity and codability of the modeled activities. When live and pictorial modeling command attention and convey the same amount of response information, they produce comparable levels of observational learning in very young children (Bandura, Ross, & Ross, 1963a). Studies of verbal modeling with children who have a good grasp of language demonstrate that modeled styles of behavior can be transmitted without requiring a model's physical presence, if the modeled acts are adequately depicted verbally (Bandura & Mischel, 1965).

Learning through verbal modeling is sometimes designated as "instructions" and distinguished from modeling as though the two modes of influence represent different processes. In analyzing verbal influence on behavior, it is essential to distinguish between the *instigational* and the *modeling* effects of instructions. Words can be used to induce individuals to perform what they have previously learned or to teach them new behaviors. Instructions are most likely to promote appropriate skills when they both describe how to construct the requisite behavior and prompt it. For new activities, verbal instigation without response instruction does not achieve much of anything. Little would be gained, for example, by merely telling a novice, who had no knowledge of airplanes, to go fly an aircraft. In empirical comparisons of instructions with verbal modeling (Masters & Branch, 1969), both types of influences produce their effects through verbal modeling, and they differ only in the explicitness with which the appropriate behavior is defined. Providing an informative rule of behavior produces faster changes than having the observer infer the rule from a few examples.

In the sense that instructions provide rules for generating examples, and modeling provides examples for inducing rules, Marlatt (1972) has characterized instructions as deductive and modeling as inductive in nature. This distinction may apply in some, but not in all, instances. In prescribed skills, which must be performed in a uniform way because of custom or natural requirements, words and actions convey equivalent information. In teaching people how to drive automobiles, for example, verbal instructions and behavioral demonstrations are essentially the same. Instructions, of course, are not always generic, and modeling is not necessarily specific. More often than not instructions describe how to perform specific acts without specifying general rules of conduct. In cognitive modeling, models verbalize the rules and strategies guiding their choice of actions (Meichenbaum, 1977). Whether learning through modeling occurs inductively or deductively thus depends on what is being modeled.

A number of studies, analyzed by Rosenthal and Zimmerman (1978), have investigated the extent to which children acquire and then generalize rule-governed behavior to new situations, when they have been either instructed in the rule, have simply observed modeled performances embodying the rule, or have been provided with the rule, along with modeled exemplars. With young children, behavioral modeling (from which the rule underlying the responses must be inferred) is comparable or superior to verbal instruction in the rule for producing generalized changes. However, generalized cognitive skills are best imparted by providing rules with demonstrations of how they can be applied in certain situations (Rosenthal & Zimmerman,

1978). The same is true of interpersonal skills (Decker, 1982). Both types of guides are usually needed because people can acquire abstract principles but remain in a quandary about how to implement them, if they have not had the benefit of illustrative exemplars.

The limitation of verbal formats alone is shown by White and Rosenthal (1974), who studied acquisition of abstract principles in a natural situation over an extended period. Children achieved significant gains in knowledge when instruction was interspersed with modeled demonstration of the principles, whereas they learned little when the equivalent information was presented through verbal instruction alone. Vivid examples enhance attention and aid comprehension by providing meaningful referents for abstract notions. In addition to facilitating learning, White and Rosenthal found that behavioral exemplifications create positive attitudes toward the subject matter. This is an important generalized benefit. Instruction should develop favorable attitudes toward what one is learning (Mager, 1968). Teaching that instills a liking for what is taught fosters self-initiated learning long after the instruction has ceased.

In the social cognitive view, a common conception-matching mechanism underlies the different modes of learning. Procedures carrying different labels (e.g., instruction, modeling, coaching) may all convey similar information. Hence, a method that proves effective by itself may appear weak when added to another one because it provides redundant information (Eisler, Blanchard, Fitts, & Williams, 1978; Rosenthal & Bandura, 1978; McFall & Twentyman, 1973). Reversing the sequence in which the methods are applied might qualify or reverse their apparent efficacy. For these reasons, it is more instructive to center attention on the amount and kind of information conveyed by instructive influences than on what they are called. Too often, progress in the understanding of learning processes is retarded by diversionary disputes over labels attached to the medium by which information is conveyed.

Verbal Modeling of Thought Processes. Much human learning is aimed at developing cognitive skills in gaining and using knowledge for future use. Observers can learn thinking skills and how to apply them by inferring the rules and strategies models use as they arrive at solutions. However, cognitive skills are less readily amenable to change by modeling of strategies alone when covert thought processes have not been adequately reflected in modeled actions. In the extreme case, the model solves the problem cognitively and enacts only the final step of the solution. The observer sees the end result but not the cognitive process by which it has been achieved.

Learning cognitive skills can be facilitated simply by having models verbalize their thought strategies aloud as they engage in problem-solving activities. The covert thoughts guiding the actions are thus made observable through overt representation. Modeling both thoughts and actions has several helpful features that contribute to its effectiveness in producing generalized, lasting improvements in cognitive skills. Nonverbal modeling gains and holds attention, which is often difficult to sustain by talk alone. It also provides an informative semantic context within which to imbed verbalized rules. Behavioral referents confer meaning on cognitive abstractions. Moreover, verbalized rules and strategies can be reiterated in variant forms as often as needed to impart a cognitive skill without taxing observers' interest by using different exemplars. Varied application deepens understanding of generative rules.

Meichenbaum (1977) has devised programs for developing cognitive skills by modeling thought processes in conjunction with action strategies. Cognitive skills are usually improved more by the combined influence of thought and action modeling than by action modeling alone (Denney, 1975; Denney & Denney, 1974). The contri-

bution of verbal thought modeling when cognitive processes are only partially observable in the action will be reviewed more fully in the discussion of cognitive development.

Role of Reinforcement in Observational Learning

An issue of contention in observational learning concerns the role of reinforcement. Behavioristic theories of imitation assume that matching responses must be performed and reinforced in order to be learned (Baer & Sherman, 1964; Miller & Dollard, 1941; Gewirtz, 1971). The operant conditioning analysis relies entirely upon the standard three-component paradigm $S^d \rightarrow R \rightarrow S^r$, where S^d denotes the modeled stimulus, R represents an overt matching response, and S^r designates the reinforcing stimulus. Observational learning presumably is achieved through differential reinforcement. When responses corresponding to the model's actions are reinforced, and divergent responses are either unrewarded or punished, the behavior of others becomes a cue for matching responses.

This conceptual scheme does not provide a suitable explanation of observational learning where observers do not perform matching behavior in the same setting in which it is modeled, when neither the model nor the observers are reinforced, and whatever responses acquired through observation are first performed days, weeks, or months later. Under this set of conditions, which represents the pervasive form of observational learning, two of the factors $(R \rightarrow S^r)$ in the three-element paradigm are absent during acquisition, and the third factor (S^d, the modeling cue) is absent from the situation in which the observationally learned behavior was first performed. The operant analysis clarifies how previously learned imitative behavior can be prompted by the actions of others and the prospect of reward. However, it does not explain how new response structures are acquired through observation. It is primarily a theory of performance control rather than of learning.

In an operant conditioning analysis of imitation, Gewirtz (1971) conceptualizes observational learning as analogous to the matching-to-sample paradigm used to study discrimination learning. In this procedure, persons choose one stimulus, from among several comparison stimuli, that shares a common property with the sample stimulus. Although modeling and matching-to-sample both involve a matching process, they can hardly be equated. A person can accurately select, from among video displays of swimming, golfing, skiing, and fencing, the one that matches a sample skiing performance but be unable to ski down a mountainside. There are numerous activities we can recognize but cannot perform adequately. Discriminative observation is only one subfunction of observational learning, not the acquisition process itself.

Gewirtz's position on observational learning is somewhat indeterminate, because he alternately questions whether the phenomenon exists, or reduces it to social facilitation of previously learned responses, or offers descriptive labels (e.g., "generalized imitation," "learned-to-learn," and "discriminated operant") as explanations. To say that people learn by observation because they have "learned-to-learn" or have acquired a "discriminated-operant" does not explain how responses are organized into new structures without reinforced performance.

Some writers contend that since the entire learning history of an observer is unknown, one cannot prove the negative: that a given behavior has not been learned prior to the modeling experience. That people can learn novel responses by observation can be easily demonstrated without having to control or catalogue their entire life history. One need only model an original response, such as the word *zergebanfloger*—never before encountered because it has just been created—and test whether observers acquire it after one or more modeled exposures. It is rarely the case that the behavior being reinforced in humans has never been observed by them. Whatever activities are reinforced were probably at least partially learned through past observational experiences. Were one to apply the above argument consistently, operant researchers would have to assess every observational experience in the entire life history of a person to prove that reinforcement was responsible for the imitative behavior.

When behavior changes without reinforcement, radical behaviorists appeal to reinforcement history as the cause. The same historical repository is invoked to explain observational learning. They assume that initial matching responses emerge by chance, physical guidance, or selective reinforcement of randomly emitted behavior. Through repeated reinforcement, response similarity eventually becomes either rewarding in itself (Baer & Sherman, 1964), or it provides a discriminative stimulus that imitative behavior will be reinforced (Gewirtz, 1971). Reinforcement is thus said to create a "generalized imitation tendency" which leads people to imitate a variety of responses, many of which go unrewarded. The generalized tendency is defined as inherent reward in Baer's formulation and as an undiscriminating disposition in Gewirtz's proposal.

Evidence to be reviewed shortly contests the view that people imitate because response similarity is inherently rewarding. Gewirtz's notion that behavioral similarity is the antecedent cue for imitation also runs into explanatory difficulties. As Parton (1976) has noted, because behavioral similarity does not appear until after the imitative response has been performed, similarity cannot be the antecedent cue for imitative acts. In Gewirtz's scheme the alleged cause (response similarity) occurs after the effect (matching behavior).

An explanation that makes similarity the determiner of action runs into empirical problems, as well as the logical one of placing the effect before the cause. People are rewarded from time to time for behaving like others but not indiscriminately so. Whether imitations are rewarded, punished, or ignored depends on the models, the kinds of actions, the persons toward whom the behavior is directed, and the times and places where the modeled behavior is performed. It is not behavioral similarity *per se* that predicts likely outcomes of adopting modeled behavior. When imitating certain models is rewarded and imitating other models is nonrewarded or punished, the models become the predictive cues for selective imitation (Bandura & Barab, 1971). Often, the nature of the behavior is the predictor. If, for example, imitative cooperation is effective, but imitative aggression is ineffective, children will selectively favor modeled cooperation (Chittenden, 1972). In other instances, the situation in which the modeled behavior is expressed is the reliable predictor. Children will imitate aggression in settings in which it is rewarded but not in situations where it is likely to be punished (Bandura & Walters, 1959; Hicks, 1968).

In brief, predictors of how imitative behavior is likely to be received take many forms. Based on the different sources of predictive information, observers form outcome expectations for regulating their imitative behavior. Foresight of consequences rather than conditioned similarity is the regulatory mechanism.

Outcome expectations derived from observed or experienced consequences may provide a source of motivation for observational learning, but reinforcement history in no way explains how behavior patterns are learned by observation. The determinants of early imitations may provide an insufficient, or even a misleading, explanation of how behavioral structures are acquired through observation. Initially, the infant's imitative acts are externally cued by a model's actions. Instant mimicry can occur without much symbolic representation or learning for that matter. The difference between externally guided and delayed modeling is like the difference between drawing a picture of one's automobile when it is at hand and drawing it from memory. In the latter situation, the hand does not automatically sketch the car; rather, one must rely on memory guides, in this case mainly imaginal representations.

When time elapses between observation and performance, the absent modeled events must be internally represented in symbolic form. Hence, cognitive factors that aid long-term retention are critical determinants of observational learning. Observers who transform modeled activities into easily remembered symbols achieve substantially better acquisition and retention of modeled behavior than those who do not (Bandura, Grusec, & Menlove, 1966; Bandura, Jeffery, & Bachicha, 1974). Indeed, when modeled activities are complex, observation without cognitive transformation produces little or no learning (Bandura & Jeffery, 1973). Because delayed modeling is achieved through different processes than is externally prompted mimicry, the latter offers an inadequate explanation of the former.

Neither appeal to "reinforcement history" nor to "generalized imitative tendency" explains why adults, who have experienced countless reinforcements for matching behavior, learn nothing from observing others unless the modeled information is cognitively transformed. Nor can the benefits of cognitive factors be dismissed on the erroneous grounds that cognitive factors are inferred from the imitative behavior (Gewirtz & Stingle, 1968). On the contrary, in the studies examining cognitive mechanisms in observational learning, observers are instructed in advance to process cognitively what they see. They code and rehearse aloud to provide public records of what ordinarily are covert processes. The memory codes are thus measured in advance and independently of the motor performance.

In the social cognitive view, observational learning occurs through cognitive processing during exposure to modeled events before any responses have been performed and does not necessarily require extrinsic reward. This is not to say that mere exposure to modeled activities is, in itself, sufficient to produce observational learning. Not all stimulation that impinges on individuals is necessarily observed by them, and even if noticed, what is registered may not be retained for any length of time.

Incentives play a role in observational learning but mainly as an antecedent rather than a consequent influence. Anticipation of benefits can influence what is observed and what goes unnoticed. Knowing that a given model's behavior is effective in producing valued outcomes, or in averting punishing ones, can improve observational learning by channeling and increasing the observers' attentiveness to a model's actions. Moreover, anticipated benefits can improve retention of what has been learned through observation by motivating people to symbolize and rehearse modeled activities that they value highly.

Theories of modeling differ in the manner in which incentives affect observational learning, rather than in whether incentives play a role in the acquisition process. The issue in dispute is whether consequences act backward to strengthen preceding imitative responses and their connection to stimuli, or whether they facilitate learning anticipatorily by enhancing attentional, encoding, and rehearsal processes. Observational learning can be improved more effectively by informing observers in advance about the benefits of adopting modeled behavior than by waiting until the observers happen to imitate a model and then rewarding them for it.

Incentives are facilitative rather than necessary, because factors other than anticipated consequences can influence what people attend to. One does not have to be reinforced, for example, to listen to compelling sounds or to look at captivating visual displays. When attention is drawn to modeled activities by the events themselves, the addition of positive incentives does not increase observational learning (Bandura, Grusec, & Menlove, 1966; Rosenthal & Zimmerman, 1978). Indeed, after the capability for observational learning has been fully developed, one cannot keep people from learning something of what they have seen.

Because the belief that responses must be performed before they can be learned is deeply entrenched, radical behaviorists have attempted to reduce observational learning to operant conditioning. Evidence about the cognitive mediation of enactive learning argues for reversing the direction of the reductive analysis. When people learn through response consequences, they construct the appropriate behavior by observing the effects of their actions and inferring the structure of the behavior from bits of information so gained. Operant conditioning thus becomes a special case of observational learning. Good examples are better conveyers of response information than are the outcomes of hit-and-miss actions. Therefore, one can symbolically construct the structure of behavior more readily from observing examples than from examining the effects of one's actions.

People often show little or only sporadic attention to ongoing modeled events when they are insufficiently striking to command attention on their own. Under such circumstances, providing incentives for observational learning can raise and channel attention to modeled behavior that might otherwise go unnoticed. The consequence of the model's responses both draw attention to the modeled behavior and facilitate its learning (Yussen, 1974). Evidence that punishment improves observational learning of the punished behavior contradicts reinforcement theory and lends further validity to the view that response consequences serve as attention and memory enhancers, rather than as retrospective strengtheners of modeled actions.

Most studies of how incentives contribute to observational learning use forced exposure to a single set of modeled acts without distracters to divert attention to other events. Observers cannot help but notice what they have been shown, regardless of whether or not they are provided incentives to do so. In everyday situations many activities go on simultaneously, and persons must choose which activities, from among the alternatives, they will observe, when they will observe them, and for what length of time. The functional value of the alternatives provides one basis for determining which modeled performances are worth observing and learning. Hence, incentives will play a greater role in observational learning under conditions of self-selected exposure than when exposure is forced.

Both reinforcement and social cognitive theories assume that whether or not people choose to perform what they have learned through observation is influenced by the consequences of such actions. Social cognitive theory, however, encompasses a broad range of incentive influences including external, vicarious, and self-generated consequences. Simply demonstrating that modeled responses are performed more often if rewarded, than if not, has no bearing on the dispute over the role of reinforcement in observational learning. All theories predict that incentives facilitate performance. To identify the determinants of observational learning requires tests of acquisition in which, after exposure to novel performances, observers either describe the modeled patterns or the rules for generating them, specify their conception of the behavior, use the acquired knowledge to comprehend events, or are instructed to enact everything fully that they have observed. Prior reward increases performance of modeled behavior, but tests of acquisition reveal equivalent observational learning regardless of whether or not imitativeness has been previously rewarded (Adams & Hamm, 1973).

Nonrewarded Modeling

Modeled behavior is often performed without any immediate external rewards. This is by no means unique to modeled conduct. Human behavior, however acquired, is largely regulated by self-percepts of efficacy and anticipated consequences of prospective actions. People will, therefore, persist for some time in actions that go unrewarded on the expectation that their efforts will eventually produce results. Since, in the behavioristic view, one cannot learn by watching without being reinforced, some of its proponents have searched for a source of instantaneous reinforcement in modeling. Baer and his associates have interpreted nonreinforced modeling, which they label "generalized imitation," in terms of its acquired reward value (Baer, Peterson, & Sherman, 1967; Baer & Sherman, 1964). They assumed that behavioral similarity eventually acquires rewarding properties through repeated association of imitative acts with tangible rewards. After similarity has become reinforcing in itself, people are disposed to imitate because it is inherently rewarding.

Explaining nonrewarded modeling in terms of conditioned reward has been challenged on both conceptual and empirical grounds. If behavioral similarity is inherently rewarding, then people should display generalized imitation of all types of conduct as modeled by all kinds of people, be they children, barbers, police officers, or professors. In fact, people are highly selective in the behaviors they adopt from others. Moreover, if every matching response is automatically rewarding, what induces an observer to stop performing them? A conditioned reward interpretation would have to posit some counteracting influence to explain why people do not imitate everything they happen to see, and why they discontinue inherently rewarding activities.

In the method used to demonstrate "generalized imitation," a model tells children to imitate responses that he or she demonstrates one at a time and rewards each correct imitation (Baer & Sherman, 1964). After a while, children imitate nonrewarded responses as long as imitation of some modeled actions is rewarded. This was taken as evidence that behavioral similarity had become rewarding in itself. However, further research revealed that social pressure rather than conditioned reward was largely responsible for nonrewarded imitation under such instructed conditions. Past experiences teach children that it is usually prudent to do what adults tell them. Nonrewarded imitation is raised by prior rewards for complying with instructions unrelated to modeling and eliminated by prior reward for noncompliance with instructions (Oliver, Acker, & Oliver, 1977). As might be expected, nonrewarded imitations decline when the social pressure is removed (Bandura & Barab, 1971; Bufford, 1971; Parton, 1970; Steinman, 1970b; Waxler & Yarrow, 1970). Even in the presence of situational demands for mimicry, observing others copy rewardable responses and ignore nonrewarded ones produces the immediate cessation of nonrewarded imitations, something which would not happen if behavioral matching were inherently rewarding (Burgess, Burgess, & Esveldt, 1970).

Although coercive inducements will foster compliance, they are not the sole determinants of nonrewarded imitations. Modeled conduct is frequently performed without immediate benefit, even when the situational demands are weak or absent. This usually results from failure to distinguish between rewarded and nonrewarded classes of behavior. In regulating their imitative behavior, observers rely on cues that predict likely consequences. The role played by discrimination failures in imitation of nonrewarded acts, under noncoercive conditions, is revealed when the model's characteristics and features of the behavior serve as predictive cues (Bandura & Barab, 1971). Children extensively imitated the manual acts of a female model who rewarded them for behaving like her, but they declined to imitate similar manual actions of a male model who never rewarded their matching behavior. In the next phase of the study, the previously rewarding female model exhibited three kinds of responses of which only the original manual set was rewarded. Children continued to imitate the rewarded

manual acts. They promptly ceased imitating vocal responses by the same female model that were easily distinguishable as ones that had never been rewarded. But they continued to perform nonrewarded manual responses that were difficult to distinguish from the rewarded manual imitations. Other studies using clearly distinguishable motor and vocal responses (Garcia, Baer, & Firestone, 1971) similarly reveal that children tend to imitate only the type of behavior that is rewarded.

In the preceding experiments, children imitated selectively on the basis of model and response characteristics that were predictive of consequences. Children also regulate their imitative behavior by situational cues signifying probable outcomes. Furnell and Thomas (1976) found that children modeled a variety of responses in the presence of situational cues predictive of reward for imitation, but they ceased imitating the same responses by the same model when the situational cues signified nonreward for imitation. Moreover, the selective imitation transferred to new situational cues according to their similarity to the original predictive ones.

When coercive inducements are superimposed on differential reward, most children will perform demanded behavior even though they recognize which types of responses will be rewarded and which will be ignored (Oliver & Hoppe, 1974; Steinman, 1970a, 1970b). Showing that social demands can override the influence of differential consequences on imitation has little bearing, however, on whether discrimination difficulties account for nonrewarded imitations when such behavior has not been socially coerced.

Given a choice of imitating responses that are rewardable and those that are not, children initially exhibit a relatively high rate of nonrewarded imitations, but after recognizing the differential outcomes, they cease imitating the nonrewarded ones (Steinman, 1970b). Nonrewarded imitations are generally performed more often when they are similar to rewarded responses than when they are clearly different from them. These and other studies (Bucher & Bowman, 1974; Peterson, Merwin, Moyer, & Whitehurst, 1971) lend further support to the role of discrimination processes in nonrewarded modeling. From the social cognitive perspective, the reward of some imitative responses supports nonrewarded imitations that are indistinguishable from the rewarded one because it creates expectations of reward, rather than making behavioral similarity inherently rewarding. Gewirtz's (1971) account of nonrewarded imitations also leans heavily on discrimination failures, but his conceptual scheme relies solely on intermittent extrinsic reinforcement as the explanatory factor. People presumably imitate all types of responses because they are intermittently rewarded for some imitative responses.

Nonrewarded modeling can have many determinants. Social inducements, indistinguishability of rewardable actions, and uncertainties arising from irregular outcomes have already been mentioned. Some nonrewarded imitations are maintained by mistaken beliefs about the social effects emulative acts are likely to produce. This is especially evident in children (Bandura & Barab, 1971). Some believe that repeated emulation might eventually persuade unresponsive models to reward their emulative acts. Others deliberately perform some nonrewarded imitations to test and confirm their hypothesis about what actions secure rewards.

Modeled behavior that has personal significance can be maintained in the absence of extrinsic incentives by self-evaluative reactions. Because people admire some forms of conduct and devalue others, behavioral similarity is not invariably self-satisfying. People respond self-approvingly to modeled actions they value. Equally close matches with devalued conduct would evoke self-critical reactions and, hence, are not even attempted, let alone repeated (Hicks, 1971). In activities having self-evaluative significance, personal standards rather than behavioral similarity determine whether close matches will be rewarding or displeasing. In most studies of nonreinforced modeling, the modeled acts are usually disconnected acts and words that lack sufficient meaning to activate self-evaluative mechanisms. To explain modeling without extrinsic incentives, as it occurs in the natural environment, research needs to be extended to personally meaningful behaviors that engage self systems.

DEVELOPMENTAL ANALYSIS OF OBSERVATIONAL LEARNING

Because observational learning involves several subfunctions that evolve with maturation and experience, it depends upon prior development. Behaviorists approach this issue as a problem of teaching children to imitate. Initially, nonimitative children are trained to imitate and to generalize imitativeness by rewarding them for matching different responses exhibited by different models in different situations (Garcia et al., 1971; Harris, 1975; Koegel & Rincover, 1974; Wulbert, Nyman, Snow, & Owen, 1973). The amount of modeling can be increased by rewarding matching behavior. However, such demonstrations do not identify what exactly is being acquired during the process. Nor is reinforcement of much help in explaining why, under identical incentive conditions, children vary greatly in how long it takes them to imitate, and some do not imitate at all (Lovaas & Newsom, 1976).

There are certain features of operant research that further limit the generality of findings regarding the initial development of observational learning. Studies of learning to imitate are often confined to severely retarded children on the disputable assumption that they have never exhibited any imitative behavior. The failure to imitate responses when they are modeled under particular incentive conditions does not mean that children lack such skills. Severely retarded children who are initially non-imitative can suddenly become highly imitative upon observing another child rewarded a few times for patterning behavior after that of a model (Bandura & Barab, 1971). Nonimitative children are usually slow in producing the first matching responses, but after grasping the idea from seeing the rewarding feedback, they suddenly start imitating at a high rate. From such findings it would appear that reinforcement serves more to inform children that imitativeness is useful than to create generative imitative skills that they did not have before. When the tasks involve instantaneous mimicry of simple responses, as they often do, the performances reflect echoic memory more than observational learning. Studies aimed at elucidating the initial development of facility in observational learning would do better to examine infants' acquisition of generative modeling skills under varying delays between observation and performance.

When analyzed in terms of its constituent subfunctions, facility in observational learning is not primarily a matter of learning to imitate, nor is it a discrete skill. Rather, developing adeptness in observational learning involves acquiring multiple subskills in selective observation, symbolic coding and rehearsal, coordinating sensory-motor and conceptual-motor systems, and judging probable outcomes for adopting another's behavior. Observational learning is hindered by deficits and enhanced by proficiency in its constituent subfunctions.

Tactics of Developmental Research

Before developmental issues in modeling are addressed, the paradigms commonly used in developmental research deserve brief comment. Two approaches can be adopted in studying the nature and rate of development. Psychosocial functioning can be analyzed by how it changes with increasing age or by how it is affected by differential proficiency in the psychological functions presumed to govern children's behavior.

Age-Based Approach. Developmental changes in thought and behavior are studied mainly as a function of age. This is because some psychological functions are difficult to develop, whereas children of differing age groups can always be easily marshalled. But chronological age, of course, is not a determinant of psychosocial functioning. It is, at best, a crude indicant of level of competency that changes with maturation and new experiences. In developmental studies, chronological age is widely used as an index of cognitive development. Performances requiring cognitive skills generally improve with age, but the relationships are far from orderly. Discrepancies arise because many factors other than cognitive competency, such as motivational systems, interpersonal skills, and self-conceptions, which significantly affect performance, also change as children grow older. This mixed index of developmental level thus leaves ambiguity concerning the source of age trends in performance.

Relating changes in psychosocial functioning to age has normative value when people at any given age do not differ much on the capabilities of interest. But on most tasks the variation within a particular age often exceeds the difference between neighboring age groups. This limits the predictive value of age, except across widely disparate age groups. Whatever the intra-age variability might be, age trends have limited explanatory value because they tell us little about the psychological functions that account for the differences.

Competency-Based Approach. The understanding of how developmental factors affect psychosocial functioning can be better advanced by measuring the level of requisite skills than by assuming their presence from a person's age. Consider, for purposes of illustration, delayed modeling which requires memory skills. Research can provide a clearer understanding of the developmental determinants of modeling by selecting children of differing memory capabilities than of differing ages. However, it is much easier to study how children of different ages perform than to assess the psychological determinants postulated by a theory. The developmental field abounds with studies in which age serves as an omnibus proxy for whatever unmeasured determinants one wishes it to represent. The practice of claiming support for stage theories with studies using ages as evidence for stages of cognitive development, rather than assessing children's cognitive competencies, is firmly entrenched in developmental research. The cognitive constraints of stages are often invoked when brief influences fail to alter the young children's performances on tasks lacking meaning for them. This practice discourages examination of the determinants and mechanisms of developmental change.

Some of the subfunctions that govern observational learning require extensive experience for their development. In such instances, the capacity for observational learning is related to the level of constituent competencies as they have developed naturally. However, developmental studies need not be confined solely to competencies in subfunctions resulting from naturally occurring experiences. Another approach is to study proficiency in observational learning by children whose attentional, memorial, and enactment skills have been increased to different levels over a period of time. This is an especially effective method for identifying the developmental determinants of observational learning because the prerequisite skills have been created directly. Research that establishes the subfunctions of a developmental mechanism is well suited to treatment programs designed to cultivate competencies in children who lack them.

Ontogeny of Observational Learning

For a long time the prevailing preconception of newborns as helpless, insensitive organisms greatly underestimated their capacities. Intensive studies of infants during the first few weeks of life, in fact, have shown them to be more perceptive and more capable of learning and influencing their social environment than was previously thought. The preconception that neonates are essentially devoid of modeling capacities has undergone a similar revision.

Piaget (1951) presented one of the early accounts of imitation in terms of developmental stages. At the initial sensory-motor stages of development, imitative responses can presumably be evoked in infants only by having a model repeat the infant's immediately preceding responses in an alternating imitative sequence. The inability to represent events cognitively requires instantaneous external cueing of acts. During this period, according to Piaget, children are unable to imitate responses they have not previously performed spontaneously, because actions cannot be assimilated unless they correspond to already existing schemata. Piaget reports that when new elements are introduced, or even when familiar responses are modeled that infants have acquired but are not exhibiting at the moment, they do not imitate them. Imitation is thus restricted to action patterns that infants have already developed, that they can see themselves make, and that they have performed immediately before the model's repetition.

In the intermediate stages of imitation, which extend to about eighteen months, infants become capable of delayed imitation of modeled performances, which they cannot see themselves make. These changes are presumably achieved through experience in coordinating visual and sensory-motor schemata and differentiating the infant's own actions from those of others. Children now begin systematic trial-and-error performance of responses until they achieve good matches to new modeled patterns.

During the final Piagetian stages of imitation, which are said to begin shortly before the second year of life, children attain representational imitation. Imitative enactments eventually become internalized as images, which can then be generated independently of action. Schemata can now be coordinated internally through imaginal representation to form new patterns of modeled behavior without requiring overt provisional trials of actions. Piaget's stage characterization of imitation ends at the point where children are beginning to acquire language. The changes that could be produced by modeling would be limited if cognitive representations were confined to images. Most modeled acts are instances of rules that must be acquired and retained through the medium of language symbols. Had Piaget extended his studies of imitation into later phases of childhood, linguistic representations would doubtless have emerged as an important functional mediator in delayed modeling.

The limitations of infant imitativeness observed by Piaget in his longitudinal study of three children are not entirely corroborated by other investigators, who have examined more systematically the process of modeling during the neonatal period. Piagetian theory itself seems to cast doubt on the notion that models cannot evoke imitative responses that infants are not already performing at the moment. Piaget's theory assumes that, during the initial stages of development, infants cannot differentiate between their own behavior and the actions of others. If infants cannot distinguish modeled acts from their own, the theory must include additional assumptions to explain why an infant's own behavior can elicit matching responses but identical actions initiated by others cannot. A basic assumption of Piagetian theory is that schemata determine what can be imitated. However, since no reliable means are provided for certifying what schemata children possess, the theory presents certain difficulties in verification and prediction.

In a longitudinal study, Valentine (1930) demonstrated some years ago that infants in the first few months of life do imitate modeled acts within their physical capabilities, even though they are not performing them beforehand. Moreover, infant imitativeness,

from which modeling capabilities are often inferred, can vary markedly depending on who the models are, what they select to model, and how they do it. Infants imitate their mothers much more than they do other people. They often fail to respond to initial demonstrations but imitate the actions if repeated a number of times. Repeated social cueing will thus reveal greater infant modeling capabilities than will brief cueing. Such findings underscore the point that developmental analyses of imitation, especially naturalistic studies, partly reflect the model's influence, not only the modeling capabilities of infants.

Further evidence that infants in the early months of life possess greater modeling capabilities than those with which they have been credited is provided by studies that allow infants more opportunity to reveal their capabilities (Kaye & Marcus, 1978, 1981). Infants are unlikely to imitate novel acts precisely when they are modeled only once or twice. Precise imitations are no more instant accomplishments of infants than they are of older children, or even adults, for that matter. When acts are repeatedly modeled, infants adopt progressively more features of the behavior over a series of trials, although not in a uniform sequence, and eventually they integrate the features into accurate imitations. Some of the modeled activities involve movements that infants cannot see themselves making. The order in which particular features of modeled acts are acquired over months, given only a few trials, corresponds to the order of mastery within a series of trials in any month. Thus, when activities are modeled only briefly at each age, acquisition phases may be misconstrued as developmental stages. Six-month old infants readily learn to retrieve objects hidden behind screens by observing adult models (Kaye, 1982). Having acquired the skill through observation, they generalize it to other objects and transfer the action from one hand to the other. In this situation, the imitative strategies gained them attractive objects and mastery of environmental barriers.

When parents model different activities for their infants, what they choose to imitate depends on the familiarity and social meaningfulness of the actions (Masur & Ritz, 1984). These characteristics affect even imitations of activities in which infants cannot see themselves as they perform them. They imitate things they cannot see themselves do if these foster social interaction, but they ignore those that are not socially meaningful. Evidence that children's imitativeness varies substantially across responses, models, modeling formats, and situational circumstances (Uzgiris, 1979) is also at variance with developmental theories postulating a fixed sequence of unitary stages of imitative competencies. Complex modeling cannot be achieved without cognitive development, but the acquisition of such a skill does not necessarily occur in fixed, unitary stages.

In a study that aroused considerable controversy, Meltzoff and Moore (1977) reported that neonates imitated facial movements, even though they could not see themselves when they were making them, and where there was a delay until after the modeled activity was completed. Although the modeled acts were simple, the imitative performances were no small accomplishment for neonates, because they required at least some representational competence to achieve fleeting memory of what they had seen modeled. Moreover, they had to have some capability for intermodal coordination to convert visual information into matching actions and to recognize the likeness between what they had seen and what they had done. There is a common belief that infants, during their first few weeks of life, are not supposed to have representational transformation capabilities. Not unexpectedly, others have disputed the findings (Hayes & Watson, 1981; Jacobson & Kagan, 1979), and Meltzoff and Moore (1983) have contested the disputations as based on evidence from insensitive procedures. Further research has produced some evidence of neonatal imitation, although it is hardly a robust phenomenon (Field, Woodson, Greenberg, & Cohen, 1982; Meltzoff & Moore, 1983). Meltzoff and Moore attribute this precocious imitation to an innate ability to represent and transform perceptions to actions. To posit an inborn capability for intermodal matching does not explain why newborns do not imitate all or most of the actions they see within their physical capacity and why dogged efforts to get them to imitate yield marginal results. Competence in subfunctions and motivational mechanisms are clearly important to the understanding of infant modeling.

While the issue of delayed neonatal imitation is still somewhat unsettled, there is ample evidence that, by several months of age, infants can and do model behavior with some consistency. The determinants and processes governing this early imitativeness remain to be clarified, however. One possibility is that there exists an innate tendency for human actions to release fixed-action patterns in infants. Some neonates display fragmentary mimicry of some acts, but even this partial imitativeness seems to disappear in a short time (Abravanel & Sigafoos, 1984). Considering that mimicry is difficult to produce even with repeated stimulation, such reactions could hardly qualify as an inborn action pattern automatically triggered by modeling stimuli. Were this the case, the study of reflexive mimicry, which appears only briefly at birth, can add little to our understanding of observational learning, which develops through social interaction. A newborn's fleeting reflex that leaves no lasting effects would not be the best place to look for the origins of psychosocial modeling. In addition, appeal to an innate releasing mechanism should be viewed with reservation, because evidence from young infants argues against such an interpretation. Modeled acts often fail to elicit matching responses even though infants pay full attention to what is being modeled. When infants do imitate, their acts do not necessarily follow a stereotyped form in the likeness of a fixed-action pattern. With repeated experience they discard irrelevant features and retain what is functional, which is more in keeping with intentional than with reflexive actions (Kaye, 1982).

The development of proficiency in observational learning is grounded on social reciprocation, in which interchanges are mutually fostered. Infants possess sufficient rudimentary representational capacities and sensory-motor coordination to enable them to imitate elementary acts within their physical capabilities. Moreover, they are sensitive to external events, they can discern environmental contingencies, and they can quickly learn how to control parental behavior by their actions (Papousek & Papousek, 1977). Microanalyses of spontaneous infant-adult interactions conducted by the Papouseks reveal that early social transactions are especially conducive to developing imitativeness in newborns. Parents readily imitate a newborn's gestures and vocalizations from the very beginning, often in expressive ways that have been shown to facilitate modeling. They are especially prone to imitate, with some enthusiasm, new behavioral patterns exhibited by the infants.

The newborn, whose means of communication and social influence are severely limited, learns that reciprocal imitation is an effective way of eliciting and sustaining parental responsiveness. Uzgiris (1984) has given considerable attention to the social function of imitation in infancy. Mutual imitation serves as a means of conveying interest and sharing experiences. During the infant's first year of life the level of reciprocal imitation with the mother increases substantially, and infants double the rate with which they imitate activities initiated by the mother. For infants, modeling thus serves an important social function in promoting interactive contact with the adults who care for them. An adult's imitation of children's behavior increases their readiness to imitate new behaviors exhibited by the adult (Kauffman, Gordon, & Baker, 1978; Thelen, Dollinger, & Roberts, 1975). In fact, reciprocal imitation often proves more effective than extrinsic rewards in increasing imitativeness in infants (Haugan & McIntire, 1972).

The microanalytic studies suggest that imitation originates more in interpersonal exchange than in reflexive circular activity. The presumption of the reflexive view is that an infant's act produces its own stimulus for repetition of the act. After infants learn to imitate their own actions, the behavior of another person presumably evokes imitative responses. However, the reflexive view fails to explain how just perceiving a prior act stimulates the repetition of that act. To assume that seeing one's own action stimulates self-imitation is to beg the very question, at issue, of how and why seeing an action produces matching behavior. It could not involve an automatic reflexive mechanism because most perceptions of one's own acts do not trigger their reiteration. Moreover, one's own act is perceived differently from the same act modeled by others because of the reverse perspective. Hence, the shift from self-imitation to other-imitation cannot occur automatically. It is now well established that parents actively stimulate imitative responses from the outset, and neonates can imitate responses that do not lend themselves easily to self-imitation, because they are not fully visible to the neonates when they themselves are performing them.

An infant's biological endowment and the reciprocally rewarding interplay between parents and their newborns enables them to imitate elementary sounds and gestures. Initially, parents tend to model acts that infants spontaneously perform. As we have already seen, parents develop the modeling set by capitalizing on infant-initiated activities and reproducing them in demonstrative ways. But parents are selective in what they reproduce from the infant's acts (Pawlby, 1977), and they are quick to initiate new response patterns for imitative sequences that help to expand their infant's competencies. Successful modeling of these more complicated patterns of behavior requires development of the subfunctions that govern observational learning. It is to the developmental course of these subfunctions that we turn next.

Development of Subfunctions Governing Observational Learning

Attentional Processes. Young children present certain attentional deficiencies that limit their proficiency in observational learning. They have difficulty simultaneously attending to multiple informative cues, distinguishing pertinent aspects from irrelevancies, and maintaining attention to ongoing events long enough to acquire sufficient information about them (Cohen & Salapatek, 1975; Hagen & Hale, 1973). With increasing experience, children's attentional skills improve in all these respects. They become more proficient at appraising diverse aspects of complex events. They learn to deploy their attention selectively to the factors most relevent in gaining mastery and predictive accuracy and to ignore the inconsequential ones. Additionally, they improve their ability to sustain focused attention on the activities being learned in the presence of distractions.

In promoting observational learning, adults alter the behavior they model to compensate for the attentional limitations of children. With infants, parents gain their attention and give salience to the behavior they want to encourage by selectively imitating them. Parents tend to perform the reciprocated imitations in an exaggerated, animated fashion that is well designed to sustain the child's attentiveness at a high level during imitative sequences (Papousek & Papousek, 1977). The animated social interplay provides a vehicle for channeling and expanding infants' attention in activities that go beyond those they have already mastered. Infant expressions that are of little value for their development are largely ignored by their parents, but they deliberately encourage acts involving manipulation and speech sounds by imitating them demon-

stratively (Pawlby, 1977). Parents initiate developmentally progressive activities for infants to imitate, as well as selectively reproducing their spontaneous expressions. With increasing frequency, infants adopt new activities that parents introduce in interaction sequences.

The preceding observational studies of interaction sequences document how the salience of modeled behavior is enhanced by exaggeration and demonstrative reflection. The attention-arousing value of the modeled acts themselves also influences what infants are likely to adopt. Several investigators have studied selective attention and imitation of different modeled actions by infants at different ages and as they develop over time. They find that infants are more attentive to, and imitate more often, modeled acts when they involve objects and sound accompaniments than when they are modeled silently and without objects to draw attention (Abravanel et al., 1976; Uzgiris, 1979). Correlational analyses further reveal that the more attention infants pay to the modeled activities, the more likely they are to adopt them. With young children, parents foster modeling not only by expressively highlighting their actions but by verbally calling attention to them. When situations are structured so that children pay attention to what the parents are doing, modeling is less dependent on these extraneous attentional devices (Waxler & Yarrow, 1975).

Another line of research bearing on the attentional determinants of observational learning involves developing perceptual skills in children who lack them. The use of modeling for expanding the cognitive and behavioral competencies of autistic children exemplifies this approach. In the treatment program devised by Lovaas and his associates (Lovaas & Newsom, 1976), complex skills are gradually elaborated by modeling the activities in small steps of increasing difficulty and rewarding adoption of the demonstrated competencies. This approach has generally proven effective if applied intensively at an early age (Lovaas, 1982). However, severely autistic children experience considerable difficulty in learning because they tend to restrict their attention to only a few of the many available cues in the environment, often to minor or irrelevant details.

When presented with a multidimensional stimulus containing auditory, visual, and tactual predictive cues, normal children learn all three aspects, whereas autistic children typically fixate on one form of information and fail to learn the other forms. They have difficulty processing multiple information presented in the same modality (e.g., different sights or different sounds), as well as multiple information presented in different sensory modes (Koegel & Schreibman, 1977; Lovaas & Newsom, 1976). Since most situations require one to learn several kinds of information simultaneously, such attentional overselectivity can seriously impair learning. Children who perceive little of what goes on around them do not gain much information for expanding their cognitive competencies. If they perceive only fragments of speech sounds, they will encounter considerable difficulty in understanding and learning language. Impoverished language and cognitive development, in turn, are likely to impair attentional involvement in activities. The relationship between attentional overselectivity and deficient cognitive development is evident among retarded and autistic children and normal children of a comparable mental age (Schover & Newsom, 1976; Wilhelm & Lovaas, 1976).

Several procedures have been devised to overcome the problems created by such attentional deficits. Learning in autistic children is facilitated by exaggerating the relevant features and gradually reducing the exaggeration, while introducing the other complexities (Schreibman, 1975). Another approach to the problem is to teach the children a general set to attend to all the relevant information in a learning situation. This is achieved by having them learn the

different kinds of information separately before combining them into more complex patterns (Koegel & Schreibman, 1977). By this means, they learn to attend to multiple information presented simultaneously.

Retention Processes. In developing memory skills, children have to learn how to transform modeled information into symbolic forms and to organize it into easily remembered structures. They also have to learn how to use timely rehearsal to facilitate the retention of activities that are vulnerable to memory loss. Memory skills are difficult to master in early childhood for a variety of reasons. First, memorial processes mainly involve covert cognitive operations. Since these are not directly observable, they are difficult to teach and to improve by corrective feedback. Second, the more efficient mnemonics require reducing and organizing information by linguistic means which are, at best, poorly developed in young children. Third, memory is greatly facilitated by relating new information to what is already known. Because of their limited experiences, young children do not have much of a knowledge base to help them comprehend new experiences.

Most of the memory operations must be performed as ongoing events are experienced, and it is not until some time later, when children have to draw on what they have learned, that the advantages of remembrance become apparent. The incentives for using memory aids, even if readily available, are weak when their benefits are not only delayed but may even be unrecognized. It takes time for children to learn that they can improve their future performances by symbolizing and rehearsing their immediate experiences. This is shown in developmental studies of children's awareness of memory as a process (Brown, 1978; Flavell, 1978a). Young children lack knowledge about the factors that tax memory, they overestimate their memorial skills, they do not monitor their memory performances well, and they only gradually come to understand how cognitive activities aid retention.

In the earliest period of development, experiences are probably retained mainly in imaginal modes of representation. Infants will model single acts, but they have difficulty reproducing coordinated sequences that require them to remember how several actions are strung together (McCall, Parke, & Kavanaugh, 1977). They often start the sequence correctly and simply forget what comes next. With experience, they become more skilled at delayed modeling. Indeed, infants even as young as 18 months will enact behavior learned from televised models after some time has elapsed. Delayed performances of this type require symbolic memory.

Developmental analyses of how representational skills affect modeling are often minimally informative, or even misleading, because of the failure to distinguish between observational learning and spontaneous performance. Because children do not spontaneously perform observed activities does not mean they have not learned them. To infer modeling capabilities from what children choose to do on their own, often with little or no incentives, is to grossly underestimate the cognitive skills they possess. Modeling capabilities are best gauged by tests of observational learning in which children are instructed and encouraged to show everything they have learned. Such tests reveal that very young children have difficulty integrating modeled sequences of behavior, but with increasing age they err more in the mastery of details than in the over-all structure of the modeled activities (Leifer et al., 1971). It should be noted that cognitive capabilities and modeling involve a bidirectionality of influence. Cognitive deficits limit the impact of modeling influences, but modeling influences expand cognitive capabilities (Fenson & Ramsay, 1981; Rosenthal & Zimmerman, 1978).

As children begin to acquire language, they can symbolize the essential aspects of events in words for memory representation. Coates and Hartup (1969) investigated the effects of verbal labeling on modeling as a function of age in a test of the production-deficiency hypothesis. According to this hypothesis, young children possess, but do not use, verbal aids that would improve performance, whereas older children do so spontaneously and hence do not benefit from instructions to produce verbal mediators. Consistent with this view, Coates and Hartup found that putting modeled activities into words enhanced observational learning in younger, but not in older, children. It is evident from other findings, however, that advancing age does not guarantee the spontaneous use of cognitive aids. Inducements to use codes improve observational learning in older children and adults (Bandura, Grusec, & Menlove, 1966; Bandura & Jeffery, 1973; Gerst, 1971). Moreover, van Hekken (1969) found that it was older children who spontaneously used their cognitive skills in other learning tasks, rather than the nonsymbolizers who increased their observational learning when instructed to code modeled acts verbally. Given the symbolizing capability, resort to symbolic coding of modeled events would be determined less by how old the person is than by whether or not there were any incentives to use codes.

A number of investigators have examined developmental changes in how children represent external events in memory (Hagen, Jongeward, & Kail, 1975). Initially they tend to encode them in terms of salient physical properties. Representation of the more subtle, abstract, and semantic aspects of events becomes more prominent later in the child's development. Moreover, the complexity of symbolization increases with age so that larger amounts of relevant information are coded and integrated into general conceptions. It is not until children acquire some cognitive and linguistic skills that they can extract rules from specific exemplars and make effective use of the more complex linguistic transformations (Rosenthal & Zimmerman, 1978).

Some of the apparent deficits in memory performance of children reflect motivational rather than ability factors (Flavell, 1970; Hagen et al., 1975). When performing memory tasks, older children and adults tend to use mnemonic strategies designed to facilitate retention. Young children are disinclined to employ such cognitive aids when exposed to new information of little functional value to them. They can be prompted to use mnemonics and thereby improve their memory performance, but they discontinue the cognitive mnemonics, with resultant retention deficits, when external inducements are removed.

Developmental studies, drawing extensively as they do on traditional paradigms, focus mainly on age-related changes in memory for objects and verbal material. How children represent knowledge about action patterns and generalizable enactive skills in memory is one direction in which developmental memory research needs to be extended. We also need more research aimed at elucidating how children learn memory skills.

For reasons given earlier, comprehending memorial processes and mastering mnemonic skills is no easy task for young children. However, there are several factors that contribute to the development of these competencies. Successful response to most environmental demands requires some memory of past events. Through such experiences, children gradually come to recognize the usefulness of retaining the knowledge they have gained. It is one thing to discover the value of memory, it is another thing to know what to do to aid retention. Children are undoubtedly encouraged to use mnemonic aids partly through direct tuition. There is some evidence to suggest that they can improve their memory performances when instructed to anticipate, verbally label, and rehearse what they observe (Brown & Barclay, 1976).

The various memorial subskills can also be acquired through modeling. By observing the memory feats of others, children learn what information is worth coding, the basis on which events should be categorized, and more general strategies for processing information (Lamal, 1971; Rosenthal & Zimmerman, 1978). Learning cognitive strategies that are not directly observable can be greatly facilitated by cognitive modeling. While performing memory tasks, models can verbalize aloud the various mnemonic strategies they are using—verbally transforming, rehearsing, grouping, and semantically elaborating the information that is most relevant. Children are then encouraged to use similar mnemonic strategies as they perform relatively easy tasks requiring them to retain knowledge over a brief interval. As they gain some facility in the memory subskills, the processing demands of the tasks are increased, and the retention period is gradually lengthened.

Symbolic representation occupies a prominent role in Piaget's (1951) developmental account of imitation, as children progress from the sensory-motor to the representational level of functioning. In this view, schemata determine what behaviors a child can or cannot imitate: Acts that do not diverge much from existing schemata will be imitated, but those that differ markedly will not. The critical issue in observational learning is not how observed acts similar to preformed conceptions are acquired but how social influences create the conceptions. Schemata formation, according to Piaget, is determined by maturation and by experiences that are moderately incongruent with preexisting mental structures. People restore the balance by restructuring their schemata to accommodate the discrepant information. The striving for balance, or equilibration, as an automotivator of cognitive change is the subject of analysis later.

There are commonalities between social cognitive and Piaget's theory in their emphasis on the development of conceptual structures. Both underscore the importance of sensory-motor and conceptual-motor learning; that is, young children must develop the cognitive competencies that enable them to comprehend and symbolize observed activities and to convert thought into organized action. The two approaches differ, however, in how people abstract conceptions from exemplars, in the scope and mechanisms of modeling influences, and in what motivates adoption of modeled patterns.

In social cognitive theory, observational learning is not confined to the moderately unfamiliar. Nor is self-discovery through behavioral manipulation the only source of information, as is emphasized in Piagetian theory. Information about new ways of behaving can be extracted from observing modeled examples, as well as from the effects of one's own actions. If perceptual and motor systems are sufficiently developed, and the component skills exist, there is no reason why children cannot learn novel responses by watching others, although obviously every theory will predict that the moderately familiar is easier to learn than the markedly different. When analyzed within the multiprocess framework, deficiencies in imitative performance, which are usually attributed by Piaget to insufficiently differentiated schemata, may also result from deficient attention to modeled activities, from inadequate symbolic representation, from motor difficulties in executing the learned patterns, or from insufficient incentives. The role of incentives deserves further comment because it bears importantly on the evaluation of findings from naturalistic studies.

The level and accuracy of children's modeling of what they see and hear is partly influenced by how models respond to their behavior. Young children imitate accurately when they have incentives to do so, but their imitations deteriorate rapidly if others do not care how they behave (Lovaas, 1967). When only the children's responses are observed and recorded, deficiencies in observational learning arising from insufficient incentives may be incorrectly attributed to cognitive deficiencies in the children. Because most naturalistic studies with infants involve a two-way influence process, imitative performances reflect not only the child's competence but also the models' reactions. If models respond in the same manner to performances that differ in adequacy, children do not imitate very well, whereas they accurately reproduce behavior that is within their capabilities if models show appropriate interest.

Production Processes. Observational learning cannot be reflected at the behavioral level until the necessary physical maturation has occurred. When the motor capabilities exist, converting conceptions to appropriate actions requires development of skills in intermodal guidance of behavior. As will be recalled from the earlier discussion, transforming symbols into actions involves learning how to organize action sequences, to monitor and compare enactments against a symbolic model, and to correct evident mismatches. When children must depend on what others tell them, because they cannot completely monitor their own actions, detecting and correcting mismatches requires linguistic competencies. Deficiencies in any of these production subskills can create a developmental lag between comprehending and performing. The development of conception-matching skills governing production competence is an area that needs more study.

When young children are first learning how to pattern their behavior after that of a model, they encounter additional problems arising from their inexperience in shifting spatial orientations. In imitating a model whom the child is facing, the child must not only discern right-left and forward-backwards orientation but also enact the behavior from the perspective of the model. Otherwise, right-handed exemplifications would prompt left-handed matching responses, and forward movements would produce backward matches. To the extent that success of the imitated behavior depends on adopting the correct spatial orientation, children eventually come to recognize the importance of transposing the modeled movements. This takes time to master. Young children fail to make correct transpositions, although they get better at it with experience (Wapner & Cirillo, 1968). Problems of spatial transposition in modeling can plague even adults (Greenwald & Albert, 1968).

Motivational Processes. A developmental theory of modeling must explain not only how competencies are acquired by observation but also how often, when, and where the modeled activities will be performed. The motivational determinants of modeling during the early years of development have not received the attention they deserve. In the preoccupation with the cognitive aspects of modeling, the functional aspects of modeling have been essentially ignored (Uzgiris, 1984). Imitation is variously attributed to an intrinsic need for acting and knowing, to a desire to reproduce actions that differ partially from existing schemata, and to the esteem with which the model is held (Piaget, 1951). However intuitively appealing such motivators might sound, they are much too general to account satisfactorily for the selective imitation of different models, of the same models at different times and places, and of different actions exhibited by the same models (Bandura & Barab, 1971).

Motivational factors that influence the use to which modeled knowledge is put undergo significant developmental changes. The motivational processes involve the cognitive representation of outcomes and the development of higher incentives that foster self-maintaining engrossment in activities. Because these matters are treated fully in a later chapter, they will be discussed only briefly here. During infancy, imitation functions mainly to secure interpersonal responsiveness. Through mutual modeling with adults, infants enjoy playful intimacy and gain experience in social reciprocation. Before long, parents cease mimicking their infant's acts, but they remain responsive to instances of infants adopting modeled patterns that expand their competencies. What continues to serve a social function for young infants changes into an instructional

vehicle for parents. This transition requires infants to cognize, on the basis of observed regularities, the social effects their different imitations are likely to produce. Such outcome expectations serve as incentives for observational learning.

Infants and young children encounter difficulties in cognizing social contingencies. This is because social outcomes are usually variable, delayed and dependent on situational circumstances that are not easily discernible without extensive experience. As a result, it is often difficult to determine what produces what. Therefore, adults who mediate most of the important response effects try to synchronize their behavior with the infant's capacity to process outcome information, so as to highlight the regularities. They make the outcomes salient, recurrent, consistent, and closely tied to the infant's actions (Papousek & Papousek, 1977). With increasing cognitive development, children become more skilled at judging probable outcomes under seemingly perplexing circumstances.

What has incentive value for children also changes with experience. At the earliest level, infants and young children are motivated primarily by the immediate sensory and social effects of their actions. In the course of development, symbolic incentives and the exercise of mastery assume increasing motivational functions. Children soon learn that models are not only sources of social reward but also valuable sources of competencies for dealing effectively with the social and physical environment. The benefits of personal efficacy become powerful incentives for modeling. After children discover that modeling is a good way of improving their capabilities, they adopt the modeled skills for the sense of self-efficacy and the personal satisfaction it brings them. Development thus increases the range and complexity of incentives that motivate children to gain knowledge through modeling and to perform what they have learned.

When viewed from the developmental perspective of social cognitive theory, observational learning is part of a more general process of cognitive and social development. But observational learning is also one of the basic mechanisms by which cognitive competencies are developed and expanded. A comprehensive theory must, therefore, examine not only the cognitive determinants of observational learning but also the observational learning mechanism of cognitive development.

Gender-Role Development

Some of the most important aspects of human functioning, such as the interests and competencies people cultivate, the occupational paths they pursue, and the conceptions they hold of themselves and others are prescribed by cultural sex-typing. The stereotypic gender conceptions that people adopt have lasting effects on how they perceive and process social information and how they use their capabilities (Bem, 1981; Betz & Hackett, 1981; Spence & Helmreich, 1978). Because so much of human experience is affected by gender differentiation, the processes of sex-typing have been the subject of much developmental theorizing and research. The kinds of attributes and social roles that are culturally linked to masculine and feminine genders should be distinguished from biological sex differences. Although biological characteristics form a basis for gender differentiation, many of the social roles that get tied to gender are not ordained by biological differences. Thus, biology confines gestation to women, but it does not confine women to a permanent homemaking role. Gender-role development is, therefore, largely a psychosocial phenomenon.

Sex-typing is promoted through a vast system of socialization practices beginning at birth with infants clothed in pink or blue apparel depending on their sex. Before long boys are attired in rugged trousers, girls in pastel skirts, and they are given different hair styles as well. Children come to use differential physical attributes, hair styles, and clothing as indicants of gender

(Katcher, 1955; Thompson & Bentler, 1971). As soon as young children begin to comprehend speech, they notice that verbal labeling in masculine and feminine terms is used extensively by those around them. It does not take them long to learn that children are categorized into boys and girls, and adults into mothers and fathers, women and men. Gender labeling gives salience not only to sorting people on the basis of gender but also to the features and activities that characterize each gender. Children begin to develop a sense of their own gender identity from such experiences.

Gender-role learning requires broadening gender conceptions to include behavioral, social, and vocational aspects. Knowledge about gender roles is more difficult to grasp than is gender identity for several reasons. First, children must achieve gender differentiation before they can organize knowledge about what roles are appropriate for males and females. Second, the stylistic and role behaviors that traditionally typify male and female orientations are not uniformly sex-linked. Not all males are aggressive, nor are all females unassertive. As a result, children have to rely on the relative prevalence of exemplars. If children routinely see women performing homemaking activities, while males only occasionally try their hand at it, homemaking readily gets sex-typed as a woman's role. But if they often observe both men and women gardening, it is not as easily sex-typeable.

Much early role learning occurs in play. The forms play takes are not untouched by social influences. Parents stereotypically stock their sons' rooms with educational materials, machines, vehicles, and sports equipment, and their daughters' rooms with baby dolls, doll houses, domestic items, and floral furnishings (Rheingold & Cook, 1975). The sex-typed play materials with which children are provided channel their spontaneous play into traditionally feminine or masculine roles. Even during the first year of a child's life, fathers promote stereotypically sex-appropriate play, although they are stricter in sex-role differentiation for sons than daughters (Snow, Jacklin, & Maccoby, 1983). In their reactions to children's play, fathers are more stereotypic socializers than are mothers (Langlois & Downs, 1980). Not surprisingly, even very young children believe their parents expect them to conform to stereotypic gender roles (Albert & Porter, 1982).

Socializing agencies outside the home add their influence to the gender-role stereotyping. Peers are sources of much social learning. In the social structuring of activities, children selectively associate with same-sex playmates pursuing gender-typed interests and activities (Huston, 1983). In these interactions children reward each other for gender-appropriate activities and punish gender-inappropriate behavior (Lamb, Easterbrooks, & Holden, 1980). The sanctions work their effects. Children also get criticized by their teachers for engaging in play activities considered inappropriate for their sex, and this is especially true for boys (Fagot, 1977).

The differentiation of the sexes extends beyond the realm of attire, make-believe play, and free activities. Whenever appropriate occasions arise, parents and others instruct children in the kinds of behavior expected of girls and boys. While obviously not all parents are inflexible sex stereotypers in all activities, most accept, model, and teach the sex roles traditionally favored by the culture. In the development of career interests and pursuits, cultural practices encourage a wider range of career options for males than for females (Betz & Hackett, 1981; Hackett & Betz, 1981). Such differential practices constrict the career pursuits for which women judge themselves to be efficacious.

Superimposed on this differential tuition, which leaves few aspects of children's lives untouched, is a pervasive cultural modeling of stereotypic sex roles. Modeling serves as a major conveyer of sex-role information. Children are continually exposed to models of sex-typed behavior in the home, in schools, on playgrounds, in readers and storybooks, and in representations of society on the television screens of every household (Courtney & Whipple, 1974; Harris & Voorhees, 1981; Jacklin & Mischel, 1973; Miller & Reeves, 1976). Males are generally portrayed as directive, venturesome, enterprising, and pursuing engaging occupations and recreational activities. In contrast, women are usually cast in subordinate roles, either tending the household or performing lower-status jobs, and otherwise acting in dependent, unambitious, and emotional ways. Heavy viewers of the media display more stereotypic sex-role conceptions than do light viewers (McGhee & Frueh, 1980). Studies in which females are portrayed as behaving unlike their traditional stereotype attest to the influence of modeling on sex-role conceptions. Nonstereotypic modeling expands children's aspirations and the range of role options they consider appropriate for their sex (Ashby & Wittmaier, 1978; O'Bryant & Corder-Bolz, 1978). Repeated symbolic modeling of egalitarian role pursuits by males and females enduringly reduces sex-role stereotyping in young children (Flerx, Fidler, & Rogers, 1976).

Deeply entrenched power relations in a society are not easily altered. Under the pressure of the women's movement, some of the more flagrant masculine and feminine stereotyping by the media has been toned down, but much still remains. Rather than modeling common attributes, aspirations, and roles by both sexes, which fosters diverse and unencumbered development, women are being portrayed as emulating the more abrasive features of the masculine stereotype (St. Peter, 1979). The freedom to pursue different life paths is better served by modeling diversity, rather than by promoting masculine caricatures.

Based on these multiple sources of gender-role information, young children form a conception of the attributes that typify masculinity and femininity and the behaviors appropriate for their own sex. In identifying the determinants of gender-role learning, it is essential to distinguish between the acquisition of gender-typed behaviors and their spontaneous performance. Children do not suspend observational learning of sex-typed activities until the time they discover whether they are girls or boys. Rather, they learn many of the things that typify gender roles from the male and female models around them before they have formed a clear gender identity and have fully comprehended the social significance attached to sexual status. Nor do children watch and gain knowledge only from same-sex models, even after they have developed a clear conception of their own sex.

Children observe and learn extensively from models of both sexes, but they are selective in what they express behaviorally. In tests for acquisition, which encourage children to reveal all they have learned observationally, they display many modeled activities they have acquired but ordinarily do not express, because they judge them inappropriate for their sex (Bandura, 1965b; Bussey & Bandura, 1984; Dubanoski & Parton, 1971). Developmental research may confuse, rather than inform, when theories about sex-typed learning are tested with measures of sex-typed performance, rather than of learning.

Numerous factors govern the performance of sex-typed behavior. Prevailing social sanctions make outcomes partly dependent on the sex-appropriateness of actions. Hence, children soon learn to use sex-typing information as a predictive guide for action. The negative sanctions for cross-sex behavior are generally more severe for males than for females. Because of status and power differentials, women's emulating masculinity is usually regarded as more understandable and less deviant than men's emulating femininity. Thus, women dressed in masculine garb may elicit stares, but men who appeared for work attired in dresses would quickly find themselves in the psychiatric ward. Even in early years, boys are more likely than girls to use the sex stereotyping of the activity as a guide for action (Serbin, Connor, & Citron, 1981). The social modeling by girls is less constrained by the sex of the model and the sex-appropriateness of the behavior than is that of

boys (Bandura, Ross, & Ross, 1963c; Bryan & Luria, 1978; Raskin & Israel, 1981; Slaby & Frey, 1975).

Knowledge about the sex appropriateness of behavior patterns does not depend entirely on directly experienced sanctions. Observing what consequences befall others also conveys knowledge of gender roles for regulating conduct. In the power relationships portrayed on television, for example, aggressive behavior is much less likely to succeed for females than for males (Gerbner, 1972). Observers take heed of such recurrent messages. As children begin to adopt standards of behavior through precept and example, much sex-typed behavior is further regulated through internal standards and self-evaluative reactions to their own conduct. They perform gender-role behaviors that bring them self-pride and eschew those that violate their own standards.

Both the acquisition of knowledge about gender roles and the valuational regulators of sex-typed activities are additionally fostered through differential structuring of social relationships. The acquisition of gender conceptions and sex-typed behaviors involves reciprocal causation. Mastery of sex-typed skills fosters interactions with same-sex associates. Extensive selective association with same-sex models pursuing sex-typed activities in turn provides further opportunities to gain knowledge of the role deemed appropriate by the culture. Variations in gender-role learning are better explained by selective attention promoted through selective association than by deployment of attention to models of both sexes one is constrained to observe (Bryan & Luria, 1978).

Some writers claim that social learning theory is insufficient to explain gender-role learning, but their views are based on arguments that rely on a simplified and truncated characterization of the theory (Kohlberg, 1966; Maccoby & Jacklin, 1974). The version often presented by adherents of cognitive developmentalism is a two-element caricature resting on imitation, portrayed as simple response mimicry, and "shaping" by the automatic effects of external reinforcement. Social learning theory neither conceptualizes these two sources of influences in such narrow, decorticate terms, nor does it consider them to be the sole conveyers and regulators of human behavior.

Evidence is at variance with the judgment of Maccoby and Jacklin that neither social practices nor modeling processes are especially influential in the development of gender-linked roles. They point to findings that, in laboratory situations, children do not consistently pattern their behavior after same-sex models. However, in these studies, which usually include only one model of each sex, the modeling displays also vary in the models' personal characteristics, the sex-appropriateness of the modeled behavior, and the context in which it is displayed. To single out only the sex of the model from this array of factors is to disregard the multifaceted nature of the influence. When the modeled behavior is highly sex-typed, the sex-appropriateness of the behavior generally exerts greater influence on which observed activities children choose to perform than does the sex of the model (Barkley, Ullman, Otto, & Brecht, 1977; Raskin & Israel, 1981). As previously noted, males weigh sex-appropriateness more heavily than do females. Consequently, males are much less inclined to adopt behavior regarded as sex-inappropriate, regardless of the sex of the model displaying it. Same-sex modeling is strongest when the gender-role content of the behavior stereotypically fits the sex of the model and the sex of the observers (Bandura, 1973; Fryrear & Thelen, 1969).

When modeled activities are neither clearly sex-typed nor of obvious differential utility, the content of the behavior itself carries little predictive value on how it is likely to be received by other people. Under such conditions, children are inclined to use the sex of the model as a guide for how they might behave in similar situations. They draw on past experiences that acting like a same-sex model is likely to be better re-ceived than acting like an opposite-sex model (Miller & Dollard, 1941; Mischel, 1970).

In everyday life, judgments of sex-appropriateness are rarely based on the actions of a single model. Rather, children have ample opportunities to observe how many members of each sex behave. Perry and Bussey (1979) show that several models displaying the same behavior within each sex is a stronger conveyer of gender-linked rules of conduct than is divergent modeling. They found that the propensity for children to pattern their preferences after models of the same sex increases as the percentage of same-sex models displaying the same preferences increases. Children reject a model of their own sex known not to typify the preferences of most members of their own sex. That multiple modeling serves as a basic mechanism in the sex-typing process is further corroborated by other studies encompassing varied activities, preferences, and stylistic behaviors (Bussey & Bandura, 1984). Over a period of time, concordant gender-linked modeling can confer masculinity or femininity on previously neutral activities.

Maccoby and Jacklin (1974) view much psychological sex differentiation as rooted in biological predispositions to learn sex-typed behaviors. Innate preparedness presumably sponsors sex differences in behavior. Since, in this formulation, gender-role behavior arises neither from socialization practices nor from modeling influences, concept matching, as set forth by Kohlberg (1966), is proposed as the major process molding the differential endowments into traditionally feminine or masculine roles. Through exposure to sex-differentiated patterns, children eventually infer their gender identity, which leads them to adopt those behaviors congruent with their stereotypic gender-role conception.

Some sex differences are biologically founded. But many of the stereotypic gender roles arise more from cultural design then from biological endowment. It is highly doubtful that males are biologically prepared to preside over board rooms and women over typewriters, or that males are innately predisposed to become dentists, but females are genetically destined to become dental technicians, which requires no less stamina or manual dexterity. As a molding mechanism, gender concept-matching may be a contributing factor, but it is ill equipped to carry the major burden of gender-role socialization.

In the cognitive-developmental theory articulated by Kohlberg (1966), children infer stereotypic conceptions of gender from what they see and hear around them. Once they achieve gender constancy—a conception of their own gender as fixed and irreversible—they positively value, and seek to adopt, only those behaviors congruent with the gender concept they have acquired. Presumably children do not adopt sex-typed behaviors until after they have labeled themselves unalterably as a boy or a girl, which usually is not achieved until about age six. Gender-linked modeling is considered to be motivated by children's desire to behave consistently with their gender conception

A major problem for a theory that makes the understanding of gender constancy a prerequisite for gender-linked modeling is that children clearly differentiate and prefer sex-typed objects and play patterns long before they view themselves as unchangeably boys or girls (Huston, 1983; Maccoby & Jacklin, 1974). Moreover, growing awareness of gender constancy does not increase children's preferences for same-sex roles, activities, and peers (Marcus & Overton, 1978; Smetana & Letourneau, 1984). Nor does research, in which the emulation of multiple male and female models is studied as a function of different levels of gender understanding, offer support for the theory that the attainment of gender constancy is a precondition for same-sex modeling (Bussey & Bandura, 1984). Young children were selected who either had begun to differentiate people as male or female (gender identity), looked upon their gender as permanent over time (gender stability) or

regarded their gender as unchangeable despite alterations in appearance, behavior, or attire (gender constancy). Even children who had only a rudimentary sense of their gender identity patterned more of their behavior after same-sex than opposite-sex models. Although the amount of modeling increases with comprehension of gender constancy, this relationship disappeared when variations in age were controlled. Thus, older children display greater same-sex modeling than do younger ones, irrespective of their gender-constancy level. It seems that gender constancy reflects children's over-all cognitive competence, which increases with age, rather than providing specialized direction for gender-role development.

Same-sex modeling seems to rely on classifying males and females into distinct groups, recognizing personal similarity to one group of models, and tagging that group's behavior patterns in memory as the ones to be used to guide behavior (Bussey & Bandura, 1984). Even very young children give evidence of classificatory capabilities where social stimuli are concerned. By the time infants are six months old, they treat infant faces as a category different from adult faces, and female faces as different from male faces (Fagan & Singer, 1979). Gender labeling and differential structuring of social experiences teach children to use the sex of the model as a guide for action (Huston, 1983).

Young children thus learn to use gender as an important characteristic for classifying persons and activities and to use gender features as a guide for selective modeling, without having to wait until they realize that their gender is permanent and irreversible. Simple awareness of gender identity—that one is a boy or girl—is sufficient to foster the acquisition of information and competencies traditionally linked to one's own sex. If belief in the permanence of one's self-categorization on other personal dimensions was necessary before one could learn from proficient models, people's self-development would be retarded and stunted. Were this so, an athlete who considered football his vocational identity could not acquire football skills through modeling until he defined his identity as a football player as everlasting and irreversible.

The view that same-sex modeling can proceed on the basis of gender identity alone, and that social factors also exert selective influence on what characteristics are adopted, accord with Spence's (1984) formulation. She posits that gender identity facilitates the adoption of prototypic gender-congruent attributes, but interacting social and personal factors determine what particular constellations of gender-related characteristics are developed. When long hair and culinary skill are in vogue, men with long flowing locks who perfect cooking skills perceive themselves as masculine, just as do men with closely cropped hair who eschew the skillet. Thus, people within each sex can develop heterogeneous patterns of gender-related attributes while retaining a confirmed personal sense of masculinity and femininity.

The gender-schema theory also suggests that children's readiness to classify objects and people in gender-related terms may well develop before a conception of gender constancy is achieved (Bem, 1981; Markus, Crane, Bernstein, & Siladi, 1982; Martin & Halverson, 1981). Children learn to encode, organize, and retrieve information about themselves and others in terms of a developing gender schema. Modeling studies that measure both acquisition and spontaneous performance reveal that young children learn the behavior exhibited by models of both sexes, but they mainly perform the behavior of same-sex models (Bussey & Bandura, 1984). It would seem that same-sex modeling is not due to differential gender-schematic processing at acquisition or retention of information about the behavior patterns exhibited by the male and female models. Rather, gender self-knowledge seems to be operating more on selective retrieval and enactment of what has been learned observationally from both sexes. Measuring acquisiton and perform-

ance permits refined analyses of whether gender conception affects acquisition, organization, retention, or enactment of modeled behavior. In the studies by Bussey and Bandura, children were simultaneously exposed to models of both sexes behaving in different ways. When there is substantial leeway in what one chooses to observe, gender conception may foster selective attention to same-sex models, which affects what is learned, and serves as a basis for organizing past experiences, which affects what is retained.

Social cognitive theory posits that, through cognitive processing of direct and vicarious experiences, children come to know their gender identity, gain substantial knowledge of sex roles, and extract rules as to what types of behavior are considered appropriate for their own sex. However, unlike radical cognitivism, it does not invest gender conceptions with automatic directive and motivating properties. Acquiring a conception of gender and valuing the attributes defining that conception are separable processes governed by different determinants.

Having a concept of one's own gender does not drive one to personify the stereotype it embraces. Nor does the self-conception of gender necessarily create positive valuation of the attributes and roles traditionally associated with it. Both the valuation of certain attributes and roles and the eagerness to adopt them are strongly influenced by the value society places on them. For example, in societies revering youth and devaluating aging, self-conception as elderly does not enhance valuation or eager adoption of the negative stereotypes of old age. Similarly, societies that discriminate against women can lead many to devalue their own identity. Results of numerous studies cited earlier reveal that, while boys clearly favor male models, girls, who are fully cognizant of their gender constancy, do not display the exclusive same-sex modeling as the cognitivistic theory would have one believe.

It is not as though the environment alone provides the grist for ascertaining one's gender, but after the self-categorization as a boy or girl occurs, the development of educational, occupational, avocational, and social competencies is driven intrapsychically by a gender conception-matching process. Social realities bear hard throughout the life span on the kinds of lives men and women pursue in a given society. In centering their theory on gender conceptual learning, cognitive theorists neglect the social realities of gender-role functioning, which are of considerable import. Although children manifest same-sex modeling when there is high consensus among models within each sex, reversal of the models' social power produces cross-sex modeling in children who display stable gender identity (Bussey & Bandura, 1984). Self-conceptions do not dictate the course of self-development in a manner oblivious to social reality.

Early in their lives, when children are cognizant of their gender but not well versed in societal gender-role sanctions, the sex of models serves as an easily identifiable guide for behavior. With growing experience the probabilistic outcomes accompanying gender-linked behavior are better comprehended. As a result, modeling is increasingly guided by multidimensional rules of conduct combining gender conception, sex of the models, the sex-typed nature of the behavior, and other predictive factors. Rules of gender-role conduct vary to some degree across social contexts and at different periods in life. Moreover, sociocultural and technological changes necessitate revision of preexisting conceptions of what is sex-appropriate behavior. Gender-role learning is, therefore, an ongoing process, rather than one limited to early childhood.

The major differences between social cognitive and cognitivistic approaches to gender-role development are not in whether cognitive skills and knowledge structures affect the course of development. In both theories they do. Rather, they differ in the nature of the cognitive structures, how they develop, and in the motivators governing gender-role acquisition and expression. Gender conception and sex-typed learning are reciprocally linked, rather than gender self-labeling unidirectionally ordaining self-development. Differentiation of gender roles is a psychosocial phenomenon, rather than merely a psychic one. A comprehensive theory of how roles get linked to gender must extend well beyond gender conception to a social analysis of how institutional structures and sanctions shape gender roles. The social determinants of gender roles, which are largely ignored in cognitivistic approaches, receive considerable attention within the social cognitive perspective.

Comparative Analysis of Modeling

The role of symbolic processes in observational learning can also be evaluated using comparative studies. If species higher in the phylogenetic scale have greater capability to symbolize experience, then one would expect differences among species in their potentialities for delayed modeling. Systematic comparisons have not been conducted between different species in observational learning on tasks varying in complexity and need for memory representation. Findings of various studies that happen to use different species, nevertheless, are suggestive.

Many investigations purporting to study observational learning are, in fact, concerned more with social facilitation of preexisting response patterns than with the learning of new ones (Hall, 1963). Studies involving acquisition of novel response patterns, therefore, are most relevant to the issue under discussion. Lower species will learn simple acts through modeling if they can perform the behavior concurrently with a trained model or immediately after it has been exhibited. Observational learning is less reliable, however, if there is an appreciable lapse of time between watching and performing (Jacoby & Dawson, 1969; Oldfield-Box, 1970; Powell & Burns, 1970).

With higher species, the superiority of observational learning over learning by reinforcement is more striking (Adler &

Adler, 1978; Herbert & Harsh, 1944; John, Chesler, Bartlett, & Victor, 1968). Higher animals can, by watching, acquire complicated sequences of responses and perform them some time after the original demonstrations, a feat which requires at least short-term memory. Puppies, soon after their eyes become functional, will rapidly pick up ways to secure food by observing a skilled model, without needing any prior reinforced training (Adler & Adler, 1977). That higher animals can process and retain modeled information regarding alternative courses of action is further illustrated by Herbert and Harsh (1944). Cats who have observed mistakes, as well as correct solutions, learned to solve manipulative problems more rapidly than those who watched only skilled performances. When there are many alternatives, seeing both what fails and what succeeds conveys more response information than seeing only one successful option.

Primates possess an even higher capacity to symbolize past experiences and to use the knowledge on future occasions. They can synthesize diverse attributes as the properties of an object for imaginal memory representation. In demonstrating this capability, Premack (1976) posed questions to a chimpanzee—who had been trained to communicate using plastic forms to symbolize words—concerning the properties of an absent apple. She was able to specify the characteristics of an apple, such as its color, shape, and stem protuberance from her internal representation of it. Primates can grasp concepts for classifying objects on several abstract dimensions; they can foresee the consequences of alternative courses of action, foretell the course that people's actions will take, and improvise information to generate solutions to problems (Mason, 1976; Premack, 1983).

Some of the earliest studies of observational learning in primates were conducted by Warden and his associates (Warden, Fjeld, & Koch, 1940; Warden & Jackson, 1935). They spent many hours training rhesus monkeys by reinforcement to solve puzzles that opened doors to raisins they rel-ished. Following training, these primate models manipulated the puzzle devices while naive monkeys, presented with a duplicate set of problems, observed the skilled demonstrators. The naive observers achieved through modeling instantaneous solutions in 76 percent of the test trials! Field studies of primate social behavior provide striking illustrations of how idiosyncratic styles of behavior are acquired and transmitted to other members of the subculture through modeling (Imanishi, 1957; Kawamura, 1963). The diffusion process is greatly influenced by existing social networks and the social status of the innovator.

The most impressive evidence for delayed modeling of intricate, novel patterns of behavior comes from chimpanzees reared in human families. They sit at typewriters striking keyboards, light cigarettes with mechanical lighters, apply lipstick to their faces before mirrors, open cans with screwdrivers, bathe, soap and dry dolls, and engage in other human activities, without having had prior tutoring, but all of which they have seen modeled from time to time (Gardner & Gardner, 1969; Hayes, 1951; Hayes & Hayes, 1952; Kellogg & Kellogg, 1933).

Considerable research has been devoted to teaching primates a system of communication that can be executed manually through sign language, objects representing words, or geometric symbols on computer consoles (Gardner & Gardner, 1975; Premack, 1976; Rumbaugh, 1977). These studies reveal the advanced capacity of primates to acquire a generalized communication skill that can be used in different settings for various purposes. After being taught a large vocabulary of signs, the animals can use them to name objects and their properties, to describe relations among objects, and to get adults to do the things they want. Although primates are capable of rudimentary two-way communication with word signs, there is some controversy over whether their use of signs is grammatically ordered in the same manner as human linguistic constructions (Gardner, 1981; Terrace, 1979). Although the issue of the linguistic organization of sign sequences remains to be resolved, the symbolic modes of communication provide a means for measuring the representational capacities of primates and for mapping the knowledge they possess. To the extent that representational processes and attainments become measurable by language symbols, the role of symbolization in observational learning in animals can be investigated much more systematically. But it is at the human level, where symbolization is the most abstract, versatile, and generative, that the capacity to learn by observation is most advanced.

ABSTRACT MODELING

Much of the behavior being modeled at any given time is socially prescribed or effective only if performed in a particular way. There is little leeway for improvisation on how to drive automobiles, perform surgical operations, or bake soufflés. The highly functional patterns, which constitute the proven skills and established customs of a culture, are adopted in essentially the same form as they are portrayed. Modeling influences, however, can convey rules for generative and innovative behavior as well. Through the process of abstract modeling, observers extract the rules underlying specific performances for generating behavior that goes beyond what they have seen or heard (Bandura, 1971a; Rosenthal & Zimmerman, 1978). In abstract modeling, judgmental skills and generalizable rules are being learned by observation.

In studies of abstract modeling, people observe others perform responses embodying a certain rule or principle. The modeled responses differ on nonrelevant aspects but contain the same underlying rule. Observers are later tested for rule learning under conditions where they can behave in a way that is conceptually and stylistically similar to the model's inclination, but the situation is new and unfamiliar enough that they

cannot simply mimic the specific responses previously observed. Consequently, they must improvise what they have learned. To take an example, a model generates, from a set of nouns, sentences containing the passive construction ("The dog *is being* petted," "The window *was* opened," etc.). The modeled speech varies in content and other nonrelevant features, but its structural property—the passive voice—is the same. Children later are asked to create sentences from a different set of nouns with the model absent, and their production of passive constructions is recorded.

In abstract modeling, observers extract the common attributes exemplified in diverse modeled responses and combine them into rules for generating behavior with similar structural properties. Responses embodying the observationally derived rule resemble the behavior the model would tend to exhibit under similar circumstances, even though observers have never seen the model behaving in these new situations.

Acquiring rules through modeling for generating behavior involves at least three processes: These include extracting relevant attributes from social exemplars; integrating the information into a composite rule; and using the rule to produce new instances of the behavior. Relevant features can be extracted by repeated exposure to specific exemplars which share the common property. Exposure alone, however, does not ensure that the relevant features will be noticed. Itoh and Fujita (1982) examined eye movements of good and poor observational learners as they watched models make conceptual judgments. Successful learners widely scanned the different features of the stimulus array until they detected the one defining the judgmental rules, whereupon they focused anticipatorily on it before the model acted. Poor observational learners quickly fixated on irrelevancies, and their attention rarely strayed from them.

A number of attention-directing factors—such as the distinctiveness of the social exemplars, informative feedback, and semantic accompaniments that impart meaning to abstract events—help observers recognize the aspects that enter into the governing rules. We have already seen how behavior can be modeled to make its basic structure more recognizable. Common attributes can also be made more salient through the outcomes of the model's actions. When only the responses embodying the rule succeed for the model, the aspects common to these examples can be more easily singled out by observers than if no informative feedback is provided concerning the adequacy of the model's judgments and actions. Informative feedback for the observers, when they themselves later act on what they have learned, similarly helps them to perfect rules and apply them successfully to new situations (Henderson & Swanson, 1978).

In observational learning of difficult concepts, abstract modeling of rules is aided by providing concrete referents in conjunction with conceptual expressions. Nowhere is this better illustrated than in the acquisition of linguistic rules. When adults and children talk to each other, their utterances usually refer to meaningful ongoing events. The knowledge children possess about these events and how they relate to each other give meaning to the words and to the word-order rules by which they are organized for intelligible communication. Modeled enactments that tap conceptions of how agents, actions, and objects are causally related (e.g., showing a rider jumping a horse over a railing while verbalizing the action sequence) give meaning to linguistic rules of how words are ordered to represent the depicted relationships. Young children learn linguistic rules with greater ease when grammatical utterances correspond to ongoing activities that depict the relationships represented in the speech than if the utterances are modeled alone (Brown, 1976). Referential modeling, which presents actual events together with their abstract counterparts, plays an especially influential role in early phases of cognitive development (Zimmerman, 1983). The more limited the knowledge and personal experiences, the more abstractions require concrete referents. Complex rules must be broken down into subordinate ones and mastered first with referential aids.

Most rules of behavior embody several factors. Judgmental rules, for example, are seldom based on only a single element without regard to other considerations. Hence, observers not only have to extract the relevant factors from modeled events but also have to combine them into a functional, composite rule. This is achieved through observation by formulating different composite rules and testing them by the success with which they predict the model's response outcomes. Erroneous composites produce mismatches between anticipated and observed response outcomes. By constructing different combination rules and testing them against the results accompanying the model's actions, observers can eventually arrive at the correct composite rule.

Observers have to go through a hypothesis-testing process when modeled performances and their effects are the only information available for inferring the rules by which others make judgments and guide their actions. Models can, of course, explain the rules they are using, as well as convey them by their actions. Modeling combined with rule verbalization is usually more effective than either alone in promoting rule-governed behavior. But the benefits of providing rules are often less than one might expect (Rosenthal & Zimmerman, 1978). Either people have difficulty fully understanding abstract rules, or they do not know how to apply them in new situations. This again illustrates the importance of distinguishing between knowledge and skill. Knowing a rule does not ensure optimal performance, as any athletic instructor or grammarian will testify. Some practice is needed in generating actions from generic rules to suit changing circumstances. As the activity becomes more complex, the production skill becomes more important.

Modeling has been shown to be a highly effective means of establishing abstract or rule-governed behavior. On the basis of modeled information, people acquire, among other things, judgmental standards, linguistic rules, styles of inquiry, information-processing skills, and standards of self-evaluation (Bandura, 1971a; Rosenthal & Zimmerman, 1978). Evidence that generative rules of thought and conduct can be created through abstract modeling attests to the broad scope of observational learning.

Conceptual Learning. Events occur with tremendous diversity. Because no two things are ever completely the same, people would remain at a loss on what to expect or how to behave if they treated everything they encounter as unique. Nor could they profit from experience, because even the same event never recurs in precisely identical form. The predicament of perpetual variation is resolved by conceptualizing things together that resemble one another. By categorizing experiences on the basis of likenesses, the knowledge gained from specific happenings serves as a general guide for judgment and action. In addition to learning rules for constructing behavior, people also have to learn rules for classifying events.

When events differ in a variety of ways, as they almost always do, any one or more of the aspects can be chosen as the basis for conceptual grouping. In trying to construct a coherent and functional view of the world, people have to discover the judgmental rules that best suit different circumstances. This can be achieved through trial-and-error experiences or communicated verbally. In addition, judgmental rules are often inferred from information conveyed by people's actions. In studies of conceptual learning through modeling, children observe adults categorize multifaceted objects according to a rule that combines several attributes. Subsequent tests show that children infer the judgmental rules from the observed choices, they generalize the rules to new situations, and they retain them over time (Rosenthal & Zimmerman, 1978).

Modeling generally surpasses discovery through experimentation, and adding modeling to experimentation boosts conceptual learning. It is evident from the generality of the effects that abstract modeling produces stable changes in judgment, rather than merely producing imitations of actions that happened to be modeled.

The external facilitators of modeling mentioned earlier accelerate observational learning of judgmental rules, as do the conceptual skills of observers. Children who have some facility at mastering concepts are quicker at inferring judgmental rules from modeled actions than those who lack conceptual skills (Ito, 1975; Sukemune, Haruki, & Kashiwagi, 1977). Of particular interest, however, is evidence that modeling improves conceptual functioning, even in children who are lacking such cognitive skills. With further aids to modeling, such children might well approximate the attainments of the more developmentally advanced. In short, the level of cognitive skill should be regarded as a reciprocally contributing influence, that is itself improvable by social learning, rather than simply a limiting condition in observational learning.

The concepts that people develop for judging and dealing with their environment serve them well in most instances. But they can be encumbrances as well. Not all things categorized together are alike in all respects. Lack of sensitivity to individual variations gives rise to indiscriminate responsiveness. When conceptions are built on irrelevant characteristics, judgments and actions become inappropriate or produce adverse personal and social effects. A notable illustration is the social stereotyping of people on the basis of age, sex, race, religion, and ethnicity, just to mention a few of the conceptual divisions that have served human prejudice. In situations in which people have limited personal contact, they tend to respond toward each other in terms of their preconceptions.

The impact of modeling on stereotyping social cognition has received surprisingly little attention considering its import. There is reason to believe that modeling carries a major share of the instruction in this domain. Social exemplars provide directly observable information for social cognition, thus requiring less inference about thought processes. When stereotyping is covertly condoned but publicly disavowed, the teaching is more by example than by direct tuition. Consider gender-role stereotyping. Society professes equality between the sexes but, as we have seen, models, in its instructional materials, mass media, and institutional practices, conceptions of masculinity and femininity that create disparities in the opportunities for personal development. Such stereotyped cultural modeling affects the self-conceptions and behavior of males and females in ways that can hamper their development and psychological functioning (Bem, 1977; McArthur & Eisen, 1976).

Strategies for Seeking and Processing Information. People expend a great deal of effort exploring their environment and seeking information relevant to the pursuit of their goals. Theories attributing human inquisitiveness to an innate drive for information or to situational novelty and variety are not of much help in explaining the large differences that exist in the level and direction of human inquisitiveness. Knowledge about how to seek and organize information is gained through varied means, including direct tuition, unguided experience, and proficient modeling. Here we examine the contribution of modeling to the development of strategies for seeking and processing information. Even when knowledge is attained by enactive exploration of the environment, modeled inquisitiveness sparks exploratory curiosity in young children (Johns & Endsley, 1977). For activities that preschoolers rarely explore on their own, simply introducing novelty and variety does not overcome their indifference, whereas modeled engrossment whets their curiosity (Haskett & Lenfestey, 1974).

Modeling influences can alter how people organize their thoughts, what type of information they seek, and how they process it.

Rosenthal, Zimmerman, and Durning (1970) exposed disadvantaged children to adults who modeled different styles of inquiry regarding a variety of objects—the children sought information about the physical properties of objects, the functional uses to which they might be put, causal relationships involving the objects, or judgments of value and preference. In subsequent tests of information seeking about different matters, the children employed the general interrogative strategies they saw exemplified. They inquired about causal relationships when models sought causal information but wanted to know what things are used for when models displayed curiosity about functional matters. Analysis of the children's inquiries disclosed that they had abstracted and generalized the modeled styles of inquiry, rather than merely copied the model's utterances.

In some cultures, seeking information by direct inquiry has traditionally not been cultivated. When children fail to draw on the understanding gained by others, the children's scope of knowledge is largely confined to their own limited explorations. Restricted inquisitiveness thus hampers intellectual development. As part of a larger program of cognitive development through modeling, Henderson and Swanson (1974) demonstrated that given appropriate exemplars, Papago Indian children, who are reluctant to seek information through questioning, master styles of inquiry for finding out about causal relationships after observing Papago adults model ways of seeking causal information. They adopted and maintained the new styles of inquiry even more effectively when modeling was supplemented with environmental supports for inquisitiveness (Swanson & Henderson, 1977).

People often seek information in the search for solutions to problems. In generating and testing possible solutions, models provide a convenient source of strategies on how to deal with various matters. Children and adults who suffer deficiencies in problem solving learn effective strategies by observing how successful models go about gaining information for evaluating alternatives (Denney & Denney, 1974; Laughlin, Moss, & Miller, 1969). But young children, whose memory and inferential capabilities are easily taxed, have some difficulty inferring cognitive strategies solely from the pattern of information-seeking responses of models. However, as in other areas of cognitive functioning, verbally augmented modeling can compensate for cognitive limitations. Young children improve their competence at solving problems when the models not only exemplify solution strategies but occasionally verbalize their guiding principles for formulating questions and organizing the resultant information (Denney, 1975; Howie, 1975).

Abstract modeling figures prominently in areas of cognitive functioning that have been interpreted in terms of developmental stages, presumed to be invariant, uniform, and mutually exclusive. Moral reasoning is one such example. We shall return later to rule learning through modeling when we analyze language acquisition, changes in moral reasoning, and other forms of cognitive development from the perspectives of both social cognitive and stage theories.

CREATIVE MODELING

Creativity constitutes one of the highest forms of human expression. Without the existence of creative works, the scope and depth of human experience would be considerably impoverished. Visualize, for example, a life without art, music, and literature. Many of the innovations in science and technology have profound impact, for better or for worse, on the way of everyday life. With the aid of advanced communications technology, innovations spread rapidly beyond the societies where they have been developed to alter the ways of life in other cultures. Despite its importance, the creative process has received surprisingly little psychological study.

Because traditional conceptions of modeling have largely been limited to response mimicry, modeling has come to be viewed as the antithesis of innovation. Contrary to this common belief, innovation can emerge through the modeling process. Modeling can contribute to creative development in several ways. As we have just seen, modeling can provide the cognitive and behavioral tools for innovation. In most creative endeavors, the requisite knowledge and skills are learned by example and by practice through some form of apprenticeship. Innovators do not cease to be observational learners simply because they have gained some mastery of their craft. They continue to learn things from others that might add new dimensions to their own creative work. In addition, modeling can directly facilitate the emergence of new genres by providing ingredients for innovative syntheses and by cultivating unconventionality.

Innovative Synthesis and Development

Originality largely involves synthesizing experiences into new ways of thinking and doing things. When exposed to models who differ in their styles of thinking and behavior, observers rarely pattern their behavior exclusively after a single source, nor do they adopt all the attributes even of preferred models. Rather, observers combine various aspects of different models into new amalgams that differ from the individual sources (Bandura, Ross, & Ross, 1963c). Because they vary in what they adopt from the diversity they observe, different observers create new blends of characteristics.

In the case of social behavior, children within the same family may develop dissimilar personality characteristics by drawing upon different parental and sibling attributes. Successive modeling, in which observers later serve as sources of behavior for new members, will most likely produce a gradual modeled evolution of new patterns which bear little resemblance to those exhibited by the original models. In homogenous cultures, where all models display similar attitudes and styles of behavior, social behavior may undergo little or no change across successive generations. New patterns are most apt to arise when people see a great deal of variety around them. It is diversity in modeling that fosters behavioral and cognitive innovation.

Creative achievements do not spring from a vacuum. They are built, in part, on the preceding innovations of others. Modeling probably contributes most to creative development in the inception of new styles. Innovators achieve novelty by incorporating new elements into customary forms. Once initiated, experiences with new forms create further evolutionary changes. A partial departure from tradition thus eventually becomes a new direction. The progression of artistic and musical careers through distinct periods provides many notable examples of this process. In his earliest works, Beethoven adopted the classical forms of Haydn and Mozart, although with greater emotional expressiveness, which foreshadowed the direction of his artistic development. Wagner fused Beethoven's symphonic mode with Weber's naturalistic enchantment and Meyerbeer's dramatic virtuosity to evolve a new operatic form. Innovators in science and technology, in the same manner, draw upon the contributions of others to build something new from their own experiences.

Cultivating Unconventionality

The discussion thus far has analyzed creativity through the innovative synthesis of influences from different sources. While existing ideas and practices furnish some of the ingredients for the new, they can also retard innovation. Established ways of thinking impede the exploration of novel ideas and the perception of new relationships. As long as familiar modes are adequate, there is little incentive to consider alternatives. The unconventional is not only unexplored, it is usually negatively received when introduced by the venturesome. Both the security of the familiar and the uncertainty and hazards of the new serve as hindrances to innovation.

Modeling influences that exemplify new perspectives on common situations can foster creative performance by weakening conventional inclinations. People exposed to models who think divergently are, indeed, more innovative than those exposed to models who behave in a conventional fashion (Belcher, 1975; Harris & Evans, 1973). Seeing models approach problems in diverse ways increases observers' versatility, whereas unimaginative modeling fosters triteness or even reduces creativity (Harris & Fisher, 1973; Mueller, 1978). Although innovative modeling generally enhances the creative ideas in others, there are some limits to this influence (Zimmerman & Dialessi, 1973). When models are unusually productive and observers' skills are underdeveloped, their creative efforts may be self-devalued by unfavorable comparison. If the attainments of distinguished models are used as proximal gauges of self-adequacy rather than as distal ideals, prolific creative modeling can dishearten the less talented.

Research has clarified how novel behavioral variants can evolve at the individual level by amalgamate modeling and the experiences ensuing from new forms. Boyd and Richerson (1985) analyze the mechanisms of cultural evolution from a population view of social learning. Within their conceptual framework, environmental conditions, multiple modeling influences, and personal experiences operate interactively to change the distribution of cultural variants over time and to foster convergence toward variants that are efficacious in particular milieus. The ways in which social learning influences favor some behavioral variants over others receive detailed consideration in a subsequent chapter devoted to the social diffusion of innovations.

CHAPTER
3

ENACTIVE
LEARNING

Enactive experience is a ubiquitous tutor, however toilsome and costly the lessons learned from experience might be at times. Some cognitive and behavioral structures are largely developed in this way, and many of those acquired through modeling are refined and perfected experientially. In learning solely through response consequences, people must depend on the information conveyed by the effects of their actions. During transactions with the environment, some of their actions prove successful, others have no discernible effect, and still others produce aversive outcomes. On the basis of informative feedback, successful courses of action tend to be selected and ineffective ones discarded. Although few would deny that actions are influenced

by their effects, the process by which consequences create new structures of behavior has been the subject of considerable debate.

Learning from the outcomes of one's actions has been traditionally portrayed as a mechanistic process in which responses are shaped automatically and unconsciously by their immediate effects. However, research that examined the role of cognitive factors in human learning offered little support for the view that consequents operate as automatic imprinters. Response outcomes have several functions. First, they impart information on how behavior must be structured to achieve given purposes and point to environmental predictors of likely happenings. By examining the pattern of outcomes they have experienced, performers can arrive at conceptions and rules of behavior. Second, contingent outcomes serve as motivators by providing incentives for action. People mobilize and sustain their efforts to secure outcomes which they value highly. The third function, which is the subject of much debate, concerns the capacity of outcomes to strengthen responses automatically. A full understanding of learning from the effects of actions, therefore, requires the detailed consideration of each of these functions.

Peripheralistic theories of learning, which contend that actions are shaped directly by their outcomes, were falling into disrepute before cognitivism began its ascendency. Most learning theorists had already parted company with the peripheralistic view. For example, in analyzing the relationship between perception and learning, Lawrence (1963) conceptualized external influences as operating through a set of rules or coding operations. Miller and his associates (Egger & Miller, 1963) interpreted reinforcement according to its informative properties. Mowrer (1960) adopted imagery as an explanatory mechanism in learning. Psychological modeling was construed in terms of the transmission of information and representational guidance of action (Bandura, 1962). Unfortunately, disputes over the mechanism of learning created a jaundiced view of the phenomenon of learning itself. The concept of "learning," which had always occupied a central position in psychological theorizing and research, assumed a tainted connotation. The phenomenon of enactive learning was summarily downgraded because of its unpopular behavioristic lineage. The advent of the computer model accelerated the shift of interest from the acquisition of performance capabilities to the processing, storage, and retrieval of information.

As the concerns of psychological theorizing and research turned toward questions of how knowledge is gained and represented, the fundamental issues of how behavioral competencies are developed were trivialized or simply ignored. Tversky (1982) traces the decline and then the eventual resurrection of learning in psychology. Learning was supplanted by memory for discrete bits of information, sentences, and prose passages. Memory, in turn, was recast as a problem of comprehension. Growth of understanding then became a problem of acquiring declarative knowledge and translating it into cognitive procedures for dealing with the environment. Procedural knowledge provides production systems which embody decision rules for solving given tasks (Anderson, 1980). In this reinstated form within the information-processing framework, learning is characterized as the acquisition of knowledge and cognitive directives for how to do something.

One must distinguish between knowledge and skill. Construing learning in terms of factual and procedural knowledge is well suited for cognitive problem solving. But there are many domains of activity that require additional mechanisms to get from knowledge structures to proficient action. Knowledge and cognitive skills are necessary but insufficient for skilled performance. A novice given complete information on how to ski, a set of decision rules, and then launched from a mountain top would most likely end up in an orthopedic ward or intensive care unit of the local infirmary. We have seen earlier that the development of performance skills requires a conception-matching mechanism for transforming knowledge into skilled action. Physical enactment serves as the translating vehicle. The information provided by enactive experience is used to make corrective adjustments in spatial and temporal features of action until a close match is eventually achieved between internal conception and performance (Carroll & Bandura, 1985). Early phases of skill development involve bidirectional influences. Conceptions guide actions, and informative feedback from the effects of enactments, in turn, modify and refine conceptions.

INFORMATIONAL ANALYSIS
OF ENACTIVE EXPERIENCE

Intrinsic Response Information

In dealing with their environment, people not only perform responses but also notice the effects they produce. This informative feedback may be intrinsic or extrinsic to the actions. The sensory effects that naturally accompany the enactment of a behavioral pattern constitute the intrinsic forms. They include the sensations arising from bodily movements and sights and sounds occasioned by the actions. Many actions also produce naturally pleasant or painful experiences, as when one is warmed by donning a coat in cold weather or is burned by touching a flame.

Behavioral patterns are readily acquirable through natural consequences when they occur quickly, predictably, and are clearly observable. This makes the causal relationship between actions and their effects easily discernible, but this is not always the case. Some of the natural effects of actions are indistinct, others set physical processes in motion that take some time to produce their effects, and still others are imperceptibly cumulative. In such instances, which are by no means uncommon, natural effects are poor tutors.

Extrinsic Response Information

If people had to rely solely on what their body tells them or on the immediate sights and sounds produced by their actions, they could acquire rudimentary skills, but otherwise their level and range of competence would be quite limited. In addition to intrinsic sensory feedback, people create socially based consequences for each others' behavior. They admire, praise, and reward some endeavors, ignore others, and criticize and punish still others. Extrinsic feedback is a socially arranged effect, not a natural or necessary consequent of the behavior. As a result, the same behavior can have markedly different consequences in different societies or under different circumstances, even within the same social milieu. Unlike intrinsic response effects, which are generated by the ongoing activity itself, extrinsic effects are socially mediated and usually occur after a given behavior has been performed.

The extrinsic mode of guidance provides a social vehicle for transmitting information for creating multiform behaviors to suit numerous purposes. Because of their versatile applicability, extrinsic consequents can serve to fashion remarkably diverse styles of behavior. Depending on what is socially valued, social approval can promote the development of aggression, altruism, conformity, creativity, cooperation, competitiveness, or most any other style of behavior. Both the cultivation of human diversity and acculturation rest heavily on the social consequences of behavior. Much of the exploratory activity that builds knowledge and skills would be difficult to sustain without at least some social guides and supports.

What Is Learned: Responses or Generative Conceptions?

Learning through the effects of actions raises fundamental questions about what is acquired and how it governs response production. Behaviorists of the more radical persuasion assume that it is motor responses that are selected from the ongoing stream of behavior and automatically reinforced by their effects. Such a view not only fits poorly with the empirical evidence regarding human learning, but it glosses over some sticky issues concerning what exactly is being reinforced. Consequences occur almost invariably after a response has ceased to exist. In animal experiments, a response produces food after the response has disappeared. In verbal conditioning, experimenters must withhold their social rewards until after judging whether particular utterances fall within the rewardable class. In social applications of incentive systems, tangible rewards are not presented until minutes, hours, or even days after the requisite activities have been completed. The tenets of radical behaviorism are formulated in terms of three external elements—antecedent stimuli, responses, and consequences—impinging upon each other to forge stimulus-response relations. Theorists who formulate laws about functional relationships between solely external physical events have the problem of explaining how something that no longer exists can be reinforced. This dilemma can be resolved only by postulating some kind of enduring residue of the absent response.

One could argue that responses leave momentary neural traces, which get reinforced by succeeding outcomes. Such an explanation, however, places exceedingly complex demands on a neural mechanism for encoding and evaluating environmental events. Consider some of the executive functions it would have to perform. Actions are often influenced by outcomes that are considerably delayed in time, with countless influences and actions intervening during the interval. Somehow, the neural system would have to select the appropriate neural traces from the profusion of inputs and hold them in abeyance until the outcomes arrive some time later.

It is difficult to conceive of how a neural system would mediate conceptual learning and judgment if it registered only the exact neural traces of external stimuli. It might be argued that only the common features of stimuli are registered. But most complex concepts do not have a fixed set of defining features (Mervis & Rosch, 1981). The concept of "modes of transport" encompasses cars, trains, bicycles, aircraft, boats, and many animals which are capable of being ridden by humans. The instances of the concept, which could be reinforced while learning it, such as a horse and an airliner, differ in countless features that produce markedly dissimilar patterns of neural impulses. The afferent data generated by exposure to objects that could serve as a mode of transport under particular conditions does not, in itself, contain the information for developing a conception of transport vehicles. Nor does outcome feedback that a horse and an airplane are vehicles of transport provide much generalizable information for categorizing a new mode of transport, such as a boat. What must be learned is the generalizable rules governing conveyance capabilities. Once the rules underlying the concept have been comprehended, the rules can be applied to new instances never encountered before.

Conceptual judgments entail reasoning from propositional knowledge. Suppose, for example, children who had grasped the transport concept were asked to judge whether or not a board in a river constituted a suitable human transport. In a theory that ignores conscious deliberation, the neural system would have to summon up its repository of neural traces of transport modalities and compare them against the new item, only to discover that the repository does not contain it. In actuality, to render an accurate judgment, the children would have to determine whether the board shares some attributes with any of the conveyances in the heterogeneous transport class (i.e., floating watercraft) and draw on their knowledge of whether this particular board was large enough to support a person. The judgment would differ for small and large boards, supporting small and large riders, and navigating quiet and turbulent waters in a standing or recumbent position.

In the preceding example, accurate judgments require inferential use of relevant sources of knowledge. This knowledge base involves networks of propositions that include conceptions of the properties of events and the cognized relations among them. People, of course, have some consciousness of what they know. They can judge things at a glance without having to go through a laborious mechanical process of checking each item against a huge repository of contents. Behavioristic theories are reluctant to grant the organism a working memory and reasoning skills, let alone the capacity for consciousness of its own knowledge. Even if the responses that have already gone before the reinforcers arrive could be reinforced, via their neural traces, they could not provide the necessary information for correct responses in novel instances. This necessitates inference from generic knowledge that has been abstracted from specific experiences. The medium of inference is neural, but the inferring is a generative cortical activity.

Similar explanatory problems are encountered by theories that portray motor skills as being governed by memory and perceptual traces automatically imprinted by feedback from individual acts. In such theories, learning can occur only by performing responses which produce the feedback stimuli that lay down the traces. The notion that feedback stimuli implant enduring traces for response production and correction implies that each movement has its own internal representation. Given the boundless variety of movements that are performed, a one-to-one mapping between stored traces and specific acts would create an immense storage problem (Schmidt, 1975). Moreover, since enactments of a skill must be constantly varied to suit changing conditions, a fixed internal generator of behavior would be more of a hindrance than an aid. Skilled performance requires a generic conception, rather than a specific representation. Situational requirements help to specify how conception is best implemented into specific courses of action. A golfer who has mastered the fundamentals of the golf swing will adjust the basic swing depending on the type of club, the distance from the hole, and whether the ball lies on the side of a hill, in the rough, or in the dreaded sandtrap. Subrules specify the enactment adjustments needed in each of these situations.

People are not unselective recipients of stimuli, nor do they learn only by doing. They learn by extracting the basic structure of behavioral patterns from information conveyed by modeled performances, instructions, and extrinsic feedback, as well as from sensory information returning from a movement. In theories depicting neural traces as executing responses and neurophysiological feedback loops as correcting them, the abstracting and generative functions of cognitive activity, which are central for understanding how skills are acquired and executed, receive little attention. One must distinguish between systems that subserve different purposes and personal exercise of those systems.

Enactive Learning as a Conception-Matching Process

In the social cognitive view, environmental influences affect behavior through a symbolization process. That is, transitory occurrences have lasting effects because the information they convey is processed and transformed into symbols. From the effects of their actions, people derive and verify their conceptions of appropriate behavior, rather than learn specific responses. The conceptions specify how to combine elements into appropriate patterns and what to do at various times and decision points in the sequential execution of behavior. A skill is thus represented mainly by rules for generating requisite patterns and sequences of action. Cognitive theories of human performance have traditionally assumed that a skill is represented in a motor schema. Although schemata and conceptions are closely analogous, the term schema has been used in many different ways and is often simply defined as a general cognitive structure, leaving much indefiniteness about its exact properties and how it gives rise to response patterns. Schemata are widely invoked as explanatory devices, but their presence and nature are rarely assessed independently of their effects. Conceptions, which embody rules of action, provide explicit guides for the production of organized patterns of behavior. Thus, in teaching novices the skills required to fly an airplane, instructors convey through words, demonstration, and corrective feedback, the rules of what to do rather than trying to imprint schemata in their totality in some ill-defined way. Anderson (1983) calls attention to the ambiguity of how schemata are acquired and how action is derived from a schema, which is conventionally defined as an undetailed plan or general structure. Procedural rules are needed that furnish the details for performance. Some of the theorists who interpret skill learning in terms of schema formation define a schema more precisely as a set of rules for producing response patterns (Pew, 1974; Schmidt,1975).

Generative conceptions are used to produce behavior patterns which share the same basic characteristics but may differ in other respects. Learning must be generative in nature, because skilled activities are seldom performed in exactly the same way; they must be varied to fit different circumstances. After children grasp the conception of a triangle, they can draw large or small ones, with either hand or foot, and create triangular paths and enclosures with materials, even though they have never produced some of these triangular constructions in this particular way before. It is because people learn generative conceptions, rather than specific acts, that human skills have remarkable flexibility and utility.

Reinforcement theories of learning assume that it is environmental consequences that automatically select and strengthen responses from among those the organism possesses. In the social cognitive view, outcomes change behavior in humans largely through the intervening influence of thought. Consequences serve as an unarticulated way of informing performers of what they must do to produce certain results. By observing the differential outcome of their actions, people eventually construct conceptions of new behavioral patterns and the circumstances in which it is appropriate to perform them. A generative conception serves two functions: It provides the rules for producing appropriate response patterns, and it provides the standard for improving performance on the basis of perceived discrepancies between conception and execution.

Within this theoretical framework, enactive learning is a special case of observational learning. In learning by direct experience, people construct conceptions of behavior from observing the effects of their actions; in learning by modeling, they derive the conceptions from observing the structure of the behavior being modeled. The rate of learning from observing skilled models and from observing the feedback of one's own performances differs substantially. The structure of complex behavior can be symbolically constructed more readily from observing the behavior displayed in an already integrated form than from attempting to construct it gradually by trying different actions and examining how well they work. When people fail to recognize the effects their actions produce, or they inadequately process the outcome information provided by variations in actions over time, they do not learn much, although the consequences are repeatedly impinging upon them.

In the social cognitive analysis, the various modes of learning (e.g., modeling, enactive exploration, conditioning, verbal instruction) are regarded as different ways of conveying information about the rules of behavior and the predictive relationships between events in the environment. These different modes of learning vary in the type, amount, and organization of information they convey, but their behavioral effects are presumed to be mediated by a common conception-matching process. Because similar subprocesses underlie the different modes of learning, one need not require a separate theory for each form of tutelage. However, the different modes must be studied in their own right, because they vary in how much they rely on the constituent subprocesses.

Central Regulatory Processes

The question of whether feedback affects behavior directly, or operates through central mechanisms, has been the subject of considerable debate over the years. Much of the research on this topic is concerned with the role of intrinsic sensory consequences in the development and regulation of behavior. Evidence from several lines of investigations lends support to the view that outcomes influence actions mainly through the central representation and regulation of action patterns. Unfortunately, the studies of intrinsic sensory feedback are largely confined to simple, discrete acts, on the assumption that understanding how an arm movement is performed will ultimately provide answers to how complex skills are mastered. Adams (1984) argues cogently for why research on isolated acts cannot reveal much about the mechanisms governing the organization of complex behavior patterns. He regards cognitive representation as important for the structuring of behavior. Feedback experiences aid the translation of cognition to action. The nature of the behavior is less of a problem in studies of extrinsic feedback, which typically analyze cognitive and behavioral skills of greater complexity.

Feedback Delay.

It takes some time for visual, auditory, and kinesthetic information that has been produced by responses to be fed back and evaluated by the performer. When responses are performed slowly, the sound, sight, and feel of what one is doing can be used to alter the direction of the behavior while it is in progress. However, when behavior is enacted swiftly, which is often the case, the peripheral feedback lags too far behind the response to direct the next action. The behavior must, therefore, be antecedently guided by action plans, rather than by immediate sensory con sequences.

Although the response feedback often cannot be used effectively while the action is in progress, nevertheless it aids learning in the ways noted earlier: Feedback provides information for refining the conception of the appropriate behavior, and it indicates the types of corrective adjustments needed to improve subsequent performances. Many actions produce predictable effects. Predictive knowledge provides the basis for anticipatory regulation of behavior. Applying

brakes sharply on a slippery road surface will cause a car to slide sideways, and steering the car in a direction opposite to the skid will accelerate the spin. Once this knowledge has been acquired, drivers know how to prevent such mishaps and what corrective actions must be taken instantly should a skid occur, without having to figure out what to do from bodily sensations. As the regularities of events become noticeable with experience, the mode of control changes from error correction, based on the immediate consequences of faulty performances, to anticipatory actions that prevent the errors (Pew, 1974).

Learning Without Sensory Feedback.

Studies of learning and performance without peripheral sensory feedback also have bearing on central control mechanisms. The role of sensory information in the regulation of behavior has been examined extensively in deafferentation studies with animals. In such experiments, kinesthetic feedback is surgically eliminated by severing the nerves that carry nerve impulses from the limbs. This results in the loss of somatic sensations for determining limb position. Young animals that can neither feel their movements nor see what they are doing can develop and maintain simple response patterns given inducements to do so (Taub, 1977). Such findings are especially damaging to the peripheral chaining theories of learning that assume that one act is directed by the sensory feedback from a preceding act.

The results of deafferentation studies have not gone unchallenged. Some writers have argued that severing nerve fibers in the sensory roots of the spinal cord does not remove all the sensory feedback from the limbs. The possibility exists that some sensory information may be carried through afferent fibers in ventral or motor pathways which remain intact, although this issue is in dispute (Adams, 1977; Taub, 1977). Sensory information can, of course, be conveyed through a number of different sensory modalities. Proponents of peripheral theories argue that even if deafferentation completely eliminates tactile and proprioceptive cues arriving from body movements, performers can use visual or auditory response feedback to guide their action. Therefore, the role of sensory feedback in the development and regulation of skilled behavior is best elucidated by eliminating different amounts and sources of sensory information. It has been shown that animals deafferentated at birth can learn purposive actions without guidance from kinesthetic and visual feedback (Taub, 1977). But other sources of feedback still exist. When deprived of sight and feel, organisms may become adept at using sound and more subtle sources of information in guiding their actions.

If it were shown conclusively that coordinated behavior can be developed and executed in the absence of sensory feedback, caution would still have to be exercised in generalizing the findings to skill learning in humans. In animals, the main components of rudimentary activities, such as walking, grasping, and the like, may be innately programmed to a large extent. If so, the response patterns would not depend much on sensory consequences for their development. Even though gross limb movements can be performed with little or no sensory feedback, there is loss in finer movement (Summers, 1981). The animals remain clumsy and poorly coordinated. Learned skills in humans typically require complex integration of behavioral components and fine coordination of action sequences. When informative feedback is eliminated, delayed, or distorted, improvements in intricate performances are retarded (Carroll & Bandura, 1985), and execution of established skills deteriorates (Bilodeau, 1966; Smith & Smith, 1966).

Learning Without Responses and Direct Sensory Feedback. The preceding research was concerned with whether behavior can be developed by performing responses without experiencing their sensory effects. The paramount role played by central mechanisms in the acquisition of skills is most clearly revealed in studies of observational learning. Conceptions of skilled behavior can be abstracted from modeled activities in the absence of motor responses and direct feedback. The observational paradigm is, therefore, especially well suited for studying the central mechanisms of learning and performance regulation. We saw earlier that modeling is one of the most effective ways of conveying the knowledge required for skill acquisition. But full mastery of intricate skills usually depends on a complex interplay between central processing of performance information and feedback from enactments (Carroll & Bandura, 1982, 1985).

In improvement of skill through cognitive rehearsal, whatever feedback comes into play is internally generated because no responses are performed overtly. A skier practices cognitively skiing down the mountainside numerous times while seated motionless in a chair (Suinn, 1983). Any sensations that might arise from the minimal innervation of relevant muscle groups would differ markedly from the sensation created by the actual performance of hurtling down a mountainside. In cognitive rehearsal, it is the perceived mismatches between conception and the form of the visualized enactments that provide the basis for modifying cognized performances in the right direction. Here the matching process is concerned more with the form and timing of actions, instead of their exact feel.

The prevailing theories of skill learning have been slow to acknowledge the phenomenon of observational learning (Stelmach, 1976). Learning, therefore, tends to be portrayed as a process in which motor schemata are formed from sensory information arising solely from trial-and-error responses. Performances are said to be improved by reducing the differences between the expected sensory consequences of correct actions and the inflow of sensory information from the actual performance. The role of cognition in the development and regulation of skilled performance generally gets lost in the concern with proprioception and the mechanics of sensory and motor physiology.

The implementation of rules of action involves neural discharges to activate appropriate motor systems, but the rules are not reducible to the discharges. The correction and improvement of behavioral enactments is achieved, in large part, through cognitive comparison processes involving cognitive representations, enactments, and outcomes, which involve more than feedback loops between motor outflow and sensory inflow. Social cognitive analyses, therefore, place greater emphasis on cognitive mechanisms of action. Studies aimed at elucidating how thought activates and orchestrates the neurophysiological mechanisms of action are needed to complement the research on how sensory feedback affects behavior. In explaining human learning in neurophysiological terms, by far the most challenging issue is how people bring into being those cortical activities that represent the processes and products of thought.

By way of summary, the several lines of evidence reviewed thus far yield consistent support for the central organization of behavior: Responses often occur too rapidly to allow peripheral feedback to guide them while in progress. Behavior can be learned without performing responses and executed without direct peripheral feedback. From the information conveyed by response consequences, people develop generative conceptions of behavior that enable them to produce novel variations of a given form of behavior that they have never before performed. Research on learning from extrinsic effects, to be discussed shortly, further substantiates the view that correlated experience affects performances through central processing, rather than by direct action on the behavior itself.

The process of learning solely from response consequences might be summarized as follows: Initially, performers are entirely dependent on response outcomes for information about what behavior might be most appropriate. They have no other way of knowing what best to do, unless they draw on knowledge gained from other situations as a guide for action. Such inferential reasoning undoubtedly operates in the initial selection of responses. People may be clueless but not without thoughts, however novel the situation might be. Based on information derived from the outcomes of their exploratory efforts, they gradually construct a conception of the behavior and its predictable effects. As the cognitive representation is being formed, organization and sequential integration of response patterns shifts from peripheral to central regulation. At this stage of learning, people rely more on their conceptual action rules than on the sensory effects of specific responses to tell them what to do. But even at this higher level of organization, skilled performance is never totally independent of peripheral feedback. With continuing practice, activities that have structural regularities are integrated into larger subunits of behavior. Errors are most likely to occur at transition points between organized subunits. As a skill is being established, it is the results of these integrated sequences, rather than the effects accompanying each specific act, that are monitored and evaluated. Higher-order rules, which specify how successive subunits are organized into more elaborate patterns, further facilitate the acquisition and retention of generative skills.

Human behavior is regulated by multilevel systems of control. Once behavior patterns become routinized, they no longer require higher cognitive control. Their execution can be largely regulated by the lower level sensory-motor system. However, when routinized behavior fails to produce expected results, the cognitive control system again comes into play. Both the behavior and the changing environmental circumstances are closely monitored to identify the source of the problem. New solutions are considered and tested. Control reverts to the lower control system after an adequate means is found and becomes the habitual way of doing things. The various processes involved in the automation of cognitive and behavioral skills will be taken up in a later chapter.

ENACTIVE LEARNING AND CONSCIOUSNESS

In learning from extrinsic consequences, actions produce outcomes that are arbitrary, rather than natural consequents of the behavior. It is by social, not natural, design, for example, that work performances bring forth paychecks and evaluative reactions from others. The issue of whether or not such learning can occur without awareness of the relationship between actions and outcomes has been hotly debated over the years. The models of human nature embraced by different theories influence what role, if any, is assigned to consciousness in learning.

Alternative Theoretical Viewpoints

In the view of radical behaviorism, behavior is automatically shaped and regulated by its immediate consequences (Skinner, 1963). Thought does not enter into the determination of new behavioral structures. It should be noted that this approach adopts a narrower conception of learning than do most other theories. Radical behaviorists define learning as changes in the probability of a response. Much of their basic experimentation is, therefore, concerned more with raising and lowering the rate with which preexisting responses are emitted than with acquisition of cognitive and behavioral competencies. Outcomes serve mainly to point out the functional utility of the responses one already possesses. In other theoretical approaches, learning is concerned with the structure, as well as the function, of behavior. Moreover, learning is evidenced not only in structural changes in behavior but also in the conceptions and rules that govern them. A full understanding of learning thus requires analysis of the structure of thought, as well as of action. Generative rules of behavior are not easily acquirable by differential outcomes alone. Hence, applications of reinforcement practices to complex human learning have to rely heavily on socially medicated guidance in the form of verbal instruction, physical prompting, and rule provision through modeling. Outcomes serve to enhance involvement in activities, to channel attention to significant features, and to convey information for constructing rules of action, rather than stamp in the surface features of behavior.

Radical behaviorists explain conscious thought in learning in two ways, neither of which grant it any causal efficacy. In the first, they regard awareness of how actions affect outcomes to be a result rather than a determinant of learning. People presumably recognize the relationship between their actions and outcomes from observing the rise in the frequency of their behavior produced automatically by reinforcement. The second solution to awareness is to treat it simply as a verbal operant that is automatically shaped by its consequences (Verplanck, 1962). Since words and actions are regarded as independent response systems, almost any type of relationship can be obtained between them depending on how they are reinforced. Words and actions will correspond when people are rewarded for saying and doing the same things, whereas words and actions will diverge when people are rewarded for saying one thing but for doing another. In the present discussion, awareness refers to knowledge of how outcomes relate to actions, not simply public utterances about them. Given sufficient inducement, students may be willing to say that not studying produces high grades, but they know and behave otherwise. Demonstrations that people can be rewarded to say one thing, but do another, hardly verify that awareness is irrelevant to learning.

Disputes about the role of awareness in learning raise the more fundamental issue of consciousness. Consciousness is generally defined as awareness of external events and of what one is thinking, feeling, and doing. Part of conscious life is concerned with what is happening in the here and now. But people also dwell a great deal on past events, and they anticipate, plan, and worry about the future. Indeed, in their thoughts people often live more in the past and in the future than in the present.

Cognitively-oriented theorists are somewhat divided on how awareness affects learning. There are those who contend that no learning can occur without awareness (Dulany, 1968; Spielberger & DeNike, 1966). The knowledge extracted from covariations between actions and outcomes creates the intention or self-instruction to perform functional acts; the strength of the tendency depends on the valuation of the incentives.

Theories modeled on the computer also assign a prominent role to cognition in human behavior. Within this perspective, psychological functioning is analyzed as a chain of component processes, with information entering a perceptual system, which is then processed and acted on by stored programs drawing on repertoires of subroutines. Consciousness is not part of the lexicon of a computer model of human functioning. Computers do not engage in reflective thought as people do when they extract relevant information from their experiences to gain new knowledge and to revise aspects of their preexisting knowledge. Lacking a comprehensive knowledge system concerning the nature of events, computers may execute irrelevant lines of inference, which yield patently nonsensical results, without the slightest recognition of what has happened. Computers are not exploratory or knowledge seeking. They do not deliberate about their past successes and failures or worry about, and plan for, the future. Nor do they undermine their performances by self-doubt or boost them by resolute self-assurance. Looking only at the mechanics of computer simulation of human thinking may convey the impression that cognitive activity is essentially nonconscious mechani-

cal thought. It is easy to lose sight of the fact that it is the knowledge and reasoning skills of creative human minds that computers mimic with nonconscious efficiency.

In analyzing theories of cognition, Coulter (1983) takes issue with the model of unconscious cognitivism which reduces thought to a body unconsciously performing computations rather than a person engaging in deliberation. Action is often the outcome of computational activities, but it is a person who brings about those activities. It is not as though a person is simply a repository for an automatic thinking device without presiding over its operation or even being cognizant of what it is doing. Deliberation involves the exercise of personal agency. As we argued earlier, to posit self-perceiving and self-guiding functions is not to invoke a dualistic system of mental and cortical activities.

Social cognitive theory views learning through response consequences as essentially a cognitive process relying on the abstractive, reflective, and generative nature of human thought. Although people do not monitor all the mechanics of proficient information processing, they do so to some extent when such cognitive skills are first being acquired. For example, children do not learn the cognitive operations of subtraction and division unconsciously. Even after some proficiency has been achieved, people do not become thoughtless during the learning process. They make conscious judgments about how their actions affect the environment. By varying their actions and observing the resultant effects, they eventually figure out what performances are needed to produce given outcomes. As we shall see shortly, they learn little, if anything, from consequences if they do not recognize them as flowing from their actions.

Gauging Cognitive Determinants of Affect and Action

The early introspectionists assumed that human behavior can be best understood by describing the elementary contents of sensory experiences. However, this introspective approach proved unfruitful because it was faulty in both conception and method. One cannot learn much about the cognitive determinants of behavior by having people describe the elementary sensations they experience to external stimulation. The structure and functional properties of cognition, rather than elementary sensations, are most relevant to an understanding of human behavior. Free-floating introspection was much too indefinite and misfocused to reveal how thought affects human affect and action. Because of this tainted legacy, for years researchers shied away from verbal indicants of thought and regarded as suspect any data yielded by such methods. Scientific advances required not only a more precise measure of thought processes but also acknowledgement that people can serve as the contributing agents, as well as the objects, of study; they are the ones who have direct access to their ongoing thoughts. The focus of inquiry centers on how information conveyed by environmental events is processed and transformed for memory representation and how the acquired knowledge is used for response production and guidance.

Characteristics of Thought Probes.
Thought probes can vary on several dimensions that significantly affect the quality of the data they yield (Ericsson & Simon, 1980). First, and foremost, is their timing in relation to the actions of interest. Thoughts may be tapped immediately prior to, concurrently, immediately after, or long after the behavior is performed. It is the thoughts measured prior to action that provide the most valid data for elucidating how thoughts function as causal antecedents of affect and action.

A major problem with retrospective probes is that people's reconstructions of what they were thinking when they performed at an earlier time are subject to various distortions. To begin with, it is difficult to recall, after the fact, exactly what thoughts occurred at different points in time. Indeed, people may be given the correct rule of action, use it to generate appropriate behavior, yet later fail to recall it (Weinstein & Lawson, 1963). In such instances, the retrospections erroneously portray learning as occurring without awareness of the production rule. Memory is not only incomplete, it often contains creative embellishments as well. To complicate further the veridicality of retrospection, insights gained through subsequent experiences color recollection of earlier thoughts. Assessing thoughts before, rather than after, the performance not only eliminates the problem of fallible memory but also removes any ambiguity about the directionality of influence.

The second feature of thought probes concerns their specificity. They may center on certain kinds of thoughts or on whatever comes to mind. Thoughts contain far too many irrelevancies to be reported in their entirety (Wright, 1980). Nondescript probes leave the screening of thoughts to the vagaries of people's intuitions about what is worth reporting from their ongoing ideation. Effective thought probes, therefore, must be sufficiently particularized to ensure that the relevant cognitions are being tapped for all participants.

Thought probes also vary in their inferential demands. Such probes should neither implant ideas nor modify the course of thinking by the process of the measurement itself. Both the problems of inculcation and assessment reactivity are minimized, if not eliminated altogether, by having persons describe what they are thinking, rather than have them speculate about their experiences. A technique that simply taps the natural thoughts attended to does not affect the course of subsequent thought and action, whereas inferential inquiries, which call for causal speculations that did not occur at the time of performance, can be misinformative and distort subsequent thinking (Ericsson & Simon, 1980; Karpf & Levine, 1971).

The evidence taken together specifies the nature of the inquiry technique best suited for clarifying functional relationships between thought and action. Thoughts should be tapped antecedently or concurrently with performance using particularized probes of actual thoughts as they naturally occur. Candid reporting is encouraged. Retrospective intuitions about causality, which are more apt to produce new thoughts than reports of the relevant past ones, can shed little informative light on the cognitive determinants of action.

Depending on which functions of thought are being explored, inquiry techniques can be implemented in a variety of ways. Thinking processes may be assessed continuously by having people verbalize their thoughts aloud as they perform given tasks (Ericsson & Simon, 1980; Genest & Turk, 1982). This method is well suited for revealing how action strategies are devised, tested, and altered in efforts to solve problems. Designated classes of thoughts may be systematically measured at important junctures in behavioral processes (Bandura, 1982a). Such selective thought assessment sheds light on how certain kinds of thoughts affect behavioral choices and motivational processes. Thoughts can also be sampled randomly at significant times over extended periods during the course of everyday activities (Hurlburt, 1979; Williams & Rappaport, 1983). This approach can furnish data on the interrelationship of thoughts and actions, provided that independent measures are obtained of what people are doing at the time, and the temporal order of thought and action is accurately specified. Cognitive event recording, in which persons indicate whenever a certain type of thought occurs, provides still another means of examining how thinking affects ensuing action and emotional arousal (Schwartz, 1971).

Research into the causal efficacy of conscious cognition need not be confined to analyzing co-variations between learning and verbally assessed awareness as it naturally occurs. As in the study of other causal processes, awareness can be deliberately imparted and its effects on actions measured. The problems of incomplete reporting and faulty recall do not arise when awareness is varied systematically. We shall see later that induced awareness markedly affects learning.

Veridicality of Indicants of Private Experience. Given that suitable thought probes are used, the question remains as to how well language depicts what one is thinking. Measuring thoughts by means of self-reports assumes that the verbal descriptions of private experience mean similar things to different people. Consensual meaning is, of course, well ingrained early in life. This is achieved by repeated social labeling of private experiences that have been reliably evoked by distinct external events. It does not require all that many trials to bite into a lemon and to be told, as one's face puckers up, that the taste is sour, to grasp the consensual meaning of a sour taste experience. There is every reason to suppose that lemon juice evokes similar taste sensations in different persons.

While language is not entirely devoid of ambiguity, it is not so uncertain and its experiential referents so indeterminate that private experience is unknowable through it. Many inner states do have some outer expressive correlates that give some indication of the internal effects the situational elicitors are known to produce. Persons who cried out when they stepped on a jagged piece of glass would unquestionably be experiencing an inner state of pain. Similarity of inner experiences and the uniformity of social labeling practices make unobservable inner events at least partially knowable through self-report.

The preceding remarks should not be misinterpreted to mean that consciousness is equated with the verbalizable. There is a difference between experiential events and the tools for gauging them. One can have consciousness, implicit knowledge, and explicit understanding of events without words. But verbalized thoughts provide an important vehicle for elucidating the causal interplay between thought, affect, action, and environmental factors. The question is sometimes raised as to whether thoughts may some day be measured directly by electrophysiological techniques. While this is not inconceivable, it seems unlikely. Electrophysiological devices can detect cortical activity, but they cannot distinguish among the things people think, know, and believe. Therefore, verbal probes are apt to remain substantially more informative than are neurophysiological ones. There is clearly much to be gained from further refinements of verbal indices of thought.

Proponents of radical behaviorism are quick to find fault with verbal indicants of thought processes. They point to the metaphysical problem of identifying private realities that are accessible only to the persons experiencing them. Thoughts are not always easy to put into words. Even if readily reportable, people can, and indeed may, misrepresent what they are thinking. Numerous people are outfitted by ophthalmologists with suitable corrective eyeglasses on the basis of their verbal reports of the relative clarity of printed and pictorial stimuli. They can be easily outfitted with defective eyeglasses by reporting the blurred stimuli as the clearer ones. However, such a possibility would hardly constitute justification for renouncing the ophthalmological enterprise.

The problem of misrepresenting one's knowledge is not unique to verbal indices. Given reasons to do so, people can deceive others by their actions as they can by their words. They can easily alter their actions to misrepresent what they have learned or really believe. People usually learn more than they represent in action due to production deficiencies or to insufficient incentives. When certain activities are nonrewarded, devalued, or punished, verbal accounts provide better measures of what people have acquired than do their performances (Bandura, 1965b; Farber, 1963). The role of thought and awareness in learning is, therefore, best studied under conditions in which learners have no incentives either to distort their reports of what they know and believe or to lead researchers astray by de-

ceptive actions. The limitations ascribed to self-reports of thought processes often arise more for reasons of the theoretical orthodoxy, that thought cannot influence action, than for its lack of predictive or explanatory power. Data yielded by verbal probes often reveal impressive functional relationships between verbalized thoughts and actions, whereas environmental events are weak predictors. Psychological endeavors in quest of explanatory and predictive power should not exclude good predictors because they happen to rely on verbal indicants of cognitive determinants.

Contingency Learning and Awareness

Numerous studies have investigated whether outcomes change behavior without conscious involvement or through an awareness of which actions produce rewarding outcomes. Initially, investigators relied upon retrospective reports of awareness based on responses to progressively more suggestive questions. Results yielded by these kinds of thought probes indicated that learning can occur without awareness, albeit slowly and inefficiently, but awareness markedly accelerates the acquisition process (Krasner, 1958). However, subsequent research revealed that the apparent learning without awareness was rather a result of the defective assessment procedure. More sensitive probes detect more actual awareness (Dawson & Reardon, 1973), and many people who have been fully aware of the rule relating actions to outcomes at the time of learning fail to recall it when they are interviewed later (Weinstein & Lawson, 1963). In any event, informative causal analyses require that the postulated cause be measured before, rather than after, the effect. When awareness is measured after the fact, it can always be argued that performers learned without awareness but that they later recognized the rule from the evident increases in their performance.

The role of awareness in learning is best clarified, not by confounded retrospective reports, but by microanalysis of the relationship between emergent awareness and subsequent behavior while learning is in progress. Studies in which people's thoughts are probed at periodic intervals throughout the learning session reveal that behavior is unaffected by its consequences without awareness of what is being rewarded (Dulany, 1968; Sallows, Dawes, & Lichtenstein, 1971; Spielberger & DeNike, 1966). Once the correct solution is recognized, learning performance suddenly rises if the incentives are valued.

If awareness is assessed after a number of trials have elapsed, it can still be argued that participants figured out the correct responses toward the end of the series of trials, after their responses have been increased noticeably by reinforcement in the absence of awareness. Some evidence was reported to suggest just this, for when recognition of the rules of reward is measured after long intervals, awareness appears to precede behavior change; however, when measurements are made after short intervals, performance gains seem to have preceded awareness for the persons who later recognize their correct responses (Kennedy, 1970, 1971). Cognitive theorists disputed the latter findings on the grounds that people were improperly classified (Brewer, 1974). Those who reported correct or correlated hypotheses were considered aware if they were certain of their judgments, but they were classified as unaware if they were tentative about their judgments. What was considered unaware learning tends to disappear when persons with tentative correct hypotheses are not misclassified as unaware. Moreover, studies in which thought probes are conducted at each learning trial reveal no learning without awareness (Gholson, 1980; Karpf & Levine, 1971; Phillips & Levine, 1975).

The way in which certainty of a person's judgment can affect detection of awareness is an issue of some interest. People may be partially aware and change their behavior accordingly, but they withhold stating their tentative judgments until they become more sure of them, for fear of appearing stupid should they err. In such instances, inquiries that encourage people to report their conjectures, however provisional or implausible they may appear at first, would eliminate any vestige of supposed unaware learning. To the extent that errors of measurement occur, the errors are invariably in the direction of misrepresenting awareness as a state of unawareness. People cannot claim to know what they do not. But they can delay disclosing what they do know until they have tested and confirmed their judgments during subsequent trials. Performance improvements guided by undisclosed provisional judgments would appear as unaware learning.

When the appropriate behavior and its outcomes are clearly observable, the role of consciousness in human learning is studied in terms of whether and when awareness has been gained. The question of whether learning must be consciously mediated could be answered decisively using tasks that prevent awareness because the action-outcome relationship cannot be observed. Awareness is precluded when either the acts are unobservable, but their outcomes are observable, or the acts are noticeable, but their outcomes are not. Unfortunately, such conditions impose severe constraints on the kinds of behaviors that can be studied. For the most part, they would have to be simple actions that might require little or no thought to produce them. Unobservable actions are easier to come by than are imperceptible outcomes.

Hefferline and his associates altered simple, unobservable responses by varying their outcomes (Hefferline, Bruno, & Davidowitz, 1970). In these studies, visibly imperceptible muscular contractions, detected by the experimenter through electronic amplification, were rewarded either by money or by termination of unpleasant stimulation. The apparently unperceived responses increased when they were reinforced and decreased after reinforcement was withdrawn. The authors report that none of the participants could retrospectively identify the responses that produced the outcomes, although they generated various hypotheses about what might work best to produce them. If their bodily movements were unaffected by actions prompted by these conjectures, one would have to conclude that the human organism has evolved so that its behavior is unconsciously responsive to money! Before drawing this seemingly implausible conclusion, alternative possibilities deserve consideration.

Awareness is not an all-or-none phenomenon. It is possible to achieve some improvement in performance on the basis of inexact hypotheses if these are partially correlated with the correct solution (Adams, 1957). If, for example, participants in a verbal learning study believe that comments about household items are the rewardable responses, when actually references to kitchen appliances are of the correct response class, they are likely to generate some correct responses. Similarly, in nonverbal behavior some observable activity, which itself is not entirely appropriate, may at times activate the relevant unseen responses. Awareness can thus exist with different degrees of accuracy, depending on how closely the chosen hypothesis corresponds to the correct one. Small changes occurring without awareness may well result from partially correlated hypotheses. The operation of correlated hypotheses must, therefore, be closely examined in analyzing the determinants of performance gains.

If response consequences promote learning largely through their informative function, then induced awareness should produce a rapid gain in performance, whereas having to extract the same information from the consequences of one's acts would be a slow learning process. This is indeed the case. People who are simply informed in advance of the appropriate behavior change instantly. Those who perform responses and are selectively rewarded for the correct ones take a long time before they hit upon the correct solution, and many do not change at all because they never figure out what is required (Merbaum & Lukens, 1968).

To sum up, although the issue is not yet conclusively resolved, there is little evidence that outcomes function as automatic shapers of human behavior (Bandura, 1969a; Brewer, 1974). Further evidence will be presented later showing that the association of neutral events with aversive experience does not automatically produce learning of emotional reactions. Some adherents of the automaticity view claim evidence for unaware learning by pointing to anecdotal reports obtained from a few people using delayed probes. Most of the data from participants in these studies had to be discarded because their behavior was either too variable or too unresponsive to social consequences (Rosenfeld & Baer, 1969, 1970). If some future experimental procedure were to reveal unaware learning, which survived close methodological scrutiny and replication, such evidence would hardly redeem the principle of reinforcement in its traditional form. Rather, it would simply raise the question of why reinforcement is only occasionally automatic but most of the time has no effect unless cognitively mediated. Proponents of automatic reinforcement argue for its universality, rather than for its occasional possibility.

Even if new methodologies established that some elementary responses can be learned without awareness of what is being rewarded, this would not mean that complex behavior can be similarly acquired. As an illustration, consider a task involving a complex rule for producing the correct behavior. Suppose that persons are presented with words of varying lengths and told that their task is to provide the correct number corresponding to each word. Let us select an arbitrary rule that gives the "current number" by subtracting the number of letters in a given word from 100, dividing the remainder by 2, and then multiplying the result by 5. Correct responses are derived from a high-order rule requiring a three-step transformation of the external stimulus. To create accurate responses, one must perform several cognitive operations in a particular sequence. Unthinking organisms are unlikely to show any consistent gains in accurate performance, however long they labor at the task.

A considerable body of evidence documents that consequences principally serve as informative and motivational influences, rather than as automatic response strengtheners. The notion of "response strengthening" is metaphoric. After response patterns have been acquired, how often they are used can be altered by varying the outcomes they produce, but the responses are not strengthened any further. For example, people will drive automobiles to places that provide recreational rewards, but the rewards do not add bits of strength to driving responses. The dubious status of both automaticity and response strengthening makes it more fitting to speak of *guidance* of behavior by anticipated incentives than *reinforcement* of behavior by reinforcers. Outcomes inform and motivate people, rather than shape their actions.

It is fortunate that outcomes do not automatically strengthen every response they follow. If behavior were reinforced by every momentary effect it produced, people would be overburdened with so many competing response tendencies that they could become immobilized. Moreover, intelligent action often requires the disregard of momentary effects. Anticipatory thought, which is so essential for purposiveness and pursuit of astute courses of action, would be rendered functionless by the overriding rule of instant effects. Limiting learning to events that are sufficiently telling to gain recognition has considerable adaptive value. For lower organisms possessing limited symbolizing capacities, there are evolutionary advantages to being biologically equipped so that even minimal experience will reliably produce essential behavior without requiring much, if any, symbolic processing of experience. However, extensive innate preprogramming, which makes it easy to shape behavior by noncognized experience, extracts a huge price by its behavioral fixedness. Outcomes can facilitate the stereotyped behavior characteristic of a species

and bring it under the control of new stimuli, but, unlike the extraordinary serviceability of cognitively based learning, it is exceedingly difficult to get animals to behave in new ways. It comes as no surprise that most of the research on learning with animals is concerned with altering the rate of responses they naturally perform, rather than building new behavioral structures (Bolles, 1972a). The latter requires some capacity for symbolic coding and organization of experience.

In evaluating the role of conscious thought in human behavior, one must distinguish between skill acquisition and skill execution. Cognitive processing plays an especially influential role during the acquisition of knowledge and skills. Although it is difficult to learn without being cognizant of events and without cognitively processing information from one's experiences, once cognitive and behavioral skills are well established, they are usually executed without much conscious deliberation. Evidence that people perform common routines without being conscious of what they are doing has no bearing on the issue of the role of conscious thought in the original development of the skills.

Self-Awareness of One's Thinking Processes

In a controversial paper, Nisbett and Wilson (1977) put forward the view that people know the results of their thinking, but they do not have direct access to their own cognitive processes. When asked to explain the reasons for their actions, people generate post hoc rationalizations based on their intuitive theories of plausible causes. Self-reports may occasionally appear accurate because intuitions happened to fit the causal factors operating in that particular situation. This sweeping generalization was quickly challenged on both conceptual and empirical grounds.

The notion that thought processes are inaccessible presupposes that valid methods exist for certifying what the nonconscious processes are. Unless the operative processes are known, there is no way of verifying that people either do or do not have access to them. Nisbett and Wilson vest the certifying criteria in the authority of the investigators' theory about what was going on. Thus, for example, if certain influences are believed to change behavior by altering causal attributions, and persons act in expected ways but do not explain their behavior in terms of altered attributions, then they are said to be unaware of their cognitive processes. The issue of who is unaware of what is not that easily resolvable. Theoretical presumption is an uncertain indicant. Nor are the factors that researchers vary, necessarily, the causes of the observed changes in behavior. This is because social influences usually contain many ingredients. Their effects may result from factors that were deliberately varied or from simultaneously occuring influences that were not only unintended but unrecognized.

The investigators' conjectures can hardly be regarded as the authentic process against which to judge whether or not others are aware of the thoughts governing their actions. Consider some examples. Nisbett and Wilson cite studies in which people changed their behavior but later failed to report the cognitive processes the investigators believed to have been operating (Storms & Nisbett, 1970; Valins & Ray, 1967). In fact, the behavioral changes were questionable, and methodologically superior studies were unable to replicate the original findings (Bootzin, Herman, & Nicassio, 1976; Singerman, Borkovec, & Baron, 1976; Kellogg & Baron, 1975; Kent, Wilson, & Nelson, 1972; Rosen, Rosen, & Reid, 1972; Sushinsky & Bootzin, 1970).

The study of Valins and Ray (1967), cited as evidence that people misconstrue the determinants of their behavior, illustrates the fallability of theoretical presumption and inferential judgments concerning the processes underlying change. Valins and Ray reasoned that if phobics are led to believe that the things they had feared no longer upset them, they will judge themselves as nonfearful and will behave more boldly. To test this process of cognitive self-reevaluation, snake phobics received false feedback, via earphones, that their heart rate did not change in reaction to slides of snakes but that their heart rate accelerated to the word shock, which had previously been paired with mild shock. Those who received false feedback, suggesting that they were no longer frightened by snakes, behaved more boldly, but they did not report any less fear. Presumably, subjects' explanations of fearful motivation do not jibe with their actions. In actuality, fear arousal has no consistent relationship to phobic behavior. Therefore, asking people to judge their fear has little to say about whether or not they can specify the things that led them to behave more boldly.

It is a well-established finding that events paired with pain become danger signals, whereas other events, in the same setting, that are never followed by pain become safety or relief signals. Gaupp, Stern, and Galbraith (1972) contended that, by the differential pairing of events, Valins and Ray were converting phobic stimuli into safety signals, rather than changing self-attributions. Indeed, Gaupp and his associates showed experimentally that if slides of snakes signal safety, they reduce physiological arousal and lead to bold behavior regardless of whether phobics were given the false feedback that their hearts were calm, were told that the sounds they had heard via the earphones were merely extraneous noises, or got to hear their actual heartbeats. Thus, Valins and Ray had unknowingly created conditions that activated processes quite different from those they believed they were studying. The validity of the investigators' hypothesized processes, rather than people's accessibility to their thought processes, becomes the issue in question.

Arbitrary Labeling of Thought Processes and Products. Nisbett and Wilson assume that people have no consciousness of their thinking processes but that they are aware of the results of their own thinking.

There are two points of ambiguity concerning these supposedly dichotomous cognitive domains. First, no adequate criteria are provided for distinguishing cognitive processes from their products, which renders essentially untestable the proposition that only the products of thinking processes are available to consciousness. As Smith and Miller (1978) note, in interpreting research findings, Nisbett and Wilson sometimes designate the same types of cognitions as products in some studies and as process in others. Thinking proceeds through different steps. It is, therefore, difficult to draw sharp distinctions between process, intermediate steps of the process, and cognitive products in ongoing thought. Consider the following three-step sequence of cognitive operations: $14 \times 3 - 7 + 12$. The result of the first step—the multiplication operation—would be a conscious product if people were asked for their thoughts then, but it would become a nonconscious process if they were asked for their thoughts only at the end of the triple cognitive operation. Thus, whether something is a cognitive product or an intermediate step in a process arbitrarily depends on when the thought probe is made.

The second source of puzzlement about the process-product dichotomy concerns their peculiar relation and the odd status of the intuitive causal theories. Nisbett and Wilson contend that behavior is related to nonconscious cognitive processes, whereas conscious thoughts are general conjectures that may bear little relationship to actions. If conscious thoughts are products of influential nonconscious thinking, then they too should be related to behavior. For example, a nonconscious mental addition should produce a conscious sum. By what means, and for what purposes, would nonconscious cognitive operations that regulate behavior be barred from consciousness, leaving people with largely irrelevant or misleading conscious thoughts? If conscious thoughts are just plausible causal intuitions that do not reflect inaccessible cognitive processing, are unaffected by demonstrably effective influences, and are unrelated to how people behave, why is human consciousness cluttered with such disconnected and functionless causal thinking? How would one explain the evolution of consciousness? Why would natural selection favor a nonfunctional consciousness that could be so misleading and so impervious to the very influences that affect human behavior?

Probing Techniques and Dependence of Action on Thought. While the conceptual issues are intriguing and debatable, the empirical findings Nisbett and Wilson cite as evidence that actions are not regulated by conscious thoughts actually have limited bearing on the issue. In the studies reported, people are asked to explain, after the fact, the reasons for their actions. Even in these retrospective conjectures, often they are not asked what their thoughts had been in the situation in which they have found themselves. Rather, they are presented with preselected factors and asked to judge how much these factors may have influenced their behavior. Forcing people to fit their explanations into a few preselected categories may reveal little about the participants' actual thought processes.

For reasons given earlier, analyses of causal thought must assess the thoughts occurring before or while actions are being performed, rather than asking participants, after they have undergone a varied set of experiences, to speculate about what may have caused their earlier behavior. Direct probes of what people are thinking during an experience tap the cognitions to which they have access, whereas retrospective probes, requiring them to speculate about the causes of their past behavior, lead them to draw on all sorts of information and beliefs in formulating answers. Such conjectures may bear little resemblance to the thoughts that actually occurred during the task. After completing a protracted negotiation, it is unlikely that negotiators could accurately recall the exact thoughts guiding a particular statement, although they would be fully conscious of what they were thinking at the time they made the statement.

Moreover, to determine if what people are thinking affects what they are doing requires a microanalysis of the concordance between thoughts and subsequent actions within an individual, rather than a comparison of the average differences in the recollections of groups of people. One cannot elucidate the functional relationship between thought and action by relating the averaged group retrospections to an averaged group action.

In previous sections we have examined the influential role of awareness in learning from response outcomes. Nisbett and Wilson argue that, in such structured learning paradigms, the use of restricted response options and evident outcomes makes the contingencies highly plausible causes. This characterization of the paradigms is at variance with the facts, however. Difficulty in achieving unaware learning has been demonstrated under varied conditions with children and adults, in delimited and free-responding situations, and with wide variations in the type and subtlety of outcomes. Even in the more structured paradigms, most of the participants usually fail to recognize causal relaions and do not learn even though they may occasionally hit upon the correct response and are promptly rewarded. Intuitions about plausible causes are of little value in predicting which participants will learn and exactly when they will hit upon the correct solution, whereas their ongoing thoughts about which actions are likely to produce the outcomes are excellent predictors of their behavior.

In a comprehensive analysis of retrospective thought probes, Ericsson and Simon (1980) document why the types of probing techniques used by Nisbett and Wilson are ill suited to yield valid indices of conscious causal thoughts. Often the wrong contents are measured by the wrong questions at the wrong time. They summarize a great deal of evidence showing that when thoughts are assessed with refined procedures concurrently or immediately after performance, people verbalize cognitive processes that relate to how they behave. When they are asked to report their actual thoughts, rather than to speculate about causality, the assessment procedure itself does not change the course of cognitive processes or behavior.

Investigations of metacognition concerning thoughts about one's cognitive activities further document how people organize, monitor, and regulate their cognitive processes in efforts to deal effectively with their environment (Brown, 1978; Flavell, 1979). To think about the adequacy of one's cognitive activities requires consciousness of them. Metacognitive functioning thus depends on accessibility of thinking and flexible use of one's thinking skills. People channel and monitor their attention, draw on their knowledge of cognitive strategies, personal capabilities, and task demands in considering courses of action, and they evaluate and revise their thinking when their efforts fail to produce desired results. Such metacognitive skills improve with experience and can be taught by cognitive behavioral means (Brown, 1978; Meichenbaum & Asarnow, 1979).

The evidence, taken as a whole, indicates that appropriate thought probes provide a rich source of data for revealing cognitive processes and their functional relation to action. While people are not fully conscious of every aspect of their thinking, neither is their thinking largely unconscious. People generally know what they are thinking. They form judgments, put them to the test, reflect on the results of their actions, and alter their judgments accordingly.

Nisbett and Wilson reason that, since people are largely unaware of their cognitive processes and since their reports about the causes of their behavior are plausible conjectures that others are also likely to invoke, the verbalized thoughts of the performers are no better than the intuitions of others in predicting how the performers will behave. The validity of this claim is highly questionable. Studies using appropriate antecedent probes would have little difficulty in demonstrating the predictive superiority of performers' thoughts over observers' conjectures. When certain responses are rewarded from among those freely expressed, people promptly increase the appropriate responses just after they figure out what is being rewarded. The sudden change in performance is highly predictable from knowledge of performers' thoughts (Dulany, 1968; Spielberger & DeNike, 1966), whereas observers would remain at a loss in predicting exactly when a significant performance change will occur. Even in studies using retrospective but well-designed probes, performers are more accurate in reporting what factors influenced their reactions than are observers who know the performers and the influencing events sufficiently well to guess what their reactions might be (Wright & Rip, 1981).

Recall can be markedly biased by what questions are asked and how they are phrased (Loftus, 1979). Adair and Spinner (1981) illustrate how many of the retrospective probes used by Nisbett and Wilson divert people's attention away from relevant factors or ask them to speculate about irrelevant ones. To be presented with irrelevant factors at the end of an experiment and to be asked to rate how much influence they may have exerted measures people's susceptibility to deceptive social influence, rather than their accessibility to their thought processes at the time the task was performed. Suggestive inquiries about irrelevancies will most likely yield conjectures that bear little relationship to earlier actions.

To explore more adequately self-awareness of one's thinking, investigators have conducted similar studies or improved replications of those reported by Nisbett and Wilson and have reanalyzed the aggregately reported data by relating people's thoughts about what influenced them to their actions. The findings of these efforts reveal that people have knowledge about what influenced their behavior, whereas Nisbett and Wilson found no indication of such self-awareness (Guerin & Innes, 1981; Smith & Miller, 1978; White, 1980; Wright & Rip, 1981). Smith and Miller sum up the matter well when they conclude that the more fruitful line of inquiry is not whether self-reports can ever reflect thought processes but under what conditions will they do so.

Conceptions that dismiss the human capacity to monitor and use consciously one's own thinking discourages research into the nature and function of human consciousness. If this aspect is deemphasized or excluded from analysis, humans may, indeed, appear to be organisms thrust about by nonconscious forces in findings of psychological research. Theories that include a functional consciousness in their model of human nature foster venturesome research that can illuminate how people exercise influence over what they do.

Acknowledging the reach of human consciousness can stimulate research in domains where one would not ordinarily tread. In so doing, one can discover interesting things. For example, sleep is widely regarded as the utmost level of nonconsciousness. However, in their study of dreaming, Brown and Cartwright (1978) report evidence that people maintain some self-awareness, even when they presumably lapse into nonconscious sleep. Awakenings during periods of rapid eye movements (REM) reveal a high incidence of dreaming whereas dreams are reported less often during quiet sleep (Dement, 1976). Rapid eye movements thus provide a behavioral indicator of dreaming. If sleep in fact represents a state of nonconsciousness, the self-awareness of dreaming raises an intriguing paradox. How could a nonconscious organism be conscious of its dream activity? Brown and Cartwright show that sleepers are more self-watchful than is commonly assumed. They instructed subjects to depress a microswitch taped to their palms whenever they experienced imagery while sleeping. Signalled self-awareness of dreaming coincided with REM sleep, and awakenings confirmed the occurrence of dreaming. Some dreaming also occurred outside of REM sleep. Regardless of the state of sleep, awakenings yielded dream contents at the time of signals of experienced imagery but rarely did so during nonsignalled awakenings. LaBerge and his colleagues (LaBerge,

Nagel, Dement, & Zarcone, 1981) provide further evidence that people can be conscious of their dreaming while fully asleep. Their signals of when they become aware they are dreaming correspond to physiological indications of dream events. Apparently, reflective consciousness can be extended even to the cognitive scenarios of sleep.

COGNITIVE SUBPROCESSES IN ENACTIVE LEARNING

The influential contribution of cognitive factors to learning from response outcomes is well documented in research analyzing the component processes necessary for learning. It should be noted, however, that much of this research is concerned with learning judgmental rules for choosing between things and classifying things rather than with learning rules governing skilled performance. Induction of rules for making correct decisions and for producing skilled action patterns undoubtedly shares basic processes as far as the knowledge component is concerned. But the development of behavioral subskills and their organization into component performances entail additional production subprocesses, as we saw earlier in the analysis of observational learning. Because judgments lend themselves more readily to study than do performance skills, the role of thought in the development of performance skills receives comparatively less attention.

The most informative studies use microanalytic procedures in which thoughts are assessed as they occur, trial by trial, during the process of learning. Results of these investigations show that both children and adults formulate conceptions for guiding their actions and test their conceptions against feedback from their responses. Erroneous conceptions that produce faulty performances are discarded; partially correct conceptions are successively refined on the basis of differential response feedback until the right one is hit upon; conceptions that produce good results are retained

(Dulany & O'Connell, 1963; O'Connell & Wagner, 1967; Phillips & Levine, 1975; Pratt, 1972). Because of the close concordance between thought and action, people's verbalized conceptions prove to be excellent predictors of their performance. Consistent with previous findings, these studies provide little evidence of unaware learning.

This is not to say that all learners are equally adept at gaining knowledge from the effects of their actions. Inducing rules from enactive experiences requires several subskills. To begin with, rule induction partly depends on people's knowledge base, which provides the guidance for selecting possible rules or constructing new ones if the appropriate rules are not already available. The acquisition process is further aided by the use of effective strategies for quickly narrowing down possible solutions to the appropriate ones. This is achieved through a verification process in which people test provisional rules indirectly by assessing the outcomes of corresponding actions. This requires matching a conception against varied response outcomes. Because many factors can influence what effects actions produce, people have to figure out how relevant factors affect the probabilistic relationship between actions and outcomes. The outcomes of action under different circumstances must, therefore, be closely monitored and the information synthesized and retained over a series of experiences. Moreover, learners have to remember what rules they tried and how well they worked; otherwise they will find themselves recycling their previously discarded notions. Deficits in any of these component skills—coming up with alternatives, formulating rule-induction strategies, monitoring situational factors and response outcomes, retaining outcome information, and matching conception to action—can impair enactive learning.

Young children have limited experience to draw upon in formulating possible rules of action. Their chances of hitting upon the appropriate conception is further reduced because they process only a small proportion of the information available to them in the situation (Schonebaum, 1973). Moreover, they do not use the most efficient strategies for narrowing the alternatives. Instead of simultaneously considering several alternatives and eliminating all the logically disconfirmed ones, on the basis of each response outcome, young children simply adopt a stereotyped preference, irrespective of outcomes, or they tend to consider only one factor at a time (Phillips & Levine, 1975; Tumblin & Gholson, 1981). When task demands are simplified, stereotypic responders learn quite well (Gholson, 1980). But when there are many irrelevancies, and the correct rule includes a combination of factors, a piecemeal approach makes learning a slow, tedious process. As a further source of difficulty, children are not always that attentive to the effects of their actions, nor do they necessarily keep close track of their past experiences. The greater the demands for retaining information from prior outcomes, the harder it is to learn by direct experience alone. For these various reasons, children have some difficulty formulating appropriate conceptions of behavior and are slow in abandoning erroneous ones, despite repeated disconfirming feedback. In the face of failure, they readily fall back on stereotyped responses and simply persevere with them.

Proponents of stage theories assume that young children perform poorly and fail to profit from the consequences of their actions because the tasks exceed their cognitive capabilities. These capabilities presumably develop gradually through experience and maturation in a stage-like progression of qualitatively different ways of thinking. The rate of learning is obviously related to the level of cognitive development. The main issue of contention is whether development is best characterized by the level of competence of cognitive subfunctions or by global forms of thinking. Social cognitive theory analyzes learning in terms of the cognitive competencies necessary for acquiring knowledge and performance skills. Viewed from this perspective, a developmental profile of cognitive subfunctions would be a

better predictor of how well people learn and the source of their learning deficits than categorizing them into global stages. Analysis in terms of cognitive subfunctions can also help to explain the large differences in learning found among children assigned to the same stage of cognitive development.

It also follows in the delineating of cognitive subfunctions that improvement of cognitive subskills should enhance adeptness at learning from the effects of actions. When learning deficiencies stem from inadequate perception of ongoing events, attentional skills must be developed that expand children's use of the situational and outcome information available to them. If they quickly forget what they have observed, they do not have relevant information to process. The development of memory skills helps children to remember what actions in response to what cues produced what outcomes, so they have available the information needed to formulate conceptions and rules of behavior. Additional problems may arise from what they do with the outcome information that is perceived and retained. Development of reasoning skills can teach children how to apply decision rules to the information they gain to come up with appropriate solutions. These component skills are best developed initially with simpler tasks and then extended to more complex ones requiring greater processing and memorial demands.

Deficits in learning from consequences, commonly attributed to stage-dependent immaturity, can be improved if young children are taught the constituent cognitive skills for processing outcome information (Brainerd, 1977; Eimas, 1970). Such findings indicate that it is more fruitful to explore the cognitive subprocesses that underlie learning than to ascribe learning difficulties to global cognitive deficits. The research also calls into question the practice of treating individual differences in pre-existing cognitive competencies as qualitatively different types of thinking that can only mature gradually. Adults also vary in the extent to which they have mastered the constituent skills for extracting rules of behavior from outcome information. Those who are inept in ferreting out what is relevant in their experiences or who use faulty inferential reasoning do not profit much from experience. When they are taught how to process outcome information more effectively, they learn more rapidly from the consequences of their actions (Eimas, 1970).

Learning proceeds most rapidly when outcomes follow actions immediately, regularly, and without other confusing occurrences. In many studies of enactive learning, outcomes are closely linked to actions, which makes the governing rules easy to learn. It is clearly more difficult to learn under probabilistic conditions, where the same actions do not always produce the same outcomes and where the environmental factors on which the outcomes depend occur along with many irrelevant ones to obscure causal relationships. It is to these common, noisier situations, which allow considerable leeway for thought to distort perception of what causes what, that we turn next.

The Power of Belief over Consequent

The capacity of thought to alter how outcomes affect behavior can be analyzed by pitting the power of belief against experienced consequences. Such studies show that beliefs about how probabilistic outcomes are related to actions can weaken, distort, or even nullify the effects of response consequences. Kaufman, Baron, and Kopp (1966) rewarded persons for performing manual responses, but they gave them different information about the rule governing reward. One group was correctly informed that their performances would be rewarded once a minute on the average (variable-interval schedule), whereas other groups were misled into believing that their behavior would be rewarded either every minute (fixed-interval schedule) or after they had performed 150 responses on the average (variable-ratio schedule). Beliefs about the prevailing rules of reward were more influential in regulating behavior than the outcomes themselves. Although everyone was actually rewarded on the same schedule, those who thought they were being rewarded once every minute produced very low rates of response (mean = 6); those who thought they were rewarded on a variable-ratio schedule maintained an exceedingly high response output (mean = 259) during the same period; while those who were correctly informed that their behavior would be rewarded every minute on the average displayed an intermediate level of responsiveness (mean = 65). Findings such as these have been reliably replicated (Baron, Kaufman, & Stauber, 1969; Frazier, 1973). That beliefs can produce markedly different performances under the same actual consequences has also been shown when people are rewarded for responding after a fixed time has elapsed, but they are neither informed nor misinformed about it. Those who believe they are rewarded for performance attainments are almost four times as productive as those who believe they are rewarded after a certain amount of time has passed (Lippman & Meyer, 1967). People regulate their level and distribution of effort in accordance with the effects they expect their actions to have. As a result, their behavior is better predicted from their beliefs than from the actual consequences of their actions.

The preceding studies varied or measured beliefs about how often behavior is likely to be rewarded. The same physical consequences can also have markedly different effects on behavior depending on people's beliefs about why they occur. People increase actions that produce physically aversive effects when they believe these unpleasant outcomes signify that they are being accurate, but they curtail such actions when they believe that these same outcomes indicate errors (Dulany, 1968). Behavior is similarly enhanced or reduced by physically pleasing consequences, depending on whether they are believed to signify correct or incorrect solutions. Neither pleasant nor aversive consequences have much, if any, effect when their occurrence is believed to be unrelated to the behavior. The meaning of outcomes also overrides their utility in influencing children's learning (Mc Kaughan, 1974).

Enactive Learning and Illusory Contingencies

Because knowledge of the effects of one's actions aids learning and effective functioning, people are prone to look for regularities in the occurrences of events. Accurate processing of information about outcomes is no simple task under the variable conditions of everyday life. In the flow of events a host of activities, experiences, and situational circumstances occur in ever changing patterns. Usually many factors enter into determining what effects, if any, given actions will have. Actions, therefore, produce outcomes probabilistically rather than certainly. Depending on the particular conjunction of factors, the same course of action may produce given outcomes regularly, occasionally, or only infrequently.

The difficulty in judging what type of behavior works well arises not only because a given course of action does not always produce the outcomes. Similar outcomes can occur for reasons other than the person's actions, which further complicates inferential judgment. Effects that arise independently of one's actions distort the influence of similar effects produced by the actions, but only on some occasions (Watson, 1979). Given a strong cognitive set to perceive regularities, even chance joint occurrences of events can be easily misjudged as genuine relationships of low contingent probability.

When actions are followed by events that are not causally related to the prior acts, people often erroneously perceive contingencies that do not, in fact, exist. This is because they are easily swayed by the evidence of joint occurrences, without comparing whether the outcomes are more likely to occur if the behavior is performed than if it is not (Jenkins & Ward, 1965; Ward & Jenkins, 1965). The more often the noncontingent happenings occur, the more confident people are about the causal rules they conjure up, and the more they behave as though their actions influence the outcomes (Jenkins & Ward, 1965; Wright, 1962). Moreover, joint occurrences tend to be better recalled than instances when the effect does not occur. The proneness to remember confirming instances, but to overlook disconfirming ones, further serves to convert, in thought, coincidences into causalities. In doing so, people subjectively impose regularities on events that occur together by chance. Illusory contingencies can nonetheless be as effective as authentic ones in creating behavior patterns. These are times when illusorily-based action can create reality-based support for it. People who have an erroneous belief in their causal efficacy may thereby develop skills and resilient self-assurance on which genuine success depends. Illusory control can thus be partially converted to behavioral control of outcomes.

The preceding studies illustrate how readily causalities are read into chance joint occurrences of events. Most performances comprise an assortment of actions, but the outcome may depend on only some of them. People may mistakenly believe that the entire behavior pattern is required to produce the outcomes. Because of such conjointedness, behavior that exerts no effect whatsoever on outcomes is developed and consistently performed (Bruner & Revusky, 1961).

The conditions under which chance joint occurrences are easily misjudged to be causally related have received little study. We have already seen that how often events occur, which are not caused by the behavior, is one determinant. Frequent events have a greater possibility of occurring together by chance along with the ongoing behavior. Anecdotal evidence suggests that the potency of events may be another influential factor. When happenings are of minor consequence, there is little incentive either to pay much attention to them or to figure out why they have occurred. This is not the case with potent incidents, especially painful ones. In such situations, people actively seek their predictors, so they can foresee when the events are most likely to occur and try to gain some control over them. The distinctiveness of events, quite apart from their potency, may also contribute to a perception of illusory causality. When actions are followed by a series of happenings, those that are especially noticeable have a greater likelihood of being linked to the actions than less salient occurrences that do not draw attention.

AMBIGUITY AND VARIABILITY OF OUTCOME INFORMATION

Constructing conceptions of behavior and the environment solely on the basis of response outcomes is a slow and often difficult process. This is because of the ambiguity and variability of most performance outcomes, especially when they are mediated by the behavior of others. Consider the uncertainty of the information conveyed by the negative effects that flow from actions. A person behaves in a certain way, and adverse consequences ensue. Knowing that a particular course of action is ineffective eliminates one alternative. But such information provides little guidance on what other courses of action, from among many remaining possibilities, might prove efficacious. Negative feedback is least informative when the appropriate behavior involves a novel synthesis of constituents selected from numerous alternatives. Because of its unusualness, there is little likelihood of hitting upon it or even some remote resemblance to it. In such instances, one can expend a great deal of time and effort discovering countless ways in which to behave ineffectually.

Information conveyed by positive response outcomes is not entirely unambiguous, either. It often requires a series of activities, rather than any single act, to produce results. Favorable outcomes indicate that a composite performance works, at least to some extent, but they do not specify whether the entire performance or only some aspects of it produce the effects. During initial phases of learning, performers may, and often do, attribute importance to the wrong aspects of their ongoing behavior. It is only by varying their actions and observing the differences in results that they come to comprehend the nature of effective courses of action. When small differences in performance produce noticeably different results, the outcomes can be highly informative concerning the form appropriate behavior should take. Some investigators have postulated complex neural feedback loops to explain the learning of rewarded responses without intrinsic sensory feedback, on the assumption that extrinsic outcomes can inform organisms as to whether their behavior has succeeded or failed but can tell them nothing about the form their behavior takes (Taub, 1977). This assumption is open to question. By comparing the different results accompanying varying action patterns, people can discover the structure of functional behavior.

Learning from enactive experience does not ensure that the best alternatives will be sought and developed. Most situations do not involve dichotomous outcomes in which a specific course of action either works or fails. Rather, different solutions are possible which vary, often widely, in adequateness. Hitting upon a sufficient alternative is likely to dissuade the search for an even better one. Superior solutions, therefore, do not get discovered, and the skills needed to achieve them remain undeveloped. More often than not, enactive experience alone fashions sufficient, rather than optimal, skills. For this reason, the findings of studies including only one correct solution exaggerate the informativeness of positive outcomes. Greater attention needs to be devoted to the conditions under which reward operates as a barrier to discovery. In a series of studies in which alternative solutions are possible, Schwartz (1982) has found that once people hit upon a solution that works, they keep using it without considering other alternatives. Past successes constrain the range of options considered in similar situations in the future. However, challenges to discover optimal solutions encourage more exploratory thinking and strategies for action.

Socially mediated consequences of behavior depend on the availability, preferences, and momentary preoccupations of other people. Hence, the same behavior may produce particular effects on some occasions but not on others, and even when the effects do occur, they may differ depending on the persons involved in the transactions. It is difficult to construct a conception from enactive experience of what behavior is appropriate when actions have such variable effects. The feedback is ambiguous on whether it is the behavior, the situational circumstances, or the persons providing the consequences that accounts for the divergent outcomes.

The prevalence of mixed outcomes is not due solely to the fact that significant persons cannot always be present to mediate the actions of others or that they are not always consistent in their reactions. It is due also to the inherent complexity of social functioning. What is highly functional in dealing with some situations can be ineffective, or even detrimental, in other circumstances. Learners must, therefore, discern regularity in the seeming confusion of effects by sorting out their experiences of how outcomes correlate with actions in the situations they confront and for the people with whom they interact. This requires estimating conditional outcome probabilities encompassing actions, places, times, and people. Even with their advanced symbolization capabilities, people are not all that skilled in deciphering causally uncertain information (Brehmer, 1980; Klayman, 1984; Nisbett & Ross, 1980). This is an issue to which we shall return later.

Experience is a more dependable teacher —provided it does not wreck the organism— when the effects of action are salient, powerful, and occur instantly with regularity. It does not require many encounters with fire to learn that touching a flame will result in painful burns. However, most actions do not produce such striking, instantaneous consequences. Many effects are slowly cumulative. Those that are socially mediated usually occur some time after the behavior has been performed. Delayed effects lose their informative value when their relationship to behavior is obscured by intervening experiences.

Augmenting the Instructiveness of Outcome Information

Learning from direct experience can be facilitated by increasing the informative value of the outcomes that flow from different courses of behavior. Some of the facilitators involve situational arrangements that increase the likelihood that the appropriate behavior will be attempted. Others call attention to certain structural features of functional ways of behaving. Others clarify the conditional relations between action and likely outcomes. And still others heighten and accelerate the consequences so that otherwise slowly cumulative effects become evident.

Proximating Distal Effects. When the effects of behavior are delayed, the activities that occur during the intervening period create some confusion as to what produces what. To learn from outcomes appearing long after the behavior, one must attend to disparate events, code them, recall them, and integrate them cognitively. When actions and their full effects are widely separated in time, distal outcomes are often difficult to link to their behavioral causes, or they are easily misjudged as resulting from actions that occur more closely in time.

Infants and young children, especially, have difficulty in recognizing that what they do has effects later and in representing such knowledge symbolically. During the first few months of life, infants do not possess the attentional and memorial capabilities to profit much from contingent experiences, even when the effects of their actions are delayed briefly (Millar, 1972; Watson, 1979). There is some evidence to suggest that, during the initial months of life, providing infants with opportunities to effect changes in the physical environment develops more competent infant learners than do efforts to influence the social environment (Gunnar, 1980). Manipulating physical objects usually produces immediate, predictable effects. After shaking a rattle repeatedly and hearing the resultant sound, infants cannot help but notice that their actions produce environmental effects.

Younger infants have difficulty learning, even from the physical effects of their actions, if the effects are displaced in time and space. This is shown in studies by Millar and his associates on how attentional strategies reflecting cognitive competencies affect learning of manual responses through perceptual feedback. Younger infants are as adept as older ones in learning when their actions and the sounds and sights they produce are spatially contiguous, so that infants can easily attend to both sets of events (Millar & Schaffer, 1972). But younger infants fail to learn when the source of the feedback is spatially displaced. They watch what they are doing, but, having difficulty remembering where the delayed effects occur, they do not notice and relate them to their actions. Older infants, by contrast, adopt an effective attentional strategy for integrating actions and outcomes—they manipulate objects while, at the same time, looking where they expect the effects to appear. If younger infants are provided with an external cue that tells them where to look for the effects of their actions, they become more observant of the happenings around them and learn from them (Millar, 1974). Such findings suggest that deficits in infant learning may often reflect failures in the deployment of attention, rather than cognitive incapacities to integrate contingent events.

The social effects of infants' behavior, depending as they do on the availability and vagaries of others, are not only more delayed and variable, but they often occur independently of the infants' behavior. That is, others frequently attend to and initiate activities with infants, regardless of what the infants may be doing at the time. A cry may bring others instantly, some time later, or not at all. Others often appear in the absence of crying. It is difficult to learn from such mixed social experiences, in which actions do not always produce social reactions, and social reactions often occur on their own through the initiative of others (Watson, 1979).

Experiences in which effects appear independently of action not only retard learning in infants but impair future learning in situations where outcomes can be controlled through action (Finkelstein & Ramey, 1977; Ramey & Finkelstein, 1978; Watson, 1971). Infants who have learned to activate physical events are more competent learners in new situations and on new tasks than those for whom the same physical events have occurred on their own, regardless of what the infants did. Noncontingent happenings teach them that salient aspects of their environment are uncontrollable. So they make little effort to master activities that would enable them to exercise influence over their immediate environment.

Microanalyses of familial interactions show that parents often structure contingent experiences in ways that help infants discover that their actions affect the environment and the behavior of others (Papousek & Papousek, 1979). This can be achieved in several ways. Parents establish close eye contact with the infant to ensure adequate attentiveness. They react quickly in animated ways to their infant's actions to create highly noticeable proximal effects. Further, to aid the perception of contingent relationships between actions and outcomes, the transactions are often repeated in rapid succession. Should the contingencies escape the infants' notice during the initial transactions, they have many additional opportunities to discover them without having to draw on an infirm memorial capability.

These types of social arrangements enable newborns and infants to learn that their actions can produce environmental effects. As infants' mobility develops, the instant effects of their acts on the physical environment provide clear evidence of causal agency. A toy that is dropped or is used as a percussion instrument produces interesting sounds and sights. Infants soon discover to their delight that they can create outcomes by their actions, especially if a parent is present to retrieve flung objects promptly. Proximal contingent experiences, whether they occur directly or through the actions of others, create a causal cognitive set to look for correlations between events when the behavior is less clearly related to its effects. A causal set and the growing knowledge of causal dependencies accelerate subsequent enactive learning.

The ability to detect contingencies is impaired in children and adults who maintain a tenuous contact with reality because of autistic self-preoccupation. In such instances, the impact of distal outcomes on behavior diminishes with increasing delay (Renner, 1964). The instructive value of contingent experience is increased by linking effects closely to actions. This very strategy is widely employed in educational and therapeutic applications of incentives. Initial efforts at mastering new skills are rewarded immediately. As knowledge and competencies are developed, the specially arranged benefits are gradually reduced and provided at later and later intervals.

Reinforcement theorists, who disavow the causal efficacy of thought, contend that consequences must be instantly contingent on behavior to affect it or that the behavior must be shepherded by chains of external cues serving as temporary proxies for the eventual consequent. Such a view is at variance with our knowledge of human functioning. After symbolic skills are developed, people can cognitively bridge delays between action and later outcomes. They profit from the distal effects of their behavior without requiring a stream of external cues to keep telling them what they must do to gain eventual benefits.

Channeling Attention. As will be recalled from the discussion of modeling, judging and classifying events constitutes one important aspect of human cognition. In observational learning, models aid observers to infer judgmental rules by demonstrating how to select the predictors from the available information and how to combine them to form the correct rule. In enactive learning, however, people have to figure all this out on their own. All they have for guidance are the positive and negative effects of their judgmental actions. By sampling and testing different predictors, they can discard erroneous ones and eventually identify the appropriate judgmental rule scheme.

If the bases for judging events are subtle or complex, learners may have to discard a large number of erroneous notions before they happen to hit upon the correct solution. This need not be so. Conceptual learning from judgmental outcomes can be accelerated by initially making the relevant factors so salient that they receive early consideration (Trabasso & Bower, 1968). After a concept has been grasped through the use of attention channelers, the factors can be gradually made more subtle and imbedded in redundant and irrelevant information. For example, children will learn sooner to judge things in terms of hardness by first judging items that are otherwise alike, varying only in how soft or hard they are, than if they have to discover the importance of the hardness property from judging items that differ only slightly in hardness and vary on other dimensions, such as color, size, and form. The learning task becomes considerably more complex when the judgmental rule incorporates several predictors. These situations are fraught with ambiguities that would ordinarily require a lot of response outcomes to clarify the governing rule. Programs designed to foster rule learning, therefore, shift from simple, gross contrasts of the factors of interest to successively finer differences between the things being judged as similar or dissimilar (Lovaas, Koegel, & Schreibman, 1979).

Actuating Appropriate Behavior. In promoting learning without the benefit of modeling or verbal guides, response information can be communicated only by providing consequences for actions. If the behavior involves novel patterns that rarely, if ever, occur spontaneously, the learners do not produce much in the way of rewardable actions. To try to create new structures of behavior by rewarding remote approximations of them is a tiresome endeavor.

The method of successive approximations was devised as the means of creating more complex behavior. In this approach, behavior is gradually elaborated into complex forms by rewarding behavioral attainments in small steps. In arguing against the use of instructions to circumvent the shaping of behavior by response consequences, Skinner (1963) points out that nonverbal organisms cannot be so instructed. Learning by response consequences is thus presumed to be the primary mode of acquisition. It is true that infants and young toddlers cannot be instructed verbally. But they can, and are, effectively instructed by informative modeling. They are quick to pick up what they see others do. Even higher animal species learn considerably faster by modeling than by shaping by response feedback (John et al., 1968; Warden, Fjeld & Koch, 1940; Warden & Jackson, 1935).

It is not the case, as Skinner (1963) claims, that verbal instruction is concerned with what happens to behavior later rather than with its acquisition. Novices can acquire much of the behavioral repertoire on how to navigate an automobile by being told and shown how to do it. In contrast, unless the instruction were conducted in a vast open plain, shaping driving skills by means of differential consequences is most likely to unshape the driver, the trainer, the automobile, and the surrounding environment. The issue in question is not the universality of consequential influences: All organisms are responsive to the effects of their actions. Rather, it is the exclusive allegiance to a single medium of communication. There exist superior ways of conveying to thinking organisms information about the structure of complex behavior.

Theories not only prescribe what psychological processes should be studied in depth but also how one goes about altering human behavior. Early applications of incentive systems were guided by the then prevalent belief that consequences modify behavior unconsciously, so that reinforcers had to occur instantly to be effective. Participants in change programs were, therefore uninformed about why they were being rewarded, and, in an effort to ensure the immediacy of effects, rewards were instructively presented, as soon as the requisite responses appeared. The net effect was a tedious shaping process that produced, at best, mediocre results in an ethically questionable manner. The view of reinforcement as furtive control remains firmly entrenched to this day in many public and professional circles, even though it no longer fits current theory, empirical evidence, or professional practice.

The realization that reinforcement is an unarticulated way of informing individuals about what to do encouraged the use of supplemental modes of instruction that capitalize on human cognitive capabilities. Not surprisingly, people change more rapidly if told what types of behavior are functional than if they have to discover them from observing the consequences of their own actions. If the necessary competencies are lacking, they can be developed with greater ease through verbal instruction, physical guidance, and graduated modeling than by relying solely on the successes and failures of unguided performance (Ayllon & Azrin, 1964; Bandura, 1969a; Lovaas, 1977). Instructive aids greatly augment the influence of contingent experience by conveying explicit conceptions of new behavior patterns and how they can be best executed.

Incentives provide an effective means of regulating response patterns that have already been learned, but, used by themselves, incentives are not an especially efficient way of creating cognitive and behavioral competencies. People, of course, rarely learn behavior in their everyday life that they have never seen performed by others. Modeling is thus ever present as an instructive influence. Because people constantly draw on the informative examples around them, it is difficult to determine whether reinforcement creates the new behavior or activates and refines what was already partly learned by observation. The latter is most likely the case.

Accelerating and Simulating Distal Outcomes of Technologies

Psychological perspectives on how outcomes promote different styles of behavior must be extended beyond the immediate effects of actions. If human beings are to survive, their social and technological practices cannot be fashioned on the basis of current effects alone, because practices that bring present benefits can usher in perilous futures. People create technologies that greatly increase their control of their environment. These technologies restructure the patterns of human lives. We are dealing here with rapid changes of huge magnitude, many of which can have pervasive effects not only on current life but on that of future generations. For example, the phenomenal advances in computer-based technologies are transforming how people conduct their work and the affairs of their daily lives. Technological innovations require new knowledge and competencies and render dysfunctional the ways they are supplanting. As machines take over physical labor, the occupational pursuits with a future require cognitive competencies rather than manual skills.

Modern technologies help to keep us healthy, feed us, shelter us, transport us, educate us, entertain us, and free us from the drudgery and the wear and tear of physical labor. But many technological innovations that provide current benefits also entail hazards that can take a heavy future toll on human beings and the environment. Nuclear reactors can furnish abundant energy but also radioactive contamination of the environment; chemical insecticides increase food yields but inject toxic substances into food chains that produce illnesses requiring advanced medical technologies to alleviate; agribusiness can produce crops efficiently through cultivation practices that erode and deplete the precious top soil; drugs that give people relief from pain and distress may impair their health in ways that do not become evident until years later; automobiles provide ready transport and access to attractive places but, in so doing, spew pollutants into the air that take their toll on human health and ravage the ecosystem through acid rain.

The capacity to extrapolate future consequences from known facts enables people to take corrective actions that avert disastrous futures. It is the expanded time perspective and symbolization of the future afforded by cognition that increases the prospects of human survival. Had humans been ruled solely by instant consequences, they would have long destroyed most, if not all, of the environmental supports of life. This is not to say that the immediate rewards of activities promoted for short-term gain do not jeopardize people's long-term chances of survival. They do. In commenting on the perils of the foreshortened perspective, Wenk (1979) enumerates the many factors that work to underweigh the future in social decisions. The public is often too enticed by short-term benefits to balance them against long-term consequences; politicians have to cater to short-term issues to ensure their political survival; the incentive systems of industry are strongly oriented toward performances that bring profits at quarterly intervals; the media probe solutions to current crises rather than enlightened planning for the future. But human accomplishments also testify to the fact that beneficial innovations are often guided by envisioned futures. Immediate consequences, unless unusually powerful, do not necessarily outweigh distal ones (Mischel, 1974). Our descendents will continue to have a future only because those who foresee the detrimental long-term consequences of current practices mobilize public support for changes that favor survival behavior. This is achieved largely by currently representing the form that harmful consequences would take were they to reach their full expression in the distant future.

Some dire forecasts are warranted. But many are misjudgments based on linear projection errors, when it is assumed that detrimental conditions will continue to increase at the same or an accelerating rate. Extrapolation of trends often proves faulty because people do not remain idle in the face of foreboding. They do things to arrest and reverse what they foresee to be hazardous trends. The adverse projected futures are thus forestalled.

Fashioning technological innovations on the basis of projected consequences presupposes knowledge of what form the effects are likely to take. Serious threats to human welfare arise when the ability to create new technologies outstrips the knowledge of their full effects. In such instances, people know not what they are unleashing by their creations. Because ecological life supports are in delicate balance, even frivolous technologies can produce effects that pose grave threats. If the chlorofluorocarbons used to disperse the contents of aerosol cans do, in fact, damage the ozone layer, which absorbs much ultraviolet radiation, a seemingly innocuous convenience can endanger health and ecosystems.

The potential risks of technological innovations are especially difficult to gauge when the interrelatedness of events is poorly understood. Purposeful efforts to secure expected benefits in one area may trigger widespread, unforeseen hazards in other aspects of life. The construction of the Aswan Dam in Egypt provides one example of good technological intention that has wrought widespread and lasting harm (George, 1972; Heyneman, 1971; Kassas, 1972). It profoundly affected the lives not only of the thousands of people who were uprooted and displaced but also of those far removed from it. The ecology of the region has been permanently changed much for the worse. The Nile no longer delivers the tons of silt and natural fertilizers needed for the cultivation of crops. To replenish the natural fertilizer, chemical fertilizer has to be produced at high cost and with chemical pollution. The salinity of the farmland is increasing. With each passing year, the adverse agricultural repercussions will mount. The increasing salinity of the Eastern Mediterranean, due to the reduced flow of the Nile, is permanently altering food chains and aquatic life. This has damaged the fishing industry. Without the counterflow of the Nile, the Egyptian shoreline is eroding at a rapid rate. The impounded water is a breeding ground for serious parasitic diseases, which are now widely spread by irrigation systems. Knowledge is too incomplete and forecasting involves too much guesswork to be able to foresee the full interdependent and cumulative effects of a massive environmental alteration. However, some of this social and ecological havoc was probably foreseeable had the broader ecological effects been given more serious attention.

Development of methods for analyzing the risks of modern technologies has become a matter of considerable interest. In these methods of risk analysis, some of which are reviewed by Rasmussen (1981), risk is computed in terms of the likelihood of a harmful event occurring within a specified time combined with the severity of the harm. In activities for which there is much experience to draw on, future risks can be estimated from past incidence rates. Barring any major changes in the technology or operating practices, the actuarial method can provide a reasonably good estimate of the chances that a harmful event will happen. The more challenging task is to estimate risks for new technologies, as, for example, nuclear power plants. In such situations, a complex system is separated into its basic components and their interrelations. Risks are estimated by combining the probabilities of malfunction by the various components of the system for different concatenations of possible failures. The component failure probabilities are known to some extent from the past performance of similar components in familiar systems or from extensive experimentation.

Risk analysis involves a good deal of guesswork. The dynamics of new complex systems are inadequately understood, creating uncertainty about potential hazards and risk estimates used. Even if the system is technically sound, mishaps often arise from human error, which is difficult to estimate, because any number of factors can impair human performance on any given day. However, there is much more to the hazards of new technologies than the immediate damage caused by failures of the technical systems themselves. As just noted, it is the broader, adverse impact on the ecosystem and human life that constitutes the more serious consequences. These may not even enter into the calculations of the risk analysts because their assessments are usually confined to the more direct hazards, which are easily quantifiable and which may fail to anticipate some critical hazards.

There is a notable difference between risks as analysts compute them and as the public perceives them. Starr, Rudman, and Whipple (1976) report that a major determinant of perceived risk is people's judgments of their own efficacy to manage potentially dangerous aspects of situations. If they believe they can control them, they feel relatively safe and take chances regarded as much too risky by those who judge themselves to be less efficacious. Most people do not suffer mishaps themselves, but they repeatedly observe media reports of others who do. Such biased comparison leads people to overestimate their own efficacy and to underestimate their personal risk (Slovic, Fischhoff, & Lichtenstein, 1982).

Similar efficacy determinants undoubtedly operate in the perceived risk of social technologies. People who distrust the judgmental efficacy of risk analysts or their impartiality are likely to be swayed more by their own intuition than by the analysts' probability calculations. Periodic reports about technologies, which were supposed to provide wondrous human benefits, causing widespread harm only reinforce public skepticism of expert judgment. With many uncertainties about potential sources of dysfunctions and about the scope of hazards, it is not uncommon for experts to disagree in their appraisals of the likelihood, magnitude, and duration of technological hazards. As a result, conflicts arise between personal estimates of risks and those of the policymakers and experts. Because safeguards that reduce risks escalate costs, the issue of what level of risk is acceptable is a further source of conflict. To complicate matters even further, the benefits and risks are often inequitably distributed, so that some groups bear most of the hazards while others get most of the benefits. Disputes over which course of action to follow get resolved in one way or another by social persuasion and political action.

Heightened awareness of potentially harmful effects increases the likelihood that corrective actions will be taken before conditions deteriorate to dangerous levels. Hazardous substances, for example, are usually banned before people fully pollute or poison themselves. However, people are not easily moved by the abstract notions of distant consequences when patterns of living bring current benefits but, while doing so, gradually impair the future quality of life. People have a remarkable capacity to adapt to the gradually worsening conditions of life. Those who have a vested interest in existing practices erect impediments to change.

Exemplification of Harmful Effects. Several methods are used to bring anticipated consequences to bear on current behavior in efforts to forestall human and ecological harm. The force of anticipated consequences can be boosted by concrete, vicarious exemplifications of potential hazards. Misfortunes that happen to others in their milieu from applications of the technology, and diseases produced by exposure to hazardous substances, are used to convert public concern to preventive action on a large scale. Telling examples can be quite persuasive. However, many injurious effects are slowly cumulative and may take decades before they are first detected. Methods for assessing human and ecological hazards are needed to identify risky practices before massive irreparable harm has been done.

In the health field, epidemiological methods are used to determine whether exposure to a certain substance may be injurious to health. By analyzing the incidence rates of a specific disease among people who have had different amounts of exposure to suspected substances, one may be able to identify the factors contributing to the occurrence of that disease. As Peto (1979) notes, the epidemiological method can yield informative results when exposure levels are reconstructable with some confidence, as in the duration and amount of cigarette smoking, or when high rates of a disease occur among the occupational groups having had extensive contact with certain toxicants, such as lead or asbestos. However, the epidemiological approach to health risks encounters problems when the levels of exposure are difficult to assess retrospectively. Moreover, this approach cannot detect risk factors until many people have begun to manifest the ravages of disease. When it takes years before the harm done becomes noticeable, younger cohorts may have already jeopardized their health by regular exposure to the deleterious substances.

Toxicological methods, which speed up the cumulative effects in animals with massive dosages, are used to identify potentially injurious substances before the public has had extensive exposure to them. Physically harmful practices are changed, in large part, by modeling noxious effects in animals who have had concentrated exposure to substances or to environmental conditions that would, otherwise, have taken a long time to produce their injurious effects. The carcinogenicity of the things people consume and the environmental conditions to which they are exposed are assessed in this way. Several concerns arise when generalizing from the massive doses for animals to the human use of small amounts of a substance over a long time (Neal, 1981; Peto, 1979). If doses are too large, they may produce serious side effects quite apart from those being examined. The body may be able to reduce absorption of small doses of toxicants and repair injuries, whereas heavy doses may overwhelm biological repair mechanisms. Moreover, different species may differ in their susceptibility to hazardous substances.

Biochemical methods have been devised for assessing the capacity of different substances to cause injury to microorganisms and cell cultures (Ramel & Rannug, 1980). Such tests permit rapid screening for potential harmfulness of the numerous chemicals introduced into the environment that would be much too costly and time-consuming to test with animals. With an adequate understanding of biological systems, the chemical properties of particular substances, and the mechanisms of toxic action, computer simulation can supplement toxicological tests of how people are likely to be affected by the substances. The producers of profitable, suspect products are quick to challenge the validity of both epidemiological and toxicological methods.

Arousing concern about distal consequences does not, in itself, necessarily rouse corrective action. Excessively threatening portrayals can activate avoidance of unpleasant forecasts (Janis, 1967). People also take comfort in the belief that future advances in technology will provide solutions for the problems technological innovations are creating. Making deleterious futures proximal by cognitive and vicarious means is most likely to alter immediately rewarding practices when aroused concern is coupled with guidance to choose beneficial alternatives (Leventhal, 1970). By provision of guides for constructive options, concerns are more likely to be channeled into constructive courses of action.

Mimicking Outcomes via Physical Modeling.

Considerable emphasis has been given thus far to the modeling of detrimental consequences because of their serious import. Physical modeling has been extensively used for other purposes, as, for example, designing mechanical systems and testing their performance. Aeronautical designers do not build aircraft and thrust them into the air to determine how well they can fly. Before the advent of computer modeling, aircraft designers could improve the structure of planes by building models and subjecting them to stringent tests in wind tunnels. In many instances, computer modeling, which can simulate processes and effects much more extensively, swiftly, and efficiently, has supplanted physical modeling. Given a complete computer representation of a construction, with an appropriate robotic output system, the computer can produce the physical models should they be desired (Hyman, 1973).

Computer Modeling of Processes and Outcomes.

Computers provide a ready means of estimating the effects of technical and social changes through computational enactments without having to carry out actual trials. A process model of the system is constructed incorporating the major factors and their interrelationships based on a theory of how it works in actuality. After the model has been translated into a simulation program, it permits the user to vary different levels and configurations of the relevant factors and to observe the effects of the simulated changes. In simulated enactments, the changes are performed electronically, and their results are observed. If the program faithfully represents how the real-world events operate, the computational enactments will simulate what outcomes are likely to occur under varying conditions. Such information provides a basis for planning and designing better systems.

Computers can serve as powerful tools to greatly extend human ability to manipulate, test, redesign, and refine physical and social systems for desired purposes (Sloman, 1978). Freed from the severe reality constraints of physical enactments, many of which are prohibitively risky, costly, and time consuming, one can easily vary key factors across a wide range of levels and combinations to gain understanding of how a system is likely to operate under different conditions. Computer modeling is being widely applied in diverse areas. In computer-aided design, for example, designers can simulate buildings, airplane fuselages and the like, alter key features of the structures, subject them to different types of stresses, and test their ability to withstand them. The outcomes can be pictured graphically in a few minutes. Similarly, applications of computer modeling to social systems enable innovators to change certain features of organizations and policies and observe their probable effects.

Like other technologies, computer simulations have their hazards as well. Whether computational enactments inform or mislead depends on the validity of the simulation program. This requires a sound theory, which specifies the variables and processes relevant to the system being analyzed. If the theory on which the program is built is faulty, the simulations can seriously miscalculate outcomes and trends. Changes in assumptions regarding the constituent variables or their interrelatedness in the model can markedly alter projected outcomes. Even if the theory is sound, simulations will err if the operating program represents it inadequately.

Empirical validation of computer simulations often presents thorny problems that are not easily solvable (Lehman, 1977). If computers are to serve as reliable tools for understanding the performance of complex systems, simulated outcomes should match real-world occurrences under comparable conditions. Such tests of predictive accuracy require that the real systems and their performance effects are available for comparison. Unfortunately, the real data are often lacking, especially for social systems where huge costs, deeply entrenched customs, and politics curtail social experimentation. As a result, the program performance is usually validated against an isolated real occurrence (Taylor, 1978). Unless predictive accuracy is tested across a number of actual occurrences, the generality of the operating model remains unknown. Nor does a good fit between simulated and real performances necessarily validate the theory embodied in the program, unless there is also a good match between the simulated and real subprocesses governing the effects.

4

SOCIAL DIFFUSION
AND INNOVATION

Understanding how new ideas and social practices spread within a society, or from one society to another, has important bearing on personal and social change. Extraordinary advances in the technology of communications, which vastly expand the range of social influence, have transformed the social diffusion process. The video system feeding off telecommunications satellites has become the dominant vehicle for disseminating symbolic environments. Further developments in cable systems, which permit two-way communication; in laser transmission with its enormous information-carrying capacity; and in computer delivery systems possessing huge storage of choices, provide diverse symbolic environments to serve almost any purpose. These remarkable converging developments in the technology of communications are restructuring institutional practices and how people conduct their lives. Social practices are not only being widely diffused within societies, but ideas, values, and styles of conduct are being modeled worldwide. The electronic media are coming to play an increasingly influential role in transcultural change.

Pattern of Diffusion

The process of social diffusion has been examined most extensively with regard to the adoption of innovations (Rogers, 1983). An innovation is any idea, practice, or device that is perceived by people to be new. By examining how psychosocial factors affect the pace and pattern of adoptions, one can delineate the determinants and mechanisms governing social diffusion. Diffusion of innovation follows a common pattern. New ideas or practices are introduced by notable example. Initially, the rate of adoption is slow because new ways are unfamiliar, customs resist change, and results are uncertain. As early adopters convey more information about how to apply the new practices and their potential benefits, the innovation is adopted at an accelerating rate. After a period in which the new practices spread rapidly, the rate of diffusion slows down. Several factors may contribute, either singly or in combination, to this decelerating growth. When adoptions are widespread, the number of remaining potential adopters begins to decrease. A shrinking source means declining adoptions. If the innovative practice proves disappointing or detrimental to some of the adopters, their negative reactions may dissuade others from trying it. Innovations, of course, do not exist by themselves; they must compete for their survival. The appearance of alternative forms of the innovation siphons off some potential adopters. Often the alternatives are imitations of the original successful innovation. Cumulative frequencies of adoptions over time approximate an S-shaped curve. After sufficient trial, the use of the innovation either stabilizes or declines, depending upon its relative functional value.

In analyzing the speed and pattern of diffusion, adoption is usually plotted over time, and the diffusion curve is segmented into innovators, early adopters, later adopters, and, finally, laggards. Researchers then examine how people at the successive stages of adoption differ in their attributes. Less refined analyses simply compare early and late adopters, or adopters and nonadopters. While much attention is centered on the personal determinants of adoptive behavior, to provide a broad understanding of this matter a theory must also encompass a large set of social and economic factors that create the opportunities to learn new ways or constrain innovative modeling and provide incentives or disincentives for innovation.

It is easy to section diffusion curves but difficult to interpret them. Differences between early and later adopters are often assumed to arise from their personal characteristics or their social and economic circumstances. Late adopters and laggards presumably wait to see the benefits gained by the innovators before trying new things themselves. In fact, some of the variations in the time of adoption may result from differences in when people were first exposed to new ideas, technologies, or fashions. Accessibility to information must be disentangled from people's receptivity to it. Some late adopters may be highly receptive to the new ideas, but they were simply late in learning about them. Temporal analyses of diffusion may, therefore, yield misleading results if individuals are not equated for the time and the amount of initial exposure.

The segment structures of a diffusion curve lose significance if they are confounded with variations in the time of exposure. This confounding can be reduced by measuring adoption from the time of a person's first exposure, rather than from when the innovation was introduced. However, the time of adoption may be confounded by the source of the information if early adopters learn about new things from the media, and late adopters learn about them through word-of-mouth or from others who adopt the innovation.

Some of the more complex innovations are not adoptable, for best results, in the exact form in which they were developed. Various features may have to be altered to make them suitable to an adopter's particular circumstances (Rice & Rogers, 1980). Moreover, adopters may add new features of their own devising that improve the prototype. Even the originators of the innovation may continue to alter it by further experimentation and by getting feedback from early adopters' experiences with it. In an interactive, evolving process, some of the people may have adopted the innovator's original prototype, others the innovator's revised prototype, others their own revision of the innovator's prototype, and still others may be appropriating the adopters' adaptations. Diffusion curves do not mean much unless the aggregate scores represent the spread of the same innovation over time.

DETERMINANTS OF THE DIFFUSION PROCESS

Social cognitive theory distinguishes between two separable processes in the social diffusion of innovation: the acquisition of knowledge concerning the innovation and the adoption of that innovation in practice. Acquisition is distinguished from adoption because it is governed by different determinants. In acquisition, modeling serves as the major vehicle for transmitting information about new styles of behavior and their likely effects. The factors that determine observational learning, which have been discussed earlier, apply to the rapid promulgation of innovations. The psychosocial factors determining whether or not people will put into practice what they have learned will be analyzed at length in subsequent chapters and will only be summarized here.

Modeling Determinants of Diffusion

Symbolic modeling usually functions as the principal conveyer of innovations to widely dispersed areas. This is especially true in the early stages of diffusion. Newspapers, magazines, radio, and television inform people about new practices and their likely risks or benefits. Early adopters, therefore, come from among those who have had greater access to media sources of information about innovations (Robertson, 1971). After novelties have been symbolically introduced, they are further disseminated to group members through personal contact with the local adopters (Rogers & Shoemaker, 1971). When the influence operates through direct modeling, adoptive behavior tends to spread along existing interpersonal networks. If the behavior is highly conspicuous, however, it can be learned from those who model it by people who are unacquainted with one another.

Dispersed occurrences of similar practices do not necessarily reflect modeling processes. Common circumstances can produce similar behavior in different places without there having been any communication between them. Such occurrences reflect concurrent origination rather than social diffusion. A modeling process is indicated by several criteria. First, there is close resemblance of the key features between the modeled pattern and the occurrences elsewhere. When the modeled practices include a novel combination of elements, there is no mistaking the source, because there is little chance that unique resemblances could appear in so many places by sheer coincidence. Second, the modeled practices and the similar ones appear temporally close together, with the events being modeled preceding in time. Third, the diffusion follows a differential spatial pattern—similar practices appear in locales where the novel behavior has been modeled but not in the places where it was never displayed. Fourth, modeling influences spark an accelerating rise in similar practices as widespread adoptions create increasing modeling instigators for further occurrences of the new behavior. And finally, the rate of adoptions varies as a function of factors that are known to facilitate or check modeling.

The conditions associated with different innovations are too diverse to permit rigid application of some of the foregoing indicants of a modeling process. Consider the criteria of temporal and geographical patterning of occurrences. In some forms of social diffusion, a long time may elapse between modeling and adoption, because the first opportunity to use what has been learned does not arise until much later. Hershey and West (1984) provide a good illustration of delayed adoption in their study of social diffusion through the modeling of a political campaign strategy. A group opposed to abortion helped to defeat a senator whose views differed with theirs on this issue, with a campaign tactic combining several distinctive features. It involved leafletting in church parking lots on the Sunday before the election, with a specially designed brochure. The brochure was also distributed that weekend by mail to likely supporters who had been located earlier by a thorough telephone identification program. The modeled campaign tactic, for which the originator claimed success and became the consultative diffusion source, could not be adopted until the next election two years later. In the next senatorial election, this particular strategy was modeled in six different states with minor variations to fit local races. However, the voter-identification component, which required more effort, resources, and access to a computer, was diffused less extensively.

In some modeling influences, the criterion of geographical patterning of occurrences is not applicable. When television models new practices on the screens in virtually every home, it is hard to find matched locales untouched by television's influence. Not all innovations, of course, are promoted through the mass media. Some rely on informal personal channels. Physical proximity, of course, does not necessarily mean close social relations. For innovations that are advocated personally and are not publicly visible, as was the case for clock thermostats to conserve energy, the innovation diffuses through social networks of friends and work associates, who live in dispersed locales, rather than spatially as a function of geographic proximity (Darley, 1978).

Dual-Link Model. It has been commonly assumed in the theory of mass communication that modeling influences operate through a two-step diffusion process. Influential persons pick up new ideas from the media and pass them on to their followers through personal influence. This dual-link model grew out of research by Katz and Lazarsfeld (1955) showing that radio and newspapers had negligible effects on people's voting behavior. Rather, their voting decisions were swayed by the opinions of associates who, in turn, were influenced by the media. Some communication researchers have interpreted such findings to mean that nonmedia influences are supreme, so that the media can only reinforce change but cannot initiate it (Klapper, 1960).

Different sources of influence are too diverse in nature to have fixed relative strengths. Depending on their quality, media influences may be subordinate to, equal to, or outweigh nonmedia influences. The view that diffusion is exclusively a filter-down process is disputed by a large body of evidence concerning modeling influences. Human judgment, values, and conduct can be altered by televised modeling without having to wait for an influential intermediary to adopt and model what has been shown. Watt and van den Berg (1978) tested several alternative theories about how media communications relate to public attitudes and behavior: Media influence people directly; media influence opinion leaders who affect others; media have no independent effects; they set the public agenda for discussion by designating what is important but do not otherwise influence the public; media reflect public attitudes and behavior rather than shape them. The direct-flow model from media to the public received the best empirical support. In this study, the behavior was highly publicized and could bring benefits without risks. When the activities being advocated require the investment of time and resources, and failures can be costly, people seek verification from other sources before they act.

Chaffee (1982) reviews substantial evidence that calls into question the prevailing view that interpersonal sources of information are necessarily more persuasive than media sources. People seek information that may be potentially useful from different sources. Neither informativeness, credibility, nor persuasiveness are uniquely tied to interpersonal or to mediated sources. How extensively different sources are used depends, in large part, on their accessibility and the likelihood that they will provide the kinds of information sought.

Multi-Pattern Diffusion. Modeling affects the adoption of innovations in several ways. It instructs people about new ways of thinking and behaving by demonstration or description. Learning about new things does not rely on a fixed order of sources. The relative importance of interpersonal and media sources of information in initiating the adoption process varies for different innovations and for the same innovation at different stages in the adoption process (Pelz, 1983). Except for simple practices, no single source ever provides complete information on the nature of the innovation, its likely benefits and costs, and complete instruction on the skills and social changes needed to implement it successfully.

Models motivate as well as inform. People are initially reluctant to embark on new undertakings that involve costs and risks until they see the advantages that have been gained by early adopters. Modeled benefits accelerate diffusion by weakening the restraints of the more cautious potential adopters. As acceptance spreads, the new ways gain further social support. Models also display preferences and evaluative reactions, which can alter the observers' values. Changes in evaluative standards affect receptivity to the innovation being modeled. Models not only exemplify and legitimate innovations, they also serve as advocates for them by directly encouraging others to adopt them.

Modeling influences can, of course, impede as well as promote the diffusion process (Midgley, 1976). Modeling negative reactions to a particular innovation, as a result of having had disappointing experiences with it, dissuades others from trying it. Even modeled indifference to an innovation, in the absence of any personal experience with it, will dampen the interests of others. In a crowded and ever changing marketplace of notions and novelties, success must come fast. During the brief period of its launch, widespread disregard of an innovation brings its quick demise.

Innovations that are inherently satisfying or highly functional do not require much modeling to diffuse them. To cite a familiar example, television was guaranteed worldwide growth by its capacity to provide instant entertainment. Advertisements directed at television buyers center on the distinguishing features of particular brands reflecting minor modifications, not on the value of the device itself. For many innovations the benefits are marginal, or they are socially conferred by public fancy, rather than deriving naturally from the innovations. In such instances, adoption depends on promotion by the media and early modeling by persons who, because of their popularity or status, can exert broad influence. The adoption rates of innovations that depend for their value on the vagaries of public fancy are difficult to predict.

Efforts to delineate the determinants and mechanisms of social diffusion should not becloud the fact, as Zaltman and Wallendorf (1979) have noted, that not all innovations are useful, nor is resistance to them necessarily dysfunctional. In the continuous flow of innovations, the number of poorly tested or disadvantageous ones far exceeds those with truly beneficial possibilities. Both personal and societal well-being are well served by initial wariness to new practices which are being promoted by hollow or exaggerated claims. The designations "venturesome" for early adopters and "laggards" for late adopters are fitting in the case of innovations that hold promise. However, when people are mesmerized by alluring appeals into trying disadvantageous innovations, the more suitable designation is "gullibility" for early adopters and "astuteness" for resisters. Rogers (1983) has criticized the prevalent tendency to conceptualize the diffusion process from the perspective of the promoters. This tends to bias the search for explanations of nonadoptive behavior in negative personal characteristics of nonadopters.

There is no single pattern of social diffusion. The media can implant ideas for change either directly or through adopters. Analyses of the role of mass media in social diffusion must distinguish between their effects on learning and their effects on performance and examine how different sources of influence affect these separable processes. In some instances the media both teach new forms of behavior and create motivators for action by altering people's preferences, perceptions of personal efficacy, and outcome expectations. In other instances, the media teach, but other adopters provide the motivation to perform what has been learned observationally. In still other instances, the effect of the media may be entirely socially mediated. People who have had no exposure to it can be influenced by adopters who have had the exposure and then themselves become the transmitters of the new ways. The latter pattern is more likely to obtain for the print media, which have a more limited audience, than for the ubiquitous video media.

Dispersion patterns can also vary widely depending on the nature of the innovation, the skills and resources it requires, the associational networks that exist for spreading the innovation, and the social constraints and incentives that impinge upon the activity. Within these various patterns of social diffusion, the media can serve as originating, as well as reinforcing, influences.

Sabido (1981) reports ingenious applications of social learning principles in Mexico that are designed to promote society-wide changes through televised modeling. One project addressed the problem of illiteracy. In an effort to reduce widespread illiteracy, the government launched a national self-instruction program. People with reading skills were urged to organize self-instruction groups in which they would teach others how to read with instructional material that had been developed for this purpose. However, these national appeals produced a disappointing social response. Sabido then selected the soap opera, which has a large, loyal following, as the best format for reaching and motivating people with problems of illiteracy. The main story line in the dramatic series centered on the interesting and informative experiences of a self-instruction group.

The program incorporated the major factors known to enhance the impact of modeling. To capitalize on prestigious modeling, the most popular soap-opera performer was cast in the role of the instructor. Actors in the learner roles were cast to represent different segments of the population to enhance further the positive influence of the televised modeling through model similarity. Music and melodramatic embellishments gave dramatic intensity to the story to ensure high attentional involvement of the viewers. As an additional vicarious motivator, the dramatic series depicted the substantial benefits of literacy for self-development and for national efficacy and pride. Epilogues, summarizing the modeled messages, aided the symbolic coding of information for memory representation. It is of little value to motivate people if they are not provided with appropriate guides and social supports for action. To facilitate media-promoted changes, the series often used real-life settings showing the actors obtaining the instructional material from an actual distribution center and eventually graduating in an actual graduation ceremony. The epilogues informed the viewers of this national self-education program and encouraged them to take advantage of it.

A prior interview study had revealed several negative self-beliefs that had dissuaded people from enrolling in the national program. Many believed that reading skills could be acquired only when one is young, others believed they personally lacked the capabilities to master such a complex skill, and still others felt that they were unworthy of educated persons' devoting their time to them. These dissuading misbeliefs were modeled by the actors and corrected by the instructor as she persuaded them to join a self-study group. In the dramatic series, which included humor, conflict, and engrossing discussions of the subjects being read, the models overcame obstacles to self-directed learning and gained progressive mastery and self-pride in their accomplishments.

Millions of viewers watched this series faithfully. In the assessment of effects, compared to nonviewers, viewers of the dramatic series were much more informed about the national literacy program and expressed more positive attitudes about helping each other to learn. The rate of enrollment in the national self-instruction program was 99,000 in the year preceding the televised series, 840,000 during the year of the series, and 400,000 in the year following the series.

A similar televised modeling format served to promote society-wide family planning in an effort to reduce the nation's burgeoning population growth. A creative format of contrasting modeling was used to portray the process and benefits of family planning. The positive family life of a small family was contrasted with the burdens of a huge family and the accompanying impoverishment and distress. Much of the drama focused on the married daughter from the huge family, who herself was beginning to experience severe marital conflicts and distress over a rapidly expanding family. The young couple was shown gaining control over their family life and the accruing benefits with the help of a family-planning center. At the end of some of the programs, viewers were informed about existing family-planning services to facilitate media-promoted changes. Records of the family-planning centers revealed a 32 percent increase in the number of new contraceptive users over the number for the previous year of operation, before the series was televised. People reported that the television portrayal served as the impetus for consulting the centers. National sales of contraceptives rose between 4 percent and 7 percent in the preceding two years, whereas they increased by 23 percent in the year the program was aired.

Changes corresponding to the introduction of televised influence must be interpreted with caution, because some of the changes may be due to other social influences operating concurrently. Symbolic modeling can have substantial impact if it serves as a vehicle for bringing people to existing community settings, which then provide the extensive guidance and incentives needed to realize personal changes. The Sabido projects explicitly linked symbolic modeling to community services. The synergistic effect of modeling combined with the national effort enlisted numerous participants, whereas the national effort alone gained relatively few recruits.

Adoption Determinants

The acquisition of knowledge and skills regarding innovations is necessary but not sufficient for their adoption in practice. A number of factors determine whether people will act on what they have learned. Environmental inducements serve as one set of regulators. In the consumer field, for example, advertising appeals are repeatedly used to stimulate consumers to purchase new products. Fashion industries saturate the market with new styles and reduce the availability of the fashions they wish to supplant. The outpouring of inducements from the various media for new products, technologies, ideas, and social practices increases the likelihood that potential adopters will be moved to try the advocated innovations.

Adoptive behavior is highly susceptible to incentive influences. Some of the motivating incentives derive from the utility of the adoptive behavior. People who have the means embrace innovations that produce tangible benefits, whereas they discard those that do not work well. The greater the relative benefits provided by an innovation, the higher is the incentive to adopt it (Ostlund, 1974; Rogers & Shoemaker, 1971). But benefits cannot be experienced until the new practices are tried. Therefore, when deciding whether or not to adopt an innovation, people have to act on the basis of anticipated benefits and possible detriments. Since innovations involve some uncertainty, good estimates of likely outcomes are not easy to come by. Promoters, of course, try to get people to adopt new practices by altering their preferences and beliefs about likely outcomes, largely by enlisting vicarious incentives. Advocates of new technologies create expectations that they offer better solutions than can established ways. Vicarious incentives increase adoptive decisions. Vicarious motivators abound in advertising. Positive appeals depict adoptive behavior as resulting in a host of benefits. Negative appeals portray the adverse consequences of failure to pursue the recommended practices. Vicarious punishment, however, is a less reliable means of promoting adoptive behavior than is the prospect of reward. The factors governing the motivating effects of vicarious incentives are examined in a later chapter.

The social and economic incentives for innovation have been studied extensively in industrial adoptions of technologies designed to increase productivity. Downs and Mohr (1979) present an incentive model integrating a number of factors that can affect organizational innovativeness. In this model, the inducement to innovate varies as a function of the ratio of perceived benefits to costs. The relative benefits are then moderated by the fiscal and staff resources needed to implement the new practices and by factors that reduce the value attached to benefits and costs. Among the perceived benefits included are the expected profits and how they might change over time, the prestige deriving from an organization's foresightfulness, and the improved functioning of the organization. The disincentives for innovation are similarly varied —the managerial time and costs of appraising the profitability of the innovation, the equipment and labor costs of implementing the innovation, and the social costs of disarranging organizational routines and structures. In addition to these dissuaders, other considerations may detract from utility estimates.

Forecasting is a risky business. Innovations involve many uncertainties, and the information used to judge probabilistic outcomes is not always the most reliable. Decision makers will not be stirred to action by images of benefits if they place low confidence in their cost-benefit estimates. The more they distrust their judgmental efficacy, the less inclined they are to venture in new directions. The more weight they give to potential risks and the costs of

getting rid of an innovation should it fail to live up to expectations, the weaker is their incentive to innovate.

Downs and Mohr (1979) acknowledge that combining potential motivators in a composite model does not mean that decision makers weigh and integrate all these factors in deciding what to do. Nor do the economic incentives, realizable through innovation, operate as forcefully as an economically oriented theory of motivation might lead one to expect. Mansfield (1968) found that the diffusion of major industrial techniques is faster the more profitable they are and the less capital investment they require. But it usually takes years before technologies of proven value have been adopted by firms that could reap financial rewards by innovating their practices. This is because personal and social factors retard adoption of successful innovations.

When faced with uncertainties and indefinite information, instead of computing cost-benefit ratios, people fall back on simpler rules which ignore many of the factors that should serve as incentives or disincentives for adoptive behavior (Kahneman, Slovic, & Tversky, 1982). Moreover, self-interest and organizational benefits of change do not always coincide. As March (1982) notes, cost-benefit analyses are often used to rationalize choices which reflect the personal preferences of those who wield power in a group, rather than necessarily to maximize benefits. In organizations containing competing factions, an innovation that might increase the power of one faction is resisted by rival factions that perceive change as detracting from their influence (Zaltman & Wallendorf, 1979). As long as uncertainties exist about the possible level of future benefits, potentially valuable innovations can be resisted or applied in compromising ways that sacrifice group gains for personal and factional benefits. Adoptive behavior is often swayed more by seeing what one's successful competitors are doing than by a detailed cost-benefit analysis. If other knowledgeable people are adopting new ways, they must be worth trying. Widespread modeling of beneficial innovations can also counteract dysfunctional social resistance. The more organizations modeling successful innovations, the stronger is the inducement for holdouts to adopt them (Mansfield, 1968).

Many innovations serve as a means of gaining social recognition and status. Early adoption of innovations that prove advantageous can enhance status and prestige. Indeed, status incentives are often the main motivators for adopting new styles and tastes. In many instances, however, the variant styles do not provide different inherent benefits, or, if anything, the most innovative styles are the most costly. Status is thus gained at a price. People who strive to distinguish themselves from the common and the ordinary adopt new styles in clothing, grooming, recreational activities, and conduct, thereby achieving distinctive status. As the popularity of the new behavior grows, it loses its status-conferring value until eventually it, too, becomes commonplace. It is then discarded for a new form. Widespread modeling thus instigates further inventiveness to preserve status differentiations.

Fads can be distinguished from fashions largely in terms of the benefits supporting the adoptive behavior. When innovations serve primarily to gain social recognition and standing, as is typical of fads, they show a quick rise in popularity and an abrupt decline as their novelty is effaced by over-use. Fashions, in contrast, enjoy a longer life span because they provide more enduring benefits. The automobile is an example of a novelty that eventually became a permanent fixture. Innovations that have intrinsic functional value survive as part of common practices until something better comes along.

Adoptive behavior is also partly governed by self-evaluative reactions to one's own behavior. People espouse what they value and regard as praiseworthy, but they resist accepting innovations that violate their social and moral standards or conflict with their firmly held beliefs. They eschew things that clash with their self-conception. The more compatible an innovation is with prevailing social norms and value systems, the greater is its adoptability (Rogers & Shoemaker, 1971). However, self-evaluative sanctions do not operate in isolation from the pressures of social influence. People are often led to behave in otherwise personally devalued ways by using strategies that circumvent negative self-reactions. This is done by changing appearances and meanings through advantageous labeling and portrayal. In marketing, for example, new products are presented in ways that appear compatible with people's cherished values and whatever is in vogue at the time. Consumer conformity is promoted in the name of individualism. To get women to smoke, marketing managers have exploited the women's movement by portraying smoking as an expression of women's liberation with catchy phrases such as, "You've come a long way, baby." Products and industrial practices that degrade the environment are advertised in the name of conservation. Expedient social labeling similarly promulgates behavior that has moral and ethical implications. People who are ordinarily considerate are often willing to adopt reprehensible social practices after they have been socially construed as serving humane purposes (Bandura, 1979).

Innovations spread at different rates and patterns because they differ in the skills and resources they require for successful adoption. Such prerequisites serve as additional factors controlling the diffusion process. Rogers and Shoemaker (1971) have identified several attributes of innovations that affect their adoptability. Meta-analysis, which summarizes the size of effects obtained from many studies, supports two of the attributes already mentioned—relative benefit and compatibility—as well as a third attribute, complexity (Tornatzky & Klein, 1982). Whether or not an innovation is complex depends on adopters' competencies. Hence, complexity must be viewed relative to preexisting competency, rather than as an absolute property of an innovation. Innovations that are difficult to understand and use receive more reluctant consideration than simpler ones.

The amenability of an innovation to brief trial is another relevant characteristic that can affect the ease of adoption. Innovations that can be tried on a limited basis are more readily adoptable than those that have to be tried on a large scale with substantial effort and costs. Innovations involve uncertainties about the future and whether their potential benefits will be realizable when transplanted by adopters to their own milieu. In making adoptive decisions, people have to consider the costs of discontinuing the new technologies or practices should they prove disappointing. The more costly the innovations are to undo, the greater the reluctance to adopt them. Resistance to innovation stemming from apprehension over uncertain outcomes can be overcome by a provisional trial on a limited basis. However, this strategy for surmounting initial resistance does not lend itself to innovations that require extensive investment of resources and reorganization that is not easily reversible. In such instances, the evident benefits accruing to other adopters must serve the persuasive function.

People will not adopt innovations even though they are favorably disposed toward them if they lack the money, the skills, or the accessory resources that may be needed. The more resources innovations require, the lower is their adoptability. The study by Havens and Flinn (1975) of transcultural diffusion of agricultural technologies in Colombia illustrates the constraints imposed by financial resources on adoptive decisions. Landowners who could afford the technologies adopted them. They prospered and bought more land. Those who had little cash flow, could not get the credit, or could not amortize the debt if given a loan did not adopt the innovations, even though they were well disposed toward them. About a quarter of them lost their minifarms to become urban laborers, and those who continued to farm eked out a marginal existence.

Some innovations are more subject to social prohibitions, which wield additional influence over which ones are adopted and the speed with which they spread. Social disincentives impede the diffusion process.

SOCIAL NETWORKS AND FLOW OF DIFFUSION

People are enmeshed in networks of relationships that include occupational colleagues, organizational members, kinships, and friendships, just to mention a few. People are linked not only in a direct fashion by personal relationships. Because acquaintanceships overlap different network clusters, many people become linked to each other indirectly by interconnected ties. Indeed, Milgram (1969) has shown that it requires less than ten intermediate acquaintances to link up any two persons who do not know each other, provided that certain information is given about the target person (e.g., Boston stock broker) to decide whom to select from one's collection of acquaintances to reach the target person.

Social structures comprise clustered networks of people with various ties among them, as well as persons who provide connections to other clusters through joint membership or a liaison role. Clusters vary in their internal structure, ranging from loosely knit ones to those that are densely interconnected. Networks also differ in the number and pattern of structural linkages between clusters. They may have many common ties or function with a high degree of separateness. In addition to their degree of interconnectedness, people vary in the positions they occupy in particular social networks. The opinions and behavior of those who possess status and prestige are likely to have greater impact on what spreads through a social network than the activities modeled by peripheral members.

Rogers assigns a prominent role to communication networks in the diffusion of innovation (Rogers & Kincaid, 1981). Information regarding new ideas and devices is often conveyed through multilinked relationships. Traditionally, the communication process has been conceptualized as one of unidirectional persuasion flowing from a source to a recipient. Rogers emphasizes the mutuality of influence in interpersonal communication. People share information, give meaning by mutual feedback to the information they exchange, gain understanding of each other's views, and influence each other. Specifying the channels of influence through which innovations are dispersed provides greater understanding of the diffusion process than simply plotting the rate of adoptions over time.

Granovetter's (1983) analyses of the strength of structural relationships suggests that innovations may be diffused most extensively through weak social ties. The reason for this seemingly paradoxical effect is as follows. People who have strong tries to each other tend to have much the same views on matters (Byrne, 1971) and to interact mainly with each other. In contrast, those with weak ties are apt to travel in more diverse social circles where they can learn different things. One is more likely to learn about new ideas and practices from brief contacts with numerous acquaintances than from frequent contact in the same circle of close friends. To the extent that the linkages between cohesive groups rely on weak ties, they serve to broaden and extend diffusion paths. That weak ties do, indeed, extend social interconnectedness is revealed when people are asked to reach someone who is unknown to them through a chain of intermediate acquaintances (Lin, Dayton, & Greenwald, 1978). Using weak ties increases the chance that the contact will be realized.

Not all people with weak ties are necessarily socially mobile. Those who lack close relationships because they do not interact much with others provide little in the way of linkages among different groups. It is acquaintances who interact with members of other groups who broaden diffusion paths. Weak and strong ties serve different functions in the spread of innovations. Weak ties may increase one's access to diversity, but

the social influences operating within closely knit networks hold sway over what gets adopted from that diversity. One must, therefore, distinguish between the configuration of social ties and the psychosocial factors governing adoptive behavior. While structural interconnectedness provides potential diffusion paths, psychosocial factors are likely to determine the fate of what diffuses through those paths. In other words, it is the transactions that occur within social relationships, rather than the ties themselves, that explain adoptive behavior.

The impact of network structures on diffusion of innovation is considerably more complex than it may appear at first glance. Much attention is centered on how best to measure network linkages (Burt, 1980). There is also the thorny question of which particular social networks provide the pathways for the spread of an innovation. People pursue most of their activities in social contexts where they make hundreds of acquaintances. One can extract from these various transactions a multitude of social networks built around any number of personal pursuits. For example, in addition to the usual ties of friendship and occupation, there are commuting networks, shopping networks, neighborhood networks, athletic networks, and saloon networks, each with its own structural linkage. A person who occupies a central position in one network may be in the periphery of another. To complicate matters further, different social networks may come into play at different stages of diffusion. In tracing adoptions of a new drug by medical communities, Coleman, Katz, and Menzel (1966) found that the influences operated through professional ties in the initial phase of diffusion and through friendship ties in subsequent phases.

Most of the research on diffusion paths relies on people's reports of whom they talk with most frequently. Sometimes the paths are reconstructed from adopters' recollections of who informed them about the innovation. Reports of communication links and retraced pathways raise questions about the reliability of network data and how well they reflect the actual structural linkages. Perception of social influence is not always accurate, especially when multiple sources are involved, and recollections may be faulty. If a topic involves sensitive matters, the respondents may withhold information about the persons with whom they discuss things. In asking only about close relationships, the sociometric inquiry disregards weak ties, which, as we have seen, often serve as important links in chains of communication. Because casual acquaintances can be numerous, such dyadic links are simply ignored, otherwise collecting and analyzing network data becomes a task of immense proportions. Full representation of social linkages is, therefore, sacrificed for procedural feasibility. Measures that truncate diffusion paths do not provide the best test of how network variables contribute to the spread of innovations.

There is not much prospect that more complete and objective measures of communication networks are in the offing. It would require total surveillance of an entire community to chart who says what to whom. Direct observation of communication networks is feasible in laboratory studies of small groups but not in the everyday environment. Brief time samples of social interactions yield an incomplete picture of chains of communication, as do logs of social transactions, because they omit the numerous informal communications of daily life. Because of these inherent methodological complexities, greater advances have been made in devising computerized methods for extracting quantitative network indices from the multitude of dyadic links found in sociometric data (Rogers & Kincaid, 1981) than in improving the quality of the sociometric data itself.

Progress in understanding how social networks contribute to diffusion requires theoretical specification of which networks are most relevant for any given innovation. The network structures should be measured before the diffusion begins. In this way, network characteristics can serve as predictors of the rate and pattern of adoptive behavior. The goal is to explain and predict adoptive behavior, rather than simply to reconstruct the paths by which it spreads. The recurring issue of the generality or specificity of assessment arises in network analysis as well. Does one measure from whom people generally get their information or those to whom they turn for information specific to the topic of the innovation? The general sociometric assessment inquires about, Whom do you talk with most frequently?, whereas the particularized sociometric assessment inquires about, Whom do you talk with about (the topic of the innovation)? There is no single social network in a community that serves all purposes. Different innovations engage different networks. Thus, as Marshall (1971) has shown, birth-control practices and agricultural innovations diffuse through quite different networks within the same community. Adoption rates are better predicted from a network that subserves the particular innovation than from a more general communication network (Rogers & Kincaid, 1981).

To acknowledge that different kinds of innovations are not all diffused by the same social network is not to say that there is no generality whatsoever to the diffusion function of network structures. If a particular social structure subserves varied activities, it can help to spread the adoption of innovations in each of those activities. Moreover, if an innovation is highly functional and does not require many resources, it can be widely diffused through a large number of networks. In tracking the diffusion of an energy-saving clock thermostat, Darley (1978) found that initial adopters diffused it to friends and professional colleagues but not to neighbors who lacked close ties with each other. High utility not only transcends the particular function of a social network, but it also supplants the role of prestige and social position in swaying adoptive decisions. Prestige gained through sound past judgment is likely to carry the greatest weight when the benefits of an innovation are uncertain. In such situations, people turn to those who seem to be in the know for guidance. Innovations providing evident benefits serve as their own persuaders. If advantageous innovations are widely publicized through the media, they can be adopted directly without requiring interaction among adopters.

The over-all evidence from studies examining different factors that can affect adoptive behavior indicates that the course of diffusion is best understood by considering the interactions among psychosocial determinants, properties of innovations, and network structures. Structural and psychological determinants of adoptive behavior should be included as complementary factors in a theory of diffusion, rather than be cast as rival theories of diffusion.

Some efforts have been made to assess the extent to which network factors contribute to the adoption of innovations (Rogers & Kincaid, 1981). Networks are usually represented by the number of social ties, rather than by the pattern of linkages. The evidence generally shows that people with many social ties are more apt to adopt innovations than those who have few ties to others. Adoption rates increase as more and more people in one's personal network adopt an innovation. But the effects of social connectedness on adoptive behavior are open to alternative explanations. Multilinked relations may foster adoption of innovations because they convey more factual information, mobilize stronger social influences, or both. It may be, however, that people with close ties are more receptive to new ideas than those who are socially estranged. Moreover, in social transactions, people see their associates adopt innovations, as well as talk about them. Multiple modeling alone can increase adoptive behavior (Bandura & Menlove, 1968; Perry & Bussey, 1979). Although sociometric assessments are framed in terms of whom people talk with, the measures of social ties reflect the incidence of both modeling and interpersonal influence. Researchers have compared the relative contribution of network factors and personal characteristics to adoptive behavior. Both factors emerge as determinants, but reports of their relative predictive power are of dubious reliability because the measures leave much to be desired. This is especially true when the social network or the personal determinants rely on indefinite omnibus measures, rather than on the particularized measures most relevant to a certain innovation.

Advances in communications and computer technologies provide the means for creating new structures that link people together in widely dispersed places. Interactive computer networking can interconnect numerous people in ways that transcend the barriers of time and space (Hiltz & Turoff, 1978). Large funds of information become readily accessible by this means. In computerized network systems, participants communicate with each other by sending and receiving information at the place and time of their own convenience. The computer stores the collective entries which can be updated and altered for use at any time by members of the network. Through this electronic interactive format, people can exchange information, share new ideas, and transact any number of pursuits. Computerized networking provides a ready vehicle for creating diffusion structures, expanding their membership, extending them geographically, and disbanding them when they have outlived their usefulness.

People behave differently in computer-mediated networks than in face-to-face interchanges. This is because the social influences that regulate how people interact with each other in direct social relations are much weaker and lack immediacy in computerized communications. Kiesler, Siegel, and McGuire (1984) document the many ways in which depersonalization of communication alters the nature of interactions and decision making. The force of status and prestige is attenuated so that members participate more equally in the computer-mediated system. If the interchanges are conducted anonymously, participants behave more uninhibitedly, expressing views and feelings they would not personally voice to each other. The combined effect of expanded participation, reduced social avenues of influence, and lack of prompt feedback makes it difficult to coordinate and guide the flow of information.

Television is being increasingly used to forge large, single-link structures in which many people are linked directly to the media source but who may have little or no direct relations with each other. For example, television evangelists attract loyal followers who adopt the transmitted precepts as guides for how to behave in situations involving moral, social, and political issues. Although they share a common bond, most members of an electronic community may never see each other. Political power structures are being changed by the creation of new constituencies tied to a single media source, but they have little interconnectedness. Mass marketing techniques, using computer identification and mass mailings, create special-interest constituencies that bypass traditional political organizations in the exercise of political influence. If media sources can get people together, they can link their constituencies socially as well.

SOCIAL EFFECTS OF DIFFUSED INNOVATIONS

Analysis of the diffusion of innovation must distinguish between the psychosocial factors governing individual adoptive behavior and the impact of widespread adoptions on the society at large. Significant innovations create new industries, alter institutional practices, and restructure the patterns of life. The development of the computer is a recent notable illustration. But benefits are usually bought at the price of some undesirable social effects, not all of which are foreseeable. For example, interactive television and home computers will enable people to teleshop, bank, vote and register their opinions about specific issues, and transact all kinds of business from their homes. The information about people's tastes, habits, values, and financial status gets stored in a central computer to which others have quick access. The invasion of personal privacy becomes a matter of social concern. Computerized records of people's actions will make it possible to determine how particular social influences affect human behavior. Requirements for informed consent will have to be devised to protect people against unwarranted experimentation without their knowledge. Many employees will work in their homes with a computer linked to their firm, rather than commute to a workplace. Computerized transactions of work and personal affairs without straying from the confines of the home increase social isolation. Television is the forerunner of communications technology, and it has restructured the nature of community interactions. Introducing television to places that have never had television reception significantly reduces the number of community settings in which people participate (Williams, 1985). The more the media dominate people's lives, the more they learn from the media, and the less they learn from each other.

The societal effects of innovations have received their greatest attention in programs designed to diffuse Western technologies to societies regarded as underdeveloped. Many of the adopted technologies and new practices do help to improve people's lives. However, some of the exported practices produce adverse consequences for the recipient cultures, rather than enrich them. Much criticism has been leveled at the ideological doctrines guiding the transcultural change (Goss, 1979; McPhail, 1981; Rogers & Adhikarya, 1979). Technical programs often seek to "develop" and "modernize" societies in the Western image through a unidirectional flow of influence. Modernity has come to be defined largely in terms of urbanization and industrialization, to the neglect of community self-development tailored to fit the indigenous conditions. This industrial type of "modernization" fosters dependence on foreign imports, technologies, and services.

When new technologies are introduced

without restructuring the social conditions which control access to them, development programs intended for the public good may, in fact, exacerbate societal problems. Recall the study by Havens and Flinn (1975) showing that the introduction of an agricultural technology widened social and economic disparities and drove some people off their land into cities in search of work as laborers. Rather than increasing social and economic participation in the affairs of the society by all sectors, development programs, which do not facilitate access to technical innovations, may unwittingly distribute benefits in ways that magnify and entrench the disparities of power in the society. In subsequent intracultural development, the advantaged sector, which enhances its expertise and means enough to assume many of the functions of the outsiders, tends to monopolize the future benefits of "modernity."

Goss (1979) argues that diffusion programs should be evaluated in terms of social distribution of benefits, as well as in terms of their aggregate utility. A distribution index, by itself, does not necessarily provide much guidance for how to select innovations that can best serve local needs and how best to implement the innovations. Verdicts about the worthwhileness of innovations ultimately rest on value systems. The same distribution of benefits can be viewed favorably or unfavorably, depending on whether it is judged from a utilitarian perspective or an equity perspective. The inequities in the distribution of benefits from agricultural technology to farmers noted in cross-cultural applications are even more striking intraculturally. The high costs of mechanized farming with fertilizers and insecticides result in the foreclosure of family farms at a rapid rate, in favor of corporate landowners who can produce crops more abundantly and more cheaply for the general public. A utilitarian might argue that sacrificing the livelihood of inefficient family farmers is justified because it brings the greatest benefits to the greatest number of consumers. The marketplace becomes the

major regulator and moral arbiter. But the judgmental issue is not quite so straightforward. Just as the distribution indicator changes depending on which constituencies are included, the utility functions change depending on the range and time course of the consequences evaluated. The farming practices that are most efficient and profitable in the short-run diminish the productivity of the land by eroding the top soil and creating public-health hazards by introducing toxins from pesticides into the environment and food chain.

When diffusion of innovations is viewed from an equity principle, however, new practices and technologies can be applied in ways that improve human well-being without disserving the less advantaged sectors or undermining the welfare of future inhabitants. One must distinguish between adverse consequences that are inherent to the innovation and those that flow mainly from the social structure into which they have been injected. Pesticides that are inherently toxic increase crop yields but create widespread health hazards, regardless of whether rich or poor farmers spray them around. In many instances, however, adverse effects result, not from an innovation itself, but from arrangements in the social system that subvert its use. If a diffusion program is to aid equitable development, it may require some social reorganization as well, so that introducing the innovation will enable the less advantaged members to share some of the benefits, rather than have their livelihood uprooted.

Gotsch (1972) documents how the same innovation creates different distribution of benefits in different social structures. The innovation of tubewells enabled farmers to grow a second crop using irrigation during the arid summer season. In the social system of Pakistan much factional dissension existed among farmers, which impeded the cooperative pooling of resources needed to purchase the innovation. The development agencies gave the subsidized credit to the more advantaged sector, so that the larger landholders installed the profitable irrigation system, whereas virtually none of those with small landholdings did. In the more cooperatively structured system of Bangladesh, the owners of minifarms formed cooperatives to install, in partnership, the technology they could not afford on their own and nearly doubled their benefits. Thus, technology widened the disparity between social and economic classes in one society and produced shared benefits in another one.

Development agencies are usually created to propagate technical innovations. Their location and operating procedures determine the ease of access to innovations and where the innovations will spread (Brown, 1981). Such agencies generally offer the greatest assistance to those who are better off, because they tend to be more knowledgeable, have the capital, or are good loan risks, and they command the social power to get preferred treatment. In an effort to produce more equitable benefits, Roling, Ascroft, and Chege (1976) instructed development agencies to identify less advantaged farmers who had consistently passed up agricultural innovations. After they were taught the innovation and were given loans, virtually all adopted the innovation and passed it on to others. Their previous nonadoptive behavior reflected access barriers, rather than personal resistances, to innovation.

Analyses of transcultural diffusion of innovations often confound at least three issues that need to be disentangled. These include the values and doctrines guiding development programs, the manner in which a development program is implemented, and the nature and scope of the theory of diffusion itself. When innovations transform sociocultural patterns without serving the people well, the fault lies primarily in the doctrine of the diffusion program. In such instances, the innovations being injected into the culture serve the interests of the outsiders better than they do the inhabitants of the host country.

When an innovation is highly functional in the recipient society, but it benefits a few at the expense of many because of the failure to create widespread access to the innovation, the fault lies mainly in its implementation. The development or modification of social agencies to assure opportunities for access should be considered as much a part of the innovation as the technology itself. Otherwise, developers become technocrats for hire, altering communities without much regard to the social consequences of their activities. The social component of a diffusion strategy is often addressed in sweeping terms calling for the need to transform the entire social system. The society may well need major changes. But since developers view direct societal change as outside their purview, wide-reaching prescripts provide excuses for evading otherwise achievable changes in agencies that superintend a particular innovation to spread its benefits. When efforts to diffuse a functional innovation produce unwanted consequences because the guiding theory neglects the critical determinants and processes of diffusion, the fault lies in the theory. Problems of doctrine and implementation should not be confused with problems of theory.

Conceptions of cross-cultural application of the diffusion model are sometimes criticized as being excessively psychological. In such evaluations, psychological tends to be equated with an individualistic focus and a motivational perspective, in which personality dispositions are thought to govern adoptive behavior. We have seen in an earlier chapter that there is no monolithic psychological theory. Rather, psychological theories come in varied forms, and they differ markedly as to their models of casuality. Social cognitive theory subscribes to neither the individual focus, nor the dispositional premise of causality. It analyzes human motivation and behavior from a social cognitive perspective in which personal and social factors act bidirectionally to produce effects. To understand the psychological mechanisms by which psychosocial factors affect adoptive behavior is hardly an impediment to developing and implementing diffusion programs. Whatever the modes and channels of influence might be, the aggregate adoption rates represent the outcomes of particular confluences of influences operating on particular individuals. Influences are only probabilistically related to adoptive decisions. Hence, knowledge of how particular influences affect adoptive behavior provides better guidelines for diffusion programs than acting in ignorance of the operative psychological mechanisms. Lack of such knowledge results in prescriptive ambiguity on how to achieve desired results reliably. When transcultural diffusion programs produce inequitable distribution of benefits, such outcomes stem more from failure to address the social and power structures superintending the flow of diffusion than from a psychological bias of diffusion theory. Defective theories can spawn faulty programs, but theory should be judged on its merits, rather than by its disciplinary affiliation. It is not psychology, sociology, or economics that govern human behavior, but rather conjunction of determinants, however they may be arbitrarily apportioned to the different disciplines.

Development of significant innovations usually requires great investment of time, effort, and resources. The pattern of human progress will be partly determined by the innovative endeavors to which societies allocate their resources. Variations in incentive systems create large imbalances in what gets innovated and socially diffused. The incentives are most favorable for technical innovations that can yield good financial returns to commercial organizations willing to spend the time and money to develop them. Hence, they make large investments in research and development and in marketing what they produce. To maintain incentives for innovation, a lengthy patent life is granted that ensures a long period of financial benefits.

What is commercially most profitable is not necessarily socially most beneficial. Innovations that bring a low rate of return to commercial firms, but high social benefits, are likely to remain underdeveloped or undeveloped, unless society is willing to subsidize them (Mansfield et al., 1977). The neglect is greatest in the case of psychosocial technologies. Much of the public is apprehensive that such techniques will inevitably be misused for social control, and governmental officials are not all that keen on subsidizing the development of methods for reorganizing social systems. Nor do psychosocial technologies hold much commercial interest, because psychological knowledge usually designates processes and social techniques for effecting personal and social change, rather than producing a continual flow of marketable products. As a result of seriously imbalanced development, the capacity to create physical technologies with potentially harmful consequences outstrips the social capacity to manage them effectively.

SOCIOCULTURAL DIFFUSION

Societies are continuously faced with pressures to change some of their traditional practices in efforts to improve the quality of life. These benefits cannot be accomplished without displacing some entrenched customs and introducing new social organizations and technologies. The benefits of change thus carry costs. The basic processes governing diffusion of innovations within a society operate similarly in the intercultural promulgation of new ideas and practices. There are some notable differences, however. Foreign practices are rarely adoptable in their entirety. Rather, imported elements are usually synthesized with indigenous patterns into new forms of mixed origins. In many instances, it is functional equivalents rather than exact replicas of foreign ways that are adopted. In addition to reshaping borrowed elements, advocates of new practices are likely to encounter stronger opposition in the diffusion of behavior from one culture to another than they do within the same culture.

Obstacles to Change

Adopting new practices initially creates negative effects that serve as barriers to change. Some of these are inherent in the acquisition process itself, during early stages of transition. To learn new ways of living requires expending much time and effort and disrupting secure routines. People are reluctant to go through the tedious process of developing new habits. Any insecurities they harbor concerning their competencies are reactivated. Adoption of innovations involving complex skills that are not easily teachable is slow (Rogers & Shoemaker, 1971). In addition to the demands for new competencies, uncertainties about the effects of an innovation arouse apprehensions about its unfamiliar ways.

When there is delay between innovative behavior and its benefits, willingness to try new practices is reduced. If innovations proved immediately beneficial, change would be welcomed. But methods cannot be transplanted from one milieu to another without some experimentation. Preliminary applications are usually plagued with problems and temporary setbacks. It is only after corrective adjustments have been made that success may be achieved in the new contexts. Even after the new practices have been adopted to local conditions and needs, the advantages that may accrue from innovations do not become evident until they have been tried for a while. Some of the benefits of new practices, such as the reduction of the future incidences of disease, are not readily noticeable to the populace, who are not in the habit of perusing epidemiological graphs and projection curves. Future incidence rates are not the kinds of events that impel the public to action. The more delayed and the less observable the outcomes, the weaker are the incentives for the adaptive behavior. The preceding chapter has reviewed different strategies for converting abstract futures into more concrete, current motivators.

Appraising costs and benefits is further complicated because societal functions are closely interrelated. Often a favorable change in one area of functioning produces unforeseen adverse effects in other areas of life. Because innovations have mixed effects and promoters generally overstate their value, people are understandably wary of forsaking practices of established utility for new ones of possibly superior but of uncertain benefit. Those with limited means or insecure status can ill afford to risk failure. As a result, most adhere to traditional ways until they have observed innovations to be rewarding for the more willing adopters.

Innovations vary in how discordant they are with the prevailing values and practices. Innovations that clash with existing values and social structures provide additional impediments to the adoption and diffusion of innovations. Some customs are fortified by beliefs and moral codes that portend hazardous consequences for the new ways. Hygiene practices that cause health problems, for example, are difficult to supplant when people are frightened by traditional beliefs that the advocated changes will have adverse effects. The power exerted by belief over behavior derives partly from the social and moral sanctions applied to conduct that violates strongly held belief systems.

Even greater obstacles to sociocultural change can be created by privileged groups that benefit from the existing social arrangements and thus have a vested interest in preserving them. They support efforts of change that enhance their well-being but actively oppose those that jeopardize their social and economic status. They mount counterinfluence by bringing coercive pressure to bear on less advantaged members, who have the most to gain from reforms and are, therefore, more receptive to them. Under these circumstances, little change will result unless adopters are protected from unauthorized coercion, and conditions are arranged so that the new practices provide some benefits for all concerned. This can be partly achieved by arranging interdependent contingencies, which tie people's benefits to progress toward common goals.

If a privileged minority continues to undermine or block reforms, then institutional sanctions must be invoked if any change is to be achieved. Desired social reforms must be backed by legal directives carrying penalities for defiance. But privilege is not so easily contravened. Enforcement of change presupposes that the implementing agencies exercise some control over rewarding resources given to communities and their leaders, that they possess the power to impose negative sanctions, and that they have sufficient social support to withstand the political repercussions of challenging privileged groups. To avoid such problems, social agencies usually rely on authorities who are beholden to the very vested interests opposing changes which do not suit them. Without outside audit of, and accountability for, the results being achieved, vested local interests exploit programs for change to their own advantage.

Ingredients of Diffusion Programs

If efforts aimed at producing sociocultural change are to succeed, instructional and motivational factors are required to overcome the initially unfavorable conditions associated with adopting new ways. A successful diffusion program has four phases: (1) selecting an optimal setting for introducing innovations; (2) creating the necessary preconditions for change; (3) implementing a demonstrably effective program; and (4) dispersing the innovations to other areas through the aid of successful examples. Each of these phases is discussed in turn.

Among the different social segments of a society, some are more receptive to new ways than others. Foisting new practices on those who oppose them is likely to do more harm than good. Such campaigns waste a lot of effort and resources with discouraging results that only impede later applications, when conditions may be more advantageous. Innovations are best introduced in settings where members are willing to try them, at least on a provisional basis. Their successes can later serve as demonstration models for those who resist adopting the innovations because of their uncertain consequences. Modeled benefits carry substantially more force than exhortations in overcoming resistance to innovation.

The preconditions for change are created by increasing people's awareness and knowledge of the innovations. They need to be provided with information about the purpose of the new practices, their relative advantages, and how adopting them is likely to affect their lives. Both personal and media presentations serve to inform and arouse interest in new practices. Failure to tailor information about the innovation to the particular desires and cognitive capabilities of would-be adopters hampers a diffusion program at the outset (Rogers & Adhikarya, 1979).

Programs of sociocultural change often fail because they do not proceed beyond the precondition stage aimed at informing people and altering their attitudes toward the innovations. Focus on attitude change as the principal means of promoting innovations assumes that attitudes determine behavior. This approach has proven only partially successful. Evidence to be discussed later shows that experiences accompanying changes in behavior alter attitudes. Hence, both attitudinal and behavioral changes are best accomplished by creating conditions that foster the desired behavior. After people behave in new ways, their attitudes accommodate to their actions. It might be argued, however, that it is exceedingly difficult to induce behavioral changes that contradict entrenched attitudes and beliefs. Such a view assumes that there is a tight linkage between beliefs and behavior. In fact, different behaviors can be construed as consistent with the same belief. If the new practices are advantageous, adopters either alter their attitudes to coincide with their new behavior or they construe their behavior in a manner consistent with their traditional beliefs. Indeed, the process of innovation of beneficial practices, which depart markedly from tradition, usually undergoes a history of initial rejection, followed by qualified acceptance, and, eventually, widespread adoption with reinterpretation in terms of customary beliefs.

Persuasion alone is not enough to promote adoptive behavior. To ensure social change, one must, in addition, create optimal conditions for learning new ways, provide positive incentives for adopting them, and build supports into the social system to sustain them. Persuasion and positive incentives are widely used as motivators when the changes being implemented depend on the consent of those whose lives are being affected. In authoritarian societies, coercive methods are also used as inducements for the changes sought by those who wield power. The acceleration of change through coercion is achieved at the price of regimentation. There are other social costs as well. By arousing opposition, enforced change is difficult to maintain without continued social surveillance. All too often central authorities are too similar in their views, and pressures for concurrence are too strong, to ensure that their collective judgments receive adequate critical examination. When the system does not allow for the critical evaluation of decisions by outsiders, there is greater risk of misjudgment that can have ruinous effects (Barnett, 1967).

Implementing a program of sociocultural change requires transmitting the requisite competencies to potential adopters. This is an especially critical aspect of the process when innovations involve new technologies and ways of doing things, rather than merely modifying existing practices. If new patterns of behavior are to be learned, potential adopters must be provided with competent models who impart the necessary skills and who are especially emulatable.

There are many ways of implementing modeling principles, some of which are more effective than others. The three-facet approach—modeling, guided enactment, and self-directed application of acquired skills—yields the most impressive results (Goldstein, 1973; Rosenthal & Bandura, 1978). Complex skills must be broken down into constituent subskills and organized hierarchically to ensure optimal progress in learning. The activities are then modeled in easily mastered steps. Videotaped modeling and other symbolic media serve as convenient aids to actual demonstrations in teaching new practices. Effective modeling incorporates the many factors known to affect the component processes of observational learning.

Modeling is now increasingly employed, but in many instances its potential is not fully realized because programs of change either fail to provide for guided mastery of modeled activities, or they lack an adequate transfer program that serves to strengthen newly acquired skills under favorable conditions. After adopters understand the new ways through modeling, they must be provided with the necessary guidance and ample opportunities to perfect the modeled activities under simulated circumstances where they need not fear making mistakes or appearing maladroit. Various mastery aids are used whenever needed to assist people through difficult performances at each step in the process. Modeling with guided enactment is conducted in this stepwise fashion until the most difficult activities are performed skillfully and spontaneously.

Some efforts have been made to assess the relative contribution of the different facets of participant modeling to psychological changes. Modeling alone produces significant improvements in behavior, but the addition of guided enactment substantially increases the power of the method (Bandura, Blanchard, & Ritter, 1969; Blanchard, 1970a; Meichenbaum & Goodman, 1971; Ritter, 1969). Using mastery-induction aids whenever performers encounter difficulties accelerates the process of change (Bandura, Jeffery, & Wright, 1974; Williams, Dooseman, & Kleifield, 1984). People achieve rapid, continuous progress when they have the benefit of mastery aids, whereas progress is slow and disappointing without them.

Modeling with guided mastery is ideally suited for creating new skills, but these skills are unlikely to be plied unless they prove useful in everyday life. It is one thing to acquire skills, it is another to use them effectively under different circumstances. Success requires not only skills but also a strong self-belief in one's capabilities to master problems. Perceived self-efficacy affects every phase of the change process—whether or not people even consider changing their ways, how hard they try should they choose to do so, their resiliency following setbacks, and how well they maintain the gains they have achieved (Bandura, 1982a). People must experience sufficient success using what they have learned to believe in themselves and in the functional value of what they have adopted. This is best achieved by a transfer program, in which newly acquired skills are first tried in natural situations likely to produce good results, and then extended to more unpredictable and difficult circumstances. After new skills have been shown to be functional through repeated success, they are habitually used even though they do not always produce quick results.

Latham and Saari (1979) demonstrate the application of mastery modeling to organizational change. Supervisors have a strong impact on the morale and productivity of an organization. Supervisory success is achieved by enlisting the concerted efforts of others. Supervisors are often selected for their technical proficiency, whereas their supervisory success depends on their social competencies to inspire and guide others. To ameliorate problems arising from supervisory ineptness, Latham and Saari used videotape modeling to convey the necessary skills, such as how to recognize good work, bolster interest, correct faulty work habits in ways that build competence, make constructive use of employee complaints, and lessen social conflicts. Supervisors then perfected these various skills by guided role-playing and instructive feedback. Mastery modeling produced enduring improvement in supervisory competencies. Supervisory skills, developed through mastery modeling, in turn improve the organizational climate and performance as reflected in reduced absenteeism and turnover, as well as higher productivity (Porras, Hargis, Patterson, Maxfield, Roberts, & Bies, 1982). Since managerial styles tend to diffuse throughout an organization (Sims & Manz, 1982), establishing good leadership practices can yield generalized benefits.

Innovations must produce benefits if they are to gain wide acceptance. Unfortunately the benefits of many innovations do not become evident until they have been applied for some time. Such lags pose special motivational problems. Advocates may, for example, be faced with the task of getting skeptical people to adopt and continue social practices for a long time, before they can obtain any convincing evidence that the programs really bring good results. As Erasmus (1961) has noted, innovations are most readily accepted when they produce prompt, observable benefits and when the causal relationship between new practices and results can be easily verified.

When the advantages to be gained from innovations are considerably delayed, it is necessary to provide current incentives to sustain adoptive behavior until its intrinsic value becomes apparent. The temporary, substitute incentives may include financial compensation, special privileges, social recognition, advancement in rank, and other status-conferring rewards. Aspirations translated into explicitly attainable goals also serve as motivators for promoting desired changes (Locke & Latham, 1984). Many diffusion failures that are attributed to resistance arising from incompatible beliefs probably result from insufficient guidance and incentives to adopt unaccustomed practices.

Initiating the dissemination phase can benefit greatly from the aid of vicarious motivators. There is nothing more persuasive than seeing effective practices in use.

Successes achieved through innovation by initial adopters can be used to encourage others to try the new ways themselves. The greater the demonstrable benefits, the greater the dispersive power of example. At this stage, communications media can play an important role in fostering change by stimulating interest in new practices, teaching the needed skills, and publicizing the results.

In cultures where people teach more by example than by exhortation, as in the Chinese culture (Munro, 1975), modeling is regarded as the principal means of transmitting values, knowledge, and skills, Honor is the highest reward. Model villages and members who excel in the valued knowledge and skills are singled out and honored in efforts to spread the practices to other areas. Oshima (1967) illustrates how the adoption of advanced agricultural and production technologies was hastened in Japan by offering subsidies as incentives for villages willing to serve as demonstration models. The model villages were then used to publicize the benefits of the new methods. When the incentives of modeled success are insufficient to overcome resistance, direct incentives can aid the diffusion process. For example, federal grants are given to states and localities as incentives to adopt new policies and programs. Policies with fiscal incentives for adopting them diffuse to states faster than those without such incentives (Welch & Thompson, 1980).

Just as persuasive exhortations are not enough to implant innovations, nor are they sufficient to disperse them even if they are to yield major benefits. Instructive guidance and positive incentives to innovate must also be provided for prospective adopters. This point is well illustrated in the research by Fairweather and his co-workers (Fairweather, Sanders, Cressler, & Maynard, 1969) aimed at diffusing a successful, community-based model of treatment for chronic psychiatric populations, as an alternative to prevailing institutional approaches. It is difficult to alter the practices of established systems, even ones that are only marginally effective, by internal changes alone. Those who administer them either have a vested interest in preserving existing arrangements or are wary of trying new approaches. This is especially true where the benefits of reforms receive little public notice, but the failure of efforts to change are widely publicized, often with social repercussions that can jeopardize statuses or careers.

Successful innovations alone do not guarantee acceptance and diffusion of new structures and practices. Dysfunctional systems persist even though better alternatives are available, when there is no adequate performance evaluation and system of accountability and when change may incur risks. Under such circumstances, agencies can be changed or replaced faster by devising successful programs on a limited scale outside the traditional structure. Officials may be willing to risk a demonstration trial, whereas they understandably resist large-scale changes when there is some uncertainty about the costs and benefits of innovations. With demonstrated success, the power of superior alternatives can then serve as the instrument of influence. If officials are held answerable for the results of their programs, ineffective practices cannot be long defended after new ones have been tried and proven better.

Psychiatric hospitals become populated with chronic residents. The longer they remain in the hospital, the more their competencies deteriorate as they settle into a dependent patient role. Their interpersonal ties to family members and others grow more distant or are eventually severed altogether. Many lack the financial, social, and vocational resources to adjust to life on the outside by themselves. If discharged, most return to the hospital after a short time. In a comprehensive outcome study, Fairweather found that neither the patients' personal characteristics nor the amount and type of treatment they had received predicted whether they would achieve a successful community adjustment (Fairweather et al., 1969). However, one notable predictor did emerge: The more supportive the environment to which they returned, the better they managed their lives on the outside. Since a socially oriented approach seemed called for, Fairweather created a semi-autonomous residence in the community where the people lived together and operated a commercial painting and janitorial business. Within this supportive subcommunity, they collectively managed their daily affairs and led an active, constructive life. In contrast, very few in a matched group, treated in a neighboring psychiatric hospital, could make it on the outside. The subcommunity model proved more humane, substantially more effective on measures of personal, social, and vocational functioning, and less costly than the prevailing institutional treatments. Nevertheless, this superior alternative to hospitalization gained few adopters.

Fairweather and his co-workers tested three diffusion strategies: providing neuropsychiatric hospitals with detailed information about the structure and benefits of the subcommunity model, offering them on-site workshops, or training their personnel on how they can create such a system (Tornatzky, Fergus, Avellar, Fairweather, & Fleischer, 1980). The results show that mental health bureaucracies are not easily persuadable, even by evident success, without instructive guidance and incentive to change. Information alone and workshops won virtually no adopters, whereas instructive guidance achieved a modest rate of adoption.

Persuading officials to adopt innovations that could supplant the very system they operate is far from the best strategy of diffusion. Unless they have little personal investment in their own practices, which is highly unlikely, their behavior is apt to be swayed more by anticipated threats than by potentialities of the innovation. Innovations can be promoted faster by persuading higher officials who oversee service systems, and thus have greater allegiance to cost-effectiveness considerations, to commit some of their resources to innovations of demonstrated value. The diffusers train the necessary personnel and help to establish the alternative system in different settings. This type of diffusion model provides both the guidance and incentives for change.

Social progress would be greatly facilitated if, as a standard policy, some resources were regularly allocated for developing and testing innovations in social services. Development funding is a vital feature of production industries, which must improve what they produce to survive. Changeability of organizations is partly determined by degree of incentive to innovate. In public agencies that enjoy monopolies over given functions, the practices that evolve are more likely to serve the interests and convenience of the staff than to maximize benefits for those the agencies are designed to serve. This is because better service to others often means harder work for the staff without increased compensation. Improvements in service organizations are achieved more rapidly by rewarding superior accomplishments of alternative systems than by criticizing deficient performances by a single system. Providing alternatives creates strong incentives for organizations to increase the effectiveness of their operations, for otherwise they lose their patronage. When services are provided by a single public agency, bureaucratic barriers to change can be lessened by creating a mechanism under public jurisdiction empowered to contract with outside specialists to devise and test better ways of doing the job. Performance assessments of how well an agency is meeting stipulated performance standards provide additional incentives to improve the quality of human services.

Communications, Innovations, and Diffusion of Ideas and Skills

The scope of social diffusion is greatly enlarged by coupling the evolving capabilities of several communications technologies. The video system can portray and edify almost every aspect of life. Two-way cable systems enable people to summon up all kinds of information and to transact activities by communicating with remote computers. Through laser pulses of light, the fiberoptic system of transmission can deliver thousands of communications simultaneously. Computer systems with huge storage capacities can provide ready access to different information and services. And satellite communication systems make it possible to distribute information instantaneously nationwide or transnationally. When these complementary technical capabilities are linked, they provide an interactive communication system with tremendous potential to inform, to teach, and to transact activities.

These technological advances create a multitude of channels for serving almost any interest and taste. The potential to provide diversity of video environments is greeted by the public with much enthusiasm. However, the economic realities of the marketplace wither the vision of bountiful choices. It is highly expensive to fill channels with specialized contents that may appeal to relatively small audiences. What gets telecast depends on what is profitable in the telecommunications marketplace. Fragmented audiences do not constitute a large enough market to support specialized interests. Consequently, broadcasters compete for a profitable share of the mass market with a plethora of programs that do not differ from each other all that much. Even with a plentitude of channels, the forces of the marketplace are more likely to spawn more of the same contents targeted at the commonest of interests than to expand the diversity of cultural productions (Littunen, 1980). The same was true for the multiplication of radio channels: It produced a largely standardized content, rather than a varied bill of fare, packaged for stations run by a few corporate owners (Le Duc, 1982). Radio is a much cheaper and adaptable medium than television, in that radio time can be easily filled with talk and music, whereas televised productions are costly and unwieldly. There are not many moneyed groups who can afford the huge capital investment and expense of operating a broadcasting system.

This inevitably concentrates control of televised fare in a few broadcasting companies.

Constraints on diversity also operate in societies that pattern their broadcasting system on a public, rather than on a commercial, model. Most lack the resources to fill the broadcasting schedules of a few channels, let alone a multitude of channels. Creating more channels does not increase the capacity to produce more programs for those channels. When the telecasting system is run by the state, political and bureaucratic forces get into the act in ways that restrict the range of choices offered to the public. In countries ruled by a single party, those who hold political power use the broadcasting system for indoctrination and to perpetuate their reign.

New telecasting services are emerging that offer some diversity in programming, but for a fee. People who can afford it gain access to specialized bodies of knowledge and to a variety of information services. Inequity of access widens the gap between rich and poor. In the absence of a public-service requirement, telecasting services are likely to be distributed mainly to the major broadcast markets of the nation which are most profitable. Inequitable distribution widens the gap between different sectors of society.

Satellite Telecasting and Transcultural Modeling

Television can serve as an effective instrument for human development and enrichment. It can teach people competencies, enlarge their perspective, and inform them on matters that affect their lives (Schramm, 1977; Schramm & Lerner, 1976). In practice, however, television is used more for commercial purposes than for personal and cultural development. Even in nations where broadcsting systems are under public ownership, multinational advertisers mount pressures toward commercialization of broadcasting. It is hard to resist the large revenues that advertising firms are willing to pay networks to advertise their products. With dependence on advertising revenue, marketing considerations begin to shape broadcasting decisions, and public service gets sacrificed. In the economics of the commercial system, televised productions must deliver the right kinds of viewers to sponsors at an attractive profit to broadcasters. Programs incurring high production costs or attracting audiences that do not fit categories advertisers wish to influence are discontinued, even though they enjoy widespread popularity (Brown, 1971).

Debates over the role of electronic media in intercultural change are concerned with the amount, content, and direction of the flow of televised influences. Most countries adopt television systems without having adequate production resources to supply their own programming needs. Consequently, they face the choice of either filling their television screens with imported reruns or restricting their broadcasting day. In the face of public pressure for longer viewing hours, most choose the former course at the cost of promoting foreign values and life styles, some of which may be traditionally devalued in the recipient society (Katz & Wedell, 1977). A few nations that are dominant internationally and possess the money and technical means to produce television programs furnish much of the input for the television systems of the world. At present, the United States, which has an abundant stock of packaged programming available at low cost, is the major foreign exporter of televised environments.

Development of domestic production capabilities does not necessarily reduce dependence upon imported fare. It is much cheaper to air foreign reruns than to create programs domestically (Lee, 1980; Schiller, 1971). The net result is that imports tend to supplant some of a society's own national culture. People throughout the world—European, Asian, African, and South American—are viewing primarily the American television serials of yesteryear. Importation of foreign programs has declined somewhat, but even nationalistic fervor has been unable to stem the flow. In most third-world countries the imports constitute half or more of the local television fare. Television has a voracious appetite, requiring a huge supply of programs to fill each broadcasting day. Viewers of different societies may cherish their national culture, but they are reluctant to part with too many of the imported television serials. What has been dubbed "media imperialism" entails a two-way transaction in which exporters with plentiful video stocks happily supply desirous foreign customers.

Some nations permit no encroachment on their culture and air only what they themselves produce. Others that can supply most of their own major television needs attempt to resist excessive foreign intrusions on their home screens by limiting the amount of outside programming. The importing countries often delete program contents they consider objectionable. For example, American television trades heavily on physical violence. Countries that have a lower tolerance for human brutality try to delete excessive portrayals of violence from the imports (Comstock & Rubinstein, 1972). Although meant as entertainment, the imported fare can serve as electronic acculturators to the customs and life styles portrayed in the television environments. Instigation of novel felonious acts in foreign countries by exported programs, as when airing the barometric bomb scenario triggered airline extortion threats by viewers in different countries a day or two after it was shown (Bandura, 1973), illustrates the potential influence of cross-cultural modeling on aggression.

Different sections of this book document the many ways in which television influences human thought, values, and conduct. Television enlarges the range of models available to members of other societies for better or for worse, depending upon what values and conduct are exemplified. The impact of foreign television on the habits of a society can be assessed by recording the appearance and spread of styles of behavior alien to the native culture until introduced by transcultural modeling. Because television occupies a large part of people's lives, the study of acculturation in the electronic era must be broadened to include electronic acculturation.

From social cognitive theory, one would expect the power of foreign televised modeling to vary with the international prestige of the exporting nation and the functional value of the modeled practices in the new cultural setting. Susceptibility to foreign modeling is increased when people consider the indigenous culture as backward or inferior, thus prompting aspiring members to accept foreign conduct as exemplifying modernity. The rate and frequency of adoption is enhanced by the effectiveness of modeled patterns in securing desired outcomes.

Direct satellite communication is becoming the new vehicle of transcultural influence. Video transmissions can be sent directly via satellites to home television sets equipped with satellite antennas. This technological advance has rekindled vigorous debate about new modes of transcultural power and cultural protectionism. When satellite signals reach the public via earth relay stations, nations can exercise some control over what is sent through their airways. If viewers pick up directly, without state encroachment, whatever satellites transmit, the messages carried by satellite channels can have worldwide impact. Whoever controls the electronic traffic and fare gains the power of global influence.

It requires huge financial resources and rocket technology to launch communication satellites into synchronous orbit at a fixed location. Countries that cannot afford their own domestic satellite system must compete with other bidders to lease satellite transponders from those who own them. Access barriers to this technology can be eased by having several countries share the operation of a satellite system. The issues of public interest, however, are not only who owns the delivery systems but the purposes to which they are put and the types of influences they deliver. A recurrent concern in the field of communications is that the symbolic environments being transmitted globally will be concentrated in the hands of the economically and politically powerful. Shifting from a terrestrial to a satellitic delivery system does not alter the usual social forces determining the content of what is transmitted. Much of the electronic traffic involves transnational business and entertainment provided by advertisers for marketing purposes. Little of it is explicitly designed to inform and edify in public service. As superpowers get into the act, some of the electronic traffic will contain ideological messages serving the battle for control of transnational opinion.

Direct satellite telecasting increases the power of one society to influence the values and behavior patterns of another. Removal of geographic and governmental barriers to access to foreign influence thus sparks debates about its impact on national cultures. Will cultural diversity give way to cultural homogenization in the image of those who dominate what flows through satellite channels? Should international policies prohibit the uninvited targeting of selected populaces for influence? Do societies have a right to protect their national sovereignty from foreign intrusions which, if left entirely unchecked, are likely to erode the national culture through imbalance of power?

Cultural interchange is hardly new. Societies have been influencing each other for ages through military conquests, colonizing expeditions, and communication by word and image. Yet, dominant cultures are not always the originators of what gets diffused. The British picked up the smoking habit from the American Indians during a colonizing expedition and then spread the habit worldwide. However, satellite telecasting involves a quantum leap in reach, speed, and pervasiveness of intercultural contact. This is because video environments beamed into homes command much of people's attention daily in every society. For example, worldwide reading of American newspapers and magazines is miniscule, but worldwide viewing of American television programs is all-reaching.

Advocates of unrestricted flow of intercultural communication, such as Pool (1979), argue that it should not only be permitted but that introjecting clashing values is socially desirable. As he describes cultural evolution, cultural development is usually prompted by outside influences and benefits from them. The adoption of cultural contents is selective and adaptive. That is, appropriated foreign elements are modified to fit the local culture and eventually become part of the cultural heritage for which preservationists then become guardians. Reasoning from the perspective of cultural Darwinism, Pool argues that telecasting diversity into the cultural marketplace expands human choices. From among the diversity, the best cultural products will survive.

Knowledge of the dynamics of power and social change supports a view of satellite telecasting that is neither as sanguine as that of the advocates of laissez-faire, nor as alarmist as that of the protectionists. As many writers have argued cogently and have shown empirically, the problem with the free-flow scenario is that the flow of intercultural influences is hardly free (Lee, 1980; Littunen, 1980; McPhail, 1981; Schiller, 1971). Those who command economic and political power are in the ranks of the senders of televised messages, whereas nations that are economically and technically less advanced tend to be the receivers. Thus, the televised environments produced by Anglo-American sources appear daily on the home screens of other nations, but American television imports less than 2 percent of its programs from abroad (Varis, 1984). Imbalance of power in the flow of televised influences arouses concern in societies that do not wield it but can be changed by the cultures that dominate televised environments.

Power regulates the direction in which influence flows intraculturally, as well as interculturally. The disadvantaged and minority groups in societies decry the fact that they are barred by privation and custom from contributing to media environments and tend to be ignored or negatively stereotyped by those who do. Others who feel that the video media should be used for human betterment decry the overcommercialization of television to the neglect of public service. The imbalance of power over what gets televised arouses much dispute intraculturally.

The cultural evolutionist view of telecasting assumes not only that there is free access to the marketplace of media environments, but that the adopted cultural elements are the best ones for human well-being. The assumption of survival of the "bestest" is as questionable as the freeness of intercultural flow of communication. Most of the fads and fashions which are widely adopted do more for the economic evolution of the promoters than for the advancement of human welfare. The global diffusion of the smoking habit, which most societies are now trying to eradicate, is but one example that argues against the notion of survival of the bestest. Adoption is often determined more by what is socially prestigious than by what is superior.

Media environments contain more than fantasies for human diversion. In the many nations where broadcasting is a major tool of marketing, media advertisers promote high-consumption life styles that deplete resources faster than they can be regenerated and that court ecological calamities. It is easy to promote lavish consumption as the mark of elite culture or as the earthly enjoyments of the popular culture. But it is difficult to persuade consumers who feast on resources built up over many generations to sacrifice some of their excesses for the benefit of future generations. Cultural productions that edify and enhance competencies do not often make it into media environments because they are not profitable to those who sell advertising time. Such cultural products are not even entrants in the media marketplace of ideas, although they may serve the culture better than crime serials that are good vehicles for selling deodorants.

Direct satellite telecasting increases the potential for intercultural influence, but it hardly pronounces a requiem for national cultures as some of the rhetoric on this issue suggests. Broadcasters will not divert their limited satellite channels to beam programs uninvitedly into the homes of foreign countries. Intrusive telecasting faces the multiple barriers of governments guarding their sovereignty, huge costs with lean returns, and language differences. Most people will continue to receive their foreign televised fare after it has been dubbed into the nation's language from domestic earth receiving stations using satellites as the relay system of transmission.

Cultural intrusion poses more serious problems for countries that share the same language, and their residents prefer the televised fare of a powerful neighbor that completely dominates the flow of televised influences. Canada is one such country that has had considerable difficulty developing and preserving a cultural identity. To avoid being engulfed by the American media environment, the Canadian government sets quotas on foreign programs, and the broadcasting system carries the American programs but deletes the commercials (Lee, 1980). However, the efforts at cultural protectionism do not work all that well. The quotas are rather generous and can be circumvented, and home satellite antennas will enable Canadians to pick up directly American telecasts intended for their own domestic consumption. Even where language barriers exist, direct satellite broadcasting increases the potential for neighboring cultural influence. The more affluent and bilingual members of a society can introduce, via direct satellite pick up, foreign ways of life into the elite culture. Some of these values and habits may eventually make their way into the popular culture. Prestigious modeling by those who have privileged access to foreign media facilitates such a diffusion pattern.

Most countries are in a quandary regarding the structure and function of their telecasting system. They wish to preserve their cultural identity, but they lack initiative or resolve in providing the resources needed to gain self-sufficiency in programming. This forces dependence on outsiders for televised fare and creates domestic disputes over the level of importation of media environments. Some of the imported contents benefit the indigenous culture, while others change viewers' values and behavior patterns in ways that do not serve the culture well. Even the domestically produced fare begins to imitate the foreign styles. Huge programming costs have promoted development of regional co-production systems operated by nations with shared values and life styles. Although such cultural partnerships lessen dependence on foreign fare, they do not supplant it.

The commercial model of telecasting relieves society of operating costs by providing advertising revenues, but it achieves this at the price of altering the function of telecasting from fulfilling cultural purposes to subserving marketing ones. Unless a society provides a viable public-service channel, sufficiently funded, to fill it with productions that edify and entertain, domestic cultural programming does not show up much in the media environment. Viewers prefer sleek imports to a pauperized public-service system that, for want of an audience, comes to cater to elite tastes. As a result, imports from dominant cultures and domestic imitations form a major part of the popular media culture. Foreign domination of a society's media environment entrusts the electronic acculturation of its inhabitants to outsiders. Direct satellite telecasting adds a new dimension to the flow of transcultural influence that poses challenges on how to deal with this new technology in ways that foster cultural integrity.

Diffusion in the Marketplace

Among innovative behaviors, none have been scrutinized more intensively than those in the consumer field. Much time and money is spent devising marketing appeals designed to gain quick acceptance of new products. Because of the important role played by initial adoptions in the diffusion process, much of the research is aimed at determining whether those who are quick to try new things possess distinguishing characteristics. If certain identifiable types of individuals are the first to adopt new ideas and products, then the diffusion process could be launched by tailoring and directing promotional appeals at them through the media they habitually use. These early adopters would, in turn, influence others by publicizing use of the product.

As previously noted, the primary determinants of adoptive behavior are the influences closely tied to it—the environmental inducements, the anticipated satisfactions, the observed benefits, the experienced functional value, the perceived risks, the self-evaluative derivatives, and various social barriers and economic constraints. These influential determinants will vary across products. Those that are publicly conspicuous, as in the case of the clothing one wears, will be subject to greater social influence than products that are used privately. In the case of highly expensive items, economic factors may outweigh social ones. For this reason, adoption determinants are not generalizable across products, unless they fall in the same class. There is little reason to expect that someone who is innovative in Paris fashions will also be innovative in dishwashing detergents. Specificity of innovation is by no means confined to products. It applies equally to the spread of new ideas, as in the innovation and diffusion of public policies across states (Gray, 1973).

Adoptive behavior, then, is best analyzed in terms of psychosocial determinants rather than types of people. Some of the marketing research, however, is predicated on the assumption that purchasing new products is determined, to a significant extent, by personality traits that promote innovative behavior. As is generally the fate of global trait measures, they have not enjoyed much success in predicting adoption of new products or fashions. Nor is there much consistency of who will be the trendsetter across products, except for closely related

commodities (Robertson, 1971). Some researchers are, nevertheless, encouraged to pursue this line of research by marginal results of weak methodologies. Behavioral measures of adoption based on actual purchase dates are not commonly used. Rather, self-reports of personal attributes and innovativeness are correlated with either purchase claims or intentions to buy. Discrepancies exist between claimed and actual adoption dates, and intentions are not always executed. Biasing factors usually distort different sets of self-report measures in similar directions. People who prize a given fashion are apt to claim earlier and greater adoption than is really the case. In contrast, those who have been influenced to do something that is socially or personally devalued will underrate how quickly and how much they adopted it. Correlations between self-report measures are, therefore, likely to be inflated.

It is often concluded from weak and conflicting findings that refinement in dispositional measures will produce better results in predicting consumer behavior. For example, Midgley and Dowling (1978) place much faith in the existence of a generalized trait of innovativeness which presumably fosters adoption of new products. However, trait measures of innovativeness have not enjoyed much predictive success. Midgley and Dowling argue that the trait is viable but the measures of it are faulty. They advocate an aggregated measure of innovativeness assessed in terms of either the number of new products purchased recently or the readiness to purchase new products regardless of the experience of others. There are several reasons to doubt that a general measure of innovativeness will remedy the usual indefinite relation between trait and behavior. People are selective in what they adopt, rather than merely behaving as innovative or noninnovative types. Since they purchase some products but reject others, an averaged measure that does not typify proclivity toward either class of products will not necessarily improve prediction. The generalized trait approach diverts attention to search for moderators that might explain how the same trait of innovativeness can spawn both adoption and rejection of new products.

Some of the problems of prediction reside in theories espousing factors that do not wield much influence over adoptive behavior as well as in the quality of measures. Measures of psychosocial factors that bear on a particular product class provide the more valid measures of adoptive behavior. The substance of these determinants is not captured in omnibus questionnaires in which the items have to be stated indefinitely to suit all purposes. Many of the predictors involve social influences and the specific attributes of innovations that vary from product to product. We saw earlier that adoptability of innovations partly depends on the interactive relation between personal and innovation attributes. Ostlund (1974) found that perceptions of a product's utility, risks, compatability, and skill requirements were related to adoption of the product, whereas personality traits commonly believed to be conducive to innovativeness had little predictive value.

Another marketing strategy is to group people by what they perceive to be the benefit of a certain product. Advertising appeals can then be tailored to the different market segments depending on their psychological profile. The problem with these profile-matching approaches, especially if perceived benefits are measured in terms of attitudes, is that they are often too unreliable to have predictive utility (Yuspeh & Fein, 1982). Small changes in the context or format of the assessment classify the same people differently. Consequently, marketing strategies tend to be tailored to more dependable factors, such as demographic classifications by age, sex, and socioeconomic level, which predict consumer behavior.

Readers will recognize many of the controversies of traditional theories of personality—dispositional determinants, trait

and profile predictors, aggregation, psychodynamic versus actuarial predictors—in marketing theory and in research on the life span of a product's sales. The predictors that such approaches favor do not seem to carry much weight. In contrast, particularized measures of relevant psychosocial determinants of consumer behavior contribute to prediction. Improvements in prediction, however, do not necessarily ensure control over the diffusion process. Some factors that strongly influence purchase decisions, such as income, are easily measured but are not manipulatable. The knowledge that relative benefits expedite adoption does not help marketing specialists much if the products they are trying to promote do not provide much in the way of new benefits. Advertising appeals may raise initial sales by suggesting illusory benefits, but they risk creating discontented adopters, who discourage others from trying the product.

In sum, modeling and other forms of persuasory appeals serve as the principal conveyances of influence, but those who have access to instruments of influence can exercise only partial control over the diffusion process. Not everything that is modeled becomes popular. The dispositional characteristics are of limited value in predicting who, from among the large assortment of potential adopters, will be the most receptive. Social and economic factors, which partly regulate adoptive behavior, set limits on the power of persuasion. Nevertheless, by operating on the determinants they can control, marketers help shape public tastes and life styles.

The impact of this influence on human welfare provokes spirited debates. Members of the business community argue that, by introducing beneficial products and disseminating information about them, marketing practices serve to enrich the quality of life. Social critics—pointing to the superficiality of commercially contrived wants, the wastefulness of extravagant consumption, and the corrupting influence of deceptive persuasion—contend that the benefits consumers may derive are not without personal and social costs.

Diffusion of Aggression

Many instances of social diffusion involve activities that are not only socially allowed but are also commercially promoted. The adoption process, as revealed by incidence rates, is similar for activities that are socially disallowed. The spread of new styles of collective protest and aggression, for example, conforms to the generalized diffusion pattern (Bandura, 1973). However, the rate with which disapproved patterns are adopted is generally slower, and the extent of their adoption is much lower. As a rule, there is a greater time lag in widespread adoption of dissocial than of prosocial styles of behavior. There are a lot of counterinfluences to overcome for behavior that carries heavy costs.

Collective Protest. Modes of collective protest that effect change are not ' only adopted by other people facing similar difficulties, but they also tend to spread to other troublesome areas. The civil rights movement, which itself was modeled on Gandhi's crusade of nonviolent resistance (King, 1958), provided the model for other protest campaigns aimed at eliminating injustices and detrimental social practices. The model of nonviolent collective protest spread to the Vietnam antiwar movement, to other disadvantaged groups, and to the antinuclear movement.

The turbulent sixties witnessed the rapid diffusion of more aggressive styles of collective protest. The urban riot in the Watts area of Los Angeles quickly grew into a national phenomenon following a common pattern of burning property, looting, and sniper fire in city after city (Kerner, 1968). The aversive conditions of life in the ghettos of the cities provided the preconditions for violent responses. The particular location and timing of riots seemed to depend on a precipitating event of police provocation. Almost every urban riot was sparked by a

provocative police encounter with a ghetto resident that provoked onlookers to retaliatory violence (Levy, 1968). The fact that fortuitous encounters served as the precipitants of riots made it difficult to predict, from the adverse preconditions alone, which cities would experience a civil disturbance and when it might happen (Caplan, 1970; Lieberson & Silverman, 1965). Modeling, however, was a good predictor of the form the collective protest would take.

The campus protest movement at Berkeley against the Vietnam War served as the model for the sit-in method of protest in universities throughout the country (Gurr, 1979). The peaceful sit-in was supplanted by progressively more violent forms of protest, graduating to disruptions of university functions, and eventually to the trashing of buildings. Modeling influences can substantially alter the personal attributes that correlate with militant action over time. In the student protest movement, socially minded students at prominent universities established the mode of protest. Like most forms of prestigious modeling, the pattern was eventually adopted by students with diverse characteristics at different educational institutions. When modeling influences gain force over time, different personal correlates of activisim will emerge for the participants in the early and late stages of the diffusion of aggression (Kahn & Bowers, 1970; Mankoff & Flacks, 1971). Personal characteristics exert less sway over aggressive actions when they come under the force of modeling and group influence (Larsen, Coleman, Forges, & Johnson, 1971).

Aggressive and Terrorist Tactics. Airline hijacking provides a graphic example of the rapid diffusion and decline of aggressive tactics. Air piracy was unheard of in the United States until an airliner was hijacked to Havana in 1961. Prior to that incident, Cubans were hijacking planes to Miami. These incidents were followed by a wave of hijackings, both in the United States and abroad, eventually involving over 70 nations. Thereafter, hijackings declined in the

United States but continued to spread to other countries, so that international air piracy became relatively common (Bandura, 1979). An inventive hijacker, D. B. Cooper, devised an extortion technique in which he exchanged passengers for a parachute and a sizeable ransom (*San Francisco Chronicle*, 1971). He then parachuted from the plane in a remote area. News of this episode temporarily revived a declining phenomenon in the United States, as others became inspired by his successful example. Within a few months, there were 18 extortion hijackings using parachutes. Publicized arrests fostered innovative improvements in this hijacking strategy, requiring new countermeasures. Once an ingenious technique that promises instant riches becomes well known, it is difficult to check its use until it fades from public consciousness. After several years, air piracy both in the United States and abroad dropped precipitously, for reasons to be discussed shortly.

Sometimes it is the fictional media that furnishes the salient example for the spread of an aggressive style of conduct. The television program *Doomsday Flight* provides an excellent illustration because of its novel modeled strategy. In this plot, an extortionist threatens airline officials that an altitude-sensitive bomb will be exploded on a transcontinental airliner in flight as it descends below 5,000 feet for its landing. In the end, the pilot outwits the extortionist by selecting an airport located at an elevation above the critical altitude. Extortion attempts using the same barometric-bomb plot rose sharply for two months following the telecast (Bandura, 1973). Moreover, a day or two after the program was rerun in different cities in the United States and abroad, airlines were subjected to further extortion demands of money to get the extortionists to reveal the placement of altitude-sensitive bombs allegedly planted in airliners in flight. Planes were rerouted to airports at high elevations, and some extortion demands were paid by airline officials, only to learn that the airliner contained no bomb. A rebroadcast of the program in Anchorage made an Alaskan viewer $25,000 richer, and a rerun in Sydney made an Australian instantly wealthy, after collecting $560,000 from Qantas. He added considerable force to his threat by directing Qantas officials to an airport locker where he had placed a sample barometric bomb he had built.

In Brazil a new model of political collective bargaining was devised when a United States ambassador was abducted and later freed in exchange for political prisoners. This practice quickly spread across Latin America as other consular and ambassadorial envoys were kidnapped in Argentina, Brazil, Guatemala, Uruguay, and the Dominican Republic and held hostage for the release of political prisoners (Bandura, 1973). Canada and Turkey, which also contain dissident political factions, soon joined the South and Central American countries in consular abductions.

There are several explanations for why similar acts occur close together in time in widely dispersed places. It might be argued that the likeness in events is sheer coincidence and that, in fact, they are not products of a modeling process. The stylistic similarity of tactics, often novel, and the rapid growth of episodes close in time would argue against merely chance matchings. A second possible explanation is that the rash of aggressive incidents is directed by a group of conspiring advocates. The spread of collective aggression is sometimes aided by visits from militant spokesmen, without organized strategic collusion. However, modeled tactics are frequently adopted in widely dispersed places by persons who neither know each other nor are following the dictates of common advocates.

It is difficult to document conclusively the determinants of collective phenomena. Nevertheless, evidence that the temporal diffusion of collective violence can be well predicted, from variables known to affect modeling, indicates that modeling influences play a significant role in the process. Pitcher, Hamblin, and Miller (1978) conducted time-series analyses of outbreaks of many different forms of collective violence (e.g., lynchings, vandalism of Jewish buildings, airliner hijackings, agrarian protests) using measures of the rate of instigative modeling and the rate of inhibitory punishment to predict the temporal course of similar violent events. The relative strength of these two sets of determinants predicted the rise and fall of violent occurrences equally well, regardless of the particular form of collective violence.

Temporal Lags in Sparking Diffusion

Salient examples are usually slower in sparking widespread diffusion of dissocial or antisocial behaviors than prosocial innovations. The differential consequences and social inducements associated with different conduct most likely account for the variation in time between exemplification and subsequent adoptions. As we have seen, early adoption of innovations that are socially valued can gain benefits for the user and, in many instances, social recognition. In contrast, behavior that is forbidden by law or by custom carries with it the risk of punishment. Therefore, it requires the cumulative impact of striking examples to reduce restraints sufficiently to initiate a substantial rise in the modeled behavior. Even under weakened inhibitions, antisocial conduct requires the coexistence of strong aversive inducements or anticipated benefits before the behavior will be adopted. People do not ordinarily perform risky behavior until they have some incentive to do so, and the conditions seem right.

Because people are reluctant to undertake activities for which they could be punished, timidity and perceived inefficacy are not the marks of those who inaugurate collective protest and aggression. Rather, the initiators of collective protest believe in their efficacy to influence the course of events with militant action (Bandura, 1973; Caplan, 1970; Lipset, 1966). After aggression begins to spread, the disinhibiting effects of widespread modeling and the anticipated benefits may prompt aggressive

action even in the more diffident. The personal characteristics conducive to collective action are, therefore, obscured when studies fail to distinguish between the initiators and those who become adopters at later periods in the diffusion process.

The discrepancy between anticipation and actual experience affects how long people continue to participate in aggression. The media usually report the more dramatic aspects of collective protest, rather than the intervening long hours of boredom and fatigue spent by the protesters. Such selective glimpses convey the sense of camaraderie and principled dedication but not the pressures of conformity, the feeling of estrangement from the larger community, and the discouragement over the failure to achieve quick results (Keniston, 1968). Many participants who are drawn into protest activities mainly by their apparent exciting nature drop out after experiencing at firsthand what the activities involve. Also, a new style of behavior rapidly loses its positive value through over-use. When the same rhetoric and tactics are used repeatedly, protest activities take on the quality of staged productions, rather than genuine expressions of principle. As leaders reduce their authenticity by trite rhetoric, their appeals tend to be viewed as manipulative and are increasingly resisted. Finally, in some instances collective protest and aggression decline because they succeed in securing the desired reforms. This removes the need for further protest.

Linear Projection Error. The effect of formal countermeasures on diffusion patterns is of interest both theoretically and for its implication concerning social policies. The course of collective aggression is often misjudged on an error of linear projection, when it is assumed that aggressive acts will continue to escalate. Expecting mounting problems, control agencies often resort to excessive countermeasures, just at the point at which the behavior is on the wane, thus prolonging the strife for a time. Formal countermeasures tend to be instituted after a phenomenon is already on the decline, because society does not fully recognize it has a serious problem on its hands until the incidence rates reach a point where they become highly noticeable. Even then, there is usually an appreciable lag between public recognition and institutional action. Hence, by the time society mobilizes its legislative and legal machinery, the behavior is usually brought under control by informal means. When this happens, the decline is credited to the countermeasures when, in fact, they may have temporarily bolstered a waning phenomenon.

Airliner hijacking provides one illustration of temporal lag. The electronic inspection of passengers and carry-on luggage was introduced about a year after hijackings had dropped sharply but for other reasons. Airline personnel had developed improved ways of identifying and thwarting hijackers, thus greatly reducing their chances of success. In addition, the extensive diffusion of hijacking had prompted international agreements, so that hijackers could no longer find any place to land their pirated aircraft. This produced a sharp decline in hijackings before the electronic surveillance systems were installed.

The pattern described above is by no means unique to aggression. From time to time there has been a rise in the number of persons using heroin for the first time (de Alacron, 1969; Dupont & Greene, 1973; Hughes, Barker, Crawford, & Jaffe, 1972). During each cyclical change, the incidence of new heroin users rises sharply and then declines rapidly, leaving many chronic addicts in its wake. Data published by Hughes and his colleagues show that the most severe legal penalties for possession and sale of narcotics are usually instituted well after the incidence of new users has declined. The authors provide evidence that informal social controls are playing the major role in curtailing further spread of addictive behavior. Rising drug costs, due to high demand and heroin seizures during the peak period, discourage new users who might otherwise be tempted to try it. After a community accumulates a substantial number of heroin addicts, it begins to experience the deleterious effects of criminal addiction. Drug use that has been grudgingly tolerated by a community as a new subcultural style is repudiated when it degenerates into criminally oriented activity (Dupont & Greene, 1973; Hughes et al., 1972). As the dangers of drug abuse become more visible, as evidenced by the arrest and debilitation of acquaintances, others are less willing to risk experimenting with drugs. Increased media reports of drug arrests and the hazards of addiction serve as additional dissuaders.

Epidemiological intervention strategies try to halt the spread of heroin use in its early stages (Hughes & Crawford, 1972). This approach seeks to identify quickly the newly addicted and to treat them so that they do not transmit the habit to others. By concentrating the initial efforts on the most influential spreaders, the course of the diffusion process can be altered. There are many obstacles, however, to implementing such a program. Heroin use is generally spread through friendship networks by persons who are in the early stages of experimentation and have not yet experienced the aversive consequences of addiction (Brown, Greene, & Turner, 1976). Early users who find that heroin gives them pleasant experiences and are naive about their capability to control the use of the substance have little desire to change. Because each initiator inducts only a few new users, to check the diffusion process would require finding a large number of spreaders and persuading them to give up what they like doing.

Triggering Lethal Acts by Publicized Fatalities

Evidence from diverse lines of research reveals that exposure to media violence can heighten aggression (Bandura, 1973; Liebert, Sprafkin, & Davidson, 1982; Murray, 1980). Such findings present some basis for examining whether publicized fatalities may trigger lethal acts as well. Incidents of media-inspired crimes against property and homicides are not all that uncommon (Hendrick, 1977). Consider a few examples. An adolescent ruminates on reports of Speck's mass murder of nurses and Whitman's mass shooting of students, until one day the adolescent himself goes on a killing spree in a beauty salon (*The New York Times*, 1966). A brooding, jealous husband recounts how he sought out and shot his former friend after observing how easy it is to kill a human being after seeing numerous reruns of Oswald shot on television (*Portland Press Herald*, 1963). An elderly retiree embarks on a brief robbery career when, in his words, television robbery "looked so easy that it became a fixation" (*San Francisco Chronicle*, 1975).

Aberrant acts are generally produced by the confluence of several unusual factors, such that, if any one of them were absent, the event would not have occurred. In a large population, some of the viewing public may experience the necessary preconditions to which the media influence adds the triggering ingredient for the lethal action. In the rhetoric on this topic, the issue of media effects is often miscast and debated in terms of whether the media influence functions as the sole cause of behavior. Because behavior requires the coexistence of multiple determinants, the pertinent issue is whether the media influences operate as an important ingredient in the multiple causation of behavior, rather than as the sole cause of human action.

Phillips (1985) has applied time-series analyses to quantify the prevalence of media-instigated acts of violence. In this approach, the rate of violent acts occurring a week after a publicized violent incident is compared with the rate the week before, on the same days of the week. The matching procedure controls for weekday, monthly, and seasonal fluctuations, and for time trends in violent behavior. Analysis of the social impact of natural events publicized in the media provides a natural kind of experiment, if certain conditions obtain: The comparison periods before and after the event are well matched; sound measures of the effects are available; there is good theoretical specification of other factors that can cause such effects for applying the appropriate statistical controls; and sound measures of the other possible causes are available as well. The value of this approach is limited when the effects are poorly measured and statistical controls for other potential causes are dictated more by availability of data than by theoretical specification. Analyses that meet most of the methodological requirements show that violence publicized in the media triggers a brief, sharp rise in violent acts that usually peaks three or four days afterwards.

Suicides by movie stars and other celebrated people have been known to set off a wave of suicides. For example, in the month after Marilyn Monroe committed suicide, the level of suicides rose by 12 percent (Phillips, 1974). Fame brings widespread public notice of self-inflicted death. Publicized suicides even by less famous people spark suicides as well. Hence, the idea planted by publicized example, rather than celebrity status, seems to be the important instigating factor. Publicized accounts of suicides stimulate a brief rise in suicides a few days later (Phillips, 1977, 1985). It is suspected that some suicides are disguised as motor-vehicle accidents to avoid the stigma of suicide for the family and the nonpayment of life-insurance claims. Deaths of drivers alone in a vehicle in single automobile crashes increase just after a publicized suicide, whereas fatalities from multiple auto crashes do not, nor do minor auto injuries either. The effect of publicized suicides on vehicular fatalities is replicated across different regions and times (Bollen & Phillips, 1981). The more publicity devoted to a suicide, the greater the rise in automobile fatalities in the following week. Closeness in age to the publicized suicide increases its instigative impact.

Variations in the form of the exemplified fatalities produce corresponding variations in the instigated acts. Whereas reports of a single suicide increase single auto fatalities, publicizing a murder-suicide briefly increases fatal auto crashes where passengers are present, an action by which a driver bent on murder can commit both suicide and homicide in the guise of an accident. Similarly, fatal crashes of private planes with passengers on board rise sharply after publicized murder-suicides, but plane crashes with the pilot flying alone do not. Such findings suggest that some multifatality crashes may be murder-suicides made to appear as airplane accidents.

Reported natural deaths of famous people do not affect suicide rates (Phillips, 1974). This suggests that rises in self-inflicted deaths just after a highly publicized suicide reflect a modeling process, rather than merely grief over the news of the deaths of celebrities. Phillips finds that suicides that are reported but not prominently featured do not have such an instigative effect. Thus, it is possible to inform the public of newsworthy events without spreading the tragedy that one is reporting. Unfortunately, newspapers and newscasting, especially at local levels, thrive on the exploitation of human tragedy. The generality of the modeling phenomena is further revealed in studies showing that acts of violence that command national attention stimulate, similarly, a brief rise in homicides (Phillips, 1983). The more publicized the violent events, the greater the rise in homicides.

The evidence taken as a whole reveals that the degree of the rise in media-instigated acts of violence co-varies with the amount of publicity given an incident, the geographic area where the incident is most publicized, age similarities, and the particular form the publicized fatality takes. Such multiple co-variations lend credence to the activation of a modeling phenomenon. The rise lags by a couple of days rather than occurring instantly. Several factors may account for the brief lag. Media influences affect conduct through cognitive processing and in interaction with other determinants operating in a person's life. Anecdotal reports suggest that when ideas picked up from the media get translated into violent action, they generally do so through a ruminative process in which the ideas come to dominate the person's consciousness and are elaborated to fit personal circumstances. It is highly unlikely that the media influence occurs synchronously with the coexistence of all the other factors needed to prompt aberrant behavior immediately following the exposure. By keeping the idea alive, however, cognitive revivication increases the chances that the right combination of factors may occur together or be created by a person bent on violence. The decision to commit suicide or homicide is not taken lightly, nor is it without conflict. It takes time to weaken restraints sufficiently for aberrant thought to gain expression in violent action. Even a decision to act requires the time and the resources to carry it out. All these factors create a time lag during which the modeling process set in motion by a media influence can become realized.

Diffusing Health Practices

Analyses of the determinants of health reveal that psychosocial factors, in interaction with biological factors, play a crucial role in human health and illness. Psychosocial factors can affect neuroendocrine and other physiological systems in ways that impair bodily functions and alter vulnerablity to infectious agents. Some of the mechanisms mediating these effects are analyzed in other sections of this book. The present discussion is concerned mainly with the impact of life-style habits on health and how habits contributing to bodily dysfunctions can by altered at a community-wide level.

In a comprehensive analysis of mortality rates within and between countries, Fuchs (1974) has shown that expenditures for medical care have only a small impact on life expectancy. However, improvements in the quality of preventive medicine and immunization programs affect how long people will live. Apart from genetic endowment, which is unchangeable, physical health is largely determined by life-style habits and environmental conditions. People suffer physical impairments and die prematurely mostly because of preventable bad habits. They eat too much, thus accumulating pounds that strain their physiological systems; or they eat the wrong things, such as fatty foods that clog the arteries or excessive salt that drives up the blood pressure; their sedentariness weakens their cardiovascular capabilities and physical fitness; their heavy drinking degenerates their liver if it doesn't maim or kill them on the highway before then; their inadequate skills for coping with stress produce wear and tear on the body; and their cigarette smoking creates a major health hazard for cancer, respiratory disorders, and heart disease. With regard to injurious environmental factors, industrial and agricultural practices inject carcinogens and harmful pollutants into the air we breath, the food we eat, and the water we drink, all of which take a heavy toll on the body. From the psychobiologic perspective on health, changing life-style habits and environmental practices yield the largest health benefits.

Fries and Crapo (1981) have marshalled a large body of evidence that the upper limit of the human life span is set biologically at about 100 years. People come equipped with reserves in organ functions far in excess of what they need. As they grow older, they experience a gradual decline in the large reserve of physiological functions. This increases susceptibility to disease and debility. The elimination of infectious diseases has increased life expectancy, so that minor dysfunctions have more time to develop into chronic diseases. Thus, the goal is to maximize the duration of the life span during which people remain healthy and psychologically adept. As Fries and Crapo explain, this requires retarding the decline in physiological functions and forestalling the development of chronic disease. Psychosocial factors largely determine how much of the potential life span is realized and the quality of the life that is lived.

The biomedical approach to health, which is strongly oriented more toward bodily dysfunctions, can have only a limited impact on the quality of health in a society. Disease-oriented services may retard the progression of debilities and provide some relief from ailments. But a broader socially oriented approach is needed to enhance and maintain physical well-being in the society at large. People's health is largely in their own hands rather than in those of physicians. To prevent the ravages of disease, people must be provided with the knowledge and skills to exercise control over their habits and the environmental conditions that impair their health.

In an innovative program of research, Maccoby and Farquhar (1975) drew on knowledge of epidemiology, communications, and social learning of self-regulatory skills to reduce the risk of cardiovascular disease in entire communities. Successful self-directed change rests on the various factors discussed earlier in the social cognitive model of diffusion. The first concerns motivational preconditions. Aversive experiences usually serve as forceful inducements for personal change. Tension, discomfort, and pain motivate people to consider programs that might bring them relief from personal distress. For people considering adopting habits conductive to health, or forsaking detrimental ones that have not yet produced any pain or recognizable adverse effects, these aversive motivators of change may be relatively weak.

Not only are the aversive motivators weak, but the process of change itself often creates temporary discomforts. Many detrimental habits are immediately rewarding, whereas the adverse effects are slowly cumulative and delayed. People may enjoy smoking now, but they do not suffer the full negative consequences until years later. Smokers experience discomfort when they first give up cigarettes, until their smoking urges abate, and they begin to feel better.

In fostering self-directed change it is necessary to enlist potential sources of motivation and to develop new ones. Maccoby and

Farquhar used the mass media at a community level to inform the public about how personal habits affect the risk of premature heart disease and about how to alter risk-related behaviors of long standing. Multimedia campaigns serve to arouse interest in health programs and to translate the likely future debilities of detrimental habits into current concerns.

People need to be provided not only with reasons to change but also with the means to do it. Effective self-regulation of behavior requires certain skills. People have to learn how to monitor the behavior they seek to change, how to set themselves proximal goals to motivate and guide their efforts, and how to arrange incentives for themselves to put forth the effort necessary to accomplish the changes they seek. We shall consider in a later chapter the different subfunctions of self-directedness and the mechanisms through which they produce their effects.

To teach self-regulatory skills, Maccoby and Farquhar devised self-help manuals providing explicit guides for reducing weight, exercising, eliminating smoking, and changing dietary patterns to decrease consumption of saturated fat, salt, cholesterol, and alcohol. In follow-up assessments, residents in the control community showed little change on the factors related to cardiovascular disease, whereas residents in two communities, who received the media program in self-directed change, achieved a net risk reduction of about 20 percent (Farquhar et al., 1977; Meyer et al., 1980). Participants at high risk, who had more to change, achieved even greater risk reductions. The risk index included smoking, systolic blood pressure, plasma cholesterol, and weight. In one of the treatment communities, a subset of residents at high risk for heart disease also received personalized instructions by health personnel using modeling and guided practice of self-regulatory skills. The addition of personalized instruction increased diffusion of information in the community about ways of preventing heart disease (Meyer, Maccoby, & Farquhar,

1977), it accelerated reduction in risk factors, and contributed to effective maintenance of those changes in subsequent years. The added benefits of personalized influence were especially evident in refractory habits, such as smoking. As people change, they serve as diffusers of health habits to others in the community. Perhaps for this reason, at least some personalized instruction improves long-term maintenance of changes.

People effect self-directed change when they understand how personal habits contribute to their well-being, are taught how to modify them, and have the self-belief in their capabilities to mobilize the necessary effort. However, personal change occurs within a network of social influences. Depending on their nature, social influences can aid, retard, or undermine efforts at personal change. When changes are promoted mainly by outsiders, community efforts may decline after the projects cease.

Influences rooted in indigenous sources generally have greater sustaining power than those applied by outsiders for a limited time. A major benefit of community-mediated programs is that they can mobilize the power of established community networks of influence for transmitting knowledge and cultivating beneficial patterns of behavior. There are several ways in which a community-mediated approach is a potentially powerful vehicle for promoting both personal and social change. It provides an effective means for creating the motivational preconditions of change, for enlisting natural social incentives for adopting and maintaining beneficial habits, for modeling and improving self-regulatory skills, and for diffusing new patterns of behavior across groups and over time. Indigenous adopters usually serve as more influential exemplars and persuaders than do outsiders.

The work of Alinsky, an astute community organizer, exemplifies successful community mobilization for social change (Alinsky, 1971; Peabody, 1971). Because he was teaching subordinated groups of people how to change inequitable social practices, a central feature of Alinsky's model is concerned with how to organize and exercise collective power. The organizational efforts in this approach are aimed at building community self-determination. Outside organizers enter the community as consultants by invitation only. The residents play a major role in selecting common goals for which broad support is enlisted by appeal to their self-interests. To ensure that local power bases survive over time, indigenous leadership is developed along with efficient problem-solving mechanisms.

To capitalize on the benefits of personal influence and to extend the applicability of their diffusion model, Farquhar and Maccoby have adopted an organizational-dissemination system (Farquhar, 1984). The program of self-directed change is applied in ways designed to create self-sustaining structures within the community for promoting health. Persons in the community, who serve as the local organizers, are taught by the project staff how to coordinate and implement the health program using existing social, occupational, and educational networks. By teaching communities how to take charge of their own change, self-directedness is fostered at the community level, as well as at the personal level.

It is better not to develop injurious habits than to try to get rid of them once they become firmly entrenched. Some of the habits that create growing health risks are acquired early in life. Therefore, efforts to promote public health must address the youth, as well as adults. The school provides a natural setting for preventive programs, especially for habits plied by peers, such as smoking, drinking, and drug use. The programs that have proven most effective strip substance abuse of its glamorous image, document how the substance adversely affects current physiological functioning, as well as increases long-term health risks, and model strategies for resisting adoption of the substances (Evans et al., 1981; McAlister et al., 1980; Telch, Killen, McAlister, Perry, and Maccoby, 1982). Older peers model tactics for resistance, and children practice role-playing counterarguments to peer pressures. In this way, students develop a sense of efficacy to resist and the skill for doing it. Peer persuaders produce larger and more lasting effects than do adults (Luepker, Johnson, Murray, & Pechacek, 1983). Follow-up assessments reveal that the combined effect of value change with resistant modeling cuts substantially the rates with which adolescents adopt smoking. Drinking and drug habits can also be changed by this means.

Health programs modeled on community efforts to reduce risk factors are being increasingly applied and tested (Lasater, Elder, Carleton, & Abrams, 1984; Blackburn et al., 1984; McAlister et al., 1982). The evidence from studies where sufficient time has elapsed indicates that the preventive community efforts not only reduce risk factors but morbidity and mortality as well (Puska, Nissinen, Salonen, & Tuomilehto, 1983). Fewer people die of cardiovascular disease in a community where health habits are changed than in a matched community not receiving the health-promoting program, or in the society at large. With further improvement in how knowledge of self-directedness and community recruitment are implemented, even greater changes in self-injurious habits may be achieved.

Not all adoption failures are due to deficiencies in diffusion strategies. Some people lack the financial resources to exercise much control over their own health, even if given the knowledge and skills to do so. Poor people struggling to survive in disease-infested environments do not have the luxury of making large changes in life style. Most people who have the means to exercise control over their health are poorly informed on how personal habits can impair their health. Even in the more publicized health risks, they may know that smoking increases risk of lung cancer but not know that it also contributes to arterosclerosis, emphysema, bronchitis, as well as retarding fetal development.

Diffusion influences directed at life styles do not operate in isolation. Those who seek to improve health habits run into formidable competition. Millions of dollars are spent annually by the tobacco, dairy, liquor, pharmaceutical, and fast-food industries on lobbying and advertising campaigns to promote the very unhealthful habits the community campaigns seek to change. Adoption rates partly reflect the pervasiveness and strength of competing influencers of public consumer habits.

Some people prefer a life of excess, knowing full well it risks infirmities, to one of moderation that ensures longevity relatively free of disease. They are willing to trade heightened pleasure for a shortened life that may spare them chronic infirmities. In commenting on the diseases of self-abuse, a noted comedian, who sipped generously of life's pleasures, remarked that had he known he would live so long he would have taken better care of himself!

Life styles that do not infringe on the welfare of others should be matters of personal choice rather than social prescription. Preventionists argue that pleasure and longevity are not necessarily incompatible. For example, nutritious styles of cooking, in which meat and fish are combined with fresh vegetables and other flavorsome ingredients, can provide greater eating delight than a hunk of beef saturated with fat. Good health education expands culinary horizons rather than diminishes pleasure. Moderation in substance use provides the pleasures without the self-impairment. The health risks of substance abuse are not entirely private. Heavy prenatal use of alcohol, drugs, and tobacco by pregnant women can retard fetal development and cause abnormalities in newborns (Little & Streissguth, 1981).

Health-diffusion programs provide people with knowledge and the means to exercise choice rather than dictate how they should live. It is in a society's interest to do so for both humanitarian and economic reasons. Diseases caused by preventable, injurious habits impair human lives and impose financial burdens on the whole society. Many people pursue unhealthful habits not through informed choice but because they do not know their effects or how to change their own behavior. Disadvantaged and minority groups suffer most from deficits in knowledge and means. By providing a more equitable distribution of psychobiologic knowledge, diffusion programs help to close the knowledge gap between advantaged and disadvantaged segments of society. Huge sums of money and medical services are spent on the ravages of diseases, but little is spent on preventing them. Lengthened life span ushering in progressive diseases of unhealthy living, and societal values that people are entitled to health care whether they can afford it or not, call for radical restructuring of health services. It does not cost much to inform the public and to teach people how to exercise control over their own health. Failure to do so diminishes the quality of life in later years and imposes mounting financial burdens on society.

CHAPTER
5

PREDICTIVE KNOWLEDGE AND FORETHOUGHT

There are certain regularities in the occurrence of most events in the physical and social environment. Knowledge of conditional relations thus enables one to predict, with varying accuracy, what is likely to happen if particular events occur. This permits foresightful action. To function effectively, people must anticipate the probable effects of different incidents and courses of action and regulate their behavior accordingly. Without anticipatory capacities, they would be forced to act blindly in ways that often prove to be fruitless, if not injurious. Information about the outcomes likely to flow from different occurrences and actions is conveyed by environmental cues. One can be informed about what to expect by the distinctive features of places, persons, and things; by social signals in the words and actions of others; and by functional rules that codify observed regularities.

In the earliest period of child development, environmental events, except those that are inherently aversive or attractive, exert no influence on behavior. However, predictive signals are not treated indifferently for long. Through direct and vicarious experiences, children quickly gain increasing knowledge about everyday events that has predictive value for selecting and guiding their actions. Environmental cues can predict either other environmental occurrences or what outcomes particular actions are likely to produce. Both forms of predictive knowledge are highly useful in the transactions of everyday life.

Some of the rules linking predictors to outcomes are derived from experiencing directly the effects of different incidents and actions. Observational experiences, involving inferences about predictors from the experiences of others, also contribute substantially to this type of knowledge. Individuals, of course, need not personally rediscover the workings of the physical and social world. Each culture contains a vast storehouse of precepts and rules which are transmitted to its members in codified form by social, educational, and legal agencies. After people come to regard, by one way or another, certain cues as reliable predictors of effects, they guide their actions partly by them. They fear and shun things that, in their judgment, portend aversive experiences but like and seek out those that hold promise of pleasantness. They restrain their conduct under circumstances that threaten punishing consequences but perform the same activities freely in settings signifying desirable outcomes.

Humans do not simply react to stimulus events. They interpret the events and organize the information derived from them into beliefs about what leads to what. Causal beliefs, in turn, affect which features of environmental events are attended to and how they are cognitively processed and interpreted. Environmental cues affect the likelihood of particular actions through their judged predictive function, not because they have been automatically linked to responses by having occurred together. In the social cognitive view, contingent experiences create expectations or beliefs rather than stimulus-response connections.

AROUSERS OF VISCERAL AND EMOTIONAL REACTIONS

Environmental cues can become arousers of physiological and emotional reactions by occurring in a predictive relation. Thus, if a formerly neutral event reliably forecasts physiological reactions activated through physical stimulation, eventually the neutral event alone tends to arouse the physiological reactions or some component of them. Although some physiological reactions are more susceptible to expectancy learning than others, most forms of visceral reactions can be brought under the influence of envi-

ronmental cues by contingent experiences. As a result, environmental events that were previously innocuous can quicken the heart rate, heighten sweating and muscular tension, increase gastrointestinal secretions, raise the blood pressure, and intensify the level of brain activity.

External signals that have psychological significance can exert an even more profound influence on the body's physiological mechanisms. The study of psychoneuroimmunologic relations provides a notable example. Disease often results from malfunction of the body's immunological system. Deficient production of antibodies weakens the body's capacity to resist infectious agents or to destroy the body's own cells that have been altered by infections. There is some suggestive evidence that stress and psychosocial factors can impair immunologic functioning in ways that increase vulnerability to infectious agents (Jemmott & Locke, 1984).

The more direct evidence that psychological factors can influence immune function is provided by experiments designed to alter immunological reactivity through learning influences. Changes in antibody production and in proliferation of lymphocytes are associated with autoimmune disease and infection. To the extent that immunological reactivity is subject to cortical influence, creating psychological activators of immunological reactions should alter susceptibility to infectious diseases and the speed of recovery from them. Evidence shows that environmental factors can affect immunological functioning through learning. Ader and Cohen (1981) associated a neutral external cue with injections of cyclophosphamide (a drug that decreases production of immune cells that destroy normal tissues of one's own body) or the cue was never associated with cyclophosphamide. The external cue that had been associated with the therapeutic drug facilitated immunosuppression in the animals and thus delayed development of autoimmune disease and mortality.

Environmental signals can activate compensatory physiological reactions in anticipation of receiving drugs that attenuate their effects. This suggests a learning mechanism for drug tolerance. In a series of studies Siegel (1983) demonstrates that the analgesic effects of drugs are regulated extensively by the predictive value of environmental events. Morphine taken in a new situation reduces pain, whereas the same dose of morphine taken in a setting in which it was previously administered is a relatively ineffective pain killer. The more consistently a drug is associated with a particular setting, the stronger is the anticipatory physiological counterreaction, and the less effective is the effect of the drug. Thus, development of morphine tolerance depends, in large part, on learning situational predictors that activate drug-compensatory reactions. Tolerance to alcohol and barbiturates is similarly mediated by expectations aroused by predictive cues.

The situational specificity of drug tolerance is most strikingly revealed in the effects of large doses of heroin. After experiencing sublethal doses of heroin, most animals survive a heroin overdose if it is administered in that same setting, whereas most of them die from the same overdose if it is administered in a situation never associated with heroin. Compensatory reactions in anticipation of drug injection in the familiar setting enabled the animals to withstand the noxious effects of opiate overdose. High doses of opiates raise the risk of fatalities if taken in new settings. Following detoxification in a treatment facility, drug addicts often find themselves reexperiencing compensatory withdrawal symptoms upon return to their drug-associated environment, thereby risking return to their habit. Laboratory studies bear this out: Formerly addicted animals are more likely to relapse if given access to the drug in the addiction environment, which tends to activate compensatory withdrawal symptoms, than in an unfamiliar environment. Solomon (1980) gives special emphasis to the interaction of opponent processes in motivation in which evocation of one hedonic effect activates an opposite hedonic

effect. Siegel's research indicates that opponent physiological reactions elicited naturally by drugs can be activated anticipatorily in the presence of cues previously associated with taking the drug.

According to behavioristic explanations of how predictive relations between events are learned, stimuli become automatically connected to responses by their temporal contiguity. However, as researchers introduced more cues into learning situations and varied their predictive relation to outcomes, it became readily evident that the critical learning factor is not temporal contiguity, but rather the amount of predictive information imparted by the cues and the amount of attention given to them. In a series of informative studies, Rescorla (1978, 1980) demonstrated that the extent to which environmental events became activators depends on the relative probabilities that the outcome will occur both in the presence of these events and in their absence. Both types of probabilistic information must be considered, because a cue is a poorer predictor if certain outcomes always occur in its presence but also sometimes in its absence, than if the outcomes occur always and only in its presence. The higher the contingency, the greater the predictive value of the cue and the stronger is its impact.

In everyday life, of course, predictors are rarely perfect, nor do they occur only singly. Happenings are usually predictable by a variety of cues which differ in their degree of forecasting value. Once persons discover that a particular cue is relatively effective in predicting what is likely to happen, they do not learn the predictive value of accompanying cues, even though these other ones are also repeatedly associated with the outcome and may be equally informative. As a rule, anything that reduces the predictive value of environmental signals, by lowering or obscuring their correlation with outcomes, diminishes their activating potential. It is only after people recognize the fallibility of their predictive system that they pay attention to the disregarded predictors.

Past experience influences how attention

is deployed and what is learned in situations containing multiple predictors that are equally informative. Prior experience that a cue lacks predictive value leads people to pay little attention to it, so they are slow in learning to use it when it later becomes a reliable predictor of outcomes. Conversely, a cue that has been predictive in the past will override other redundant predictors. Both of these effects have been demonstrated by Lanzetta and Orr (1980, 1981) in studies in which a neutral cue accompanied slides of fearful facial expressions, happy expressions, or passive expressions, as joint predictors of painful events. Although objectively the neutral cue was equally predictive in all three expressive contexts, it was largely ignored when it competed with fearful expressions, which usually forebode painfulness and hence were selected as the predictor of painful occurrences. The neutral cue became the dominant predictor in the context of joyful expressions, which ordinarily do not indicate aversive outcomes, and it shared predictive functions with passive expressions, which do not bias attention one way or the other.

Thought does more than simply aid in recognition of environmental predictors. Because thought serves diverse functions, it introduces further complexities into human expectancy learning. People can develop anticipatory responses on the basis of what they are told without having to undergo conditional experiences. In such instances the predictive relation between events is fashioned cognitively. Even when expectancy learning results from direct encounters with the environment, people do not always extract the correct probabilistic information from their experiences. Cognitive biases can distort how relations between events are perceived and structured. Moreover, recognition of predictors may be necessary but insufficient for self-activation. Knowledge that events occur contingently can bring about different anticipatory reactions depending upon other accompanying thoughts regarding the outcomes. We shall return to these various issues later.

Symbolic Affective Learning

Affective learning is not confined to firsthand experiences. It is not uncommon for individuals to develop strong emotional reactions toward places, persons, and things without having any personal contact with them. Such reactions are often formed though associative symbolic experiences in which emotion-laden symbols provide the basis for affective learning.

Words that arouse emotion are widely used as vehicles for affective learning (Staats, 1975; Staats & Staats, 1963). Remarks that conjure up feelings of revulsion and dread can create new fears and hatreds; conversely, remarks arousing positive reactions can be used to foster likes and attractions. Studies in which affective learning was measured in terms of evaluative ratings (Staats & Staats, 1957, 1958) aroused some controversy as to whether participants had altered their evaluations or were merely saying what they believed was expected of them (Page, 1969; Staats, 1969). However, subsequent research using physiological indicants confirms that associative experiences with affect-laden words do leave emotional effects. When insulting comments are repeatedly paired with a neutral tone, before long the occurrence of the tone alone is viscerally arousing (Gale & Jacobson, 1970). The affective impact is evident in subtle effects that are not easily subject to the influence of social expectation (Arenson, Lannon, Offermann, & Kafton, 1982).

Affective learning can also be promoted by arousing pictures. Geer (1968), for example, established autonomic reactions to formerly neutral sounds by pairing them with frightening photographs. The role of learning processes in the development of affective arousers is perhaps nowhere more dramatically evident than in the marked cross-cultural variations in the physical attributes and adornments that become sexual arousers. What arouses people in one society—corpulence or skinniness; upright hemispheric breasts or long pendulous ones; shiny white teeth or black pointed ones; distorted ears, noses, or lips; wide hips or slim ones; light skin color or dark—may be neutral or aversive to members of another social group (Ford & Beach, 1951). A bold experiment by Rachman (1966) on how fetishes might be acquired throws some light on symbolic learning of sexual arousal through the pictorial mode. After a photograph of women's boots was regularly associated with erotic slides, men exhibited sexual arousal (as measured by penile volume increases) to the boots alone and generalized the sexual responses to shoes of a similar color. Needless to say, these sexual reactions were promptly eliminated.

Evaluative reactions developed toward a particular object may transfer along established associative networks, thus resulting in more widespread effects. This is shown by Das and Nanda (1963). After associating neutral syllables with the names of two aboriginal tribes, the investigators created either positive or negative reactions to the syllables by pairing them with affective words. Through the past association, the tribes came to be viewed positively or negatively in accordance with the evaluative reactions developed to the syllables. Affective learning through indirect association is commonly used to create likes and dislikes.

Vicarious Affective Learning

Although many emotional propensities are learned from direct experience, they are also frequently acquired through observation. Some intractable fears arise not from personally injurious experiences but from seeing others respond fearfully toward, or be hurt by, threatening objects. Similarly, evaluative reactions toward places, persons, or things often originate from exposure to modeled attitudes. Because of their pervasiveness, vicarious influences greatly expand the scope of affective learning.

In vicarious affective learning, events become evocative through association with emotions aroused in observers by the affective expressions of others. Observers get aroused by displays of emotion conveyed by vocal, facial, and postural cues of models. Such affective social cues acquire arousal value largely through correlated interpersonal experiences. That is, when others close to one are happy, anxious, angry, or despondent they are likely to behave in ways that make those around them feel good or miserable. As a result of contingent affective experiences, the emotional expressions of models generate anticipatory arousal in observers.

After the capability for vicarious arousal is developed, people can learn to respond emotionally toward formerly neutral events by observing them evoke affective reactions in models (Berger, 1962). For example, a formerly neutral event that foretells painful happenings to others can itself make observers anxious when encountered on subsequent occasions. In this process, events become arousing predictors by means of the joys and sufferings of others. Defensive behavior, as well as emotional arousal, can be created by vicariously mediated correlation between events. The mechanisms governing vicarious affective learning are addressed in a later chapter.

Developmental theories often draw sharp distinctions between associative and cognitive processes, with the implication that young children learn by association and older ones by cognitive processing of information. As we have seen, cognitive factors markedly affect learning that is widely regarded as purely associative. And associative factors, such as the regularity and the closeness in time that events occur together, affect how easily correlations between events can be extracted.

It is evident from the preceding discussion that affective learning is much more complex than is commonly believed. Emotional reactions can be activated by intricate combinations of internal and external cues that may be either closely related to, or temporally remote from, physical experiences. Predictive cues can acquire potential on a vicarious basis or by association with thought-produced arousal, further adding to the complexity of the learning process.

Once cues become evocative, this function transfers to other classes of events that are similar physically, to semantically related cues, and even to highly dissimilar cues that happen to be associated in people's past experiences.

Fear Arousal and Protective Action

A great deal of human emotion and behavior is activated by cues which have become threatening by either direct or symbolic association with painful experiences. If adequately grounded in reality, apprehensive thought can serve useful functions. It encourages development of coping skills and fosters protective behavior aimed at preventing or forestalling unpleasant, if not hazardous, outcomes. However, frightful and extreme anticipations which are overgeneralized and based upon flimsy conditional probabilities raise havoc with psychological functioning. They produce heightened anxiety arousal, create somatic dysfunctions, promote elaborate self-protective behavior, and constrain pursuit of potentially rewarding activites.

Dual-Process Theory. For years defensive behavior has been explained in terms of a dual-process theory (Dollard & Miller, 1950; Mowrer, 1950). According to this view, the pairing of neutral cues with painful experiences converts the neutral cues to threats that are themselves capable of arousing a fear drive that motivates defensive behavior. Defensive behavior that forestalls or removes threatening cues is, in turn, reinforced by reducing the fear they arouse. The contiguous pairing creates the fear drive, while the reduction of fear strengthens the instrumental defensive acts. To eliminate defensive behavior, it was considered necessary to eradicate the underlying fear. Many therapeutic efforts, therefore, have been keyed to extinguishing fear arousal.

This theory, although still widely accepted, has been found seriously wanting (Bolles, 1975; Herrnstein, 1969; Schwartz,

1978). Autonomic arousal constitutes the principal index of fear. The view that defensive behavior is controlled by autonomic arousal is disputed by several lines of evidence. To begin with, the differential latencies of autonomic and skeletal response systems pose serious problems for the postulated causal sequence. Since autonomic reactions take much longer to activate than avoidant responses, the latter cannot be caused by the former. Indeed, in laboratory investigations, defensive reactions to predictive threatening cues are performed instantly, even before autonomic reactions can be elicited. A cause cannot appear after the effect it supposedly causes. Psychological principles need not be reduced to physiological ones, but a postulated psychological mechanism concerning the relationship between autonomic arousal and defensive behavior cannot violate what is known about the physiological systems that subserve them. Consistent with the differential fleetness by which the two systems become activated, evidence suggests that routine defensive acts prevent the fear arousal rather than being motivated by it.

Autonomic arousal is not required to learn defensive behavior. Surgical removal of autonomic feedback in animals may retard how quickly some of them initiate defensive behavior, but most learn it rapidly without having normal autonomic functioning (Wynne & Solomon, 1955). Autonomic arousal may thus facilitate, but is not necessary for, learning defensive behavior. Maintaining defensive behavior is even less dependent upon autonomic feedback. Depriving animals of autonomic function after defensive behavior has been developed does not increase how quickly such activites can be eliminated (Rescorla & Solomon, 1967). Nor does blocking a noticeable form of autonomic arousal by giving drugs to phobics lessen their phobic behavior when they are exposed to threats (Katz, Stout, Taylor, Horne, & Agras, 1983). Experiments in which autonomic arousal and defensive behavior are measured concurrently provide little support for the view that arousal causes defensive acts. They are often performed even when fear arousal is absent and can persist long after automatic reactions to threatening signs have been eliminated (Black, 1965; Notterman, Schoenfeld, & Bersh, 1952; Rescorla & Solomon, 1967). Assessments conducted during treatment of phobic disorders reveal no consistent relationships between changes in anxiety arousal and phobic behavior (Leitenberg, Agras, Butz, & Wincze, 1971). Elimination of phobic behavior can be preceded by increases in autonomic arousal, by reductions in autonomic arousal, or by no change in autonomic arousal. It is not uncommon for fear arousal to diminish only after phobic behavior has been eliminated (Barlow, Leitenberg, Agras, & Wincze, 1969). In these cases, behavioral change precedes reduction in autonomic arousal.

Further evidence that avoidance behavior is not peripherally regulated by physiological arousal is provided by studies showing that neither the pattern nor the magnitude of change in autonomic arousal accompanying treatment correlates significantly with the degree of behavioral change (O'Brien & Borkovec, 1977; Orenstein & Carr, 1975; Schroeder & Rich, 1976). The failure to find any consistent relationship cannot be discounted, as is sometimes done, by invoking a time lag between autonomic reduction and behavioral change. How can a postulated factor serve as a cause of behavior if it does not operate until long after the behavior has repeatedly occurred?

In the dual-process theory, fear reduction occasioned by escape from threatening cues presumably reinforces the defensive behavior. When defensive behavior successfully averts painful outcomes, the threatening cues that presumably motivate the self-protective action are no longer associated with aversive experiences. It would follow from the conditioning model, upon which the dual-process theory is based, that cues should lose their fear-arousing potential by occurring repeatedly without anything untoward happening. Successful defensiveness should, therefore, extinguish the fear and

then, itself, promptly cease. The refractory nature of defensive behavior does not bear this out.

Research not only confirms that fear is not the motivator of defensive behavior but also casts doubt on the notion that fear reduction strengthens defensive behavior. Whether or not defensive behavior removes threatening cues has variable effects on performance of the behavior. The aversiveness of a threatening cue is not the important factor; what is important is that its removal predicts safety (Bolles, 1975). Resort to defensive behavior can, therefore, be increased by any events it produces that bode safety. Many protective acts are performed routinely without arousal because they signify safety.

Rarely, in everyday life, do defensive acts infallibly prevent aversive events from happening. Rather, some acts portend less likelihood of aversive outcomes than do others, although unpleasantness will be experienced occasionally even with the best of means. At these times, it is the lowered probability, rather than the absence of aversive happenings, that is being sought. Defensive behavior can be acquired and maintained by its relative success in reducing the frequency of aversive experiences, even in the absence of threatening cues to arouse fear and to provide a source of negative reinforcement (Herrnstein, 1969).

Social Cognitive Mechanisms. In the social learning analysis, correlated experiences create expectations that regulate action, rather than a drive state that prompts action. Fear arousal and defensive behavior are largely coeffects, rather than causally linked. Aversive experiences, of either a personal or a vicarious sort, can instill belief in one's inefficacy to control painful outcomes that gives rise to both fear arousal and defensive conduct. For example, being bitten severely by a dog can instill belief in one's inefficacy to control their dangerousness and can simultaneously produce dislike, fear, and avoidance of dogs. Until effective coping skills are developed, threats will produce much arousal and various defensive maneuvers. As soon as persons gain a means for averting painful outcomes, their fear arousal promptly disappears as they apply the coping device whenever the need arises (Notterman, Schoenfeld, & Bersh, 1952). Once they become adept at self-protective behavior, they perform it in potentially threatening situations without waiting until they feel frightened. Should their habitual devices fail, they reexperience heightened fear arousal until they develop new means of coping that reduce their sense of vulnerability. The nature of the relationship between arousal and avoidant behavior, therefore, varies depending on how well perceived coping efficacy and coping skills match situational requirements.

Appraisal of personal capabilities and potential hazards is not always accurate or rational. In fact, it is faulty beliefs that most often agitate the viscera and promote aberrant behavior. The manner in which self-percepts of coping efficacy and outcome expectations govern fear arousal and defensive behavior is thoroughly reviewed in subsequent chapters and will not be discussed here.

Acquired threats activate defensive behavior because of their predictive, rather than their aversive, qualities. They signal the likelihood of painful outcomes unless one takes protective measures. Defensive behavior, in turn, is maintained by its success in forestalling or reducing the occurrence of aversive events. To illustrate how anticipatory thought can regulate defensive behavior without having to be spurred by emotional arousal, consider a situation in which a protective act performed anytime during the month averts a boiler explosion. A person will perform such an act whenever it is most convenient to do so, rather than waiting for an agitated viscera as a signal to act and then depending on a drop in arousal to do so in the future. To cite a common example of this process, electricians, who know they run the risk of electrocution if they fail to flip a circuit breaker before repairing an electrical outlet, will perform this self-protective response without having to depend upon autonomic arousal to prompt them to action. Indeed, if people had to rely upon the nondescript stirrings of their viscera to impel them to take self-protective action against potential threats, their survival would be in considerable jeopardy.

Once established, defensive behavior is difficult to eliminate even when the hazards no longer exist. This is because protective avoidance prevents individuals from learning that what they perceive to be dangerous is actually quite safe. When expected adversities do not follow a defensive act believed to forestall them, their nonoccurrence is viewed as a confirming consequent that the defense works rather than being seen as a nonhappening. The nonoccurrence of expected adversities functions as a positive outcome (Crandall, 1963; Crandall, Good, & Crandall, 1964). Hence, the failure of anticipated calamities to materialize becomes confirmatory evidence strengthening the belief that the defensive maneuvers forestalled them. This process of subjective confirmation is captured by the apocryphal case of a compulsive who, when asked by his therapist why he snapped his fingers ritualistically, replied that it kept ferocious lions away. When informed that obviously there were no lions in the vicinity to ward off, the compulsive replied, "See, it works!"

Beliefs that have little basis in reality would ordinarily be amenable to change through accurate information. But expectations of vulnerability are not entirely groundless. Situations usually contain uncertainties, and circumstances can arise that swamp coping capabilities. Some animals do bite, automobiles crash from time to time, and assertiveness is sometimes punished, despite the best of efforts. When injurious consequences occur irregularly and unpredictably, beliefs about one's coping capabilities and potential hazards are not easily altered. If self-doubting persons do not fully trust what they have been told, as happens in severe cases, they continue to behave in accordance with their beliefs rather than risk painful consequences, however improbable they may be. What such individuals need in order to relinquish their erroneous beliefs are powerful disconfirming experiences, which verbal assurances alone do not provide. Mastery experiences facilitated by participant modeling have proven highly effective for achieving rapid reality testing (Bandura, 1976b; Rosenthal & Bandura, 1978). This approach provides both powerful disconfirmatory tests that ceasing defensive behavior does not bring injurious consequences, and confirmatory tests that one can exercise control over potential threats.

Tripartite View of Fear. Lang (1977) proposed a conception of fear as a tripartite response that can be represented verbally, physiologically, and motorically. These three modes of expression are believed to be only loosely coupled, thus permitting varied patterns of interconnectedness. It has been shown that reports of fear, visceral reactions, and avoidant acts may cohere, diverge, or remain independent of each other. Findings such as these led Eriksen (1958, 1960) to characterize verbal, physiological, and motoric systems as operating partially independently of each other. It should be noted, however, that even the so-called components themselves are diverse and complexly interactive. Physiological indices are often poorly interrelated (Lacey, 1967). There is much specificity to actions, and when they do cluster, different social settings yield different behavioral co-variations (Wahler, Berland, & Coe, 1979). Because responsiveness within each of the three systems is so multifaceted and variable, any tripartite pattern obtained with a particular set of modality indices can change markedly if other indices of the same modalities are selected.

Discordances across the three systems can arise from various sources. The modalities differ in their susceptibility to influence. Bold words, for example, come much easier than bold deeds. As a result, an influence may be sufficient to alter what people say but insufficient to affect what they do. The modalities differ in their susceptibility to extraneous influences, as well as to those selected for study. Trivial movements can speed heart rate but not affect what people say or do. High sensitivity to extraneous factors contributes to the unreliability of psychophysiological measures (Arena, Blanchard, Andrasik, Cotch, & Myers, 1983). Concerns about how one is evaluated may lead people to censor what they say while, simultaneously, heightening their autonomic reactions (Weinberger, Schwartz, & Davidson, 1979). And finally, differences in the units and accuracy of measurement will contribute to disparities between modalities.

The multisystem notion is primarily a conception of the construct of fear, not a theory about its causes, mechanisms, or effects. Indeed, to make affect, action, and cognition all constituents of fear essentially precludes meaningful theoretical analyses of its origins and functions. For example, if fear is defined in terms of acts of avoidance, the theoretical issue of whether fear motivates avoidant behavior is reduced to the empty question of whether avoidant behavior determines itself. Similarly, if fear is characterized as fearful thoughts, this renders untestable the proposition that thoughts generate fear because they become the same thing.

The field of attitude change presents similar conceptual problems when attitudes are endowed with cognitive, affective, and behavioral components. If attitudes embrace behavior, to ask whether attitudes influence behavior would be to ask whether behavior influences itself. While standard definitions of attitude proclaim its multifaceted qualities, theoretical analyses and empirical tests restrict it to evaluative cognitions. It then becomes meaningful to explore how attitudes affect action. The same is true of fear. In definition, it may be endowed with multifaceted representations, but in theorizing about it and the tests to verify it, fear is conceptualized as an emotion of fright indexed by autonomic arousal or feelings of agitation. Theories about whether or not fear mediates self-protective action and whether thoughts arouse fear thus become testable.

The biological capability for independent expression both within and between modalities has considerable adaptive value. If the modalities were totally conjoined, a fearful thought would regularly trigger flight, while an annoying one would prompt physical assault, neither of which would be especially advantageous under most circumstances. If visceral arousal and action were firmly wedded to each other, arousal would routinely trigger immobility or avoidant behavior, which would severely curtail people's ongoing activities. It is because people can confront and cope with stressful situations, despite perturbing arousal, that they are able to overcome inappropriate fears and to function adequately, even in the face of realistic threats. If, through preset linkage, actions set off corresponding thoughts, people would have limited opportunity to think about matters that differ from what they happen to be doing at the moment. Leeway for varied patterning of thought, affect, and action permits development of functional dependencies and disuniting malfunctional ones, whereas fixed coupling would be most maladaptive.

Two-Factor Theory. According to the two-factor theory of emotion proposed by Schachter (1964), different emotions have a similar physiological state. How people experience the undifferentiated visceral reactions depends on how they interpret the causes for them. When people experience arousal for which they have no plausible explanation, their cognitive appraisal of situational factors will determine what emotion they feel. Physiological arousal will be labeled and felt as anger in hostile contexts and as euphoria in joyful contexts. There are limiting conditions to variable cognitive self-labeling of the same arousal state. The source of the arousal must be ambiguous. If external instigators are apparent, arousal states are less susceptible to arbitrary

relabeling by social influences that suggest otherwise. Persons who are viscerally agitated at the sight of a growling dog cannot be easily talked into believing they are experiencing euphoria. Moreover, the social factors that influence cognitive appraisal must occur before the rise in arousal, otherwise the arousal will be attributed to whatever has just happened. Given people's strong propensity to interpret events, it is unlikely that they will experience arousal for long without producing an explanation for it. From this perspective, anxiety is a joint effect of two separate factors, visceral arousal and cognitive self-labeling of the internal state as anxiety.

Most theories of emotion assign an important role to cognitive appraisal in determining how visceral reactions are experienced phenomenologically. However, there is some dispute over the aspect of the theory involving misattribution or mislabeling of the arousal. The issue in contention is whether people who are physiologically aroused, but misinformed about what caused it, can be made to feel their arousal as different emotions in different emotional contexts, such as hostile, comic, or frightening ones (Marshall & Zimbardo, 1979; Maslach, 1979; Schachter & Singer, 1979). Evidence suggests that unexplained arousal tends to be experienced as negative affect. Most people do not find joy in uncertainty, and, as Maslach (1979) suggests, it signifies a lack of personal control which can be highly disconcerting. Unexplained arousal, therefore, does not lend itself readily to mislabeling as a positive affect. We have seen earlier that efforts to reduce anxiety and phobic behavior by misattributing arousal created by threats to neutral sources have also met with little success.

Sometimes people have several emotional experiences in close succession; thus, the residual arousal of one source merges with the next. If people have been emotionally aroused by a particular experience, they tend to respond more intensely to new incitements, as though the residual affect was combined and reinterpreted in line with the new experience (Zillman, 1983). For example, prior sexual arousal may intensify aggression to subsequent anger arousal. Other evidence suggests, however, that in many instances the enhanced reactions may be due to something about the prior activation (Reisenzein, 1983) or to cognitive disinhibition (Malamuth & Donnerstein, 1982), rather than to misattribution of transferred arousal. The operation of alternative mechanisms points to a need to measure whether residual arousal is, in fact, added and relabeled, rather than simply to assume misattribution from changes in behavior.

In a review of Schacter's two-factor theory, Shaver and Klinnert (1982) question the centrality of cognitive appraisal in a theory of emotion, because subhumans and infants express their emotions in recognizable ways without self-labeling. They argue that a comprehensive theory of emotion should begin by explaining what animals have in common with humans. However, it might also be argued that commonalities constitute only a small part of the story. Both animals and human infants display rudimentary affective reactions, but human emotions become highly differentiated and are less dependent on immediate external instigators. Chronic worriers often agitate their viscera, even in tranquil surroundings by imagining possible calamities. What differentiates species may be of greater social import than are rudimentary commonalities. For example, if animals and infants do not experience envy of another's success, researchers would fail to understand envious feelings by studying what is common to all species. Because animals exhibit rudimentary communication, one would not necessarily give priority to the kinds of communicative expression used by all species. Otherwise, a theory of generative speech, which is the hallmark of human communication, would have to fit a theory that explained communication only by vocal and gestural cues.

From the social cognitive perspective of social learning—which posits an interactional model—thought, affect, and action operate as complexly interacting factors, rather than as loosely linked components or as conjoint events (Bandura, 1978a, 1982a). Thought plays a broader role in human emotion than simply interpreting visceral reactions. In everyday life, physiological arousal itself is often generated cognitively by arousing trains of thought (Beck, 1976; Schwartz, 1971). Thought thus creates physiological arousal, as well as providing affective labels for it. Arousal can, in turn, influence thought. The prominent role of self-referent thought in human anxiety will be discussed at some length in a later chapter. Research that speaks to the role of cognitive functions in affective learning is considered next.

Cognitive Functions in Affective Learning

Affective learning through paired experiences has been traditionally viewed as a conditioning process, wherein formerly neutral stimuli are directly and automatically connected to affective responses evoked by primary stimulation. Thus, if a child has been hurt in an attack by a dog, the mere sight of a dog is likely to provoke fear and anticipatory avoidance. It should be noted that conditioning is simply a descriptive term for learning resulting from paired experiences, not an explanation of how changes come about. Originally, conditioning was assumed to result automatically from stimulus events occurring together in time. Closer examination has revealed that it is, in fact, cognitively mediated.

People learn little, if anything, from repeated paired experiences, unless they recognize that the events are correlated (Dawson, 1973; Dawson & Furedy, 1976). Awareness determines learning of predictors, rather than being a concomitant or a result of such learning. This is shown by studies of how awareness, induced through prior instruction, affects the acquisition of anticipatory physiological reactions to a cue signalling a painful event (Chatterjee & Eriksen, 1962). In these studies, persons are either informed that a particular cue will be followed by a painful event, or they are led to believe that the occurrence of the painful event is not related in any consistent way to the cue. Aware persons quickly learn anticipatory physiological reactions to the predictive cue, whereas the unaware ones show no evidence of learning, even though both groups repeatedly undergo the same paired stimulation. That awareness is critical for affective learning is also corroborated by studies using tasks that mask relations between events. Misleading explanation for the purpose of the task directs attention to recurring cues but impedes recognition that one of the cues predicts the occurrence of painful events. Affective learning occurs reliably when awareness is induced, but unaware people never learn what predicts painful outcomes despite repeated correlated experiences (Dawson & Biferno, 1973; Dawson & Reardon, 1973).

Further evidence of the cognitive regulation of anticipatory affective reactions is provided by studies aimed at eliminating an existing emotional proclivity by inducing awareness. The emotional reactions of people who are told that predictive signals are no longer informative because the associated painful outcomes have ceased are compared with the emotional reactions of people who are not told that the threat no longer exists. Induced awareness promptly eliminates fear arousal and avoidance behavior in the informed participants, while the uninformed lose their fear only gradually (Bandura, 1969a).

Self-Arousal Functions

It is because affective reactions can be cognitively stimulated that thought plays such a central role in the physiological and phenomenal experience of emotion. People can easily make themselves nauseated by imagining sickening experiences. They can become sexually aroused by conjuring up erotic fantasies. They can frighten themselves by scary thoughts. And they can work themselves into a state of anger by ruminating about social slights and mistreat-

ment. In systematic analyses of cognitively generated emotion, people conjure up neutral or affect-laden thoughts in a pattern of their own choosing, while changes in their visceral reactions are continuously measured. Visceral arousal is heightened by self-induced emotional thoughts and restored to normal by neutral or relaxing thoughts (May & Johnson, 1973; Schwartz, 1971). The incomparable Satchel Paige, whose extended baseball career provided many opportunities for anxious self-arousal, vividly described the power that one's thoughts can exert over visceral functioning when he advised, "If your stomach disputes you, lie down and pacify it with cool thoughts."

Thoughts about stressful events can be as arousing as experiencing the actual events themselves. Thinking about painful stimulation produces subjective discomfort and physiological reactions similar to those induced by the actual physically painful stimulation (Barber & Hahn, 1964). The same is true of stress reactions to events that people have learned to fear. Phobics become as viscerally agitated by thoughts about dreaded objects as by actual exposure to them (May, 1977). Phobic thinking, which is easily triggered and difficult to turn off, can thus take a heavy toll of the visceral system.

In the social cognitive analysis, so-called conditioned reactions are considered to be largely self-activated on the basis of learned expectations, rather than automatically evoked. The critical factor, therefore, is not that events occur close together in time, but that people learn to foresee from predictive cues what is likely to happen and to summon up anticipatory reactions. Several lines of evidence, some of which have already been reviewed, lend validity to this self-arousal interpretation of associative emotional learning.

For people who are aware that certain events forebode distress, such events activate fear-arousing thoughts, which in turn produce emotional responses. Those who fail to notice, for one reason or another, that certain cues foreshadow painful experiences do not conjure up these arousing thoughts. As a result, the predictive cues rarely evoke emotional responses, even though repeatedly paired with unpleasant experiences. When contingency awareness and emotional reactions are measured concurrently throughout the course of learning, the findings show that awareness precedes affective learning. Anticipatory reactions to predictive cues do not occur reliably until the point at which awareness is achieved (Dawson & Biferno, 1973). The sudden disappearance of previously learned emotional responses, after attained awareness that the threat has ceased, can also be explained in terms of self-arousal processes. Once such knowledge has been gained, antecedent events no longer activate frightening thoughts, thus removing the cognitive source of emotional responses.

Because of people's capability for cognitive self-arousal, emotional responses can be developed toward formerly neutral events by cognitive means in the absence of physically painful experiences. Several investigators report findings bearing on this matter (Bridger & Mandel, 1964; Grings, 1973). In these experiments, individuals are told that a certain cue will sometimes be followed by painful stimulation, but, except for a sample experience, this never happens. Perturbing thought must, therefore, produce the affect. As the trials progress, the formerly neutral cue becomes arousing through its association with thought-produced emotional responses.

The role of awareness in emotional learning has been examined extensively with the advent of more sensitive inquiry techniques, but the self-arousal component has received comparatively little attention. Although it is difficult to learn, without awareness, which features of the environment carry predictive value, the presence of awareness alone does not guarantee anticipatory arousal (Dawson & Furedy, 1976; Furedy, 1973). People can be aware that certain events are predictive, but they can act on that knowledge in ways that either raise or lower their level of arousal. Knowing when painful events are going to happen ordinarily heightens stressful anticipations. But when recurring painful outcomes are uncontrollable, people often resort to attentional and cognitive coping strategies designed to lessen their internal distress. They divert their attention to more serene matters, generate palliative thoughts, induce self-relaxation, and divest the situation of some of its intimidating features by cognitive restructuring of their meaning (Bandura & Rosenthal, 1966; Lazarus, 1980; Miller, 1979).

Awareness and cognitive self-arousal are separable factors, and both must be measured to gain a full understanding of affective learning. The types of thoughts people engage in will determine the strength and persistence of their anticipatory reactions. The more they believe that events are related, and the more severe the effects they conjure up, the stronger their anticipatory reactions will be (Dawson, 1966). Thus, awareness with fearful ideation will heighten arousal, whereas awareness with palliative ideation will attenuate arousal.

Some writers contend that the extent to which fear is subject to cognitive control may vary, depending upon whether it was established symbolically or through direct experience. Bridger and Mandel (1964) report that fear is learned just as readily regardless of whether neutral cues are associated only with the threat of painful outcomes or with the threat combined with actual painful experiences. Fear that develops through actual painful experiences, however, is less susceptible to change by cognitive means. Thought-induced fear diminishes rapidly with the knowledge that the physical threat will no longer be forthcoming. By contrast, fear originating in painful experiences persists for some time, despite awareness that the physical threat no longer exists.

If fears arising from ideational and experiential sources were shown to differ reliably in their modifiability, several factors could account for the results. One possibility is that emotional responses contain dual components, as Bridger and Mandel suggest.

One of the components—created by cognitive self-arousal—is modifiable by altering one's thoughts. The second component may be a nonmediated one that is directly evoked by external cues and, hence, requires repeated disconfirming experiences for it to be eliminated. An alternative possibility is that perturbing thoughts arising from pain are more tenacious than those created by threat alone.

Some writers assume that certain fears are not mediated by thought, not because of evidence that fear arousal appears without frightening cognitions, but because reassurances of safety do not promptly eradicate fear (Bridger & Mandel, 1964; Ohman & Hugdahl, 1979; Seligman, 1971). This view assumes that telling frightened people that things are safe will instantly banish their scary thoughts. Unfortunately, dreadful apprehensions are not that easily disposable. Just as telling people to stop thinking about giraffes may fix them in mind, so telling them they will no longer get hurt may keep their thoughts centered on painful events for a while, especially when vivid reminders of past unpleasantness keep recurring. When people have undergone repeated painful experiences, situational threats are likely to activate fearful trains of thought, which are not readily subject to voluntary control. Aversive thoughts, which are instantly triggered and difficult to turn off, will sustain arousal for a long time. Acrophobics, who are told that they can look down safely from the rooftop of a tall building because of protective railings, may be unable to expel quickly thoughts about the horrendous things that could conceivably happen. Here fearfulness is still cognitively mediated, but phobics are unable to control their thoughts, however safe the situation might appear. Claims that fears are not cognitively mediated require assessment of what, if anything, people are thinking prior to, and while, they are experiencing fear arousal.

Lest too much be made of the notion of differential modifiability, it bears noting that fear born of physical pain is not necessarily more unyielding to cognitive influence than is fear born of threat of pain. Contrary to the findings of Bridger and Mandel, other researchers provide evidence that fear is equally changeable by cognitive means regardless of whether it was induced physically or cognitively (Katz, Webb & Stotland, 1971). What does contribute to persistency of fear is the experience that threats forebode the occurrence of aversive events but their severity is unpredictable. Uncertainty invites anticipations of the worst possible happenings.

The powerful cognitive regulation of fear reactions in laboratory situations contrasts with the tenacity of defensive behavior in everyday life. The tenacity of fears acquired naturally is not fully known because those that are responsive to social persuasion usually do not come to public attention. In fact, naturally acquired fears are quite amenable to change (Jersild & Holmes, 1935). If only the refractory cues are noticed, the biased focus will create the erroneous belief that all naturally acquired fears are refractory. Whatever variations there are in persistency are probably due, in large part, to the severity and predictability of aversive consequences. In laboratory situations, relatively weak threats are completely removed by experimenters, who exercise full control over the occurrence of painful outcomes. By contrast, the things people fear excessively are ordinarily innocuous, but they do occur occasionally with harmful results despite assurances to the contrary. Even laboratory-produced fears of considerably less injurious outcomes can persist when there is some chance they may happen. Hence, the probability of injury, however low, can negate the potential influence of factual knowledge on action. For this reason, intense fears are rarely eliminated by reassuring information alone. Rather, frightening expectations often require experiences that build a sense of coping efficacy. Rapid changes are best achieved, not by sheer repetitive exposure, as nonmediational theories suggest, but by cultivating coping skills for rendering what is feared predictable and controllable (Bandura, 1982a; Miller, 1979).

Nonmediational theories of affective learning assume that paired events must be registered in the nervous system of the organism. It is conceivable that in studies that reduce awareness by diverting attention to irrelevant events, the predictive cues may not be registered sufficiently to produce learning. Neural responses to afferent input can be substantially weakened by focusing attention on competing events. In neurophysiological studies (Hernandez-Peon, Scherrer, & Jouvet, 1956), for instance, auditory neural responses to a loud sound were virtually eliminated in cats when they gazed at mice, sniffed fish odors attentively, or received shocks that disrupted their attentiveness. Similarly, instructions that lead people to attend selectively to particular cues and to disregard others result in stronger cortically evoked responses to occurrences of favored stimuli (Donchin & Cohen, 1967).

If people confine their attention to extraneous features or irrelevant events, they may neither experience nor recognize the predictive cue. The absence of anticipatory learning in such circumstances may be attributed wrongly to lack of conscious recognition when, in fact, it reflects deficient sensory registration of stimulus events. Proof that awareness is necessary for learning to occur would require evidence that, despite adequate neural registration of paired stimulation, anticipatory responses are not learned, unless the predictive relation between the events has been recognized. These conditions are fulfilled in studies demonstrating that anticipatory learning does not occur without awareness, even when individuals are forced to attend to predictive and nonpredictive cues equally, but give this equal attention for misleading reasons (Dawson & Biferno, 1973). The learning deficits result not from failure to recognize the recurrent events but from failure to realize that one of them is a predictor of outcomes.

Direct Holistic Activation of Emotional Reactions

Zajonc (1980) has proposed what is commonly regarded as a noncognitive view of affective arousal. Actually, Zajonc's conception of the relationship between thought and affect is hardly the radical departure from cognitivists' views it is usually made out to be. This is because Zajonc posits various relationships between thought and affect—that they are partially independent, that affect precedes thought, that some appraisal precedes affect, and that thought and affect are inseparably fused, so that rarely are thoughts affectless or affects without thought. The notions that thought and affect are independent and that affect precedes cognitive appraisal in human emotional reactions are usually singled out by commentators and are those with which cognitivists take issue (Birnbaum, 1981; Lazarus, 1982; O'Malley, 1981). However, the dispute is greatly exaggerated because Zajonc acknowledges that events must be interpreted, at least minimally, before affect is aroused, which indicates that some appraisal precedes affective arousal. Clearly, some initial reading of a situation is necessary because it is difficult to become emotional about nondescript events. The point at issue, therefore, is not whether affective arousal is devoid of appraisal, but rather how much and in what form is the interpretative activity needed to generate emotional reactions.

In Zajonc's view, affect is activated by preferenda, which embody vague, holistic features of objects and internal states of persons. Instant reactions to strangers are said to typify preferenda at work. People are certainly known to react with instant likes or dislikes to strangers, but such reactions generally stem from selective attention to distinct cues tied to strong expectations. In a case to be cited later, a woman who had a painful experience with a blind date sporting a bow tie thereafter reacted with anxious suspicion the moment she set eyes on bow-tied gents. Or consider the following case of a man for whom blonde locks are the basis for instant evaluative reactions: "I have trouble with blondes. Everytime I go for a girl and she is blonde she turns out to be a golddigger. I notice on TV whenever they have a golddigger she is blonde. Should I pass up all blondes from now on?"

Cognitive appraisal need not involve a protracted analysis of the physical features of objects as it is portrayed by Zajonc. As the above examples illustrate, cognitive appraisal or misappraisal, as the case may be, can center on minimal information that renders judgments only all too swiftly. Prototypes, defined by a few key features, and simple heuristics also serve to bring about speedy judgment. Cognitivists would advise Zajonc's rabbit, which has encountered a snake, not to waste time conducting a detailed feature analysis of the elongated beast. A simple guide—run from anything unfamiliar that moves—is more likely to keep the rabbit out of the reptile's digestive system than to wait for an autonomic emotive system that reacts slowly to tell the rabbit to flee. Shape, noise, and movement, which are instantly interpretable, provide valuable information for appraising the perilousness of given situations. The notion that affect is governed more by holistic preferenda than by informative cues is not easily testable until preferenda are more explicitly designated.

Zajonc sees a need for a special mode of encoding and activating affect because, in his view, affective reactions possess unique properties. Actually, the properties he lists are not unique. Affect is basic: So is the cognitive propensity to differentiate and categorize events. Affective reactions are said to be quick and inescapable: So are nonaffective cognitive reactions. Don't visualize a giraffe. A visualized giraffe will inescapably pop into mind. Affective judgments are presumably irrevocable: So are many nonaffective judgments. Once a person grasps the notion of gravity, the belief that one will fall upon jumping from a high

place is essentially irrevocable. Conversely, strong, affective reactions, such as long-standing phobias, can be acknowledged as groundless and promptly discarded through mastery experiences (Bandura, Reese, & Adams, 1982). Attitudes are resistant to verbal persuasion: This is more of a commentary on the efficacy of method than on the intractability of affect. Attitudes and proneness to affective arousal are changed more fundamentally by persuasion through mastery modeling than by getting rid of affect (Bandura, Blanchard, & Ritter, 1969). Affective judgments implicate the self, whereas cognitive judgments, presumably, concern qualities residing in objects: Cognitive self-referent judgment, such as one's stamina, also implicates the self. Affect relies on nonverbal means of communication: Human emotions can be more reliably and powerfully activated by words than by facial expressions. Affective reactions need not depend on cognition: Nor do highly routine acts and choices. The daily routine of brewing coffee does not require that thoughts guide each step in the process. Affective reactions may become separated from content: Contents also often take leave of affect. Travelers remember vistas while the perturbing hassles of travel fade from memory.

Theories concerning the relation between thought and affect usually define affect in terms of emotional arousal. The data Zajonc brings to bear on this matter mainly concern judgments of preference. Indeed, he often presents the cognitive-affect issue in terms of two types of cognitions—"hot" cognition (affective judgment) and "cold" cognition (feature discrimination)—rather than as two different systems of expression. In this analysis, cognition is equated with feature analysis of objects. To confine cognition to this simple function hardly does justice to the multiform way in which cognition arouses affect. The thought that stirs the passions includes views about persons and events that bestir emotional reactions, perturbing self-appraisals, and cognitive enactments of emotive scenarios. Judgments of preference or liking should also be distinguished from affective reactions because preferences do not necessarily involve emotional arousal. A transit rider may prefer a window to an aisle seat but remain emotionally unstirred by either location. The common affects addressed by theories of emotion, be they anger, fear, joy, despair, or grief, are highly visceral expressions. Other evidence that emotion is detached from interpretive processes has been questioned on the grounds that the things being measured are not emotions (Lazarus, 1984; Zajonc, 1984).

Zajonc cites experiments showing that people like familiar stimuli slightly more than new ones, but they have difficulty telling which ones they had seen before. Such data are taken as evidence that affect is largely independent of cognition. Recollections do not necessarily reflect the thought processes operating at the time events were encountered. Moreover, so-called cold cognitions can be just as discrepant from recollections of the past events that engendered them as are affective judgments. There is little evidence that people can accurately identify the sources of their nonemotive cognitions. Sources fade from memory but cognitive contents remain. And finally, judgment of liking is an easier task than judging whether one has seen something before, which requires comparing each perception against a collection of remembered experiences.

Disputes about the determinants of emotion are difficult to resolve when conceptions rest on presumptive processes that are hard to specify in observable terms. The notion that emotional reactions are triggered directly by pure sensory input (Zajonc, 1984) requires decisive evidence that sensory experiences undergo no interpretation whatsoever. People select and process sensory information, rather than simply react to whatever impinges on their sense organs. If people reacted emotionally to sights and sounds without interpreting them at all,

they would find themselves emoting indiscriminately. The notion that emotional reactions are triggered by primitive unconscious appraisal (Lazarus, 1984) similarly requires convincing evidence for unconscious interpretation.

Substantial evidence exists from an earlier dispute about unconscious affective encoding of events (Eriksen, 1958, 1960; Goldiamond, 1958). These studies were conducted to test claims that the unconscious mind readily perceives threatening stimuli occurring below the level of awareness and reacts to them emotionally. People were presented neutral words and explicit sexual words at a scarcely perceptible level, during which time their autonomic reactions and conscious perceptions were concurrently recorded. Little evidence was found for unconscious affective responding to emotionally charged stimuli, in the absence of conscious recognition. Both affective and cognitive systems are equally insensitive to perturbing stimuli presented faintly, but, as the stimuli become more perceptible, the cognitive system is more sensitive to them than is the affective one (Dulany & Eriksen, 1959). One can make a persuasive case for the view that affective arousal requires at least some minimal interpretation of events. The more radical conception that affective arousal requires no interpretation whatsoever will doubtless continue to be the subject of much debate.

Inborn Learning Biases

It is a truism that differences exist in the case with which different behavior patterns and environmental contingencies can be learned. Some of these variations are due to the physiological limitations of the sensory-motor and cortical structures with which organisms are innately endowed. They cannot be influenced by sensory information if they lack the appropriate receptors, nor can they learn repertoires of behavior that exceed their physical capacities. Moreover, the neural systems with which organisms are equipped limit how much central processing of information and central organization of behavior they can achieve.

Biological Preparedness. Seligman and Hager (1972) have put forth the interesting notion that genetic endowment also provides a specialized associative apparatus that determines how readily an organism can be influenced by experience. According to this principle of preparedness, organisms are biologically constructed, through evolutionary selection, to associate certain events more easily than others. They learn biologically primed associations with minimal output but the unprepared associations painstakingly, if at all. The ease of association varies for different species and is, presumably, even highly specific to events.

Substantial evidence can be marshalled to support specialized biological preprogramming in subhuman species (Hinde & Hinde-Stevenson, 1973; Seligman & Hager, 1972). Thus, for example, illness will readily create aversions to novel tastes and odors in many animals, but painful shock will not; shocks will establish avoidance of sounds and sights, where illness will not (Garcia & Koelling, 1966). Arbitrary responses, which compete with ones that are more natural to a species, are difficult to establish and to sustain. Moreover, animals may persist in performing natural responses even though they prevent them from gaining food rewards (Breland & Breland, 1961). Different species are equipped with preferred types of defensive reactions, which are easily elicited and strengthened, but it is difficult to teach them less natural modes of defense to physical threats (Bolles, 1975). Based on these lines of evidence, Seligman and Hager argue against general mechanisms of learning serving diverse purposes, in favor of event-specific associative biases.

Evidence that learning in lower species operates under severe biological constraints does not mean that human learning is also governed by event-specific mechanisms. Because of both advanced human capacity to symbolize experience and limited inborn programming, humans are capable of learning an extraordinary variety of behaviors under unusually diverse circumstances. They can fly through the atmospere in airplanes and spacecraft, speed on the ground with automobiles and cycles, navigate through water in submarines, and burrow underground in tunnels. There is little reason to believe that learning to fly airplanes, to drive automobiles, to pilot submarines, and to dig tunnels is governed by different innate linkages. People learn to pursue numerous roles and occupations, to create diverse social systems, and to espouse sundry ideologies without requiring specific associative mechanisms for each class of activities. Moreover, they can thrive in all types of habitats—tropical, temperate, polar, soggy, or arid. Such remarkable versatility calls for generalists, rather than innately programmed specialists.

The innate preprogramming that enables animals to deal in a stereotyped fashion with the recurring demands of a limited habitat would not be evolutionarily advantageous for humans, who must often cope with exceedingly complex and rapidly changing circumstances. Under such diverse and highly variable conditions of living, generalizable mechanisms of learning, which rely heavily on experiential organization of behavior, have greater evolutionary value than do fixed, inborn mechanisms, except in the regulation of rudimentary biological functions. Humankind cannot wait for a protracted succession of survivors of atomic holocausts to evolve a specific preparedness for avoidance of nuclear bombs.

Researchers who are concerned with biological constraints sometimes question traditional investigations of animal learning on the grounds that arbitrary responses and contingencies are selected for study. In a thoughtful review of the preparedness concept, Schwartz (1974) argues that it is precisely because of this arbitrariness that analysis of animal learning has any relevance to human learning. People organize and regulate their behavior largely on the basis of individual experience. Analyses of how behavior is wrought from experience and regulated by arbitrary influences can, therefore, tell us more about how socially structured influences affect human conduct than studying genetically predisposed actions of lower organisms.

Ease of Learning and Co-variant Properties of Events.

Variations in the ease of learning do not necessarily reflect only inborn preparedness. As we have already seen, anticipatory action involves learning about the predictive relations between events. Some predictors can be learned more readily than others because the events occur close together in time and space in ways that facilitate recognition of predictive relationships (Testa, 1974). The salience of the predictors, their number and degree of intercorrelation, the intensity of the outcomes, and how many things intervene between them also affect how readily predictive relations can be discerned. Clearly, not all relations between events are learnable with equal ease. The influential factor in the rate of most human learning is the recognizability of external co-variation, rather than selective internal associability. Rate of learning is also markedly affected by experiential preparedness. Experience makes predictive cues more salient, furnishes prerequisite competencies, builds incentives, and instills attentional and cognitive biases that may either facilitate or retard learning of probabilistic relationships.

Variations in ease of learning that are sometimes ascribed entirely to selective biological preparedness may also partly reflect co-variant properties of events. In studies creating taste aversions, for example, food flavors were associated either immediately with shock or, after appreciable delays, with nausea. The aversive events thus differ not only in their nature but also in when they occur. By delaying shock, Krane and Wagner (1975) were able to induce taste aversions that had previously been achievable only by gastric upset. Delayed shocks produced aversion to sweetened water, while immediate shocks did not. By contrast, immediate shocks accompanied by bright, noisy cues produced aversion to water, but delayed shocks proved ineffective. The authors attribute the variations in aversive learning to the fact that a trace of food flavor persists for some time, whereas the stimulus trace of sights and sounds disappears when they cease. Learning abilities unique to the adaptive requirements for a particular species do, of course, exist. However, the principal determinants of learning affect the rate with which aversions are acquired and how long they will be expressed, in much the same way across species and tasks (Logue, 1979).

It is difficult to create in animals an aversion to a taste that has previously produced no ill effects unless aversive outcomes are repeatedly experienced. Even a single experience, whether recent or distant, that establishes a substance as safe can make it relatively immune to the effects of gastric illness (Kalat & Rozin, 1973). Yet humans often develop aversions, after a nauseating experience, to tastes that are not only familiar but especially liked. A stomach upset misattributed to a bearnaise sauce can render it nauseating even though it has been a revered taste (Seligman & Hager, 1972). Alcoholics can develop temporary aversions to their favorite alcoholic beverages which they have repeatedly consumed, by pairing their smell and taste with drug-induced nausea or even with other discomforts that do not arise from physical illness (Rachman & Teasdale, 1969).

Humans are prone to revivify nauseous experiences cognitively, regardless of the familiarity of tastes that have been associated with gastric illness. Indeed, once a taste becomes associated with nausea in one's mind, whether justifiably or not, it is difficult to think of that substance without recalling the nauseant feeling. Hence, aversions can be created in humans by thought-induced nausea as effectively as through emetic drugs. With people, cognitive revivification and judgmental processes, which determine which particular element of taste in the aggregate of taste sensations is singled out as the likely malefactor, assume importance.

Selective Associability and Phobias.
Some explanations of the origin of human fears assign considerable importance to innate preparedness. According to Seligman (1971), people are biologically predisposed to fear things that have threatened human survival through the ages. As testimony to innate preparedness, phobias are said to be commonly acquired by only a single or a few frightening experiences, they are difficult to eliminate, they are unaffected by thought, and they are largely restricted to objects that have endangered survival. Thus, people become phobic of animals and insects but not of pajamas or grass.

Evidence concerning the origins and intractability of phobias is far from clear. Accounts of how phobias develop depend inevitably upon retrospective reports, rather than on actual knowledge of the totality of aversive experiences phobics have suffered. Recollections single out salient precipitating events, which may convey misimpressions that one or two frightening experiences produced a full-blown phobia. While some phobias may arise from traumatic experience, they often result from mounting everyday stresses that eventually overwhelm coping capabilities (Bandura, Adams, Hardy, & Howells, 1980).

We have previously noted that selective factors also provide an exaggerated image of the intractability of phobic conditions. If only refractory phobic conditions, for which professional help is sought, are studied, as is typically the case, they appear unusually resistant to change because the more common tractable ones go unexamined. Even in extreme forms, it is debatable how much of the intractability reflects the power of the treatment and how much it reflects the phobic condition itself. Weak methods make little dent on severe phobias, whereas powerful methods can eliminate them rapidly (Rosenthal & Bandura, 1978).

Studies examining the role of thought patterns in severe anxiety and phobic reactions reveal that, far from being reflexive conditioned reactions, they are usually triggered by frightening cognitions (Beck, Laude, & Bohnert, 1974; Laude & LaVigne, 1974). These irrational thought precipitants center on coping inefficacies that signify vulnerability to injury and gross exaggerations of the potential harmfulness of situations. Sometimes the phobic object itself is cognitively transformed as when sight of a flying insect arouses thoughts of hideous monsters remembered from a science fiction movie.

Psychological Properties of Phobeogenic Events.
In the social cognitive view, all events are not equally susceptible to becoming objects of phobic dread. There are certain properties of events—agential hurtfulness, intensity, unpredictability, and uncontrollability—that make them especially phobeogenic. Among the things that are correlated with aversive experience, animate ones are more apt to produce phobias than are inanimate ones. This is because animate threats, by virtue of their ability to act and roam around, can appear at unpredictable times and places and inflict injury despite self-protective efforts. Thus, limp pajamas and stationary grass, which lack injurious agency, cannot easily become aversive, whereas animals, which roam around and are quite capable of inflicting bodily harm, can readily be made scary through a painful experience. It is, therefore, not entirely surprising that an aversive experience that created fear of an animal (Watson & Rayner, 1920) produced no fear of inanimate objects such as curtains, wooden blocks, and a wooden duck, none of which have agentive, hurtful capabilities (Bregman, 1934; English, 1929). There is nothing much a curtain or a wooden duck can do on its own. Inanimate things can become objects of phobic avoidance if they are believed to harbor pernicious agents. Obsessive compulsive people who believe they will become infected by bacteria or viruses residing on whatever has been touched go

to great lengths to avoid common objects in fear of contamination, and they spend exhausting hours in protective cleansing rituals (Rachman & Hodgson, 1980).

In addition to injurious agency, unpredictability and uncontrollability are other important properties of phobeogenic events. Predictable aversive events are less frightening than those one cannot foretell when or where they might happen, thus making it difficult to distinguish safe from unsafe circumstances. Similarly, ability to exercise control, or even the perception that one can do so, greatly reduces the threat of potentially painful events (Averill, 1973; Bandura, 1982a; Miller, 1979, 1980a). Active, unpredictable threats, over which one has only partial control, give more cause for generalized anxiety than equally aversive threats that are predictable, immobile, and safe, as long as one chooses to stay away from them. It is in the properties of events, then, rather than in the experiences of one's ancestors, that answers to the selectivity of human phobias are most likely to be found. However, properties of events do not reflexively activate associative mechanisms. The impact of events on fear reactions is, in large part, dependent on cognitive processing, which defines the threatening quality of particular objects under different circumstances.

Some phobias arise not from fear that external objects may inflict injury but from fear of untrustworthy control over one's own actions, which could injure oneself or others. In these instances, it is one's own agency that is feared. The phobic preoccupation centers on thoughts that one is liable to behave in ways that bring social and physical catastrophies (Beck et al., 1974). Lapses in consciousness will produce fatal traffic accidents, and foolish actions will bring public humiliation. Perceived inefficacy in controlling oneself and unpredictability as to where and when self-control might fail create a profound sense of vulnerability and generalized phobic dread.

Traumatic linkage can produce aversions to events lacking agentive properties. Acute suffering may fashion such a powerful relation between events that people cannot refrain from cognitively revivifying the aversive experiences when confronted with the reminders, however hard they try. In one case illustrating this process (Rachman & Seligman, 1976), a woman with impaired vision, who as a child was repeatedly taunted by peers rubbing vegetables and plants in her face, developed a strong aversion to vegetables and had nightmares about them. A further example of traumatic linkage, originating in a gruesome military experience, is provided by Little and James (1964). A soldier had shot two enemy soldiers while being taken captive near enemy lines. In making his escape, he burst through a doorway in a farm house only to find a dozen enemy troops in the process of awakening. He stood guard over them for ten strained hours, shot their sergeant, who kept urging the soldiers to rush their captor, and brought in the prisoners as night fell. For 18 years following his discharge, he was unable to open and walk through a doorway if he could hear voices on the other side. His severe phobia was eventually eliminated through repeated symbolic reenactment of the traumatic military episode.

The preparedness formulation calls attention to the need to explain why some types of phobias are more prevalent than others, but there is reason to doubt that it provides the answer. Among the various human anxieties, those related to sexual activity rank high. It would be difficult to find evolutionary benefits to impotence or frigidity. One rarely, if ever, encounters mushroom phobias, nor are lasting affective reactions easily established toward them (Ohman, Fredrikson, Hugdahl, & Rimmo, 1976), even though, through the ages, the poisonous forms have taken a sufficiently heavy toll of undiscriminating diners to have instilled a phobic preparedness for this fungus. In the course of evolution, more people have probably drowned than died of snake bites, but snake phobias are more prevalent than phobic dread of water. Snakes acquire threat value through a combination of experiences, including fearful parental modeling reinforced by frightening personal experiences, and portrayals of reptiles as menacing creatures (Bandura, Blanchard, & Ritter, 1969). Through these various means, they come to be viewed as hurtful, unpredictable as to their whereabouts in rural areas, and difficult to control should they strike. If vast quantities of water could suddenly sneak up and innundate people at any time and place, water would similarly become a prevalent source of phobic dread.

Freud's famous case of Little Hans, who exhibited among other things a phobia of horses, has been cited as an example of an evolutionarily prepared phobia (Seligman, 1971). In point of fact, this case illustrates the explanatory weakness of the preparedness notion. Hans had undergone a number of experiences that sensitized him to horses: He had been frightened at seeing horses being beaten at a merry-go-round; he was warned to avoid horses, for they might injure him; he was frightened when a friend was hurt while playing horses; and in the episode that immediately preceded the onset of the phobic behavior, Hans was terrified at witnessing a bus accident in which he believed a large bus-horse was killed. The phobia is said to be prepared because Hans allegedly developed a fear of horses but not of transport vehicles. In fact, he was phobic of transport vehicles.

There were three important elements in the final, traumatic incident—large horse, heavily loaded transport vehicle, and horse and vehicle traveling at high speed. The occurrence and intensity of Hans's phobic reactions varied as a function of the specific patterning of these three predictive cues. He was more frightened of large dray horses than of small horses, more frightened of heavily loaded vehicles than of empty ones, and more frightened when a horse-drawn cart made a turn which increased the risk of turning over. Indeed, transport vehicles were as much, or more, of a factor in Hans's fear than were horses *per se*. As he described it, "I'm afraid of buses and luggage-carts, but only when they're loaded up, not when they're empty. When there's one horse and the cart's loaded full up, then I'm afraid; but when there are two horses and it's loaded full up, then I'm not afraid" (Freud, 1955, pp. 90–91). Preparedness fails to explain not only the discriminative patterning of Hans's phobic behavior but also why he feared heavily loaded vehicles and locomotives as well, a phobia which reflects generalization from the transport-vehicle incident, rather than evolutionary selectivities from pretechnological times.

To evaluate systematically the predictive utility of the preparedness tenet, DeSilva, Rachman, and Seligman (1977) compared the acquisition and modifiability of phobias judged to be either evolutionarily prepared or unprepared. Judged preparedness failed to predict suddenness and age of onset of the disorder, severity of impairment, or susceptibility to change. Indeed, arbitrary fears can be exceedingly resistant to change (Rachman & Seligman, 1976).

Disentangling Experiential and Biological Preparedness. A number of laboratory tests have been conducted on whether presumed innate predisposition affects the speed with which anticipatory autonomic reactions to threats are learned and eliminated. In these studies, shock is associated directly, vicariously, or by verbal threat, alone, with pictures of evolutionarily significant objects, such as snakes and spiders, or biologically indifferent ones, such as houses, flowers, and geometrical forms. The basic assumption of the preparedness principle is that innately primed linkage ensures rapid learning of threats; otherwise, preparedness would lack survival value because perilous threats usually permit few errors. Speeding automobiles do not give many second chances to careless pedestrians who happen to get in the way. An evolutionary legacy that did not facilitate acquisition of fears, but only slowed their extinction, would place the bias at the wrong end because slow learning of dangers is likely to extinguish the organism. The assumption of rapid acquisition receives little empirical support in laboratory findings. Neither repeated shock nor observing others suffering direct painful experiences makes people fear prepared objects any faster than arbitrary ones (Hygge & Ohman, 1978; Ohman, Erixon, & Lofberg, 1975; Ohman & Hugdahl, 1979). But paradoxically, verbal threats are sometimes more effective than painful experiences in establishing fear of prepared objects, which supposedly are insensitive to cognitive influence.

The knowledge that shocks have been discontinued is generally less effective in eliminating autonomic reactions to prepared than to arbitrary objects. However, even here, findings conflict across studies and depend on whether momentary orienting responses or anticipatory reactions are examined. Knowledge of safety may affect autonomic reactions differentially the moment the objects appear, but assurance produces similar reductions in anticipatory reactions, whether triggered by prepared or by arbitrary objects. In some studies, fear is just as persistent toward geometrical forms as toward snakes on every type of reaction measured, whether orienting, anticipatory, or hindmost (Ohman et al., 1976). Fears established toward prepared objects are quite reducible by cognitive means (McNally, 1981). Moreover, if correlated experiences are provided so that pictures of snakes and flowers come to signal safety from painful events, both of these objects are equally effective in diminishing fear toward other threats (McNally & Reiss, 1982). In the preparedness view, one would not expect that an object biologically predisposed for fear could be so readily transformed into a fear reducer and be just as tranquilizing as a dainty flower. Despite repeated disconfirmation of the effects of presumed preparedness on rate of learning and mixed results on rate of fear extinction, these findings continue to be cited as evidence of biologically prepared learning.

A preparedness mechanism that does not help humans learn from the pain or calamities of others to fear dangers any faster and that has variable effects on the persistence of anticipatory arousal is not exactly the most reliable basis on which to rest survival chances. Forethought and advanced capacity to profit from the injuries of others, both of which are hallmarks of human adaptiveness, are more likely to ensure progeny than is reliance on blind associations. It is much wiser to trust one's survival to forethought concerning the properties of human creations because cultural evolution introduces new objects—guns, bombs, automobiles—that are considerably more prevalent and perilous than tigers.

Even if it had been found that innate preparedness carried the burden of autonomic learning delegated to it, ambiguities would still remain regarding evolutionary implications. This is because autonomic arousal is not causally linked to any particular type of action. From the standpoint of survival, the important factor is not that organisms become easily upset but that they make hasty retreats from perilous situations, which can cost them life or limb. It is smart protective action rather than internal discomposure that is of central concern to healthy longevity. Moreover, organisms who can guide their behavior on the knowledge of what is safe and what is dangerous are better equipped to survive and flourish than those who continue to cringe needlessly, knowing full well that what they have come to fear is now perfectly safe. Functional thought is evolutionarily advantageous.

Verification of innate preparedness in humans is much more complicated than it might at first appear. Studies usually confound experientially and biologically based susceptivities to different threats. For example, social influence instills many repulsive affective associations toward reptiles but few toward geometrical forms. If reliable differences were found in acquisition and persistence of fear toward objects varying in phobeogenic properties, the question remains whether the explanation lies in affect-laden cognitions instilled socially in the here and now, or in the snake bites suffered by some ancestors generations ago. Psychological preparedness underscores the need for additional control techniques. Confounding of innateness and social experience can be minimized by comparing how rapidly fear develops toward objects that have equal agentive, hurtful properties and activate the same level of affective cognitions but differ in whether the valence of the objects is primarily allied to evolutionary history or to social experience. In comparing the rate of fear learning involving shifty snakes, a person wielding a gun provides a better control than merely a gun itself, which has no agential properties. Efforts to disentangle biologically and experientially prepared learning further corroborate that biological preparedness does not affect learning (Hugdahl & Karker, 1981). Experiential preparedness remains an explanatory contender for slower extinction of phobias when stimuli of shifty animals depicted negatively by the culture are compared with inanimate objects which have harmful potential but which lack any agential properties.

Innumerable studies have shown that painful experiences readily create experiential preparedness to fear selected types of objects and events. By varying the pattern of positive and negative experiences, one can carve out particular domains of sensitivities (Hoffman, 1969). Even after acquired fears are completely eliminated, the sensitivities remain. Years later, stressful experiences arising from unrelated sources can reinstate fearful reactions toward former threats in the experientially sensitized domains.

FORETHOUGHT AND ACTION

The same behavior often has different effects depending upon, among other factors, the time, the place, and the persons toward whom it is directed. Driving through a busy intersection on a red light, for example, will have painfully different consequences than crossing on a green light. When variations in certain situational, symbolic, and social cues are regularly associated with differential response outcomes, such cues come to serve as activators and guides for action.

People, therefore, pay close attention to the aspects of their environment that predict outcomes but ignore those that do not. The capacity to regulate one's actions on the basis of predictors of response consequences provides the mechanism for foresightful behavior.

Cues acquire predictive value by being correlated with differential response consequences. Traditional accounts of this process focus mainly on direct experience in which responses are rewarded or punished only in the presence of certain cues but not in other contexts. In this mode of learning, enactive experience provides the information for gaining knowledge about the rules governing outcomes. Once the predictive information is extracted, people guide their actions on their judgments of probable consequences.

The effects that actions have are, in large part, socially mediated. Predictive social cues, therefore, play an especially significant role in the regulation of human conduct. Children often behave quite differently in the presence of one parent, in accordance with that particular parent's disciplinary practices. Hyperaggressive boys will aggress freely around a lenient parent, but they rarely do so in the presence of the parent who tolerates no aggression (Bandura & Walters, 1959).

In a formal study of how behavior is socially signalled, Redd and Birnbrauer (1969) had an adult reward a group of reclusive children only for playing cooperatively, while a second adult rewarded them equally, regardless of how they behaved. Later, the mere appearance of the contingently rewarding adult evoked cooperative play, whereas the noncontingent adult had no influence on the children's social behavior. When the adults reversed their rewarding practices, their power to elicit cooperative play by their mere presence changed accordingly.

People generally regulate their behavior on the basis of rules embodying subtle social cues. Consider the common example of parents who are quick to issue commands to their children but who do not always see to it that their requests are heeded. Eventually, children learn to ignore demands voiced in mild or moderate tones. The parents' mounting anger becomes a predictive signal that compliance will be enforced, so that only shouts produce results. Consequently, many households are run on a fairly high decibel level.

The predictive value of cues is undoubtedly established and maintained in many instances through direct personal experiences linking response outcomes to situational circumstances. However, people's symbolic capacity enables them to gain such information without having to perform a given behavior, under all types of circumstances, to discover the probable outcomes that each situation signifies. Much rule learning is, in fact, achieved through explanations that describe the circumstances under which particular actions are rewardable and punishable. One does not have to commit transgressive acts and suffer legal consequences, for instance, to learn the conditions under which given types of conduct are forbidden by law.

People often behave appropriately without either personal experience or explanation of probable response consequences. This is because information about predictors of outcomes is also derived vicariously by observing how the behavior of others is received in different situations. The three sources of information—enactive, symbolic, and vicarious—operate in an interrelated fashion. What one sees and has been told facilitates extraction of rules from personal experiences. Although actions are frequently guided by judgments based on what one has observed or been told, the maintenance of the predictive value of cues established verbally or vicariously ordinarily requires periodic confirmation through direct experience.

Modeled Predictors

Of the numerous predictive cues that influence behavior at any given moment, none is more common or informative than the actions of others. People applaud when others clap, they laugh when others laugh, they exit from social events when they see others leaving, they dress like the fashion setters do, and in countless other situations, their behavior is prompted and channeled by modeling influences.

The actions of others acquire predictive value through correlated consequences, in much the same way as do nonsocial physical and symbolic predictors. Modeling cues prompt similar conduct when behaving like others produces rewarding outcomes, but they elicit divergent behavior when actions dissimilar to the model prove more beneficial (Miller & Dollard, 1941). Because people usually model behavior of proven value, following good examples is much more efficacious than laborious trial and error. Thus, by relying on the actions of knowledgeable models, people can act appropriately in different situations without having to discover what conduct is acceptable from the shocked or pleased reactions of onlookers to their groping performances. The dictum "When in Rome do as the Romans do" underscores the considerable value of modeling cues.

The power of example to activate and channel behavior has been abundantly documented in both laboratory and field studies (Bandura, 1969a; Rosenthal & Bandura, 1978). One can get people to behave altruistically, to volunteer their services, to delay or to seek gratification, to show affection, to behave punitively, to prefer certain foods and apparel, to converse on particular topics, to be inquisitive or passive, to think innovatively or conventionally, and to engage in almost any course or action by having such conduct exemplified. Even the rate of engagement in a given activity, such as how much alcohol or food is consumed, is strongly influenced by social modeling (Caudill & Marlatt, 1975; Garlington & Dericco, 1977; Rosenthal & McSweeney, 1979). The kinds of models prevailing within a given social environment thus affect which human qualities, from among many alternatives, will be selectively activated.

Correlates of Modeling

People differ in how readily their behavior is influenced by modeling cues, and not all models are equally effective in eliciting the types of behavior they themselves exemplify. Responsiveness to modeling influences is largely determined by three sets of factors, which in turn derive their activating power largely from correlative relationships with response outcomes. These are the attributes of models, the attributes of observers, and the functional value of what is modeled.

Model Attributes. Models who have status, competence, and power are more effective in prompting others to behave similarly than are models of lower standing. The force of prestigious modeling is shown in a field study about behavioral contagion among children at summer camp (Lippitt, Polansky, & Rosen, 1952). Observers recorded how often children modeled the actions of their peers when the peers were making no effort to get others to follow their example. A few boys with the most power served as the major sources of social behavior. Their actions set the style for others. The influence of prestigious modeling is most convincingly demonstrated when identical actions are modeled but the prestige of the model is systematically varied (Lefkowitz, Blake, & Mouton, 1955). In one such study, pedestrians were more likely to cross a street on a red light when they saw a presumably high-status person dressed as an executive do so, than when the same transgression was performed by the same person dressed in patched trousers, scuffed shoes, and a blue denim shirt.

Possession of social power to affect the rewarding outcomes of others adds force to modeling influences, as does high standing in a prestige hierarchy. Children are much more likely to model the preferences and actions of the adults who control and dispense rewarding resources than the preferences and actions of the recipients of rewards (Bandura, Ross, & Ross, 1963c). The same is true if children themselves have previously been the beneficiaries of the models' rewards (Chartier & Weiss, 1974; Mischel & Grusec, 1966).

That possession of rewarding power enhances models' cueing efficacy is further revealed by pitting rewarding power against an opposing source of influence. When exposed to several male and female models, who all display high consensus in their behavioral preferences, children selectively follow the actions of the same-sex models (Perry & Bussey, 1979). However, power inversions override the influence of gender, thus increasing the inclination to adopt the behavior of opposite-sex models who control resources (Bussey & Bandura, 1984). Boys are more prone to emulate power than are girls. That the cross-sex modeling is produced by filmed models, who can in no way affect observers' lives, indicates that signs of power may operate by conferring utility on the behavior of powerholders, rather than by simply instilling expectations that imitation will curry favor with the powerholders. The exercise of punitive power is quite another matter, especially when observers are at the receiving end of it. If anything, punitiveness, which arouses apprehension and avoidance, tends to reduce reliance on such models as guides for action (Chartier & Weiss, 1974).

It is not difficult to understand why signs of status and power enhance the cueing function of modeled conduct. The behavior of models who have gained distinction is more likely to be successful, and hence to have greater functional value for observers, than that of models who are relatively low in vocational, intellectual, or social competence. Unless gained through bequest, possession of extensive valued resources suggests exceptional resourcefulness and competence to have acquired them. When adopting the styles of behavior of different models produces different results, the models' characteristics assume informative value in signifying the probable effectiveness of the behavior they exemplify.

When people are uncertain about the wisdom of modeled courses of action, they must rely on such cues as general appearance, speech, style, age, symbols of socioeconomic success, and signs of expertise as indicators of past successes. The effects of a model's status tend to generalize from one area of behavior to another, as when prominent athletes express preferences for breakfast cereals as though they were nutrition experts. Because status casts a broad aura of expertise, observers may be initially swayed more by indicants of high educational status than by attributed specific competence in the particular activity (Huang & Harris, 1973). Unfamiliar persons, likewise, gain influence by their similarity to models whose behavior has proven successful in the past.

People need not rely solely on power and status symbols for judging the likely utility of modeled actions. They often have ample opportunities to observe directly the relative competence of models as they deal with their environment. Because model competence is a highly reliable indicant of an adroit performance, modeling cues gain cogency from knowledge about capableness. When this attribute is varied experimentally, the higher the apparent competence of the model the more observers are guided by the model's actions (Kanareff & Lanzetta, 1958; Rosenbaum & Tucker, 1962). To the extent that observers achieve good results by adopting modeled solutions, they raise their estimate of the models' competence and are even more prone to use their behavior as a guide (Greenfeld & Kuznicki, 1975).

Observer Attributes. Some attention has been devoted to identifying the types of people who are most responsive to modeling influences. Those who lack confidence in their own ability and hold themselves in low esteem, and who often fail in their own attempts while finding modeled actions helpful, are especially prone to adopt the behavior of successful models (Akamatsu &

Thelen, 1974; Rosenbaum, Chalmers, & Horne, 1962; Turner & Forehand, 1976). Differential responsiveness to modeling cues does not reflect a generalized personality disposition that operates irrespective of the functionality of modeled behavior. People with low self-esteem may be initially a bit quicker than those with high self-esteem to rely on highly competent models as guides for action, but they do not differ in their responsiveness to models of moderate or low competence (Rosenbaum, Horne, & Chalmers, 1962). If the solutions of others are superior to one's own, it stands to reason that modeling guides will gain high utility.

It would be a mistake to conclude that it is mainly the uncertain, dispirited, and inefficacious who profit most from example. These prosaic correlates are based largely on results of studies in which unfamiliar models exhibit simple responses that have little or no functional value for observers, beyond the immediate situation. In everyday life, perceptive and efficacious people emulate idealized models and those whose behavior is highly useful. It is exceedingly unlikely that dull students, who lack assurance in their ability, would profit more from observing skillful performances by ski instructors, brain surgeons, computer operators, pianists, or inventive researchers than would understudies who are bright and self-assured. When modeling is explicitly used to develop competencies, the more talented and venturesome are apt to derive the greatest benefits from observing proficient models. The personal correlates of aspirational modeling, where persons have a clear idea of what they wish to become and select models exemplifying the valued skills, will differ markedly from the correlates of alien or insecure modeling, where people turn to others because the situation is entirely foreign to them or because they distrust their own capabilities.

Functional Value. Reliance on models as guides for action depends heavily on the functional value of their behavior. There are several ways in which the utility of modeled actions is determined. Observers try what they see and judge how well it works for them. We have seen in an earlier chapter how persons regulate their behavior discriminately, on the basis of distinguishable characteristics of modeled activities that are predictors of outcomes. They are highly responsive to social cues for courses of action that are likely to bring them success, but they ignore those that fail to secure them benefits.

Observing the response outcomes of others, similarly, conveys information about the probable functional value of what is modeled. However, since observed outcomes are not unequivocal indicators of how one might fare with similar actions, judging utilities from vicarious information involves a number of inferential processes. This is the subject of a later chapter.

Generalizations about the personality correlates of modeling must be accepted with reservation because the functional value of modeled behavior overrides the influence of either model or observer characteristics. A model's attributes exert greatest influence when the modeled behavior is observable, but its consequences remain unknown. The probable value of modeled conduct must, therefore, be judged from outward appearances and signs of achievement. Because the informative value of these cues rests on past correlative experiences, they are not always reliable predictors of how useful the behavior might be under current circumstances. One would not expect behavior that has been activated by anticipations based on model attributes to survive for long in the face of actual unfavorable consequences. A prestigious or attractive model may induce a person to try a given course of action, but if the behavior should prove unsatisfactory, it will be discarded and the model's reputation and future influence will be diminished. Studies conducted under conditions in which modeled response outcomes are not evident may, therefore, exaggerate the role played by model attributes in the continuing social guidance of behavior.

Induction of Rules from Abstract Modeling

We have seen in an earlier chapter that models do much more than simply provide specific cues for action. In their transactions with the environment, they exemplify the rules for constructing response patterns and for predicting likely outcomes. By analyzing the choices models make and the consequences they experience, observers can discover generalizable rules of action (Rosenthal & Zimmerman, 1978). Since rule induction from abstract modeling has already been discussed at some length, it will not be reviewed here.

Discussions about the role of modeling in complex judgment often treat vicarious influences as if models act but remain speechless. Society, of course, is not populated with mute models. While modeling efficacious actions, especially in didactic situations, those who have gained competence describe how they select information, how they weigh it, and what rules they use for judging events and solving problems. Complex judgmental rules are mastered easily when models verbalize the predictive knowledge they possess, as well as exemplify it in their actual judgments.

Models influence judgmental styles not only by the strategies they model but also by how they evaluate their own decision making. This is illustrated by Brockner and his associates in studies of judgmental modeling in entrapping conflict situations (Brockner et al., 1984). People often find themselves in predicaments in which they have invested much time, effort, and money in what turns out to be a losing course of action. They have to decide whether to acknowledge the mistake and cut their losses or to invest additional resources with the hope of recouping something from their investment. In efforts to convince themselves and others of their sound judgment, people often try to turn a mistake around, only getting themselves even more deeply entrapped in a losing proposition. Observers adopt modeled entrapping judgments, despite their evident costs, if models justify their errant judgments as risks worth taking. In contrast, observers profit from models' experiences and avoid similar mistakes when models question the adequacy of their own judgment. Thus, the force of judgmental modeling is determined by justifications, as well as by evident results.

INFERENTIAL THOUGHT AND EXTRACTION OF RULES

Environmental cues that predict outcomes are usually part of a bewildering variety of irrelevant bits of information. To complicate judgment further, many of the rules governing outcomes require combining and weighing information conveyed by different sets of cues. To illustrate this inferential process, let us consider a task in which people unfamiliar with drinking customs are asked to judge the appropriateness of drinking alcohol under varying conditions. Relevant factors would include the time of day, the setting, the social circumstances, and the amount of alcohol consumed. These four relevant cues, as well as many irrelevant ones (e.g., the type of liquor drunk, the beverages mixed with it, the sex of the drinker, etc.), are portrayed in varying combinations in sets of videotaped situations. Let us arbitrarily designate as "acceptable" imbibing under circumstances showing an adult drinking moderate amounts of liquor at mealtime or in the evening, and let us call heavy solitary drinking during the daytime, at home or at work, "inappropriate." As individuals try to figure out which factors are relevant on the basis of their provisional suppositions, they receive feedback as to whether or not their judgments are accurate.

At first, they draw on their past knowledge to select certain aspects as the basis for their judgments. Most of their initial judgments might be faulty because they would not have hit upon the compound rule instantly. A few of their judgments, however,

are likely to prove successful because the factors selected as relevant will appear as part of the correct configuration in some of the situations portrayed. By comparing how the features of the situation differ in the positive and negative instances, other cues common to the positive instances will be noticed and tested. On the basis of further informative feedback, individuals will continue to revise their suppositions until they eventually extract all the relevant cues and integrate them into a composite rule that defines socially appropriate drinking behavior. In the present example, the predictive configuration includes the joint presence of time, place, and quantity features.

The judgmental process becomes more complicated when multiple cues must not only be combined but also weighted differentially. To continue with the above example, the amount drunk is a heavily weighted factor that overrides the importance of the other pertinent cues. A solitary lunchtime drink is regarded as socially acceptable but getting soused at lunchtime is not. Because social sanctions differ across settings and times, the rules predicting probable outcomes vary accordingly. Afternoon drinking may be acceptable on weekends but not during working days. Special circumstances can radically alter factor weights. Heavy imbibing at an Oktoberfest constitutes an appropriate pattern of drinking behavior, whereas light sipping would be regarded disapprovingly as a sign of uptightness.

Subprocesses in Learning Predictive Rules. In gaining predictive knowledge, individuals must discern relevant factors, weigh them appropriately, and combine them into generalizable rules of action. As indicated in the preceding example, learning predictive rules involves several component processes. The relevant cues must be identified from among numerous irrelevancies through selective attention. The cues must then be integrated by a rule. This can be achieved by instructive modeling or tuition, by drawing on knowledge gained from past experiences, or, if the appropriate rule is unavailable, by constructing different compound rules and testing their accuracy against informative feedback. Rule induction from feedback about outcomes depends on faithful memory of which solutions worked and which did not. Thus, by testing and revising their suppositions, individuals eventually combine the relevant factors into correct rules. Readers will recognize these basic subprocesses as similar to some of those governing observational and enactive learning of behavioral and cognitive skills. However, since forecasting the effects of action patterns differs markedly from being able to perform them skillfully, separate bodies of knowledge are needed that specify how the basic subprocesses are enlisted for these diverse purposes.

It should be emphasized that most rules of action are conveyed by instruction rather than discovered by direct experience. This is easy to lose sight of because, despite its prevalence, such preceptive learning receives little attention in psychological theorizing and research. Behavior theories tend to stress learning through one's own successes and failures. The Piagetian approach emphasizes gradual development of conceptual skills on the basis of one's own improvised experiences. Theories of inferential thinking center heavily on the alteration of judgment through correctness feedback.

Inferential thinking has been studied from diverse perspectives, each examining different aspects of the process. Some investigators focus attention on how people select cues provided by exemplars to form working hypotheses and how they then test and alter them on the basis of outcome feedback until the correct rule is discovered. Other researchers explore how the characteristics of cues and the form of their relation to future happenings affect the ease with which predictive rules can be discerned from the probabilistic information conveyed by multiple cues. Still others analyze the heuristic rules people use to simplify the difficult task of ascertaining probabilities from the large amounts of uncertain information that readily taxes the limits of human integrative and memorial capability.

Selecting Predictors and Testing Predictive Rules

In trying to predict future happenings, any number of factors might be considered. A first step toward understanding human judgment requires knowledge about the factors governing choice of possible predictors (Bourne, 1966; Trabasso & Bower, 1968). Cues can be singled out for attention on the basis of inherent salience, preparatory set, or learned bias and knowledge structures. It is difficult to achieve predictive accuracy when irrelevancies abound and pertinent information is conveyed by subtle properties of events that easily go unnoticed. Under such circumstances, there are many opportunities to go astray. Conditions that reduce irrelevancies and heighten the salience of relevant cues facilitate acquisition of predictive knowledge.

People do not pay equal attention to everything they see and hear. Cues acquire importance mainly by what has worked in the past. When a certain type of cue has been found to be a good predictor, not only is the value of that specific cue learned, but more generalized predictive knowledge is gained about a wide range of cues representing the same underlying property (Lawrence, 1963). Acquired biases exercise selective influence on what factors are most likely to be considered important when new situations are encountered.

The more predictors an event has, the easier it is to find a relevant one, and the quicker some predictive accuracy is achieved. However, predictive success retards, if not obstructs, learning of alternative predictors. Cues that co-vary do not add to predictability because they provide the same information about likely outcomes. When their relation to the events of interest is limited, such redundancy is not very helpful. Any one of the predictors will do, but they all do equally modestly. After one of them has been found to work, there is an inclination to cease testing the predictive value of the redundant ones, even though they are equally informative (Lovaas, Koegel, & Schreibman, 1979; Trabasso & Bower, 1968). Predictors that are independent of each other but relate to the future events increase predictive accuracy. Each provides some useful information for estimating what is likely to happen.

A second major aspect of inferential judgment involves testing the validity of whatever predictors are singled out for attention. Theories about how this occurs differ in some of the specifics, such as whether potential predictors are tested separately and then combined or tested in combinations, whether people learn from successes as well as from errors, and how heavily they use their memory of what worked and what did not in validating their hypotheses (Bourne, Ekstrand, & Dominowski, 1971; Trabasso & Bower, 1968). Nevertheless, the various theories postulate an essentially similar verification process. Possible predictors are tested in the order of their assumed predictive value. If judgments based on the initially dominant factor prove incorrect, the other possibilities are tried until the correct one is discovered. The lower the appropriate predictor happens to be in the subjective ranking, the longer it takes to discover its value. That preexisting biases guide the verification process receives support from studies showing that cue-preference rankings, assessed independently of judgment tasks, predict the speed with which different judgment problems are solved (Suchman & Trabasso, 1966). Matches between perceptual preferences and the type of information relevant to solutions expedite accurate judgment, whereas mismatches between what is preferred and what is predictive give rise to a lot of faulty judgments.

Studies comparing proficient and inept rule learners shed light on optimal strategies for discovering rules through outcome feedback (Bruner, Goodnow, & Austin, 1956; Bourne, 1965). Skilled learners use a two-phase strategy. In the first phase, they construct a provisional composite rule including several potentially relevant predictors. This permits simultaneous cognitive processing of several predictors to narrow the search to a subset which appears relevant. It is unlikely that the correct rule will be hit upon from the outset. In the next phase, learners identify the structure of the rule through more detailed tests, altering one factor at a time in the composite, and either discarding or retaining it depending on the accuracy of their judgments. In contrast, less adept learners are more likely to begin with a fragmentary rather than with a composite hypothesis. They make less effective use of feedback information, often neglecting to make changes after an error, and they tend to alter several factors simultaneously, making it difficult to determine what accounts for successes and failures in judgment. One can learn little from such rambling, sequential processing of information.

Human judgment, of course, is not always as systematic as the optimal model implies, nor is memory infallible for what seemed to work and what did not on different past occasions. Haphazard or distorted sampling of predictive factors, due to unmotivating, stressful, or otherwise disruptive conditions, and faulty memory impair inferential thinking. Resort to deficient judgmental strategies becomes readily evident when the available information is only moderately predictive and when, to achieve even this modest degree of success, the relevant factors must be combined into a complex rule (Brehmer, 1974). After unsuccessfully trying rules that have worked for them in the past, people tend either to resample what has already been disconfirmed or to fall back on inadequate cognitive strategies, rather than to construct and to test new working rules systematically.

Most events are predictable from a combination of indicants, not from an isolated bit of information. Physicians judge the presence of a particular illness from a collection of symptoms, rather than from any one symptom alone. In judging likely reactions of parents to coercive behavior, children consider a constellation of factors, including the mood and sex of the parent and the circumstances under which the behavior is put to use (Bandura & Walters, 1959). In more complex judgmental situations several factors must be weighed and combined into a predictive rule. Mastering simple and compound rules relies on similar strategies of verification. However, not only are compound rules considerably more difficult to discover, but they often require constructing new rules, rather than merely sampling those one already possesses.

Characteristics of Predictors and Predictive Rules

Induction of predictive rules has been studied extensively in terms of the characteristics of the cues and the form of their relationship to environmental events (Brehmer, 1974; Hammond, Stewart, Brehmer, & Steinmann, 1975). Much of this research has been conducted within the general framework of Brunswik's (1952) probabilistic functionalism. In this view, causal dependencies in the environment contain many sources of ambiguity and uncertainty. Cues are usually related probabilistically, rather than invariably, to future events, which leaves some degree of uncertainty. Events are typically multidetermined. Hence, a given environmental event often has more than one predictor, and the same cues may predict, with varying degrees of accuracy, more than one environmental event. The fact that the same predictor may foretell multiple effects, and the same effect can have multiple predictors, introduces considerable ambiguity as to what is likely to lead to what. To achieve high predictive accuracy requires combining and weighing multiple cues into complex relational rules.

Informativeness of Predictors. The cues that convey predictive information vary in their number, dependability, and

degree of interrelatedness (Hammond & Summers, 1972). Some cues can predict events with a high degree of certainty, others are much less reliable, while still others offer no useful information whatsoever. It is easier to comprehend and to deal foresightedly with realities that have dependable predictors. When the validity of cues is low, simple rules can be deciphered without too much difficulty, but more complex rules prove elusive because low co-variation between events makes it hard to reject or to confirm the value of any particular rule (Brehmer, 1974). In complex judgments, the level of predictive accuracy people achieve corresponds quite closely to how predictable the outcomes are from the information available (Brehmer, 1976). Misjudgments, therefore, reflect the interaction of judgmental predilections and task unpredictability, rather than solely personal deficiencies of inferential thinking. Even supremely rational and skillful thinkers will do poorly with poor predictors.

The influential judgments that guide human behavior are not based solely on environmental cues and on how situational occurrences depend upon each other. By their actions, people often make causal contributions to the very events they are forecasting. A major predictor of likely happenings is the scope and level of one's personal competency to affect the environment. Adept persons will create substantially different happenings than will inept ones. Self-judged efficacy is, therefore, a pervasive factor that is weighed heavily in estimating probable environmental outcomes. The cognitive processing and integration of information regarded as indicators of personal efficacy is addressed in a later chapter.

Complexity of Predictive Rules. Events in the environment may be related to each other in relatively simple ways, or they may be linked complexly. The ease with which predictive rules are mastered depends on the structural dependencies of events in the environment (Brehmer, 1974). Compound rules, placing as they do heavy demands on cognitive capabilities for weighing and integrating multiple sources of information, are more difficult to learn than simple ones. Rules representing linear relationships between values of predictors and outcomes are easier to learn than are nonlinear rules. Similarly, probabilistic rules, in which predictors forecast the likelihood of future happenings but with some uncertainty, are much harder to grasp than are deterministic rules in which predictors forecast happenings unfailingly. In the probabilistic instance, an optimal rule is easily discarded because verification of it as the best guide requires not only remembering a lot of information but also estimating from these past experiences that the rule produces less error than does any other imperfect rule. People tend to search for the perfect rule that will produce success every time, rather than an optimal rule that minimizes errors.

The complexity of predictive rules is reflected not only in how highly and intricately events are related but also in the indefiniteness of the predictors themselves. Many of the activities that produce important outcomes are not defined by fixed physical properties. Moreover, the same properties may appear in activities that are considered to be of an entirely different sort and, hence, give rise to dissimilar outcomes.

Indefiniteness and commonality of attributes complicates predictive judgments. By way of example, consider the task of predicting the likely social consequences of aggressive acts. Aggression is usually defined as behavior that results in personal injury and physical destruction. However, the major defining property of aggression (i.e., injuriousness) does not specify it adequately. Not all injurious and destructive acts are considered aggressive, as when pain and damage are inflicted accidentally or as part of a person's socially sanctioned role. Loggers, who destroy trees, and wreckers, who demolish old buildings, are paid for their efforts, not punished as aggressors. Many acts that produce neither injury nor destruction are considered extremely aggressive. A person who tried to kill an unsuspecting victim by gunshot, but happened to miss, would be considered as behaving violently, although no actual injury was caused. Moreover, the same harmful act is perceived differently depending on the sex, age, attractiveness, status, and ethnic background of the injurer. Thus, whether injurious behavior is viewed as aggressive or not depends heavily on the context and on people's subjective judgments of intention and causality (Bandura, 1973; Rule & Nesdale, 1976). Predictive rules about how aggressive conduct is likely to be received must, therefore, include, in addition to injuriousness, a catalogue of factors that have little to do with the properties of the behavior itself.

If people's predictive judgment was as deficient as it appears in formal tests, their daily life would be filled with serious blunders and mishaps. Fortunately, people are more adept in using probabilistic predictors in their everyday life than they do in laboratory tests. Klayman (1984) identifies a number of factors that serve to underestimate people's capabilities in the latter situation. In laboratory situations, people often have to learn arbitrary, nonlinear relations between abstract factors. It is hard to sustain involvement in such activities. By contrast, when dealing with meaningful situations, people have greater incentive to generate ideas and to keep track of how well they work. Moreover, they have more time to test and improve the predictive accuracy of their judgment than they do in brief laboratory tests. When people are instructed to discover the optimal predictive rule, such a cognitive set may lead them to discard a good but imperfect rule they would ordinarily have retained, in favor of an unproductive pursuit of the perfect rule.

Klayman (1984) points to the fact that natural situations, however, usually provide many possible predictors for increasing one's understanding of how the environment operates. This enables people to improve their predictive accuracy by ferreting out relevant predictors, substituting strong predictors for weak ones, and otherwise refining their predictive knowledge. Although, as we have seen, people have difficulty weighting the relative importance of predictors, or figuring out rules when predictors are related to outcomes nonlinearly, they learn linear rules quite well. Klayman argues that the nondiscernment of subtleties in how things are related is not necessarily a major handicap. This is because people can predict reasonably well by combining, into a linear rule, the different predictors to which they give equal weight, even when the factors should carry different weights and are actually more complexly related (Dawes & Corrigan, 1974). The more predictors people identify and incorporate into their conceptual system, the higher the predictive accuracy they achieve.

Quality of Feedback. The search for predictive rules relies extensively on informative feedback from judgmental acts. This provides the basis for discarding faulty notions and for selecting and constructing appropriate relational rules. This testing process has been examined mainly in terms of outcome feedback, which merely indicates the correctness of a judgment. In everyday life, faulty judgments are not only labeled as incorrect, but also explanations are generally provided about the conditions under which certain things are likely to happen. Explanatory feedback, being vastly more informative than response outcomes, expedites the learning and application of predictive rules (Hammond & Summers, 1972).

In an effort to overcome the limits of human judgmental capabilities, Hammond has devised explanatory feedback systems employing interactive computer graphics (Hammond, 1971). By this means, individuals can get continuing feedback that explains in pictorial form their selection and weighting of cues and the rules they are following in making their choices. Moreover, the properties of their judgments can be easily compared pictorially against the optimal cue weights and predictive rules.

Predictive knowledge is rapidly acquired when one has the benefit of such detailed explanatory and comparative feedback.

While recognizing the superiority of explanatory feedback, one should not lose sight of the fact that aidful explanations depend on a reliable knowledge base. Someone has to identify the relevant cues and to discover the predictive rules reflecting the causal structure of the environment. A comprehensive theory of human judgment thus requires a means of finding predictive rules in the absence of foreknowledge. The informative effects of exploratory judgment provide a dependable means of discovery. A theory of inferential thinking that regards correctness feedback as a hindrance to sound judgment would be hard pressed to explain how the knowledge on which explanatory feedback depends has been gained to begin with (Hammond & Summers, 1972).

Rule Structures of Specialized Knowledge Domains. Must human judgment and decision making occurs in the context of vocational pursuits involving specialized knowledge domains. In trying to master the knowledge in their specialties, people turn to instructors, books, and what their own experiences might tell them. Unfortunately, these instructional modes are often not as systematized and comprehensive as they should be, the knowledge is presented in generalities that lack operational specificity, and the judgmental heuristics formed from personal experiences leave much to be desired as far as their accuracy is concerned. Moreover, rapid growth of knowledge creates increasing difficulties in staying abreast of new developments. Computer technology is being applied as an aid in diverse fields by organizing the judgmental knowledge in a particular domain into a symbolic reasoning program (Feigenbaum, 1977).

A great deal of professional work involves inferential judgment and symbolic problem solving. Much of the work of physicians, for example, entails diagnosing maladies from collections of symptoms and prescribing remedies based on the effects the treatments are expected to produce. The knowledge and reasoning strategies required for good judgment are in the minds of experts or scattered throughout the pages of textbooks. In making this specialized wisdom available to others as a clinical aid, researchers extract from experts the judgmental knowledge they have developed through years of practice (Shortliffe, Buchanan, & Feigenbaum, 1979). The facts and decision rules are then organized into computer programs for general use. Sets of facts are fed into the computer which reaches decisions by following the series of judgmental rules from the reasoning network gleaned from experts. The rules are tested and refined by comparing the decision-making performance of the computerized system with that of the experts on new problems. In the medical example, by providing the computer with information on a patient's history and symptoms, a physician can get a quick diagnosis of the probable malady, its severity, and suggested courses of treatment. The steps in the reasoning by which decisions are reached can be requested and displayed, a process that has instructive value in itself. If computers are supplied with relevant facts, less experienced persons approximate, or even match, the problem-solving feats of experts in the field (Shortliffe, Buchanan, & Feigenbaum, 1979). As new knowledge is gained, the judgmental system can be easily updated by substituting new decision-making factors and rules.

Computational models of reasoning are only as good as the decisional factors and inference rules programmed into the system. Ferreting out the relevant factors and the rule structures in a knowledge domain is no easy task. Johnson (1983) describes three ways to codify the operative knowledge of experts and the inference rules that they use to solve problems. One approach focuses inquiry on what they know, what they look for, and how they reason. Such reconstructions, although highly informative, are often incomplete and are sometimes cast in generalities. A second approach to gaining operational knowledge has experts verbalize aloud the steps in their reasoning as they solve problems. But, some knowledge may be neither easily verbalized nor fully demonstrated in the context of task performance. A third approach relies on statistical operations to identify the best way of combining and weighting decisional factors to yield optimal solutions to problems. In this method, decision makers who have demonstrated sound judgment make many decisions using a given set of predictors. The judgmental tasks may include simulated problems providing different combinations of information, as well as naturally occurring problems. Their decision rules can then be modeled by a regression equation reflecting how they weight the various predictors in rendering judgments.

Although the weighting practices of experts have some validity, they usually fall short of being optimal. Any decision rules extracted from the fallible judgments of experts will reflect their limitations (Slovic, 1983). Given adequate knowledge of relevant predictors and well-defined outcomes, one can determine how best to integrate and weigh predictors by how well different decision rules predict the significant outcomes rather than how well they fit judgments of experts.

The different approaches to illuminating judgmental processes complement each other. Statistical tools cannot produce much, if judgmental knowledge is deficient. The analysis of reliable sources of judgmental knowledge and the verbalized reasoning of experts provide insights into important predictors and the rules of inference by which they arrive at sound decisions. Statistical analyses can formalize and refine decision rules for judgmental situations that are recurrent. Since a formalized system is not misled by irrelevancies or subject to misweighting of relevant predictors by biases that happen to crop up, it can render better predictions than the intuitive judgments from which it has been derived (Dawes & Corrigan, 1974). A formalized rule system retains valid rules of human judgment but excludes extraneous influences, which hinder effective application of these rules.

Devising computerized computational models is one thing, but getting practitioners to use them is quite another. People are wary of computers making judgments for fear that computerized systems will become invested with the aura of expertise and then be used as decision makers rather than as decisional aids. If fed faulty or incomplete information, computers yield erroneous judgments. This is equally true of human judgment—if people ignore or misuse predictive information, or are swayed by irrelevant factors, they will err in their judgment. However, unlike computers, people can reason about their reasoning and thus monitor the adequacy of their judgment. Self-corrective capability is crucial because situations can change in ways that alter the validity of customary predictors or call for additional ones. In judging changing situations, people must draw on their knowledge and reasoning skills, monitor the accurateness of their judgments, and learn from their experiences. But they can do this better with decision aids than without them.

Reported and Enacted Indicants of Judgmental Processes. Knowledge of judgmental processes can be gained by analyzing either the judgments people make or their verbal statements about the rules they are constructing and following. Actual judgments generally correspond closely to designation of rules (Armelius & Armelius, 1976; Brehmer, 1974; Phillips & Levine, 1975). When discrepancies arise between what people say and what they do, it does not necessarily mean that actual judgments provide the more accurate representation of inferential thought processes. In commenting on this issue, Brehmer and his colleagues underscore the distinction between knowledge and the facility to use it fully (Brehmer, Hagafors, & Johansson, 1980). It requires cognitive skills and practice in using rules to make good judgments.

Disparities often occur, not because people do not know the appropriate judgmental rules, but because they are unskilled in applying what they know. This is particularly true in applying configural rules where the relative importance of a particular factor varies depending on the nature of other factors. For example, the same moderate increase in blood pressure does not constitute a large risk for future heart attack if the cholesterol level is low, but the increase becomes a serious risk in the presence of elevated cholesterol level. Configural weighting of predictive information is a difficult cognitive task. Even though people know what configural rule should be used, they tend to weight factors equally rather than differentially according to other information, often without realizing their misapplication of the rule.

Simplifying Judgmental Rules

As has already been shown, predictive judgment based on indefinite information demands attention, memory, and integrative cognitive skills. Since people possess neither perfect memories nor the best intuitive computational skills, they often resort to simpler judgmental rules for explaining and predicting events. Tversky and Kahneman (1974, 1980) provide an insightful analysis of these simplifying cognitive heuristics.

Judgment Through Likeness Matching. Human judgments are not made in a void. People interpret what they see and hear in terms of their preexisting beliefs and knowledge structures. When faced with new situations, they tend to judge them through their likeness to familiar examples, which carry predictive information gleaned from past experiences. Once an associative likeness is struck, knowledge of the familiar gives predictive significance to the new. To the extent that perceptions of similarities and knowledge structures vary from person to person, as they usually do, people's predictive judgments will differ even though they are based on the same new information. Tversky and Kahneman regard the representativeness heuristic, which operates through perceived similarity, as a basic feature of human judgment.

The knowledge structures to which new events are compared are variously labeled beliefs, scripts, stereotypes, prototypes, and schemata (Abelson, 1981; Cantor & Mischel, 1979; Neisser, 1976; Taylor & Crocker, 1980). Although the nomenclature differs, they all refer essentially to generic knowledge abstracted from examples of categories of things, actions, or situations. Predictive judgment involves inferences based on conceptions the person already holds. Once people and events are categorized, predictive judgments about them are then made in terms of what is believed to be typical of the prototype, rather than on their own particular attributes.

Judgment through likeness depends upon several factors. The content of one's generic knowledge shapes how things are judged that bear some similarity to one's prototypes. The features defining the category prototype and the matching process whereby new events are likened to familiar ones also play an influential role. Events have many features, some of which are in common with other events and some of which are distinctive. Judgments of similarity involve a matching process. The likelihood that things will be viewed as similar depends on the extent of their common and their distinctive features (Mervis & Rosch, 1981; Tversky, 1977). Events thus get categorized by how well they match the most representative example (i.e., their prototypicality), rather than in terms of how they fit a fixed set of defining characteristics. Since comparisons can be made in terms of a number of aspects, the nature of activities and situational demands influence which types of factors are likely to be considered most relevant. In judging athletic promise, one looks for different things and draws on different prototypes than when estimating probable academic achievement.

The ability to bring predictive generic knowledge to bear on whatever specific events may be encountered increases understanding and prediction of events. If each instance of the same class of events had to be approached anew, many dreary, if not painful, hours would have to be spent separately ferreting out their significances, over and over again. However, the vast benefits of generalizability depend on the validity of the conceptual scheme and on matching commonalities that carry predictive significance. When new events are associated on the basis of superficial or irrelevant aspects, misjudgments occur because the wrong predictive knowledge has been used. Similarly, matching will also yield misjudgment if the conceptual scheme from which the predictions flow is erroneous. Predictive information that conflicts with strong stereotypical conceptions is ignored, minimized, or given distorted meaning. Haire and Grunes (1950) asked students to judge a person described as a factory worker, who is strong and active, who reads about current events and is intelligent, an attribute that clashed with their stereotype. Some of them simply discounted his intelligence, others distorted it into a negative indication that he lacked initiative, others promoted him to foreman, and still others acknowledged that intelligence did not fit their view of a factory worker, but, nevertheless, placed more stock in their stereotype than in the worker's evident acumen.

Judgment Through Recallability of Instances. Intuitive judgment of the probability that certain events will occur is also influenced by the ease with which instances can be brought to mind (Tversky & Kahneman, 1974). Events that occur often are more readily recallable than those that occur infrequently. For example, heavy viewers of television, in which violent assaults abound, judge their chances of criminal victimization to be higher than do light viewers of television violence (Hawkins & Pingree, 1982). When recallability reflects actual frequencies, it provides a reasonably good basis on which to predict the likelihood of certain happenings. However, frequency and recallability are not necessarily highly correlated. Occurrences that are easily visualized and very memorable tend to distort judgment because of the readiness with which they come to mind (Tversky & Kahneman, 1974). A burglary in the neighborhood is likely to outweigh abstract crime statistics in judging the risk of criminal victimization. When people are asked to judge the likelihood of various hazards, they overestimate the more dramatic and sensational ones but underestimate the less spectacular ones (Slovic, Fischhoff, & Lichtenstein, 1980).

ON MISREADING EVENTS

The capability to predict significant happenings and to choose courses of action that secure desired outcomes and avert undesired ones has considerable adaptive value. Unfortunately, as mentioned earlier, this capability also gets people into trouble when they misjudge situations and base their actions on beliefs that are not well grounded in reality. Some of the misjudgments concern relationships between environmental happenings, others between actions and outcomes.

Misjudgment of Threats

Many people's lives are dominated by subjective dangers that give rise to apprehensive vigilance, needless distress, and constriction of activities. Fearful preoccupation often intrudes on effective performance and enjoyment of daily activities. Dysfunctional beliefs of this sort can develop in several different ways.

Coincidental Association. Of the numerous events that occur in conjunction with a painful experience, some are actually related to it, while others are only coincidental. Because of selective attention or the distinctiveness of events, it is sometimes the coincidental ones that assume predictive value. The following letter, taken from an advice column in a newspaper, provides a

striking illustration of such inappropriate expectancy learning: "My friend fixed me up with a blind date, and I should have known the minute he showed up in a bow tie that he couldn't be trusted. I fell for him like a rock. He got me to love him on purpose and then lied to me and cheated on me. Every time I go with a man who wears a bow tie, the same thing happens. I think girls should be warned about men who wear them."

In this example, the letter writer had developed a belief that bow ties are bad omens, an item one would not expect to be routinely correlated with deceitfulness. Misbeliefs would not last long were it not for the fact that they influence selection and production of experiences. Coincidental association is often converted through misbeliefs into a genuine correlation. To the extent that anticipatory distrust evokes negative counterreactions from bow-tied men, defensive behavior is perpetuated by the unpleasant experiences it creates. In this process, the inappropriate belief and its accompanying defensiveness are maintained by self-produced reality, rather than by conditions that have existed in the past but are no longer in effect. When viewed from an interactional model, people create predictors, as well as cognitively process predictive features. It is not as though people are inert forecasters of inevitable outcomes.

Inappropriate Generalization. Irrational defensive behavior often occurs through overgeneralization from painful experiences to innocuous events that are similar either physically or semantically to the traumatic event. In the often quoted study by Watson and Rayner (1920), for example, a young boy not only learned to fear a rat that was associated with a frightening noise but also generalized the fear widely to other furry objects such as rabbits, dogs, fur coats, cotton, wool, and even human hair. As a rule, the more similar innocuous cues are to those originally associated with aversiveness, the stronger are the generalized reactions.

Innocuous events can acquire aversive potential through generalization on the basis of semantic similarity. To cite a clinical example, Walton and Mather (1963) report the case of a woman who became so obsessed about being dirty that she spent much of her time in exhausting cleansing rituals. This obsessive compulsive behavior began with her severe guilt feelings of "dirtiness" because of her love affair with a married man. Eventually, a wide range of things related to urogenital activities and anything that might be soiled provoked acute distress.

Perceived Self-Inefficacy. Aversiveness is a potential, not a fixed, property of events, which inevitably descends upon whoever encounters them. Judging the likelihood of aversive happenings does not rely solely on reading external signs of danger or safety. Rather, it involves a transaction between personal capabilities and potentially hurtful aspects of the environment. A potentially aversive milieu will be judged as relatively safe by people skilled in coping but as hazardous by inept ones. Persons who judge themselves as lacking coping capabilities, whether the self-appraisal is objectively warranted or not, will perceive all kinds of dangers in situations and exaggerate their potential harmfulness.

In human fear, the overgeneralization from adverse experience that is of major import is the judgment of coping self-efficacy. When a few mishaps are misread as signs of basic coping inefficacy, all kinds of situations become fraught with danger. To understand people's judgments of external threats it is, therefore, necessary to analyze their judgments of their own coping capabilities which, in large part, determine the subjective perilousness of environmental events.

Research on perceived self-efficacy further underscores the need for an interactional model of forethought. People's thoughts about their self-efficacy influence how well they perform and thus the outcomes they are likely to experience. In stud-ies examining a wide range of activities, when variations in perceived self-efficacy are partialled out, the outcomes expected for given accomplishments do not account for much of the variation in human behavior (Barling & Abel, 1983; Barling & Beattie, 1983; Godding & Glasgow, 1985; Lee, 1984a; Wheeler, 1983). If they believe themselves incapable of requisite attainments, they foresake the endeavor, and their beliefs about the outcomes such accomplishments could bring have little effect on their behavior.

Misjudgments Governing Decisions and Actions

Misjudgments that result in faulty decisions and actions can arise from failure to consider pertinent information, misperceptions of relevant information, or from deficient cognitive processing of the information that has been gleaned. Predictive judgment is most errant when the factors used to make inferences are not the most reliable, and cognitive biases further distort how the extracted information is coded and interpreted.

Deficient Utilization of Predictors. Severe problems in personal development and functioning occur when important aspects of the environment either repeatedly go unnoticed or are misperceived. For example, attentional dysfunctions have been found to be a persuasive impediment in childhood autism (Schreibman & Koegel, 1982). When presented with a task containing a set of cues, each of which predicts likely outcomes, normally functioning children learn the informative value of all of them, whereas autistic children usually attend to only one aspect without learning anything about the others. On later occasions if the cues are presented separately, autistic children fail to use them as guides for action, just as though they had never encountered them before, unless the cue happens to be the one on which they had focused during the repeated exposure.

Autistic children display the marked attentional deficit regardless of how many informative cues are available, whether they are expressed in different modalities (i.e., auditory, visual, tactile), or within the same sensory mode. No particular modality is consistently preferred, suggesting that their failure to learn predictive aspects of their environment stems from difficulty in dealing with multiple information, rather than from a sensory deficiency. If previously ignored cues are correlated separately with response outcomes, autistic children eventually learn their predictive value.

Attentional dysfunctions can impair psychological functioning in several ways. One is that they limit generalized use of skills (Lovaas et al., 1979). This is because the same set of cues does not always recur together at different times and places. Effective action under changeable circumstances, therefore, requires broad knowledge of the different aspects of the environment that have predictive value. Overdependence on only a few predictors dissuades children from functional action when those particular cues happen to be absent. The tasks of everyday life provide not only multiple informative cues but many irrelevant ones as well. Attentional overselectivity often results in inappropriate action when some minor or unreliable aspect of the environment is erroneously invested with predictive significance (Rincover & Koegel, 1977). Autistic children are aided in gaining knowledge of their environment when others accent for them the important features and gradually introduce new complexities with ample corrective feedback.

Observational learning provides a mechanism for rapid acquisition of social and cognitive competencies. Without close attention to modeling guides, competencies cannot be easily developed. In his work with autistic children, Lovaas (1977) found that they pay little attention to modeling influences, but they draw on example when modeled actions are made obviously predictive of valued outcomes. Autistic children who lacked communicative speech matched therapists' speech with a high degree of accuracy when doing so produced positive outcomes. When they were equally generously rewarded, but without regard to the quality of their speech, their utterances progressively deteriorated until they bore little resemblance to the linguistic features modeled for them by therapists. After the benefits of matching therapists' speech was reinstated, the children used modeling cues as communicative guides. Autistic children evidently are not insensitive to environmental events when they are made clearly predictive of valued outcomes.

Because of the importance of symbolic communication in human relationships, deficient or inappropriate responsiveness to verbal cues can have adverse social consequences. In their treatment of adult psychotics, Ayllon and his associates provide many illustrations in their treatment of adult psychotics of how the cueing function of language can be negated and restored by altering its outcome correlates (Ayllon & Haughton, 1962). Bizarre outcome relations can create idiosyncratic meanings that would be inexplicable without knowing the conditions of social learning. Lidz, Cornelison, Terry, and Fleck (1958) report a case in which sibling schizophrenics believed, among other strange things, that the word *disagreement* meant constipation. This peculiar conceptual behavior is quite understandable considering the social practices that prevailed in this household. Whenever the sons disagreed with their mother, she informed them that they were constipated and required an enema. The boys were then undressed and given enemas, a practice that endowed disagreement with a most unusual meaning.

Utilization of situational predictors is affected by stress, as well as by the response outcomes associated with them. People under strong threat are less able to distinguish critical from irrelevant features of the environment than when under mild threat, and those prone to high emotional arousal are the most adversely affected by stress in this regard (Rosenbaum, 1953, 1956).

Misjudgment by Assumed Likeness.

Because similarities generally aid predictive accuracy, perceived likenesses often override more valid sources of information. Tversky and Kahneman (1974) document the many ways this type of cognitive bias leads people astray. When given individuating or specific information, people tend to base their judgments on the stereotype aroused by the specific description and to ignore information about base rates, the prior likelihood of occurrence. The neglect of base-rate probabilities, once specific information is given, occurs even when the specific description that prompts the similarity matching is irrelevant.

The ease with which superficial similarities can distort predictive judgment has been shown in a series of studies conducted by Gilovich (1981). Both coaches and sportswriters overrated a college athlete's prospect of success in professional football when irrelevant association with the name of a professional superstar was introduced. In judging how the United States should respond to a totalitarian threat toward a small nation by another country, students advocated a more interventionist course of action when the international crisis was likened to another Munich, representing political appeasement to Nazi Germany, than when it was likened to another Vietnam, representing a disastrous military entanglement. Gilovich adds a new twist to Santayana's adage that those who forget the past are condemned to repeat it: Those who see unwarranted likeness to the past are disposed to misapply its lessons.

Misjudgment through Biased Perspective.

People's personal experiences are of necessity limited and biased by the particular circles in which they move and by the activities in which they engage routinely. Nevertheless, they make quick judgments about various matters without giving adequate consideration to the unrepresentativeness of their personal experiences (Tversky & Kahneman, 1974). Biased perspectives spawn inaccurate judgment. Nisbett and Ross (1980) provide an extensive analysis of how misapplication of preexisting beliefs and simplifying modes of reasoning give rise to faulty judgment.

Like other cognitive capabilities, skill in applying statistical rules can be developed. Memory aids and instruction in the rules relating predictors to outcomes improve human judgment (Kuylenstierna & Brehmer, 1981). Even so, probabilistic reasoning is far from optimal. Suboptimal judgment reflects both the fallibility of human reasoning and the imperfection of instruction. People can learn rules but put them to poor use because they do not recognize their applicability to the situations they encounter. Operative understanding comes through guided experience in applying a given rule to different situations. In studies designed to demonstrate that probabilistic reasoning is a teachable skill, Krantz, Fong, and Nisbett (1983) demonstrated that teaching abstract rules with applications to everyday examples produces greater use of the rule than does either abstract rule instruction or examples alone. The untutored made little use of statistical rules.

Kahneman and Tversky (1979) present several methods for correcting some of the common errors of intuitive judgment. It will be recalled that a major judgmental bias is the tendency to be swayed unduly by information (often meager and unreliable) about a particular case and to underweigh or ignore information about typical outcomes of similar cases. This type of error can be reduced by setting the judgment between the impression of the specific case and what is known to be generally true of similar cases. The less dependable the specific information, the more the judgment should be regressed toward the average or base rates for that class. Thus, in estimating the likelihood of becoming a successful novelist, one should consider the typical success rate for writers and then adjust the judgment upward or downward, depending upon available information distinguishing the particular writer from others in this reference class.

In many instances, correcting intuitive misjudgment by adjusting toward the class value is easier prescribed than applied because applying base-rate corrections is far from a simple matter. It requires, among other things, selecting an appropriate reference class from possible alternatives, knowing the average and range of outcomes for the reference class, choosing only the relevant individuating information, and knowing its predictive value. These factors themselves are often poorly understood or misjudged. For example, in estimating which new consumer product, from the many that are introduced, has the best chance of becoming a hit, neither the class referents nor the individuating predictors are all that definite. One will err with statistical reasoning if one's intuitions about appropriate reference classes and base rates are amiss. Uncertainty about which predictors and reference classes might be most pertinent for a particular undertaking fuels disagreements among experts.

Correcting for intuitive judgment through base-rate considerations becomes even more complex when events are rapidly changing than when they are static, thus rendering past referential probabilities misleading (Einhorn & Hogarth, 1981). An important part of good judgment is skill in ferreting out information on whether to reason statistically or causally. Consider the law of large numbers, which counsels that greater weight be given to the outcomes of many instances than to those of a few instances, because highly deviant occurrences are likely to be less prevalent in a larger sample. Suppose a diner recently experienced a few bad meals in an otherwise large number of delicious ones in a favorite restaurant. If the disappointing fare was due to random fluctuations in the kitchen, then reasoning statistically from past probabilities will bring the diner back to enjoy many future delicious meals. If, however, there has been a change in the kitchen and the culinary skills of the new chef leave much to be desired, then acting on statistical reasoning will ensure dining disappointments, whereas reasoning causally will steer one to delicious meals elsewhere. Failure to use statistical rules does not necessarily reflect cognitive deficiencies.

People generally overestimate the adequacy of their knowledge, especially in areas of limited familiarity. In addition to possessing incomplete, if not unreliable knowledge, they tend to use what they do know in ways that lead them to overestimate the validity of their judgments. They favor confirmatory evidence but disregard contradictory evidence. Instances in which actions produce positive outcomes are easily remembered, whereas it is difficult to remember also all the instances when actions failed to produce the outcomes or when the outcomes occurred without the actions, and to figure out the probabilistic relationship between actions and outcomes. As a result, outcome information is more likely to be represented in memory as frequency of successes than as probability of successes (Einhorn & Hogarth, 1978; Estes, 1976). The predictiveness of a relevant factor can be altered or even nullified by other conditions. Such conditional predictive relationships are best identified by seeking disconfirming evidence. Nor do people examine fully the tenuous assumptions on which their judgments of outcomes rest. Unwarranted overconfidence can be reduced by having people specify their implicit assumptions, examine contradictory evidence they usually neglect, and create probability distributions for their outcome estimations (Kahneman & Tversky, 1979; Koriat, Lichtenstein, & Fischhoff, 1980; Lichtenstein & Fischhoff, 1980).

Benefits of Affirmative Misjudgment

It is commonly assumed that misjudgment begets dysfunction, whereas unerring judgment optimizes benefits. Acting on gross misjudgment is usually a costly matter. However, lesser positive misjudgments are not necessarily harmful, nor is veridical judgment always beneficial. Indeed, much human progress and well-being rest on judgments that are not entirely veridical. Evidence for the benefits of positive misjudgments that do not stray unduly from what is possible comes from a variety of sources.

Human effort and actions are extensively regulated by self-judgments of efficacy. What people can do depends largely on the skills they possess and on self-beliefs that govern the amount of effort and perseverance they bring to bear on a task. Vigorous, sustained effort may produce extraordinary attainments where less concerted efforts yield ordinary performances, if not failures. Operative capabilities, therefore, are a changeable rather than a fixed property. Since what people can do depends partly on how hard they work at it, those who overestimate their capabilities are not necessarily being irrational. Rather, they are inclined to regard that probabilistically low attainments are realizable through sustained high effort. If self-percepts of efficacy always reflected only what persons can do normally, they would rarely fail, but they also would not risk challenges that lead them to expect more of themselves and, as a consequence, to surpass their ordinary performances.

Advantageous Self-Judgment of Capabilities. Self-percepts that slightly exceed what one can normally do at any given time are most conducive to self-development. Belief in one's capabilities for difficult attainments is likely to promote the perseverance needed to succeed, whereas disbelief in one's capabilities is apt to foreordain failure. When people err in their self-appraisals, they usually overestimate their capabilities (Bandura, 1977b; Schunk, 1981). The occasions when performances fall short of elevated self-percepts become evident instances of misjudgment. But exaggerated self-percepts that raise performance to the point where disparities between self-perception and action do not occur come to be regarded as instances of veridical self-judgment. Performance is usually accepted uncritically as the marker of reality against which to gauge the accurateness of judgment. In actuality, performance attainment is a probabilistic, rather than a fixed, event, and a given performance under particular circumstances is not necessarily representative of the best one can do. When judgment and action diverge, it is arguable whether the self-appraisal is faulty or the specific performance is unrepresentative. Because illusory self-percepts can give rise to congruent, extraordinary performances, the specification of veridical judgment is more complex than a cursory analysis might suggest. For activities in which errors carry no heavy costs, the risk of a shortcoming is a modest price for the substantial benefits of heightened mastery.

Competence has traditionally been viewed as mainly a matter of developing cognitive, social, and behavioral skills. It has been assumed that skill development reduces vulnerability to human distress and dysfunction. However, on closer inspection it has become evident that coping skills are necessary, but insufficient, for effective functioning. The skills and self-beliefs of anxious, avoidant, and depressed people have been compared with those who are unburdened by such problems. The findings generally show that these groups differ little in their actual skills, but they differ substantially in their perceived self-efficacy. People who shun social interactions are just as socially skilled in structured situations as are the more sociable ones, but the sociable ones judge their interpersonal adeptness more highly (Glasgow & Arkowitz, 1975). It remains to be seen whether differences continue to reside more in self-perception than actual social skills when people have to initiate and structure social contacts, rather than just respond to prearranged ones. Depressed persons display realistic self-appraisals of their social competencies, whereas the nondepressed view themselves as more adept than others see them (Lewinsohn, Mischel, Chaplin, & Barton, 1980). In the course of treatment, the depressed begin to manifest self-enhancing distortions in appraising their competencies much as the nondepressed do. One can, of course, point to instances in which distorted self-appraisal is part of severe dysfunction. Psychotic depression characterized by self-blame for the world's ills and a sense of total worthlessness is one example.

Misjudgment of Causal Agency. In their everyday life, people continually cause effects through their actions. Since they make all kinds of things happen in their immediate environment, there is every reason for them to believe that their actions will continue to have at least some effect in whatever new situations they may encounter. Indeed, considering that the outcomes people experience depend heavily upon how they behave, it would require an unusually obtuse organism to fail to gain some sense of causal agency. Not surprisingly, people are prone to view good outcomes as dependent on their actions, even when they are determined by other factors.

Research has clarified some of the conditions fostering an illusory sense of causal efficacy. In these studies people judge how much control they exerted over outcomes in situations where their actions actually have no effect whatsoever on when the outcomes occur. Despondent mood and thinking dampen misbelief in one's power to produce desired effects (Alloy & Abramson, 1979). Nondepressed persons tend to overestimate their control over desirable outcomes, when they occur often, and underrate their causa-

tion of bad outcomes. Depressed people are quite realistic in judging that they exercise little control. When nondepressed people are made temporarily depressed, they become realists in judging their low personal control, whereas when depressed people are made to feel happy they overestimate how much control they exert over positive events (Alloy, Abramson, & Viscusi, 1981). Even prior failure experiences do not shake the misbeliefs of nondespondent people that they make things happen (Alloy & Abramson, 1982). Thus, in situations in which actions exert no effect on positive outcomes, the depressed appear as realists about themselves, the nondepressed as confident illusionists.

Nondespondent people do not approach new situations with an indiscriminate rosy glow of casual efficacy. Their self-judgments are partly governed by competence-related cues that summon up past experiences and self-knowledge of capabilities. In examining this process, Langer (1975) has shown that people are easily misled into overestimating their causal efficacy by cues indicative of skill and prospective success. When elements that increase the likelihood of success on tasks of skill are introduced into chance activities, people feel confident they have gained some influence over outcomes entirely determined by chance. Such things as choice, familiarity, active involvement, and practice on chance tasks, even though completely irrelevant to what will happen, create a set that carrying out these rituals of skill operates to provide some measure of control over chance outcomes. However, a depressed outlook nullifies the power of superficial skill cues to induce a spurious sense of casual agency (Golin, Terrell, & Johnson, 1977; Golin, Terrell, Weitz, & Drost, 1979).

Judgments of causality are strongly influenced by the frequency with which actions and outcomes appear together. Confirming instances are given much weight. Nonconfirming instances—the outcome appears without the action or the action occurs without the outcome—are generally given less consideration (Jenkins & Ward, 1965). Selective recall of successes inflates judgment of causal efficacy. The tendency to overweigh successes in judging personal causation is increased when experiences occur over time, leaving judgments about past happenings and their causes to the vagaries of imperfect memory and cognitive biases.

An important indicant of casual efficacy is evidence that one can alter outcome probabilities by varying one's behavior. When a given course of action is noticeably more successful than others in securing desired outcomes, people are fairly accurate in judging how much control they can command (Alloy & Abramson, 1979). A sense of causal agency arises largely from successes in producing effects through intentional action. Action is, therefore, apt to be more suggestive of causal efficacy than is inaction. In accord with this expectation, Alloy and Abramson found that nondespondent people develop a greater sense of personal control when they secure rewards through action than if they gain the same rewards by nonresponse.

As evident from these comparative studies, successful functioning requires both the skills and the self-beliefs that ensure optimal use of these capabilities. Because most efforts do not bring quick results, success requires robust self-assurance. The motivational benefits of reasonably overoptimistic self-appraisals are interestingly revealed in studies in which self-percepts of efficacy have been illusorily boosted (Weinberg, Gould, & Jackson, 1979; Weinberg, Yukelson, & Jackson, 1980). People who are led to believe they are highly capable are spurred by inflated self-appraisal to greater efforts that enable them to surpass their usual performances.

Optimistic self-percepts of efficacy reduce stress reactions in taxing situations, as well as enhance motivation. This affective benefit not only spares wear and tear on the viscera, but it lessens the likelihood that performances will be impaired by disruptive arousal. There is a third benefit to advantageous self-appraisal. Performance successes are determined by both personal and situational factors. To the extent that performers are generous in crediting good outcomes to their capabilities, they experience a high level of positive self-evaluation (Abramson & Alloy, 1980). Self-deprecation of one's own efforts begets discouragement.

Misjudgments of Social Sanctions and Collective Efficacy.

The threat of legal sanctions is extensively used in social efforts to deter criminal conduct. In a later chapter we shall have occasion to see that the chances of being apprehended and punished for committing criminal acts is exceedingly low. Occasional penalties for profitable illegal activities cannot act as much of a deterrent. However, legal deterrents rely upon perceived, rather than on actual, risk of punishment. It turns out that lawabiders greatly overestimate the likelihood that illegal acts will be punished, whereas those who take up antisocial pursuits hold a more realistic view of the risks (Claster, 1967; Parker & Grasmick, 1979). In the maintenance of the social order, misjudgment helps to keep much of the citizenry lawful.

Many people devote their lives to social and political activism by their unwavering conviction that by collective effort they will eventually bring about fundamental changes in society. While such convictions often go unrealized, they sustain reform efforts that achieve lesser but nonetheless important social changes. In the effort for social change, success is better measured by gains than by victories. Were social activists to be entirely realistic about the prospects of success, they would either forego the endeavor or fall easy victim to discouragement. Realists may adapt well to existing realities, but dedicated visionaries effect changes in those realities.

These findings taken as a whole indicate

that it is the successful, the sociable, the nondespondent, the lawabiding, and the social reformers who display positive "distortions" in judging their capabilities and the likely outcomes of their efforts. Such misjudgments furnish the hope and self-incentives for pursuits that hold promise of bringing personal attainments and satisfactions. If not unrealistically exaggerated, optimistic self-appraisals prompt and sustain the type of outlook and effort needed to realize personal aspirations.

INCENTIVE MOTIVATORS

If people acted with foresight on the basis of informative cues but remained unaffected by the results of their actions, they would be too insensible to survive very long. Behavior is, in fact, extensively regulated by its effects. Actions that bring rewards are generally repeated, whereas those that bring unrewarding or punishing outcomes tend to be discarded. Human behavior, therefore, cannot be fully understood without considering the regulatory influence of response consequences.

Research on how outcomes regulate behavior has been predominantly concerned with immediate external effects. But external consequences, as influential as they often are, are not the only kind of outcomes that determine human behavior. People partly guide their actions by both observed consequences and the consequences they create for themselves. These three regulatory incentive systems, based on external, vicarious, and self-produced outcomes, will be analyzed separately. The present chapter is concerned with external outcomes that are directly experienced.

EXPLANATION OF OUTCOME DETERMINANTS

Outcome determinants of action have always occupied a central position in theories relying upon feedback regulatory mechanisms. However, it is within the operant framework that almost all the causes of behavior are rooted in response consequences (Skinner, 1969, 1974). That actions are influenced by their effects is now acknowledged in most theories that aspire to explanatory and predictive power. They differ in how large a role they assign to this determinant and in the mechanisms through which it operates.

Automatic Mechanism

Behavior theories have traditionally distinguished between antecedent and consequent regulation of actions. This differentiation rests on the assumption that actions are directly strengthened and weakened by their immediate consequences. Because the likelihood of a behavior occurring is affected by events that follow it does not mean that control resides in those events. Indeed, since consequences follow actions, making the actual consequences the controlling agents is to place the cause after the effect. Radical behaviorists seek to resolve the problem of backward causation by placing the cause of behavior in the implants of past consequences. However, studies of how outcomes enter into the determination of human behavior call into question such an automatic mode of operation. Recall from the earlier discussion that outcomes influence behavior largely through their informative and incentive value, rather than by serving as automatic response strengtheners. For the most part, response outcomes influence behavior antecedently by creating expectations of similar outcomes on future occasions. The likelihood of particular actions is increased by anticipated reward and reduced by anticipated punishment.

Behavior is related to its outcomes at the level of aggregate rather than momentary consequences (Baum, 1973). That is, people do not respond to each bit of feedback as an isolated experience. Rather, they process and synthesize feedback information from sequences of events over time to gain knowledge of what is needed to produce certain kinds, patterns, and rates of outcomes. Because outcomes affect actions largely through the mediation of thought, conse-

quences alone often produce little change in behavior until people become aware of what actions are being rewarded or punished (Brewer, 1974). Once expectation of reward has been created, a lot of behavior can be maintained by only occasional reward in the absence of better alternatives.

We saw earlier that in studies pitting belief against consequent, persons' erroneous beliefs about how often and why outcomes flow from certain actions can exert a greater influence on behavior than the outcomes themselves (Dulany, 1968; Kaufman, Baron, & Kopp, 1966). Erroneous beliefs override the influence of actual outcomes most readily when consequences are not only irregular but also delayed, thus making errors in judgment more difficult to detect (Frazier, 1973). In everyday circumstances, actions usually produce mixed effects, they occur closely or far removed in time, irrelevancies abound, and many factors influence the probabilistic relation between actions and outcomes. Such bewildering patterns provide a fertile ground for misjudgment. When people are left to their own devices to figure out the bases on which their actions are rewarded, they infer different rules of reward. Even though exposed to the same outcome contingency, they display marked differences in behavior, which are highly predictable from their beliefs (Lippman & Meyer, 1967).

The widely accepted dictum that behavior is governed by its consequences fares better for anticipated than for actual consequences. As people experience some success in producing effects by their actions, they behave on the basis of the outcomes they expect to prevail in the future. In most instances, customary outcomes are good predictors of behavior because what people anticipate is accurately derived from and, therefore corresponds closely to, prevailing rules of reward. Belief and actuality, however, do not always coincide. This is because people partly derive their beliefs about how much control they can exert over outcomes from the observed outcomes experienced by others, from what they read or are told, and from other indicators of likely consequences.

People may accurately assess existing rules of reward but fail to act in accordance with them because of false hopes that their actions may eventually bring favorable results. In one study, some children persisted in modeling behavior that was never rewarded, in the mistaken belief that their continued imitation might change the adults' reward practices (Bandura & Barab, 1971). People often lead themselves astray by erroneous beliefs when they assume wrongly that persistence or certain changes in their behavior will alter the likelihood of future consequences.

When belief differs from actuality, which is not uncommon, behavior is weakly controlled by its actual consequences until repeated experience instills realistic beliefs. It is not always one's beliefs that change in the direction of social reality. Acting on erroneous beliefs can alter how others behave, thus shaping the social reality in the direction of the mistaken beliefs (Snyder, 1981). In most human transactions the influence process is best represented by bidirectional causality between belief and social reality.

Cognitive Mechanisms

Remarkably diverse events can act as motivators of human behavior. In the social learning view, these multiform incentives operate largely through the common mechanism of anticipatory thought. Response consequences affect the motivation to perform given activities by creating beliefs about the effects actions are likely to have under different circumstances. People select courses of action within their perceived capabilities and sustain their efforts partly on the basis of such outcome expectations. Because of their cognitive capacity to foresee the likely outcomes of prospective actions, people can sustain their efforts by symbolic motivators over a long time perspective. Infrahuman species, likewise, be-

have in anticipation of outcomes, but, due to their limited symbolic capacities, they require external reminders of distal outcomes that they cannot keep in mind, and they depend mainly on somatically based incentives. The weaker the symbolic capabilities, the more external cues have to be substituted for anticipatory thought.

Anticipatory outcome determinants of action are often conceptualized in terms of expectancies. Tolman (1932) was one of the early theorists to argue that reinforcement builds expectancies rather than strengthens habits. For Tolman, expectancy was not a causal cognition but simply a descriptor of an action sequence in which an organism acts "as if" it expects its behavior to produce a specific consequence. Most contemporary theories view expectancies as cognitions, usually indexed by subjective estimates of the likelihood that particular events will occur.

A number of theorists have explained motivation in terms of the expectancy-valence model (Atkinson, 1964; Fishbein, 1967; Rotter, 1954; Vroom, 1964). All these formulations assume that strength of motivation is jointly a function of the belief that particular actions will produce specified outcomes and the value placed on those outcomes. They differ mainly in what additional determinants are combined with expectancy and valence. Atkinson adds an achievement motive; Fishbein adds perceived social pressures to perform the behavior and proneness to compliance; and Vroom adds belief that the behavior is achievable through effort.

In its basic version, the expectancy-valence theory predicts that the higher the perceived outcome expectancy and the more valued the outcomes, the greater is the motivation to perform the activity. Results of numerous laboratory and field studies show that outcome expectations obtained by adding or multiplying these factors predict performance (Mitchell, 1974; Schwab, Olian-Gottlieb, & Heneman, 1979). However, much of the variance in performance remains unaccounted for. This has stimulated a spirited debate about the scope of the expectancy-valence model, its major assumptions, and the methodologies used for assessing and combining the components.

According to maximizing-expectancy models, people seek to optimize their outcomes. Questions have been raised, however, concerning the assumptions about how decisions are usually made. Several authors have argued convincingly that people are not as systematic in considering alternative courses of action and in weighing their likely consequences as such models assume (Behling & Starke, 1973; Simon, 1976). Alternatives are often ill defined. People rarely examine all the feasible alternatives or give detailed thought to all the consequences of even the options they do consider. More typically they pick, from a limited array of possibilities, the course of action that looks satisfactory, rather than search studiously for the optimal one. Moreover, they are sometimes inconsistent in how they order alternatives, they have difficulty assigning relative weights to different types of outcomes, they let the attractiveness of the outcomes color their judgments of how difficult it might be to attain them, and they opt for lesser outcomes because they can get them sooner. When faced with many alternatives and possible outcomes, they use simplifying decision strategies that may lead them to select alternatives that differ from those they would have had they weighed and ordered the various factors as presupposed by the maximizing model.

The issue in question is not the rationality of the judgmental process. People have incomplete or erroneous information about alternatives and their probable consequences, they process information through cognitive biases, and what they value may be rather odd. Decisions that are subjectively rational to the performer, given the basis on which they were made, may appear irrational to others. Subjective rationality often sponsors faulty choices. There are too many aspects to a judgmental process in which one can go astray to achieve objective ration-

ality (Brandt, 1979). The main issue in dispute concerns the correspondence between the postulated process and how people actually go about appraising and weighing the probable consequences of alternative actions.

The types of incentives singled out for attention is another dimension on which expectancy theory often departs from actuality. Some of the most valued rewards of activities are in the satisfaction derived from fulfilling personal standards, rather than in tangible payoffs. Because incentive theories tend to neglect the self-evaluative outcomes of action, self-reactive incentives rarely receive the consideration they deserve in the cost-benefit calculation. Predictiveness is sacrificed if influential self-incentives are overlooked. With regard to the scope of the model, even the elaborated versions include only a few motivational processes. In actuality, forethought concerning outcomes influences effort and performance through a variety of intervening mechanisms.

People act on their judgments of what they can do, as well as on their beliefs about the likely effects of various actions. There are many activities, which, if done well, guarantee cherished outcomes, but they are not pursued by persons who doubt they can do what is needed to succeed. Self-perceived inefficacy can nullify the most enticing outcome expectations. Conversely, a strong sense of personal efficacy can strengthen and sustain efforts in the face of uncertain outcomes.

In activities that call upon competencies, perceived self-efficacy mediates how outcome expectations influence personal decisions and expenditures of effort. Vroom (1964) partially addresses this issue by including in his model beliefs that hard work will bring forth good performances. However, as will be shown later, judgments of self-efficacy depend on much more than effort considerations. This is because quality and effectiveness of performance are not controlled merely by effort. People judge their capability for challenging attainments more in terms of their perceptions of the skills and strategies they have at their command than solely by how much they can exert themselves. Performances that call for ingenuity, resourcefulness, and adaptability depend more on adroit use of skills than on dint of effort. People who cope poorly with stress expect that marred performances in threatening situations will be determined by their self-debilitating habits rather than by the efforts they make. Indeed, the harder they try, the more poorly they may do. Expectancy theorists most likely singled out effort as the exclusive determiner of performance accomplishments because the theory has often been concerned with the level at which people perform their routine activities. Therefore, the aspect of self-efficacy that becomes the most relevant in routine repetitive activities is people's perceived perseverant capabilities, that is, whether or not they can exert themselves sufficiently to achieve certain levels of productivity.

For outcomes requiring prolonged endeavor, people need more than visions of valued payoffs to sustain them in their efforts. To ensure success, self-regulatory mechanisms relying on proximal subgoals and self-evaluative incentives must be pressed into service to provide a continuing source of self-motivation. The same outcome expectations will have different motivational impact depending on the self-regulatory influences enlisted in the process.

Desire for cherished but hard-to-get outcomes can dominate people's outlooks and lead them to disregard most of the dissuading consequences of their chosen pursuits. Through selective attention they rivet their sights on hoped-for outcomes, a process which helps to sustain them in the face of objectively dismal prospects. A more impartial weighing of alternatives would prescribe a quite different course of action. In short, people act on outcome beliefs, but their actions are not always designed to optimize benefits. They usually make choices on outcome considerations arrived at informally through cognitive biases, rather than by methodical calculation of the costs and benefits of alternative actions.

DEVELOPMENT OF INCENTIVE FUNCTIONS

Social cognitive theory distinguishes between two broad classes of motivators of behavior: those which are biologically based and those which are cognitively based.

The *biologically based* motivators include physiological conditions arising from cellular deficits and external aversive stimuli that activate behavior through their physically painful effects. It should be noted, however, that activities related to cellular needs and other biological functions reflect the pull of external incentives, as well as the action of bodily conditions. The sight of appetizing food prompts people to eat even though they are not that hungry. Eating customs rather than hours of food deprivation determine when they hunger for food. Through relational learning, even infants become active and fuss when they expect to be fed, rather than on the basis of how hungry they actually are (Marquis, 1941).

Sexual motivators similarly depend heavily on incentive factors. Humans are sexually stirred by external and symbolic arousers, rather than by the press of an internal sex drive. With advancing evolutionary status, hormonal activation of sexual behavior has given way to social arousers (Beach, 1969; Ford & Beach, 1951). In the lower mammalian species, sexual activities are closely regulated by gonadal hormones; among primates sexual responsiveness is partially independent of hormone secretions; and human sexual arousal is exceedingly variable and relatively independent of hormonal conditions. To produce sexy rodents requires injections of sex hormones, whereas exposing them to erotic pictures of mice endowed with sex appeal would have no stimulating effects. To produce sexy humans, one relies on erotic displays rather than on hormonal injections.

Cross-cultural studies disclose further that certain regions of the body, the physical characteristics, the gestures, and the sensory stimuli that function as sexual arousers all vary considerably from society to society.

What is erotically stimulating in one culture may be neutral or repulsive to members of another social group. A similar diversity exists for the age at which sexual interest first emerges. As these few examples illustrate, incentive mechanisms play a substantial role in the regulation of human behaviors that cater to organic needs. Physiological conditions do, of course, affect the activating potency of incentives.

The second major source of inducements involves *cognitively based* motivators. Through symbolic representation of foreseeable consequences, future outcomes can be converted into current guides and motivators of behavior. Here, the instigator to action is forethought rather than the sight of the actual incentives. The outcome expectations may be material (e.g., consumable, physically painful), sensory (e.g., novel, enjoyable, or unpleasant sensory stimulation), token (e.g., grades, money), or social (e.g., positive and negative interpersonal reactions).

A second cognitively based source of motivation, which will be analyzed in a later chapter, operates through the intervening influences of internal standards and self-evaluative reactions to one's own performances. Goals and standards serve as cognitive representations of desired futures. By making self-satisfaction conditional on fulfilling selected goals, people give direction to their actions and create self-incentives to persist in their efforts until their performances match their goals.

Primary Incentives

What people find motivating changes as a result of developmental experiences. At the outset, infants are responsive mainly to immediate primary instigators involving food, aversive stimuli, and physical contact. The potency of primary incentives tied to bodily needs, such as food and drink, is strengthened by deprivation and weakened by satiation. However, the motivating stimuli do not arise solely from deprivation. The motivating force of physiological deprivation partly depends on external arousers (Bolles, 1975). Thus, food deprivation in the sight of food or at the time of day when eating is anticipated is highly activating, whereas food deprivation alone is not.

Events that derive their motivating power from aversiveness activate courses of action designed to relieve pain and discomfort. The strength of aversive motivators depends on the intensity of the pain-producing stimuli. As Miller (1963) has pointed out, any stimuli of high intensity can serve as drives to action. Cognitive factors can raise or lower the intensity of aversive motivators (Turk, Meichenbaum, & Genest, 1981), as they affect motivators arising from physiological deprivation. Primary incentives are not only important in their own right; they also contribute to the development and support of symbolic incentives.

Sensory Incentives

Many human activities are regulated by the sensory feedback they provide. Infants, for example, repeatedly perform acts that produce new sounds and sights (Rheingold, Stanley, & Doyle, 1964; Stevenson & Odom, 1964). Novelty and change generally increase, and repetitiveness reduces, the effectiveness of discrete sensory events. Similarly, older children and adults spend long hours playing musical instruments that create sounds they find pleasing. Although most sensory effects are intrinsically related to the actions, the affective valence of the sensory feedback is usually a product of learning. Neither atonal music nor cubistic art is innately pleasing. However, through repeated exposure, prototypes and structural properties of events are learned which serve as references for experiencing what is seen and heard as enjoyable or displeasing. Matches are pleasing, whereas mismatches are usually experienced as displeasing.

Various theories have been proposed to explain how sensory events operate as motivators (Eisenberger, 1972; Fowler, 1971). Some theorists have posited curiosity and exploratory drives that are aroused by novel stimuli and reduced by continued exposure to them (Berlyne, 1960; Harlow, 1953). Other theorists have postulated a need to sustain an optimal level of sensory stimulation (Fiske & Maddi, 1961; Leuba, 1955). People will, therefore, do things to increase sensory input if they experience a deficit and to reduce the input if sensory stimulation exceeds the optimal level.

Theories that place the burden of explanation on innate drives encounter a number of difficulties. In the prototypical studies designed to confirm a curiosity drive, animals enclosed in a sound-proof and light-proof box performed responses that opened a window affording them a view of different activities (Butler, 1954, 1958). As Brown (1953) points out, the animals' actions could not have been motivated by a curiosity drive roused by novel stimuli, because the animals did not see the novel stimuli until after they had already performed the behavior. Miller and his associates (Myers & Miller, 1954) and Mowrer (1960) pointed to other possible motivators of exploratory behavior. Monotony and sensory deprivation create boredom and sometimes arouse anxiety, both of which are aversive. Organisms will do things to escape boredom and to reduce apprehension. Thus, in many situations, seeking a change in stimulation might reflect the push of boredom, rather than the pull of novelty.

People are not always questing for novelty and stimulus change. Whether they seek novelty or familiarity varies greatly across activities. Sports fans will spend money, time, and effort to see their favorite team in an athletic contest, but few, if any, would do so to watch repeated reruns of a game they had already seen. In contrast, a symphony that played nothing but new selections, in the belief that people are driven by a search for novelty, would be bankrupt in short order. It is the oft-repeated repertoires that fill concert halls. In the history of creative endeavors, whether it be art, music, film, or other activities, avant-garde forms typically receive a cool, if not hostile reception, until eventually they become familiar

through repeated exposure, usually appended to familiar works. Even then, the public often patronizes these newer forms, which it neither likes nor understands, to maintain cultural pretensions.

The amount and type of stimulation people seek is predicted better from the *content* than from the sheer *amount* of sensory input that activities provide. The same is true of lower species. Monkeys confined in a drab box will work for opportunities to view other monkeys, movies, and electric trains or to hear sounds from a monkey colony, but they prefer utmost boredom to sensory stimulation that disturbs them (Butler, 1954, 1958). Findings such as these, showing that valence overrides quantity of stimulation, are at odds with theories cast solely in terms of a drive for optimal activation.

According to other theories, sensory input is motivating because it creates a discrepancy between preexisting knowledge or expectation and current experience (Piaget, 1960). Incongruity motivates exploratory efforts to resolve the conflict. Moderate discrepancies are presumed to be motivating, whereas larger ones are not. Motivation arising from informational discrepancy is analyzed in a later chapter and will not be considered here, except to acknowledge some of the problematic aspects of this type of explanation. Discordances often prompt reappraisals of feedback information, rather than spur exploration and curiosity. Without an independent measure of what people know and what constitutes a moderate level of discrepancy, there is little basis for predicting whether informative feedback will spark curiosity or leave persons unmoved. Studies in which the discrepancy levels are varied do not provide consistent support for the view that moderate mismatches are most preferred or provide the strongest impetus for learning (Wachs, 1977). Another issue concerns the nature of the internal comparison process itself. It has been amply documented that disparity between informative feedback and internal standards creates motivational inducements that can sustain extended involvement in activities. Whether the motivational mechanism involves discrepancy from states of knowledge or from personal standards needs to be differentiated.

To sum up, sensory events can become motivators through a variety of means—some may be intrinsically pleasing or aversive, many satisfy acquired preferences and tastes, others provide escape from boredom or distress, and still others create motivating internal discordancies. Rather than novel stimuli automatically arousing a curiosity drive that propels behavior, activities are largely selected and motivated anticipatorily by the sensory effects they are expected to produce.

Social Incentives

In the course of development, physically rewarding experiences often occur in conjunction with expressions of interest and approval of others, while unpleasant experiences are associated with disapproval. By such correlation of events, social reactions themselves become predictors of primary consequences and thereby become incentives. People will do things for approval and refrain from actions that arouse the wrath of others. By reversing the physical correlates, one could make smiles foreboders of suffering and scowls forewarners of pleasure. The effectiveness of social reactions as incentives thus derives from their predictive value, rather than inhering in the reactions themselves. For this reason, the approval or disapproval of people who exercise rewarding and punishing power is more influential than similar expressions by individuals who cannot affect one's life. Indiscriminate praise that never carries any tangible effects becomes an empty reward, and disapproval that is never backed up with any tangible consequences becomes an empty threat devoid of motivating value.

Several factors contribute to the power of social incentives. The same social expressions can predict an array of possible rewarding or punishing experiences. Disapproval, for example, may result in such

unpleasant effects as physical punishment, deprivation of privileges, penalties, dismissal from a job, withdrawal of love, or ostracism. An event that signifies diverse possible consequences will have greater potency than if it portends only a single effect. Moreover, social reactions are not invariably accompanied by primary experiences: Praise does not always bring material benefits, and reprimands do not always result in physical suffering. Unpredictability protects social and symbolic incentives from losing their effectiveness (Mowrer, 1960). Because of intermittency and diversity of correlates, social reactions retain their incentive function even with minimal primary support.

Development of social incentives is crucial for successful human relationships and accomplishments. Most endeavors produce tangible results only after extended effort. The encouragement and commendation of associates help to support goal-directed activities in the interim. Social reactions also provide a convenient way for people to influence each other without having to resort continuously to physical consequences. Indeed, it is difficult to conceive of a society populated with people who are completely unmoved by the respect, approval, and reproof of others.

Monetary Incentives

All societies use money as a powerful generalized incentive. Its motivating value derives from the fact that money can purchase most anything people desire—commodities, properties, human services, health care, privileges, and even social influence. As a result, people are attracted to occupations that pay well, they labor daily at tasks they may not entirely enjoy for the pay it brings them, they mobilize their collective power to negotiate favorable pay rates, and they become apprehensive about economic conditions that devalue the money they already possess.

Monetary incentive systems have changed substantially over the years. Initially, piece-rate incentives were widely used as the preferred means of motivating task performance. However, as employees have gained collective bargaining power, they have negotiated wage systems in which compensation was tied only loosely to performance. Payments have become linked to time rates (e.g., hourly, weekly, monthly, or yearly) which, in turn, are determined by such factors as job level, competing offerings, and seniority, rather than by actual accomplishments. As money lost some of its incentive function by becoming less tied to performance, the burden of motivating performance has fallen more heavily on social and personal incentives. Varied sources of influence are enlisted for this purpose, including informal social relations, group pressures, threats to job security, personal advancement, self-fulfillment, organizational goal-setting, and intergroup competition. Because of the personal and social rewards people derive from their work, many like their jobs even though they are dissatisfied with their pay.

Efforts to restore the motivating power of money have evolved various incentive systems designed to reward productivity (Lawler, 1971). Some of the variants combine fixed payment with either individual merit raises or group bonuses. Performance improves if it brings higher pay. But poorly implemented merit systems, in which merit pay is based on subjective or biased appraisals (Hammer, 1979), arouse the thorny problems associated with inequitable reward.

In group-incentive systems the proceeds of collective ventures are either divided equally among group members or are allocated in proportion to their contribution to the total effort. In studies comparing different monetary systems, persons paid on a fixed hourly basis set lower goals for themselves and accomplish less than those rewarded on the basis of individual or group performance. Group incentives that reward merit are more motivating than when proceeds are allotted equally (Farr, 1976b; Weinstein & Holzbach, 1973). Although

group-incentive systems foster commitment and productivity, they are seldom used because those who own organizations are not particularly eager to part with more of their profits. Small group bonuses provide little incentive for raising performance norms.

Professional and creative endeavors place a premium on personal initiative by tying monetary rewards intimately to level and quality of performance. Physicians and lawyers, for example, determine their own incomes by the number of clients they serve and the fees they charge. Similarly, authors and recording artists gain fortunes through sales of their books and records, and celebrities in different fields book themselves on profitable speaking and concert tours. People vie for popularity in activities that bring lavish rewards. Social scientists who warn that high pay will ruin the interest and motivation of salaried workers rarely counsel low reward of professional services and creative efforts. Many people, of course, take a more relaxed attitude toward work and are not all that interested in working hard for money. A growing number are sacrificing money and material luxuries for other things in life they value (Campbell, 1981).

Activity Incentives

The early influential theories of reinforcement, which were closely allied with biological drives, assumed that outcomes affect behavior by satisfying or reducing a physiological drive (Hull, 1943; Dollard & Miller, 1950). As a result, much of the theorizing and experimentation on this topic centered on consumables and pain reduction. Premack (1965, 1971) conducted a series of ingenious experiments that both challenged the drive-reduction mechanism and expanded greatly the types of tangible incentives that could be used as motivators.

Activities differ in their relative value. Premack showed that, for any given pair of activities, people will perform the less preferred one if this gives them an opportunity to engage in the more preferred one.

For example, if reading is preferred to arithmetic, individuals will labor at arithmetic to get a chance to read; but if arithmetic is preferred to reading, individuals will read for a chance to engage in arithmetic activities. The motivating power of a preferred activity can be promptly eradicated by changing its relative value by satiation or linkage to a more highly valued activity. Similarly, by altering value relations, a given activity can become a punisher if it is made conditional on performing a much preferred activity. Thus, the same activity can become an instrumental act, a motivator, or a punisher depending on its relative value. Further evidence suggests the need for refinements in the relational principle because the motivational value of activity incentives depends upon other factors as well, such as how much performance is required and how much access it affords to another valued activity (Allison, 1978). When high-performance demands provide only limited access to other valued activities, such an arrangement offers little incentive.

Testing the generalizability of Premack's theory across populations and domains of activity presents some difficulties when different assessment techniques yield different preference rankings for a given set of activities. Measures of preference derived from ranking the likability of each activity, the choices made between paired activities, and the amount of time one engaged in alternate activities under conditions of unlimited access, often produce dissimilar orderings (Whitehurst & Domash, 1974). Until valid measures are devised, it is difficult to determine from conflicting results whether the theory itself or, rather, the ordinal ranking of preferences is at fault. This problem is circumvented in practice by using only clearly preferred activities or an array of activities as incentives.

The motivating power of a contingent activity does not reside in its intrinsic properties but is derived relationally. Although experiential value is not totally independent of somatic states, evidence that the motivating properties of the same outcome can be instantly transformed by relational arrangements argues for an incentive, rather than a drive reduction, mode of operation.

Premack's research spoke to several other issues of concern to traditional theories of reinforcement. In such approaches, positive and negative "reinforcers" are defined as events that increase and reduce, respectively, the frequency of preceding acts. To define an event by the effects it is supposed to produce, rather than by independent criteria, creates explanatory circularity and renders the theory unfalsifiable. If a change in behavior defines a reinforcer, whenever outcomes fail to alter behavior they can be dismissed as not being genuine reinforcers. Meehl (1950) offered a way out of the circularity by defining a reinforcer independently of the behavior it is designed to change, on the assumption that outcomes work transsituationally. If, for example, money is verified as a reinforcer because it increases the frequency of a particular act, then it can serve to increase other acts as well. However, this transsituational solution provided only partial rescue because incentives do not necessarily affect all types of behavior. There are many things people will refuse to do for money. If money seems to work in some instances but not in others, the negative instances would refute the theoretical proposition that reinforcers automatically alter behavior. Premack disputed the assumption that outcomes retain their incentive properties across situations. His definition of incentive value avoided the problem of circularity without requiring that incentives possess transsituational power. Through prior transitive ordering of the value of different incentives, one can specify beforehand which incentives will change which acts.

Activity incentives are widely used in everyday life. Parents often make television, play activities, and outings contingent on children's completing academic or other tasks. Adults mobilize and channel their efforts by deferring breaks and leisure activities until they have achieved a certain amount of progress on a task. Evidence that contingent activities serve as motivators has encouraged the use of more natural incentives in treatment and remedial programs for people handicapped by deficient motivation and self-defeating behavior patterns (Homme, 1970). Moreover, activity incentives can be selected that have developmental value of their own. McLaughlin and Malaby (1974) used this approach with children plagued by growing academic difficulties because they rarely did their classroom work. When completing academic assignments gave them free time to read books and pursue self-selected projects, the children regularly completed most of their language and math assignments during the course of the year.

Status and Power Incentives

Most groups are structured in terms of status and power relations. Social power provides a measure of control over the resources and the behavior of others. Thus, through symbolic display and exercise of the power individuals possess, they wield jurisdiction over the group's life, enjoy the material rewards, social recognition, and privileges associated with high social rank, extract obedience, and are better able to further their personal interests and desires.

Because of the general benefits, people will go to great lengths to gain and hold positions of power. Aspiring executives take on burdensome work loads to scale the ranks of their organization. In aggressive gangs, where status and social power are tied to fighting prowess, members fight challengers within their own group and from rival gangs. Threats to status provoke quick, aggressive counteraction in efforts to preserve the existing power relations (Short, 1968; Wolfgang & Ferracuti, 1967; Yablonsky, 1962).

Although status and social incentives have some common features, they differ in several important respects. In the case of status, a required level of competence gains one a rank that carries with it a wide array of benefits, as long as that position is occupied.

In the case of social rewards, certain actions win approval without necessarily altering rank in the status hierarchy. In other words, one can be praised without being promoted in a status or power hierarchy.

Status incentives operate as more powerful motivators of behavior than does social approval of particular response patterns (Martin, Burkholder, Rosenthal, Tharp, & Thorne, 1968). To lose a specific reward for neglecting or mismanaging some task is of no great import. But when a few foolhardy or faulty actions can cause a demotion in rank and forfeiture of a large array of benefits, the threat of loss of status creates general pressure for exemplary performance. The pressure for performance is especially intense when the number of status positions is limited, when they carry huge benefits, and when there are many eager competitors for them. To reduce the level of competitiveness and stress, many organizations create seniority systems and due-process safeguards against easy demotion.

In addition to providing strong motivational inducements, status incentive systems foster valued patterns of behavior by their inherent modeling influences (Martin et al., 1968). Most social ranking is based on skill in activities valued highly by the particular group. By designating the competencies required for different positions, members who aspire to higher status have symbolic and actual models of what they must do to gain more privileged ranks.

Status undoubtedly derives its incentive value, in large part, from the social and material benefits associated with it. However, people strive for social ranks even in the absence of material benefit. For example, children will buy positions of leadership that heap responsibilities on their shoulders while bringing them little in the way of external rewards (Phillips, Phillips, Wolf, & Fixsen, 1973). For some individuals, the attraction of status and power may be of a personal nature. Effective exercise of leadership provides self-satisfaction, especially if the group endeavor serves worthy purposes. In situations involving potentially aversive events, the perception and exercise of personal control diminishes stress (Averill, 1973; Miller, 1979). Self-efficacious individuals, therefore, prefer to run things, rather than to entrust their welfare and peace of mind to less competent persons.

Reinforcement or Reciprocal Exchange?

Theories that subscribe to the automaticity view of reinforcement assume that consequences have to be instantaneously contingent upon behavior to affect it. Immediacy of effects is undoubtedly important for young children who have difficulty linking outcomes to actions when a delay or other activities intervene. After cognitive skills are developed, however, people can cognitively bridge delays between behavior and subsequent outcomes without mistaking what is being rewarded or punished. Human functioning would be thrown into considerable disarray if actions were swayed by every momentary effect they happened to produce. It is because behavior is selected, organized, and sustained by cognized future outcomes that it retains coherence and direction, despite dissuading momentary effects.

Most incentive practices involve a process of mutual exchange or social contracting. Positive incentives affirm that if individuals do certain things, they are entitled to specified rewards and privileges. In the case of negative sanctions, censurable conduct carries punishment costs. Behaviorists typically portray the process in terms of unidirectional impact, but it is basically one of social exchange. Most human interactions are, of course, governed by such conditional agreements, although they are often couched in the language of reinforcement. Describing them differently does not change their nature, but it does affect how incentives are used and what effects they have.

Incentive motivation involves a two-way transaction rather than a one-sided process. Whether it is seen as the exercise of personal influence or an accommodation to social influence depends on power differen-

tials and on which side of the process is emphasized. When participants have a voice in incentive arrangements, as most employees and performers do when negotiating contracts and fees, both parties are influencers and being influenced at the same time. Possession of valued competencies and collective power increases the potential for reciprocal influence. If, however, incentive structures are imposed on people without their concurrence, they resist change, they continually devise ways to circumvent the system, and they are quick to discard the activities when the external inducements are weak. One-sided impositions often fail to produce lasting change (Kazdin, 1977), where two-way transactions succeed (Besalel-Azrin, Azrin, & Armstrong, 1977).

Self-Evaluative Incentives and the Rewards of Personal Efficacy

Development of an expanding array of incentives has thus far included physical, social, and symbolic forms. In skilled activities, performers see the results of their actions. Such knowledge of results can serve two functions: First, it provides information concerning the accuracy of performance. If the feedback is sufficiently detailed, it specifies what aspects of the performance need to be corrected or improved. Second, results of actions convey signs of progress which can be either encouraging or disheartening depending on the level and direction of performance change.

Signs of progress affect motivation through self-evaluative mechanisms rather than directly. Whether or not a given level of progress will become a source of personal satisfaction depends upon the internal standards against which it is appraised. The same sign of progress will arouse disappointment when judged against a self-standard seemingly out of reach, but satisfaction when measured against a personal standard that is more easily fulfilled. Feedback about progress, in turn, affects the goals set for future performance, thus providing a continuing source of self-motivation (Cummings, Schwab, & Rosen, 1971; Locke, Cartledge, & Koeppel, 1968). Skilled and creative endeavors depend heavily on this highly evolved form of personal incentive, the rewards of personal efficacy. People invest vast amounts of time and energy in the pursuit of taxing activities that bring them self-satisfaction. What may appear like grueling work to others is for them a labor of self-fulfillment.

EXTRINSIC AND INTRINSIC INCENTIVES

There has been some reluctance, both within professional circles and among the public, to acknowledge the influential role that extrinsic incentives play in the regulation of behavior. Some believe that behavior should be performed for its own sake and not be tainted by reward. Others see behavior as being motivated by innate drives for exploration and competence, which they believe can be thwarted by social influences. Concerns are voiced that incentive practices may impede development of self-directedness and diminish inherent interest in activities.

Self-motivation and self-directedness require certain basic tools of personal agency that are developed, in part, through the aid of external incentives. Many of the activities through which competencies are built are initially tiresome and uninteresting. As piano players, and the much larger ranks of former piano players, will attest, there is little joy in practicing the rudiments of the keyboard, especially when one's peers are at play. It is not until some proficiency is acquired that the activity becomes rewarding. Without the aid of positive incentives during early phases of skill acquisition, potentialities are likely to remain undeveloped. Instead, more often than not, coercion and threats are brought to bear, which instill antipathies rather than competencies. One way to ensure the prerequisite learning is to support children's efforts until their skills are developed to the point where they produce naturally rewarding effects.

Distinctions are often drawn between extrinsic and intrinsic motivators as though they were antithetical. What is commonly referred to as intrinsic motivation includes several types of contingencies between actions and their effects. These different patterns, as depicted in Figure 4, arise through variations in the locus and inherentness of the outcomes of action.

In extrinsic motivators, the outcomes originate externally, and their relationship to the behavior is arbitrary. It is not in the natural course of things that work should produce paychecks, that good performances should evoke praise, or that reprehensible conduct should bring legal penalties. Approval, money, privileges, penalties, and the like are socially arranged, rather than natural consequences of behavior. When these outcomes are no longer forthcoming, the behavior declines unless it acquires other functional value.

Intrinsic motivation, as the concept is commonly used, comprises three types of relationships between behavior and its effects. In one intrinsic form, the consequences originate externally, but they are naturally related to the behavior. Touching a hot plate produces a painful burn, stepping out of the rain reduces wetness, watching television provides audiovisual stimulation, and striking piano keys generates melodic sounds. Because the sensory effects are intrinsic to the acts, they serve as highly effective regulators of behavior.

		CONTINGENCY	
		Natural	Arbitrary
LOCUS	External	Intrinsic	Extrinsic
	Internal	Intrinsic	Intrinsic

FIGURE 4. Variations in the locus and inherentness of the outcomes of actions that distinguish extrinsic motivators from intrinsic motivators.

Pleasing sensations sustain actions; aversive ones suppress them.

In the second intrinsic form, behavior produces naturally occurring outcomes that are internal to the organism. Responses that generate physiological effects directly, rather than through the action of external stimuli, typify this type of contingent relation. Physical exertion creates fatigue, sustained tension of the musculature can induce painful headaches and other somatic effects, and relaxation exercises can relieve tension. Although most thoughts acquire their potential to activate bodily states through extrinsic pleasurable and painful experiences, cognitive activities can also produce physiological effects directly. Perturbing thoughts can generate aversive arousal; tranquilizing thoughts can reduce it.

The self-evaluative mechanism provides the third form of intrinsic motivation. In most activities from which people derive lasting enjoyment, neither the behavior itself nor its natural feedback is rewarding. Rather, people's self-reactions to their own performances constitute the principal source of reward. To cite an uncommon example, there is nothing inherently gratifying about playing a tuba solo. To an aspiring tuba instrumentalist, however, an accomplished performance is a source of considerable self-satisfaction that can sustain much tuba blowing. Improvements in athletic, artistic, and intellectual pursuits similarly activate self-evaluative reactions that create personal incentives for performance. The evaluative consequences are internally generated, but the contingencies are arbitrary, in that any activity can become invested with self-evaluative significance. What is a source of self-satisfaction for one person may be devalued or of no self-consequence for another.

The capability for self-motivation by adopting challenging standards for oneself is established partly by intrinsic influences. Self-evaluative regulation of behavior requires skill acquisition, adoption of performance standards, and self-generation of evaluative consequences. After some proficiency, judgmental standards, and self-motivating functions are developed, qualitative variations in performance become sources of personal satisfaction or dissatisfaction. The focal role played by self-evaluative mechanisms in the regulation of human thought and conduct receives detailed consideration in a later chapter.

When people speak of intrinsic motivation as evidenced by behavior being performed for its own sake, the designation is shrouded in ambiguity. Action is not animated by itself. Rather, action ascribed to intrinsic motivators is largely regulated by the effects that either flow naturally from it or arise from internal standards. Behavior is not its own reward, but it can provide its own rewards. To mountaineers, the act of crawling over slippery rocks in foul weather is not inherently joyful. It is personal triumphs over lofty peaks that provide the exhilaration. Remove the personal challenges and crawling over rocks becomes quite boring. Pursuit of activities is lasting and is least susceptible to the vagaries of situational inducements when effects are either intrinsically related to the behavior or are self-provided.

Incentives and Cultivation of Intrinsic Interest

Most of the things people enjoy doing for their own sake had little or no interest for them originally. Children are not born innately interested in singing operatic arias, playing tubas, solving mathematical equations, writing sonnets, or propelling shot-put balls through the air. But with appropriate learning experiences, almost any activity, however silly it may appear to many observers, can become imbued with consuming significance.

The process by which people develop interest in activities for which they initially lack skill, interest, and self-efficacy is an issue of some significance. Positive incentives are often used to promote such changes. In the view of some writers, however, rewarding people for engaging in an activity is more likely to reduce than to increase subsequent interest in it (Deci, 1975; Lepper & Greene, 1978).

According to Deci's cognitive evaluation theory (Deci, 1975; Deci & Ryan, 1980), people are born with a need for competence and self-determination. This innate drive motivates them to seek out novelties, challenges, and incongruities to conquer. Extrinsic rewards reduce intrinsic motivation in two ways: They alter people's perceptions of the causes of their behavior from personal to external sources, and they lower their feelings of competence. Rewards that appear controlling but are uninformative about competence weaken intrinsic motivation, whereas those that signify competence boost it.

Lepper (1981) approaches the topic of intrinsic motivation from the perspective of attribution and self-perception theory (Bem, 1972). In this view, people's perceptions of the causes of their behavior influence how they will behave in the future. They judge their motivation partly from the circumstances under which they behave. If they perform activities for external rewards, an extrinsic reason for performance is provided so they infer lesser personal interest. However, if they perform without external inducement, they judge themselves to be intrinsically motivated. According to Lepper and Greene (1978), reductions in interest become demonstrable if four conditions are met: The relation between performance and reward is plain to see; there is sufficient preexisting interest in the activity to permit room for attributional shifts of causality; the situation is free of social surveillance, demands, or expectation of continued reward that could sustain task involvement; and finally, there are no performance improvements that could provide sources of satisfaction.

In social cognitive theory, growth of intrinsic interest is fostered through self-evaluative and self-efficacy mechanisms (Bandura, 1981a, 1982a). People display enduring interest in activities at which they feel self-efficacious and from which they derive self-satisfaction. Both of these self-functions rely on standards. Personal standards can contribute to enhancement of interest in activities in at least three ways. Challenging standards enlist sustained involvement in activities needed to build competencies. When people aim for and master valued levels of performance, they experience a sense of satisfaction (Locke, Cartledge, & Knerr, 1970). The satisfactions derived from goal attainments foster intrinsic interest. Standards also serve as an important vehicle for the development of self-percepts of efficacy. Without standards against which to measure their performance, people have little basis for judging how they are doing or for gauging their capabilities. A sense of personal efficacy in mastering tasks is more apt to spark interest in them than is self-perceived inefficacy in performing competently.

The nature of the relation between the growth of self-efficacy and interest warrants systematic investigation. There may exist some temporal lag between newly acquired self-efficacy and corresponding growth of interest in activities that are disvalued or even disliked. In the temporal lag pattern, self-efficacy fosters mastery experiences which, over a period of time, provide self-satisfactions conducive to growth of interest. If, in fact, effects follow such a temporal course, then increased interest would emerge as a later, rather than as an instant, consequent of enhanced self-efficacy. The threshold notion suggests an alternative pattern. At least moderate self-efficacy may be required to generate and sustain interest in an activity, but additional increases in self-efficacy above the threshold level do not produce further gains in interest (Bandura & Schunk, 1981). Indeed, supreme self-assurance may render activities unchallenging and thus uninteresting. Harackiewicz, Sansone, and Manderlink (1985) report evidence that perceived self-efficacy mediates task enjoyment, but these factors are not linearly related. Temporal lag and threshold effects are by no means incompatible. In fact, both probably operate in the developmental process.

Conception of Intrinsic Motivation

Each of the preceding theories assigns perceived competence a mediating role in intrinsic interest, but they differ in several important respects. In Deci's cognitive evaluation theory, interest reflects an inborn competence drive. In Lepper's attribution theory, interest is a product of retrospective judgments about the causes of one's performance. In social cognitive theory, interest grows from satisfactions derived from fulfilling challenging standards and from self-percepts of efficacy gained through accomplishments and other sources of efficacy information.

Intrinsic motivation is a highly appealing but elusive construct. Intrinsic motivation is usually defined as the performance of activities without any apparent external reward. More exclusionary criteria than persistence without noticeable incentives are needed to substantiate intrinsic motivation. This is because behavior is extensively regulated by informative cues and anticipated outcomes. The physical and social structures of situations, their material content, the expectations of others, and a host of other external factors all exert substantial influence on behavior. How long one persists in a given activity will vary depending upon the alternatives available in the situation. People will appear intrinsically motivated to engage in a particular activity when they do not have anything better to do, but they appear intrinsically unmotivated for the same activity when they have more attractive options. The activation and persistence of behavior is, therefore, best understood as a continuous interaction between personal and situational sources of influence. Any theory of motivation must consider a large set of interactive processes if it is to provide an adequate explanation of human behavior.

Most human behavior is maintained by anticipated rather than by immediate outcomes. Athletes, students, and entertainers put in long, hard hours of preparatory work for the prospect of fame and fortune, even though their endeavors bring little in the way of immediate, tangible rewards. Reliable criteria have yet to be provided to determine whether an activity is pursued because of an inherent motive or for anticipated future benefits. In actuality, instances in which people are internally driven without any forethought of what their actions will produce are hard to find.

To complicate conceptual matters further, the terms intrinsic interest and intrinsic motivation are often used interchangeably, and both are usually inferred from the level of performance. There is a major difference between a motive, which is an inner drive to action, and an interest, which is a fascination with something. Interests should not be confused with motives. People spend countless hours watching television without extraneous reward, but one would hardly regard such viewing as impelled by an intrinsic competency drive.

Theories in which motivation is inferred from the very behavior it supposedly causes are fraught with difficulties. This is because behavior is affected by many different factors. Investigators usually interpret decreases in performance after incentives are withdrawn as evidence of reductions in intrinsic motivation. However, rewards can decrease later performance through a variety of processes without transforming motivational systems. One decremental process operates through the effects of incentive contrast. Because the motivating potential of incentives is determined relationally, abrupt withdrawal of rewards is not a neutral event. Nonreward, after a behavior has been consistently rewarded, functions as a punisher that reduces performance until people become accustomed to the new reality (Buchwald, 1959b). In this process, incentive changes temporarily affect motivation by altering the meaning and valence of outcomes.

Another decremental process that can affect later involvement in an activity is satiation and tedium. When incentives are used to get people to perform the same activity over and over again, they soon tire of it. In efforts to equate the amount of monotonous repetitiveness experienced by persons who are either rewarded or nonrewarded, situations are so arranged that rewards do not increase performance. This solves the problem of differential satiation, but it undermines the relevance of the research because the reason for using incentives is to enhance behavioral functioning. What is the point of using incentives if they do not enhance performance at the time they are applied? Research findings have limited applicability to either theory or practice when the effects of the incentives being studied do not operate as incentives.

When interest in activities is measured at several points in time, there is less risk of misinterpreting temporary changes in interest as transformation of intrinsic motivation. In studies specifically addressed to this issue, children show a drop in interest immediately after rewards are withdrawn, but when they are tested later they show as much or more spontaneous interest in the formerly rewarded activity than they did originally (Feingold & Mahoney, 1975; Sagotsky & Lewis, 1978; Vasta & Stirpe, 1979).

In Deci's (1975) theory, rewards diminish intrinsic motivation when they appear controlling but increase it when they convey information about competency. Distinctions are easy to draw, but actual incentive systems are difficult to classify because they usually embody a number of different properties. Consider a concert pianist who demands a huge performance fee. Is the fee controlling, and, if so, is the pianist controlling the impresario or is the impresario controlling the pianist? Does a high fee signify competence, or is box-office popularity based on other factors? Research in this area rests on intuitive and post hoc classifications of incentive systems. Until objective criteria are provided for classifying rewards as controlling, informative, or expressive of some other aspect of a rewarding transaction, the theory is not easily testable.

The controlling-informative dichotomy by no means exhausts the properties of incentives that may affect interest and motivation. Indeed, we shall see shortly that challenges motivate people to develop and exercise their competency, and they serve as a major determinant of interest. Challenges can be created by incentives, by assigned goals, or by self-standards. In evaluating incentive systems, one must distinguish between the compensation of an incentive and its challenge. To someone working on an assembly line, the incentive system pays but does not challenge. To business executives, the challenge of achieving a certain profit can make their work just as interesting for them as reaching summits does for mountaineers. The more extrinsic incentives provide challenges, the more likely they are to infuse interest in an activity.

Originally, rewards requiring performance achievements were regarded as more controlling, and hence more detrimental, than rewards that make no performance demands. This supposition did not fare well empirically, because rewarding people regardless of how they behave, although clearly less controlling, is more likely to dampen their interest (Bates, 1979; Farr, 1976a; Farr, Vance, & McIntyre, 1977; Greene & Lepper, 1974; Phillips & Lord, 1980). Rewards demanding performance accomplishments, which generally increase interest, were then redefined as being informative. Inconsistencies exist across studies in the classification of similar types of incentives as predominantly controlling or as informative. The variable usage illustrates the vagueness of the controlling-informative distinction. Evaluation of whether this scheme can serve as an organizing principle awaits explicit criteria for assessing the controlling and informative properties of incentives.

Incentive structures that tie compensation and acclaim to standards of excellence are controlling in that they demand certain competencies of those who desire the benefits. But these are the very incentive structures that are well suited for enlisting personal challenges. Cultivating competencies enables people to exercise personal control over outcomes. Just as incentive structures are not necessarily the foes of self-determination, neither is information about competency necessarily the interest builder it is made out to be. The effects on motivation depend on whether that competency feedback conveys good or bad news. Feedback about progress and exemplary attainments is beneficial to interest, whereas feedback of deficient performances can create internal barriers to self-determination by undermining perceived self-efficacy. Perceived competency is clearly an important mediator of interest and motivation. However, the effects incentive systems have on perceived competency need to be examined systematically.

People react oppositionally to manipulation by others. If rewards used manipulatively reduce involvement in activities, the result may reflect oppositional reaction (Brehm, 1966), rather than any loss of interest or motivation. Incentives are more likely to arouse resistance when they are used as coercive inducements than when presented as supportive aids or as encouragements to exercise personal control through accomplishments. It is unlikely that concert pianists lose interest in the keyboard because they are offered high performance fees. Rather, it is more likely that they would feel devalued and insulted by low fees.

It might be noted parenthetically that conceptualizations of intrinsic motivation contain an interesting paradox. On the one hand, intrinsic motivation is said to be the wellspring of motivity. On the other hand, it is contended that incentives, constraints, deadlines, and directives, all readily sap intrinsic motivation. If this were so, such a motivator would be thoroughly undermined by the countless extrinsic pressures impinging constantly on people in their daily lives. If intrinsic motivation is so easily wiped out by extrinsic influences, it could hardly function as a pervasive motivator of behavior.

Bestowal of reward is a social act that not only arouses positive or negative reactions in others, but it can also lower or raise the valuation of the activities themselves. These results depend on whether the rewarders convey the impression that the activity is uninteresting or that it eventually becomes enjoyable for its own sake after some proficiency is attained. The same incentives can thus have different effects on behavior depending upon the message conveyed by the rewarders.

Verification of Intrinsic Drives. Drive theories become testable if drives are measured independently of the behavior they supposedly activate. If variations in task performance are taken as evidence of variations in strength of a competency drive, the circularity strips the theory of predictive value. Unless the strength of a drive is measured separately from its postulated effects, the functional properties ascribed to it are not empirically verifiable.

In attribution theory, causal ascriptions are regarded as the intervening determinant of performance. However, in empirical tests, the attributions actually evoked by extraneous rewards are seldom measured. Because rewards can alter performance through a variety of mechanisms, evidence that rewards capable of affecting causal judgments influence performance provides a weak empirical test. The evidence of a dual linkage between incentive practices, causal judgment, and interest in the activity constitutes the strong test of the theory. The need to assess, rather than simply to presume, the mediating link is borne out by developmental studies examining how rewards affect attributions. Young children actually attribute more intrinsic interest to an activity when it is rewarded than when it is not (Kun, 1978; Karniol & Ross, 1976). Morgan (1981) found that rewards reduce the interest of children, regardless of whether they subscribed to the additive principle that rewards raise interest or to the discounting principle that rewards detract from interest. These findings challenge the notion that, in young children, rewards reduce interest through a discounting attributional process. Morgan offers an explanation that seems more in keeping with the known judgmental capabilities of young children: In their social learning experiences, children quickly learn a simple principle that adults use rewards to get children to do unpleasant or boring things. If adults offer rewards the task must be uninteresting.

Older persons may be more inclined to see rewards as detracting from interest in activities that require little in the way of competence. However, their causal reasoning is not so limited that the only conclusion they can draw from being rewarded for performing interesting activities is that they must lack interest in them. In fact, a variety of attributional judgments are possible. Because people know what they like, when needlessly rewarded, they are more likely to make inferences about the values, obtuseness, or manipulativeness of the rewarder than about their own interests. Skilled performers give greater credit to their capabilities when paid than when not (Salancik, 1975). In the entertainment, athletic, and business fields, talented practitioners, who command high fees and salaries, are much more likely to judge that they are paid well because they are highly competent, than that they behave competently because they are paid well.

The effects of extraneous rewards on interest have received extensive study. Results show that such rewards can increase interest in activities, reduce interest, or have no effect (Kruglanski, 1975; Lepper & Greene, 1978; Morgan, 1984a). In evaluating the role of incentives in human functioning, it is important to distinguish between whether incentives are used to manage performance or to promote competencies.

Task-Contingent Incentives. Extrinsic rewards are most likely to reduce interest when they are given for merely performing

over and over again an activity that is already of high interest (Bates, 1979; Condry, 1977; Lepper & Greene, 1978). With this type of loose contingency, rewards are gained regardless of the level or quality of performance. However, even under the limiting conditions when rewards are believed to reduce interest, incentives sometimes enhance interest (Arnold, 1976; Davidson & Bucher, 1978), boost low interest but diminish or have no affect on high interest (Calder & Staw, 1975; Loveland & Olley, 1979; McLoyd, 1979), or reduce low interest but do not affect high interest (Greene, Sternberg, & Lepper, 1976).

Conflicting findings occur when a given factor exerts a weak influence, with the result that other factors can easily alter or override its effects. Many possible contributors have been studied, often with inconclusive results. They include how closely rewards are linked to performance; the level of preexisting interest and ability; the size, salience, and value of rewards; the type of activity; and how intrinsic motivation is measured and the settings in which it is assessed. That the effects of task-contingent reward remain somewhat unsettled is of no great social import because rewards are rarely showered on people regardless of how they behave. Nor is there much call for incentive systems for activities people find highly interesting and thus readily pursue on their own without extrinsic motivators.

Competency-Contingent Incentives. A controversy over the effects of superfluous rewards on high interest has led to neglect of the more important issue of whether incentives for performance attainments cultivate interest and perceived efficacy. Rewards for task mastery, which promote the development and exercise of personal efficacy, should be distinguished from performance-contingent rewards gained for performing routine activities. A garment worker paid on a piece-rate basis for sewing shirts day in and day out is unlikely to develop growing fondness for sewing, despite the high degree of contingency between performance and reward.

There are several ways in which incentives for mastering tasks can contribute to the growth of interest and self-efficacy. Positive incentives foster performance accomplishments. The resultant acquisition of knowledge and skills that enable one to fulfill personal standards of merit tends to heighten perceived self-efficacy. Incentives for competency do this better than noncontingent incentives (Schunk, 1983b). Success in attaining desired outcomes by surmounting challenges additionally verifies existing competencies. This is because people usually do not perform at their best even though they possess the constituent skills. Incentives that lead them to try hard help them find out what they are able to do. By mobilizing great effort, incentives can help to substantiate talents even though no new skills are acquired in the process.

Rewards also have informative value regarding efficacy when competencies are difficult to judge from performances alone, which is often the case. In such instances the magnitude of the reward serves as social validation of competency. To complicate further the competence-validation process, most activities are multifaceted. For example, baseball players must consider such factors as their batting, fielding, base stealing, production of runs, and their impact on the team's morale. Self-perceived adequacy may vary depending on how different aspects of an activity are subjectively weighted. Because of these ambiguities, level of reward imparts social information about the quality of performance. In this process, competent performances are perceived as the reason for the rewards, rather than the rewards being viewed as the cause of competent performances (Karniol & Ross, 1977). Studies of how the experience of causal efficacy affects children's interest show that personal causation of rewarding outcomes heightens interest in the instrumental activity (Kun, Garfield, & Sipowicz, 1979; Nuttin, 1973). Attaining rewarding ends enhances attraction of the means.

Several lines of research confirm that positive incentives promote interest when they either enhance or authenticate personal efficacy. Both children and adults maintain or increase their interest in activities when they are rewarded for performance attainments, whereas their interest declines when rewarded for undertaking activities irrespective of how well they perform (Boggiano & Ruble, 1979; Ross, 1976). The larger the extrinsic reward for performances signifying competence, the greater is the increase in interest in the activity (Enzle & Ross, 1978). When rates of pay are tied to levels of competency, greater interest in the activity is produced if competency is generously rewarded than if it is meagerly compensated. In the absence of competency information, variations in pay rate have little effect on interest (Rosenfield, Folger, & Adelman, 1980). In naturalistic applications of incentives (Lopez, 1981), the greater people's sense of personal efficacy for performance attainments, the more their interest increases under a bonus-pay system. When material reward for performance attainments is accompanied by either self-verbalization of competence or social feedback of competence, both children and adults sustain high interest in the activity (Pretty & Seligman, 1984; Sagotsky & Lewis, 1978). Even incentives for undertaking a task, rather than for performing it well, can raise interest if engaging in the activity provides information about personal competence (Arnold, 1976). That perceived competency is central to interest receives further support from evidence that interest is enhanced by feedback alone about competency, even without the bestowal of any tangible rewards (Rosenfield et al., 1980). Social comparative evidence of competence contributes to interest as well. Young children make little use of comparative appraisal, but older children display much greater interest in an activity if they surpass their peers than if they do less well (Boggiano & Ruble, 1979).

Performance accomplishments gained through self incentives are also well suited for building interest. Personal standards provide challenges, and self-directed mastery heightens self-percepts of efficacy. Thus, habit changes achieved with the aid of self-reward instill a stronger sense of personal causation than if the same changes are produced by external reward (Jeffrey, 1974). Moreover, people sustain much higher interest in activities if each component of the self-motivation system—performance standards, level of reward, bestowal of reward—is personally determined rather than externally set (Enzle & Look, 1979). These findings, as well as those of Dollinger and Thelen (1978), suggest further that if many external constraints are placed on the exercise of self-reward, it may lessen involvement in the activities, unless new skills are being acquired in the process.

Beyond Extrinsic Incentives

The preceding discussion should not be misinterpreted as advocating the wholesale use of extraneous incentives. One can point to instances in which material incentives are applied thoughtlessly and more for purposes of social regulation than for personal development. Incentives should be used, if necessary, mainly to cultivate skills and enduring interests. To reward people materially for activities that already hold high interest for them, or that they would pursue for symbolic rewards, is not only inappropriate but contraindicated by incentive theory. The introduction of superfluous or excessive rewards invites unnecessary difficulties when the time comes to fade them out. Rather, incentives encourage participation in activities that people would otherwise disregard and in which they would thus never develop any interest. As involvement and skills in the activities increase, social, symbolic, and self-evaluative rewards assume the incentive functions (Bandura, 1969a).

Incentives are not the only, nor necessarily the best, means of cultivating interest. As indicated earlier, involvement in activities

through goal setting can build intrinsic interest. Proximal subgoals serving valued aspirations are well suited for enlisting the sustained involvement in activities that builds competencies, self-efficacy, and interest where they are lacking. Subgoals provide reliable proximal incentives for cultivating skills. Subgoal attainments furnish rising indicants of mastery for enhancing self-percepts of efficacy. By contrast, distal goals are too far removed in time to provide sufficiently clear markers of progress to ensure a growing sense of self-efficacy. Self-appraisal of efficacy is indeed less veridical under distal goals than under proximal ones (Manderlink & Harackiewicz, 1984). The standards against which performance attainments are compared also affects how much self-satisfaction is derived from them. When performances are measured against distal goals, accomplishments may prove disappointing because of wide disparities between current performance and lofty future standards. As a result, interest fails to develop even though skills are being acquired in the process.

That proximal self-motivation can build intrinsic interest in devalued activities receives support from a study in which children who were grossly deficient and uninterested in mathematics pursued a program of self-directed learning under conditions involving proximal subgoals, distal goals, or no reference to goals (Bandura & Schunk, 1981). Under proximal subgoals, children progressed rapidly in self-directed learning, achieved substantial mastery of mathematical operations, and developed a sense of personal efficacy and intrinsic interest in arithmetic, which initially held little attraction for them. Distal goals had no demonstrable effects. The higher the perceived self-efficacy, the greater was the interest in arithmetic activities. The value of proximal subgoals in cultivating interest is further corroborated by Morgan (1984b) in a study designed to improve the academic activities of college students over an extended period.

Like any other form of influence, goals

can be applied in ways that breed dislikes, rather than nurture interests. Personal standards, which serve as guides for valued aspirations, and personal challenges promote interest. But if goals assigned by others impose severe constraints and burdens, they may become onerous prescripts that can render the pursuit aversive. Because the motivational effects of goals depend on their properties, propositions regarding goal setting must be qualified by the types of goals used. Mossholder (1980) reports that goals enhance interest in dull tasks by infusing them with challenge, but reduce interest on interesting tasks. Self-development, however, would be poorly served if aspirations and challenges become dysfunctional for activities that normally hold some interest. Fortunately, this is not the case. An interesting activity with a rising standard for success, which continues to present challenges, enhances intrinsic interest, whereas the same activity with a low level of challenge does not (McMullin & Steffen, 1982). If subgoals for an interesting activity pose little challenge because they are easily attainable, then distal goals which are viewed as less readily achievable may hold greater interest (Manderlink & Harackiewicz, 1984). Routine successes with no corresponding growth of competence are not especially good sources of enjoyment. In the studies in which proximal goals cultivate perceived efficacy and intrinsic interest, each proximal subgoal presents new challenges in mastery of new subskills (Bandura & Schunk, 1981).

Csikszentmihalyi's (1975) conception of intrinsic interest places considerable emphasis on structuring activities in ways that present constant challenges and thus enlist continuing involvement. Csikszentmihalyi (1979) examined what it is about activities that fosters deep engrossment and enjoyment in different types of life pursuits. He found that almost any activity can be made intrinsically interesting by selecting challenges that match one's perceived capabilities and getting feedback about how one is

doing. The most important structural feature of computer games that captivates players for hours on end is whether or not the activity has a challenging goal (Malone, 1981).

Activities can be creatively structured in ways that capture and build interest (Hackman & Lawler, 1971; Malone, 1981; Malone & Lepper, 1985). This is achieved by building positive features into tasks that make them enjoyable to do, creating challenges through goal setting, adding variety to counteract boredom, encouraging personal responsibility for accomplishments, and providing feedback about progress. Knowledge of how these various factors enlist cognitive motivators provides guidance for creating effective learning environments. The less interestingly activities are structured, the more one has to rely on extrinsic incentives as motivators.

In exploring cognitive mediators of interest, it is all too easy to overlook the broader social determinants of human interests. The enthusiasm of models imparts interest to activities that might otherwise be regarded indifferently. Biographical study of lives reveals that examples of people who seek challenges and become actively engaged in what they do leave deep impressions on others and often set the course of other people's life pursuits. Modeling influences carry important implications for developing and channeling human interests.

Multiform Incentives in Psychological Functioning

Although what people find to be rewarding undergoes developmental changes, human behavior is regulated by different combinations and levels of incentives throughout life. Many activities are governed by their physical effects. People go to great lengths to reduce or eliminate aversive conditions and to gain physical comfort, sexual gratification, appetizing foods, and the like. Large segments of behavior are maintained by sensory feedback of the sights, sounds, and tactile sensations they produce.

People do a lot of things for money or to gain access to enjoyable activities. Social commentators who decry the use of extrinsic incentives rarely forswear such rewards for themselves when it comes to salary increases, book royalties, and performance fees, for fear the currency of the realm will sap their interest. Valued rewards are accepted as though innocuous to oneself but harmful to others. People will go to great lengths to secure the positive regard of others or to avoid social censure. It would be a rare, unfeeling person who could remain totally indifferent to the sentiments of others. Indeed, sometimes they will exert greater effort to produce benefits for others than for themselves (Haruki & Shigehisa, 1983).

Many of the outcomes experienced in daily interchanges are mediated by the actions of others. Through persuasive or coercive behavior people can obtain valued goods and services, get others to perform onerous tasks for them, alter regulations to their own liking, eliminate conditions that adversely affect their well-being, and resist pressures for courses of action that do not serve their interests. In such instances, social behavior is rewarded by its success in influencing the conduct of others.

People also do a lot of things to please themselves. Much time and effort is expended in activities for the personal satisfaction derived from accomplished performances. One's self-regard often outweighs the inducements of money, social recognition, and physical comfort in determining how one behaves. Developmental experience thus expands the range of effective incentives and alters their priority but does not replace those incentives that may be considered lower in a multiform system.

Predictability of Outcomes

Human transactions are partly governed by incentive rules. Some outcomes are socially arranged according to time schedules, while others are linked to performance

(Ferster & Skinner, 1957). The rewards associated with most activities that become part of daily routines, such as household meals, trips on public buses and airliners, and recreational pastimes, are available only at certain times. This enables people to regulate their behavior temporally so that they need not waste their time or tax their patience doing things when the outcomes they seek are unavailable.

Temporal scheduling of outcomes is well suited for organizing activities but not for sustaining them for a given period. For the latter purpose, performances must be rewarded on the basis of quality or productivity, rather than only at certain times. Creative endeavors are typically rewarded in terms of standards of excellence, whereas in production and service enterprises, outcomes are tied closely to the level of productivity. When outcomes depend upon one's own efforts, behavior is well maintained.

Another dimension on which performance outcomes vary is their predictability. Individuals whose behavior has been consistently rewarded come to expect quick results and are easily discouraged should their efforts fail. In contrast, those who have been rewarded irregularly tend to persist, despite setbacks and only occasional success. Unpredictable outcomes produce behavior that is highly resistant to change because one's efforts are sustained by the belief that they will eventually prove successful. Behavior is most persistent when it is rewarded at a low, variable level and when better means of secured desired outcomes are lacking.

STRUCTURAL VARIATIONS IN INCENTIVE SYSTEMS

The influence of human functioning through incentives is not simply a matter of dealing with isolated persons and acts. Incentive systems are socially structured to give coherence and direction to social life. Moreover, most human strivings involve social interdependencies within particular group structures designed to promote valued human qualities and accomplishments. Because the social context is an important determinant of incentive effects, the full understanding of the role that incentives play in human functioning requires social analysis.

Innumerable studies have been conducted on individualistic incentive systems in which people's outcomes depend upon their own actions, regardless of how others behave. Despite the prevalence of collective endeavors, the effects of group incentives on group functioning have received surprisingly little attention. Social life involves extensive interdependence between actions and outcomes. Many outcomes that are highly valued can be achieved only through the coordinated efforts of others. This makes the rewards of individuals partially or fully dependent on the performances of other members. Incentive systems are also sometimes structured so that transgressions by individuals affect how other members of the group with which they are closely affiliated are treated.

Socially structured incentives affect more than behavior. They can profoundly influence people's self-percepts of efficacy, their sense of community, and the level of self-satisfaction and self-esteem they derive from what they do. Evaluation of incentive systems should, therefore, address the type of psychological and social life they foster, as well as behavioral functioning. Performance accomplishments can be promoted in ways that enrich the quality of people's lives or in ways that degrade them.

Differential Effects of Individual and Group Incentives

Incentives do not necessarily affect group functioning in the same way as they affect the behavior of individuals. This is because group-oriented incentives activate other sources of social influence which, depending on their nature, amplify or weaken the power of incentives. When incentives are applied in a social setting, the behavior modeled by other participants emerges as an influence in its own right. The co-varying changes that incentives produce in modeled behavior alter how group members behave. Due to concomitant modeling influences, the same incentive system is much more effective if prominent members of the group respond favorably than if they are less responsive (Schwartz & Hawkins, 1965). Indeed, seeing others respond oppositionally to incentive inducements can nullify the usual effects of reward (Ditrichs, Simon, & Greene, 1967).

Efforts to influence the level of group performance through incentives also cause group members to react to each other in ways that may carry more force than the incentives themselves. Mutual social supports boost the power of incentives by providing performance aids and heightening group dedication and aspiration. Social changes are resisted when they arouse apprehension, conflict with entrenched customs, and threaten status and power structures. Influential group members can negate incentive systems by disapproving of the social changes that the incentives have been designed to bring about.

Group structural determinants come into play as well. When people see other group members profit from their labors without contributing their fair share, they feel exploited. The productive ones slaken their own efforts, even though it reduces rewards to themselves and to the group, rather than suffer the exploitation (Kerr, 1983). Some discontent may arise, though to a lesser extent, even without big disparities in relative contributions. Ross (1981) has shown that people observe and recall more of their own contribution to a collective effort than that of their co-participants. Consequently, they generally take more credit for a group accomplishment than their co-participants grant them. Because the self-focused bias in evaluating personal contribution is pervasive, group ventures can easily arouse feelings of insufficient recognition or exploitation.

Most group endeavors require specialized roles and skills. Therefore, not all members contribute equally to group accomplishments. If different amounts of effort by participants provide equal reward, the more creative or prolific contributors will perceive the incentive system as unfair. Even when rewards are tied to the relative contributions of each member, motivational problems arise if disparities in benefits are viewed as unreasonably disproportionate to the degree of contribution to the group effort. Within a medical group, nurses may concur that physicians should receive higher pay but regard as unfair the huge disparity in income. Incentive systems perceived as inequitable breed discontent and dissension. Since objective measures of relative contributions and proportionality of reward allocation are hard to devise, group incentives leave ample room for dissatisfaction.

Hierarchical Incentive Structures

Organizations typically link major rewards and privileges to rank. In these hierarchical structures, members are stratified into various positions on the basis of such characteristics as education, seniority, or specialized competencies. We have seen earlier that, because of their many benefits, social ranks serve as powerful incentives for the development and deployment of skills. Hierarchical structures are not unique to any particular type of social system. Group effort requires competent direction and coordination, whatever the guiding principles of a society might be. Those who manage organizations gain increased status and benefits, otherwise the added responsibilities would hold little interest for them. It comes as no surprise, therefore, that even societies organized on supposedly egalitarian principles have their privileged ranks (Stavrianos, 1976).

Although most group enterprises use rank incentives, they figure most prominently in work organizations. What particular form the organizational structuring takes differs across societies in accordance with their national ideologies (Tannenbaum,

Kavcic, Rosner, Vianello, & Wieser, 1974). Rank incentives are well suited for attracting hardy, talented persons to positions of leadership, but they create problems as well. The ranking criteria must reflect the competencies necessary for the activity, otherwise the incentive system becomes suspect. Unless persuasively justified, large status differences dissatisfy and alienate subordinates. The disaffection is greatest when much power and privilege is vested in upper echelons, when large differences exist in compensation that arouse strong feelings of inequity, when opportunities for personal advancement are limited, and when subordinates have little say in the formulating and implementing policies that affect their welfare (Tannenbaum et al., 1974). Members display greater satisfaction and personal commitment to their organization when status and pay inequalities are less pronounced and when they have a participative role in its management. The organizational challenge is to reward merit and to structure people's relationships to their work and associates in ways that do not breed disaffection.

Impact of Structural Variations on the Effects of Group Incentives

Interdependent incentive systems vary on several dimensions that affect group functioning significantly. In one form, independent actions by any member produce group rewards. When individuals enjoy the benefits of someone else's labors, they come to expect somebody else to do the work, with the result that both individual and group performances progressively deteriorate (Glaser & Klaus, 1966). The social effects are quite different, however, when individuals are punished, rather than rewarded, for somebody else's behavior. If transgressive actions by any member bring punishment on the entire group, associates are quick to enforce the rules on each other in order to spare themselves common suffering. Coercive social systems exploit such negative interdependencies to impel group members to police themselves (Bettelheim, 1943).

In many situations people work together but are rewarded differentially, depending on their skills and contribution to the collective effort. Such incentive systems enhance group productivity, provided that the individual rewards are judged equitable and that ample opportunities exist for personal advancement. Otherwise, the disparities inherent in hierarchical rewards for collective accomplishment create dissatisfaction in people at lower levels (Tannenbaum et al., 1974). Under conditions of restricted opportunities for mobility, subordinates have little incentive to exceed minimally acceptable performances.

Some patterns of group life involve both performance and outcome interdependencies. Through coordination of specialized skills and functions, groups achieve outcomes which they share among themselves. Because personal benefits depend upon the level of the group's performance, collective efforts are well maintained (Farr, 1976b; Glaser & Klaus, 1966). Additionally, this form of incentive system fosters in its members commitment to, and responsibility for, the collective enterprise. The interpersonal effects are important because incentives influence group performance partly through the mutual social influences they activate in the group. When benefits are not tied to quality or productivity, peer pressures develop against high performance (Lawler, 1973). However, when personal benefits vary according to the group's performance, incentives mobilize support of peers in the service of the activity.

Results of comparative studies show that cooperative structures, in which members encourage and teach each other, generally promote higher performance attainments than do competitive or individualistic ones (Johnson, Maruyama, Johnson, Nelson, & Skohn, 1981). Adding competition between groups to cooperative effort within the groups does not seem to enhance group achievement. However, intergroup competition is more likely to heighten intra-group effort, and thus boost productivity, when outcomes of some importance are at stake.

Structural factors also affect people's self-evaluations and the esteem with which they hold themselves and their associates (Ames, 1984). Less talented members fare much better in successful cooperative systems than in competitive ones. They judge themselves more capable, they feel more deserving of reward, and they are more self-satisfied. These personal benefits do not come at costs to highly capable members when the group effort works well. Skilled performers evaluate themselves just as positively as they do in competitive systems. When cooperative efforts fail, however, the more skilled feel less satisfied than if rewarded independently, and they view those who perform poorly as less deserving of reward. The less able performers also think less well of themselves under these circumstances. In competitive reward systems, successes of skilled members spell failures for the less able. The victors enhance their self-evaluation, losers suffer self-devaluation. The negative impact may be lessened if different people find different things at which they can excel. In any event, the combined findings suggest that both performance attainments and favorable self-evaluations are best achieved through rewarded cooperative effort that is organized to work well.

Group-incentive systems can be further differentiated in terms of who determines and manages them. In self-governing systems, the group members themselves play an active role, either directly or through their representatives, in deciding which values and activities will be promoted or discouraged. In more authoritarian systems, the norms and rules defining how people are expected to behave emanate from those who hold power. Self-influence, which arises from commitment to personal standards and self-evaluative reactions to one's own performances, is more likely to be activated by self-involvement in decision making than by external dictates. Hence, participation generally improves group functioning (Willner, Braukmann, Kirigin, & Wolf, 1978).

Societal Structuring by Individualistic or Collectivistic Incentives

Societies and subgroups within them differ in the extent to which incentives are structured on an individual or a collective basis. Those that value self-development and individual achievement favor individualistic incentive systems. These include hierarchical incentives, opportunities for personal advancement, and generous social and material rewards for pursuit of personal success, however it might be self-defined. Social arrangements in which one's outcomes are personally determined encourage self-initiative, self-interest, and self-evaluation based on how one's progress compares with one's prior attainments. In many activities, however, people cannot exercise control over outcomes entirely independently of each other because rewards are limited and there are many competitors for them. Social comparison and competitiveness thus encroach on individualistic systems.

Group-incentive systems are most prevalent in societies espousing a collectivist ethic (Bronfenbrenner, 1970). In such systems, self-interest is subordinated to group welfare. This is achieved by tying personal well-being to group functioning so that members are affected by each other's behavior. Individual benefits are based on group accomplishments, and censurable behavior by individual members reflects negatively on the entire group. Incentives for collective achievement are introduced by creating competition among subgroups within the larger system. When people share the consequences of their decisions and actions, their interests are best served by committing their efforts to common goals, by helping each other, and by assuming mutual responsibility. This is not to say that collective systems are devoid of differential reward and privilege. High achievers, in whatever activities the society values, and the bureaucratic elite enjoy many privileges and luxuries.

Because different social goals require different incentive practices, no single structure can be prescribed as the best. Individualistic incentives are well suited for creating independent, self-seeking people. If, on the other hand, a society wishes to promote a sense of shared responsibility and concern for others, then group incentives are more appropriate. The adverse effects of excessive individualism or collectivism can be mitigated through the use of individual and group incentives. In such systems, people's outcomes are determined by both personal attainments and group accomplishments.

GENERALITY AND STABILITY OF CHANGE

Social cognitive theory distinguishes among three basic processes of change, namely, the *acquisition, generality,* and *stability* of psychological functioning. Acquisition is concerned with the development of knowledge and skills that govern thought and action. Generality has to do with how widely acquired capabilities are used. It can take varied forms—generality across different situations, toward different persons, and across modalities of thought, affect, and action. Stability is concerned with how well changes are sustained over time.

A multiprocess analysis of change is required because not only are the three facets partially independent, but they are governed by somewhat different determinants. The conditions needed for cultivating skills differ, in many respects, from the factors that determine when and where they will be used. Achieved changes do not automatically generalize nor do they necessarily last. A given set of influences might create changes that are circumscribed and transitory, generalized but short-lived, circumscribed but enduring, or both generalized and enduring.

Substantial knowledge, much of which

has already been reviewed, exists on how to achieve psychological changes with some degree of consistency. However, the realization of broad, stable changes, which depends on self-directive capabilities and on the functional value of what is learned, often presents difficult challenges. This is because behavior is often subjected to inconsistent and conflicting influences in everyday transactions. For behavioral propensities to survive requires intransigence in the face of discordant influences.

Alternative Conceptions of the Sources of Generality and Stability

Operant theory reduces issues of the generality and stability of psychological functioning to external stimulus control. When behavior is reinforced under certain stimulus conditions, it generalizes to other similar situations and to other similar responses. Because behavior is considered to be dependent on external reinforcement, if it is to generalize to different settings and to survive for long, it requires continuing reinforcement. Like any action pattern, in the operant scheme of things the generality and stability of functioning involve no special processes beyond those of stimulus control supported by differential reinforcement (Johnston, 1975). The research stimulated by this perspective is, therefore, confined largely to the role played by situational cues and extrinsic incentives.

In the social cognitive view, persons are active agents who exercise some influence over their own motivation and actions. This is not to minimize incentives as important determinants of how people will behave at different times and in different places. They are clearly influential factors. But the achievement of general and stable functioning depends on more than situational rewards and punishments. Social cognitive theory expands what constitutes rewards for action and posits varied factors, both personal and situational, that contribute to the

generality and stability of human behavior. In addition to the conventional incentives, the rewards of personal efficacy—the satisfactions and benefits derived from mastering events—figure prominently in the generality and steadfastness of human pursuits. Much behavioral control is exercised through self-regulatory functions. These involve, among other things, values and internal standards, self incentives, self-percepts of efficacy, generative cognitive skills, and other tools of personal agency. These sources of self-influence receive detailed discussion in later chapters and will, therefore, be mentioned only briefly here.

Acquisition of Functional Skills

Generality and persistence are often discussed as though these features of behavior are unmitigated virtues. They are not. It is difficult to achieve generalized, enduring changes when the activities being rewarded are primarily for the convenience or benefit of others. This is not an entirely lamentable state of affairs. If one could instill, through brief application of reward, lasting behavioral changes that benefitted the promoters but not the recipients, people would be amenable to wholesale, arbitrary control. Because reinforcement practices serve as incentives for, rather than as implanters of, behavior, people retain what is useful for them and discard what is not.

With activities that are personally inconvenient or uninteresting but nevertheless important to the general welfare, sanctions and incentive supports must be provided on a continuing basis. Every society adopts incentive structures for this purpose. The same is true of many service and production activities that are entrepreneurial rather than socially prescribed. No methods exist for making menial labor intrinsically interesting so that workers will perform the same routine day after day for little or no pay. Were it possible to do so, people would be exploited by those who possess the power to engineer whatever intrinsic interests served their purposes.

Incentives promote broad, enduring changes when they sponsor generalizable skills that have functional value, irrespective of time and place. Thus, for example, children may initially require social encouragement to learn to read, but after they become proficient at it, they read on their own for the enjoyment and useful information it provides. Learning effects are irreversible. The discontinuation of extraneous incentives does not expunge what has been learned. Accomplished readers do not revert to illiteracy when the social supports that helped them learn how to read are later discontinued. However, complex skills are better acquired, generalized, and maintained if one can get valued things with them than if they bring only arbitrary rewards (Hart & Risley, 1968, 1980). Once people have developed communicative, cognitive, manual, and social competencies, they use them under varied circumstances because such skills enable them to deal effectively with their environment.

Even the most serviceable skills may be abandoned in environments where they no longer bring any results. Under such adverse conditions, the decline in functioning reflects disuse, rather than loss, of acquired competencies (Lovaas, Koegel, Simmons, & Long, 1973). The resultant decreases in behavior are reversible, so that unused skills are quickly reinstated in responsive social environments.

Approximating the Discordance of Everyday Life

In the early phases of learning skills and eradicating dysfunctions, progress is greatly aided by providing coherent learning experiences with positive feedback. Unfortunately, the natural social environment is not that harmonious and supportive. Indeed, it is often inconsistent, contradictory, and inattentive. Therefore, to ensure that newly acquired skills generalize and endure even under these less favorable circumstances re-

quires instituting transitional practices that gradually approximate those of the natural social environment. Much research has been conducted on how incentive systems can increase the likelihood of achieving generalized change. This knowledge has not only clarified some of the processes governing behavioral generality but also has provided guides for how to promote it. Although the specific strategies take different forms (Stokes & Baer, 1977), they all essentially serve as a method for demonstrating that particular skills have wide functional value.

One way of conveying information about functional utility is to reward similar behavior under dissimilar conditions. The patterns of generality achieved by this means will depend on which aspects of the environment are varied. Situational generality is promoted by rewarding similar behavior in varied settings and under changing circumstances (Friedman, Filipczak, & Fiordaliso, 1977; Handleman & Harris, 1980; Rincover & Koegel, 1977). Interpersonal generality is facilitated by rewarding similar behavior toward different people (Marburg, Houston, & Holmes, 1976). Verifying the functional utility of particular skills across places, times, and people increases the likelihood that the skills will be widely used for diverse purposes.

Human actions are organized, rather than existing as isolated elements. A change in one behavior can, therefore, significantly affect other response tendencies. In exploring this issue, Wahler and his associates have used cluster analysis of intercorrelations between different activities to identify the patterning of human behavior (Wahler, Berland, & Coe, 1979). The clusters obtained provide a basis for predicting the direction and scope of psychological change if one of the constituted behaviors is altered. Thus, if, in school settings, cooperativeness is positively linked with scholastic achievement and good peer relations but negatively linked to aggression, then cultivating cooperativeness will raise the former and lower the latter behavioral proclivities. Because social environments differ in what they value and foster, the types of behaviors that become related to each other differ from person to person, and even for the same person, in different social settings. How behaviors cluster in the home may differ with how they cluster in the school. Whatever the co-variant behaviors are in any given case, increasing a particular response pattern tends to increase positively correlated activities and to reduce negatively correlated ones.

Incentive practices affect generality across modalities, as well as the transfer and patterning of action. In studies of phobic dysfunctions to be reviewed shortly, enactive mastery experiences not only eliminate phobic behavior but also reduce fear arousal and alter phobic thinking (Bandura, 1982a). Rewarding verbal expressions increases corresponding actions (Lovaas, 1964; Loew, 1967; Slaby & Crowley, 1977). However, intermodal transfer is most reliably achieved by rewarding consistency across different modes of expression. If people are repeatedly rewarded for doing what they say, words become functionally related to deeds, so that verbal pledges later affect action in new situations (Israel, 1978). Similarly, in language development, teaching speech comprehension may facilitate production of grammatical speech. But these different linguistic functions are best mutually enhanced by cultivating both of them rather than by relying on automatic transfer from language comprehension to speech production (Harris, 1975).

There is much variability within, as well as between, modalities of expression. In the realm of action, people typically exhibit different patterns of behavior, as, for example, performing some forms of aggression but not others (Bandura & Walters, 1959; Mischel, 1968). In the physiological mode, the various indices of autonomic reactivity, such as sweating, heart rate, and blood pressure, do not correlate all that highly (Lacey, 1967). Rewarding congruity in reactivity can enhance generality of expression within a modality as well. If persons are rewarded only when they raise both their heart rate and blood pressure, these two forms of autonomic reactivity become linked; but if rewards are given only when one type of autonomic response goes up and the other goes down, the physiological reactions become dissociated (Schwartz, 1972). Incentives can thus delimit and dissociate physiological functioning, as well as integrate and expand it.

In the social environments of everyday life, activities rarely produce instant benefits. If people come to expect quick successes, they become easily dissuaded by adverse experiences. Because the outcomes of actions are often diverse, distant, and uncertain, courses of behavior have to be sustained by expectations of eventual benefits and by satisfactions derived from how the activity is performed. Perseverance is strengthened by incentive practices that link actions expectantly to future outcomes and thereby render behavior relatively insensitive to its immediate discouraging effects. When there is a low probabilistic relationship between actions and desired outcomes and when better means are lacking, an occasional reward can sustain prolonged efforts that are undeterred by repeated failure.

Learning complex skills requires prompt feedback that conveys information about underlying rules and the adequacy of performance. Rewarding feedback is frequently used for this purpose because it can both inform and motivate. While immediate reward aids learning, it weakens perseverance. Therefore, after skills are acquired, transitional incentive practices must serve to reduce vulnerability to discouragement. These practices take many forms. Behavior becomes highly persistent when progressively more effort is needed to achieve results. Lengthening the delay between action and outcomes also builds perseverance. Changing the basis on which benefits are gained, from specific performances to general level of functioning, further encourages continuing exercise of personal efficacy in a wide array of activities. Such transitional practices can enhance durability of personal change in the natural environment after the incentives used to foster it originally have been discontinued (Kazdin, 1984; Stokes & Baer, 1977). It bears repeating, however, that no psychological alchemy exists for infusing durability in behavior patterns that incur costs without any personal benefits.

The routes to competence and success are usually long and difficult. When desired outcomes are not readily attainable, social and symbolic rewards help to support people's efforts. Many of the human pursuits that have considerable import are directed at long-range outcomes that may take years to realize. Participation in such endeavors is sustained by signs of progress and by the mutual social rewards of close associates committed to the same cause (Bandura, 1973; Keniston, 1968).

Strengthening Coping Self-Efficacy

In most intractable fears and inhibitions what is feared in fact is quite safe. Nonetheless, unceasing avoidance not only precludes any dealings with the subjective threats but bars participation in many enjoyable activities in which the threats might conceivably appear, however remote the possibility (Bandura, 1978c). For example, the lives of snake phobics are often severely constricted by defensive avoidance of social, recreational, and vocational activities that might occasion exposure to a snake. But even restricting daily activities does not ensure them relief from distress. Most are plagued by intrusive ruminations and recurrent nightmares in which menacing reptiles figure prominently. Similarly, the constricted lives of obsessive compulsives are spent endlessly scrubbing themselves and their households, ruminating about safety, and executing elaborate rituals to safeguard against imagined threats (Rachman & Hodgson, 1980). Overcoming phobias and compulsions can thus have pervasive ramifications in everyday life.

Participant modeling has proven to be one of the most effective means of achieving rapid reality testing, which provides the cor-

rective experiences for change (Bandura, 1977b). Restored functioning, in turn, brings widespread benefits that expand and bolster personal changes. People displaying intractable fears are, of course, not about to do what they dread. In applying participant modeling, therapists, therefore, create an environment in which phobics can perform successfully despite their incapacities. This is achieved by enlisting a variety of performance-mastery aids, including modeling of threatening activities, graduated subtasks, enactment for progressively longer periods, joint performance with the therapist, protective aids that reduce the likelihood of feared consequences, and varying the severity of the threat itself (Bandura, Jeffery, & Wright, 1974). As treatment progresses, the supplementary aids are withdrawn so that clients cope effectively unassisted. Self-directed mastery experiences, designed to provide varied confirmatory tests of coping capabilities, are then arranged to authenticate and strengthen a sense of coping self-efficacy.

Within a relatively short time, participant modeling achieves widespread psychological changes. It eliminates phobic behavior, reduces fearful behavior in areas not specifically treated, and enables people to pursue enjoyable activities they formerly shunned. The beneficial effects typically generalize across all modalities—in addition to restoring behavioral capabilities, personal mastery diminishes anxiety arousal, instills positive attitudes, and eradicates perturbing ruminations and nightmares. That mastery of threats profoundly affects dream activity is a particularly striking accompanying improvement. Generalized benefits have been obtained with different types of phobias (Bandura, Blanchard, & Ritter, 1969; Bandura, Jeffery, & Gajdos, 1975; Biran & Wilson, 1981; Ferguson, Taylor, & Wermuth, 1978; Lassen & McConnell, 1977), obsessive-compulsive disorders (Rachman & Hodgson, 1980), and sexual dysfunctions (Nemetz, Craig, & Reith, 1978). The favorable changes remain very much in evidence months and years later.

The nature and pattern of changes accompanying eradication of phobic behavior indicate that generality is mediated through self-regulatory mechanisms, rather than being automatically controlled by stimulus similarity (Bandura, Adams, & Beyer, 1977; Bandura, Jeffery, & Gajdos, 1975). In the course of treatment, participants acquire generalizable skills for coping with threats and strong beliefs in their coping efficacy. This enables them to improve their functioning in areas that may bear little similarity to the specifically treated one. While generalized improvements are, of course, most noticeable in areas that resemble the treated domain, they are by no means bound by stimulus similarity. The nature and scope of the changes people achieve is predictable from the generality of their self-percepts of efficacy.

After a fear has been overcome, additional self-directed mastery experiences strengthen self-percepts of coping efficacy and further enhance the generality of change (Bandura, Jeffery, & Gajdos, 1975; Smith & Coleman, 1977). It should be noted that self-directed mastery refers to unaided performance of activities after functioning has been restored, not whether or not someone is present once persons can do things on their own (O'Brien & Kelley, 1980).

Extrapolations from attribution and self-perception theories to the field of behavioral change often imply that people must labor unaided or under inconspicuously managed prompts, if they are to convince themselves of their personal capabilities (Kopel & Arkowitz, 1975). Such prescriptions require qualification. Misappraisals which lessen the impact of success can be easily minimized without sacrificing the substantial benefits of powerful mastery aids. This is achieved by providing opportunities for self-directed accomplishments after useful skills have been established. Any lingering doubts people may have, either about their capabilities or about the risks of particular courses of action, can be dispelled in this manner. The more varied the circumstances under which events have

been mastered independently, the more strongly personal efficacy can be substantiated and the less likely the success experiences are to be discounted. Lasting changes can be achieved best by enactive mastery using dependable mastery aids initially to develop capabilities, then removing external aids to verify personal efficacy, and finally using self-directed mastery to strengthen and generalize self-percepts of efficacy.

Mastery experiences that perfect skills and strengthen perceived self-efficacy can reduce vulnerability to dysfunction, as well as facilitate generality. People who are skilled in dealing with potential threats will have fewer aversive experiences than those who are less adept. Those who are fully assured of their coping efficacy, after having had many successful interactions with what they previously feared, will not be much affected by a few unpleasant encounters. At most, such experiences, unless highly aversive, will foster avoidance of realistic threats, which has adaptive value. If, however, people have only limited contact after treatment with what they had feared, a few later mishaps are likely to destroy their newly acquired efficacy and reinstate defensive behavior. Thus, exploiting opportunities for self-directed mastery after behavioral functioning is restored can effectively reduce the likelihood of later mishaps and weaken their impact should they occur.

If new patterns of behavior, however competently executed, often produce aversive consequences, then the changes will be short lived unless the pernicious environmental conditions are altered. No psychological methods exist for rendering people permanently insensitive to the adverse effects of their actions. Such imperviousness would not, indeed, be desirable because, if people remained totally unaffected by the results of their actions, they would function in a grossly maladaptive way.

Once unwarranted fears are removed, people do not behave recklessly. Overcoming a phobic dread of automobiles does not dispose persons to wander heedlessly into onrushing traffic on busy thoroughfares.

Rather, rigid avoidance is supplanted by flexibly adaptive behavior that is cognitively controlled by judgments of the probable consequences of prospective actions.

Inauguration into New Relationships and Social Milieus

Small changes in behavior aided by positive incentives can cause lasting personal changes when they inaugurate individuals into new social relationships. The incentive and modeling influences within this new social reality expand and sustain the new patterns of behavior. Baer and Wolf (1970) demonstrate the operation of this process in programs designed to ameliorate severe behavioral deficits. To cite one example, through their social support, adults help withdrawn children to relate to peers until they achieve mutually rewarding interactions with them. After lonely children derive satisfaction from their peer relationships, they maintain their sociability even though adults discontinue their social support for interactive behavior.

In many situations, determination of the people with whom one must interact, whether they be classmates, teachers, or supervisors, is socially structured rather than personally determined. Because of their characteristics or heavy demands on their attention, others may not always be adequately responsive. This is no cause for despair. Because social transactions involve mutual influence, individuals can exercise some control over how their efforts are received. When children, who get ignored in classrooms, are taught how to seek feedback and gain recognition for their work, they cultivate a much more supportive environment for their intellectual development. Teachers praise their good work more often, and the children, in turn, improve the quality of their academic performances (Stokes, Fowler, & Baer, 1978). Those who are resourceful in encouraging social responsiveness in others also tend to be viewed as more intellectually adept and likeable (Cantor & Gelfand, 1977). Behavior is more readily generalized and sustained when people are skilled in recruiting social supports for their efforts. Such a strategy teaches people how to create their own circumstances.

Initiatory influences are most powerful when they branch people into new life paths. This is well documented by studies of children from impoverished backgrounds who go on to college and professional careers (Ellis & Lane, 1963; Krauss, 1964). In these families the parents themselves cannot provide the necessary resources and preparatory skills. However, a key role in setting the course of the children's intellectual development during their formative years is usually played by a parent or a family acquaintance who values education highly. The values thus instilled are further developed by teachers whom the children admire. These evolving preferences lead to selective association with college-oriented peers who, by their interest and example, promote the attitudes, achievement standards, and cognitive skills conducive to intellectual pursuits.

The inaugural process sometimes involves even more radical changes in social milieus. We saw earlier that groups vary in how extensively they touch personal lives of their members and in their degree of physical and psychological closeness. Closed social systems that wield substantial rewarding and coercive power can create profound and enduring changes in belief and behavior. Induction into such closed milieus often is achieved by use of highly attractive rewards as affiliative inducements (Bandura, 1982c). In their recruitment practices, cults often shower the initiates with unconditional love and friendship (Lofland, 1978). To the insecure and confused, this sense of community and the meaning and direction that dedicated groups give to a person's life may serve as a major basis for attraction. Others may be drawn to a group by the worthy purposes it is designed to serve. In lives that have gone awry through fortuitous induction into deleterious collectives, these groups initially traded heavily on mesmerizing images of utopian societies (Powers, 1971; Watkins & Soledad, 1979; Winfrey, 1979).

Self-Regulatory Capabilities

Because people constantly preside over their own behavior, they are in the best position to bring self-influence to bear on their actions whenever need be. In exercising personal control, people adopt internal standards, monitor their actions, and use self incentives to mobilize and sustain their efforts until they accomplish what they set out to do. As has been previously noted, extrinsic incentives and other situational influences affect actions in large part through the exercise of personal agency. So even incentive influences, commonly regarded as purely external, depend on self-regulatory influence for their impact.

The regulation of behavior by self-influence is extensively reviewed in a later chapter. Applications of knowledge generated by this line of research show that people can extend and sustain changes in their behavior with the aid of self-regulatory skills (Nellans & Israel, 1981; Rhode, Morgan, & Young, 1983; Sanders & James, 1983). The causal attributions people are given for their behavior can also augment the durability and generality of change. Social influences designed to instill self-evaluative standards produce more lasting changes than can be produced by simply rewarding desired behavior patterns (Miller, Brickman, & Bolen, 1975). Regardless of how behavioral changes have been created, attributing them to personal inclinations produces greater generalization to new settings and different forms of the behavior than does ascribing the behavior to external inducement or having been socially praised for it (Grusec, Kuczynski, Rushton, & Simutis, 1978; Grusec & Redler, 1980).

Evidence that causal attributions stabilize and generalize behavior leaves unanswered questions about the mechanisms linking perceived causality to action. In a social cognitive analysis, ascribing behavior to personal agency conveys self-evaluative standards and boosts perceived self-efficacy. Perry and his associates provide some evidence that evaluative self-standards are, indeed, altered by causal ascriptions (Perry, Perry, Bussey, English, & Arnold, 1980). Children who were told they were good self-controllers become self-critical if they transgressed in situations that appear manageable.

It is most difficult to sustain changes over an extended period in behavior that is instantly rewarding and thus becomes refractory to control. This creates special problems when the behavior also produces adverse effects that do not wield much influence because they are delayed and slowly cumulative. Regulation of overeating by obese persons is a perfect case in point. Maintenance strategies that are effective in other forms of behavior are relatively unsuccessful with obesity (Stunkard & Penick, 1979; Wilson & Brownell, 1980). Fading out arbitrary incentives works with social and cognitive competencies because other sources of reward—the natural benefits of the new skills—support the activities. Booster treatments, in which people return for supplementary instruction periodically, also do not do much to improve maintenance. People who have allowed their eating behavior to get out of control and have regained the pounds they had shed cannot benefit all that much from periodic contacts.

Self-regulation over an extended period requires effective means for controlling one's own behavior and an internal standard, which specifies the occasions when self-influences should be applied. In testing this type of model of self-regulation with overeating (Bandura & Simon, 1977), people were taught how to reduce the amount of food they consume. After they achieved the desired reduction in weight, the special self-influence procedures were suspended. However, they continued to keep track of their weight using a preselected amount of weight gain as the cue to reinstate self-influence until they returned to their desired weight level. By temporarily reinstating self-corrective influences, weight gains were promptly arrested and the behavioral trend reversed. As a result, weight never strayed too far beyond the desired level.

In successful maintenance of change, self-corrective efforts do not have to be applied continuously, otherwise the self-direction may become more bothersome than the problem itself. Rather, self-influence is reinstituted only at the first signs of deteriorating self-regulation. Because habits that serve one well normally become a regular part of one's daily life, self-correctives are needed only on those occasions when things go awry. Maintenance processes are, therefore, best clarified by analyzing ongoing self-regulation, rather than by changing behavior and then simply reassessing it weeks, months, or years later. Continued analysis sheds light on how self-regulatory mechanisms operate and the conditions under which they malfunction, whereas measuring only the end points of the process does not.

In the preceding discussion, self-regulatory efforts are used to sustain a given level of functioning. Novelists managing how much they write each day, and students how much they study, are other examples of achieved stabilities in behavior. The tools of self-directedness can be used to promote growth as well as stability. By fostering self-development, the self-regulatory mechanisms operate in the same fashion but with a progressively rising standard that builds on enlarging skills.

DISINCENTIVES AND DETERRENTS

People cannot exercise unlimited freedom, because their actions would repeatedly infringe on the freedom and welfare of others. Thus, for example, if motorists had no traffic codes they would continuously immobilize each other in traffic jams and maim each other, whereas adopting a few sensible rules greatly enhances everyone's well-being. In all societies, members institute certain customs and rules by which they live. But since people favor their self-interest and are not much enamored of social demands and limits, they inevitably come into conflict with one another in their everyday lives. Some of their actions may be personally upsetting, others may be injurious, and still others may constitute serious breaches of conduct that undermine the social order. Much social effort is directed at instilling self-restraints that aid observance of social prohibitions. Negative sanctions are often enlisted for this purpose.

Sources of Behavioral Restraints

Restraint over behavior can arise from two different sources: social restraints and internal restraints. *Social restraints* are rooted in threats of external punishment. Negative consequences, which are observed or directly experienced, convey information about the circumstances under which particular kinds of behavior are social disapproved. In situations involving risk of punishment, behavior is partly regulated by anticipated negative consequences. Restraints arising from external threats rely on cognitive appraisals of situational factors that signify risks. Hence, restraints vary in strength depending on situational factors believed to predict the likelihood of threatened consequences.

At first, control is necessarily external. Young children rely on the guidance and direction of others to keep them out of trouble. It is not long, however, before they begin to adopt internal standards of behavior which serve as guides and deterrents for their actions. *Internal restraints* operate through anticipatory self-censure of one's own conduct. The operation of internal control is manifested in two principal ways. First, individuals resist performing acts that are contrary to their standards, even when their behavior is unlikely to be detected. Second, if they do temporarily yield to strong inducements for transgressive conduct, they react with self-reprimands. Successful socialization is aimed at substituting internal control and direction for external sanctions and demands. Indeed, if a society had to rely solely on external agents to keep its members abiding by rules, it would require continuous, massive surveillance of their daily activities.

The deterrent efficacy of negative sanctions is often discussed in terms of the types of people, rather than the interactive determinants of conduct. In these dispositional categorizations, persons who have internalized prosocial standards are portrayed as highly unlikely to transgress, regardless of whether or not external penalties exist. Those who lack internal standards, or have internalized dissocial ones, are depicted as readily transgressing unless constrained by threatened punishment. Those who have tenuous internal controls are bolstered in their resolve to exercise restraint over forbidden conduct by the prospect of punishment in their efforts.

Self-imposed sanctions certainly play a crucial role in reducing proneness to transgressive behavior, but the typological approach neglects the complexities of behavioral regulation. Human affairs are governed by a continuous interaction of self-imposed and social sanctions. Because different domains of behavior are often regulated by separate standards rather than by an all-encompassing one, the above typology can be represented in one and the same individual. Thus, the same person may curb cruel actions toward others by self-censuring reactions regardless of external consequences, forego cheating on income taxes because of threatened penalties by tax collectors, and use forbidden drugs and engage in socially prohibited sexual behavior despite social threats of punishment.

Even in activities that are ordinarily strongly self-regulated, self-sanctions may be insufficient to override unusually powerful inducements that happen to arise, thus requiring the restraining aid of external consequences. Moreover, self-regulatory mechanisms can be temporarily disengaged from censurable conduct through a variety of self-exonerative operations. Social sanctions that make it difficult to divest oneself of personal responsibility discourage the dissociation of acts from self-evaluative consequences.

Functions of Social Sanctions

Social sanctions serve two quite different functions. In their first use, evaluative social reactions provide one means of transmitting standards of behavior, thus serving an educative role. Approving and disapproving responses convey information about the behavior patterns that are socially regarded as right and wrong. Social sanctions are not necessarily adopted as personal standards. The types of methods used, the manner in which they are applied, and the quality of human relationships involved affect the likelihood that the values of others will be accepted as the standards for regulating one's own actions.

The second major use of sanctions is for purposes of social control. When threatened consequences are used for deterrence, costs are superimposed on whatever benefits the disapproved behavior provides, in the hope that the threatened penalties will override the expected gains and thus curb the behavior. Punishment affirms what not to do but, in itself, provides no guidance for what to do. Therefore, how punishment, even if sufficiently inhibiting, alters future behavior depends on the availability of alternatives and the benefits associated with them.

Punishment is often used as a method of social control when the conditions maintaining the prohibited behavior are either unknown or, if known, difficult to modify. For example, most people feel that solutions to widespread social conditions that breed crime are beyond their control—they cannot eliminate poverty, and unemployment, abolish discriminatory maltreatment, and vitalize disintegrating families. So they try to deter criminal behavior fostered by such conditions by increasing police forces and legal penalties. When causes are known, but the remedies are expensive, prevailing societal ideologies partly determine the extent to which resources will be used either to rectify conditions fostering transgressive behavior or to restrain and punish transgressors.

Promoting Restraints through Social Sanctions

Conditioning theories attribute the inhibitory effects of punishment to conditioning of fear to response-produced cues (Mowrer, 1960). Execution of an act generates sensory cues. If misbehavior is repeatedly punished, fear becomes linked to the cues accompanying the act and suppresses it. Empirical tests of this theory have centered mainly on the effects of timing of punishment on response suppression. It was reasoned that punishment at the beginning of an act is most restraining because the conditioned fear would be aroused at the onset, whereas if punishment occurs only on completion of the act, fear would not be aroused until after the deed is done. The findings generally showed that early punishment is more restraining than late punishment (Aronfreed, 1968).

However, theories that internalize control of action in anxiety roused by response-produced cues are beset by serious problems. Because the same bodily equipment has to perform innumerable functions, identical actions are used in both punished and rewarded activities. For example, the proprioceptive cues that accompany reaching for somebody else's money are the same as reaching for one's own, yet the latter act is unrestrained while the former one is usually inhibited. Behavioral restraints are similar, regardless of whether the transgressive hand or the innocent, inactive hand gets punished (Kaufman, 1964). Moreover, seeing others punished for prohibited acts instills self-restraints in observers even though they perform no responses at the time (Benton, 1967).

Choice of actions is governed by anticipatory thought, rather than by signals from the muscles and limbs. Confounding factors in the timing of punishment most likely explain its differential restraining effects. Prompt punishment at the moment an act is initiated conveys a much stricter prohibition than if nothing much is said until after the transgressive behavior has occurred for some time. In addition to being more forbidding, punishment at the onset of an act provides only unpleasantness, whereas being able to enjoy a pleasurable activity that is later chastised provides both rewards and unpleasantries. Punishment alone is more dissuading than if it has to compete with rewards of action.

In the conditioning view of internalization proposed by Aronfreed (1968), which follows the dual-process conception of avoidance learning, anxiety becomes attached through punishment not only to motoric cues but also to thoughts of the action and to external cues as well. Thereafter, these warning cues trigger anxiety which, due to its aversiveness, arrests the intended behavior. Operant conditioning theory strips both thought and anxiety of causal efficacy but retains external cues as the selective controllers of action. If a certain class of behavior is punished in the presence of particular stimuli, the appearance of those stimuli will suppress the behavior.

In the social cognitive analysis, restraints are governed largely by self-standards and anticipated outcomes. Regulation of conduct is, therefore, neither entirely external nor is it necessary to experience anxiety arousal to forego reprehensible actions. Thought can guide action without having to depend upon being stirred up emotionally. Anticipated self-censure for violating one's own standards and anticipated social censure for violating societal codes serve as the principal restraining mechanisms. It is not that thoughts of misdeeds activate anxiety that has been conditioned to them, but that thoughts of the adverse personal and social consequences of misdeeds lead persons to restrain transgressive actions.

Modes of Negative Sanctions and Self-Restraints

Negative sanctions may involve either withdrawal of rewarding events or presentation of aversive ones. Sanctions in the latter category may take the form of physical punishment, verbal reprimands, or other aversive outcomes. Those in the former category involve levying fines and depriving persons for a time of things they like, such as enjoyable activities, privileges, and social rewards. Although both types of sanctions represent forms of punishment, they have somewhat different effects on behavior and on social relationships.

Punishment restrains forbidden conduct when the threats appear credible, but, if severe, punishment also carries risks of unintended detrimental effects (Bandura, 1969; Walters & Grusec, 1977). Painful experiences can suppress more than just the socially prohibited actions. Punishments, especially if applied without clarifying explanation, can create inhibitions that generalize to socially desirable patterns as well. Once developed, such vulnerability to fear and inhibition is not easily eliminated (Hoffman, 1969). Moreover, when developmental discontinuities exist in cultural demands, as, for example, in sexual activities, behavior that has been prohibited in childhood is expected later in life. Even at a given time, activities that are forbidden in certain situations are permitted in others. Effective functioning, therefore, requires adaptability to changing circumstances. Restraints instilled through painful experiences can create behavioral inflexibility (Whiting & Mowrer, 1943).

Aversive punishment also activates avoidance of the punishers. In the absence of social constraints or interpersonal rewards that create strong psychological ties, punishments that are too weak to suppress behavior will prompt transgressors to stay away from the punishers (Azrin & Holz, 1966). Interpersonal avoidance reduces opportunities for constructive social influence. Punishment can also drive persons to associate with people who model and encourage the very troublesome patterns of behavior that the punishment was designed to curtail (Bandura & Walters, 1959). Patterson, Dishion, and Bank (1984) verify this process in the development of aggressive deviancy in boys. They found that parental reliance on punitive modes of control promotes coercive behavior in their children, which evolves into a physically aggressive style of behavior. Because such conduct alienates the aggressors from most of their peers, the youngsters gravitate to an antisocial peer group.

Another possible, unintended effect of punitive sanctions is negative modeling. In an all-too-common disciplinary scenario, parents spank their children for mistreating and hitting others. The punitive modeling is not lost on the children, who tend to adopt similar styles of behavior in their own dealings with others. Thus, parents who favor coercive discipline have children who likewise use coercive means with peers (Hoffman, 1960). That familial violence breeds violence is confirmed by studies of child abuse (Silver, Dublin, & Lourie, 1969; Sweet & Resick, 1979). Children who suffer brutal treatment at the hands of punitive parents are themselves inclined to use assaultive behavior with their own future children. Evidence from laboratory studies showing that children who are subjected to punishment treat others in a similar fashion lends support to modeling as a causal factor (Gelfand, Hartmann, Lamb, Smith, Mahan, & Paul, 1974; Mischel & Grusec, 1966).

Negative sanctions involving withdrawal of rewarding events can reduce prohibited behavior with minimal aversiveness and adverse side effects. This is particularly true if previously agreed-upon sanctions are applied promptly, straightforwardly, and unemotionally. The outcomes thus come to be regarded as more or less natural, inevitable consequences of misconduct, rather than as arbitrary or malevolent treatment. When restoration of rewards is made contingent on constructive conduct, this type of sanction can both restrain transgressive behavior and provide positive guidance.

Sanctions that rely solely on the punishing consequences of actions place the burden of control on others. As a result, deterrents that rest solely on external constraints require extensive social surveillance for their success. Negative sanctions exert more dependable and enduring influence on human behavior when they are used in ways that instill and bolster personal standards of conduct. Social sanctions can foster self-control by modeling standards, by applying them consistently, by raising awareness of and a sense of personal responsibility for the effects caused by transgressive actions, and by providing opportunities for self-direction. In this broader function, sanctions operate in concert with precept and example.

Cognitive Mediation

The contribution of cognition to the impact of disciplinary sanctions on self-regulation has been studied extensively with regard to reasoning. Reasoning is used to convey several types of information—it instructs on how to behave, it labels misconduct as inappropriate, it identifies events that motivate it, and it specifies the consequences it is likely to bring upon the wrongdoer and others. Studies of socialization practices show that punishment combined with reasoning is more effective than punishment alone (Sears, Maccoby, & Levin, 1957). High use of reasoning that appeals to behavioral standards and to empathetic concern for the suffering inflicted on others is associated with self-regulatory capabilities (Bandura & Walters, 1959; Hoffman, 1970; Perry & Bussey, 1984).

Correlational studies leave unsettled the question of the direction of causality. Does reasoning foster self-regulatory skills, or are persons who are skilled in guiding their own behavior easily influenced by reasoning and thus do not require more forceful sanctions? Laboratory studies of this issue have examined how reasoning affects the impact of negative sanctions on the development of self-restraint in children (Cheyne & Walters, 1970; Parke, 1974; Walters & Grusec, 1977). Reasons combined with negative consequences generally produce stronger and more lasting self-restraints than negative consequences alone. When a transgressive act is punished, it is unclear whether that particular act or that general type of behavior is considered unacceptable. Discipline that is used as an occasion for explaining a rule of conduct is more effective in creating self-regulation of similar activities than if the specific act is simply punished (LaVoie, 1974). Aversive experience may thus extract compliance in a given situation, whereas cognitive guides provide a basis for regulating future conduct under changing circumstances.

The extent to which the influence of negative sanctions is enhanced by reasoning depends on its content and on a person's cognitive capabilities. Appealing to abstractions is likely to be lost on young children who lack the experience to comprehend them. They are swayed more by reasons centered on the tangible consequences of misdeeds than on abstract rules (Parke, 1974). As children gain social experience and knowledge about what is right, they become more responsive to abstract appeals to rules and moral directives (Cheyne & Walters, 1970; LaVoie, 1974).

The social consequences that transgressors might bring on themselves through their actions do not materialize if they can avoid detection. But the injury and suffering such actions cause others occur regardless of whether or not the wrongdoer is discovered. Thoughts of punishing consequences gain force through self-interest. However, if the punishment is seen as avoidable or easily tolerable, it may be less restraining than concerns over possible injuries to others. There is some evidence to suggest that negative sanctions, accompanied by reasons arousing empathy for the victims, may promote stronger self-restraints than those that try to impress on wrongdoers that their conduct is likely to bring negative consequences to themselves (Walters & Grusec, 1977). The effectiveness of appeals to empathy increases with age (LaVoie, 1974). Qualitative differences in the use of reasoning are evident when comparing families of hyperaggressive to prosocial adolescents (Bandura & Walters, 1959). The former families emphasize the punishments misconduct can bring one; the latter families stress the injury and suffering misconduct inflicts on others.

Restitutive Sanctions. Appeals to reason do not guarantee increased self-restraint, especially when transgressions bring benefits that cannot be easily eliminated. For example, people are not easily talked out of using aggression that enables them to control others and to gain rewards, which are otherwise unavailable to them. Foxx and Azrin (1972) examined extensively the power of restitutive overcorrection as a negative sanction that both underscores offenders' responsibility for the effects of their actions and benefits those who suffer the woes of harmful conduct. Having transgressed, wrongdoers are required to undo the damage they have caused and make reparations to the sufferers. The restitutive tasks are used primarily to instill personal responsibility and social awareness, rather than to inflict pain. Those who aggress have to help clean up, bandage, and care for their victims; those who wreck property have to clean up the debris and repair the damage.

By tying restitution closely to the misconduct, the sanction becomes just, whereas arbitrary penalties make it easy for offenders to shift attention from their misconduct to disputes about the fairness of the punishment. Restitutive sanctions often produce rapid, enduring reductions in detrimental behavior that is refractory to change (Foxx & Bechtel, 1982; Ollendick & Matson, 1978). However, if restitutive demands far exceed the transgression or are imposed vindictively, they are more likely to fuel interpersonal resentment than to instill a heightened sense of personal responsibility and empathy for victims.

The principle of restitutive sanction is reflected in alternative-sentencing programs for unlawful offenses which lend themselves to this type of consequence. These are usually nonviolent offenses. Rather than being jailed or simply being put on probation, transgressors are required to perform community services or to pay off their liabilities to victims through work programs. For example, a physician who was convicted of defrauding a public-health program, in addition to being fined, had to provide medical services at an Indian reservation for a year. Restitutive sanctions differ in whether they require payment of money or performance of social services, whether the restitutive activity corresponds to the criminal offense or is unrelated to it, and whether the sanction is used alone, combined with other penalties, or is a condition for parole (Martin, 1981). Fitting the restitutive activity to the offense is apt to increase its corrective impact because it testifies to the injuriousness of the offense. Having arsonists work in a hospital burn unit and drunk drivers work in a physical rehabilitation unit is better suited to instill concern over the suffering transgressive conduct inflicts on victims than is community service in recreational centers.

Restitutive penalties may effectively deter unlawfulness and benefit society and victims more than costly incarceration, which only imposes further burdens on society. For the most part, the public regards restitution to be an acceptable sanction, offenders regard it as fair, fulfillment of contracts is high, and it costs society much less than incarceration or probation (Martin, 1981). It is often claimed that offenders who have to rectify the damage they have caused tend to stay out of future trouble. However, systematic comparison of recidivism rates accompanying different sanctions is needed before any results are accepted, because restitutive sentences may have been given to offenders who are the quickest to change their ways. Assessment of the corrective power of restitutive sanctions should distinguish between the different forms these sanctions can take.

Some retributionists may object to restitutive penalties on the grounds that the law should extract payment in pain rather than in rectification of damage. In this view, vengeful punishment should impose the equivalent amount of pain and suffering on offenders as they inflicted on their victims, whatever the social costs and effects might be. Restitutive penalties are hardly painless. Moreover, they can both serve retributive purposes and benefit society. Restitutive punishment has greater moral justification than repaying cruelty with cruelty. One can, of course, point to many instances in which the damage cannot be undone or be fully compensated. Even in such cases, both society and the force of criminal sanctions may be better served by curtailing the freedom of offenders and requiring them to compensate their victims or dependents as much as possible, than by inflicting pain, but otherwise absolving offenders of any responsibility toward those whom they have victimized. Unachievability of complete redress should not preclude at least partial redress. In efforts to lessen the burden on victims, societies devise institutional compensators. Insurance carriers pick up the tab for many of the losses and injuries caused by criminal conduct and simply pass on the costs to the law abiders. The displaced system of redress punishes the wrong people.

Severity of Sanctions, Causal Attributions, and Self-Standards

Results of several lines of research show that behavioral restraints increase with severity of punishment (Aronfreed, 1968;

Azrin & Holz, 1966; Cheyne & Walters, 1970). For response patterns that bring some rewards, weak sanctions have little effect, moderate ones are partially restraining, while severe sanctions substantially reduce prohibited behavior. The consistency of punishment similarly affects self-restraints (Parke, 1970). Courses of action that are consistently punished hold little interest. However, people who have learned that benefits of disapproved acts can be obtained at the risk of occasional punishment are not easily deterred by negative sanctions.

The notion that the severity of punishment enhances self-restraints has been the subject of some debate. According to dissonance theory, mild sanctions are more effective than severe ones in fostering internal control. If persons can be induced to comply with a prohibition under mild threat, they experience cognitive dissonance because of the inconsistency between their compliance and an insufficient external cause for it. They reduce the aversive dissonance by convincing themselves that the forbidden activity was not all that attractive after all. Compliance gained by strong threat does not produce self-control by devaluation of forbidden activities because the restraint is seen as being externally enforced.

Proponents of the self-perception and attribution theory, similarly, regard strong threats as impeders of internalization, but they ascribe the effects to cognitive appraisal of causality rather than to the press of a dissonant drive state (Lepper, 1981). Compliance under mild threat will lead people either to infer from their action a lack of interest in the activity or to ascribe their compliance to internal causes. In contrast, forceable threats will promote external attributions for compliant behavior. In this view, self-control is best developed by using the minimum social pressure needed to gain compliance. How causal attributions govern self-restraint in the face of enticements has not been spelled out by the proponents. If the effects depend on a change in self-perception, then anticipated self-devaluation for behaving counter to one's self-conception would be the governing mechanism.

In a procedure commonly used to test whether mild threats diminish the allure of forbidden activities, children are warned not to play with a certain toy they had previously ranked as second in attractiveness, because the experimenters would be annoyed (mild threat) or would become very angry (severe threat) should they disobey. Children are then left alone to play with the same set of toys, whereupon they again rate the toys for attractiveness. Mildly threatened children are generally more inclined than the severely threatened to devalue the forbidden item (Lepper, 1981). However, questions have been raised concerning the generality of the devaluation effect. For lower-class children, who generally experience harsher discipline, a severe threat seems to produce a greater devaluation of what is forbidden (Biaggio & Rodrigues, 1971; Ostfeld & Katz, 1969). With regard to compliance, children are less prone to transgress on future occasions if they have exercised self-control under mild rather than severe threat (Freedman, 1965).

The latter findings seem to be at variance with those showing that firm sanctions ordinarily instill stronger self-restraint than weak ones. Studies of family socialization practices reveal that self-directedness and self-esteem in children are promoted neither by parental punitiveness nor by parental coyness in influence (Baumrind, 1973; Coopersmith, 1967; Perry & Perry, 1983). Rather, parents provide guidance for competence, they set explicit standards of conduct, and they are firm about enforcing them. Findings of experimental studies are difficult to compare because they differ in sanctions, transgressive behavior, and strength of allurements. In studies that instill restraints by actual consequences, several activities are prohibited, and children are left alone with only forbidden objects, a situation which severely taxes their self-restraint. In studies using only verbal threats, children are provided with a set of attractive items and only their second-favorite item is forbidden. It is easy to forsake an activity of secondary attraction when something even better is freely available. For example, little, if any, threat would be required to get people to decline their second-choice job or their second-choice college when they are free to pursue their first choice. Situations highly instigative of transgression, without the presence of any better alternatives, provide a more stringent test of personal control.

A mild threat of displeasure that produces total compliance in everyone does not attest to the power of mild sanctions but rather to the weakness of the allurements. It also raises questions about what role, if any, behavioral compliance plays in the devaluation process. Although all the mildly threatened children conform, a sizeable percentage of them, ranging anywhere from 35 percent to 64 percent, maintain or raise their valuation of the forbidden object. Severe threats typically increase valuation, but here, too, full conformity is accompanied by mixed valuations. Thus, changes in valuation seem to bear little relationship to how children actually behave. Verbal prohibition alone can alter the perceived attraction of forbidden objects by the values it conveys. Adults do not usually get violently upset about trivial things. Severe threats suggest the object is valuable, whereas mild threats may diminish its value. In all three theories emphasizing causal judgments (i.e., dissonance, self-perception, attribution), compliant behavior is a critical ingredient in the devaluation process: Compliance is needed to arouse cognitive dissonance and to provide the data for self-perception and for causal attribution. Whether the prohibition itself may be producing most of the effects needs to be tested.

Several other aspects of this research deserve a brief comment as well. Devaluation of forbidden activities is postulated as a mechanism that mediates self-restraint. However, studies of the change in perceived attractiveness of activities and subsequent resistance to transgression surprisingly do not examine how the two events relate to each other (Freedman, 1965; Pepitone, McCauley, & Hammond, 1967). Evidence that severity of threat with compliance is weakly related to valuation but does affect later conforming behavior argues against valuation serving as the mediator of self-restraint. There is also a certain arbitrariness about the explanations themselves. Most of the research in this area was guided by, and interpreted as, verifying dissonance theory, which regards an aversive drive aroused by incongruity to be the critical causal factor. As attribution theory came into vogue, the same findings are cited as verifying self-perception and attribution theory, both of which eschew drives as causal mediators. When postulated mediators remain unmeasured, incompatible mechanisms can be claimed to be verified by the same data. The suitability of theoretical transplants on preexisting data is difficult to evaluate. Rigorous tests of attributional theory require demonstrating that certain social influences alter causal contributions and that they, in turn, govern behavior.

Targeting activities of secondary interest for control may be ill suited for clarifying the determinants and mechanisms of self-restraint, as it operates in more enticing situations. Nevertheless, this approach provides an interesting strategy for establishing self-control. In an informative study, Lepper (1973) showed that compliance under mild threat increases children's resistance to transgression in other temptation situations. Thus, personal triumphs over weak temptations achieved under conditions of minimum sanction can strengthen self-regulatory capabilities for managing subsequent stronger temptations.

Social labeling of persons can change their self-perceptions in ways that lead them to behave in accordance with their new self-percepts. Thus, children who are told they are good resisters of temptation or good ecologists are less likely to violate social prohibitions, and they litter their environment less (Miller, Brickman, & Bolen, 1975; Toner, Moore, & Emmons, 1980). That so-

cial labeling produces enduring changes, whereas telling children they are expected to behave better does not, suggests that social expectations and demands do not account for the effects. As shown earlier, ascribing behavior to personal agency augments self-regulation by enlisting self-evaluative standards and strengthening perceived self-efficacy. Standards of conduct can also be instilled and strengthened by serving in the role of a model. Having children model resistance to transgression increases their own self-control when they themselves later encounter temptation situations (Toner, Moore, & Ashley, 1978).

Self-restraint is a matter of evaluative standards and self-regulatory skill. Later, we shall see that people's perceptions of their self-regulatory efficacy predicts their future success in managing behavior that is refractory to control. Social sanctions should be judged by their impact on personal standards and on perceived regulatory self-efficacy, rather than solely by transgressions in the same setting where the sanctions had been applied. Exercise of restraint over transgression under conditions of minimal sanctions is more likely to strengthen a sense of personal efficacy than if such acts are checked by compelling external constraints. As happens all too often, ready resort to force undermines the educative function of negative sanctions.

Variable Effects of Negative Sanctions for Social Control

The effectiveness of negative sanctions for controlling behavior depends on a number of factors (Axelrod & Apsche, 1983; Bandura, 1969a; Walters & Grusec, 1977). The benefits derived from the prohibited activities and the availability of alternative means of securing desired outcomes are especially influential. In addition, the severity of the threatened consequences and the likelihood that the transgressions will be detected and punished affect how people will respond to negative sanctions.

When alternative means are available for people to get what they want, actions carrying high risk of punishment are readily discarded (Azrin & Holz, 1966). However, negative sanctions serve as precarious external inhibitors when the behavior brings rewards and when alternative means of getting desired outcomes are unavailable, less attractive, or not within the individual's self-perceived capabilities. Under such conditions, punishment must be applied with considerable force and consistency to be a deterrent. Even then, it produces, at best, temporary and selective control. Behavior that is personally functional, but socially prohibited, is readily performed in settings in which the chance of punishment is low, and it promptly reappears in formerly risky situations after negative sanctions are removed (Bandura & Walters, 1959).

Punishment is informative, as well as inhibitory. People can profit from the failures of others, as well as from their own mistakes. Under positive inducements and limited options, threats lead people to adopt less risky forms of transgressive behavior or to refine the prohibited behavior so as to improve its chances of success (Hill, 1955). To the extent that the substitutes or refinements raise the transgressor's confidence that punishment can be eluded, transgressive behavior will be performed on future occasions. The most effective solution is to combine negative sanctions for transgressive behavior with development of positive alternatives. However, this dual strategy is not applied very often because it is easier simply to punish transgressors than to spend the time, effort, and resources needed to develop new competencies and prosocial standards of behavior.

When forceful perseverance in a course of action can eventually bring success, punishment is likely to escalate rather than curtail the behavior. This escalative effect is most evident in coercion and aggression. Recurrent aggressors become well versed in skills for controlling others through force.

In interpersonal encounters, they respond to counterattacks with progressively more punitive reactions to force acquiescence (Edwards, 1968; Toch, 1969). In homes of hyperaggressive children, family interactions rely mainly on escalating mutual punitiveness (Patterson, 1976). Antagonistic behavior by children evokes punitive counterreactions from parents. The counterreactions, in turn, intensify the children's aversive behavior in an escalating power struggle. In this process of escalating coercion, each member provides aversive instigation for the other, and each is periodically reinforced for behaving punitively by overpowering the other through more painful counterreactions. Mutually punitive systems of this sort can be converted to more wholesome ones by teaching the parents nonpunitive sanctions for aborting escalative aggression and by helping family members develop mutually rewarding patterns of behavior (Patterson & Reid, 1973).

The use of punishment as a technique for social control, similarly, carries the risk of escalating collective aggression when grievances are justifiable and when challengers possess substantial coercive power (Bandura, 1973; Gurr, 1970). When legitimate demands and constructive efforts to produce needed reforms are repeatedly thwarted by those who benefit from inequitable practices, more intense collective protests are mounted. Warranted changes may be temporarily blocked by suppressive countermeasures at high costs to society and at the risk of enlarging the ranks of the challengers. If challengers can mobilize sufficient collective power, escalative coercive action eventually succeeds in changing social practices that lack sufficient justification to withstand concerted protest.

Sanctions of Supernatural Agents

So far, we have been dealing with the sanctions of kinships, associates, and agents of social systems. In most societies large segments of the populace subscribe to beliefs involving supernatural agents, who play a paramount role in their thinking and conduct. Some of these involve polytheistic systems which include a variety of deities personifying different aspects of life. Others are monotheistic systems based on a single supreme deity.

Religious doctrines, whatever theistic structure they represent, give meaning and purpose to life and provide extensive rules of conduct supported by supernatural sanctions. Adherence to religious codes is believed to bring worldly rewards or a blessed afterlife, whereas violations of them bring worldly suffering and eternal punishment through deistic agency. Because the doctrines encompass diverse domains of behavior, and the deity is present in all places at the same time, belief in deistic sanctions can provide a transsituational source of behavioral guidance and control. Unlike socially mediated sanctions, which are circumventable through clever means, neither thought nor conduct can escape deistic surveillance and consequences. The stronger the faith, the stronger is this source of behavioral influence.

The power of threatened supernatural sanctions in regulating human behavior is most strikingly revealed in cultures subscribing to beliefs that the spirits of the dead continue to exercise rewarding and punishing power over the fate of the living. In the war-like culture of the Dani in the New Guinea highlands, men regularly engage in intertribal warfare as the central activity of their life (Gardner & Heider, 1969). They do not fight for land, food, or conquest of opponents; rather, fighting serves a social and spiritual purpose. Fighting is instigated and perpetuated largely by feared consequences of unavenged spirits. It is believed that the spirit released when a dead warrior is cremated has the power to cause accidents, sickness, crop damage, and other misfortunes for its living relatives until it is avenged by the taking of an enemy life. As a further method of the Dani's placation of malicious spirits, a finger of a young girl is amputated and burned, with the result that females in this culture lose several fingers before they reach adulthood. Since the form, time, and place of the punishment by spiritual agents is unspecified, it is easy to seize upon adversities and maladies as the penalties for feintheartedness.

While the Dani spirits punish conciliatory behavior, the Tahitian ancestral spirits punish aggressiveness (Levy, 1969). The Tahitians are an affable people who are slow to anger, quick to get over any ill feelings and, on the infrequent occasions when they are provoked to action, they aggress ineptly by design. Aggression in this pacific society is discouraged through fear of punishment, especially by appeal to spirits who are believed to punish aggressors by making them sick and suffer mishaps. This belief is culturally enforced from time to time. When people get sick or suffer accidents, the misfortunes are designated as spiritual punishments for prior misdeeds. Ascribing untoward happenings to divine retribution gives force to supernatural sanctions.

LEGAL SANCTIONS AND DETERRENCE

Many forms of behavior are personally advantageous but harm others or infringe on their rights. Without some social controls, everyone's well-being and freedom would be continuously in jeopardy. The best deterrent to forbidden conduct is the development of prosocial alternatives sufficiently attractive to supplant antisocial patterns. Indeed, most law-abiding behavior relies more on deterrence through preferable prosocial options than on threats of legal sanctions. Thus, for example, people who possess satisfying income-producing skills are not much tempted to obtain money through burglaries, robberies, or bank hold-ups. However, when inducements to criminal acts are strong, when personal sanctions against such conduct are weak, and when people lack socially acceptable means of getting what they want, fear of punishment serves as a major deterrent to transgressive conduct.

The threat of punishment can act as a deterrent in two ways (Packer, 1968; Zimring & Hawkins, 1973). In *direct deterrence*, transgressors are punished to reduce their propensity to commit criminal acts in the future. In *vicarious deterrence*, transgressors are punished to discourage others from engaging in similar criminal conduct. The example of punishment is designed to create a widespread, deterrent effect. The present chapter analyzes the deterrent force of legal sanctions. The factors governing the strength of vicarious influence and the mechanisms by which consequences to others affect self-restraints are discussed in the next chapter.

Multifaceted Conception of Deterrence

The role of legal sanctions in criminal conduct must be analyzed within a larger conceptual system of how human behavior is regulated. Deterrents for criminal conduct have three major sources: the restraints of self-sanction, of social sanction, and of legal sanction. *Legal sanction* depends on beliefs about the likelihood that transgressive acts will be punished. If threatened legal consequences are to serve as deterrents, they must be credible. In transgressions that are readily detectable, such as income-tax evasion, the prospect of legal penalties keeps most people law abiding and spawns legitimate ways of circumventing heavy tax payments. However, for most criminal activities there is little risk of being apprehended and convicted of wrongdoing. Of the many crimes committed, about half of them do not even come to the attention of enforcement agencies because they are never reported. Only a fraction of reported crimes produce arrests. Of those arrested, only a fraction are prosecuted because of insufficient evidence. Of the cases brought to trial, many are dismissed, most of the apprehended bargain for lesser charges, which are granted for providing incriminating information about others or to avoid long, costly trials, and some are convicted. Of those who happen to be convicted, only a small fraction are sent to prison.

Although arrest and punishment rates obviously vary for different crimes, Zimring and Hawkins (1973) estimate that only about 1 percent of the total crimes committed result in prison sentences. Even if other penalties are considered, given the considerable progressive shrinkage from committed crimes to reports, arrests, and convictions, most criminal conduct clearly goes unpunished. Transgressors have little reason to alter their behavior when there is little chance of being caught and punished. The threat of punishment is probably least credible in communities in which crimes are commonplace but arrests and convictions are infrequent.

When one considers the low risk of legal penalties, the challenging question is not the occurrence of criminal acts, but why they are not much more prevalent. A distinction must, of course, be drawn between actual and perceived risks. Because deterrence depends on beliefs, infrequent punishment that is widely publicized can reap deterrent benefits by leading people to overestimate the chances of punishment. Overestimating legal risks dampens temptation. Studies of the perceived likelihood of legal punishment for various offenses lends some validity to this interpretation (Jensen, 1969; Parker & Grasmick, 1979). People who are not in the habit of breaking the law share a distorted perception of legal threats, in which they greatly overestimate the risks of getting caught and punished for unlawful acts. In contrast, offenders judge personal risks to be lower and more in line with the actual probabilities (Claster, 1967).

The heavy social costs of being charged and convicted of a crime constitute the second major deterrent that exerts a powerful restraining effect. They represent the informal *social sanction* for illegal conduct. For persons who enjoy a favorable status in their vocational and community life, a criminal offense can have devastating social consequences on their reputations and livelihoods. The fine for shoplifting may be trivial, but an arrest for shoplifting can ruin a career. Criminal stigmatization imperils future opportunities (Zimring, 1971). Moreover, transgressive conduct that violates widely held norms gives rise to a variety of lesser, though unpleasant, social consequences. Many people are, therefore, well behaved, even when there are low risks of punishment and trifling legal penalties, because pervasive social consequences can flow from public knowledge about the criminal offense itself.

Because a personal stake tends to be interpreted narrowly, writers often convey the impression that the behavior of those who are not in the mainstream of society is checked mainly by visions of police and prisons. Criminal conduct is widely restrained by a personal stake in one's own physical well-being. Assailants get beat up and robbers get shot. Those who pursue antisocial careers have to live up to the social codes of their own subculture, which disallow some forms of criminal conduct. As the saying goes, there is honor even among thieves. Persons will refrain from criminal behavior for fear of both injury by those they victimize and censure from their peers, although they repudiate societal codes and are self-assured that they will not fall into the hands of the police.

Self-sanction arising from moral standards is the third source of deterrents that promotes law-abiding behavior. In this personal mode of control, criminal acts are deterred by anticipatory self-condemnation were the individual to engage in the misconduct. Once such self-sanctions are developed, laws and enforcement agents are no longer required to deter the individual from antisocial conduct. This is the most effective form of deterrence because antisocial behavior is renounced, even in situations in which there is little or no risk of getting caught. In the absence of self-sanctions rooted in societal standards, whenever personal desires conflict with societal codes, external threats, in the form of legal and social sanctions, and extensive social surveillance are needed to ensure that the rights and welfare of others are not completely disregarded.

A comprehensive theory of criminal deterrence must include the restraints of self-sanction, social sanction, and legal sanction. In addition to *negative deterrents*—the personal, social, and legal costs of wrongdoing—the considerable role played by *positive deterrents* to criminal conduct must be included in the conceptual scheme. In positive deterrents the benefits of prosocial behavior override the enticements to antisocial behavior. It is now a well-established principle that disallowed patterns of behavior are more effectively eliminated by fostering positive means of gaining benefits than by punishing forbidden means. To achieve explanatory power, a theory of deterrence must encompass the different regulatory mechanisms through which transgressive behavior is controlled.

Gauging Deterrence Effects

The deterrent value of criminal sanctions does not lend itself to neat experiments in which enforcement factors and penalties are varied systematically in identical communities. Investigators, therefore, try to estimate deterrent effects from naturalistic data of unknown reliability. Much of the research on criminal deterrence correlates legal sanctions and socioeconomic indices with crime rates. Among the legal sanctions, special attention is given to the certainty and severity of punishment, the two principal ways in which a society tries to raise the costs of criminal conduct. Research of this type, if based on reliable data, can provide some information bearing on matters of social policy, but it cannot shed much light on deterrence processes. This is because the research encompasses only a limited set of proxy variables and depends almost exclusively on correlational analyses, which leave ambiguities about the exact nature and direction of causality.

Progress in understanding the determinants and mechanisms of criminal deterrence requires research that measures the extent to which the different negative deterrents—personal, social, and legal—

contribute to the control of transgressive acts. Multiple determination of behavior cannot be erased by dividing people up into different one-dimensional types, each supposedly deterred by moral, social, or legal sanctions but not by more than one of these. The prevalent belief that a large segment of the populace is so well socialized that it requires no legal sanctions finds little support in surveys of middle-class adults (Wallerstein & Wyle, 1947). Many males and some females admit offenses that amount to felonies, while almost all acknowledge one or more offenses sufficiently serious to draw a sentence of at least one year. Illegal activities that are widely condoned are undoubtedly even much more frequent.

The contribution of positive deterrents to the control of crime similarly requires assessing people's skills for socially acceptable pursuits, the benefits that can be secured by these alternate means, and the opportunities that exist to pursue them. When a broad set of determinants is measured, the likelihood of transgressive acts is better predicted by functional value of the behavior, moral standards, and fear of social censure than by fear of legal consequences (Tittle, 1977). Such findings suggest that transgressive conduct is restrained more by consideration of self-generated and social consequences than by legal threats. One can define deterrence as suppression of criminal behavior by legal threats, but one can hardly disregard the multiple, nonlegal determinants that, in fact, strongly influence the incidence of criminal offenses. The way in which personal competencies and different sources of restraint combine to control misconduct will vary across individuals, transgressive acts, and situations. Acts that bring into play multiple sources of restraint are more easily deterrable than those that rely primarily on legal threats.

Deterrent effects are especially difficult to study because they are reflected in the nonoccurrence of transgressive acts. As we have already seen, there are any number of reasons why people might refrain from transgressing. Rather than measuring the principal sources of deterrence successes, investigators examine only crime rates, which actually represent deterrence failures. In a thoughtful analysis of this issue, Meier and Johnson (1977) make it clear that deterrent effects cannot be fully understood unless both successes and failures are analyzed. Because social factors can alter the relative strength of the various deterrents, legal sanctions may have gained restraining force even though offense rates remain unchanged or are even increasing. For example, with relaxation of social mores, forbidden conduct that was formerly restrained mainly by personal and social sanctions may now be checked by legal threats. Were it not for the legal sanctions, the offenses might otherwise be much higher. This would be a case in which legal sanctions are exerting a significant effect, even though there has been a rise in the number of offenses. Conversely, growing cultural devaluation of an objectionable behavior can usher in strict laws along with a drop in offenses, but the heightened personal and social sanctions are largely responsible for the decline. In the latter instance, the change in the law and rate of offenses, rather than being causally linked, are both coeffects of shifts in social values. When changes in norms and social practices precede modifications in the law, as is typically the case, the deterrent effects are mistakenly credited to the legal sanctions. As these examples illustrate, failure to assess how the strength of each of the three types of sanctions has changed can yield misleading conclusions about the impact of legal penalties.

The measures of illegal conduct on which much of the research on criminal deterrence rests is another major source of concern. Crime rate is usually defined as the number of offenses reported per capita; certainty of punishment is the percentage of reported crimes for which offenders are caught and convicted; and severity of punishment is the average prison sentence for different offenses. Reporting practices vary across localities and over time, and only a fraction of the actual offenses are ever reported. The measure of the incidence of criminal behavior is thus seriously flawed (Cook, 1980; Gibbs, 1975). Such measures are plagued by many other problems as well: Police may alter the crime reports which reflect on their efficiency; the prevalent practice of plea bargaining results in conviction on a lesser crime; and juvenile offenders, who commit a sizeable share of the offenses, do not appear in imprisonment rates. Because of the dubious status of police crime data, some researchers rely on victimization surveys, in which people are interviewed as to whether or not they have been the victims of offenses.

Deterrent effects are often evaluated by correlating variations in legal sanctions with crime rates. In correlations based on aggregate measures, it is unknown whether the people who perceive a lower risk of punishment are the ones committing the crimes. There is also ambiguity about the time lag between changes in legal penalties and how soon they are expected to affect crime rates. There are hazards in making causal inferences from aggregate data. Moreover, time lags between the commission of crimes, the apprehension, and the adjudication of cases create uncertainties at what points in time the indices should be related. To complicate matters further, imprisonment rates may confound possible reductions in crimes due to the deterrence effect, with reductions resulting from the removal of repeated offenders from circulation. It should also be noted that white-collar crime, which extracts a continuing, heavy toll from the society, shows up more in the price of commodities than in official crime statistics. Nor do such data include the injuries caused to large numbers of people by unlawful organizational practices that are sufficiently profitable to take the risks (Geis & Monahan, 1976; Rosenberg, 1984). Studies abound on how to deter free-lancing transgressors, but they are virtually nonexistent on how to deter organizational misconduct that is harmful for the society.

Econometric models of criminal conduct, which are generating much research on deterrence, are based on the rationalistic premise that offenders seek to maximize their expected gains by calculating costs and benefits (Ehrlich, 1979). However, in empirical tests of such models, important determinants of illegal behavior are either not included or are represented by crude substitute indices that may reflect any number of factors. Sophisticated statistical methodology cannot make up for truncated models of deterrence and disputable measures of its components. For example, the social and material benefits of criminal acts are unknown, and the estimates of personal costs are confined to what is easily measurable—the length of imprisonment. Personal and social costs of wrongdoing are conspicuously absent from the severity indices, even though they may figure more prominently in the regulation of antisocial conduct than legal sanctions (Tittle, 1977). Although the decision to engage in criminal activities presumably depends upon weighing the relative costs and benefits of illegal and lawful behavior, the lawful means available to individuals, which help to keep most of us law abiding, are not assessed, except for the gross indices of national employment and the like.

A utilitarian model with adequate measures might lend itself well to crimes of profit, but it is unclear how gains are computed for interpersonal crimes, such as assaults and rapes, or for offenses involving drunkenness, illegal gambling, and use of prohibited drugs. When one considers that many homicides and other crimes are committed by intoxicated offenders, it is doubtful that their actions are governed by thoughtful cost-benefit calculations and by profit-maximizing considerations. This is not to say that anger arousal and inebriation abolish all thoughts of consequences. Rather, such altered states can weaken cognitive control of behavior because less thought is given to the prospective consequences.

Recklessness is commonly excused by blaming it on alcohol when, in fact, its disinhibitory effects may be due more to self-exonerating thought than to the pharmacological action of alcohol itself. Males who are led to believe they have drunk alcoholic beverages behave more aggressively and display greater sexual arousal to erotic films and to depictions of rape and sadistic aggression toward women than those who think they have drunk nonalcoholic beverages, regardless of whether their drinks contained alcohol or not (Briddell, Rimm, Caddy, Krawitz, Sholis, & Wunderlin, 1978; Lang, Goeckner, Adesso, & Marlatt, 1975; Wilson & Lawson, 1976). Alcohol itself had little effect on social behavior. In these studies, alcohol decreases inhibition toward sex and aggression through cognitive rather than physiological means. Since most aroused or intoxicated individuals do not commit crimes, outcome considerations help to predict the likelihood that criminal acts will be performed in such states. It will be recalled from the earlier discussion of expectancy theories that people base their actions partly on outcome judgments, but their anticipatory thought does not necessarily take the form of optimizing calculations.

The model of limited, rather than optimal, rationality is supported by the research of Caroll (1978), who had adult and juvenile offenders and nonoffenders make decisions about committing crimes with different payoffs and penalties and with different chances of succeeding or getting caught. In their decisions, people consider only a few aspects of the situations, rather than engage in thoughtful weighting of all relevant factors. People are swayed much more heavily by the payoffs of crimes than by the penalties that might be incurred, and they give greater weight to the prospect of success than to the likelihood of apprehension. Prison inmates think the same way (Peterson & Braiker, 1981). In considering criminal activities, they anticipate the benefits of crime but give little thought to possible punitive consequences. Thus, criminal judgments are not all that different from the way people generally go about making decisions—they single out and overweigh a few factors and engage in only a partial examination of other alternatives. They tend to reflect more on benefits than on punishments.

Deterrence theory is formulated in terms of beliefs about the prospective costs and benefits of alternative courses of action. The prospects of success depend largely on the skillfulness with which activities are executed. To test the premises of this theory, therefore, requires microanalysis of how individuals' judgments of their capabilities and likely outcomes affect the behavioral choices they make. In practice, with few exceptions, empirical studies of deterrence employ the wrong measures with the wrong paradigms. Investigators relate group crime rates to crude indices of certainty and severity of punishment, rather than to personal beliefs about the risks and gains of different criminal acts. Belief and actuality are not all that highly correlated. Rather than relating persons' self-efficacy and outcome beliefs to their actions, investigators correlate variations in legal penalties and crime rates averaged across time or jurisdictional units (states, counties, cities), or they examine how the frequency of different types of crimes co-varies with the legal penalties associated with them. Whereas the theory is formulated in terms of an individual's choice of behavior, it is tested with groups as the unit of analysis. The omission of efficacy and outcome beliefs and the aggregation of data across people create major incongruities between deterrence theory and the data used to test it.

Some efforts have been made to clarify the relation between perceived risk of legal sanctions and unlawful behavior. Paternoster and his associates have criticized much of this research because it relates current perceived risk to past criminal conduct (Paternoster, Saltzman, Waldo, & Chiricos, 1983). This is the wrong causal ordering for verifying a legal deterrence effect. In a longitudinal study, they found that unlawful conduct strongly affects perceived risk of arrest. As people commit illegal acts and get away with it, they see less risk of legal punishment. However, the deterrence effect of perceived legal sanction appears weak. Perhaps this is because the chances of being caught are seen to be relatively low. It may also be that perceived risk of arrest fluctuates, so that the measured beliefs are not the ones guiding illegal conduct over the course of a year. Other evidence argues against such an interpretation. Analysis relating beliefs to illegal action, even over a short time span, finds little evidence that fear of legal punishment acts as the disincentive to forbidden conduct (Minor & Harry, 1982). These and other findings suggest that most people behave lawfully either because illegal pursuits hold little attraction for them or because they are deterred primarily by anticipated personal and social sanctions.

Certainty and Severity of Legal Sanctions

Few would doubt that the threat of legal sanctions deters unlawful conduct. Removal of all legal penalties for tax evasion would rapidly deplete the Federal treasury. If men could rape with impunity, the incidence of sexual assaults would, in all likelihood, increase. If car theft carried no legal punishment, much of the populace would soon find itself dispossessed of their prized automobiles. The issue of primary interest does not center on whether legal threats deter unlawful behavior but on whether increases in the level of legal penalties achieve further reductions in the incidence of crime.

Although the results are by no means unequivocal, findings of correlational studies generally show that increased certainty of arrest and punishment is associated with reduced likelihood of criminal behavior (Erickson & Gibbs, 1976; Jensen, Erickson, & Gibbs, 1978; Palmer, 1977; Tittle & Rowe, 1974). The correlations are generally in the low-to-moderate range, with higher relationships obtained for property crimes than for assault and homicide (Blumstein, Cohen, & Nagin, 1978; Geerken & Gove, 1977). Econometric analyses have produced conflicting findings. This is because researchers often include different causal factors in the deterrence model, they make different assumptions about how the various factors they include affect crime, and they use different analytic methods. As a result, they arrive at different conclusions (Brier & Fienberg, 1980; Ehrlich, 1973). Unless one has a sound theory to guide selection of potential determinants of criminal conduct and suitable measures of those determinants, even the most sophisticated analytic procedures cannot provide reliable answers.

Showing that certainty of punishment covaries with crime rates does not necessarily mean that legal threats are the cause of good behavior. A high volume of crime diminishes the ability of police to catch offenders through overload of work and thus lowers arrest rates (Logan, 1975). To complicate analysis of causality, the arrest and crime rates may both be caused by a third factor, that is, social and moral imperatives may be largely responsible for both strict enforcement and lawful behavior. Indeed, some suggestive evidence to this effect has been reported (Erickson, Gibbs, & Jensen, 1977). The more reprehensible people view a particular offense, the less inclined they are to commit it. The relationship between severity of punishment and lawfulness shrinks markedly when the influence of perceived reprehensibility is removed. Erickson and his colleagues argue that a condemnatory social attitude toward certain crimes deters such offenses, enlists citizen participation in curbing unlawfulness, and pressures enforcement agencies to catch and punish those who happen to transgress. Variations in the prevailing values in different states and counties may similarly account for much of the correlation between arrest certainty and offense rates. In this regulatory process, strict enforcement affirms the moral values of the citizenry, rather than the legal threat functioning as the primary deterrent.

Multivariate correlational analyses are increasingly used to estimate how much different factors contribute to changes in crime rates when the effects of the other factors are simultaneously controlled. To be most informative, such analyses require theoretical specification of the relevant causal factors and their causal priority. Analyses that fail to include the influence of social standards may exaggerate the contribution of legal sanctions if a good part of the relationship between legal sanctions and illegal conduct is due to social standards, which affect both factors. Thus, the relationship between legal sanctions and transgressive behavior may change considerably, depending on what other determinants are included in the analysis and the order in which their independent contribution is assessed. Without a sound theory to serve as a guide, multivariate correlational analyses can yield diverse conclusions. Because different types of sanctions can affect each other, they probably act together to regulate criminal activities.

There is little evidence that increasing the severity of punishment affects crime rates, except for homicide (Erickson & Gibbs, 1976; Tittle, 1969). It would seem that, for many people, the pervasive social consequences of being convicted of a crime are sufficiently threatening that adding more severe penalties does not yield further deterrent benefits. The policy implications of this finding are not inconsequential. It is much easier to pass laws that impose stiffer sentences on offenders than to devise effective means for catching them. Urban domains are so vast that even a sizeable expansion of police forces still leaves widely dispersed locales unpatrolled most of the time and thus does not really improve the chances of deterring or apprehending wrongdoers. A study in which contiguous areas of a city received their usual patrols, no patrols, or substantially increased patrols

revealed no differences in arrest or crime rates over a period of a year (Kelling, Pate, Dieckman, & Brown, 1975). These findings are consistent with those of correlational studies showing that enlarging the size of police forces does not reduce crime rates (Levine, 1975). The effect of police on crime is better analyzed by relating offense rates to how many police are on patrol and what they do there than to how many are on the payroll. Whether more vigorous policing deters criminal activities is in dispute because analyses rest on conjectural indices of police behavior, rather than on direct examination of how vigorously police enforce the laws (Jacob & Rich, 1980; Wilson & Boland, 1978).

Unusually large rises in crime often prompt expanded police coverage of troublesome areas. Where the locale is circumscribed, as in subway trains and stations, saturation coverage can reduce the incidence of offenses (Chaiken, Lawless, & Stevenson, 1974). However, since escalating unlawful conduct typically drops due to informal social controls before legal penalties are increased (Bandura, 1973; Dupont & Greene, 1973), it is difficult to determine how much of the decline is creditable to police surveillance and how much to social countermeasures growing out of public concern. Large infusions of police forces in certain precincts can temporarily reduce crime in the targeted area, but offenders may displace some of their criminal activities to adjacent areas or become bolder over time, as they become more familiar with the police and their patrol patterns (Chaiken, 1978).

Interrupted time-series analysis provides a quasi-experimental method of evaluating the impact of legal sanctions. In this approach, the magnitude and duration of changes in offenses following the introduction of strict penalties are compared with changes in offense rates plotted over a long time. Such analyses often show that unusual rises in offenses are followed by drops, even without special enforcement. Thus, for example, a publicized crackdown on speeding may be followed by lower traffic deaths, but similar declines occur after a period of high traffic fatalities even without heightened legal threats (Ross & Campbell, 1968). Apparently, the publicity about fatalities, rather than the sterner threats, encouraged more careful driving. Even when people have to submit to police checks without having aroused any suspicion, such as when roadblocks are used to spot drivers under the influence of alcohol, severe penalties produce a temporary drop in traffic accidents, but the deterrence effect quickly dissipates (Ross, 1982). The initial publicity greatly exaggerates the risk of being arrested and convicted for drunk driving. Public clamor often creates tough laws that neither the police nor the courts are all that keen to enforce permanently, because they have to contend with more pressing demands on their already overtaxed resources. Tough laws that are poorly enforced do not have much lasting deterrent force. Because the chances of being apprehended are very low, people quickly learn that the legal threat carries little actual risk. Before long they revert to their usual habits.

To achieve even a marginal increase in the certainty and severity of punishment imposes heavy burdens on enforcement systems and on society at large. With only a small fraction of lawbreakers being apprehended and brought to trial, court dockets are so overloaded that it takes months and years to try a case. Prisons are so overcrowded that they pose serious dangers to inmates and their keepers alike. Longer prison terms do not have much effect on crime rates, but ironically they can weaken the system of legal sanction. Overloaded courts and crammed prisons encourage plea bargaining in exchange for lesser charges and waiver of prison sentences. If mandatory sentences are too excessive for the offenses committed, both judges and juries are less willing to convict wrongdoers in cases where they feel a lengthy prison sentence would, in the long run, do society more harm than good. The more severe the punishment, the lower are the conviction rates and the less likely are offenders to be sent to prison (Erickson & Gibbs, 1976; Kerr, 1978). While the public demands surer and stiffer penalties, it defaults on the costs that would be required for additional police, courts, judgeships, jails, prisons, and subsistence for the families of inmates during their extended imprisonment. Most law breaking is clandestine. To achieve higher detectability of criminal acts requires methods of social and electronic surveillance that encroach on privacy and civil liberties. Much of the public expects law to curb the problems of the human condition. But, as we have noted, enlarged expenditures on enforcement systems do not necessarily buy more deterrence.

It might be argued that long prison terms reduce crime because habitual lawbreakers cannot pursue criminal activities while locked up. This would be a logical consequence, provided that stiff terms did not alter conviction and sentencing practices and that offenders removed from circulation were not replaced by new recruits. The adage that every solution has a problem applies to the remedy of social quarantine as well. Petty offenses and bizarre crimes may be committed individually, but most criminal activities involve a collective effort. Some analysts speculate that it is the less competent and foolhardy who are apprehended, only to be replaced by new recruits who will ply their criminal trade more skillfully (Cook, 1977). Arresting a small number of drug smugglers or organized burglars will not dent their ranks if the illegal enterprise brings huge profits. Because of ready substitution of criminal functionaries, social quarantine of offenders does not necessarily reduce crime rates. There are inherent limits to crime reduction that can be achieved by lengthy imprisonment even for crimes that are performed individually. Because arrest and conviction rates are very low, lengthening the period of incarceration for those who happen to get caught makes little dent in the overall crime rate (Cohen, 1983).

Evidence that crime is deterrable by legal punishment does not necessarily mean that it offers a practical solution to the problem. Criminal practices are mainly the pursuit of young people. If criminal pursuits are to hold little interest for youths, they must adopt prosocial standards of conduct, self-regulatory skills, and competencies supportive of prosocial lifestyles. Investing in social supports for prosocial development holds much greater promise of reducing crime than spending huge sums of money trying to catch, convict, and punish offenders who have become immersed in a life of crime.

The widespread public belief that the solution to the control of crime is swift, certain, and severe punishment neither recognizes the inordinate costs and the difficulties in applying these prescriptions nor the marginal returns that heightened legal threats yield. In the view of many legal scholars (Packer, 1968; Zimring & Hawkins, 1973), the criminal sanction is a cumbersome and very costly way of trying to regulate human conduct. While the presence of legal penalties can help to deter unlawful acts when persons would otherwise be tempted to transgress, increasing the level of legal sanctions yields diminishing returns at heavy costs to society. A realistic view of the limits of legal sanctions might encourage more serious consideration of alternative forms of deterrents that enlist the power of social and moral sanctions in the service of societal lawfulness.

Beliefs about Legal Risks and Lawfulness

As we have seen, the deterrent effect of legal sanctions rests on beliefs regarding the prospect of being caught and punished for wrongdoing. The benefit of this psychological mechanism of control is that high perceived risk helps bolster lawfulness despite low actual risk of legal penalties. Even if actual risks were raised somewhat through infusion of huge sums of money and more law enforcers, such changes would not, in themselves, necessarily affect the incidence of criminal conduct, unless they altered public beliefs. Because beliefs about risks and benefits have causal efficacy, studying the fac-

tors that influence such beliefs and how they regulate transgressive acts holds promise of clarifying some of the psychological mechanisms of deterrence. Strategies for reducing misconduct through legal threats should be judged partly in terms of their effectiveness in strengthening beliefs that transgressions are likely to bring penalties.

In discussing the policy implications of research on deterrence, Meier (1978) sets forth the view that efforts to deter crime through legal threats should be aimed at strengthening beliefs that transgressions carry high risk. Since certainty of punishment is more deterring than its severity, beliefs about the chances of arrest and conviction are most likely to bolster self-imposed restraints. However, it should be remembered that legislated sanctions express societal values, as well as serve as deterrents. To treat pernicious conduct lightly may well encourage it by conveying a permissive societal attitude toward it, even though the legal threat itself has little deterrent effect. When the legal consequences are light compared to the seriousness of the offenses, sanctions run the risk of condoning criminal conduct. Some writers place much greater credence on the value of legal sanctions to articulate collective moral imperatives than on the direct deterrent value of legal threats (Chein, 1975). In this indirect route of influence, legal prohibitions strengthen moral standards which, in turn, deter transgressive conduct.

For most people, beliefs about risks regarding criminal conduct are instilled and strengthened more by information about the experiences of others and by reports of the efficacy of enforcement systems than through direct experience. Legal deterrents, therefore, require widespread publicity. To segments of the populace that have little, if any, personal acquaintance with crime, widely publicized accounts of arrests and convictions of offenders amplify the threat of legal sanctions by conveying the impression that it is difficult to evade arrest for wrongdoing. For example, the arrest rate for burglary in newspaper reports is about five times greater than the actual rate of arrests (Parker & Grasmick, 1979). Selective information, which gives salience to arrests but little notice to the magnitude of successful evasions, promotes overestimation of the hazards of wrongdoing.

Announcements by public officials that more police will be deployed to a troublesome area or that the law will be enforced more vigorously also serve to raise perceived risks. Such presentations by the media, targeted at beliefs, can reduce crime rates even though the actual chances of arrest remain unchanged (Meier, 1978; Ross, 1973). Publicized community programs, in which residents organize in a common effort to combat crime in their neighborhoods similarly raise perceived risks. In organizing themselves for crime prevention and condemning criminal activities, community residents also increase the force of social sanctions.

A belief-oriented approach to legal deterrents presents special challenges in locales where crime is prevalent but arrests are infrequent. To residents of such areas, illusory legal threats have little credibility. If such threats are to have any force where crime has become commonplace, they must be backed up by actual consequences from time to time. A limited enforcement capability can lend some credibility to legal threats through saturation coverage of particular areas at uncertain times by nonuniformed patrols, thus making it difficult to figure out when it is relatively safe and when it is hazardous to commit offenses. Unpredictability of safety from arrest creates a generalized sense of jeopardy. But without positive deterrents and active neighborhood participation in curbing misconduct, such tactics are unlikely to have much impact.

CHAPTER
7
VICARIOUS MOTIVATORS

People do not live as isolates in a private world. As social beings, they observe the conduct of others and the occasions on which it is rewarded, ignored, or punished. Hence, they can profit from the successes and mistakes of others, as well as from their own direct experiences. We have seen in an earlier chapter how the symbolic capacity to learn cognitive and behavioral skills through observation is of considerable functional value. This same symbolic capability enables people to regulate their actions advantageously on the basis of knowledge gained vicariously about the likely benefits and risks of different courses of action. Indeed, if human behavior depended solely on personally experienced consequences, most people would not survive the hazards of early development. Of those who managed to outlive their mistakes, each would have to rediscover, through tiresome trial

and error, what works and what fails in everyday transactions with their environment. Fortunately, people are spared many hazards and much tedium by their capacity to benefit from the experiences of others.

Consideration of vicarious motivators contributes importantly to the understanding of human behavior in several ways. Observed outcomes can alter behavior just as directly experienced consequences can. As a general rule, seeing certain courses of behavior succeed for others increases the tendency of observers to behave in similar ways, whereas seeing behavior punished decreases the likelihood that they will use similar means.

Of even greater importance is the evidence that observed outcomes can affect the level of motivation by changing the value and force of external incentives. The value of a given incentive depends largely on its relation to other incentives, rather than solely on its intrinsic qualities (Premack, 1965). Research on how the valence of external incentives is determined relationally shows that the same outcomes can be either rewarding or punishing depending upon the type, frequency, and generosity of prior outcomes. Rewards function as punishers when compared with even more attractive past rewards, but they function as positive incentives when contrasted with prior nonreward or punishment (Buchwald, 1959a, 1959b, 1960).

Incentives can be altered by social comparison, as well as by comparison with what one has experienced in the past. Incentive contrast, resulting from the disparity between observed and personally experienced consequences, affects people in a similar way as disparity with past personal outcomes. People weigh their own consequences against those others gain for similar behavior. Observed outcomes provide a standard for judging the equity and value of the outcomes of one's own behavior. The same compliment is likely to be discouraging to persons who have seen similar performances by others more highly acclaimed but experienced as rewarding when others have been less generously praised. Some of the factors determining likely responses to inequitable treatment will be discussed later.

Relational properties of incentives affect not only behavior and motivation but also the level of personal satisfaction or discontent. Sensitivity to differential treatment is developed early in life when children are often treated unequally before they can fully understand the reasons for it. Children see their older siblings or their own peers staying up later, doing more interesting things, and enjoying greater freedom. They are not easily placated by explanations about the apparent inequity, even if they understand that certain rewards and privileges are linked to age and competence. Inequities become even more upsetting when they are based on arbitrary favoritism. The perturbing aspects of differential treatment are extended and fueled in later years by in-equities in services, in social recognition, in wages, and in occupational advancement. Equitable rewards foster a sense of well-being; inequitable treatment breeds discontent and resentment. The emotional effects of perceived inequity further underscore the importance of social comparative aspects of incentive practices.

The comparative appraisal of outcomes is not a passive process in which observers simply compare their own outcomes to those they see others accrue. People differ widely in their life situations and in the types of benefits and penalties they experience. The others with whom personal comparisons are made must, therefore, be selected from a wide array of possible choices. For example, teachers might judge their salaries in relation to those of their colleagues, regional or national salary levels, or with how members of other occupations are compensated. Self-satisfaction will be strongly affected by the types of comparisons made. Inequitable comparisons breed discontent; favorable ones generally produce self-satisfaction. Those who select comparative referents that create unrealistic reward expectations suffer much self-dissatisfaction.

VICARIOUS REWARD

Seeing that the actions of others produce good results increases the likelihood that observers will behave in a similar way. But observing modeled acts can, in itself, lead others to engage in similar activities (Bandura, 1962; Kaplan, 1972; Phillips, 1968). Therefore, verification that vicarious incentives make a causal contribution requires evidence that observing a model rewarded enhances imitativeness over and above seeing the same modeled conduct occur with no evident consequences.

Results of numerous studies show that rewarded modeling is generally more effective than modeling alone in fostering similar patterns of behavior. The influence exerted by observed consequences, however, varies with how highly observers value the outcomes and with the type of behavior being modeled. Given both insignificant behavior that is easily noticeable and high situational inducement to peform it, people will behave imitatively, regardless of whether or not the model has been rewarded. Under the latter circumstances, observed rewards provide no additional information on how best to behave, beyond that conveyed by the modeled acts alone. Situational performance demands obscure the influence of vicarious incentives.

Observed positive outcomes are more likely to foster adoption of activities that involve effort and other unpleasant aspects, thus requiring additional incentives if they are to be performed. To cite a few examples, people will more readily adopt stringent standards that reduce self-gratification, (Bandura, Grusec, & Menlove, 1967b), select nonpreferred foods (Barnwell, 1966), sacrifice material goods (Presbie & Coiteux, 1971), divulge personal problems that they would ordinarily keep to themselves (Marlatt, 1972), and pursue courses of action they formerly resisted (Clark, 1965), if they see models praised for exhibiting such conduct than if models receive no recognition for their actions.

If a person experiences consequences in a group setting, the observed outcomes can affect the behavior of the group as a whole. Even mild praise or reprimand can lead other group members to adopt praiseworthy acts and to avoid censurable ones (Kazdin, 1981; Kounin, 1970). Vicarious influence achieves multiplicative effects because it can touch large numbers of people simultaneously. Moreover, persons who have been vicariously influenced become models for others in their immediate environment. These secondary effects of reinforced modeling further amplify the scope of vicarious influence. In televised modeling, which has a vast reach, even if the behavior of a small proportion of viewers is altered, it can create widespread effects. This is well illustrated in the use of reinforced modeling of consumer behavior in national advertising campaigns. Even a 5 percent in-crease in buyers brings large profits because it represents many thousands of people.

Most complex behavior is governed by rules that are not easily discernible from exemplars alone. Rules of speech, standards for judging events, and decision strategies must often be extracted from information conveyed by subtle features in modeled behavior that contains many irrelevancies as well. Seeing modeled actions selectively rewarded, depending upon whether or not they embody a certain rule, helps observers to identify relevant features and to grasp the underlying rule (Bandura, 1971a; Rosenthal & Zimmerman, 1978). As we shall see later, additional information about the parameters of the rule provided by modeled response consequences greatly facilitates acquisition of rule-governed behavior.

Observed rewards exert little impact when the modeled conduct is so markedly inappropriate to the sex, status, or social role of observers that they cannot be easily persuaded to adopt it (Bandura, 1965b; Dubanoski, 1967). In this type of conflicting situation, two sources of counterinfluence may operate, either separately or together. If others are rewarded for behavior that violates the observers' own internal standards, the observers are deterred from modeling such conduct by their anticipated self-devaluative reactions. Even if the rewarded behavior is not regarded as personally objectionable, so that there is little internal resistance, observers may be deterred from adopting it by fear of social disapproval for behaving inappropriately. When there is high consensus on the appropriateness of conduct, an instance where unacceptable actions are rewarded is more apt to be viewed by observers as an eccentricity than as a social sanction that applies to their own life. It would take repeated vicarious reward of influential models to legitimize incongruous conduct.

The social impact of vicarious outcomes depends heavily on their informativeness. If they convey little new information, they will have weak, if any, effect. The correct way of behaving in many situations is defined by social convention, rather than by the natural effects of the behavior. Indeed, many of the "proper" ways of doing things are inconvenient or even uncomfortable. Natural consequences would not prescribe the wearing of neckties in sweltering heat. When the correct ways have been designated by fiat, people rely on the social effects of modeled actions in learning conventional rules of behavior. However, in activities drawing on knowledge and skills for their success, there is an intrinsic relation between competency and its effects. That is, skilled performances clearly work better than defective ones in managing the physical and social environment. The correct way to handle a sailboat is evident from how the vessel moves. Observers can judge for themselves from the natural results of differing competency the usefulness of what is modeled. Therefore, the information conveyed to observers by praise for skilled performances and criticism of faulty ones is redundant with the evident benefits or costs that the behavior naturally produces. Under such circumstances, vicarious extrinsic consequences do not create much additional influence. Nor are they apt to have much effect when arbitrary and intrinsic outcomes conflict, as when actions that are highly effective in securing valued rewards are socially disapproved.

The type of behavior being rewarded helps to explain some of the variable effects of vicarious outcomes. However, the value of the observed outcomes is, perhaps, an even more important determinant. In laboratory studies the rewards that models receive generally include, at most, mild praise. Seeing models briefly commended by strangers for insignificant behavior mainly affects observers who are eager to please others (Marlowe, Beecher, Cook, & Doob, 1964). Such studies cannot shed much light on the extent to which people, in fact, guide their actions partly by the experiences of others.

Unlike laboratory situations, which favor arbitrary, verbal consequences, in everyday life vicarious motivators often have significant impact on people's lives. As we have seen in an earlier chapter, the diffusion of innovation relies extensively on the observed effectiveness of new modes of behavior and social practices. Industries adopt technical innovations that have proven successful, whereas they show little interest in things that make a poor showing. New policies that provide improved solutions for social problems spread nationwide (Gray, 1973; Poel, 1976). Political candidates favor the same campaign strategies that have won elections for others in the past (Hershey, 1984). The television industry slavishly copies whatever program formats happen to attract large audiences (Brown, 1971). In collective efforts to produce social change, tactics of others that have achieved some success are much more readily adopted by people seeking solutions for their own problems than if these tactics had been observed to be ineffective (Bandura, 1973).

Distinguishing between Vicarious and Implicit Outcomes

Often times several people perform similar activities, but some individuals are singled out for attention while others are not. Those whose efforts go unrecognized are more likely to be disheartened than inspired by seeing others receiving recognition to which they also feel entitled. In studying this process, Sechrest (1963) had pairs of children solve similar problems concurrently, and, although both achieved correct solutions, the performance of only one of the pairmates was praised or criticized. Seeing their own accomplishments ignored, but praised in others, served as an implicit punishment that depressed the subsequent efforts of the slighted ones. However, children who observed their own peformances accepted without comment, while others were criticized, intensified their efforts much as if they had been rewarded. When children are treated inequitably on repeated occasions, initially they try harder, but if their efforts continue to go unrecognized they become demoralized (Ollendick, Dailey, & Shapiro, 1983; Ollendick & Shapiro,

1984). Older children, who make greater use of social comparison information, are more adversely affected than younger ones. Inequitable treatment in which others are favored not only discourages those who are slighted, but it may devalue the rewards bestowed on the favored ones (Sharpley, 1982, 1984; Sharpley, Irvine, & Hattie, 1980).

Implicit outcomes should be distinguished from vicarious ones because they represent different phenomena (Bandura, 1971b). In the vicarious form, people observe the outcomes accruing to others without themselves engaging in similar activities at the time. In the implicit form, all people perform similar behavior concurrently, but some are rewarded while others are not. When some are praised, while others are ignored for the same deserving performances, the slighted persons not only observe the others' outcomes, they also experience immediate, direct consequences for their own behavior. The consequences become rewarding or punishing by comparison. Inequitable reward is discouraging, whereas observed reward is motivating.

VICARIOUS PUNISHMENT

Societies actively promote the behaviors they prize and try to discourage those they devalue. A large part of this acculturation process is fostered through the influence of vicarious sanction. Although devalued behavior is diminished most effectively by cultivating constructive alternatives, exemplary punishment is used extensively for deterrent purposes. Seeing others experience aversive outcomes tends to decrease observers' inclinations to behave in similar or related ways.

Measurement of Vicarious Inhibitors

Measuring the impact of observed punishment poses special problems because it involves two sets of influences that operate in opposing directions: The power of modeled actions to facilitate similar behavior in observers is checked by the suppressive effects of observed punishment. When these counteracting influences have comparable strength, those who have seen the conduct punished may display the same low incidence of the behavior as those who have not seen the modeled conduct. If the model displays novel response patterns that are rarely performed, vicarious punishment that completely suppressed what the observers learned would produce no modeled behavior and thus match the zero baseline of nonexposed persons. However, the behavior would exceed zero if the punishment only partially nullified the facilitative effects of modeling. For this reason, modeling alone, rather than a nonexposed group, provides the appropriate baseline for evaluating the impact of punished modeling.

The decremental effects of observed punishment have been demonstrated in several ways. In one approach, using a reversal design, the observers' behavior is measured during successive periods when the acts of models are punished or ignored. By this means, Wilson and his colleagues (Wilson, Robertson, Herlong, & Haynes, 1979) studied the effects of vicarious punishment on aggression in the classroom. Students did not act aggressively when a peer's aggressive acts were punished, but they aggressed freely when they saw the peer's aggression go unpunished. In a related approach, behavioral changes are measured simultaneously from multiple baselines where one set of behaviors is vicariously punished and another set is not. An illustrative study by Crooks (1967) applying this design reveals that animals have a notable ability to learn from the painful experiences of a member of their own species. Monkeys actively avoided a harmless object after they had observed a monkey verbalize distress (actually presented via a tape recorder) upon touching the object, but the observers played freely with objects that were never accompanied by vocalizations of distress. These findings testify to how adaptive knowledge about potentially dangerous activities can be gained solely through observational experience.

Another way to gauge the effects of observed punishment is to compare changes in behavior produced by different vicarious outcomes under different incentives. In one such study (Bandura, 1965b), children who observed an aggressive model punished performed fewer imitative aggressive responses spontaneously than those who observed the model rewarded or undergo no evident consequences for his actions. Children were then rewarded for imitative aggression to activate into performance what they had learned through observation but had inhibited. Boys performed all the aggression they had learned when they saw the modeled aggression well received. However, when models were punished for aggressive actions, boys performed less than they had learned, but they readily displayed the aggression they had inhibited once it was rewarding to do so. By contrast, girls, for whom physical aggression is traditionally regarded as sex-inappropriate, and hence negatively sanctioned, partially inhibited imitative aggression even though it was portrayed as acceptable, and they almost completely inhibited such behavior when they saw it punished in others. Their learning was not manifested in action until they had received direct assurance that it was acceptable to behave aggressively.

That vicarious punishers affect the relationship between knowledge and action is shown further in studies comparing observers' spontaneous performances with what they demonstrate when simply asked how the models behaved. Compared to no vicarious consequences, vicarious reward enhances, whereas vicarious punishment suppresses, observers' spontaneous performances of modeled behavior. Observers who have seen modeled behavior punished are much less likely to act on what they have learned than if they have seen the modeled behavior rewarded or ignored (Cheyne, 1971; Levy, McClinton, Rabinowitz, & Wolkin, 1974; Liebert & Fernandez, 1970; Liebert, Sobol, & Copemann, 1972).

Another method for assessing how observers are influenced by seeing the adverse effects of other people's behavior is to use vicarious compound outcomes. Rosekrans and Hartup (1967) studied imitative aggression in children who had observed the aggressive behavior of a model consistently rewarded, consistently punished, or successively rewarded and punished. Seeing modeled aggression both rewarded and punished produced less imitative behavior than consistent reward, but more than consistent punishment. The capacity of observed rewards to enhance performance was thus weakened by observed punishment. Consistent vicarious punishment, in turn, reduced imitative behavior to the near zero baseline of children who had not observed the aggressive acts modeled.

Efforts to deter personally functional but socially disapproved behavior by punishment generally produce limited results. Such behavior is likely to be restrained when risk of punishment is high, but it is readily performed when punitive threats are weak. The same is true for the restraining effect of vicarious negative sanctions. In the studies cited above, seeing others punished for behaving aggressively reduced similar aggressive acts by observers, but it did not discourage other forms of aggression (Bandura, Ross, & Ross, 1963b). When behavior is controlled mainly by intimidation, its expression varies depending on whether or not sanctioning agents are present. Hicks (1968b) had children observe a televised aggressive model with an adult who responded approvingly, disapprovingly, or nonevaluatively toward the model's conduct. Later, in the adult's presence, children who previously heard him praise the modeled aggressive conduct displayed much imitative aggression; those who heard him condemn the aggressor seldom behaved aggressively; and when the adult had shown no reaction the children were moderately aggressive. However, when the sanctioning adult was absent, children paid no heed to his prior evaluative reactions and displayed the same amount of imitative aggression, regardless of whether he had previously approved, condemned, or showed indifference toward the modeled actions.

Transgressive Behavior and Vicarious Sanctions

The inhibitory effects of vicarious punishment have been examined most extensively in the deterrence of forbidden conduct. In these studies prohibitions are verbally imposed, after which people observe filmed models either rewarded, punished, or experiencing no consequences for engaging in inviting, but socially prohibited, activities. Later, the observers find themselves in a similar tempting situation, and how quickly and how often they themselves perform forbidden acts is measured.

People who have seen models punished for violating prohibitions are less inclined to transgress than if they see the modeled violations either rewarded or simply ignored (Walters, Leat, & Mezei, 1963; Walters & Parke, 1964; Walters, Parke, & Cane, 1965). The weaker the threatened consequences and the stronger the instigation to engage in the forbidden activities, the more likely is transgressive modeling to foster infractions by others (Blake, 1958). Results of a study by Benton (1967) indicate that, under some conditions, observed and directly experienced punishment may be equally effective in deterring transgressive behavior. Children who observed peers punished for engaging in prohibited activities later showed the same degree of self-restraint in tempting situations as did the punished transgressors.

Arbitrary prohibitions against activities ordinarily considered socially acceptable are unlikely to arouse much moral agonizing in offenders. Ritter and Holmes (1969) investigated the power of transgressive modeling to reduce inhibitions when either external threat or self-censure served as the major restraining influence. People who were deterred from disapproved actions mainly by fear of external punishment readily deviated after they saw a model transgress with-out reprimand, whereas those who regarded such conduct as morally objectionable were only minimally affected by transgressive modeling. This does not mean that after self-sanctions have been developed, transgressive modeling loses all its disinhibitory potential. Censurable behavior can be modeled in ways that morally sanction it, thereby weakening observers' self-restraint (Bandura, 1973; Berkowitz, 1965). If is it widespread, transgressive modeling can eventually alter observers' own standards of conduct.

Hoffman (1970) has argued that self-control can be weakened, but not instilled, by vicarious influences. The evidence cited for this view comes from studies in which children who have received strong prohibitions without exposure to transgressive models rarely deviate (Stein, 1967). As previously noted, the prohibition's inhibitory effect can be demonstrated only if children not exposed to transgressive models transgress enough so that vicarious influence can decrease the forbidden behavior. Rewarding a transgressive model can undermine prior prohibitions, but modeled resistance to temptation or punishment of transgressive modeling cannot further inhibit what is already fully inhibited by the prohibition itself. When enticements to commit forbidden behavior are given more force by repeated encouragement to violate prohibitions, modeled resistance to transgression lastingly strengthens observers' self-control (Grusec, Kuczynski, Rushton, & Simutis, 1979). Others have similarly showed that resistive modeling bolsters self-restraint (Bussey & Perry, 1977).

The influence of vicarious sanctions is best studied under conditions in which the prohibited activities are sufficiently attractive to tempt transgressions. Zimmerman and Kinsler (1979) varied the strength of social prohibitions and whether or not children had seen on videotape a child punished for engaging in a forbidden activity. Children who saw a peer model punished refrained from similar behavior regardless of whether it was prohibited strongly, mildly, or not at all. However, children who had no exposure to the modeled sanctions refrained when social prohibitions were strong but transgressed quickly under milder prohibitions. For young children, even strong social prohibitions have no lasting effects, whereas similar prohibitions with vicarious sanctions do.

People often respond self-critically to their own actions that others may consider permissible or even commendable. Modeled self-censure, which is exemplified most prevalently in achievement and transgression, can also have an inhibitory impact on observers. Seeing models criticize some of their own performances as not laudatory leads observers to deny themselves rewards for similar attainments (Bandura, 1971b; Herbert, Gelfand, & Hartmann, 1969). With regard to transgressive behavior, Porro (1968) found that when children saw a model praise herself for violating prohibitions, most of them later engaged in forbidden activities, whereas relatively few children transgressed who had observed the same model respond self-critically toward her own transgressions.

It is generally easier to disinhibit than to inhibit behavior through vicarious means. This is because negative sanctions are usually applied to behavior that is rewarding for the user but is prohibited for the convenience, benefit, or welfare of others. Self-interest thus has to accommodate to traffic codes, property rights, tax statutes, and a host of social conventions. Conflicts also arise when otherwise acceptable and enjoyable activities are socially discouraged because they interfere with self-development of competencies requiring toilsome efforts. Television viewing is commonly restricted to further children's mastery of academic subjects, piano keyboards, and the like. So rules and norms of conduct are devised to curtail what infringes on the well-being of others and to promote what is toilsome but socially valued.

By disregarding prohibitions, people can get what they want more expeditiously than by following irksome rules. Those who lack prosocial alternatives can secure, by transgressive means, rewards that might otherwise be denied them. Therefore, it does not require much successful modeling of transgressive conduct to reduce vicariously restraints over forbidden but pleasurable activities. In contrast, inhibitions are more difficult to establish and sustain by either direct or vicarious sanctions when they require relinquishing behaviors that are personally functional.

As the preceding discussion indicates, the answer to why behavior is more easily disinhibited than inhibited resides in the properties of the behavior being controlled, rather than in the properties of the inhibitory process itself. It requires less influence to get people to pursue enjoyments that others may disapprove than to foresake enjoyments. However, one could readily demonstrate that inhibition is easier to produce vicariously than is disinhibition by selecting activities that do not hold much interest for observers. For example, self-sacrifice is more likely to be quashed by vicarious punishment than swelled by vicarious reward.

Disinhibition through Absence of Anticipated Sanctions

When models engage in functional or enjoyable activities that are ordinarily inhibited by social prohibitions, seeing the behavior go unpunished increases similar conduct in observers in much the same way as observing models rewarded (Bandura, 1965b; Walters & Parke, 1964; Walters, Parke, & Cane, 1965). To the extent that the absence of anticipated punishment conveys social acceptability, observers reduce their restraints, so that weaker inducements are needed to goad behavior that violates social codes but serves one's self-interests.

Because consequences derive their value in relation to other outcomes, the omission of anticipated negative outcomes is indeed a significant consequence. For this reason, in personally valued but socially prohibited activities, distinctions between rewarded and nonrewarded modeling may be more rhetorical than real. Persons who expected to be punished for violating a law, but got off free, would hardly react as though they experienced no outcomes. When anticipated consequences exist, observed nonreactions from significant others are likely to operate as a favorable outcome in the context of expected punishment and as a punisher in the context of expected reward.

Behavior may be socially prohibited for reasons of either convention or morality (Turiel, 1977). Whether particular activities fall under the realm of convention or morality depends, in large part, on the gravity of the consequences of the conduct. Many rules of proper conduct are adopted and enforced for social convenience, group benefit, or because they serve those in advantaged positions, rather than because of the inherent goodness or harmfulness of the behavior itself. Rules governing conduct which fall in the domain of social convention are more difficult to justify, to enforce, and to receive compliance. It is activities likely to produce serious injurious consequences that tend to be regarded as moral imperatives. Thus, under most circumstances, the killing of one human being by another is considered morally wrong in all societies. However, moralities are not always easily distinguished from social conventions. Conventional rules often govern conduct that can cause some harm or violate the rights of others, and moralities vary in their weightiness.

Changes in the consequences of an activity can alter its moral status. For example, most societies subject sexual behavior to a stringent code of morals and socialization practices in efforts to deter premarital and extramarital sexual relationships. The serious social consequences of extramarital entanglements, the breakup of homes, and unwanted pregnancies in children who have reached reproductive maturity, provided moral justifications for prohibitions and restrictions of sexual behavior. Contraceptives have greatly alleviated the hazards of unplanned pregnancy by dissociating procreation and copulation. Liberalized styles

of unmarried couples living together diminished the interpersonal costs of sexual mobility. Some of the original basis for the morality surrounding sexuality has thus gradually eroded. With increasing liberalization of sexuality, for many persons, especially the unattached and those preferring informal cohabitation arrangements, sexual activities have become more a matter of convention than of morality.

Increase in the injurious consequences of an activity can transform it from the realm of convention into that of morality. The development of military nuclear technology with its awesome annihilative capacity has moved the issue of nuclear armaments from the category of conventional deterrence strategies to a serious moral issue (Churchill, 1983). Moral reasons are being marshalled for and against the build up of ever deadlier nuclear arsenals, their threatened use as a deterrence policy, and their actual use as a retaliatory reaction.

Disinhibition of Aggression

Disinhibitory modeling has been the subject of extensive study in the area of aggression because of its social import. Results of laboratory and field studies show that children and adults tend to behave more punitively if they have seen others act aggressively than if they have not been exposed to aggressive models (Bandura, 1973; Liebert, Sprafkin, & Davidson, 1982; Murray, 1980). The disinhibitory power of modeling is enhanced when observers are angered or otherwise emotionally aroused, when they have developed aggressive styles of conduct, when the exemplified aggression goes unpunished or gets good results, when the aggression is socially justified, when the victim invites attack through actions that facilitate attribution of blame, and when the injuries suffered by the victim are minimized or sanitized (Bandura, 1973; Baron, 1977; Berkowitz, 1965).

Because of the prevalence of, and massive exposure to, televised violence, much of the research on disinhibition of aggression has grown out of interest in the effects of symbolic modeling. Behavioral restraints are reduced most rapidly by moral justifications that make injurious conduct socially and personally acceptable. Analyses of televised programs reveal that violent conduct is portrayed, for the most part, as permissible, successful, and relatively clean (Halloran & Croll, 1972; Larsen, 1968). Witnesses to the violence in the dramatic presentations are more likely to approve of such behavior or to join in the assaults rather than to seek alternative solutions. Violence not only is shown to pay off but is readily used by superheroes, who dispose of their adversaries in a quick, perfunctory way as though slaying human beings was of no great concern.

When good triumphs over evil by violent means, viewers show greater disinhibition of aggression than when aggressive conduct is not legitimized by admired media characters (Goranson, 1970). Dramatic requirements that villainous characters succeed for a time in their aggressive exploits reduce the inhibitory potential of terminal punishment. The message is not that aggression does not pay but rather that its benefits are pretty good except for an occasional mishap, which might be avoided. Given that aggressive life styles are portrayed as prevalent, socially acceptable, and highly functional, it is not surprising that viewing violence is conducive to aggressive conduct.

Television journalism devotes much time to reporting violent events (Singer, 1970). Since most people rely solely on the electronic media for their news, especially television, its reach and impact are greater than those of the written word. Television has, therefore, become a force of some interest. Unlike fictional violence, which has been examined extensively, how viewers might be affected by newscast portrayals of aggression has received little attention. Although freedom of the press is constitutionally protected, there undoubtedly exists some apprehension that, should adverse effects be demonstrated, such evidence may fuel efforts to muzzle the messengers.

There are several ways in which newscasts of violence can serve as an instrument of influence (Bandura, 1973). If televised reports convey detailed information about acts and strategies of aggression, they can contribute to the spread of the very methods they report through the instruction they provide. In addition, media reports of violent episodes can influence restraints over aggression by how the consequences are portrayed. Because each point in audience ratings means millions of dollars in advertising revenue, the visual displays accompanying news reports are selected to attract and hold viewers, as well as to inform. The outcomes of aggression, especially collective actions, are easily misrepresented when dramatic pictorials are favored over less interesting but important consequences. Thus, showing people running off with appliances and liquor from looted stores during an urban riot is more likely to promote aggression in viewers living under similar circumstances than showing the terror and suffering caused by the massive destruction of one's neighborhood.

Exposure to newscasts of violence can disinhibit aggression in viewers (Wilkins, Scharff, & Schlottmann, 1974). The evidence indicates that the degree of justification given to violent activities by the narration stories determines how strongly aggressive restraints are affected. Meyer (1971) found that people who watched a news film with a voice-over justification of a military execution subsequently behaved more punitively than those who observed the same news event either with no commentary or with narration portraying the killing as unjustified.

Televised reports of violence, depending on what they accent, may sometimes affect the course of collective aggression for better or for worse by their power to bestow legitimacy (Bandura, 1973). Because of the scarcity of newscast time, only a few items from the vast array of newsworthy events can be presented. Selection is similarly involved in which violent episodes are reported, since only a few aspects of an event can be covered. One can highlight the social conditions that provoke strife, the specific tactics of aggression used, the immediate or delayed consequences for aggressors, the injuries suffered by the victims, the pronouncements of leading protagonists, or the countermeasures employed by societal agents. The effects of media presentations are likely to vary depending on what aspects are selected for public display and how they are characterized in accompanying commentaries. Ball-Rokeach (1972) attaches special significance to media expressions of evaluative reactions to violent events. The reason for this is that relatively few viewers experience sufficient inducement to use the violent strategies they have seen, but the transmitted justifications and evaluations can help to mobilize public support for policy actions favoring either social control or social change that have widespread social and political ramifications. Because of its potential influence, the communication system itself is subject to constant pressures from different factions within society seeking to sway it to their idealogy.

Disinhibition of Sexual Behavior

Sexual behavior has been subject to many cultural taboos. Consequently, the effects of sexual modeling on sexual arousal and behavior have only recently received systematic study. Sexual modeling can effect sexual behavior in several ways. It can teach amorous techniques, reduce sexual inhibitions, alter sexual attitudes, and shape sexual practices in a society by conveying norms about what sexual behaviors are permissible and which exceed socially acceptable bounds.

Much of the research conducted in this area has been confined to the physiological and behavioral effects of viewing erotic films. Because provocative poses and the sight of nudity alone can be sexually arousing, both the erotogenic body cues and the amorous activities of the filmed partners contribute to the arousal generated by sex-

ual modeling. However, even attention to erotogenic body cues can be disinhibited through modeling. In a study conducted by Walters, Bowen, and Parke (1964), as people watched a film of nudes in provocative poses they saw a moving spot of light on the film supposedly indicating the eye movements of a previous observer. For some viewers, the spot of light roved mainly over the breast and genital areas, whereas for other viewers the light roamed largely over the background of the picture, thus giving the impression that the observer was avoiding the display of nudity. When the viewers' own eye movements were later recorded while viewing slides of naked people, those who had been exposed to a supposedly sexually uninhibited voyeur looked longer at the nudes than did viewers who had observed the sexually inhibited voyeur.

Exposure to sexual modeling produces transitory increases in sexual arousal and behavior. It also increases sexual fantasies which can serve as a source of self-arousal on later occasions. The more graphic the sexual modeling, the more erotic are the observers' fantasies (Sachs & Duffy, 1976). Contrary to the stereotype that women are turned on by romance and men by physical sex, erotic modeling has similar effects on sexual arousal and fantasies of both males and females (Sachs & Duffy, 1976; Schmidt, 1975). With massive exposure, ritualized erotica gradually loses its potency as a sex arouser (Reifler, Howard, Lipton, Liptzin, & Widmann, 1971). However, the existence of many devoted consumers of erotica suggests that variety counteracts satiation effects.

The short-term arousal produced by seeing couples engage in sexual activities tends to activate established modes of sexuality (Brown, Amoroso, & Ware, 1976; Mann, Sidman, & Starr, 1971; Schmidt, 1975; Schmidt & Sigusch, 1970). Exposure to erotic modeling temporarily increases masturbation in single persons who habitually do it and in other sexually conversant people who lack willing mates. Among married couples and sexually experienced persons with available partners, viewing erotic modeling increases sexual intercourse shortly thereafter or during the next day or so.

Most laboratory studies of disinhibitory sexual modeling are conducted with volunteer college students who probably exhibit more liberal attitudes and less sexual anxiety than either the general population or students who shun exposure to erotica. It is in sexually inhibited persons that erotica can have its greatest effects by functioning both as a sex arouser and disinhibitor. For those who already express their sexuality freely, erotica serves only as a transitory arouser (Fisher & Byrne, 1978). Sexual modeling has been shown to have long-term effects when used for therapeutic purposes with persons suffering from sexual anxieties and dysfunctions. As will be shown later, modeling of mutual pleasure alleviates sex anxieties, creates more favorable attitudes toward sex, and sparks inactive sex lives.

Fear that pornography may trigger sex offenses receives little support in the crime statistics of countries like Denmark, which has removed all restrictions on pornography (Kutchinsky, 1975). For sex offenders and avid consumers of erotica, pornographic material is a stimulant for masturbation, whereas in nondeviant persons erotica is more likely to prompt sex relations with available partners (Kant, 1971).

The effects of erotica on sexual attitudes and behavior depend, of course, on what form of sensuality is modeled—tender, bizarre, coercive, or abusive. The issue of concern is whether deviant or abusive erotica might contribute to sexual transgressions. Thoughts of erotic material serve as sexual self-arousers on later occasions. Exposure to violent erotica stimulates rape fantasies (Malamuth, 1981a). Masturbation stimulated by deviant sexual fantasies makes the deviant sexual activity more sexually arousing (McGuire, Carlisle, & Young, 1965). Moreover, some users of erotica, including sexual offenders, report modeling the sexual activities they have seen (Kant, 1971).

Erotica and Aggression

The effects of erotic modeling extend beyond sexual behavior. To the extent that sexual modeling serves as a source of arousal and generalized disinhibition, it can heighten aggressiveness in situations where such actions are considered acceptable. The findings generally show that, by eliciting positive affect, pleasant erotica either does not affect or reduces aggressions, whereas pornographic sexuality tends to increase aggressiveness, especially in irritated viewers (Baron, 1977; Malamuth, Feshbach, & Jaffe, 1977; Ramirez, Bryant, & Zillmann, 1982).The latter effect was originally attributed to heightened emotional arousal. Irritated viewers may misread their residual sexual arousal. However, evidence points to a more enduring impact of pornography. Different forms of erotica foster different levels of aggression even though they are equally arousing, and aggression remains heightened even after sexual arousal dissipates (Donnerstein, 1980; Malamuth, Feshbach, & Jaffe, 1977). Zillmann and Bryant (1984) found that massive exposure to hard-core pornography alters sexual standards and attitudes toward women. Massively exposed viewers regard the hard-core fare as less offensive and more enjoyable, they perceived uncommon sexual practices as more prevalent than they really are, they show greater sexual callousness toward women, they devaluate issues of importance to women, and they are more lenient toward rape offenses. Women viewers are affected by pornographic content in much the same way as are men. Violent erotica increases the acceptability of violence toward women and the acceptance of rape myths that women desire sexual assault (Malamuth & Check, 1981). Changes in sexual standards and devaluation of women leave lasting effects.

Violent Erotica

Content analyses reveal an increase in abusive behavior toward women in pornographic depictions (Malamuth & Donnerstein, 1984). Research has added to our understanding of how violent erotica affects viewers. Males exposed to modeled sexual assault behave more punitively toward women than if exposed to modeled sexual intimacy devoid of aggression (Donnerstein, 1980). Violent erotica often depicts women initially resisting but eventually relishing being raped. Such portrayals reinforce rape myths and weaken restraints over harshness toward women by indicating they enjoy being manhandled. Depictions of rape as pleasureable to women heighten punitiveness toward women regardless of whether males are angry or not (Donnerstein & Berkowitz, 1981). Even depictions of rape as traumatic to women increase punitiveness toward women by angered men, but not by unangered men. Violent erotica does not increase intermale aggression.

In studies designed to evaluate the role played by the aggressive component in violent erotica, Zillman, Bryant, and Carveth (1981) found that nonaggressive erotica (bestiality) enhanced aggression to the same degree as did violent erotica (sadomasochism). They ascribed the detrimental effects of violent erotica to the combined effects of arousal and unpleasantness rather than to display of aggression. Arousal and unpleasantness can heighten punitiveness (Zillman, Bryant, Comisky, & Medoff, 1981); however, the evidence indicates there is more to the story.

The effects of modeled sexual assaults are strongly influenced by how the victims' reactions are portrayed. Showing women experiencing orgasmic pleasure while being raped stimulates greater punitiveness than if they are depicted expressing pain and abhorrence. Depictions of traumatic rape foster less aggression, even though they are as arousing and more unpleasant, than depictions of rape as pleasurable. Sexual violence promotes greater punitiveness toward women than does nonsexual violence (Donnerstein, 1983). Being shown bizarre sexuality featuring bestiality and sadomasochism in a reputable place may be interpreted as signifying a permissive attitude toward conduct that is normally socially condemned. Other forms of human harshness may seem less objectionable when sexual assault has been portrayed positively or has gone uncensured.

Analyses of component-arousal cues in sexual displays, as measured by penile tumescence, point to the potential hazards of violent erotica (Abel, Barlow, Blanchard, & Guild, 1977; Abel, Becker, Blanchard, & Flanagan, 1981). Nonrapists are sexually aroused by depictions of mutually enjoyable sex but not by traumatic rape. Rapists show equally high sexual arousal to depictions of rape and consenting sex and some arousal to nonsexual aggression. Sadistic rapists, who enjoy torturing their victims, are highly aroused by nonsexual aggression and by rape, but they are not turned on by mutually enjoyable sex. Arousal patterns thus provide a measure not only of the proclivity to rape but even the form it is likely to take. High sexual arousal to nonsexual violence identifies sadists. By variation in the age of the persons and degree of violence in the depictions, the arousal patterns can identify the rapist whose victims are most likely to be children or elderly women and whether sex or aggression is the source of sexual arousal (Avery-Clark & Laws, 1984).

Malamuth (1981b) has identified several correlates of the proclivity to rape in men. About one third of college men admit that there is a likelihood that they would rape if fully assured of not getting caught. Their attitudes and sexual arousal patterns are similar to those of actual rapists: They subscribe to rape myths that women invite sexual assault by their dress and behavior and that they secretly enjoy it; they are sexually aroused by rape depictions in which the victim abhors the assault; and they behave more punitively toward women in situations where aggression is acceptable. Even students who disavow rape and who are turned off by traumatic rape depictions are sexually stimulated by depictions of rape if the women victims are shown experiencing sexual arousal resulting in orgasm (Malamuth & Check, 1983).

Because violent erotica fosters devaluation and punitiveness, it may well serve as a stimulant for sexual assaults by males who are sexually aroused by modeled violence toward women. The disinhibitory potential of violent erotica is increased when it incorporates certain elements that weaken the operation of internal controls, as in portrayals of acts of rape. These elements typically include dehumanizing women, attributing the blame for rape to women's sexual enticements or to assailants' uncontrollable sexual instincts, mimimizing the trauma women suffer or turning it into orgasmic euphoria, and sanctioning expression of masculinity and power through sexual domination (Griffin, 1971).

Although both sexual and aggressive modeling teach and disinhibit behavior in much the same way, the social effects in these two areas of functioning differ markedly. Because of the harmful consequences of physical aggression, a society has to exercise control over the injurious actions of children and adults alike. Humane living requires reducing social influences that promote cruelty and destructiveness. By contrast, most cultures, including our own, present discontinuities in the socialization of sexual behavior. Overt sexual expression is prohibited during childhood and adolescence, yet it is not only expected but considered essential to a satisfying heterosexual relationship in adulthood. Therefore, the more successfully inhibitory training is achieved in early formative years, the more likely is heterosexual behavior to serve as a source of guilt and anxiety in adulthood. Given the prolonged negative conditioning of sexual attitudes and behavior, many people regard the availability of erotica either as innocuous or as an aid to counteract dysfunctional inhibitions. However, the research delineating the forms of erotica that heighten aggressiveness does set some boundary conditions for innocuous and potentially harmful effects.

The long-standing public controversy over pornography has escalated since cable television systems and video cassettes are disseminating the fare to larger segments of the population. Prohibitionists argue that it degrades women and promotes sexual transgressions. Libertarians argue that people differ in what they regard as obscene, and suppression of sexual expression jeopardizes other types of expression. Society has the right to regulate obscene materials that can cause harm, but disputes arise over which forms should be subject to regulation and which should be free from governmental interference. Efforts to resolve conflicts over erotica by appeals to courts for regulatory guidelines leave all factions displeased. On the one hand, as views of morality are liberalized, the scope of constitutional protection is expanded to include sexual material the prohibitionists regard as obscene. On the other hand, recent rulings that what is obscene should be judged by local community standards disturb libertarians because of the ambiguity of what constitutes a community and the chilling effect of variable standards being applied to the same contents in the prosecution of pornography in different locales (Schauer, 1975). Uncertainty regarding standards can create unforseeable violations of the law.

OPERATIVE MECHANISMS

There are several mechanisms by which seeing the effects actions produce for others can alter the the thoughts, feelings, and behavior of observers. Vicarious events vary in a number of aspects, including the type of behavior being modeled, the characteristics of models and sanctioning agents, the type, intensity, and consistency of consequences, their justifiability, the contexts in which they occur, and the reactions of models to the outcomes they experience. Because these factors have diverse effects, no single mechanism can adequately explain the many psychological changes resulting from exposure to vicarious consequences. Which mechanisms will be activated by any given vicarious influence will depend upon which combination of factors is present in the situation.

INFORMATIVE FUNCTION

The consequences experienced by others convey information to observers about the kinds of actions that are likely to prove effective or detrimental. Having gained knowledge observationally about the contingencies operating in the environment, people are inclined to do the things they have seen succeed and avoid those they have seen fail. Vicarious consequences exert their influence through judgments of probable outcomes for similar courses of action. Consistent with this notion, Bussey and Perry (1976) found that, in guiding their actions, children rely more on what happens to an adult model if the outcomes they and the adult had previously experienced were correlated than if they were unrelated.

Judgments of outcomes are usually based on several sources of information that vary in their relative predictiveness and interactive complexity. Observers must weigh and integrate information extracted from what they have observed in making their inferences. Therefore, to predict the effects of vicarious consequences, one must consider not only the nature of the observed outcomes but also other informational elements in modeled events affecting the probability that similar actions will produce similar results for observers.

Model Similarity and Commonality of Outcomes

Most social functioning is structured so that patterns of behavior permitted for some members are prohibited for others depending upon such factors as their age, gender, race, social rank, and legitimized roles. Thus, for example, autocratic behavior may produce benefits for bosses but antagonism if underlings were to act in a similar manner. As a general rule, the more alike observers are to models in status and characteristics, the greater is the likelihood that similar actions will produce comparable results. Therefore, observers use model similarity as one piece of information for judging likely commonality of response outcomes. In the case of gender, for example, the consequences of same-sex models operate as more influential performance guides for observers than those of opposite-sex models (Bussey & Perry, 1976). Vicarious consequences will be least influential in promoting response patterns when observers have reason to believe that what is acceptable for the models is inappropriate or not permissible for them, or vice versa.

Model characteristics do not necessarily predict the observers' likely outcomes in all types of behavior and circumstances. When outcomes are mediated by other people, the same actions produce different effects, depending on who performs them. Aggression can bring material rewards, subservience, or painful retaliation because those toward whom it is directed respond differently depending on who is doing the aggressing. Thus, model cues gain their greatest predictive value when the effects of actions are socially mediated and tied to social status.

Many forms of behavior produce their effects directly. In these instances, success depends on the adequacy with which the behavior is executed, not on who does it. Cyclists will succeed in riding bicycles if they perform the correct actions, regardless of their age, race, sex, or social standing. There are also many activities involving socially-mediated outcomes that produce similar rewards or punishments regardless of who does them. Victors of contests are entitled to the prizes bestowed. Although the consequences are socially mediated, they are not tied to social status. In both of the preceding instances the effectiveness of modeled behavior, rather than the models' characteristics, provides observers the most relevant information for judging probable response consequences. Finally, there are some behaviors that are so well conceived and easy to execute successfully that they are adopted even from highly dissimilar models.

Contextual Predictors of Outcomes

The same behavior is often treated differently depending upon when and where it is expressed and the persons toward whom it is directed. Judgments of probable outcomes are, therefore, made not only in terms of actions and the assumed commonality of sanctions but also on the basis of situational factors that provide some indication of how a behavior is likely to be received. When people are rewarded for certain acts in one context, but ignored or punished for displaying the same type of behavior in a different situation, observers gain knowledge about situational demands (McDavid, 1964; Wilson, 1958). The different vicarious consequences help observers to identify what aspects of the environment signify what is appropriate and what is inappropriate in the setting. Predictive knowledge increases the likelihood of behavior in situations that portend favorable reception but decreases it in settings that forewarn adverse consequences.

How easily observers can identify signs in the environment that indicate the likely effects of actions depends on the degree to which environmental cues are correlated with observed response outcomes. If, for example, being assertive to people in authority is consistently punished, whereas being assertive to persons of lower rank is consistently rewarded, the predictive relation between authority status and outcomes is very high. Given this highly informative relationship, it would not take observers long to discern that being assertive to authorities is unwise.

In everyday life, environmental contin-gencies are rarely so predictable. Being assertive may produce poor results with some authorities but good results with others. Nor are the effects of assertiveness all that uniform when dealing with persons of lower rank. Therefore, in judging vicarious consequences, observers must deal with probabilistic information conveyed by modeled behavior and by situational factors of varying predictiveness. The relative usefulness of informative behavior or situations depends on which of these is a better predictor of the observed outcomes.

A vicarious event contains three sets of relationships that carry the probabilistic information about the consequences of action: the relation between actions and outcomes, between situations and outcomes, and between actions and situations. McDavid (1962, 1964) has examined the rate of observational learning by varying the co-occurrences of these factors. For different observers, the modeled behavior was performed either only in one particular setting—often in that setting, but sometimes in other settings as well—or it occurred randomly in different settings. When modeled behavior is rewarded regardless of where it is displayed, the behavior, not the setting, carries the useful information about probable response consequences. When the modeled behavior is rewarded only in a particular setting, then it is the situation which conveys the predictive information. When either acts or situations are highly informative, outcome contingencies are easily learned vicariously. Observational learning is most difficult when observers see the modeled behavior rewarded with moderate frequency in a particular setting. Observers who misread what they see and who select an uninformative setting as the only predictor extract a misleading guide for their own actions.

Under most circumstances neither behavior nor situation is the sole conveyer of outcome information. Rather, both factors serve as indicators of likely consequences. Since actions are not invariably effective and situational reactions are not always consistent, observers have to decide how much predictive weight to give to these different elements of information. Consequences to the model provide observers with a basis for deciphering the circumstances under which particular courses of action are most likely to succeed, fail, or have no effect.

Performance Ambiguity

The informative value of observed outcomes varies depending upon the amount of reliable knowledge that observers already possess. Observed consequences are especially informative when there is much uncertainty about what behavior is the most appropriate because the situation is unfamiliar or ambiguous. People who are unsure about the best way to behave will use the experiences of others as a guide for their own actions (Thelen, Dollinger, & Kirkland, 1979). To the extent that observers have already developed highly successful means of dealing with familiar situations, they will be guided more by their own knowledge than by the experiences of others.

This is not to say that vicarious influence operates only under uncertainty. Quite the contrary. Research on how ambiguity affects modeling has been concerned with simple choice responses, rather than with the development and refinement of skill. Among the profusion of models in everyday life, some of the modeled patterns are much more effective than those observers habitually use. If they can reap greater benefits from the new modeled ways, they will adopt them. In improving their skills, people continue to draw on the expertise of others, even though they already know what to do and may do it fairly well. Personal development would be stunted if observational learning ceased once a way of dealing with a certain situation was hit upon. In most circumstances, receptivity to modeled information is governed more by the relative functional value of what is modeled than by situational familiarity. By continually observing the successes and failures of others, observers become more knowledgeable

about what works best under what circumstances. Moreover, vicarious influences motivate, as well as inform. Success of others can inspire people to pursue similar courses of action where there is little ambiguity about the outcome.

Performance Complexity

When modeled actions are relatively simple, they can be easily learned by observing them regardless of the effects they produce. However, in complex activities, which often require learning the rules underlying modeled actions, observers are aided greatly by the extra information supplied by vicarious consequences about the relevant dimensions of the rules. In a study examining this very issue, Hirakawa and Nakazawa (1977) found that vicarious consequences facilitate the abstraction of rules of behavior for complex tasks but not for simple ones. Although vicarious consequences may not supply much information for learning simple rules of behavior, even in this case they do convey valuable information about whether or not it is wise to perform what has been learned (Spiegler & Liebert, (1973).

Valence of Vicarious Consequences

In evaluating the impact of vicarious consequences, it is important to distinguish between learning and performance effects. When acts have been modeled only once, observers learn much of what they have seen regardless of whether the model is rewarded, punished, or ignored (Bandura, 1965b; Lerner & Weiss, 1972). But if models have been reinforced on several occasions, having seen the consequences of earlier performances can alter observers' attentiveness to the models' subsequent behavior.

The valence of vicarious consequences can affect the level of attentiveness to the behavior of others. Modeled activities that have no evident effects do not command much attention, whereas positive and negative consequences heighten and draw attention to the actions producing these results. It will be recalled that attentional processes play a central role in observational learning. By enhancing attentiveness, vicarious consequences can indirectly affect the course of observational learning, provided that there are repeated opportunities to observe modeled performances, that observers value the consequences, and that they believe comparable behavior will produce similar results for them.

Although observed punishment generally serves as an inhibitor of performance, it can aid observational learning of the very behavior being punished by heightening and focusing attention to it. Indeed, Yussen (1974) has shown this to be the case. When attentional involvement is low, both vicarious reward and punishment increase attentiveness to the modeled behavior which, in turn, enhances observational learning.

Powerful vicarious consequences affect the memorability of events, as well as attentiveness to them. Seeing others experience potent outcomes is likely to prompt covert rehearsal of appropriate behavior to instill the information for future use. Negative consequences, however, do not always enhance attention or rehearsal. If too severe, they become so disturbing to observers that they elicit avoidance rather than vigilance (Bandura & Rosenthal, 1966). Observers can easily avoid what the performers cannot, simply by turning their attention elsewhere.

As previously noted, a number of factors in modeling situations, other than response consequences, can command attention. When modeled actions are conspicuous and individuals must observe them, the consequences depicted cannot add much to an already high level of attentiveness, so their effects on observational learning are variable. In some studies, observed praise and criticism both increase observational learning (Cheyne, 1971; Liebert & Fernandez, 1970); in others, observed praise heightens observational learning, but observed criticism

does not (Liebert, Sobol, & Copemann, 1972); and in still others, neither type of outcome enhances acquisition of responses more than observation of nonreinforced modeling (Peed & Forehand, 1973).

The diverse results are not entirely surprising considering that the rule underlying the modeled responses was relatively simple, observers had to attend to each modeled response without competing distractors, and the resultant consequences were restricted to mild verbal reactions. Any effects obtained when observers are forced to watch are probably attributable more to differential cognitive processing and rehearsal of modeled information than to selective attention. Modeled information that has been observed, symbolically coded, and rehearsed is more likely to be remembered than information that goes uncoded and unrehearsed. In modeling in everyday life, where attentional constraints are minimal, people are exposed to diverse behavior patterns which compete for attention. By selectively drawing attention, response consequences partly determine which modeled activities from among many will be noticed and learned.

Evidence that observed punishment can inhibit modeled behavior, but can also facilitate its acquisition, has important social implications. Punishment does not erase what has been implanted. With the passage of time, knowledge endures, but its original source is usually difficult to recall. A similar process operates in the differential recall of modeled acts and their consequences. Observers better retain modeled acts that were punished than acts that drew no reactions, but they forget the negative consequences (Spiegler & Weiland, 1976). Should appropriate circumstances arise, what has been learned can be easily put into practice.

As the preceding discussion shows, vicarious consequences vary in how much and what kind of information they convey about probable response consequences. The information may be entirely new, partially correlated with that of other sources, redundant, or contradictory. The more independent information vicarious consequences provide, the greater the impact they are likely to have on observers.

MOTIVATIONAL FUNCTION

Observed outcomes not only inform, they can also motivate. Seeing others rewarded or punished functions as a motivator by arousing expectations in observers that they, too, are likely to experience similar outcomes for comparable performances. Although all observed consequences are informative, they are not all motivating. If a particular outcome has no incentive value for observers, then exposure to the vicarious influence will have negligible effects. Thus, seeing students achieve high grades with great effort conveys the same outcome information to students and nonstudents alike, but it is the students who are most likely to be motivated by the observed benefits. Differences in incentive preferences explain why some observed outcomes are motivating while others are not, or why even the same observed outcomes may provide a different incentive with changing levels of deprivation.

In the social cognitive view, vicarious outcomes affect motivation through two cognitive mechanisms. First, they create outcome expectations that can serve as positive or negative incentives for action. However, knowing what outcomes result from a given course of action is unlikely to spur observers to action if they doubt they can do it. Thus, motivation is also mediated by self-percepts of efficacy, the second mechanism. Seeing other people succeed or fail affects observers' judgments of their own capabilities (Brown & Inouye, 1978). People mobilize greater effort and persist longer on a task if they are confident they can do it than if they judge themselves to be inefficacious.

Frequency and Magnitude of Observed Outcomes

Variations in the amount, type, and frequency of observed outcomes provide equivalent information about what kinds of activities produce rewards. But such variations in incentives have different motivational effects as reflected by the vigor and persistence with which observers themselves behave. A number of studies have been conducted in which models are rewarded either continuously or intermittently, after which both models and observers are tested for how long they persevere when their own actions are no longer rewarded. Variations in the frequency of reward generally have similar effects on observers and performers (Braun, 1972). As a rule, observers are more persistent in the face of failure when they have seen the efforts of others rewarded only occasionally than when they have seen others frequently rewarded (Berger & Johansson, 1968; Borden & White, 1973). The motivational impact of exposure to vicarious outcomes can last over a relatively long period (Hamilton, 1970).

Perseverance is affected by how much, as well as by how often, others are rewarded (Kerns, 1975). The larger the observed rewards, the greater is their motivational influence. Of special interest is evidence that vicarious outcomes foster the greatest perseverance when tenacious effort is seen to produce infrequent but sizeable rewards. The motivation of people who aspire to achievement in athletic, business, scientific, and professional enterprises is doubtless partly sustained, when their labors bring few rewards, by the example of others gaining recognition and fortune through dogged effort.

Seeing sustained effort eventually pay off demonstrates the usefulness of perseverance when rewards are hard to come by. Successes by others raise observers' outcome expectations and judgments of their own performance capabilities. If, however, successes come easily to others, but rarely to oneself, the discrepant experiences undermine confidence in one's abilities and produce despondency (Davies & Yates, 1982). After a while, observers conclude that they either lack the necessary competence in the activity or that the situation has changed so that the behavior is no longer rewarded. In either case, there is little point in pursuing the endeavor.

Model Similarity

Whether or not observers themselves are motivated by seeing perseverance pay off is affected, of course, by social comparison processes. Evidence that dissimilar persons succeed from time to time does not necessarily persuade observers that they, too, can attain such outcomes through their efforts. If, for example, the successes of models with superior ability are viewed by observers as beyond their reach, however hard they might try, the vicarious incentives will not serve as motivators for them. Vicarious rewards are most apt to heighten motivation when observers perceive themselves to be similar to the models on relevant attributes (Berger, 1971; Paulus & Seta, 1975).

One might point to evidence that the successes of eminent models often inspire and motivate neophytes in like pursuits despite huge disparities in competence and status. Distal vicarious incentives do provide purpose for long-term endeavors. But it is probably the more proximal successes of similar peers that operate as recurring motivators in day-to-day activities. Visions of fame and fortune eventually achieved by others would not have much sustaining power if the efforts of those around one met with repeated failure.

Just as vicarious successes can heighten and sustain motivation, vicarious failures can weaken it. Here, too, the strength of the effect depends on social comparison processes. A study by Brown and Inouye (1978) speaks to both the comparative process and the mediating role of perceived self-efficacy.

Observers maintained a high sense of efficacy and did not slaken their efforts, despite repeated failure, after exposure to a failing model whom they believed to be of lower ability. However, observing a model of comparable ability fail had a devastating effect on observers' self-efficacy and persistence. The more their self-efficacy was undermined by the vicarious failure, the quicker they gave up when they encountered difficulties.

Because of their motivational effects, vicarious incentives play an important role in both personal development and social change. Seeing others eventually succeed provides incentives for individuals to undertake difficult tasks. Moreover, showing that success is possible through perseverance helps to sustain effort in the face of setbacks. Without the benefit of observed accomplishments, initial personal failures—which inevitably occur in difficult endeavors—more readily create discouragement and resignation.

Comparative Power of Direct and Vicarious Outcomes

The relative strength of observed and directly experienced consequences is an issue of interest. Their comparative efficacy partly depends on whether effects are measured in terms of learning or performance.

Learning Effects. By attending to the pattern of successes and failures of others, observers can learn what behavior is most appropriate in given situations. Observers generally learn faster than reinforced performers, especially on tasks that place greater demands on conceptual, rather than on manual, skills (Berger, 1961; Hillix & Marx, 1960; Kanfer, 1965; Rosenbaum & Hewitt, 1966). Enhancement of learning by the observational mode is also more evident in activities requiring extensive cognitive processing, as, for example, complex performances (Klein & Posner, 1974). The use of modeling to convey the structure of behavior provides large practical benefits as well. Learning by direct experience requires providing consequences for each person's actions, whereas modeling can promote learning simultaneously in large numbers of observers, thus yielding the substantial dividend of multiplied benefits. Direct experience is better used to refine and perfect skills than to build them from the outset.

The relative superiority of vicarious experience most likely stems from its fewer attentional demands. Performers may have difficulty discovering what effects their actions are having because they must devote at least some of their attention to creating, selecting, and enacting different courses of behavior. Their ongoing self-evaluations and emotional reactions to the consequences of their actions may further divert their attention from what produces what. Observers, on the other hand, can give their undivided attention to discovering correct rules and solutions. It is easier for observers to construct a cognitive representation of complex behavior, unhampered by the attentional demands of simultaneously figuring out the correct behavior, enacting it, and dealing with the effects it produces. When the observers experience the same consequences for errors as the performers, they often learn less well (Craig, 1967).

Motivational Effects. Direct incentives have greater motivational power than vicarious ones when it comes to maintaining behavior over time. For example, one would not advise employers to maintain the productivity of their employees by having them witness a group of workers receiving pay checks at the end of each month. Seeing others rewarded may raise motivation temporarily, but it is unlikely, by itself, to have much sustaining power. Observing other people's outcomes, however, can exert substantial continuing influence on the motivating strength of direct incentives. Because both direct and vicarious incentives inevitably occur together in everyday life,

their interactive effects, rather than their independent ones, are of primary interest.

Interaction of Vicarious and Direct Incentives

Seeing how others are treated introduces comparative judgment into the operation of incentive influences. That is, the observed outcomes accruing to others provide a standard for judging whether one's own usual outcomes are equitable, beneficent, or unfair. The same incentive can thus function as a reward or as a punisher, depending on whose outcomes are selected for comparison.

The psychological effects of different patterns of direct and vicarious outcomes have received surprisingly little attention considering the prevalence of their joint influence. Seeing the efforts of others succeed from time to time can enhance the motivating strength of direct incentives. This is especially true when performances must be sustained by hope for a long time because direct rewards come only occasionally. Thus, people who have been rewarded both directly and vicariously persevere longer in the face of nonreward than those who have experienced only direct outcomes. However, the interactive power of incentives varies depending on the extent, direction, and duration of the discrepancy between the outcomes received and observed. Negative disparities temporarily intensify efforts to secure the more favorable benefits achieved by others (Bruning, 1965). But persistent inequitable treatment, which gives rise to feelings of deprivation, exploitation, and injustice, has more diverse and profound effects. How people interpret unfair treatment, the amount of power they possess, and the modifiability of reward systems emerge as critical determinants of responses to social inequities.

Effects of Inequitable Treatment. When grievance procedures exist and complaints carry a low risk of reprisal, people try to remedy unfairness. Those who possess social power may resort to coercive measures to force desired improvements by using such means as protest, strikes, and boycotts. Discontent arising from privation is often given as a principal cause for collective aggression. The view that privation alone breeds violence has not fared well under close scrutiny. Severe privation is more likely to produce feelings of hopelessness and apathy than acts of aggression. If measured in absolute terms, the poor of today are deprived compared to their contemporaries but much better off than even the advantaged of yesteryear, who had no electricity, labor-saving devices, television sets, life-saving medical technologies and wonder drug therapies. While the disadvantaged slowly improve their lot in life, the more affluent members of society usually make even more rapid progress, so that the disparity between groups widens. Hard-won gains become relative losses (Pettigrew, 1963). Thus, betterment of social conditions can produce discontent.

Theories of collective aggression have, therefore, come to emphasize relative deprivation, rather than absolute level of aversive conditions, as the instigator of collective aggression. Although aggression is more likely to be provoked by relative than by absolute deprivation, most people who feel relatively deprived do not resort to violent action. Inequitable privation alone is a weak predictor of social protest (Bandura, 1973; McPhail, 1971). Additional social learning factors determine whether relative deprivation will result in aggression or other behaviors. Under conditions of limited power and high punishment for protesting, discontented people lower their aspirations and become resigned to inequitable treatment. Comparative studies indicate that inequitable treatment provokes protest not in those who have lost hope, but in the more efficacious members who believe themselves capable of influencing the course of events by their collective effort (Bandura, 1973).

Whether or not disparity between observed and experienced outcomes creates discontent and protest depends upon the adequacy of social justifications. Social ranking and reward for ability is generally accepted because it provides incentives for self-development and benefits society if the skills are put to good use. However, when social ranking is by birthright, inheritance of wealth, race, ethnicity, or other extraneous factors, people are more likely to view themselves as victims of inequity. Disparities in reward or status judged to be warranted are accepted without indignation, whereas lesser inequities regarded as unjustified are resented. Inequity in outcomes that people believe to be rightfully theirs is most conducive to assertive action.

Inequitable treatment is often structured to minimize its negative effects. Greater rewards for others is accepted as deserved for activities that carry greater responsibility, incur high personal costs, or require specialized skills. Indeed, some professions justify their exorbitant fees by large personal costs required to develop the necessary skills. An early investment presumably entitles one to be richly compensated for a lifetime. Another prevalent attitude is that activities which are intrinsically satisfying merit lower compensation. As a result, members of some occupations get less than they deserve for their services without their voicing much complaint.

Discrepancies in outcome are also willingly accepted when people are graded by custom into social ranks and rewarded by rank rather than by performance. To further discourage unfavorable social comparison, the differential rewards are usually kept as private rather than as public matters. In the interests of preserving their self-esteem, which could suffer if close associates were compensated more generously, most of the people involved favor the secrecy. Because hierarchical arrangements create incentives for personal development and reduce discontent in the lower echelons, such systems are widely employed. When mobility aspirations are socially discouraged, individuals are even less inclined to make the inter-rank comparisons that could arouse dissatisfaction with their lot in life.

Even arbitrary inequities are likely to be tolerated if subordinates are cast into groups and are led to believe that possessing stereotypical attributes makes them less deserving of equal treatment. People are commonly sorted on the basis of sex, race, religion, or ethnicity. Out of any large group, some members will behave in ways that reinforce conventional stereotypes. Negative stereotypes repeated often enough are eventually accepted although they may have little foundation. Even the victims of discrimination, who see that the imputed attributes do not fit them, may nevertheless assume that the stereotypes apply to other members of the class. Those who do not conform to the preconceptions are viewed as exceptional cases. Once established, stereotypical beliefs can be effectively preserved by their occasional confirmation. For years, stereotyping practices have justified inequitable compensation of women for achievements that were comparable to those of men. Effectively rationalized discrimination has more devastating personal consequences than acknowledged unfairness because its victims devalue themselves. Social change is difficult to achieve when the people who practice discrimination feel no personal wrongdoing, and the victims blame themselves for their plight (Gray-Little & Teddlie, 1978).

Negative reactions to inequities, which are openly acknowledged to be unwarranted, can still be attenuated by promises of rectification. Inequities become more tolerable when people are led to expect that unfair practices will be corrected within the foreseeable future and that eventually opportunities will be created that promise improved benefits. Hope thus reduces the provocation of otherwise incensing inequities. Remedial measures sustain expectations that warranted benefits will eventually be realized. However, genuine changes can be institutionally thwarted for a long time while assuaging resentment by displacing responsibility for current inequities to past practices, blaming the maltreated for impatience in demanding reforms that may be costly, and temporizing promised rectifications with token changes.

The nature and strength of reactions to inequities considered to be unjust are partly determined by the amount of coercive power the discontented possess and the likely costs of coercive action. In important matters, corrective measures are not that readily available because those who benefit from inequitable practices resist attempts to change them. When the discontented possess coercive power and are safeguarded against punitive reprisals, they resort to coercive measures in efforts to force desired improvements.

Variations in the scope and severity of mistreatment affect whether discontented people will attempt to force changes in specific practices within a system or more radical changes of the social system itself. Using a multideterminant approach, Gurr (1970) examined the level of civil disorder in western nations as a function of three sets of factors. The first is the level of social discontent arising from economic decline, oppressive restrictions, and social inequities. The second factor is a traditional acceptance of force to achieve social change. Some societies disavow aggressive tactics; in others, mass protests and coups d'etat are considered acceptable ways of forcing change. The third factor is the balance of coercive power between the system and the challengers as measured by the amount of military, industrial, labor, police, and foreign support the protagonists can marshal on their side. The analysis revealed that when aggressive tactics are considered acceptable, and challengers possess coercive power, they will use collective force to change inequitable practices within the system without there being much discontent. Revolutionary violence, however, required that there be widespread discontent and that the challengers possess strong coercive power, while tactical traditions are of less importance.

Inequity, Productivity, and Quality of Performance. The preceding discussion has analyzed the conditions under which people respond to inequitable treatment by trying to change exploitative social practices by force. How people react to perceived inequities, when they can neither leave nor change the situation in which they find themselves, is also a subject of considerable interest. This is most widely exemplified by the inequitably underrewarded, who find themselves trapped in dissatisfying work situations for lack of any better alternatives. Adams's (1965) equity theory has provided a major impetus for research on behavioral reactions to unfair compensation. Walster, Walster, and Berscheid (1978) have extended equity theory to diverse areas of human life.

According to Adams, people are motivated to achieve congruence between their perceived contribution and the rewards they receive because inequity creates tension. Perceived inequity arises when the ratio between one's contribution and one's reward is less favorable than that achieved by others. Provided that people do not reduce their feelings of inequity by distorting perceptions of their efforts or outcomes, or by choosing somebody else against whom to compare themselves, they change the productivity or quality of their work to bring it in line with their outcomes. In the prototypical experiment designed to test predictions from this theory, people perform a task for pay after being told that they are either qualified, unqualified, and thus presumably overpaid, or overqualified for the job. Compared to the equitably paid, the overpaid increase, and the underpaid reduce, the quality or productivity of their work (Adams, 1965).

That people should lower the level or quality of their performances when they feel unfairly compensated is fully understandable. The interpretative controversy centers on why the overpaid should feel the necessity to compensate. Creating perceived inequities by telling people that they are unqualified does more than just instill feelings of unfairness. To be told that one is unqualified provides a challenge to prove one's competence by superior work. It can also cause insecurities about keeping the present job, receiving a pay cut, or finding future work (Lawler, 1968). Insecurity leads people to work harder to safeguard their job and pay arrangement.

Results of studies controlling these other effects of perceived inadequacy suggest that the challenges to competence and security, rather than the distress about overpayment, may be the critical determinants of performance. When perceived inequity is produced by varying the level of pay, rather than by the perceived level of qualification, the overpaid are not especially moved to raise their performance, and the underpaid become less diligent in their work (Lawler, 1968). Although people are highly sensitive to being underpaid, overcompensation is more likely to raise the beneficiaries' estimates of their capabilities than to make them feel overpaid (Moore & Baron, 1973). These findings are consistent with other studies showing that advantageous inequity heightens positive self-evaluation rather than raises efforts to restore equity (Gray-Little & Teddlie, 1980).

Abundant resources and prosperity lessen concern and discontent over disparities in compensation. Although people cannot help but feel some dissatisfaction over receiving less than they judge they deserve, it suggests greed or insecurity concerning one's self-worth to become overly exercised about some disparity in reward if they are fully enjoying the comforts of life. Those who are moved to complain are, therefore, more likely to cast their protests in terms of rectifying injustice than in pursuing personal gain. It is a different matter when inequities exist under conditions of material deprivation. Martin (1981) speculates that shrinking resources heighten sensitivity to intergroup inequities.

Unfair compensation becomes a matter not only of injustice but of aversive everyday existence. As deprivation increases in severity, the disadvantaged compare their meager compensation upwardly with that of dissimilar prosperous groups, as well as with those who occupy a similar status. Under adverse economic conditions, inequities among groups exacerbate conflicts for available resources.

Leventhal (1980) argues for a broader view of equity and justness than simply matching rewards to contributions. Personal need is also suggested as an important part of a standard of justness. The view that one measure of a society is how it treats its disadvantaged members reflects social concern over merciless meritocracy. Leventhal mentions equality of benefits regardless of contributions as another possible standard of justness. However, when those who contribute much receive no more benefits than those who contribute little, group productivity declines so that there is not all that much left to share. Different rules of justness will produce different reactions to how the returns of collective effort should be distributed. The extent to which inequalities in rewards are considered unjust and intolerable depends on the prevailing social ideologies. People who subscribe to egalitarian ideologies are more disturbed by large intergroup disparities in pay than are members of societies in which social ranking by birthright is a well-established tradition (Scase, 1974).

EMOTIVE FUNCTION

People commonly display emotional reactions while undergoing rewarding or painful experiences. Observers are easily aroused by such emotional expressions. This capacity for vicarious arousal plays a vital role in the development and modification of emotional reactivity. On the positive side, it enables people to learn what might be pleasurable or distressful, without having to go through the same experiences themselves. In addition to its immediate functional value, vicarious arousal is an integral aspect of human empathy. Empathy with the suffering of others helps to facilitate altruistic acts and to curb interpersonal aggression (Hoffman, 1977; Rushton, 1980). These effects are of no small social benefit.

Like any other capabilities, vicarious arousal can bring misery as well as benefits. Many of the dysfunctional fears and aversions, which plague people's lives, stem mainly, or in part, from distressing vicarious experiences. People come to dislike particular places, persons, or things with which they have had little or no direct contact by repeated exposure to modeled antipathies (Bandura, 1965a). Once acquired, fears and antipathies become self-perpetuating through the negative actions they promote.

Emotional learning through the experiences of others involves two separable processes. First, there is the process of vicarious arousal. If any affective learning is to occur, the model's joy, pain, anger, or distress must activate emotional reactions in observers. Although necessary, arousal alone is insufficient. Emotive models can arouse others but leave no lasting effects. Hence, the second constituent process is concerned with how the events, associated with vicariously generated emotions, gain emotion-arousing potential themselves. Thus, for example, in seeing dogs inflict painful injuries on others, observers not only become frightened, they also come to fear dogs themselves. The mechanisms by which emotive modeling create new patterns of emotionality are examined in the sections that follow.

Vicarious Arousal

In the occurrences of everyday life, vicarious instigators usually include both emotive modeling and the situational events that arouse the models. By way of example, a snarling dog is the situational arouser, the frightened expression of a passer-by is the emotive modeling. In an incisive analysis of vicarious arousal, Berger (1962) restricts the phenomenon of vicarious instigation to the arousal produced by the modeled expressions rather than by the situational events. These two sources of arousal are easy to separate conceptually but difficult to dissociate in practice. The emotional state of another person is not directly observable. Hence, its presence, quality, and intensity must be inferred from stimuli impinging on the models and their reactive expressions signifying emotional arousal. As Berger points out, observers may be vicariously instigated by erroneous inferences from situational events, as when parents respond fearfully to seeing their child fall, even though the child is unhurt and unperturbed. Similarly, bystanders may react apprehensively to hearing a scream although, unknown to them, the cry of distress is feigned.

Berger reasons that a scream that provokes fear in observers might represent pseudo-vicarious instigation because the vocal cue may serve merely as a conditioned fear stimulus for the observer, independently of the model's emotional state. The basis for this distinction is debatable, however. Expressive cues are the observable indicants of the model's emotional state. It is precisely because such social cues have come to signal emotion that observers can be at all aroused by the experiences of others. There are, however, instances in which synchronous arousal in observers and models does not necessarily arise through vicarious instigation. An environmental cue that has general signal value can directly activate emotional reactions in different people. When workers become fearful upon hearing a fire alarm in their building, they may be reacting similarly, but independently, to the same nonsocial cue. However, assessing causal contributors to arousal is no easy task, because the force of even nonsocial instigators can be greatly augmented or diminished by how others react. The same fire alarm is substantially more arousing if others react with panic than if they respond calmly or ignore it altogether. Vicarious instigation is most convincingly demonstrated when the model's affective expressions are the sole instigators of the observers' emotional reactions. This condition obtains when the situational events that arouse the model are either unobservable by, or neutral for, observers.

Arousing Expressive Cues. Information about a model's emotional state is communicated partly through facial, vocal, and gestural cues. These observable reactions, especially facial expressions, serve as indicators and vicarious arousers of emotion (Izard, 1971; Yamaguchi, Harano, & Egawa, 1978). Miller and his colleagues conducted a series of studies of cooperative avoidance that reveals both the communicative and the functional value of expressive signs (Miller, Banks, & Ogawa, 1962, 1963; Miller, Murphy, & Mirsky, 1959). Monkeys first learned to avoid shock, signaled by a light, by pressing a bar. The animals were then placed in different rooms so that the model could see the forewarning light come on, while the observer had the bar to forestall the shock. The model therefore had to communicate distress by facial and other expressions via video to the observing partner, who could take the protective action necessary to avoid shock for both of them. Modeled expressions of distress in anticipation of the shock elicited fear in the observing companion, as reflected in elevated heart rate and prompt avoidance responding. Even color slides of an animal showing fear or pain provoked avoidance responses in observers, thus confirming the central role of facial expressions in vicarious arousal. Emotional responses could be vicariously aroused not only by the sight of their partner but also, through generalization, by an unfamiliar fearful monkey. Moreover, seeing another monkey express fear reinstated avoidance behavior in observers even after their fear had been thoroughly extinguished.

Vicarious activation affects more than just peripheral autonomic functions and defensive actions; it produces neurophysiological changes in the central nervous system as well. Observing others engage in injurious activities releases brain chemicals that serve as neurotransmitters (Welch & Welch, 1968).

Humans possess a greater capacity to communicate affect nonverbally because they can be more facially expressive and can draw on a richer repertoire of expressive gestures than can infrahumans. Research on social referencing gives documentation that infants use adult facial signals of emotion as a source of information in appraising unfamiliar people and things in ambiguous situations (Feinman, 1982; Klinnert, Campos, Sorce, Emde, & Svejda, 1983). They then guide their actions on the basis of such information. Infants will cross the visual illusion of a table edge when the mother mimics smiles but halt their crawl if she mimics fear or anger. Infants similarly look to their mothers' emotional expressions when deciding whether to approach unfamiliar toys and strangers or to stay clear of them. Smiles encourage contact, fearful displays are read as warning for avoidance. However, when situations are clearly designated as safe or as dangerous by nonsocial cues (Sorce, Emde, Campos, & Klinnert, 1985) or by familiarity with the objects (Gunnar & Stone, 1984), emotive signals are largely disregarded as guides for action. Their predictive value under conditions of uncertainty, rather than their innate signal value, seems important.

Developmental analyses of social referencing tend to emphasize perceptual skills in discriminating emotional expressions. Perceptual skills are necessary but insufficient for emotive guidance. Unless emotional expressions convey predictive information, simply noticing them is unlikely to affect behavior. Children require correlated experiences that endow emotive signals with predictive value. Through social learning, the smiles of people who have proven dependable can signify safety, while their fears forebode danger. Consistent with this analysis, infants are more inclined to use their mothers' happy or fearful expressions in interpreting strange events than the same facial signals by strangers (Zarbatany & Lamb, 1985).

Development of the Signal Value of Expressive Cues. How people interpret bodily movements has been the subject of serious study and popular treatises on "body language." But how such cues become indicators of specific emotions has received much less attention. The communicative value of expressive cues undoubtedly reflects both evolutionary development and learning experience. The ability to read signs of happiness, fear, and anger has considerable adaptive value in guiding actions toward others. Those who are insensitive to, or misread, how others are feeling are apt to behave inappropriately, which can cause untold problems.

People can produce facial expressions indicative of pleasant or unpleasant experiences, and they can judge with some accuracy whether pleasant or unpleasant emotions are being experienced from facial expression (Ekman, 1973; Ekman & Oster, 1979). This does not mean, however, that specific emotions are connected to specific bodily movements or that expressive cues necessarily reflect an emotional state. In studies of vicarious instigation discussed previously, models arouse observers by feigning pain reactions (Berger, 1962).

Research into the physiology of different emotions also bears on the assumption of a specific linkage between emotional states and bodily movements. Tests have been conducted on whether different emotions are associated with distinct cardiovascular patterns when the emotions are socially instigated, revivified in imagery, or aroused by films. Although people feel myriad emotions, they tend to be associated with similar patterns of visceral arousal and hormonal secretions (Frankenhaeuser, 1975; Levi, 1972; Patkai, 1971). Others have reported some small differences in blood pressure and heart rate for different emotions (Ax, 1953; Schwartz, Weinberger, & Singer, 1981). Ekman and his associates report that voluntary changes in facial muscles, characteristic of different emotions, and relived emotions are accompanied by some difference in autonomic reactions—compared to happiness, fear and anger race the pulse and anger raises skin temperature (Ekman, Levenson, & Friesen, 1983). However, there is little in the over-all evidence to indicate that different facial muscle movements and relived emotions trigger distinct autonomic reactions. Sadness, happiness, surprise, and disgust, which are markedly different emotions, do not produce any differences in autonomic responses that are consistent for both facial expressions and relived emotions. Fear and anger differ slightly from each other for facial expressions but not for relived emotions. The autonomic undifferentiation is more striking than the differentiation, as is the inconsistency across different ways of inducing emotion.

When the findings are considered as a whole, the extensive similarities in the autonomic correlates of different emotions overshadow any small differences. The differences obtained are not always reproduced from study to study, which suggests that uncontrolled factors co-varying with emotion inductions may be responsible for some of the differences. Adequate tests of whether qualitatively different emotions produce distinct autonomic reactions require that the emotions be equated in their intensity. Otherwise, the differences could be due to uncontrolled variations in intensity, rather than to the type of emotion experienced. For example, it is hard to compare the autonomic concomitants of fear and anger when people are frightened by threat of grave physical injury or annoyed with snide remarks (Ax, 1953). A snide remark is a much weaker instigator of emotion than threat of serious injury. Moreover, it is essential to demonstrate that different instigators of the same emotion (e.g., different ways of provoking fear) produce the same autonomic pattern (Duffy, 1962). Comparing the autonomic concomitants of a single fear instigator with a single anger instigator provides a weak test of the physiological differentiation of emotions.

All emotions are generally characterized by elevation in autonomic arousal. Some fluctuations in autonomic arousal will occur due to uncontrolled factors. The reliability of differences between patterns of autonomic reactions accompanying different emotions is rarely tested objectively. Consequently, a few small differences among otherwise large similarities in autonomic patterns for different emotions are interpreted as evidence of both specificity of autonomic linkage by some people and generality of autonomic activation by others. Even if it were reliably established, with appropriate controls, that a certain emotion produced a few more heartbeats than other emotions, it is doubtful that such a small difference in an otherwise common elevated pattern would be sufficiently distinguishable to serve as the cue specifying the emotion. Extensive visceral commonality cannot be the source of different expressive movements.

Ekman (1973) posits an innate linkage between particular facial movements and different emotions. For example, fear is said to elicit the same facial expressions in all societies. However, universal facial expressions can be modified by cultural display rules which lead people to distort or inhibit their facial expressions. When facial expressions do not fit emotional experiences, the discrepancies arise from social control. Cultural influences certainly shape emotional expression. However, when a posited control mechanism can make evidence of diversity compatible with universality, disputes over a universal linkage between emotional experience and facial expression are not easily resolved empirically unless a reliable method is provided for measuring the nature and degree of social control. Observers read more than just bodily movements when judging what emotions, if any, others might be experiencing. People also express their feelings in words that particularize their state of internal arousal. Words, like actions, can be used to feign or to conceal emotion, as well as to reveal it. But vicarious arousal does not rest on observers' accurate deciphering of expressive cues.

The widespread belief that affect is communicated primarily by nonverbal means is not uniformly supported by research. When observers have access to verbal, vocal, and body expressions during social transactions, they read emotions more accurately from what the performers say and how they say it than from their facial expressions and gestures (Krauss, Apple, Morency, Wenzel, & Winton, 1981). However, the relative informativeness of verbal, vocal, and motoric indicants of affect can change substantially, depending on social customs and sanctions which designate the appropriate mode of expression under particular circumstances.

People develop conceptions about the causes of different emotions through direct and vicarious correlative experiences linking antecedent events to emotional reactions. Judgments of emotional experience are therefore strongly influenced by what observers see as the situational instigators and how they interpret them. Public insult and appreciative applause are more distinctive definers of the emotion a recipient is feeling than the increased heart rate that both situations produce. Emotional arousal in threatening situations is judged as fear, arousal produced by thwarting as anger, and arousal resulting from irretrievable loss of what is valued as sorrow (Hunt, Cole, & Reis, 1958). Situational instigators thus give emotional specificity to visceral commonality. The same facial expression may take on different meanings in different social contexts. A sad face on a clown may elicit laughter from others in the happy context of a circus ring but tears in the sad context of the loss of a job. The relative weight given to expressive and contextual information depends on its clarity and cogency (Ekman, 1982).

Expressive cues arouse humans largely through cognitive mediation. The evidence for this comes from several lines of research. Gestures of pain are vicariously arousing if observers know beforehand that models will undergo hurtful experiences, but the same gestures alone have little emotional impact (Craig & Lowery, 1969). The interpretations placed on emotion-provoking events similarly affect vicarious

arousal. Seeing a filmed brutal fight elicits stronger autonomic reactions in observers if they look upon it as a vengeful or intentional beating than as a fictional enactment (Geen & Rakosky, 1973). In a series of experiments, Lazarus and his associates measured people's autonomic reactions to a film portraying a primitive puberty ritual in which a boy underwent a crude circumcision (Lazarus, Speisman, Mordkoff, & Davison, 1962). Sobs and other expressions of pain generated less vicarious arousal when accompanied by sound-track commentaries minimizing the aversiveness of the operation than when the commentary mentioned the suffering and hazards of such operations.

One of the earliest developmental studies of vicarious arousal provides information on how experience and cognitive skills that come with age affect the social transmission of emotion (Dysinger & Ruckmick, 1933). Movie scenes of danger and tragedy elicited the greatest physiological reactions among young children, but responsiveness decreased progressively with increasing age. The authors explain the inverse relationship in terms of the greater ability of older children to distinguish fantasy from reality and to attenuate distress by forecasting eventual favorable outcomes. Not surprisingly, autonomic reactions to erotic scenes increased with age.

Mandler (1975) puts it succinctly when he explains that expressive actions do not necessarily "express" some underlying emotion. Rather, such expressions gain signal value through correlation with situational instigators that often produce distinct emotional experiences. If stimuli that observers have previously experienced as painful are seen to produce grimacing and reflexive withdrawal actions in others, then facial grimaces and retractions will come to function as pain cues. Since people in all walks of life and cultures are likely to grimace when hurt, particular facial expressions and movements can have similar signal value across cultures. Social and cognitive factors determine not only what emotions observers are likely to feel, but even whether express-ive cues arouse any emotion at all.

Vicarious Arousal through Correlated Experience.

Learning experiences largely determine whether observers will be roused or unmoved by the emotional expressions of others. Expressive displays most likely acquire arousal-provoking capacity through correlated social experiences. That is, when individuals are in high spirits they treat others amiably, which generates positive feelings. As a result of such occurrences, smiles and other expressions of happiness come to signify a positive state of affairs. Conversely, when individuals are dejected, ailing, distressed, or angry, the people around them are likely to suffer in one way or another. Expressive signs of anger or despondency forebode aversive experiences.

Results of a study by Church (1959) underscore the importance of correlated experience in vicarious arousal. He found that cries of pain by an animal evoked strong emotional arousal in animals who had suffered pain together; the cries had less impact on animals who had undergone equally painful experiences, but never in conjunction with suffering by another member of the same species; and cries of pain left unmoved animals who had never been subjected to painful treatment. That sensitivity to expressive displays grows out of social learning experiences receives further support from Miller, Caul, and Mirsky (1967). They found that monkeys reared in total social isolation during their infancy were unresponsive, either behaviorally or physiologically, to the facial expressions of emotion by other monkeys. Thus, even primates require common social experiences to develop the capacity for vicarious arousal. There is little in the preceding findings to suggest that facial expressions or vocalized pain cues are innate, vicarious instigators of emotion.

Past correlated experiences heighten vicarious arousal because they make what happens to others predictive of what might happen to oneself. For this reason, the injuries and delights of strangers are less vicariously arousing than the suffering and joy of close associates. Vicarious instigators gain their power through similarity either in performance roles or attributes. In role similarity, seeing models undergo emotional experiences in performance situations that observers themselves are likely to face in the future has much greater emotional impact than if the observed activities have no personal relevance (Craig & Lowery, 1969). In attribute similarity, it is the possession of similar characteristics that enhances vicarious arousal (Krebs, 1975). These may involve sex, age, race, or socioeconomic status. However, not all shared characteristics heighten vicarious arousal (Brown, 1974). It is the attributes that observers, rightfully or wrongfully, assume to be predictive of similar outcomes that serve as the influential, vicarious instigators.

Research conducted by Lanzetta and his co-workers amply document that correlative experience plays a central role in creating empathetic and disempathetic proclivities. Past congruent experiences in which modeled pleasure has signaled reward for oneself and modeled distress has signaled pain heighten an observer's empathetic reactions to the model's emotional expression alone. Observers who have undergone discordant experiences (e.g., model's joy brings suffering to oneself) respond indifferently or disempathetically to the model's joy and suffering (Englis, Vaughan, & Lanzetta, 1982). Different levels of vicarious arousal to the emotional experiences of others are easily activated when observers expect cooperative or competitive interactions, which from past experience foretells concordant or discordant outcomes, respectively. The joy and distress of a cooperative model elicit corresponding reactions from observers, whereas displays of joy by a competitive model distress observers, and displays of distress calm them (Lanzetta & Englis, 1982). The differential empathy to modeled affect generalizes to situations in which the model and the observers no longer experience any outcomes together. Similarly, observers respond empathetically to the emotional experiences of models depicted as in-group members and disempathetically to those portrayed as out-group members, in the absence of having shared any experiences with them (McHugo, Smith, & Lanzetta, 1982). If a sense of mutuality has been created, so that the joys and distresses of an out-group member foretell similar experiences for the observers, similarity of outcomes transforms disempathy to empathy. However, this empathetic responsiveness does not necessarily generalize to other out-group members.

It is not unusual for people who have shared severe adversity and misery to become indifferent or callous to the suffering of others. There are several possible explanations for this apparently paradoxical effect. Repeated painful experiences may eventually desensitize emotional reactions to pain. Such experiences also create standards for evaluating the hardships of others. To someone who has undergone intense suffering, the lesser adversity of others pales by comparison and thus reduces vicarious responsiveness. Another possible explanation is that a self-protective reaction has been developed as a result of hypersensitivity to human distress. If, through past suffering, persons experience acute distress upon seeing others hurt, they can perfect attentional and cognitive ways to tune out vicarious arousers, and this detachment leaves them seemingly unfeeling and uncaring (Bandura & Rosenthal, 1966). In many service professions, where each day brings endless lines of troubled people, some depersonalization of human suffering is essential for effective functioning (Maslach, 1979). If physicians, psychotherapists, dentists, and lawyers fully experienced the agonies suffered by their clients, their viscera could not withstand the wear and tear for long.

Mediating Mechanisms. In the social cognitive analysis, vicarious arousal operates mainly through an intervening self-arousal process. That is, seeing others react emotionally to evident instigators, or having foreknowledge of them, activates emotion-arousing thoughts and imagery in observers. Because of their capacity for cognitive self-arousal, people can generate physiological reactions to cues that are only suggestive of a model's emotional arousal; their physiological reactions to these same expressive cues can vary markedly depending on what they know about the situational causes of the model's reactions; and they can neutralize the impact of human suffering by mobilizing tranquilizing trains of thought.

Cognitive self-arousal can take two forms: personalizing the experiences of another or taking the perspective of another. In the personalizing form, observers get themselves emotionally aroused by imagining things happening to themselves that either are similar to the model's or have been generalized from previous positive and aversive experiences. Correlated prior experiences facilitate vicarious arousal not only because they bestow predictive significance on the model's plight. They also provide concrete and readily accessible reminders of past joys, pains, and sorrows for enhancing the activating power of vicarious influences.

In the perspective-taking form, observers come to experience the emotional states of others by adopting their perspective. Research conducted within this framework has been concerned primarily with how role-taking skills develop and affect social behavior (Flavell, 1968; Iannotti, 1978). However, experimental evidence is lacking on how vicarious arousal can be affected by putting oneself in a model's place. What little evidence does exist suggests that personalizing modeled experiences is more vicariously arousing than role-taking. Stotland (1969) found that observers react more emotionally to the sight of a person in pain if, at the time, they imagine how they themselves would feel than if they imagine how the other person feels. Studies of the development of empathetic understanding corroborate the importance of personalization (Hughes, Tingle, & Sawin, 1981). Young children who focus on their own emotional reactions to the experiences of others gain better understanding of others' emotions than if they focus on how others might feel. Stotland regards the ability to visualize oneself undergoing the experiences to which others are being subjected as a fundamental aspect of the empathy process. This imaginative self-involvement is facilitated by recall of similar past experiences. Empathetic facility requires the requisite skills for cognitive self-arousal and a rich fund of past experiences to draw upon.

Vicarious Self-Arousal and Empathy

In personality and developmental theories, vicarious arousal is typically conceptualized in terms of empathy. It is treated either as a process in which people experience the emotions of others or as a trait indexed by sensitivity to vicarious arousal. Much of the research conducted within this tradition is devoted to devising measures of empatheticness, tracing its origins, and examining its behavioral correlates. Several kinds of developmental changes have been identified in children's empathic responsiveness as they gain experience and cognitive skills (Hoffman, 1977; Zahn-Waxler & Radke-Yarrow, 1979). They begin to see others as differentiable from themselves and to show growing awareness that others have feelings, thoughts, and other inner experiences. As their knowledge of the causes of affective states and their inferential capabilities increase, they become better able to put themselves in the place of others and to vivify emotional reactions through vicarious self-arousal. Contingent learning experiences build sensitivity to the more abstract and subtle cues of human joys and distresses. This enables people to become highly aroused by the signs and symbols of modeled emotions in certain predicaments without requiring the actual presence of emoting models.

As in most global constructs, reliable determinants and correlates of empathy are hard to come by because empathy is not a unitary phenomenon. Rather, it incorpo-rates several processes, such as social perspective-taking, imaginative self-involvement, and emotional responsiveness, not all of which are that closely related to each other. A collection of diverse capabilities, which may vary in their rate and level of development across individuals, cannot yield neat antecedents and correlates. In everyday transactions, vicarious arousers take many forms, vary in strength, and can elicit a variety of empathetic responses to the state of another person (Strayer, 1980). People are more inclined to respond altruistically to the plight of another when they are in a positive mood than if they are in a negative frame of mind (Rosenhan, Salovey, Karylowski, & Hargis, 1981). Fluctuations in the affective state of the observer will, therefore, produce further variations in altruistic responsiveness.

Even if empathy were a unitary factor, its relationship to social behavior would still be variable because empathetic arousal is only one of many factors influencing how people are likely to respond to the emotional reactions of others. For example, empathic sensitivity presumably promotes altruism and curbs aggression. High empathizers, who become easily distressed by human suffering, can reduce their own discomfort by alleviating the suffering of others. Krebs (1975) summed it up well when he said that, because of their capacity for vicarious arousal, people can be hedonistic without being selfish. Whether or not high empathizers will, in fact, be moved to altruistic acts by human suffering is partly contingent on other determinants such as social inducements, situational constraints, potential costs, availability of skills and resources needed to help others, assigned responsibilities, the characteristics of the sufferers, and their relationship to the empathizers. Although empathic sensitivity usually facilitates helping behavior (Gaertner & Dovidio, 1977; Krebs, 1975; Staub, 1978), if the means are lacking, high empathy may have the opposite effect. In the absence of helpful skills, high empathizers tend to avoid involvement with sufferers because it only upsets them (Stotland, Mathews, Sherman, Hansson, & Richardson, 1978).

The same issues of globality and multidetermination arise in studies of the inhibitory effects of empathetic arousal on aggression. To the extent that aggressors or viewers of assaults vicariously experience the suffering inflicted on victims, their resulting distress would tend to inhibit aggression. However, when measured as a general trait, empathy tends to be weakly and inconsistently related to aggression (Feshbach & Feshbach, 1969; Mehrabian & Epstein, 1972; Sawin, 1979). General training in taking the perspective of another designed to heighten empathetic sensitivity does not affect aggressiveness either (Iannotti, 1978).

Specific indicants of vicarious distress to the suffering of victims of aggression predict subsequent aggression, whereas global measures of empathy do not (Ekman, Liebert, Friesen, Harrison, Zlatchin, Malmstrom, & Baron, 1972; Sawin, 1979). In the studies of altruism cited above, the level of vicarious self-arousal to others' distress predicts how much help the observers will give. These findings suggest that measures of vicarious distress to empathy instigators associated with the behavior one wishes to explain hold greater promise for clarifying the role of vicarious affect in altruism and aggression than measures of empathy as a general trait.

Vicarious Emotional Learning

If the emotional expressions of others aroused observers only fleetingly, it would be of some interest but of little psychological import. What gives significance to vicarious influence is that people can acquire enduring attitudes and emotional dispositions toward things associated with the model's arousal. They learn to fear the things that frightened models, to dislike what repulsed them, and to enjoy what pleased them. It is this learning legacy of vicarious arousal that will be examined next.

The paradigm of vicarious emotions devised by Berger (1962) has helped to clarify some aspects of how people learn through the emotional reactions of others. In this laboratory procedure, observers hear a neutral tone and then see a model react with pain, ostensibly in response to a shock, which is actually feigned. Observers repeatedly witness the pairing of the tone and modeled distress. They begin to react physiologically to the tone alone, even though they themselves have never experienced any pain in conjunction with it. The more salient the model's pain reactions are, and the more consistent they are with the situational instigators, the more strongly observers come to fear the formerly neutral cue (Berger, 1962; Kravetz, 1970, 1974). Under natural conditions, arousal has many sources, so a variety of vicarious instigators, such as seeing persons distressed over failure or subjective threats, can promote vicarious emotional learning (Bandura, Blanchard, & Ritter, 1969; Craig & Weinstein, 1965). Just as vicarious arousal is subject to cognitive modulations, so is vicarious emotional learning. To achieve vicarious learning, observers have to recognize the events that foretell painful experiences for the model (Vaughan & Lanzetta, 1980). Unaware observers do not profit from the modeled occurrences even though they are repeatedly exposed to them. Observers thus learn from the emotional experiences of others by extracting predictive information, rather than by being mechanically conditioned.

Level of Emotionality. Exposure to the emotional experiences of others does not invariably leave lasting effects. We noted earlier that vicarious emotional learning cannot occur unless observers are aroused by what they see. Hence, the observers' level of emotionality, as reflected in induced states of arousal and in their emotional proneness, would be expected to facilitate vicarious acquisition and retention of physiological reactivity. Research, in which varying levels of arousal have been induced in the observers before they are exposed to emotive modeling, shows that vicarious learning and extinction of emotional reactions are related to level of emotionality but not in a simple linear fashion (Bandura & Rosenthal, 1966). Observers who have been moderately aroused acquire autonomic responses vicariously in the most rapid and enduring fashion, whereas those who have been either minimally or markedly aroused achieve the weakest vicarious learning. The curvilinear relationship obtained with induced arousal is further confirmed by correlations between observers' proneness to anxiety arousal and their vicarious learning. Proneness to emotionality is positively related to vicarious learning under elevated arousal but negatively related under marked arousal.

Further results of this study suggest that the facilitative and disruptive effects of arousal level on vicarious learning are mediated through attentional and cognitive mechanisms. Modeled anguish proved so upsetting to observers who were already beset by high personal arousal that they diverted their attention from the sufferer to distractions in the environment, and they conjured up distracting thoughts to escape the discomfort produced by the painful expressions being modeled. In the natural environment, physical detachment affords more efficient self-protection from the suffering of others than cognitive distraction. Those wracked by poverty, disease, and psychological derangements are usually physically segregated and given little thought by the more advantaged members of society. The plight of the forsaken cannot have much social impact if they are out of sight and out of mind.

Past Aversive Experience. People who have suffered pain are more likely to personalize the suffering of others and thus be more strongly affected by it. In studies examining this issue, observers who have undergone prior painful experiences learn more through socially mediated suffering than observers who have experienced only mild unpleasantness or none at all (Greco, 1973; Ogston & Davidson, 1972). However, if models show no signs of pain in hurtful situations, the effects of prior experience will not be activated (Hygge, 1978). Social cognitive theory posits that it is socially correlated, rather than simply prior, experience that wields the greatest influence on vicarious emotional learning. The findings of Lanzetta and his co-workers cited earlier speak to this issue: The degree of correlation between the prior experience of models and observers is the critical determinant of vicarious affective learning.

Sociopathy and Emotional Learning. A common assumption is that people who engage in sociopathic behavior lack sensitivity to other people's feelings (Cleckley, 1964). Because of their weak empathy they can exploit and hurt others without experiencing much distress or remorse. Studies of socially mediated learning reveal that, indeed, sociopaths are not overly affected by the plight of others (Aniskiewicz, 1979; House & Milligan, 1976; Sutker, 1970). Although the results are not always consistent, the predominant finding regarding vicarious arousal to signs of pain is that sociopaths show weaker autonomic reactivity to observed suffering than nonsociopaths. The differences are even more evident in their lack of capacity to learn from the pain experienced by other persons. Through vicariously elicited emotions, nonsociopaths develop emotional reactions to situational events that forebode painful experiences, whereas individuals with strong sociopathic tendencies are deficient in anticipatory learning. Persons who fail to learn predictors of pain from the injuries suffered by others are likely to repeat painful mistakes.

Vicarious Acquisition of Intractable Fears

When fear and distress are modeled in response to real dangers, socially mediated arousal serves useful social purposes. In the studies discussed earlier, for example, participants were able to spare themselves a great deal of pain by observing and acting with foresight on the information provided by the distress of others. However, if modeled fears are irrational, as is often the case, vicarious arousal creates much needless distress and wasted effort in self-protection against nonexistent threats.

Psychological theories that view learning solely in terms of direct experience cannot account for intense fears in the absence of injurious encounters with the feared objects. To cite but one example, snake phobics rarely, if ever, have been bitten or otherwise hurt by a snake, yet they dread them (Bandura et al., 1969; Bandura, Jeffery, & Gajdos, 1975). Efforts to explain such phenomena either appeal to questionable assumptions about generalization from other injurious experiences or attribute the fear to forbidden impulses that have presumably been displaced and projected outward.

Intractable fears often arise not from personally injurious experiences but from seeing others respond fearfully toward, or be hurt by, threatening events. Support for the influential role of vicarious experiences comes from studies showing that modeling of phobic reactions, usually by parents, is a prevalent factor in the development of phobic disorders. Children who fear dogs differ little from their nonfearful peers in injurious experiences with such animals, but their parents tend to display a phobic dread of dogs (Bandura & Menlove, 1968). Similarly, Windheuser (1977) found a close match between mothers' phobic reactions and the phobias that plague their children. In the personal history of clients suffering from severe agoraphobia, agoraphobic reactions to stress had been habitually modeled by other family members (Bandura, Adams, Hardy, & Howells, 1980).

That intense and persistent fears can be acquired by observational experiences alone receives strong support from experimental studies by Mineka and her associates (Cook, Mineka, Wolkenstein, & Laitsch, 1985; Mineka, Davidson, Cook, & Keir, 1984). Most monkeys reared in the wild display a fear of snakes, whereas monkeys reared in a

laboratory do not. In Mineka's studies, lab-reared monkeys who were fearless of snakes, became highly fearful of them after having observed adult monkeys behave fearfully in the presence of a snake. The observers generalized the marked fear and avoidance to new settings and showed no diminution of fear when tested months later. The more intense the modeled fear reactions, the stronger was the vicariously acquired fear.

This is not to say that phobias spring solely from vicarious experience or that direct experience plays only a secondary role in the process. Intractable fears usually have multiple origins (Bandura, 1977a; Rachman, 1977). Analysis of the etiology of snake phobias is illustrative of this point (Bandura et al., 1969). Parental modeling of a phobic dread of snakes often sets the stage by creating sensitivities and apprehensions regarding reptiles. To young children, seeing their parents alarmed even at the mere mention of snakes conveys the impression that they are not only exceedingly dangerous, but even adults are vulnerable to being injured by them. Having become apprehensive about snakes, these children are frequently selected by their peers as targets for scary pranks involving live or dead snakes and toy specimens. Although not a single phobic in the study had ever been hurt by a snake, occasional surprise encounters with snakes proved very frightening to them, given their growing fearfulness, even though they kept their distance. Phobic reactions arising from such experiences are frequently reinforced by terrifying filmed or televised modeling in which snakes are shown stalking their prey, crawling menacingly toward sleeping people, wrapping themselves around animals or people and crushing them slowly to death, or in which people are shown being thrown into a pit of writhing snakes. Such exposures fuel recurrent nightmares.

As their fear develops, phobics increasingly dwell on potential threats and constrict their lives by avoiding social, recreational, and vocational activities that might occasion exposure to a snake, however remote the possibility. Unyielding avoidance prevents reality testing which could provide corrective experiences for change. But even elaborate defensive constraints do not ensure serenity for phobics. They are plagued by dire ruminations and disturbing nightmares over which they can exercise little control. Phobic thinking thus provides a powerful self-generated source of distress for magnifying the subjective danger of reptiles.

The vicarious induction of fears has more profound societal consequences than direct experience because the vicarious mode, especially televised modeling, can affect the lives of vast numbers of people. A notable example is the public's growing fear of becoming a victim of violence. Physical assaults against strangers do not occur often. Nevertheless, they arouse widespread anxiety. There are several aspects of criminal victimization that enable accounts of a few incidents to instill widespread public fear. The first is unpredictability. One cannot predict when or where one might be victimized. The second factor is the gravity of the consequences. They may involve crippling injury, or death. People would not restrict their activities if the threat were merely loss of one's wallet or watch. However, they are unwilling to risk being maimed for life or killed, even though the chance of being victimized by a stranger is extremely low. The third factor is the sense of helplessness. People feel a lack of control over whether or not they might be victimized. The risk of personal injury and death from driving an automobile is much higher. But people fear the streets more than their cars, because they believe they can exercise personal control over the chance of injury by how they drive.

It takes only one rape or a few armed robberies to instill widespread fear. As a result of heightened fear over personal safety, people are leading more confined lives— they live behind locked doors, they avoid many downtown areas and public parks, they desert their streets at night, and more and more of them are arming themselves.

The stronger their fear of victimization, the more they limit their activities (Garofalo, 1979). Women and the elderly, who feel the most vulnerable, experience the highest fear.

Because most people have little, if any, exposure to assaultive behavior in their everyday life, their perceptions of criminal victimization are strongly shaped by what they see on television and read in newspapers. American telecasts and newspapers tend to overreport violent crimes as newsworthy events (Singer, 1971). Dwelling on crime greatly magnifies perceptions of danger lurking in one's surroundings. As a newspaper reporter once remarked, he could create a "crime wave" in a week by himself, simply by emphasizing criminal incidents on the front page. Because more viewers of telecasts bring larger advertising revenues, show business intrudes on news business. The fictional world of television is populated even more heavily with villainous and assaultive characters (Gerbner, Gross, Signorielli, & Morgan, 1980).

That heavy viewing of violence can frighten viewers has been shown in a comparison of how light and heavy viewers of television perceive their social reality (Bryant, Carveth, & Brown, 1981; Pingree & Hawkins, 1981). Heavy viewers are more distrustful of others and overestimate their chances of being criminally assaulted than light viewers. To check the possibility that heavy viewers may be more fearful of falling victim to crime because they are living in more violent neighborhoods, Doob and Macdonald (1979) measured people's media usage and fear of victimization in high- and low-crime neighborhoods in both urban and suburban areas. Heavy exposure to televised violence proved to be the most frightening to residents in high-crime urban neighborhoods. Since suburbanites stay clear of areas that they believe threaten their personal safety they, of course, have much less to fear. Heath (1984) found that the amount of fear instilled by sensational crime reports depends on the social and geographic distance between the readers and the victims. Media reports of victimizations in one's own locality that appear unpredictable and uncontrollable are the ones that strike fear in a populace. Brief media reports of general incidence rates, of hazards that have little personal relevance or are personally controllable are more apt to heighten perceptions of societal dangers than of personal risks (Tyler & Cook, 1984).

Fear Reduction through Vicarious Triumphs

Fears and inhibitions can be substantially reduced, if not eradicated, through the power of modeling. Such disinhibitory effects are evident when observers engage in feared or prohibited activities after seeing others perform similar actions without any untoward consequences. This type of change is most strikingly illustrated in the treatment of intractable phobias by modeling influences. After repeatedly observing efficacious models, anxious people lose some of their fears, resume activities they formerly avoided, and develop more favorable attitudes toward the things they have abhorred (Bandura, 1971c). Similar changes are achieved regardless of whether the modeling is presented as live, filmed, or cognitive modeling in which people visualize themselves or others coping successfully with threatening situations (Bandura & Menlove, 1968; Cautela, Flannery, & Hanley, 1974; Hersen, Kazdin, Bellack, & Turner, 1979; Rosenthal & Reese, 1976).

Treatments based on modeling principles have been applied to a wide range of fears with generally good results. Phobic disorders of long-standing have been ameliorated with modeling (Rosenthal & Bandura, 1978; Gelfand & Hartmann, 1977; Rachman, 1972; Thelen, Fry, Fehrenbach, & Frautschi, 1979). Filmed modeling is successful in alleviating children's anxieties about hospitalization and surgical procedures (Melamed & Siegel, 1975), in reducing their fear of dental treatment (Melamed, 1979), and in enabling adult dental phobics to complete restorative

work on teeth pitted with caries after years of neglect (Shaw & Thoresen, 1974). These favorable results indicate that filmed modeling in preparation for medical treatments could go a long way to reduce people's stressful anticipation about the procedures they are soon to undergo.

In the area of achievement anxiety, cognitive modeling portraying coping strategies lowers distress and debility in anxiety-prone people by altering their attentional and thought patterns so that they deploy their skills more effectively to meet the demands of the task (Rosenthal, 1980; Sarason, 1975b). Interpersonal anxiety can be similarly alleviated through modeling. Videotapes of sexual behavior reduce sexual anxiety and increase sexual activities in people suffering from sexual dysfunctions (Nemetz, Craig, & Reith, 1978; Wincze & Caird, 1976). Timid children and adults, who lack assertiveness and shy away from social encounters, overcome their inhibitions by modeling successful ways of relating to others (Kazdin, 1978; O'Connor, 1969, 1972).

Disinhibitory modeling contains a number of elements, including threatening events, modeled coping strategies, and their consequences. Studies examining the causal contribution of these elements to change reveal that exposure to threats alone does not reduce phobic behavior, but observation of efficacious modeling does (Bandura, Grusec, & Menlove, 1967b; Kazdin, 1978). The major benefits of vicarious influences apparently derive from the information they convey about coping capabilities and strategies and about the likely consequences of modeled ways.

Potentiating Factors. A number of modeling variables affect the disinhibitory power of vicariously derived information. Diversified modeling, in which people of widely differing characteristics handle feared events effectively, has more impact on observers than the successes of a single model (Bandura & Menlove, 1968; Kazdin, 1974a, 1976). When vicarious influence relies on only a few exemplars, similarity to the model in personal attributes facilitates disinhibition (Kazdin, 1974b; O'Sullivan & Gilner, 1976). However, age differences, which imply superior coping skills and judgment, produce variable disinhibitory effects depending on the direction of the discrepancy. Observing peers and even younger models succeed in their coping efforts reduces fear, whereas seeing the triumphs of older models, who presumably are more competent, is less effective (Bandura & Barab, 1973; Kornhaber & Schroeder, 1975).

Modeling formats may rely on mastery models, who perform calmly and faultlessly, or on coping models, who begin fearfully but gradually overcome their difficulties by determined coping efforts (Meichenbaum, 1971). Variations on the coping-mastery dimension have produced somewhat mixed results. In some studies, coping surpasses mastery modeling (Kazdin, 1974d; Meichenbaum, 1971); in others, coping modeling aids disinhibition, when it is combined with model similarity, but not by itself (Kazdin, 1974b); and in still other studies, coping and mastery modeling are equally effective (Kato & Fukushima, 1977; Klorman, Hilpert, Michael, LaGana, & Sveen, 1980). Coping modeling contains two separable factors: Models display decreasing fear as they struggle with the task, and they demonstrate techniques for managing difficult situations. Instruction in coping techniques is more helpful than emotive modeling. Therefore, whether coping modeling is weaker, equipotent, or stronger than mastery modeling will depend, in large part, on the number of serviceable coping strategies these two forms of modeling convey.

If modeling initial apprehension aids disinhibition by increasing model similarity, it is possible to capitalize on the motivational benefits of likeness by historical modeling without temporarily exacerbating distress by emotive displays. For instance, while demonstrating effective ways of coping, models can describe, and even show, how they have previously suffered from similar fears but have overcome them by determined effort. In this approach, which is a common rehabilitative practice especially in self-help groups, modeled mastery of problems is described historically, rather than enacted in the present.

Models can exhibit coping strategies both by their actions and by voicing their thoughts about how to analyze task demands, find alternative solutions, monitor the effects of their actions, correct errors, and deal effectively with stress. In complex activities, the thinking skills guiding actions are, in many respects, more informative than the modeled actions themselves. People who lack problem-solving skills benefit more from observing people model self-guiding thoughts in conjunction with actions than from seeing the actions alone (Sarason, 1975b).

The adequacy of modeled thoughts and action strategies is conveyed by the results they are shown to produce. Hence, the direction and amount of influence models wield over observers' fears depend largely on the success of their coping strategies. Modeled performances are more influential when they bring good results than when their effects remain ambiguous (Kazdin, 1974c, 1976). Were models to bring punishment on themselves by their actions, the vicarious experience would exacerbate rather than reduce observers' fears.

Mediating Mechanisms. Evidence will be reviewed in a later chapter to show that fear arousal is mediated by the perceived predictability and controllability of potentially aversive events. People who judge themselves to be ineffectual in coping with threatening situations magnify hazards and generate frightening thoughts about what is likely to happen to them. Not knowing when or where threats might occur gives rise to perpetual anxious anticipations. If people can predict and exercise control over aversive events, they have little reason to fear them.

What phobic thinking renders frightful, informative modeling demagnifies and makes predictable and personally controllable. Modeling by itself, produces the best results when the situations the observers regard as hazardous occur repeatedly and when effective ways of managing them are modeled. Through focused, instructive modeling, observers gain probabilistic information about what they fear and acquire coping strategies that are useful in whatever situations might arise. Such experiences boost perceived coping self-efficacy.

That modeling reduces fear through its effects on self-percepts of efficacy receives support from several studies designed to elucidate various aspects of this mechanism of change. Both live and cognitive modeling enhance perceived self-efficacy in phobics. Self-percepts of efficacy predict how well people cope with threats and how much fear arousal they experience (Bandura, Adams, Hardy, & Howells, 1980; Bandura, Reese, & Adams, 1982). They experience high fear on tasks in which they perceive themselves to be inefficacious, but, as the strength of their self-judged efficacy increases, their fear arousal declines. The means by which potentiating modeling factors boost perceived coping efficacy will receive detailed consideration later.

Modeled Suffering and Pain Tolerance

Pain is a psychobiologic event that can be exacerbated or lessened by psychological influences. Because pain is subject to cognitive modulation, pain threshold and tolerance is modifiable by the discomfort models display while undergoing painful experiences (Craig, 1978, 1983). Observers exposed to models tolerating painful stimulation without undue distress accept high levels of shock before experiencing them as painful, whereas observers exposed to models displaying low pain tolerance find even weak shocks painful. Even nonaversive stimulation is made painful by modeled hurting. Modeled pain tolerance also affects capability to perform intellectual tasks under pain. People who have seen models persevere under pain work much longer and solve more

problems when they themselves are in pain than if they had seen models give up quickly (Turkat & Guise, 1983; Turkat, Guise, & Carter, 1983). Children's ability to cope with chronic clinical pain seems to be similarly affected by parental modeling of styles to cope with pain (Turkat, 1982).

When expressions of pain in response to increasing shock are studied under different vicarious conditions, larger increases in aversive stimulation are needed to produce discomfort in observers exposed to forbearing models than in those who have seen others easily hurt (Craig, Best, & Ward, 1975). Modeled coping reactions thus alter sensory sensitivity to painful stimulation. The altered sensitivities to painful events remain long after the modeling influence is over. On physiological indicators of discomfort, observers of forbearing models accept more intense shocks without suffering any greater visceral distress (Craig & Neidermayer, 1974). The combined findings of Craig's research indicate that modeling affects not only the subjective experience of pain but also sensory sensitivity to painful stimulation and physiological systems that are implicated in pain.

If models show no discomfort whatsoever to painful stimulation, they convey the erroneous impression that the events causing pain are painless. Unexpectedness of painful experiences, and unpreparedness for them, creates a cognitive source of distress over and above the physical discomfort produced by the external events themselves. Unperturbed modeling may therefore increase the aversiveness of painful events. Vernon (1974) provides some evidence bearing on this issue with hospitalized children receiving preoperative injections. Observing peers who react nonchalantly to injections increased children's distress to injections, but even modeled mild discomfort lessened their stress reactions when compared to the absence of any preparatory modeling.

The preceding findings are not inconsistent with those reported by Craig and his associates. Craig's stoic models are not impassive. They express some discomfort, although, as in the Vernon study, they show weaker pain reactions than the events ordinarily evoke. As aversive stimulation increases for models and observers alike, the models display somewhat more discomfort. In other words, it is forbearance, not falsity, that is modeled.

Janis and his associates have similarly shown that preparatory information about surgical procedures and pain experiences, coupled with instructions about how to cope with pain, can increase stress tolerance and hasten postoperative recovery (Janis, 1958). The benefits derive more from the coping strategies than from the preparatory information about what to expect (Langer, Janis, & Wolfer, 1975). Indeed, Miller (1980b) has shown that when people lack effective means for controlling aversive events, providing a lot of information about the predicaments they are to undergo only heightens their anticipatory distress. Under such circumstances, it is best to distract oneself from impending painful experiences. In contrast, people who possess coping capabilities are benefitted by knowing what to expect, because such information enables them to take ameliorative action. In dealing with aversive situations, active copers seek information about aversive events; ineffective copers avoid it.

The mechanisms through which vicarious influence modulates the experience of pain is an intriguing question. Neurophysiological models of pain distinguish between the sensory signals of pain and the affective experience of pain, both of which are subject to cognitive control (Melzack & Wall, 1982). One possibility is that modeling affects reports of pain but not the sensory experience of pain itself. Results of studies measuring physiological signs of pain, however, dispute such an interpretation. Forbearing models not only reduce observers' pain expressions but also lower their sensory sensitivity and their physiological agitation to aversive stimulation (Craig & Prkachin, 1978). Modeling produces genuine changes in the amount of discomfort experienced internally.

There are many psychological ways of lessening pain and raising pain tolerance. Consciousness has a very limited capacity. If it is occupied with competing ideation, then pain sensations become less noticeable. Dwelling on the pain one is experiencing not only vivifies it but can exacerbate it by arousing distressing thoughts that heighten pain through bodily tension. Diverting attention from pain sensations by thinking of other things can make pain more tolerable (McCaul & Malott, 1984). Performance of grueling activities relies heavily on this very strategy. For example, attentional diversion enables long-distance runners to press on even though their body is wracked in pain. Were they to focus on their mounting aches, they would cease running before long. In chronic clinical pain, engrossment in meaningful activities that are attentionally demanding diverts attention from pain sensations in a more enduring fashion than arbitrary trains of thought conjured up to engage one's consciousness. Arbitrary thought patterns may serve as distractors for a short time, whereas engrossing activities can fully occupy one's consciousness for hours on end without requiring deliberate effort because the continuity of the activity captures attention.

Other cognitive strategies for pain control involve thinking about pleasant events during painful stimulation; imagining that the body area being stimulated aversively is insensitive or is experiencing something other than pain; or reinterpreting the situation producing the pain as a nonpainful one (Grimm & Kanfer, 1976; Hilgard & Hilgard, 1975; Weisenberg, 1977). When pain sensations are hard to displace from consciousness, they are easier to bear if their meaning is transformed. The more cognitive strategies are used, the greater is the pain reduction (Chaves & Barber, 1974).

Self-relaxation serves as another means of alleviating pain by reducing muscular tension and visceral arousal. Thus, after acquiring self-relaxation skills, sufferers of tension headaches can prevent headaches or reduce their severity, should they occur, by relaxing their musculature in stressful situations (Blanchard, Ahles, & Shaw, 1979). Pain from other origins, such as menstrual, lower back, and phantom limb, has similarly been abated by self-relaxation (Sanders, 1979).

Cognitive coping skills, which instill a sense of personal control, have also proven effective in relieving pain. But the best results are obtained by flexible use of the full array of coping strategies. These include attention diversion, self-relaxation, positive imagery, calming self-instruction on how to prepare for and handle painful situations, cognitive reappraisal of aversive events, and self-affirmation of one's capabilities (Meichenbaum & Turk, 1976; Turk & Genest, 1979). Such cognitive analgesics can work as well as or better than drugs.

Although the strategies are varied, evidence suggests that their effects on pain sensitivity and tolerance may be largely mediated through perceived coping efficacy. Attentional distractors increase pain tolerance more if they are personally controlled than if the same distractors are presented at the same time by others (Kanfer & Seidner, 1973). The mere belief that one possesses a self-relaxation technique to relieve discomfort increases ability to withstand pain, even though the belief is unfounded (Neufeld & Thomas, 1977). In numerous laboratory studies, people who are led to believe they can exercise some control over aversive stimuli are able to endure more severe pain with less physiological distress than those who believe they lack personal control, although all receive the same aversive stimuli (Averill, 1973; Miller, 1979, 1980a).

Studies measuring self-precepts of efficacy provide the most direct evidence that cognitive analgesics may work, in part, by instilling a sense of efficacy in managing one's pain. Reese (1983) found that the more training in cognitive coping techniques raised people's perceived efficacy in controlling and reducing pain, the less pain they experienced subjectively, and the longer they tolerated it. The way in which perceived coping efficacy ameliorates pain is analyzed in a later chapter.

VALUATIONAL FUNCTION

Human behavior is partly governed by value preferences and evaluative standards. It is through this internal source of guidance that people give direction to their lives and derive satisfactions from what they do. Values and internal standards of behavior are extensively developed and altered through the experiences of others. Because values and standards are central to human affairs, the valuational function of vicarious consequences is, in many respects, more fundamental than the enlightenment they provide about environmental contingencies.

Internal Standards. One of the major mechanisms through which standards of behavior are socially transmitted relies on modeled self-evaluative reactions. As people engage in activities they express, from time to time, reactions to their own behavior according to their personal standards. They react self-approvingly when their behavior matches or surpasses their standards but self-critically when it falls short or violates their internal standards. Through repeated exposure to modeled self-reactions, observers eventually extract the underlying standards and often use them as guides for their own future behavior (Bandura, 1976a; Masters & Mokros, 1974). The processes by which this is achieved receive detailed consideration in the next chapter.

The evaluative reactions that people express toward others also reflect their personal standards, not just momentary whims. Observers can, therefore, gain more from vicarious experiences than simply knowledge of the probable consequences of different courses of action. They can figure out the standards of conduct exemplified in the social reactions to a model's behavior as they do from observing the model's own self-evaluations. Internalization of standards is an especially important function of vicarious experience because it creates the capability for self-directedness.

Value Preferences. People act in terms of value preferences. They do things that bring about what they like and those that prevent or remove what they dislike (Rokeach, 1980). Values can be both developed and altered vicariously through the positive and negative experiences of others. For example, children are more apt to develop a taste for things they previously disliked if the preferences being modeled are rewarded than if they are not (Barnwell, 1966). In an ingenious experiment, Duncker (1938) demonstrated the long-term effects of modeled pleasure on food preferences. Young children consistently selected chocolate with a pleasant lemon flavor over a sugar with a disagreeable medicinal taste. They later heard a story in which a stalwart hero abhorred a tart substance, which tasted like the children's favored food, but enthusiastically relished a sweet tasting substance. The modeled reactions altered the children's preferences for foodstuffs and reversed their habitual liking for chocolate in favor of the medicated sugar in tests conducted over a period of several days. Brief recall of the story reinstated the vicariously-created preferences after they had declined.

Modeling is an effective way of introducing young children to unfamiliar tastes and developing preferences for foods they have previously held in disfavor (Birch, 1980; Harper & Sanders, 1975). The food preferences of animals can be influenced in much the same way. Kittens seeing their mothers eating atypical food—forsaking meat for mashed potatoes—acquire a lasting preference for mashed potatoes that is most unusual for their species (Wyrwicka, 1978).

That evaluations created vicariously can affect actions is shown most directly in thera-peutic applications of modeling. Loathsome evaluations of long standing are changed to neutral or even favorable ones through modeling of positive reactions toward disliked phobic objects. The degree of change in evaluative reactions predicts the amount of behavioral change (Bandura & Barab, 1973; Bandura et al., 1969; Blanchard, 1970a).

Research on behavior subject to inhibitory socialization extends the generality of the valuative effects of modeling. Sexual modeling creates more favorable attitudes toward sex, especially less familiar practices that have previously met with disapproval (Howard, Liptzin, & Reifler, 1973; Mann et al., 1971; Nemetz et al., 1978). In the area of aggression, exposure to televised violence increases preferences for aggressive solutions to interpersonal conflicts (Dominick & Greenberg, 1972; Leifer & Roberts, 1972).

Image Makers and the Symbolic Environment. During the course of their daily lives, people have direct contact with only a small sector of the environment. In their daily routines, they travel the same limited routes, visit the same familiar places, and see the same group of friends and associates. As a result, people form impressions of many social realities, with which they have little or no contact, from symbolic representations of society, mainly by the mass media. To a large extent, people act on their images of reality.

Because of its appeal and pervasiveness, television has become an influential source of acculturation. According to Gerbner (1972), a leading communications researcher, the message system of television has certain ideological orientations that find expression in the values, attitudes, and behavior it depicts. Image makers help to shape the popular culture. Recurrent televised scenarios convey notions about the basic structure of society and the power relations within it. Analyses of televised programs reveal that, through their portrayal of social roles and human relations, the media cultivate social stereotyping by sex, age, and race (Busby, 1975; Gerbner & Gross, 1976).

In this era of electronic campaigning, image politics, orchestrated by pollsters, computer programmers, and television producers, has become the major vehicle for influencing the electorate. It is easier to shape images by portraying favorable personal characteristics than to change attitudes by examining issues. Image management is more effectively achieved by contrived media portrayals than by public appearances. Professional image makers draw heavily on the mass media to heighten the attraction of their candidates to voters (Nimmo, 1976). Pollsters probe the public's likes, dislikes, fears, concerns, and hopes. On the basis of this information, campaign staffs cast their candidate in a positive image and their opponents in a negative image through mass-marketing techniques using television, ads, radio spots, and personalized mailers targeted to specific categories of voters identified by computers. The more voters rely on television for their information, the more their voting decisions are influenced by candidates' imaged qualities than by their position on issues (McLeod, Glynn, & McDonald, 1983).

Electronic campaigning significantly alters how candidates do their politicking, as well as the content of media messages. They have to spend much of their time preparing television and radio spots, staging media events likely to be reported in newscasts, and raising large sums of money to buy expensive media time. Rising campaign costs increase dependence on special interest dollars. The polling operations and new tools of politics continue to be used during the time the victor is in office to ensure future electoral success.

Shaping Consumer Habits through Vicarious Influence.

Acculturation to consumer habits is heavily promoted through commercial advertising. When promoters cannot directly elicit and reinforce the behavior they desire, as is the case in persuasion through the mass media, they seek to encourage it by altering viewers' evaluations, preferences, and outcome expectations. Advertisers cannot personally instruct and reward a brunette for dyeing her hair blond, but they can increase the likelihood of their hair dyes being purchased, by creating the impression that blondness increases social attractiveness. Since the potency of vicarious influences can be increased by showing modeled acts bringing rewards, vicarious outcomes figure prominently in advertising campaigns. Thus, drinking a certain brand of beer or using a particular shampoo wins the loving admiration of beautiful people, enhances job performance, masculinizes self-conception, actualizes individualism and authenticity, tranquilizes irritable nerves, invites social recognition and amicable reactions from total strangers, and arouses affectionate overtures from spouses.

In the positive appeals, buying what the advertisers suggest produces any number of benefits. The types of vicarious outcomes, model characteristics, and modeling formats that are selected vary depending on what happens to be in vogue at the time. When the public was down on conformity, advertisers sought to promote conformity in smokers by portraying selection of their brand of cigarettes as an expression of individualism. The graphics in the ad show the lover of their brand taking "independent action" by exiting on a deserted off-ramp away from the mass of faceless freeway drivers. Since social acceptance and affection are common desires, scenarios involving social attraction have been widely used through the years to sell all manner of products.

In the same way, model characteristics are varied to boost the persuasiveness of commercial messages. Prestigious models are often enlisted to capitalize on the high regard in which they are held. The best sellers depend on what happens to be popular. When environmental conservation was in vogue, Ansel Adams, the foremost nature photographer, was shown promoting automobiles amidst the splendor of Yosemite valley, which is ironically suffering from the pollution and ravages of the automobile. When jogging was a major public pastime, James Fixx, who wrote a bestseller on running, was enlisted to sell breakfast food. As emphasis has shifted to life styles and "relating," advertisers have made their products a conspicuous part of sportive life styles and sharing precious moments in life. Whatever sport is in season, its superstars are busy endorsing products right and left. Celebrity status in the film and television world also sells well by exploiting the sway of attractiveness.

Drawing on evidence that similarity to the model enhances imitation, some advertisements portray common folk achieving wonders with the wares advertised. Because vicarious influence increases with multiplicity of modeling, the beers, soft drinks, and snacks are being consumed with gusto in the advertised world by groups of wholesome, handsome, fun-loving models. Eroticism is another stimulant that never goes out of style. Therefore, seductive appeals, mainly by winsome females, do heavy duty in efforts to command attention and to make advertised products more attractive to potential buyers. Sexual modeling alters the perceived qualities of products and increases favorable attitudes toward them, provided the model and the product are not grossly mismatched and the sexual titilation is not too crassly exploitive (Kanungo & Pang, 1973; Peterson & Kerin, 1979; Smith & Engel, 1968).

Negative appeals portray the detrimental personal and social consequences which result from failure to use the advertised products. Ignoring mouth washes or particular shampoos brings social rejection from the scourge of bad breath or dandruff. Failure to purchase a certain brand of tires endangers the lives of wives driving treacherous roads in torrential rainstorms. In offering remedies for the fear they arouse, marketing managers often use modeling to create aversions to natural characteristics, as when perspiratory odor is made to seem repellent and the skin discoloration of aging is labeled "ugly." Negative modeling is a less reliable vehicle for selling products. Depicting repellent outcomes tends to arouse unpleasant emotions that may lead viewers to avoid the disturbing material (Janis, 1967) or, inadvertently, to endow the advertised product itself with negative valence. People are more inclined to act on fear-arousing appeals if, in addition to being frightened, they are told what remedial actions they should take (Leventhal, 1970).

Controversy over the impact of televised commercials on children's health habits has made advertising a topic of serious research, which hitherto was of interest mainly to marketing managers. Capitalizing on people's affinity for sweets, the food and confectionary industries target children with frequent ads promoting highly-sugared foods such as candies, sweetened snacks, cereals, and beverages. Sugar-rich foods are not only low in nutrients, they put on pounds, decay teeth, and contribute to health problems in adult life. Exposing children to commercials touting sugared foods indeed increases their preference for, and consumption of, such foods (Jeffrey, McLellarn, & Fox, 1982; Roberts, 1978; Goldberg, Gorn, & Gibson, 1978). With repetition of ads, altered food preferences generalize to nonadvertised sugared products. Ads for nutritious foods can increase children's choices of fruit over sweets (Cantor, 1981).

The eating and drinking habits modeled in televised programs can similarly shape viewers' habits. The eating patterns shown on television are not the type to keep people slim and healthy (Kaufman, 1980). Alcohol is the main drink. Such portrayals are not lost on young viewers. Exposure to televised drinking increases the likelihood of children serving liquor to adults in simulated situations (Rychtarik, et al., 1983). High exposure to liquor advertising is a predictor of adolescent drinking behavior (Atkin, Hocking, & Block, 1984).

In the process of shaping consumer preferences, televised commercials model social relationships, occupational roles, and life styles that can have unintended social effects. Ads contribute to social stereotyping of people. For example, in the world of television commercials, women mainly perform domestic duties. Men not only lead more varied occupational and leisure lives, but even in domestic ads, they are usually presented as the authorities telling women what to do and testing women's preferences for products (Courtney & Whipple, 1974). Commercials presenting women in nontraditional roles increase girls' knowledge about occupations, lower their occupational stereotyping by sex, and raise their preference for jobs historically confined to males (O'Bryant & Corder-Bolz, 1978). The elderly also tend to be socially stereotyped as simpletons or as leading vacuous lives plagued by bowel irregularities, slack dentures, arthritis, and tired blood.

Food commercials aimed at young children use them to influence parental shopping patterns. Exposure to televised commercials increases children's attempts to get parents to buy advertised products (Brody, Stoneman, Lane, & Sanders, 1981; Galst & White, 1976). Televised advertising sets off family conflict when parents deny children's requests for advertised products (Atkin, 1978). Parental refusal of things children want creates greater unhappiness in children who have seen the items advertised than in the ones who have not (Goldberg & Gorn, 1978). The latter finding suggests that commercial advertising can increase social discontent by creating or strengthening desires that many people do not have the means to satisfy.

Conferral of Social Status. In the vicarious effects discussed above, exemplified consequences alter observers' valuation of the objects with which the models interact. Some of the behavioral changes accompanying observed outcomes may be mediated by changing the model's social status itself.

Individuals who possess high status are generally emulated more than those of subordinate standing. Status can be conferred on people by the way in which their behavior is reinforced (Hastorf, 1965). Punishment tends to devalue models and their behavior, whereas the same models assume emulative qualities when their actions are lauded.

To examine how vicarious consequences affect the attractiveness and status of models, Zajonc (1954) exposed children to symbolic models who exhibited either affiliative or authoritarian styles of behavior, which either succeeded or failed. Exemplified effectiveness had pronounced impact on children's valuations, regardless of how the models behaved. Children admired the models' attributes and preferred to pattern their behavior after them when they succeeded, but they disliked these same attributes and regarded the models as unworthy of emulation when they failed.

Observing the successfulness of models alters not only their attractiveness but also the extent to which observers actually pattern their own behavior after them (Bandura, Ross, & Ross, 1963b). Aggressors were selected as preferred models for emulation when their behavior was effective in amassing rewards, whereas they were disvalued and rejected when they heaped punishment upon themselves by such actions. Imitative aggressiveness was increased with boosts in model status and reduced with lowered model status. The generality of these findings is extended by Shafer (1965), who measured modeling as a function of reversal of the model's status. Children readily adopted the behavior of models presented as celebrities but discarded the modeled patterns of behavior after the models were discredited as being imposters.

In conflicts of power and injustice, observed punitive treatment enhances rather than lowers the victim's social status in the eyes of many observers. People who risk punishment for upholding beliefs and conduct cherished by a group or for challenging social practices that violate the professed values of society gain the admiration of sympathizers. For this reason, authorities are usually careful not to discipline challengers or transgressors in ways that might make martyrs of them.

Vicarious experiences can alter how people value those wielding influence, as well as the recipients of it. People who reward others lavishly are usually considered insincere, ingratiating, or lacking standards, all of which detract from their influence. Valuation is changed even more strongly by the exercise of punitive power. Restrained and principled use of coercive power commands respect. When societal officials misuse their power to reward and punish, they undermine the legitimacy of their authority and arouse strong resentment. Seeing inequitable punishment is, therefore, more likely to generate opposition than compliance in observers. Indeed, leaders of protest movements sometimes attempt to rally supporters to their causes by selecting tactics calculated to provoke authorities to excessively punitive actions (Bandura, 1973; Searle, 1968; Spiegel, 1970). Such actions transform the original disputed issue into collective protests against the officials' practices and the institutions they serve. When violence is used to provoke repressive countermeasures to breed public disaffection with the system, the official overreaction may be a greater detriment to society than the violent acts themselves.

The emotional reactions models express about outcomes of their actions can also affect the impact of vicarious consequences on observers. In a study conducted by Lerner and Weiss (1972), for example, models' expressions of delight or displeasure with the rewards they had received outweighed the value of the observed rewards in influencing other children's performance of similar activities. Modeled displeasure reduced the effectiveness of highly valued vicarious rewards, whereas modeled satisfaction enhanced the vicarious influence of relatively unattractive rewards. Observers persist longer in the face of nonreward if they have seen models display elation over success and annoyance over failure than if the

models remain impassive to the results of their efforts (Berger & Johansson, 1968).

The effects of models' emotional reactions probably operate, at least in part, through valuational functions. People do not get aroused about inconsequential matters. High affective reactivity may thus confer significance to the modeled activities or to the accompanying consequences. In threatening situations, however, emotional reactions tend to diminish a model's status and perceived effectiveness by conveying a sense of insecurity. This is illustrated in studies of aggression that is commanded. Individuals readily defy demands to act punitively after they observe peer models resist such orders (Milgram, 1965). However, modeled defiance is less effective in reducing obedient aggression if resisters become emotionally upset than if they are unperturbed by their disobedience (Powers & Geen, 1972). Nervous defiance apparently conveys the impression that the challengers either lack conviction in the stand they have taken or that they are faint-hearted.

Influenceability Function. People usually see not only the consequences experienced by models but also the manner in which they respond to their treatment. The exemplified responsiveness is an integral part of vicarious events that must also be considered in explaining the effects of observed outcomes. Observers' susceptibility to influence by direct consequences is increased by prior exposure to modeled responsiveness to social approval, and it is reduced by modeled resistance to attempts to influence them by social approval.

In their daily affairs, people have to reckon not only with power structures but also with constant efforts to influence their behavior in one direction or another. Although they will do many things for praise and material rewards, they also value their integrity and sense of freedom. How models respond to social rewards and sanctions can change how observers' judge the causes of behavior, what value they place on the outcomes, and how much latitude of action they perceive in similar situations. Positive responsiveness suggests to observers that the models' actions reflect, at least in part, their own desires, rather than merely the dictates of others. When modeled actions are seen as reflecting personal preferences, observed outcomes appear more as helpful incentives than as social coercers. In contrast, when models are resistant, it appears as though rewards are being used to force them to act in ways that others desire. Obedience to manipulative reward is apt to generate self-devaluative reactions. As a result, observers become reluctant to trade their perceived freedom and integrity for social rewards when they themselves become the objects of influence.

Ditrichs, Simon, and Greene (1967) provide evidence regarding this point. Observers increased a behavior that brought them approval when they had previously seen models respond positively to praise, whereas they remained unresponsive to praise after they had seen models resist similar attempts to influence them. Modeled resistance thus overrode the usual sway of observed praise. This is not to say that observers are necessarily more impressed by how others react to positive incentives than they are by the incentives themselves. The relative influence of these two factors undoubtedly varies depending upon the nature of the behavior, the status of the models, the appropriateness of their reactions, the value of the incentives, and the prestige of the influencers.

People resist coercion and punitive control more often than they resist valued incentives. Although the example of punishment is prevalent, the degree to which its inhibitory power is weakened by modeled resistance has received surprisingly little attention. Since behavior that is socially prohibited usually has some appeal, modeled opposition is probably more effective in negating the influence of observed punishment than of observed reward.

Proponents of operant conditioning interpret vicarious effects in terms of discriminative stimulus control. From this perspective, the consequences of a model's actions merely serve as discriminative stimuli signifying which class of responses are likely to be reinforced (Gewirtz, 1971). These cues presumably control how observers themselves will behave on future occasions. This sort of explanation acknowledges the informative value of observed outcomes. However, it confounds two processes—information transmission and mechanism of response regulation—that must be distinguished. This can be illustrated by first considering an example of direct reinforcement. If driving responses in the presence of red and green signal lights are differentially reinforced, the lights become informative cues about the probable effects of different driving acts at busy intersections. As a result, people stop on red and go on green, although some drivers will ignore them if they think it is safe to do so. It is arguable where the control of action ultimately resides—in the stimulus or in human judgment—nevertheless, the external cues are both informative and physically present to aid the regulation of behavior.

The metaphor of stimulus control offers little to clarify the lasting effects of vicarious influences. If control resides in discriminative cues they must be physically present to exercise their influence. Previously observed consequences to the model are informative, but they cannot function as discriminative cues because they are no longer present when observers act on later occasions. The moment the rewarding and punishing consequences end, they cease to exist as cues. Operant analysis fails to explain how actions can be externally controlled by nonexistent stimuli. The successes and failures of others provide information for judgments about self-efficacy and probable outcomes. People act upon such judgments long after the modeled outcomes have disappeared. Modeled exemplification of consequences is the mode of information transmission, and the observer's inferential judgment is the mechanism of response regulation. Thus, the same model performing the same responses with the same outcomes can have markedly different effects on different observers, because each draws different inferences from what they have observed. Observers' judgments predict how they are likely to behave after seeing the same vicarious outcomes (Brown & Inouye, 1978). To assign control to history of reinforcement does not adequately specify the present causes of behavior. Such an explanation assumes that external stimuli are imprinted directly on the organism without any cognitive mediation. In fact, external events usually affect behavior through cognitive processing of the information they convey. Hence, behavior is often better predicted by current judgment than by past stimulus conditions.

LEGAL DETERRENTS THROUGH VICARIOUS INFLUENCE

The legal system of deterrence rests largely on the restraining function of exemplary punishment. In fact, legal sanctions would have limited value if their sole purpose was to modify the future behavior of the small number of transgressors who happen to be apprehended and convicted of wrongdoing. Because the actual risk of punishment is so low, the power of legal threats resides mainly in their vicarious deterrent effect. Publicized examples raise the perceived risk of punishment, thereby deterring people should they encounter circumstances that tempt them to transgressive acts. It may be recalled from an earlier discussion that deterrence is more readily achieved by heightening the perceived risks of transgression than by trying to alter the actual risks (Meier, 1978).

Experimental studies document that exemplary punishment strengthens restraints in others against forbidden conduct. However, a number of personal and social factors modify its impact. The prevalence of transgressive modeling is one such factor. Modeling influences can reduce as well as raise the deterrent efficacy of threatened le-

gal consequences. As already noted, the chances of being caught and punished for criminal conduct are relatively low. In locales in which transgressions are common, people have personal knowledge of numerous crimes being committed without offenders being detected or apprehended. Such exposure to unpunished transgressions weakens observers' restraints against legally forbidden behavior. The larger the number of unpunished transgressors and the higher their status, the greater is their disinhibitory impact on others (Lefkowitz, Blake, & Mouton, 1955; Russell, Wilson, & Jenkins, 1976). As might be expected, people transgress most readily when prohibitions are weak and others have been seen violating them with impunity, whereas strong threats combined with modeled compliance discourage forbidden conduct (Blake, 1958). Exposure to rule-abiding models reduces the amount of conflict observers experience in tempting situations and also strengthens their self-restraint (Ross, 1971).

As is true of direct punishment, the restraining power of vicarious sanctions depends on the availability of behavior options. People are easily dissuaded from transgressive conduct by exemplary punishment if they have alternative prosocial means of getting what they want. Punishment that is observed to occur infrequently has an especially weak restraining effect on people whose range of options for securing valued rewards is limited largely to antisocial means. Under threats of punishment, they are likely to resort to safer criminal alternatives or to change their techniques to avoid being caught.

The level of instigation to forbidden conduct is another factor that affects the restraining efficacy of vicarious sanctions. Weakly motivated behavior is readily deterred by threatened consequences. However, in the face of powerful instigation, people tend to act without paying much heed to the negative effects their actions may produce. High instigation similarly negates the deterring influence of rule-abiding modeling. Kimbrell and Blake

(1958) found that under strong provocation individuals disregard prohibitions and the example of compliant models. But when the level of instigation is not so strong as to impel violations, persons who observe rule-abiding models are less disposed to engage in forbidden activities than those who have been exposed to unpunished transgressors.

Multiple Effects of Legal Sanctions.

The discussion so far has centered on the inhibitory effects of exemplary punishment and on the undermining of legal sanctions by transgressive modeling. We saw earlier that vicarious consequences do much more than modify restraints through fearful anticipation. The same is true of legal sanctions. Seeing certain forms of behavior repeatedly punished can endow the behavior itself with negative value and help build personal standards of conduct. Deterrents arising from self-standards are considerably more effective in keeping forbidden conduct in check than are external threats that carry a low risk. People constantly preside over their own conduct, whereas enforcement agents are rarely present in situations inviting transgressive behavior.

The forms of behavior made subject to criminal sanctions and the severity and manner in which they are applied can affect the credibility of the legal system itself. Legal sanctions are best used to prohibit socially injurious conduct, not to impose partisan morality on others. Nevertheless, the law is commonly used to control behavior that might better remain a matter of personal choice. Thus, unconventional beliefs, life styles, and personal habits that may displease, but do not harm, others are often subjected to legal consequences. Legal prohibitions against conduct that some segments of society regard as immoral, but that many people endorse, receive low compliance at the high cost of stigmatizing nonconformists and discrediting enforcement systems. To preserve its credibility, the law eventually accommodates to changing customs by making permissible what was formerly forbidden, as the practice becomes more widely spread. The rule of law breaks down when legal sanctions are misused as a coercive weapon by entrenched power groups, or when the law lags too far behind social change.

Observed punishment is informative, as well as inhibitory. One can profit from the failures of others. When better options are lacking and the prohibited behavior holds some prospect of success, witnessing the failures of others will more likely lead people to refine the disallowed behavior to improve its chances of success than to give it up. Airline hijacking provides a good illustration of this process. An inventive hijacker devised an extortion technique involving exchange of passengers for money and a parachute, which he used to bail out over a remote area (*San Francisco Chronicle*, 1971a). Others, inspired by his success, copied the hijacking technique but were captured with the aid of signal devices planted in the parachutes to allow easy tracking by pursuing planes. The Air Force announced publicly that this failure should serve as a lesson to others. It did. The next hijacker brought his own parachute aboard and, after sending the interceptor planes astray by casting off the bugged parachute, bailed out safely with half a million dollars (*San Francisco Chronicle*, 1972). Another hijacker successfully eluded the interceptor planes by parachuting into a jungle in Central America (*Palo Alto Times*, 1972b). Given the prospect that failure can be converted into profitable success by slight modifications of technique, the parachute mode of hijacking continued even though subsequent extortionists were killed or apprehended in the process. They ceased only after an automatic locking device was installed on the exit doors of planes.

Air piracy to foreign countries, which was already common before the strategy of extortion with a parachute, added the demand for ransom money, once the idea got planted. Some of the early attempts were foiled, however, by armed federal agents disguised as money couriers. These failures did not stop ransom demands. After a hijacker succeeded by having officials in the nude deliver money aboard the aircraft, nude couriers were incorporated as an element in the hijacking-extortion strategy.

The deterring power of exemplary punishment is probably strongest for those who need it least. Included here are the people who pursue rewarding life styles that make criminal alternatives uninviting, who have too high a stake in their community to risk the devastating consequences of criminal stigmatization, and who are infrequently exposed to transgressive modeling. Those who lack prosocial options and see others securing rewards unlawfully with little risk of apprehension do not give much thought to legal statutes. The best mode of prevention requires a dual approach combining legal sanctions with the cultivation of more functional alternatives. To punish without providing any positive options is a costly and unreliable means of social control.

Capital Punishment and Deterrence

The use of exemplary punishment for deterrent purposes takes its most extreme form in capital punishment. Indeed, since incarceration can afford society protection against homicidal assailants, the only justification for the death penalty, apart from retribution purposes, is that it will deter future murders. Public support for the death penalty fluctuates with incidents of heinous killings and changes in level of fear of crime in the society. Whatever the public sentiment might be at a given time, prescribing death as a remedy for homicide creates ambivalences and paradoxes. Many people favor the death penalty in the abstract, but they are reluctant to advocate it in a particular case, once the individual has been personalized (Ellsworth, 1978). Actions that culminate in violence are unlikely to arouse much in the way of restraining imagery of gas chambers or gallows as proponents of capital punishment contend, unless executions are carried out publicly to provide horrid reminders. The public wants to

instill the imagery of death as a restraining influence, while at the same time keeping executions hidden from public view. Public executions were discontinued because of concern over their brutalizing effects. Advocates of the death penalty are also inclined to oppose any restrictions of guns, which are favorite murder weapons (Vidmar & Ellsworth, 1974).

The issue is not whether the threat of punishment by death can deter homicide, but whether the death penalty deters homicides more effectively than does life imprisonment. The unique deterrent power of the death penalty has been vigorously debated over the years. Abolitionists argue that there is no evidence that capital punishment deters murder any better than life imprisonment (Bedau, 1967). Given the already severe punishment of protracted imprisonment, the added penalty of death may not necessarily increase the deterrent power of legal sanctions. In judging the magnitude of punishment, many people, in fact, view the death penalty as no more severe than life imprisonment without parole (Hamilton & Rotkin, 1979). The evidence regarding deterrence is not inconsistent with these perceptions. Homicide rates do not differ in neighboring states with and without capital punishment or in the same state before and after the death penalty has been abolished. Such comparisons, of course, are subject to criticism, given the difficulty of matching states and time periods on all factors that can affect the incidence of homicides.

The kinds of crimes legally designated as punishable by death have been narrowed markedly over the years. Abolition of the death penalty does not lead to a differential rise in crimes no longer punishable by execution as compared to those that are. Reinstatement of the death penalty does not have a discernible effect on the rate of capital crimes. Nor does the incidence of capital crimes differ consistently before and after publicized executions. Neither police nor inmates and their keepers are any safer in states that retain the death penalty than in states that have abolished it. Regardless of what methodology is used, the results are highly consistent in showing that executions do not deter homicides.

In the absence of evidence for a unique deterrent effect, putting to death inmates, against whom society is already protected by their imprisonment, serves mainly retributive or economic purposes. Executions provide revenge, and they are cheaper than lifetime incarceration. The fact that many people would continue to support executions, even if they were shown conclusively to have no deterrent effect (Vidmar & Ellsworth, 1974), suggests that a good deal of vengeance masquerades under deterrent justifications.

Advocates of capital punishment present the counterargument that the uniquely deterrent force of the death penalty has not been adequately tested, at least in recent years, because, although many states have the death penalty, they rarely execute anyone. In a highly controversial study Ehrlich (1975a, 1975b) concluded, from analyses of how law enforcement and economic factors contribute to changes in homicide rates, that execution has a small deterrent effect on murder rates. However, this conclusion did not withstand methodological scrutiny and efforts to replicate the findings have failed to provide any evidence that executions create additional deterrence to homicides (Archer, Gartner, & Beittel, 1983; Blumstein, Cohen, & Nagin, 1978). Social factors have a large effect on homicide rates, but executions do not. Societies are not at liberty to vary systematically whether they execute murderers or imprison them for life. Correlational analyses based on inadequately tested assumptions and questionable measures yield conflicting conclusions. Given this state of affairs, the empirical dispute over the special deterrent efficacy of execution does not lend itself readily to definitive resolution.

Considering the gravity of executions by society, advocates must show that the threat of execution is a superior deterrent to life imprisonment. The unintended social consequences of death penalties also demand attention. Occasionally, innocent persons are executed. The penalty of death is irrevocable. Taking human life entails complicated legal processes of appeal to protect the innocent from execution. The protracted appeals of condemned prisoners reduce the courts' capacity to adjudicate other forms of criminality. Because condemned defendants are found innocent from time to time, efforts to curtail judicial review are, and should be, vigorously opposed.

The brutalizing effect of societal killings is another matter of serious concern. Executions devalue human life. When society executes offenders, it conveys a dual message condemning murder but also morally sanctioning violence by modeling the very abhorrent behavior it wishes to discourage in others. To gain public support for capital punishment, a society must create persuasive moral justifications for the taking of human life. Modeling moral justifications for killing can weaken inhibitions over aggression. Thus, a killing that is morally justified heightens human cruelty more than if it is not sanctified (Meyer, 1971). Violent conduct is further legitimized, and thereby disinhibited, when respected agents of society resort to violent means, although more humane alternatives are available. Some researchers report that any immediate inhibitory impact of executions is quickly offset by a rise in homicides above the levels before the executions (Phillips, 1980; Zeisel, 1982). In a study of longer-term effects, Bowers and Pierce (1980) conclude that executions stimulate people to kill. Homicides rise above expected rates in the month following an execution, and this instigating effect on potential killers may extend into the second month, as well. However, other time-series analyses reveal that executions neither deter nor instigate homicides (McFarland, 1983). The questionable deterrence of capital punishment must be weighed against the moral and aggression-sanctioning costs. The task of justifying executions as deterrents is becoming increasingly more difficult as the discriminatory use of capital punishment is publicized, and large segments of society contest the morality of the practice.

Because death rows contain many prisoners, and new ones continue to be added, enforcement of the death penalty would require daily executions. However, society is spared this ghastly task by periodic court rulings that find unconstitutional features in capital-punishment laws. In states that impose the death penalty, only a small fraction of those who have committed capital crimes are, in fact, executed. Discretion is exercised throughout the criminal process by prosecutors, judges, and juries. As a result, poor people and unpopular minorities were more likely to be sentenced to death than the more advantaged who had been convicted for similar crimes. Execution rates of those sentenced to death revealed selective influences operating in the commutation of death sentences based on the race and socioeconomic level of offenders, the quality of lawyers they can afford, the race of victims, and other factors (Johnson, 1957; Wolfgang, Kelly, & Nolde, 1962; Wolfgang & Riedel, 1973). Selective executions for similar crimes expose society's biases in administering its system of justice.

Nontotalitarian societies adopting the death penalty resort to scenarios that preserve the death penalty but spare them the gruesome task of frequent executions. Court rulings against discriminatory enforcement of the death penalty have commuted death sentences to life imprisonment. Laws are then amended to make death mandatory for certain crimes. While the constitutionality of the new statutes is being contested, death rows again fill up. The mandatory statutes are, in turn, challenged on the grounds that aggravating and mitigating circumstances must be given consideration, thus setting in motion the process for commuting the death sentences of another wave of prisoners. Laws are rewritten to provide further guidelines for the exercise of discretion in the imposition of the death penalty. Such quasi-mandatory statutes allow for the reappearance of discriminatory sentencing practices. To apply the death penalty evenhandedly would require exacting statutory guidelines and unusual invulnerability to bias in prosecutors, jurors, and judges, who are hardly without prejudices. Capital statutes continue to be reformed, but human bias continues to influence who gets indicted, convicted, and sentenced to death and who does not for similar crimes (Bowers, 1983; Paternoster, 1983). Discrimination in which murderers the society executes invites new legal challenges.

The real death threat for serious crimes is not in penal death chambers but in the markedly higher likelihood of death at the hands of police and victims during the commission of a crime (Sellin, 1961). Television and newspapers provide daily reminders in gruesome detail that violent criminality is often a ticket to the morgue. However, there is little in the cross-cultural data of homicide rates to support the view that providing people with the weapons to shoot each other deters violent crime. The gun appears no more effective than the gallows in curbing violent assaults. If anything, ready access to firearms increases the likelihood of people shooting each other accidentally, mistakenly, impulsively, or deliberately.

Difficult social problems that breed public fear become highly politicized, and they prompt resort to legal solutions that are politically expedient but socially ineffective. The problems thus get displaced on courts which then become the objects of hope, hostility, and distrust for different factions of society. The public campaigns that are mounted from time to time on behalf of capital punishment probably do more to advance the political careers of the promoters than to protect society or to increase reverence for human life.

8

SELF-REGULATORY MECHANISMS

In previous chapters we have analyzed how behavior is regulated by external outcomes, either observed or experienced firsthand. If actions were determined solely by external rewards and punishments, people would behave like weathervanes, constantly shifting direction to conform to whatever momentary influence happened to impinge upon them. They would act corruptly with unprincipled people and honorably with righteous ones, and liberally with libertarians and dogmatically with authoritarians. In actuality, except when subjected to coercive pressures, people display considerable self-direction in the face of many competing influences. Anyone who attempted to change a pacifist into an aggressor or a religious devotee to an atheist would quickly come to appreciate the force of self-reactive influence in the regulation of human behav-

ior. The notion that environment controls behavior takes on considerable indefiniteness of meaning on close scrutiny. In social transactions people become each other's environments. The same act can be taken as behavior or environment depending arbitrarily on which side of the ongoing exchange one happens to look at first. Even if one person acts to suit another's every preference, then the other person is exercising considerable control over the social environment.

Theories that seek to explain human behavior as solely the product of external rewards and punishments present a truncated image of human nature because people possess self-directive capabilities that enable them to exercise some control over their thoughts, feelings, and actions by the consequences they produce for themselves. Psychological functioning is, therefore, regulated by an interplay of self-generated and external sources of influence.

Behavior is commonly performed in the absence of immediate external reward or punishment. Many activities are directed toward outcomes projected into the future. People do things to gain anticipated benefits or to avert future trouble. The anticipation of distal outcomes provides general direction for choosing activities, and it raises the level of involvement in them. But most anticipated outcomes are too far off, or too general, to sheperd specific actions in immediate situations that present many uncertainties and complexities. People have to create for themselves proximal guides and self-motivators for courses of action that lead to distal attainments. In the exercise of self-directiveness, people set certain standards of behavior for themselves and respond to their own actions self-evaluatively. Because of their symbolizing and self-reactive capabilities, human beings are not at the mercy of immediate external prompts to tell them how to behave.

The act of writing provides a familiar example of a behavior that is continuously self-regulated through self-evaluation. When writing a paper or manuscript, writers do not have someone sitting beside them, selectively reinforcing each written statement until a satisfactory version has been produced. Rather, they adopt a standard of what constitutes an acceptable piece of work. They generate ideas and rephrase them in thought several times before anything is committed to paper. Authors successively revise provisional expressions until they are satisfied with what they have written. The more exacting their personal standards, the more corrective improvements they make (Simon, 1979c). Self-editing often exceeds the external requirements of what would be acceptable to others. Indeed, some people are such critical self-editors that they essentially paralyze their own writing efforts because they judge most of what they produce to be inadequate. Those who adopt more lenient standards exercise less self-correction.

SUBFUNCTION IN SELF-REGULATION

Self-regulation is not achieved by a feat of willpower. It operates through a set of subfunctions that must be developed and mobilized for self-directed change (Bandura, 1977a; Kanfer, 1977). Neither intention nor desire to change alone has much effect if people lack the means for exercising influence over their own behavior (Bandura & Simon, 1977). The constituent processes of the mechanism for self-regulation by self-reactive influence are summarized in Figure 1 and are discussed at some length in the sections that follow.

Self-Observation Subfunction

People cannot influence their own actions very well if they are inattentive to relevant aspects of their behavior. Activities may vary on a number of dimensions, some of which are listed in Figure 5. Depending on their values and on the functional significance of activities, people attend selectively to certain aspects of their behavior and ignore nonrelevant aspects. For example, they monitor their speed in track sports; the quality, quantity, or originality of their work in achievement situations; and the sociability and morality of their conduct in interpersonal situations.

In the flow of transactions with the environment, many factors compete for attention. People may attend most closely to what is going on around them, to what others do, to what they themselves are doing, or to the effects of their behavior. If they want to exert influence over their actions, they have to know what they are doing. Success in self-regulation, therefore, partly depends on the fidelity, consistency, and temporal proxim-

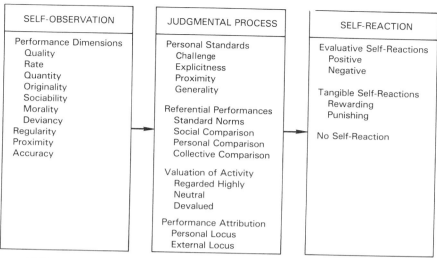

SELF-OBSERVATION	JUDGMENTAL PROCESS	SELF-REACTION

Performance Dimensions
  Quality
  Rate
  Quantity
  Originality
  Sociability
  Morality
  Deviancy
Regularity
Proximity
Accuracy
	Personal Standards
	  Challenge
	  Explicitness
	  Proximity
	  Generality
	
	Referential Performances
	  Standard Norms
	  Social Comparison
	  Personal Comparison
	  Collective Comparison
	
	Valuation of Activity
	  Regarded Highly
	  Neutral
	  Devalued
	
	Performance Attribution
	  Personal Locus
	  External Locus
		Evaluative Self-Reactions
		  Positive
		  Negative
		
		Tangible Self-Reactions
		  Rewarding
		  Punishing
		
		No Self-Reaction

FIGURE 5. Subprocesses involved in the self-regulation of behavior by internal standards and self incentives.

ity of self-monitoring. Kazdin (1974a) and Nelson (1977) review evidence concerning some of the factors that affect the accuracy and effects of self-observation. Reliable self-monitoring requires sustained, focused effort. Since people's attentiveness to their ongoing behavior fluctuates widely, they are not always all that self-observant. The more multifaceted the behavior, and the more concurrent events compete for attention, the greater are the inaccuracies in self-observation.

The process of self-monitoring is not simply a mechanical audit of one's performances. Preexisting self-conceptions exert selective influence on which aspects of one's ongoing behavior are given the most attention, how they are perceived, and how performance information is organized for memory representation. Mood states also affect how one's performances are self-monitored and cognitively processed. For example, when people are in a despondent mood they interpret events negatively and recall unpleasant experiences easily, whereas in a positive mood they take a more favorable view of matters and bring positive ex-

periences more easily to mind (Clark & Isen, 1982; Kuiper, MacDonald, & Derry, 1984; Teasdale, 1983). Depressive cognitive processing of experiences, in turn, exacerbates depressive mood. Self-monitoring of behavior that bears on competence and self-esteem is especially likely to activate affective reactions that can distort self-perceptions at the time the behavior is occurring and later recollections of it. We shall return to the issue of perceptual and memorial distortion of performance information in analysis of dysfunctions of the self-regulatory system.

Self-Monitoring and Self-Reactive Influence

Self-observation serves at least two important functions in the process of self-regulation: It provides the information necessary for setting realistic performance standards and for evaluating ongoing changes in behavior. But there are additional dynamic ways in which paying close attention to one's thought patterns and actions can contribute to self-directed change.

Self-Diagnostic Device

Habitual patterns of behavior become so routinized that people often act without much awareness of what they are doing. If they observe their behavior and the circumstances under which it occurs, they begin to notice recurrent patterns. By analyzing regularities in the co-variation between situations and their thoughts and actions, people can identify the psychologically significant features of their social environment that serve as instigators for them. For those who know how to alter their behavior, the self-insights so gained can set in motion a process of corrective change.

Efforts to unravel the causes of behavior traditionally rely upon incomplete and hazy reconstructions of past events. Systematic self-observation provides a self-diagnostic device for gaining a better sense of what conditions lead one to behave in certain ways. Diagnostic self-monitoring need not be confined simply to observing natural occurrences. Significant determinants can be identified more effectively through personal experimentation (Neuringer, 1981). By systematically varying things in their daily lives and recording the accompanying personal changes, people can discover how those factors influence their psychological functioning and sense of well-being. In Neuringer's view, a science of self can be partly based on systematic self-study.

Self-Motivating Device

When people attend closely to their performances, they are inclined to set themselves goals of progressive improvement, even though they have not been encouraged to do so. Goal setting enlists evaluative self-reactions that mobilize efforts toward goal attainment. Numerous studies which differ considerably in their choice of subjects, behavior patterns, and self-monitoring procedures have addressed the issue of whether self-observation changes the behavior being observed. The findings are quite variable. Self-observation sometimes increases the behavior being noted, sometimes reduces it, and oftentimes has no effect.

One can bring some order to this heterogeneity by considering the intervening mechanism of self-directedness. Studies in which self influences have been measured antecedently show that knowledge of how one is doing alters one's subsequent behavior to the extent that it activates self-reactive influences in the form of self-set goals and self-evaluative reactions (Bandura & Cervone, 1984). The types of goals people set for themselves and the strength of their commitment to them are, in turn, determined by people's perceptions of their capabilities (Bandura & Cervone, 1986; Locke, Frederick, Lee, & Bobko, 1984). A number of factors, some relating to the persons, others to the behavior, and still others to the nature and type of self-monitoring can affect the likelihood that observing how one behaves will enlist self-reactive influence.

Temporal Proximity. One such factor is how close in time the self-monitoring is to the changeworthy behavior. Self-directed change is more readily achieved by bringing consequences to bear on present behavior than on its remote effects. Immediate self-observation provides continuing information and thus the best opportunity for self-evaluation to influence the behavior while it is still in progress. When attention focuses on the more distal effects of actions, people may feel pleased or disappointed with their efforts, but such evaluative reactions cannot alter past behavior. Thus, for example, obese individuals are more successful in regulating their weight by monitoring their daily caloric intake than by periodically weighing the pounds that excessive calories have added (Romanczyk, 1974; Romanczyk, Tracey, Wilson, & Thorpe, 1973). Intermittent self-monitoring, because it is only partially informative, also produces less effective self-regulation than continuous attention to one's own performance (Mahoney, Moore, Wade, & Moura, 1973).

Informativeness of Feedback. A second factor is the informativeness of performance feedback. Evaluative self-reactions cannot be much aroused if one does not have a clear idea of how one is doing. Self-observation enhances performance when there is clear evidence of progress, but it has little effect when signs of progress are somewhat vague (Agras, Leitenberg, & Barlow, 1968; Leitenberg, Agras, Thompson, & Wright, 1968). When the behavior is not especially striking or occurs often, even close attentiveness to it is not too informative unless the instances are noted (Kazdin, 1974b).

Motivational Level. Motivational level is still another factor mediating the effects of self-observation. People who desire to change the behavior they are monitoring are the most prone to set goals for themselves and to react self-evaluatively to the progress they are making. Low motivation is accompanied by unreactive self-observation. Self-monitoring is thus more likely to improve behavior in motivated than in unmotivated individuals (Komaki & Dore-Boyce, 1978; Nelson, 1977).

Valence. Valence of the behavior will affect the type and strength of evaluative self-reactions that self-observation is apt to elicit. Behavioral attainments in valued domains produce self-satisfactions and raise aspirations that can augment change; devalued behaviors are apt to be reduced by activating self-displeasure; and neutral behaviors are likely to undergo little alteration because they do not arouse much in the way of self-reactions (Kanfer, 1970). Studies have been conducted in which the same behavior is arbitrarily assigned a positive, a negative, or a neutral value, and then individuals monitor their performance of it. For activities that are easily modifiable, self-monitoring does, in fact, produce the expected differential patterns of change. Valued behavior increases, devalued behavior decreases, and neutral behavior does not change (Kazdin, 1974b; Sieck & McFall,

1976). Self-observation has similar differential effects when the valence of the behavior has already been established through natural experience rather than being arbitrarily assigned by others (Cavior & Marabotto, 1976).

Focus on Successes or Failures. Behavior and perceived self-efficacy are altered more effectively by rewarding improvement than by punishing deficiencies. To the extent that attending to one's accomplishments is encouraging and observing repeated failures is discouraging, the degree of change accompanying self-monitoring will partly depend on whether successes or failures are being observed. Such differential effects have, indeed, been reported. Self-monitoring successes increases desired behavior, whereas observing failures causes little change or lowers performance accomplishments (Gottman & McFall, 1972; Kirschenbaum & Karoly, 1977). Self-monitoring shortcomings is accompanied by self-devaluation of one's attainments, diminished self-reward, and anxiety, all of which tend to undermine performance.

Amenability to Control. Behavior varies greatly in its amenability to voluntary control. Rate of speaking and pulse rate, for example, can be made equally observable, but it is much easier to quicken one's speech than one's heart beats. Self-monitoring alone can produce lasting changes in activities that are relatively easy to modify by deliberate effort (Johnson & White, 1971; Richards, 1975). But self-observation has, at best, only transient effects on behavior that is highly resistant to change. Optimal goals, powerful self incentives, and other self-regulatory aids must be brought to bear on refractory behavior if self-directed efforts are to succeed.

It is evident from the foregoing discussion that self-observation is not simply a mechanical tracking and registry process. It often enlists self-reactive influences. Consequently, self-monitoring is not easily separable from other constituent processes of self-regulation. Some of the behavioral effects of self-monitoring are undoubtedly mediated through self-evaluation. This is not to say that any informal goal setting which might be prompted by self-observation necessarily produces optimal goals. If they are set too high, are too vague, or are too remote, immediate performances prove too disappointing to sustain high effort for long. Perhaps, for this reason, the behavioral effects of self-observation tend to be relatively weak and are not always consistent. Information on the type of covert goals, if any, activated by attending to one's behavior is, therefore, central to predicting the effects self-monitoring will have.

JUDGMENTAL SUBFUNCTION

Observing how one is behaving is the first step toward doing something to affect it, but, in itself, such information provides little basis for self-directed reactions. Actions give rise to self-reactions through a judgmental function that includes several subsidiary processes. Whether a given performance will be regarded favorably or negatively depends upon the personal standards against which it is evaluated.

Development of Internal Standards

Self-directedness requires internal standards for judging and guiding one's actions. Such standards are developed from information conveyed by different modes of social influence. They can be established by direct tuition, by evaluative social reactions to one's behavior, and by exposure to the self-evaluative standards modeled by others.

Precept and Evaluative Follow-Through

People form standards for judging their own behavior partly on the basis of how significant persons in their lives have reacted to it. Sociological perspectives on the self have tended to emphasize this particular mode of acquisition (Cooley, 1902; McCall, 1977). Parents and others subscribe to certain standards for judging what is worthy and good. They are generally pleased when children meet or exceed valued standards and disappointed when their performances fall short of them. As a result of such differential reactions, children eventually come to respond to their own behavior in self-approving and self-critical ways, depending on how it compares to the evaluative standards set by others. This process is by no means confined to children. Adults also partly draw on the evaluative reactions of others whose views they value in forming standards for judging their own behavior (Kanfer & Marston, 1963).

Standards can be acquired through direct teaching, as well as through the evaluative reactions of others toward one's actions (Liebert & Ora, 1968; Rosenhan, Frederick, & Burrowes, 1968). In this form of transmission, standards are drawn from the tutelage of persons in one's social environment or those prescribed in the writings of influential figures. As in other forms of influence, direct tuition is most effective in fostering development of standards when it is based on shared values and is supported by feedback from one another. If there is little consistency in the standards being advocated, people experience uncertainty about what values to adopt for themselves. The dilemmas created by diversity are not necessarily undesirable, especially in activities that are not vital to the general well-being of society. Diversity permits people greater leeway to construct their own standards of behavior. Societies differ in the extent to which they favor collective or individualistic standards. Most try to strike the best balance between the two, promoting a unifying set of standards in domains essential for societal functiong while, at the same time, allowing individuals latitude to develop their own personal standards in the other areas of their lives.

Advocating certain standards of behavior, even if they are widely shared, does not ensure their adoption. Thus, if parents preach altruism but pay no attention to how their children treat others, the precepts soon lose their force. Effective tuition requires some social validation through behavioral consequences. Violation of valued standards brings negative reactions for those around one, whereas behaving in accordance with standards is positively received. Even occasional feedback, if consistent, can increase the effectiveness of direct tuition (Bandua, 1976a). When efforts are made to ensure that children abide by the standards being taught, they are much more likely to adopt and act upon them on their own (Drabman, Spitalnik, & O'Leary, 1973). In many instances, however, instruction is ineffective for transmitting performance standards because it is accompanied by inconsistent or inadequate follow-through.

Acquisition of Standards through Modeling

People not only prescribe self-evaluative standards for others, but also exemplify them in responding to their own behavior. There are substantial cultural and individual differences in what people consider praiseworthy and in the types of self-reactions they exhibit in their own life. Some follow stringent standards of conduct and reward themselves sparingly. Others are quite self-satisfied with ordinary or even mediocre performances.

The influence of models in transmitting evaluative standards has received substantial attention. In experimental analyses of this process, children observe models performing a task in which the models adhere to either high or low performance standards for self-reward. The findings show that children tend to adopt evaluative standards modeled by others, they judge their own performance relative to those standards, and they reward themselves accordingly (Bandura & Kupers, 1964). Children exposed to models who set high standards reward themselves only when they achieve superior performances, whereas children exposed to models favoring low self-

standards reward themselves for minimal performances. As a result of adopting different standards, the same performance attainment makes one child very pleased but leaves another one dissatisfied.

Adult standards are affected by modeling influences in the same way as those of children (Marston, 1965). Adoption of modeled standards by adults is especially evident when people have had little personal experience in a particular domain of activity (Rakestraw & Weiss, 1981). They use the adopted standard to regulate their effort and to judge the adequacy of their performances. Self-evaluation is affected by modeled standards, regardless of prior experience with the activity.

Further evidence for the power of example in transmitting evaluative standards is reported by Thelen and Fryrear (1971a, 1971b) in studies in which modeling of stringent standards was pitted against information about how well others have performed the task. Children who had observed models who did not reward themselves unless they did better than the normative level later judged their own performances worthy of self-reward only when they surpassed the norms. Modeling influences can leave lasting effects on personal standards, even though the activity has never been performed in the interim (Thelen, Fryrear, & Rennie, 1971).

When observers have only the modeled self-evaluative actions to go on, they have to infer the underlying standard from how models react to their own behavior in different situations. If changes in circumstances produce variations in modeled self-reactions, the underlying standard is more difficult to discern. In everyday life, of course, models not only react self-evaluatively but also often voice the standards they are using to judge the adequateness or goodness of their behavior. The impact of modeling influences is increased when standards are expressed in word as well as in action (Liebert, Hanratty, & Hill, 1969).

Different people may model different

standards. Divergent modeling adds further to the complexity of the process of social transmission. Many selective factors operate in determining which self-evaluative standards will be adopted from the profusion of modeling influences. The adoption of high standards is of particular social and theoretical interest. This is because competencies are cultivated through the pursuit of excellence—but so are human miseries when people judge themselves by lofty standards they cannot fulfill. It does not ask much of a theory to account for why people would opt for lenient standards that demand little of them. It is self-stringency that presents the explanatory challenge. Exacting standards require considerable investment of time and effort in activities. If the standards are excessively high, most performances not only prove disappointing, but many beget self-criticism. Reluctance to emulate exacting standards is, therefore, understandable. Nevertheless, it is not uncommon for people to subscribe to high standards. Indeed, universities, concert halls, athletic fields, and the various professions are heavily populated with members who are self-satisfied only with superior performances in the tasks they undertake. That is how they achieve extraordinary feats.

Competence Discrepancies and Modeling of Standards.

People differ widely in ability. They must, therefore, select from among many modeled alternatives the standards that will serve as a gauge against which to evaluate their own behavior. This is a matter of some import, because self-motivation and self-satisfaction depend to a large extent on the level of one's personal standards. Much research has been conducted on how people evaluate their ability through comparison with the performances of others (Suls & Miller, 1977). People who are of comparable or slightly higher ability provide the most informative social comparison. But adoption of standards involves more complicated factors than does ability evaluation. People of equal ability do not necessarily subscribe to the same per-

formance standards. When evaluating ability, there is little incentive to seek comparisons with those having low competence because their performances convey little useful information about one's own capabilities. However, people are not averse to adopting low performance standards since they create more lenient self-demands and lesser self-dissatisfaction.

In the absence of social inducements for emulating excellence, people ordinarily favor performance standards that are not too taxing for their ability over standards that can be matched only through great effort. Children readily adopt standards displayed by either less able models, who are satisfied with mediocre performances, or moderately competent models whose standards are within the children's reach (Bandura & Whalen, 1966). However, children reject the lofty standards of adept models and, instead, set their own requirement within their range of capabilities.

High standards are widely emulated, despite some of their vexing effects, because they are actively cultivated through a vast system of social supports. People are praised, admired, and honored for adhering to exemplary standards and criticized for being self-satisfied with mediocre or faulty performances. Vicarious influences supplement direct sanctions as another source of social support for standard setting behavior. Observing others being recognized and rewarded publicly for seeking excellence fosters emulative behavior.

Social environments contain numerous modeling influences, which may be either compatible or conflicting. As will be shown later, social transmission of standards is facilitated by consistency in modeling. The effects of multiple modeling on social learning are most often discussed in the context of conflicting influences between adults and peers. There are several factors that might predispose children toward peer standards when these conflicts arise. Similarity in competence makes the peers more appropriate reference models for the children

(Davidson & Smith, 1982). Because adult aspirations may be relatively high, were children to adopt them, they would judge their lesser accomplishments as substandard and thus experience many self-disappointments.

The potential conflict between adult and peer modeling is usually reduced, if not obviated, by selective peer association. Parents impart the values and standards of conduct that influence their children's associational preferences. As a result, children tend to choose peer associates whose behavioral norms are compatible with and reinforce familial standards (Bandura & Walters, 1959; Elkin & Westley, 1955). Parents who do not themselves model but value self-development promote such aspirations in children by encouraging them to associate with peers who are achievement oriented (Ellis & Lane, 1963; Krauss, 1964).

Social conditions that foster emulation of standards usually occur in combination with each other, rather than alone. Adoption of high standards is markedly affected when other influential factors are systematically varied (Bandura, Grusec, & Menlove, 1967a). Thus, children who are exposed only to adult models adhering to a stringent performance standard are much less inclined to self-reward low attainments than if they are exposed to conflicting standards— high ones exemplified by adults and low ones by peers. Children are also more likely to impose high standards on themselves when they see adult models praised for adherence to high standards. In addition, the children who experience an indulgent relationship with adult models tend to be more lenient with themselves.

Analysis of various combinations of determinants reveals that the tendency for peer modeling to reduce the impact of adult modeling is counteracted by social recognition of adherence to high standards. The most stringent pattern of self-reward is displayed by children when all three conditions prevail. Children observe social recognition bestowed upon adult models for holding to high standards, they are not exposed to conflicting peer norms, and the adult models are disinclined to behave indulgently toward the children. Under these social conditions, children rarely considered performances below the adults' standards worthy of self-reward, even though they seldom attained or surpassed that level. The adoption of, and continued adherence to, unrealistically high standards is especially striking, considering that the children were alone and at liberty to reward themselves whenever they wished, without anyone there to judge their actions. By contrast, children disregarded stringent standards when they were modeled in the context of adult indulgence, peer self-leniency, and were not socially recognized.

Discrepancies in Modeling Influences.
The process of learning performance standards is complicated by inconsistencies in the standards exemplified by different people and by the same person on separate occasions. Divergent modeling itself, however, does not create problems in observational learning. As previously noted, the behavior of some models may be considered so unsuitable, objectionable, or unrewarding that they are disregarded as sources of standards, even though they may be very much in evidence. Selectivity amidst diversity reduces the actual range of models that exert significant influence.

Effective psychological functioning requires both generalization and appropriate discrimination in the activation of self-evaluative standards, depending on the nature of the activities and the conditions under which they are performed. To hold to the same standards without considering the circumstances requires rigid imperatives. As long as variations in the evaluative standards modeled by others are predictable and the reason for the discrepancies is understood, what appears to be capriciousness is, in fact, a consistent pattern of self influence. Observers can learn standards of conduct by selective modeling, as well as where and when to apply them appropriately. Inconsistent standards are most likely to generate conflict when people know what is expected, but they see others differ in how much they adhere to the standards. Discrepancies in modeling under such conditions reduce adoption of standards (Allen & Liebert, 1969; Hildebrandt, Feldman, & Ditrichs, 1973; McMains & Liebert, 1968).

Contradictions between Example and Tuition.

Although standards can be conveyed by either example or tuition alone, these two modes of influence usually operate jointly. People do not always practice what they preach. In families, for instance, some parents lead austere lives but are lenient in what they ask of their children. Others are self-indulgent while expecting their children to adhere to exacting standards of achievement requiring long hours of work and sacrifice. Contradictions between what is taught and what is modeled arise repeatedly in other settings as well.

Transmission of standards has been studied by having adults prescribe either high or low standards for children while requiring either much or little of themselves for self-reward (Hildebrandt et al., 1973; McMains & Liebert, 1968; Rosenhan et al., 1968). Children tend to adopt stringent standards and to reward themselves sparingly when high standards are consistently prescribed and modeled. When adults both practice and teach leniency, children are quite self-satisfied with mediocre performances.

Discrepant practices may take different forms. In the hypocritical practices, models impose exacting standards on others but lenient ones on themselves. In the magnanimous forms, they set higher standards for themselves than for others. Any contradiction between edict and exemplification will reduce the likelihood that high standards will be adopted. Of the two types of inconsistencies, hypocrisy has the stronger negating effects. Leniency fosters lesser standards, whereas hypocrisy encourages children to abandon performance standards and to reward themselves on the basis of expediency.

Hypocritical inconsistencies undermine adoption of performance standards by arousing resentment and opposition in those upon whom the heavier demands are imposed. Such contradictions also provide self-exonerating justifications for violating precepts. If models do not abide by what they preach, why should others do so? However, factors which lend justification to inequitable standards can reduce oppositional reactions. Competence is one such factor. It is excusable for models of limited ability or means to expect higher performances of others. But it is incensing for competent models to practice self-leniency while advocating stringency for others. As a consequence, hypocritical practices lower models' attractiveness and increase rejection of the standards they propagate (Ormiston, 1972).

Modeling Facilitators.

The power of modeling is enhanced by model characteristics signifying personal efficacy, which holds true in the transmission of high performance standards as well. Exemplified standards carry more force when models possess status (Akamatsu & Farudi, 1978) and social power (Grusec, 1971; Mischel & Liebert, 1967). Observer characteristics also contribute to the modeling process. Children who prefer personal control are more inclined to adopt high modeled standards than those who see their behavior as externally regulated (Soule & Firestone, 1975). When exposed to conflicting standards, children who value achievement tend to reject lenient performance standards and opt for challenging ones (Stouwie, Hetherington, & Parke, 1970).

Generalization of Performance Standards

Development of performance standards would be of limited value if they never generalized beyond the specific activity for which they had been established. Indeed, a principal goal of social development is to foster generalizable standards that could serve to guide the self-regulation of behavior in a variety of activities, including new ones that occur in the future.

Generic standards are best established by

varying the types of activities that are performed but prescribing a similar performance standard for self-evaluation (Bandura & Mahoney, 1974). The common standard is thus separated from the specific activities in the same way that rules are extracted from particular exemplars that may otherwise differ in content. The development of achievement standards typifies this process. Adults who subscribe to high standards expect children to excel in whatever academic subjects they are pursuing. After children adopt a general standard of excellence as the measure of adequacy, they tend to apply it on future occasions to their performance in new academic activities.

The generalizability of learned skills enables people to adapt to many new situations. As a result, what is learned in a specific activity tends to be applied to other situations as well unless, of course, it is disadvantageous to do so. There is some evidence that performance standards are, to some extent, generalizable, even when they have been acquired on a single task. Children who adopt, through modeling, high standards tend to apply similar standards on later occasions, even with different activities in dissimilar settings (Lepper, Sagotsky, & Mailer, 1975; Sagotsky & Lepper, 1982).

As is evident from the preceding discussion, people do not passively absorb standards of behavior from whatever influences happen to impinge upon them. Rather, they extract generic standards from the numerous evaluations that are prescribed, modeled, and taught by different individuals, or by even the same person at different activities and in different settings. People must, therefore, process the conflicting information to form general standards against which to judge their own behavior. The standards provide the basis for the mechanism of self-directedness.

Successive Transmission of Standards

Cultural standards of behavior are transmitted from generation to generation partly through a succession of social and symbolic models. The process of successive transmission is well illustrated in an early study conducted by Jacobs and Campbell (1961). In this experiment a group of people adopted an arbitrary norm for judging environmental events. The original models were then removed one by one from the group, and new members were gradually introduced. These new members became unwitting transmitters of the arbitrary norm to still new entrants. Although some deviation from the original standard occurred with successive groups, new members perpetuated remnants of it for four or five generations after the total replacement of the original models.

The manner in which self-evaluative standards may be passed on through a succession of models has been demonstrated by Mischel and Liebert (1966). Children who had adopted high adult standards later modeled and applied the same standards to peers. Marston (1965) has likewise shown that observing models reward their performance either generously or sparingly affects not only how liberally adult observers rewarded their own behavior but also how generously they reward others.

The laboratory findings corroborate field studies, which provide data on the cultural modeling of standards, although more than simply modeling is involved in the cultural adoption process (Hughes, Tremblay, Rapoport, & Leighton, 1960). In those homogeneous communities where the ethic of self-betterment predominates, people adhere to high self-demands and take pride and pleasure in their accomplishments. By contrast, in neighboring communities, where patterns of self-gratification prevail, people reward themselves generously without much regard to how they behave.

Familial and Social Transmission Models. Psychological theories have traditionally assumed that behavioral standards are transmitted through parent-child relationships. In a provocative paper, Reiss (1965) contrasts theories based on the familial transmission model with those emphasizing institutionally organized systems, and he offers several reasons why the familial model cannot adequately explain the socialization process. Assuming, at least, a 20-year difference between generations, a long time intervenes between parents' imparting values and standards to their children and those values being passed on to succeeding descendants. This would produce an exceedingly slow rate of social change, whereas, in fact, extensive society-wide shifts in normative behavior often occur within a single generation. Reiss, therefore, argues that the parent-child relationship cannot be the major agency of cultural transmission. Rather, standards of behavior are primarily disseminated by institutionally organized systems (e.g., educational, religious, political, and legal agencies) and regulated by collectively enforced sanctions. Innovation, in Reiss's view, originates at the social level, whereas changes emerging within the family are of lesser social consequence. Thus, for example, racial segregation in public accommodations and infringement of voting rights were changed more rapidly by invoking Supreme Court decisions than by waiting for prejudiced parents to inculcate in their children acceptant attitudes which they would display toward minority groups when they became restaurateurs and motel operators thirty or forty years later.

Consistent with Reiss's main thesis, social cognitive theory assumes that values and standards arise from diverse sources of influence and are prompted by institutional backing. Because social agencies possess considerable power to reward and punish, collectively enforced sanctions can produce rapid and widespread changes in behavior. However, a social systems' theory is insufficient by itself to explain why there is so much variation in standards, even in relatively homogeneous subgroups. Differences arise because parents, teachers, and others must be the ones who implement institutional prescriptions for the youth of a society. Those who, for whatever reason, do not subscribe to the institutionally sanctioned codes will undermine the broader social transmission effort. Barring strong sanctions, parents often resist adopting new values for some time.

A comprehensive theory of social transmission must also explain what produces and sustains the behavioral standards promulgated by the cultural institutions. They are products of influences wielded by members of the society. Changes in social systems are often initiated by determined advocates acting on values modeled largely from individuals who have opposed prevailing social practices (Bandura, 1973; Keniston, 1968; Rosenhan, 1970).

In discussing the limitations of personality theories of socialization, Reiss states that, in such approaches, social change can arise only when there is a breakdown in transmission between generations. This criticism is applicable to theories assuming that parental values are introjected by children *in toto* and then are later passed on unmodified to their progeny. Actually, social learning is a continuous process in which acquired standards are elaborated and modified, and new ones are adopted. Children repeatedly observe and learn the standards not only of parents but also of siblings, peers, and other adults. Moreover, the extensive symbolic modeling provided in the mass media serves as a prominent extra-familial source of influence. Hence, children's values and standards are likely to reflect amalgams of these diverse sources, rather than simply the unaltered familial heritage. Even if standards of conduct arose solely from familial sources, significant changes could emerge across generations through familial transmission because the standards children develop are composites from different admixtures of parental and sibling values at each generation. The composites differ from the individual sources (Bandura, Ross, & Ross, 1963c). Although some of the criticisms levied by Reiss against the familial transmission model are debatable, his contention that social institutions play a heavier role in perpetuating and changing values than familial influences is well taken.

Social Referential Comparisons

For most activities there are no absolute measures of adequacy. The time in which a given distance is run or a given score is obtained on achievement tasks provides insufficient information for self-appraisal, even when measured against an internal standard. Thus, a student who achieves a score of 115 points on an examination, and whose aspiration is to be in the upper 10 percent of a certain group, would have no basis for meaningful self-appraisal without knowing how others have performed. When adequacy is defined rationally, appraisals of one's own behavior require comparisons among three major information sources: performance level, internal standards, and the performances of others.

Normative Comparison. The referential comparisons with others may take different forms for different tasks. For some regular activities, standard norms based on representative groups are used to determine one's relative standing. Normative attainments, expressed in terms of percentiles or departures from the mean, are provided for different age groups, educational levels, sexes, and geographical locales. The value of such norms for self-appraisal depends on the representativeness of the sample on which they are based and on their appropriateness as a standard of comparison in any given case. If the normative group is atypical of those for whom it is intended, the norms are misleading. If individuals compare themselves against inappropriate norms, they will misjudge their attainments.

Social Comparison. More often people compare themselves to particular associates in similar situations. This may involve certain classmates, work associates, or people in other settings engaged in similar endeavors.

Performance judgments will therefore vary substantially depending upon the level of ability of those chosen for social comparison. Positive self-appraisal is enhanced by comparison to the lesser attainments of others and diminished by using the accomplishments of the more talented as the relative standard of adequacy (Karoly & Decker, 1979; Simon, 1979b). Surpassing those known to be of lesser ability has dubious merit. For this reason, people ordinarily choose to compare themselves with those whom they regard as similar or slightly higher in ability. Faring well in the latter types of social comparisons is most likely to give rise to favorable self-appraisals. Such comparison choices have value because they provide realistic challenges, ensure some degree of success, and create motivational incentives for improvement of abilities.

Comparison choices sometimes reflect defensive overevaluation at one extreme or gross self-devaluation at the other. In the former pattern, individuals boost their self-appraisals by selecting social referents whom they can easily surpass, while downgrading the accomplishments of the more talented who threaten their precarious self-evaluations. In the contrasting devaluative pattern, individuals continually make unfavorable self-appraisals by pitting themselves against the extraordinary attainments of the most talented. We shall return to these problems when we consider dysfunctional self-evaluation systems.

Self-Comparison. One's previous behavior is continuously used as a reference against which ongoing performance is judged. In this referential process, self-comparison supplies the measure of adequacy. Past attainments affect self-appraisal mainly through their effects on standard setting. Evidence from research on level of aspiration shows that people try to surpass their past accomplishments (Festinger, 1942; Lewin, Dembo, Festinger, & Sears, 1944). After a given level of performance has been attained, it is no longer challenging, and people seek new self-satisfactions by means of progressive improvement. Hence, people tend to raise their performance standards after success and to lower them to more realistic levels after repeated failure. However, the use of simple tasks that call for little effort limits the generality of the results. This is because, in everyday life, most performance accomplishments require arduous effort over an extended period. People do not necessarily expect to surpass each past accomplishment in an ever-rising series of triumphs. Having surpassed a demanding standard through laborious effort does not automatically lead people to raise their aspiration (Bandura & Cervone, 1986). Those who have a high sense of self-efficacy set themselves more challenging goals to accomplish. But some are left with self-doubts that they can muster the same level of laborious effort again, and they set their sights on trying to match the standard they had previously pursued. Having driven themselves to success, others judge themselves inefficacious to repeat a demanding feat and lower their aspirations.

People who are prone to psychological distress often exhibit quite unrealistic standard setting. Many of them continue to adhere to lofty performance standards well beyond their reach, even though they repeatedly fail in their efforts (Sears, 1940). Compared to nondepressed persons, the depressed set higher performance standards for themselves in the face of declining improvements, but lower their goals in response to increasing improvements (Simon, 1979b).

There is a widely shared view that social learning practices should be structured so that people come to judge themselves in reference to their own capabilities and standards, rather than by comparing themselves against others. Self-comparison provides the benefits of personal challenge and success experiences for self-development without the cost of invidious social comparison. However, in competitive, individualistic societies, where one person's success is an-

other person's failure, social comparison inevitably enters into self-appraisal.

Continued progress in a valued activity does not necessarily ensure perpetual self-fulfillment. The strides at which activities are mastered can drastically alter self-evaluative reactions (Simon, 1979b). Successes that surpass earlier ones bring a continued sense of self-satisfaction. But people derive little satisfaction from small improvements, or even devalue them, after having made larger strides. Early successes that reflect large gains in proficiency can thus be conducive to later self-dissatisfaction even in the face of continuing self-improvement. In short, self-discontent can be created by self-comparison just as it can by social-comparison.

Collective Comparison. The referential performances against which one partly judges one's own behavior take other forms in societies organized around collectivist principles. In these social systems it is group performance rather than individual accomplishment that is evaluated and publicly acclaimed (Bronfenbrenner, 1970). Comparison processes still operate under collective arrangements, but self-appraisal is primarily based on one's relative contribution to the group accomplishment and how well it measures up to the standard adopted by the group. Collective achievement is spurred by creating competition between groups.

Valuation of Activities

Another important factor in the judgmental component of self-regulation concerns the valuation of activities. People do not care much how they do in activities that have little or no significance for them, and they expend little effort on devalued activities. It is mainly in areas affecting one's welfare and self-esteem that performance appraisals activate self-reactions.

Simon (1979a) studied variations is self-evaluative reactions to performance attainments on tasks differing in their relevance to personal merit. People are more self-approving for high attainments and more self-critical for low performances on a task they believe taps intellectual creativity than if they believe it taps nonintellectual skills. Thus, the more relevant performances are to one's sense of personal adequacy, the more likely self-evaluative reactions are to be elicited in that activity.

After people have repeatedly engaged in an activity that they initially regarded with indifference and have received feedback on how well they did, they begin to respond self-evaluatively to their performances (Simon, 1979a). Indeed, in everyday life people imbue remarkably varied activities, many seemingly trivial in character, with high evaluative significance, as when they invest their self-esteem in how far they can throw a shot-put ball.

The preceding research illustrates how self-evaluative reactions can be engaged for an otherwise neutral activity simply by construing it in personally significant ways. Self-regulatory processes can be similarly disengaged, or even reversed, by cognitive restructuring of the behavior. Ordinarily, destructive conduct is personally controlled by anticipatory self-censure, but reprehensible behavior can be made honorable by portraying it in the service of beneficial or moral ends. Such cognitive restructuring not only eliminates self-generated deterrents but engages self-reward in the service of destructive behavior (Bandura, 1979; Kelman, 1973; Sanford & Comstock, 1971).

Performance Attribution

Self-reactions also vary depending on how people perceive the determinants of their behavior. There exists substantial research on causal attributions for success and failure on achievement tasks (Frieze, 1976; Lefcourt, 1976; Weiner, 1979). However, the self-evaluative reactions aroused by different causal judgments of performance have received relatively little attention. People are most likely to take pride in their ac-

complishments when they ascribe their successes to their own abilities and efforts. They do not derive much self-satisfaction, however, when they view their performances as largely dependent on external factors. Thus, children who take credit for their achievements reward themselves more generously for success and deprive themselves more for failure than children who view their performances as externally determined (Cook, 1970).

Self-reactions to faulty and blameworthy conduct similarly depend on causal judgments. People respond self-critically to faulty performances for which they hold themselves responsible but not to those they perceive as due to unusual circumstances, to insufficient capabilities, or to unrealistic demands (Weiner, Russell, & Lerman, 1978). In the latter instances, external conditions are considered to be at fault. Finding situational causes to reduce self-censure is used most extensively when people judge behavior on their part that is socially injurious. Evidence will be reviewed later on how people dissociate self-evaluative consequences from their reprehensible conduct through social arrangements that obscure personal responsibility for their actions and lay blame on circumstances or on the victims.

A number of factors influence judgments about the causes of actions. As alluded to above, some of these concern the external circumstances under which the activities have been carried out. The greater the situational pressures and the external aids and supports, the less likely performances are to be credited to oneself (Bem, 1972). Similarly, deficient performances that have been ascribed to transitory internal conditions, such as debilitating moods, fatigue, or maladies (Frieze, 1976), are unlikely to activate evaluative self-reactions. In addition to situational and personal factors, prior social learning experiences can create judgmental biases toward how the determinants of different kinds of behavior are viewed.

Attributional predilections have been examined most extensively in sex differences in self-appraisal of achievement behavior.

Although findings vary across tasks and age levels, the evidence generally shows that girls are more prone than boys to attribute their successes to external causes and to ascribe their failures to themselves in stereotypically male activities (Parsons, Ruble, Hodges, & Small, 1976). These differences in causal attribution may stem from a combination of developmental influences, each of which can foster the underestimation of personal capabilities. The first concerns the pervasive cultural modeling of sex-role stereotypes, which casts women into predominantly nonachieving roles. To the extent that girls adopt the stereotype conception, they will harbor self-doubts about their own proficiency on achievement tasks. Peers also operate as important influences in this regard. Even by the early preschool years, children already subscribe to the stereotype of different intellectual capabilities for boys and girls (Crandall, 1978). By behaving in ways that are more conducive to intellectual success for boys than for girls, peers help to create validation for the conventional stereotypes.

Self-appraisals are influenced by the evaluative reactions of other significant people. There is some evidence that parents and teachers have different achievement expectations, and they vary their attributional explanations for successes and failures, depending on the sex of the child. They tend to expect less of girls academically, to center criticism on the intellectual aspects of their academic work, and to judge their failures as reflecting ability rather than motivational problems (Dweck, Davidson, Nelson, & Enna, 1978; Dweck & Goetz, 1978; Parsons et al., 1976). Girls, whose sense of competence has been undermined by such experiences, would be less inclined to credit their achievements to their own capabilities.

Developmental experiences that can affect causal judgments vary as a function of sex, socioeconomic level, and ethnic status, but no two people are treated alike. Variations in configurations of social learning experiences across individuals will produce different judgmental orientations in causal judgments of behavior.

SELF-REACTIVE INFLUENCES

Development of evaluative standards and judgmental skills establishes the capability for self-reactive influence. This is achieved by creating incentives for one's own actions and by responding evaluatively to one's own behavior, depending on how it measures up to an internal standard. Thus, people pursue courses of action that produce positive self-reactions and refrain from behaving in ways that result in self-censure. The self-motivating incentives may be either tangible outcomes or self-evaluative reactions.

In the social cognitive view, self incentives affect behavior mainly through their motivational function (Bandura, 1977a). When people make self-satisfaction or tangible gratifications conditional upon certain accomplishments, they motivate themselves to expend the effort needed to attain the requisite performance. Both the anticipated satisfactions of desired accomplishments and the dissatisfactions with insufficient ones provide incentives for actions that increase the likelihood of performance attainments.

In many areas of social and moral behavior the personal standards that serve as a basis for regulating one's conduct are relatively stable. That is, people do not change from week to week in what they regard as right or wrong or as good or bad. However, in areas of functioning involving achievement behavior and the cultivation of competencies, the personal standard that is selected as the mark of adequacy progressively rises as skills are developed and challenges are met (Bandura & Cervone, 1986).

Standards do more than simply provide a criterion of adequacy for maintaining a given level of behavior. As noted above, they also represent aspirations that affect self-motivation when they are cast in the form of goals. Later we shall have occasion to examine in some detail the properties of goals that are most likely to activate the self-evaluative mechanism governing self-motivation.

Tangible Self-Motivators

People get themselves to do things they would otherwise put off or avoid altogether by making tangible incentives dependent upon performance attainments. By making free time, relaxing breaks, recreational activities, and other types of tangible self-reward contingent upon a certain amount of progress in an activity, they mobilize the effort necessary to get things done. The weaker the external demands for performance, the heavier is the reliance on self-regulation. This is nowhere better illustrated than in the writing habits of successful novelists. They must depend on their own self-discipline because they have no resident supervisors issuing directives and overseeing daily writing activities. As Wallace (1977) clearly documents, novelists influence how much they write by making the pursuit of other activities contingent on either completing a certain amount of writing each day or writing for a designated length of time. Most acclaimed novelists wrote regularly for a fixed number of hours a day. Once he launched upon a novel, Jack London wrote a thousand words per day, 6 days a week, whether inspired or not. Hemingway, who closely monitored his daily writing output, demanded more of himself on days preceding his fishing trips (Plimpton, 1965). As these examples illustrate, in self-directed pursuits, people have to exercise considerable personal discipline if they are to accomplish what they seek. But even in activities that are externally prompted, self-regulatory skills partly determine how effectively people can mobilize their efforts and resources to do them.

Numerous studies have been conducted in which children and adults regulate their own behavior by arranging tangible incentives for themselves. The results show that people who reward their own attainments usually accomplish more than those who perform the same activities under instruction but without self incentives, are rewarded noncontingently, or monitor their own behavior and set goals for themselves without rewarding their attainments (Ballard & Glynn, 1975; Bandura & Perloff, 1967; Bellack, 1976; Felixbrod & O'Leary, 1973; Glynn, 1970; Jeffrey, 1974; Litrownik, Franzani, & Skenderian, 1976; Mahoney, 1974b; Martin, 1979; Montgomery & Parton, 1970; Nelson & Birkimer, 1978; Speidel, 1974; Wall, 1982). One of the factors that differentiates people who succeed in regulating their behavior on their own from the unsuccessful ones is the effective use of self incentives (Perri & Richards, 1977; Rozensky & Bellack, 1974).

Self incentives are at least as effective or even better motivators than externally arranged incentives (Bandura & Perloff, 1967; Brownell, Colletti, Ersner-Hershfield, Hershfield, & Wilson, 1977; Lovitt & Curtiss, 1969; Tirrel, Mount, & Scott, 1977; Weiner & Dubanoski, 1975). However, the relative power of these two incentive systems is partly determined by predelictions for personal or external control. Persons who are self-directed do not respond well to external rewards. Rather, they use self incentives more effectively and regulate their behavior better by this means than those who rely on external incentives as guides and motivators of their actions (Bellack, 1972, 1975; Switzky & Haywood, 1974; Rozensky & Bellack, 1976). This is not to say that the externally-directed cannot benefit from self incentives. Regulatory processes are reciprocal rather than unidirectional. Repeated success in influencing one's behavior through self incentives can build a sense of self-directedness (Jeffrey, 1974).

In some studies children select the achievement levels they consider worthy of self-reward (Bandura & Perloff, 1967). The higher the goals they set for themselves, the harder they must work to gain self-satisfaction. Of particular interest is the prevalence with which children prescribe difficult goals for themselves. Although at liberty to select any goal, many children choose a standard which requires more than the minimum effort. Some select the highest achievement level as the minimal performance meriting self-reward. Still others raise their initial standard to a higher level without a corresponding increase in the amount of self-reward, thereby demanding of themselves more work for the same compensation. Many children show the same self-stringency when they have the choice of how generously to reward their attainments (Weiner & Dubanoski, 1975).

Why do people demand of themselves high levels of performance when no one requires them to do so? One possible explanation is in terms of the constraints of self-evaluation. Once achievement standards have been adopted through example and precept, self-regard becomes conditional upon valued attainments. Conflicts arise when material gains can be increased by resorting to behavior that has a low self-regard value. On the one hand, there is the temptation to maximize reward with minimum effort simply by lowering standards. On the other hand, rewarding oneself for mediocre or undeserving performances incurs self-esteem costs.

People will deny themselves material rewards over which they have had full control, rather than incur self-disapproval for unmerited self-reward. Such behavior is at variance with utility theories that explain behavior in terms of maximizing reward, unless such formulations include the self-esteem costs of rewarding oneself for devalued behavior. When activities lack personal value to activate self-evaluative reactions, or peer influences undermine adherence to performance standards, most children opt for standards that require the least amount of effort for self-reward (Felixbrod & O'Leary, 1974; Santogrossi, O'Leary, Romanczyk, & Kaufman, 1973).

Self-imposition of stringent standards is not necessarily a common phenomenon. But however often it occurs, it is self-stringency, rather than self-lenience, that challenges the explanatory power of a theory. Much more is asked of a theory to explain why people forego rewards that are under their control than why they treat themselves to them. As will be shown later, the social supports for adherence to performance standards have been examined in some detail. However, the personal supports, which do not lend themselves as readily to study, have not received the attention they deserve. People do not behave just to please the public. They also seek to please themselves, even though it may require hard work and temporary self-denial of material benefits.

Behavior is also modifiable through negative self-sanctions. However, desired changes are prompted better by self incentives for accomplishments than by self disincentives for faulty performances (Humphrey, Karoly, & Kirschenbaum, 1978; Masters & Santrock, 1976). Several factors may account for the lesser effectiveness of self-punishment. Negative self-reactions can arouse disruptive thoughts and affect that divert attention from the task and reduce interest in it. Moreover, selectively focusing on one's deficiencies can detract from any perceived efficacy derived from performance improvements gained by negative self-inducement. Evidence that the discontinuance of self incentives produces a smaller decline in performance after self-reward than after self-punishment (Humphrey et al., 1978) suggests that changes in interest and self-efficacy, rather than transiently aroused affect, are the more likely mediating factors.

Development of Self-Regulatory Skills for Self-Directedness

Evidence that people can exercise self-influence has provided the impetus for the development of self-regulatory techniques. In these programs of self-directed change, people are taught how to alter refractory behavior by monitoring their activities and marshalling environmental supports, cognitive aids, and suitable self incentives for the changes they desire (Coates & Thoresen, 1979; Kanfer, 1980; Karoly, 1977; Mahoney & Thoresen, 1974; Rosenbaum & Drabman, 1979). Self incentives provide the proximal motivators in this multifaceted approach. Results of such applications show that both children and adults can improve their knowledge and competencies with the aid of self incentives, just as well as when others provide the incentive for change. Negative self incentives have also been used with some success to reduce faulty patterns of thought and behavior of long standing (Thoresen & Mahoney, 1974).

Personal change is often difficult to achieve because it tends to be associated, at least initially, with unfavorable conditions of reinforcement. Refractory activities such as excessive drinking, overeating, and defensive behavior are powerfully maintained by their immediate rewarding effects, whereas their detrimental consequences accumulate slowly and are not experienced for some time. Efforts to control such behaviors produce immediate discomfort, while the benefits are delayed considerably. To an obese person, the delectable taste of a hot fudge sundae easily outweighs the effects of the imperceptible increase in weight it produces. To a chain smoker, the immediate distress accompanying cigarette withdrawal is an infinitely more powerful motivator for smoking than the health benefits experienced several months hence for nonsmoking. Self incentives are, therefore, used to provide immediate motivational inducements for self-controlling behavior, until the benefits that eventually accrue assume the rewarding function. As a general rule, efforts at self-directed change of refractory behavior are more successful with the aid of self-managed incentives than without them (Bellack, 1976; Mahoney, 1974b).

Much of the knowledge of self-regulation is derived from studies of problematic behavior, such as overeating, smoking, studying, and the like. Generalizations about self-regulatory capabilities can be easily distorted by selectively examining only the most refractory cases, while ignoring the vast population of people who achieve notable successes in regulating their own behavior. Consider the theory constructed to explain the refractory nature of overeating: Food is a powerful primary reinforcer that produces instant gratification; households are filled with foodstuffs that whet the appetite; people have to eat it at periodic intervals; food is advertised, displayed, and prepared in the most appetizing forms; social custom continuously forces food on people; and it is a handy tranquilizer for deprivation and distress. These powerful conditions presumably compel overeating and swamp people's efforts at self-regulation. Were one to present this theory to the proverbial Martians, they would fully expect all earthlings to be very obese. Yet, most people manage to stay reasonably slim amidst all this appetizing fare. Smoking is another case in point. Smoking is presumably intractable because it is compelled by two types of dependencies—nicotine dependence, in which each puff sends a nicotine shot to the brain, and psychological dependence, which creates a craving for cigarettes. The high relapse rates of those smokers who have sought professional help supposedly attest to the intractable nature of smoking.

Interviews with people about their smoking and weight histories reveal that a sizeable percentage cure themselves of smoking and obesity (Schachter, 1982). The milllions of people who have quit smoking on their own testify to human self-regulatory capabilities. Schachter offers several explanations for why self-cures are substantially higher than clinical cures. The most inefficacious people turn to therapists for help. Unless the treatment is very powerful, success rates are low with people who present many personal and social barriers to change. Intractable behavior rarely yields to a single attempt at self-regulation. Renewed effort following failed attempts is what is more likely to bring success. A life-course analysis reveals successes achieved after repeated tries, whereas the results of therapy represent the outcome of only one particular attempt. Repeated tries will produce a higher success rate than will any single effort. Another possibility is that successful self-regulators have developed better methods of self-influence than those provided by many therapists.

Full understanding of self-regulatory mechanisms requires examination of naturally occurring self-directed change, as well as the treatment of refractory cases. Naturalistic studies show that successful self-regulators are highly skilled in enlisting the component subfunctions of self-regulation—they track their behavior; they set proximal goals for themselves; they draw from an array of coping strategies, rather than relying on a single technique; and they arrange incentives for their efforts (Perri & Richards, 1977; Perri, Richards, & Schuetheis, 1977). Moreover, they apply multifaceted self-influence more consistently and more persistently than ineffectual self-regulators. Successes achieved through sustained self-directed effort would be expected to strengthen beliefs in one's self-regulatory capabilities. Rozensky and Bellack (1974) confirmed in laboratory tests that people who are effective in regulating their behavior on their own are better at sustaining their efforts by positive self-influence than ineffectual self-regulators, who tend to be less self-rewarding and more self-punishing for comparable performances. When the methods developed by skilled self-regulators are given to others to change their own problematic behavior, the naturally evolved ones produce better results than those used in standard practices (Heffernan & Richards, 1981).

Self-Evaluative Motivators

Most people value their self-respect and the self-satisfaction derived from a job well done more highly than they value material rewards. The self-regulation of behavior by self-evaluative reactions is a uniquely human capability. We have noted in an earlier chapter that evaluative reactions acquire significance through their correlation with aversive and pleasurable experiences. Although the manner in which self-evaluations gain their incentive value has received little study, there is every reason to believe that they, too, acquire their valence through correlation with tangible consequences. People usually gratify themselves and think pleasing trains of thoughts when they feel a sense of self-pride, whereas they treat themselves badly and cogitate distressingly when they judge themselves self-critically. As a result, negative self-evaluations come to signify aversiveness, and positive self-evaluations signify rewarding experiences. If people did not treat themselves differently following self-approving and self-critical evaluations, such expressions would have no incentive power.

Self-evaluation figures centrally in people's lives in several ways. Human behavior is extensively regulated through self-evaluation, which provides a personal guidance system for action. Ongoing behavior is continuously assessed and modified in terms of evaluative standards of adequacy. Indeed, it is difficult to imagine how people could function effectively in their daily pursuits if they never evaluated how they were doing.

Self-evaluation not only gives direction to behavior, it also creates motivators for it. Evaluative self incentives are repeatedly recruited in the service of behavior that reflects on personal competence. By making self-satisfaction conditional on performances that match a personal index of merit, people get themselves to put forth the effort necessary to accomplish what they value (Bandura & Cervone, 1983). Those who are self-satisfied only with superior performances exert greater effort for longer periods on tasks than those who are content with lesser attainments (Simon, 1979c). Researchers have also compared performance under conditions in which persons are, or are not, encouraged to respond self-evaluatively to their performances on neutral tasks, which ordinarily might not enlist personal standards. Self-evaluative reactions heighten persistence and level of achievement in both children (Masters & Santrock, 1976) and adults (Kanfer, 1977; Schneiderman, 1980). Evaluative self-reward can foster more rapid learning than material self-reward (Masters, Furman, & Barden, 1977).

In most instances, people exert influence on their own behavior by enlisting both evaluative and tangible self incentives. Thus, novelists influence how much they write by making leisure-time activities contingent on completing a certain amount of work, but they revise and improve what they write by their self-evaluative reactions to their productions.

Evaluative self-sanctions also figure prominently in the self-regulation of conduct in the domain of morality. The anticipation of self-reproach for behavior that violates one's moral standards provides a source of motivation to keep behavior in line with standards in the face of opposing inducements. Self-restraints are brought to bear on transgressive behavior that will bring self-condemnation (Bandura & Walters, 1959). Individuals who have adopted standards that make cruel or tyrannical behavior a source of personal pride are not troubled by self-censure for acts that most others disavow (Toch, 1969; Yablonsky, 1962). Lacking self-reprimands for hurtful conduct, they are deterred from such acts mainly by threats of reprisal.

As evident from the preceding discussion, self-regulation of behavior through self-reactive influence cannot be reduced to reflexive mechanics in which feedback signals are compared to a criterion, and, if incongruity exists, the organism is automatically redirected on the correct path. Human self-regulation operates in terms of adopted general guides rather than minutely prescriptive rules. The more complex the activities to be self-regulated, and the less particularized the decision rules, the more judgmental factors enter the process. The process of self-regulation requires judgment within a set of guidelines, which cannot be completely prescriptive, because

there are too many variable elements in situations. Thus, thought often overrides the effects of immediate feedback, and how events are construed even affects whether the self-reactive system will become engaged in a particular endeavor. These higher control functions are usually subsumed by an executive control system in multilevel cybernetic analogues. This issue is not whether one can formalize properties of human self-regulation represented by a cybernetic analogue with executive control functions (Carver & Scheier, 1981). Rather, it is in the variable operation of executive functions where human self-regulation differs most from the rule-following routines of the analogue system. The challenge is to explain and formalize how the higher cognitive control system operates in the self-regulation of behavior by self-evaluation.

Incomplete preprogramming has some decided benefits. A wholly automated psychocybernetic self system would produce completely predictable responsiveness but at the heavy price of rigidity. When environmental demands vary across places, persons, and times, as they typically do, what is functional under one set of circumstances becomes dysfunctional under different circumstances. Adaptive functioning, therefore, requires considerable versatility. An automaton that is self-guided by instant feedback to a fixed internal comparator would get itself into serious difficulties or even direct itself out of existence.

Phenomenological Aspects of Self-Evaluation

In addition to serving as guides and incentives for behavior, self-evaluations are of considerable interest in their own right. They affect how much satisfaction people gain from what they do. We have already seen that self-satisfaction is determined not only by one's accomplishments but also by the standards against which accomplishments are measured. Performances that leave one person happy can leave another dissatisfied because their standards differ.

High standards that cannot be fulfilled easily beget great self-disappointment.

Self-Concept. The self-concept and self-esteem, both of which are central constructs in phenomenological theories of personality (Rogers, 1959; Wylie, 1974), are characterized largely in terms of self-evaluation. In traditional assessments of self-concepts, people are presented with descriptive statements in the form of adjective check lists, Q-sorts, or inventories, and they are asked to rate which statements apply to them. The different responses are then summed to provide a global measure of the person's self-concept.

Social cognitive theory defines a negative self-conception in terms of proneness to devalue oneself and a positive self-conception as a tendency to judge oneself favorably. Competencies and evaluative standards vary for performances in different realms (e.g., social, intellectual, vocational, and athletic) and are likely to produce different self-evaluations. Individuals may, for example, regard themselves highly in their vocational speciality, moderately positively in social relationships, and negatively in athletic pursuits. A person's self-conceptions may vary even in different aspects of the same sphere of activity. With people's increasing experience, their self-conceptions become more differentiated across activities (Mullener & Laird, 1971). For this reason, measures of self-evaluation in particular areas of functioning are more meaningful than a conglomerate index.

Self-Esteem. Self-esteem is also defined and gauged largely in terms of how people evaluate themselves (Coopersmith, 1967). Those who express a sense of unworthiness are said to have low self-esteem, whereas persons who express self-pride are said to hold themselves in high esteem. Self-esteem can stem from evaluations based on competence or on possession of attributes that have been culturally invested with positive or negative value. In esteem arising from competence, people derive their sense of self-pride from fulfilling their standards of merit. Those who meet or surpass their standards feel pleased with themselves, whereas those who fail to measure up to their standards are displeased with themselves.

Others frequently voice evaluations reflecting their likes and dislikes and attitudes towards stereotyped attributes, rather than in response to evident competencies. Such social judgments can influence how the recipients evaluate themselves. Thus, children are often rejected and deprecated when they fail to live up to the ideals of others or remind others of things they dislike. The role played by personal competence and social evaluation in the development of self-esteem receives support from the studies of Coopersmith (1967). He found that children who exhibited high self-esteem had parents who were accepting, who set clear standards of behavior, and who provided their children with considerable support and latitude to acquire competencies that can serve them well in the situations they encounter.

Cultural stereotyping is another way in which social judgments affect perceptions of self-worth. People are cast into valued or devalued groups on the basis of their ethnic background, race, sex, or physical characteristics. Those who possess socially disparaged characteristics and who accept the stereotyped evaluations of others will hold themselves in low regard, despite their talents. It is the unfortunate persons combining ineptness, exacting standards, and disparaged attributes who are the most likely to harbor a pervasive sense of worthlessness.

The different sources of self-devaluation call for different corrective measures. Self-devaluation rooted in incompetence requires cultivation of skills and realistic standards of achievement. Self-devaluation resulting from belittling social evaluations requires new social experiences that affirm one's self-worth. Self-devaluation stemming from discriminatory disparagement of attributes requires modeling and rewarding a sense of pride regarding those attributes. When self-evaluation arises from multiple sources, multiform corrective measures are needed, as, for example, fostering pride in one's racial characteristics and also cultivating competencies that instill a high and resilient sense of personal efficacy.

Values. Psychological theories attribute some of the variation in behavior to differences in values. There are several ways in which values can exert influence on conduct. One mode operates through incentive preferences. People differ in the value they place on approval, money, material possessions, social status, and freedom from restrictions. Values affect behavior because prized incentives can motivate the actions required to secure them; disvalued incentives do not. The higher the incentive value people attach to certain outcomes, the more effort they will expend if they judge themselves capable of obtaining them.

Value can be invested in activities themselves, as well as in extrinsic incentives. The value is not inherent in the behavior itself but in the positive and negative self-reactions to the behavior. Evaluative self-reaction thus provides a second mechanism by which values influence conduct. The evaluative standards represent the values; the anticipatory self-pride and self-criticism for actions that correspond to, or fall short of, adopted standards serve as the regulatory influences.

Dysfunctional Self-Evaluative Systems

When analyses of self-regulation dwell mainly on performance standards, conditional self-evaluations, and motivation of effort, the process sounds like the self-infliction of encumbrances. In actuality, self-directedness provides an important and continuing source of personal satisfaction, interest, and self-esteem. Without aspirations and evaluative involvement in activities, people remain unmotivated, bored, uncertain about their capabilities, and dependent upon momentary external stimulation for their satisfactions. Life without any elements of challenge can be rather dull. However, internalization of dysfunctional standards of self-evaluation can serve as a source of chronic misery. Extreme examples readily spring to mind of individuals who drive themselves relentlessly in pursuit of unachievable goals and whose ever-rising standards negate any sense of self-fulfillment along the way.

Stringent standards breed self-created stress and despondency. All people have their ups and downs from time to time, but those who are burdened with unrealistic performance standards find it hard to gain satisfaction from what they do, because they rarely measure up. To make matters worse, such standards are often accompanied by unfavorable comparisons with the extraordinary achievements of others. As an unidentified pundit once remarked, "If you compare yourself with others, you may become vain or bitter; for always there will be greater and lesser persons than oneself." Yet social comparison is inevitable, especially in societies that place a high premium on competitiveness and individual achievement. Ironically, it is the talented who have high aspirations, which are possible but exceedingly difficult to realize, who are especially vulnerable to self-dissatisfaction despite notable achievements. Boyd (1969) gives a graphic portrayal of this phenomenon: "Each violinist in any second chair started out as a prodigy in velvet knickers who expected one day to solo exquisitely amid flowers flung by dazzled devotees. The 45-year-old violinist with spectacles on his nose and a bald spot in the middle of his hair is the most disappointed man on earth." Linus, the security-blanketed member of the Peanuts clan, also alluded to this phenomenon when he observed: "There is no heavier burden than a great potential."

When people's own behavior is a source of self-inflicted distress, they seek relief through behavior designed to avert or lessen the discomfort. Dysfunctional self systems thus generate personally aversive conditions conducive to deviant behavior. Some people whose accomplishments bring them a sense of failure resort to self-anesthetization with alcohol or drugs; others escape into grandiose ideation where they achieve in fantasy what is unattainable in reality; many renounce pursuits having self-evaluative implications and gravitate to groups embracing anti-achievement norms; others protect themselves against self-condemnation for their self-alleged faults by imputing persecutory schemes; and, tragically, still others are driven by relentless self-disparagement to suicide.

Dysfunctional Self-Evaluation in Depression

In its more extreme forms, harsh standards of self-evaluation give rise to depression, feelings of worthlessness, and lack of purposefulness. Chronic self-disparagement is, in fact, the chief feature of depression. Ernest Hemingway, who died by suicide, suffered from this type of self-generated tyranny (Yalom & Yalom, 1971). Throughout his life he imposed upon himself demands that were unattainable, pushed himself to extraordinary feats, and constantly demeaned his accomplishments. The depth of self-inflicted misery and despair of severely depressed persons is poignantly revealed when their experiences are examined over an extended period. Binswanger (1958) provides a detailed account of one such case. This woman was constantly tormented by the relentless pursuit of unattainable standards. As a child she would weep for hours if she did not outrank all others in what she was doing. But even peerless attainments brought no satisfaction because she had her sights set on magnificent achievements that would ensure her undying fame. Living by the motto, "Either Caesar or nothing," she looked upon her performances as dismal failures, although judged by any other standards they were clearly superior. Not only was she cruel to herself, but she constantly judged others harshly by the same extraordinary standards. As her paralyzing despair began to destroy her effectiveness, she became deeply preoccupied with a sense of worthlessness and futility. Only death could provide a welcome relief from her torment, which she sought through repeated suicide attempts.

Substantial progress has been made in clarifying how the constituent processes of self-evaluation operate to produce depression (Kanfer & Hagerman, 1981; Rehm, 1982). Dysfunctions can occur in each of the self-regulatory subfunctions—in how personal experiences are self-monitored and cognitively processed, in the evaluative self-standards that are adopted, and in the evaluative self-reactions to one's own behavior. Problems at any one of these points can create self-dissatisfactions and dejection. Dysfunctions in all aspects of the self system are most apt to produce the most chronic self-disparagement and despondency.

Self-Monitoring. People who are prone to depression tend to misperceive their performance attainments or to distort their memory of them in self-slighting directions. In contrast, the nondepressed are more inclined to distort personal experiences in a self-enhancing fashion. Thus, despite gaining the same pattern of outcomes, depressed persons underestimate their successes but are very much aware of their failures, whereas the nondepressed remember their successes well but recall fewer failures than they have actually experienced (DeMonbreun & Craighead, 1977; Nelson & Craighead, 1977; Wener & Rehm, 1975). The nondepressed similarly overrate their social skills and the degree of control they exercise over positive outcomes (Alloy & Abramson, 1979; Lewinsohn, Mischel, Chaplin, & Barton, 1980). In studies relating depressive mood to recollection of past experiences, the more depressed people are, the more they underestimate how well they have performed (Buchwald, 1977). Temporarily induced positive and negative mood biases remembrance of past successes and failures in much the same way (Wright & Mischel, 1982).

Other results of the preceding studies

suggest that the distortions in self-monitoring exhibited by depressed persons occur in recollections rather than in perception of their performances. The perceptual accuracy is somewhat at variance with a common observation that the depressed misperceive, as well as misremember, how well they performed and the outcomes they achieved. Indeed, it is on the basis of such evidence that Beck (1976) postulated a depressogenic self-schema that leads depressed persons to anticipate, select, and interpret transactions with their environment in self-deprecating ways. The negative biasing effects on memory also appear in recollections of self-evaluative reactions (Gotlib, 1981). Depressed persons exaggerate their past self-criticisms and minimize their self-commendations.

The apparent discrepancy in the findings regarding perceptual accuracy most likely stems from the methods used to study how depressed persons monitor and process self-referent information. In laboratory situations, persons typically perform a task involving discrete trials, and the experimenter tells them whether they succeeded or failed on each try. There is little else going on in the situation to create ambiguities about the causes of their successes and failures, which would require inferential judgment. Nor do their actions have any effect on the future course of events. Even the recollections are measured shortly after performance without any intervening experiences to create confusion over what has happened earlier. It is hard to misperceive, or even to misremember, events that are conspicuous, well defined, and uncluttered.

The conditions of everyday life differ from those created in laboratories in several important respects. First, successes and failures are largely self-defined in terms of personal standards. The higher the self-standards, the more likely will given attainments be viewed as failures, regardless of what others might think. Second, the presence of many interacting influences, including the attainments of others, create further leeway in how one's performances

and outcomes are cognitively appraised. We shall see shortly that the depressed tend to exhibit self-standards and judgmental biases that would leave anyone feeling self-dissatisfied and inadequate. Third, transactions with the environment involve a continuously interactive process. In social interchanges, depressed persons elicit morose, hostile, and rejecting behavior in others (Coyne, 1976a). So it is not only that the depressed have a gloomy view of their environment, they also create gloomy social environments for themselves to view. The negative social reactions they produce in those with whom they interact provide some social validation for their negative self-percepts. This is a further illustration of how, in a reciprocal model, self-percepts foster actions that generate information, as well as serve as a filtering mechanism for self-referent information in the self-maintaining process.

One might expect that selective over-attention to failures and personal deficiencies would, in itself, be depressing. But apparently negative self-monitoring alone is not enough. O'Hara and Rehm (1979) found that people who self-monitored only unpleasant experiences for a full month did not differ in their daily mood or physical activity from those who attended solely to pleasant experiences or to both types of incidents. Except for events that carry great weight, it is not experience *per se,* but how they match expectations, that governs their emotional impact.

Standard-Setting. The satisfactions people derive from what they do are determined to a large degree by their self-evaluative standards. A sure way of inducing self-discouragement and a sense of personal inadequacy is to judge one's ongoing performances against lofty, global, or distal goals. This is not to say that high aspirations are necessarily detrimental to self-esteem. High aspirations can be self-motivating, rather than self-discouraging, provided that ongoing performances are measured against attainable subgoals through which aspirations are eventually realized.

Compared to nondepressed persons, the depressed tend to set higher standards for themselves relative to their attainments and to evaluate their performances as poorer for similar accomplishments (Golin & Terrell, 1977; Loeb, Beck, Diggory, & Tuthill, 1967; Schwartz, 1974). This aspect of the depressive process becomes even more apparent when standard-setting is studied as a function of variations in the rate of performance improvement (Simon, 1979b). Unlike the nondepressed, whose standards are realistically tied to accomplishments, the depressed set higher goals for themselves in the face of declining improvement and are thus more self-dissatisfied, even though their actual performances are the same. The people who overaspire and belittle their actual accomplishments are most vulnerable to depression.

Goal stringency is a relational characteristic, not a matter of absolute level. Whether the goals people set for themselves are realistic or not depends on whether they have the capabilities to match them. Goals that surpass attainments do not necessarily breed depression. As long as people believe they can fulfill them, the disparity is more of a motivating challenge than a cause for despondency. Depression is most likely to arise when personal standards of merit are set well above one's perceived efficacy to attain them (Kanfer & Zeiss, 1983). Perceived inefficacy to accomplish desired goals debilitates motivation, as well as creates discontent, whereas unfulfilled goals are motivating when they are regarded as reachable (Bandura & Cervone, 1983, 1986).

Depressive reactions are often precipitated by promotion to higher ranks, although such an event might appear to be cause for joy. People who strive for standards that are not easily fulfilled are especially prone to promotion depression. High positions carry heavy responsibilities for diverse activities that can be managed effectively only through the efforts of others. New demands arouse uncertainties concerning perceived efficacy to fulfill them. Those who are unskilled in guiding the work of others, or whose stringent standards make it difficult for them to delegate responsibility, because they believe they are the only ones capable of doing the work well, try to do it all themselves. The net effect is a burdensome work load that diminishes any pleasure the work may hold.

Performance Appraisal. The likelihood of depressive reactions is heightened when lofty standards are combined with a penchant for processing performance information in self-belittling ways. Depressed persons are not especially charitable to themselves in how they judge their performance determinants. In causal appraisals of their performances, nondepressed persons favor a self-enhancing bias: crediting successes to themselves and failures to situational factors. Such favorable appraisals serve to heighten positive affect. The depressed, while not always discounting their contributions to successes, nevertheless are quick to attribute failures to themselves (Kuiper, 1978; Rizley, 1978; Peterson & Seligman, 1984). Self-blame begets self-punishment.

Judgments of adequacy involve social comparison processes. Depression-prone individuals also tend to use social comparative information in self-depreciating ways. When exposed to the high attainments of others, the depressed judge their own accomplishments as less praiseworthy than the nondepressed (Ciminero & Steingarten, 1978). Self-devaluation for performances that fall below the level achieved by others is especially evident in depressed females (Garber, Hollon, & Silverman, 1979).

Evaluative Self-Reaction. People who judge themselves unfavorably are not inclined to treat themselves pleasantly. Numerous studies have compared the self-reactions of depressed and nondepressed persons following comparable levels of performance (Gotlib, 1981; Lobitz & Post,

1979; Nelson & Craighead, 1977; Rehm, 1982). The depressed generally evaluate themselves less favorably and reward themselves less than the nondepressed, who are more inclined to savor their successes. The depressed are also inclined to punish themselves more severely for poor performances.

The focus of the preceding studies is on how depression-prone individuals react to what they do. Repeated self-disparagement can produce a dysphoric mood. Dysphoric mood can, in turn, affect self-reactions to one's accomplishments. When different moods are temporarily induced, people are more self-approving of their performances when in a joyful mood but more self-punishing when in a despondent mood (Jones & Thelen, 1978). Feelings of self-worth, which are less changeable than transient moods, also affect self-rewarding reactions. Both children and adults who hold themselves in low regard are less self-rewarding and more self-punishing for similar accomplishments than those who have high self-esteem (Heaton & Duerfeldt, 1973; Neistein & Katovsky, 1974; Reschly & Mittman, 1973).

Although research confirms that dysfunctions in each self-regulatory component can contribute to the depressive process, the results are not always consistent (Coyne & Gotlib, 1983). Several factors, which differ across studies, may create discrepancies in findings. First, the amount and type of self-regulatory dysfunction that is found will vary depending on the severity of the depression being studied. Second, the evaluative significance of the task determines the extent to which self-evaluative mechanisms will become engaged in any given activity (Simon, 1979a). Third, some investigators misconstrue judgments of response accuracy as self-evaluative reactions. Accuracy judgments provide the basis for evaluative self-reactions, but they can hardly be equated (Bandura, 1971b). There are many occasions when people judge their responses as accurate but not as deserving of self-praise, because the task is trivial or devalued. At other times, they judge their responses to be incorrect but see no cause for self-criticism, because the task is inordinately difficult or insignificant to them.

There is more than one process through which one can become depressed. Some persons adopt modest standards and judge their behavior accurately but experience despondency because they lack the necessary skills or socially valued attributes for gaining satisfaction and self-esteem (Lewinsohn, 1975). Others become chronically despondent when they lose, by death or rejection, persons on whom they have become heavily dependent for their well-being. Still others become dejected when they perceive themselves as incapable of exercising control over important events in their lives (Miller & Seligman, 1982). Referential standards are still involved, to some extent, even in the latter instances because dissatisfaction with one's life situation depends on what one desires. Felt privations arising from disparity between actual and desired outcomes breed discontent, but when they are combined with perceived responsibility for the adversities experienced, they breed despondent self-derogation.

Because depression can have multiple determinants, any group of depressed persons will yield variable results. For this reason, theories also need to be tested by varying the conditions believed to be conducive to depression, rather than simply comparing depressed and nondepressed people. Some of the conditions, of course, may not be easily producible in laboratory situations. Under these circumstances, a research strategy relying on prediction is informative. Persons who either possess or lack the predisposing self-evaluative dysfunctions are compared in how they react to created or naturally occurring distress. Using this approach, Heiby (1983a, 1983b) corroborated the proposition that a well-developed self system reduces vulnerability to depression arising from adverse events in life and losses in social regard. Moods in high self-rewarders are unaffected by variations in how often their attainments are socially praised. In contrast, low self-rewarders become depressed when their proficient performances bring them less commendation from others than they have come to expect. Adverse life events are also more depressing to those who lack a positive self-evaluative system to sustain them through difficult times. O'Hara, Rehm, and Campbell (1982) found that women who displayed an evaluation self system that was negatively biased were especially vulnerable to depression following childbirth. These findings suggest that self-regulatory dysfunctions are contributors to, rather than merely concomitants of, depression.

Successful treatment of despondency stemming from dysfunctional self-evaluation addresses each aspect of the self-regulatory process (Jackson, 1972; Rehm, 1982). To foster more accurate self-appraisal, clients record their daily positive experiences, which they would ordinarily minimize when left to memory. To alter performance standards that create self-discouragement and a sense of personal inadequacy, clients adopt explicit, attainable subgoals for their daily activities. This provides the accomplishments needed for a sense of competence and self-satisfaction. To supplant devaluative self-reactions, clients are taught how to reward and commend themselves for their attainments. This type of treatment reduces depressed mood, increases interpersonal responsivity, and instills a more positive outlook on life.

Treatments which remedy only part of the dysfunctional self system generally work as well as those altering all the subfunctions, although in some studies, fostering more generous self-reward amplifies the benefits (Rehm, 1982; Tressler & Tucker, 1980). However, treatments directed at the evaluative self processes are more effective in alleviating depression than those aimed at improving social functioning, indicating that the benefits derive from changes in the self system. When the subfunctions of self-regulation operate conjointly, it is difficult to alter them independently. Consequently, a treatment that addresses only certain facets of a self system may undesignedly be activating other subfunctions that are the object of explicit attention in a multifaceted approach. For example, focusing solely on positive self-monitoring can prompt unbidden goal setting and more positive self-reaction. Changes in subfunctions must, therefore, be measured, rather than simply be assumed to have occurred isolatedly from what was socially prescribed.

Other Effects of Dysfunctional Self-Evaluation

Problems of self-evaluation appear, either directly or indirectly, in other types of behavior disorders. People who have experienced a decline in ability due to ageing or physical injury, but continue to adhere to their usual performance standards, suffer considerable self-devaluation. What brought them satisfaction in the past now leaves them with a sense of failure. As a result, they begin to lose interest in activities and become increasingly apathetic.

Demanding self-standards can also take a heavy toll on the viscera, as attested to by the prevalence of ulcers, hypertension, and coronaries among the intensely ambitious. Those who are unskilled in managing self-inflicted stress are more likely to drive themselves to debility or to drink than to success. Researchers have examined the role of goal setting in the Type A behavioral orientation, which is considered to be a risk factor in coronary disease. People displaying this coronary-prone behavior are competitive, hard-driving, under constant time pressure, and easily angered (Cooper, Detre, & Weiss, 1981; Friedman & Rosenman, 1974). In laboratory studies where performance attainments do not differ, compared to the more easy going Type B individuals, Type A individuals display elevated goal setting, greater reluctance to alter their overaspiration in the face of failure experiences, and a penchant for evaluating themselves against the best performers (Grimm & Yarnold, 1984; Matthews & Siegel, 1983; Snow, 1978). Males who have suffered coronaries are prone to set high performance standards for themselves which they often fail to reach (Rime & Bonami, 1976). Peptic ulcers are also an affliction of overaspiring self-drivers (Raifman, 1957).

So far we have discussed the personal misery that can result from austere self-evaluation standards. Deficient or deviant standards also create problems, although the resulting adverse effects are more likely to be experienced by others, rather than personally. If adequate self-standards are lacking, people exercise little self-directedness. As a result, they become highly dependent on external prompts and guides for their actions. Unprincipled individuals who pursue an ethic of expediency and those who take self-pride in excelling at antisocial activities facilely resort to injurious conduct unless deterred by external sanctions. These are issues to which we shall return later.

CONCEPTUAL BYPASS OF THE SELF SYSTEM

The notion that people can exercise some influence over their behavior and shape their environment is dissonant with theories that view actions as the products of environment. The operation of a self system in human functioning, therefore, does not go unchallenged. Adherents of unidirectional environmental determinism have proposed alternative conceptions of self-regulatory processes that would make behavior explainable without having to postulate any self-generated influences. Much of the controversy centers on whether self incentives facilitate change through motivational function or for some other reason (Bandura, 1976a; Catania, 1975).

Disavowal of Self-Influence by Renaming and Exteriorization

One solution offered by radical behaviorists to self influences is to redefine and exteriorize them. According to Catania

(1975), self incentives enhance behavior because they promote "self-awareness" that one has achieved a rewardable performance. This type of analysis essentially amounts to explanation by describing one of the constituent processes—self-monitoring—in self-regulation. It is true that attainments that match or exceed internal standards signify occasions for self-reward. But to say that people pursue activities over a long time just because they will notice later that they have met their standard, places the cause after the effect. People do not sustain and enhance their effort by self incentives because they will notice their attainments in the future but because they withhold desired incentives from themselves until they achieve the requisite performances. To secure the self-withheld rewards, they organize and deploy their efforts more effectively. *Regulation,* not the *awareness,* of the contingency between attainments and self-reward is the critical factor.

The weight of the evidence is heavily against attributing the effects of self incentives to self-monitoring. Simply observing and recording one's own behavior has no consistent behavioral effects (Kazdin, 1974a; Nelson, 1977). When knowledge of performance alone produces some change, it does so by getting people to set goals for themselves and thus to engage their self-evaluative reactions in the pursuit of those goals (Bandura & Cervone, 1983, 1986). Many of the studies previously reviewed include controls for the effects not only of self-monitoring but of goal setting as well. People who set goals, monitor their performances, and reward themselves for designated attainments typically surpass their counterparts who also set goals and monitor their progress but do not enlist self incentives.

Some of the reasons given by radical behaviorists for why self incentives cannot affect behavior have rested on questionable assumptions about how outcomes affect actions. We have already examined a fundamental difference between social cognitive theory and radical behaviorism in how these two theories view "reinforcement." Social cognitive theorists stress the informative and motivating function of prospective outcomes; radical behaviorists believe that outcomes automatically strengthen the responses they have followed. These differences extend as well to explanations of how self incentives work. Self-rewards enhance performance because they motivate anticipatorily, not because they automatically reinforce backwardly. That is, by making desired self incentives conditional upon attaining a certain level of performance, people create the self inducements necessary to produce these performances.

Ignoring the antecedent motivational function of self incentives, Catania (1975) argues that since the performance attainments have already occurred, the self-reward is superfluous. This reasoning, if consistently applied, undermines the very reinforcement theory that radical behaviorists embrace. One can just as well argue that, in externally reinforced behavior, since the responses have already occurred, the external reinforcers which follow them are also superfluous. Attempts to dismiss the effects of self incentives as due solely to self-awareness creates other conceptual inconsistencies. Behaviorists consider awareness to be a by-product, rather than a determinant, of performance. Being aware of aspects of one's behavior does not cause the behavior of which one is aware. Thus, in positing that self-awareness causes behavioral changes, Catania appears to be abandoning a basic tenet of his own theory.

Catania argues further that people cannot influence their behavior through self incentives because organisms can only reinforce responses, not themselves. This dichotomization, which disembodies responses from the organism producing them, brings to the fore a fundamental issue that is rarely discussed in behavioristic explanations of reinforcement. We have noted earlier that consequences almost always occur after the response has ceased to exist, whether this involves rewarding an animal for having pressed a bar, commending someone for having done well, or paying people for completing work assignments. How can performances that are no longer in existence be reinforced? In actuality, one cannot reinforce responses. One can only reinforce an organism for having selected and performed certain types of behavior.

Operant theorists have always argued against explaining behavior in terms of events that may occur in the future. Indeed, since in this approach people cannot affect their actions by thought, anticipated outcomes have no causal efficacy. However, in explaining increases in self-rewarded behavior, some adherents of this view appeal to remote rewards of prospective behavior but neglect the personal determinants of behavior that operate in the here and now (Rachlin, 1974).

Placement of the cause of behavior in future reinforcers, while disavowing the causal efficacy of anticipatory thought, creates explanatory strains on how an organism with functionless thought can be motivated and guided by these far-off reinforcers. The metaphor, in which external cues transport behavior across time and place, is typically used as the explanatory device. Human actions are presumably orchestrated by a continuous chain of external stimuli strung out over time that carry the behavior to its eventual payoff. A self incentive becomes simply the stimulus bridging the delay between behavior and its far-off reinforcers (Rachlin, 1974). Thus, for example, engaging in free-time activities, something which novelists withhold from themselves until they have written a designated amount each day (Wallace, 1977), is nothing but a salient stimulus. When Jack London made his visits to the local saloon contingent upon writing 1000 words a day, the rollicking saloon activities presumably held no incentive value for him. They were merely cues for yet-to-come royalties, which would, in turn, serve as tokens to buy commodities, which may themselves be only cues for even more far-off rewards. After all, people may covet the symbolic value of a yacht, a Rolls Royce, or an estate more than the items themselves.

Operant theorists provide no reliable criteria for identifying the remote reinforcer to which the vast collection of external cues are chained.

The notion that people can bridge long delays by being steered along by chains of external cues assumes that there is something worthwhile to be gained at the end. Operant procedures create a chain of performances by beginning at the rewarding end and then working backwards. But this is not the way human endeavors operate. Individuals do not become physicians by beginning with an affluent medical practice, then working their way backwards to a medical degree, to being admitted to a medical school, then mastering pre-med courses, then being accepted at an undergraduate college, after having wound their way through the public school labyrinth. Having retraced their steps, they would then be led forward from one stand-in cue to another, until they reached the point of being licensed healers relishing the luxurious life.

People embark on new courses of action toward uncertain futures based on beliefs about where their actions might lead and what they might bring them. The products of many tiresome endeavors are disappointments, rather than long-term rewards. Explanations in terms of ultimate external reinforcement, even if it could be reconciled with operant principles, still leaves unexplained what sustains arduous goal-directed activities toward futures that may turn out to be empty or full of adversity. People are often motivated by false notions of what their efforts will eventually bring them, but operant theory does not allow for such cognitive determinants of action. External, conditioned reinforcers may be put forth as temporary stand-ins for the eventual payoff, but this hardly provides a satisfactory explanation. It simply begs the question of what guides and sustains effortful, goal-directed behavior during the intervals when conditioned reinforcers are nowhere in sight. If persons could not cognitively bridge delays between actions and their eventual effects, any break in the external chain of cues, however brief, would abort goal-directed pursuits.

Several operant investigators have conducted studies designed to show that self incentives are merely proxy cues for distant outcomes and thus presumably operate differently from external incentives regulating behavior. The methodological and interpretive problems with this research have been extensively reviewed elsewhere (Bandura, 1981b). The authors (Castro & Rachlin, 1980; Nelson, Hayes, Spong, Jarrett, & McKnight, 1983) claim support for the view that self incentives are merely signals that steer a person to future outcomes even though, in different studies, variations in significant distal consequences have no effect; there are no control groups in which people perform without "cueing" themselves, therefore no demonstration of cueing function is possible; the factors varied have no consistent effect, so no claims can be made for anything; and failure to include external reward conditions, as well as self-reward conditions, precludes any judgment as to whether external and self incentives operate through similar or different processes. Research which includes externally administered consequences (Castro, de Perez, de Albanchez, & de Leon, 1983) yields the anomalous result that the best way to help people achieve the changes they seek is to punish them for making the changes, whereas rewarding of progress has no effect. Such findings are not only called into question by common evidence, but they dispute even the operant view of how consequences affect behavior, a theory to which the authors seem to give their allegiance. Thus, efforts to demonstrate that self incentives cannot be motivators end up as refutations of the operant theory of reinforcement.

Contrary to the cueing perspective, results of a large body of evidence reviewed earlier in this chapter show that people who create incentives for themselves usually outperform those who merely record their progress toward distant outcomes. Giving oneself tokens of no value for attaining a subgoal—certainly conspicuous cues—has no demonstrable effect on behavior, whereas monetary self-reward for similar attainments improves performance (Flaxman & Solnick, 1975). The incentive motivation theory of self-reward further predicts that the higher the value of self-rewards, the more motivating they will be, even though they are equally conspicuous cues. And finally, self-punishment, which hardly lacks vividness, reduces rather than increases the behavior toward which it is directed (Humphrey et al., 1978).

In the social cognitive analysis, anticipated eventual benefits create some incentive for pursuing a long-term course of action, but it is the proximal self influences that provide the needed incentives and guides along the way to override the lure of competing activities. Lest one's vision be dulled by preoccupation with consumable rewards, it should be noted that not all self-reward has to be material, nor does it have to be exclusively in the service of distant material payoffs. People often do things that carry no extrinsic rewards to please themselves. They also often forego material rewards attainable only by conduct that violates their personal standards, thus producing self-condemnation. When they act on moral imperatives that challenge prevailing social practices, they are willing to suffer severe punishment, rather than yield to the injustices and tyranny of oppressors.

The criteria that together constitute a self-rewarding event include self-bestowal of freely available rewards contingent upon performances that meet adopted standards (Bandura, 1976a). Some of the behaviorists' dismissals of self influence ignore certain defining criteria of self-rewarding events, thus likening two incentive systems that differ in important ways. For example, Goldiamond (1976) regards external- and self-regulation as one and the same because, in both instances, people produce consequences for themselves by their actions. These two systems presumably only differ in who defines the adequacy of the efforts—the performer or somebody else. However,

there is an even more fundamental difference that should not be overlooked. In external regulation, others control the incentives so that they can be secured only by performing the behavior demanded by others; in self-regulation the incentives are controlled by the individuals themselves so that they could have them anytime they wish without performing at all. There is a marked difference between conforming to the demands of others and behaving in accordance with one's own standards. Withholding freely available rewards until self-acceptable performances have been achieved is a critical aspect of self-regulation. To ignore this important difference is to neglect the very essence of self-directedness.

Occasionally, the behaviorists' dismissal of self influence results from the failure to distinguish between self-reward and intrinsic reward. It may be recalled that, in the intrinsic form, the consequences flow naturally from the behavior. Drinking quenches thirst, donning warm clothing reduces chilliness, and running gets where one wants to go faster than walking. The benefits can be obtained only by performing the required actions, whereas in self-reward the benefits can be had without performing, but the person chooses to withhold them until fulfilling a selected standard. Self- and external-reward appear indistinguishable when intrinsic reward is misconstrued as self-reward, as in the case when Goldiamond (1976) considers scratching maintained because it relieves irritation as an instance of self-reward. If scratchers could gain relief without scratching but withheld relief for themselves until they completed a certain activity, this example would constitute an instance of self-regulation through contingent self-reward.

Some of the adherents of operant theory misconstrue the conception of self-motivation through incentives by confusing two issues: having control over incentives and choosing to use them selectively (Castro, de Perez, de Albanchez, & de Leon, 1983). People can have control over their money but choose when and how they will spend it. They have free access to their supply of liquor but decide when they will treat themselves to a drink. Contrary to Castro and his associates, there is nothing incompatible with having full control over rewarding resources and exercising that control as one chooses. Indeed, it is because people are able to do whatever they wish with the rewards they control that they can be agents of their own motivation. Castro's assertion that, in the social cognitive conception of self-motivation, incentives have an absolute value simply has no foundation in fact. The value of incentives varies relationally, rather than inheres as a fixed property.

In sum, writers who question the legitimacy of self-influence ignore focal defining properties of self-reward, judge it in terms of a backward strengthening function that rests on very shaky empirical grounds, misconstrue the process, or are talking about a different phenomenon altogether. Moreover, the arguments they put forward are often inconsistent with, and undermining of, the very behavioristic theory they espouse.

Another explanation that is routinely invoked, whatever the psychological phenomena may be, is that of "demand characteristics." This is a descriptive term used as though it were an explanation. To designate changes as demand effects does not explain them. It simply begs the question because one still must explain how "demands" work. All forms of influence (e.g., instructions, persuasive appeals, conditioning, modeling, reinforcement, or environmental arrangements) represent demands, in the sense that they provide inducements and guides for behavior. Influences can vary in a number of ways—in informativeness, strength, explicitness, coerciveness, source, intentionality, and whether they operate directly or through cognitive processing. Social influences are, therefore, better explained in terms of these distinguishable properties, rather than in terms of whether demands are involved.

Characterizing the effects of self incen-

tives as manifestations of social demand (Jones, Nelson & Kazdin, 1977) receives little support from experiments including controls of such factors (Bandura, 1976a). In studies varying both social demands and contingent self-reward, behavior that is difficult to maintain is increased by self incentives but unaffected by increasing social pressure to engage in the activities (Flaxman & Solnick, 1975). Moreover, behavioral standards developed by modeling on a specific task operate over a long period in dissimilar situations, with different persons, and on different tasks (Lepper, Sagotsky, & Mailer, 1975; Sagotsky & Lepper, 1982). Such evidence is not easily explainable in terms of situational demands.

Disavowal of Self-Influence by Selective Regress of Causes

Another common behavioristic solution to self-influence is to apply a selective regression of causes. By locating a past environmental factor that might affect self-reactions, self-generated influences are thereby converted into simple operants. As Stuart (1972) succinctly put it, "The behaviors commonly ascribed to self-control can be functionally analyzed as a special subset of operant responses which are, in fact, under situational control" (p. 130). The organism thus becomes simply a repository of self-control responses waiting to be externally activated, but it otherwise possesses no capacity to generate guides and incentives for its own actions. But causal regression is a no more convincing way to dispose of self-generated influences than renaming, because for every environmental cause that is invoked, one can find a prior personal cause of that environment.

Some conceptual regression of self influences to situational causes treat reciprocally interacting factors as if they were autonomous rivals of causation. This view is exemplified by Jones, Nelson, and Kazdin (1977), who consider external influences to be "plausible rival interpretations" of the changes people achieve by creating incentives for themselves. The situational contenders in these unidirectional analyses assume several different forms. A favorite external candidate is "reinforcement history." As Jones and his colleagues (1977) note, self-regulation partly depends upon prior learning of how to judge and set standards of performance. This is certainly true. Values and generic standards of self-reward are created from diverse experiences.

Having earlier external origins, of course, in no way detracts from the fact that, once established, self influences operate as current contributory causes of behavior. Ascribing a capability to past experiences cannot substitute for the present influences arising through exercise of that capability, any more than one could attribute Shakespeare's literary masterpieces to his prior instruction in the mechanics of writing. A unidirectional environmentalist might well argue that literary creations are products of the sum total of past situational influences. No one would argue with the view, however empty its predictive value, that human ingenuity incorporates some aspects of past experience. A social cognitive analysis, however, emphasizes the reciprocally interacting influences of personal and environmental factors in the innovating process. By their actions, people partly determine the nature of their experiences; through their capacity to manipulate symbols and to engage in reflective thought for innovative action, they can generate novel ideas that transcend their experiences, and they can fashion new environments for themselves and others.

In studies of self-regulatory processes, behavioral standards are transmitted through evaluative feedback, tuition, or modeling. In applications of self-incentive practices, information on how to set performance goals and how to regulate one's own behavior are usually conveyed by instruction. To proponents of one-sided determinism, instruction about self-influence exteriorizes the locus of regulation (Jones et al., 1977). Externalizing the determinants in instructions, as in embodying control in reinforcement histories, fails to do justice to the reciprocate complexities of the regulatory process. One must distinguish between the mechanics and the agency of behavior regulation. An environment may provide information for developing self-regulatory skills, but the recipients extract the information they need and decide when and how to use the acquired skills.

Instructions are merely sources of information that become influences through cognitive processing, not through reflexive adoption. If people always did what they were told, human behavior could be externally orchestrated at will. In fact, people often disregard instructions or improvise on them to create their own performance guides (Bandura & Simon, 1977; Dubbert & Wilson, 1984). To exteriorize self-mediated determinants of behavior is to sacrifice explanatory and predictive power. Jones and his co-workers found that if they told children to adopt stringent standards they work harder than if told to be more lenient with themselves (Jones & Evans, 1980; Jones & Ollendick, 1979). The authors interpret the verbal induction of differential standards by verbal means as a "continuum of external cues." The external-cues interpretation, however, cannot account for the variations in behavior within the stringent and lenient conditions. Variations in performance when the externally prescribed standards are the same can be explained by taking into account the standards people set for themselves and their commitment to them (Bandura & Cervone, 1986; Locke, Frederick, Lee, & Bobko, 1984). A major challenge to the study of self-regulatory processes, whether they involve self-observation, goal setting, cognitive rehearsal, or self incentives, is that people do not simply react reflexively to situational influences; they actively process and transform them to their own liking.

We saw earlier that if people are to influence their actions through self incentives, they have to know what they are doing and to measure their behavior against personal standards of what constitutes a worthy performance. Hence, self-monitoring and goal setting are indispensible constituents of the process, rather than being ancillary components that can be arbitrarily plugged in or disconnected from the self-regulatory system. Jones and his collegues (1977) speculate about how self-observation, goal setting, and situational demands may account for the effects of contingent self-reward. An issue of contributory influence need not be cast in terms of rival determinants. The large body of evidence reviewed earlier shows that personal changes that have been facilitated by self incentives usually exceed those resulting from either self-monitoring or goal setting alone or in combination with each other.

RECIPROCAL INFLUENCE OF EXTERNAL FACTORS ON SELF-REGULATORY FUNCTIONS

Social cognitive theory does not regard self-generated influences as autonomous regulators of behavior but as contributors to the triadic system of reciprocal causality. People shape their environment by their own self-regulated actions. Environmental influences can, in turn, affect the operation of a self system in at least three major ways: They contribute to the development of subfunctions in self-regulatory systems; they provide partial support for adherence to internal standards; and they facilitate selective activation and disengagement of self-regulatory processes.

Development of Self-Regulatory Subfunctions

Skill in monitoring one's own behavior develops through experience. People learn from social influences and the effects of their actions not only how and what to observe. They also gain knowledge about themselves and task demands. Such knowledge can affect what they do (Bandura,

1982a; Brown, 1978; Flavell, 1981). But self-observation is a bidirectional process. Beliefs and expectations affect what is perceived (Neisser, 1976), and self-conceptions and affective states influence what people tend to observe about themselves and how often and accurately they do so (Markus & Sentis, 1982; Snyder, 1979).

The internal standards by which behavior is evaluated do not emerge in a vacuum. They are established by precept, social evaluation, and modeling. Here, too, the role of personal factors in the development of generic standards should not be overlooked. People do not passively incorporate whatever they hear or see. They must process the disparate information that impinges upon them to form their own standards. Associational preferences add another reciprocal element to the acquisition process. The people with whom one regularly associates partly influence the standards of behavior that one adopts. Value orientations, in turn, selectively influence one's choice of associates and activities.

The self-reactive function is also partially a product of experience. There are many evaluative and tangible ways that people can respond to themselves when their behavior corresponds or runs counter to their personal standards. Past modeling and disciplinary experiences leave their mark on the type and strength of self-reactions people display to their own conduct (Aronfreed, 1968; Bandura & Walters, 1959; Sears, Maccoby, & Levin, 1957).

External Supports for Self-Regulation

In analyzing the regulation of behavior through self-reactions, one must distinguish between two sources of incentives operating in the process. First, there are the conditional self incentives that provide guides and proximal motivators for given courses of action. Second, there are the more distal incentives for adhering to internal standards. The way in which self incentives serve as proximal motivators of behavior has already been amply documented. In this section we shall examine the issue of why people abide by standards that impose performance demands on themselves and cause at least temporary self-denial. The challenging questions requiring explanation are why people deny themselves rewards that they control, why they adhere to exacting standards requiring difficult performances, and why they punish themselves. The supports for self-directedness can take varied forms.

Personal Benefits. Exercising influence over one's behavior can result in a number of benefits. Some of these benefits are extrinsic to the behavior; others derive from changes in the behavior itself. People often use self incentives to improve skills and competencies that serve them well in their everyday life. The personal gains accrued from improved proficiency make adherence to internal standards worthwhile. Given that they possess the necessary skills, people can do what needs to be done more effectively with self incentives than without them, even though the external inducements remain the same. In these ways self-directedness enables people to exercise better control over their lives. When self-regulatory skills are lacking, people defer tasks to the last moment, do them minimally, or not at all. Skills that can be cultivated only through sustained effort remain underdeveloped. Moreover, when people procrastinate on required tasks, thoughts about what they are putting off continuously intrude on, and detract from, their enjoyment of other activities. Those who can mobilize themselves to get things done are spared such intrusive self-reminders.

People are especially motivated to exercise self-influence when the behavior they seek to regulate is aversive or potentially so. Control of overeating brings relief from the discomforts, maladies, and social costs of obesity. Completing academic assignments makes educational pursuit less aversive and spares them failing grades. Performing the tasks of one's trade well and on time makes vocational pursuits less stressful and more secure. When deficient self-regulation produces aversive outcomes, efficacious self-influence that reduces aversiveness creates an intrinsic source of reward for current efforts.

Because self-regulation involves brief self-denial, it does not necessarily create an adverse state of affairs, as it might appear to on first sight. Singling out the temporary self-privation from the total effect of self-influence, as is commonly done, overemphasizes the negative aspects of the process. A different picture emerges if one compares the over all, rather than the momentary effects, of self-influence. Self-directedness provides both the temporarily withheld rewards, as well as the many benefits of increased proficiency. To ask little of oneself makes life less taxing, but at the cost of forfeiting competencies and repeated hassles over failure to do what needs to be done. For activities that have personal value, self-directedness can produce the greatest over all benefits. Thus, on closer analysis, the exercise of momentary self-denial becomes less perplexing than it might originally appear. If, however, the behavior being self-regulated benefits others but is of little value to the performer, adherence to standards will require more in the way of extraneous support.

Social Reward. If societies relied solely on inherent benefits to sustain self-directedness, many activities that are tiresome and uninteresting until enough proficiency is acquired would never be mastered. Upholding standards is, therefore, socially promoted by a vast system of rewards including praise, social recognition, honors, and awards. Few accolades are bestowed on people who self-reward mediocre performances. Social encouragement fosters adherence to high performance standards (Brownell et al., 1977).

Vicarious influence greatly expands the sphere of influence of social reward in promoting standards of excellence. Praising people affects not only their standard-setting behavior, it also conveys that self-directedness as an attribute is desirable to others as well. Indeed, seeing performers publicly recognized for upholding excellence aids emulation of high standards, even under social conditions that tend to lower aspirations (Bandura et al., 1967a).

Reference groups are chosen in large part on the basis of shared values. The self-evaluations of members are influenced by actual or anticipated reactions of associates whose judgment they value. When the immediate reference group is small, individuals appear to be "inner-directed" because their self-evaluations are not much influenced by the views of most people (Riesman, 1950). In fact, members of such groups are highly responsive to the few whose good opinion they prize. Individuals are rare who regard their behavior so highly that the reactions of their associates have no effect on their self-evaluation.

Modeling Supports. Modeling is an excellent vehicle for transmitting knowledge and skills, but it is infrequently studied as a maintainer of standards. Human behavior has been shown to be extensively regulated by the actions of others. There is every reason to expect that seeing others master tasks through self-directedness makes observers more inclined to abide by performance standards in their own pursuits.

Negative Sanctions. When people acquire or apply standards to themselves erratically, unmerited self-reward often draws negative social reactions. Rewarding oneself for inadequate or undeserving performances is more likely than not to evoke criticism from others. Lowering one's standards is rarely considered praiseworthy, unless they are unrealistically perfectionistic. Adherence to performance standards is strengthened when unmerited self-reward is even occasionally disapproved. The higher the certainty of negative sanctions for undeserving self-reward, the greater is their capacity to sustain standards (Bandura & Mahoney, 1974).

Development of self-regulatory skills is central to treatment programs for children who are unable to control their behavior. This is achieved through a series of transitional steps in which children first gain some measure of control with the aid of external incentives. Then they are taught how to judge their own behavior relative to a standard. After gaining proficiency in self-appraisal, they judge their own actions and reward themselves accordingly. The external aids are then gradually reduced until children eventually guide their own behavior with self-evaluative reactions. During the early phases of treatment, praise and occasional sanctions are required to get children to adhere to standards (Drabman et al., 1973). After codes of conduct have been adopted, personal sanctions operate as well as social ones in fostering adherence to them. The anticipation of thought-produced distress for behaving in personally disapproved ways provides an internal incentive to abide by one's standards of conduct. This process will shortly be considered in more detail.

Contextual Supports. Situations differ in the standards of behavior espoused in them. Self-leniency in settings fostering pursuit of excellence is likely to draw disapproval, which eventually endows the situation with predictive significance. As a result, situational cues indicating that undeserving self-reward is frowned upon can, in themselves, bolster adherence to performance standards. Environments where high performance standards were favored foster adherence to those standards, even after sanctions for unmerited self-reward have been discontinued (Bandura, Mahoney, & Dirks, 1976).

Although self-regulatory functions are developed and occasionally supported by external influences, this does not negate the fact that exercise of that function partly determines how people behave. When tasks require sustained effort and competing attractions abound, environmental inducements alone often fail to produce change, whereas the same inducements prove successful with the addition of self incentives. Competencies developed through the aid of self incentives enable people to activate environmental influences that would otherwise not even come into play. This is because most environmental influences are only potentialities until actualized by appropriate action. In still other instances, the behavior fashioned through self-directed effort transforms the environment.

Because personal and environmental determinants affect each other in a reciprocal fashion, attempts to assign causal priority to either of these two sources of influence are reduced to a "chicken-or-egg" debate. Situational factors prompt self-influences which, in turn, alter the situational determinants. For example, overweight individuals who refrain, through self-influence, from buying an assortment of chocolates on a shopping tour create a different environment for themselves than those who head home with a generous supply of high-caloric delicacies. A full explanation of self-regulatory processes must include the self-control determinants of environments, as well as the environmental determinants of self-control. A quest for the ultimate environmental determinant of self-regulated behavior becomes a regressive contest that can yield no victor because, for every ultimate environmental cause that is invoked, one can find prior actions that helped to produce it. Promotion systems for occupational pursuits, grading schemes for academic endeavors, and reverence for slimness are human creations, not decrees of an autonomous, impersonal environment.

Self-Inflicted Punishment

Self-punishment, a prevalent aspect of the human condition, is more perplexing than the temporary imposition of self-privation. Considering that people seek pleasure and go to great lengths to avoid pain, the self-infliction of pain would appear on first examination to be an aberration. However, investigations into the origins and functions of self-punishment suggest that it is not so unusual.

The Origins and Precursors of Self-Criticism. During the early years when children lack personal standards, they do not apply negative sanctions to their own behavior. When they misbehave, parents usually take steps not only to discourage future misconduct but to foster adoption of guiding values as well. Expressions of self-criticism following wrongdoing typically arise during disciplinary incidents. This is because self-rebuke often lessens parental displeasure and reinstates parental approval. Children learn to voice self-criticism if it restores the positive regard of significant adults (Grusec, 1966; Grusec & Ezrin, 1972; Sears, Maccoby, & Levin, 1957). In the initial development of self-reactive tendencies, self-reprimands probably serve more as ways of managing the displeasure of others than as expressions of internalized standards.

In their early childhood play, the approvals and admonishments children hand out to each other and to dolls or stuffed animals often reflect adult attitudes and values that parents have not attempted to teach directly. In these instances, children evaluate themselves and others in accordance with standards they have acquired through modeling. Laboratory studies showing that children will adopt self-punitive behavior through exposure to self-critical models provide further evidence for this process (Herbert, Gelfand, & Hartmann, 1969). Because standards arising from example are formed more through self-selection than through social imposition, they are more likely to be accepted as one's own.

Reduction of Thought-Produced Distress. With the development of personal standards, self-punishment acquires the capacity to alleviate thought-produced distress. When people perform inadequately or violate their own standards of conduct, they tend to engage in self-critical and other aversive thoughts. Self-punishment provides one means of relief. Having criticized or punished themselves for reprehensible conduct, individuals are likely to discontinue further upsetting ruminations about their past behavior. Self-punishment can reduce distressing thoughts about self-disappointing performances, as well as about moral conduct. Like transgressive conduct, faulty performances can cause disconcerting thoughts that are reducible by self-criticism.

People thus inflict punishment on themselves because it provides them with relief from thought-produced anguish, which is enduring and is often more painful than the self-reprimand itself. This process is most vividly illustrated in cases where individuals have tormented themselves for years over minor transgressions and do not rest easy, until making some type of restitution. They return money stolen in their youth, admission prices to activities they sneaked into without paying, and objects pilfered from hotels (*Palo Alto Times,* 1976; *Peninsula Times Tribune,* 1980). Sometimes the costs of conscience exceed the actual damages, as in the case of a transgressor who sent $100 to repair minor damages to a door in a theatre caused by what he regarded as his "stupid vandalism" (*Palo Alto Times,* 1978).

In psychotic disorders, self-punishment is often powerfully maintained by delusional contingencies that have little relationship to reality. In a case to be cited later, a psychotic religionist, who regarded trivial acts as heinous sins, could gain relief from his self-contempt and tormenting visions of hellish torture only by torturing himself for long hours (Bateson, 1961).

Self-Protective Value. Self-punishment often serves as an effective means of lessening negative reactions from others. When certain behavior is almost certain to evoke disciplinary actions, self-punishment may be the lesser of two evils. Stone and Hokanson (1969) show how self-punitive behavior can, indeed, be effectively maintained by its self-

protective and stress-reducing value. When adults could avoid painful shocks by administering shocks of lesser intensity to themselves, they increased self-punitive responses and became less physiologically perturbed. Depressed individuals, who are highly prone to self-criticism, inflict more self-punishment and experience faster drops in autonomic arousal after punishing themselves than the nondepressed (Forrest & Hokanson, 1975).

Why self-punishment should be autonomically tranquilizing is perhaps best explained in terms of the benefits of perceived control over aversive events. Being able to exercise some control over external threats reduces perturbing anticipation, thereby diminishing their aversiveness. People experience self-inflicted pain as less aversive than pain inflicted by others (Vernon, 1969). Depression-prone persons, who tend to view themselves as blameworthy, may expect more severe reprimands from others and thus be more relieved by control through self-punishment.

Self-punishment that is successful in averting anticipated threats can prevent reality testing, so that it persists in ever-escalating intensities long after the threats have ceased to exist. Sandler and Quagliano (1964) document the durability of anticipatory self-punishment in studies with animals. After monkeys had learned to press a lever to avoid shock, conditions for learning self-punishment were introduced. The animals could prevent shock by pressing the lever, but, by doing so, they administered a weaker shock to themselves. The strength of the self-administered shock was then gradually increased until it equalled the one being avoided. However, the animals did not reduce their self-punishment, even though it no longer was the lesser of two evils. After the original avoided shock was permanently abolished, the animals continued to punish themselves, needlessly, with the same shock intensities that they had previously worked hard to avoid. These findings show how self-punishment can become dissociated from current reality through its capacity to forestall anticipated threats, which in fact, no longer exist. To observers who witness the self-inflicted punishment without knowing its functional origin, the behavior appears absurdly useless or driven by some obscure masochistic pleasure.

Social Rewards. Self-punishment can be used to extract compliments from others. By criticizing and belittling themselves, people can get others to enumerate the self-disparagers' praiseworthy qualities and achievements and to reassure them of their future successes. Self-criticism is socially rewarded by such reassurances. For dependent persons who lack attractive attributes, this process can evolve to a depressive cycle in which self-disparagements become the chief means of securing consideration and reassurance from others (Coyne, 1976b). As people begin to tire of the constant self-criticism, their reassurances give way to rebuffs, thus requiring more extreme self-disparagements to gain further reassurances. Occasional responsiveness to drastic behavior serves only to strengthen it.

The work of Lovaas and his associates suggests that a similar reciprocal process may operate in physically self-injurious behavior, which is especially prevalent among autistic children (Lovaas & Newsom, 1976). In unresponsive environments, children with impoverished social skills may resort to self-injurious acts to force others to pay attention to them. If, over time, progressively more intense self-punitiveness is needed to secure attention, as is often the case with aversive behaviors, high rates of self-injury can be maintained by only sporadic attention. Any withdrawal of social responsiveness readily prompts self-injurious acts. Autistic children also resort to self-injury as a way of getting others to stop making demands on them (Carr, Newsom, & Binkoff, 1976). They start hitting themselves when requests are made of them but promptly cease when the requests are discontinued. As the preceding discussion illustrates, not all self-punishment represents self-censure.

Interplay between Personal and External Influence

After self-reactive capabilities are developed, behavior usually produces two sets of consequences: self-evaluative reactions and external outcomes. The personal and external outcomes that result from certain courses of action may operate as complementary or opposing influences on behavior.

People commonly experience conflict when they are socially or materially rewarded for behavior they themselves devalue. The anticipated self-reproach for violating one's standards provides motivation to keep behavior in line with one's standards in the face of opposing inducements. An example of a conflict of this type, in which self influence prevailed, is well demonstrated by a worker who found a wallet containing $34,500 in a telephone booth at a major airport. He spent three days tracking down the owner, shipped the wallet to him at his own expense, and declined a reward. As he described it: "The money is something, but the feeling inside is worth a heck of a lot more than the money" (*Peninsula Times Tribune*, 1979). One need not seek striking cases for evidence of this process. In laboratory studies in which people are paid to sacrifice quality for quantity, those who subscribe to standards of excellence continue to strive for quality, even though they reduce their prospects of monetary reward (Simon, 1979c).

When self-devaluative consequences outweigh the force of external rewards for socially accommodating behavior, the external influences are relatively ineffective. There is no punishment more devastating than self-contempt. If certain courses of action produce rewards greater than the anguish of self-censure, the result can be cheerless compliance. People, however, possess cognitive skills for reconciling upsetting discrepancies between standards and conduct. The processes by which losses of self-respect for devalued conduct are reduced will be analyzed later.

Another type of conflict between external and self-produced consequences arises when individuals are punished for behavior they highly value. Principled dissenters and nonconformists often find themselves in this predicament. Here, the relative strength of self-approval and external censure determines whether the behavior will be restrained or expressed. Should the threatened consequences be severe, people hold in check self-praiseworthy acts when there is a high risk of penalty but perform them readily when the chances of escaping punishment are good. There are individuals, however, whose sense of self-worth is so strongly invested in certain convictions that they will submit to prolonged maltreatment, rather than accede to what they regard as unjust or immoral. Thomas More, who was beheaded for refusing to compromise his resolute convictions, is a notable example from history. One can cite many other historical and contemporary figures who have endured considerable punishment for unyielding adherence to ideological and moral principles.

Another common situation is one in which the external rewards for pursuing certain activities are minimal or nonexistent, so that individuals have to sustain their efforts largely through self-encouragement. This is illustrated by innovators who, despite repeated failures, persist in endeavors that provide neither rewards nor recognition over long periods, if ever. In order to continue activities that require time and effort, people must be sufficiently convinced of the worth of what they are doing to self-reward their efforts and not be much concerned about the opinions of others.

Behavior is especially susceptible to external influences in the absence of countervailing internal standards. People who are not much committed to personal standards adopt a pragmatic orientation, tailoring their behavior to fit whatever the situation seems to call for (Snyder & Campbell, 1982). They become adept at reading social cues, processing and retaining social information, and varying their self-presentation. This is

not to say that principled individuals are above social influence. External influence will have its greatest impact on behavior when it is compatible with personal standards. Under these conditions, rewardable acts are a source of self-satisfaction and punishable ones are self-censured. In studies pitting values against outcomes, the same external rewards can enhance, diminish, or have no effect on behavior, depending on whether it is personally valued, devalued, or viewed neutrally (Dulany, 1968; Ekman, Krasner, & Ullmann, 1963; Lilliston, 1972). To enhance the compatibility between personal and social influences, people generally select associates who share similar standards of conduct and thus ensure social support for their own system of self-evaluation.

SELECTIVE ACTIVATION AND DISENGAGEMENT OF INTERNAL CONTROL

Development of self-regulatory capabilities does not create an invariant control mechanism within a person, as implied by theories of internalizaton that incorporate entities such as conscience and superego as continuous internal overseers of conduct. Self-evaluative influences do not operate unless activated, and there are many factors that exercise selective control over their activation. Therefore, the same behavior is not uniformly self-rewarded or self-punished, irrespective of the circumstances under which it is performed.

The processes by which self-sanctions are acquired have been examined in some detail. However, the selective activation and disengagement of internal control, which have considerable theoretical and social import, have only recently received systematic study. These processes figure most prominently in patterns of behavior that serve the user in some way but injure others.

After social and moral standards of conduct have been adopted, anticipatory self-condemnation for violating personal standards ordinarily serves as self-deter-

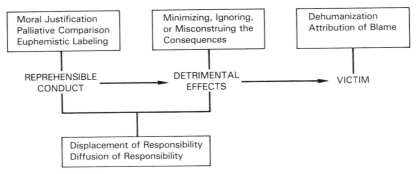

FIGURE 6. Mechanisms through which internal control is selectively activated or disengaged from conduct at different points in the process.

rents against reprehensible acts. Individuals normally refrain from conduct that produces self-devaluative consequences. They pursue activities that serve as sources of self-satisfaction and self-esteem. Self-deterrence is likely to be activated most strongly when the causal connection between reprehensible conduct and its injurious effects is unambiguous. There are various means, however, by which self-evaluative reactions can be dissociated from censurable behavior. Figure 6 shows the several points in the process at which the disengagement may occur.

Moral Justification

One set of disengagement practices operates on the nature of the behavior itself. People do not ordinarily engage in reprehensible conduct until they have justified to themselves the morality of their actions. What is culpable can be made honorable through cognitive restructuring. In this process, reprehensible conduct is made personally and socially acceptable by portraying it in the service of moral ends.

Radical shifts in destructive behavior through moral justification are most strikingly revealed in military training. People who have been taught to deplore killing as morally condemnable can be transformed rapidly into skilled combatants, who feel little compunction and even a sense of pride

in taking human life. The task of converting socialized men into dedicated combatants is achieved not by altering their personality structures, aggressive drives, or traits. Rather, it is accomplished by restructuring the moral value of killing, so that it can be done free from self-censuring restraints (Kelman, 1973; Sanford & Comstock, 1971). In justifying warfare, one sees oneself fighting ruthless oppressors who have an unquenchable appetite for conquest, protecting one's way of life, preserving world peace, saving humanity from being subjugated to an evil ideology, and honoring the country's international commitments. Such restructuring of circumstances is designed to get even considerate people to regard violent means as morally justifiable to achieve humane ends. Violence is made morally defensible when alternative means are said to have been exhausted, and the suffering caused by the violent countermeasures is greatly outweighed by the human suffering inflicted by the foe.

Moral redefinition of killing is nowhere more dramatically illustrated than in the case of Sergeant York, one of the phenomenal fighters in the history of modern warfare (Skeyhill, 1928). Because of his deep religious convictions, he registered as a conscientious objector, but his numerous appeals were rejected. At camp, his battalion commander quoted chapter and verse from the Bible to persuade him that under appropriate conditions it was Christian to fight and kill. A marathon, mountainside prayer finally convinced him that he could serve both God and country by becoming a dedicated fighter.

Soldiers are returned to civilian life without putting them through a resocialization process designed to reinstate self-sanctions against killing. Upon discharge, moral standards are promptly reengaged, so that behaving cruelly is again deterred by self-condemning reactions.

Over the years, much destructive and reprehensible conduct has been perpetrated by decent, moral people in the name of religious principles, righteous ideologies, and nationalistic imperatives. Individuals espousing high moral principles are inclined to resist arbitrary social demands to behave punitively, but they will commit aggression against people who violate their personal principles (Keniston, 1970). Throughout history many have suffered at the hands of self-righteous crusaders bent on stamping out what they consider evil. Acting on moral or ideological imperatives does not reflect an unconscious defense mechanism, but rather a conscious offense mechanism.

Although moral restructuring can be easily used to support self-serving and destructive behavior, it can also serve militant action aimed at changing inhumane social conditions. By appealing to morality, social reformers are able to use coercive, and even violent, tactics to force social change. Vigorous disputes arise over the morality of collective action directed against institutional practices. Those in privileged positions are not easily persuaded to make needed changes that conflict with their own self-interests; thus, their entrenchment invites social activism. Challengers define their coercive actions as morally justifiable means to eradicate harmful social practices. Established authorities, in turn, condemn such disruptive activism as representing impatient resort to aggressive solutions when alternative avenues are open to rectify grievances.

There are those who argue for a high moral threshold as a criterion of coercive ac-

tivism (Bickel, 1974). In this view, unlawful conduct is justified only if traditional means have failed, and those who break the law do so publicly and then willingly accept the consequences of their transgressive behavior. In this way, specific unjust practices can be challenged while maintaining respect for the judicial process itself. It is presumably the suffering endured by the aggrieved protesters that shakes the moral complacency of compassionate citizens and thereby mobilizes the widespread support required to force warranted reforms. If challengers demand amnesty for unlawful conduct, it not only defeats the purpose of conscientious disobedience, but it is morally wrong. If individuals do not have to accept responsibility for their actions, violent tactics and threats of force will be quickly used whenever grievances arise. It is further argued that illegal defiance of the rules in a representative society fosters contempt for the principle of democratic authority. Anarchy would flourish in a climate in which individuals acted on private moral principles and considered coercive tactics acceptable when they disliked majority decisions.

Challengers refute such moral arguments by appeal to what they regard as a higher level of morality, derived from communal concern. Their constituencies may be expanded to include all people, both at home and abroad, victimized either directly or indirectly by injurious institutional practices. From the protesters' perspective, they are acting under a moral imperative to stop the adverse treatment of people who are outside the system and who, therefore, have no way of modifying its policies. The disadvantaged members, even within the system, lack the resources and means to influence it in significant ways. Some are disenfranchised, most have no voice in decision making, and legal efforts to remedy their grievances are repeatedly thwarted. Even if the judicial procedures were impartially administered, few could afford the heavy expenses and the protracted time required to exhaust legal remedies. Not only is one not obliged to obey authorities who preside over inequitable systems that protect them with layers of bureaucratic barriers and coercive power, so the reasoning goes, but one is morally right to disobey them. When leaders secure widespread support from a populace that benefits from exploitive policies, the social activism of an aggrieved minority is more likely to arouse demands for coercive social control rather than sympathy for them. Indeed, people in advantaged positions excuse high levels of violence for social control, but they are quick to condemn dissent and protest for social changes as acts of violence (Blumenthal, Kahn, Andrews, & Head, 1972). Submitting to the punitive consequences of their disruptive protest, challengers argue, places institutional procedures above the welfare of human beings and simply allows the system to perpetuate its exploitation of the disadvantaged.

As the preceding discussion shows, people can easily marshal moral reasons for coercive actions for social control or for social change. In conflicts of power, one person's violence is another person's benevolence. One group's terrorists are another group's freedom fighters. This is why moral appeals against violence usually fall on deaf ears. Because the mass media, especially television, provide the best access to the public, they are increasingly used as the principal vehicles of justification. Struggles to legitimize and gain support for one's causes and to discredit those of one's opponents are now waged more and more through the electronic media (Ball-Rokeach, 1972). For this reason, there is growing public concern about restricted access to the media and concentration of its ownership in fewer hands.

Euphemistic Labeling

Actions can take on very different appearances depending on what they are called. Euphemistic language thus provides a convenient device for masking reprehensible activities or even conferring a respectable status upon them. Through convoluted verbiage, pernicious conduct is made benign and those who engage in it are relieved of a sense of personal agency. That euphemistic language has disinhibitory power is clearly shown by Diener and his associates in a study on interpersonal aggression (Diener, Dineen, Endresen, Beaman, & Fraser, 1975). Adults behaved more than twice as aggressively when the assault of a person was called a game than when it was called aggression.

In an insightful analysis of the language of nonresponsibility, Gambino (1973) identifies the different varieties of euphemisms. One form, palliative expressions, is most widely used to make the reprehensible respectable. Through the power of hygienic words, even killing a human being loses much of its repugnancy. Soldiers "waste" people rather than kill them, CIA operatives "terminate (them) with extreme prejudice." When mercenaries speak of "fulfilling a contract," murder is transformed by admirable words into the honorable discharge of duty. Sanitizing euphemisms, of course, perform heavy duty in less loathsome but unpleasant activities that people are called upon to do from time to time. In the language of some government agencies, people are not fired, they are "selected out," as though they were receiving preferential treatment. In teaching business students how to lie in competitive transactions, some instructors speak euphemistically of "strategic misrepresentation" (Safire, 1979). The television industry produces and markets some of the most brutal forms of human cruelty under the sanitized labels of "action and adventure" programming (Baldwin & Lewis, 1972). The nuclear power industry has created its own specialized set of euphemisms for the injurious effects of nuclear mishaps; an explosion becomes an "energetic disassembly," a reactor accident is a "normal aberration," and plutonium contamination is merely "infiltration" (*San Fransisco Chronicle*, 1979a).

The agentless passive form serves as a linguistic device for creating the appearance that culpable acts are the work of nameless forces, rather than people (Bolinger, 1982).

It is as though people are moved mechanically but are not really the agents of their own acts. Even inanimate objects are sometimes invested with agentive properties, "The telephone pole was approaching. I was attempting to swerve out of its way when it struck my front end" (*San Francisco Chronicle*, 1979b). Gambino further documents how the specialized jargon of a legitimate enterprise can be misused to lend an aura of respectability to an illegitimate one. In the Watergate vocabulary, criminal conspiracy became a "game plan," and the conspirators were "team players" calling for the qualities and behavior befitting the best sportsmen. The disinhibitory power of language can be boosted further by colorful metaphors that change the nature of culpable activities.

Advantageous Comparison

Judgments of behavior partly depend on what it is compared against. Self-deplored acts can be made righteous by contrasting them with flagrant inhumanities. The more outrageous the comparison practices, the more likely are one's reprehensible acts to appear trifling or even benevolent. Promoters of the Vietnamese war and their supporters, for example, minimized the slaying of countless people as a way of checking massive communist enslavement. Given the trifling comparison, perpetrators of warfare remained unperturbed by the fact that the intended beneficiaries were being killed at an alarming rate. Domestic protesters, on the other hand, characterized their own violence against educational and political institutions as trifling, or even laudable, by comparing it with the carnage perpetrated by their country's military forces in foreign lands. In social conflicts, injurious behavior usually escalates with each side lauding its own behavior but condemning that of their adversaries as heinous.

Cognitive restructuring of behavior through moral justifications and palliative characterizations is the most effective self-disinhibitor because it not only eliminates self-generated deterrents but engages self-reward in the service of injurious enterprises. What was once morally unacceptable becomes a source of self-pride.

Displacement of Responsibility

Another set of dissociative practices operates by obscuring or distorting the relationship between actions and the effects they cause. People will behave in ways they normally repudiate if a legitimate authority acknowledges responsibility for the consequences of the conduct (Diener et al., 1975; Milgram, 1974). Under conditions of displaced responsibility, people view their actions as springing from the dictates of authorities, rather than their being personally responsible for them. Since they are not the actual agent of their actions, they are spared self-prohibiting reactions. Displacement of responsibility not only weakens restraints over one's own detrimental actions but diminishes concern over the well-being of those mistreated by others (Tilker, 1970).

Exemption from self-devaluation for heinous deeds has been most gruesomely revealed in socially sanctioned mass executions. Nazi prison commandants and their staffs felt little personal responsibility for their unprecedented inhumanities. They were simply carrying out orders. Impersonal obedience to horrific orders was similarly evident in military atrocities, such as the My Lai massacre (Kelman, 1973). In an effort to deter institutionally sanctioned atrocities, the Nuremberg Accords were established, declaring that obedience to inhumane orders, even from the highest authorities, does not relieve subordinates of the responsibility of their actions. However, since victors are disinclined to try themselves as criminals, such decrees have limited deterrence without an international judiciary system empowered to impose penalties on victors and losers alike.

In studies of disinhibition through displacement of responsibility, authorities explicitly authorize punitive actions and hold themselves fully accountable for the consequences. However, responsibility for reprehensible behavior is rarely assumed so explicitly, because no one wants to be answerable for such acts. To minimize loss of self-respect and risk to themselves, superiors more often invite and condone reprehensible conduct in insidious ways to create a sense of their own ignorance for what is happening. Moreover, the intended purpose of sanctioned destructiveness is usually disguised so that neither issuers nor perpetrators regard their actions as censurable. When reproachful practices are publicized, they are officially dismissed as only isolated incidents arising through misunderstanding of what, in fact, had been authorized.

A number of social factors affect the ease with which responsibility for one's actions can be surrendered to others. High justification and social consensus about the morality of an enterprise aid in the relinquishment of personal control. The legitimacy of the authorizers is another important determinant. The higher the authorities, the more legitimacy, respect, and coercive power they command, and the more amenable are people to defer to them. Modeled disobedience, which challenges the legitimacy of the activities, if not the authorizers themselves, reduces the willingness of observers to carry out the actions called for by the orders of a superior (Milgram, 1974; Powers & Geen, 1972).

It is difficult to continue to disown personal agency in the face of evident harm following directly from one's actions. People are, therefore, less willing to obey authoritarian orders for injurious behavior when they see firsthand how they are hurting others (Milgram, 1974; Tilker, 1970).

Obedient functionaries do not necessarily cast off all responsibility for their behavior as though they were mindless extensions of others. If this were the case, they would act like automatons, only when told to. In fact, they are much more conscientious and self-directed in the performance of their duties. It requires a strong sense of responsibility to be a good functionary. In situations involving obedience to authority, people carry out orders partly to honor the obligations they have undertaken (Mantell & Panzarella, 1976). One must, therefore, distinguish between two levels of responsibility: duty to one's superiors and accountability for the effects of one's actions. The self system operates most efficiently in the service of authority when followers assume personal responsibility for being dutiful executors while relinquishing personal responsibility for the consequences of their behavior. Followers who disowned responsibility without being bound by a sense of duty would be quite unreliable.

Diffusion of Responsibility

The deterrent power of self-reactions is weakened when the link between conduct and its consequences is obscured by diffusing responsibility for culpable behavior. This happens in several ways. Responsibility can be diffused by division of labor. Most enterprises require the services of many people, each performing fragmentary jobs that seem harmless in themselves. The fractional contribution is easily isolated from the end product, especially when participants exercise little personal judgment in carrying out a subfunction that is related by remote, complex links to the end result. After activities become routinized into programmed subfunctions, attention shifts from the import of what one is doing to the details of one's fractional job (Kelman, 1973).

Group–decision making is another common bureaucratic practice that enables otherwise considerate people to behave inhumanely, because no single individual feels responsible for policies arrived at collectively. Where everyone is responsible no one is really responsible. Social organizatons go to great lengths to devise sophisticated mechanisms for obscuring responsibility for decisions that will affect others adversely. Collective action is still another diffusion expedient for weakening self-restraints. Any harm done by a group can always be ascribed, in large part, to the behavior of other members. People, therefore, act more harshly when responsibility is obfuscated by a collective instrumentality than when they hold themselves personally accountable for what they do (Bandura, Underwood, & Fromson, 1975; Diener, 1977; Zimbardo, 1969).

This is not to say that shared responsibility has no legitimate purpose. In efforts to serve diverse constituencies, actions beneficial to one group may be detrimental to another. Because differences are not always reconcilable, someone will inevitably be hurt, whatever is done. Those who must make tough decisions and perform society's nasty duties are at least spared some personal distress by sharing the accountability. They could not function for long if they had to bear the full load alone.

People often behave in harmful ways, not because responsibility is diffused by formal organizational arrangements, but because they all routinely engage in activities that contribute to negative effects. They pollute the air they breathe with their automobiles and degrade their environment to produce the vast amounts of energy and products they consume. As a result of collective action, good environmentalists can also be good polluters by blaming others for degrading the environment. The more detrimental the collectively produced effects, the less people feel personally responsible for them (Shippee & Christian, 1978).

Disregard or Distortion of Consequences

Additional ways of weakening self-deterring reactions operate through disregard or misrepresentation of the consequences of action. When people choose to pursue activities harmful to others for personal gain or because of social inducements, they avoid facing the harm they cause or minimize it. They readily recall prior information given them about the potential benefits of the behavior but are less able to remember its harmful effects (Brock & Buss, 1962, 1964). People are especially prone to minimize adverse consequences when they act alone and thus cannot easily escape responsibility (Mynatt & Herman, 1975). In addition to selective inattention and cognitive distortions, the misrepresentation may take more active forms. For example, the tobacco industry hires scientists to discredit evidence that heavy smoking increases health risks. As long as the detrimental results of one's conduct are ignored, minimized, or distorted, there is little reason for self-censure to be activated.

It is relatively easy to hurt others when their suffering is not visible and when causal actions are physically and temporally remote from their effects. Mechanized warfare, in which masses of people can be put to death by destructive forces released remotely, illustrates such depersonalized behavior. Even high personal responsibility is a weak restrainer without feedback about the pain others suffer (Tilker, 1970). In contrast, when people can see and hear the suffering they cause, vicariously aroused distress and self-censure serve as self-restraining influences. For example, in his studies of commanded aggression, Milgram (1974) obtained diminishing obedience as the victims' pain became more evident and personalized.

Most organizations involve hierarchical chains of command in which superiors formulate plans and intermediaries transmit them to executors, who then carry them out. The farther removed individuals are from the end results, the weaker is the restraining power of the foreseeable effects. Kilham and Mann (1974) make an interesting observation that the disengagement of internal control is easiest for the intermediaries in a hierarchical system—they neither bear responsibility for major decisions nor are they a party to their execution. In performing the transmitter role they model dutiful behavior and further legitimize their superiors and their practices. Consistent with these speculations, intermediaries are much more obedient to destructive commands than those who have to carry them out and face the results (Kilham & Mann, 1974).

Dehumanization

The final set of disengagement practices operates at the point of recipients' consequences. The strength of self-evaluative reactions partly depends on how the perpetrators view the people toward whom the behavior is directed. To perceive another as human enhances empathetic or vicarious responsiveness through perceived similarity. The joys and suffering of similar persons are more vicariously arousing than those of strangers or individuals who have been divested of human qualities. Personalizing the adverse effects experienced by others also makes their suffering much more salient. As a result, it is difficult to mistreat humanized persons without risking self-condemnation.

People will mistreat animals and kill them for game, for food, or simply because they are nuisances without experiencing any empathetic reactions or self-devaluation. Self-sanctions against mistreatment of people can be similarly disengaged or blunted by divesting them of human qualities. Once dehumanized, they are no longer viewed as persons with feelings, hopes, and concerns but as subhuman objects demeaningly stereotyped as "gooks," "fags," or "niggers." Subhumans are presumably insensitive to maltreatment and influenceable only through more primitive methods. If dispossessing disfavored people of their humanness does not blunt self-reproof, it can be fully eliminated by attributing bestial qualities to them. They become "degenerates," "pigs," and other bestial creatures. Over the years slaves, women, manual laborers, and religious and racial minorities have been treated as chattel or as subhuman objects (Ball-Rokeach, 1972).

Studies of interpersonal aggression give vivid testimony to the self-disinhibitory power of dehumanization (Bandura, Underwood, & Fromson, 1975). Dehumanized individuals are treated more than twice as punitively as those who have been invested with human qualities and more severely than those who have been depicted impersonally. When punitiveness fails to achieve results, this is likely to be taken as further evidence of the unworthiness of dehumanized persons, thus justifying their even greater maltreatment. Analyzing the cognitive concomitants of punitive behavior reveals that dehumanization fosters different self-exonerative patterns of thought. People seldom condemn punitive conduct and generate self-disinhibiting justifications for it when they are directing their behavior toward individuals who have been deprived of their humanness. By contrast, people strongly disapprove of punitive actions and rarely excuse their use when they interact with individuals depicted in humanized terms.

Many conditions of contemporary life are conducive to impersonalization and dehumanization (Bernard, Ottenberg, & Redl, 1965). Bureaucratization, automation, urbanization, and high social mobility lead people to relate to each other in anonymous, impersonal ways. In addition, social practices that divide people into in-group and out-group members produce human estrangement that fosters dehumanization. Strangers can be more easily cast as insensate than can personal acquaintances.

Under certain conditions, the exercise of institutional power changes the users in ways that are conducive to dehumanization. This happens most often when persons in positions of authority have coercive power over others and when adequate safeguards for constraining the behavior of powerholders are lacking. Kipnis (1974) identifies several processes by which power can devalue others in the eyes of the powerholder. It is easy for persons who wield control over others and institutional practices and who receive a lot of ingratiating flattery to develop an inflated view of themselves. When persons preside over institutions measured in terms of products and profits, material gains tend to be valued more highly than the people who produce them. This is evident in athletic and artistic endeavors. Once such activities have been commercialized into big business, performers come to be regarded as disposable commodities to be used only as long as they bring in the currency.

Kipnis (1974) documents the devaluating effects of unilateral power, even when briefly exercised. Compared to student supervisors, who had to rely on their persuasive skills, those who could influence the behavior of workers through money thought less of their ability and performances, viewed them as objects who had to be manipulated to get things done, and had less desire to associate with them. That wielding power over others strengthens manipulative attitudes and fosters devaluation of those subject to control is replicated by Zimbardo's simulated prison experiment (Haney, Banks, & Zimbardo, 1973). College students, who had been randomly designated as guards, began to treat their charges in degrading tyrannical ways. In involuntary institutions even methods of treatment can be perverted into methods of punishment, when the people who run them are granted coercive power and the safeguards of due process are lacking (Opton, 1974).

People who have subordinate status often organize into groups in efforts to reduce power imbalances. They use the collective power of numbers not only to improve their lot in life but also to preserve their sense of self-worth and human dignity. Professional athletes represent some of the more recent groups seeking to change their status from properties that are drafted, traded, and sold by franchise owners to employees with some choice of teams and salaries (Garvey, 1979).

Psychological research tends to focus extensively on how easy it is to bring out the worst in people through dehumanization and other self-exonerative means. The sensational negative findings receive the greatest attention. Thus, for example, the aspect of Milgram's research that is routinely cited is the evidence that good people can be talked into performing cruel deeds. To get people to carry out punitive acts, the overseer had to be physically present, repeatedly ordering them to act as they voiced their concerns and objections. Orders to escalate punitiveness to more intense levels are largely ignored or subverted when remotely issued by verbal command. As Helm and Morelli (1979) note, this is hardly an example of blind obedience triggered by an authoritative mandate. Moreover, what is rarely noted is the equally striking evidence that people steadfastly refuse to behave punitively, even in response to strong authoritarian commands, if the situation is personalized a bit (e.g., they can see the victim or they must aggress directly). The emphasis on the negative is understandable, considering the prevalence and harmfulness of people's inhumanities to one another. However, of considerable theoretical and social significance is the power of humanization to counteract injurious conduct. Studies examining this process reveal that, even under conditions that weaken self deterrents, it is exceedingly difficult for individuals to behave cruelly toward others when they are characterized in ways that personalize and humanize them (Bandura, Underwood, & Fromson, 1975). Affirmation of common humanity can bring out the best in others.

The moderating influence of humanization is most strikingly revealed in situations involving lethal violence. Most abductors find it very difficult to harm their hostages after they have gotten to know them personally. Gangs often have to rely on out-of-town hit men because members who know the victims personally are unable to pull the trigger. Most people support the death penalty in the abstract, but the more they know about particular cases, the less they favor executing them (Ellsworth, 1978). As Ellsworth explains it, in the absence of personal information, people conjure up an image of the most heinous criminal, an image that disposes them to favor punishment by death.

As in other disengagement mechanisms, there are certain conditions under which some emotional detachment can serve humane purposes. Members of the helping professions must deal continually with people who experience considerable pain and suffering. Physicians and surgeons see multitudes of suffering patients. Most of the people with whom psychotherapists deal lead tormented lives. Those who staff social welfare programs see seemingly endless lines of people ravaged by poverty, disease, and years of societal maltreatment or neglect. Were they to empathize fully with the suffering of their clients, they would be too overwhelmed emotionally to be able to help them. Some moderating of the personalization of other people's suffering serves to reduce impairing or incapacitating personal distress (Maslach, 1982).

In dealing with recurrent human problems day in and day out, it is all too easy to routinize and depersonalize services to the point where people are treated like subhuman objects. Boredom and apathy set in when one's perceived self-efficacy to render significant benefits declines. Maslach and her associates (Maslach & Jackson, 1982; Maslach & Pines, 1977) have identified three aspects to this type of "burnout syndrome": depersonalization, emotional exhaustion, and a low sense of personal accomplishment in one's work. Health and social service workers seem most vulnerable. In such cases, respect and "detached concern" for clients is replaced by indifference, if not callousness. Quality of service deteriorates, as does staff morale. Maslach presents a strong case that such self-debilitation, which is an occupational hazard of most service professions, is rooted more in the nature and structure of stressful work than in the attributes of the practitioners. Among the factors identified as contributory to human debilitation and depersonalization are prolonged intense contact with people in distress; few breaks with nonpersonal work to reduce the emotional strain; unvaried work routines; lack of personal control over the policies and practices of one's work environment; little feedback of how one is doing on the job; inability to quit thinking about the job during off-hours; and lack of social support from colleagues to ease the burden. Exposure to the cynical and dehumanizing views of other workers concerning troubled people accelerates this process.

Attribution of Blame

Attributing the blame to those who are being maltreated is still another expedient that can serve self-exonerative purposes. Detrimental interactions usually involve a series of reciprocally escalative actions, in which the victims are rarely faultless. One can always select from the chain of events an instance of the adversary's defensive behavior and view it as the original instigation. Injurious conduct thus becomes a justifiable defensive reaction to beligerent provocations. At the societal level, adverse social practices breed human failings, which can then be used as self-confirming evidence of the victims' defects or worthlessness. But here, too, those who are victimized are not entirely faultless because, by their behavior, they contribute partly to their own plight. Victims can, therefore, be blamed for bringing suffering on themselves. Self-exoneration is similarly achievable by viewing one's reprehensible behavior as forced by circumstances, rather than as a personal decision. By blaming others or circumstances, not only are one's own actions excusable, but one can even feel self-righteous in the process.

Observers of victimization can be disinhibited in much the same way as perpetrators by the tendency to infer culpability from misfortune. Seeing victims suffer maltreatment for which they are held partially responsible leads observers to derogate them (Lerner & Miller, 1978). The devaluation and indignation aroused by ascribed culpability, in turn, provides moral justification for even greater maltreatment. That attribution of blame can give rise to devaluation and moral justification illustrates how the various disengagement mechanisms are often interrelated and work together in weakening internal control.

Evidence suggests that these mechanisms of self-disinhibition facilitate sexually assaultive behavior toward women. Rapists and males who acknowledge a proclivity to rape subscribe to myths about rape embodying the various mechanisms by which moral self-censure can be disengaged (Feild, 1978; Malamuth, 1981b). These beliefs hold rape victims responsible for their own victimization because they have supposedly invited rape by sexually provocative appearance and behavior and by resisting sexual assault weakly. Men blame rape victims more than women do. Trivialization and distortion of consequences to rape victims is another disengagement mechanism that comes into play. Men who are prone to sexual assault believe that women secretly enjoy being raped. Anticipatory self-censure is eliminated when the traumatic effects of sexual assault are twisted into pleasurable ones for the victim. Such self-disinhibiting patterns of thinking predict proclivity to rape, whereas sexual attitudes, frustration, and quality of sex life do not (Briere & Malamuth, 1983).

Cross-cultural studies reveal that aggressive sexuality is an expression of the cultural ideology of male dominance (Sanday, 1981). Rape is prevalent in societies where violence is a way of life, male supremacy reigns, aggressive sexuality is valued as a sign of manliness, and women are treated as property. Rape is rare in societies that repudiate interpersonal aggression, endorse sexual equality, and treat women respectfully. Cultural ideologies that attach prestige to male dominance and aggressive sexuality weaken self-censure for sexual abuse of women. Cultural practices that belittle the role of women, and a flourishing pornography industry that dehumanizes them, both contribute further to the self-disinhibition of aggression toward women (Malamuth & Donnerstein, 1983).

Justified abuse can have more devastating human consequences than acknowledged cruelty. Maltreatment that is not clothed in righteousness makes the perpetrator, rather than the victim, blameworthy. But when blame is convincingly ascribed to victims, they may eventually come to believe the degrading characterizations of themselves (Hallie, 1971). Moreover, ascriptions of blame are usually accompanied by discriminatory social practices that create the

very failings that serve as excuses for maltreatment. Vindicated inhumanity is, thus, more likely to instill self-contempt in victims than inhumanity that does not attempt to justify itself.

Gradualism and Self-Disinhibition

The aforementioned self-disinhibitory devices will not instantaneously transform a considerate person into an unprincipled, callous one. Rather, the change is usually achieved through gradual disinhibition in which people may not fully recognize the changes they are undergoing. Initially, individuals are prompted to perform questionable acts that they can tolerate with little self-censure. After their discomfort and self-reproof have been diminished through repeated performances, the level of reprehensibility progressively increases until eventually acts originally regarded as abhorrent can be performed without much distress. Escalative self-disinhibition accelerates if the people being subjected to maltreatment are divested of human qualities (Bandura, Underwood, & Fromson, 1975).

Analyses of disengagement mechanisms usually draw heavily on examples from military and political violence. This tends to convey the impression that selective disengagement of self-sanctions occurs only under extraordinary circumstances. Quite the contrary. Such mechanisms operate in everyday situations in which decent people routinely perform activities having injurious human effects to further their own interests or for profit. Self-exonerations are needed to neutralize self-sanctions and to preserve self-esteem. For example, institutionalized discrimination, a practice which takes a heavy toll on its victims, requires social justification, attributions of blame, dehumanization, impersonalized agencies to carry it out, and inattention to the injurious effects it causes. Different industries, each with its public-spirited vindications, cause harmful effects on a large scale, either by the nature of their products or the environmental contaminants they produce.

Self-Disinhibition and Self-Deception

The issue arises as to whether self-disinhibition involves self-deception. Because of the incompatibility of being simultaneously a deceiver and the one deceived, many philosophical analyses dispute whether literal self-deception exists (Bok, 1980; Champlin, 1977; Haight, 1980). It is logically impossible to deceive oneself into believing something, while simultaneously knowing it to be false. Hence, the analytic task is redirected to explain phenomena that are commonly misconstrued as self-deception. Writers who assume that self-deception is a genuine phenomenon usually try to resolve the paradox by creating split selves and rendering one of them unconscious. However, the self-splitting solution annihilates such a phenomenon, rather than explains it. The split-self conceptions fail to specify how a conscious self can lie to an unconscious self without some awareness of what the other self believes. The deceiving self has to be aware of what the deceived self believes because deception, by definition, entails deliberate misrepresentation. Self-deception presupposes both an awareness of what beliefs are held in order to concoct a deception and the intent to deceive oneself into believing what one knows to be false (Champlin, 1977). Different levels of awareness are sometimes proposed as another possible solution to the paradox. It is said that "deep down" people really know what they believe. This attempt to reacquaint the split selves only reinstates the paradox of how one can be the agent and the object of deception at the same time. People, of course, often misconstrue events, they lead themselves astray by their biases, and they display unawareness. But the latter phenomena should not be confused with lying to oneself.

People's values and beliefs affect what information they seek and how they interpret what they see and hear. Most strive to maintain or enhance their positive self-regard. Therefore, they do not go looking for evidence of their culpability or adverse effects of their actions. Selective self-exposure and distorted interpretations of events, which confirm and strengthen preexisting beliefs, reflect biased self-persuasion, not a case of self-deception. To be misdirected by one's preconceptions does not mean that one is lying to oneself.

Self-deception is often invoked when people choose to ignore possibly countervailing evidence. It could be argued that they must believe its validity in order to avoid it, otherwise they would not know what to shun. This is not necessarily so. Staunch believers often choose not to waste their time scrutinizing opposing arguments because they are already convinced of the fallacy of the arguments. When confronted with evidence that ostensibly disputes their beliefs, they question its credibility, dismiss its relevance, or twist it to fit their views. However, if the evidence is sufficiently persuasive, they alter their original beliefs to accommodate the discrepant evidence. More interesting are people who harbor self-doubts concerning their beliefs and avoid seeking certain evidence, because they have an inkling the evidence might disconfirm what they wish to believe. Indeed, they may engage in all kinds of maneuvers, both in thought and in action, to avoid finding out the actual state of affairs. Suspecting something is not the same as knowing it to be true. Inklings can always be discounted as possibly being ill founded. As long as one does not find out the truth, what one believes is not personally known to be false. Both Haight (1980) and Fingarette (1969) give considerable attention to processes whereby people avoid a painful truth by either not taking actions that would reveal it or not spelling out fully what they are doing or undergoing that would make it known. Under conditions of uncertainty, shunning evidence that permits one to believe what one wants to believe is wishful thinking, which is not the same as believing what one knows to be false. Nor is clinging to a belief in the face of contradictory evidence that one disbelieves or reinterprets a case of self-deception.

Self-disinhibition involves more than the reduction of self-censure. People are also concerned about how they appear in the eyes of others when they engage in conduct that is morally suspect. This adds an interpersonal evaluative factor to the process. Haight (1980) argues that, in much of what is called self-deception, persons are aware of the reality they are trying to deny, but they create the public appearance that they are deceiving themselves. Others are thus left uncertain about how to judge and treat persons who seem to be sincerely deluding themselves in efforts to avoid an unpleasant truth. The public pretense is designed to head off social reproof. When people are caught up in the same painful predicament, the result may be a lot of collective public pretense.

The mechanisms of self-disinhibition involve cognitive and social machinations but not literal self-deception. In moral justification, for example, people may be misled by those they trust into believing that injurious means are morally right because the means will check the human suffering of tyranny. The persuasive depictions of the perils and benefits may be accurate, exaggerated, or just pious rhetoric masking less honorable purposes. The same persuasory process applies to self-disinhibition by dehumanizing and blaming adversaries. In the rhetoric of conflict, opinion shapers ascribe their foes with irrationalities, barbarities, and culpabilities (Ivie, 1980) that color public beliefs. In these different instances, those who have been persuaded are not lying to themselves. The misleaders and the misled are different persons. When the misleaders are themselves operating under erroneous beliefs, the views they voice are not intentional deceptions. They seek to persuade others into believing what they themselves believe. In social deception, public declarations by others may belie their private beliefs, which are concealed from those being deceived.

In self-disinhibition by ignoring, minimizing, or misconstruing the social effects of their actions, people lack the evidence to disbelieve what they already believe. The issue of self-dishonesty does not arise as long as one remains uninformed or misinformed about the outcomes of one's actions. When self-disinhibition is promoted by diffused and displaced responsibility, functionaries carry out the orders of superiors and often perform only a small subfunction, at that. Such arrangements enable people to think of themselves merely as instruments, rather than as agents, of the entire enterprise. If they regard themselves as minor cogs in the intricate social machinery, they have little reason to believe otherwise concerning their initiatory power. This is not to say that disengagement of self-censure operates flawlessly. If disbeliefs arise, especially at the point of moral justification, people cannot get themselves to behave inhumanely, and if they do, they pay the high price of self-contempt.

Alternative Perspectives on Disengagement of Personal Control

Behaviorists, for whom control ultimately resides in the environment, ascribe reductions in restraints to situational disinhibitors. They view social factors that promote detrimental conduct, such as anonymity, group action, and diffused responsibility, as discriminative cues that such behavior will go undetected or unpunished. Mistreating persons who have been devalued and faulted for their misfortune would presumably carry a lower risk of punishment than would maltreatment of those who are valued or considered blameless.

While people often do behave in ways designed to gain favor and avoid the displeasure of others, they also act in terms of their own personal standards. Consequently, external rewards often do not increase behavior, and external punishments often fail to reduce it. People commonly resist acts they consider to be transgressive or immoral, despite strong social pressures and rewards. They are known to make amends on their own for past undetected transgressions that would forever have remained so. When they act on moral imperatives that challenge prevailing social practices, they suffer and even die for principles they value. These types of actions do not lend themselves to explanations in terms of external payoffs. Rather, it is self-respect rooted in personal standards that wields decisive influence.

In an elaboration of deindividuation theory, Zimbardo (1969) explains lapses in self-control as losses of one's individuality. Deindividuation is defined as an internal state characterized by reduced self-awareness and self-evaluation and by diminished concern over the reactions of others. Lowered self-consciousness weakens cognitive control over behavior, thereby facilitating impulsive acts.

People can be deindividuated by a variety of conditions, including anonymity, immersion in a group, diffused responsibility, high emotional arousal, intense sensory stimulation, and physiological conditions that alter states of consciousness. The postulated determinants that have been examined most closely, group immersion, anonymity, and emotional arousal, tend to reduce restraints, especially if other factors conducive to disinhibition are also present (Bandura, 1973; Diener, 1977; Dipboye, 1977; Zimbardo, 1969). Verification of the internal deindividuation link in the causal chain is a much more complicated matter. This requires measuring changes in self-consciousness and concern over personal and social evaluation at the time the impulsive actions are occurring. Attempts to link the indicants of deindividuation (assessed after the fact) either to situational conditions or to disinhibited behavior have so far produced inconclusive results (Diener, 1977). However, it is doubtful that retrospective reports by persons who have acted in censurable ways truly reflect their thought patterns at the time they were misbehaving. There is evidence that heightened self-attentiveness inhibits disapprovable acts (Diener, 1980; Wicklund, 1975). However, people who value aggressiveness increase, rather than reduce, their aggression when they pay close attention to what they are doing (Carver, 1975).

It should be recognized that this line of research presents especially difficult methodological problems. One cannot interrupt people as they act unrestrainedly to measure their perceptions of themselves and others without aborting the disinhibitory process. To measure the cognitive concomitants of external disinhibitors prior to action can alter the very phenomenon being studied. Tests of theories in this domain, therefore, rest mainly on success in predicting degree of behavioral disinhibition under particular constellations of influences. This leaves theoretical issues somewhat unsettled when alternative theories predict the same covariation between antecedent conditions and behavioral disinhibition but for different reasons. Evidence regarding the mediating process becomes critical.

In view of the importance of self-exonerative and self-justificatory processes in self-disinhibition, a full explanation of how internal control is disengaged must also consider the self-regulatory mechanisms discussed earlier. In an integrative effort in this direction, Diener (1980) has proposed a modified theory of deindividuation that deemphasizes altered states of consciousness and gives greater weight to self-awareness and self-regulation based on personal and social standards. According to the revised formulation, group situations, or even nonsocial conditions, which divert attention from oneself, reduce people's awareness of themselves as individuals. Inattentiveness to one's own behavior, in turn, diminishes self-regulation and forethought. The lowered level of self-regulation increases susceptibility to immediate situational influences.

Although deindividuation and social cognitive theory posit some overlapping determinants and processes of self-disinhibition, they differ in certain important respects. Deindividuation views culpable behavior as resulting from loss of cognitive control. Social cognitive theory encompasses a broad range of disinhibitory factors that affect both impulsive and principled conduct. People frequently engage in destructive activities, not because of reduced self-control, but because their cognitive skills and self-control are all too well enlisted through moral justification and self-exonerative devices in the service of destructive causes. The infamous extermination procedures of Nazi concentration camps were perfected in laboratories using human victims (Wechsberg, 1967). In the Nazi value system, where the enslavement and execution of Jewish people were viewed as meritorious acts of patriotism, camp commandants proudly compared execution rates as if they were industrial production figures (Andrus, 1969). This monstrous death industry required a methodical program of research and efficient and dedicated management.

The massive threats to human welfare are generally brought about by deliberate acts of principle, rather than by unrestrained acts of impulse. It is the principled resort to destructiveness that is of greatest social concern but is the most ignored in psychological theorizing and research. Given the existence of so many self-disinhibiting devices, a society cannot rely entirely on individuals, however honorable their standards, to provide safeguards against harmful conduct. Humaneness requires, in addition to benevolent personal codes, social systems that uphold compassionate behavior and discourage cruelty. If societies are to function more humanely, they must create effective organizational safeguards against the misuse of institutional justificatory power for exploitive and destructive purposes.

CHAPTER

9

SELF-EFFICACY

The preceding chapter examined the processes by which people regulate their behavior through internal standards and self-evaluative reactions to their own behavior. Now we turn our attention to another important facet of a self system, namely, the role of self-referent thought in psychosocial functioning. Among the different aspects of self-knowledge, perhaps none is more influential in people's everyday lives than conceptions of their personal efficacy. This chapter addresses the centrality of the self-efficacy mechanism in human agency.

Psychological theories and research tend to focus on issues concerning either acquisition of knowledge or performance of response patterns. As a result, the processes governing the interrelationship between knowledge and action have been largely neglected (Newell, 1978). Some of the recent efforts to bridge this gap have been di-

rected at the biomechanics problem—how efferent commands expressing action plans guide the production of appropriate response patterns (Stelmach, 1976, 1978). Others have approached the matter in terms of algorithmic knowledge, which furnishes guides for executing action sequences (Greeno, 1973; Newell, 1973). Social cognitive theory examines the transformation mechanism in terms of conception-matching processes whereby symbolic representations are translated into appropriate courses of action.

Knowledge, transformational operations, and constituent skills are necessary but insufficient for accomplished performances. Indeed, people often do not behave optimally even though they know full well what to do. This is because self-referent thought mediates the relationship between knowledge and action. The issues addressed in this line of inquiry are concerned with how people judge their capabilities and how their self-percepts of efficacy affect their motivation and behavior.

Recent years have witnessed increasing convergence of theory and research on the influential role of self-referent thought in psychological functioning (DeCharms, 1978; Garber & Seligman, 1980; Lefcourt, 1976; Perlmuter & Monty, 1979; Rotter, Chance, & Phares, 1972). Although the research is conducted from a number of different perspectives under a variety of labels, the basic phenomenon being addressed centers on people's sense of personal efficacy to exercise some control over events that affect their lives.

Perceived Self-Efficacy as a Generative Capability

Efficacy in dealing with one's environment is not simply a matter of knowing what to do. Nor is it a fixed act that one does or does not have in one's behavioral repertoire, any more than one would construe linguistic efficacy in terms of a collection of words or a colony of fixed sentences in a verbal repertoire. Rather, efficacy involves a generative capability in which cognitive, social, and behavioral subskills must be organized into integrated courses of action to serve innumerable purposes. Success is often attained only after generating and testing alternative forms of behavior and strategies, which requires perseverant effort. Self-doubters are quick to abort this generative process if their initial efforts prove deficient.

There is a marked difference between possessing subskills and being able to use them well under diverse circumstances. For this reason, different people with similar skills, or the same person on different occasions, may perform poorly, adequately, or extraordinarily. Collins (1982) selected children who perceived themselves to be of high or low mathematical self-efficacy at each of two levels of mathematical ability. They were then given difficult problems to solve. While mathematical ability contrib-

uted to performance, at each abilit[y] children who regarded themselves [effi]cacious were quicker to discard faulty strategies, solved more problems, chose to rework more of those they failed, did so more accurately, and displayed more positive attitudes toward mathematics. As this and other studies show, perceived self-efficacy is a significant determinant of performance that operates partially independently of underlying skills (Locke, Frederick, Lee, & Bobko, 1984; Schunk, 1984).

Competent functioning requires both skills and self-beliefs of efficacy to use them effectively. Operative efficacy calls for continuously improvising multiple subskills to manage ever changing circumstances, most of which contain ambiguous, unpredictable, and often stressful elements. Even routinized activities are rarely performed in exactly the same way. Initiation and regulation of transactions with the environment are, therefore, partly governed by judgments of operative capabilities—what people think they can do under given circumstances. Perceived self-efficacy is defined as people's judgments of their capabilities to organize and execute courses of action required to attain designated types of performances. It is concerned not with the skills one has but with judgments of what one can do with whatever skills one possesses.

Judgments of personal efficacy are distinguished from response-outcome expectations. Perceived self-efficacy is a judgment of one's capability to accomplish a certain level of performance, whereas an outcome expectation is a judgment of the likely consequence such behavior will produce. For example, the belief that one can high jump six feet is an efficacy judgment; the anticipated social recognition, applause, trophies, and self-satisfactions for such a performance constitute the outcome expectations.

An outcome is the consequence of an act, not the act itself. Serious confusions arise when an act is misconstrued as an outcome of itself, as when jumping six feet is viewed as a consequent. An act must be defined by the criteria that state what it is, for example, a leap upward of a designated height. To regard a six-foot high jump as an outcome would be to misinterpret the specification criteria of an act as the consequences that flow from it. If an act is defined as a six-foot leap, then a six-foot leap is the realization of the act, not a consequent of it. Failure to complete a designated act (e.g., knocking off a crossbar by failing to jump six feet) cannot be the outcome of that act because it was never fully executed. The failed jump is an incomplete act that produces its own divergent collection of outcomes, be they social, physical, or self-evaluative.

Outcome expectations are also sometimes misconstrued as the effectiveness of a technique (Maddux, Sherer, & Rogers, 1982; Manning & Wright, 1983). Means are not results. An efficacious technique is a means for producing outcomes, but it is not itself an outcome expectation. For example, an effective cognitive skill for solving problems can be put to diverse uses to gain all kinds of outcomes. Useful means serve as the vehicles for exercising personal efficacy.

Efficacy and outcome judgments are differentiated because individuals can believe that a particular course of action will produce certain outcomes, but they do not act on that outcome belief because they question whether they can actually execute the necessary activities. Thus, expectations that high grades gain students entry to medical school and that medical practice yields high incomes will not steer undergraduates into premedical programs who have serious self-doubts that they can master the science requirements.

Dependence of Expected Outcomes on Performance Efficacy Judgments

In transactions with the environment, outcomes do not occur as events disconnected from actions. Rather, most outcomes flow from actions. Hence, how one behaves largely determines the outcomes one experiences. Similarly, in thought, the types of outcomes people anticipate depend largely on their judgments of how well they will be able to perform in given situations. Drivers who judge themselves inefficacious in navigating winding mountain roads will conjure up outcomes of wreckage and bodily injury, whereas those who are fully confident of their driving capabilities will anticipate sweeping vistas rather than tangled wreckage. The social reactions people anticipate for asserting themselves depend on their judgments of how adroitly they can do it. Tactless assertiveness will produce negative counterreactions, whereas adept assertiveness can elicit accommodating reactions. In social, intellectual, and physical pursuits, those who judge themselves highly efficacious will expect favorable outcomes, self-doubters will expect mediocre performances of themselves and thus negative outcomes.

As the above examples illustrate, one cannot sever expected outcomes from the very performance judgments upon which they are conditional. One must distinguish between the source of outcome expectations and their role in regulating behavior. Because outcomes emanate from actions in no way detracts from the regulatory influences of those envisioned outcomes. It is because people see outcomes as contingent on the adequacy of their performances, and care about those outcomes, that they rely on self-judged efficacy in deciding which courses of action to pursue. Physical and psychological well-being is better served by action based on self-appraisal of efficacy than by mindless leaps into action without regard to one's capabilities.

For activities in which outcomes are either inherent to the actions or tightly linked by social codes, outcome expectancies cannot be disjoined from the self-judged performances from which they flow. Physical injury from a poorly executed gymnastic routine typifies inherent linkage; money gained as the prize for winning an athletic contest typifies prescribed social linkage. It is because expected outcomes are highly dependent on self-efficacy judgments that expected outcomes may not add much on their own to the prediction of behavior. If you control for how well people judge they can perform, you account for much of the variance in the kinds of outcomes they expect. Hence, in analyses that statistically control for the effects of the various factors, perceived self-efficacy predicts performance much better than expected outcomes in such diverse activities as phobias, assertiveness, smoking cessation, athletic feats, sales performances, and pain tolerance (Barling & Abel, 1983; Barling & Beattie, 1983; Godding & Glasgow, 1985; Lee, 1984a, 1984b; Manning & Wright, 1983; Williams & Watson, 1985).

Outcome expectations can be dissociated from self-efficacy judgments when either no action can produce a selected effect or extrinsic outcomes are loosely linked to level or quality of performance. Such structural arrangements permit social biases to come into play, so that the same performance attainments may produce variable and often inequitable outcomes. In prejudicially structured systems, variations in performance, however skillfully executed, may have little or no effect on some desired outcomes. Thus, for example, when athletes were rigidly segregated by race, black athletes could not gain entry to major league baseball no matter how well they pitched or batted.

Expected outcomes are also partially separable from self-efficacy judgments when extrinsic outcomes are fixed to a minimum level of performance, as when a designated level of productivity produces a fixed pay but better performance brings no additional monetary benefits. When effects are socially linked to some minimal standard, performance exerts only partial control over outcomes. However, in most everyday activities, variations in performance produce concurrent changes in outcomes. Indeed, even small variations in performance can produce markedly different effects, as when a slight swerve of an automobile on a crowded freeway can cause an instant collision.

SELF-EFFICACY MECHANISM IN HUMAN AGENCY

Function and Diverse Effects of Self-Efficacy Judgment

Self-percepts of efficacy are not simply inert estimates of future action. People's beliefs about their operative capabilities function as one set of proximal determinants of how they behave, their thought patterns, and the emotional reactions they experience in taxing situations. Self-beliefs thus contribute to the quality of psychosocial functioning in diverse ways.

Choice Behavior. In their daily lives people have to make decisions all the time about what courses of action to pursue and how long to continue what they have undertaken. Decisions involving choice of activities and certain social milieus are partly determined by judgments of personal efficacy. People tend to avoid tasks and situations they believe exceed their capabilities, but they undertake and perform assuredly activities they judge themselves capable of handling (Bandura, 1977b). Any factor that influences choice behavior can have profound effects on the course of personal development. Advantageous self-percepts of efficacy that foster active engagement in activities contribute to the growth of competencies. In contrast, perceived self-inefficacies that lead people to shun enriching environments and activities retard development of potentialities and shield negative self-percepts from corrective change.

Reasonably accurate appraisal of one's own capabilities is, therefore, of considerable value in successful functioning. Large misjudgments of personal efficacy in either direction have consequences. People who grossly overestimate their capabilities undertake activities that are clearly beyond their reach. As a result, they get themselves into considerable difficulties, undermine their credibility, and suffer needless failures. Some of the missteps, of course, can produce serious, irreparable harm.

People who underestimate their capabilities also bear costs, although, as already noted, these are more likely to take self-limiting rather than aversive forms. By failing to cultivate personal potentialities and constricting their activities, such persons cut themselves off from many rewarding experiences. Should they attempt tasks having evaluative significance, they create internal obstacles to effective performance by approaching them with unnerving self-doubts.

The efficacy judgments that are the most functional are probably those that slightly exceed what one can do at any given time. Such self-appraisals lead people to undertake realistically challenging tasks and provide motivation for progressive self-development of their capabilities. Accurate self-appraisal is supported by promoting choice of actions with high likelihood of success. However, we shall see shortly that many factors can contribute to misjudgments of self-efficacy.

Effort Expenditure and Persistence. Judgments of efficacy also determine how much effort people will expend and how long they will persist in the face of obstacles or aversive experiences. The stronger their perceived self-efficacy, the more vigorous and persistent are their efforts. When beset with difficulties, people who are plagued by self-doubts about their capabilities slacken their efforts or give up altogether, whereas those who have a strong sense of efficacy exert greater effort to master the challenge (Bandura & Cervone, 1983, 1986; Brown & Inouye, 1978; Schunk, 1984b; Weinberg, Gould, & Jackson, 1979). Strong perseverance usually pays off in high performance attainments. Because knowledge and competencies are achieved by sustained effort, perceived self-inefficacy that leads people to give up easily is personally limiting.

There is a distinction between the effects of strength of perceived self-efficacy on effort during learning and during execution of established skills. In approaching learning tasks, those who perceive themselves to be highly self-efficacious in the undertaking may feel little need to invest much preparatory effort in it. However, in applying skills already acquired, a strong belief in one's self-efficaciousness intensifies and sustains the effort needed to realize difficult performances, which are hard to attain if one is doubt-ridden. In short, self-doubt creates the impetus for learning but hinders adept use of previously established skills. Salomon (1984) provides some evidence bearing on this issue. He found that children's high perceived self-efficacy as learners is associated with a high investment of cognitive effort and better learning from instructional media children consider difficult, but it is associated with less investment of effort and poorer learning from media they believe to be easy. Thus, some uncertainty can benefit preparation. Self-development is aided by a strong sense of self-efficacy to withstand failures, tempered with some uncertainty (construed in terms of the challenge of the task rather than fundamental doubts about one's capabilities) to spur preparatory acquisition of knowledge and skills.

Thought Patterns and Emotional Reactions. People's judgments of their capabilities also influence their thought patterns and emotional reactions during actual and anticipated transactions with their environment. Those who judge themselves inefficacious in coping with environmental demands dwell upon their personal deficiencies and cognize potential difficulties as more formidable than they really are (Beck, 1976; Lazarus & Launier, 1978; Meichenbaum, 1977; Sarason, 1975a). Such self-referent misgivings create stress and undermine effective use of the competencies people possess by diverting attention from how best to proceed to concern over personal failings and possible mishaps. By contrast, persons who have a strong sense of efficacy deploy their attention and effort to the demands of the situation and are spurred by obstacles to greater effort. Perceived self-efficacy also

In
ns,
ly
eir
ose ✓
ed
efi-

im-
ied
elf-
ate
eo-
set
ter-

efficacious act, think, and feel differently from those who perceive themselves as inefficacious. They produce their own future, rather than simply foretell it.

Relationship between Self-Efficacy Judgment and Action

Although self-efficacy judgments are functionally related to action, a number of factors can affect the strength of the relationship. Perceived efficacy alone can affect level of motivation, but it will not produce new-fangled performances if necessary subskills for the exercise of personal agency are completely lacking. Of course, people rarely express vacuous self-efficacy because they are disinclined to judge themselves as highly efficacious in activities for which they have no capabilities whatsoever. However, people usually possess many of the basic subskills for fashioning new performances. The more difficult the tasks, the greater the need for perseverant effort in generating and testing alternative forms of behavior. If some of the subskills are lacking, efficacy-sustained effort promotes their development. Conversely, misbeliefs in one's inefficacy may retard development of the very subskills upon which more complex performances depend. Perceived self-efficacy thus contributes to the development of subskills, as well as draws upon them in fashioning new behavior patterns.

Disincentives and Performance Constraints. Persons may possess the constituent skills and a strong sense of efficacy that they can execute them well, but they still choose not to perform the activities because they have no incentives to do so. In such instances, discrepancies arise from disincentives to act upon one's self-percepts of efficacy. Nor will perceived self-efficacy be expressed in corresponding action if people lack the necessary equipment or resources to perform the behavior adequately. Efficacious artisans and athletes cannot perform well with faulty equipment, and efficacious executives cannot put their

est and involvement in activities; they intensify their efforts when their performances fall short of their goals, make causal ascriptions for failures that support a success orientation, approach potentially threatening tasks nonanxiously, and experience little in the way of stress reactions in taxing situations. Such self-assured endeavor produces accomplishments. In marked contrast, those who regard themselves as inefficacious shy away from difficult tasks, slacken their efforts and give up readily in the face of difficulties, dwell on their personal deficiencies, which detracts attention from task demands, lower their aspirations, and suffer much anxiety and stress. Such self-misgivings undermine performance and generate a good deal of distress.

The notion that people can influence by self-referent thought how they behave does not sit well with those who find behavioristic tenets more to their liking (see Rachman, 1978). They divest self-percepts of efficacy of any determinative properties, as if self-percepts simply reside as passive predictors of future behavior in the host organism. The question arises as to how, in behaviorist theory, future behavior gets realized by an organism that can forecast the future but has no capacity for self-influence. External stimuli and implants of past stimuli must steer the organism to eventual attainments. In contrast to this view, research shows that people who regard themselves as highly talents to good use if they lack adequate financial and material resources. Physical or social constraints further impose limits on what people can do in particular situations. When performances are impeded by disincentives, inadequate resources, or external constraints, self-judged efficacy will exceed the actual performance. When there are such discrepancies, it is not that people do not know their capabilities but that execution of their skills is hindered by external factors.

Consequences of Misjudgment. The seriousness of missteps also influences the veridicality of self-efficacy judgments. Situations in which misjudgments of capabilities carry no consequences provide little incentive for accurate appraisal of self-efficacy. When such judgments are made publicly, modesty or self-flattery can take precedence over accurateness because concern over what others might think becomes more important than how well one performs on some future occasion. When people have to choose between courses of action that have significant personal consequences, or have to decide how long they will continue a thwarting activity that consumes their time, effort, and resources, then accurate self-appraisals serve as valuable guides for action.

Temporal Disparities. The time elapsing between assessments of self-efficacy and action is another factor affecting the degree of relationship. In the course of their daily lives, people's competencies are repeatedly tested, if not expanded, thus prompting periodic reappraisals of self-efficacy. Strong self-percepts, which are changeable only through compelling disconfirmation, can predict how people will behave years later. But weaker self-percepts of efficacy are sensitive to new information, and even firmly established ones are alterable through powerful negating experiences.

The relationship between self-referent thought and action is most accurately re-

vealed when they are measured in close temporal proximity. To relate actions to dated judgments of self-efficacy creates artifactual discordances if people are acting on altered self-percepts. Proximal self-percepts more accurately represent existing relations to behavior than earlier ones, if they have been revised in the interim. The relevant factor, of course, is the potency of intervening experiences, not the amount of time elapsed.

Faulty Assessments of Self-Percepts or Performance. Causal processes are best clarified by a microanalytic approach in which self-referent thought is measured in terms of particularized self-percepts of efficacy that may vary across activities and circumstances, rather than in terms of a global disposition assayed by an omnibus test. Measures of self-percepts must be tailored to the domain of psychological functioning being explored. This methodology permits microanalysis of the degree of congruence between self-percepts of efficacy and action at the level of individual tasks.

Efficacy judgments vary on several dimensions that have important performance implications: They differ in *level*. The self-judged efficacy of different persons may be limited to simple tasks, extend to moderately difficult ones, or include even the most taxing performances within a particular domain of functioning. Perceived self-efficacy also differs in *generality*. People may judge themselves efficacious only in certain domains of functioning or across a wide range of activities and situations. Domain-linked assessments reveal the patterning and degree of generality of people's perceptions of their efficacy. In addition, perceived self-efficacy varies in *strength*. Weak self-percepts of efficacy are easily negated by disconfirming experiences, whereas people who have a strong belief in their own competence will persevere in their coping efforts despite mounting difficulties. Hence, the degree of correspondence between self-efficacy judgment and performance will vary depending on strength of the belief in one's capabilities. The stronger the perceived self-efficacy, the more likely are persons to select challenging tasks, the longer they persist at them, and the more likely they are to perform them successfully. Strength of self-efficacy is not necessarily linearly related to choice behavior (Bandura, 1977b). A certain threshold of self-assurance is needed to attempt a course of action, but higher strengths of self-efficacy will result in the same attempt.

The most informative efficacy analysis requires detailed assessment of the level, strength, and generality of perceived self-efficacy commensurate with the particularity and precision with which performance is measured. In comparative studies, particularized measures of self-percepts of efficacy surpass global measures in explanatory and predictive power (Barrios, 1985; Kaplan, Atkins, & Reinsch, 1984; McAuley & Gill, 1983; Walker & Franzini, 1983). Behavior must also be adequately assessed under appropriate circumstances. Ill-defined global measures of perceived self-efficacy or defective assessments of performance will yield discordances. Disparities will also arise when efficacy is judged for performances in actual situations but performance is measured in simulated situations that are easier to deal with than the actualities.

Perceived self-efficacy is concerned with generative capabilities not with component acts. Self-percepts of efficacy are usually measured in terms of variable use of the subskills one possesses under different situational demands. For example, in measuring driving self-efficacy, people are not asked to judge whether they can turn the ignition key, shift the automatic transmission, steer, accelerate and stop an automobile, blow the horn, monitor signs, read the flow of traffic, and change traffic lanes. Rather, they judge, whatever their subskills may be, the strength of their perceived self-efficacy to navigate through busy arterial roads, congested city traffic, onrushing freeway traffic, and twisting mountain roads. The motor components of driving are trivial, but the generative capability of maneuvering an au-tomobile through congested city traffic and speedy freeways is not.

Misweighting Requisite Subskills. Performance tasks can vary widely in difficulty and in the subskills they require. Different activities make different demands on cognitive and memory skills, on manual facility, strength, endurance, and stress tolerance. Even the same activity may tap different abilities under different circumstances. Delivering a prepared speech requires less in the way of generative and memory skills than producing one spontaneously. The more knowledgeable and critical the audience, the greater are the demands on skills for managing stress. Discrepancies between self-efficacy judgment and performance will arise when either the tasks or the circumstances under which they are performed are ambiguous. When performance requirements are ill-defined, underestimating task demands produces errors in the direction of overassurance; overestimating task demands will produce errors in the conservative direction.

Judgment of perceived self-efficacy for cognitive activities presents special problems because the cognitive operations required to solve particular tasks are not always readily apparent from what is most easily observable. When complex cognitive operations are imbedded in seemingly easy tasks, which is often the case, appearances may be quite misleading (Bandura & Schunk, 1981). Moreover, solving problems typically requires applying multiple cognitive operations. Even if these operations are readily recognizable, judgment of cognitive capabilities for a given activity is complicated if some of the constituent operations are thoroughly mastered while others are partially understood. Selective attention to elements already mastered will highlight competencies, whereas focusing on what is less well understood will highlight shortcomings. Even equal attentiveness to all aspects of the task will produce some variation in judgments of self-efficacy depending on how much weight is given to the differentially mastered cognitive skills.

Obscure Aims and Performance Ambiguity. Self-percepts of efficacy do not operate in a vacuum. To regulate effort effectively, performers must have some idea of the performances they are seeking to attain and have at least some information about what they are doing. Otherwise, they are at a loss to know how much effort to mobilize, how long to sustain it, and when to make corrective adjustments in their strategies. When aims are clear and level of performance is discernible, self-percepts of efficacy operate as influential regulators of performance attainment (Bandura & Cervone, 1983). However, when people are not aiming for anything in particular or they cannot monitor their performance, there is little basis for translating perceived efficacy into appropriate magnitudes of effort. The problem of performance ambiguity arises when aspects of one's performances are not personally observable (Carroll & Bandura, 1982; Feltz, 1982) or when the level of accomplishment is socially judged by ill-defined criteria so that one has to rely on others to find out how one is doing. In the latter situations, if designating feedback is lacking for tasks on which performers cannot judge their output, they are left in foggy ambiguity. In most everyday pursuits, such problems do not arise because people have aims in mind, and they do not need others to tell them their performances because they can see for themselves how they are doing.

Faulty Self-Knowledge. In most of the situations discussed thus far, self-appraisals of efficacy are reasonably accurate, but they diverge from action because people do not know fully what they will have to do, lack information for regulating their effort, or are hindered by external factors from doing what they can. However, discrepancies often arise from misjudgments of self-efficacy rather than from performance ambiguities or constraints (Bandura & Schunk, 1981; Schunk, 1981). Faulty self-judgments can result from a variety of sources.

In new undertakings people have insufficient experience to assess the veridicality of their self-appraisals and hence must infer their performance capabilities from knowledge of what they can do in other situations, which may be misleading. Self-efficacy will also be misjudged when personal factors distort self-appraisal processes. The distortions may occur at the level of perception, during cognitive processing, or during recall of efficacy-relevant experiences. At the initial perceptual point in the process, people may misperceive their failures and attainments. They may perceive their ongoing experiences accurately but introduce distortions by how they cognitively select, combine, and weigh the multiform efficacy information available to them. Finally, distortions in memory of efficacy-relevant experiences and the circumstances under which they occurred will produce faulty self-appraisals. We shall return to these issues later. Whatever the sources of distortion might be, when people act on faulty self-efficacy judgments they suffer adverse consequences.

In the case of habitual routines, people develop their self-knowledge through repeated experience to the point where they no longer need to judge their efficacy each time they perform the same activity. They behave in accordance with what they know they can or cannot do without giving the matter much further thought. However, significant changes in task demands or circumstances prompt self-efficacy reappraisals as guides for action under altered conditions.

There are decided benefits to suspending further self-efficacy appraisals in routine performances that have proven highly successful. If people had to judge their capabilities anew each time they were about to drive their automobiles or to prepare a familiar dinner, they would spend much of their cognitive life in redundant self-referent thought. There are considerable personal costs, however, when self-judged inefficacy leads to routine thoughtless avoidance of activities and situations that can enrich one's life. Langer and her associates (Langer, 1979) document the self-debilitating effects that result when people erroneously judge themselves as incompetent and begin to behave ineffectually without giving much further thought to their capabilities.

SOURCES OF SELF-EFFICACY INFORMATION

Self-knowledge about one's efficacy, whether accurate or faulty, is based on four principal sources of information: performance attainments; vicarious experiences of observing the performances of others; verbal persuasion and allied types of social influences that one possesses certain capabilities; and physiological states from which people partly judge their capableness, strength, and vulnerability to dysfunction. Any given influence, depending on its form, may draw on one or more sources of efficacy information.

Enactive Attainment

Enactive attainments provide the most influential source of efficacy information because it is based on authentic mastery experiences (Bandura, Adams, & Beyer, 1977; Biran & Wilson, 1981; Feltz, Landers, & Raeder, 1979). Successes raise efficacy appraisals; repeated failures lower them, especially if the failures occur early in the course of events and do not reflect lack of effort or adverse external circumstances. The weight given to new experiences depends on the nature and strength of the preexisting self-perception into which they must be integrated. After a strong sense of self-efficacy is developed through repeated successes, occasional failures are unlikely to have much effect on judgments of one's capabilities. People who are assured of their capabilities are more likely to look to situational factors, insufficient effort, or poor strategies

as the causes. When they ascribe poor performance to faulty strategies rather than to inability, failure can raise confidence that better strategies will bring future successes (Anderson & Jennings, 1980). Failures that are overcome by determined effort can instill robust percepts of self-efficacy through experience that one can eventually master even the most difficult obstacles.

Once established, enhanced self-efficacy tends to generalize to other situations, especially those in which performance has been self-debilitated by preoccupation with personal inadequacies (Bandura, Adams, & Beyer, 1977; Bandura, Jeffery, & Gajdos, 1975). As a result, behavioral functioning may improve across a wide range of activities. However, the generalization effects occur most predictably in activities that are most similar to those in which self-efficacy was enhanced.

Vicarious Experience

People do not rely on enactive experience as the sole source of information about their capabilities. Self-efficacy appraisals are partly influenced by vicarious experiences. Seeing or visualizing other similar people perform successfully can raise self-percepts of efficacy in observers that they too possess the capabilities to master comparable activities (Bandura, Adams, Hardy, & Howells, 1980; Kazdin, 1979). They persuade themselves that if others can do it, they should be able to achieve at least some improvement in performance. By the same token, observing that others perceived to be similarly competent fail despite high effort lowers observers' judgments of their own capabilities and undermines their efforts (Brown & Inouye, 1978).

There are several conditions under which self-efficacy appraisals are especially sensitive to vicarious information. The amount of uncertainty about one's capabilities is one such factor. Perceived self-efficacy can be readily changed by relevant modeling influences when people have had little prior experience on which to base evaluations of their personal competence. Lacking direct knowledge of their own capabilities, they rely more heavily on modeled indicators (Takata & Takata, 1976). This is not to say that a great deal of prior experience necessarily nullifies the potential influence of social modeling. Quite the contrary. Mixed experiences can instill self-doubts, and tasks and associates change from time to time so that social comparative information continues to carry diagnostic value. Moreover, modeling influences that convey effective coping strategies can boost the self-efficacy of individuals who have undergone many experiences confirming their inefficacy (Bandura, 1977b; Bandura, Reese, & Adams, 1982). Even the self-assured will raise their perceived self-efficacy if models teach them better ways of doing things.

The effects of vicarious information on self-efficacy appraisals will also depend on the criteria by which ability is evaluated (Festinger, 1954; Suls & Miller, 1977). Activities that produce clear external information about the level of performance provide a factual basis for judging one's capabilities. High jumpers, for example, can assess their proficiency and rate of improvement from the heights they clear. However, most performances do not, in themselves, provide sufficient information to gain knowledge of one's capabilities. A student who scores 117 on an examination has little basis for judging whether it is a good or a poor performance. When factual evidence for performance adequacy is lacking, personal efficacy must be gauged in terms of the performances of others. Because most performances are evaluated in terms of social criteria, social comparative information figures prominently in self-efficacy appraisals.

Although vicarious experiences are generally weaker than direct ones, vicarious forms can produce significant, enduring changes through their effects on performance. People convinced vicariously of their inefficacy are inclined to behave in ineffec-tual ways that, in fact, generate confirmatory behavioral evidence of inability. Conversely, modeling influences that enhance perceived self-efficacy can weaken the impact of direct experiences of failure by sustaining performance in the face of repeated failure (Brown & Inouye, 1978; Weinberg, Gould, & Jackson, 1979). A given mode of influence can thus set in motion processes that augment its effects or diminish the effects of otherwise powerful influences.

Verbal Persuasion

Verbal persuasion is widely used to try to talk people into believing they possess capabilities that will enable them to achieve what they seek. Social persuasion alone may be limited in its power to create enduring increases in self-efficacy, but it can contribute to successful performance if the heightened appraisal is within realistic bounds. People who are persuaded verbally that they possess the capabilities to master given tasks are likely to mobilize greater sustained effort than if they harbor self-doubts and dwell on personal deficiencies when difficulties arise. To the extent that persuasive boosts in self-efficacy lead people to try hard enough to succeed, they promote development of skills and a sense of personal efficacy. Persuasory efficacy attributions, therefore, have their greatest impact on people who have some reason to believe that they can produce effects through their actions (Chambliss & Murray, 1979a, 1979b). However, the raising of unrealistic beliefs of personal competence only invites failures that will discredit the persuaders and will further undermine the recipient's perceived self-efficacy.

It is probably more difficult to produce enduring increases in perceived efficacy by persuasory means than to undermine it. Illusory boosts in self-efficacy are readily disconfirmed by the results of one's actions. But those who have been persuaded of their inefficacy tend to avoid challenging activities and give up quickly in the face of difficulties. By restricting choice behavior and undermining effort, self-disbeliefs can create their own validation.

Physiological State

People rely partly on information from their physiological state in judging their capabilities. They read their somatic arousal in stressful or taxing situations as ominous signs of vulnerability to dysfunction. Because high arousal usually debilitates performance, people are more inclined to expect success when they are not beset by aversive arousal than if they are tense and viscerally agitated. Fear reactions generate further fear through anticipatory self-arousal. By conjuring up fear-provoking thoughts about their ineptitude, people can rouse themselves to elevated levels of distress that produce the very dysfunctions they fear. Treatments that eliminate emotional arousal to subjective threats heighten perceived self-efficacy with corresponding improvements in performance (Bandura & Adams, 1977; Barrios, 1983). Physiological indicants of efficacy are not limited to autonomic arousal. In activities involving strength and stamina people read their fatigue, windedness, aches, and pains as indicants of physical inefficacy (Taylor, Bandura, Ewart, Miller, & DeBusk, 1985).

Cognitive Processing of Self-Efficacy Information

Information that is relevant for judging personal capabilities—whether conveyed enactively, vicariously, persuasively, or physiologically—is not inherently enlightening. Rather, it becomes instructive only through cognitive appraisal. A distinction must, therefore, be drawn between information conveyed by environmental events and information as selected, weighted, and integrated into self-efficacy judgments. A host of factors, including personal, social, situational, and temporal circumstances under which events occur, affect how personal experiences are cognitively appraised. For this reason, even noteworthy performance attainments do not necessarily boost perceived self-efficacy.

Nor are self-percepts that have served protective functions for years quickly discarded. Those who question their coping efficacy are more likely to distrust their positive experiences than to risk encounters with threats they judge they cannot adequately control. When experience contradicts firmly held judgments of self-efficacy, people may not change their beliefs about themselves if the conditions of performance are such as to lead them to discount the import of the experience. In such instances, producing enduring, generalized changes in self-efficacy requires powerful confirmatory experiences in which people successfully manage task demands that far exceed those commonly encountered in their daily lives (Bandura, 1977b).

The cognitive processing of efficacy information involves two separable functions: The first concerns the types of information people attend to and use as indicators of personal efficacy. Each of the four modes of conveying information has its distinctive set of efficacy indicators. The second concerns the combination rules or heuristics they employ for weighting and integrating efficacy information from different sources in forming their self-efficacy judgments.

Enactive Efficacy Information. Many factors can affect level of performance that have little to do with capability. Therefore, there is no simple equivalence of performance to perceived capability. Appraisal of self-efficacy is an inferential process in which the relative contribution of ability and nonability factors to performance successes and failures must be weighted. The extent to which people will alter their perceived efficacy through performance experiences will depend upon, among other factors, the difficulty of the task, the amount of effort they expend, the amount of external aid they receive, the circumstances under which they perform, and the temporal pattern of their successes and failures.

To succeed at an easy task is redundant

with what one already knows, whereas mastery of a difficult task conveys new efficacy information for raising one's efficacy appraisal. Successes achieved with external aid carry less efficacy value because they are likely to be credited to external factors rather than to personal capabilities. Similarly, faulty performances under adverse conditions will have much weaker efficacy implications than those executed under optimal circumstances.

Cognitive appraisals of effort expended may further affect the impact of performance accomplishments on judgments of personal efficacy. People come to view effort as inversely related to capabilities (Nicholls & Miller, 1984). Success with minimal effort on a challenging task signifies a high level of ability, whereas analogous attainments gained through hard labor connote lesser ability and are thus less likely to raise perceived self-efficacy. Effort also figures importantly in self-appraisal of capabilities from failures (Trope, 1983). Poor performance with only feeble expenditure of effort tells little about what one can do. Performance levels on difficult tasks speak more strongly to underlying capabilities when much effort has been exerted under conditions conducive to maximum performances. Failure under such conditions signifies limited capability. The rate and pattern of attainments furnish additional information for judging personal efficacy. Individuals who experience periodic failures but continue to improve over time are more apt to raise their perceived efficacy than those who succeed but see their performances leveling off compared to their prior rate of improvement.

Studies conducted within the attributional framework (Bem, 1972; Frieze, 1976; Weiner, 1979) have examined how causal judgments regarding factors such as effort and task difficulty affect performance. In a social cognitive analysis, these types of factors serve as conveyors of efficacy information that influence performance largely through their intervening effects on self-percepts of efficacy. Thus, people infer high self-efficacy from successes achieved through minimal effort on difficult tasks, but they infer low self-efficacy if they had to work hard under favorable conditions to master relatively easy tasks. Perceived self-efficacy influences the types of causal attributions people make for their performances. Children who regard themselves as highly efficacious ascribe their failures to insufficient effort, whereas those who regard themselves as inefficacious view the cause of their failures as stemming from low ability (Collins, 1982). That perceived self-efficacy is both a determiner of causal attributions and a mediator of their effects on performance is shown in an evaluation of causation by path analysis (Schunk & Gunn, 1984). Self-efficacious children tend to attribute their successes to ability, but ability attributions affect performance indirectly through perceived self-efficacy.

As already alluded to, inferential processes operate similarly in self-efficacy appraisal based on performance failures. Deficient performances are unlikely to lower perceived efficacy much, if at all, when failures are discounted on the grounds of insufficient effort, adverse conditions, despondency, or physical debilitation. People who hold a low view of themselves are prone to the opposite judgmental bias, crediting their achievements to external factors, rather than to their own capabilities (Bandura, Adams, Hardy, & Howells, 1980). Here the problem is one of inaccurate ascription of personal competency to situational factors. In such cases, the boost in self-efficacy requires mastering challenging tasks with minimal external aids, which verifies personal capabilities (Bandura, 1977b).

Having phobics verbalize aloud their thought processes during mastery experiences sheds some light on the cognitive processing of enactive efficacy information (Bandura, 1983b). They register notable increases in self-efficacy when their experiences disconfirm misbeliefs about what they fear and when they gain new skills to manage potential threats. They hold weak self-percepts of efficacy in a provisional status, testing their newly acquired knowledge and skills before raising judgments of what they are able to do. If, in the course of completing a task, they discover something that appears intimidating about the task, or suggests limitations in their mode of control, they lower their perceived self-efficacy despite their successful performance. In such instances, apparent successes leave them shaken rather than emboldened. As they gain increasing ability to predict and manage potential threats, they develop a robust self-assurance that serves them well in mastering new challenges.

Perceived efficacy is affected not only by how performance successes and failures are interpreted but also by biases in the self-monitoring of the performances themselves. In any given endeavor, some performances surpass, others match, and others fall below one's typical attainments. Such variability allows some leeway in which performances are closely observed and best remembered. People who selectively attend to and recall the more negative aspects of their performances are likely to underestimate their efficacy even though they may process correctly what they remember. In such instances the problems reside in faulty attentional and memory processes, rather than in the inferential judgments made about the causes of one's successes and failures.

Selective self-monitoring can also magnify percepts of self-efficacy if only one's successes are especially noticed and remembered. Research on self-modeling provides suggestive evidence bearing on this enhancement effect (Dowrick, 1983). In these studies persons exhibiting deficient skills are helped, by a variety of aids, to perform at a level that exceeds their usual attainments. The hesitancies, mistakes, and external aids are then edited from the videotape recordings to show the persons performing much more skillfully than they are normally capable. After observing their videotaped successes, they display substantial improvement in performance compared to their baseline level or to other activities that are filmed but not observed. Conversely, observing one's defective actions reduces the quality of performance. Seeing oneself perform errorlessly can enhance proficiency in at least two ways: It provides distinctive information on how to perform appropriately, and it strengthens self-beliefs in one's capability. In a study designed to separate these effects, Gonzales and Dowrick (1983) found that self-observed apparent skillfulness, wherein good endings were spliced to errant performances in videotapes, produced similar improvements to self-observed actual skillfulness. These findings suggest that self-modeling of skillfulness may operate largely by enhancing perceived self-efficacy.

Vicarious Efficacy Information. Cognitive processing of vicariously derived information will similarly depend on the indicants of self-efficacy conveyed by modeled events. We noted earlier that people judge their capabilities partly by comparing their performances with those of others. Similarity to a model is one factor that increases the personal relevance of modeled performance information for observers' perceptions of their own efficacy. Persons who are similar or slightly higher in ability provide the most informative comparative information for gauging one's own capabilities (Festinger, 1954; Suls & Miller, 1977). Neither outperforming those of much lesser ability, nor being surpassed by the greatly superior convey much information about one's own level of competence. In general, modeled successes by similar others raise, and modeled failures lower, self-appraisals of efficacy.

In judging personal efficacy through social comparisons, observers may rely on similarity either in the model's past performances or in the model's attributes that are presumably predictive of the ability in question. The influential role of prior performance similarity on vicarious efficacy appraisal is revealed in a study by Brown and Inouye (1978). Observers who believed themselves to be superior to a failing model maintained a high sense of personal efficacy and did not slacken their effort at all, despite repeated failure. In contrast, modeled failure had a devastating effect on observers' self-judged efficacy when they perceived themselves of comparable ability to the model. They expressed a very low sense of personal efficacy and gave up quickly when they encountered difficulties. The lower their perceived self-efficacy, the quicker they gave up.

Some writers have commented on the apparent paradox that one uses prior knowledge of similarity to ascertain similarity in capabilities (Goethals & Darley, 1977). The paradox exists only if old and new activities are identical and situational demands remain invariant. This is rarely the case. Both the activities and the situations in which they are performed vary to some degree. Therefore, in arriving at a self-efficacy appraisal, observers must extrapolate from past performance similarities and knowledge of the model's attainments in the new situations. To cite an example, students judge how well they might do in a chemistry course from knowing how peers, who performed comparably to them in physics, fared in chemistry.

Efficacy appraisals are often based, not on comparative performance experiences, but on similarity to models on personal characteristics that are assumed to be predictive of performance capabilities (Suls & Miller, 1977). People develop preconceptions of performance capabilities according to age, sex, educational and socioeconomic level, race, and ethnic designation, even though the performances of individuals within these groups are extremely varied. Such preconceptions usually arise from a combination of cultural stereotyping and overgeneralization from salient personal experiences. Attributes invested with predictive significance operate as influential factors in comparative self-appraisals. Thus, the same physical stamina modeled by a female raises women's perceived physical efficacy and muscular endurance, whereas that of a male model does not (Gould & Weiss, 1981). Attribute similarity generally increases

the force of modeling influences even though the personal characteristics may be spurious indicants of performance capabilities (Rosenthal & Bandura, 1978). For example, similarity in age and sex to coping models emboldens phobic observers, although these characteristics do not really affect how well one can perform the feared activities. Such misjudgments reflect overgeneralization from activities in which these attributes would predict performance, at least to some extent. Indeed, when model attributes irrelevant to the new task are salient and overweighted in their predictive value, these irrelevant model characteristics sway observers more than relevant ability indicants (Kazdin, 1974b). When the successes of models who possess similar attributes lead others to try things they would otherwise shun, spurious indicants can have beneficial social effects. But comparative self-efficacy appraisals through faulty preconceptions often lead those who are uncertain about their abilities to judge valuable pursuits to be beyond their reach. In such instances, judging efficacy by social comparison is self-limiting, especially if the models have verbalized self-doubts about their own capabilities (Gould & Weiss, 1981).

Diversified modeling, in which different people master difficult tasks, is superior to exposure to the same performances by a single model (Bandura & Menlove, 1968; Kazdin, 1974a, 1975, 1976). If people of widely differing characteristics can succeed, then observers have a reasonable basis for increasing their own sense of efficacy. Observers also generally benefit more from seeing models overcome their difficulties by determined effort than from observing facile performances by adept models (Kazdin, 1973; Meichenbaum, 1971). Showing the gains achieved by intensified effort not only reduces the negative effect of temporary setbacks but also demonstrates that perseverance eventually brings success. Such displays help to create the cognitive set that failures reflect insufficient effort rather than lack of ability.

Social comparison serves functions other

than ability appraisal, which can influence the choice of models. The performances of others are often selected as standards for self-improvement of abilities. For this purpose, performers choose to compare themselves with proficient models possessing the competencies to which they aspire. We saw earlier in the analysis of self-evaluative reactions how level of self-satisfaction is affected by comparative choices. Competitive comparisons with superior performers give rise to self-deprecation and despondency, whereas comparisons with the less talented produce favorable self-evaluations. People who are insecure about themselves will avoid social comparisons that are potentially threatening to their self-esteem. When threatened, they tend to compare themselves either with subordinates who make them look good or with eminent figures who are much too far removed to pose any serious evaluative threats.

Vicariously derived information can alter perceived self-efficacy through ways other than social comparison. Competent models can teach observers effective strategies for dealing with challenging or threatening situations. This contribution is especially important when perceived inefficacy reflects skill deficits rather than misappraisals of the skills one already possesses. In addition, modeling displays convey information about the nature of environmental tasks and the difficulties they present. Modeled transactions may reveal the tasks to be more or less difficult, and potential threats more or less manageable than observers originally believed. Adoption of serviceable strategies and altered perceptions of task difficulty will change perceived self-efficacy.

Modeled performances designed to alter coping behavior emphasize two aspects—predictability and controllability—that are conducive to the enhancement of self-percepts of efficacy (Bandura et al., 1982). In demonstrating predictability, models repeatedly engage in threatening activities in ways that exemplify how feared persons or objects are most likely to behave in each of many different situations. Predictability reduces stress and increases preparedness for coping with threats (Averill, 1973; Miller, 1981). When modeling controllability, the model demonstrates highly effective techniques for handling threats in whatever situation might arise. What phobic thinking renders frightening instructive modeling makes predictable and personally controllable.

There are some conditions under which the influence of modeled strategy information can alter the usual efficacy effects of social comparative information. Seeing a skilled person fail by use of insufficient strategies can boost self-efficacy in observers who believe they have more suitable strategies at their command. Observed failure is most likely to raise perceived self-efficacy when seeing what has not worked raises the observer's confidence in other alternatives. Conversely, observing a similar person barely succeed despite the most adroit tactics may lead observers to reevaluate the task as much more difficult than they had previously assumed. To delineate how factors in modeled portrayals affect self-efficacy appraisals, research should concern itself with strategy exemplification and task designation, as well as with comparative ability indicants.

Persuasory Efficacy Information. For many activities, people cannot rely solely on themselves in evaluating their ability level because such judgments require inferences from probabilistic indicants of talent about which they may have limited knowledge. Self-appraisals are, therefore, partly based on the opinions of others who presumably possess evaluative competence. People, of course, do not always believe what they are told concerning their capabilities. Skepticism develops from personal experiences that often run counter to what one has been told. Were this always the case, performers would eventually turn a deaf ear to their persuaders. But there are many occasions when individuals are persuaded to try things they avoid or to persist at tasks they were ready to discontinue, only to discover, much to their surprise, that they were capable of mastering them. This is because performance attainments on many tasks are determined more by how hard one works at them than by inherent capacity. Mixed experiences with persuasory efficacy appraisals are common because they are used for flattery, perfunctory encouragement, or manipulative "hype," as well as for realistic assessments of how well recipients can manage prospective situations. Consequently, persuasory efficacy appraisals have to be weighted in terms of who the persuaders are, their credibility, and how knowledgeable they are about the nature of the activities.

The impact of persuasory opinions on self-efficacy is apt to be only as strong as the recipient's confidence in the person who issues them. This is mediated through the perceived credibility and expertness of the persuaders. The more believable the source of information about one's performance capabilities and task demands, the more likely are judgments of personal efficacy to change. People are inclined to trust evaluations of their capabilities by those who are themselves skilled in the activity, have access to some objective predictors of performance attainments, or possess a rich fund of knowledge gained from observing and comparing many different aspirants and their later accomplishments (Crundall & Foddy, 1981; Webster & Sobieszek, 1974). Skill in a given pursuit does not necessarily confer competence in gauging talent for it. For performers who realize this, evidence of extensive experience in judging talent is apt to be the more persuasive indicant of evaluative competence. Others often voice opinions of what performers can do without being thoroughly acquainted with the difficulty of the tasks or with the circumstances under which they will have to be performed. Therefore, even the judgments of otherwise credible advisors may be discounted on the grounds that they do not fully understand the demands of the task.

Attempts to boost perceived self-efficacy persuasively often take the form of evaluative feedback about ongoing performances. That such feedback can affect judgments of one's capability and subsequent accomplishments is shown by Schunk (1982a, 1983d). In these studies children who lack arithmetic skills are periodically given different attributional feedback for their rate of progress in a self-paced learning program. The same progress credited to underlying talent or concentrated effort raises perceived cognitive efficacy and accelerates mastery of arithmetic skills more than feedback implying either lesser ability, thus calling for harder work, or no feedback at all. The more the encouraging feedback instills efficacious self-beliefs, the more effort children exert and the more they accomplish.

Persuasory efficacy appraisals are most likely to become believable when they are slightly beyond what individuals can do at the time because better performances are achievable through extra effort. Those who are persuaded they can succeed are more likely to expend the necessary effort than if they are troubled by uncertainties. Performance successes raise the perceived evaluative competence of the persuaders. Inflated persuasory appraisals that mislead performers to failure quickly undermine the evaluative credibility of the persuaders.

Physiological Efficacy Information.
The information conveyed by physiological arousal similarly affects perceived self-efficacy through judgmental processes. A number of factors, including appraisal of the sources of arousal, the level of activation, the circumstances under which arousal is elicited, and past experiences on how arousal affects one's performances, are likely to figure in the cognitive processing of emotional reactivity. Activities are often performed in situations containing varied evocative stimuli. This creates ambiguity about what caused the physiological reactions. The efficacy import of the resultant arousal on self-efficacy will, therefore, vary depending on the factors singled out and the meaning given to them. Speakers who

ascribe their sweating to the physical discomforts of the room read their physiology quite differently from those who view it as distress reflecting personal failings.

Self-appraisal of efficacy from arousal cues raises a number of intriguing developmental questions. How do young children come to view bodily states as emotional conditions? How do they learn to tell what emotion they are experiencing? How do they learn that arousal cues signifying particular emotions are predictive of level of functioning? In the social cognitive view, knowledge concerning bodily states is acquired, in large part, through social labeling processes. Arousing experiences contain three significant events, two of which are publicly observable—*affective elicitors* give rise to *internal arousal* and *expressive reactions*. The internal arousal itself cannot play a differentiating role in the social labeling because the arousal is unobservable to others. Moreover, phenomenologically different emotions appear to have too many similar physiological reactions to be differentiable by the person experiencing them. Adults must, therefore, infer the presence of bodily states in young children from their expressive reactions and from environmental elicitors known to produce particular types of emotions. Drawing on these observable events, adults describe and differentiate the emotions children are experiencing (e.g., happy, sad, angry, fearful) and explain their causes. Thus, parents label children's bodily tension and other expressions of somatic agitation as fear in threatening situations and as anger in irritating or thwarting situations. Through repeated social linkage of elicitors, expressive reactions, and internal arousal, children eventually learn to interpret and to differentiate their affective experiences. Different personal interpretations of internal arousal (e.g., "frightened," "fired up") will have different impact is on perceived self-efficacy.

The self-efficacy implications of arousal derive from past experiences with how labeled arousal affects performance. For people who generally find arousal facilitory, arousal will have a different efficacy meaning than for those for whom arousal has been debilitating. Indeed, high achievers view arousal as a facilitator, whereas low achievers regard it as a debilitator (Hollandsworth et al., 1979). The judgmental process is complicated by the fact that it is not arousal *per se* but rather its level that carries the greater weight in judging operative capabilities. As a general rule, moderate levels of arousal facilitate deployment of skills, whereas high arousal disrupts it. This is especially true of complex activities requiring intricate organization of behavior.

What constitutes an optimal level of arousal depends not only on the nature of the task but on the causal inferences concerning the arousal. People vary in their judgmental sets. Those who are inclined to perceive their arousal as stemming from personal inadequacies are more likely to lower their perceived efficacy than those who regard their arousal as a common transitory reaction that even the most competent people experience. Accomplished theatrical performers, who become anxious before a performance but lose their apprehensiveness once the play gets under way, are likely to ascribe their anticipatory arousal to normative situational reactions rather than to personal deficiencies. Sir Laurence Olivier, the renowned actor, has used self-efficacy orations to combat stage fright by appearing on stage before a show begins and proclaiming behind the curtain that he is a superb actor whose performance will captivate the audience. Given a predilection to attribute arousal to personal deficiencies, the heightened attention to visceral cues can result in reciprocally escalating arousal (Sarason, 1975a).

By influencing what people focus their attention on, salient situational factors partly determine how physiological arousal is judged. Thus, visceral arousal occurring in situations containing threatening cues is interpreted as fear, arousal in thwarting situations is experienced as anger, and that resulting from irretrievable loss of valued objects as sorrow (Hunt, Cole, & Reis, 1958).

Moreover, residual arousal from a prior experience may be misassigned to a prominent element in a new situation, as when residual sexual arousal is misjudged as anger in the presence of anger-provoking cues (Tannenbaum & Zillmann, 1975; Zillmann, 1978). Even the same source of physiological arousal may be interpreted differently in ambiguous situations depending on the emotional reactions of others in the same setting (Mandler, 1975; Schachter & Singer, 1962). Because of their selective attention to threatening cues, those who perceive themselves to be inefficacious are especially prone to misjudge arousal arising from other sources as a sign of coping deficiencies.

Much of the preceding discussion has centered on how affective arousal may be read as one indicant of coping self-efficacy. The research of Bower (1981, 1983) shows that mood states can affect cognitive processing and retrieval of experiences. People can learn things faster that are congruent with the mood they are in, and they recall things better if they are in the same mood as when they learned them. Intense moods exert stronger effects than weak ones, except for despondency which retards most everything. It is assumed that emotional arousal primes affective themes, thus making congruent information more salient, learnable, and memorable. Memory involves an associative network of concepts and propositionally encoded events. In Bower's network theory of how emotional arousal affects thought processes, emotions become associated in memory with different events, thus creating multiple linkages within the associative network. Activating a particular emotion unit in the memory network will facilitate recollection of events linked with it.

Mood-biased recollection can similarly affect people's judgments of their personal efficacy. If sad mood readily leads to thoughts of past failings, self-percepts of efficacy will be diminished, whereas if a positive mood activates thoughts of accomplishments, perceived self-efficacy will be boosted. Evidence appears to be consistent with this view. People judge their capabilities in social, academic, and athletic pursuits higher under hypnotically-induced positive mood than under a neutral state, and they regard themselves as least self-efficacious in a negative mood (Kavanagh & Bower, 1985). The impact of mood on self-percepts of efficacy is widespread, rather than confined to the particular domain of functioning in which happiness or sadness was experienced. Revivified strong mood colors self-efficacy judgment more than visualizing success or failure with little affect (Kavanagh, 1983). In dealing with cognitive tasks, persons act in accordance with their mood-altered percepts of self-efficacy, choosing more challenging tasks in an efficacious than in an inefficacious frame of mind. Despondency can thus lower self-percepts of efficacy that give rise to ineffectual performance breeding even deeper dependency. In contrast, by raising perceived efficacy that gets more out of one's talents, good mood can set in motion an affirmative reciprocal process.

In areas of functioning involving physical pursuits, physiological sources of efficacy information may take on special significance. The way in which such information is cognitively processed can affect how active a life people lead. Those who read their fatigue, aches, and lowered stamina as signs of declining physical capacity are likely to curtail their activities more than those who regard such signs as the effects of sedentariness.

The cognitive processing of physiological information also figures prominently in psychological recovery from physical disorders (Ewart, Taylor, Reese, & DeBusk, 1983; Taylor, Bandura, Ewart, Miller, & DeBusk, 1985). For example, patients who have had a heart attack are likely to base their level of activity on their perceived cardiac capability, which they infer from observable signs such as fatigue, shortness of breath, pain, and reduced stamina. Since different physical conditions, including sedentariness, can produce these same effects, such signs are easily misread as evidence of cardiac impairment.

When patients perform treadmill tests, those who selectively focus on exercise-induced symptoms at the terminal phase of the test will perceive a debilitated cardiac capability, whereas those who focus on the strenuous workloads they have accomplished will perceive a robust cardiac capability. Differential cognitive processing of physiological information can lead to quite different perceptions of one's physical capabilities.

Integration of Self-Efficacy Information

The preceding discussion explored the efficacy implications of single dimensions of information within each of the four modalities. In forming their efficacy judgments, people have to deal not only with different configurations of efficacy-relevant information conveyed by a given modality, but they also have to weigh and integrate efficacy information from these diverse sources. The weights assigned to different types of efficacy information may vary across different domains of activity. There has been little research on how people process multidimensional efficacy information. However, there is every reason to believe that efficacy judgments are governed by some common judgmental processes.

Studies of judgmental processes show that people have difficulty weighing and integrating multidimensional information (Slovic, Fischhoff, & Lichtenstein, 1977; Slovic & Lichtenstein, 1971; Tversky & Kahneman, 1974). As a result, they tend to rely on simple judgmental rules. This often leads them to ignore or to misweigh relevant information. When subjective descriptions of their judgmental processes are compared with their actual judgments, the findings show that people tend to underestimate their reliance on important cues and overweigh those of lesser value.

Although common cognitive processes probably operate in both efficacy and nonpersonal judgments, forming conceptions of oneself undoubtedly involves some distinct processes as well. The persons are

rare who are entirely dispassionate about themselves. Self-referent experiences are more likely than experiences involving other persons or objects to pose threats to self-esteem and social valuation. Such threats can produce self-exaggeration or self-belittlement of personal capabilities. Affect can have different effects on personal and social judgment. Thus, depressive mood can lower judgments of personal controlling efficacy but inflate judgments of the efficacy of others under identical outcome feedback (Martin, Abramson, & Alloy, 1984). Activation of self-referent processes may distort self-monitoring, retention, or processing of multidimensional efficacy information.

RELATED VIEWS OF PERSONAL EFFICACY

The role of self-referent thought in psychosocial functioning has been the subject of considerable interest in a number of approaches to human behavior. The theoretical perspectives differ, however, in how they view the nature and origins of self-percepts and the intervening processes by which they affect behavior.

Self-Concept

Self-appraisal has traditionally been conceptualized in terms of the self-concept (Rogers, 1959; Wylie, 1974). The self-concept is a composite view of oneself that is formed through direct experience and evaluations adopted from significant others. In these approaches, self-concepts are measured by having people rate in one way or another descriptive statements that they think apply to themselves. The principal thesis that self-concepts determine psychological functioning is then tested by correlating the self-concepts, or the disparities between actual and ideal selves, with various indices of adjustment, attitudes, and behavior.

Examining self processes in terms of the

self-concept contributes to understanding how people develop attitudes toward themselves and how their self-attitudes may affect their outlook toward life. There are several features of self theories of this type, however, that detract from their power to explain and to predict how people are likely to behave in particular situations. For the most part, self theories are concerned with global self-images. A global self-conception does not do justice to the complexity of self-efficacy percepts, which vary across different activities, different levels of the same activity, and different circumstances. A composite self-image may yield some modest correlations, but it is not equal to the task of predicting with any degree of accuracy the intraindividual variability in performance. Self theories have had difficulty explaining how the same self-concept can give rise to diverse types of behavior.

Self-esteem is another facet of self-referent thought that should be distinguished from perceived self-efficacy because the two concepts represent different phenomena. Self-esteem pertains to the evaluation of self-worth, which depends on how the culture values the attributes one possesses and how well one's behavior matches personal standards of worthiness. Perceived self-efficacy is concerned with the judgment of personal capabilities. Judgments of self-worth and of self-capability have no uniform relation. Individuals may regard themselves as highly efficacious in an activity from which they derive no pride (skilled combat soldier) or judge themselves inefficacious at an activity without suffering a loss of self-worth (e.g., inept skater). However, in many of the activities people pursue, they cultivate self-efficacies in what gives them a sense of self-worth. Thus, both self-esteem and self-efficacy contribute in their own way to the quality of human life.

Effectance Motivation

In seeking a motivational explanation for exploratory and manipulative behavior, White (1959, 1960) postulated an "effect-ance motive," which is conceptualized as an intrinsic drive for transactions with the environment. The effectance motive presumably develops through cumulative acquisition of knowledge and skills in dealing with the environment. In these conceptual papers, White argues eloquently for a competence model of child development. The theory deals at some length with nonorganic motivators of behavior. However, there are a number of points on which the theory requires clarification. The process by which an effectance motive emerges from effective transactions with the environment is not spelled out. In this formulation, successful action builds effectance motivation. But there is no place in the theory for the effects of failure experiences, which are by no means insignificant (Harter, 1978). Harter (1981) has broadened this line of theorizing within a developmental framework.

Verification of the existence of an effectance motive is difficult because the motive is inferred from the exploratory behavior it supposedly causes. Without an independent measure of motive strength, one cannot tell whether people explore and manipulate things because of a competence motive to do so or for any number of other reasons. It will be recalled from the earlier analysis of exploratory behavior that theorists have argued about whether it is the push of boredom and apprehension or the pull of novelty that rouses organisms to action (Berlyne, 1960; Brown, 1953; Harlow, 1953; Mowrer, 1960). Proponents of behavioral approaches have been able to explain and to alter some forms of exploratory behavior by response consequences without recourse to an underlying drive (Fowler, 1971). However, theories concerned solely with external prompts to action are hard pressed to explain the directedness and persistence of behavior over extended periods when immediate situational inducements are weak, absent, or even negative. This type of sustained involvement requires self-regulatory capabilities that operate anticipatorily.

The theory of effectance motivation has

not been formulated in sufficient detail to permit extensive theoretical comparisons. Nevertheless, there are several issues on which social cognitive and effectance formulations clearly differ. In the social cognitive view, choice behavior, effort expenditure, and affective arousal are governed in part by percepts of self-efficacy rather than by a drive. Because self-efficacy judgments are defined and measured independently of performance, they provide a basis for predicting the occurrence, general ity, and persistence of behavior, whereas an omnibus motive does not. People will approach, explore, and try to deal with sit uations within their self-perceived capabilities, but, unless externally coerced, they will avoid transactions with aspects of their environment that they perceive as exceeding their coping capability.

These alternative views also differ on the origins of personal efficacy. Within the framework of effectance theory, the effectance drive develops gradually through prolonged transactions with one's surroundings. This theory thus focuses almost exclusively on the affects produced by one's own actions. In social cognitive theory, perceived self-efficacy results from diverse sources of information conveyed vicariously and through social evaluation, as well as through direct experience. These differences in theoretical approach have significant implications for how one goes about studying the role of perceived self-efficacy in motivation and action.

Judgments of personal efficacy do not operate as dispositional determinants independently of contextual factors. Some situations require greater skill and more arduous performances, or carry higher risk of negative consequences, than others. Efficacy judgments will vary accordingly. Thus, for example, the level and strength of perceived self-efficacy in public speaking will differ depending on the subject matter, the format of the presentation, and the types of audiences to be addressed. Therefore, analyses of how self-beliefs of capabilities affect actions rely on microanalytic measures, rather than on global indices of personality traits or motives of effectance. It is no more informative to speak of self-efficacy in global terms than to speak of nonspecific social behavior.

In effectance theory, affecting the environment arouses feelings of pleasure and efficacy. Although this may often be the case, as we have already seen, performance attainments do not necessarily enhance perceived efficacy. It depends on how the determinants of the performances are cognitively appraised and how they measure up against internal standards. Nor does the exercise of personal mastery necessarily bring pleasure or raise self-esteem. When competencies are used for harmful purposes, performers may feel self-efficacious in their triumphs but remain displeased with themselves. A theory of effectance must, therefore, consider the important role played by personal standards and cognitive appraisal in the affective and self-evaluative reactions to one's own performances. The manner in which internal standards and self-percepts of efficacy operate as interrelated mechanisms of personal agency is addressed in the next chapter.

Effectance motivation presumably comes into play only under certain limited conditions (White, 1959), a point that is often overlooked in overextensions of the theory to wide realms of behavior. The effectance motive is believed to be aroused when the organism is otherwise unoccupied or is only weakly stimulated by organic drives. In the words of White (1960), effectance promotes "spare-time behavior." In the social cognitive view, self-efficacy judgments enter into the regulation of all types of performances, except for habitual patterns that have become routinized.

Yarrow and his associates (Yarrow et al., 1983) have recast effectance motivation in a more testable form. They call it mastery motivation and construe it as a striving for competence which, in turn, is defined as effective action in dealing with the environment. Mastery motivation is manifested in attentiveness, exploratory behavior, and persistence in goal-directed activities. Developmental tests of this motive system yield equivocal findings: Behavioral indices of mastery motivation are weakly related to each other and become more heterogeneous with increasing age; the same mastery behavior shows little consistency even over a short time; and indices of mastery motivation are not consistently linked to competence. However, the authors place a positive interpretation on this substantial disconnectedness: Weak relationships between indices of the same motive are taken as evidence that mastery motivation is multifaceted. Increasing heterogeneity indicates that the motive becomes more differentiated with age. Lack of behavioral continuity indicates that the motive undergoes developmental transformation. The unsteady linkage between mastery motivation and competence suggests that they create each other interactively.

An alternative conclusion is that striving for competence is not driven by an omnibus mastery motive but rather is motivated by the varied benefits of competent action. What is competent functioning differs across time, milieus, and domains of activity. Competence requires appropriate learning experiences, rather than emerging spontaneously. Hence, people develop different patterns of competencies and deploy them selectively depending on environmental demands. A functional analysis of striving for competence explains this phenomenon better than one cast in terms of an omnibus mastery motive.

Outcome-Expectancy Theories

With the ascendency of cognitive views of behavior, the concept of expectancy assumed an increasingly prominent place in explanations of human behavior. Psychological theories postulating that expectations influence actions focus almost exclusively on outcome expectations. Irwin's (1971) theory of intentional behavior and motivation is cast in terms of act-outcome expectancies. In Bolles's (1975) view, learning essentially involves the acquisition of expectancies that particular cues or responses will give rise to certain outcomes. Rotter's (1966) conceptual scheme centers on causal beliefs about the relation between actions and outcomes. In a similar vein, Seligman (1975) sets forth the view that people behave resignedly because they acquire expectancies that they cannot affect environmental outcomes through their actions. According to expectancy-valence theories, performance level is a multiplicative function of the expectancy that behaving in a particular way will lead to a given outcome and the value of that outcome (Atkinson, 1964; Feather, 1982; Vroom, 1964).

The heavy emphasis on outcome expectations can be traced in large part to the Tolmanian roots of this line of theorizing. Tolman formulated his conceptual system at a time when competing theories sought to resolve controversies about learning by explaining how animals learn to solve mazes. The prevailing theories viewed learning as habit acquisition, whereas Tolman interpreted learning as development of expectations that behavior will produce certain outcomes (Tolman, 1932, 1951). The question of whether animals could find their way to the end of the runway was, of course, never at issue. Therefore, what the animals expected to find in the goal box was considered to be the major determinant of their choice behavior. Self-efficacy judgment was understandably neglected because animals are not in the habit of influencing their efforts by thoughts about what they can or cannot do. In contrast, humans, who engage in considerable self-reflective thought, boost or undermine their efforts by beliefs about their capabilities. Any theory of human behavior must, therefore, consider the influential role played by self-referent thought.

The self-efficacy portion of social cognitive theory departs from the Tolmanian tradition in several notable ways. While acknowledging the role of outcome expectations, it also posits a self-referent expectancy system in the regulation of human behavior. The outcomes people expect in given situations depend heavily on their judgments of the types of performances they will be able to produce. Moreover, social cognitive theory, in its broad form, is concerned with the acquisition of cognitive and behavioral skills, as well as with knowledge of what leads to what. The prevalent emphasis on contingency learning, to the relative neglect of skill acquisition, reflects the legacy of this historical focus on learning in animals. Learning was indexed by choice responses in maze running or by variation in response rate, rather than in terms of the acquisition of new ways of behaving.

Some of the theorizing and experimentation on expectancies concerning the controllability of outcomes bear some likeness to the notion of perceived self-efficacy. According to the theory of personality proposed by Rotter (1966), behavior varies as a function of generalized expectancies that outcomes are determined either by one's actions or by external forces beyond one's control. Such expectations about the instrumentality of behavior are considered to be largely the products of one's reinforcement history. Much of the research within this tradition is concerned with how behavior is influenced by individual differences in the tendency to perceive events as being either personally or externally determined (Lefcourt, 1976, 1979; Phares, 1976; Rotter et al., 1972). In general, people who believe their outcomes are determined by their behavior tend to be more active than those who perceive events more fatalistically.

External causality is defined largely in terms of beliefs that outcomes are dependent on chance factors. Gurin and her associates have argued that lack of personal control is often due, not to chance or whimsy, but to unresponsiveness of social systems and the systematic obstacles they set up (Gurin & Brim, 1984; Gurin, Gurin, & Morrison, 1978). A social system can be unresponsive because no available courses of action provide an adequate solution to a problem. More often, however, a social system is unresponsive because it is negatively biased against certain classes of people but rewards the competence of other members. Institutional bias either bars access to, or imposes a higher competence requirement for, the attainment of valued outcomes. These different meanings of unresponsiveness are illustrated in the changing social practices of administrative organizations. At one time, executive positions were closed to minorities and women, no matter how talented they were. Later, the extraordinarily talented could gain entry into lower echelons. Today, differential competence requirements for entry into subordinate ranks may be minimal, but they still operate strongly at top executive levels. We shall return later to some of these issues in the discussion of collective efficacy and system modifiability.

It is widely assumed that beliefs in personal determination of outcomes create a sense of efficacy and power, whereas beliefs that outcomes occur regardless of what one does result in apathy. It should be noted, however, that Rotter's (1966) conceptual scheme is primarily concerned with causal beliefs about the relation between actions and outcomes rather than with personal efficacy. Perceived self-efficacy and beliefs about the locus of outcome causality must be distinguished. Convictions that outcomes are determined by one's own actions can be either demoralizing or heartening, depending on the level of self-judged efficacy. People who regard outcomes as personally determined, but who lack the requisite skills, would experience low self-efficacy and view the activities with a sense of futility. Thus, for example, a child who fails to grasp arithmetic concepts and expects course grades to be dependent entirely on skill in the subject matter has every reason to be demoralized. It is when people possess competencies that beliefs in personal determination of outcomes will create a sense of power.

DEVELOPMENTAL ANALYSIS OF SELF-EFFICACY

We noted earlier that accurate appraisal of one's own capabilities is highly advantageous and often essential for effective functioning. Those who seriously misjudge what they can do are apt to behave in ways that produce detrimental consequences. Very young children lack knowledge of their own capabilities and the demands and potential hazards of different courses of action. They would repeatedly get themselves into dangerous predicaments were it not for the guidance of others. They can climb to high places, wander into rivers or deep pools, and wield sharp knives before they develop the necessary skills for managing such situations safely (Sears, Maccoby, & Levin, 1957). Adult watchfulness and guidance see young children through this early formative period until they gain sufficient knowledge of what they can do and what different situations require in the way of skills. With development of cognitive capacities, self-efficacy judgment increasingly supplants external guidance.

Beginnings of Perceived Causal Efficacy

A comprehensive theory must explain the origin of social cognition, as well as its nature, function, and developmental course. Self-referent thought is initially derived from action and from observing the experiences of others. Children's experiences with their environment provide the initial basis for developing a sense of causal efficacy. However, newborns' immobility and limited means of action upon the physical and social environment restrict their domain of influence. The initial experiences that contribute to development of a sense of personal agency are tied to infants' ability to control the sensory stimulation from manipulable objects and the attentive behavior of those around them. Infants behave in certain ways, and certain things happen. Shaking a rattle produces predictable sounds, energetic kicks shake their cribs, and screams bring adults.

Realization of causal efficacy requires both self-observation and recognition that one's actions are part of oneself. By repeatedly observing that environmental events occur with action but not in its absence, infants learn about contingent relations between actions and effects. Infants who experience success in controlling environmental events become more attentive to their own behavior and more competent in learning new efficacious responses than infants for whom the same environmental events occur regardless of how they behave (Finkelstein & Ramey, 1977; Ramey & Finkelstein, 1978). Repeated experiences of inefficacy in influencing events impair development of a sense of causal agency and responsiveness in situations where actions would produce results (Garber & Seligman, 1980).

Development of perceived self-efficacy requires more than simply producing effects by actions. Those actions must be perceived as part of oneself. The self becomes differentiated from others through differential experience. Thus, if self action causes pain sensations, whereas seeing similar actions by others does not, one's own activity becomes distinct from that of all others. Infants acquire a sense of personal agency when they begin to perceive environmental events as being personally controlled—a growing realization that they can make events occur.

During the initial months of life, the exercise of influence over the physical environment may contribute more to the development of a child's sense of causal efficacy than influence over the social environment (Gunnar, 1980b). This is because manipulating physical objects produces quick, predictable, and easily observable effects, thus facilitating perception of personal agency in infants whose attentional and representational capabilities are limited. In contrast, causal agency is more difficult to discern in noisier social contingencies, where actions have variable social effects, and some of them occur independently of what the infants are doing. However, with the development of representational capabilities, infants can begin to learn from probabilistic and more distal outcomes. Before long the exercise of control over the social environment begins to play an important role in the early development of self-efficacy.

Growth of Self-Efficacy

Familial Sources of Self-Efficacy. Children must gain self-knowledge of their capabilities in broadening areas of functioning. They have to develop, appraise, and test their physical capabilities, their social competencies, their linguistic skills, and their cognitive skills for comprehending and managing the many situations they encounter daily. Development of sensory-motor capabilities greatly expands the infants' available environment and the means for acting upon it. These early exploratory and play activities, which occupy much of their waking hours, provide opportunities for enlarging their basic skills.

While developing their capabilities during this initial period of immaturity, most of the infants' gratifications must be mediated by adults. Neonates have to depend on others to feed them, clothe them, comfort them, entertain them, and to furnish the play materials for their manipulative exploration. Because of this physical dependency, infants quickly learn how to influence the actions of those around them by their social and verbal behavior. Many of these transactions involve the exercise of proxy control in which young children get adults to effect changes that the children themselves cannot bring about. Efficacy experiences in the exercise of personal control are central to the early development of social and cognitive competence. Parents who are responsive to their infants' communicative behavior, who provide an enriched physical environment, and who permit freedom of movement for exploration have infants who are relatively

accelerated in their social and cognitive development (Ainsworth & Bell, 1974; Yarrow, Rubenstein, & Pedersen, 1975). During the course of development, infant and environment operate as reciprocal interactants. Parental responsiveness increases cognitive competence, and infant capabilities elicit greater parental responsiveness (Bradley, Caldwell, & Elardo, 1979).

Acquisition of language provides children with the symbolic means to reflect on their experiences and thus to begin to gain self-knowledge of what they can and cannot do. Once children can understand speech, parents and others comment on the children's performance capabilities to guide them in foreseen situations where the parents may not be present. To the extent that children adopt efficacy appraisals of others, they can affect the rate of personal development by influencing whether and how children approach new tasks. Thus, for example, overprotective parents, who are oversolicitous and dwell on potential dangers, undermine development of their children's capabilities (Levy, 1943), whereas the more secure are quick to acknowledge and to encourage their children's growing competencies.

The initial efficacy experiences are centered in the family, but as the growing child's social world rapidly expands, peers assume an increasingly important role in children's developing self-knowledge of their capabilities. It is in the context of peer interactions that social comparison processes come most strongly into play. At first the closest comparative age-mates are siblings. Families differ in number of siblings, how far apart in age they are, and in their sex distribution. Different family structures, as reflected in family size, birth order, and sibling constellation patterns, create different social references for comparative efficacy appraisal. Firstborns and only children have different bases for judging their capabilities than children with older brothers and sisters. Ordinal position can exert differential effects on achievement efficacy

(Zajonc & Markus, 1975) and on social efficacy. Comparative efficacy appraisals for siblings close in age will differ from those for siblings spaced farther apart in age. Siblings of the same sex force more competitive ability evaluations than those of the opposite sex. The potential for rivalrous comparisons favoring the older sibling is strongest between same-sexed siblings who are not too far apart. Close age spacing may, therefore, create pressures on younger members to differentiate themselves from older siblings by developing dissimilar personality patterns, interests, and vocational pursuits (Leventhal, 1970). The evaluative habits developed in sibling interactions undoubtedly affect the salience and choice of comparative referents in self-ability evaluations in later life.

Peers and the Broadening and Validation of Self-Efficacy.

The nature of children's efficacy-testing experiences changes substantially as they move increasingly into the larger community. In peer relationships they both broaden the scope of, and make finer discriminations in, self-knowledge of their capabilities. Peers serve several important efficacy functions. Those who are most experienced and competent provide models of efficacious styles of behavior. A vast amount of social learning occurs, for better or for worse, among peers. In addition, agemates provide the most informative points of reference for comparative efficacy appraisal and verification. Children are, therefore, especially sensitive to their relative standing among the peers with whom they affiliate in activities that determine prestige and popularity.

Peers are neither homogeneous nor selected indiscriminately. Children tend to choose close associates who share similar interests and values. Selective peer association will promote self-efficacy in directions of mutual interest, leaving other potentialities underdeveloped (Bandura & Walters, 1959; Bullock & Merrill, 1980; Ellis & Lane, 1963; Krauss, 1964). The influences are undoubt-

edly bidirectional—affiliation preferences affect the direction of efficacy development, and self-efficacy, in turn, partly determines choice of peer associates and activities. Because peers serve as a major agency for the development and validation of self-efficacy, disrupted or impoverished peer relationships can adversely affect the growth of personal efficacy. Perceived social inefficacy can, in turn, create internal obstacles to favorable peer relationships (Wheeler & Ladd, 1982). Development of personal efficacy in coercive styles of behavior may likewise be socially alienating. Thus, children who readily resort to aggression perceive themselves as highly efficacious in getting things they want by such means (Perry, Perry, & Rasmussen, 1985).

School as an Agency for Cultivating Cognitive Self-Efficacy.

During the crucial formative period of children's lives, the school functions as the primary setting for the cultivation and social validation of cognitive efficacy. School is the place where children develop their cognitive competencies and acquire the knowledge and problem-solving skills essential for participating effectively in society. Here their knowledge and thinking skills are continually tested, evaluated, and socially compared. The motivated, who learn quickly, are adequately served by the prevailing educational practices. Teachers who are well versed in their subject matter and have a high sense of efficacy about their teaching capabilities can motivate low achievers and enhance their cognitive development (Aston, 1985; Gibson & Dembo, 1984). However, there are numerous critics who believe that for many children, the school falls short of accomplishing its purposes. Not only does it fail to prepare the youth adequately for the future, but all too often it undermines the very sense of personal efficacy needed for continued self-development. Recurring difficulties encountered with low-achieving students eventually take their toll on teachers' sense of instructional efficacy (Dembo & Gibson, 1985).

There are a number of school practices that, for the less talented or ill prepared, tend to convert instructional experiences into education in inefficacy. These include lock-step sequences of instruction, which lose many children along the way; ability groupings which further diminish the self-efficacy appraisal of those cast into subordinate ranks; and competitive practices where many are doomed to failure for the success of a relative few.

Classroom structures affect perceptions of cognitive capabilities, in large part, by the relative emphasis they place on social-comparative versus self-comparative appraisal. Rosenholtz and Rosenholtz (1981) show that self-appraisals of less able students suffer most when the whole group studies the same material and teachers make frequent comparative evaluations. Under such a uniform structure, which highlights social comparative standards, students rank themselves according to capability with high group consensus. Once established, reputations are not easily changed. In a diversified classroom structure, individualized instruction tailored to students' knowledge and skills enables all of them to expand their competencies and provides less basis for demoralizing social comparison. As a result, students are more likely to compare their rate of progress to their personal standards than to the performance of others. They have greater leeway in selecting others with whom to compare, should they choose to do so. Personalized classroom structure produces higher perceived capability and less dependence on the opinions of teachers and classmates than the monolithic structure.

Children have to learn to face displeasing realities concerning gaps in their knowledge and competencies. However, classroom practices that undermine students' perceived self-efficacy, and thereby lower their future academic performances, partly contribute to these personal realities. A major aim of research in the scholastic domain is to clarify how different types of educational practices and structures affect the development of social and cognitive competencies. Educational practices should be gauged not only by the skills and knowledge they impart for present use but also by what they do to children's beliefs about their capabilities, which affects how they approach the future. Students who develop a strong sense of self-efficacy are well equipped to educate themselves when they have to rely on their own initiative.

Growth of Self-Efficacy through Transitional Experiences of Adolescence. Each period of development brings with it new challenges for coping efficacy. As adolescents approach the demands of adulthood, they must learn to assume full responsibility for themselves in almost every dimension of life. This requires mastering many new skills and the ways of adult society. Learning how to deal with heterosexual relationships and partnerships becomes a matter of considerable importance. The task of choosing what lifework to pursue also looms large during this period. These are but a few of the areas in which new competencies have to be acquired. The ease with which this transition from childhood to adulthood is made depends, in no small measure, on the assurance in one's capabilities built up through prior mastery experiences.

Self-Efficacy Concerns of Adulthood. Young adulthood is a period when people have to learn to cope with many new demands arising from lasting partnerships, marital relationships, parenthood, and careers. As in earlier mastery tasks, a firm sense of self-efficacy is an important motivational contributor to the attainment of further competencies and success. Those who enter adulthood poorly equipped with skills and plagued by self-doubts find many aspects of their adult life stressful and depressing.

By the middle years, people settle into established routines that stabilize self-percepts of efficacy in the major areas of functioning. However, the stability is a shaky one because life does not remain static. Rapid technological and social changes constantly require adaptations calling for self-reappraisals of capabilities. In their occupations, the middle aged find themselves pressured by young challengers. Situations in which people must compete for promotions, status, and even work itself force constant self-appraisals of capabilities by means of social comparison with younger competitors (Suls & Mullen, 1982).

For those whose livelihood and self-esteem rest mainly on physical strength, as in athletic careers, reduced physical adeptness brings early forced retirement. This requires redirection of life pursuits posing new challenges to personal adequacy. A life devoted almost exclusively to professional sport, to the neglect of competencies required for other occupational pursuits, is not easy to redirect (McPherson, 1980). To find oneself unemployed with abrupt loss of income and status and poorly equipped with skills necessary for another occupation creates severe personal strains.

During the middle years, people have to confront seriously the limits of their capabilities. Most will have gotten as far as they will in their jobs. They see time and opportunities to realize the ambitions that sustained them over the years slipping away. Visions of a future lacking variety and prospects for new accomplishments may give rise to midlife strains, especially for people who harbor doubts that what they are doing is worthwhile.

Reactions to taking stock of one's life in the middle years take varied forms. Most people scale down their ambitions and try to pursue their vocation as competently as they can. Because even the same pursuit changes somewhat over time, opportunities for self-development still remain. Many who find themselves in routine jobs do them perfunctorily and seek satisfaction through development of capabilities in avocational pursuits. Still others restructure their lives to be more challenging and fulfilling. They change careers, mates, and locales (Chew, 1976) or simply drop out for a life free of performance demands and responsibilities.

Reappraisals of Self-Efficacy with Advancing Age. The self-efficacy problems of the elderly center on reappraisals and misappraisals of their capabilities. Discussions of aging focus extensively on declining abilities. Advancing age is said to produce losses in physical stamina, sensory functions, intellectual facility, memory, and in the ability to process information. Many physical capacities indeed decrease as people grow older, thus requiring reappraisals of self-efficacy for activities in which the mediating biological functions have been significantly affected. However, people are equipped with excess physiological reserve so that some loss of reserve with aging does not necessarily impair the level of psychosocial functioning (Fries & Crapo, 1981). Gains in knowledge, skills, and expertise compensate for some loss in physical capacity. Nevertheless, such evidence does not easily dispel the stereotype of deterioration evoked by vivid images of emaciated senility.

In cultures that revere youth and negatively stereotype the elderly, age becomes a salient dimension for self-evaluation. Once age assumes great significance, changes in performances over time, stemming largely from social factors, are easily misattributed to biological ageing. The widespread belief in intellectual decline is a good case in point. Longitudinal studies reveal no universal or general decline in intellectual abilities until the very advanced years, but in cross-sectional comparisons of different age groups the young do surpass the old (Baltes & Labouvie, 1973; Schaie, 1974). The major share of age differences in intelligence is due to differences in the experiences across generations rather than to biological ageing. To paraphrase Schaie, cultures age as do people. Many age differences are partly the product of cultural changes. It is not so much that the old have declined in intelligence but that the young have had the benefit of richer experiences enabling them to function at a higher level. When the elderly are taught to use their intellectual capabilities, their improvement in cognitive functioning more than offsets the average decrement in performance over two decades (Baltes & Willis, 1982). Because people rarely exploit their full potential, elderly persons who invest the necessary effort can function at the higher levels of younger adults. By affecting level of involvement in activities, perceived self-efficacy can contribute to the maintenance of cognitive functioning over the adult life span.

Misappraisals of performance declines in terms of biological ageing undoubtedly occur in other areas of functioning as well. Decreases in sexuality with age resulting from stress or boredom may be misattributed mainly to loss of sexual capabilities. Perceived sexual inefficacy, in turn, diminishes sexual activity. Even declines in physical stamina may partly reflect decrements in self-perception of efficacy. In laboratory studies of this mediating mechanism, reductions in perceived physical self-efficacy, induced vicariously through exposure to supposedly superior performances of competitors, lower observers' physical endurance (Weinberg et al., 1979; Weinberg, Yukelson, & Jackson, 1980). The more perceived physical efficacy is diminished, the greater is the decline in physical stamina. The incomparable Satchel Paige alluded to the self-limiting effects of age-typing when he queried: "How old would you be if you didn't know how old you was?" Although most people enjoy good health, illnesses in the later years of life take their toll on both psyche and body. The damage to self-percepts of efficacy is no small matter.

As in earlier periods of development, the major sources of efficacy information provide the elderly with the basis for reappraising their personal efficacy. They evaluate their performance attainments and compare them to their level of functioning at earlier periods of their life (Suls & Mullen, 1982). The accomplishments of others provide a further gauge of self-efficacy. The

different age trends in intellectual ability, which have been revealed by longitudinal and cross-sectional comparisons, can have quite different impact on how much change is perceived in intellectual functioning. The elderly who weigh self-comparison in functioning over the course of time more heavily than social comparison with younger cohorts are less likely to view themselves as declining in capabilities than if younger cohorts are used extensively in comparative self-appraisals. In exploiting the needs, physical changes, and common ailments associated with ageing, the television industry stereotypes the elderly either as idle simpletons or as leading impoverished, hypochondriacal lives. The stereotypes of infirm old persons shape cultural expectations and evaluative reactions of inefficacy in regard to the elderly.

A declining sense of self-efficacy is apt to set in motion self-perpetuating processes that result in declining cognitive and behavioral functioning. People who are insecure about their efficacy not only curtail the range of their activities but undermine their efforts in those they undertake. The result is a progressive loss of interest and skill. In societies that emphasize the potential for self-development throughout the life span, rather than psychophysical decline with ageing, the elderly are most likely to lead productive, self-fulfilling lives.

Interrelatedness of Efficacy Influences

The preceding discussion centered mainly on how major social systems contribute to the growth of self-efficacy for developmental tasks that become crucial at differe nt periods of life. These diverse efficacy influences, of course, operate in an interrelated fashion. This is perhaps best illustrated in the emergence of sex differences in achievement efficacy. Although the findings vary across tasks and age levels, the evidence generally shows that girls view themselves as less efficacious than boys at intellectual activities that have been stereotypically linked with males (Parsons, Ruble,

Hodges, & Small, 1976). These differences stem from a combination of developmental influences, each of which fosters underestimation of the capabilities of girls. The first concerns the pervasive cultural modeling of sex-role stereotypes. Whether it be the television medium, children's play materials and instructional literature, or the social examples around them, children see women cast predominantly in nonachieving roles (Jacklin & Mischel, 1973; McArthur & Eisen, 1976; Sternglanz & Serbin, 1974; Weitzman, Eifler, Hokada, & Ross, 1972). Girls who adopt the stereotypic conception will mistrust their proficiency on achievement tasks. Even by early preschool years children already subscribe to the sexual stereotype of differential intellectual capabilities (Crandall, 1978). To the extent that children's own stereotyping leads them to behave in ways more conducive to intellectual success in boys than in girls, they create further social validation for the preconceptions.

We have previously noted that self-appraisals are influenced by evaluative reactions of others. There is some evidence to suggest that parents and teachers have different achievement expectations and vary their explanations for successes and failures depending on the sex of the child. They tend to expect less of girls, to center criticism on the intellectual aspects of their academic work, and to judge their failures more as a result of ability than of motivation (Dweck, Davidson, Nelson, & Enna, 1978; Parsons et al., 1976). The cumulative effect of these diverse influences is to create a sense of inefficacy that can only serve to hinder self-development of intellectual capabilities.

Development of Self-Appraisal Skills

With cognitive development through exploratory experiences, tuition, and social comparison, children gradually improve their self-appraisal skills. The self-knowledge gained by applying self-appraisal skills enables them to make efficacy judgments on their own to guide their actions in whatever situations may arise. How children learn to use diverse sources of efficacy information in developing a stable and accurate sense of personal efficacy is a matter of considerable interest.

Accurate appraisal of one's capabilities depends on a number of constituent skills that develop through direct and socially mediated experience. While engaging in activities, children must attend simultaneously to multiple sources of efficacy information conveyed by the nature of the task, circumstances, characteristics of the performances, and the results they produce. Since the activities are performed on repeated occasions, children must be able to transcend particular instances and to integrate efficacy information from performance samples extended over time. This places heavy demands on their ability to monitor ongoing events, to evaluate the causes of fluctuations in performances and outcomes, and to represent and retain efficacy information derived from many prior experiences under varying circumstances.

Research on development of metacognitive skills has explored how children gain knowledge about cognitive phenomena, such as thoughts about themselves as cognizers, about task goals and strategies for achieving them (Brown, 1978; Flavell, 1978a, 1979). Gaining self-knowledge of capabilities as a doer, as well as a thinker, greatly expands the number of constituent skills that must be appraised. Personal efficacy entails improvisation of multiple cognitive, social, and manual skills. In addition to appraising the versatility of their skills, children have much to learn about the difficulty of environmental tasks, the abilities they require, and the types of problems likely to arise in executing different courses of action. Incongruities between self-efficacy and action may stem fro m misperceptions of task demands, as well as from faulty self-knowledge. With wider experience, children gain better understanding of themselves and their everyday environment, which enables them to judge their efficacy in particular areas of functioning more realistically.

Because of their limited cognitive skills and experience, young children lack knowledge of their cognitive and behavioral capabilities. They have difficulty in attending simultaneously to multiple sources of efficacy information, in distinguishing between important and minor indicants, and in processing sequential efficacy information. As a result, their self-appraisals are apt to be quite dependent on immediate, salient outcomes and hence relatively unstable.

As children become more proficient with age in appraisal skills, reliance on immediate performance outcomes declines in importance when judging what they can do. These changes are accompanied by developmental increases in children's use of more diverse, less salient, and sequential efficacy information (Parsons, Moses, & Yulish-Muszynski, 1977; Parsons & Ruble, 1977). With experience they begin to understand how expenditure of effort can compensate for lack of ability (Kun, 1977). Through more extensive use of efficacy information across tasks, time, and situations, older children judge their capabilities and limitations more accurately. As children get older they begin to use inference rules or heuristics in processing efficacy information, as, for example, inferring that the more effort is expended, the less the capability.

We saw earlier that people judge their capabilities partly through social comparison with the performances of others. Measuring personal efficacy by social comparative information involves greater complexities than self-appraisals based on direct experience. Comparative appraisals of efficacy require not only evaluation of one's own performances but also knowledge of how others do, cognizance of nonability determinants of their performances, and some understanding that it is others, like oneself, who provide the most informative social criterion for comparison. With development, children become increasingly discriminative in their use of comparative efficacy informa-

tion. Developmental analyses conducted by Morris and Nemcek (1982) show that effective use of social comparative information lags behind perception of ability rankings. Except for the very young (e.g., three-year-olds), who do not discern differences in ability, with increasing age children are progressively more accurate in appraising their own abilities and those of their peers. However, not until about age six do they realize that it is the performances of others who are like themselves, but slightly better, that are most informative for comparative purposes.

A problem of future research is to clarify how young children learn what type of social comparative information is most useful for efficacy evaluation. Such knowledge is probably gained in several ways. One process undoubtedly operates through social comparison of success and failure experiences. Children repeatedly observe their own behavior and the attainments of others. We know from the work of Morris and Nemcek that, at least in some areas of functioning, children begin to discern differences in ability at a very early age. Given that they can rank ability, they would soon learn that neither the successes of the very superior nor the failures of inept peers tells them much about how well they are likely to perform new activities. Rather, it is the attainments of others similar to themselves that are most predictive of the children's own operative capabilities. Acting on appropriate comparative self-appraisal thus maximizes the likelihood of success. Attribute similarity would also gain informative value for comparative appraisal of ability through differential experiences. To the extent that children with similar characteristics achieve comparable performance levels, using the performances of similar peers is likely to yield more accurate self-appraisal than using the accomplishments of dissimilar peers.

Children do not rely solely on the behavioral consequences of comparative efficacy inferences in learning to select similar others for self-ability evaluation. They receive direct instruction from time to time about the appropriateness of various social comparisons. Because of their limited experience, young children are quick to try what they see others doing, even though it is well beyond their reach. Faulty performances can undermine their developing sense of efficacy or, if the activities are potentially dangerous, result in injury. To minimize such consequences, parents explain to their children who is appropriate for comparison and who is not for gauging their capabilities.

Measuring efficacy judgments as a function of age can shed some light on developmental trends in children's use of efficacy information in self-appraisals. However, such research does not clarify how proficiency in self-appraisal develops. Knowledge about the determinants and processes of efficacy evaluation can be advanced by experiments designed to increase efficacy-appraisal skills where they are lacking. Cognitive modeling provides one effective means for increasing children's understanding of the efficacy value of relevant sources of information.

In cognitive modeling (Meichenbaum & Asarnow, 1979), models verbalize aloud their thoughts as they solve problems and form judgments. The usually covert thought processes are thus made fully observable. In applying cognitive modeling to developing efficacy judgment, models would identify efficacy-relevant cues and verbalize rules for interpreting and integrating the efficacy information while performing different tasks. Functional rules for judging social comparative information can be modeled in a similar fashion.

Research aimed at building efficacy-appraisal skills offers therapeutic benefits, as well as knowledge about developmental processes. Many children are severely handicapped by perceived inefficacy stemming from frequent misconstrual of performance difficulties arising from nonability factors as due to personal limitations and from inappropriate social comparisons. They have much to gain from changing judgmental orientations that lead them to belittle their capabilities.

GENERALITY OF THE SELF-EFFICACY MECHANISM

Microanalytic Research Strategy

In testing propositions about the origins and functions of perceived self-efficacy, a microanalytic methodology is employed (Bandura, 1977b). Individuals are presented with self-efficacy scales representing tasks varying in difficulty, complexity, stressfulness, or in some other dimension, depending on the particular domain of functioning being explored. They designate the tasks they judge they can do and their degree of certainty that they can execute them. This methodology permits a microanalysis of the degree of congruence between self-percepts of efficacy and action at the level of individual tasks.

The question arises as to whether self-efficacy probes can affect performance by creating public commitment and pressure for consistency. Various safeguards are included to minimize any possible motivational effects of the assessment itself. With such safeguards behavior and emotional reactions are the same regardless of whether people do or do not record their self-percepts of efficacy (Bandura, 1982d; Bandura & Cervone, 1983; Brown & Inouye, 1978; Gauthier & Ladouceur, 1981; Weinberg, Yukelson, & Jackson, 1980; Reese, 1983). Veridical self-appraisal is best achieved under conditions that reduce concern over social evaluation (Telch, Bandura, Vinciguerra, Agras, & Stout, 1982). When social evaluation of people's efficacy judgments is made salient, they are inclined to become conservative in their self-appraisals. This reduces, rather than increases, the degree of concordance between self-efficacy judgment and action.

Of central interest to self-efficacy theory is the dynamic interplay between self-referent thought, action, and affect. A special merit of the microanalytic approach is that particularized indices of self-efficacy provide refined predictions of human action and affective reactivity.

Causal Analysis of Self-Percepts of Efficacy

Psychological theories postulate mediatory mechanisms through which external factors affect behavior. Experimental tests of causation may vary in the number of linkages they verify between the relevant events. The weakest test provides evidence that behavior co-varies with changes in external factors believed to affect the postulated mediator without measuring the mediator independently. Such co-variation increases confidence in the theory, but it does not firmly establish its validity, because the co-variation can be mediated by other mechanisms capable of producing similar effects. Research is much more persuasive when it relies on assessed mediation than on presumptive mediation. A postulated mediator is not directly observable; nevertheless, it should have observable indicants other than the actions it presumably governs. The most stringent test of a theory provides evidence of dual linkage in the causal process—changes in relevant external factors are linked to an independently measured indicant of the internal mediator, and it, in turn, is linked to changes in behavior.

Studies of the causal contribution of perceived self-efficacy to behavior test all of the postulated linkages in the causal process. In the most refined tests, changes in perceived self-efficacy are closely monitored as external influences are applied, until perceived self-efficacy is raised to preselected levels, whereupon behavior is measured (Bandura, Reese, & Adams, 1982). The efficacy-action link is corroborated by microlevel relationships between particular self-percepts of efficacy and corresponding action, or by macrolevel relationships between aggregated self-percepts of efficacy and aggregated behavior. Because perceived self-efficacy is systematically varied rather than merely correlated, the findings speak to the issue of causality.

In one experiment (Bandura, Reese, & Adams, 1982), the level of perceived self-efficacy was raised in phobics from virtually nonexistent to low, moderate, or high levels through enactive mastery of progressively more threatening activities. A second experiment provided an even more stringent causal test by creating different levels of perceived self-efficacy vicariously. In the vicarious mode of efficacy induction, persons observe coping strategies being modeled, but they themselves do not execute any actions. Observers, therefore, have to rely solely on what they see in forming generalized perceptions of their own capabilities.

The findings of these studies lend validity to the thesis that self-percepts of efficacy operate as cognitive mediators of performance. Increasing levels of perceived self-efficacy both across groups and within the same individual gave rise to progressively higher performance accomplishments. The efficacy-action relationship is replicated across different phobic dysfunctions and in both intergroup and intrasubject comparisons, regardless of whether self-percepts of efficacy were raised by enactive mastery or by vicarious influence. Microanalyses of efficacy-action congruences reveal a close fit between performance and self-percepts of efficacy on individual tasks. People successfully execute tasks that fall within their enhanced range of perceived self-efficacy, but they shun or fail those that exceed their perceived coping capabilities.

That self-percepts of efficacy are not simply reflective imprints of past actions when efficacy is enhanced by enactive mastery is revealed in fine-grain analyses of performance attainments and changes in perceived self-efficacy at each step in the change process (Bandura, Reese, & Adams, 1982). Self-percepts of efficacy often exceed, only occasionally match, and sometimes remain below past performance attainments, depending on how deeds are cognitively appraised. When people are fully assured of their capabilities, they remain unshaken in their perceived efficaciousness and persevere doggedly, even though they fail repeatedly on problems that are unsolvable (Brown & Inouye, 1978). Had self-percepts of efficacy been simply reflectors of past performance, they would have suffered a marked decline as would performance. Because people are influenced more by how they read their performance successes and failures than by their performance attainments *per se*, it is not uncommon for perceived self-efficacy to predict future behavior better than past performance (Bandura & Adams, 1977; Bandura, Adams, Hardy, & Howells, 1980; Bandura, Reese, & Adams, 1982; Colletti, Supnick, & Payne, 1985; Kendrick, Craig, Lawson, & Davidson, 1982; McIntyre, Lichtenstein, & Mermelstein, 1983; Schunk, 1984b; Williams, Dooseman, & Kleifield, 1984). Past behavior affects future actions partly through its effects on perceived self-efficacy, and perceived self-efficacy can affect actions independently of past behavior or arousal.

Findings from the vicarious mode are especially well suited for demonstrating the causal contribution of perceived self-efficacy to performance. Individuals simply observe models' performances, make inferences from the modeled information about their own coping capabilities, and later behave in accordance with their self-judged efficacy. In observational modes of self-efficacy induction, motoric mediators are not present to complicate analysis of causal relationships.

The issue of causality has been examined by a number of other research designs and efficacy-enhancing procedures as well. One such approach measures the performances of people with the same ability level but who differ in their perceptions of their capabilities. Recall the study by Collins (1982), who selected children of high and low perceived mathematical self-efficacy within each of two levels of mathematical ability. Children who judged themselves as self-efficacious were more successful in solving mathematical problems than those of equal ability who lacked a sense of efficacy.

Even a trivial factor devoid of information to affect competency can nevertheless alter the level of perceived self-efficacy, which is then reflected in differential perseverance. Studies of anchoring effects show that arbitrary reference points from which judgments are adjusted either upward or downward can affect the judgments (Tversky & Kahneman, 1974). Because adjustments from the anchor are usually insufficient, judgments remain biased. Thus, a randomly selected low number as a starting point will lead people to estimate a smaller crowd in a stadium than if the arbitrary starting number is large. Cervone and Peake (1985a) demonstrate a similar anchoring influence on self-judged efficacy. Judgments made from a randomly selected, high reference point of ability create higher perceived self-efficacy as a problem solver than judgments made from a low reference point. The higher the instated self-percepts of efficacy, the longer people persevere on difficult and unsolvable problems. In a related study (Cervone & Peake, 1985b), efficacy judgment was biased simply by having people judge their perceived self-efficacy in relation to ascending or descending levels of possible attainments; the initial levels in these sequences serve as anchoring influences that lower or raise perceived self-efficacy, respectively. Elevated self-percepts of efficacy heightened effort, whereas lowered self-percepts lessened effort on troublesome problems.

Modification of self-percepts of efficacy through verbal persuasory modes of influence also sheds empirical light on the issue of causality. Studies in which perceived efficacy is altered by arbitrary feedback typify this approach. Weinberg and his associates reveal that changes in physical stamina in competitive situations are partly mediated through self-percepts of efficacy (Weinberg, Gould, & Jackson, 1979; Weinberg, Yukelson, & Jackson, 1980). Perceived self-efficacy is raised by false feedback that one has triumphed in a competitive trial and diminished by feedback that one has been outperformed by a competitor. The lower the illusorily instated self-percepts of physical efficacy, the weaker the competitive endurance in new physical activities. Of particular interest is evidence for the power of self-efficacy belief over brawn. Self-percepts of efficacy, illusorily boosted in females and illusorily diminished in males, obliterate large preexisting sex differences in actual physical strength (Weinberg et al., 1979).

Still another approach employs a contravening design in which a procedure that ordinarily impairs functioning is applied, but in ways that raise perceived self-efficacy. The changes accompanying psychological ministrations may result as much, if not more, from instilling beliefs in self-efficacy as from the particular skills imparted. To the extent that people's beliefs in their coping efficacy are strengthened, they approach situations more assuredly and make better use of the talents they have. Procedures that by themselves could exacerbate a debilitation when presented in ways that enhance self-efficacy may produce beneficial results. Holroyd and his associates (Holroyd et al., 1984) told persons suffering from tension headaches that headaches would abate by relaxing facial muscles. In a series of biofeedback sessions some of the participants were trained to relax their facial muscles, whereas other participants were unbeknowingly trained to tense their facial muscles which, if anything, should aggravate the condition. At the end of each session they received false feedback that they had achieved either a great deal of control over their facial muscles or little control. Regardless of whether people were tensing or relaxing, success feedback instilled a strong sense of efficacy that they could prevent the occurrence of headaches in different stressful situations. The higher the perceived efficacy, the fewer headaches they experienced. The actual amount of change in muscle activity achieved in treatment was unrelated to the incidence of subsequent headaches.

Results of these diverse causal paradigms with different populations and domains of functioning provide convergent evidence that perceptions of personal efficacy contribute to level of psychological functioning. A substantial body of research, examined next, further clarifies the role of perceived self-efficacy in human thought, affect, and action.

Predictive Generality across Modes of Influence

The aim of a comprehensive theory is to provide a unifying conceptual framework which can encompass diverse modes of influence that have been shown to alter behavior. The greatest benefits psychological ministrations can bestow are not solutions to a specific problem but the tools with which to effect solutions on one's own in whatever future situations might arise. In any activity, skills and self-beliefs that ensure their optimal use are required for successful functioning. If self-efficacy is lacking, people tend to behave ineffectually, even though they know what to do.

In social cognitive theory, perceived self-efficacy operates as one common mechanism of behavioral change—different modes of influence alter coping behavior partly by creating and strengthening self-percepts of efficacy. This does not mean that other mechanisms do not also come into play in promoting change. Commonality of mechanism does not imply exclusivity of mechanism. Research designed to clarify particular mechanisms governing behavior should be distinguished from studies aimed at maximizing the amount of variance explained in behavior by combining a host of factors that contribute to it. In the social cognitive view, perceived efficacy operates in concert with other mechanisms analyzed in this book in the regulation of behavior.

Perceived Self-Inefficacy and Phobic Dysfunction. Because behavior is partly governed by self-referent thought, perceived inefficacy can give rise to severe psychological dysfunctions. People who are burdened by acute misgivings about their coping capabilities suffer much distress and expend much effort in defensive action (Bandura, 1978b). They cannot get themselves to do things they find subjectively threatening even though they are objectively safe. They may even shun easily manageable activities because they see them as leading to more threatening events over which they will be unable to exercise adequate control. As a result, their lives are constricted by defensive avoidance of social, recreational, and vocational activities that might expose them to the threats, however remote the possibility. But even restricting daily activities does not ensure relief from stress. They are repeatedly tormented by distressing thoughts and intrusive ruminations about possible calamities.

Some human debilities stem not so much from insecurities about particular coping skills but from perceived inefficacy in controlling oneself or brief lapses in one's mental functioning. Actors visualize themselves forgetting their lines, singers their lyrics, and concert soloists their musical selections. In such well-rehearsed activities, the inefficacy concerns involve control of memory lapses, rather than skillful execution of the activities. Some performing artists give up promising careers because of their inordinate concern over blacking out in the midst of a performance (Zailian, 1978). In other activities the inefficacy concerns may center more on the ability to control potentially dangerous lapses in attentional and motor aspects of performance than on momentary cognitive failings.

Inefficacy sometimes involves perceived vulnerability to total loss of personal control, rather than momentary lapses in functioning. Such persons believe they will lose consciousness or be unable to restrain themselves from behaving in grossly inappropriate ways. Thus, individuals who doubt they can resist jumping or retaining consciousness when looking down from heights will be reluctant to venture upward. Aerophobics, who perceive themselves as vulnerable to disintegrative loss of control while cruising aloft, remain grounded. However,

a few participant modeling trips that convince them they are fully capable of controlling themselves in the aircraft will get them airborne, even though they do not give up their beliefs that airliners occasionally crash or make hazardous crash landings due to mechanical malfunctions.

The explanatory and predictive power of self-efficacy across modes of influence has been tested in a series of experiments in which snake phobics whose lives were adversely affected by their phobia received treatments relying on enactive, vicarious, emotive, and cognitive modes of influence (Bandura & Adams, 1977; Bandura, Adams, & Beyer, 1977; Bandura, Adams, Hardy, & Howells, 1980). This type of disorder permits the most precise tests of mechanisms of change because participants rarely, if ever, have contact with reptiles while the treatment is in progress. Consequently, the changes accompanying treatment are not confounded by uncontrolled experiences arising from periodic contact with the threats between sessions. In each study in this series, the level, strength, and generality of self-efficacy for a variety of threatening tasks was measured prior to and after treatment.

In the treatment employing enactive mastery as the principal vehicle of change, phobics are assisted by performance mastery aids to confront and deal with threats (Bandura, Blanchard, & Ritter, 1969; Bandura, Jeffery, & Wright, 1974). As treatment progresses, the provisional aids are withdrawn, and self-directed mastery experiences are then arranged to authenticate and strengthen personal efficacy. In the vicarious mode of treatment, phobics merely observe the model exercising control over progressively more threatening activities without any adverse effects. In the third treatment tested, which draws heavily on a cognitive modality (Kazdin, 1973a), phobics generate cognitive scenarios in which multiple models of differing characteristics cope with and master threatening activities. As a further test of the generality of efficacy theory, an emotive-oriented procedure was also examined. In this desensitization treatment, people visualize threatening scenes while deeply relaxed, until they no longer experience any anxiety arousal (Wolpe, 1974). The imaginal conquest of fear and acquisition of a self-relaxation coping skill can boost perceived coping self-efficacy.

Results of these studies confirm that different modes of influence all raise and strengthen self-percepts of efficacy. Behavior corresponds closely to level of self-efficacy change regardless of the method by which self-efficacy is enhanced. The higher the level of perceived self-efficacy, the greater are the performance accomplishments. Strength of efficacy also predicts behavior change. The stronger the perceived efficacy, the more likely are people to persist in their efforts until they succeed. Consistent with self-efficacy theory, enactive mastery produces the highest, strongest, and most generalized increases in coping efficacy. This finding is corroborated by other comparative studies demonstrating that enactive mastery surpasses persuasory (Biran & Wilson, 1981), emotive (Katz, Stout, Taylor, Horne, & Agras, 1983), and vicarious (Feltz, Landers, & Raeder, 1979) influences in building self-percepts of efficacy.

Self-efficacy theory explains rate of change during the course of treatment as well (Bandura & Adams, 1977). Although participants master the same challenges, they vary in how much perceived self-efficacy they derive from their successes. Self-percepts of efficacy formed at different points in treatment predict well subsequent coping successes on tasks the phobics had never done before.

The degree of relationship between self-percepts of efficacy and action can be quantified in several ways. First, correlations can be computed between aggregate scores of perceived self-efficacy and performance attainments. Second, at a more particularized level of analysis, degree of congruence between self-percepts and action can be gauged by recording whether or not persons judge themselves capable of performing each of the various tasks using a cutoff strength value and computing the percent of accurate correspondence between self-efficacy judgment and actual performance on individual tasks. Dichotomizing self-efficacy judgments on the basis of a minimal strength value inevitably loses some predictive information. Third, a more refined microanalysis of congruence is provided by computing the probability of successful performance as a function of strength of perceived self-efficacy. All three indices reveal a close relationship between self-percepts of efficacy and action, whether efficacy is developed by enactive mastery, vicarious experience, cognitive coping, or elimination of anxiety arousal (Bandura, 1977b, 1982b; Cervone, 1985).

Influences that operate through nonperformance modes are of particular interest because they provide no behavioral information for judging changes in one's self-efficacy. Persons have to infer their capabilities from vicarious and symbolic sources of efficacy information. Even in the case of enactively instated self-efficacy, it bears noting that performance is not the genesis of the causal chain. Performance includes among its determinants self-percepts of efficacy. We know from the research of Salomon (1984), for example, that self-perceived learning efficacy affects how much effort is invested in given activities and what levels of performance are attained. Thus, judgments of one's capabilities partly determine performance accomplishments which boost perceived self-efficacy in a mutually enhancing process (Taylor, Bandura, Ewart, Miller, & DeBusk, 1985). It is not as though self-percepts of efficacy affect future performances but play no role whatsoever in earlier performance attainments. Because perceived self-efficacy and performance affect each other, measuring the influence of perceived efficacy on future performance with the effects of past performance partialled out of the correlation underestimates the actual relationship. Past performance partly reflects the influence of perceived efficacy, so partialling out past performance also inappropriately removes the effect of prior, perceived efficacy from the effect of subsequent perceived efficacy on behavior. Questions about causal ordering of factors arise for enactively based influences when interactive processes are treated as linear, sequential ones, and causally prior self-efficacy determinants of past performance accomplishments go unmeasured.

Perceived Self-Efficacy in the Self-Regulation of Pain. Self-management of pain is a markedly different area of functioning that illustrates further the generality of the self-efficacy mechanism across modes of influence. Pain is a complex psychobiologic phenomenon, influenced by psychosocial factors, rather than simply a sensory experience arising directly from stimulation of pain receptors. The subjective experience of pain depends not only on sensory stimulation but also on what one attends to, how the experience is cognitively appraised, and on self-activation of physiological systems by means of various coping techniques. The same intensity of pain stimulation can thus give rise to varying subjective experiences of pain.

That psychosocial factors can significantly influence pain is revealed in analgesic placebo responses. Placebo pills can bring pain relief to many people. The analgesic potency of placebos closely mimics the pharmacologic properties of drugs, producing additive effects, dose-level effects, and greater pain relief from a placebo injection than from a placebo pill (Evans, 1974). Misbeliefs about the substance being taken can counteract the usual pharmacologic action of drugs, as well as invest inert substances with analgesic potency (Wolf, 1950). For example, nausea is eliminated by an emetic that ordinarily induces nausea and vomiting if it is presented to patients as a drug that alleviates stomach upset. In the latter instances, beliefs override physiological reactions activated by the pharmacologic action of drugs. Psychological coping techniques enable people to reduce even more effectively the amount of pain they experience and the amount of analgesic medication they require (Neufeld & Thomas, 1977; Turk, Meichenbaum, & Genest, 1981).

Research has clarified some aspects of the physiological mechanisms mediating pain reduction. The brain possesses an endogenous system that produces endorphins and enkephalins that play an important role in the regulation of pain. These are morphine-like substances the body uses to relieve pain. Studies by Levine and his associates indicate that the endorphinergic systems can be activated by psychological means (Levine, Gordon, & Fields, 1978; Levine, Gordon, Jones, & Fields, 1978). Patients experiencing postoperative dental pain are administered either morphine or a placebo intravenously. About one third of the patients achieve pain relief from the placebo. Naloxone is an opiate antagonist that attaches to opiate receptors and impedes endorphins from blocking the transmission of pain impulses. Administration of naloxone produces a sudden rise in pain in patients who achieved relief from the placebo but does not affect the placebo non-responders. Such findings indicate that placebo analgesia is mediated by endorphin release. The pain relief achieved by psychological means is thus just as real and explainable in terms of opioid activation as is the pain relief gained through pharmacologic analgesics.

There are several ways in which perceived self-efficacy can bring belief from pain. People who believe they can alleviate pain are likely to mobilize whatever ameliorative skills they have learned and to persevere in their attempts. If pain mounts, the self-inefficacious are likely to give up quickly, whereas those who believe they can exercise some control over their pain will be more tenacious in their efforts. A sense of coping efficacy also cuts down on distressing anticipations that create aversive physiological arousal and bodily tension which only exacerbate sensory pain and discomfort. Dwelling on pain sensations makes them more noticeable and thus more difficult to bear. Perceived self-efficacy can moderate pain by diverting attention from pain sensation to ameliorative activities. The more attentionally demanding the coping activities, the less attention pain sensations can command. To the extent that pain sensations are supplanted in consciousness they are felt less.

That perceived self-efficacy may mediate the potency of different psychological analgesics was put to test by Reese (1983). People received one of three modes of treatment for alleviating cold pressor pain produced by placing one's hand in ice water. In the cognitive mode, they were taught cognitive techniques, including attention diversion, pleasant imagery, coping self-instruction, and dissociation; in the motoric mode they used muscular self-relaxation to cope with pain; in the ministration drawing on the placebo modality, they were administered a placebo described as a medicinal analgesic. Each of these treatments increased perceived self-efficacy to cope with and ameliorate pain. The more self-efficacious the persons judged themselves to be, the less pain they experienced in later cold pressor tests, and the higher was their pain threshold and pain tolerance.

Coping by cognitive means proved more effective than muscular relaxation in controlling pain which, in turn, was better than placebos. Research by Neufeld and Thomas (1977) reveals that the benefits of relaxation stem more from boosts in perceived coping efficacy than from the muscular exercises themselves. Mere belief, created by the false feedback that one is a skilled relaxer for controlling pain, increased pain tolerance in the absence of any differences in actual muscular relaxation. In the study by Reese (1983), it was the participants for whom placebo medication raised perceived self-efficacy that the placebo was an effective analgesic. Perceived self-efficacy in controlling pain predicted not only positive placebo responders but negative placebo responders as well. Participants who continued to distrust their pain controlling efficacy after receiving the placebo medica-

tion became even less tolerant of pain.

That perceived self-efficacy makes pain easier to manage is corroborated by studies of acute and chronic clinical pain. Women who had been taught relaxation and breathing exercises to reduce pain during their first childbirth differed in how much control they believed they could exercise over pain while giving birth (Manning & Wright, 1983). Their perceived self-efficacy predicted how well they managed pain during labor and delivery. The higher their perceived self-efficacy, the longer they tolerated labor pain before requesting medication and the less pain medication they used. Shoor and Holman (1984) document the influential role of perceived self-efficacy in managing the chronic pain of arthritis. When patients are equated for degree of physical debility and other relevant factors, those who believe they can exercise some influence over their pain and how much their arthritic condition affects them lead more active lives and experience less pain.

The evidence discussed above testifies to the effectiveness of psychological means of pain control. Their analgesic potency depends, in part, on the extent to which they provide people with pain coping skills and strengthen their perceived self-efficacy in exercising some control over their pain. The analysis needs to be pursued further to identify the mechanisms by which self-percepts of efficacy enhance pain tolerance. There is some reason to believe that psychological techniques may produce analgesic effects mainly through nonopioid mechanisms. Stress can activate endogenous opioids that block pain transmission (Bolles & Fanselow, 1982). It is not the physically painful stimulation, *per se*, but the psychological stress over its uncontrollability that seems to be the important factor in opioid activation (Hyson, Ashcraft, Drugan, Grau, & Maier, 1982).

Pain sensations can be blocked at the level of physiological transmission or psychological awareness. Because a high sense of coping efficacy makes aversive situations less stressful, it may reduce stress-activated opioids. While there may be less opioid blockage of pain, a high efficaciousness that occupies consciousness with engrossing matters can block awareness of pain sensations by a nonopioid cognitive mechanism. The attentional resources available at any given moment are severely limited. Therefore, it is hard for people to attend to more than one thing at a time. Effective diversion of attention to absorbing matters could attenuate perception of pain sensations without implicating endorphins.

Analgesic reactions may be mediated primarily by a nonopioid mechanism when people have effective means of coping with painful conditions, but by an opioid mechanism when they lack coping techniques for attenuating pain or for blocking it from awareness. Most likely both mechanisms operate in the regulation of pain, but their relative contribution to pain sensitivity and tolerance may vary with degree of controlling efficacy and stages of coping. A strong sense of efficacy increases pursuit of pain-producing activities, as in arthritis, or willingness to bear mounting pain stimulation (Reese, 1983; Shoor & Holman, 1984). The exercise of self-efficaciousness may heighten pain stimulation to the point where psychological analgesics no longer work effectively, thus activating opioid mechanisms in later stages of coping.

Predictive Generality across Domains of Functioning

The preceding discussion has examined the explanatory and predictive generality of self-efficacy theory across different modes of influence applied to the same type of dysfunction. Diverse lines of research applying different modes of influence to varied domains of functioning also address the issue of perceived self-efficacy as a common mechanism mediating psychosocial changes. A few examples will suffice to illustrate the scope of the endeavor.

Perceived self-efficacy predicts degree of change in diverse types of social behavior, coping behavior, stress reactions, physiolog-ical arousal, depression, pain tolerance, physical stamina, behavioral self-regulation, self-motivation, achievement strivings, athletic attainments, and career choice and development. Many of these areas of research will be discussed more fully because they clarify different aspects of the self-efficacy mechanism.

In these diverse lines of research, predictive success is achieved across time, settings, performance variants, expressive modalities, types of self-efficacy probes, and quite different domains of psychological functioning (Bandura, 1982a). Moreover, microanalyses reveal that self-percepts of efficacy predict variations in the level of affective and performance changes produced by different modes of influence, variations in performance between persons receiving the same mode of influence, and even variations within individuals about particular tasks they are likely to master or fail (Bandura, 1977b; Bandura, Adams, Hardy, & Howells, 1980). Convergent evidence from divergent domains and procedures lends broad support to the notion that perceived self-efficacy operates as an influential mechanism in human agency.

Achievement Strivings

People expend effort and persevere despite difficulties to gain things they value. Such strivings for achievement are mediated through several cognitive mechanisms. They are fostered in part by an extensive system of extrinsic incentives in the form of approval, social recognition, privileges, power, and money. This motivator operates through outcome expectations for prospective feats. People also motivate themselves to notable accomplishments by the goals and the standards of excellence they set for themselves. Both outcome expectations and personal aspirations depend on perceived self-efficacy (Bandura & Cervone, 1983; Locke, Frederick, Lee, & Bobko, 1984). People are disinclined to strive for rewards requiring performances they judge themselves incapable of attaining. Nor do they passionately aspire to goals they judge they can never fulfill, unless they are bent on self-inflicted misery. The way in which perceived self-efficacy operates as a mediator of personal strivings is extensively reviewed in the next chapter. The present discussion centers mainly on efficacy analyses of cognitive achievement.

Numerous studies have been conducted in which self-percepts of efficacy are enhanced in children who have major deficits in cognitive skills by self-directed learning supplemented with goal structures, causal attributional feedback, social comparison information, self-verbalization of strategies, and positive incentives (Bandura & Schunk, 1981; Relich, 1983; Schunk, 1981, 1982a, 1982b, 1983a, 1983b, 1983d, 1984a). As children master cognitive skills, they develop a growing sense of cognitive efficacy. These various supplementary influences augment the changes accompanying self instruction. Enhanced perceived self-efficacy predicts increased persistence in seeking solutions, higher level of cognitive achievement, and more intrinsic interest in activities formerly disliked. Regression analyses show that self-efficacy contributes to achievement behavior beyond the effects of cognitive skills. This is consistent with the findings of Collins (1982) showing that perceived self-efficacy is partially independent of cognitive skills but contributes significantly to performances requiring such skills. Self-perceived capabilities similarly mediate adult achievement strivings (Covington & Omelich, 1979).

The task of creating learning environments conducive to development of cognitive skills rests heavily on the talent and self-efficaciousness of teachers. Evidence indicates that classroom atmospheres are partly fashioned by teachers' beliefs in their capabilities to promote learning even in difficult students. Gibson and Dembo (1984) found that teachers who are highly assured of their instructional efficacy devote more classroom time directly to academic learning, stick with students when they fail to help them succeed, and then praise them for their accomplishments. In teachers who doubt their instructional efficacy spend more time on nor pastimes, readily give up on students n t... do not get results, and are prone to criticize. Over time, such instructional orientations can substantially affect students' perceptions of their learning capabilities and academic achievements (Ashton, 1985).

Self-Efficacy Determinants of Career Development and Pursuits

The choices people make during formative periods that influence the direction of their development shape the course of their lives. Such choices foster different competencies, interests, and affiliative preferences and set boundaries on the career options that can be realistically considered. Hackett and Betz (1981) provide a causal model of career development in which perceived self-efficacy functions as a major mediator. Most occupational pursuits depend on cognitive and social competencies that may require years to master. Hackett and Betz document the diverse ways in which institutional practices and socialization influences contribute to developmental paths by the types of competencies and self-beliefs they cultivate. Experiences during this formative period of life leave their mark on personal efficacy which can, in turn, set the future direction of a life course by affecting the choices made and the successes attained.

One of the important issues addressed in this line of research is how the career interests and pursuits of women are constricted by their self-beliefs that traditionally male occupations are inappropriate for them because they lack the capabilities to master the requisite skills. Efficacy analyses of career decision making in college students (Betz & Hackett, 1981) reveal that males perceive themselves to be equally efficacious for traditional male and female vocations. In contrast, females judge themselves highly efficacious for the types of occupations traditionally held by women but in efficacious in mastering the educational requirements and job functions of vocations dominated by males. These different perceptions of personal efficacy are especially striking because the groups do not differ in their actual verbal and quantitative ability on standardized tests. It is not the subskills that selected college students possess but how they perceive and use them that makes the difference.

Regardless of sex, the higher the level of perceived self-efficacy, the wider the range of career options seriously considered and the greater the degree of interest shown in them. The latter results are consistent with those reported by Collins (1982), who found that perceived self-efficacy predicted interest better than actual ability. Occupational preferences are determined more by perceived self-efficacy than by the valued outcomes believed to be attainable by different occupational pursuits (Wheeler, 1983). Perceived self-inefficacy not only constricts the range of career options considered but generates indecisiveness about those regarded as viable (Taylor & Betz, 1983).

Betz and Hackett (1983) have devoted special attention to perceived mathematical self-efficacy because modern technologies have made quantitative skills increasingly important to a wide range of career options and to professional advancement. Avoidance of careers that may require some quantitative competency is determined more by perceived mathematical efficacy than by actual mathematical ability (Hackett & Betz, 1984). Self-inefficacy barriers in this domain can thus be especially limiting. Perhaps because mathematics is sex-typed as a masculine activity, women harbor a lower sense of mathematical efficacy than men and tend to shy away from science-based college majors. Using a path analysis to identify causal links, Hackett (1985) found that gender, which reflects the influence of gender-role socialization, and high-school preparation affect perceived self-efficacy in quantitative capabilities. Perceived self-inefficacy in dealing with numbers, in turn, affects students' anxiety about mathematics and the relatedness

to science and math of the college major they choose.

The causally prior contribution of perceived efficacy to socialization practices and educational preparation remains an important problem for future research to determine through longitudinal analyses. It follows from the present model of career development that the parents' own career-related efficacy will influence what vocational options they consider viable for their offspring. Students' differential self-percepts of efficacy for mastering occupational entry requirements are likely to influence what types of courses they choose in high school.

Computer literacy is becoming an increasingly important factor in career development and advancement. Even a brief check of the regular patrons of computers shows that computer skills have become highly masculinized. Boys are much more likely than girls to master computers, which boys see as necessary for their future (Hess & Miura, 1985). Socialization influences that breed perceived inefficacy in the use of computer tools are thus creating new career barriers for women. These are not easily overcome. Even at an early age, girls distrust their efficacy to program and operate computers, despite instruction and the school's encouragement to acquire such skills (Miura, 1984b). The lower the perceived efficacy in computer activities, the lesser the interest in acquiring computer competencies. Sex differences in perceived self-efficacy to master computer coursework extend to the college level. Regardless of sex, college students lacking a sense of computer efficacy are computer avoiders. They show less interest or inclination to pursue computer course work and see computer literacy as less relevant to their future careers (Miura, 1984a).

Societal practices require of women a robust sense of self-efficacy to pursue nontraditional vocations. In preparing for and entering careers dominated by men, they must believe strongly in themselves.

Self-doubts are often difficult to override even in socially endorsed endeavors, but doubly so when nontraditional pursuits receive minimal support or are regarded with disfavor by many people. Stereotyping and discriminatory practices create additional obstacles. Progress in a career requires considerable sustained effort to produce the types of results that contribute to advancements and personal fulfillment. This is difficult to achieve if one has to fulfill the heavy demands arising from the dual workloads of career and household.

Career pursuits require more than the specialized knowledge and the technical skills of one's trade. A high sense of personal efficacy is required to enlist the perseverant effort needed for a successful job search (Kanfer & Hulin, 1985). Success on the job further depends on self-efficacy in dealing with the social realities of work situations. Hackett, Betz, and Doty (1985) have identified a number of skills that subserve this broader function. These include the ability to communicate well, to relate effectively to others, to plan and manage the demands of one's job, to exercise leadership, and to cope with stress effectively. One's level of perceived self-efficacy in these skills can aid or impede career advancement quite apart from the technical skills one possesses.

Self-Efficacy Mediation of Skilled Performance

It is not uncommon for individuals of distinguished abilities to perform deficiently, even though they possess superior skills and have strong incentives to do well. In such instances, problematic self-efficacy often serves as a major obstacle to performance. That a firm sense of self-efficacy is a key to optimal performance has long been recognized in athletic circles. After capabilities are perfected and practiced extensively, perceived self-efficacy can be the difference between a good or poor showing in athletic contests. This is because, with relatively comparable capabilities, a small lapse

in effort or accuracy makes a major difference in outcome. Even more talented athletes beset by self-misgivings can be easily surpassed by less capable competitors who are assured of their abilities.

Athletic superstars give considerable weight to the contribution of perceived self-efficacy to skilled performance. King (1979) put it well when she observed that in tennis "more matches are won internally than externally." The performance dividends of perceived self-efficacy are equally evident in collective competitive accomplishments. Whether or not a team performs up to its potential depends partly on whether its members execute their functions in a highly efficacious frame of mind. Whatever the contests might be, coaches acknowledge that the game is a matter of ability and hard work, but above all, it is a matter of self-assurance. Adept motivators can get a team to play beyond what one would normally expect of its members.

The various methods used to create athletic competencies, such as modeling and proficient enactment, have been shown to be self-efficacy builders as well (Feltz, Landers, & Raeder, 1979; Gould & Weiss, 1981). Many practice routines are designed as much to boost perceived self-efficacy as to perfect skill. The benefits of "psyching up" strategies may also operate partly through this mechanism. As Wilkes and Summers (1984) have shown, immediate cognitive preparation emphasizing self-efficacy to succeed improves performance, whereas simply visualizing either optimal techniques or maximal performances has little effect. Physical injuries can produce problematic self-efficacy or "head problems" in talented athletes. The injury mends, but the lingering uncertainties of self-efficacy hinder optimal execution of skills.

The preceding remarks are not meant to imply that perceived self-efficacy can substitute for talent. Athletes who survive competitive selection possess natural ability for their chosen pursuits. Tuition and repeated practice convert talent into skill. However, a capability is only as good as its execution. Neither talent nor cultivated subskills guarantee distinguished performance. What athletes do with what they have and know is partly determined by their beliefs in their capabilities. It is hard to perform well with a low opinion of one's comparative ability. Thus, athletes of comparable abilities but differential self-assurance do not perform the same. Gifted athletes plagued by self-doubts perform far below their potential, and less talented but highly self-assured athletes outperform more talented competitors who lack faith in their abilities. Such variations between capabilities and accomplishments underscore the contribution of perceived self-efficacy to athletic adeptness.

Competitive sports also reveal the fragility of self-percepts of efficacy. A series of failures that can undermine perceived self-efficacy send professional athletes into performance slumps. Because of self-misgivings, they do not execute their skills well, even though they have perfected them and their very livelihood rests on their doing well. An insightful baseball catcher once described vividly the process of a self-efficacy slump when he remarked that a hitting slump begins at the bat, goes to the head, and ends in a chronically upset stomach.

Anecdotal evidence that self-percepts of efficacy mediate athletic performance receives support in laboratory experiments which concern the issue of causality (Weinberg et al., 1979; Weinberg et al., 1980; Weinberg et al., 1981). In these studies, adults perform a muscular strength task during which their perceived physical efficacy is is raised or lowered by fictitious feedback that they either surpassed or fell short of the performance of a competitor. Later they compete on a muscular endurance task either simultaneously or alternately with their competitor who performs well. Lowering people's perceived physical efficacy diminishes the amount of physical power they muster during the contest. Those who feel assured of their physical efficacy are undaunted by setbacks, while further weakening the muscular power of those who judge themselves inefficacious. The higher the illusorily instated self-percepts of physical efficacy, the greater is the competitive endurance in new physical activities. In simultaneous competition, which renders comparative ability appraisals especially salient, altered self-percepts of efficacy are more closely related to performance than in successive competition. Self-percepts of physical efficacy raised vicariously similarly boost physical stamina (Gould & Weiss, 1981).

In field studies, the higher the perceived self-efficacy, the better athletes are likely to perform in such diverse sports as track (Morelli & Martin, 1982), tennis (Barling & Abel, 1983), diving (Feltz, 1982), and gymnastics (Lee, 1982; McAuley & Gill, 1983). When athletic tasks are performed for the first time, preexisting self-efficacy predicts initial performance (Feltz & Albrecht, 1985), but, given adequate performance feedback, initial experience with a new task is likely to prompt reappraisals of self-efficacy, so that it is the updated self-percepts that affect subsequent performance (Weinberg et al., 1981). Perceived self-efficacy also affects how much anxiety athletes experience. In analyzing many potential determinants of athletic anxiety, Leland (1983) found that perceived self-efficacy to execute requisite athletic feats emerged as the major predictor of precompetition anxiety, whereas a measure of anxiety proneness accounted for little of the variation in apprehensiveness. Perceived physiological arousal seems to affect athletic performance only indirectly, through perceived self-efficacy (Feltz & Albrecht, 1985). The distinction drawn earlier between preparatory and performance efficacy is especially pertinent to athletics. In preparing for contests, coaches raise some doubts to get athletes to practice seriously, but just prior to contests they try to raise perceived self-efficacy persuasively so that players can get the most out of themselves.

Evidence that self-percepts of efficacy can significantly affect motor performance has bearing on the pursuit of transcendent athletic accomplishments. Self-perception blocks can hinder even the most gifted from realizing their potential. For years each athletic activity has had a performance level that has been widely regarded as a physical barrier, seemingly unattainable short of a Herculean effort. To cite but one example, for many decades even the most fleet of foot could never quite conquer the four-minute mile. Analysis of the effects of breaking a transcendent record reveal a common pattern. Regardless of whether the athletic performance is on the ground, in the air, or in water, occurs in simultaneous or successive competition, or is executed by males or females, immediately after a barrier is broken, it is surpassed by others at a rapidly accelerating rate. Once extraordinary performances are shown to be doable, they become commonplace.

Resiliency of Perceived Self-Efficacy. Self-efficacy mediation of superior performances is by no means confined to athletic activities. People's staying power is continually taxed in highly competitive fields. Self-efficacy demoralization operates in temporary, and the more enduring, slumps in most endeavors. Self-misgivings can set in fast after a few failures or setbacks. The important matter is not that failure rouses self-doubt, which is a natural immediate reaction, but rather the degree and speed of recovery from adversity. Some people quickly recover their sense of efficacy, others lose faith in their capabilities. It is resiliency of perceived self-efficacy that counts.

Examples of these processes abound in scholarly productivity. There are certain characteristics of scientific enterprises that are especially conducive to undermining personal efficacy. Unlike many activities, which continue to be prized if performed well, scientific fashions undergo cyclic changes. New ideas and paradigms are introduced, some of which gain popularity. Unless the new conceptions have basic value, their growing popularity creates the very conditions for their demise. It is

difficult to sustain professional interest over a long period in ideas that have become commonplace. To further threaten their longevity, popularity invites criticism from those who are vying for professional recognition or leadership. As a result, many of today's "hot ideas" become tomorrow's footnotes. Researchers who pursue what is no longer in vogue may find their work poorly received, even though it is of superior quality. Those who remain unshaken in their self-belief either continue their line of work, develop new aspects of their conceptions that rekindle professional interest, or they change what they are doing. But many experience scholarly slumps from which they never recover. Fortunately, conceptions that deepen understanding of significant phenomena and create the means for predicting and changing them usually weather temporary fluctuations in professional interest.

Perceived Self-Regulatory Efficacy

The exercise of influence over one's own behavior is not achieved by a feat of willpower. Self-regulatory capabilities require tools of personal agency and the self-assurance to use them effectively (Bandura, 1982a). People who are skeptical of their ability to exercise adequate control over their motivation and behavior tend to undermine their efforts in situations that tax capabilities. Relapses in the self-regulation of refractory behavior provide a familiar example.

Marlatt and Gordon (1980) have postulated a common relapse process for heroin addiction, alcoholism, and smoking in which perceived self-regulatory efficacy operates as a contributing factor. The common precipitants of breakdowns in self-control typically include inability to cope with negative emotions, social pressures to use the substance, and interpersonal conflict. Such experiences undermine perceived efficacy to resist use of the substances (Barrios & Niehaus, 1985). People who have the skills and assurance in their coping efficacy mobilize the effort needed to succeed in high-risk situations. Mastery of problem situations further strengthens self-regulatory efficacy. In contrast, when coping skills are underdeveloped and poorly used because of disbelief in one's efficacy, a relapse will occur. Selective recall of the pleasures, but not the adverse effects, of the substance creates further strains on efforts at self-regulation. Faultless self-control is not easy to come by even for pliable habits, let alone for dependence on addictive substances. The self-diagnostic significance given to occasional slips can bolster or undermine self-regulatory inefficacy. Having labeled themselves as powerless, people abandon further coping efforts, resulting in a total breakdown in self-control.

Studies of behavior that is amenable to change but where the changes are difficult to sustain over a long time indicate that perceived self-inefficacy increases vulnerability to relapse. In this research investigators measure the self-judged efficacy of cigarette smokers to resist smoking under various social and stressful inducements after they had quit smoking through various means (DiClemente, 1981; Colletti, Supnick, & Payne, 1985; McIntyre, Lichtenstein, & Mermelstein, 1983; Walker & Franzini, 1983). Although all participants stop smoking, they do not exhibit the same level of self-efficacy that they can resist craving for cigarettes. Compared to abstainers, relapsers express lower self-efficacy at the end of treatment about their ability to resist cigarettes in situations that commonly prompt smoking. The higher the perceived self-regulatory efficacy, the more success there is in checking smoking during the follow-up period. The predictiveness of perceived self-efficacy is confirmed with biochemical measures of tobacco use (Colletti, Supnick, & Payne, 1985; Godding & Glasgow, 1985; Killen, Maccoby, & Taylor, 1984). Neither demographic factors, history of smoking behavior, nor degree of physical dependence on nicotine differentiates relapsers from abstainers. Evidence that past successes and failures in breaking the smoking habit are unrelated to perceived self-efficacy after treatment (Reynolds, Creer, Holroyd, & Tobin, 1982) indicates that self-percepts of efficacy are not simply reflections of past coping experiences.

In a microanalysis of the relation between self-percepts of efficacy and smoking behavior, Condiotte and Lichtenstein (1981) assessed, at the completion of treatment, people's perceived capability to resist the urge to smoke in a variety of situations. Perceived self-regulatory efficacy predicted, months later, which participants would relapse, how soon they would relapse, and even the specific situations in which they would experience their first slip. Moreover, perceived self-efficacy at the end of treatment predicts how participants are likely to respond to a subsequent relapse, should it occur. Highly self-efficacious persons are inclined to regard a slip as a temporary setback and reinstate control; the less self-efficacious peers display a marked decrease in perceived self-efficacy and relapse completely. Measures of perceived self-efficacy can be used to gauge progress and guide optimal timing of new challenges and mastery tests. By identifying areas of vulnerability, people can be taught how to deal effectively with risky situations that get them into trouble and tax their self-regulatory capabilities.

Coping skills and belief in one's self-regulatory ability are built, in large part, through mastery experiences. Substance abuse poses special challenges in this regard. Triumphs over slips can strengthen perceived coping efficacy, but, in so doing, they may foster periodic lapses into old habits through assurance that one can always reinstate control. In studying the effects of controlled relapse, Cooney, Kopel, and McKeon (1982) had participants in a smoking-cessation program smoke a cigarette and then resume control, while others were told to avoid the cigarette because control is unachievable after relapse. Controlled relapse strengthened, and abstinence admonitions lowered, perceived self-efficacy in coping with slips. But the participants who practiced reinstating control resumed smoking sooner. It is also noteworthy that, whereas perceived self-efficacy for resisting inducements is a consistently good predictor of enduring abstinence, perceived self-efficacy for overcoming slips is not.

Programs aimed at abstinence build self-efficacy to resist inducements to use the substance and try to strengthen resistance by lowering perceived self-efficacy to handle the substance—one drink leads to a drunk, as the warning goes. This strategy poses its own risks. Should a slip occur, which is not uncommon among former substance abusers, the instilled diminished self-efficacy for recovery encourages total abandonment of self-regulatory efforts. The challenge is how to strengthen both resistive and recovery self-efficacy so that self-belief in each of these capabilities serves the purpose of abstinence. This may require instilling strong resistive self-efficacy and only moderate recovery self-efficacy, sufficient to counteract judgment of complete self-inefficacy should a slip occur, but not so strong as to embolden trial of the substance.

Interactive Perceived Efficacy and Health Behavior

Social environments may place constraints on what people do or may aid them to behave optimally. Whether their endeavors are socially impeded or supported will depend, in part, on how efficacious others perceive them to be. The impetus for interpersonal judgments of efficacy is strongest in close relationships involving interdependent consequences. This is because actions of a partner based on faulty self-percepts of efficacy can produce detrimental consequences for all concerned. Since risky actions are also the means of securing valued benefits, veridical mutual judgments of efficacy provide a reliable basis to promote advantageous endeavors and to dissuade foolhardy ones. Full understanding of how perceptions of efficacy affect courses of action in close social interdependencies requires analysis of interactive efficacy determinants.

Recovery from a heart attack offers an important problem in which to study both the impact of interactive efficacy and the contribution of self-percepts of efficacy to health-promoting habits. In recovering from a heart attack the restoration of perceived physical efficacy is an essential ingredient in the process. The heart heals rapidly. But psychological recovery is slow for patients with uncomplicated myocardial infarction who believe their cardiac capability is too impaired to resume their customary activities. They avoid physical exertion and recreational activities they previously enjoyed, they are slow to resume vocational and social life on the belief they will overburden their debilitated cardiac capacity, and they fear that sexual activities will do them in. The rehabilitative task is to restore a sense of cardiac efficacy so that postcoronary patients can lead full, productive lives.

Physicians typically use one or more of the four principal sources of efficacy information in efforts to convince postcoronary patients of their cardiac robustness. Enactive efficacy information is compellingly conveyed by strenuous treadmill exercises. Vicarious efficacy information is provided by enlisting the aid of former patients who exemplify active lives. Persuasive efficacy information is furnished by informing patients about what they are capable of doing. The meaning of physiological efficacy information is explained to ensure that patients do not misread their physiology, for example, by misinterpreting cardiac acceleration as portending a reinfarction or misattributing common bodily disturbances to an impaired heart. Patients who regard themselves as physically efficacious perform heavier workloads on the treadmill, and treadmill exercises and explanatory consultation, in turn, augment perceived physical efficacy (Ewart, Taylor, Reese, & DeBusk, 1983). Perceived physical capability is a better predictor of resumption of an active life than cardiovascular capacity as reflected in peak heart rate on the treadmill.

Psychological recovery from a heart attack is a social rather than individual matter. Wives' notions about their husbands' cardiac and physical capabilities can aid or retard the recovery. In a study exploring this process (Taylor, Bandura, Ewart, Miller, & DeBusk, 1985), several weeks after patients had experienced a myocardial infarction their self-percepts of physical efficacy were measured for physical exertion, cardiac capability, emotional stress, and sexual activities before and after treadmill exercises. Judgments of cardiac efficacy are especially interesting because postinfarction patients are likely to base their level of activity on how robust they perceive their heart to be. Spouses' judgments of their husbands' physical efficacy were also measured with three levels of involvement in the treadmill activity—when she was uninvolved in the treadmill exercises; when she was present to observe the husband's stamina as he performed treadmill with increasing workloads; or when she herself performed strenuous treadmill exercises to experience personally the physical demands of the task, after having observed her husband do the same. In the informative consultation with the medical staff, which followed the treadmill activity, couples received information about the patient's cardiac functioning and its relation to physical, vocational, and sexual activity. Their stamina on the treadmill is presented to patients as a generic indicant of their cardiovascular robustness; that is, the workloads they performed far exceed the strain that everyday activities might place on their cardiovascular system.

Treadmill activities increased patients' perceptions of their physical and cardiac efficacy. Wives who were either uninvolved in, or merely observers of, the treadmill activity continued to perceive their husbands' cardiovascular capabilities as impaired, even after receiving medical counseling to the contrary. In contrast, wives who personally experienced the strenuousness of the treadmill activity raised their perceptions of their husbands' physical and cardiac efficacy after they observed their husband's treadmill attainments and received medical counseling. The joint beliefs of patients and wives in the patients' cardiac capabilities was a consistently good predictor of cardiovascular functioning on treadmill tests conducted months later. Perceived cardiac efficacy predicted future level of cardiovascular functioning with initial treadmill performance partialled out, whereas initial treadmill performance did not with perceived efficacy partialled out. Wives who judge that their husbands have a robust heart are much more likely to encourage them to resume an active life than those who believe the heart is impaired and vulnerable to further damage. Pursuit of an active life improves patients' ability to manage energetic activities without overtaxing the cardiovascular system.

There is a good deal of research to indicate that perceived self-efficacy mediates health behavior. Unless people believe they can master and adhere to health-promoting habits, they are unlikely to devote the effort necessary to succeed. Thus, those who consider themselves incapable of kicking the smoking habit do not even try, despite grim health warnings, whereas the more self-efficacious override their cravings and break their smoking habit (DiClemente, Prochaska, & Gilbertini, 1985). The improvements patients with pulmonary disease derive from various behavioral and cognitive treatments partly depend on the degree to which their beliefs about their physical efficacy have been raised (Kaplan, Atkins, & Reinsch, 1984). The more efficacious they judge themselves to be, the more physically active they become, and the greater the respiratory volumes and capacities they achieve. That health behavior is mediated through changes in perceived self-efficacy is further documented in the studies reviewed earlier on control of tension headaches and self-management of pain.

The diverse ways in which the exercise of perceived self-efficacy improves physiological functioning can combine to contribute significantly to psychological and physical well-being. A field experiment designed to retard or reverse deteriorative functioning in the elderly provides testimony for the health benefits of controllability (Langer & Rodin, 1976; Rodin & Langer, 1977). Elderly residents in a nursing home who were given personal control over their daily activities were happier, more actively interested and sociable, and physically healthier than those for whom the staff structured their activities.

Persuasive communications are widely used to get people to adopt health practices designed to prevent illness. In such health messages, appeals to fear depicting the ravages of disease are used as motivators, and recommended preventive practices are provided as guides for action. The early emphasis on fear arousal proved counterproductive in that it fostered avoidance of the grisly messages and undermined people's perceived ability to control health threats (Beck & Frankel, 1981; Leventhal, 1970). People need knowledge of potential dangers to warrant action, but they do not have to be frightened to act, anymore than students have to be scared out of their wits to study or homeowners to insure their households.

What people need is knowledge about how to regulate their behavior and firm belief in their personal efficacy to turn concerns about future maladies into effective preventive actions. Beck and Lund (1981) studied the persuasiveness of health communications in which the seriousness of periodontal disease and susceptibility to it were varied. Patients' perceived efficacy that they could stick to the required hygienic routine was a good predictor of whether they adopted it, whereas fear arousal predicted neither intention nor behavior. The perceived inefficacy barrier to preventive health is all too familiar in peoples' resignation concerning different health risks over which they can exercise control. For instance, obese persons who judge themselves incapable of shedding their excess pounds permanently are disinclined to mount the effort needed to do so, however perturbed they might be about the health and personal costs of obesity. The self-inefficacious not only forego preventive practices, but if they judge themselves incapable of managing pain, they are prone to avoid corrective treatment as well (Klepac, Dowling, & Hauge, 1982). To be most effective, health communications should instill in people the belief that they have the capability to alter their health habits. Communications that explicitly do so increase people's determination to modify habits detrimental to health (Maddux & Rogers, 1983). To strengthen the staying power of instilled self-beliefs, the communications should emphasize that success requires perseverant effort so that people's sense of personal efficacy is not undermined by a few setbacks.

Self-Efficacy of Fear Arousal

Perceptions of self-efficacy affect emotional reactions as well as behavior. This is especially true of anxiety and stress reactions to unfamiliar or potentially aversive events. Self-efficacy theory suggests an alternative way of looking at human anxiety. Psychodynamic theories generally attribute anxiety to intrapsychic conflicts over the expression of forbidden impulses. The threat posed by the impulse is presumably displaced and projected outward. The external object of anxiety is considered to be of limited significance because the threat can be projected onto any number of things. In this approach, anxiety is rooted in the prohibited impulse.

Conditioning theory assumes that formerly neutral events acquire fear-provoking properties by association with painful experiences. This theory externalizes the cause in the stimulus: It is the stimulus that is said to become aversively valenced. Painful experiences change perceptions of oneself and the meaning of external stimuli, not the stimuli themselves. If a person develops a phobia of mountain driving as a result of a mishap on a hairpin turn, it is not the mountain road that is changed by the aversive experience. Rather, it is perceived competence in driving and anticipatory thought patterns that undergo change.

From the social cognitive perspective, it is mainly perceived inefficacy to cope with potentially aversive events that makes them fearsome. To the extent that people believe they can prevent, terminate, or lessen the severity of aversive events, they have little reason to be perturbed by them. But if they believe they are unable to manage threats safely, they have much cause for apprehension. Hence, experiences that increase perceived coping efficacy can diminish fear arousal and increase commerce with what was previously dreaded and avoided.

A sense of controllability can be achieved either behaviorally or cognitively (Averill, 1973; Lazarus, 1981; Miller, 1979). In behavioral control, individuals take action that forestalls or attenuates aversive events. In cognitive control, people believe they can manage environmental threats should they arise. These two forms of controllability are distinguished because the relationship between actual and perceived coping efficacy is far from perfect. Indeed there are many competent people who are plagued by a sense of inefficacy, and many less competent ones who remain unperturbed by impending threats because they are self-assured of their coping capabilities.

Behavioral Control. The effects of behavioral control on fear reduction and stress responses have been amply documented with both children and adults. Ability to exercise behavioral control over potentially aversive events eliminates or decreases autonomic reactions to them (Gunnar-vonGnechten, 1978; Miller, 1979). There are times when people can exercise control over when they experience painful events, but they cannot alter the painfulness of the events themselves. Even this limited form of behavioral control can diminish the aversiveness of stressful incidents by reducing uncertainty about when they will happen (Averill, 1973). When threats are severe and occur without forewarning, people maintain anxious vigilance and dwell a great deal on the possible dangers. Because fear-arousing thoughts about impending threats augment their aversiveness, the more people dwell on them, the more distressed they become.

People's fear of even potentially dangerous events over which they exercise no personal control will vary depending on their perceived efficacy to protect themselves against the impact of those events should they ever occur. For example, those who perceive themselves as helpless against the hazards of earthquakes will dread them. Most others, who believe they can minimize or avoid injury by taking immediate protective action, will rarely dwell on earthly tremors. Seafarers who expect to drown helplessly should an ocean liner meet with a mishap will conjure up frightful consequences, whereas those who believe they can manage safely in lifeboats until rescued are more likely to visualize gourmet spreads, vintage wines, and escape from daily cares.

Behavioral control over events makes them predictable, thus reducing uncertainty, which in itself can be ameliorative. Therefore, it might be argued that it is predictability rather than behavioral mastery that reduces stress. However, behavioral control decreases arousal over and above any benefits derived from the ability to predict the occurrence of stressors (Gunnar, 1980a; Miller, 1981). Forewarning with an effective means of forestalling or attenuating painful events is much less frightening than forewarning alone. If anything, having foreknowledge of when aversive events will occur without being able to do anything about them increases anticipatory stress reactions. Predictability can signal safety during periods when forewarnings are absent, as well as danger when they are present (Seligman & Binik, 1977). Predictability can thus have opposite effects at different points in time—raising anticipatory arousal prior to unpleasant events while reducing arousal during safe interim periods. Whatever tranquilizing potential predictability may have, it is as a predictor of safety, not as a predictor of danger (Gunnar, Leighton, & Peleaux, 1984; Weinberg & Levine, 1980). Knowing when one is not in danger allows one to relax.

Being able to exercise control over potential threats can diminish arousal because the capability can be used to reduce or to prevent painful experiences. But there is much more to the process of stress reduction by behavioral control than simply curtailing painful events. In some forms of behavioral mastery, ordinarily frightening events occur undiminished, but they become non-threatening when activated personally. A mechanical toy that is frightening to infants when it is turned on by others can be instantly transformed into a pleasant one when the infants activate it themselves (Gunnar-vonGnechten, 1978). Here it is the exercise of personal agency, not the curtailment of events themselves, that reduces fear. And in situations in which the opportunity to wield control exists but is unexercised, it is the self-knowledge that one can exercise control should one choose to do so rather than its application that reduces anxious arousal (Glass, Reim, & Singer, 1971).

A strong sense of controlling capability renders situations less intimidating and can thereby lessen stress reactions to encountered threats. Such a generalized ameliorative effect of controllability is strikingly revealed in a developmental study by Mineka, Gunnar, and Champoux (1985). Initial rearing experiences in which monkeys exercised control over access to food, months later reduced fearful reactions to the sight of novel threats and increased venturesomeness in an unfamiliar environment. The same threat was highly intimidating to monkeys who had been reared under conditions in which they could not develop a sense of control because the food was simply given to them independently of their behavior.

Cognitive Control. A painful experience has two components of arousal to it: discomfort produced by aversive external events and thought-produced distress. The thought component—the arousal generated by repetitive, perturbing ideation—accounts for much of human distress. As noted earlier, people who judge themselves inefficacious dwell upon their coping deficiencies and view trying situations as fraught with danger. They not only magnify the severity of possible threats but worry about perils that rarely, if ever, happen. As a result, they experience a high level of cognitively generated distress. Elevated arousal, in turn, heightens preoccupation with personal inefficacy and possible calamities.

Anticipatory thought that does not exceed realistic bounds has functional value in that it motivates development of competencies and plans for dealing with foreseeable threats. But to those who distrust their coping self-efficacy, the anxious anticipation can become a preoccupation that often far exceeds the objective hazards. In an analysis of acute anxiety reactions, Beck, Laude, and Bohnert (1974) found that, almost without exception, frightful cognitions occur just prior to the onset of anxiety attacks. The ideation often centers around profound coping inefficacy that results in dreadful physical and social catastrophes. For example, in anticipation of delivering lectures, a college instructor works himself into a panic by imagining a scenario in which disastrous teaching performances lead to vociferous complaints by students causing him to be fired and repeatedly rejected in efforts to secure a teaching position and ending up as a derelict on skid row. Spell-binding lectures are hard to deliver when one's thoughts revolve around personal inefficacies resulting in calamity-filled consequences. In these terrifying cognized scenarios, people perceive themselves as inept, defenseless individuals who cannot control themselves, disintegrate physically and mentally, lose their source of livelihood through their blunders, and otherwise behave in ways that are publicly humiliating and ostracizing.

There is some evidence to suggest that intense anxiety reactions first arise under either conditions of acute distress or mounting everyday problems that overwhelm coping capabilities (Bandura et al., 1980).

Such disintegrative experiences leave individuals with a strong sense of coping inefficacy. The resulting "head problem"—profound perceived inefficacy—becomes a major cause of the continuing self-debilitation. The original undermining stressors may have diminished or ceased altogether, but the perceived inefficacy problem lingers. Once perceived coping efficacy is destroyed, even mild distress in taxing situations forebodes disintegrative loss of personal control.

The way in which self-referent thought arouses anxiety and debilitates performance has been examined extensively in the area of achievement anxiety. Sarason (1975b, 1978) and Wine (1971) have shown that in evaluative situations, people who are prone to anxiety about achievement impair their performances by dwelling on their deficiencies rather than attending to the task at hand. In contrast, those who are not prone to anxiety are spurred by evaluative pressures to better performances by mobilizing their efforts and concentrating on the requirements of the task. Anxiety-prone individuals can lower their distress and debility by altering, through the aid of instruction (Wine, 1971) or coping modeling (Sarason, 1975b), their attentional and thought patterns. Distressing ideation is supplanted by cognitive rehearsal of coping strategies for dealing with stressors. As a result, they deploy their skills more effectively to meet the demands of the situation. Thus, it is not arousal *per se* but self-evaluative rumination that is detrimental to performance (Morris & Liebert, 1970). The arousing and performance-debilitating effects of negative self-referent thought are further documented by Meichenbaum (1977) and by Lazarus and Launier (1978) in other areas of functioning.

Because stress-inducing thought plays a paramount role in human torment, self-percepts of coping efficacy can reduce the level of arousal before, during, and after a trying experience. In laboratory studies of perceived control, people who are led to believe that they can exercise some control over aversive events display less autonomic arousal and performance impairment than those who believe they have no personal control, even though both groups are subjected to the same painful stimulation (Averill, 1973; Miller, 1979, 1980). Mere belief in coping efficacy similarly increases ability to withstand pain (Neufeld & Thomas, 1977; Reese, 1983).

Most laboratory studies underestimate the stress-reducing effects of perceived personal control because people are led to believe they have some control over aversive events, but, in fact, they experience the same prearranged aversive stimulation regardless of how well they perform (Averill, 1973). Even though an enhanced sense of efficacy produces superior coping behavior, it can have no effect whatsoever on the aversiveness of the laboratory environment because it is fixed beforehand. In the face of repeated disconfirming experience, persuasively instilled beliefs about personal control will not survive for long (Glass, Singer, Leonard, Krantz, & Cummings, 1973). In everyday life, perceived self-efficacy sustains determined coping efforts that actually increase performance success. By promoting effective action, perceived self-efficacy can set in motion reciprocal processes that not only alter the aversiveness of the environment itself but genuinely cultivate skills and personal efficacy through repeated successes.

Self-Efficacy as a Mediating Mechanism. That perceived self-efficacy operates as a cognitive mechanism by which controllability reduces psychophysiological arousal receives support from three different lines of research. One approach relates strength of perceived efficacy to degree of subjective distress while coping with threats following treatments designed to enhance coping efficacy (Bandura & Adams, 1977; Bandura, Beyer, & Adams, 1977; Bandura, Adams, Hardy, & Howells, 1980). People experience high anticipatory and performance distress on tasks in which they perceive themselves to be inefficacious, but as the strength of their self-judged efficacy increases, their fear arousal declines. At high strengths of self-efficacy threatening tasks are performed with virtually no apprehensiveness. Studies in which perceived self-efficacy is induced to differential levels (Bandura, Reese, & Adams, 1982) provide further support to the notion that fear arousal arises from perceived coping inefficacy. Here the data of interest are the amount of distress phobics experience at different levels of perceived self-efficacy while performing the same task. The less efficacious subjects judge themselves to be, the more fear they experience, regardless of whether self-percepts of efficacy are enhanced enactively or vicariously, or whether the analysis involves anticipatory or performance fear based on intrasubject or intergroup increases in perceived efficacy.

The generality of the relationship between perceived inefficacy and stress reactions is further corroborated in a second line of research using physiological indices of arousal (Bandura, Reese, & Adams, 1982). Elevation in blood pressure and cardiac acceleration were measured in severe phobics during anticipation and performance of intimidating tasks corresponding to strong, medium, and weak strength of perceived self-efficacy. Individuals were viscerally unperturbed while coping with tasks they regarded with utmost self-efficacy. However, on tasks about which they were moderately insecure concerning their coping efficacy their heart rate accelerated and their blood pressure rose during anticipation and performance of the activities. Phobics promptly reject tasks in their range of weak self-efficacy as too far beyond their coping capabilities even to attempt them. Their anticipatory visceral reactions changed when they declined to perform tasks they judged would overwhelm their coping capabilities. Cardiac reactivity subsided, but blood pressure remained elevated. After self-percepts of efficacy were

strengthened to the maximal level, everyone performed all previously intimidating tasks without any visceral agitation.

Heart rate is likely to be affected more quickly than blood pressure by personal restructuring of stressful demands, which may explain the differential pattern of physiological reactivity at the extreme level of self-inefficaciousness. There exists some evidence that catecholamines (epinephrine and norepinephrine) are released at different times in response to external events (Mefford, Ward, Miles, Taylor, Chesney, Keegan, & Barchas, 1981). Heart rate is especially sensitive to momentary changes in hormonal patterns with epinephrine, which is rapidly discharged, having a more pronounced effect on cardiac activity than on arterial pressure.

Understanding of the physiological mechanisms through which perceived self-efficacy may operate was carried one step further by analyzing the microrelation between strength of perceived self-efficacy and the neuroendocrine processes governing stress reactions (Bandura, Taylor, Williams, Mefford, & Barchas 1985). Phobics were presented coping tasks in their high, medium, and low ranges of perceived self-efficacy, during which continuous blood samples were obtained to determine the amount of epinephrine and norepinephrine released into the blood. High perceived self-efficacy elicited low levels of these catecholamines, whereas moderate self-efficaciousness produced substantial increases in plasma epinephrine and norepinephrine. The phobics instantly rejected tasks they judged themselves totally incapable of doing, whereupon their hormonal releases declined suddenly. After they became highly self-efficacious through mastery experiences, they executed all the coping tasks without producing any differences in catecholamine level.

Microanalyses, whether conducted at the level of phenomenal experience, autonomic reactivity, or hormonal release, thus provide converging evidence for close linkage between self-percepts of efficacy and level of psychophysiological arousal. Perceived self-inefficacy is accompanied by high endocrine activity, autonomic activity, and subjective distress. Evidence that strengthening perceptions of coping efficacy to maximal level eliminates stress reactions to the previously intimidating tasks indicates that the arousal resulted from the degree of perceived match between coping capabilities and task demands, rather than from properties inhering in the tasks themselves. The crucial role played by controllability in human arousal is further shown in the level of catecholamines released during the course of enactive mastery treatment (Bandura et al., 1985). During the initial phase of treatment, when phobics lacked a sense of controlling efficacy, even the mere sight or minimal contact with the phobic object produces high catecholamine release. After they become fully efficacious in managing potential threats, their catacholamine levels remain low during the most stressful transactions with phobic objects. If these same high stressors are presented, but the individuals are told to relinquish their controlling strategies, catecholamines suddenly rise to high levels. It will be recalled from the earlier discussion that autonomic arousal to stressors is reduced by self-knowledge that one can wield control over them even though that controlling capability is unexercised. Choosing not to exercise control at a particular time, but being able to do so whenever one wants to, should be distinguished from being deprived of all means of control while subjected to stressors. Relinquished control leaves one completely vulnerable, whereas usable control leaves one in full command.

Interactive but Asymmetric Relation.
Social learning posits an interactive, although asymmetric, relation between perceived self-efficacy and fear arousal, with coping efficacy exercising the much greater sway. That is, perceived self-inefficacy in coping with potential threats leads people to approach such situations anxiously, and experience of disruptive arousal may further lower their sense of efficacy that they will be able to perform skillfully. People are much more likely to act on their self-percepts of efficacy inferred from many sources of information rather than rely primarily on visceral cues. This is not surprising because self-knowledge based on information about one's coping skills, past accomplishments, and social comparison is considerably more indicative of capability than the indefinite stirrings of the viscera. For example, accomplished actors interpret their brief nervousness before a play as a normative situational reaction, rather than as an indicant of personal incapability, and they are not dissuaded by their viscera from going on stage and performing well. They know what they can do once they get started. Given a sufficient level of perceived self-efficacy to take on threatening tasks, phobics perform them with varying amounts of fear arousal depending on the strength of their perceived self-efficacy.

Substantial benefits in psychological functioning accrue because behavior is not automatically controlled by fear. People have fearful anticipations about many of the things they do in their life pursuits that fall at the lower limits of their self-judged efficacy. If fear arousal inevitably triggered avoidant action, the populace would find itself in phobic immobility. Entertainers could not go on stage, relief pitchers could not venture on the mound, and students could not get themselves to examination rooms. Because people can perform activities at weaker strengths of perceived efficacy, despite high anxiety, they are able to overcome inappropriate fears and function effectively even in the face of anticipated aversive consequences. Thus, perceived coping efficacy predicts phobic behavior much better than fearful anticipations (Lee, 1984a, 1984b; Williams & Watson, 1985). Perceived self-efficacy retains its predictiveness of phobic behavior when variations in anticipatory and performance anxiety are partialled out, whereas the relationship between anxiety and phobic behavior essentially disappears when the influence of perceived self-efficacy is controlled (Williams, Dooseman, & Kleifield, 1984; Williams, Turner, & Peer, 1985). Studies of academic activities corroborate the generality of this finding (Hackett & Betz, 1984). Perceived self-inefficacy predicts avoidance of academic activities whereas anxiety does not.

Conditioned-anxiety theory posits a unidirectional causality in which self-percepts of efficacy are construed as epiphenomenal by-products of conditioned fear (see Rachman, 1978). However, a large body of evidence disputes such a view. Self-percepts of efficacy predict phobic behavior well but, as we have seen earlier, fear arousal bears no uniform relationship to phobic behavior. A good predictor cannot be an epiphenomenal reflector of a poor predictor. The studies of perceived control already examined also have direct bearing on this issue. The same aversive stimulation produces differential fear arousal depending on instilled misbeliefs about one's efficacy to control the painful stimuli (Geer, Davison, & Gatchel, 1970; Glass, Reim, & Singer, 1971). Such findings corroborate the power of self-belief, rather than conditioned fear. Repeated failures create stress reactions when they are ascribed to personal inefficacy, but the same painful experiences leave people unperturbed if ascribed to external factors (Wortman, Panciera, Shusterman, & Hibscher, 1976). Frightening events are promptly transformed to pleasant ones when their occurrence is personally controlled (Gunnar-vonGnechten, 1978). Controlling efficacy established with appetitive events reduces fear arousal to novel threats (Mineka, Gunnar, & Champoux, 1985).

Self-efficacy theory does not posit uniform concordance between behavior and fear arousal, as is sometimes assumed (Craske & Craig, 1984). The relationship between action and arousal in transactions with potential threats varies depending on the strength of perceived coping efficacy. People perform activities with little accompanying arousal at strong perceived self-efficacy but with elevated arousal in their moderate efficacy range; at the upper limits of their perceived coping capabilities they display performance impairments and heightening arousal.

One can, of course, have arousal even during performance with a relatively strong sense of efficacy if the activity is objectively dangerous. When faulty performance can have disastrous effects, any self-doubts concerning one's efficacy will be accompanied by some arousal while executing the task. The smaller the margin of error, the greater the demands for a strong sense of personal control. For example, efficacious soldiers will experience some fear in military combat because even small misjudgments may produce tragic results. But even in objectively dangerous situations, other things being equal, those who have a strong sense of controlling efficacy are less likely to dwell on possible mishaps and will experience objective dangers as less agitating than those who distrust their coping capabilities. Herpetologists who regard themselves as fully efficacious in controlling behavior of reptiles will not scare themselves with visions of injury or death from commerce with poisonous reptiles, although they remain acutely cognizant of the venomous threat.

Perceived Self-Inefficacy, Futility, and Despondency

Inability to influence events and social conditions that significantly affect one's life can give rise to feelings of futility and despondency, as well as to anxiety. Self-efficacy theory distinguishes between two judgmental sources of futility. People can give up trying because they seriously doubt they can do what is required. Or they may be assured of their capabilities but give up trying because they expect that their efforts will not produce any results due to an unresponsive, negatively biased, or punitive social environment. These two separate sources of futility have quite different causes and remedial implications. To change efficacy-based futility requires development of competencies and strong percepts of self-efficacy. In contrast, to change outcome-based futility necessitates changing the social environment so that people can gain the benefits of the competencies they already possess.

In any given instance, behavior can be predicted best by considering both self-efficacy and outcome beliefs. Different patterns of self-efficacy and outcome beliefs are likely to produce different psychological effects. A strong sense of personal efficacy and a responsive environment that rewards performance achievements fosters assured, active responsiveness. Consider then the pattern combining strong self-efficacy with low environmental responsiveness. Efficacious individuals who cannot achieve positive outcomes by their actions will not necessarily cease trying. Those of low perceived self-efficacy will give up readily should their efforts fail to produce results. But self-efficacious individuals will intensify their efforts and, if necessary, try to change inequitable social practices.

The pattern in which competency goes unrewarded or is punished underscores the need to differentiate two levels of control: control over outcomes and control over the social systems that prescribe what the outcomes will be for different kinds of behavior. Piece-rate workers may control their income by how hard they work but exercise no control over the unit pay rate the system sets. Gurin and Brim (1984) and Lacey (1979) address this issue of control over social systems, which typically receives scanty notice in psychological analyses of controllability. Conditions combining high self-efficacy and environmental unresponsiveness tend to generate resentment, protest, and collective efforts to change existing practices (Bandura, 1973; Short & Wolfgang, 1972). Should change be hard to achieve, given suitable alternatives, people will desert environments that are unresponsive to their efforts and pursue their activities elsewhere.

The joint influence of self-efficacy and outcome beliefs provides a basis for differentiating conditions conducive to apathy from those likely to induce despondency. When people have a low sense of personal efficacy and no amount of effort by themselves or by comparative others produces results, they become apathetic and resigned to a dreary life. The pattern in which people perceive themselves as ineffectual but see others like themselves enjoying the benefits of successful effort is apt to give rise to self-disparagement and depression. The evident success of others makes it hard to avoid self-criticism. In studies instilling different perceptions of self-efficacy and the success of others, the condition that combines perceived self-inefficacy for securing valued outcomes that are readily attainable by others is most conducive to depressive mood and cognitive debilitation (Bloom, Yates, & Brosvic, 1983; Davies & Yates, 1982). Males are easily depressed by such conditions because they start out with a high perceived efficacy and repeated failure takes a heavy toll on their sense of competence. Low perceived self-efficacy and knowledge that others do not often gain valued outcomes does not produce depression. Under fatal threats, of course, as in life-threatening illnesses, perceived inefficacy in managing one's life is sufficient by itself to make one depressed (Devins et al., 1982).

The original theory of learned helplessness formulated by Seligman (1975) focused solely on response-outcome expectancies. People give up and become depressed if their actions cannot affect what happens to them. Because they expect future responses to be futile, they no longer try even in situations where they can achieve results through their own behavior. Findings of many studies have shown that repeated failure produces diverse effects: Some people give up, others sustain their efforts, and still others intensify their efforts to succeed. The answer to these variable effects on depression does not seem to lie in expectancies about the relation between actions and outcomes (Huesmann, 1978). Abramson, Seligman, and Teasdale (1978) have proposed a reformulated theory that shifts the causal locus of resignation and despondency from beliefs that actions cannot affect outcomes (response-outcome noncontingency) to beliefs that one cannot produce the required performances. If one cannot produce the actions, one cannot control the outcomes that depend on them. Whether or not repeated failure makes people depressed depends on whether they ascribe their failures to personal deficiencies or to external or more transient factors. The theory singles out three dimensions in judgments about the causes of failure that represent the depressing explanatory style. Internality: Are failures ascribed to personal or to external factors? Stability: Are the ascribed causes enduring or transient? Generality: Are the causes believed to operate in many situations or only a few? Attributing one's failures to personal deficiencies of a generalized and enduring nature, which can be most debilitating and depressing, constitutes a profound sense of self-inefficacy. Biases toward ascribing the occurrence of bad events to basic personal deficiencies increase proneness to depression (Peterson & Seligman, 1984).

The adequacy of performance attainments depends upon the personal standards against which they are judged. A comprehensive theory of depression must, therefore, be concerned not only with the perceived causes of failures but also with the internal standards by which attainments will be self-judged as successes or as failures to begin with. Depressive reactions often arise from stringent standards of self-evaluation which make otherwise objective successes seem to be personal failures. Individuals who are prone to depression impose upon themselves high performance demands and devalue their accomplishments because they fall short of their exacting standards (Kanfer & Hagerman, 1980; Rehm, 1977; Simon, 1979b). Stringency of standards, of course, cannot be gauged independently

of capabilities. The same performance standard is easy when it matches capabilities but difficult when it exceeds capabilities. People plagued with depression perceive their self-efficacy as falling short of their minimal standards of personal merit, whereas for the nondepressed their perceived self-efficacy corresponds more closely to their standards (Kanfer & Zeiss, 1983).

In addition to personal standards, as we have previously seen, the valuation of the activity also influences affective reactions to one's own performances. Failure is unlikely to induce depression when performers do not invest their self-esteem and sense of self-worth in the tasks. Pole vaulters will not grieve over their inability to win foot races, and runners will not become despondent over their inability to vault over high bars. Such experiences are likely to foster disinterest rather than depression. It is failure in personally valued activities that is the common source of depression.

A theory must specify when perceived self-inefficacy will produce anxiety and when it will give rise to despondency. The nature of the outcomes over which personal control is sought is one differentiating factor. People experience anxiety when they perceive themselves ill equipped to manage potentially painful events, which will make them vulnerable to harm. Inadequate control over *aversive outcomes* is central to anxiety. People are saddened and depressed by their perceived inefficacy to control highly valued outcomes. Irreparable loss or failure to gain desired *rewarding outcomes* figures prominently in despondency. In extreme cases, individuals become so chronically preoccupied with self-deprecation and their sense of worthlessness that the pursuit of personal satisfaction becomes futile (Beck, 1973). There are certain situations, of course, in which perceived self-inefficacy in gaining highly valued outcomes can be anxiety provoking as well. When the valued outcomes one seeks also serve to forestall future aversive events, as when failure to secure a job jeopardizes one's livelihood, perceived inefficacy is both distressing and depressing. Because of the interdependence of events, both apprehension and despair often accompany perceived personal inefficacy.

Undermining Self-Efficacy by Relinquishing Personal Control

When personal control is easy to exercise and enables one to deal effectively with everyday events, it is highly desired. Indeed, in laboratory studies in which aversive stimuli can be controlled by simple responses requiring neither skills nor expenditure of effort, and entailing no risks, controllability is decidedly preferred (Miller, 1979). But there is an onerous side to personal control that is rarely, if ever, incorporated in most of the paradigms designed to study personal control. Self-development of efficacy requires mastering knowledge and skills attainable only through long hours of arduous work. This often necessitates sacrifice of many immediate gratifications. Moreover, the maintenance of proficiency in these endeavors, which constantly change with social and technological advances, demands continued investment of time, effort, and resources.

In addition to the work of self-development, in many situations the exercise of personal control carries heavy responsibilities and risks. For example, presidents of corporations are granted considerable controlling power, but they must bear personal responsibility for the negative consequences of their decisions and actions, some of which have widespread repercussions. These burdensome aspects can dull the appetite for personal control. Attractive incentives, privileges, and heady social rewards are, therefore, needed to get people to seek control involving complicated skills, laborious responsibilities, and great risks.

Proxy Control. People are often willing to relinquish control over events that affect their lives to free themselves of the performance demands and hazards that the exercise of control entails. Rather than seeking personal control, they seek their security in proxy control—wherein they can exert some influence over those who wield influence and power. Part of the price of proxy control is restriction of one's own efficacy and a vulnerable security that rests on the competencies and favors of others.

Perceived self-inefficacy fosters dependence on proxy control, which further reduces opportunities to build the necessary skills for efficacious action. The influential role of comparative self-ability evaluation in proxy control is revealed in studies by Miller and her associates (Miller, 1980). People who are led to believe they possess superior coping ability handle potential threats by themselves, whereas those who believe themselves to be less skilled readily yield control to others to cope with the aversive environment. The dependent ones enjoy the protective benefits without the performance demands and attendant stresses, while the controllers do the work and suffer the distress over task demands and risks of failure.

People who are in the habit of exercising personal control do not like to place their fate in the hands of others, even when it may be advantageous for them to do so. The competitive, hard-driving individuals of the Type A variety are constantly struggling to master task demands under a sense of time urgency (Glass & Carver, 1980). Relentless struggle for control increases risk of coronary disease. Miller, Lack, and Asroff (1985) found that people who exhibit Type A behavior would rather suffer aversive experiences than relinquish control to people who cope more competently, whereas Type B individuals readily give up control under similar circumstances. Type A females are willing to yield control provisionally to someone who is more skilled, if they can reclaim it at will. But many Type A males will not surrender control even provisionally.

Underminers of Personal Efficacy. The preceding discussion has focused on personal inefficacy arising from the costs and demands of efficacious behavior. Many factors operate in everyday life to undermine efficacious use of the knowledge and skills that people possess. In a program of research on illusory incompetence, Langer (1979) has given us a better understanding of how people give up personal control, either by making erroneous inferences from their experiences or by inadvertent action. At the time the actions are taken, people do not perceive themselves as relinquishing control, nor do they realize that their actions may hinder their future competence. Since the self-debilitation goes largely unnoticed, there is little reason to resist it.

We have already discussed conditions in which failure experiences may lead people to judge themselves as incompetent so that they give up and become apathetic in situations in which they could, in fact, produce effects through their actions. Even situational factors that often accompany poor performance can, in themselves, arouse a sense of incompetence that is unwarranted. For example, the mere presence of a highly confident individual undermines effective use of routine skills. Attending to what is strange in new tasks, rather than what is familiar and within one's range of competence, may similarly hinder performance.

People often relinquish control by their actions because it is the easier thing to do at the time. Langer (1979) documents the various conditions under which this is likely to happen. In some instances, the effort involved in mastering an activity seems to outweigh its potential benefits. In others, people foster self-induced dependencies when they can obtain outcomes more easily by having somebody else do things for them. When people are cast in subordinate roles or are assigned inferior labels implying limited competence, they perform activities at which they are skilled less well than when they do not bear the negative labels or the subordinate role designations.

The intervening mechanism through which demoralizing conditions undermine effective use of well-established skills remains to be clarified. Studies in which self-percepts are measured under induced illusory self-efficacy suggest that perceived inefficacy, with its concomitant effects on choice behavior, effort expenditure, persistence, and self-debilitating thought, may be the operative mechanism (Weinberg et al., 1979; Weinberg et al., 1980). The lower the illusorily instated self-percepts of efficacy, the more is competitive performance debilitated. Even the mere sight of a formidable-looking opponent instills lower self-percepts of efficacy than one who looks less impressive. As might be expected, preexisting self-percepts of efficacy have the greatest impact on initial competitive performance, whereas socially induced self-percepts affect the subsequent course of competitive endurance (Weinberg, Gould, Yukelson, & Jackson, 1981). The power of self-efficacy belief over brawn is underscored further by evidence that self-percepts of physical efficacy illusorily raised in females and illusorily diminished in males obliterate large, preexisting sex differences in physical strength (Weinberg et al., 1979).

COLLECTIVE EFFICACY

The discussion thus far has focused mainly on the personal effects of perceived self-efficacy. People do not live their lives in social isolation. Many of the challenges and difficulties they face reflect group problems requiring sustained collective effort to produce any significant change. The strength of groups, organizations, and even nations lies partly in people's sense of collective efficacy that they can solve their problems and improve their lives through concerted effort. Perceived collective efficacy will influence what people choose to do as a group, how much effort they put into it, and their staying power when group efforts fail to produce results. As will be shown shortly, collective efficacy is rooted in self-efficacy, so that research on personal efficacy does not necessarily reflect an individualistic bias in psychology. Inveterate self-doubters are not easily forged into a collectively efficacious force.

Collective Efficacy and Social Change

The task of social change has never been an easy one. Those who seek to alter social systems and their practices encounter opposition from powerholders and influential vested interests. Should challengers resort to forceful social protest, punitive sanctions can be brought to bear against them. Numerous obstacles and coercive threats deter attempts to alter social conditions that adversely affect human lives.

It is often said that hopelessness breeds militant social action. However, the evidence seems to dispute this view. Consistent with efficacy theory, studies of social and political activism indicate that detrimental conditions do not instigate forceful action in those who have lost hope but rather in the more able members whose efforts at social and economic betterment have met with at least some success (Bandura, 1973). Consequently, they have reason to believe that some changes can be brought about through forceful group action.

Among the members of dissident groups, those who protest social inequities, as compared to nonparticipants, are generally better educated, have greater self-pride, have a stronger belief in their ability to influence events in their lives, and favor coercive measures, if necessary, to improve their living conditions (Caplan, 1970; Crawford & Naditch, 1970). In many nations, university students, rather than the severely underprivileged segments of the society, are the spearhead of political activism (Lipset, 1966). They are the ones who often initiate the protest movements that eventually force social reforms and topple governments. Results of comparative studies indicate that people who are most disposed to social action generally come from family backgrounds in which the exercise of social influence has been modeled and rewarded (Keniston, 1968; Rosenhan, 1970). However, modeling influences, which serve as a major vehicle of social diffusion, can substantially alter the personal and social correlates of activism over time. Those who initi-

ate collective action usually differ in characteristics from later adopters, who need greater assurance that they have something to gain through militant action.

Research that measures perceptions of personal efficacy speaks more directly to the issue of whether perceived efficacy serves as a mechanism through which social discontent gives rise to social activism. In these studies, perceived self-efficacy is conceptualized in similar ways—as persons' beliefs that they can affect political and social events by their efforts—but there is variation in how self-efficacy is measured. Many investigators use survey items that were designed to tap two elements of perceived political efficacy (Campbell, Gurin, & Miller, 1954). The first is personal efficacy, as indicated by individuals' judgments that they have a say in what government does, that they can influence how government works by voting, and that they are capable of understanding how the system operates. The second element, the system's responsiveness, is gauged in terms of judgments that the political system is unresponsive to people's needs and that public officials are uncaring. Other investigators use variants of one or both of these themes. Still others emphasize vicarious sources of efficacy in which the successes and failures of others instill beliefs in the utility or disutility of militant action (Muller, 1972).

Because this research relies on global indices of perceived efficacy that often blend mixed contents (Balch, 1974), the obtained relationships vary somewhat in size but are fairly consistent in direction. The higher the perceived efficacy, the greater is the propensity to social activism (Forward & Williams, 1970; Marsh, 1977; Muller, 1972, 1979). The likelihood of militant action is highest when personal efficacy is combined with political cynicism and distrust of the system, and legitimate means for accomplishing social change are perceived as ineffective.

Global indices are limited in what they can reveal about determinants and causal processes of collective action. Rather than being globally dispositional, self-percepts of efficacy may vary widely across domains of activities, circumstances, and social subsystems. Hence, sharper empirical tests of theory will require particular, multifaceted measures of people's judgments of their capabilities to fashion and execute strategies to influence the course of events. Social changes are typically achieved in concert with others; therefore, people need to be tested for their perceptions of the groups' efficacy to effect change, as well as their own personal efficacy to execute their function in a collective endeavor. Enlisting and merging divergent efforts for large-scale collective action entails structural arrangements that can obtain different performances from the same participants. For this reason, perceived collective efficacy may be insufficiently represented by the sum of the perceived personal efficacies of participants. In the arena of social activism, perceived collective efficacy is reflected in judgments about group capabilities to make decisions, to enlist supporters and resources, to devise and carry out appropriate strategies, and to withstand failures and reprisals.

Underminers of Collective Efficacy

Rapidly changing conditions, which impair the quality of social life and degrade the physical environment, call for wide reaching solutions to human problems and greater commitment to shared purposes. Such changes can be achieved only through the mutual effort of people who have the skills, the sense of collective efficacy, and the incentives to shape the direction of their future environment. As the need for efficacious group action grows, so does the sense of collective powerlessness.

One can point to a number of factors that serve to undermine the development of collective efficacy. Modern life is extensively regulated by complex physical technologies that most people neither comprehend nor believe they can do much to influence. Pervasive dependence on the technologies that govern major aspects of life imposes dependence on highly specialized technicians. The social machinery of society is no less challenging. Layers of bureaucratic structures thwart effective social action. Even the more efficacious individuals, who are not easily deterred, find their efforts blunted by mazy organizational mechanisms that diffuse and obscure responsibility. Rather than developing the means for shaping their own future, most people grudgingly relinquish control to technical specialists and to public officials.

Effective action for social change requires merging diverse self-interests in support of common goals. Disagreements among different constituencies, who have a personal stake in the matters of concern, create additional obstacles to successful group action. The recent years have witnessed growing social fragmentation into constituencies with narrow interests. Pluralism is taking the form of militant factionalism. As a consequence, it is easier to enlist diverse factions to block courses of action than to merge them into a unified force for social change.

In addition to the difficulties in enlisting shared purposes and collective effort in their service, the institutions that are the objects of change mount their own forceful countermeasures. Because of the many conflicting forces that come into play, attempts to produce socially significant changes do not bring quick successes. Even if desired reforms are officially adopted, their implementation is forestalled by defeated factions using legal challenges in an effort to restore some of the power and privileges they have lost. Long delays between action and noticeable results discourage many of the advocates along the way, even though changes of long-term significance may eventually occur. A sense of collective efficacy is difficult to develop and to sustain when the effects of group effort are not so noticeable.

To complicate matters further, life in the societies of today is increasingly affected by transnational interdependencies (Keohane

& Nye, 1977). What happens in one part of the world can affect the welfare of vast populations elsewhere. There are no handy direct mechanisms by which people can exercise reciprocal influence on the transnational systems that affect their daily lives. Profound global changes—burgeoning populations, shrinking resources, deteriorating environments—are creating new realities requiring transnational remedies. National self-interests and the fear of infringement of sovereignty create obstacles to fashioning transnational mechanisms for effecting change.

The subject of collective efficacy calls for a broad and comprehensive research effort. Advancement in this field of study requires the development of suitable tools for measuring perceptions of group efficacy to achieve varying levels of results. The greatest progress can be made in elucidating the development, decline, and restoration of collective efficacy, and how it affects group functioning, if measures of perceived group efficacy are tied closely to explicit indices of group performance.

National surveys have been conducted periodically of people's general sense of political efficacy, their confidence in their social institutions, and how they view the competence of those they choose to lead them. While such omnibus measures leave much to be desired, they do provide evidence of a growing erosion of perceived efficacy of the citizenry and its social institutions to solve human problems (Guest, 1974; Lipset & Schneider, 1983).

Factional Efficacy and Collective Endeavor

In analyzing the impediments to human endeavors, it is all too easy to lose sight of the fact that human influence, whether individual or collective, operates in reciprocal rather than in unidirectional ways (Bandura, 1978a; Endler & Magnusson, 1976; Pervin & Lewis, 1978). Although the degree of reciprocality may vary from one domain of activity to another, social transactions are rarely unilateral. The amount of imbalance of social power partly depends on the extent to which people exercise the influence that is theirs to command. The less they bring their influence to bear on others, the more control they relinquish to them.

The internal barriers created by perceptions of collective inefficacy are especially pernicious because they are more demoralizing and behaviorally self-debilitating than external impediments. People who have a sense of collective efficacy will mobilize their efforts and resources to cope with external obstacles to the changes they seek. But those convinced of their collective inefficacy will cease trying, even though changes are attainable through concerted effort.

The "social system" is not a monolith. Rather, it comprises numerous constituencies, each vying for power and lobbying for its own interests in shifting coalitions. In this continual interplay one and the same faction is transmuted from a challenger of the system to an influential confederate in the system opposing rival factions, depending on the issues at stake. Thus, for example, the tobacco constituency fights the "system" in federal efforts to curtail smoking, but it becomes the "system" fighting the efforts of challengers to curtail federal subsidies to tobacco growers. Whether people want government in or out of their lives depends on the particular interests being serviced.

The rise of narrow-interest groups flexing their factional efficacy does not jibe with the diagnoses of growing public apathy and feelings of helplessness. Clearly there exists a paradox to be explained. Viewed from the efficacy perspective, in the absence of shared imperatives, growing factional efficacy undermines the exercise of collective efficacy through mutual immobilization. Efficacious factional initiatives, often fragmented and rivalrous, create an overload of programs and regulations, force divisive issues on officeholders, weaken their capabilities to deal with them satisfactorily, and obfuscate a sense of purpose (Atkin, 1980; Barton, 1980; Fiorina, 1980). Thus, people are exercising greater factional influence but achieving less collectively and becoming more discontented. Since changing the officeholders does not eliminate the social problems people face, they become disillusioned about the prospect of effecting significant change in their social and economic way of life by the institutional means available to them.

Achievement of collective efficacy requires cogent means of relating factional interests to shared purposes. The unifying purposes must be explicit and attainable through concerted effort. Because success calls for sustained effort over a long time, proximal subgoals are needed to provide incentives and evidence of progress along the way. As a society, we enjoy the benefits left by those before us who collectively resisted inhumanities and worked for social reforms that permit a better life. Our own collective efficacy will, in turn, shape how future generations will live their lives. Considering the pressing worldwide problems that loom ahead, people can ill-afford to trade efficacious endeavor for public apathy or mutual immobilization. The times call for a commitment of collective effort rather than litanies about powerlessness that instill in people beliefs of inefficacy to influence conditions that shape their lives.

10

COGNITIVE REGULATORS

If human behavior always co-varied closely with the occurrence of external events, there would be no need to postulate any internal determinants. Laws of behavior relating external stimuli to responses would be sufficient. However, such regularities are hard to come by because persons contribute causally to their own motivation and action. Behavior is, therefore, a product of both self-generated and external sources of influence. Most external influences affect behavior through intermediary cognitive processes. Cognitive factors partly determine which environmental events will be observed, what meaning will be conferred on them, whether they leave any lasting effects, what valence and efficacy they will have, and how the information they convey will be organized for future use. By symbolically manipulating the information derived from personal and vicarious experiences, people can comprehend events and generate new knowledge about them.

Human thought is a powerful tool for understanding and dealing effectively with the environment. It furnishes a vast store of knowledge in the form of abstract representations of experiences. Such representational knowledge is put to heavy use in forming judgments and in constructing and selecting courses of action. Some of the highest forms of human motivation arising from aspirations and evaluative standards are rooted in symbolic representations of valued futures and cognitive comparison processes. Thought also provides the means for monitoring and regulating one's efforts to manage and shape the events of daily life. Some attention has already been given throughout this book to the diverse ways in which cognitive functions subserve human motivation and action. These and other issues receive further consideration in this chapter.

REPRESENTATION AND USE OF KNOWLEDGE

The power of thought resides in the human capability to represent events and their interrelatedness in symbolic form. Whatever fund of knowledge is acquired can be drawn upon, as needed, to derive new understanding and to guide judgment and action. Cognitive representations have several properties that amplify their functional value. One of these is abstractness. If each event encountered was represented in exactly the form in which it was experienced, people would possess vast amounts of fragmentary information of little value because no two events are identical. Whatever information was acquired would be useless in dealing with new situations. However, knowledge is represented in terms of abstracted similarities and shared meanings, rather than in details of discrete events. By embodying generalities, abstract conceptual codes have wide applicability (Anderson & Bower, 1973).

Another important property of cognitive representation is the extensive conceptual linkages in people's knowledge. These interrelationships provide a rich conceptual structure for comprehending events and for guiding judgment and action. Recall the earlier example in which a person must judge whether or not a board in a river is a safe mode of transport. A correct judgment can be made by drawing on different sources of knowledge and their interrelationship: the flotation properties of the board; and how the size and weight of the navigator, the turbulence of the water, the speed and direction of the current, and the upright and reclining riding positions alter the risks of nautical mishaps. The solution is derived from the configurations of knowledge, rather than from any single proposition.

Form of Representation

Cognitive representations preserve information about events. The particular forms in which knowledge is represented are the subject of a lively debate. Proponents of the dual-code theory maintain that information is coded in imaginal and linguistic representations. According to Paivio (1971), a leading proponent of the dualist view, the two representational systems are functionally independent but partially interconnected. Concrete information conveyed nonverbally is processed and represented in imaginal form, whereas verbal information is represented in linguistic form. The knowledge that people possess is activated selectively and operated on cognitively in the form of images and words. Other theorists contend that information, however conveyed, is retained in an abstract propositional form that is not tied to any particular modality (Anderson, 1978; Pylyshyn, 1973). They acknowledge that people do think in terms of images and words and that the mode in which information is presented, whether visually or linguistically, can affect the level of acquisition and retention. But, they argue, it is information represented in abstract conceptual form that is used to generate images and linguistic expressions. The images and words are merely transformations of the underlying propositionally encoded information.

Propositionalists dispute the view that imaginal and linguistic codes constitute the primary systems of representation (Anderson, 1978; Pylyshyn, 1981). The gist of their critique is as follows: When people are exposed to information conveyed verbally, they remember the meaning of what they hear and read, rather than the exact strings of words. People extract the same meaning from verbal accounts of events even when they are cast in different linguistic forms. Moreover, understanding derives, in part, from the interrelationships among concepts and encoded events which can be represented best as networks of propositions.

The imaginal coding system is similarly

criticized on several grounds. Imagists disclaim that images are pictures in the head, but, by likening images to pictures, they create confusions about the nature of the imagery system. Physical displays must be interpreted rather than simply registered in raw sensory form. Hence, the same display can be seen as different things under different cognitive sets. When exposed to visual displays, people extract and remember the meaning of what they saw, not replicas of the physical displays. Evidence of cross-modal integration of knowledge, in which information presented in one mode is comprehended in a different mode, suggests a common representational system.

Among the arguments levied against specialized representational systems, some rest on disputable characterizations of the dualist view but others pose explanatory challenges. To equate linguistic coding with learning word strings verbatim is to focus on the medium to the neglect of the verbal products distilled from it. In the cognitive processing of verbal contents, people extract and verbally code meanings and rules, rather than memorize collections of sentences. Thus, linguistic codes embody conceptions and propositions, not the exact string of words by which they were conveyed. Much of the dispute over verbal and propositional coding rests on trivializing the verbal code.

If the linguistic system is essentially propositional in nature, the issue of interest is whether imagery constitutes a separate representational system or is derivative from propositionally encoded information. Evidence that information conveyed in one modality is retrievable in a different modality argues for a common representational system. However, to infer a single amodal representational system from evidence of learning across modalities assumes that imaginal and verbal expressions are activated completely independently. In fact, verbal descriptions typically evoke imagery, and pictorial displays evoke thoughts expressed in linguistic symbols (Paivio, 1975). For example, try to encode the verbal description of a giraffe munching on the upper leaves of a tree without experiencing the corresponding imagery. Because words and pictures are separated procedurally by researchers does not mean that thoughts and imagery are dissociated experientially by the recipients of the presentations.

Much is made of the picture metaphor in critiques of imaginal coding. It is true that images are often described in terms of quasi-picturable qualities, but proponents of imagery theories are not positing a homunculus viewing pictures projected in the head (Kosslyn, 1980; Shepard & Podgorny, 1978). The functional relations among imaged events are assumed to be analogous to the relations among the same events as actually perceived. No one claims that perception of objects projects pictures in a person's head. The neural processes activated by centrally aroused perceptions (i.e., images) would be analogous to the internal processes accompanying perception of external objects. Nor are images tied entirely to specific perceptions. Since no two objects, actions, or events of the same class are identical, imaginal coding requires abstraction of commonalities. Thus, images are abstractions rather than exact replicas.

It is commonly said that humans must convert their seemingly countless experiences into general knowledge; otherwise, they would be overwhelmed by massive bits of information defying all efforts at retrieval. People certainly extract generalities from particulars, but they retain and need the particulars as well. An abstract representation cannot recreate a specific event in all its rich detail because the particularized information is not contained in the abstract code. A dog can be represented abstractly by a set of configural features: four legs, an elongated body, a head with ears, and a tail. However, dogs come in exceedingly varied shapes, sizes, hairiness, and tail and facial features. The proverbial Martian given the abstract canine representation would be at a loss to depict or recognize an Afghan

Hound, a Komondor, a Dachshund, a Whippet, a Cocker Spaniel, a Pekingese, or a Great Pyrenees. A given species may be a prototype of minor variants within it, but the abstract code is relatively nondescript for a particular species. If instructed to visualize a friend, one imaginally retrieves a specific, full-bodied friend, not a prototypic or generic friend with the skeletonized features common to one's circle of friends who vary in size, shape, sex, and personal attributes. People retain detailed information about different persons, places, things, and events that have touched their lives. Symbolic representations thus embody both generic and highly specific information (Lindsey & Norman, 1977; Tulving, 1983).

Attempts to resolve controversies about the form in which knowledge is represented have been fraught with difficulty because of the way in which the amodal propositional system is typically characterized. It is said that the basic representation is formless, is inaccessible to consciousness, and that it begets the images and linguistic expressions of consciousness. Moreover, the medium in which information is coded is considered inseparable from the processes by which the abstract representations are accessed and operated on to express the acquired knowledge in words or images. By positing different conversion processes, a single amodal representational system can be made to mimic the behavioral predictions of rival representational systems. A representational system which is formless, personally inaccessible, and combinable with conversion processes to match the predictions of other coding systems does not enable researchers to resolve theoretical disputes decisively. Given this indeterminacy, many researchers have questioned whether there is much to be gained from pursuing the issue of amodal versus multimodal coding. Rather, they center their attention on how information is transformed into different symbolic codes and how imaginally and linguistically coded knowledge guides human judgment and action.

Representation of Contingency Structures

How people cognize relationships between environmental events and between their actions and outcomes forms an important part of their propositional knowledge. It provides the basis for their hopes and fears, for their foresightful actions, as well as for their errant and bizarre behavior. It has been shown previously that contingent experiences create lasting effects mainly by fostering abstract knowledge structures, rather than by forging specific associations. People will learn little from repeated, paired experiences unless they recognize that the events are correlated. They come to fear those they believe forebode suffering and are cheered and comforted by those they believe signify pleasant happenings. Moreover, they are not much affected by the consequences of their behavior if they fail to recognize the probabilistic relation between their actions and the outcomes they experience. However, after people gain predictive contingency knowledge, they guide their actions partly by it.

Most events are determined by constellations of factors that do not always co-appear in the same medley or in the same relative strengths. Hence, events are typically related to each other probabilistically rather than invariantly. Such causal uncertainty leaves much room to err in judging why things happen. We have seen how, under laboratory conditions, people can form faulty causal beliefs that override the influence of actual consequents in the regulation of their behavior: Erroneous beliefs about how actions produce outcomes weaken, distort, or nullify the effects of response consequences (Kaufman, Baron, & Kopp, 1966); the meaning conferred on physically aversive and physically pleasing outcomes exerts markedly greater influence on behavior than the actual physical properties of the outcomes (Dulany, 1968); false hopes sustain behavior that can bring no success (Bandura & Barab, 1971); and people often form illusory beliefs about how much control they exercise over outcomes (Alloy & Abramson, 1979).

Beliefs instilled by influences created in the laboratory are much too weak to reveal the full power that illusory and delusory beliefs can exert over action. In some of the more severe behavior disorders, psychotic acts are so powerfully controlled by bizarre autistic contingencies that the behavior remains impervious to the most intense physical consequences. This process is graphically illustrated (Bateson, 1961) in a patient's account of his psychotic experiences. The patient, who had received a scrupulously moralistic upbringing, considered innocuous conduct sinful enough to provoke the wrath of God; hence, many of his innocent acts aroused dreadful apprehensions, leading him to perform, for hours on end, torturing atonement rituals designed to forestall the imagined disastrous consequences. Both the inducements for the self-torturing rituals and their rewarding consequences were internally created. The patient's acceptance of medicine, an act he later considered as rebellious distrust of the Almighty, aroused dreadful hallucinations of hellish torture, which could be banished only by enacting the arduous, bizarre rituals. Reduction of acute distress through the nonoccurrence of subjectively feared, but objectively nonexistent, threats provides a source of reinforcement for many forms of psychotic behavior. Given powerful contingencies created and confirmed in thought, behavior is refractory to social influence even in the face of severe penalties and blatant disconfirming experiences. The punishments administered to the patient by the attendants were pale compared with his imagined Hadean torture. When the prophecies of divine inner voices failed to materialize, the patient discounted these disconfirming experiences as tests by the Almighty of the strength of his religious convictions.

Grotesque homicidal actions provide further illustrations of how behavior can come under the powerful control of bizarre beliefs. Every so often tragic episodes occur in which persons are led by delusional beliefs to commit acts of violence. Some follow divine inner voices commanding them to murder. Others are instigated by paranoid suspicions to protect themselves from people who are supposedly conspiring to harm them. And still others are motivated by grandiose convictions that it is their heroic responsibility to eliminate evil persons in positions of power.

A study of the assassins of American presidents (Weisz & Taylor, 1970) shows that, with one exception, the murderous assaults were partly under delusional control. The assassins acted by divine mandate, through alarm that the president was in conspiracy with treacherous foreign agents to overthrow the government or on the conviction that their own adversities resulted from presidential persecution. Misbeliefs can be corrected before they get delusional if the person reveals them to others he trusts. But assassins tend to be extreme loners. Being unusually seclusive in their behavior, they effectively shielded their erroneous beliefs from corrective social influences. Deteriorating personal functioning along with marked seclusiveness breeding autistic persecutory resentments are distinguishing characteristics of psychotic murders (Bandura, 1973). When delusional constructions take precedence over social reality, irritants can trigger homicidal action.

Cognitive Guidance and Automaticity

The earlier analyses of skill acquisition dealt mainly with the mechanisms by which representational rules of action, constructed from observed examples, response outcomes, and from tuition, guide production of suitable behavior. Representational knowledge is especially influential in early and intermediate phases of skill development. Such knowledge informs on how appropriate subskills must be selected, coordinated, and sequenced to suit particular purposes. The initial conversion of symbolic representations to proficient attainments requires close attention to the details of enactments. After skills become routinized through repeated execution, they are performed in recurring situations without requiring prior thought guides, unless something goes awry. Consider a common example. When learning to drive a car with a manual transmission, knowledge of the required operations and the order in which to do them guides the driver's behavior. After driving becomes a well-integrated routine, people think of other matters while driving along the streets and freeways, although their driving may momentarily occupy their thoughts whenever unfamiliar or hazardous situations arise.

Attending to the mechanics of what one is doing after proficiency is achieved tends, if anything, to disrupt skilled performance by fractioning its continuity. Partial disengagement of thought from proficient action has considerable functional value. If one had to think before carrying out every routine activity, it would consume most of one's attention and create a monotonously dull inner life. There are obviously substantial benefits to being able to think about and to do different things at the same time.

Distributed Consciousness and Automaticity

Automatization of skills should be distinguished from consciousness of one's performances. It is a common error to equate automatization with unconsciousization. Different activities can be performed simultaneously, if they are regulated by different subsystems. One can drive an automobile and converse at the same time because the visiomotor subsystems superintending driving differ from the audiovocal subsystems subserving conversation, and thoughts can flit back and forth. Attention can be distributed across activities using noncompeting modalities. But one cannot drive speedily on a crowded freeway while gazing attentively at passengers in the back seat without joining the ranks of highway casualties. Driving skills eventually become routinized

to the point where the mechanics of driving no longer require attention, but drivers must remain acutely conscious of how they are maneuvering their vehicle in the flow of traffic or on winding roads. People can simultaneously perform even activities that vie for control processes, albeit with some sacrifice in accurateness, by rapidly shifting attention between them. Because different activities are not punctuated identically, they do not demand close attention at the same instant. With practice, proficiency can be gained in shifting attention at key junctures in the execution of concurrent activities.

Nature of Automatization

The automatization of complex skills involves at least three major subprocesses. The first process is *mergerization,* whereby the essential elements of an activity are combined into progressively larger units. When a skill is being learned, some thought and attention must be devoted to how to execute each step. During this initial period, when the activity is fractionated and some thought must be given as to what to do at each step and transition point in an enactment, performance is slow and poorly coordinated. As familiarity with the activity is gained through repeated performance, segments are merged into progressively larger ones until eventually the entire sequence of operations is fully integrated. Once the routine is put together through the aid of thought and extensive practice, there is no longer any need to think about the subparts and how they should be spatially and temporally coordinated. Thought is thus freed for other purposes. The merging subprocesses in automaticity have been analyzed in some detail by LaBerge (1981) in the development of reading skills and by Neves and Anderson (1981) in the automatization of cognitive skills. In the latter analysis, knowledge is translated into specific production rules that, through repeated application, are combined into a composite production system.

Behavioristic theories generally explain merging of constituent activities as a process of serial chaining. Through repeated association sensory feedback from prior actions presumably cues the next action segment in the sequence. However, as noted earlier, most skills are executed too rapidly for sensory feedback from actions to have time to trigger succeeding actions. The process of mergerization involves central organization and guidance, rather than serial coupling by means of peripheral feedback. Mergerization occurs in the perception of ongoing behavior, as well as in the execution of skills. When exposed to a flow of action, observers initially segment it into small units (Newtson, 1976). As activities become predictable, behavior is encoded in larger units. Should unexpected elements arise in the action sequence, observers revert to finer segmentation of the behavior they are observing in an effort to understand it better. Variations in cognitive set also markedly alter the units into which behavior is segmented (Cohen & Ebbesen, 1979). The fact that people shift at will their perceptual organization of behavior further argues against a peripheral chaining process.

Actions, of course, are not performed in a vacuum. Automatization of skills also involves gaining knowledge about the properties of tools, the demands of the task, the nature of environment, and how to adjust enactments to these external realities. In new transactions with the environment, people either draw on helpful rules of action given to them or figure out on their own what best suits particular circumstances. With repeated experience of success in certain types of situations, eventually the situation rather than prior judgment prescribes the action. Novice drivers initially tap their knowledge about how to negotiate steep hills safely, but after maneuvering many heights the mere sight of a precipitous grade will prompt them to gear downward. What was originally thought-governed behavior shifts to situationally prompted enactment of a fully integrated routine. This second subprocess of automaticity involves the *routinized linkage of whole action patterns to contexts*, rather than the internal integration of the action patterns themselves. This form of routinization arises where highly predictive relations exist between situations and the actions they require. It is doubtful, however, that initiation of even the most habitual behavior is ever completely thoughtless. Claims that routinized actions are thoughtless rest on subjective impressions, rather than on conclusive empirical evidence that such actions are executed without a single preceding or accompanying thought.

The third subprocess in the automatization of skills is a *shift in the locus of attention* from the execution of the action pattern to its correlated effects. While a skill is being mastered close attention is paid to specific aspects of the performance. Actions produce correlated effects that provide an indirect means of monitoring one's behavior. Actions can be felt and outcomes can be seen. To continue with the driving example, turning a steering wheel a given amount alters the course of the car in a predictable direction, shifting to different gear positions produces corresponding accelerating and breaking effects, and applying brakes with different forces on slippery surfaces produces characteristic skid patterns. While performers are learning what to do, they are also gaining knowledge about what effects are linked to particular actions. Such knowledge about co-variations between actions and effects enables them to know what they are doing and what corrective adjustments they are making by tracking the observable effects of their performances.

In activities that are partially unobservable because major segments of the skill occur outside the field of vision, performers depend heavily on correlated effects of their actions to detect and correct what they are doing. For example, by knowing what actions produce what effects, golfers and tennis players monitor their performances indirectly by observing where the balls fly. On tasks providing little implicit feedback about how one is doing, regulation of routine performances deteriorates when extrinsic performance feedback is withheld (Bandura & Cervone, 1983; Smith & Smith, 1966). In executing established skills, the effects of performance rather than the performance itself are closely monitored. The shift in the locus of attention with automatization is often misinterpreted as obliviousness to what one is doing. As the foregoing discussion indicates, complex behavior does not fall into neatly dichotomized categories of activities that are either completely thoughtless or thoroughly consciously mediated. Rather than representing a unitary process, most activities contain both consciously mediated and nonmediated components.

Cognitive guidance plays a different role in learning than it does in skilled performance. To learn without the aid of instructive thought and awareness of what one is doing is difficult, but once skills are fully developed they are typically executed without much conscious deliberation. Evidence that people perform common routines having predictable effects without paying much attention to specific aspects of their performance has no bearing on the role of thought and performance awareness in the original mastery of the skill.

Costs of Routinization.
The utility of routinized information processing and enactment is widely heralded. Among its benefits it frees attention, a distinctly limited capacity, from habitual routines to activities requiring judgment, production, and close monitoring (Shiffrin & Dumais, 1981). Routinization is, indeed, advantageous when the ways that have been automatized are the optimal ones and remain so under changing circumstances. Since all too often this is not the case, routinization extracts some costs. There is little to be gained from habitualizing deficiencies. Once people adopt habitual ways of thinking and acting, they often pay little attention to the informative aspects of their environment that call for discerning responsiveness (Abelson, 1981; M. Bandura, Langer, & Chanowitz, 1984; Chanowitz & Langer, 1980). A familiar cue readily sets off habitual thoughts and behavior patterns despite the presence of more relevant bases for action.

Psychosocial functioning can be seriously impaired when stereotyped reaction based on superficial similarities of events replaces thoughtful action. Varied remedial procedures have been designed to supplant stereotyped responding with flexibly adaptive behavior that is cognitively regulated by judgments of the probable effects of prospective action. People are made aware of their hampering routinisms and develop better ways of managing the demands of everyday life. Analyses of automaticity center mainly on routinized actions performed unthinkingly. However, a common feature of human distress is the automaticity of perturbing thought patterns (Beck, 1976). In this process, events to which people have become sensitized promptly activate stereotyped self-inefficacious, phobic, angry, jealous, or depressive thoughts. Reasoned thought is restored by challenging such habitual ideation and arranging experiences that disconfirm them. We shall return later to the methods used for this purpose.

Rule-Governed versus Rule-Conforming Behavior.
Distinctions are often drawn between rule-governed and rule-conforming behavior. In the former case, prescriptive rules guide behavior; in the latter case, descriptive rules codify regularities in behavior (Gumb, 1972). It is the prescriptive rules of the performer that hold much psychological interest because they provide the means for the production and adaptive regulation of behavior. The descriptive rules of external observers are of lesser import. This is because virtually every routine activity can be shown to conform to some type of rule. Preparing a main course for dinner, writing a letter, and dressing for different occasions all involve sequentially organized actions, each of which can be characterized as following a rule or a set of rules. To say that behavior is rule-conforming is to say very little that is distinctive.

Whether behavior is rule-governed or rule-conforming varies as competencies are being acquired, proficiently executed, and improvised to better suit changing circumstances. During the acquisition phase much human behavior is guided by provisional rules as alternatives are formulated and tested. Rules are also used, rather than merely accorded with, in the early stages of application when acquired rules subserve the construction of suitable forms of behavior. However, after proficiency is attained, people perform well without having to refer to the rules by which they organized the skilled behavior. If adopted ways prove unsuccessful, rule-conforming execution is likely to give way to rule-guided exploration until better ways are found and perfected.

It will be recalled from an earlier chapter that human behavior is regulated by multilevel systems of control. Routinization entails reduction in the degree of cognitive involvement or shifts of control to subsystems that do not require acts of thinking, rather than a shift from conscious thinking to unconscious thinking. For example, to find the solution initially to the product of 7 and 13 minus 9, a person must perform the operations cognitively. But after having solved the problem repeatedly, the solution becomes part of one's knowledge and is given instantly without having to go through the tedious cognitive computations each time. Changes in degree of cognitive involvement and control systems are often misconstrued as unconsciousization of thinking.

THOUGHT AS SYMBOLIC CONSTRUCTIONS

Tools of Thought

Symbols that represent events, cognitive operations, and relationships serve as the vehicles of thought. Thinking depends to a large extent upon language symbols, although other specialized symbols are also used, as, for example, numerical and musical notations. By manipulating symbols that convey relevant information, one can gain understanding of causal relationships, expand one's knowledge, solve problems, and deduce the consequents of actions without actually performing them. The functional value of thought rests on the close correspondence between the symbolic system and external events, so the former can be substituted for the latter. Thus, cognitively subtracting the number 2 from 10 yields the same outcome as physically performing the operation by removing two objects from a group of ten.

Symbols, being much easier to manipulate than their physical counterparts, greatly increase the flexibility and power of cognitive problem solving. Symbols provide the vehicle of thought; cognitive representations of experiences and knowledge provide the substance for the thinking; rules and strategies provide the cognitive operations for manipulating knowledge. Thoughts are symbolic constructions, and thinking is the process of operating on the fund of knowledge one possesses to realize different purposes.

The process by which people learn to solve problems symbolically has received comparatively little attention, despite its central role in human functioning. Because thought is a private activity, it must be explored through indirect means. Cognitive skills are usually developed by initially performing operations on actual objects and then translating the external procedures into covert symbolic ones of increasing complexity and abstraction. In being taught arithmetic principles, for example, children first learn the formal operations of addition and subtraction by physically combining and withdrawing actual objects and receiving feedback on whether they were right or wrong. Pictorial representations are also used in early phases as concrete referents in the acquisition of arithmetic principles. After children have learned to solve problems through physical manipulation, the objects are symbolized by numbers. Correct solutions are now achieved by manipulating numerical symbols on paper, where each step in the cognitive operation can be checked and corrected. The activity at this stage is still partially overt, in that the intermediate outcomes in the sequential operation are publicly observable, but the operations by which each step is achieved are executed internally. At the beginning of this transitional phase, performers may be encouraged to verbalize their ongoing thought processes to correct misunderstandings. Eventually solutions are generated entirely cognitively by having children think through the problem without any external aids or external monitoring at intermediate points in the thought process.

In this way thought processes gradually become independent of immediate concrete referents. Symbols can then be manipulated to produce thoughts that are not necessarily limited to those directly translatable to external events. Many fantasies and unusual ideas in fact involve novel symbolic constructions that transcend the bounds of reality. One can easily think of cows jumping over the moon and elephants riding on flies, even though these events are physically impossible. The remarkable flexibility of symbolization and its independence from the constraints of reality expand the scope of thought.

After people acquire knowledge and cognitive skills for operating on it, they can think creatively, formulate alternative solutions to tasks at hand, and evaluate the probable immediate and long-range consequences of different courses of action. The result of weighing how much skill and effort are required and the relative risks and benefits involved influences which actions are chosen from among the various alternatives. This is not to say that the decisions are necessarily good ones or that reason always prevails. Decisions may be based on inadequate assessment of information and misjudgment of anticipated consequences. Moreover, people often know what they ought to do but are swayed by immediately compelling circumstances or emotional factors to behave otherwise.

Cognitive Skills and Strategies for Problem Solving

Coping with the demands of everyday life would be exceedingly trying if good solutions to problems could be found only by performing actions and suffering the consequences. Fortunately, cognitive skills enable people to conduct most problem solving in thought rather than in action. They design airliners, for example, without having to continue building them until they happen to hit upon a structure that can be airborne and not disintegrate under the rigors of stratospheric flying. Rather, they consider the relevant information, apply appropriate cognitive operations to it, and generate suitable solutions. The alternatives are initially tested by symbolic exploration and are either discarded or retained on the basis of calculated consequences. It is the solution emerging from this cognized process judged to be the best one, within given reality constraints, that is actually implemented. This is not to say that careful deliberation always precedes action. But the capability to think ahead fosters at least some thought before leaping into uncertain situations. Those who adopt a problem-solving mode of thinking are better able to manage their everyday affairs and to accomplish their goals. People are quite susceptible to their own ill-planned, if not completely thoughtless, behavior when faced with conflictful, stressful, or complicated demands that severely tax their coping resources.

Subprocesses of Problem-Solving Thinking. Writers who have presented systematic analysis of problem solving generally agree on the basic cognitive operations needed to achieve successful solutions (Anderson, 1980; D'Zurilla & Goldfried, 1971; Spivack, Platt, & Shure, 1976). The various theories differ mainly in the number of subprocesses posited. Decomposition of problem solving into sequential reasoning steps by Brim and his associates (Brim, Glass, Lavin, & Goodman, 1962) is illustrative of a comprehensive approach to this subject. They analyze problem solving in terms of the following six subprocesses: (1) identifying the nature of the problem, (2) seeking information relevant to it, (3) generating alternative solutions from the available knowledge, (4) evaluating the likely outcomes associated with each course of action, (5) selecting the best means for implementing the chosen solution, and (6) enacting the plan and revising it, if necessary, based on the results it is producing. The subprocesses of problem-solving thinking are easy to delineate but, as we shall see, difficult to carry out.

Problem-solving thinking skills must be distinguished from the knowledge base upon which they operate. Before any solutions can be considered, the nature of the problem must be identified. This requires knowledge of how to size up problems and to ferret out their major causes. Similarly, to develop suitable alternatives and to gauge accurately their likely outcomes requires a fund of information relevant to the problem. Difficulties in solving problems often arise more from deficiencies in knowledge than from inadequacies of thinking skills (Glaser, 1984). Experienced persons not only have greater knowledge than novices to bring to bear on problems, they also know how to secure information needed to arrive at good solutions. Life is too short and errors are too costly to acquire such diagnostic knowledge through trial-and-error experience alone. Rather, people draw on the judgments and problem-solving skills modeled and taught by others. Modeling improves observers' skills in seeking information needed to evaluate their alternative courses of action (Krumboltz & Thoresen, 1964).

The informal acquisition of judgmental knowledge, often derived from scattered sources over an extended time, is being systematized in some areas of problem solving through computer decision aids gleaned from expert models (Clancey, 1984; Feigenbaum, 1977; Shortliffe & Fagan, 1983). In such systems the requisite knowledge and judgmental rules are obtained by intensive inquiry of experts as they solve problems. Heuristic decision aids are most suitable for problem-solving domains in which valid bodies of knowledge exist, so that there is consensus among experts. If experts do not agree among themselves, one lacks a reliable basis for selecting judgmental rules and a standard against which to validate the program. Several experts can make the same faulty judgments in less well-known domains. Therefore, this mode of structuring knowledge for problem solving must rest on the established validity of expert judgment. In most of the problematic situations people face in their everyday life they have to use whatever knowledge and reasoning skills they possess without the benefit of well-specified information.

Generating alternative solutions and evaluating their outcomes are considerably more difficult than may appear at first glance. People have neither the time nor the endurance to conduct exhaustive information searches before making a decision. The value of additional information must be balanced against the cost of obtaining it (Spetzler & Stael von Holstein, 1975). Instead, a small set of alternatives is usually considered from which the choices can be made. Moreover, it is not an easy matter to evaluate the results likely to be gained by alternative courses of action. To begin with, the likely outcomes of different solutions are often uncertain because outcomes vary depending on the resources available, the skill with which activities are executed, and any number of foreseeable and unforeseen circumstances. Probabilistic judgment requiring weighting and integrating information about factors affecting what outcomes will occur is not exactly a human forte (Slovic, Fischhoff, & Lichtenstein, 1977). To complicate further the decision process, solutions typically produce mixed results. Potential benefits of alternative solutions must, therefore, be considered against the likely costs. There is also the problem of weighing short-run results against long-range outcomes, which are not always in accord. And finally, strong idiosyncratic preferences can lead people to act against their better judgment.

The model of the judicious problem solver, who selects the best alternative by performing calculations about the utility of all feasible alternatives, falls far short of actuality. Faced with many possible options, incomplete, uncertain, and mixed outcome knowledge, and cognitive limitations in integrating probabilistic information, people typically simplify the task by considering only a few alternatives and relying on intuitive judgmental rules for estimating outcomes (Kahneman & Tversky, 1979; Simon, 1976). Because there is always some uncertainty about outcomes when a course of action is first chosen, and further choices have to be made along the way, decisions are often made provisionally and altered on the basis of new information gained from preliminary results. Given the usual uncertainty about outcomes, one is wise to heed the advice of the American Indian proverb: "Never test the depth of the water with both feet."

In efforts to overcome cognitive limitations and misguiding personal biases, decision aids have been devised that provide knowledge, judgmental rules, and integrated outcome estimates (Feigenbaum, 1977; Hammond, 1971; Slovic, Fischhoff, & Lichtenstein, 1977). It is one thing to devise decision aids; it is another thing to get people to use them. In the absence of close performance evaluation, people quickly revert to their own intuitive methods in which they place excessive confidence.

Verbal Modeling of Thinking Skills for Problem Solving. Problem-solving skills involve more than just the sequential execution of cognitive operations in the likeness of computational exercises that generate predictable results. People often deal poorly with the problems confronting them, even though they know the rules for accomplishing satisfactory solutions. In previous chapters we examined how self-misgivings and evaluative apprehensions can disrupt

optimal use of cognitive skills, whereas a strong sense of self-efficacy enables people to make the most of their capabilities. Moods can affect self-referent thinking which, in turn, affects how well people execute what they know. A comprehensive approach to problem solving must therefore consider how self-referent thinking impinges on problem-solving thinking as people experience successes, setbacks, and failures in the search for adequate solutions.

In developing thinking skills people are either left to their own devices to discover some heuristics from the results of their actions, or they are taught rules and strategies by didactic modes of instruction. Cognitive modeling is another mode of tuition that is especially well suited not only to teach problem-solving rules of thinking but also how best to manage intrusive self-referent impediments (Meichenbaum, 1980). Children acquire cognitive skills better from observing models verbalize their thought processes as they solve problems than from didactic instruction of the same rules and strategies (Schunk, 1981). People whose performances are easily debilitated through perturbing self-preoccupation use their cognitive skills more effectively after learning from verbalizing models how to manage intrusive thinking (Sarason, 1975b).

Collective Problem Solving

Many of the common human problems stem from adverse social conditions that cannot be altered effectively by individual action alone. The ills of life arising from social inequities, poverty, crime, social fragmentation, environmental pollution, and the progressive degradation of the productive capacity of the environment are not eliminated by individual action. Group problems require group solutions. The basic components of collective problem solving are similar to those operating at the individual level. However, collective determination of priorities, selection of action strategies, and implementation of solutions entail additional processes peculiar to group functioning. Collective problem solving is, therefore, not reducible to the same processes as individual problem solving.

The decisional processes for determining priorities among alternatives are considerably more complex at the collective level. Individual self-interests often conflict with long-run, group benefit. Even if some social consensus exists, conflicts of interests and values inevitably arise among different constituencies over the types of changes preferred and the means by which they should be pursued. Group selection of alternatives requires devising mechanisms for clarifying the consequences of the alternatives, for ascertaining collective preferences, and for resolving conflicts among different constituencies. Those who are skilled in discerning and translating diverse self-interests into common proximal goals forge consensus most effectively (Hornstein et al., 1971).

People are eager to act as decision makers, but they generally show less concern for evaluating the full consequences of their preferred solutions. As a result, social practices are often instituted without self-corrective assessments that provide the basis for enhancing beneficial effects and reducing adverse unintended consequences. When performance indices are used, their corrective potential is sometimes diminished by selecting indicators that are more likely to further certain factional self-interests than to promote the common good. Collective decision making will not, in and of itself, ensure advancement of valued goals unless means and effects are given serious consideration as well.

Progress in attaining common aims requires suitable strategies and organized collective effort in implementing them (Zaltman, Kotler, & Kaufman, 1972). New solutions often disrupt entrenched practices and activate resistance from vested interests, who perceive the changes advocated as threatening to their customs, status, and power. Attempts to produce sweeping changes at the same time pose widespread threats and thus mobilize many opposers, whereas changing one thing at a time can effect greater progress because of sustained concerted effort and lessened opposition (Huntington, 1968). Devising means of surmounting countermeasures to change, some of which may take discrediting and coercive forms, constitutes another important aspect of group efforts to alter the structure or function of social systems.

If estimating the likely outcomes of alternative solutions is difficult in the individual case, it is doubly difficult in the group situation. The potential benefits are hard to measure because varied and conflicting influences typically come into play, with the relative power of the contending factions determining whose preferences will prevail. The same is true for reckoning with potential costs. It is often said that every social solution has a problem. In many instances, the costs are unforeseen and become evident only after a given practice has been in effect for some time. When untoward effects arise indirectly through interdependent changes and are slowly cumulative, the causes of the outcomes are hard to detect, let alone to verify. Uncertainties about future consequences of alternative courses of action invite discord. A further complicating factor in collective decision making is that the mixed results accompanying a given solution differ for different groups. Some benefit substantially, others marginally, and still others may bear the brunt of the costs. There are no fixed guides for decisions when alternative solutions produce differential outcomes for different constituencies. Cost-benefit analyses will yield different answers depending on the personal values assigned to the various benefits and costs. In the final analysis, collective decision making is swayed by the amount of social influence and power the various constituencies can wield.

As in the case of individual judgment, evidence of how decisions are made in organizations does not exactly jibe with standard decisional theories. In masterly fashion, March (1982) describes the actuality. People involved in decision making maintain a healthy skepticism about the types of information that are said to yield optimal choices. They view much of the information as tainted by the biases of those gathering it; they do not place heavy stock in guesses about future outcomes in a future that contains many uncertainties; they know that highly touted advice has proven misleading much too often to be taken unreservedly. Rather than adopting a systematic problem-solving mode, in which future outcomes of a large set of alternatives are calculated and ordered in terms of subjective value, decision makers are inclined to apply rules derived from past experiences or to model the decision rules used by others. Collective decisions are orchestrated by trading favors, exercising power, and forming coalitions with conflicting interests. In this process, information is gathered and used partly to convey competence and to add legitimacy to decisions that have been made already.

INTENTIONS AND GOALS

A great deal of human behavior is directed and sustained over long periods in the absence of immediate external inducements. In these instances the guides and incentives to action are rooted largely in cognitive activities. In social cognitive theory, intention plays a prominent role in the self-regulation of behavior. An intention is defined as the determination to perform certain activities or to bring about a certain future state of affairs. Intentional regulation of behavior operates principally through two cognitively based sources of motivation, both relying on cognitive representational mechanisms. One form operates anticipatorily through the exercise of forethought. We saw earlier that the capacity to represent future consequences in thought provides a necessary condition for one cognitive source of motivation. Through cognitive representation of future outcomes individuals can generate current motivators for courses of action that are instrumental in attaining the outcomes they value.

A second cognitively based source of motivation relies on goal setting and self-evaluative reactions to one's own behavior. This form of self-motivation, which operates largely through a cognitive comparison process, requires standards against which to evaluate ongoing performance. By making self-satisfaction conditional on a selected level of performance, individuals create their own incentives to persist in their efforts until their performances match internal standards. Intentions, whether expressed in determination to engage in a specific course of action or to attain certain levels of performance, increase the likelihood that sought futures will be realized.

Behavioristic theorists might argue that goal-directed behavior is fully explainable without reference to goals or intentions. To illustrate the different theoretical perspectives, let us consider a specific example. An adventuresome host intends to treat a dinner guest several days hence to a salmon soufflé to be prepared for the first time on the basis of a recipe only recently committed to memory. The intention to serve the soufflé provides direction and inducement for an organized set of activities spanning a considerable period of time. This includes shopping in advance for the ingredients thought to be necessary, later assembling the kitchen utensils and ingredients, preparing the soufflé mixture from memory, and timing the baking of the soufflé based on the chef's knowledge of how long it takes to produce a magnificent puff.

An analysis of goal-directed behavior that excludes intentions from among its set of determinants has to rely on an unwieldy cueing-transport metaphor as the explanatory device. That is, the chef's actions are presumably orchestrated by a chain of environmental stimuli strung out over time that lead to the final primary reward. Somewhere along the line an external soufflé cue initiates the chain of actions; other situational cues later bring the chef to a shopping center; once in the supermarket a series of cues transport the chef to the vegetable, fish, and cheese departments, whereupon the salmon, shallots, parmesan cheese, oregano, butter, and eggs somehow gain selective power to activate reaching and purchasing responses without the guidance of thought. Some time later a temporal cue directs the chef to the kitchen where, from among the numerous culinary cues, the soufflé relevant ones gain sufficient salience to activate the preparatory responses for creating the soufflé mixture. The externalization of cognitive guides to action encounters considerable difficulty at the mixing bowl, because the soufflé mixture is created from memory. If thought is disavowed as a regulator of action, one is at a loss to explain the incorporation and precise blending of ingredients. The explanatory burden usually falls upon the indefinite but omnific "history of reinforcement."

In an operant theorist's interpretation of intention, Day (1976) reduces intention to external contingency control in which action is dictated by environmental cues and consequents. The human organism becomes mainly a host to responses, but otherwise it cannot affect its own behavior by foresight of consequents or by other means of self-direction. This type of analysis rests on faith in the explanatory and predictive efficacy of contingency control, which was shown earlier to be seriously wanting. Skinner (1974) argues, on the one hand, that intentions cannot act as causes of behavior but, on the other hand, that "operant behavior is the very field of purpose and intention" because persons act to bring about certain happenings. Acts do produce outcomes, but, as Porpora (1980) explains, in the operant view, behavior is performed because it was reinforced in the past, not for the sake of a goal. From this viewpoint, behavior is governed by the history of reinforcement rather than by the goals sought. As already noted, intentional behavior requires cognitive representation of prospective goals and judgments about the means best suited to attain them. To disavow the causal efficacy of forethought is to strip the organism of its goal-directed capacity.

The same behavior can serve different purposes. A motorist, for example, might drive an automobile to the same shopping center to shop for groceries, for clothing, for literary material, or for any number of other purposes. Intention cannot be inferred from actions; otherwise, it would provide a circular explanation in which the same event is taken as evidence of both cause and effect. Rather, intention must be defined independently of the behavior it regulates. In the social cognitive analysis of intention, the affirmation of what one will do and the course of action one actually pursues are separate events. One might try to infer intentions from environmental stimuli. However, it would be an immense task, indeed, to try to figure out, from among the multitude of cues that continuously impinge on people, which ones may give direction to their actions. Even if informative external cues could be identified, the question of whether the cues affect behavior directly or through the mediation of intention would be left unanswered.

One can gain access indirectly to people's intentions by having them report beforehand what they intend to do at specified times. Verbalized intentions provide a basis for predicting the direction of human action. Causality is even more convincingly tested by creating different types of intentions and measuring their behavioral effects. In experimental analyses of intentional determinants of action, goal intentions are varied by suggestions or other indirect means, and their effects on motivation and choice of action are assessed (Locke, Shaw, Saari, & Latham, 1981; Ryan, 1970). It might be argued that people do not always adopt suggested goals or adhere steadfastly to them. This is doubtless true. If people set their own goal intentions or change them, then their altered self-set intentions serve as the better predictors of what they are most likely to do (Bandura & Cervone, 1986). Even if predictions of behavior were based solely on initial intentions, one would err sometimes, whereas if one completely disregarded intentions one would often misjudge what others will do.

Several theorists have proposed explanatory models in which intentions are included among the determinants of behavior (Dulany, 1968; Fishbein & Ajzen, 1975; Ryan, 1970). Such models vary in the type of factors presumed to affect the likelihood that people will act on their intentions. Much progress has been made in delineating the conditions under which intentions guide actions. Goal intentions are of greater import than simple action intentions because they serve to structure and guide human endeavors over long periods of time.

Mechanisms of Goal Intentions

The goals by which behavior is regulated have diverse psychological effects. It is to these various effects and the mechanisms through which goal intentions operate that we turn next.

Motivational Effects. Among the different effects of goals, the motivational ones have received greatest attention (Locke & Latham, 1984). Social cognitive theory posits that goals enhance motivation through self-reactive influences. When individuals commit themselves to explicit goals, perceived negative discrepancies between what they do and what they seek to achieve create self-dissatisfactions that serve as incentives for enhanced effort. The motivational effects do not derive from the goals themselves but rather from the fact that people respond evaluatively to their own behavior. Goals specify the conditional requirements for positive self-evaluation. The more self-dissatisfied people are with substandard performances, the more they heighten their efforts (Bandura & Cervone, 1983, 1986; Locke, Cartledge, & Knerr, 1970).

Activation of self-evaluation processes through internal comparison requires both personal standards and knowledge of the level of one's own performance. Neither knowledge of performance without standards nor standards without performance knowledge provides a basis for self-evaluative reactions. Self-motivation is apt to be low when discrepancies are precluded by the absence of one of the necessary comparative factors. Studies in which goal level and performance feedback are varied yield results that are consistent with this formulation (Bandura & Cervone, 1983; Becker, 1978; Strang, Lawrence, & Fowler, 1978). Simply adopting a goal, whether an easy or challenging one, without knowing how one is doing, or knowing how one is doing in the absence of a goal, has no appreciable motivational effects. Nor are people motivated by knowing that their performances match easy goals. Rather, it is knowledge of performance in relation to attainable challenging goals that is most motivating. These patterns of effects are obtained in such diverse areas of functioning as cognitive activities, physical stamina, and conserving electrical energy.

When people engage in an ongoing activity and are informed of their performance attainments, some will set goals for themselves spontaneously. Analysis of performance effort as a function of self-set goals under conditions of feedback alone is also consistent with the view that both knowledge of performance and a standard of comparison are needed to produce motivational effects (Bandura & Cervone, 1983). Those who set no goals achieve no change and are outperformed by those who aim to sustain their performance gain, and the latter, in turn, are outperformed by those who set themselves the more challenging goal of bettering their past attainments. Self-set goals are not in themselves motivating without knowledge of one's performance.

The form of the relationship between degree of perceived discrepancy and performance motivation is not linear. Performances that fall markedly short of standards are too discouraging and lead people to abandon goals by undermining their perceived self-efficacy for attaining them. Moderately discrepant performances, which do not jeopardize the perceived attainability of standards, activate self-dissatisfaction that spurs efforts to achieve valued standards that appear attainable through extra effort. Attainments that fall just short of challenging standards are also highly motivating when they strengthen self-beliefs that, through greater effort, standards can be matched or even surpassed. Most successes do not bring lasting satisfaction; having accomplished a given level of performance, people generally motivate themselves by setting greater challenges that create new discrepancies to be mastered (Bandura & Cervone, 1986; Campbell, 1982; Simon, 1979b). Thus, notable attainments bring temporary enjoyment, but people enlist new challenges as self-motivators for further accomplishment.

Increases in motivation by means of goal setting are reflected in more than just the sheer amount of effort expended on an activity. Goals increase and channel attention to relevant aspects of activities. They also enhance cognitive processing of information arising from the increased involvement in ongoing activities. When given unlimited time, people who adopt high goals work much longer at a task and master more of it than those who adopt easy goals or are simply encouraged to do their best. However, differential goals result in different levels of task mastery even when a fixed time is set (LaPorte & Nath, 1976). When a definite time is allotted, challenging goals facilitate learning more by mobilizing attentional and cognitive factors than by increasing perseverance.

Self-Efficacy Effects. Goals not only provide direction and create incentives for action, they also figure prominently in the development of self-efficacy. Without standards against which to measure their performances, people have little basis for judging how they are doing, nor do they have much basis for gauging their capabilities. Temporally proximal goals serve this function especially well (Bandura &

Schunk, 1981). Subgoal attainments provide indicants of mastery for enhancing self-percepts of efficacy. By contrast, distal goals are too far removed in time to provide sufficiently clear markers of progress along the way to ensure a growing sense of personal efficacy.

Self-motivation through internal standards and perceived self-efficacy operate as interrelated rather than as separate mechanisms of personal agency. Goal attainments build self-efficacy. People's judgments of their capabilities, in turn, affect their aspirations, how much effort they mobilize in pursuit of adopted goals, and how they respond to discrepancies between their performances and what they seek to achieve. The self-assured are much more likely than self-doubters to set themselves challenging standards by which they raise their level of motivation. By doing so, they expand their knowledge and skills which further increases their sense of personal efficacy.

Whether negative goal discrepancies are motivating or disheartening will be partly influenced by perceptions of personal efficacy for goal attainment. People who harbor self-doubts are easily discouraged by failure, whereas those who are assured of their capabilities intensify their efforts when their performances fall short and persist until they succeed. If investment of greater effort still falls short of the mark, the highly self-efficacious are more apt to judge the subgoal as too large, rather than distrust their own capabilities. To the extent that perceived self-inefficacy leads people to give up readily in the face of difficulties and to shun challenging goals that serve to expand capabilities, they deny themselves the mastery experiences needed to build robust self-assurance.

Research examining the self-reactive influences that occur when performance falls short of one's internal standard reveals that the effects of goal systems on motivation are mediated through self-evaluative and self-efficacy mechanisms activated by cognitive comparison (Bandura & Cervone, 1983). Self-reactive influences are highly predictive of motivation when both comparative factors are present—a goal and performance feedback of progress toward it. The more self-dissatisfied persons are with a substandard performance, the more they increase their subsequent effort; the stronger their perceived self-efficacy that they can meet their standard, the more they intensify their effort. When one of the comparative factors for activating self-reactive influences is lacking (i.e., persons perform without either goals or feedback about their progress), the relationship of self-reactive influences to motivation depends on available partial information or on information that performers subjectively supply for themselves. When people aim for a challenging standard but have to guess how they are doing, the stronger their perceived self-efficacy for goal attainment and the more pleased they are with whatever they surmise their performance to be, the more they heighten their efforts. Similarly, when they receive feedback about a significant accomplishment in the absence of an aspiring standard, the more pleased they are to sustain that same level of improvement, the more effortfully they behave. Self-evaluative reactions thus operate differently when there are different patterns of comparative information. With goals and feedback of substandard performance, self-dissatisfaction affects effort. With either goals alone or performance feedback alone, effort is governed by level of self-satisfaction.

The two self-reactive influences even predict changes in performance motivation over time. The self-dissatisfied but also self-efficacious greatly accelerate their performance effort, those who are either self-dissatisfied or self-efficacious sustain their performance effort, whereas those who judge themselves inefficacious to fulfill the goal and are satisfied with a substandard gain slacken their efforts and show a substantial decline in performance. The latter findings are congruent with results of field studies (Carroll & Tosi, 1970) showing that difficult goals increase effort in self-assured persons but lower effort in those doubting their capabilities. Moreover, the efforts of the self-assured are less easily disrupted by difficulties and setbacks than the efforts of those who harbor self-misgivings. The multiple functions that self-percepts of efficacy serve in motivation by means of goal systems is further revealed by Locke and others (Earley, 1986; Locke, Frederick, Lee, & Bobko, 1984; Taylor, Locke, Lee, & Gist, 1984). Perceived self-efficacy for goal attainment raises the level of self-set goals, strengthens commitment to goals, and enhances performance.

Depending on their direction and magnitude, goal discrepancies can raise the motivating potential of one of the self-reactive factors while simultaneously lowering the motivating potential of the other (Bandura & Cervone, 1986). Thus, attainments that fall markedly short of a standard increase self-dissatisfaction but lower perceived self-efficacy for goal attainment. Perceived inefficacy leads people to set their sights lower. A decrement in self-efficacy sufficient to prompt adoption of a lower standard would serve to reduce negative self-reactions. Smaller negative discrepancies reduce self-dissatisfaction but strengthen self-percepts of efficacy. When attainments closely approach the standard, performers who judge themselves to be highly efficacious may set their sights even higher, thus creating further motivational inducements for themselves. When attainments surpass the standard, there is no cause for self-dissatisfaction. Motivation under suprastandard performance is governed by perceived self-efficacy and the level of the subsequent challenges people set for themselves to accomplish. Thus, the motivational impact of goal structures is best understood by considering the dynamic interplay between self-evaluation, perceived self-efficacy, and self-set standards.

Interest Enhancement Effects. Attaining challenging goals creates self-satisfaction and a sense of fulfillment. Level of self-satisfaction tends to be proportional to the discrepancy between valued aims and actual attainments; that is, the closer attainments match goal intentions, the greater are the positive self-reactions (Bandura & Cervone, 1986; Locke, Cartledge, & Knerr, 1970). The satisfactions derived from goal attainments contribute to the growth of interest. Accordingly, working toward explicit attainable goals enhances interest and personal involvement in activities, whereas trying to do one's best without a specifiable goal does not. Proximal goals, which confer self-efficacy through progressive attainments of challenging subgoals, are most conducive to the cultivation of intrinsic interest (Bandura & Schunk, 1981; Morgan, 1984b).

Setting goals does not necessarily stimulate interest and self-satisfaction, even though it improves performance (Latham & Yukl, 1976; Umstot, Bell, & Mitchell, 1976). It depends on whether goals are used to expand competencies, to master challenges with the skills at one's command, or to raise performance output. Thus, in work situations requiring repetitive execution of the same tedious activities, adopting goals will heighten productivity. However, doing more of a tedious activity will not increase the liking of it. Heightened productivity without increased benefits can also arouse resentments over felt inequity or cause open resistance if improved performance simply raises standards even higher. If goals become onerous dictates they breed disaffection rather than bring personal satisfaction. It is on tasks involving self-improvement or a contribution to valued endeavors that the relationship between goal setting, effective performance, and interest enhancement are most likely to obtain. People, of course, tend to read self-evaluative significance into most things they do (Simon, 1979a). Even on tasks that might appear inconsequential they view their performance as reflecting their astuteness and competence, and they are pleased by performance improvements. Therefore, the conditions necessary for goal setting to generate personal involvement encompass a vast range of activities.

Goal Properties and Self-Motivation

Goal intentions do not automatically activate the self-influence mechanisms that govern performance. Indeed, one need only point to the predictable failure of most good intentions as evidence that not all goal setting enhances motivation. Certain properties of goals determine the likelihood that self-evaluative reactions will be enlisted in any given activity.

Goal Specificity. The degree to which goals create incentives and guides for action is partly determined by their specificity. Clear standards regulate performance by designating the type and amount of effort required to attain them, and they foster self-satisfaction and perceived efficacy by furnishing unambiguous signs of personal accomplishments. General intentions, which do not designate a performance level, provide little basis for regulating one's effort or for evaluating how one is doing.

The regulative function of goals differing in specificity has been examined extensively, although the goals in these studies are usually assigned, rather than set entirely by the persons themselves. However, evidence to be reviewed shortly suggests that assigned and self-selected goals yield similar relationships. Clear, attainable goals produce higher levels of performance than general intentions to do one's best, which usually have little or no effect (Locke et al., 1981). Specific performance goals serve to motivate the unmotivated and to foster positive attitudes toward the activities (Bryan & Locke, 1967).

Goal Challenge. The amount of effort and satisfaction that accompany variations in goals depends upon the level at which they are set. When self-satisfaction is contingent upon attainment of challenging goals, more effort is expended than if easy ones are adopted as sufficient. For activities that are readily amenable to voluntary control, the higher the goals, the higher the performance level (Locke, 1968). On difficult tasks, however, one would not expect goal level to be linearly related to performance attainment, and this is indeed the case (Baron & Watters, 1981). When goals are set unrealistically high, most performances prove disappointing. Strong effort that produces repeated failure weakens perceived self-efficacy, thereby reducing motivation to perform the activity.

Although theorists agree that goal difficulty raises performance, they differ in how they view the nature of that relationship. According to Atkinson (1957), performance is the product of the subjective probability of success and the value of attaining it. These two determinants are assumed to be inversely related so that hard goals have a low success expectancy but high value; easy goals have a high success expectancy but low value. This theory predicts a curvilinear relationship between goal difficulty and performance, with both effort and performance being higher for goals of moderate difficulty (i.e., when the probability of goal attainment is at .50) than for easy or very difficult ones. On the assumption that success expectancy and the value of success are not related linearly, Heckhausen (1977) posits a success probability at about .30 as being maximally motivating.

In contrast to Atkinson's view, Locke (1968) postulates an increasing linear function between goal level and performance. A large body of evidence shows that the higher the goals, the harder people work to attain them and the better is their performance. People pursuing high goals typically outperform those aiming for moderate goals. However, the linear relationship is assumed to hold only if the goals are accepted. Most people, of course, eventually reject performance goals they consider unrealistically demanding or well beyond their reach. However, people remain surprisingly steadfast to goals they have little chance of fulfilling, even when given normative information that others reject them as unrealistic (Erez & Zidon, 1984). When assigned goals are beyond their reach and failure to attain them carries no cost, people try to approximate high standards as closely as they can, rather than abandon them altogether and thus sustain their performances (Garland, 1983; Locke, Zubritzky, Cousins, & Bobko, 1984). Consequently, they achieve notable progress, even though the accomplishment of distal goal aspirations eludes them. This characterizes most of the strivings of everyday life—long-range aspirations exceed current attainments, but personal and social advancements are realized in the process of striving. These findings run counter to expectancy-value theories which predict declining performance as goals become more and more difficult to attain. Unattainable standards are more likely to be abandoned when failure to meet them brings aversive consequences and one can choose the activities in which to invest one's efforts.

Proponents of expectancy-valence models interpret evidence that harder goals produce higher performances as support for their theory. To the extent that the incentive value of goal attainment is higher for difficult than for easy goals, people will exert more effort to succeed at high goals (Matsui, Okada, & Mizuguchi, 1981). However, in experiments in which different determinants of performance effort are varied, goal difficulty and perceived capability predict effort, whereas goal valence and expectancy of success do not, when other factors are controlled (Mento, Cartledge, & Locke, 1980). High valence and expectancy of success increase the likelihood that assigned goals will be accepted as personal goals. Valence and success expectancy thus affect performance indirectly, through their influence on goal acceptance, rather than operating directly on performance. When success expectancy affects performance directly, its independent contribution is small compared to that of personal goals (Garland, 1984).

Social cognitive theory distinguishes between distal goals and proximal subgoals.

End goals serve a general directive function, but specific subgoals determine people's immediate choice of activities and how hard they will work on them. For example, sprinters who aspire to break a particular record will deploy much of their free time to the track. But their efforts in practice sessions are best mobilized and sustained by setting a series of proximal subgoals, each surpassing preceding levels of performance. Attainable subgoals leading toward ultimate goals create the most favorable conditions for continuing self-motivation.

The relationship between probability of goal attainment and effort expenditure will differ for subgoals and for end goals. Proximal subgoals that are challenging but clearly attainable through extra effort are likely to be most motivating and self-satisfying. Therefore, a high level of self-motivation can be sustained through progressively rising subgoals, even though the long-range goals are exceedingly difficult to realize (Jeffery, 1977). In an ongoing pursuit, however, the perceived difficulty of an ultimate goal does not remain constant. The pattern and rate of progress toward a goal in the distant future alters subjective estimates of eventual success. As one comes closer to realizing distal goals, their attainment appears less formidable than when originally viewed from far down the line.

Goal Proximity. The effectiveness of intentions in regulating behavior depends greatly on how far into the future they are projected. A proximate standard of comparison serves to mobilize self-influences and direct what one does in the here and now. In addition to enlisting motivating self-reactive influences, proximal subgoals also reduce the risk of self-demoralization that can occur if current accomplishments are gauged against lofty distal aspirations. Distal goals alone are too far removed in time to provide effective incentives and guides for present action. Ordinarily there are too many competing influences at hand for thoughts of far-off futures to exert much control over current behavior. By focusing on the distant future, it is all too easy to put off matters in the present—one can always begin in earnest in the tomorrows of each day. This habitual tendency to temporize, which often trades immediate gratifications for more burdensome futures, is captured well in the adage: The more dilatory the persons, the more they expect to do tomorrow.

Exercising influence over behavior in the present increases the likelihood that desired futures will be realized. The stronger are the current inducements for actions that compete with goal-directed activities, the greater is the need to enlist self-influence through proximal subgoals. This general principle figures prominently in the practices of Alcoholics Anonymous. Recovering alcoholics commit themselves to the immediate goal of not drinking today, rather than to the future goal of never drinking again.

Much of the research on goal setting involves activities that are readily amenable to voluntary control. Evidence of intentional control of easily manageable behavior may not be fully generalizable to goal-directed activities that are difficult to sustain over an extended time. The self-regulative value of proximal intentions is best tested with behavior that is refractory to change. One study of goal proximity in self-directed change focused on reducing excessive eating by people burdened with severe obesity (Bandura & Simon, 1977). Obese people who adopted daily subgoal limits for how much they ate achieved substantial continuing reductions in both eating behavior and weight. In contrast, those who pursued distal weekly goals rarely attained them, achieved relatively small reductions in eating behavior, shed no pounds, and did not differ in these respects from people who monitored their eating without benefit of reductive goals. Interestingly, many of the people who were assigned the distal goals adopted, on their own, proximal daily goals in an effort to gain control over their own behavior. Those who improvised proximal subgoals for themselves attained substantial control over their eating behavior and lost significant amounts of weight.

Studies in which goal setting has failed to enhance self-directed change in refractory behavior have relied almost exclusively on distal goals (Mahoney & Thoresen, 1974). Unless participants on their own segment remote goals into proximal subgoals, the prospects of success are limited. Goal proximity should be distinguished from specificity of planning which includes not only temporal variation in goals but also prescribes more onerous busywork in planning, monitoring, and recording progress for proximal than for distal plans (Kirschenbaum, Humphrey, & Malett, 1981; Kirschenbaum, Tomarken, & Ordman, 1982). Self-influence requiring excess busywork is usually less faithfully applied, with less beneficial results. The motivating potential of goal proximity is best revealed by varying only whether performance is compared to close or distant standards without including other co-varying, confounding factors.

Efforts to clarify how goal proximity operates in self-regulatory mechanisms ordinarily present difficulties because, even though encouraged to set themselves distal goals, people are prone to convert them into more helpful proximal ones. They simply partition desired future attainments into more easily realizable subgoals (Bandura & Simon, 1977). Spontaneous goal transformations were precluded in a project in which young children, who were grossly deficient in mathematical skills, pursued a program of self-directed learning using goals varying in temporal proximity (Bandura & Schunk, 1981). The children could not transform distal into proximal self-motivators because, not knowing how to divide, they could not partition the entire instructional enterprise into smaller subunits! With daily subgoals, children progressed more rapidly in self-directed learning, achieved higher mastery of basic mathematical operations, and developed greater perceived self-efficacy and intrinsic interest in mathematics. Distal goals contributed little either to personal accomplishments or to

self development. Evidence from several studies attests to the motivating potential of proximal subgoals, whether they are suggested or spontaneously generated or whether the self-sustained behavior is tractable or very difficult to produce.

Differential reactions to prescribed distal goals illustrate the dual self processes of exercising and undergoing influence. When socially encouraged to adopt distal goals for their performances, many people improvise their own more helpful proximal goals. Even when encouraged to raise their level of performance on an ongoing activity, without any reference to goals, people vary as to whether they create their own goals by themselves (Bandura & Cervone, 1983). Those who set no goals for themselves achieve little change in performance, those who set goals to sustain their level of effort make modest improvements, while those who set themselves goals to better their past attainments accomplish large performance gains. As such findings show, a major challenge to the investigation of self-regulatory processes, whether they involve self-monitoring, goal setting, cognitive rehearsal, or self-generated incentives, is that people do not simply react to situational influences. They often transform them into self-influences that differ from what others intend. Theories that attempt, through regressive causal analysis, to reduce self-regulatory processes to situational control overlook the fact that people are not only objects of change but also act as agents who give new form to situational influences. Such bidirectionality of influence supports a reciprocal model of self-regulation.

To sum up, self-motivation is best maintained by explicit proximal subgoals that are instrumental in achieving larger future ones. Subgoals provide present guides and inducements for action, while subgoal attainments produce the efficacy information and self-satisfactions that sustain one's efforts along the way. Persistence that leads to eventual mastery of an activity is thus ensured through a progression of subgoals, each with a high probability of success. Reliance on goal proximity as a motivational device does not imply any restriction in the future time perspective of aspirations. Personal development is best served by combining distal aspirations with proximal self-guidance.

Self-motivation through self-reactive influence is doubtless a significant ingredient in a variety of motivational phenomena that come under different names. Achievement motivation is one such phenomenon. High achievers tend to make self-satisfaction contingent upon attainment of challenging goals; low achievers adopt easy goals as sufficient. The higher the performance standards people set for themselves, the more likely they are to excel in their attainments. The research of Matsui, Okada, and Kakuyama (1982) indicates that achievement motivation influences performance indirectly through its effects on goal setting. The relationship between achievement motivation and performance disappears when the difficulty of self-set goals is controlled. The goals people set for themselves predict their performance level and self-satisfaction better than the traditional personality measures of need for achievement (Arvey & Dewhirst, 1976; Ostrow, 1976; Yukl & Latham, 1978). Evidence that high need achievers select high goals does not necessarily reflect unidirectional dispositional causality, as is commonly assumed. Personal standards of excellence may lead people to endorse achievement statements on personality tests, rather than such endorsements verifying an achievement motive that fuels aspiring standards. Evidence that standard setting is a better predictor of behavior than indices of achievement motives lends causal priority to standard setting.

Self-reactive influence through goal setting also contributes to the motivational effects of extrinsic feedback and incentives. Incentives can motivate partly by activating personal goals for progressive improvement. Indeed, a series of studies conducted by Locke and his associates shows that incentives increase performance to the extent that they encourage people to set motiva-ting goals for themselves (Locke, Bryan, & Kendall, 1968). In research reporting mixed results on whether incentives influence performance partly by their effect on self-set goals, performers were given no information about their level of performance (Pritchard & Curtis, 1973). Self-evaluative motivators are not effectively activated under such conditions. Self-set goals with performance information enhance effort; self-set goals alone do not (Bandura & Cervone, 1983). People are stirred to action by the prospect of valued outcomes, but by applying evaluative standards to their ongoing performances, they strive to perform successfully to please themselves as well.

People impose goal structures on activities that reflect their basic orientations to achievement situations. This process has been the focus of research on how people's conceptions of intelligence affect the goals they pursue, which, in turn, determine the quality of their intellectual functioning (M. Bandura, 1983; Dweck & Elliot, 1983). Two major conceptions have been identified. In one perspective, intelligence is construed as an *incremental skill* that can be continually enhanced by acquiring knowledge and perfecting one's competencies. People with this orientation adopt a learning goal. They seek challenging tasks providing opportunities to develop their competencies. Errors are regarded as a natural, instructive part of the process—one learns from mistakes. Personal progress carries precedence over social comparison of capabilities. Effort is rewarded by growth of personal efficacy.

In the contrasting perspective, intelligence is construed as a more or less *stable entity*. Since quality of performance is considered from this view as diagnostic of intellectual capability, errors and performance insufficiencies carry personal threat and social evaluation of competence is of much concern. Consequently, people adopting the entity view prefer performance goals on tasks minimizing errors and demonstrating proficiency at the expense of learning something new. They are prone to measure their capabilities by comparison with the achievements of others. Effort is rewarded by validation of intellectual status. These differential orientations are also reflected in coping with obstacles. Children who view intelligence as an entity and perceive themselves as deficient in it are easily debilitated by failures, whereas those subscribing to an incremental view take failures in their stride. When the former children are encouraged to adopt a learning goal, they manage failure much more effectively.

Strength of Goal Commitment

Goals and intentions are unlikely to have much impact on future behavior if there is little personal commitment to them. Goal commitment is defined as the resolve to pursue a course of action that will lead to selected outcomes or performance attainments. Goal commitment is affected by a number of factors, including valuation of the activity, the perceived attainability of the goals, and binding pledges. When accomplishments in weakly valued activities fall far short of goals, the goals are more apt to be deserted rather than efforts to reach them intensified. This is especially true if failure in goal attainment undermines perceived efficacy to accomplish it (Bandura & Cervone, 1983). Even in prized pursuits goals perceived to be unattainable short of a herculean effort will be abandoned for more realistic ones.

Goal commitment can be strengthened by pledges that bind one to a designated future performance (Kiesler, 1971). The motivational effects of pledging oneself to some future course of action derive, in large part, from the costs of reneging on an agreement. Committing oneself to certain goals creates anticipated consequences that operate against readily abandoning them. Some of these potential consequences are social, others are personal. Commitments that carry responsibility to others generate social pressures to follow through. Thus, a person who agreed to deliver a public lecture but did not bother to appear would in-

cense both the organizers and the stranded audience. Failure to meet commitments, depending on their nature, brings penalties, social disapproval, or loss of reputation concerning personal reliability.

Prior decisions often eliminate the chance of pursuing alternative courses of action. Preliminary commitment decisions and acts that reduce future response options force behavior in the chosen direction. For this reason small commitments that will eventually lead to large ones are often sought first (Freedman & Fraser, 1966). For similar reasons, people are inclined to avoid making decisions until pressured by circumstances, they temporize as long as they can, or they make decisions tentatively so they can back out of their agreements. The higher the social costs, the more strongly one is bound to the committed behavior, however much the original decision might be regretted.

If goal commitment invariably constrained freedom through reduction of options, it would be shunned like the plague. However, the impact of goal commitment on freedom depends on whether current or future options are considered and whether the commitment is to the cultivation of competence or an accommodation to social demands. In channeling their efforts into pursuits that build knowledge and competencies, individuals temporarily sacrifice other activities but thereby expand the range of future options available to them. Those who fail to develop essential competencies find many options barred to them. Goal commitments that facilitate realization of desired futures are not difficult to enlist, except perhaps in the early phases of endeavor when efforts seem burdensome, the journey long, and eventual success uncertain. It is goals requiring people to work harder without bringing them noticeable or adequate benefits that create problems of commitment.

So far the discussion has centered on how pledges can maintain a chosen course of action through the social pressures and constraints they create. When people pledge themselves personally to some future action or goal, commitment also creates motivational inducements by enlisting self-evaluative influences. Given a strong commitment to valued goals, failure to exert the necessary effort tends to arouse self-reproof that can serve as a personal constraint against reneging. Pledges to oneself, however, are more easily revocable than social ones, when the goals do not involve basic personal concerns. In such instances, self-dissatisfactions over unfulfilled intentions can be reduced by diminishing the importance of the goal, by finding extenuating circumstances, or by putting off conscientious effort to a later time. But in activities that touch on fundamental values, personal commitments carry considerable force because failure to live up to one's standards carries strong self-censure. People do not take lightly commitments to their moral standards of conduct or to the standards by which they judge the adequacy of their accomplishments.

Strength of goal commitment will partly determine the amount of effort expended in the pursuit. When the level of initial commitment is low or the process of change has unpleasant aspects, as it usually does, people have difficulty sustaining their efforts unless conditions are arranged to increase their behavioral commitment. The way in which intentions are affirmed is one influential factor (Kiesler, 1971). Public commitment enhances self-involvement in a chosen course of action by creating expectations in others that pledged actions will be forthcoming. Failure to follow through requires embarrassing explanations, if not more serious consequences. Constraints on behavior are weaker in the case of privately held intentions because there are no social consequences with which to contend. Degree of goal commitment also varies depending upon the amount of external pressure exerted by others on decisions to pursue a given course of behavior. When people act under social directives, they do not view themselves as personally responsible for fulfilling future goals if they did not have much choice in their selection. Rather, it is commitment under conditions of perceived choice that mobilizes self-evaluation in support of goal adherence.

Justifications and Goal Commitment.
The effects of justifications for actions on perceived volition and goal commitment deserve comment because of some theoretical differences on this issue. Conceptions of motivation based on attribution and cognitive consistency theories (Weiner, 1972; Zimbardo, 1969a) generally assume that the fewer the external justifications to perform a given behavior, the more one is committed to pursue it. Presumably, when people have insufficient external reasons for their actions they tend to attribute them to intrinsic interest in the activity itself.

Whether external justifications will or will not undermine perceived choice and commitment depends on the nature of the justifications. From the social cognitive perspective, commitment arises less from lack of justification than from personally persuasive reasons. Different types of justifications will have different effects on perceived choice and goal commitment. In laboratory studies, external justifications are usually created by offering money or applying coercive pressures to engage in the activity. One can more readily get people to commit themselves to a course of action through reason, anticipated natural benefits, or moral justifications than by money or coercion. Indeed, some of the most steadfast commitments to future goals result from compelling justifications. Thus, for example, people can become militantly committed to social reforms after being persuaded of the human suffering and immorality of institutionalized inequities (Bandura, 1973; Short & Wolfgang, 1972). Those who have been victimized by harmful social practices gain commitment to social change as a result of their painful experiences. If people are pressured by arbitrary social and material incentives to pursue an activity, then commitment to it will remain low, unless new experiences derived from self-involvement in the activity provide better reasons for engaging in it. Depending on their nature, external justifications can increase commitment to future courses of action or lessen personal responsibility for them.

Self-Determination of Goals and Goal Attainment.

Degree of participation in goal setting can affect strength of commitment to goal attainment. When people play a significant role in selecting goals, they hold themselves responsible for progress toward these goals and thereby engage self-evaluative mechanisms in the process. When goals are imposed by others, individuals do not necessarily accept them or feel obligated to meet them. Self-evaluative inducements for goal attainment may, therefore, be weaker when performance standards are prescribed by others.

The effects of assigned versus collaborative goal setting have been examined extensively in relation to job performance (Latham & Yukl, 1975; Locke & Schweiger, 1979). People perform better with goals, but while participative goal setting tends to increase satisfaction, it has little effect on performance. Several factors may explain why allowing people to participate in determining their own goals fails to improve their performance. If assigned and participatively set goals lead people to select different goals, then the effects of participation become confounded with variations in goal level. However, even when goal level is equated, assigned, and participatively set, or even self-set, goals produce equivalent increases in performance (Latham & Marshall, 1982). Once people get immersed in an activity, it appears as though the goal itself becomes more salient than how it was set. It may be that goals set unilaterally enlist weaker commitment than participatively set goals when there is some reluctance to pursue an activity wholeheartedly. Commitment through self-involvement then becomes more important.

People are rarely of one mind on a matter, and group deliberation rarely forges joyous unanimity. For members whose preferences differ from the prevailing view, participative decision making will not bring them an increased sense of personal determination. As Locke and Schweiger point out, groups can be quite autocratic and their dictates highly constraining. Moreover, opportunities for participative decision making by a group do not necessarily mean that most members exercise their influence in the formulation of group goals. In fact, a few influential members usually determine, in large part, what gets decided. Subordinate members may assent to decisions without feeling any personal commitment to them. So, unless there is a high level of involvement by all concerned in the formulation of collective goals, the differences between participative and prescriptive decision making are more illusory than real.

Field studies of how goals are set are often conducted in organizational settings, containing many evaluative and modeling influences. When supervisors set goals with expectance of evaluative feedback, they create strong external pressure for improvements in performance that can obscure the effects of evaluative self-motivation arising from personal commitment. Although setting goals in itself increases performance, concern over evaluation of one's work by others and the productivity of co-workers affect performance in social settings (White, Mitchell, & Bell, 1977). Whether self-determination of goals enhances goal commitment and likelihood of goal attainment, therefore, is best studied under conditions in which people set their own goals and external pressures to perform the activity are minimal. When environmental constraints are reduced, the influence of self-evaluative motivators becomes most evident.

Intentions and Amenability of Behavior to Voluntary Control

The impact of goals and intentions on action is partly determined by how susceptible the behavior is to voluntary control. Activities that can be easily increased or reduced at will may exaggerate the motivational force of goals. Even when goals are shown to enhance difficult performances, questions remain concerning their power to sustain performance gains over time. Organizational applications of goal-setting strategies measure productivity over extended periods, but, as we have just noted, the motivational effects of goals are inevitably confounded by constraints of the work environment and by the sanctions of supervisory personnel. Because of the flow of activities on a job, employees have to keep up a certain level of performance whether or not they are personally motivated to do so. Should their efforts slacken, supervisors will exert pressure on them to meet at least a minimally acceptable level of productivity. Nevertheless, evidence that goals augment effort over and above the common organizational inducements attests to the continuing motivational impact of performance goals (Dockstader, 1977; Latham & Kinne, 1974).

The upper limits of the influence of goals and intentions on performance are tested with habit patterns that are unusually resistant to change. The obese whose fondness for fattening foods strain their efforts to shed pounds, and alcoholics who readily lose control over their consumption of alcohol, are two familiar examples. When the activities to be self-regulated are intractable, goals are most likely to have a sustaining influence if they are set in close temporal proximity to the behavior (Bandura & Simon, 1977). The sustaining power of goal setting thus depends partly upon the nature of the goals. The more refractory the behavior, the greater the need for explicit, proximal, and attainable goals.

Cognitive Disequilibrium as an Automotivator

Cognitive motivation has been explained by some theorists in terms of an inborn motivating mechanism to understand things. According to Piaget (1960), people are inherently motivated to advance their cognitive development. During ongoing activities, they encounter discrepancies between the schemata they already have and perceived events. The resulting cognitive perturbations motivate exploration of the source of the discrepancy, until internal schemata are altered to accommodate the contradictory experiences. Events that differ markedly from what one knows or expects are too bewildering, and those that differ minimally are too familiar to arouse interest and exploration. It is moderately discrepant experiences that presumably arouse cognitive conflict that prompt cognitive reorganization. Piagetian theory thus proposes cognitive perturbations by moderately discrepant experiences as the basic automotivator for cognitive learning.

Equilibration models have been tested empirically in terms of attentional preferences for novelty or complexity, and by responsiveness to social influences designed to alter existing modes of thinking. In the preference studies, typically conducted with infants, a familiar standard is created by repeated preexposure to a particular stimulus pattern, after which stimuli that vary from it in configuration or complexity are presented. Familiar events do not hold much interest for infants. However, the findings are more variable at higher levels of discrepancy between familiar and novel events. Infants are often most attentive to moderately novel or complex events, but studies also show that the more novel and complex the stimuli, the more infants attend to them (McCall & McGhee, 1977). A comprehensive review of a substantial body of literature on this topic by Wachs (1977) provides neither strong nor consistent evidence that it is the moderately discrepant stimulation that is either the most preferred or the best promoter of cognitive learning. This conclusion is tempered, however, by reservations over whether discrepancy levels were adequately operationalized in relation to participants' cognitive schemata.

Until objective criteria are specified for determining preexisting cognitive standards and for specifying which events are minimally, moderately, or maximally discrepant from them, the equilibration model of self-motivation does not lend itself readily to empirical test. All too often either the cognitive standards or the discrepancies, or both, are judged intuitively, rather than measured objectively beforehand. These procedural ambiguities permit easy dismissal of findings that do not fit theoretical expectations. When inquisitiveness heightens with increasing novelty and complexity of stimulation, discordant stimuli simply get redefined as falling within the intermediate range. If highly novel activities are pursued until mastered, the resultant learning tends to be discounted as "superficial." If moderate mismatches between conceptions and evidence fail to arouse and sustain efforts to change, the discrepancy is faulted as not being within the optimal range. Some proponents of the equilibration model have added further qualifiers that render it difficult to test, even if discrepancy levels are adequately operationalized. Langer (1969) maintains that it is the cognitive perturbations children spontaneously produce by themselves rather than those externally activated by discrepant events that are the effective instigators of cognitive change. Moreover, the cognitive conflict is said to be often unconscious, which makes it even less accessible to study. Unless independent measures of self-perturbation are provided, the posited incongruity motivator is incapable of verification.

Gauging discrepancy between schemata and external influences is less troublesome with older children, who can be tested for what they know and theory specifies graded levels of thinking. In such studies, which explore cognitive change through discordant influence, cognitive conflict is created by exposing children briefly to views, at graded discrepancies, which are contradictory to those they hold. Some researchers find that children are more inclined to adopt views that involve only small shifts from their own than those that are more highly discordant (Rest, Turiel, & Kohlberg, 1969; Turiel, 1966). Others find that the more highly dis-

cordant influences are as effective, or even more so, in fostering cognitive changes (Arbuthnot, 1975; Matefy & Acksen, 1976; Walker, 1982). Kupfersmid and Wonderly (1982) address other conceptual and empirical problems associated with the equilibrium model. Although motivational inducements presumably spring from cognitive conflict between beliefs held and the information conveyed by situations encountered, surprisingly little effort has been made to verify the causal links between discrepant influences, indicants of internal conflict, and the quest for new understanding. What little evidence there is on this point shows that discrepant influences foster cognitive changes, but the changes seem unrelated to level of cognitive conflict (Zimmerman & Blom, 1983). Discordant notions that are not discounted or otherwise explained away may provide an impetus for inquiry. But the latter findings question whether internal conflict is necessary for the acquisition of knowledge. There are, of course, many other motivators for bettering one's knowledge and thinking skills.

Simply demonstrating that children are bored by what they already know and easily discouraged by information that exceeds their cognitive-processing capabilities is a mundane finding that can be explained without requiring an elaborate automotivating mismatch mechanism. But arousal of interest is by no means confined to events that differ only slightly from what one already knows. Moreover, a moderate discrepancy of experience alone does not guarantee cognitive learning. As for the pedagogical implications of motivation through cognitive disequilibrium, they are much the same as those of any other theory: Children can most readily learn what is only slightly beyond what they already know or can do.

There are several reasons why an automotivational system of the type under discussion might be viewed with some reservation. An automatic self-motivator explains more than has ever been observed. If disparities between perceived events and mental structure were, in fact, automatically motivating, learning would be unremitting and much more unselective than it really is. As a rule, people do not pursue most activities that differ moderately from what they know or can do. Indeed, if they were driven by every moderately discrepant event encountered in their daily lives, they would be rapidly overwhelmed by innumerable imperatives for cognitive change. Effective functioning requires selective deployment of attention and inquiry. A teacher may be motivated by instructional failures to gain a better understanding of how children learn but show little interest in pursuing knowledge about the workings of the internal combustion engine because of mechanical difficulties with a car. Distinguished intellectual accomplishments are gained through a single-mindedness of purpose that disregards the countless puzzlements encountered in other aspects of daily life. When faced with contradictions between facts and their conceptions, people often discount or reinterpret the "facts," rather than change their way of thinking. If they were motivated by an innate drive to know, they should all be highly knowledgeable about the world around them and continually progressing toward even higher levels of reasoning. The evidence does not seem to bear this out.

In the social cognitive view, people function as active agents in their own motivation. Evaluating self-motivation through cognitive comparison requires distinguishing between standards of what one knows and standards of what one desires to know. It is the latter standards, together with perceived self-efficacy, that exert selective influence over which of many activities will be actively pursued. Aspirational standards determine which discrepancies are motivating and which activities people will strive to master. It will be recalled that strength of self-motivation varies curvilinearly with the level of discrepancy between standards and attainments: Relatively easy standards are insufficiently challenging to arouse much interest or effort; moderately difficult ones maintain high effort and produce satisfactions through subgoal achievements; while standards set well beyond a person's reach can be demotivating by fostering discouragement and a sense of inefficacy. It bears noting that self-motivation, although of considerable importance, is only one of several sources of incentives for developing competencies. Cognitive and behavioral skills that enable people to manage their environment are perfected rapidly because of their generalizable value. The insulated cognitivism of the equilibration model, which construes human beings as striving mainly to achieve harmony in thought, minimizes the fact that thought is a tool for guiding effective transactions with the environment. Reasoning skills have a broader purpose than lessening perturbations of the cognitive system. The social origin and social function of cognitive competencies are issues to which we shall return later.

COGNITIVE DEVELOPMENT

The typical changes that occur in the development of cognitive competencies is an issue of considerable interest and debate in developmental psychology. Developmental theorists who subscribe to fixed stage theories portray cognitive development as a succession of typological changes occurring in an invariant sequence of discrete, global modes of thinking. Piagetian theory exemplifies this approach (Piaget, 1950; Piaget & Inhelder, 1969). During the sensory-motor stage, which covers the first two years of life, infants learn perceptual-motor coordinations, that objects in the environment still exist even though out of sight, and that their actions can affect the environment. The next stage, ranging from two to seven years, is characterized by preoperational thought. Language enables children at this stage to use words to represent events, but their thinking is egocentric and is easily swayed by physical appearances. Because they do not understand rules and mental operations, they lack the capability to generalize and classify that requires combining information. In the succeeding stage of concrete operational thinking, spanning ages seven to eleven, children can abstract and generalize from particulars, but their reasoning is still closely tied to concrete events. In the final stage in the developmental sequence, formal operational thinking, normally achieved by age fifteen, although not universally attained, individuals are capable of full abstract, logical reasoning. The characterization of cognitive development within this conceptual framework is rooted in a model of logical structure powered by a cognitive-consistency drive.

Progression from concrete to abstract reasoning certainly characterizes some aspects of cognitive development. However, changes in cognitive functioning are more diversified and require much more than an intrapsychic autoregulator to achieve. Cognitive development encompasses multifaceted developmental sequences that often begin and extend over varying periods of time. Cognitive functioning relies on knowledge structures and cognitive skills for ferreting out relevant information, transforming it for memory representation, and operating on it for selected purposes. Different activities entail different types of knowledge and judgmental rules. Moreover, tasks vary in how heavily they draw on various cognitive skills. Hence, even small changes in the structure of tasks can alter how children with particular cognitive competencies will perform. Knowledge structures and cognitive skills develop over time, but they do not all develop at the same time in the likeness of unitary stages. The modes by which cognitive systems are transformed also vary. Cognitive learning is fostered through tuition, modeling, and performance feedback, rather than confined to the influence of mismatching experiences of unguided action. Most of the cognitive skills and structures used in daily pursuits are cul-tivated socially, rather than transform themselves asocially.

Discrete Global Structures or Specialized Cognitive Competencies

Virtually all theories of cognitive development assume that children become more skilled at abstract reasoning as they grow older. They also share the view that the ability to abstract rules and to manipulate information symbolically predicts the level of intellectual functioning. It is the notion that thinking undergoes discrete global changes that is in dispute and that has come under increasing criticism from several quarters. Some writers question the explanatory value of stages on the grounds that they are not identified independently from the types of intellectual performances they purportedly explain (Brainerd, 1978). Problems of circularity arise when cognitive stages are inferred from styles of thinking and then are invoked as the determinants of similar thinking styles. To demonstrate that concrete thinkers tend to think concretely on related tasks and abstract thinkers tend to think abstractly shows that thinking skills have some generality, but it hardly establishes stage structure as the regulating system of the reasoning performances.

Attempts to verify a stage theory are beset with difficulties unless the theory links stage structures to identifiable conditions that produce them. The causal contribution of the structures can then be tested by varying conditions that create them and measuring whether the accompanying changes in cognitive functioning correspond to what the theory predicts. Unfortunately, Piagetian theory does not lend itself to this dependable form of empirical verification. This is because the determinants of cognitive stages are said to involve intricate interactions between maturational and experiential factors that operate over a long time and are neither specifiable nor systematically producible. Successive modes of thinking will appear spontaneously over time through common experiences, without any need for special environmental conditions. Faced with indefinite and unproducible stage determinants, researchers working within this framework end up inferring cognitive stages from intellectual performances or, more often, simply using age as the indicator of the stage of cognitive development, on the assumption that particular modes of thinking typically manifest themselves at certain ages. Because many factors change with age, considerable ambiguity exists about what exactly is being varied by age grouping and what age trends and correlates reflect.

Psychoanalytic theory provides an earlier example of how postulating unproducible developmental determinants discouraged the type of experimental inquiry that can deepen understanding of the phenomena in question. Consider the psychoanalytic theory of modeling phenomena. In this view, two sets of conditions induce children to adopt adult characteristics (Freud, 1925, 1948). Dependent identification is believed to occur through threatened loss of love which motivates the child to introject parental characteristics. In the defensive form of identification, tailored mainly for boys, Oedipal anxieties about castration for incestuous wishes toward the mother and rivalrous feelings toward the father are reduced by emulating the characteristics of the intimidating father. Based on these two prototypical determinants of modeling, for example, a youngster's emulation of a baseball player would require either a threatened loss of love from the brawny model or an Oedipal entanglement with his spouse. We saw earlier that there are much easier, dependable, and producible ways to promote modeling.

Because neither cathectic bonds nor Oedipal complexes are creatable under controlled conditions, experimental analysis of modeling phenomena were essentially precluded within this theoretical framework. The correlational approaches on which researchers relied were plagued with so many methodological problems that it was difficult to bring empirical evidence to bear on the validity of this theory of modeling (Bandura, 1969b, 1973; Bronfenbrenner, 1958). Only after modeling was conceptualized as governed by producible conditions of theoretical import was a large body of knowledge established regarding the determinants, mediating mechanisms, and diverse effects of modeling. This knowledge guided development of effective modeling procedures for cultivating human competencies (Rosenthal & Bandura, 1978). An experimental approach to cognitive development does not mean that cognitive change can, or must be, compressed into a few hours. Experimental developmental research can study systematically the growth of cognitive competencies as a function of differential conditions applied over an extended period.

Cognitive stages presumably comprise qualitatively different modes of thinking that are uniform within each stage. Higher stages are achieved by transforming lower ones. The assumption of stratified uniformities of thought, however, is at variance with empirical findings. The level of cognitive functioning commonly varies across different domains of content (Feldman, 1980). Because of different experiences and understandings, people think concretely about some matters but abstractly about others. Moreover, their mode of thinking may vary even among different measures of the same cognitive skill. For example, children's conservation judgments of whether quantities remain invariant with changes in shape differ depending on the materials used in the test of conservation (Brown & Desforges, 1979; Uzgiris, 1964). Variations in the level of cognitive functioning cannot spring from a uniform thought structure. Flavell (1978b) summed up this multiformity well when he said, "However much we may wish it were otherwise, human cognitive growth may simply be too contingent, multiform, and heterogeneous—too variegated in developmental mechanisms, routes, and rates—to be accurately categorized by any stage theory of the Piagetian kind" (p. 187).

Another assumption of stage theory is that cognitive changes form an invariant sequence progressing from concrete modes of thinking to abstract forms. Social influences may affect the rate with which changes occur, but they do not alter the order of succession. Almost every theory would agree that understanding of concrete events precedes abstractions about them. Indeed, as Hamlyn (1971) notes, since the development of understanding proceeds from the particular to the abstract, it is inconceivable that this type of sequence could be otherwise, unless one assumes innate endowment of refined ideas. But progression from concrete to abstract is only one of many developmental dimensions embodying cognitive acquisition sequences. Similarly, to characterize developmental progression as a change from simple to complex skills is to say little that is distinctive, because it would be difficult to find a theory that assumes otherwise.

Cognitive functioning involves knowledge, much of it specialized, and cognitive skills for operating on it. Most intellectual activities contain hierarchical sequences in which complex cognitive skills are formed through integration of simpler subskills. This is not simply a cumulative process, because once acquired, knowledge and subskills can enter into a variety of new integrations. Because skills are hierarchically structured, acquisition sequences are necessarily ordered. Writers, for example, cannot compose essays before they learn words. The theoretical question at issue is not hierarchical organization but the nature and source of hierarchical structures: Are they a natural unfolding of modes of thinking, or are they prescribed by the structure of the cognitive activities? Feldman (1980) argues forcefully that it is more fruitful to look for inherent sequentialities in the structure of task domains than in the minds of children.

Different cognitive domains have their own optimal acquisition sequences. Acknowledging the diversity of cognitive functioning promotes psychological analyses of knowledge structures, the judgmental rules they embody, and the differential demands they place on perceptual, representational, organizational, and memorial subprocesses. It is not as though acquisition of formal operational thinking in the adolescent years—the endstate of cognitive development in Piagetian theory—ensures intellectual achievements, whatever forms they might take. In fact, Piagetian cognitive stages are poor predictors of cognitive functioning in adults (Tumblin & Gholson, 1981). Stratification by cognitive stages does not help much in predicting adult attainments on cognitive tasks, and there is much variability in attainments among individuals categorized as being within the same cognitive stage.

The multiplicity of developmental sequences and their variable temporal patterning are amply documented in research on cognitive functioning conducted within the life-span framework (Baltes, 1982; Schaie, 1979). Over the course of life, some forms of cognitive functioning increase, others decline, and still others remain relatively stable. This variation in cognitive functioning is more profoundly affected by social factors than by biological ageing, until very old age when physical systems begin to give out. An expanded perspective toward cognitive development gives salience to many important, but neglected, dimensions of cognitive functioning as they manifest themselves in the growth of occupational, avocational, and social competencies. These cognitive attainments require the acquisition of domain-specific knowledge coupled with specialized judgmental rules. The rules of reasoning that children develop to judge conservation of quantities cannot tell us much about how physicians develop expertise in diagnostic reasoning. There are commonalities in the subprocesses of rule acquisition and problem-solving reasoning, but there is no single set of omnibus rules that represents the knowledge of diverse domains.

Social Determinants of Cognitive Development.

The influence of social factors in the development of cognitive competencies receives little attention in Piagetian theorizing and research. This omission is understandable, considering that the theory, following as it does a biological growth model, depicts cognitive change as largely dependent on maturational organization aided by the information ensuing from common activities, but otherwise requiring little in the way of specialized experiences to materialize. As a result, the theory says comparatively little about specific determinants of cognitive stages but much about how cognitive stages reign over intellectual functioning.

In the view of Piagetian developmentalists, maturational factors and self-discovery experiences, occurring when children are ready to understand them, produce cognitive growth. Their thinking is not changeable to any significant degree through specialized instruction (Duckworth, 1979). Rather, they must discover for themselves that their beliefs are discrepant with the results of their actions and resolve the cognitive conflict by reorganizing their thinking. This process of change is thus largely an intrapsychic affair in which social influence plays, at best, a minor role. The views of others, if perceived as divergent, may stir cognitive conflict, but they do not alter styles of thinking.

Within the social cognitive perspective, social factors play an influential role in cognitive development, and the pursuit of competence is entrusted to a varied array of motivators, rather than solely to the drive of cognitive perturbations. The conditional dependence between certain events is naturally so highly structured that it is clearly evinced across an unusually wide range of circumstances. Understanding of these types of relationships in the physical world can be gained through repeated experiences without requiring social mediation. Because virtually all objects when dropped will fall on every occasion in every culture, such invariant regularity quickly produces almost universal comprehension of terrestial gravitation. But, as Feldman (1980) explains at some length, acquisition of much of the knowledge that people need to function competently in their various occupational, avocational, and social pursuits depends to a considerable extent on specialized learning conditions, not on impersonal universal ones. Most of this valuable information is authored and imparted socially. For example, the models who figure prominently in children's lives do not merely cause cognitive perturbations. They serve as indispensable sources of knowledge that contribute to what and how children think about different matters. Children's intellectual self-development would be stunted if they could not draw on this heritage of knowledge in each realm of functioning and instead had to rediscover bits of it through perturbations of their own activity.

Efforts have been made to determine whether modeling reasoning skills that children lack changes their level of reasoning by imparting knowledge or by triggering cognitive conflict which sets in motion changes in thinking to resolve the incongruities. Many of these studies are concerned with the principle of conservation, which reflects a child's ability to recognize that a given property remains the same despite external changes that make it look different (e.g., the amount of water is the same regardless of whether it is poured into a short, wide beaker or into a tall, narrow one). Young children tend to judge things on the basis of appearance. Modeling accurate reasoning produces equivalent cognitive change in children, irrespective of whether or not things are added to heighten the cognitive conflict (Charbonneau & Robert, 1977; Lefebrve-Pinard & Reid, 1980). Modeling that effectively conveys abstract rules of judgment improves children's reasoning skills, regardless of how much they may be internally conflicted (Zimmerman & Blom,

1983). These types of findings suggest that the acquisition of cognitive skills is affected more by the amount of knowledge imparted than by internal disequilibrium. People do not have to wait until they feel inner conflict to seek knowledge and to improve their cognitive skills. They develop competencies for the anticipated social benefits, for the control over life events that skills afford, and for the fulfillment of internal standards, as well as for the resolution of perplexities.

Ample documentation has been provided that abstract rules of reasoning through modeling or direct tuition enhance the cognitive skills of children who allegedly have not reached the stage of readiness to profit from such social experiences (Brainerd, 1978; Robert, 1981; Rosenthal & Zimmerman, 1978). Lest these findings be dismissed as evidence of mere mimicry, it should be noted that the cognitive performances meet stringent criteria of genuine understanding. Children make accurate judgments, they explain the reasons for their judgments, they apply their reasoning skills to new or unfamiliar tasks embodying the rule of reasoning, and they retain their acquired competencies over time. Moreover, the cognitive performances of children who master abstract rules of reasoning through modeling are indistinguishable from those who acquire them spontaneously in the course of their everyday experiences (Kaneko, Tanaka, & Matsui, 1983; Sullivan, 1967). This growing body of evidence is not easily dismissable by tautological arguments that cognitive change is a slow process, so if instructive influence produces cognitive changes in a short time, the changes must not be "genuine." One can, of course, point to circumstances where superficial influences produce circumscribed change. But it is studies providing a more substantial didactic fare that speak most persuasively to the issue of whether reasoning skills can be socially cultivated.

Given the evidence for social determination of cognitive functioning, care must be taken that faulty performances not be attributed too readily to cognitive deficiencies.

The ease with which cognitive change is achieved reflects the adequacy of the instruction as well as the capabilities of the learners. Improved methods of instruction, which give full consideration to the subprocesses governing learning, enhance the rate with which cognitive skills are acquired. This is not to imply that children of any age can be taught everything. All learning requires certain prior capabilities. The issue in question is whether the requisites for cognitive change, which all theories acknowledge, are specialized cognitive skills or graded cognitive structures.

Piagetian developmentalists subscribe to the view that cognitive change requires maturation and cumulative spontaneous experiences and thus takes a long time. Hence, cognitive competencies developed through specialized instruction tend to be regarded as suspect, even though the cognitive feats meet the exacting criteria of genuine understanding. Research designed to gain understanding of children's learning potential and the subprocesses of cognitive functioning is often pejoratively labeled as the "American" preoccupation with accelerating change. In fact, the acquisition of cognitive competencies is not studied experimentally for the pragmatic purpose of rushing children through "stages" but to advance knowledge of the determinants and processes of cognitive functioning.

Portraying cognitive development as spontaneous self-discovery moving toward ever higher stages of intellect arouses appealing imagery of socially unfettered exploration. However, the constraining nature of stage doctrines is rarely given much thought. Such approaches cast children into prefixed types, thus lending themselves readily to social stereotyping by stage classification. After children have been so categorized, they tend to be viewed in terms of the category stereotype, rather than by the individuality of their knowledge and cognitive skills. As a result, classification practices often do more harm than good.

Theories and social practices free of typological stage thinking explore the potentialities for cognitive development and the diversity of cognitive functioning, while keeping the cognitive limitations and uniformities in proper perspective. Through guided learning, children can master the conceptual tools needed to gain new knowledge and to deal intelligently with the varied situations they encounter in their everyday life. When cultivation of cognitive competencies through instructive means is misrepresented as rushing children through cognitive stages, guided learning takes on a pernicious connotation. Stage theories lend themselves to excusing weak instructional programs that are supposed to foster intellectual development. Deficiencies in cognitive learning become readily attributable to lack of "cognitive readiness." As Sullivan (1969) has observed, rather than creating environments conducive to learning, some adherents of stage doctrines are inclined to wait for children to become ready for learning. For many it can be a long wait.

Piagetian theory emphasizes spontaneous learning by doing, tailoring contents to the constraints of cognitive readiness, and eschewing socially guided learning. But otherwise it does not offer much in the way of explicit educational prescriptions. When results obtained by different instructional approaches are compared, the Piagetian claims for the superiority of action-based learning are not borne out (Brainerd, 1978; Lawton & Hooper, 1978). However, the issue of their relative efficacy is not all that easily resolvable empirically, because the measures of intellectual change can be challenged as inadequately reflecting critical cognitive functions, and the purity of the instructional programs can be disputed. It is easy to polarize positions in theoretical discourse but difficult to sustain rigidly, in practice, the stance that knowledge is acquirable through the effects of action but unteachable by demonstration and other expository means. In actual practice, socially guided learning encourages self-directed inquiry, and so-called spontaneous self-discovery inevitably draws on many didactic aids. Cognitive development is thus exten-

sively fostered by the many determinants and mechanisms already reviewed at length which are commonly enlisted in programs based on different theoretical allegiances.

MORAL JUDGMENT

The domain of moral reasoning further illustrates the different perspectives of stage theory and social cognitive theory toward cognitive development. Stage theorists assume that different types of moral thinking appear as integrated wholes in discontinuous stages forming an invariant sequence. Piaget (1948) favors a developmental sequence progressing from moral realism, in which rules are seen as unchangeable and conduct is judged in terms of damage done, to relativistic morality, in which conduct is judged primarily by the performer's intentions. In the latter stage, well-intentioned acts that produce much harm are viewed as less reprehensible than ill-intentioned acts that cause little harm. Moral absolutism stems from unquestioning acceptance of adult prescripts and the egocentric outlook of young children, and moral relativism develops from increasing personal experiences and reciprocal relationships with peers.

Kohlberg (1969, 1976) postulates a six-stage sequential typology beginning with punishment-based obedience, evolving through instrumental hedonism, approval-seeking conformity, respect for authority, contractual legalistic observance, and culminating in principled morality based on standards of justice. Because the stages constitute a fixed developmental sequence, individuals cannot learn a given form of moral judgment without first acquiring each of the preceding modes in order. The presumption is that exposures to moral reasoning that are too discrepant from one's dominant stage have little impact because they are insufficiently understood to activate any changes. Judgmental standards of lesser complexity are similarly rejected because they have already been displaced in attaining more advanced forms of thinking. Views that diverge slightly above one's stage presumably create the necessary cognitive disequilibrium in observers, which is reduced by adopting the higher stage of moral reasoning.

A universal, although not inborn, latent preference for higher modes of thinking is posited to explain why people do not preserve their equilibrium simply by adhering to their own opinions and rejecting conflicting ones (Rest, Turiel, & Kohlberg, 1969). What makes higher stage reasoning morally superior is not entirely clear. In thoughtful reviews of the stage theory of morality, Locke (1979, 1980) identifies and refutes alternative bases of hierarchical superiority. It is not that higher stages of reasoning are cognitively superior because, in most of their judgments, people do not use the highest mode of thinking they understand and most prefer. On the matter of stage progression, if people are actuated by an inherent drive for higher ways of moral thinking, it is puzzling why they rarely adopt the uppermost level as their dominant mode, even though they comprehend it (Rest, 1973). It is similarly arguable that higher stage reasons are morally superior. By what logical reasoning is a morality rooted in law and order (Stage 4) morally superior to one relying on social regard and concern for others (Stage 3)? Oppressed minorities and those subjected to the rule of apartheid would not think so. Nor would writers who argue that responsibility and concern for others should be the guiding rule of morality (Gilligan, 1982).

Higher stage reasoning cannot be functionally superior because stages provide the rationale for supporting either side of a moral issue, but they do not prescribe particular solutions. Developmental stages determine the reasons given for actions, not what actions should be taken. Different modes of thinking can justify stealing, cheating on income taxes, and military bombing of foes. Immorality can thus be served as well, or better, by sophisticated reasoning as by simpler reasoning. Indeed, the destructive social policies advocated by enlightened graduates of renowned academies is better explained by the social dynamics of group thinking than by the collective level of moral maturity (Janis, 1972). When people reason about moral conflicts they commonly face in their environment, Kohlberg and his associates find that moral reasoning is more a function of the social influences operating in the situation than of persons' stages of moral competence (Higgins, Power, & Kohlberg, 1984).

Kohlberg (1971a) underscores the point that his hierarchical stages of reasoning are concerned with form, not content. However, the end point of moral reasoning, Stage 6, is heavily infused with values such as justice, equality, and respect. Unlike the preceding stages, where it is acknowledged that a given mode of thinking can support either side of a moral issue, at the endpoint stage, thought is said to certify what courses of action are morally right. Because movement through the stages is said to be achieved naturally by the sway of reasoning, empirical "is" thus becomes philosophical "ought." However, the evidence for the cultural universality of the "is" has not gone uncontested (Locke, 1979; Simpson, 1974). Other theorists argue that Kohlberg's moral prescriptions reflect personal preferences, rather than objective standards or the dictates of reason (Shweder, 1982). Some moral philosophers, who can hardly be faulted for lacking principled reasoning, regard the principle of justice as only one among other moral principles that either compete for the role of chief yardstick of morality or share a pluralistic system of judgment (Carter, 1980; Codd, 1977). If, however, principled reasoning is defined as using justice as the supreme judgmental rule, it becomes a conceptual truth incapable of empirical disproof (Peters, 1971). The common finding is that adults comprehend different moral principles but use them selectively depending on circumstances and the domain of functioning. Moral development produces multiform moral thinking, rather than following a single developmental track.

Empirical analyses of Kohlberg's theory generally rely on a test that includes only a few moral dilemmas sampling a narrow range of moral conflicts. To contend that a few sketchy items verify moral truths is to invest a simple assessment tool with extraordinarily revelatory power. A test that can offer only a limited glimpse of moral predicaments may provide a shaky empirical basis on which to found a theory of morality or to classify people into moral types. A person's propensity for principled moral reasoning will vary depending on the information included in the depicted moral conflicts. For example, the moral dilemmas devised by Kohlberg are ambiguous about the likely consequences of transgressive behavior. When information about different types of consequences are added to the dilemmas, as the severity of consequences increases, people favor self-interest over principled reasoning (Sobesky, 1983). How often people offer principled solutions for moral conflicts may partly reflect the gravity of the consequences they happen to imagine for the sketchy portrayals, rather than their competence for principled reasoning.

Skeletonized abstract principles do not provide much guidance for judgment or action until they are fleshed out with relevant details that are inevitably laden with evaluative biases. For purposes of illustration, consider the example given by Peters (1971) on judging what is just payment for service rendered under a given set of circumstances. The abstract principle of justness does not yield a uniform answer. For instance, what is a just fee for a surgeon? Different people can arrive at different judgments from the same principle of justness, depending on what factors they consider relevant and how they weigh them (e.g., the amount and expense of past training required, operating costs, the effort and risks involved, the surgeon's financial needs, the benefits to patients, and the patients' financial status). The judgmental thicket becomes even more ensnarled if remuneration for other occupations, such as poorly paid teachers and exhorbitantly paid superstar singers, is considered.

Given the prescriptive ambiguity of abstract principles, it is not surprising that cognitively facile people can find ways to serve their self-interests under the cloak of justice or social contract. The advantaged members of a society have considerable say in how justice is defined at the operational level. If the view that form and content of thought are independent is consistently applied, then principled reasoning can be used to support destructive acts, as well as humane ones. To pit petty theft against human life, as in the oft-quoted conflict of the husband faced with stealing a drug to cure his wife's cancer, is not all that much of a dilemma. The operation of principled reasoning would be more interestingly revealed were one to pit the taking of a human life, as in the assassination of a Hitler to prevent the massacre of countless human beings. Kohlberg's (1971b) prescriptive stance—that moral education in the classroom should consist of moving children through the stages of moral reasoning, even regardless of parental wishes—draws understandably heavy fire, as does the claim that the moral viewpoint of his theory represents moral rightness (Aron, 1977; Wonderly & Kupfersmid, 1980).

A major problem with sequential typologies is that people hardly ever fit them. Because differing circumstances call for different judgments and actions, unvarying judgment is a rarity. A person's moral judgments typically rely on reasoning from several different "moral standards," rather than being based on only one type of moral standard. Stage theorists classify people into types according to their model form of reasoning, although they usually display co-existing mixtures of reasoning that span several stages. Most people get categorized as being in varying degrees of transition between stages. People not only display substantial variability in their moral reasoning at any given period, but many years elapse from the time they first adopt a new standard of morality to the time when they come to use it as a preferred one (Colby, Kohlberg, Gibbs, & Lieberman, 1983). Fischer (1983) comments that such evidence is at variance with stage theory, which depicts changes in thinking as occurring by pervasive transformations of preceding modes of thought. Rather than exhibiting wholistic reorganization of their moral thinking, people gradually adopt new moral standards, eventually discard simpler ones, and draw from among a co-existing set of standards in judging different moral predicaments.

One might question the practice of treating reasoning that draws on more than one moral standard as evidence of moral immaturity evolving toward justness as the ultimate standard of morality. Different moral standards are not necessarily contradictory. Hence, adoption of a certain standard need not require jettisoning another. To judge the morality of conduct by a system of complimentary standards, such as justness and compassion, reflects a high level of moral reasoning, rather than transitional immaturity in thinking. Indeed, Peters (1966) argues that justice is necessary but not sufficient for a moral system. He points out that people can be brutal but entirely impartial or just in their brutality. A society that subscribes to standards of both justness and compassion will be more humane than a society concerned solely with justness.

Socialization of Moral Judgment

There are some universal features to the socialization of standards of conduct. People vary in what they teach, model, and sanction with children of differing ages. At first, guidance of behavior is necessarily external and highly concrete. To discourage hazardous conduct in children who do not understand speech, parents must rely on physical guidance. They structure situations physically to reduce the likelihood of problem behavior, such as injurious aggression, and should it arise they try to check it by offer-ing competing activities or by disciplinary action. Sometimes they pair simple verbal prohibitions with physical intervention, so that eventually a "no" alone will suffice as a restrainer. As children mature, social sanctions increasingly replace physical ones as influential guides for how to behave in different situations. Parents and other adults explain standards of conduct and the reasons for them. Social sanctions that disapprove transgressive acts and commend valued conduct add substance to the standards. It is not long before children learn to discriminate between approved and disapproved forms of conduct and to regulate their actions on the basis of anticipated social consequences.

Parents cannot always be present to guide their children's behavior. Successful socialization requires gradual substitution of symbolic and internal controls for external sanctions and demands. The mechanisms by which social and cognitive factors affect the development of internal standards have been addressed in an earlier chapter and will not be reviewed here. After individuals adopt standards of conduct, their self-demands and self-respect serve as major guides and deterrents.

As the nature and seriousness of possible transgressions change with age, parents and other significant adults in the child's life add new aspects to the moral persuasion. For example, they do not appeal to legal arguments when handling preschoolers' misconduct, but they do explain legal codes and penalties to preadolescents to influence future behavior that can have serious legal consequences. It is hardly surprising that adolescents are more likely than young children to consider legalities in their reasoning about transgressive acts.

That parents react differently to their children's misconduct at different ages is corroborated by Denney and Duffy (1974). They measured the responses of parents and their children to simulated transgressions scored according to Kohlberg's stage designations. Parents increase their level of moral reasoning as their children get older.

Even when variations in age are controlled, the more abstract the parent's moral reasons in dealing with misconduct, the higher is their children's level of moral reasoning. Parent-child congruence in the rules used to judge the morality of transgressive conduct is further corroborated by Leon (1984). Mothers differ in how they integrate information into moral judgments, ranging from a simple unidimensional rule based solely on damage, to a composite linear rule combining intent and damage, to a more complicated nonlinear rule that weighs damage differentially depending on intent. The types of judgmental rules young boys employ are much like those of their mothers in form and complexity. Parents facilitate discernment of their moral rules not only by modeling moral judgments but also by explaining in disciplinary contexts the factors on which they base their judgments.

Adoption of internal standards does not necessarily encompass every domain of activity or completely supplant other forms of control. Even the most principled individuals may, in some domains and under some circumstances, regulate their behavior mainly by anticipated social consequences. Moreover, during the course of development, children learn how to get around moral consequences of culpable behavior that brings personal benefits. They discover that they can reduce the likelihood of reprimands by invoking extenuating circumstances for their misdeeds (Bandura & Walters, 1959; Sears, Maccoby, & Levin, 1957). As a result, different types of vindications become salient factors in moral judgments. Even very young children are quite skilled in using mitigating factors to excuse harmdoing (Darley, Klosson, & Zanna, 1978). Later they learn to weaken, if not completely avoid, self-censure for reprehensible conduct by invoking self-exonerating justifications. A theory of moral reasoning must, therefore, be concerned as well with how cognitive processes can make the immoral inconsequential or even moral.

Parents, of course, are not the exclusive source of children's standards of moral judgments and conduct. Other adults, peers, and symbolic models, who are by no means uniform in their moral perspectives, play influential roles as well. Children exposed to adult and peer models who exemplify conflicting standards adopt different standards of conduct than if adults alone set the standard or if adults and peer models subscribe to the same moral standards (Bandura, Grusec, & Menlove, 1967a; Brody & Henderson, 1977). To complicate matters further, the standards acquired through modeling are affected by variations in the judgments displayed by the same model over time and by discrepancies between what models practice and what they preach (Bryan & Walbek, 1970). Modeled moral standards are more readily discerned and adopted if a model's judgments are guided by a common standard than if they follow different standards (Harvey & Liebert, 1979). To the developing child, televised modeling, which dramatizes a vast range of moral conflicts that transcend viewers' immediate social realities, constitutes another integral part of social learning. The values modeled in print can similarly impart moral standards for judging conduct (Walker & Richards, 1976). Symbolic modeling influences the development of moral judgments by what it portrays as acceptable or reprehensible conduct and by the sanctions and justifications applied to it.

As the preceding comments indicate, with a child's increasing age, social practices are altered to promote developmental changes in how conduct is judged and regulated. A varied array of interacting societal influences contribute to the development of moral perspectives. To attribute changes in moral judgment chiefly to internal reorganization of thought by stage-regulated mental perturbations for modifications channeled by latent preferences for higher moral stages is to make light of the prominent role social influences play in cultivating moral standards and commitments. It is not that stage theory takes no notice of social factors. It does, but it grants them a narrow function—the views of others serve mainly as external perturbators for autoregulated change. In fact, they do much more. People impart moral standards and provide a great deal of social support for moral commitments.

Developmental trends obviously exist in moral reasoning and judgment, as they do in everything else, but the conditions of social learning are much too varied to produce uniform moral types. Even at the more advanced levels, some behaviors come under the rule of law, others under social sanctions, and still others under personal sanctions. When statistical controls for other causal factors are not applied, developmental changes, which have been attributed to stagelike unfolding or moral modes of thought, may reflect changes in general intelligence, information-processing skills, educational level, and socialization practices with which moral reasoning correlates (Kay, 1982). Evidence of age trends, which every theory predicts, is often accepted as validating stage theories of morality. The validity of stage propositions, however, demands much more than age trends: They assume (1) that there is uniformty of judgment when a person is at any given stage, (2) that a person cannot evaluate conduct in terms of a given moral principle without first adopting a series of preceding principles, and (3) that attainment of a given judgmental principle replaces preceding modes of thought by transforming them. These presumptions do not fare well when compared to empirical findings.

Social Modification of Moral Standards

Moral reasoning involves interpreting available information in moral predicaments in accordance with personal standards for evaluating the rightness or wrongness of conduct. The standards for moral reasoning are much more amenable to social influence than stage theories would lead one to expect. Numerous studies have been conducted in which children with differing moral perspectives are exposed to divergent views of models who use either malevolent intentions or severity of harm as the standard for judging the reprehensibility of conduct. Such modeling influences alter how heavily children weigh intentions and harm when they judge transgressive acts: Children who had previously judged wrongdoing mainly by intentions judge conduct by the harm caused; and those who previously evaluated wrongdoing by the amount of harm that was caused adopt intentions as the principal indicant of reprehensibility (Bandura & McDonald, 1963; Cowan, Langer, Heavenrich, & Nathanson, 1969; Le Furgy & Woloshin, 1969). These altered moral perspectives are reflected in moral reasoning, as well as in the judgments made, they generalize across transgressive situations and different patterns of intentions and damages, and they endure over time (Dorr & Fey, 1974; Schleifer & Douglas, 1973). Although the modeled perspectives of both adults and peers are persuasive, the moral reasoning of adults is usually the more influential (Brody & Henderson, 1977; Dorr & Fey, 1974).

Efforts aimed at altering moral reasoning have relied heavily on the influence of example. Exposure to others modeling an opposing view can alter moral judgments in several ways. By favoring certain judgmental standards, models call attention to the factors the standards embody. The views models express also provide supporting justifications for reweighing various factors in making decisions about the wrongness of certain acts. Things that were regarded as minor may become important and *vice versa*. In areas of morality, for which society places a premium on socially acceptable attitudes, public opinions may differ substantially from those that are privately held. Expression of moral convictions by models provides the social sanctions for others to voice similar opinions. Modeling of opposing viewpoints can thus effect changes in moral judgments through attentional, cognitive, and disinhibitory mechanisms.

As in other areas of functioning, modeling influences do not invariably alter moral reasoning. The lack of effects can result from either comprehension deficits or performance preferences. People cannot be influenced much by modeled opinions if they do not understand them. Preexisting knowledge and cognitive skills place limits on what can be learned from brief exposure to opposing opinions. There is substantial difference, however, between making social influence dependent on cognitive processing skills and making it dependent on concatenated unitary thought.

When models voice opinions, they transmit their ideas and preferences. But modeling does not itself guarantee that the views so learned will be articulated by the learner. Where apparent uninfluenceability reflects performance preferences, modeled standards have been learned but are simply not expressed because they are personally or socially disfavored. The ease with which judgmental standards can be shifted in one direction or another depends upon the conceptual skills they require and the consequences they generate. In addition, judgmental standards vary in how easily they can be discerned, which affects the facility with which they can be learned. It is much easier to recognize damage than to infer the historical antecedents or intentions of actions. When information about intentions is provided in ways that aid its recall, young children use the intentions of wrongdoers to judge culpability (Austin, Ruble, & Trabasso, 1977). The claim, sometimes attributed to social learning theory, that different moral standards are equally modifiable has no foundation. Some judgmental changes are obviously more difficult to achieve than others. It might also be noted in passing that, contrary to what is sometimes alleged (Murray, 1983), social learning theory has never proposed the implausible assumption that erroneous reasoning in matters of fact is just as producible by social influence as accurate reasoning. Once children have learned to reason in accord with evident fact (e.g., changing the shape of a clay ball does not change its mass), they will not revert to fallacious reasoning by exposure to arguments they know to be untrue.

Some efforts have been made to test the equilibration mechanism of developmental change within Kohlberg's framework by exposing children to moral arguments that increasingly diverge from the views children already hold. In the initial investigations of stage constraints on moral change, children were presented with a few hypothetical moral dilemmas (e.g., stealing a drug to save a wife dying of cancer), and they were given conflicting moral advice by persons using reasons from different stages (Rest, Turiel, & Kohlberg, 1969; Turiel, 1966). The investigators report that children reject modeled opinions below their dominant mode of thinking, are unaffected by those that are too advanced, but are likely to adopt modeled views one stage above their own.

Subsequent research indicates that the restricted changeability of moral reasoning may lie more in the weakness of the modeling influence used than in constraints of the child's stage. One can easily fail to produce cognitive changes by using weak influences. Theories predicting null results should apply social influences repeatedly in their most powerful form. Children do not remember the essential details of moral situations presented to them briefly, but they show good recall with greater exposure (Austin, Ruble, & Trabasso, 1977). Fleeting information that goes by unrecognized or unrecalled cannot affect thinking. In the abovementioned studies, not only is the modeling influence unusually brief, but the models disagree in their views by advocating opposing solutions. Although results are not entirely uniform (Walker, 1983), models who are consistent in how they judge different moral predicaments generally have greater impact on children's moral reasoning than models who disagree with each other (Brody & Henderson, 1977; Keasey, 1973). When the modeled views are consistent, children's moral perspectives are changed more by exposure to moral reasoning two stages above their own than by reasoning one stage more advanced (Arbuthnot, 1975; Matefy & Acksen, 1976). These findings are in accordance with substantial evidence in social psychology showing that the more discrepant supportive reasoning is from one's own views, the more one's attitudes change (McGuire, 1969). Immaturity, of course, places some limits on the power of discrepant influences. Young children cannot be influenced by reasoning so advanced that it is completely incomprehensible to them.

Children also adopt modeled modes of reasoning labeled as more primitive in the stage hierarchy, but the findings are mixed on how well they adhere to them over time. Here, too, the variable adherence may reflect more how persuasively modeling is used than stage constraints. The views of a lone model, or one who disagrees, can be easily discounted as atypical. It is consensual multiple modeling that carries the strong persuasive impact necessary to override preexisting orientations. Viewers are likely to conclude that if everyone firmly believes something, there must be some truth to it. It could be argued that judging by the intentionality of actions does not necessarily represent a higher level of reasoning. In judging morality of nuclear warfare, for example, the awesome destructiveness of a nuclear attack should be the overriding consideration, rather than intentions of the launchers of such attacks. To give utmost priority to the devastating consequences of a nuclear strike would hardly be considered "regressive" or "primitive" thinking. Rather, to judge as moral well-intended conduct that can destroy much of the planet would reflect blind reverence for intention and personal principle.

Evidence that there are some age trends in moral judgment, that children fail to adopt standards they do not fully comprehend or about which there is disagreement, and that they are disinclined to stick to views considered immature for their age can be adequately explained without requiring elaborate stage propositions.

Evidence that moral reasoning can be changed by exposure to modes of thinking that invert or skip stages is at variance with the contention of stage theory that, to alter how one thinks about moral issues, one has to pass through an invariant sequence of stages, each displacing lower ones along the way from which there can be no return. Acknowledging the intraindividual diversity of moral reasoning, some stage theorists (Rest, 1975) have redefined stage progression as a shifting distribution of mixed modes of thinking that are affected by many environmental factors. Such a view reduces the mismatch between the theoretical conception and the actuality. But it raises the issue of what purpose is served by adhering to a stage doctrine stripped of its major defining properties of change by structural displacement, steplike discontinuity, uniformity of cognitive structure, and judgment unarbitrated by either the situational factors or the domain of activity? If stage progression is recast as a multiform, gradualistic process cultivated by environmental influences, such a model differs little from developmental theories that do not invoke stages.

Apparent deficiencies in moral reasoning, often attributed to cognitive limitations or insensitivity to certain moral issues, have also been shown to depend partly on how moral thought is assessed (Chandler, Greenspan, & Barenboim, 1973; Gutkin, 1972; Hatano, 1970; Leming, 1978). The same individuals express different types of moral judgments depending on how morally relevant factors are presented: whether children judge verbal accounts or behavioral portrayals of transgression, whether they judge common or outlandish moral conflicts, whether they reveal their moral orientations in abstract opinions or in the severity of the sanctions they apply to different acts, and whether they judge the transgressive acts of others or give moral reasons for how they would behave if faced with similar moral dilemmas. The view that stages constrain people to think in a uniform way receives little support in the notable variability of moral thinking, even with small changes in how moral conflicts are presented and how judgments are rendered.

Moral Judgment as Application of Multidimensional Rules

In the social cognitive view, moral thinking is a process in which multidimensional rules or standards are used to judge conduct. Situations with moral implications contain many decisional ingredients that not only vary in importance but may be given lesser or greater weight depending upon the particular constellation of events in a given moral predicament. Among the many factors that enter into judging the reprehensibility of conduct are the characteristics of the wrongdoers, such as their age, sex, ethnic and social status; the nature of the transgression; the contexts in which the conduct is performed and the perceived situational and personal motivators for it; the immediate and long-range consequences of the action; whether it produces personal injury or property damage; whether it is directed at faceless agencies and corporations or at individuals; the characteristics of the victims and their perceived blameworthiness. In dealing with moral dilemmas people must extract, weigh, and integrate the morally relevant information in the situations confronting them.

Moral rules or standards of conduct are fashioned from varied social sources, including precepts, evaluative social reactions, and models of moral commitments. From such diverse experiences people learn which factors are morally relevant and how much weight to attach to them. Factors that are weighed heavily under some combinations of circumstances may be disregarded or considered of lesser import under a different set of conditions. With increasing experience and cognitive competence, moral judgments change from single-dimensional rules to multidimensional and configural rules of conduct.

Researchers who approach moral thinking as a process of information integration have studied the rules by which children weigh and combine information in making moral judgments (Lane & Anderson, 1976; Leon, 1980). When presented with situations varying in degree of maliciousness and harm, children do not reason dichotomously, that is, using harm when young and intention when older. Rather, they apply varied integration rules in which the different factors are combined additively, multiplicatively, or configurally. However, additive rules seem to predominate. Children at all ages use both intention and harm in forming their judgments, with developmental changes in the weight given these factors being gradual rather than stagelike (Grueneich, 1982; Surber, 1977). Detailed analysis of the rules people apply to information containing many factors can clarify better the processes governing moral judgment than can global attributional analyses of whether outcomes are attributed to personal causation or to external circumstances.

More work remains to be done on how people deal with large sets of morally relevant factors, how social influences alter the weight they give to different factors, and what types of combinatorial rules they use. We noted earlier that humans are not all that adept at integrating diverse information. As in other judgmental domains, when faced with complexities, most people probably fall back on judgmental heuristics that give too much weight to a few moral factors while ignoring other relevant ones. Consistent social feedback can produce lasting changes in the rules used to judge the morality of action (Schleifer & Douglas, 1973). However, in everyday life social consensus on morality is difficult to come by, thus creating ambiguity about the correctness of judgment. In the absence of consistent feedback, reliance on convenient heuristics may become routinized to the point where moral judgments are rendered without giving much thought to individuating features of moral situations. The susceptibility of moral judgment to change depends in part on the effects of the actions it fosters. People alter what they think by experiencing the social effects of their actions.

Relation between Moral Reasoning and Conduct

An issue that has received surprisingly little attention is the relationship between moral reasoning and moral conduct. The study of moral reasoning would be of limited interest if people's moral codes and thoughts had no effect on how they behaved. In the stage theory of moral maturity, the structure of moral thought is not linked to particular conduct. This is because each level of moral reasoning can be used to support or to disavow transgressive behavior. People may act prosocially or transgressively out of mutual obligation, for social approval, for duty to the social order, or for reasons of principle. A person's level of moral development may indicate the types of reasons likely to be most persuasive to that person, but it does not ensure any particular kind of conduct.

The implications for human conduct of the stage theory of moral maturity are difficult to test empirically because conflicting claims are made about how moral reasoning is linked to behavior. On the one hand, it is contended that the level of moral reasoning does not sponsor a certain kind of behavior (Kohlberg, 1971a). Hence, in studies designed to alter moral perspectives through exposure to moral argument, the same level of reasoning is used, for example, for and against stealing (Rest, Turiel, & Kohlberg, 1969). On the other hand, a positive relationship is claimed between level of moral reasoning and moral conduct—the higher the moral reasoning, the more likely is moral conduct, and the greater is the consistency between moral judgment and conduct (Kohlberg & Candee, 1984).

Studies on whether stages of moral reasoning are linked to characteristic types of conduct are inconsistent in their findings (Blasi, 1980; Kurtines & Greif, 1974). Some researchers report that moral conduct is related to the level of moral reasoning, but others have failed to find such a relationship. Some of the studies routinely cited as corroborating such a link have not withstood replication. Others are seen under close scrutiny as contradicting it or as uninterpretable because of methodological deficiencies (Kupfersmid & Wonderly, 1980). Moreover, relationships may disappear when controls are applied for other differences between persons at varying levels of moral reasoning, such as general intelligence (Rushton, 1975).

Efforts to verify the link between moral thought and action have raised disputes about the designation of moral conduct. Kohlberg and Candee (1984) argue that it is performers' intentions that define their actions as moral or immoral. If the morality of conduct is defined by the intentions voiced by transgressors, then most behavior that violates the moral codes of society will come out laundered as righteous. People can easily find moral reasons to redefine their misdeeds as, in reality, well-intentioned acts. They become more adept at self-serving justifications as they gain cognitive facility. Presumed intent always enters in as one factor in the social labeling of behavior (Bandura, 1973), but intention is never used as the sole definer of conduct. A robber who had a good intent would not thereby transform robbery into nonrobbery. A theory of morality must explain the determinants and the mechanisms governing transgressive conduct, not only how perpetrators justify it. This requires a broader conception of morality than is provided by a rationalistic approach cast in terms of skill in abstract reasoning.

In social cognitive theory, how moral thought affects conduct is not entirely an intrapsychic affair. Rather, it involves a reciprocality of influence between thought, conduct, and social factors. People are ordinarily deterred by anticipatory self-censure from engaging in behavior that violates their moral principles. This process of self-regulation, which involves moral standards, judgments, and self-generated affective consequences, operates interactively within a network of social influences. Under social circumstances in which transgressive behavior cannot easily be excusable by oneself, actions are likely to be congruent with moral standards. But exonerative moral reasoning and social circumstances can weaken internal control. People display different levels of injurious behavior and offer different types of moral reasons for it, depending on whether they find themselves in social situations that are conducive to humane or to hurtful conduct (Bandura, Underwood, & Fromson, 1975).

Because almost any conduct can be morally justified, the same moral principles can support different actions, and the same actions can be championed on the basis of different moral principles. However, moral justification is only one of many mechanisms that affect the operation of moral standards. The preceding chapter reviewed at length how the self-regulation of moral conduct is weakened or nullified by psychosocial mechanisms that disengage moral thought from action. These include, in addition to moral justification of immorality, linguistic obfuscations, social arrangements that obscure personal agency and the harm actions cause, and social depersonalization of others. Under such circumstances even normally considerate people may behave in ways that violate their own moral principles.

LANGUAGE DEVELOPMENT

A great deal of human thought is linguistically based. Hence, the processes by which language develops are of major interest. Initially, children acquire knowledge about objects and about the relationships between them through nonlinguistic processing of direct and vicarious experience. Such understanding helps to impart meaning to linguistic symbols. By relating the utterances they hear to what they understand to be going on at the time, children begin to grasp what the different linguistic forms signify (Bowerman, 1973; Macnamara, 1972). The establishment of the linguistic system in children creates an intricate bidirectional influence between cognitive development and language acquisition. Schlesinger (1982) underscores this interactive relationship in distinguishing between interpreting events and figuring out how to categorize them. Children's understanding of environmental events gives meaning to words, and the way in which others verbally categorize things delimits what gets included under those words in forming concepts. Words that mark variations in things of a like class call attention to subtle differences between them and thus foster a more differentiated perception of things. After children learn the names for things and how to represent conceptual relationships in words, language can influence how children perceive, organize, and interpret events. Language thus becomes not only a means of communication but also shapes the form of thought. The rules for encoding semantic relations in words are originally learned from discourses regarding concrete events of high interest and meaning to children. As children master linguistic competencies, language becomes more abstract and is no longer dependent on immediate referents. This greatly extends the power of language as a tool of thought.

There has been considerable debate about how much of language is inborn and about the mechanisms by which young children extract linguistic rules from the speech they hear around them. Proponents of the strong nativistic view (Chomsky, 1965; McNeill, 1970) argue that people are innately equipped with grammatical categories, such as "subject," "verb," and "object," which predetermine discovery of the meaning of linguistic input. Presumably, some minimal exposure to speech alone is sufficient to elicit linguistic competence without requiring any specific guidance. Actually, language acquisition depends on a considerable amount of semantic and linguistic input information adapted to children's cognitive capabilities. Despite repeated exposure to speech, it takes children almost a year and a half to master intelligible single-word utterances to represent salient events they experience over and over again. Moreover, putting two words together in an appropriate order does not come easily to them. It is not that they are underdeveloped neurophysiologically to acquire language, because children can master lexical items and multiword utterances at a very early age, if provided with enriched language stimulation that matches their cognitive level (Swenson, 1983).

Although the rate of language acquisition increases with growing experience, children's speech remains incomplete, ill formed, and semi-grammatical for some time. The problem is not that young children lack an understanding of what is being addressed. In fact, they demonstrate nonlinguistic comprehension of everyday events in the way they anticipate, discriminate, and manage them. However, they have considerable difficulty putting their knowledge and intentions into words in grammatical sentences. Variations in the quality of the verbal environment produce large differences in the rate of language acquisition, even though the natural linguistic output would be more than sufficient to elicit the various linguistic forms, if they were as strongly preprogrammed as nativistic theories would lead one to expect.

Many students of language consider it more fruitful to treat rules of grammar as acquirable through the cognitive processing of the linguistic and semantic information provided in the environment than as largely elicitable from innate knowledge by minimal linguistic input. Even researchers who favor the nativistic position now generally rely less on innate programming to produce syntactic competence. Linguistic proficiency is a complex skill that requires extensive experience in which children's cognitive capabilities, linguistic input, and semantically aidful contexts are coordinated in ways conducive to learning. Young children gain little from exposure to semantically and syntactically complicated utterances that convey little meaning because the things to which they refer are absent at the time or are referentially ambiguous.

There are other aspects of language that may be over attributed to innate determinants. Speech is universal, and all languages have common grammatical categories. However, the existence of common features does not necessarily mean that language is largely innate. Other skills that are universally functional will be found in all cultures. An innate propensity for tools, for example, is rarely proposed to explain why all people use tools (Rosenthal & Zimmerman, 1978). There are basic uniformities in the structure of environmental events in every culture, such as agents performing actions, objects acted upon, and actions producing effects. The commonality of events will produce universal conceptual categories and relations. Utterances used to represent these recurring event structures will, therefore, contain similar syntactic features in different cultures (e.g., a noun phrase with a verb phrase). The degree of semantic complexity will produce regularities in the order in which children master different syntactic features.

Transformational grammarians distinguish between "deep" structure and constructions derived from it as "surface" structure. The transformations are achieved by reordering, adding, or deleting elements from kernel sentences. Hall (1969) has questioned this depth metaphor, arguing that both the starting structure and constructions derived from it are simply rewordings of the same meaning, as in the transformation of the active into the passive voice (e.g., "The dog chased the cat" and "The cat was chased by the dog"). Meaning can be worded in different ways, and one type of paraphrase is not any deeper than another. He advocates a change in terminology from "deep" structure to "source" structure to avoid the value implications that a starting paraphrase is primal and its derivative paraphrasings are superficial. While acknowledging the value of specifying transformational relationships in linguistic structure, Hall (1969) notes that there are limits to the generality of this approach. Transformationalists contend that, by applying adequate transformational rules, one can produce all the "well-formed" sentences of a given language from simple declarative sentences. However, if analyses are restricted to "well-formed" sentences, one runs the risk of circularity, that is, such sentences will indeed conform to a set of rules. Winter (1965) describes grammatical forms which cannot be derived from kernel sentences. Hall (1969) reminds us that people's everyday speech often violates the established rules of grammar. He argues that such utterances are not derivable from a single syntactic kernel, nor can they be dismissed as imperfect expressions of it. A theory of language acquisition must explain anomalous speech forms, as well as those that conform to rules.

In trying to comprehend speech, listeners have to separate an utterance into its parts and to figure out the sense in which the words are used. Clark (1983) documents the problems that arise in parsing and interpreting utterances when words are used in ambiguous or innovative ways. The meaning of such utterances cannot be specified by lexical rules because they do not embody novel meanings of words. Consider one of Clark's examples in which a noun is used as a verb, *George managed to porch the newspaper yesterday.* To understand the speaker's intended meaning, the listener must consider the context in which the expression was used and draw on common knowledge of how carriers deliver newspapers. As Clark convincingly points out, with expressions used in unconventional senses the intended meaning cannot be derived solely from the linguistic properties of what is said. Achievement of understanding also requires intentional parsing of speech that relies on contextual information and coordinated knowledge for its meaning.

In Clark's view, anomalous expressions are a customary part of the language. Indeed, many of them are not only considered acceptable but are widely modeled and emulated in particular social circles. For example, in the modern argot, people do not interact, they *network*; corporations *P. R. the public* in efforts to gain for themselves a favorable public image. The computer jargon is spawning many odd usages of words: Rest breaks in activities are *downtimes*; level of productivity is *throughput capacity*; and things that are easy to use are *user-friendly*. As anomalous expressions gain shared referents through widespread usage, some of them become conventional forms.

It is generally acknowledged that language has an inborn component. Generative language is unique to humans. Chimpanzees can be taught signs representing objects and be prompted to string a few of them together in a loose order, but this rudimentary communication bears little resemblance to the characteristics of human speech. People are endowed with information-processing capacities for extracting linguistic rules and using them to encode and convey information. The inherent capability to categorize, to abstract general characteristics from particular instances, to generalize across features of similarity, and to discriminate by features of dissimilarity provides the basic apparatus for discerning the regularities in language. Moreover, neonates can discriminate voices from other kinds of sounds, and infants show increasing sensitivity to different intonational patterns (Jusczyk, 1981). These basic perceptual facilities aid in segmenting the flow of speech into recognizable units. To learn what utterances signify, children have to be able to recognize similarities and differences in speech sounds.

Language is the product of multiple determinants operating through a number of mediating processes. One set of determinants concerns the *cognitive skills* that children need to process linguistic information. This requires capabilities to perceive the essential elements of speech, to recognize and remember sequential structures, to abstract rules from exemplars, and to select the appropriate words and production rules to generate intelligible utterances. These all involve intricate cognitive subskills. In trying to decipher speech, children have to figure out how the arrangement of spoken words relates to what they know about what is going on at the time. Thus, the second set of determinants of language acquisition pertains to children's fund of *nonlinguistic knowledge* in different areas of discourse. Young children have some understanding of common occurrences before they talk about them. Such knowledge provides the source for conjectures about what the words mean and how they have to be arranged to convey the child's understood conceptual relations. Linguistic knowledge is hard to come by, unless notions about words and structures are considered and then put to the social test. As in other areas of functioning, the rate of language acquisition is likely to be better predicted from a person's knowledge that is most pertinent to the area of discourse than from global cognitive structures. The complexity of *linguistic input* and semantic accompaniments constitutes the third set of factors governing language acquisition. The speech to young children has to be structured in ways that facilitate language acquisition. *Interpersonal factors*, which figure prominently in the pragmatics or functions of speech, serve as a further source of influence on language development. These various determinants will be examined shortly in some detail.

When viewed from the broader perspective of communication, the process of language acquisition involves much more than syntactic analysis. Cognitive and social factors are an integral part of the process. However, in the concern over the form of speech, its social function was long neglected. The concern with how linguistic knowledge is acquired overshadowed the issues of how such knowledge gets translated into proficient speech and how expressive language is developed as a tool for effective communication. Contemporary theorizing and research in psycholinguistics has been considerably expanded to encompass cognitive and social determinants of both linguistic and communicative competence.

Simplistic Conceptions of Learning

Until recently, it was commonly assumed that social factors had only a secondary influence on language development. This conclusion was largely based on a simplistic view of social learning processes. For example, psycholinguistic theorizing and research regarding modeling processes have been essentially confined to verbal mimicry. By restricting their analyses to children's repetition of what they hear, researchers concluded that by imitation one can learn only specific utterances, not the grammatical rules of speech. Actually, it is abstract modeling, which operates through perceptual, representational, and productive processes, rather than simple verbal mimicry, that is most germane to the development of generative grammar. Rather than simply copying specific utterances, children extract syntactic rules from the modeled utterances embodying these rules, which then enables them to generate an almost infinite variety of new sentences that they have never heard.

The contribution of social factors to language development has also been downplayed because of certain observations (Ervin, 1964; Lenneberg, 1962; Menyuk, 1964). During initial language learning, children usually convert adult speech to simpler grammars. They can acquire linguistic rules without engaging in any overt speech. In addition, it has been claimed that children do not imitate speech forms that are more linguistically advanced than the grammar they display in their spontaneous utterances. It was, therefore, argued that limitation cannot produce new grammatical forms. Many psycholinguists viewed social feedback in learning theory as essentially confined to extrinsic reward and punishment. Social feedback was discounted as playing a significant role in grammatical learning, on the grounds that adults are more inclined to approve of the factual accuracy of children's utterances than their grammatical correctness. And finally, it is argued that language is acquired too rapidly to occur by direct tuition.

Many of the above criticisms are valid when applied to theories of imitation that emphasize verbatim repetition of modeled responses and that assume that learning requires reinforced performance (Skinner, 1957). It is evident from the material already discussed in earlier chapters that the social cognitive interpretation of modeling is compatible with rule-learning theories proposed by psycholinguists. Both conceptualizations assign special importance to the process of abstracting grammatical rules from diverse utterances. The differentiation made by psycholinguists between language competence and production corresponds to the distinction made between acquisition and performance in social cognitive theory. Since observational learning does not require performance, it provides a medium for the rapid acquisition of competencies.

Some of the limitations ascribed to learning theory have resulted from the failure to distinguish between response mimicry and observational learning. Consider the widely cited argument that imitation cannot serve as a vehicle of language learning, because spontaneous imitations diminish during the second year of life, when language is developing at an accelerating rate. Parents initially encourage infants' mimicking of sounds and simple acts when they are very young as a way of building mutuality, but parents cease doing so as the children grow older. Children quickly learn to quit mimicking everything they see or hear. However, the decline in indiscriminate mimicry does not mean that humans cease observational learning after age two. On the contrary, as children's attentional, representational, and productive skills develop with age, their capabilities for observational learning are greatly enhanced.

The role of modeling in grammatical learning has also been questioned on the grounds that children often display ungrammatical speech unlikely to have been modeled by any adults with whom they have had contact (e.g., "I runned"). Many of these errors represent children's overgeneralizing from regular to irregular grammatical constructions from the rules they have learned. Such novel utterances arise because the children model rules too well. The misapplications of the rules are easily eliminated by corrective feedback to teach the exceptions to the rules (Sherman, 1971). The linguistic environment, of course, is not populated solely with adults. Young children also frequently model the language of their peers, who are not the best of grammarians (Hamilton & Stewart, 1977).

Other reservations concerning modeling determinants of linguistic competency arose from the limitations of methodology. For example, Ervin (1964) reasoned that imitation cannot contribute to children's language development, because they cannot imitate linguistic forms exceeding their existing grammatical competence. However, evidence of more refined procedures disputes this observation. One method parents use to promote language development is to expand their children's previous utterances by replacing deletions or adding more complex linguistic elements. Through this process, young children pick up new linguistic forms from the modeled expansions and use them in their own speech (Bloom, Hood, & Lightbown, 1974; Kemp & Dale, 1973; Slobin, 1968; Nicolich & Raph, 1978). The more parents engage in reciprocal imitation, which enhances its social function, the more readily children adopt their parents' modeled expansions (Folger & Chapman, 1978). Children's utterances represent efforts to communicate about meaningful activities that command their attention. Perhaps because of the greater attentional involvement of the children, parental linguistic modeling, which expands children's utterances, increases their spontaneous use of the selected linguistic forms more effectively than similar parental modeling that is not linked to children's prior speech (Hovell, Schumaker, & Sherman, 1978).

Instructive modeling by means of linguistic elaboration of children's utterances can clearly serve as a device for language acquisition. Another form of linguistic modeling that accelerates language acquisition involves replying to children's speech by recasting it into a new syntactic form without altering the meaning of what is said. By using this type of modeling, Nelson (1977a, 1977b; Baker & Nelson, 1985) selectively promoted children's mastery of advanced syntactic forms they had lacked. He attributes the success of modeled recastings to the fact that they provide conspicuous contrasts between the child's speech forms and those of the model for cognitive comparison. The juxtaposition aids recognition of modeled syntactic rules. Like modeled expansions, recastings address children's immediate communicative concern and are thus well suited to catch attention and enlist motivation to improve one's linguistic competence.

Introducing grammatical complexities in modeled speech increases the intricacy of expressive speech, even in children who already possess substantial linguistic knowledge (Greeson, 1981; Harris & Hassemer, 1972). Parents model new linguistic forms, as well as restructure and elaborate on their children's ill-formed utterances. Longitudinal microanalyses of the effects of the speech modeled by parents show that modeling is an important vehicle of language acquisition (Moerk & Moerk, 1979).

Brown and Hanlon (1970) report that parents rarely use contingent approval to correct their children's ungrammatical utterances. However, this does not mean that parents do not engage in syntactic corrections. We know from the work of Vasta (1976) that the best way to remedy faulty performances is to model the correct forms. As the evidence on expansions demonstrates, modeled corrections of children's ill-formed constructions improve and extend their linguistic competence. Although modeled feedback is a prevalent device, parents use a variety of strategies conducive to language acquisition (Moerk, 1983; Snow, 1977). We shall return to this issue.

There has been some speculation about whether imitation, comprehension, and production form a developmental causal sequence in language acquisition. It is generally agreed that consistent production of novel instances of a syntactic rule requires comprehension of the rule. Most of the disputes center on the role that imitation plays in language development. Different theorists contend that imitation fosters comprehension or that comprehension fosters imitation, or that imitation and comprehension are causally unrelated (Bloom, Hood, & Lightbown, 1974; Fraser, Bellugi, & Brown, 1963; Ervin, 1964; Whitehurst & Vasta, 1975). In the social cognitive perspective, imitation serves as a social means of promoting understanding of syntactic relations and skills in productive speech, rather than operating as a causal link in a three-stage process. Vocal mimicry does not require comprehension. Children can repeat what they hear without understanding the form and the meaning of their utterances. Elicited imitation mainly reflects the capacity for short-term memory and how linguistic knowledge affects the reconstruction of modeled speech.

Imitative utterances do not instate grammars. It is through observational learning that children extract syntactic rules from the speech they hear around them. However, in the initial phase of language development, vocal imitation develops articulatory skills in forming words. It also provides much needed practice in selecting appropriate words and combining them linguistically to represent conceptual relationships. Moreover, errors in imitative utterances reveal linguistic deficiencies and thus provide good occasions for instructive feedback. By corrective modeling and other techniques, which draw children's attention to the structural features of speech and their meaning, such transactions facilitate the observational learning of linguistic rules. In initial stages of learning, requiring immediate mimicry of utterances can impede extraction of the rules they embody by diverting attention to the demands of vocalization. Children more easily acquire a linguistic form and make more generalized productive use of it if they observe the rule modeled repeatedly than if they immediately mimic what they hear (Courtright & Courtright, 1976).

Linguistic modeling with meaningful referents can produce both rule learning and some translation of linguistic knowledge into grammatical speech, without requiring verbal imitation (Brown, 1976; Morgulas & Zimmerman, 1979). However, the development of skill in expressive language proceeds faster if children engage in imitative speech and receive instructive feedback (Novak, 1978). Evidence that verbal imitation alone does not increase productive use of comprehended rules (Brown, 1979) suggests that it is the opportunities imitative speech provides for instructive feedback that fosters productive proficiency. The more complex the syntactic forms, the greater is the benefit of the instructive transactions occasioned by imitative utterances.

Knowledge of linguistic rules does not ensure the productive use of them. As will be recalled from earlier chapters, the acquisition of knowledge and skilled performance is governed by different subprocesses. To gain productive proficiency, one must develop skills in converting conceptions to intelligible, grammatical utterances. Language proficiency is best developed by linguistic modeling combined with speech production and instructive feedback, especially through the use of corrective modeling. Children thus gain skill in using speech for communicative purposes in conformance to linguistic rules.

Clark and Hecht (1983) posit a process for matching production to comprehension that is similar to the conception-matching process of social cognitive theory. According to their analysis, children adopt from modeled utterances representations of linguistic forms, which they use as a standard of comparison for their own productions. Clark and Hecht cite several lines of evidence that children indeed possess linguistic standards derived from adult speech. Children recognize and correctly distinguish between proper forms of speech before they can produce them accurately. They understand well-formed adult utterances better than the telegraphic forms they display (Shipley, Smith, & Gleitman, 1969). When children correct their own speech in response to signs of other people's noncomprehension, they tend to alter mainly the faulty elements of their utterances in the direction of adult speech, rather than engage in random variations in search of a suitable form (Kasermann & Foppa, 1981). To make such systematic corrections on their own, they have to know what they said wrong and have a grammatical standard to know how to correct it. Thus, the evidence indicates that children monitor what they say and make corrective adjustments to achieve closer matches to their standard for comprehension (Evans, 1985). Mismatches between representations and productions motivate corrective improvements in expressive language. With growing experience, the standards adopted incorporate new linguistic complexities, which prolong the process of language acquisition. As is true of other skills, after much practice, language production becomes automatic.

Many factors mediate the relationship between comprehension and speech production. The incentives for acquiring speech proficiency take many forms. Social considerations affect expressive language. Therefore, scant productive use of comprehended linguistic forms does not necessarily reflect deficiencies in speech generation. The problem may be less in the generation of a certain form of speech than in the social rules of speech about where and when it is appropriate to use it. For example, children who fully understand the passive form, but who do not use it in their speech even when given cues to do so, speak in the passive voice after observing adult models speak that way (Morgulas & Zimmerman, 1979). In such instances, modeling conveys normative information about the appropriateness of different styles of speech in different social contexts. Even very young children evidence surprisingly good grasp of the social rules of speech and adjust their language accordingly (Rice, 1984). When children do not display a particular syntactic structure in their spontaneous speech, it may be that they do not understand it, they understand it but cannot produce it, or they understand and can express it, but, for social reasons, they do not use it.

Modeling Determinants of Language Development

Significant progress has been made in our understanding of how children come to comprehend and use language through social learning processes. Much information has been gained from observational studies and correlational analyses of the relationship between social influences and language acquisition. Experimental microanalyses of the processes governing language acquisition speak most directly to the issue of causality. In learning to communicate symbolically, children must acquire appropriate verbal symbols for objects and events and syntactic rules for representing relationships among them. The process of acquiring language involves not only learning grammatical relations between words but also correlating the linguistic forms with the events to which they apply. This requires integrating two relational systems—linguistic and perceptual—both relying on a common base of understanding. Language learning, therefore, depends extensively on nonlinguistic understanding of the events to which the utterances refer. For this reason, it is difficult to transmit linguistic forms that children do not already know by verbal modeling alone.

Adults, of course, do not converse abstractly with young children who have a poor grasp of speech. Verbal expressions that convey grammatical relations are usually matched to meaningful ongoing activities about which children already have some knowledge. Grammatical features of speech are more informative and distinguishable when the semantic referents to the utterances are present than when they are ab-sent. Young children, for example, are helped to comprehend plural forms if they hear singular and plural labels applied to single and multiple objects, respectively.

In the initial stages of speech acquisition, when children have little or no understanding of language, they have to learn the referents to which the words apply. Children infer the appropriate referents from coordinated matching of the word with the defining properties of the object class or event class (Clark, 1973). This is not an easy task for them. If different objects are present when adults apply a label for one of them, the child may pick the wrong referent. Moreover, objects and events have many properties. Even a simple object, such as a cup, includes color, decoration, shape, size, and functional properties. Because of the multifaceted nature of events, words can be ambiguous as far as the property to which they refer. Thus, for example, children have to figure out that the word *cup* refers to a vessel with a handle and to identify the properties that distinguish cups from other drinking vessels and utensils with handles. Unless the ambiguity in labeling is removed, the child may attach the word to irrelevant properties of the object.

Understanding of the word-referent relation is greatly facilitated by structuring social interactions so they direct the child's attention and give priority to the property of the object to which the adult is referring. Bullock (1979) has shown that young children learn property terms faster when adults coordinate their lexical modeling with activities that draw attention to the relevant aspects of events than if the activities draw attention to the events without highlighting the aspects to which the terms refer. It helps to use the most prototypical examples in establishing conceptual categories and the labels for them. This increases the likelihood that children will attach the word to referents that typify the semantic category. After the correct labeling has been accomplished with highly prototypical features, the conceptual category must be linguistically delimited by exposure to mistakable examples of lesser likeness and adult labeling that designates whether or not they are instances of the concept.

Learning the meaning of words is complicated by the fact that different things have some common features (e.g., dogs and cats) and similar things have some dissimilar features (e.g., greyhounds and pekingeses). Clark (1973) provides an analysis of the process by which children learn the domain of words and the order in which they ascribe distinguishing semantic features to them. Initially, children identify the meaning of a word with only a few general features. If a salient feature is applied too broadly in early speech, it creates a confusing overextension of words, as when all creatures with four legs and fur are referred to as *doggies*. With growing experience, children add more specific aspects of meaning to words which specify them more precisely. Dogs bark, whereas cats, which are also four-legged and furry, meow. Adoption of distinguishing semantic features delimits the word class. The acquisition and restructuring of word meanings is influenced by salient perceptual information, correlative activities, and discriminative labeling, all of which draw attention to prototypical features of the things for which a given word is used.

Conceptual categories vary in their level of abstraction (Rosch, 1978). They range from specific classes to superordinate levels of classification (e.g., spaniel, dog, animal). It is easier to learn the labels for specific object classes because the members share many attributes. The more abstract classes have fewer common attributes. For example, spaniels bear a close resemblance to each other, whereas dogs come in different shapes and sizes, and animals are even more varied in their attributes. Children have to learn the hierarchical order of these classifications, as, for example, the inclusion relation that all dogs are animals but not all animals are dogs (Markman & Callahan, 1983).

Acquisition of language rules is also greatly facilitated by linking linguistic modeling to semantic referents. In a study by Brown (1976), young children, who had little or no understanding of constructions in the passive voice, heard a model narrate a story in the passive form in which animals engaged in a series of activities. While describing the incidents, the model performed the corresponding activities with toys, or showed pictures portraying the same activities, or used no referential aids. Modeling with the enacted referents substantially increased children's comprehension of passive constructions. Linguistic modeling without accompanying referents improved comprehension in children who already had a partial understanding of passive constructions, whereas modeling with enacted referents facilitated learning of the grammatical form, even in children who did not previously know it. Moeser (1977) similarly found that an artificial language is learned faster with semantic referents than without them. Seeing things happen provides a more informative clue to the meaning of accompanying utterances than seeing the same events pictured (Brown, 1976). Static portrayals may leave ambiguities about agents and objects and agent-action relationships. Enactive referents also produce faster productive use of a novel modeled rule than pictorial referents or suggestive but incomplete referents of either form (Leonard, 1975). However, if pictorial referents convey semantic relations clearly, children do not have much difficulty extracting the linguistic rules from modeled utterances and then drawing on the rules to comprehend speech in new situations (Whitehurst, 1977; Whitehurst, Ironsmith, & Goldfein, 1974).

When events in the referential system correspond closely to those in the linguistic system, the congruity undoubtedly facilitates extraction of the rules embodied in modeled utterances. The task is considerably more difficult when the structure of the modeled utterances incompletely matches or mismatches what is going on at the time. Such situations create greater need for feedback to children's comprehension of speech to correct evident misunderstandings. Modeling complex syntactic rules without any accompanying semantic referents has little effect on children's attention to the structural properties of the modeled speech (Bandura & Harris, 1966). This is achieved by creating distinct contrasts between other forms of speech and the new form and providing feedback for successful use of the latter. A complicated rule can also be transmitted by verbal modeling alone if it is used in speech that is semantically simplified—words that children know are used to describe events with which they are thoroughly familiar (Brown, 1976). The semantically rich content gives salience to the modeled word-order rules that represent it.

The power of referents to engage children's attention and interest partly determines the rate of vocabulary acquisition as well. Children are more likely to incorporate in their vocabulary new modeled names for accompanying edible and active objects than the names for passive objects or names unassociated with any concrete referents (Stewart & Hamilton, 1976). Children similarly adopt more thoroughly the word-order rule for producing passives if the modeled constructions accompanying pictorial referents involve vivid action verbs (e.g., *kick*) than nonactive verbs (e.g., *read*) that attract less attention (deVilliers, 1980). Learning the meaning of words that are applied to abstract referents, such as fairness, altruism, or freedom, would pose the greatest difficulties. Initial language acquisition requires referents, but after some linguistic competence has been achieved, further learning becomes less dependent upon immediate, semantic referents.

The rate of language acquisition is affected by the complexity of the model's language relative to the children's cognitive capabilities. Children can gain little from modeled speech that exceeds their ability to process what they hear. Linguistic rules must be initially modeled in simplified, as well as in semantically enriched forms to make them more easily learnable. Indeed, parents usually adjust their speech to their children's linguistic competence in an effort to facilitate language acquisition. Rules for organizing words into sentences are discovered more easily from short, simple utterances than when they are obscured by ponderous verbiage. When addressing young children, parents use utterances that are shorter, more repetitive, and grammatically simpler than when they speak to older children (Baldwin & Baldwin, 1973; Moerk, 1974; Snow, 1972). Parents also speak slower, which eases the processing of linguistic input, and they use exaggerated intonation as an attention-focusing device. Even young children will simplify their speech when they are talking to younger children (Shatz & Gelman, 1973). Linguistic simplification partly depends on signs of noncomprehension from listeners. Adults are more likely to simplify their speech when children indicate they do not understand what is being said than when they seem to comprehend it (Bohannon & Marquis, 1977).

The simplification is not confined to syntax. Language acquisition is facilitated by semantic simplification in which adult utterances express, using highly concrete referents, elementary semantic relations that children already comprehend to some extent (Furrow, Nelson, & Benedict, 1979). Semantic complexities are gradually introduced as children come to understand things better. Moreover, Snow (1977) maintains that some of the adjustments in parental speech are designed to impart the social rules of conversation. Parents use interrogatives extensively with infants to elicit at least a minimal response from them, and parents keep the interaction going by filling in for them before they are able to vocalize much of anything. These rudimentary interchanges build skills in being the speaker or the listener, an accomplishment necessary for sustaining the flow of conversation to gain information about things. As children's conversational skills improve, their parents speech style changes to a more genuine reciprocal communication.

In summary, experimental investigations reveal that modeling, supplemented with semantic aids and devices to focus attention on key linguistic features, is a highly effective way of promoting language acquisition. Sequential analyses of verbal interchanges between parents and their young children show that parents are active language teachers (Moerk, 1976). Their instructive and corrective strategies include repetitive modeling of more advanced linguistic forms, restructuring and elaborating the child's constructions in modeled feedback, simplifying structures, varying the content around the same structure, rephrasing utterances, prompting, questioning, informing, answering, labeling, pictorial structuring, and accenting grammatically significant speech elements.

It has been widely assumed that much linguistic knowledge must be innate because parental speech is too jumbled and ungrammatical to enable children to learn linguistic rules from what they hear. It is ironic that an innate device that supposedly provides children with the rules of grammar should leave adults speaking so ungrammatically. Although some adult speech is ill-formed, the evidence cited above disputes the claim that the speech parents direct to their young children is a discomposed and confusing verbal morass. Quite the contrary. Parents tailor their language to the children's level of cognitive and linguistic capabilities. It is not as though children are inundated with speech but are otherwise left to their own devices to ferret out the rules of grammar. Rather, parents do much of the abstraction for them by structuring linguistic information in ways that make grammatical rules more easily learnable (Moerk, 1983). As children increase their linguistic competence, parents diminish their instructive activities. Variations in the instructive aspects of parental speech correlate with the rate of children's language development (Furrow,

Nelson, & Benedict, 1979). The results of laboratory studies, in which these instructive aspects of modeled speech are systematically varied, corroborate the causal impact of the adults' speech on children's acquisition and productive use of linguistic rules.

Functional Determinants of Language Development

Much of the preceding discussion has been concerned with how modeled speech is structured and semantically enriched to enhance language acquisition. Mechanisms of language acquisition may be intriguing to students of language, but children adopt language because they can do useful and wondrous thing with it. Intelligible speech provides many benefits which function as incentives for acquiring communicative competence. Obviously, infants do not use vocalizations to gather and exchange information. In the initial prelinguistic phase, vocal expressions mainly serve interpersonal purposes. It will be recalled from the earlier discussion on the ontogeny of observational learning that reciprocal imitation is a highly effective way for infants to maintain enjoyable contact with adults. Most of this social interaction involves vocal imitation. When adults repeat the infants' vocal expressions, the infants' rate of spontaneous vocalizations increases substantially (Haugan & McIntire, 1972). Experience with this type of verbal interplay can enhance the infants' responsiveness to parental linguistic modeling for later language acquisition.

As children begin to recognize the communicative function of speech, their expressive language is influenced by different modes of feedback. We have already seen how language skills can be improved by elaborative and corrective modeling in adult response to incomplete or ungrammatical utterances by children. If children possess sufficient linguistic knowledge, even signs of noncomprehension by adults can serve to correct faulty expressive speech, as shown by Kasermann and Foppa (1981). When adults indicate they do not understand what children are trying to say, and what the children are saying is in some way incorrect, then the children correct their own speech in the direction of more advanced forms of language. They add better referents when the ones they had used were ambiguous or inadequate; they add or correct grammatical elements when their prior utterances were grammatically incomplete or inaccurate. In contrast, when adults display noncomprehension of children's linguistically correct utterances, the children simply repeat themselves or delete their redundancies to make what they are saying more understandable to the adult.

Adults do not make arbitrary rewards contingent upon correct grammar, but this does not mean that grammatical accuracy has no differential effects. Children's language is affected more strongly by its natural consequences than by arbitrary, extrinsic ones. The most effective natural consequences are the benefits derived from influencing the social environment. Success in getting others to do things that bring one different benefits is better achieved by grammatical speech than by unintelligible utterances. The demands for communicative accuracy, although minimal initially, increase as children grow older.

Changes in children's expressive language have been studied when elaborated forms of speech are made highly useful in securing valued outcomes (Hart & Risley, 1978). In these naturalistic studies, young children with limited language skills can get attractive things they want, or assistance with tasks, provided they ask for things in informative ways using appropriate modifiers and compound-sentence structures. If they do not know the speech forms, they are initially modeled for them in the context of the requests for assistance, whereupon they are encouraged to use the elaborated speech forms. A variety of attractive things are made available to create many natural opportunities for language instruction. Formal assessments reveal that children do not pick up advanced speech forms for verbal approval alone, but they quickly adopt them when they can get what they want that way (Hart & Risley, 1968). Moreover, they generalize these elaborated styles of speech across settings, occasions, activities, and people, and they continue to use them after conditions have changed so that simpler speech would do (Hart & Risley, 1974, 1975). In longitudinal assessments (Hart & Risley, 1980), children who are taught the value of informative speech display marked increases in the spontaneous use of elaborated language during a preschool year, whereas children who have not had this type of instructive experience change little in the amount and quality of their expressive language during the year. Hart and Risley attribute the effectiveness of this motivational system to the fact that language is developed through natural interactions initiated by the children relating to activities that arouse their interest and provide strong incentives to improve their communicative skills. They receive modeled guidance if needed. These are the optimal conditions for learning.

Children use language to gain needed information about things, as well as to gain access to them. Their interest in information grows as they begin to perceive relationships between environmental events and between their actions and outcomes. It is not long before they learn that knowledge which enables them to predict and control events can be very useful. Transmission of information about the workings of the environment requires elaborated language to represent the events of interest. This provides additional incentive for children to enlarge their communicative skills, so they can ask about things and understand what people tell them. The more conceptually complex the subject matter, the greater the demands it makes on linguistic skills. As the function of language expands with the child's development, the nature and function of the parents' language changes as well. Their speech is tailored less to aid language acquisition and more to guide their children's behavior, to inform them about things, and to expand their cognitive and social competencies (Gleason & Weintraub, 1978).

Children find language useful in guiding their actions and in explaining their own behavior to themselves and to others. This can make a big difference in how others treat them. The consequences of verbally guided action further underscore the many benefits of linguistic competencies. Acting on misunderstandings of what other people say can have adverse effects, as can miscommunications that lead others astray. The outcomes of actions create informative feedback for improving one's understanding and use of speech.

MODES OF THOUGHT VERIFICATION

People form conceptions about themselves and the world around them by acquiring information from direct and vicarious experiences about the regularity in events. By representing the information derived from such experiences symbolically, they gain knowledge about the properties of objects, about proximal and distal relationships between events, about their own nature and capabilities, and about how to predict what is likely to happen under a certain set of conditions. Effective cognitive functioning requires means of distinguishing between accurate and faulty thinking. Thoughts about the adequacy of one's thoughts are formed through a verification process. As we have noted, knowledge about oneself and the environment is represented in symbolic constructions. Judgments concerning the validity and functional value of one's thoughts are formed by comparing the goodness of the match between thoughts and some standard of verity. Good matches

corroborate thoughts; mismatches tend to refute them. This verification by matching can take different forms depending on what is used as the indicant of how things are. These forms include enactive, vicarious, persuasory, and logical verification.

Enactive Verification

Enactive verification relies on the adequacy of the fit between thought and the result of one's actions. People derive much of their knowledge from direct experience of the effects of their actions. It does not require many encounters with flames set by matches, for example, to come to know the properties of matches and that striking them will cause things to burn. Based on experiences of when things will or will not burn, people develop conceptions about fire and the conditions under which it is likely to occur. Conceptions of causality, personal agency, and so on are developed through a process of this type.

Theories of cognitive development generally focus on feedback from enactive experimentation as the major vehicle for verifying and correcting conceptions of events. In Piagetian theory, for example, the degree of the match between beliefs and results of actions informs on the adequacy of the belief. Moderate incongruences prompt changes in beliefs. Although behavioristic and Piagetian conceptions of psychological functioning are typically presented as antithetical, they share the assumption that knowledge is gained through one's own activity. However, Piagetians emphasize information gained by self-generated activity, whereas behaviorists place higher value on socially guided activity.

Thought is easily verifiable enactively when thought-guided actions produce immediate, consistent effects that are readily observable. Thus, beliefs about how to get to a particular place are unmistakably substantiated if they get one there and easily disconfirmed if they lead one astray. But the ways of Nature and society are not always that straightforward. Most events are complexly related so that actions produce mixed results, depending on the constellation of determinants operating at any given time. The long-term results of actions often differ from their immediate effects, which creates problems about what to believe. When contingencies are socially structured, and results depend on the vagaries of others, the same actions can have diverse effects with different persons or with the same person on different occasions. Confirmation for all kinds of misbeliefs can be found in the mixed and variable results of one's own activity. Undoubtedly, much knowledge is gained through action, but direct experience is not the only way to assess the adequacy of one's understanding.

Vicarious Verification

As has been extensively documented in preceding chapters, knowledge about the nature of things is frequently gained from vicarious experience. In this mode of verification, observing the effects produced by somebody else's actions serves as a way of checking one's own thoughts. The earlier analysis of comparative self-appraisal documents how people draw on the successes and failures of others to confirm and alter their beliefs about their own capabilities (Bandura, 1981a; Festinger, 1954; Suls & Miller, 1977). Because in most activities, appraisal of one's own capabilities depends more on how well others perform in similar situations than on the performance alone, vicarious verification is especially influential in the development of self-knowledge.

Vicarious verification is not simply a serviceable supplement to enactive experience. The increasing presence of televised environments in people's lives provides vast amounts of information, of variable accuracy, about places, persons, and things that extend beyond the confines of their personal experiences. Symbolic modeling through print and televised means greatly expands the range of verification experiences that cannot otherwise be attained by personal action because of social prohibitions or the limitations of mobility, time, resources, and capability. The experiences of others not only provide the means for testing the correctness of one's beliefs, but vicarious influences can alter the informative value of direct experience (Brown & Inouye, 1978). Psychological theories formulated before the revolutionary advances in communications technology may present a less-than-adequate account of how thought patterns are formed and authenticated under contemporary conditions of life.

Televised representations of social realities reflect ideological bents in their portrayal of human nature, social relations, and the norms and structure of society (Adoni & Mane, 1984; Gerbner, 1972). Heavy exposure to this symbolic world may distort perceptions of reality in the direction of the televised representations. In numerous domains, compared to light viewers, the beliefs of heavy viewers match the televised world more closely than the actual social realities, even when other possible contributing factors are simultaneously controlled (Hawkins & Pingree, 1972). Laboratory studies showing that media portrayals shape beliefs clarify further the direction of causality: The televised influence is the source of the changes in viewer's beliefs (Flerx et al., 1976; O'Bryant & Corder-Bolz, 1978; Siegel, 1958). Some disputes about the vicarious cultivation of beliefs have arisen over findings that heavy viewers of television programs, many of which have their share of assaultive and villainous characters, are less trustful of others and exaggerate their chances of being victimized than light viewers (Gerbner, Gross, Morgan, & Signorielli, 1981; Hirsch, 1980).

Like any other social influence, televised portrayals do not have a universal impact, nor do they operate independently of their content. Televised influence is best defined in terms of the contents people watch, rather than the sheer amount of television viewing. High television exposure is more likely to be related to beliefs of social danger and mistrust if heavy viewing centers on a violent fare (Pingree & Hawkins, 1981). Vicarious cultivation of misconceptions is most clearly revealed in studies demonstrating causality by varying experimentally the amount of exposure to televised violence (Bryant, Carveth, & Brown, 1981). Heavy exposure heightens viewers' beliefs that they themselves will become victims of violence. Heath (1984) further demonstrates the value of using particularized rather than global indices of media influences. She found that it is not the sheer number of crime reports but their nature that affects fear of victimization. A lot of sensational newspaper reports of local crimes and ones in which assailants apparently picked their victims randomly instills strong fear of crime, whereas reading about crimes in distant places or those provoked by the victim does not. Laboratory research, in which story elements are systematically varied, replicates the fear-provoking effects of crime locality and randomness of victimization.

The measure of fear of personal victimization also needs refinement. Such measures are usually limited to fear of criminal assault in one's immediate neighborhood. However, people's activities are not confined just to their dwelling place. Assessment of fear of personal victimization must be expanded to include other urban areas and the extent to which they are deliberately avoided because they are perceived to be dangerous places. The full impact of televised construction of reality on fear of personal victimization is best understood by examining how people's lives are constricted by fear of different urban areas and other environs.

The symbolic environment of television often diverges in significant ways from actual social reality. Hence, to see the world as the televised messages portray it is to harbor some misconceptions. Indeed, many of the shared misconceptions about occupational pursuits, ethnic groups, minorities, the elderly, social and sex roles, and other aspects of life are at least partly cultivated through symbolic modeling of stereotypes (Buerkel-Rothfuss & Mayes, 1981; McGhee & Frueh, 1980; Tan, 1979). Verification of thought by comparison with televised versions of social reality can thus foster collective illusions.

The psychological mechanisms by which vicarious experience shapes human thought and action have been extensively reviewed in earlier chapters. This large body of knowledge additionally identifies the various personal, social, and media factors that affect susceptibility to vicarious experience. There are also several interacting factors that bear on the issue of vicarious cultivation of belief systems. One of these concerns the pluralistic nature of media systems. Vicarious experience gains power to shape public conceptions if there is ideological uniformity in the televised images and messages. However, if varied ideas and ways of life are portrayed, no particular view enjoys a monopolistic influence. Availability of pluralistic influences does not necessarily produce diversity of vicarious experiences at the individual level. Selective viewing can give rise to personal uniformity even amidst diversity. For this reason, in evaluating vicarious influences on the public's conceptions of reality, it is *what* people watch, rather than merely *how much* they watch, that must be minimized.

Vicarious influences compete not only with each other within the media but also with direct experience. The more people depend on television for their information about matters the more their conceptions of reality are shaped by it (Ball-Rokeach & DeFleur, 1976). It is commonly assumed that vicarious influence has the strongest impact when observers either do not have opposing beliefs or the modeled version of reality confirms their preconceptions. While this is often the case, because vicarious and actual experiences operate interactively, personal experiences and preconceptions are not unidirectional controllers of vicarious effects. Vicarious influence can attenuate, or even negate the usual sway of personal experience (Brown & Inouye, 1978). Faced with conflicting sources of information, people often dismiss their personal experiences as exceptions to the rule and regard televised versions of reality as the more representative. Tyler (1980) analyzed how personal and indirect experiences are weighted differently and integrated to form beliefs about crime. Indirect sources of information conveyed by media and informal accounts by others were often given heavier weight than first-hand experiences. The impact of experiences on belief depended on the perception of their informativeness, although their affectivity and memorability were also important. Gerbner's notion of cultural "mainstreaming" assumes that by repetitive exposure to televised portrayals of social reality vicarious experience can counter, at least to some extent, the influence of direct experience (Gerbner et al., 1981). People from divergent backgrounds may thus develop converging conceptions of life from heavy viewing of a common televised world.

Persuasory Verification

A third mode of verification relies on comparing one's thoughts to the judgments of others. In many domains of knowledge, there is no easy way to check the validity of one's thinking. Some of these cognitive realms concern complex matters involving a lot of specialized information, which limits how much any one person can get to know about them. Consequently, views will differ from person to person, depending on their fund of experiences and level of expertise.

In other domains, the relevant information takes many forms, it varies in reliability, and the different facets may assume high or low importance depending on how they are valued subjectively. This provides a murky "factual" basis for assessing the adequacy of judgment. The same "facts" can be combined and weighted in a way that supports divergent beliefs. Still other areas of thinking concern metaphysical ideas that cannot be subjected at all to empirical confirmation, as, for example, beliefs about deities and divine agency. When experiential verification is either difficult or impossible, people evaluate the soundness of their views by comparing them to the judgments of others. Because discordant belief jeopardizes social acceptance and favorable evaluation by peers, social validation of thought patterns assumes considerable import (Zimbardo, Ebbesen, & Maslach, 1977).

Social verification can foster conventional, unorthodox, or even bizarre thought patterns depending upon the shared beliefs of the reference groups with which one affiliates. Pluralistic systems provide diverse social standards of reality for judging the "correctness" of one's own views on different matters. Groups seeking mass followings devise effective communication modes to promote their particular beliefs and images of reality. In the past, the print media were widely used for this purpose. Because of its greater potential for collective influence, the video system feeding off telecommunication satellites has become the dominant vehicle for influencing collective thought.

Bizarre views of reality have the greatest power to authenticate bizarre beliefs in totalistic milieus where members are cut off from corrective outside influences. Aberrant views flourish when access is denied to information that invalidates them. Such totalistic systems usually combine charismatic leaders, whose views become imperatives, with mutual solidarity and intolerance of dissent, and suspicion of outsiders is cultivated to discredit their opinions (Bromley

& Shupe, 1979). The extreme perversion of communal power leading to collective madness is most tragically illustrated in the Jonestown settlement, where followers poisoned themselves in a mass death. In the beginning, Jim Jones used messages about love and egalitarian utopias to gain and hold followers in the People's Temple. As his image as faith healer and prophet began to tarnish and members began to defect, the humanitarian themes turned into messages of fear and hate designed to implant suspicion and dread of the outside world. In the isolated jungle settlement of Jonestown, where Jones exercised total control, "for hours on end, and sometimes all night, Jones used the camp loudspeakers to amplify his nightmare vision" of outside mercenaries invading their compound and torturing, killing, or imprisoning them in concentration camps (Winfrey, 1979). He preached that, since their destruction was inevitable, they should follow the only dignified escape available—revolutionary mass suicide through which they would be reincarnated and reunited to form the utopian society that had eluded them.

Logical Verification

In the course of development, people acquire rules of inference. They can then detect certain errors in thought by logical verification. Thoughts convey information about events. If the information contained in these propositions is accepted as valid, they create logical implications that can be used to gauge the correctness of propositions derived from them. In this mode of verification, the logic of thought provides a means of checking the validity of one's reasoning. The products of reasoning must match the logical consequences that follow deductively from other propositions.

Knowledge can provide information about new situations, as well as be evaluated by rules of inference. By deducing consequences from propositions that they have found to be true, people can derive knowledge about things that extend beyond their experience. Thus, if one knows that a persimmon is a deciduous tree and that deciduous trees shed their leaves in the autumn, then one can arrive at the knowledge that a persimmon tree will remain bare during the winter, without having to observe its foliage throughout the different seasons. In analyzing knowledge by deduction, Powers (1978) notes that deductive reasoning does not create new knowledge. The understanding derived reflects integration of what is already known. But in reasoning from what is already known, one can comprehend what was once unfamiliar.

Logical reasoning operates through a number of subprocesses. The knowledge forming premises must be cast into a propositional format, different sources of propositional knowledge must be combined in a logical relationship, and deductive rules must be applied to the composite information to yield a logical conclusion. As in any multifaceted cognitive skill, one can err at any step of the process, and, indeed, deductive reasoning is often flawed. The errors of reasoning may stem from several sources (Falmagne, 1975). Logical reasoning will yield erroneous conclusions if any part of the propositional knowledge on which it is based is faulty. People commonly form strong beliefs about things on the basis of insufficient or inadequate evidence. They are quick to overgeneralize from limited experiences. Inaccurate suppositions, due largely to nonlogical factors, will provide inferences that are deductively valid but factually erroneous. Even if the propositional knowledge is sound, judgmental errors will arise if the knowledge is linguistically misformulated or faulty deductive rules are applied. In the latter instance, the facts are sound but the reasoning is illogical. To add a further source of error, reasoning is hardly dispassionate. Prejudices and preferences often intrude on reasoning processes. People are, therefore, more prone to appeal to informal judgmental rules that disregard or misweigh relevant facts than to rules of logic. They are probably misled more by their biases concerning what they are reasoning about than by their logical intuitions.

FAULTY THINKING AND HUMAN DISTRESS

The capacity to think vastly expands human capabilities, but, if put to faulty use, it can also serve as a major source of personal distress. Many human dysfunctions and the ensuing torments stem from problems of thought. This is because, in their thoughts, people often dwell on painful pasts and on perturbing futures of their own invention. They burden themselves with stressful arousal through anxiety-provoking rumination. They debilitate their own efforts by self-doubting and other self-defeating ideation. They constrain and impoverish their own lives through phobic thinking. They drive themselves to despondency by harsh self-evaluation and depressogenic modes of thinking. And they often act on misconceptions that get them into trouble.

The preceding chapters have analyzed many lines of evidence on how cognition regulates different facets of human functioning and is itself modified by experience and reflection. Cognitive representations serve as guides for action, and cognitive motivators operating through forethought provide incentives for it. Self-referent thought functions as a major factor in self-regulatory mechanisms mediating stress reactions and coping behavior. Much of the theorizing and research done by cognitive behavior therapists centers on the capacity of perturbing ideation to produce anxiety and despondency (Beck, Laude, & Bohnert, 1974). That thought contributes to affect receives support from experiments showing that self-induced stressful thoughts trigger autonomic arousal (May, 1977; Schwartz, 1971).

Cognitive Therapies for Faulty Thinking

Earlier chapters addressed the origins of dysfunctional modes of thinking and the various means by which they can be altered. In most of these approaches, faulty thinking that gives rise to distress and problem behavior is successfully altered through informative corrective experiences. Thus, for example, phobic thinking is rapidly eradicated by mastery experiences that instill strong self-beliefs of coping efficacy. Other approaches seek to change faulty thinking mainly through verbal, persuasory means.

The major premise of the rational-emotive treatment devised by Ellis is that emotional disturbances are caused by irrational beliefs about oneself and the world (Ellis & Grieger, 1978). He has singled out a set of core beliefs as the major source of human suffering—beliefs such as one must be loved by everyone, one must be supremely competent in all undertakings, and one's value must be judged by one's deeds. Therapists attempt to eradicate such beliefs by persuasion, logical challenge, exhortation, and by prescribing activities that negate irrationality. Through such a process, perfectionists, who are hard on themselves, will adopt the view that it is all right to be imperfect, and self-devaluators will dissociate their self-evaluations from their behavior.

Ascertaining the efficacy of rational-emotive therapy is no easy task because it is said to employ virtually every method that has been shown to influence human behavior. However, the proposition that correcting flawed thinking through rational restructuring improves psychological functioning is testable. Findings of controlled studies suggest that efforts to modify faulty ideation solely by rational analysis and verbal restructuring generally have weak impact on human distress and problem behavior (Mahoney, 1974a; Zettle & Hayes, 1980). Clinical applications of this approach that prescribe actions as well as dispute misbeliefs doubtless produce better results. The benefits of the combined procedure probably derive more from the corrective assignments to behave differently than from the exhortations to think better.

In the cognitive perspective posited by Ellis, human affect and action spring from a small set of global beliefs. Substantial bodies of evidence already reviewed indicate that cognition operates in much more particularized, multifaceted, and reciprocal ways within causal processes. Social labeling of irrationalities is another issue around which differences arise. Given the usual murky factual basis of beliefs, who is to say which beliefs are rational and which are irrational? If carried to an extreme by believers, most of the thought patterns in Ellis's catalogue of irrationalities would be widely accepted as such, but labeling some cognitive functions as psychological hang-ups needing to be eradicated might be contested. For example, Ellis (1973) regards self-evaluation as a dysfunctional human creation that only impairs performance and breeds distress. People should not judge themselves by their conduct, he argues; rather, their value derives from their aliveness.

Self-evaluative functions are neither good nor bad. Whether they impair, inspire, restrain, or liberate depends on their form and the purposes to which they are put. To sever deeds from self-evaluative standards assuages emotional distress but carries with it potential social costs. Perpetrators of inhumanities would be comforted by the view that their abominable deeds should in no way detract from their sense of worthiness. An Adolph Hitler should feel just as worthy as an Albert Schweitzer. Talking tyrants out of their self-evaluative "irrationalities" would lessen their self-censuring reactions but would likely heighten the suffering they inflict on their victims. This is not to say that personal valuation should derive entirely from how one behaves. Humans should value themselves for their being, but should self-evaluation enjoy total immunity from the nature of one's conduct?

Selective experience with distressed persons can instill misbeliefs in theorists that irrationalities are sure to beget human distress and dysfunction. This is because therapists see mainly people whose misbeliefs make them anxious and depressed. Visionaries and unshakeable optimists, whose misbeliefs foster hope and sustain their effort in endeavors beset with immense obstacles, do not flock to psychotherapists. People embark on career paths believing themselves fully capable of reaching the upper ranks, even though objective probabilities show such a belief to be ill founded. For most, their expectations go unrealized, but their misbelief has served them well by sustaining their resolve during the difficult times of developing competency and pursuing their careers. Similarly, the efforts of social reformers rest on illusions about the amount of social change their collective actions will accomplish. Although their fondest hopes are likely to be unrealized during their lifetime, nevertheless their concerted efforts achieve some progress and strengthen the perceived efficacy of others to carry on the struggle. For those leading impoverished, oppressed lives, realism can breed despair. Recall the findings cited earlier that it is nondistressed persons who are positive illusionists, and, following successful treatment, those who have been formerly anxious and despondent display similar self-enhancing distortions. Clearly, the relationship between illusion and psychological functioning is a complex one.

Beck (1976) ascribes psychological dysfunctions to disordered thought, but he emphasizes faulty habits of thinking more than global, irrational beliefs. Among the common errors in thinking Beck singles out are those in which people misread social realities by jumping to erroneous conclusions from flimsy evidence. They fixate on some fragment of their experience but ignore the important aspects. They overgeneralize from particular incidents, as when an isolated failure is taken as proof of complete incompetence. They magnify the significance or seriousness of events, seeing all kinds of catastrophic consequences flowing from ordinary mistakes or setbacks. They personalize happenings that have little, if anything, to do with themselves. They think in a dichotomous fashion. For example, one is either bright or dumb, bold or cowardly, saint or sinner. Faulty cognitive processing of social realities builds idiosyncratic self-schemata which, in turn, negatively distort interpretation and recall of experiences concerning oneself and the environment.

In treating psychological dysfunctions from this perspective, faulty habits of thinking are analyzed and corrected by examining the evidence for and against the misbeliefs. In addition to critical examination of thinking processes, performance-based experiences are used extensively to disconfirm fallacious thinking. For example, after examining the reasons for their immobility, depressed persons are helped through aided performance to deal with tasks they previously considered insurmountable. What appeared hopelessly difficult is thus shown to be attainable through graduated steps. Through such mastery experiences they eventually see themselves as efficacious rather than as inept. Persons who have had a long history of depression derive considerable benefit from this mode of treatment (Rush, Beck, Kovacs, & Hollon, 1977). Combining corrective action with cognitive restructuring achieves greater changes than either factor alone (Taylor & Marshall, 1977).

Meichenbaum (1977) depicts human dysfunction as arising mainly from self-debilitating internal dialogues. That is, people talk themselves into fear, anger, failure, and despondency. However, rather than disputing faulty thinking, Meichenbaum seeks to supplant it by teaching constructive self-talk as a coping strategy. The rationale for focusing on self-instruction as the locus of change derives from Luria's (1961) theory of verbal self-regulation. Luria proposed a three-stage process in the internalization of verbal self-control. Children's behavior is initially regulated by verbal instructions from others. Later, children guide their own actions by overt self-instruction and eventually by covert self-instruction. Although self-guiding speech is a major part of Meichenbaum's approach, it embraces a broader conceptual scheme akin to a personal scientist model (Meichenbaum & Cameron, 1982). Cognitions are viewed as hypotheses to be evaluated rationally and tested empirically by the results of behavioral assignments carried out in the natural milieu. Self-talk, depending on its nature, either aids or hinders the behavioral experimentation.

Some research has been devoted to the self-regulatory function of covert speech (Zivin, 1979). Naturalistic studies tapping spontaneous speech during ongoing transactions raise the usual questions about the direction of causality. Some researchers have concluded from analyses of spontaneous utterances that while self-speech typically precedes or accompanies action, it is often too diffuse and nonspecific to guide it (Roberts, 1979). However, the functional role of self-speech is better clarified by examining how differential pretraining in verbal self-influence affects action. Studies investigating control of simple motor acts following cursory pretraining in role utterances have yielded conflicting findings, especially with young children (Fuson, 1979). The evidence more consistently shows that self-instruction enhances performance when complex tasks requiring thought are used, when extensive pretraining is provided in cognitive self-guidance, and when persons have at their disposal numerous cognitive strategies they can use flexibly, depending on task demands and what works best for them (Meichenbaum & Goodman, 1979). Considerable research by Mischel (1973, 1981) shows that if children are taught effective cognitive strategies they can be quite successful in regulating their own behavior. Cognitive self-influence can regulate action through several different processes. Most explanations emphasize the informative and directive nature of its content. These functional properties are clearly important, but we shall see shortly that there are other processes as well through which training in verbal self-influence can affect action.

Drawing on Luria's developmental sequence, Meichenbaum (1974) devised a set of treatment procedures for developing cognitive self-regulatory skills. In this approach, the therapist thinks aloud strategies of action while modeling coping behavior. The modeled self-talk includes a variety of self-guides, such as analysis of task requirements, symbolic rehearsal of a plan of action, self-instructions for performance, coping self-talk to counteract disruptive thought patterns, and self-praise for attainments. Following the cognitively elaborated modeling, the therapist instructs participants while they practice performing the activities. Fading procedures are then used to establish self-instructional control by having participants perform tasks while instructing themselves at first aloud, then quietly, and eventually covertly.

The procedure combining modeled verbal self-guidance with overt-to-covert self-instructed performance has been applied successfully to a variety of dysfunctions. Some of the components, such as a working rationale, cognitive strategies for diagnosing and solving problems, coping self-statements, and self-praise, are used in all applications of this method. In activities involving stressors and pain, other components, such as attention diversion, self-relaxation, reappraisal and cognitive transformation of events, are added. The composite method achieves significant improvements in varied areas of functioning that may require reducing cognitive and behavioral impulsiveness (Kendall & Finch, 1979; Meichenbaum, 1979); coping with anger, stress, and pain (Meichenbaum & Jaremko, 1983; Novaco, 1979; Turk, Meichenbaum, & Genest, 1981); and acquiring cognitive and social skills.

Varying different facets of the self-talk component does not appear to produce consistent changes in results (Jaremko, 1979).

Several factors may account for such findings. It may be that some of the factors convey redundant information about cognitive strategies for effective action. Outcomes will not be much affected by deletions and additions of redundant aids. A second possibility is that people may already possess many of the requisite cognitive skills, but they make little use of them. The finding is well-established that impaired intellectual functioning often arises more from disuse than from deficits of cognitive competencies (Flavell, 1970). Intensive instruction in verbal self-guidance may provide the means for eliminating disruptive self-referent thought and the motivation for putting into practice known strategies. When part of a method appears to work as well as the complete one, the similarity in results may be due to reduced adherence to the broader method. If people are prescribed many things to do, they may abandon most of them because it is too much bother. A broader method will fail to produce superior results if it is not fully adopted and consistently applied. A further plausible explanation lies in the self-efficacy mediator of change. The pursuits chosen and how well skills are executed partly depends on perceived self-efficacy. Like other modes of treatment, self-guidance training is a self-efficacy builder. The more it raises people's belief in their coping capabilities, the greater are their performance attainments (Fecteau & Stoppard, 1983). Different facets of a method may be roughly equivalent in their efficacy-raising potential.

Although cognitive self-guidance is a multifaceted procedure, the outcomes it produces are often ascribed to self-instructive thought, whereas the reciprocal effects of successful action on thought receive little attention. When treatment is viewed from an interactive perspective, action is used to change thought, as well as thought serving to change action. A component analysis of the self-regulatory approach attests to the influential contribution of enactive mastery. Greater increases in behavioral functioning are achieved by verbal techniques combined with enactive mastery than by verbal techniques alone (Meichenbaum & Goodman, 1971). The following discussion addresses itself to the interactive model of psychological change.

Distinguishing between Mechanisms and Modes of Change

According to the basic tenet of cognitive therapy, to alter how people behave one must alter how they think. To endow thought with causal efficacy need not imply a unidirectional cognitive determinism. Although thought enters into the determination of action, obviously action is not governed solely by thought. Nor is faulty thought necessarily best modified by talk alone.

There is a common misconception that the modality of treatment must match the modality of dysfunction: Behavioral dysfunctions presumably require an action-oriented treatment; emotional distress requires an emotive-oriented treatment; and faulty thinking requires a cognitively-oriented treatment. In fact, powerful experiences can effect changes in all modalities of functioning—motor, cognitive, and affective. A person who had the misfortune to be mauled by a Doberman pinscher, for example, would avoid them like the plague, show visceral agitation at the mere sight of them, develop phobic thinking about them, and loathe them. Powerful enactive mastery experiences similarly eliminate defensive behavior, physiological stress reactions, and faulty thought patterns (Bandura, Blanchard, & Ritter, 1969; Bandura, Reese, & Adams, 1982; Biran & Wilson, 1981). Indeed, performance-mastery experiences achieved through a few hours of participant modeling can even profoundly affect dream activity, eradicating nightmares of long standing (Bandura, Jeffery, & Gajdos, 1975). Such evidence indicates that nightmarish dreaming is more amenable to change by coping mastery than by interpretive dream analysis. In short, the strength of influences rather than the modality in which they are conveyed is more likely to determine the scope of change.

Developments in the field of psychological change reveal two major divergent trends. On the one hand, explanations of psychological change rely increasingly on cognitive mechanisms. On the other hand, performance treatments operating through mastery experiences are proving most powerful in producing cognitive, affective, and behavioral changes. For example, most of the treatments devised to eliminate fearful and defensive behavior have been implemented either through enactive mastery or in symbolic versions in which phobics cope with threats presented in imaginal, vicarious, or verbal forms. Regardless of the methods being compared, treatments using enactive mastery as the principal vehicle of change achieve results superior to those based on symbolic forms of the same approaches (Bandura, 1977a). When those who have benefitted only partially from symbolic treatments subsequently receive enactive mastery, their functioning is fully restored, regardless of the severity of their condition (Bandura, Blanchard, & Ritter, 1969; Biran & Wilson, 1981; Thase & Moss, 1976). Verbal, vicarious, and imaginal attainments are clearly no substitute for masterly action. The apparent divergence between cognitive theory and enactive practice can be reconciled by distinguishing between process and means. Cognitive processes mediate psychological change, but the cognitive events can be developed and altered most readily by enactive mastery.

There is a good deal of evidence that cognitive behavioral therapies effect improvements in varied dysfunctions (Dush, Hirt, & Schroeder, 1983; Kendall & Hollon, 1979). The question of theoretical interest is not whether such methods work, especially if supplemented with a variety of performance aids, but rather the power of cognitive restructuring through verbal means alone to alter behavior. Therapeutic power is best gauged by comparing cognitive restructuring with methods of proven strength, rather than with untreated controls or with weak treatments.

Biran and Wilson (1981) treated phobics either with enactive mastery or with cognitive restructuring that included the three major variants of this procedure—irrational beliefs were corrected as phobics verbalized their thoughts while visualizing threatening situations, they were taught how to supplant self-debilitating ideation with coping self-talk, and how to relabel situations to make them less intimidating. Enactive mastery instilled a strong sense of coping efficacy, diminished physiological stress reactions, and eradicated phobias in virtually everyone. Cognitive restructuring created a weaker and less realistic sense of coping efficacy, did not affect stress reactions, and produced few cures; but when the phobics were given enactive mastery, almost all were cured.

Others have found enactive mastery to be considerably more powerful than multi-faceted cognitive restructuring not only in eradicating phobic behavior but in eliminating agoraphobic thinking as well (Emmelkamp, Kuipers, & Eggeraat, 1978). While imagining threatening situations, phobics can supplant scary thoughts with bold internal dialogues, only to revert to phobic thinking when actual threats are confronted. In contrast, people who gain a strong sense of coping efficacy through enactive triumphs over actual threats have little reason to engage in phobic thinking. Altering thought through enactive experience accords with social psychological approaches that use behavior change to alter attitudes (Abelson et al., 1968; Festinger, 1957).

The efficacy information conveyed by enactive mastery experiences can easily preempt the weaker redundant information provided by verbal restructuring (Rosenthal & Bandura, 1978). Perhaps for this reason adding cognitive restructuring to enactive mastery does not usually promote greater behavioral change than enactive mastery

alone (Emmelkamp, van der Helm, van Zangen, & Plochg, 1980; Emmelkamp & Mersch, 1982; Ladouceur, 1983; Williams & Rappoport, 1983). Whether these findings are generalizable to nonphobic dysfunctions remains to be seen.

Triadic Reciprocality and Cognitively-Oriented Change

Cognitive behavior therapy does not rely solely on verbal analysis of thought processes. To correct faulty ways of thinking, new ways of behaving are prescribed as an integral part of this approach. However, guides for fashioning this aspect of the treatment are undeveloped. Selecting the enactive experiences best suited to disconfirm faulty thought patterns, therefore, rests largely on intuition. When the enactive part of the treatment is implemented only verbally, corrective courses of action are structured for persons to pursue, but they are left to their own devices to carry them out. It is one thing to prescribe corrective action; it is another thing to get people to carry it out, especially when it involves onerous or threatening aspects. The successes achieved will depend on a number of factors: the extent to which individuals are provided with the cognitive and social skills and the self-beliefs of efficacy required to perform effectively, judicious selection and structuring of performance tasks to disconfirm misbeliefs and to expand competencies, incentives to put behavioral prescriptions into practice, and social supports for personal change.

Outcomes are uncertain when distressed persons have to create by themselves the environmental conditions necessary for their own change. Conditions conducive to personal change are more reliably achieved by enlisting the aid of significant others in the treatment. In fact, when enactive modes of treatment are well developed, nonprofessionals can serve as well or better than professionals in guiding mastery experiences that promote rapid change (Mathews et al.,

1977; Moss & Arend, 1977). A cognitively-oriented treatment combining verbal restructuring, simulated practice, and socially aided enactment will produce better results than if corrective action is verbally prescribed but its realization is left unguided.

Cognitive treatments have come under fire from radical behaviorists (Ledwidge, 1978). They raise the spectre of disembodied mentalism. They relabel thought as behavior and argue that behavior cannot cause behavior, only influences outside the organism can. They point to evidence that cognitive methods are no more effective, and often less so, than behavioral techniques. If one looks carefully beneath the surface of such critiques, cognition assumes a quite different form and function. Thoughts are brain processes, not disembodied mental states. To christen thought as behavior is to stretch the definition of behavior to the point where it ceases to have any meaning. Nor is it easy to uphold the dichotomous view that there exist pure cognitive and behavioral treatments. One would be hard pressed to find a "behavioral" method that does not rely, at least in part, on cognitive conveyance, or a "cognitive" method that is devoid of any performance elements.

Within the model of triadic reciprocality, action, cognition, and environmental factors act together to produce changes. Distressed people create perturbing social realities by how they behave, as well as by misreading what they encounter in their everyday life (Coyne, 1982). The causal contribution of cognition is, therefore, best understood and used in concert with behavioral and environmental interactants. The successful treatment of phobic disorders illustrates this point. Phobias are rarely eradicated by thought analysis alone, and although performance successes are forceful persuaders, they do not necessarily ensure generalized changes. The impact that performance attainments exert depends on what is made of them. Among driving phobics, all of whom have been helped to navigate the same difficult routes, some judge themselves thoroughly efficacious and drive around unimpededly; others retain some self-misgivings about their capabilities and drive in a circumscribed fashion; while still others judge their capabilities as confined to the particular route mastered but remain otherwise immobilized by their perceived inefficacy, despite their performance successes (Bandura et al., 1980). The degree and generality of change is mediated by self-percepts of efficacy gleaned from performances, rather than changes being directly forged by the performed responses. When self-referent thought attenuates the force of performance accomplishments, this does not mean that enactive mastery should be abandoned for talk. Rather, analysis of how people are reading their performances provides guides for how to structure mastery experiences to make them more persuasive. In the case of the self-inefficacious drivers, having them succeed on diverse routes, under diverse circumstances, with different field workers quickly persuaded them of their capabilities. Those who judge themselves fully efficacious on the basis of a few performance successes do not require such repetitive proof of coping capabilities.

By analyzing thinking patterns one can best discern the type and amount of enactive experiences needed to alter self-debilitating thought in any given case. The locus of intervention thus involves thought and behavior concurrently rather than singling out one factor as a unidirectional source of change. Psychological changes can, of course, be effected without attending to cognitive processing of experiences, by programming massive mastery experiences that eventually persuade even the most recalcitrant self-doubters. By ignoring cognitive interactants, one sacrifices understanding of the mechanisms mediating change, retards the rate of progress which depends on optimally persuasive behavioral tests, and jeopardizes generalization of change.

Because of the interactive relationship between thought, affect, and action, psychological influences are not exclusively cognitive or behavioral. Nor does their strength depend simply on adding or deleting cognitive and behavioral elements as though they were independent modules of influence. Rather, they act bidirectionally to shape the course of personal and environmental change. It is only fitting that this work should close with the opening theme that has served as an integrating causal principle throughout this volume, namely, the triadic reciprocality of influence.

REFERENCES

ABEL, G. G., BARLOW, D. H., BLANCHARD, E. B., & GUILD, D. (1977). The components of rapists' sexual arousal. *Archives of General Psychiatry, 34,* 895–908.

ABEL, G. G., BECKER, J. V., BLANCHARD, E. B., & FLANAGAN, B. (1981). The behavioral assessment of rapists. In J. Hays, T. Roberts, & K. Solway (Eds.), *Violence and the violent individual* (pp. 211–230). Jamaica, NY: Spectrum.

ABELSON, R. P. (1981). Psychological status of the script concept. *American Psychologist, 36,* 715–729.

ABELSON, R. P., ARONSON E., McGUIRE, W. J., NEWCOMB, T. M., ROSENBERG, M. J., & TANNENBAUM, P. H. (1968). *Theories of cognitive consistency: A sourcebook.* Chicago: Rand McNally.

ABRAMSON, L. Y., & ALLOY, L. B. (1980). Judgment of contingency: Errors and their implications. In A. Baum & J. E. Singer (Eds.), *Advances in environmental psychology* (Vol. 2). *Applications of personal control*, pp. 111–130. Hillsdale, NJ: Erlbaum.

ABRAMSON, L. Y., SELIGMAN, M. E. P., & TEASDALE, J. D. (1978). Learned helplessness in humans: Critique and reformulation. *Journal of Abnormal Psychology, 87,* 49–74.

ABRAVANEL, E., LEVAN-GOLDSCHMIDT, E., & STEVENSON, M. B. (1976). Action imitation: The early phase of infancy. *Child Development, 47,* 1032–1044.

ABRAVANEL, E., & SIGAFOOS, A. D. (1984). Exploring the presence of imitation during early infancy. *Child Development, 55,* 381–392.

ADAIR, J. G., & SPINNER, B. (1981). Subjects' access to cognitive processes: Demand characteristics and verbal report. *Journal for the Theory of Social Behaviour, 11,* 31–52.

ADAMS, C. R., & HAMM, N. H. (1973). A partial test of the "contiguity" and "generalized imitation" theories of the social modeling process. *The Journal of Genetic Psychology, 123,* 145–154.

ADAMS, J. A. (1976). Issues for a closed-loop theory of motor learning. In G. E. Stelmach (Ed.), *Motor control: Issues and trends* (pp. 87–107). New York: Academic Press.

ADAMS, J. A. (1977). Feedback theory of how joint receptors regulate the timing and positioning of a limb. *Psychological Review, 84,* 504–523.

ADAMS, J. A. (1984). Learning of movement sequences. *Psychological Bulletin, 96,* 3–28.

ADAMS, J. K. (1957). Laboratory studies of behavior without awareness. *Psychological Bulletin, 54,* 393–405.

ADAMS, J. S. (1965). Inequity in social exchange. In L. Berkowitz (Ed.), *Advances in experimental social psychology* (Vol. 2, pp. 267–299). New York: Academic Press.

ADER, R., & COHEN, N. (1981). Conditioned immunopharmocologic responses. In R. Ader (Ed.), *Psychoneuroimmunology* (pp. 281–319). New York: Academic Press.

ADLER, H. E., & ADLER, L. L. (1978). What can dolphins (*Tursiops truncatus*) learn by observation? *Oteology, 30,* 1–9.

ADLER, L. L., & ADLER H. E. (1977). Ontogeny of observational learning in the dog (*Canis Familiaris*). *Developmental Psychobiology, 10,* 267–271.

ADONI, H., & MANE, S. (1984). Media and the social construction of reality: Toward an integration of theory and research. *Communication Research, 11,* 323–340.

AGRAS, W. S., LEITENBERG, H., & BARLOW, D. H. (1968). Social reinforcement in modification of agoraphobia. *Archives of General Psychiatry, 19,* 423–427.

AINSWORTH, M. D. S., & BELL, S. M. (1974). Mother-infant interaction and the development of competence. In K. Connolly & J. Bruner (Eds.), *The growth of competence* (pp. 97–118). London: Academic Press.

AKAMATSU, T. J., & FARUDI, P. A. (1978). Effects of model status and juvenile offender type on the imitation of self-reward criteria. *Journal of Consulting and Clinical Psychology, 46,* 187–188.

AKAMATSU, T. J., & THELEN, M. H. (1974). A review of the literature on observer characteristics and imitation. *Developmental Psychology, 10,* 38–47.

ALBERT, A. A., & PORTER, J. R. (1982). Children's perception of parental sex-role expectations. *The Journal of Genetic Psychology, 140,* 145–146.

ALINSKY, S. D. (1971). *Rules for radicals.* New York: Random House.

ALLEN, M. K., & LIEBERT, R. M. (1969). Effects of live and symbolic deviant-modeling cues on adoption of a previously learned standard. *Journal of Personality and Social Psychology, 11,* 253–260.

ALLISON, J. (1978). Beyond the relational principle of reinforcement. *Journal of the Experimental Analysis of Behavior, 29,* 557–560.

ALLOY, L. B., & ABRAMSON, L. Y. (1979). Judgment of contingency in depressed and nondepressed students: Sadder but wiser? *Journal of Experimental Psychology, 108,* 441–487.

ALLOY, L. B., & ABRAMSON, L. Y. (1982). Learned helplessness, depression and the illusion of control. *Journal of Personality and Social Psychology, 42,* 1114–1126.

ALLOY, L. B., ABRAMSON, L. Y., & VISCUSI, D. (1981). Induced mood and the illusion of control. *Journal of Personality and Social Psychology, 41,* 1129–1140.

ALLPORT, F. H. (1924). *Social psychology.* Cambridge, MA: Riverside.

ALLPORT, G. W. (1961). *Pattern and growth in personality.* New York: Holt Rinehart & Winston.

AMES, C. (1984). Competitive, cooperative, and individualistic goal structures: A cognitive-motivational analysis. In R. E. Ames & C. Ames (Eds.), *Research on motivation in education: Student motivation* (Vol. 1, pp. 177–207). New York: Academic Press.

ANDERSON, C. A., & JENNINGS, D. L. (1980). When experiences of failure promote expectations of success: The impact of attributing failure to ineffective strategies. *Journal of Personality, 48,* 393–407.

ANDERSON, J. R. (1978). Arguments concerning representations for mental imagery. *Psychological Review, 85,* 249–277.

ANDERSON, J. R. (1980). *Cognitive psychology and its implications.* San Francisco: Freeman.

ANDERSON, J. R. (1983). *The architecture of cognition.* Cambridge, MA: Harvard University Press.

ANDERSON, J. R., & BOWER, G. H. (1973). *Human associative memory.* New York: Wiley.

ANDERSON, R. C. (1978). Schema-directed processes in language comprehension. In A. M. Lesgold, J. W. Pellegrino, S. D. Fokkema, & R. Glaser (Eds.), *Cognitive psychology and instruction* (pp. 67–82). New York: Plenum.

ANDRUS, B. C. (1969). *The infamous of Nuremberg.* London: Fravin.

ANISKIEWICZ, A. S. (1979). Autonomic components of vicarious conditioning and psychopathy. *Journal of Clinical Psychology, 35,* 60–67.

ANTROBUS, J. S. (1979). Matters of definition in the demystification of mental imagery. *The Behavioral and Brain Sciences, 2,* 549–550.

ARBUTHNOT, J. (1975). Modification of moral judgment through role playing. *Developmental Psychology, 11,* 319–324.

ARCHER, D., GARTNER, R., & BEITTEL, M. (1983). Homicide and the death penalty: A cross-national test of a deterrence hypothesis. *The Journal of Criminal Law & Criminology, 74,* 991–1013.

ARENA, J. G., BLANCHARD, E. B., ANDRASIK, F., COTCH, P. A., & MYERS, P. E. (1983). Reliability of psychophysiological assessment. *Behaviour Research and Therapy, 21,* 447–460.

ARENSON, S. J., LANNON, P. B., OFFERMANN, L. R., & KAFTON, A. (1982). The validity of attitude change by classical conditioning. *The Journal of Social Psychology, 117,* 243–248.

ARMELIUS, B. A., & ARMELIUS, K. (1976). *Combination rules in multiple-cue probability learning. II. Performance, confidence and development of rules.* (Umea Psychological Reports No. 101). University of Umea, Sweden.

ARNOLD, H. J. (1976). Effects of performance feedback and extrinsic reward upon high intrinsic motivation. *Organizational Behavior and Human Performance, 17,* 275–288.

ARON, I. E. (1977). Moral philosophy and moral education: A critique of Kohlberg's theory. *School Review, 85,* 197–217.

ARONFREED, J. (1968). *Conduct and conscience.* New York: Academic Press.

ARONFREED, J. (1969). The problem of imitation. In L. P. Lipsitt & H. W. Reese (Eds.), *Advances in child development and behavior* (Vol. 4, pp. 209–319). New York: Academic Press.

ARVEY, R. D., & DEWHIRST, H. D. (1976). Goal-setting attributes, personality variables, and job satisfaction. *Journal of Vocational Behavior, 9,* 179–190.

ASHBY, M. S., & WITTMAIER, B. C. (1978). Attitude changes in children after exposure to stories about women in traditional or nontraditional occupations. *Journal of Educational Psychology, 70,* 945–949.

ASHTON, P. (1985). Motivation and the teacher's sense of efficacy. In C. Ames & R. Ames (Eds.), *Research on motivation in education: The classroom milieu* (pp. 141–171). New York: Academic Press.

ATKIN, C. K. (1978). Observation of parent-child interaction in supermarket decision-making. *Journal of Marketing, 42,* 41–45.

ATKIN, C., HOCKING, J., & BLOCK, M. (1984). Teenage drinking: Does advertising make a difference? *Journal of Communication, 34,* 157–167.

ATKIN, J. M. (1980). The government in the classroom. *Daedalus, 109,* 85–89.

ATKINSON, J. W. (1957). Motivational determinants of risk-taking behavior. *Psychological Review, 64,* 359–372.

ATKINSON, J. W. (1964). *An introduction to motivation.* Princeton, NJ: Van Nostrand.

AUSTIN, J. H. (1978). *Chase, chance, and creativity: The lucky art of novelty.* New York: Columbia University Press.

AUSTIN, V. D., RUBLE, D. N., & TRABASSO, T. (1977). Recall and order effects as factors in children's moral judgments. *Child Development, 48,* 470–474.

AVERILL, J. R. (1973). Personal control over aversive stimuli and its relationship to stress. *Psychological Bulletin, 80,* 286–303.

AVERY-CLARK, C. A., & LAWS, D. R. (1984). Differential erection response patterns of sexual child abusers to stimuli describing activities with children. *Behavior Therapy, 15,* 71–83.

AX, A. F. (1953). The physiological differentiation between fear and anger in humans. *Psychosomatic Medicine, 15,* 433–442.

AXELROD, S., & APSCHE, J. (Eds.). (1983). *Effects of punishment on human behavior.* New York: Academic Press.

AYLLON, T., & AZRIN, N. H. (1964). Reinforcement and instructions with mental patients. *Journal of the Experimental Analysis of Behavior, 7,* 327–331.

AYLLON, T., & HAUGHTON, E. (1962). Control of the behavior of schizophrenic patients by food. *Journal of the Experimental Analysis of Behavior, 5,* 343–352.

AZRIN, N. H., & HOLZ, W. C. (1966). Punishment. In W. K. Honig (Ed.), *Operant behavior* (pp. 380–447). New York: Appleton-Century-Crofts.

BAER, D. M., PETERSON, R. F., & SHERMAN, J. A. (1967). The development of imitation by reinforcing behavioral similarity to a model. *Journal of the Experimental Analysis of Behavior, 10,* 405–416.

BAER, D. M., & SHERMAN, J. A. (1964). Reinforcement control of generalized imitation in young children. *Journal of Experimental Child Psychology, 1,* 37–49.

BAER, D. M., & WOLF, M. M. (1970). The entry into natural communities of reinforcement. In R. Ulrich, T. Stachnik, & J. Mabry (Eds.), *Control of human behavior: From cure to prevention* (Vol. 2, pp. 319–324). Glenview, IL: Scott, Foresman.

BAKER, N. D., & NELSON, K. E. (1985). Recasting and related conversational techniques for triggering syntactic advances by young children. *First Language.*

BALCH, G. I. (1974). Multiple indicators in survey research: The concept "sense of political efficacy." *Political Methodology, 1*(2), 1–43.

BALDWIN, A. L., & BALDWIN, C. P. (1973). The study of mother-child interaction. *American Scientist, 61,* 714–721.

BALDWIN, T. F., & LEWIS, C. (1972). Violence in television: The industry looks at itself. In G. A. Comstock & E. A. Rubinstein (Eds.), *Television and social behavior: Vol. 1. Media content and control* (pp. 290–373). Washington, DC: U.S. Government Printing Office.

BALLARD, K. D., & GLYNN, T. (1975). Behavioral self-management in story writing with elementary school children. *Journal of Applied Behavior Analysis, 8,* 387–398.

BALL-ROKEACH, S. J. (1972). The legitimation of violence. In J. F. Short, Jr. & M. E. Wolfgang (Eds.), *Collective violence* (pp. 100–111). Chicago: Aldine-Atherton.

BALL-ROKEACH, S., & DEFLEUR, M. (1976). A dependency model of mass media effects. *Communication Research, 3,* 3–21.

BALTES, P. B. (1982). Life-span developmental psychology: Observations on history and theory revisited. In R. M. Lerner (Ed.), *Developmental psychology: Historical and philosophical perspectives* (pp. 79–111). Hillsdale, NJ: Erlbaum.

BALTES, P. B., & LABOUVIE, G. V. (1973). Adult development of intellectual performance: Description, explanation, and modification. In C. Eisdorfer & M. P. Lawton (Eds.), *The psychology of adult development and aging* (pp. 157–219). Washington, DC: American Psychological Association.

BALTES, P. B., REESE, H. W., & LIPSITT, L. P. (1980). Life-span developmental psychology. *Annual Review of Psychology, 31,* 65–110.

BALTES, P. B., & WILLIS, S. L. (1982). Plasticity and enhancement of intellectual functioning in old age: Penn State's adult development enrichment project. In F. I. M. Craik & E. E. Trehub (Eds.), *Aging and cognitive processes* (pp. 353–389). New York: Plenum.

BANDURA, A. (1962). Social learning through imitation. In M. R. Jones (Ed.), *Nebraska Symposium on Motivation* (Vol. 10, pp. 211–274). Lincoln: University of Nebraska Press.

BANDURA, A. (1965a). Vicarious processes: A case of no-trial learning. In L. Berkowitz (Ed.), *Advances in experimental social psychology* (Vol. 2, pp. 1–55). New York: Academic Press.

BANDURA, A. (1965b). Influence of models' reinforcement contingencies on the acquisition of imitative responses. *Journal of Personality and Social Psychology, 1,* 589–595.

BANDURA, A. (1969a). *Principles of behavior modification.* New York: Holt, Rinehart & Winston.

BANDURA, A. (1969b). Social-learning theory of identificatory processes. In D. A. Goslin (Ed.), *Handbook of socialization theory and research* (pp. 213–262). Chicago: Rand McNally.

BANDURA, A. (Ed.). (1971a). *Psychological modeling: Conflicting theories*. Chicago: Aldine-Atherton.

BANDURA, A. (1971b). Vicarious and self-reinforcement processes. In R. Glaser (Ed.), *The nature of reinforcement* (pp. 228–278). New York: Academic Press.

BANDURA, A. (1971c). Psychotherapy based upon modeling principles. In A. E. Bergin & S. L. Garfield (Eds.), *Handbook of psychotherapy and behavior change* (pp. 653–708). New York: Wiley.

BANDURA, A. (1973). *Aggression: A social learning analysis*. Englewood Cliffs, NJ: Prentice-Hall.

BANDURA, A. (1976a). Self-reinforcement: Theoretical and methodological considerations. *Behaviorism, 4*, 135–155.

BANDURA, A. (1976b). Social learning perspective on behavior change. In A. Burton (Ed.), *What makes behavior change possible?* (pp. 34–57). New York: Brunner/Mazel.

BANDURA, A. (1977a). *Social learning theory*. Englewood Cliffs, NJ: Prentice-Hall.

BANDURA, A. (1977b). Self-efficacy: Toward a unifying theory of behavioral change. *Psychological Review, 84*, 191–215.

BANDURA, A. (1978a). The self system in reciprocal determinism. *American Psychologist, 33*, 344–358.

BANDURA, A. (1978b). Reflections on self-efficacy. In S. Rachman (Ed.), *Advances in behaviour research and therapy* (Vol. 1, pp. 237–269). Oxford: Pergamon.

BANDURA, A. (1978c). On paradigms and recycled ideologies. *Cognitive Therapy and Research, 2*, 79–103.

BANDURA, A. (1979). Psychological mechanisms of aggression. In M. Von Cranach, K. Foppa, W. LePenies, & D. Ploog (Eds.), *Human ethology: Claims and limits of a new discipline* (pp. 316–356). London: Cambridge University Press.

BANDURA, A. (1981a). Self-referent thought: A developmental analysis of self-efficacy. In J. H. Flavell & L. D. Ross (Eds.), *Cognitive social development: Frontiers and possible futures* (pp. 200–239). New York: Cambridge University Press.

BANDURA, A. (1981b). In search of pure unidirectional determinants. *Behavior Therapy, 12*, 30–40.

BANDURA, A. (1982a). Self-efficacy mechanism in human agency. *American Psychologist, 37*, 122–147.

BANDURA, A. (1982b). The self and mechanisms of agency. In J. Suls (Ed.), *Psychological perspectives on the self* (Vol. 1, pp. 3–39). Hillsdale, NJ: Erlbaum.

BANDURA, A. (1982c). The psychology of chance encounters and life paths. *American Psychologist, 37*, 747–755.

BANDURA, A. (1982d). The assessment and predictive generality of self-percepts of efficacy. *Journal of Behavior Therapy and Experimental Psychiatry, 13*, 195–199.

BANDURA, A. (1983a). Temporal dynamics and decomposition of reciprocal determinism: A reply to Phillips and Orton. *Psychological Review, 90*, 166–170.

BANDURA, A. (1983b). Self-efficacy determinants of anticipated fears and calamities. *Journal of Personality and Social Psychology, 45*, 464–469.

BANDURA, A., & ADAMS, N. E. (1977). Analysis of self-efficacy theory of behavioral change. *Cognitive Therapy and Research, 1*, 287–308.

BANDURA, A., ADAMS, N. E., & BEYER, J. (1977). Cognitive processes mediating behavioral change. *Journal of Personality and Social Psychology, 35*, 125–139.

BANDURA, A., ADAMS, N. E., HARDY, A. B., & HOWELLS, G. N. (1980). Tests of the generality of self-efficacy theory. *Cognitive Therapy and Research, 4*, 39–66.

BANDURA, A., & BARAB, P. G. (1971). Conditions governing nonreinforced imitation. *Developmental Psychology, 5*, 244–255.

BANDURA, A., & BARAB, P. G. (1973). Processes governing disinhibitory effects through symbolic modeling. *Journal of Abnormal Psychology, 82*, 1–9.

BANDURA, A., BLANCHARD, E. B., & RITTER, B. (1969). Relative efficacy of desensitization and modeling approaches for inducing behavioral, affective, and attitudinal changes. *Journal of Personality and Social Psychology, 13*, 173–199.

BANDURA, A., & CERVONE, D. (1983). Self-evaluative and self-efficacy mechanisms governing the motivational effects of goal systems. *Journal of Personality and Social Psychology, 45*, 1017–1028.

BANDURA, A., & CERVONE, D. (1986). Differential engagement of self-reactive influences in cognitive motivation. *Organizational Behavior and Human Decision Processes, 38*, 92–113.

BANDURA, A., GRUSEC, J. E., & MENLOVE, F. L. (1966). Observational learning as a function of symbolization and incentive set. *Child Development, 37*, 499–506.

BANDURA, A., GRUSEC, J. E., & MENLOVE, F. L. (1967a). Some social determinants of self-monitoring reinforcement systems. *Journal of Personality and Social Psychology, 5*, 449–455.

BANDURA, A., GRUSEC, J. E., & MENLOVE, F. L. (1967b). Vicarious extinction of avoidance behavior. *Journal of Personality and Social Psychology, 5*, 16–23.

BANDURA, A., & HARRIS, M. B. (1966). Modification of syntactic style. *Journal of Experimental Child Psychology, 4*, 341–352.

BANDURA, A., & HUSTON, A. C. (1961). Identification as a process of incidental learning. *Journal of Abnormal and Social Psychology, 63*, 311–318.

BANDURA, A., & JEFFERY, R. W. (1973). Role of symbolic coding and rehearsal processes in observational learning. *Journal of Personality and Social Psychology, 26*, 122–130.

BANDURA, A., JEFFERY, R. W., & BACHICHA, D. L. (1974). Analysis of memory codes and cumulative rehearsal in observational learning. *Journal of Research in Personality, 7*, 295–305.

BANDURA, A., JEFFERY, R. W., & GAJDOS, E. (1975). Generalizing change through participant modeling with self-directed mastery. *Behaviour Research and Therapy, 13*, 141–152.

BANDURA, A., JEFFERY, R. W., & WRIGHT, C. L. (1974). Efficacy of participant modeling as a function of response induction aids. *Journal of Abnormal Psychology, 83*, 56–64.

BANDURA, A., & KUPERS, C. J. (1964). Transmission of patterns of self-reinforcement through modeling. *Journal of Abnormal and Social Psychology, 69,* 1–9.

BANDURA, A., LIPSHER, D. H., & MILLER, P. E. (1960). Psychotherapists' approach-avoidance reactions to patients' expressions of hostility. *Journal of Consulting Psychology, 24,* 1–8.

BANDURA, A., & MAHONEY, M. J. (1974). Maintenance and transfer of self-reinforcement functions. *Behaviour Research and Therapy, 12,* 89–97.

BANDURA, A., MAHONEY, M. J., & DIRKS, S. J. (1976). Discriminative activation and maintenance of contingent self-reinforcement. *Behaviour Research and Therapy, 14,* 1–6.

BANDURA, A., & McDONALD, F. J. (1963). Influence of social reinforcement and the behavior of models in shaping children's moral judgments. *Journal of Abnormal and Social Psychology, 67,* 274–281.

BANDURA, A., & MENLOVE, F. L. (1968). Factors determining vicarious extinction of avoidance behavior through symbolic modeling. *Journal of Personality and Social Psychology, 8,* 99–108.

BANDURA, A., & MISCHEL, W. (1965). The influence of models in modifying delay of gratification patterns. *Journal of Personality and Social Psychology, 2,* 698–705.

BANDURA, A. & PERLOFF, B. (1967). Relative efficacy of self-monitored and externally imposed reinforcement systems. *Journal of Personality and Social Psychology, 7,* 111–116.

BANDURA, A., REESE, L., & ADAMS, N. E. (1982). Microanalysis of action and fear arousal as a function of differential levels of perceived self-efficacy. *Journal of Personality and Social Psychology, 43,* 5–21.

BANDURA, A., & ROSENTHAL, T. L. (1966). Vicarious classical conditioning as a function of arousal level. *Journal of Personality and Social Psychology, 3,* 54–62.

BANDURA, A., ROSS, D., & ROSS, S. A. (1963a). Imitation of film-mediated aggressive models. *Journal of Abnormal and Social Psychology, 66,* 3–11.

BANDURA, A., ROSS, D., & ROSS, S. A. (1963b). Vicarious reinforcement and imitative learning. *Journal of Abnormal and Social Psychology, 67,* 601–607.

BANDURA, A., ROSS, D., & ROSS, S. A. (1963c). A comparative test of the status envy, social power, and secondary reinforcement theories of identificatory learning. *Journal of Abnormal and Social Psychology, 67,* 527–534.

BANDURA, A., & SCHUNK, D. H. (1981). Cultivating competence, self-efficacy, and intrinsic interest through proximal self-motivation. *Journal of Personality and Social Psychology, 41,* 586–598.

BANDURA, A., & SIMON, K. M. (1977). The role of proximal intentions in self-regulation of refractory behavior. *Cognitive Therapy and Research, 1,* 177–193.

BANDURA, A., TAYLOR, C. B., WILLIAMS, S. L., MEFFORD, I. N., & BARCHAS, J. D. (1985). Catecholamine secretion as a function of perceived coping self-efficacy. *Journal of Consulting and Clinical Psychology, 53,* 406–414.

BANDURA, A., UNDERWOOD, B., & FROMSON, M. E. (1975). Disinhibition of aggression through diffusion of responsibility and dehumanization of victims. *Journal of Research in Personality, 9,* 253–269.

BANDURA, A., & WALTERS, R. H. (1959). *Adolescent aggression.* New York: Ronald Press.

BANDURA, A., & WALTERS, R. H. (1963). *Social learning and personality development.* New York: Holt, Rinehart & Winston.

BANDURA, A., & WHALEN, C. K. (1966). The influence of antecedent reinforcement and divergent modeling cues on patterns of self-reward. *Journal of Personality and Social Psychology, 3,* 373–382.

BANDURA, M. M. (1983). *Children's conception of intelligence in relation to achievement goals and patterns of achievement-related cognition, affect and behavior.* Unpublished doctoral dissertation, Pennsylvania State University.

BANDURA, M. M., LANGER, E. J., & CHANOWITZ, B. (1984). Interpersonal effectiveness from a mindlessness/mindfulness perspective. In P. Trower (Ed.), *Radical approaches to social skills training* (pp. 182–204). London: Croom Helm.

BARBER, B., & FOX, R. C. (1958). The case of the floppy-eared rabbits: An instance of serendipity gained and serendipity lost. *The American Journal of Sociology, 54,* 128–136.

BARBER, T. X., & HAHN, K. W., JR. (1964). Experimental studies in "hypnotic" behavior: Physiological and subjective effects of imagined pain. *Journal of Nervous and Mental Disease, 139,* 416–425.

BARKLEY, R. A., ULLMAN, D. G., OTTO, L., & BRECHT, J. M. (1977). The effects of sex typing and sex appropriateness of modeled behavior on children's imitation. *Child Development, 48,* 721–725.

BARLING, J., & ABEL, M. (1983). Self-efficacy beliefs and performance. *Cognitive Therapy and Research, 7,* 265–272.

BARLING, J., & BEATTIE, R. (1983). Self-efficacy beliefs and sales performance. *Journal of Organizational Behavior Management, 5,* 41–51.

BARLOW, D. H., LEITENBERG, H., AGRAS, W. S., & WINCZE, J. P. (1969). The transfer gap in systematic desensitization: An analogue study. *Behaviour Research and Therapy, 7,* 191–196.

BARNETT, A. D. (1967). A note on communication and development in communist China. In D. Lerner & W. Schramm (Eds.), *Communication and change in the developing countries* (pp. 231–234). Honolulu: East-West Center Press.

BARNWELL, A. K. (1966). Potency of modeling cues in imitation and vicarious reinforcement situations. *Dissertation Abstracts, 26,* 7444 (University Microfilms No. 66–02681).

BARON, A., KAUFMAN, A., & STAUBER, K. A. (1969). Effects of instructions and reinforcement-feedback on human operant behavior maintained by fixed-interval reinforcement. *Journal of the Experimental Analysis of Behavior, 12,* 701–712.

BARON, P., & WATTERS, R. G. (1981). Effects of goal-setting and of goal levels on weight loss induced by self-monitoring of caloric intake. *Canadian Journal of Behavioural Science, 13,* 161–170.

BARON, R. A. (1977). *Human aggression.* New York: Plenum.

BARRIOS, B. A. (1983). The role of cognitive mediators in heterosocial anxiety: A test of self-efficacy theory. *Cognitive Therapy and Research, 7,* 543–554.

BARRIOS, F. X. (1985). A comparison of global and specific estimates of self-control. *Cognitive Therapy and Research, 9,* 455–469.

BARRIOS, F. X., & NIEHAUS, J. C. (1985). The influence of smoker status, smoking history, sex, and situational variables on smokers' self-efficacy. *Addictive Behaviors, 10,* 425–430.

BARTON, A. H. (1980). Fault lines in American elite consensus. *Daedalus, 109* (3), 1–24.

BATES, J. A. (1979). Extrinsic reward and intrinsic motivation: A review with implications for the classroom. *Review of Educational Research, 49,* 557.

BATESON, G. (Ed.). (1961). *Perceval's narrative: A patient's account of his psychosis, 1830–1832.* Stanford, CA: Stanford University Press.

BAUM, W. M. (1973). The correlation-based law of effect. *Journal of the Experimental Analysis of Behavior, 20,* 137–153.

BAUM, W. M. (1981). Optimization and the matching law as accounts of instrumental behavior. *Journal of the Experimental Analysis of Behavior, 36,* 387–403.

BAUMRIND, D. (1973). The development of instrumental competence through socialization. In A. D. Pick (Ed.), *Minnesota symposia on child psychology* (Vol. 7, pp. 3–46). Minneapolis: University of Minnesota Press.

BEACH, F. A. (1969, July). It's all in your mind. *Psychology Today,* pp. 33–35, 60.

BECK, A. T. (1973). *The diagnosis and management of depression.* Philadelphia: University of Pennsylvania Press.

BECK, A. T. (1976). *Cognitive therapy and the emotional disorders.* New York: International Universities Press.

BECK, A. T., LAUDE, R., & BOHNERT, M. (1974). Ideational components of anxiety neurosis. *Archives of General Psychiatry, 31,* 319–325.

BECK, K. H., & FRANKEL, A. (1981). A conceptualization of threat communications and protective health behavior. *Social Psychology Quarterly, 44,* 204–217.

BECK, K. H., & LUND, A. K. (1981). The effects of health threat seriousness and personal efficacy upon intentions and behavior. *Journal of Applied Social Psychology, 11,* 401–415.

BECKER, L. J. (1978). Joint effect of feedback and goal setting on performance: A field study of residential energy conservation. *Journal of Applied Psychology, 63,* 428–433.

BEDAU, H. A. (Ed.). (1967). *The death penalty in America: An anthology* (rev. ed.). Garden City, NY: Anchor Books.

BEHLING, O., & STARKE, F. A. (1973). The postulates of expectancy theory. *Academy of Management Journal, 16,* 373–388.

BELCHER, T. L. (1975). Modeling original divergent responses: An initial investigation. *Journal of Educational Psychology, 67,* 351–358.

BELL, R. Q., & HARPER, L. V. (1977). *Child effects on adults.* Hillsdale, NJ: Erlbaum.

BELLACK, A. S. (1972). Internal vs external locus of control and the use of self-reinforcement. *Psychological Reports, 31,* 723–733.

BELLACK, A. S. (1975). Self-evaluation, self-reinforcement, and locus of control. *Journal of Research in Personality, 9,* 158–167.

BELLACK, A. S. (1976). A comparison of self-reinforcement and self-monitoring in a weight reduction program. *Behavior Therapy, 7,* 68–75.

BEM, D. J. (1972). Self-perception theory. In L. Berkowitz (Ed.), *Advances in experimental social psychology* (Vol. 6, pp. 2–62). New York: Academic Press.

BEM, D. J., & ALLEN, A. (1974). On predicting some of the people some of the time: The search for cross-situational consistencies in behavior. *Psychological Review, 81,* 506–520.

BEM, D. J., & FUNDER, D. C. (1978). Predicting more of the people more of the time: Assessing the personality of situations. *Psychological Review, 85,* 485–501.

BEM, S. L. (1978). Beyond androgyny: Some presumptuous prescriptions for a liberated sexual identity. In J. Sherman & F. Denmark (Eds.), *The psychology of women: Future directions in research* (pp. 1–23). New York: Psychological Dimensions.

BEM, S. L. (1981). Gender schema theory: A cognitive account of sex typing. *Psychological Review, 88,* 354–364.

BENTON, A. A. (1967). Effects of the timing of negative response consequences on the observational learning of resistance to temptation in children. *Dissertation Abstracts, 27,* 2153–2154.

BERGER, S. M. (1961). Incidental learning through vicarious reinforcement. *Psychological Reports, 9,* 477–491.

BERGER, S. M. (1962). Conditioning through vicarious instigation. *Psychological Review, 69,* 450–466.

BERGER, S. M. (1971). Observer perseverance as related to a model's success. *Journal of Personality and Social Psychology, 19,* 341–350.

BERGER, S. M., & JOHANSSON, S. L. (1968). Effect of a model's expressed emotions on an observer's resistance to extinction. *Journal of Personality and Social Psychology, 10,* 53–58.

BERKOWITZ, L. (1965). The concept of aggressive drive: Some additional considerations. In L. Berkowitz (Ed.), *Advances in experimental social psychology* (Vol. 2, pp. 301–329). New York: Academic Press.

BERLYNE, D. E. (1960). *Conflict, arousal, and curiosity.* New York: McGraw-Hill.

BERNARD, V., OTTENBERG, P., & REDL, F. (1965). Dehumanization: A composite psychological defense in relation to modern war. In M. Schwebel (Ed.), *Behavioral science and human survival* (pp. 64–82). Palo Alto, CA: Science and Behavior Books.

BESALEL-AZRIN, V., AZRIN, N. H., & ARMSTRONG, P. M.

(1977). The student-oriented classroom: A method of improving student conduct and satisfaction. *Behavior Therapy, 8*, 193–204.

BETTELHEIM, B. (1943). Individual and mass behavior in extreme situations. *Journal of Abnormal and Social Psychology, 38*, 417–452.

BETZ, N. E., & HACKETT, G. (1981). The relationship of career-related self-efficacy expectations to perceived career options in college women and men. *Journal of Counseling Psychology, 23*, 399–410.

BETZ, N. E., & HACKETT, G. (1983). The relationship of mathematics self-efficacy expectations to the selection of science-based college majors. *Journal of Vocational Behavior, 23*, 329–345.

BIAGGIO, A., & RODRIGUES, A. (1971). Behavioral compliance and devaluation of the forbidden object as a function of probability of detection and severity of threat. *Developmental Psychology, 4*, 320–323.

BICKEL, A. (1974). Watergate and the legal order. *Commentary, 59*, 19–25.

BILODEAU, E. A. (Ed.). (1966). *Acquisition of skill.* New York: Academic Press.

BINDRA, D. (1974). A motivational view of learning, performance, and behavior modification. *Psychological Review, 81*, 199–213.

BINSWANGER, L. (1958). The case of Ellen West. In R. May, E. Angel, & H. F. Ellenberger (Eds.), *Existence: A new dimension in psychiatry and psychology* (pp. 237–264). New York: Basic Books.

BIRAN, M., & WILSON, G. T. (1981). Treatment of phobic disorders using cognitive and exposure methods: A self-efficacy analysis. *Journal of Consulting and Clinical Psychology, 49*, 886–899.

BIRCH, L. L. (1980). Effects of peer models' food choices and eating behaviors on preschoolers' food preferences. *Child Development, 51*, 489–496.

BIRNBAUM, M. H. (1981). Thinking and feeling: A skeptical review. *American Psychologist, 36*, 99–101.

BLACK, A. H. (1965). Cardiac conditioning in curarized dogs: The relationship between heart rate and skeletal behaviour. In W. F. Prokasy (Ed.), *Classical conditioning: A symposium* (pp. 20–47). New York: Appleton-Century-Crofts.

BLACKBURN, H. ET AL. (1984). The Minnesota Heart Health Program: A research and demonstration project in cardiovascular disease prevention. In J. D. Matarazzo, S. M. Weiss, J. A. Herd, N. E. Miller, & S. M. Weiss (Eds.), *Behavioral health: A handbook of health enhancement and disease prevention* (pp. 1171–1178). Silver Spring, MD: Wiley.

BLAKE, R. R. (1958). The other person in the situation. In R. Taguiri & L. Petrullo (Eds.), *Person perception and interpersonal behavior* (pp. 229–242). Stanford, CA: Stanford University Press.

BLANCHARD, E. B. (1970a). Relative contributions of modeling, informational influences, and physical contact in extinction of phobic behavior. *Journal of Abnormal Psychology, 76*, 55–61.

BLANCHARD, E. G. (1970b). The generalization of vicarious extinction effects. *Behaviour Research and Therapy, 7*, 323–330.

BLANCHARD, E. B., AHLES, T. A., & SHAW, E. R. (1979). Behavioral treatment of headaches. In M. Hersen, R. M. Eisler, & P. M. Miller (Eds.), *Progress in behavior modification* (Vol. 8, pp. 207–247). New York: Academic Press.

BLASI, A. (1980). Bridging moral cognition and moral action: A critical review of the literature. *Psychological Bulletin, 88*, 1–45.

BLOCK, J. (1981). Some enduring and consequential structures of personality. In A. I. Rabin, J. Aronoff, A. M. Barclay, & R. A. Zucker (Eds.), *Further explorations in personality* (pp. 27–43). New York: Wiley.

BLOOM, C. P., YATES, B. T., & BROSVIC, G. M. (1983, August). *Self-efficacy reporting, sex-role stereotype, and sex differences in susceptibility to depression.* Paper presented at the annual meeting of the American Psychological Association, Anaheim, CA.

BLOOM, L., HOOD, L., & LIGHTBOWN, P. (1974). Imitation in language development: If, when, and why. *Cognitive Psychology, 6*, 380–420.

BLUMENTHAL, M., KAHN, R. L., ANDREWS, F. M., & HEAD, K. B. (1972). *Justifying violence: The attitudes of American men.* Ann Arbor, MI: Institute for Social Research.

BLUMSTEIN, A., COHEN, J., & NAGIN, D. (1978). *Deterrence and incapacitation: Estimating the effects of criminal sanctions on crime rates.* Washington, DC: National Academy of Sciences.

BOGGIANO, A. K., & RUBLE, D. N. (1979). Competence and the overjustification effect: A developmental study. *Journal of Personality and Social Psychology, 37*, 1462–1468.

BOHANNON, J. N., III, & MARQUIS, A. L. (1977). Children's control of adult speech. *Child Development, 48*, 1002–1008.

BOK, S. (1980). The self deceived. *Social Science Information, 19*, 923–936.

BOLINGER, D. (1982). *Language: The loaded weapon.* London: Longman.

BOLLEN, K. A., & PHILLIPS, D. P. (1981). Suicidal motor vehicle fatalities in Detroit: A replication. *American Journal of Sociology, 87*, 404–412.

BOLLES, R. C. (1972a). The avoidance learning problem. In G. Bower (Ed.), *The psychology of learning and motivation* (Vol. 6, pp. 97–145). New York: Academic Press.

BOLLES, R. C. (1972b). Reinforcement, expectancy, and learning. *Psychological Review, 79*, 394–409.

BOLLES, R. C. (1975). *Learning theory.* New York: Holt, Rinehart & Winston.

BOLLES, R. C., & FANSELOW, M. S. (1982). Endorphins and behavior. *Annual Reviews of Psychology, 33*, 87–101.

BOOTZIN, R. R., HERMAN, C. P., & NICASSIO, P. (1976). The power of suggestion: Another examination of misattribution and insomnia. *Journal of Personality and Social Psychology, 34*, 673–679.

BORDEN, B. L., & WHITE, G. M. (1973). Some effects of observing a model's reinforcement schedule and rate of responding on extinction and response rate. *Journal of Experimental Psychology, 97*, 41–45.

Boring, E. G. (1957). When is human behavior predetermined? *The Scientific Monthly, 84*, 189–196.

Borkovec, T. D. (1973). The role of expectancy and physiological feedback in fear research: A review with special reference to subject characteristics. *Behavior Therapy, 4*, 491–505.

Bourne, L. E., Jr. (1965). Hypotheses and hypothesis shifts in classification learning. *The Journal of General Psychology, 72*, 251–261.

Bourne, L. E., Jr. (1966). *Human conceptual behavior.* Boston: Allyn & Bacon.

Bourne, L. E., Jr., Ekstrand, B. R., & Dominowski, R. L. (1971). *The psychology of thinking.* Englewood Cliffs, NJ: Prentice-Hall.

Bower, G. H. (1972). Mental imagery and associative learning. In L. Gregg (Ed.), *Cognition in learning and memory* (pp. 51-88). New York: Wiley.

Bower, G. H. (1975). Cognitive psychology: An introduction. In W. K. Estes (Ed.), *Handbook of learning and cognition* (pp. 25–80). Hillsdale, NJ: Erlbaum.

Bower, G. H. (1981). Mood and memory. *American Psychologist, 36*, 129–148.

Bower, G. H. (1983). Affect and cognition. *Philosophical Transactions of the Royal Society of London* (Series B), *302*, 387–402.

Bower, G. H., & Hilgard, E. R. (1981). *Theories of learning* (5th ed.). Englewood Cliffs, NJ: Prentice-Hall.

Bowerman, M. (1973). Structural relationships in children's utterances: Syntactic or semantic? In T. E. Moore (Ed.), *Cognitive development and the acquisition of language* (pp. 197–213). New York: Academic Press.

Bowers, K. S. (1973). Situationism in psychology: An analysis and a critique. *Psychological Review, 80*, 307–336.

Bowers, W. J. (1983). The pervasiveness of arbitrariness and discrimination under post-Furman capital statutes. *The Journal of Criminal Law & Criminology, 74*, 1067–1100.

Bowers, W. J., & Pierce, G. L. (1980). Deterrence or brutalization: What is the effect of executions? *Crime and Delinquency, 26*, 453–487.

Boyd, L. M. (1969, March 15). Most disappointed men in the world. *San Francisco Chronicle.*

Boyd, R., & Richerson, P. J. (1985). *Mechanisms of cultural evolution.* Chicago: University of Chicago Press.

Bradley, R. H. Caldwell, B. M., & Elardo, R. (1979). Home environment and cognitive development in the first two years: A cross-lagged panel analysis. *Developmental Psychology, 15*, 246–250.

Brainerd, C. J. (1977). Learning research and Piagetian theory. In L. S. Siegel & C. J. Brainerd (Eds.), *Alternatives to Piaget: Critical essays on the theory* (pp. 69–109). New York: Academic Press.

Brainerd, C. J. (1978). The stage question in cognitive-developmental theory. *The Behavioral and Brain Sciences, 2*, 173–213.

Brandt, R. B. (1979). *A theory of the good and the right.* Oxford: Clarendon.

Bransford, J. D., & Franks, J. J. (1976). Toward a framework for understanding learning. In G. H. Bower (Ed.), *The psychology of learning and motivation* (Vol. 10, pp. 93–127). New York: Academic Press.

Braun, S. H. (1972). Effects of schedules of direct or vicarious reinforcement and modeling cues on behavior in extinction. *Journal of Personality and Social Psychology, 22*, 356–365.

Bregman, E. O. (1934). An attempt to modify the emotional attitudes of infants by the conditioned response technique. *Journal of Genetic Psychology, 45*, 169–198.

Brehm, J. (1966). *A theory of psychological reactance.* New York: Academic Press.

Brehmer, B. (1974). Hypotheses about relations between scaled variables in the learning of probabilistic inference tasks. *Organizational Behavior and Human Performance, 11*, 1–27.

Brehmer, B. (1976). Note on clinical judgment and the formal characteristics of clinical tasks. *Psychological Bulletin, 83*, 778–782.

Brehmer, B. (1980). In one word: Not from experience. *Acta Psychologica, 45*, 223–241.

Brehmer, B., Hagafors, R., & Johansson, R. (1980). Cognitive skills in judgment: Subjects' ability to use information about weights, function forms, and organizing principles. *Organizational Behavior and Human Performance, 26*, 373–385.

Breland, K., & Breland, M. (1961). The misbehavior of organisms. *American Psychologist, 16*, 681–684.

Brewer, W. F. (1974). There is no convincing evidence for operant or classical conditioning in adult humans. In W. B. Weimer & D. S. Palermo (Eds.), *Cognition and the symbolic processes* (pp. 1–42). Hillsdale, NJ: Erlbaum.

Briddell, D. W., Rimm, D. C., Caddy, G. R., Krawitz, G., Sholis, D., & Wunderlin, R. J. (1978). Effects of alcohol and cognitive set on sexual arousal to deviant stimuli. *Journal of Abnormal Psychology, 87*, 418–430.

Bridger, W. H., & Mandel, I. J. (1964). A comparison of GSR fear responses produced by threat and electric shock. *Journal of Psychiatric Research, 2*, 31–40.

Brier, S. S., & Fienberg, S. E. (1980). Recent econometric modeling of crime and punishment: Support for the deterrence hypothesis? *Evaluation Review, 4*, 147–191.

Briere, J., & Malamuth, N. M. (1983). Self-reported likelihood of sexually aggressive behavior: Attitudinal versus sexual explanations. *Journal of Research in Personality, 17*, 315–323.

Brim, O. G., Jr., Glass, D. C., Lavin, D. E., & Goodman, N. (1962). *Personality and decision processes.* Stanford, CA: Stanford University Press.

Brim, O. G., Jr., & Kagan, J. (1980). Constancy and change: A view of the issues. In O. G. Brim, Jr. & J. Kagan (Eds.), *Constancy and change in human development.* Cambridge, MA: Harvard University Press.

Brim, O. G., Jr., & Ryff, C. D. (1980). On the properties of life events. In P. B. Baltes & O. G. Brim, Jr. (Eds.), *Life-span development and behavior* (Vol. 3, pp. 367–388). New York: Academic Press.

Brock, T. C., & Buss, A. H. (1962). Dissonance, aggression, and evaluation of pain. *Journal of Abnormal and Social Psychology, 65*, 197–202.

BROCK, T. C., & BUSS, A. H. (1964). Effects of justication for aggression and communication with the victim on postaggression dissonance. *Journal of Abnormal and Social Psychology, 68*, 403–412.

BROCKNER, J., NATHANSON, S., FRIEND, A., HARBECK, J., SAMUELSON, C., HOUSER, R., BAZERMAN, M. H., & RUBIN, J. Z. (1984). The role of modeling processes in the "knee deep in the big muddy" phenomenon. *Organizational Behavior and Human Performance, 33*, 77–99.

BRODY, G. H., & HENDERSON, R. W. (1977). Effects of multiple model variations and rationale provision on the moral judgments and explanations of young children. *Child Development, 48*, 1117–1120.

BRODY, G. H., STONEMAN, Z., LANE, T. S., & SANDERS, A. K. (1981). Television food commercials aimed at children, family grocery shopping, and mother-child interactions. *Family Relations, 30*, 435–439.

BROMLEY, D. G., & SHUPE, A. D. (1979). *"Moonies" in America: Cult, church, and crusade*. Beverly Hills: Sage.

BRONFENBRENNER, U. (1958). The study of identification through interpersonal perception. In R. Tagiuri & L. Petrullo (Eds.), *Person, perception and interpersonal behavior* (pp. 110–130). Stanford, CA: Stanford University Press.

BRONFENBRENNER, U. (1970). *Two worlds of childhood: U.S. and U.S.S.R.* New York: Russell Sage Foundation.

BROWN, A. L. (1978). Knowing when, where, and how to remember: A problem of metacognition. In R. Glaser (Ed.), *Advances in instructional psychology* (Vol. 1, pp. 77–165). Hillsdale, NJ: Erlbaum.

BROWN, A. L., & BARCLAY, C. R. (1976). The effects of training specific mnemonics on the metamnemonic efficiency of retarded children. *Child Development, 47*, 71–80.

BROWN, B. S., GREENE, M. H., & TURNER, N. J. (1976). The spread of addiction—The role of the "average addict." *American Journal of Drug and Alcohol Abuse, 3*, 521–528.

BROWN, G., & DESFORGES, C. (1979). *Piaget's theory: A psychological critique*. London: Routledge & Kegan Paul.

BROWN, H. C. (1980). From little acorns to tall oaks: From boranes through organoboranes. *Science, 210*, 485–492.

BROWN, I., JR. (1974). Effects of perceived similarity on vicarious emotional conditioning. *Behaviour Research and Therapy, 12*, 165–174.

BROWN, I., JR. (1976). Role of referent concreteness in the acquisition of passive sentence comprehension through abstract modeling. *Journal of Experimental Child Psychology, 22*, 185–199.

BROWN, I., JR. (1979). Language acquisition: Linguistic structure and rule-governed behavior. In G. J. Whitehurst & B. J. Zimmerman (Eds.), *The functions of language and cognition* (pp. 141–173). New York: Academic Press.

BROWN, I., JR., & INOUYE, D. K. (1978). Learned help-lessness through modeling: The role of perceived similarity in competence. *Journal of Personality and Social Psychology, 36*, 900–908.

BROWN, J. N., & CARTWRIGHT, R. D. (1978). Locating NREM dreaming through instrumental responses. *Psychophysiology, 15*, 35–39.

BROWN, J. S. (1953). Comments on Professor Harlow's paper. In *Current theory and research on motivation: A symposium* (pp. 49–55). Lincoln: University of Nebraska Press.

BROWN, L. (1971). *Television: The business behind the box*. San Diego, CA: Harcourt Brace Jovanovich.

BROWN, L. A. (1981). *Innovation diffusion: A new perspective*. New York: Methuen.

BROWN, M., AMOROSO, D. M., & WARE, E. E. (1976). Behavioral effects of viewing pornography. *Journal of Social Psychology, 98*, 235–245.

BROWN, R., & HANLON, C. (1970). Derivational complexity and order of acquisition in child speech. (pp. 11–53) In J. R. Hayes (Ed.), *Cognition and the development of language*. New York: Wiley.

BROWN, S. D. (1980). Videotape feedback: Effects on assertive performance and subjects' perceived competence and satisfaction. *Psychological Reports, 47*, 455–461.

BROWNELL, K. D., COLLETTI, G., ERSNER-HERSHFIELD, R., HERSHFIELD, S. M., & WILSON, G. T. (1977). Self-control in school children: Stringency and leniency in self-determined and externally imposed performance standards. *Behavior Therapy, 8*, 442–455.

BRUNER, A., & REVUSKY, S. H. (1961). Collateral behavior in humans. *Journal of the Experimental Analysis of Behavior, 4*, 349–350.

BRUNER, J. S., GOODNOW, J., & AUSTIN, G. A. (1956). *A study of thinking*. New York: Wiley.

BRUNING, J. L. (1965). Direct and vicarious effects of a shift in magnitude of reward on performance. *Journal of Personality and Social Psychology, 2*, 278–282.

BRUNSWIK, E. (1952). *The conceptual framework of psychology*. Chicago: University of Chicago Press.

BRYAN, J. F., & LOCKE, E. A. (1967). Goal-setting as a means of increasing motivation. *Journal of Applied Psychology, 51*, 274–277.

BRYAN, J. H., & WALBEK, N. H. (1970). Preaching and practicing generosity: Some determinants of sharing in children. *Child Development, 41*, 329–354.

BRYAN, J. W., & LURIA, Z. (1978). Sex-role learning: A test of the selective attention hypothesis. *Child Development, 49*, 13–23.

BRYANT, J., CARVETH, R. A., BROWN, D. (1981). Television viewing and anxiety: An experimental examination. *The Journal of Communication, 31*, 106–119.

BUCHER, B., & BOWMAN, E. (1974). The effects of a discriminative cue and an incompatible activity on generalized imitation. *Journal of Experimental Child Psychology, 18*, 22–33.

BUCHWALD, A. M. (1959a). Extinction after acquisition under different verbal reinforcement combinations. *Journal of Experimental Psychology, 57*, 43–48.

BUCHWALD, A. M. (1959b). Experimental alterations in the effectiveness of verbal reinforcement combinations. *Journal of Experimental Psychology, 57,* 351–361.

BUCHWALD, A. M. (1960). Supplementary report: Alteration of the reinforcement value of a positive reinforcer. *Journal of Experimental Psychology, 60,* 416–418.

BUCHWALD, A. M. (1977). Depressive mood and estimates of reinforcement frequency. *Journal of Abnormal Psychology, 86,* 443–446.

BUERKEL-ROTHFUSS, N. L., & MAYES, S. (1981). Soap opera viewing: The cultivation effect. *Journal of Communication, 31,* 108–115.

BUFFORD, R. K. (1971). Discrimination and instructions as factors in the control of nonreinforced imitation. *Journal of Experimental Child Psychology, 12,* 35–50.

BULLOCK, D. H. (1979). *Social coordination and children's learning of property words.* Unpublished doctoral dissertation, Stanford University, Stanford, CA.

BULLOCK, D. (1983). Seeking relations between cognitive and social-interactive transitions. In K. W. Fischer (Ed.), *Levels and transitions in children's development. New directions for child development, No. 21* (pp. 97–108). San Francisco: Jossey-Bass.

BULLOCK, D., & MERRILL, L. (1980). The impact of personal preference on consistency through time: The case of childhood aggression. *Child Development, 51,* 808–814.

BULLOCK, D., & NEURINGER, A. (1977). Social learning by following: An analysis. *Journal of the Experimental Analysis of Behavior, 25,* 127–135.

BUNGE, M. (1980). *The mind-body problem: A psychological approach.* Oxford: Pergamon.

BURGESS, R. L., BURGESS, J. M., & ESVELDT, K. C. (1970). An analysis of generalized imitation. *Journal of Applied Behavior Analysis, 3,* 39–46.

BURLESON, G. (1973). Modeling: An effective behavior change technique for teaching the blind. *The New Outlook for the Blind, 67,* 433–441.

BURT, R. S. (1980). Models of network structure. *Annual Review of Sociology, 6,* 79–141.

BUSBY, L. J. (1975). Sex-role research on mass media. *Journal of Communication, 25*(4), 107–131.

BUSSEY, K. & BANDURA, A. (1984). Gender constancy, social power, and sex-linked modeling. *Journal of Personality and Social Psychology, 47,* 1292–1302.

BUSSEY, K., & PERRY, D. G. (1976). Sharing reinforcement contingencies with a model: A social-learning analysis of similarity effects in imitation research. *Journal of Personality and Social Psychology, 34,* 1168–1176.

BUSSEY, K., & PERRY, D. G. (1977). The imitation of resistance to deviation: Conclusive evidence for an elusive effect. *Developmental Psychology, 13,* 438–445.

BUTLER, R. A. (1954). Incentive conditions which influence visual exploration. *Journal of Experimental Psychology, 48,* 19–23.

BUTLER, R. A. (1958). The differential effect of visual and auditory incentives on the performance of monkeys. *The American Journal of Psychology, 71,* 591–593.

BYRNE, D. (1971). *The attraction paradigm.* New York: Academic Press.

CAIRNS, R. B. (Ed.). (1979). *The analysis of social interactions: Methods, issues, and illustrations.* Hillsdale, NJ: Erlbaum.

CALDER, B. J., & STAW, B. M. (1975). Self-perception of intrinsic and extrinsic motivation. *Journal of Personality and Social Psychology, 31,* 599–605.

CAMPBELL, A. (1981). *The sense of well-being in America: Recent patterns and trends.* New York: McGraw-Hill.

CAMPBELL, A., GURIN, G., & MILLER, W. E. (1954). *The voter decides.* Evanston, IL: Row, Peterson.

CAMPBELL, D. J. (1982). Determinants of choice of goal difficulty level: A review of situational and personality influences. *Journal of Occupational Psychology, 55,* 79–95.

CANNON, W. B. (1945). *The way of an investigator, a scientist's experiences in medical research.* New York: Norton.

CANTOR, J. (1981). Modifying children's eating habits through television ads—Effects of humorous appeals in a field setting. *Journal of Broadcasting, 25,* 37–48.

CANTOR, N. L., & GELFAND, D. M. (1977). Effects of responsiveness and sex of children on adults' behavior. *Child Development, 48,* 232–238.

CANTOR, N., & MISCHEL, W. (1979). Prototypes in person perception. In L. Berkowitz (Ed.), *Advances in experimental social psychology* (Vol. 12, pp. 3–52). New York: Academic Press.

CAPLAN, N. (1970). The new ghetto man: A review of recent empirical studies. *Journal of Social Issues, 26,* 59–73.

CAROLL, J. S. (1978). A psychological approach to deterrence: The evaluation of crime opportunities. *Journal of Personality and Social Psychology, 36,* 1512–1520.

CARR, E. G., NEWSOM, C. D., & BINKOFF, J. A. (1976). Stimulus control of self-destructive behavior in a psychotic child. *Journal of Abnormal Child Psychology, 4,* 139–153.

CARROLL, S. J., JR., & TOSI, H. L. (1970). Goal characteristics and personality factors in a management-by-objectives program. *Administrative Science Quarterly, 15,* 295–305.

CARROLL, W. R., & BANDURA, A. (1982). The role of visual monitoring in observational learning of action patterns: Making the unobservable observable. *Journal of Motor Behavior, 14,* 153–167.

CARROLL, W. R., & BANDURA, A. (1985). Role of timing of visual monitoring and motor rehearsal in observational learning of action patterns. *Journal of Motor Behavior, 17,* 269–281.

CARTER, R. E. (1980). What is Lawrence Kohlberg doing? *Journal of Moral Education, 9,* 88–102.

CARVER, C. S. (1975). Physical aggression as a function of objective self-awareness and attitudes toward punishment. *Journal of Experimental Social Psychology, 11,* 510–519.

CARVER, C. S., & SCHEIER, M. F. (1981). *Attention and self-regulation: A control-theory approach to human behavior.* New York: Springer-Verlag.

CASTRO, L., CAIJIAO DE PEREZ, G., BUSTOS DE ALBANCHEZ, D., & PONCE DE LEON, E. (1983). Feedback properties of "self-reinforcement": Further evidence. *Behavior Therapy, 14*, 672–681.

CASTRO, L., & RACHLIN, H. (1980). Self-reward, self-monitoring, and self-punishment as feedback in weight control. *Behavior Therapy, 11*, 38–48.

CATANIA, C. A. (1975). The myth of self-reinforcement. *Behaviorism, 3*, 192–199.

CATTELL, R. B. (1966). *The scientific analysis of personality.* Chicago: Aldine.

CAUDILL, B. D., & MARLATT, G. A. (1975). Modeling influences in social drinking: An experimental analogue. *Journal of Consulting and Clinical Psychology, 43*, 405–415.

CAUTELA, J. R., FLANNERY, R. B., JR., & HANLEY, S. (1974). Covert modeling: An experimental test. *Behavior Therapy, 5*, 494–502.

CAVIOR, N., & MARABOTTO, C. M. (1976). Monitoring verbal behaviors in a dyadic interaction. *Journal of Consulting and Clinical Psychology, 44*, 68–76.

CERVONE, D. (1985). Randomization test to determine significance levels for microanalytic congruences between self-efficacy and behavior. *Cognitive Therapy and Research, 9*, 357–365.

CERVONE, D., & PEAKE, P. K. (1985a). Anchoring, efficacy, and action: The influence of judgmental heuristics on self-efficacy judgments and behavior. *Journal of Personality and Social Psychology.*

CERVONE, D., & PEAKE, P. K. (1985b). *Sequence anchoring biases in self-efficacy judgments and performance.* Unpublished manuscript, Stanford University, Stanford, CA.

CHAFFEE, S. H. (1982). Mass media and interpersonal channels: Competitive, convergent, or complementary? In G. Gumpert & R. Cathcart (Eds.), *Inter/Media: Interpersonal communication in a media world* (pp. 57–77). New York: Oxford University Press.

CHAIKEN, J. M. (1978). What is known about deterrent effects of police activities. In J. A. Cramer (Ed.), *Preventing crime* (pp. 109–135). Beverly Hills: Sage.

CHAIKEN, J. M., LAWLESS, M. W., & STEVENSON, K. A. (1974). *The impact of police activity on crime: Robberies on the New York City subway system.* New York: Rand Institute.

CHAMBLISS, C. A., & MURRAY, E. J. (1979a). Cognitive procedures for smoking reduction: Symptom attribution versus efficacy attribution. *Cognitive Therapy and Research, 3*, 91–96.

CHAMBLISS, C. A., & MURRAY, E. J. (1979b). Efficacy attribution, locus of control, and weight loss. *Cognitive Therapy and Research, 3*, 349–354.

CHAMPLIN, T. S. (1977). Self-deception: A reflexive dilemma. *Philosophy, 52*, 281–299.

CHANDLER, M. J., GREENSPAN, S., & BARENBOIM, C. (1973). Judgments of intentionality in response to videotaped and verbally presented moral dilemma: The medium is the message. *Child Development, 44*, 315–320.

CHANOWITZ, B., & LANGER, E. (1980). Knowing more (or less) than you can show: Understanding control through the mindlessness/mindfulness distinction. In J. Garber & M. E. P. Seligman (Eds.), *Human help-*

lessness: Theory and implications (pp. 97–129). New York: Academic Press.

CHAPLIN, W. F., & GOLDBERG, L. R. (1984). A failure to replicate the Bem and Allen study of individual differences in cross-situational consistency. *Journal of Personality and Social Psychology, 47*, 1074–1090.

CHARBONNEAU, C., & ROBERT, M. (1977). Observational learning of quantity conservation in relation to the degree of cognitive conflict. *Psychological Reports, 41*, 975–986.

CHARTIER, G. M., & WEISS, R. L. (1974). Comparative test of positive control, negative control, and social power theories of identificatory learning in disadvantaged children. *Journal of Personality and Social Psychology, 29*, 724–730.

Chatterjee, B. B., & Eriksen, C. W. (1962). Cognitive factors in heart rate conditioning. *Journal of Experimental Psychology, 64*, 272–279.

CHAVES, J. F., & BARBER, T. X. (1974). Cognitive strategies, experimenter modeling, and expectation in the attenuation of pain. *Journal of Abnormal Psychology, 83*, 356–365.

CHEIN, I. (1975). There ought to be a law: But why? *The Journal of Social Issues, 31*, 221–244.

CHEW, P. (1976). *The inner world of the middle-aged man.* New York: Macmillan.

CHEYNE, J. A. (1971). Effects of imitation of different reinforcement combinations to a model. *Journal of Experimental Child Psychology, 12*, 258–269.

CHEYNE, J. A., & WALTERS, R. H. (1970). Punishment and prohibition: Some origins of self control. In T. M. Newcomb (Ed.), *New directions in psychology* (Vol. 4, pp. 281–337). New York: Holt, Rinehart & Winston.

CHITTENDEN, G. E. (1942). An experimental study in measuring and modifying assertive behavior in young children. *Monographs of the Society for Research in Child Development, 7* (1, Serial No. 31).

CHOMSKY, N. (1965). *Aspects of a theory of syntax.* Cambridge, MA: MIT Press.

CHURCH, R. M. (1959). Emotional reactions of rats to the pain of others. *Journal of Comparative and Physiological Psychology, 52*, 132–134.

CHURCHILL, R. P. (1983). Nuclear arms as a philosophical and moral issue. *The Annals of the American Academy of Political and Social Science, 469*, 46–57.

CIMINERO, A. R., & STEINGARTEN, K. A. (1978). The effects of performance standards on self-evaluation and self-reinforcement in depressed and nondepressed individuals. *Cognitive Therapy and Research, 2*, 179–182.

CLANCEY, W. M. (1984). Methodology for building an intelligent tutoring system. In W. Kintsch, P. Miller, & W. Polson (Eds.), *Method and tactics in cognitive science* (pp. 920–1066). Hillsdale, NJ: Erlbaum.

CLARK, B. S. (1965). The acquisition and extinction of peer imitation in children. *Psychonomic Science, 2*, 147–148.

CLARK, E. (1973). What's in a word? On the child's acquisition of semantics in his first language. In T. E. Moore (Ed.), *Cognitive development and the acquisition of language* (pp. 65–110). New York: Academic Press.

CLARK, E. V., & HECHT, B. F. (1983). Comprehension, production and language acquisition. *Annual Review of Psychology, 34,* 325–350.

CLARK, H. H. (1983). Making sense of nonce sense. In G. B. Flores d'Arcais & R. J. Jarvella (Eds.), *The process of language understanding* (pp. 297–331). New York: Wiley.

CLARK, L. V. (1960). Effect of mental practice on the development of a certain motor skill. *Research Quarterly, 31,* 560–569.

CLARK, M. S., & ISEN, A. M. (1982). Toward understanding the relationship between feeling states and social behavior. In A. H. Hastorf & A. M. Isen (Eds.), *Cognitive social psychology* (pp. 73–108). New York: Elsevier North Holland.

CLASTER, D. S. (1967). Comparison of risk perception between delinquents and non-delinquents. *The Journal of Criminal Law, Criminology and Police Science, 58,* 80–86.

CLECKLEY, H. (1964). *The mask of sanity* (4th ed.), St. Louis, MO: Mosby.

COATES, B., & HARTUP, W. W. (1969). Age and verbalization in observational learning. *Developmental Psychology, 1,* 556–562.

COATES, T. J., & THORESEN, C. E. (1979). Behavioral self-control and educational practice: Or do we really need self-control. In D. Berliner (Ed.), *Review of Research in Education* (Vol. 7, pp. 3–45). Washington, DC: American Educational Research Association.

CODD, J. A. (1977). Some conceptual problems in the cognitive developmental approach to morality. *Journal of Moral Education, 6,* 147–157.

COHEN, C. E., & EBBESEN, E. B. (1979). Observational goals and schema activation: A theoretical framework for behavior perception. *Joural of Experimental Social Psychology, 15,* 305–329.

COHEN, J. (1983). Incapacitation as a strategy for crime control: Possibilities and pitfalls. In M. Tonry & N. Morris (Eds.), *Crime and justice: An annual review of research* (Vol. 5, pp. 1–84). Chicago: University of Chicago Press.

COHEN, L. B., & SALAPATEK, P. (1975). *Infant perception: From sensation to cognition: Vol. 1. Basic visual processes.* New York: Academic Press.

COLBY, A., KOHLBERG, L., GIBBS, J., & LIEBERMAN, M. (1983). A longitudinal study of moral judgment. *Monographs of the Society for Research in Child Development, 38* (1–2, Serial No. 200).

COLEMAN, J. S., KATZ, E., & MENZEL, H. (1966). *Medical innovation: A diffusion study.* New York: Bobbs-Merrill.

COLLETTI, G., SUPNICK, J. A., & PAYNE, T. J. (1985). The smoking self-efficacy questionnaire (SSEQ): Preliminary scale development and validation. *Behavioral Assessment, 7,* 249–260.

COLLINS, J. L. (1982, March). *Self-efficacy and ability in achievement behavior.* Paper presented at the annual meeting of the American Educational Research Association, NY.

COMSTOCK, G., CHAFFEE, S., KATZMAN, N., McCOMBS, M., & ROBERTS, D. (1978). *Television and human behavior.* New York: Columbia University Press.

COMSTOCK, G. A., & RUBINSTEIN, E. A. (Eds.) (1972). *Television and social behavior: Media content and control* (Vol. 1). Washington, DC: U.S. Government Printing Office.

CONDIOTTE, M. M., & LICHTENSTEIN, E. (1981). Self-efficacy and relapse in smoking cessation programs. *Journal of Consulting and Clinical Psychology, 49,* 648–658.

CONDRY, J. (1977). Enemies of exploration: Self-initiated versus other-initiated learning. *Journal of Personality and Social Psychology, 35,* 459–477.

COOK, M., MINEKA, S., WOLKENSTEIN, B., & LAITSCH, K. (1985). Observational conditioning of snake fear in unrelated rhesus monkeys. *Journal of Abnormal Psychology, 94,* 591–610.

COOK, P. J. (1977). Punishment and crime: A critique of current findings concerning the preventive effects of punishment. *Law and Contemporary Problems, 41,* 164–204.

COOK, P. J. (1980). Research in criminal deterrence: Laying the groundwork for the second decade. In N. Morris & M. Tomy (Eds.), *Crime and justice: Annual review of research* (Vol. 2, pp. 211–268). Chicago: University of Chicago Press.

COOK, R. E. (1970). Relation of achievement motivation and attribution to self-enforcement (Doctoral dissertation, University of California, Los Angeles). *Dissertation Abstracts International, 31,* 1560B. (University Microfilms No. 70–15, 938).

COOLEY, C. H. (1902). *Human nature and the social order.* New York: Scribner's.

COONEY, N. L., KOPEL, S. A., & McKEON, P. (1982). *Controlled relapse training and self-efficacy in ex-smokers.* Paper presented at the annual meeting of the American Psychological Association, Washington, D.C.

COOPER, T., DETRE, T., & WEISS, S. M. (1981). Coronary prone behavior and coronary heart disease: A critical review. *Circulation, 63,* 1119–1215.

COOPERSMITH, S. (1967). *The antecedents of self-esteem.* San Francisco: Freeman.

CORBIN, C. (1972). Mental practice. In W. Morgan (Ed.), *Ergogenic aids and muscular performance* (pp. 93–118). New York: Academic Press.

CORDUA, G. D., McGRAW, K. O., & DRABMAN, R. S. (1979). Doctor or nurse: Children's perceptions of sex typed occupations. *Child Development, 50,* 590–593.

COWAN, P. A., LANGER, J., HEAVENRICH, J., & NATHANSON, M. (1969). Social learning and Piaget's cognitive theory of moral development. *Journal of Personality and Social Psychology, 11,* 261–274.

COULTER, J. (1983). *Rethinking cognitive theory.* New York: St. Martin's.

COURTNEY, A. E., & WHIPPLE, T. W. (1974). Women in TV commercials. *The Journal of Communication, 24,* 110–118.

COURTRIGHT, J. A., & COURTRIGHT, I. C. (1976). Imitative modeling as a theoretical base for instructing language-disordered children. *Journal of Speech and Hearing Research, 19,* 655–663.

COVINGTON, M. V., & OMELICH, C. L. (1979). Are causal attributions causal? A path analysis of the cognitive model of achievement motivation. *Journal of Personality and Social Psychology, 37,* 1487–1504.

COYNE, J. C. (1976a). Depression and the response of others. *Journal of Abnormal Psychology, 85,* 186–193.

COYNE, J. C. (1976b). Toward an interactional description of depression. *Psychiatry, 39,* 28–40.

COYNE, J. C. (1982). A critique of cognitions as causal entities with particular reference to depression. *Cognitive Therapy and Research, 6,* 3–13.

COYNE, J. C., & GOTLIB, I. H. (1983). The role of cognition in depression: A critical appraisal. *Psychological Bulletin, 94,* 472–505.

CRAIG, K. D. (1967). Vicarious reinforcement and noninstrumental punishment in observational learning. *Journal of Personality and Social Psychology, 7* 172–176.

CRAIG, K. D. (1978). Social modeling influences on pain. In R. A. Sternbach (Ed.), *The psychology of pain* (pp. 73–109). New York: Raven.

CRAIG, K. D. (1983). A social learning perspective on pain experience. In M. Rosenbaum, C. M. Franks, & Y. Jaffe (Eds.), *Perspectives on behavior therapy in the eighties,* (pp. 311–327). New York: Springer.

CRAIG, K. D., BEST, H., & WARD, L. (1975). Social modeling influences on psycho-physical judgments of electrical stimulation. *Journal of Abnormal Psychology, 84,* 366–373.

CRAIG, K. D., & LOWERY, H. J. (1969). Heart-rate components of conditioned vicarious autonomic responses. *Journal of Personality and Social Psychology, 11,* 381–387.

CRAIG, K. D., & NEIDERMAYER, H. (1974). Autonomic correlates of pain thresholds influenced by social modeling. *Journal of Personality and Social Psychology, 29,* 246–252.

CRAIG, K. D., & PRKACHIN, K. M. (1978). Social modeling influences on sensory decision theory and psychophysiological indexes of pain. *Journal of Personality and Social Psychology, 36,* 805–815.

CRAIG, K. D., & WEINSTEIN, M. S. (1965). Conditioning vicarious affective arousal. *Psychological Reports, 17,* 955–963.

CRANDALL, V. C. (1963). Reinforcement effects of adult reactions and nonreactions on children's achievement expectations. *Child Development, 34,* 335–354.

CRANDALL, V. C. (1978, August). Expecting sex differences and sex differences in expectancies: A developmental analysis. In *Role of belief systems in the production of sex differences.* Symposium presented at the meeting of the American Psychological Association, Toronto.

CRANDALL, V. C., GOOD, S., & CRANDALL, V. J. (1964). Reinforcement effects of adult reactions and nonreactions on children's achievement expectations: A replication study. *Child Development, 35,* 485–497.

CRASKE, M. G., & CRAIG, K. D. (1984). Musical performance anxiety: The three-systems model and self-efficacy theory. *Behaviour Research and Therapy, 22,* 267–280.

CRAWFORD, T., & NADITCH, M. (1970). Relative deprivation, powerlessness, and militancy: The psychology of social protest. *Psychiatry, 33,* 208–223.

CROOKS, J. L. (1967). *Observational learning of fear in monkeys.* Unpublished manuscript, University of Pennsylvania.

CRUNDALL, I., & FODDY, M. (1981). Vicarious exposure to a task as a basis of evaluative competence. *Social Psychology Quarterly, 44,* 331–338.

CSIKSZENTMIHALYI, M. (1975). *Beyond boredom and anxiety.* San Francisco: Josey-Bass.

CSIKSZENTMIHALYI, M. (1979). Intrinsic rewards and emergent motivation. In M. R. Lepper & D. Greene (Eds.), *The hidden costs of reward* (pp. 205–216). Morristown, NJ: Erlbaum.

CUMMINGS, L. L., SCHWAB, D. P., & ROSEN, M. (1971). Performance and knowledge of results as determinants of goal setting. *Journal of Applied Psychology, 55,* 526–530.

DARLEY, J. M. (1978/79). Energy conservation techniques as innovations, and their diffusion. *Energy and Buildings, 1,* 339–343.

DARLEY, J. M., KLOSSON, E. C., & ZANNA, M. P. (1978). Intentions and their contexts in the moral judgments of children and adults. *Child Development, 49,* 66–74.

DAS, J. P., & NANDA, P. C. (1963). Mediated transfer of attitudes. *Journal of Abnormal and Social Psychology, 66,* 12–16.

DAVIDSON, E. S., & SMITH, W. P. (1982). Imitation, social comparison and self-reward. *Child Development, 53,* 928–932.

DAVIDSON, P., & BUCHER, B. (1978). Intrinsic interest and extrinsic reward: The effects of a continuing token program on continuing nonconstrained preference. *Behavior Therapy, 9,* 222–234.

DAVIS, F. W., & YATES, B. T. (1982). Self-efficacy expectancies versus outcome expectancies as determinants of performance deficits and depressive affect. *Cognitive Therapy and Research, 6,* 23–35.

DAWES, R. M., & CORRIGAN, B. (1974). Linear models in decision making. *Psychological Bulletin, 81,* 95–106.

DAWSON, M. E. (1966). *Comparison of classical conditioning and relational learning.* Unpublished master's thesis, University of Southern California, Los Angeles.

DAWSON, M. E. (1973). Can classical conditioning occur without contingency learning? A review and evaluation of the evidence. *Psychophysiology, 10,* 82–86.

DAWSON, M. E., & BIFERNO, M. A. (1973). Concurrent measurement of awareness and electrodermal classical conditioning. *Journal of Experimental Psychology, 101,* 55–62.

DAWSON, M. E., & FUREDY, J. J. (1976). The role of awareness in human differential autonomic classical conditioning: The necessary-gate hypothesis. *Psychophysiology, 13,* 50–53.

DAWSON, M. E., & REARDON, P. (1973). Construct validity of recall and recognition postconditioning measures of awareness. *Journal of Experimental Psychology, 98*, 308–315.

Day, W. F., Jr. (1976). Contemporary behaviorism and the concept of intention. In W. J. Arnold (Ed.), *Nebraska Symposium on Motivation* (Vol. 23, pp. 65–131). Lincoln: University of Nebraska Press.

Day, W. F., Jr. (1977). On the behavioral analysis of self-deception and self-development. In T. Mischel (Ed.), *The self: Psychological and philosophical issues* (pp. 224–249). Oxford: Blackwell.

De Alacron, R. (1969). The spread of heroin abuse in a community. *Bulletin on Narcotics, 21,* 17–22.

Debus, R. L. (1970). Effects of brief observation of model behavior on conceptual tempo of impulsive children. *Developmental Psychology, 2,* 22–32.

DeCharms, R. (1978). *Personal causation: The internal affective determinants of behavior.* New York: Academic Press.

Deci, E. L. (1975). *Intrinsic motivation.* New York: Plenum.

Deci, E. L., & Ryan, R. M. (1980). The empirical exploration of intrinsic motivational processes. In L. Berkowitz (Ed.), *Advances in experimental social psychology* (Vol. 13, pp. 39–80). New York: Academic Press.

Decker, P. J. (1982). The enhancement of behavior modeling training of supervisory skills by the inclusion of retention processes. *Personnel Psychology, 35,* 323–332.

Del Rey, P. (1971). The effects of video-taped feedback on form, accuracy, and latency in an open and closed environment. *Journal of Motor Behavior, 3,* 281–287.

Dembo, M. H., & Gibson, S. (1985). Teachers' sense of efficacy: An important factor in school improvement. *Elementary School Journal.*

Dement, W. C. (1976). *Some must watch while some must sleep.* San Francisco: San Francisco Book.

DeMonbreun, B. G., & Craighead, W. E. (1977). Distortion of perception and recall of positive and neutral feedback in depression. *Cognitive Therapy and Research, 4,* 311–329.

Denney, D. R. (1975). The effects of exemplary and cognitive models and self-rehearsal on children's interrogative strategies. *Journal of Experimental Child Psychology, 19,* 476–488.

Denney, N. W., & Denney, D. R. (1974). Modeling effects on the questioning strategies of the elderly. *Developmental Psychology, 10,* 458.

Denney, N. W., & Duffy, D. M. (1974). Possible environmental causes of stages in moral reasoning. *The Journal of Genetic Psychology, 125,* 277–284.

DeSilva, P., Rachman, S., & Seligman, M. E. P. (1977). Prepared phobias and obsessions: Therapeutic outcome. *Behaviour Research and Therapy, 15,* 65–77.

deVilliers, J. G. (1980). The process of rule learning in child speech—A new look. In K. E. Nelson (Ed.), *Children's language* (Vol. 2, pp. 1–44). New York: Gardner.

Devins, G. M., Binik, Y. M., Gorman, P., Dattel, M.,

McCloskey, B., Oscar, G., & Briggs, J. (1982). Perceived self-efficacy, outcome expectations, and negative mood states in end-stage renal disease. *Journal of Abnormal Psychology, 91,* 241–244.

DiClemente, C. C. (1981). Self-efficacy and smoking cessation maintenance: A preliminary report. *Cognitive Therapy and Research, 5,* 175–187.

DiClemente, C. C., Prochaska, J. O., & Gilbertini, M. (1985). Self-efficacy and the stages of self-change of smoking. *Cognitive Therapy and Research.*

Diener, E. (1977). Deindividuation: Causes and consequences. *Social Behavior and Personality, 5,* 143–156.

Diener, E. (1980). Deindividuation: The absence of self-awareness and self-regulation in group members. In P. Paulus (Ed.), *The psychology of group influence* (pp. 209–244). Hillsdale, NJ: Erlbaum.

Diener, E., & DeFour, D. (1978). Does television violence enhance program popularity? *Journal of Personality and Social Psychology, 36,* 333–341.

Diener, E., Dineen, J., Endresen, K., Beaman, A. L., & Fraser, S. C. (1975). Effects of altered responsibility, cognitive set, and modeling on physical aggression and deindividuation. *Journal of Personality and Social Psychology, 31,* 328–337.

Dipboye, R. L. (1977). Alternative approaches to deindividuation. *Psychological Bulletin, 84,* 1047–1075.

Ditrichs, R., Simon, S., & Greene, B. (1967). Effect of vicarious scheduling on the verbal conditioning of hostility in children. *Journal of Personality and Social Psychology, 6,* 71–78.

Dockstader, S. L. (1977, August). *Performance standards and implicit goal setting: Field testing Locke's assumption.* Paper presented at the meeting of the American Psychological Association, San Francisco.

Dollard, J., & Miller, N. E. (1950). *Personality and psychotherapy.* New York: McGraw-Hill.

Dollinger, S. J., & Thelen, M. H. (1978). Overjustification and children's intrinsic motivation: Comparative effects of four rewards. *Journal of Personality and Social Psychology, 36,* 1259–1269.

Dominick, J. R., & Greenberg, B. S. (1972). Attitudes toward violence: The interaction of television, family attitudes and social class. In G. A. Comstock & E. A. Rubinstein (Eds.), *Television and social behavior: Vol. 3. Television and adolescent aggressiveness* (pp. 314–335). Washington, DC: U.S. Government Printing Office.

Donchin, E., & Cohen, L. (1967). Averaged evoked potentials and intramodality selective attention. *Electroencephalography and Clinical Neurophysiology, 22,* 537–546.

Donnerstein, E. (1980). Aggressive erotica and violence against women. *Journal of Personality and Social Psychology, 39,* 269–277.

Donnerstein, E. (1983). Erotica and human aggression. In R. Geen & E. Donnerstein (Eds.), *Aggression: Theoretical and empirical reviews* (Vol. 2, pp. 127–154). New York: Academic Press.

Donnerstein, E., & Berkowitz, L. (1981). Victim reactions in aggressive erotic films as a factor in violence against women. *Journal of Personality and Social Psychology, 41,* 710–724.

Doob, A. N., & Macdonald, G. E. (1979). Television viewing and fear of victimization: Is the relationship causal? *Journal of Personality and Social Psychology, 37,* 170–179.

Dorr, D., & Fey, S. (1974). Relative power of symbolic adult and peer models in the modification of children's moral choice behavior. *Journal of Personality and Social Psychology, 29,* 335–341.

Downs, G. W., Jr., & Mohr, L. B. (1979). Toward a theory of innovation. *Administration & Society, 10,* 379–408.

Dowrick, P. W. (1983). Self modelling. In P. W. Dowrick & S. J. Biggs (Eds.), *Using video: Psychological and social applications* (pp. 105–124). London: Wiley.

Drabman, R. S., Spitalnik, R., & O'Leary, K. D. (1973). Teaching self-control to disruptive children. *Journal of Abnormal Psychology, 82,* 10–16.

Dubanoski, R. A. (1967). *Imitation as a function of role appropriateness of behavior and response consequences to the model.* Unpublished manuscript, University of Iowa, Iowa City.

Dubanoski, R. A. (1972). An empirical test of Mowrer's theory of imitation. *Psychonomic Science, 28,* 203–204.

Dubanoski, R. A., & Parton, D. A. (1971). Imitative aggression in children as a function of observing a human model. *Developmental Psychology, 4,* 489.

Dubbert, P. M., & Wilson, G. T. (1984). Goal-setting and spouse involvement in the treatment of obesity. *Behaviour Research and Therapy, 22,* 227–242.

Duckworth, E. (1979). Either we're too early and they can't learn it or we're too late and they know it already: The dilemma of "Applying Piaget." *Harvard Educational Review, 49,* 297–312.

Duffy, E. (1962). *Activation and behavior.* New York: Wiley.

Dulany, D. E. (1968). Awareness, rules, and propositional control: A confrontation with S-R behavior theory. In T. R. Dixon & D. L. Horton (Eds.), *Verbal behavior and general behavior theory* (pp. 340–387). Englewood Cliffs, NJ: Prentice-Hall.

Dulany, D. E. (1974). On the support of cognitive theory in opposition to behavior theory: A methodological problem. In W. B. Weimer & D. S. Palermo (Eds.), *Cognition and the symbolic processes* (pp. 43–56). Hillsdale, NJ: Erlbaum.

Dulany, D. E., Jr., & Eriksen, C. W. (1959). Accuracy of brightness discrimination as measured by concurrent verbal responses and GSRs. *Journal of Abnormal and Social Psychology, 59,* 418–423.

Dulany, D. E., Jr., & O'Connell, D. C. (1963). Does partial reinforcement dissociate verbal rules and the behavior they might be presumed to control? *Journal of Verbal Learning and Verbal Behavior, 2,* 361–372.

Duncker, K. (1938). Experimental modification of children's food preferences through social suggestion. *Journal of Abnormal Social Psychology, 33,* 489–507.

Dupont, R. L., & Greene, M. H. (1973). The dynamics of a heroin addiction epidemic. *Science, 181,* 716–722.

Dush, D. M., Hirt, M. L., & Schroeder, H. (1983). Self-statement modification with adults: A meta-analysis. *Psychological Bulletin, 94,* 408–422.

Dweck, C. S., Davidson, W., Nelson, S., & Enna, B. (1978). Sex differences in learned helplessness: II. The contingencies of evaluative feedback in the classroom; III. An experimental analysis. *Developmental Psychology, 14,* 268–276.

Dweck, C. S., & Elliott, E. S. (1983). Achievement motivation. In P. H. Mussen (Ed.), *Handbook of child psychology* (4th ed., Vol. 4, pp. 644–691). New York: Wiley.

Dweck, C. S., & Goetz, T. E. (1978). Attributions and learned helplessness. In J. Harvey, W. Ickes, & R. Kidd (Eds.), *New directions in attribution research* (Vol. 2, pp. 157–179). Hillsdale, NJ: Erlbaum.

Dysinger, W. S., & Ruckmick, C. A. (1933). *The emotional responses of children to the motion-picture situation.* New York: Macmillan.

D'Zurilla, T. J., & Goldfried, M. R. (1971). Problem solving and behavior modification. *Journal of Abnormal Psychology, 78,* 107–126.

Earley, P. C. (1986). Supervisors and shop stewards as sources of contextual information in goal setting: A comparison of the U.S. with England. *Journal of Applied Psychology, 71,* 111–117.

Edwards, N. L. (1968). Aggressive expression under threat of retaliation. *Dissertation Abstracts, 28,* 3470B (University Microfilms No. 68–00922).

Egger, M. D., & Miller, N. E. (1963). When is reward reinforcing? An experimental study of the information hypothesis. *Journal of Comparative and Physiological Psychology, 56,* 132–137.

Ehrlich, I. (1973). Participation in illegitimate activities: A theoretical and empirical investigation. *Journal of Political Economy, 81,* 521–565.

Ehrlich, I. (1975a). The deterrent effect of capital punishment: Question of life or death. *American Economic Review, 65,* 397–417.

Ehrlich, I. (1975b). Deterrence: Evidence and inference. *The Yale Law Journal, 85,* 209–227.

Ehrlich, I. (1979). The economic approach to crime: A preliminary assessment. In S. Messinger & E. Bittner (Eds.), *Criminology review yearbook* (pp. 25–60). Beverly Hills: Sage.

Eimas, P. D. (1970). Effects of memory aids on hypothesis behavior and focusing in young children and adults. *Journal of Experimental Child Psychology, 10,* 319–336.

Einhorn, H. J., & Hogarth, R. M. (1978). Confidence in judgment: Persistence of the illusion of validity. *Psychological Review, 85,* 395–416.

Einhorn, H. J., & Hogarth, R. M. (1981). Behavioral decision theory: Processes of judgment and choice. *Annual Review of Psychology, 32,* 53–88.

Eisenberger, R. (1972). Explanation of rewards that do not reduce tissue needs. *Psychological Bulletin, 77,* 319–339.

EISLER, R. M., BLANCHARD, E. B., FITTS, H., & WILLIAMS, J. G. (1978). Social skill training with and without modeling for schizophrenic and non-psychotic hospitalized psychiatric patients. *Behavior Modification, 2,* 147–172.

EKMAN, P. (1973). Cross-cultural studies of facial expression. In P. Ekman (Ed.), *Darwin and facial expression* (pp. 169–222). New York: Academic Press.

EKMAN, P. (1982). *Emotion in the human face.* Cambridge, England: Cambridge University Press.

EKMAN, P., KRASNER, L., & ULLMANN, L. P. (1963). Interaction of set and awareness as determinants of response to verbal conditioning. *Journal of Abnormal and Social Psychology, 66,* 387–389.

EKMAN, P., LEVENSON, R. W., & FRIESEN, W. V. (1983). Autonomic nervous system activity distinguishes among emotions. *Science, 221,* 1208–1210.

EKMAN, P., LIEBERT, R. M., FRIESEN, W. V., HARRISON, R., ZLATCHIN, C., MALMSTROM, E. J., & BARON, R. A. (1972). Facial expressions of emotion while watching televised violence as predictors of subsequent aggression. In G. A. Comstock. E. A. Rubinstein, & J. P. Murray (Eds.), *Television and social behavior. Reports and papers: Vol. 5. Television's effects. Further explorations* (pp. 22–58). Washington, DC: Department of Health, Education and Welfare.

EKMAN, P., & OSTER, H. (1979). Facial expressions of emotion. *Annual Review of Psychology, 30,* 527–554.

ELDER, G. H. (1981). History and the life course. In D. Bertaux (Ed.), *Biography and society: The life history approach in the social sciences* (pp. 77–115). Beverly Hills: Sage.

ELKIN, F., & WESTLEY, W. A. (1955). The myth of adolescent culture. *American Sociological Review, 20,* 680–684.

ELLIS, A. (1973). *Humanistic psychotherapy.* New York: McGraw-Hill.

ELLIS, A., & GRIEGER, R. (Eds.). (1978). *Handbook of rational-emotive therapy.* New York: Springer.

ELLIS, R. A., & LANE, W. C. (1963). Structural supports for upward mobility. *American Sociological Review, 28,* 743–756.

ELLSWORTH, P. (1978). *Attitudes toward capital punishment: From application to theory.* Unpublished manuscript, Yale University, New Haven.

EMMELKAMP, P. M. G., KUIPERS, A. C. M., & EGGERAAT, J. B. (1978). Cognitive modification versus prolonged exposure *in vivo*—Comparison with agoraphobics as subjects. *Behaviour Research and Therapy, 16,* 33–42.

EMMELKAMP, P. M. G., & MERSCH, P. P. (1982). Cognition and exposure *in vivo* in the treatment of agoraphobia: Short-term and delayed effects. *Cognitive Therapy and Research, 6,* 77–90.

EMMELKAMP, P. M. G., VAN DER HELM, M., VAN ZANGEN, B. L., & PLOCHG, I. (1980). Treatment of obsessive compulsive patients: The contribution of self-instructional training to the effectiveness of exposure. *Behaviour Research and Therapy, 18,* 61–66.

EMMERICH, W. (1959). Parental identification in young children. *Genetic Psychology Monographs, 60,* 257–308.

ENDLER, N. S., & MAGNUSSON, D. (Eds.). (1976). *Interactional psychology and personality.* Washington, DC: Hemisphere.

ENGLIS, B. G., VAUGHAN, K. B., & LANZETTA, J. T. (1982). Conditioning of counter-empathetic emotional responses. *Journal of Experimental Social Psychology, 18,* 375–391.

ENGLISH, H. B. (1929). Three cases of the "conditioned fear response." *The Journal of Abnormal and Social Psychology, 24,* 221–225.

ENZLE, M. E., & LOOK, S. C. (1979). *Self versus other reward administration and the overjustification effect.* Paper presented at the meeting of the American Psychological Association, New York.

ENZLE, M. E., & ROSS, J. M. (1978). Increasing and decreasing intrinsic interest with contingent rewards: A test of cognitive evaluation theory. *Journal of Experimental Social Psychology, 14,* 588–597.

EPSTEIN, S. (1983). The stability of behavior across time and situations. In R. Zucker, J. Aronoff, & A. I. Rabin (Eds.), *Personality and the prediction of behavior* (pp. 209–268). San Diego, CA: Academic Press.

ERASMUS, C. J. (1961). *Man takes control.* Minneapolis: University of Minnesota Press.

EREZ, M., & ZIDON, I. (1984). Effect of goal acceptance on the relationship of goal difficulty to performance. *Journal of Applied Psychology, 69,* 69–78.

ERICKSON, M. L., & GIBBS, J. P. (1976). Further findings on the deterrence question and strategies for future research. *Journal of Criminal Justice, 4,* 175–190.

ERICKSON, M. L., GIBBS, J. P., & JENSEN, G. F. (1977). The deterrence doctrine and the perceived certainty of legal punishments. *American Sociological Review, 42,* 305–317.

ERICSSON, K. A., & SIMON, H. A. (1980). Verbal reports as data. *Psychological Review, 87,* 215–251.

ERIKSEN, C. W. (1958). Unconscious processes. In M. R. Jones (Ed.), *Nebraska symposium on motivation* (pp. 169–227). Lincoln: University of Nebraska Press.

ERIKSEN, C. W. (1960). Discrimination and learning without awareness: A methodological survey and evaluation. *Psychological Review, 67,* 279–300.

ERVIN, S. M. (1964). Imitation and structural change in children's language. In E. H. Lenneberg (Ed.), *New directions in the study of language* (pp. 163–189). Cambridge, MA: MIT Press.

ERWIN, E. (1980). Psychoanalysis: How firm is the evidence? *Nous, 14,* 443–456.

ESTES, W. K. (1971). Reward in human learning: Theoretical issues and strategic choice points. In R. Glaser (Ed.), *The nature of reinforcement* (pp. 16–36). New York: Academic Press.

ESTES, W. K. (1972). Reinforcement in human behavior. *American Scientist, 60,* 723–729.

ESTES, W. K. (1976). The cognitive side of probability learning. *Psychological Review, 83,* 37–64.

EVANS, F. J. (1974). The placebo response in pain reduction. In J. J. Bonica (Ed.), *Advances in neurology* (Vol. 4, pp. 289–296). New York: Raven.

EVANS, M. A. (1985). Self-initiated speech repairs: A

reflection of communicative monitoring in young children. *Developmental Psychology, 21,* 365–371.

EVANS, R. I., ROZELLE, R. M., MAXWELL, S. E., RAINES, B. E., DILL, C. A., GUTHRIE, T. J., HENDERSON, A. H., & HILL, P. C. (1981). Social modeling films to deter smoking in adolescents: Results of a three-year field investigation. *Journal of Applied Psychology, 66,* 399–414.

EWART, C. K., TAYLOR, C. B., REESE, L. B., & DEBUSK, R. F. (1983). Effects of early post-myocardial infarction exercise testing on self-perception and subsequent physical activity. *American Journal of Cardiology, 51,* 1076–1080.

EYSENCK, H. J., & WILSON, G. D. (1973). *The experimental study of Freudian theories.* London: Methuen.

FAGAN, J. F., & SINGER, L. T. (1979). The role of simple feature differences in infants' recognition of faces. *Infant Behavior and Development, 2,* 39–45.

FAGOT, B. I. (1977). Consequences of moderate cross-gender behavior in preschool children. *Child Development, 48,* 902–907.

FAIRWEATHER, G. W., SANDERS, D. H., CRESSLER, D. L., & MAYNARD, H. (1969). *Community life for the mentally ill: An alternative to institutional care.* Chicago: Aldine.

FAIRWEATHER, G. W., SANDERS, D. H., TORNATZKY, L. G., & HARRIS, R. N., JR. (1974). *Creating change in mental health organizations.* New York: Pergamon.

FALMAGNE, R. J. (1975). *Reasoning: Representation and process in children and adults.* Hillsdale, NJ: Erlbaum.

FARBER, I. E. (1963). The things people say to themselves. *American Psychologist, 18,* 185–197.

FARQUHAR, J. W. ET AL. (1984). The Stanford Five City Project: An overview. In J. D. Matarazzo, S. M. Weiss, J. A. Herd, N. E. Miller, & S. M. Weiss, (Eds.), *Behavioral health: A handbook of health enhancement and disease prevention* (pp. 1154–1165). Silver Spring, MD: Wiley.

FARQUHAR, J. W., MACCOBY, N., WOOD, P. D., ALEXANDER, J. K., BREITROSE, H., BROWN, B. W., JR., HASKELL, W. L., MCALISTER, A. L., MEYER, A. J., NASH, J. D., & STERN, M. P. (1977, June). Community education for cardiovascular health. *Lancet,* pp. 1192–1195.

FARR, J. L. (1976a). Task characteristics, reward contingency, and intrinsic motivation. *Organizational Behavior and Human Performance, 16,* 294–307.

FARR, J. L. (1976b). Incentive schedules, productivity, and satisfaction in work groups: A laboratory study. *Organizational Behavior and Human Performance, 17,* 159–170.

FARR, J. L., VANCE, R. J., & MCINTYRE, R. M. (1977). Further examinations of the relationship between reward contingency and intrinsic motivation. *Organizational Behavior and Human Performance, 20,* 31–53.

FEATHER, N. T. (Ed.). (1982). *Expectations and actions: Expectancy-value models in psychology.* Hillsdale, NJ: Erlbaum.

FECTEAU, G. W., & STOPPARD, M. M. (1983, December). *The generalization of self-efficacy to a cognitive-behavioural treatment for speech anxiety and the verbal persuasion source of efficacy information.* Paper presented at the annual meeting of the American Association of Behavior Therapy, Washington, DC.

FEILD, H. S. (1978). Attitudes toward rape: A comparative analysis of police, rapists, crisis counselors, and citizens. *Journal of Personality and Social Psychology, 36,* 156–179.

FEIGENBAUM, E. A. (1977). The art of artificial intelligence: I. Themes and case studies of knowledge engineering. *Proceedings of the Fifth International Joint Conference of Artificial Intelligence, 2,* 1014–1029.

FEINGOLD, B. D., & MAHONEY, M. J. (1975). Reinforcing effects on intrinsic interest: Undermining the overjustification hypothesis. *Behavior Therapy, 6,* 367–377.

FEINMAN, S. (1982). Social referencing in infancy. *Merrill-Palmer Quarterly, 28,* 445–470.

FELDMAN, D. H. (1980). *Beyond universals in cognitive development.* Norwood, NJ: Ablex.

FELIXBROD, J. J., & O'LEARY, K. D. (1973). Effects of reinforcement on children's academic behavior as a function of self-determined and externally imposed contingencies. *Journal of Applied Behavior Analysis, 6,* 241–250.

FELIXBROD, J. J., & O'LEARY, K. D. (1974). Self-determination of academic standards by children. *Journal of Educational Psychology, 66,* 845–850.

FELTZ, D. L. (1982). Path analysis of the causal elements in Bandura's theory of self-efficacy and an anxiety-based model of avoidance behavior. *Journal of Personality and Social Psychology, 42,* 764–781.

FELTZ, D. L., & ALBRECHT, R. R. (1985). The influence of self-efficacy on approach/avoidance of a high-avoidance motor task. In J. H. Humphrey & L. Vander Velden (Eds.), *Current research in the psychology/sociology of sport* (Vol. 1). Princeton, NJ: Princeton Book Company.

FELTZ, D. L., & LANDERS, D. M. (1983). Effects of mental practice on motor skill learning and performance: A meta-analysis. *Journal of Sport Psychology, 5,* 25–57.

FELTZ, D. L., LANDERS, D. M., & RAEDER, U. (1979). Enhancing self-efficacy in high avoidance motor tasks: A comparison of modeling techniques. *Journal of Sport Psychology, 1,* 112–122.

FENIGSTEIN, A. (1979). Does aggression cause a preference for viewing media violence? *Journal of Personality and Social Psychology, 37,* 2307–2317.

FENSON, L., & RAMSAY, D. S. (1981). Effects of modeling action sequences on the play of twelve-, fifteen-, and nineteen-month-old children. *Child Development, 52,* 1028–1036.

FERGUSON, J. M., TAYLOR, C. B., & WERMUTH, B. (1978). A rapid behavioral treatment for needle phobics. *The Journal of Nervous and Mental Disease, 166,* 294–298.

FERSTER, C. B., & SKINNER, B. F. (1957). *Schedules of reinforcement.* New York: Appleton.

FESHBACH, N. D., & FESHBACH, S. (1969). The relationship between empathy and aggression in two age groups. *Developmental Psychology, 1,* 102–107.

FESTINGER, L. (1942). A theoretical interpretation of

shifts in level of aspiration. *Psychological Review, 49,* 235–250.

FESTINGER, L. (1954). A theory of social comparison processes. *Human Relations, 7,* 117–140.

FESTINGER, L. (1957). *A theory of cognitive dissonance.* Evanston, IL: Row, Peterson.

FIELD, T. M., WOODSON, R., GREENBERG, R., & COHEN, D. (1982). Discrimination and imitation of facial expressions by neonates. *Science, 218,* 179–181.

FINGARETTE, H. (1969). *Self-deception.* New York: Humanities Press.

FINKELSTEIN, N. W., & RAMEY, C. T. (1977). Learning to control the environment in infancy. *Child Development, 48,* 806–819.

FIORINA, M. P. (1980). The decline of collective responsibility in American politics. *Daedalus, 109*(3), 25–45.

FISCHER, K. W. (1983). Illuminating the processes of moral development. *Monographs of the Society for Research in Child Development, 38* (1–2, Serial No. 200).

FISHBEIN, M. (Ed.). (1967). *Readings in attitude theory and measurement.* New York: Wiley.

FISHBEIN, M., & AJZEN, I. (1975). *Belief, attitude, intention and behavior: An introduction to theory and research.* Reading, MA: Addison-Wesley.

FISHER, W. A., & BYRNE, D. (1978). Individual differences in affective, evaluative, and behavioral responses to an erotic film. *Journal of Applied Social Psychology, 8,* 355–365.

FISKE, D. W., & MADDI, S. R. (Eds.). (1961). *Functions of varied experience.* Homewood, IL: Dorsey.

FLAVELL, J. H. (1968). *The development of role-taking and communication skills in children.* New York: Wiley.

FLAVELL, J. H. (1970). Developmental studies of mediated memory. In H. W. Reese & L. P. Lipsitt (Eds.), *Advances in child development and behavior:* (Vol. 5, pp. 181–211). New York: Academic Press.

FLAVELL, J. H. (1978a). Metacognitive development. In J. M. Scandura & C. J. Brainerd (Eds.), *Structural-process theories of complex human behavior* (pp. 213–245). Alphen a.d. Rijn, The Netherlands: Sijithoff and Noordhoff.

FLAVELL, J. H. (1978b). Developmental stage: Explanans or explanadum? *The Behavioral and Brain Sciences, 2,* 187–188.

FLAVELL, J. H. (1979). Metacognition and cognitive monitoring: A new area of cognitive-developmental inquiry. *American Psychologist, 34,* 906–911.

FLAVELL, J. H. (1981). Cognitive monitoring. In W. P. Dickson (Ed.), *Children's oral communication skills* (pp. 35–60). New York: Academic Press.

FLAXMAN, J., & SOLNICK, J. V. (1975, December). *Self-reinforcement and self-monitoring under conditions of high and low demand.* Paper presented at a meeting of the Association for Advancement of Behavior Therapy, San Francisco.

FLERX, V. C., FIDLER, D. S., & ROGERS, R. W. (1976). Sex role stereotypes: Developmental aspects and early intervention. *Child Development, 47,* 998–1007.

FOLGER, J. P., & CHAPMAN, R. S. (1978). A pragmatic analysis of spontaneous imitations. *Journal of Child Language, 5,* 25–38.

FORD, C. S., & BEACH, F. A. (1951). *Patterns of sexual behavior.* New York: Harper.

FORREST, M. S., & HOKANSON, J. E. (1975). Depression and autonomic arousal reduction of accompanying self-punitive behavior. *Journal of Abnormal Psychology, 84,* 346–357.

FORWARD, J. R., & WILLIAMS, J. R. (1970). Internal-external control and black militancy. *Journal of Social Issues, 26,* 75–92.

FOSS, B. M. (1964). Mimicry in mynas (Gracula religiosa): A test of Mowrer's theory. *British Journal of Psychology, 55,* 85–88.

FOURCIN, A. J., & ABBERTON, E. (1972). First applications of a new laryngograph. *The Volta Review, 74,* 161–176.

FOWLER, H. (1971). Implications of sensory reinforcement. In R. Glaser (Ed.), *The nature of reinforcement* (pp. 151–195). New York: Academic Press.

FOXX, R. M., & AZRIN, N. H. (1972). Restitution: A method of eliminating aggressive-disruptive behavior of retarded and brain damaged patients. *Behaviour Research and Therapy, 10,* 15–27.

FOXX, R. M., & BECHTEL, D. R. (1982). Overcorrection. In H. Hersen, R. M. Eisler, & P. M. Miller (Eds.), *Progress in behavior modification* (Vol. 13, pp. 227–288). New York: Academic Press.

FRANKENHAEUSER, M. (1975). Experimental approaches to the study of catecholamines and emotion. In L. Levi (Ed.), *Emotions: Their parameters and measurement* (pp. 209–234). New York: Raven.

FRANKL, V. E. (1971). Determinism and humanism. *Humanitas, 7,* 23–37.

FRASER, C., BELLUGI, U., & BROWN, R. (1963). Control of grammar in imitation, comprehension, and production. *Journal of Verbal Learning and Verbal Behavior, 2,* 121–135.

FRAZIER, J. R. (1973). Fixed ratio schedule responding as a function of contingency descriptions and reinforcement delay. *Psychological Reports, 33,* 667–672.

FREEDMAN, J. L. (1965). Long-term behavioral effects of cognitive dissonance. *Journal of Experimental Social Psychology, 1,* 145–155.

FREEDMAN, J. L., & FRASER, S. (1966). Compliance without pressure: The foot-in-the-door technique. *Journal of Personality and Social Psychology, 4,* 195–202.

FREUD, S. (1925). Mourning and melancholia. In *Collected Papers* (Vol. IV). London: Hogarth.

FREUD, S. (1948). *Group psychology and the analysis of the ego.* London: Hogarth.

FREUD, S. (1955). *The complete psychological works of . . . .* Translated by James Strachey. Vol. 10. London: Hogarth.

FREUD, S. (1963). Introductory lectures on psychoanalysis. In J. Strachey (Ed. and Trans.), *The standard edition of the complete psychological works of Sigmund Freud* (Vols. 15 and 16). London: Hogarth. (First German edition published 1917).

FREUD, S. (1964). *New introductory lectures on psychoanalysis.* In *Standard edition* (Vol. 22). London: Hogarth. (First German edition published 1933).

FRIEDMAN, M., & ROSENMAN, R. H. (1974). *Type A behavior and your heart.* Greenwich, CT: Fawcett.

FRIEDMAN, R. M., FILIPCZAK, J., & FIORDALISO, R. (1977). Within-school generalization of the preparation through responsive educational programs (PREP) academic project. *Behavior Therapy, 8,* 986–995.

FRIES, J. F., & CRAPO, L. M. (1981). *Vitality and aging: Implications of the rectangular curve.* San Francisco: Freeman.

FRIEZE, I. (1976). The role of information processing in making causal attributions for success and failure. In J. S. Carroll & J. W. Payne (Eds.), *Cognition and social behavior* (pp. 95–112). Hillsdale, NJ: Erlbaum.

FRYREAR, J. L., & THELEN, M. H. (1969). The effect of sex of model and sex of observer on the imitation of affectionate behavior. *Developmental Psychology, 1,* 298.

FUCHS, V. (1974). *Who shall live? Health, economics, and social choice.* New York: Basic Books.

FUREDY, J. J. (1973). Some limits on the cognitive control of conditioned autonomic behavior. *Psychophysiology, 10,* 108–111.

FURNELL, J. R. G., & THOMAS, G. V. (1976). Stimulus control of generalized imitation in subnormal children. *Journal of Experimental Child Psychology, 22,* 282–291.

FURROW, D., NELSON, K., & BENEDICT, H. (1979). Mothers' speech to children and syntactic development: Some simple relationships. *Journal of Child Language, 6,* 423–442.

FUSON, K. C. (1979). The development of self-regulating aspects of speech: A review. In G. Zivin (Ed.), *The development of self-regulation through private speech* (pp. 135–217). New York: Wiley.

GAERTNER, S. L., & DOVIDIO, J. F. (1977). The subtlety of white racism, arousal, and helping behavior. *Journal of Personality and Social Psychology, 35,* 691–707.

GALE, E. N., & JACOBSON, M. B. (1970). The relationship between social comments as unconditioned stimuli and fear responding. *Behaviour Research and Therapy, 8,* 301–307.

GALST, J. P., & WHITE, M. A. (1976). The unhealthy persuader: Reinforcing value and children's purchase-influencing attempts at the supermarket. *Child Development, 47,* 1089–1096.

GAMBINO, R. (1973, November–December). Watergate lingo: A language of non-responsibility. *Freedom at Issue* (No. 22), 7–9, 15–17.

GARBER, J., HOLLON, S. D., & SILVERMAN, V. (1979, December). *Evaluation and reward of self vs. others in depression.* Paper presented at the meeting of the Association for the Advancement of Behavior Therapy, San Francisco.

GARBER, J., & SELIGMAN, M. E. P. (Eds.). (1980). *Human helplessness: Theory and applications.* New York: Academic Press.

GARCIA, E., BAER, D. M., & FIRESTONE, I. (1971). The development of generalized imitation within topographically determined boundaries. *Journal of Applied Behavior Analysis, 4,* 101–112.

GARCIA, J., & KOELLING, R. A. (1966). Relation of cue to consequence in avoidance learning. *Psychonomic Science, 4,* 123–124.

GARDNER, B. T. (1981). Project Nim: Who taught whom? *Contemporary Psychology, 26,* 425–426.

GARDNER, B. T., & GARDNER, R. A. (1975). Evidence for sentence constituents in the early utterances of child and chimpanzee. *Journal of Experimental Psychology: General, 104,* 244–267.

GARDNER, R. A., & GARDNER, B. T. (1969). Teaching sign language to a chimpanzee. *Science, 165,* 644–672.

GARDNER, R., & HEIDER, K. G. (1969). *Gardens of war.* New York: Random House.

GARLAND, H. (1983). Influence of ability, assigned goals, and normative information on personal goals and performance: A challenge to the goal attainability assumption. *Journal of Applied Psychology, 68,* 20–30.

GARLAND, H. (1984). Relation of effort-performance expectancy to performance in goal-setting experiments. *Journal of Applied Psychology, 69,* 79–84.

GARLINGTON, W. K., & DERICCO, D. A. (1977). The effect of modeling on drinking rate. *Journal of Applied Behavior Analysis, 10,* 207–212.

GAROFALO, J. (1979). Victimization and the fear of crime. *Journal of Research in Crime and Delinquency, 17,* 80–97.

GARVEY, E. R. (1979). From chattel to employee: The athlete's quest for freedom and dignity. *The Annals of the American Academy of Political and Social Science, 445,* 91–101.

GAUPP, L. A., STERN, R. M., & GALBRAITH, G. G. (1972). False heart-rate feedback and reciprocal inhibition by aversion relief in the treatment of snake avoidance behavior. *Behavior Therapy, 3,* 7–20.

GAUTHIER, J., & LADOUCEUR, R. (1981). The influence of self-efficacy reports on performance. *Behavior Therapy, 12,* 436–439.

GEEN, R. G. (1978). Some effects of observing violence upon the behavior of the observer. In B. A. Maher (Ed.), *Progress in experimental personality research* (Vol. 8, pp. 49–92). New York: Academic Press.

GEEN, R. G., & RAKOSKY, J. J. (1973). Interpretations of observed aggression and their effect on GSR. *Journal of Experimental Research in Personality, 6,* 289–292.

GEER, J. H. (1968). A test of the classical conditioning model of emotion: The use of nonpainful aversive stimuli as unconditioned stimuli in a conditioning procedure. *Journal of Personality and Social Psychology, 10,* 148–156.

GEER, J. H., DAVISON, G. C., & GATCHEL, R. I. (1970). Reduction of stress in humans through nonveridical perceived control of aversive stimulation. *Journal of Personality and Social Psychology, 16,* 731–738.

GEERKEN, M., & GOVE, W. R. (1977). Social control, deterrence, and perspectives on social order. *Social Forces, 56,* 408–423.

GEIS, G., & MONAHAN, J. (1976). The social ecology of violence. In T. Lickona (Ed.), *Man and morality* (pp. 342–356). New York: Holt, Rinehart & Winston.

GELFAND, D. M., & HARTMANN, D. P. (1977). The prevention of childhood behavior disorders. In B. B. Lahey & A. E. Kazdin (Eds.), *Advances in clinical child psychology* (Vol. 1, pp. 361–395). New York: Plenum.

GELFAND, D. M., HARTMANN, D. P., LAMB, A. K., SMITH, C. L., MAHAN, M. A., & PAUL, S. C. (1974). The effects of adult models and described alternatives on children's choice of behavior management techniques. *Child Development, 45,* 585–593.

GENEST, M., & TURK, D. C. (1982). Think-aloud approaches to cognitive assessment. In T. V. Merluzzi, C. R. Glass, & M. Genest (Eds.), *Cognitive assessment* (pp. 233–269). New York: Guilford.

GEORGE, C. J. (1972). The role of the Aswan high dam in changing the fisheries of the southeastern Mediterranean. In M. T. Farvar & J. P. Milton (Eds.), *The careless technology: Ecology and international development* (pp. 159–178). Garden City, NY: The Natural History Press.

GERBNER, G. (1972). Communication and social environment. *Scientific American, 227,* 153–160.

GERBNER, G., & GROSS, L. (1976). Living with television: The violence profile. *Journal of Communication, 26,* 173–199.

GERBNER, G., GROSS, L., MORGAN, M., & SIGNORIELLI, N. (1981). A curious journey into the scary world of Paul Hirsch. *Communication Research, 8,* 39–72.

GERBNER, G., GROSS, L., SIGNORIELLI, N., & MORGAN, M. (1980). Aging with television: Images on television drama and conceptions of social reality. *Journal of Communication, 30*(1), 37–47.

GERST, M. S. (1971). Symbolic coding processes in observational learning. *Journal of Personality and Social Psychology, 19,* 7–17.

GEWIRTZ, J. L. (1971). Conditional responding as a paradigm for observational, imitative learning and vicarious-reinforcement. In H. W. Reese (Ed.), *Advances in child development and behavior* (Vol. 6, pp. 273–304). New York: Academic Press.

GEWIRTZ, J. L., & STINGLE, K. C. (1968). The learning of generalized imitation as the basis for identification. *Psychological Review, 75,* 374–397.

GHOLSON, B. (1980). *The cognitive-developmental basis of human learning: Studies in hypothesis testing.* New York: Academic Press.

GIBBS, J. P. (1975). *Crime, punishment, and deterrence.* New York: Elsevier.

GIBSON, S., & DEMBO, M. H. (1984). Teacher efficacy: A construct validation. *Journal of Educational Psychology, 76,* 569–582.

GILLIGAN, C. (1982). *In a different voice: Psychological theory and women's development.* Cambridge, MA: Harvard University Press.

GILOVICH, T. (1981). Seeing the past in the present: The effect of associations to familiar events on judgments and decisions. *Journal of Personality and Social Psychology, 40,* 797–808.

GLASER, R., (1984). Education and thinking: The role of knowledge. *American Psychologist, 39,* 93–104.

GLASER, R., & KLAUS, D. J. (1966). A reinforcement analysis of group performance. *Psychological Monographs: General and Applied, 80*(13).

GLASGOW, R. E., & ARKOWITZ, H. (1975). The behavioral assessment of male and female social competence in dyadic heterosexual interactions. *Behavior Therapy, 6,* 488–498.

GLASS, D. C., & CARVER, C. S. (1980). Helplessness and the coronary-prone personality. In J. Garber & M. E. P. Seligman (Eds.), *Human helplessness: Theory and applications* (pp. 223–243). New York: Academic Press.

GLASS, D. C., REIM, B., & SINGER, J. (1971). Behavioral consequences of adaptation to controllable and uncontrollable noise. *Journal of Experimental Social Psychology, 7,* 244–257.

GLASS, D. C., SINGER, J. E., LEONARD, H. S., KRANTZ, D., & CUMMINGS, H. (1973). Perceived control of aversive stimulation and the reduction of stress responses. *Journal of Personality, 41,* 577–595.

GLEASON, J. B., & WEINTRAUB, S. (1978). Input language and the acquisition of communicative competence. In K. E. Nelson (Ed.), *Children's language* (Vol. 1, pp. 171–222). New York: Gardner.

GLYNN, E. L. (1970). Classroom applications of self-determined reinforcement. *Journal of Applied Behavior Analysis, 3,* 123–132.

GODDING, P. R., & GLASGOW, R. E. (1985). Self-efficacy and outcome expectancy as predictors of controlled smoking status. *Cognitive Therapy and Research.*

GOETHALS, G. R., & DARLEY, J. M. (1977). Social comparison theory: Attributional approach. In J. M. Suls & R. L. Miller (Eds.), *Social comparison processes: Theoretical and empirical perspectives* (pp. 259–278). Washington, DC: Hemisphere.

GOLDBERG, M. E., & GORN, G. J. (1978). Some unintended consequences of TV advertising to children. *The Journal of Consumer Research, 5,* 22–29.

GOLDBERG, M. E., GORN, G. J., & GIBSON, W. (1978). TV messages for snack and breakfast foods: Do they influence children's preferences? *The Journal of Consumer Research, 5,* 73–81.

GOLDIAMOND, I. (1958). Indicators of perception: I. Subliminal perception, subception, unconscious perception: An analysis in terms of psychological indicator methodology. *Psychological Bulletin, 55,* 373–412.

GOLDIAMOND, I. (1976). Self-reinforcement. *Journal of Applied Behavior Analysis, 9,* 509–514.

GOLDSTEIN, A. P. (1973). *Structured learning therapy.* New York: Academic Press.

GOLIN, S., & TERRELL, F. (1977). Motivational and associative aspects of mild depression in skill and chance tasks. *Journal of Abnormal Psychology, 86,* 389–401.

GOLIN, S., TERRELL, F., & JOHNSON, B. (1977). Depression and the illusion of control. *Journal of Abnormal Psychology, 86,* 440–442.

GOLIN, S., TERRELL, F., WEITZ, J., & DROST, P. L. (1979). The illusion of control among depressed patients. *Journal of Abnormal Psychology, 88,* 454–457.

GONZALES, F. P., & DOWRICK, P. W. (1983, October). *Ef-*

fects of video self-modeling in "feedforward" training hand/eye coordination. Unpublished manuscript, University of Alaska, Anchorage, Alaska.

GORANSON, R. E. (1970). Media violence and aggressive behavior: A review of experimental research. In L. Berkowitz (Ed.), *Advances in experimental social psychology* (Vol. 5, pp. 2–31). New York: Academic Press.

GOSLIN, D. A. (1969). *Handbook of socialization theory and research.* Chicago: Rand McNally.

GOSS, K. F. (1979). Consequences of diffusion of innovations. *Rural Sociology, 44,* 754–772.

GOTLIB, I. H. (1981). Self-reinforcement and recall: Differential deficits in depressed and nondepressed psychiatric inpatients. *Journal of Abnormal Psychology, 90,* 521–530.

GOTSCH, C. H. (1972). Technical change and the distribution of income in rural areas. *American Journal of Agricultural Economics, 54,* 326–341.

GOTTMAN, J. M., & McFALL, R. M. (1972). Self-monitoring effects in a program for potential high school dropouts: A time-series analysis. *Journal of Consulting and Clinical Psychology, 39,* 273–281.

GOULD, D., & WEISS, M. (1981). Effect of model similarity and model self-talk on self-efficacy in muscular endurance. *Journal of Sport Psychology, 3,* 17–29.

GRANOVETTER, M. (1983). The strength of weak ties—A network theory revisited. In R. Collins (Ed.), *Sociological theory 1983* (pp. 201–233). San Francisco: Jossey-Bass.

GRAY, V. (1973). Innovation in the States: A diffusion study. *The American Political Science Review, 4,* 1174–1185.

GRAY-LITTLE, B., & TEDDLIE, C. B. (1978). Racial differences in children's responses to inequity. *Journal of Applied Social Psychology, 8,* 107–116.

GRAYSON, G. (1980, November 20). "Coding" athletes to win. *St. Louis Post-Dispatch,* pp. 1, 4.

GRECO, T. S. (1973). The effects of prior situational and aversive experience on vicarious emotional arousal (Doctoral dissertation, University of Georgia, 1972). *Dissertation Abstracts International, 33,* 4506–B. (University Microfilms No. 73–5701, 98).

GREENE, D., & LEPPER, M. R. (1974). Effects of extrinsic rewards on children's subsequent intrinsic interest. *Child Development, 45,* 1141–1145.

GREENE, D., STERNBERG, B., & LEPPER, M. R. (1976). Overjustification in a token economy. *Journal of Personality and Social Psychology, 34,* 1219–1234.

GREENFELD, N., & KUZNICKI, J. T. (1975). Implied competence, task complexity, and imitative behavior. *Journal of Social Psychology, 95,* 251–262.

GREENO, J. G. (1973). Theory and practice regarding acquired cognitive structures. *Educational Psychologist, 10,* 117–122.

GREENWALD, A. G. (1980). The totalitarian ego: Fabrication and revision of personal history. *American Psychologist, 35,* 603–618.

GREENWALD, A. G., & ALBERT, S. M. (1968). Observa-

tional learning: A technique for elucidating S-R mediation processes. *Journal of Experimental Psychology, 76,* 267–272.

GREESON, L. E. (1981). Modeling, intelligence, and language development. *The Journal of Genetic Psychology, 139,* 195–203.

GRIFFIN, S. (1971, September). Rape: The all-American crime. *Ramparts,* pp. 26–35.

GRIMM, L., & KANFER, F. H. (1976). Tolerance of aversive stimulation. *Behavior Therapy, 7,* 593–601.

GRIMM, L. G., & YARNOLD, P. R. (1984). Performance standards and the Type A behavior pattern. *Cognitive Therapy and Research, 8,* 59–66.

GRINGS, W. W. (1973). The role of consciousness and cognition in automatic behavior change. In F. J. McGuigan & R. Schoonover (Eds.), *The psychophysiology of thinking* (pp. 233–262). New York: Academic Press.

GRUENEICH, R. (1982). The development of children's integration rules for making moral judgments. *Child Development, 53,* 887–894.

GRÜNBAUM, A. (1984). *The foundations of psychoanalysis: A philosophical critique.* Berkeley: University of California Press.

GRUSEC, J. E. (1966). Some antecedents of self-criticism. *Journal of Personality and Social Psychology, 4,* 244–252.

GRUSEC, J. E. (1971). Power and the internalization of self-denial. *Child Development, 42,* 93–105.

GRUSEC, J. E., & EZRIN, S. A. (1972). Techniques of punishment and the development of self-criticism. *Child Development, 43,* 1273–1288.

GRUSEC, J. E., KUCZYNSKI, L., RUSHTON, J. P., & SIMUTIS, Z. M. (1978). Modeling, direct instruction, and attributions: Effects on altruism. *Developmental Psychology, 14,* 51–57.

GRUSEC, J. E., & REDLER, E. (1980). Attribution, reinforcement, and altruism: A developmental analysis. *Developmental Psychology, 16,* 525–534.

GUERIN, B., & INNES, J. M. (1981). Awareness of cognitive processes: Replications and revisions. *The Journal of General Psychology, 104,* 173–189.

GUEST, A. M. (1974). Subjective powerlessness in the United States: Some longitudinal trends. *Social Science Quarterly, 54,* 827–842.

GUMB, R. D. (1972). *Rule-governed linguistic behavior.* The Hague: Mouton.

GUNNAR-vonGNECHTEN, M. R. (1978). Changing a frightening toy into a pleasant toy by allowing the infant to control its actions. *Developmental Psychology, 14,* 147–152.

GUNNAR, M. R. (1980a). Control, warning signals, and distress in infancy. *Developmental Psychology, 16,* 281–289.

GUNNAR, M. R. (1980b). Contingent stimulation: A review of its role in early development. In S. Levine & H. Ursin (Eds.), *Coping and health* (pp. 101–119). New York: Plenum Press.

GUNNAR, M. R., LEIGHTON, K., & PELEAUX, R. (1984). Effects of temporal predictability on the reactions of

1–year olds to potentially frightening toys. *Developmental Psychology, 20,* 449–458.

GUNNAR, M. R., & STONE, C. (1984). The effects of positive maternal affect on infant responses to pleasant, ambiguous and fear-provoking toys. *Child Development, 55,* 1231–1236.

GURIN, P., & BRIM, O. G., JR. (1984). Change in self in adulthood: The example of sense of control. In P. B. Baltes & O. G. Brim, Jr. (Eds.), *Life-span development and behavior* (Vol. 6, pp. 281–334). New York: Academic Press.

GURIN, P., GURIN, G., & MORRISON, B. M. (1978). Personal and ideological aspects of internal and external control. *Social Psychology, 41,* 275–296.

GURR, T. R. (1970). Sources of rebellion in Western societies: Some quantitative evidence. *Annals of the American Academy of Political and Social Science, 391,* 128–144.

GURR, T. R. (1979). Political protest and rebellion in the 1960's: The United States in world perspective. In H. D. Graham & T. R. Gurr (Eds.), *Violence in America: Historical and comparative perspectives* (pp. 49–76). Beverly Hills: Sage.

GUSTKEY, E. (1979, December 21). The computerized athlete is here. *San Francisco Chronicle,* pp. 67, 70.

GUTHRIE, E. R. (1952). *The psychology of learning* (rev. ed.) New York: Harper.

GUTKIN, D. C. (1972). The effect of systematic story changes on intentionality in children's moral judgments. *Child Development, 43,* 187–195.

GUTKIN, D. C. (1975). Maternal discipline and children's judgments of moral intentionality. *The Journal of Genetic Psychology, 127,* 55–62.

HACKETT, G. (1985). The role of mathematics self-efficacy in the choice of math-related majors of college women and men: A path analysis. *Journal of Counseling Psychology.*

HACKETT, G., & BETZ, N. E. (1981). A self-efficacy approach to the career development of women. *Journal of Vocational Behavior, 18,* 326–339.

HACKETT, G., & BETZ, N. E. (1984). *Mathematics performance, mathematics self-efficacy, and the prediction of science-based college majors.* Unpublished manuscript, University of California, Santa Barbara.

HACKETT, G., BETZ, N. E., & DOTY, M. S. (1985). The development of a taxonomy of career competencies for professional women. *Sex Roles, 12,* 393–409.

HACKMAN, J. R., & LAWLER, E. E., III. (1971). Employee reactions to job characteristics. *Journal of Applied Psychology Monograph, 55,* 259–286.

HAGEN, J. W., & HALE, G. A. (1973). The development of attention in children. In A. D. Pick (Ed.), *Minnesota Symposia on Child Psychology* (Vol. 7, pp. 117–140). Minneapolis: University of Minnesota Press.

HAGEN, J. W., JONGEWARD, R. H., JR., & KAIL, R. V., JR. (1975). Cognitive perspectives on the development of memory. In H. W. Reese (Ed.), *Advances in child development and behavior* (Vol. 10, pp. 57–101). New York: Academic Press.

HAIGHT, M. R. (1980) *A study of self deception.* Atlantic Highlands, NJ: Humanities Press.

HAIRE, M., & GRUNES, W. F. (1950). Perceptual defenses: Processes protecting an organized perception of another personality. *Human Relations, 3,* 403–412.

HALDANE, J. S. (1984). Life and mechanism. *Mind, 9,* 27–47.

HALL, K. R. (1963). Observational learning in monkeys and apes. *British Journal of Psychology, 54,* 201–226.

HALL, R. A. (1969). Some recent developments in American linguistics. *Neuphilologische Mitteilunger, 2,* 192–227.

HALLIE, P. P. (1971). Justification and rebellion. In N. Sanford & C. Comstock (Eds.), *Sanctions for evil* (pp. 247–263). San Francisco: Jossey-Bass.

HALLORAN, J. D., & CROLL, P. (1972). Television programs in Great Britain: Content and control. In G. A. Comstock & E. A. Rubinstein (Eds.), *Television and social behavior: Vol. 1. Media content and control.* Washington, DC: U.S. Government Printing Office.

HAMILTON, M. L. (1970). Vicarious reinforcement effects on extinction. *Journal of Experimental Child Psychology, 9,* 108–114.

HAMILTON, M. L., & STEWART, D. M. (1977). Peer models and language acquisition. *Merrill-Palmer Quarterly of Behavior and Development, 23,* 45–56.

HAMILTON, V. L., & ROTKIN, L. (1979). The capital punishment debate: Public perceptions of crime and punishment. *Journal of Applied Social Psychology, 9,* 350–376.

HAMLYN, D. W. (1971). Epistemology and conceptual development. In T. Mischel (Ed.), *Cognitive development and epistemology* (pp. 3–24). New York: Academic Press.

HAMMER, W. C. (1979). How to ruin motivation with pay. In R. M. Steers & L. W. Porter (Eds.), *Motivation and work behavior* (pp. 538–551). New York: McGraw-Hill.

HAMMOND, K. R. (1971). Computer graphics as an aid to learning. *Science, 172,* 903–908.

HAMMOND, K. R., STEWART, T. R., BREHMER, B., & STEINMANN, D. O. (1975). Social judgment theory. In M. F. Kaplan & S. Schwartz (Eds.), *Human judgment and decision processes* (pp. 271–312). New York: Academic Press.

HAMMOND, K. R., & SUMMERS, D. A. (1972). Cognitive control. *Psychological Review, 79,* 58–67.

HANDLEMAN, J. S. & HARRIS, S. L. (1980). Generalization from school to home with autistic children. *Journal of Autism and Developmental Disorders, 3,* 323–332.

HANEY, C., BANKS, C., & ZIMBARDO, P. (1973). Interpersonal dynamics in a simulated prison. *International Journal of Criminology and Penology, 1,* 69–97.

HARACKIEWICZ, J. M., SANSONE, C., & MANDERLINK, G. (1985). Competence, achievement orientation, and intrinsic motivation: A process analysis. *Journal of Personality and Social Psychology, 48,* 493–508.

HARLOW, H. F. (1953). Motivation as a factor in the acquisition of new responses. In *Current theory and re-*

search in motivation: A symposium (pp. 24–49). Lincoln: University of Nebraska Press.

HARPER, L. V., & SANDERS, K. M. (1975). The effect of adults' eating on young children's acceptance of unfamiliar foods. *Journal of Experimental Child Psychology, 20,* 206–214.

HARRIS, M. B. (1975). Modeling influences on creative behavior. *School Psychology Digest, 4,* 29–33.

HARRIS, M. B., & EVANS, R. C. (1973). Models and creativity. *Psychological Reports, 33,* 763–769.

HARRIS, M. B., & FISHER, J. L. (1973). Modeling and flexibility in problem-solving. *Psychological Reports, 33,* 19–23.

HARRIS, M. B., & HASSEMER, W. G. (1972). Some factors affecting the complexity of children's sentences: The effects of modeling, sex, and bilingualism. *Journal of Experimental Child Psychology, 13,* 447–455.

HARRIS, M. B., & VOORHEES, S. D. (1981). Sex-role stereotypes and televised models of emotion. *Psychological Reports, 48,* 826.

HARRIS, S. L. (1975). Teaching language to nonverbal children—with emphasis on problems of generalization. *Psychological Bulletin, 82,* 565–580.

HART, B., & RISLEY, T. R. (1968). Establishing use of descriptive adjectives in the spontaneous speech of disadvantaged peschool children. *Journal of Applied Behavior Analysis, 1,* 109–120.

HART, B., & RISLEY, T. R. (1974). Using preschool materials to modify the language of disadvantaged children. *Journal of Applied Behavior Analysis, 7,* 243–256.

HART, B., & RISLEY, T. R. (1975). Incidental teaching of language in the preschool. *Journal of Applied Behavior Analysis, 8,* 411–420.

HART, B., & RISLEY, T. R. (1978). Promoting productive language through incidental teaching. *Education and Urban Society, 10,* 407–430.

HART, B., & RISLEY, T. R. (1980). In vivo language intervention: Unanticipated general effects. *Journal of Applied Behavior Analysis, 13,* 407–432.

HARTER, S. (1978). Effectance motivation reconsidered: Toward a developmental model. *Human Development, 21,* 34–64.

HARTER, S. (1981). A model of mastery motivation in children—Individual differences and developmental change. In W. A. Collins (Ed.), *Aspects of the development of competence: Minnesota Symposia on child psychology* (Vol. 14, pp. 215–255). Hillsdale, NJ: Erlbaum.

HARUKI, Y., & SHIEGEHISA, T. (1983). Experimental analysis of the types of reinforcement—with special reference to social behavior theory. *Waseda Psychological Reports, Special Issue,* 63–93.

HARVEY, S. E., & LIEBERT, R. M. (1979). Abstraction, inference, and acceptance in children's processing of an adult model's moral judgments. *Developmental Psychology, 15,* 552–558.

HASKETT, G. J., & LENFESTEY, W. (1974). Reading-related behavior in an open classroom: Effects of novelty and modelling on preschoolers. *Journal of Applied Behavior Analysis, 7,* 233–241.

HASTORF, A. H. (1965). The "reinforcement" of individual actions in a group situation. In L. Krasner & L. P. Ullmann (Eds.), *Research in behavior modification* (pp. 268–284). New York: Holt, Rinehart & Winston.

HATANO, G. (1970). Subjective and objective cues in moral judgment. *Japanese Psychological Research, 12,* 96–106.

HAUGAN, G. M., & McINTIRE, R. W. (1972). Comparisons of vocal imitation, tactile stimulation, and food as reinforcers for infant vocalizations. *Developmental Psychology, 6,* 201–209.

HAVENS, A. E., & FLINN, W. (1975). Green revolution technology and community development: The limits of action programs. *Economic Development and Cultural Change, 23,* 469–481.

HAWKINS, R. P., & PINGREE, S. (1982). Television's influence on social reality. In D. Pearl, L. Bouthilet, & J. Lazar (Eds.), *Television and behavior: Ten years of scientific progress and implications for the eighties* (Vol. II, pp. 224–247). Rockville, MD: National Institute of Mental Health.

HAYES, C. (1951). *The ape in our house.* New York: Harper.

HAYES, K. J., & HAYES, C. (1952). Imitation in a home-raised chimpanzee. *Journal of Comparative and Physiological Psychology, 45,* 450–459.

HAYES, L. A., & WATSON, J. S. (1981). Neonatal imitation: Fact or artifact? *Developmental Psychology, 17,* 655–660.

HEATH, L. (1984). Impact of newspaper crime reports on fear of crime: Multimethodological investigation. *Journal of Personality and Social Psychology, 47,* 263–276.

HEATON, R. C., & DUERFELDT, P. H. (1973). The relationship between self-esteem, self-reinforcement, and the internal-external personality dimension. *The Journal of Genetic Psychology, 123,* 3–13.

HECKHAUSEN, H. (1977). Achievement motivation and its constructs: A cognitive model. *Motivation and Emotion, 1,* 283–329.

HEFFERLINE, R. F., BRUNO, L. J. J., & DAVIDOWITZ, J. E. (1970). Feedback control of covert behaviour. In K. Connolly (Ed.), *Mechanisms of motor skill development* (pp. 245–278). New York: Academic Press.

HEFFERNAN, T., & RICHARDS, S. (1981). Self-control of study behavior: Identification and evaluation of natural methods. *Journal of Counseling Psychology, 28,* 361–364.

HEIBY, E. M. (1983a). Depression as a function of the interaction of self- and environmentally controlled reinforcement. *Behavior Therapy, 14,* 430–433.

HEIBY, E. M. (1983b). Toward the prediction of mood change. *Behavior Therapy, 14,* 110–115.

HELM, C., & MORELLI, M. (1979). Stanley Milgram and the obedience experiment: Authority, legitimacy, and human action. *Political Theory, 7,* 321–346.

HENDERSON, R. W., & SWANSON, R. A. (1974). Application of social learning principles in a field setting. *Exceptional Children, 41,* 53–55.

HENDERSON, R. W., & SWANSON, R. A. (1978). Age and directed-participation variables influencing the effectiveness of televised instruction in concrete operational behavior. *Educational Communication and Technology, 26,* 301–312.

HENDRICK, G. (1977, January 29). When television is a school for criminals. *TV Guide,* pp. 4–10.

HENEMAN, H. G., & SCHWAB, D. P. (1972). Evaluation of research on expectancy theory predictions of employee performance. *Psychological Bulletin, 78,* 1–9.

HERBERT, E. W., GELFAND, D. M., & HARTMANN, D. P. (1969). Imitation and self-esteem as determinants of self-critical behavior. *Child Development, 40,* 421–430.

HERBERT, J. J., & HARSH, C. M. (1944). Observational learning by cats. *Journal of Comparative Psychology, 37,* 81–95.

HERNANDEZ-PEON, R., SCHERRER, H., & JOUVET, M. (1956). Modification of electric activity in cochlear nucleus during "attention" in unanesthetized cats. *Science, 123,* 331–332.

HERRNSTEIN, R. J. (1969). Method and theory in the study of avoidance. *Psychological Review, 76,* 49–69.

HERSEN, M., & BELLACK, S. (1977). Assessment of social skills. In A. R. Ciminero, K. S. Calhoun, & H. E. Adams (Eds.), *Handbook of behavioral assessment* (pp. 509–554). New York: Wiley.

HERSEN, M., KAZDIN, A. E., BELLACK, A. S., & TURNER, S. M. (1979). Effects of live modeling, covert modeling and rehearsal on assertiveness in psychiatric patients. *Behaviour Research and Therapy, 17,* 369–377.

HERSHEY, M. R. (1984). *Running for office: The political education of campaigners.* Chatham, NJ: Chatham House.

HERSHEY, M. R., & WEST, D. M. (1984). Senate campaigners and the pro-life challenge in 1980. *Micropolitics, 3,* 547–589.

HESS, R. D., & MIURA, I. (1985). Gender differences in enrollment in computer camps and classes. *Sex Roles.*

HEYNEMAN, D. (1971). Mis-aid to the third world: Disease repercussions caused by ecological ignorance. *Canadian Journal of Public Health, 62,* 303–313.

HICKS, D. J. (1968). Effects of co-observer's sanctions and adult presence on imitative aggression. *Child Development, 39,* 303–309.

HICKS, D. J. (1971). Girls' attitudes toward modeled behaviors and the content of imitative private play. *Child Development, 42,* 139–147.

HIGGINS, A., POWER, C., & KOHLBERG, L. (1984). Student judgments of responsibility and the moral atmosphere of high schools: A comparative study. In W. Kurtines & J. L. Gewirtz (Eds.), *Morality, moral behavior and moral development: Basic issues in theory and research* (pp. 74–106). New York: Wiley Interscience.

HILDEBRANDT, D. E., FELDMAN, S. E., & DITRICHS, R. A. (1973). Rules, models, and self-reinforcement in children. *Journal of Personality and Social Psychology, 25,* 1–5.

HILGARD, E. R., & HILGARD, J. R. (1975). *Hypnosis in the relief of pain.* Los Altos, CA: Kaufman.

HILL, B. (1955). *Boss of Britain's underworld.* London: Naldreth.

HILLIX, W. A., & MARX, M. H. (1960). Response strengthening by information and effect on human learning. *Journal of Experimental Psychology, 60,* 97–102.

HILTZ, S. R., & TUROFF, M. (1978). *The network nation: Human communication via computer.* Reading, MA: Addison-Wesley.

HINDE, R. A., & HINDE-STEVENSON, J. (1973). *Constraints on learning.* New York: Academic Press.

HIRAKAWA, T., & NAKAZAWA, J. (1977). Observational learning in children: The effects of vicarious reinforcement on the discrimination shift behavior in simple and complex tasks. *Japanese Journal of Educational Psychology, 25,* 254–257.

HIRSCH, P. M. (1980). The "scary world of the nonviewer" and other anomalies: A reanalysis of Gerbner et al.'s findings on cultivation analysis. Part I. *Communication Research, 7,* 403–456.

HOFFMAN, H. S. (1969). Stimulus factors in conditioned suppression. In B. A. Campbell & R. M. Church (Eds.), *Punishment and aversive behavior* (pp. 185–234). New York: Appleton-Century-Crofts.

HOFFMAN, M. L. (1970). Moral development. In P. Mussen (Ed.), *Carmichael's manual of child psychology* (Vol. 2, pp. 261–359). New York: Wiley.

HOFFMAN, M. L. (1960). Power assertion by the parent and its impact on the child. *Child Development, 31,* 129–143.

HOFFMAN, M. L. (1977). Empathy, its development and prosocial implications. In H. E. Howe & C. B. Keasey (Eds.), *Nebraska symposium on motivation: Vol. 25. Social cognitive development* (pp. 169–217). Lincoln: University of Nebraska Press.

HOLLANDSWORTH, J. G., JR., GLAZESKI, R. C., KIRKLAND, K., JONES, G. E., & van NORMAN, L. R. (1979). An analysis of the nature and effects of test anxiety: Cognitive, behavioral, and physiological components. *Cognitive Therapy and Research, 3,* 165–180.

HOLROYD, K. A., PENZIEN, D. B., HURSEY, K. G., TOBIN, D. L., ROGERS, L., HOLM, J. E., MARCILLE, P. J., HALL, J. R., & CHILA, A. G. (1984). Change mechanisms in EMG biofeedback training: Cognitive changes underlying improvements in tension headache. *Journal of Consulting and Clinical Psychology, 52,* 1039–1053.

HOLT, E. B. (1931). *Animal drive and the learning process* (Vol. 1). New York: Holt.

HOMME, L. (1970). *How to use contingency contracting in the classroom.* Champaign, IL: Research Press.

HORNSTEIN, H. A., BUNKER, B. B., BURKE, W. W., GINDES, M., & LEVICKI, R. J. (1971). *Social intervention: A behavioral science approach.* New York: Free Press.

HOUSE, T. H., & MILLIGAN, W. L. (1976). Autonomic responses to modeled distress in prison psychopaths. *Journal of Personality and Social Psychology, 34,* 556–560.

HOVELL, M. F., SCHUMAKER, J. B., & SHERMAN, J. A. (1978). A comparison of parents' models and expansions in promoting children's acquisition of adjectives. *Journal of Experimental Child Psychology, 25,* 41–57.

HOWARD, J. L., LIPTZIN, M. B., & REIFLER, C. B. (1973). Is pornography a problem? *Journal of Social Issues, 29,* 133–145.

HOWIE, A. M. (1975). Effects of brief exposure to symbolic model behavior on the information-processing strategies of internally and externally oriented children. *Developmental Psychology, 11,* 325–333.

HUANG, L. C., & HARRIS, M. B. (1973). Conformity in Chinese and Americans: A field experiment. *Journal of Cross-Cultural Psychology, 4,* 427–434.

HUESMANN, L. R. (Ed.) (1978). Learned helplessness as a model of depression. *Journal of Abnormal Psychology, 87,* Whole No. 1.

HUGDAHL, K., & KARKER, A. (1981). Biological vs experiential factors in phobic conditioning. *Behaviour Research and Therapy, 19,* 109–115.

HUGHES, C. C., TREMBLAY, M., RAPOPORT, R. N., & LEIGHTON, A. H. (1960). *People of Cove and Woodlot: Communities from the viewpoint of social psychiatry.* New York: Basic Books.

HUGHES, P. H., BARKER, N. W., CRAWFORD, G. A., & JAFFE, J. H. (1972). The natural history of a heroin epidemic. *American Journal of Public Health, 62,* 995–1001.

HUGHES, P. H., & CRAWFORD, G. A. (1972). A contagious disease model for researching and interviewing in heroin epidemics. *Archives of General Psychiatry, 27,* 149–155.

HUGHES, R., JR., TINGLE, B. A., & SAWIN, D. B. (1981). Development of empathic understanding in children. *Child Development, 52,* 122–128.

HULL, C. L. (1943). *Principles of behavior.* New York: Appleton-Century-Crofts.

HULTSCH, D. F., & PLEMONS, J. K. (1979). Life events and life-span development. In P. B. Baltes & O. G. Brim, Jr. (Eds.), *Life-span development and behavior* (Vol. 2, pp. 1–36). New York: Academic Press.

HUMPHREY, G. (1921). Imitation and the conditioned reflex. *Pedagogical Seminary, 28,* 1–21.

HUMPHREY, L. L., KAROLY, P., & KIRSCHENBAUM, D. S. (1978). Self-management in the classroom: Self-imposed response cost versus self-reward. *Behavior Therapy, 9,* 592–601.

HUNG, J. H., & ROSENTHAL, T. L. (1981). Therapeutic videotaped playback. In J. L. Fryrear & R. Fleshman (Eds.), *Videotherapy in mental health* (pp. 5–46). Springfield, IL: Thomas.

HUNT, J. McV., COLE, M. W., & REIS, E. E. S. (1958). Situational cues distinguishing anger, fear, and sorrow. *American Journal of Psychology, 71,* 136–151.

HUNTINGTON, S. (1968). *Political order in changing societies.* New Haven: Yale University Press.

HURLBURT, R. T. (1979). Random sampling of cognitions and behavior. *Journal of Research in Personality, 13,* 103–111.

HUSTON, A. C. (1983) Sex typing. In P. H. Mussen (Ed.), *Handbook of child psychology* (Vol. 4, pp. 387–467). New York: Wiley.

HYGGE, S. (1978). The observer's acquaintance with the models' stimulus in vicarious classical conditioning. *Scandinavian Journal of Psychology, 19,* 231–239.

HYGGE, S., & OHMAN, A. (1978). Modeling processes in the acquisition of fears: Vicarious electrodermal conditioning to fear-relevant stimuli. *Journal of Personality and Social Psychology, 36,* 271–279.

HYMAN, A. (1973). *The computer in design.* London: Studio Vista.

HYSON, R. L., ASHCRAFT, L. J., DRUGAN, R. C., GRAU, J. W., & MAIER, S. F. (1982). Extent and control of shock affects naltrexone sensitivity of stress-induced analgesia and reactivity to morphine. *Pharmacology Biochemistry & Behavior, 17,* 1019–1025.

IANNOTTI, R. J. (1978). Effect of role-taking experiences on role taking, empathy, altruism, and aggression. *Developmental Psychology, 14,* 119–124.

IMANISHI, K. (1957). Social behavior in Japanese monkeys, *Mascaca fuscata. Psychologia, 1,* 47–54.

IRWIN, F. W. (1971). *International behavior and motivation: A cognitive view.* Philadelphia: Lippincott.

ISRAEL, A. C. (1978). Some thoughts on correspondence between saying and doing. *Journal of Applied Behavior Analysis, 11,* 271–276.

ITO, H. (1975). An analysis of mediation processes in observational learning: A comparison of imaginal and verbal mediation. *Japanese Psychological Research, 17,* 182–191.

ITOH, H., & FUJITA, K. (1982). Eye movements during problem solving: Difference in scanning patterns between successes and failures. In R. Groner & P. Fraisse (Eds.), *Cognition and eye movements* (pp. 84–99). Amsterdam: North Holland.

IVIE, R. L. (1980). Images of savagery in American justifications for war. *Communication Monographs, 47,* 270–294.

IZARD, C. E. (1971). *The face of emotion.* New York: Appleton-Century-Crofts.

JACKLIN, C. N., & MISCHEL, H. N. (1973). As the twig is bent—sex role stereotyping in early readers. *The School Psychology Digest, 2,* 30–38.

JACKSON, B. (1972). Treatment of depression by self-reinforcement. *Behavior Therapy, 3,* 298–307.

JACOB, H., & RICH, J. J. (1980–81). The effects of the police on crime: A second look. *Law & Society Review, 15,* 109–122.

JACOBS, R. C., & CAMPBELL, D. T. (1961). The perpetuation of an arbitrary tradition through several generations of a laboratory microculture. *Journal of Abnormal and Social Psychology, 62,* 649–658.

JACOBSON, S. W., & KAGAN, J. (1979). Interpreting "imitative" responses in early infancy. *Science, 205,* 215–217.

JACOBY, K. E., & DAWSON, M. E. (1969). Observation and shaping learning: A comparison using Long Evans rats. *Psychonomic Science, 16,* 257–258.

JAMES, W. (1884). Absolutism and empiricism. *Mind, 9,* 281–286.

JANIS, I. L. (1958). *Psychological stress.* New York: Wiley.

JANIS, I. L. (1967). Effects of fear arousal on attitude change: Recent developments in theory and experimental research. In L. Berkowitz (Ed.), *Advances in* experimental social psychology (Vol. 3, pp. 167–224). New York: Academic Press.

JANIS, I. L. (1972). Victims of groupthink: A psychological study of foreign-policy decisions and fiascoes. Boston: Houghton Mifflin.

JAREMKO, M. E. (1979). A component analysis of stress inoculation: Review and prospectus. Cognitive Therapy and Research, 3, 35–48.

JEFFERY, K. M. (1977). The effects of goal-setting on self-motivated persistence. Unpublished doctoral dissertation, Stanford University, Stanford, CA.

JEFFERY, R. W. (1976). The influence of symbolic and motor rehearsal in observational learning. Journal of Research in Personality, 10, 116–127.

JEFFREY, D. B. (1974). A comparison of the effects of external control and self-control on the modification and maintenance of weight. Journal of Abnormal Psychology, 83, 404–410.

JEFFREY, D. B., McLELLARN, R. W., & FOX, D. T. (1982). The development of children's eating habits: The role of television commercials. Health Education Quarterly, 9, 174–189.

JEFFRIES-FOX, S., & SIGNORIELLI, N. (1979). Television and children's conceptions of occupations. In H. S. Dordick (Ed.), Proceedings of the sixth annual telecommunications policy research conference (pp. 21–38). Lexington, MA: Lexington Books.

JEMMOTT, J. B., III, & LOCKE, S. E. (1984). Psychosocial factors, immunological mediation, and human susceptibility to infectious diseases: How much do we know? Psychological Bulletin, 95, 78–108.

JENKINS, H. M., & WARD, W. C. (1965). Judgment of contingency between responses and outcomes. Psychological Monographs: General and Applied, 79(1, Whole No. 594).

JENSEN, G. F. (1969). "Crime doesn't pay": Correlates of a shared misunderstanding. Social Problems, 17, 189–201.

JENSEN, G. F., ERICKSON, M. L., & GIBBS, J. P. (1978). Perceived risk of punishment and self-reported delinquency. Social Forces, 57, 57–78.

JERSILD, A. T., & HOLMES, F. B. (1935). Methods of overcoming children's fears. Journal of Psychology, 1, 75–104.

JOHN, E. R., CHESLER, P., BARTLETT, F., & VICTOR, I. (1968). Observational learning in cats. Science, 159, 1489–1491.

JOHNS, C., & ENDSLEY, R. C. (1977). The effects of a maternal model on young children's tactual curiosity. The Journal of Genetic Psychology, 131, 21–28.

JOHNSON, D. W., MARUYAMA, G., JOHNSON, R., NELSON, D., & SKON, L. (1981). Effects of cooperative, competitive, and individualistic goal structures on achievement: A meta-analysis. Psychological Bulletin, 89, 47–62.

JOHNSON, E. H. (1957). Selective factors in capital punishment. Social Forces, 36, 165–169.

JOHNSON, P. E. (1983). What kind of expert should a system be? The Journal of Medicine and Philosophy, 8, 77–97.

JOHNSON, S. M., & WHITE, G. (1971). Self-observation as an agent of behavioral change. Behavior Therapy, 2, 488–497.

JOHNSTON, J. M. (1975, December). Generalization and its relation to generality. Paper presented at the meeting of the Association of Advancement of Behavior Therapy, San Francisco.

JONES, E. E., & NISBETT, R. E. (1972). The actor and the observer: Divergent perceptions of the causes of behavior. In E. E. Jones, D. E. Kanouse, H. H. Kelley, R. E. Nisbett, S. Valins, & B. Weiner (Eds.), Attribution: Perceiving the causes of behavior (pp. 79–94). Morristown, NJ: General Learning Press.

JONES, G. E., & JOHNSON, H. J. (1978). Physiological responding during self generated imagery on contextually complete stimuli. Psychophysiology, 15, 439–446.

JONES, G. F., & THELEN, M. H. (1978). The effects of induced mood states on self-reinforcement behavior. The Journal of Psychology, 98, 249–252.

JONES, R. T., & EVANS, H. L. (1980). Self-reinforcement: A continuum of external cues. Journal of Educational Psychology, 72, 625–635.

JONES, R. T., NELSON, R. E., & KAZDIN, A. E. (1977). The role of external variables in self-reinforcement: A review. Behavior Modification, 1, 147–178.

JONES, R. T., & OLLENDICK, T. H. (1979). Self-reinforcement: An assessment of external influences. Journal of Behavioral Assessment, 1, 289–303.

JUSCZYK, P. W. (1981). Infant speech perception: A critical appraisal. In P. D. Eimas & J. L. Miller (Eds.), Perspectives on the study of speech (pp. 113–164). Hillsdale, NJ: Erlbaum.

KAHN, R. M., & BOWERS, W. J. (1970). The social context of the rank-and-file student activist: A test of four hypotheses. Sociology of Education, 43, 38–55.

KAHNEMAN, E., SLOVIC, P., & TVERSKY, A. (Eds.). (1982). Judgment under uncertainty: Heuristics and biases. New York: Cambridge University Press.

KAHNEMAN, E., & TVERSKY, A. (1979). Intuitive prediction: Biases and corrective procedures. TIMS Studies in the Management Sciences, 12, 313–327.

KALAT, J. W., & ROZIN, P. (1973). "Learned safety" as a mechanism in long-delay taste-aversion learning in rats. Journal of Comparative and Physiological Psychology, 83, 198–207.

KANAREFF, V. T., & LANZETTA, J. T. (1958). The acquisition of imitative and opposition responses under two conditions of instruction-induced set. Journal of Experimental Psychology, 56, 516–528.

KANEKO, R., TANAKA, A., & MATSUI, M. (1983). Comparison of natural and model-trained conservers. Psychological Reports, 53, 623–630.

KANFER, F. H. (1965). Vicarious human reinforcement: A glimpse into the black box. In L. Krasner & L. P. Ullmann (Eds.), Research in behavior modification (pp. 244–267). New York: Holt, Rinehart & Winston.

KANFER, F. H. (1970). Self-regulation: Research, issues, and speculation. In C. Neuringer & J. L. Michael (Eds.), Behavior modification in clinical psychology (pp. 178–220). New York: Appleton-Century-Crofts.

KANFER, F. H. (1977). The many faces of self-control,

or behavior modification changes its focus. In R. B. Stuart (Ed.), *Behavioral self-management* (pp. 1–48). New York: Brunner/Mazel.

KANFER, F. H. (1980). Self-management methods. In F. H. Kanfer & A. P. Goldstein (Eds.), *Helping people change* (2nd ed., pp. 334–389). New York: Pergamon.

KANFER, F. H., DUERFELDT, P. H., MARTIN, B., & DORSEY, T. E. (1971). Effects of model reinforcement, expectation to perform, and task performance on model observation. *Journal of Personality and Social Psychology, 20,* 214–217.

KANFER, F. H., & HAGERMAN, S. (1981). The role of self-regulation. In L. P. Rehm (Ed.), *Behavior therapy for depression: Present status and future directions* (pp. 143–180). New York: Academic Press.

KANFER, F. H., & MARSTON, A. R. (1963). Determinants of self-reinforcement in human learning. *Journal of Experimental Psychology, 66,* 245–254.

KANFER, F. H., & SEIDNER, M. L. (1973). Self-control: Factors enhancing tolerance of noxious stimulation. *Journal of Personality and Social Psychology, 25,* 381–389.

KANFER, R., & HULIN, C. L. (1985). Individual differences in successful job searches following lay-off. *Personnel Psychology, 38,* 835–848.

KANFER, R., & ZEISS, A. M. (1983). Depression, interpersonal standard-setting, and judgments of self-efficacy. *Journal of Abnormal Psychology, 92,* 319–329.

KANT, H. S. (1971). Exposure to pornography and sexual behavior in deviant and normal groups. *Corrective Psychiatry and Journal of Social Therapy, 17,* 5–17.

KANUNGO, R. N., & PANG, S. (1973). Effects of human models on perceived product quality. *Journal of Applied Psychology, 57,* 172–178.

KAPLAN, K. J. (1972). Vicarious reinforcement and model's behavior in verbal learning and imitation. *Journal of Experimental Psychology, 95,* 448–450.

KAPLAN, J. (1971). The role of law in drug control. *Duke Law Journal,* pp. 1065–1104.

KAPLAN, R. M., ATKINS, C. J., & REINSCH, S. (1984). Specific efficacy expectations mediate exercise compliance in patients with COPD. *Health Psychology, 3,* 223–242.

KARNIOL, R., & ROSS, M. (1976). The development of causal attributions in social perception. *Journal of Personality and Social Psychology, 34,* 455–464.

KARNIOL, R., & ROSS, M. (1977). The effect of performance-relevant and performance-irrelevant rewards on children's intrinsic motivation. *Child Development, 48,* 482–487.

KAROLY, P. (1977). Behavioral self-management in children: Concepts, methods, issues, and directions. In M. Hersen, R. M. Eisler, & P. M. Miller (Eds.), *Progress in behavior modification* (Vol. 5, pp. 197–262). New York: Academic Press.

KAROLY, P., & DECKER, J. (1979). Effects of personally and socially referenced success and failure upon self-reward and self-criticism. *Cognitive Therapy and Research, 3,* 399–405.

KARPF, D., & LEVINE, M. (1971). Blank-trial probes and introtacts in human discrimination learning. *Journal of Experimental Psychology, 90,* 51–55.

KASERMANN, M. L., & FOPPA, K. (1981). Some determinants of self correction: An interactional study of Swiss-German. In W. Deutsch (Ed.), *The child's construction of language* (pp. 97–104). London: Academic Press.

KASSAS, M. (1972). Impact of river-control schemes on the shoreline of the Nile Delta. In M. T. Farvar & J. P. Milton (Eds.), *The careless technology: Ecology and international development* (pp. 179–188). Garden City, NY: The Natural History Press.

KATCHER, A. (1955). The discrimination of sex differences by young children. *Journal of Genetic Psychology, 87,* 131–143.

KATO, M., & FUKUSHIMA, O. (1977). The effects of covert modeling in reducing avoidance behavior. *Japanese Psychological Research, 19,* 199–203.

KATZ, A., WEBB, L., & STOTLAND, E. (1971). Cognitive influences on the rate of GSR extinction. *Journal of Experimental Research in Personality, 5,* 208–215.

KATZ, E., & WEDELL, G. (1977). *Broadcasting in the third world: Promise and performance.* Cambridge, MA: Harvard University Press.

KATZ, E., & LAZARSFELD, P. F. (1955). *Perso ' influence: The part played by people in the flow of mass communications.* New York: Free Press.

KATZ, R. C., STOUT, A., TAYLOR, C. B., HORNE, M., & AGRAS, S. (1983). The contribution of arousal and performance in reducing spider avoidance. *Behavioural Psychotherapy, 11,* 127–138.

KAUFFMAN, J. M., GORDON, M. E., & BAKER, A. (1978). Being imitated: Persistence of an effect. *Journal of Genetic Psychology, 132,* 319–320.

KAUFMAN, A. (1964). Increased suppression during punishment applied to the responding member. *Psychonomic Science, 1,* 311–312.

KAUFMAN, A., BARON, A., & KOPP, R. E. (1966). Some effects of instructions on human operant behavior. *Psychonomic Monograph Supplements, 1,* 243–250.

KAUFMAN, L. (1980). Prime-time nutrition. *The Journal of Communication, 30*(3), 37–46.

KAVANAGH, D. J. (1983). *Mood and self-efficacy.* Unpublished doctoral dissertation, Stanford University, Stanford, CA.

KAVANAGH, D. J., & BOWER, G. H. (1985). Mood and self-efficacy: Impact of joy and sadness on perceived capabilities. *Cognitive Therapy and Research, 9,* 507–525.

KAWAMURA, S. (1963). The process of sub-culture propagation among Japanese Macaques. In C. H. Southwick (Ed.), *Primate social behavior* (pp. 82–90). Princeton: Van Nostrand.

KAY, S. R. (1982). Kohlberg's theory of moral development: Critical analysis of validation studies with the defining issues test. *International Journal of Psychology, 17,* 27–42.

KAYE, K. (1982). *The mental and social life of babies: How parents create persons.* Chicago: University of Chicago Press.

KAYE, K., & MARCUS, J. (1978). Imitation over a series

of trials without feedback: Age six months. *Infant Behavior and Development, 1,* 141–155.

KAYE, K., & MARCUS, J. (1981). Infant imitation: The sensory-motor agenda. *Developmental Psychology, 17,* 258–265.

KAZDIN, A. E. (1973). Covert modeling and the reduction of avoidance behavior. *Journal of Abnormal Psychology, 81,* 87–95.

KAZDIN, A. E. (1974a). Comparative effects of some variations of covert modeling. *Journal of Behavior Therapy and Experimental Psychiatry, 5,* 225–232.

KAZDIN, A. E. (1974b). Covert modeling, model similarity, and reduction of avoidance behavior. *Behavior Therapy, 5,* 325–340.

KAZDIN, A. E. (1974c). Effects of covert modeling and reinforcement on assertive behavior. *Journal of Abnormal Psychology, 83,* 240–252.

KAZDIN, A. E. (1974d). The effect of model identity and fear-relevant similarity on covert modeling. *Behavior Therapy, 5,* 624–635.

KAZDIN, A. E. (1974a). Self-monitoring and behavior change. In M. J. Mahoney & C. E. Thoresen (Eds.), *Self-control: Power to the person* (pp. 218–246). Monterey, CA: Brooks/Cole.

KAZDIN, A. E. (1974b). Reactive self-monitoring: The effects of response desirability, goal setting, and feedback. *Journal of Consulting and Clinical Psychology, 42,* 704–716.

KAZDIN, A. E. (1975). Covert modeling, imagery assessment, and assertive behavior. *Journal of Consulting and Clinical Psychology, 43,* 716–724.

KAZDIN, A. E. (1976). Effects of covert modeling, multiple models, and model reinforcement on assertive behavior. *Behavior Therapy, 7,* 211–222.

KAZDIN, A. E. (1977). *The token economy.* New York: Plenum.

KAZDIN, A. E. (1978). Covert modeling—Therapeutic application of imagined rehearsal. In J. L. Singer & K. S. Pope (Eds.), *The power of human imagination: New methods in psychotherapy. Emotions, personality, and psychotherapy* (pp. 255–278). New York: Plenum.

KAZDIN, A. E. (1979). Imagery elaboration and self-efficacy in the covert modeling treatment of unassertive behavior. *Journal of Consulting and Clinical Psychology, 47,* 725–733.

KAZDIN, A. E. (1981). Vicarious reinforcement and punishment processes in the classroom. In P. S. Strain (Ed.), *The utilization of classroom peers as behavior change agents* (pp. 129–153). New York: Plenum.

KAZDIN, A. E. (1984). *Behavior modification in applied settings* (3rd ed.). Homewood, IL: Dorsey.

KEASEY, C. B. (1973). Experimentally induced changes in moral opinions and reasoning. *Journal of Personality and Social Psychology, 26,* 30–38.

KELLER, H. (1927). *The story of my life.* New York: Doubleday.

KELLING, G. L., PATE, T., DIECKMAN, D. , & BROWN, C. E. (1975). Kansas City preventive patrol experiment. In S. L. Halleck, P. Lerman, S. L. Messinger, N. Morris, P. V. Murphy, & M. E. Wolfgang (Eds.), *The Aldine crime and justice annual—1974* (pp. 196–236). Chicago: Aldine.

KELLOGG, R., & BARON, R. S. (1975). Attribution theory, insomnia, and the reverse placebo effect: A reversal of Storms and Nisbett's findings. *Journal of Personality and Social Psychology, 32,* 231–236.

KELLOGG, W. N., & KELLOGG, L. A. (1933). *The ape and the child: A study of environmental influence upon early behavior.* New York: McGraw-Hill.

KELMAN, H. C. (1973). Violence without moral restraint: Reflections on the dehumanization of victims and victimizers. *Journal of Social Issues, 29,* 25–61.

KEMP, J. C., & DALE, P. S. (1973). *Spontaneous imitations and free speech: A developmental comparison.* Paper presented at the meeting of the Society for Research in Child Development, Philadelphia.

KENDALL, P. C., & FINCH, A. J., JR. (1979). Developing nonimpulsive behavior in children: Cognitive-behavioral strategies for self-control. In P. C. Kendall & S. D. Hollon (Eds.), *Cognitive-behavioral interventions: Theory, research, and procedures* (pp. 37–79). New York: Academic Press.

KENDALL, P. C., & HOLLON, S. D. (Eds.). (1979). *Cognitive-behavioral interventions: Theory, research, and procedures.* New York: Academic Press.

KENDRICK, M. J., CRAIG, K. D., LAWSON, D. M., & DAVIDSON, P. O. (1982). Cognitive and behavioral therapy for musical-performance anxiety. *Journal of Consulting and Clinical Psychology, 50,* 353–363.

KENISTON, K. (1968). *Young radicals.* New York: Harcourt, Brace and World.

KENISTON, K. (1970). Student activism, moral development, and morality. *American Journal of Orthopsychiatry, 40,* 577–592.

KENNEDY, T. D. (1970). Verbal conditioning without awareness: The use of programmed reinforcement and recurring assessment of awareness. *Journal of Experimental Psychology, 84,* 487–494.

KENNEDY, T. D. (1971). Reinforcement frequency, task characteristics, and interval of awareness assessment as factors in verbal conditioning without awareness. *Journal of Experimental Psychology, 88,* 103–112.

KENT, R. N., WILSON, G. T., & NELSON, R. (1972). Effects of false heart-rate feedback on avoidance behavior: An investigation of "cognitive desensitization." *Behavior Therapy, 3,* 1–6.

KEOHANE, R. O., & NYE, J. S. (1977). *Power and interdependence: World politics in transition.* Boston: Little, Brown.

KERNER, O. (1968). *Report of the National Advisory Commission on Civil Disorders.* New York: Dutton.

KERNS, C. D. (1975). Effects of schedule and amount of observed reinforcement on response persistence. *Journal of Personality and Social Psychology, 31,* 983–991.

KERR, N. L. (1978). Severity of prescribed penalty and mock jurors' verdicts. *Journal of Personality and Social Psychology, 36,* 1431–1442.

KERR, N. L. (1983). Motivation losses in small groups: A social dilemma analysis. *Journal of Personality and Social Psychology, 45,* 819–828.

KIESLER, C. A. (1971). *The psychology of commitment: Experiments linking behavior to belief.* New York: Academic Press.

KIESLER, S., SIEGEL, J., & McGUIRE, T. W. (1984). Social psychological aspects of computer-mediated communication. *American Psychologist, 39,* 1123–1134.

KILHAM, W., & MANN, L. (1974). Level of destructive obedience as a function of transmitter and executant roles in the Milgram obedience paradigm. *Journal of Personality and Social Psychology, 29,* 696–702.

KILLEN, J. D., MACCOBY, N., & TAYLOR C. B. (1984). Nicotine gum and self-regulation training in smoking relapse prevention. *Behavior Therapy, 15,* 234–248.

KIMBRELL, D. L., & BLAKE, R. R. (1958). Motivational factors in the violation of a prohibition. *Journal of Abnormal and Social Psychology, 56,* 132–133.

KING, B. J. (1979, July 5). *Palo Alto Times,* D4.

KING, M. L. (1958). *Stride toward freedom.* New York: Ballantine Books.

KIPNIS, D. (1974). The powerholders. In J. T. Tedeschi (Ed.), *Perspectives on social power* (pp. 82–122). Chicago: Aldine.

KIRSCHENBAUM, D. S., HUMPHREY, L. L., & MALETT, S. D. (1981). Specificity of planning in adult self-control: An applied investigation. *Journal of Personality and Social Psychology, 40,* 941–950.

KIRSCHENBAUM, D. S., & KAROLY, P. (1977). When self-regulation fails: Tests of some preliminary hypotheses. *Journal of Consulting and Clinical Psychology, 45,* 1116–1125.

KIRSCHENBAUM, D. S., TOMARKEN, A. J.. & ORDMAN, A. M. (1982). Specificity of planning and choice applied to adult self-control. *Journal of Personality and Social Psychology, 42,* 576–585.

KLAPPER, J. T. (1960). *The effects of mass communication.* New York: Free Press.

KLAYMAN, J. (1984). Learning from feedback in probabilistic environments. *Acta Psychologica, 56,* 81–92.

KLEPAC, R. K., DOWLING, J., & HAUGE, G. (1982). Characteristics of clients seeking therapy for the reduction of dental avoidance: Reactions to pain. *Journal of Behaviour Therapy and Experimental Psychiatry, 13,* 293–300.

KLINE, P. (1972). *Fact and fantasy in Freudian theory.* London: Methuen.

KLINE, R. M., & POSNER, M. I. (1974). Attention to visual and kinesthetic components of skills. *Brain Research, 71,* 401–411.

KLINNERT, M. D., CAMPOS, J. J., SORCE, J. F., EMDE, R. N., & SVEJDA, M. (1983). Emotions as behavior regulators: Social referencing in infancy. In R. Plutchik & H. Kellerman. (Eds.), *Emotion: Theories, research, and experience:* (Vol. 2). New York: Academic Press.

KLORMAN, R., HILPERT, P. L., MICHAEL, R., LaGANA, C., & SVEEN, O. B. (1980). Effects of coping and mastery modeling on experienced and inexperienced pedodontic patients' disruptiveness. *Behavior Therapy, 11,* 156–168.

KOEGEL, R. L., & RINCOVER, A. (1974). Treatment of psychotic children in a classroom environment: I. Learning in a large group. *Journal of Applied Behavior Analysis, 7,* 45–59.

KOEGEL, R. L., & SCHREIBMAN, L. (1977). Teaching autistic children to respond to simultaneous multiple cues. *Journal of Experimental Child Psychology, 24,* 299–311.

KOHLBERG, L. (1963). Moral development and identification. In H. W. Stevenson (Ed.), *Child psychology: The sixty-second yearbook of the National Society for the Study of Education. Part I* (pp. 277–332). Chicago: The National Society for the Study of Education.

KOHLBERG, L. (1966). A cognitive-developmental analysis of children's sex-role concepts and attitudes. In E. E. Maccoby (Ed.), *The development of sex differences* (pp. 82–173). Stanford, CA: Stanford University Press.

KOHLBERG, L. (1969). Stage and sequence: The cognitive-developmental approach to socialization. In D. A. Goslin (Ed.), *Handbook of socialization theory* (pp. 347–480). Chicago: Rand McNally.

KOHLBERG, L. (1971a). From Is to Ought: How to commit the naturalistic fallacy and get away with it in the study of moral development. In T. Mischel (Ed.), *Cognitive development and epistemology* (pp. 151–232). New York: Academic Press.

KOHLBERG, L. (1971b). Stages of moral development as a basis for moral education. In C. M. Beck, B. S. Crittenden, & E. V. Sullivan (Eds.), *Moral education: Interdisciplinary approaches.* Toronto: University of Toronto Press.

KOHLBERG, L. (1976). Moral stages and moralization. In T. Lickona (Ed.), *Moral development and behavior* (pp. 31–53). New York: Holt, Rinehart & Winston.

KOHLBERG, L., & CANDEE, D. (1984). The relation of moral judgment to moral action. In W. Kurtines & J. L. Gewirtz (Eds.), *Morality, moral behavior and moral development. Basic issues in theory and research* (pp. 52–73). New York: Wiley Interscience.

KOMAKI, J., & DORE-BOYCE, K. (1978). Self-recording: Its effects on individuals high and low in motivation. *Behavior Therapy, 9,* 65–72.

KOPEL, S., & ARKOWITZ, H. (1975). The role of attribution and self-perception in behavior change: Implications for behavior therapy. *Genetic Psychology Monographs, 92,* 175–212.

KORIAT, A., LICHTENSTEIN, S., & FISCHHOFF, B. (1980). Reasons for confidence. *Journal of Experimental Psychology, 6,* 107–118.

KORNHABER, R. C., & SCHROEDER, H. E. (1975). Importance of model similarity on extinction of avoidance behavior in children. *Journal of Consulting and Clinical Psychology, 43,* 601–607.

KOSSLYN, S. M. (1980). *Image and mind.* Cambridge, MA: Harvard University Press.

KOSSLYN, S. M., PINKER, S., SMITH, G. E., & SCHWARTZ, S. P. (1979). On the demystification of mental imagery. *The Behavioral and Brain Sciences, 2,* 535–581.

KOUNIN, J. S. (1970). *Discipline and group management in classrooms.* New York: Holt, Rinehart & Winston.

KRANE, R. V., & WAGNER, A. R. (1975). Taste aversion learning with a delayed shock US: Implications for the "generality of the laws of learning." *Journal of Comparative and Physiological Psychology, 88,* 882–889.

KRANTZ, D. H., FONG, G. T., & NISBETT, R. E. (1983). *Formal training improves the application of statistical heuristics to everyday problems.* Unpublished manuscript, University of Michigan, Ann Arbor.

KRASNER, L. (1958). Studies of the conditioning of verbal behavior. *Psychological Bulletin, 55,* 148–170.

KRAUSS, I. (1964). Sources of educational aspirations among working-class youth. *American Sociological Review, 29,* 867–879.

KRAUSS, R. M., APPLE, W., MORENCY, N., WENZEL, C., WINTON, W. (1981). Verbal, vocal, and visible factors in judgments of another's affect. *Journal of Personality and Social Psychology, 40,* 312–320.

KRAVETZ, D. F. (1970). Heart rate as a minimal cue for the occurrence of conditioned vicarious autonomic responses. *Psychonomic Science, 19,* 90–91.

KRAVETZ, D. F. (1974). Heart rate as a minimal cue for the occurrence of vicarious classical conditioning. *Journal of Personality and Social Psychology, 29,* 125–131.

KREBS, D. (1975). Empathy and altruism. *Journal of Personality and Social Psychology, 32,* 1134–1146.

KRUGLANSKI, A. W. (1975). The endogenous-exogenous partition in attribution theory. *Psychological Review, 82,* 387–406.

KRUMBOLTZ, J. D., & THORESEN, C. E. (1964). The effect of behavioral counseling in group and individual settings on information-seeking behavior. *Journal of Counseling Psychology, 11,* 324–333.

KUHN, D. (1973). Imitation theory and research from a cognitive perspective. *Human Development, 16,* 157–180.

KUIPER, N. A. (1978). Depression and causal attributions for success and failure. *Journal of Personality and Social Psychology, 36,* 236–246.

KUIPER, N. A., MACDONALD, M. R., & DERRY, P. A. (1983). Parameters of a depressive self-schema. In J. Suls & A. Greenwald (Eds.), *Psychological perspectives on the self* (Vol. 2, pp. 191–217). Hillsdale, NJ: Erlbaum.

KUN, A. (1977). Development of the magnitude-covariation and compensation schemata in ability and effort attributions of performance. *Child Development, 48,* 862–873.

KUN, A. (1978, August). *Perceived additivity of intrinsic and extrinsic motivation in young children.* Paper presented at the meeting of the American Psychological Association, Toronto.

KUN, A., GARFIELD, T., & SIPOWICZ, D. (1979, March). *Causality pleasure: An experimental study of mastery motivation.* Paper presented at the meeting of the Society for Research in Child Development, San Francisco.

KUPFERSMID, J. H., & WONDERLY, D. M. (1980). Moral maturity and behavior: Failure to find a link. *Journal of Youth and Adolescence, 9,* 249–262.

KUPFERSMID, J. H., & WONDERLY, D. M. (1982). Disequilibrium as a hypothetical construct in Kohlbergian moral development. *Child Study Journal, 12,* 171–185.

KURTINES, W., & GREIF, E. B. (1974). The development of moral thought: Review and evaluation of Kohlberg's approach. *Psychological Bulletin, 8,* 453–470.

KUTCHINSKY, B. (1975). *Law, pornography and crime: The Danish experience.* London: Martin Robertson.

KUYLENSTIERNA, J., & BREHMER, B. (1981). Memory aids in the learning of probabilistic inference tasks. *Organizational Behavior and Human Performance, 28,* 415–424.

LABERGE, D. (1981). Unitization and automaticity in perception. In J. H. Flowers (Ed.), *Nebraska Symposium on Motivation* (Vol. 28, pp. 53–71). Lincoln: University of Nebraska Press.

LABERGE, S. P., NAGEL, L. E., DEMENT, W. C., & ZARCONE V. P., JR. (1981). Lucid dreaming verified by volitional communication during REM sleep. *Perceptual and Motor Skills, 52,* 727–732.

LACEY, H. M. (1979). Control, perceived control and the methodological role of cognitive constructs. In L. C. Perlmuter & R. A. Monty (Eds.), *Choice and perceived control* (pp. 5–16). Hillsdale, NJ: Erlbaum.

LACEY, H. M. (1979). Skinner on the prediction and control of behavior. *Theory and Decision, 10,* 353–385.

LACEY, H. M., & RACHLIN, H. (1978). Behavior, cognition and theories of choice. *Behaviorism, 6,* 117–202.

LACEY, J. I. (1967). Somatic response patterning and stress; Some revisions of activation theory. In M. H. Appley & R. Trumbull (Eds.), *Psychological stress: Issues in research* (pp. 14–42). New York: Appleton-Century-Crofts.

LADOUCEUR, R. (1983). Participant modeling with or without cognitive treatment of phobias. *Journal of Consulting and Clinical Psychology, 51,* 942–944.

LAMAL, P. A. (1971). Imitation learning of information-processing. *Journal of Experimental Child Psychology, 12,* 223–227.

LAMB, M. E., EASTERBROOKS, M. A., & HOLDEN, G. W. (1980). Reinforcement and punishment among preschoolers: Characteristics, effects and correlates. *Child Development, 51,* 1230–1236.

LANE, J., & ANDERSON, N. H. (1976). Integration of intention and outcome in moral judgment. *Memory and Cognition, 4,* 1–5.

LANG, A. R., GOECKNER, D. J., ADESSO, V. J., & MARLATT, G. A. (1975). Effects of alcohol on aggression in male social drinkers. *Journal of Abnormal Psychology, 84,* 508–518.

LANG, P. J. (1977). Physiological assessment of anxiety and fear. In J. D. Cone & R. P. Hawkins (Eds.), *Behavioral assessment: New directions in clinical psychology* (pp. 178–195). New York: Brunner/Mazel.

LANGER, E. J. (1975). The illusion of control. *Journal of Personality and Social Psychology, 32,* 311–328.

LANGER, E. J. (1979). The illusion of incompetence. In L. C. Perlmuter & R. A. Monty (Eds.), *Choice and perceived control* (pp. 301–313). Hillsdale, NJ: Erlbaum.

LANGER, E. J., JANIS, I. L., & WOLFER, J. A. (1975). Reduction of psychological stress in surgical patients. *Journal of Experimental Social Psychology, 11,* 155–165.

LANGER, E. J., & RODIN, J. (1976). The effects of choice and enhanced personal responsibility for the aged:

A field experiment in an institutional setting. *Journal of Personality and Social Psychology, 34,* 191–198.

LANGER, J. (1969). Disequilibrium as a source of development. In P. Mussen, J. Langer, & M. Covington (Eds.), *Trends and issues in developmental psychology* (pp. 22–37). New York: Holt, Rinehart & Winston.

LANGLOIS, J. H., & DOWNS, A. C. (1980). Mothers, fathers, and peers as socialization agents of sex-typed play behaviors in young children. *Child Development, 51,* 1237–1247.

LANZETTA, J. T., & ENGLIS, B. G. (1982). *The effect of observer expectancies on vicarious emotional responses.* Paper presented at the meeting of the Eastern Psychology Association.

LANZETTA, J. T., & ORR, S. P. (1980). Influence of facial expressions on the classical conditioning of fear. *Journal of Personality and Social Psychology, 39,* 1081–1087.

LANZETTA, J. T., & ORR, S. P. (1981). Stimulus properties of facial expressions and their influence on the classical conditioning of fear. *Motivation and Emotion, 5,* 225–234.

LAPORTE, R. E., & NATH, R. (1976). Role of performance goals in prose learning. *Journal of Educational Psychology, 68,* 260–264.

LARSEN, K. S., COLEMAN, D., FORGES, J., & JOHNSON, R. (1971). Is the subject's personality or the experimental situation a better predictor of a subject's willingness to administer shock to a victim? *Journal of Personality and Social Psychology, 22,* 287–295.

LARSEN, O. N. (Ed.). (1968). *Violence and the mass media.* New York: Harper & Row.

LASATER, T. M., ELDER, J. P., CARLETON, R. A., ABRAMS, D. B. (1984). The Pawtucket Heart Health Program: Prospects and process. *Academy of Behavioral Medicine Research.*

LASSEN, M. K., & McCONNELL, S. C. (1977). Treatment of a severe bird phobia by participant modeling. *Journal of Behavior Therapy and Experimental Psychiatry, 8,* 165–168.

LATHAM, G. P., & KINNE, S. B., III. (1974). Improving job performance through training in goal setting. *Journal of Applied Psychology, 59,* 187–191.

LATHAM, G. P., & MARSHALL, H. A. (1982). The effects of self-set, participatively set and assigned goals on the performance of government employees. *Personnel Psychology, 35,* 399–404.

LATHAM, G. P., & SAARI, L. M. (1979). Application of social learning theory to training supervisors through behavioral modeling. *Journal of Applied Psychology, 64,* 239–246.

LATHAM, G. P., STEELE, T. P., & SAARI, L. M. (1982). The effects of participation and goal difficulty on performance. *Personnel Psychology, 35,* 677–686.

LATHAM, G. P., & YUKL, G. A. (1975). A review of research on the application of goal setting in organizations. *Academy of Management Journal, 18,* 824–845.

LATHAM, G. P., & YUKL, G. A. (1976). Effects of assigned and participative goal setting on performance and job satisfaction. *Journal of Applied Psychology, 61,* 166–171.

LAUDE, R., & LaVIGNE, G. (1974). *The role of cognition in anxiety neurosis and phobic neurosis.* Unpublished manuscript, University of Pennsylvania School of Medicine.

LAUGHLIN, P. R., MOSS, I. L., & MILLER, S. M. (1969). Information-processing in children as a function of adult model stimulus display, school grade, and sex. *Journal of Educational Psychology, 60,* 188–193.

LaVOIE, J. C. (1974). Type of punishment as a determinant of resistance to deviation. *Developmental Psychology, 10,* 181–189.

LAWLER, E. E., III. (1968). Equity theory as a predictor of productivity and work quality. *Psychological Bulletin, 70,* 596–610.

LAWLER, E. E., III. (1971). *Pay and organizational effectiveness: A psychological view.* New York: McGraw-Hill.

LAWLER, E. E., III. (1973). *Motivation in work organizations.* Monterey, CA: Brooks/Cole.

LAWRENCE, D. H. (1963). The nature of a stimulus: Some relationships between learning and perception. In S. Koch (Ed.), *Psychology: A study of a science* (pp. 179–212). New York: McGraw-Hill.

LAWTON, J. T., & HOOPER, F. H. (1978). Piagetian theory and early childhood education: A critical analysis. In L. S. Siegel & C. J. Brainerd (Eds.), *Alternative to Piaget: Critical essays on the theory* (pp. 169–199). New York: Academic Press.

LAZARUS, R. S. (1981). The stress and coping paradigm. In C. Eisdorfer, D. Cohen, A. Kleinman, & M. Maxim (Eds.), *Models for clinical psychopathology* (pp. 177–214). New York: Spectrum.

LAZARUS, R. S. (1982). Thoughts on the relations between emotion and cognition. *American Psychologist, 37,* 1019–1024.

LAZARUS, R. S. (1984). On the primacy of cognition. *American Psychologist, 39,* 124–129.

LAZARUS, R. S., & LAUNIER, R. (1978). Stress-related transactions between person and environment. In L. A. Pervin & M. Lewis (Eds.), *Perspectives in interactional psychology* (pp. 287–327). New York: Plenum.

LAZARUS, R. S., SPEISMAN, J. C., MORDKOFF, A. M., & DAVISON, L. A. (1962). A laboratory study of psychological stress produced by a motion picture film. *Psychological Monographs, 76,* (No. 34, Whole No. 553).

LAZOWICK, L. (1955). On the nature of identification. *Journal of Abnormal and Social Psychology, 51,* 175–183.

LeDUC, D. R. (1982). Deregulation and the dream of diversity. *The Journal of Communication, 32,* 164–179.

LEDWIDGE, B. (1978). Cognitive behavior modification: A step in the wrong direction? *Psychological Bulletin, 85,* 353–375.

LEE, C. (1980). *Media imperialism reconsidered: The homogenizing of television culture.* Beverly Hills: Sage.

LEE, C. (1982). Self-efficacy as a predictor of performance in competitive gymnastics. *Journal of Sport Psychology, 4,* 405–409.

LEE, C. (1983). Self-efficacy and behaviour as predictors of subsequent behaviour in an assertiveness training programme. *Behaviour Research and Therapy, 21,* 225–232.

LEE, C. (1984a). Accuracy of efficacy and outcome expectations in predicting performance in a simulated assertiveness task. *Cognitive Therapy and Research, 8,* 37–48.

LEE, C. (1984b). Efficacy expectations and outcome expectations as predictors of performance in a snake-handling task. *Cognitive Therapy and Research, 8,* 509–516.

LEFCOURT, H. M. (1976). *Locus of control: Current trends in theory and research.* Hillsdale, NJ: Erlbaum.

LEFCOURT, H. M. (1979). Locus of control for specific goals. In L. C. Perlmuter & R. A. Monty (Eds.), *Choice and perceived control* (pp. 209–220). Hillsdale, NJ: Erlbaum.

LEFEBVRE-PINARD, M., & REID, L. (1980). A comparison of three methods of training communications skills: Social conflict, modeling, and conflict-modeling. *Child Development, 51,* 169–187.

LEFKOWITZ, M., BLAKE, R. R., & MOUTON, J. S. (1955). Status factors in pedestrian violation of traffic signals. *Journal of Abnormal and Social Psychology, 51* 704–705.

LE FURGY, W. G., & WOLOSHIN, G. W. (1969). Immediate and long-term effects of experimentally induced social influence in the modification of adolescents' moral judgment. *Journal of Personality and Social Psychology, 12,* 104–110.

LEHMAN, R. S. (1977). *Computer simulation and modeling: An introduction.* Hillsdale, NJ: Erlbaum.

LEIFER, A. D., COLLINS, W. A., GROSS, B. M., TAYLOR, P. H., ANDREWS, L., & BLACKMER, E. R. (1971). Developmental aspects of variables relevant to observational learning. *Child Development, 42,* 1509–1516.

LEIFER, A. D., & ROBERTS, D. F. (1972). Children's responses to television violence. In J. P. Murray, E. A. Rubinstein, & G. A. Comstock (Eds.), *Television and social behavior* (Vol. 2, pp. 43–180). Washington, DC: U.S. Government Printing Office.

LEITENBERG, H., AGRAS, W. S., BUTZ, R., & WINCZE, J. (1971). Relationship between heart rate and behavioral change during the treatment of phobias. *Journal of Abnormal Psychology, 78,*59–68.

LEITENBERG, H., AGRAS, W. S., THOMPSON, L. E., & WRIGHT, D. E. (1968). Feedback in behavior modification: An experimental analysis in two phobic cases. *Journal of Applied Behavior Analysis, 1,* 131–137.

LELAND, E. I. (1983). *Relationship of self-efficacy and other factors to precompetitive anxiety in basketball players.* Unpublished doctoral dissertation, Stanford University, Stanford, CA.

LEMING, J. S. (1978). Cheating behavior, situational influence, and moral development. *Journal of Educational Research, 71,* 214–217.

LENNEBERG, E. H. (1962). Understanding language without ability to speak. *Journal of Abnormal and Social Psychology, 65,* 419–424.

LEON, M. (1980). Integration of intent and consequence information in children's moral judgments.

In F. Wilkening, J. Becker, & T. Trabasso (Eds.), *Information integration by children* (pp. 71–97). Hillsdale, NJ: Erlbaum.

LEON, M. (1984). Rules mothers and sons use to integrate intent and damage information in their moral judgments. *Child Development, 55,* 2106–2113.

LEONARD, L. B. (1975). The role of nonlinguistic stimuli and semantic relations in children's acquisition of grammatical utterances. *Journal of Experimental Child Psychology, 19,* 346–357.

LEPPER, M. R. (1973). Dissonance, self-perception, and honesty in children. *Journal of Personality and Social Psychology, 25,* 65–74.

LEPPER, M. R. (1981). Intrinsic and extrinsic motivation in children: Detrimental effects of superfluous social controls. In W. A. Collins (Ed.), *Minnesota symposium on child psychology* (Vol. 14, pp. 155–214). Hillsdale, NJ: Erlbaum.

LEPPER, M. R., & GREENE, D. (1978). Overjustification research and beyond: Toward a means-end analysis of intrinsic and extrinsic motivation. In M. R. Lepper & D. Greene (Eds.), *The hidden costs of reward: New perspectives on the psychology of human motivation* (pp. 109–148). Hillsdale, NJ: Erlbaum.

LEPPER, M. R., SAGOTSKY, G., & MAILER, J. (1975). Generalization and persistence of effects of exposure to self-reinforcement models. *Child Development, 46,* 618–630.

LERNER, L., & WEISS, R. L. (1972). Role of value of reward and model affective response in vicarious reinforcement. *Journal of Personality and Social Psychology, 21,* 93–100.

LERNER, M. J., & MILLER, D. T. (1978). Just world research and the attribution process: Looking back and ahead. *Psychological Bulletin, 85,* 1030–1051.

LERNER, R. M. (1982). Children and adolescents as producers of their own development. *Developmental Review, 2,* 342–370.

LEUBA, C. (1955). Toward some integration of learning theories: The concept of optimal stimulation. *Psychological Reports, 1,* 27–33.

LEVENTHAL, G. S. (1970). Influence of brothers and sisters on sex-role behavior. *Journal of Personality and Social Psychology, 16,* 452–465.

LEVENTHAL, G. S. (1980). What should be done with equity theory?: New approaches to the study of fairness in social relationships. In K. J. Gergen, M. S. Greenberg, & R. H. Willis (Eds.), *Social exchange: Advances in theory and research* (pp. 27–55). New York: Plenum.

LEVENTHAL, H. (1970). Findings and theory in the study of fear communications. In L. Berkowitz (Ed.), *Advances in experimental social psychology* (Vol. 5, pp. 119–186). New York: Academic Press.

LEVI, L. (Ed.). (1972). Stress and distress in response to psychosocial stimuli. *Acta Medica Scandinavica, 191,* Supplement No. 528.

LEVINE, J. D., GORDON, N. C., & FIELDS, H. L. (1978, September 23). The mechanism of placebo analgesia. *The Lancet,* pp. 654–657.

LEVINE, J. D., GORDON, N. C., JONES, R. T., & FIELDS,

H. L. (1978). The narcotic antagonist naloxone enhances clinical pain. *Nature, 272,* 826–827.

LEVINE, J. P. (1975). The ineffectiveness of adding police to prevent crime. *Public Policy, 23,* 523–545.

LEVY, B. (1968). Cops in the ghetto: A problem of the police system. *American Behavioral Scientist, 11,* 31–34.

LEVY, D. M. (1943). *Maternal overprotection.* New York: Columbia University Press.

LEVY, E. A., McCLINTON, B. S., RABINOWITZ, F. M., & WOLKIN, J. R. (1974). Effects of vicarious consequences on imitation and recall. *Journal of Experimental Child Psychology, 17,* 115–132.

LEVY, R. I. (1969). On getting angry in the Society Islands. In W. Caudill & T. Y. Lin (Eds.), *Mental health research in Asia and the Pacific* (pp. 358–380). Honolulu: East-West Center Press.

LEWIN, K., DEMBO, T., FESTINGER, L., & SEARS, P. S. (1944). Level of aspiration. In J. McV. Hunt (Ed.), *Personality and the behavior disorders* (Vol. 1, pp. 333–378). New York: Ronald Press.

LEWINSOHN, P. M. (1975). The behavioral study and treatment of depression. In M. Hersen, R. M. Eisler, & P. M. Miller (Eds.), *Progress in behavior modification* (Vol. 1, pp. 19–64). New York: Academic Press.

LEWINSOHN, P. M., MISCHEL, W., CHAPLIN, W., & BARTON, R. (1980). Social competence and depression: The role of illusory self-perceptions. *Journal of Abnormal Psychology, 89,* 203–212.

LEWIS, M., & ROSENBLUM, L. A. (Eds.). (1974). *The effect of the infant on its caregiver.* New York: Wiley.

LICHTENSTEIN, S., & FISCHHOFF, B. (1980). Training for calibration. *Organizational Behavior and Human Performance, 26,* 149–171.

LIDZ, T., CORNELISON, A., TERRY, D., & FLECK, S. (1958). Intrafamilial environment of the schizophrenic patient: VI. The transmission of irrationality. *A.M.A. Archives of Neurology and Psychiatry, 79,* 305–316.

LIEBERSON, S., & SILVERMAN, A. R. (1965). The precipitants and underlying conditions of race riots. *American Sociological Review, 30,* 887–898.

LIEBERT, R. M., & FERNANDEZ, L. E. (1970). Effects of vicarious consequences on imitative performance. *Child Development, 41,* 847–852.

LIEBERT, R. M., HANRATTY, M., & HILL, J. H. (1969). Effects of rule structure and training method on the adoption of a self-imposed standard. *Child Development, 40,* 93–101.

LIEBERT, R. M., & ORA, J. P., JR. (1968). Children's adoption of self-reward patterns: Incentive level and method of transmission. *Child Development, 39,* 537–544.

LEIBERT, R. M., SOBOL, M. P., & COPEMANN, C. D. (1972). Effect of vicarious consequences and race of model upon imitative performance by black children. *Developmental Psychology, 6,* 453–456.

LIEBERT, R. M., SPRAFKIN, J. N., & DAVIDSON, E. S. (1982). *The early window: Effects of television on children and youth* (2nd ed.). Elmsford, NY: Pergamon.

LILLISTON, L. (1972). Verbal conditioning of value-related material. *Journal of Consulting and Clinical Psychology, 39,* 478–482.

LIN, N., DAYTON, P. W., & GREENWALD, P. (1978). Analyzing the instrumental use of relations in the context of social structure. *Sociological Methods and Research, 7,* 149–166.

LINDSEY, P. H., & NORMAN, D. A. (1977). *Human information processing* (2nd ed.). New York: Academic Press.

LIPPITT, R., POLANSKY, N., & ROSEN, S. (1952). The dynamics of power. *Human Relations, 5,* 37–64.

LIPPMAN, L. G., & MEYER, M. E. (1967). Fixed interval performance as related to instructions and to subjects' verbalizations of the contingency. *Psychonomic Science, 8,* 135–136.

LIPSET, S. M. (1966). University students and politics in underdeveloped countries. *Comparative Education Review, 10,* 132–162.

LIPSET, S. M., & SCHNEIDER, W. (1983). *The confidence gap: Business, labor and government in the public mind.* New York: Free Press.

LITROWNIK, A. J., FRANZINI, L. R., & SKENDERIAN, D. (1976). The effect of locus of reinforcement control on a concept-identification task. *Psychological Reports, 39,* 159–165.

LITTLE, J. C., & JAMES, B. (1964). Abreaction of conditioned fear reaction after eighteen years. *Behaviour Research and Therapy, 2,* 59–63.

LITTLE, R. E., & STREISSGUTH, A. P. (1981). Effects of alcohol on the fetus: Impact and prevention. *Canadian Medical Association Journal, 125,* 159–164.

LITTUNEN, Y. (1980). Cultural problems of direct satellite broadcasting. *International Social Science Journal, 32,* 283–303.

LOBITZ, W. C., & POST, R. D. (1979). Parameters of self-reinforcement and depression. *Journal of Abnormal Psychology, 81,* 33–41.

LOCKE, D. (1979). Cognitive states or developmental phases—Critique of Kohlberg stage-structural theory of moral reasoning. *Journal of Moral Education, 8,* 168–181.

LOCKE, D. (1980). The illusion of stage six. *Journal of Moral Education, 9,* 103–109.

LOCKE, E. A. (1968). Toward a theory of task motivation and incentives. *Organizational Behavior and Human Performance, 3,* 157–189.

LOCKE, E. A., BRYAN, J. F., & KENDALL, L. M. (1968). Goals and intentions as mediators of the effects of monetary incentives on behavior. *Journal of Applied Psychology, 52,* 104–121.

LOCKE, E. A., CARTLEDGE, N., & KNERR C. S. (1970). Studies of the relationship between satisfaction, goal setting, and performance. *Organizational Behavior and Human Performance, 5,* 135–158.

LOCKE, E. A., CARTLEDGE, N., & KOEPPEL, J. (1968). Motivational effects of knowledge of results. *Psychological Bulletin, 70,* 474–485.

LOCKE, E. A., FREDERICK, E., LEE, C., & BOBKO, P. (1984). Effect of self-efficacy, goals, and task strategies on task performance. *Journal of Applied Psychology, 69,* 241–251.

LOCKE, E. A., & LATHAM, G. P. (1984). *Goal setting: A motivational technique that works!* Englewood Cliffs, NJ: Prentice-Hall.

LOCKE, E. A., & SCHWEIGER, D. M. (1979). Participation in decision-making: One more look. In B. M. Staw (Ed.), *Research in organizational behavior* (Vol. 1, pp. 265–339). Greenwich, CT: JAI Press.

LOCKE, E. A., SHAW, K. N., SAARI, L. M., & LATHAM, G. P. (1981). Goal setting and task performance: 1969–1980. *Psychological Bulletin, 90,* 125–152.

LOCKE, E. A., ZUBRITZKY, E., COUSINS, E., & BOBKO, P. (1984). Effect of previously assigned goals on self-set goals and performance. *Journal of Applied Psychology. 69,* 694–699.

LOEB, A., BECK, A. T., DIGGORY, J. C., & TUTHILL, R. (1967). Expectancy, level of aspiration, performance, and self-evaluation in depression. *Proceedings of the 75th Annual Convention of the American Psychological Association, 2,* 193–194.

LOEW, C. A. (1967). Acquisition of a hostile attitude and its relationship to aggressive behavior. *Journal of Personality and Social Psychology, 5,* 335–341.

LOFLAND, J. (1978). "Becoming a world-saver" revisited. In J. T. Richardson (Ed.), *Conversion careers: In and out of the new religions* (pp. 10–23). Beverly Hills: Sage.

LOFTUS, E. F. (1979). *Eyewitness testimony.* Cambridge, MA: Harvard University Press.

LOGAN, C. H. (1975). Arrest rates and deterrence. *Social Science Quarterly, 56,* 376–389.

LOGUE, A. W. (1979). Taste aversion and the generality of the laws of learning. *Psychological Bulletin, 86,* 276–296.

LOPEZ, E. M. (1981). Increasing intrinsic motivation with performance-contingent reward. *The Journal of Psychology, 108,* 59–66.

LORD, C. G. (1982). Predicting behavioral consistency from an individual's perception of situational similarities. *Journal of Personality and Social Psychology, 42,* 1076–1088.

LOVAAS, O. I. (1964). Control of food intake in children by reinforcement of relevant verbal behavior. *Journal of Abnormal and Social Psychology, 68,* 672–678.

LOVAAS, O. I. (1966). *Reinforcement therapy* [Film]. Philadelphia: Smith, Kline and French Laboratories.

LOVAAS, O. I. (1967). A behavior therapy approach to the treatment of childhood schizophrenia. In J. P. Hill (Ed.), *Minnesota Symposia on Child Psychology* (Vol. 1, pp. 108–159). Minneapolis: University of Minnesota Press.

LOVAAS, O. I. (1977). *The autistic child: Language development through behavior modification.* New York: Irvington.

LOVAAS, O. I. (1982, September). *An overview of the young autism project.* Paper presented at the meeting of the American Psychological Association, Washington, DC.

LOVAAS, O. I., KOEGEL, R. L., & SCHREIBMAN, L. (1979). Stimulus overselectivity in autism: A review of research. *Psychological Bulletin, 86,* 1236–1254.

LOVAAS, O. I., KOEGEL, R., SIMMONS, J. Q., & LONG, J. S. (1973). Some generalization and follow-up measures on autistic children in behavior therapy. *Journal of Applied Behavior Analysis, 6,* 131–166.

LOVAAS, O. I., & NEWSOM, C. D. (1976). Behavior modification with psychotic children. In H. Leitenberg (Ed.), *Handbook of behavior modification and behavior therapy* (pp. 303–360). Englewood Cliffs, NJ: Prentice-Hall.

LOVELAND, K. K., & OLLEY, J. G. (1979). The effect of external reward on interest and quality of task performance in children of high and low intrinsic motivation. *Child Development, 50,* 1207–1210.

LOVITT, T. C., & CURTISS, K. A. (1969). Academic response rate as a function of teacher- and self-imposed contingencies. *Journal of Applied Behavior Analysis, 2,* 49–53.

LUBORSKY, L., SINGER, B., & LUBORSKY, L. (1975). Comparative studies of psychotherapies: Is it true that "everyone has won and all must have prizes"? *Archives of General Psychiatry, 32,* 995–1008.

LUEPKER, R. V., JOHNSON, C. A., MURRAY, D. M., & PECHACEK, T. F. (1983). Prevention of cigarette smoking: Three-year follow-up of an education program for youth. *Journal of Behavioral Medicine, 6,* 53–62.

LURIA, A. (1961). *The role of speech in the regulation of normal and abnormal behavior.* New York: Liveright.

MACCOBY, E. E., & JACKLIN, C. N. (1974). *The psychology of sex differences.* Stanford, CA: Stanford University Press.

MACCOBY, N., & FARQUHAR, J. W. (1975). Communication for health: Unselling heart disease. *Journal of Communication, 25,* 114–126.

MACNAMARA, J. (1972). Cognitive basis of language learning in infants. *Psychological Review, 79,* 1–13.

MADDUX, J. E., & ROGERS, R. W. (1983). Protection motivation and self-efficacy: A revised theory of fear appeals and attitude change. *Journal of Experimental Social Psychology, 19,* 469–479.

MADDUX, J. E., SHERER, M., & ROGERS, R. W. (1982). Self-efficacy expectancy and outcome expectancy: Their relationship and their effects. *Cognitive Therapy and Research, 6,* 207–212.

MADSEN, C., JR. (1968). Nurturance and modeling in preschoolers. *Child Development, 39,* 221–236.

MAGER, R. F. (1968). *Developing attitude toward learning.* Palo Alto, CA: Fearon.

MAHONEY, M. J. (1974a). *Cognition and behavior modification.* Cambridge, MA: Ballinger.

MAHONEY, M. J. (1974b). Self-reward and self-monitoring techniques for weight control. *Behavior Therapy, 5,* 48–57.

MAHONEY, M. J. (1976). *Scientist as subject: The psychological imperative.* Cambridge, MA: Ballinger.

MAHONEY, M. J., & BANDURA, A. (1972). Self-reinforcement in pigeons. *Learning and Motivation, 3,* 293–303.

MAHONEY, M. J., MOORE, B. S., WADE, T. C., & MOURA, N. G. M. (1973). The effects of continuous and intermittent self-monitoring on academic behavior. *Journal of Consulting and Clinical Psychology, 41,* 65–69.

MAHONEY, M. J., & THORESEN, C. E. (1974). *Self-control: Power to the person.* Monterey, CA: Brooks/Cole.

MALAMUTH, N. M. (1981a). Rape fantasies as a function of exposure to violent sexual stimuli. *Archives of Sexual Behavior, 10,* 33–47.

MALAMUTH, N. M. (1981b). Rape proclivity among males. *Journal of Social Issues, 37,* 138–157.

MALAMUTH, N. M., & CHECK, J. V. P. (1981). The effects of mass media exposure on acceptance of violence against women: A field experiment. *Journal of Research in Personality, 15,* 436–446.

MALAMUTH, N. M., & CHECK, J. V. P. (1983). Sexual arousal to rape depictions: Individual differences. *Journal of Abnormal Pschology, 92,* 55–67.

MALAMUTH, N. M., & DONNERSTEIN, E. (1982). The effects of aggressive-pornographic mass media stimuli. In L. Berkowitz (Ed.), *Advances in experimental social psychology* (Vol. 15, pp. 104–136). New York: Academic Press.

MALAMUTH, N. M., & DONNERSTEIN, E. (Eds.). (1984). *Pornography and sexual aggression.* New York: Academic Press.

MALAMUTH, N. M., FESHBACH, S., & JAFFE, Y. (1977). Sexual arousal and aggression: Recent experiments and theoretical issues. *The Journal of Social Issues, 33,* 110–133.

MALONE, T. W. (1981). Toward a theory of intrinsically motivating instruction. *Cognitive Science, 5,* 333–370.

MALONE T. W., & LEPPER, M. R. (1985). Making learning fun: A taxonomy of intrinsic motivations for learning. In R. E. Snow & M. J. Farr (Eds.), *Aptitude, learning, and instruction: III. Conative and affective process analysis.* Hillsdale, NJ: Erlbaum.

MANDERLINK, G., & HARACKIEWICZ, J. M. (1984). Proximal versus distal goal setting and intrinsic motivation. *Journal of Personality and Social Psychology, 47,* 918–928.

MANDLER, G. (1975). *Mind and emotion.* New York: Wiley.

MANKOFF, M., & FLACKS, R. (1971). The changing social base of the American student movement. *Annals of the American Academy of Political and Social Science, 395,* 54–67.

MANN, J., SIDMAN, J., & STARR, S. (1971). Effects of erotic films on the sexual behavior of married couples. In *Technical report of the commission on obscenity and pornography* (Vol. VIII). *Erotica and social behavior* (pp. 170–254). Washington, DC: U.S. Government Printing Office.

MANNING, M. M., & WRIGHT, T. L. (1983). Self-efficacy expectancies, outcome expectancies, and the persistence of pain control in childbirth. *Journal of Personality and Social Psychology, 45,* 421–431.

MANSFIELD, E. (1968). *Industrial research and technological innovation: An econometric analysis.* New York: Norton.

MANSFIELD, E., RAPOPORT, J., ROMEO, A., VILLANI, E.,

WAGNER, S., & HUSIC, F. (1977). *The production and application of new industrial technology.* New York: Norton.

MANTELL, D. M., & PANZARELLA, R. (1976). Obedience and responsibility. *The British Journal of Social and Clinical Psychology, 15,* 239–246.

MARBURG, C. C., HOUSTON, B. K., & HOLMES, D. S. (1976). Influence of multiple models on the behavior of institutionalized retarded children: Increased generalization to other models and other behaviors. *Journal of Consulting and Clinical Psychology, 44,* 514–519.

MARCH, J. G. (1982). Theories of choice and making decisions. *Transaction: Social Science and Modern Society, 20,* 29–39.

MARCUS, D. E., & OVERTON, W. F. (1978). The development of cognitive gender constancy and sex role preferences. *Child Development, 49,* 434–444.

MARKMAN, E. M., & CALLAHAN, M. S. (1983). An analysis of hierarchical classification. In R. Sternberg (Ed.), *Advances in the psychology of human intelligence* (Vol. 2, pp. 325–365). Hillsdale, NJ: Erlbaum.

MARKUS, H., CRANE, M., BERNSTEIN, S., & SILADI, M. (1982). Self-schemas and gender. *Journal of Personality and Social Psychology, 42,* 38–50.

MARKUS, H., & SENTIS, S. (1982). The self in social information processing. In J. Suls (Ed.), *Psychological perspectives on the self* (Vol. 1, pp. 41–70). Hillsdale, NJ: Erlbaum.

MARLATT, G. A. (1972). Task structure and the experimental modification of verbal behavior. *Psychological Bulletin, 78,* 335–350.

MARLATT, G. A., & GORDON, J. R. (1980). Determinants of relapse: Implications for the maintenance of behavior change. In P. O. Davidson & S. M. Davidson (Eds.), *Behavioral medicine: Changing health lifestyles* (pp. 410–452). New York: Brunner/Mazel.

MARLOWE, D., BEECHER, R. S., COOK, J. B., & DOOB, A. N. (1964). The approval motive, vicarious reinforcement and verbal conditioning. *Perceptual and Motor Skills, 19,* 523–530.

MARMOR, J. (1962). Psychoanalytic therapy as an educational process: Common denominators in the therapeutic approaches of different psychoanalytic schools. In J. H. Masserman (Ed.), *Science and psychoanalysis* (Vol. 5). *Psychoanalytic education* (pp. 286–299). New York: Grune & Stratton.

MARQUIS, D. P. (1941). Learning in the neonate: The modification of behavior under three feeding schedules. *Journal of Experimental Psychology, 29,* 263–282.

MARSH, A. (1977). *Protest and political consciousness.* Beverly Hills: Sage.

MARSHALL, G. D., & ZIMBARDO, P. G. (1979). Affective consequences of inadequately explained physiological arousal. *Journal of Personality and Social Psychology, 37,* 970–988.

MARSHALL, J. F. (1971). Topics and networks in intra-village communication. In S. Polgar (Ed.), *Culture and population: A collection of current studies* (pp. 160–166). Cambridge, MA: Schenkman.

MARSTON, A. R. (1965). Imitation, self-reinforcement, and reinforcement of another person. *Journal of Personality and Social Psychology, 2*, 255–261.

MARTIN, C. L., & HALVERSON, C. F. (1981). A schematic processing model of sex typing and stereotyping in children. *Child Development, 52*, 1119–1134.

MARTIN, C. L., & HALVERSON, C. F., JR. (1983). The effects of sex-typing schemas on young children's memory. *Child Development, 54*, 563–574.

MARTIN, D. J., ABRAMSON, L. Y., & ALLOY, L. B. (1984). Illusion of control for self and others in depressed and nondepressed college students. *Journal of Personality and Social Psychology, 46*, 125–136.

MARTIN, J. (1979). Laboratory studies of self-reinforcement (SR) phenomena. *The Journal of General Psychology, 101*, 103–150.

MARTIN, J. (1981). Relative deprivation: A theory of distributive injustice for an era of shrinking resources. In B. Staw & L. Cummings (Eds.), *Research in organizational behavior* (Vol. 3, pp. 53–107). Greenwich, CT: JAI Press.

MARTIN, M., BURKHOLDER, R., ROSENTHAL, T. L., THARP, R. G., & THORNE, G. L. (1968). Programming behavior change and reintegration into school milieus of extreme adolescent deviates. *Behaviour Research and Therapy, 6*, 371–383.

MARTIN, S. E. (1981). Restitution and community service sentences: Promising sentencing alternative or passing fad. In S. E. Martin, L. B. Sechrest, & R. Redner (Eds.), *New directions in the rehabilitation of criminal offenders* (pp. 470–496). Washington DC: National Academy Press.

MASLACH, C. (1979). Negative emotional biasing of unexplained arousal. *Journal of Personality and Social Psychology, 37*, 953–969.

MASLACH, C. (1982). *Burnout—The cost of caring.* Englewood Cliffs, NJ: Prentice-Hall.

MASLACH, C., & JACKSON, S. E. (1982). Burnout in health professions: A social psychological analysis. In G. S. Sanders & J. Suls (Eds.), *Social psychology of health and illness* (pp. 227–251). Hillsdale, NJ: Erlbaum.

MASLACH, C., & PINES, A. (1977). The burn-out syndrome in the day care setting. *Child Care Quarterly, 6*, 100–113.

MASON, W. A. (1976). Environmental models and mental modes: Representational processes in the great apes and man. *American Psychologist, 31*, 284–294.

MASTERS, J. C., & BRANCH, M. N. (1969). A comparison of the relative effectiveness of instructions, modeling, and reinforcement procedures for inducing behavior change. *Journal of Experimental Psychology, 80*, 364–368.

MASTERS, J. C., FURMAN, W., & BARDEN, R. C. (1977). Effects of achievement standards, tangible rewards, and self-dispensed achievement evaluations on children's task mastery. *Child Development, 48*, 217–224.

MASTERS, J. C., & MOKROS, J. R. (1974). Self-reinforcement processes in children. In H. W. Reese (Ed.), *Advances in child development and behavior* (Vol. 9, pp. 151–187). New York: Academic Press.

MASTERS, J. C., & SANTROCK, J. W. (1976). Studies in the self-regulation of behavior: Effects of contingent cognitive and affective events. *Developmental Psychology, 12*, 334–348.

MASUR, E. F., & RITZ, E. G. (1984). Patterns of gestural, vocal, and verbal imitation performance in infancy. *Merrill-Palmer Quarterly, 1984, 30*, 369–392.

MATEFY, R. E., & ACKSEN, B. A. (1976). The effect of role-playing discrepant positions on change in moral judgments and attitudes. *The Journal of Genetic Psychology, 128*, 189–200.

MATHEWS, A., TEASDALE, J., MUNBY, M., JOHNSON, D., & SHAW, P. (1977). A home-based treatment program for agoraphobia. *Behavior Therapy, 8*, 915–924.

MATTHEWS, K. A., & SIEGEL, J. M. (1983). Type A behaviors by children, social comparison, and standards for self-evaluation. *Developmental Psychology, 19*, 135–140.

MATSUI, T., OKADA, A., & KAKUYAMA, T. (1982). Influence of achievement need on goal setting, performance and feedback effectiveness. *Journal of Applied Psychology, 67*, 645–648.

MATSUI, T., OKADA, A., & MIZUGUCHI, R. (1981). Expectancy-theory prediction of the goal theory postulate, "The harder the goals, the higher the performance." *Journal of Applied Psychology, 66*, 54–58.

MAY, J. R. (1977). A psychophysiological study of self and externally regulated phobic thoughts. *Behavior Therapy, 8*, 849–861.

MAY, J. R., & JOHNSON, H. J. (1973). Physiological activity to internally elicited arousal and inhibitory thoughts. *Journal of Abnormal Psychology, 82*, 239–245.

MCALISTER, A., PERRY, C., KILLEN, J., SLINKARD, L. A., & MACCOBY, N. (1980). Pilot study of smoking, alcohol and drug abuse prevention. *American Journal of Public Health, 70*, 719–721.

MCALISTER, A., PUSKA, P., SALONEN, J. T., TUOMILEHTO, J., & KOSKELA, K. (1982). Theory and action for health promotion: Illustrations from the North Karelia Project. *American Journal of Public Health, 72*, 43–50.

MCARTHUR, L. Z., & EISEN, S. V. (1976). Achievements of male and female storybook characters as determinants of achievement behavior by boys and girls. *Journal of Personality and Social Psychology, 33*, 467–473.

MCAULEY, E., & GILL, D. (1983). Reliability and validity of the physical self-efficacy scale in a competitive sport setting. *Journal of Sport Psychology, 5*, 410–418.

MCCALL, G. J. (1977). The social looking-glass: A sociological perspective on self-development. In T. Mischel (Ed.), *The self: Psychological and philosophical issues* (pp. 274–287). Oxford, England: Blackwell.

MCCALL, R. B., & MCGHEE, P. E. (1977). The discrepancy hypothesis of attention and affect in infants. In I. C. Uzgiris & F. Weizmann (Eds.), *The structuring of experience* (pp. 179–210). New York: Plenum.

MCCALL, R. B. PARKE, R. D., & KAVANAUGH, R. D. (1977). Imitation of live and televised models by children one to three years of age. *Monographs of the Soci-*

ety for Research in Child Development, 42(5, Serial No. 173).

McCaul, K. D. & Malott, J. M. (1984). Distraction and coping with pain. *Psychological Bulletin, 95,* 516–533.

McDavid, J. W. (1962). Effects of ambiguity of environmental cues upon learning to imitate. *Journal of Abnormal and Social Psychology, 65,* 381–386.

McDavid, J. W. (1964). Effects of ambiguity of imitative cues upon learning by observation. *The Journal of Social Psychology, 62,* 165–174.

McFall, R. M., & Twentyman, C. T. (1973). Four experiments on the relative contributions of rehearsal, modeling and coaching to assertion training. *Journal of Abnormal Psychology, 81,* 199–218.

McFarland, S. G. (1983). Is capital punishment a short-term deterrent to homicide? A study of the effects of four recent American executions. *The Journal of Criminal Law & Criminology, 74,* 1014–1032.

McGhee, P. E., & Frueh, T. (1980). Television viewing and the learning of sex-role stereotypes. *Sex Roles, 6,* 179–188.

McGuire, R. J., Carlisle, J. M., & Young, B. G. (1965). Sexual deviations as conditioned behaviour: A hypothesis. *Behaviour Research and Therapy, 2,* 185–190.

McGuire, W. J. (1961). Some factors influencing the effectiveness of demonstrational films: Repetition of instructions, slow motion, distribution of showings, and explanatory narration. In A. A. Lumsdaine (Ed.), *Student response in programmed instruction* (pp. 187–207). Washington, DC: National Academy of Sciences-National Research Council.

McGuire, W. J. (1969). The nature of attitudes and attitude change. In G. Lindzey & E. Aronson (Eds.), *The handbook of social psychology* (2nd ed.): *III.* (pp. 136–314). Reading, MA: Addison-Wesley.

McHugo, G. J., Smith, C. A., & Lanzetta, J. T. (1982). The structure of self-reports of emotional responses to film segments. *Motivation and Emotion, 6,* 365–385.

McIntyre, K. O., Lichtenstein, E., & Mermelstein, R. J. (1983). Self-efficacy and relapse in smoking cessation: A replication and extension. *Journal of Consulting and Clinical Psychology, 51,* 632–633.

McKaughan, L. (1974). Propositional self-control in children. *Journal of Experimental Child Psychology, 17,* 519–538.

McLaughlin, T. F., & Malaby, J. E. (1974). Increasing and maintaining assignment completion with teacher and pupil controlled individual contingency programs: Three case studies. *Psychology, 2,* 1–7.

McLeod, J. M., Glynn, C. J., & McDonald, D. G. (1983). Issues and images: The influence of media reliance in voting decisions. *Communication Research, 10,* 37–58.

McLoyd, V. C. (1979). The effects of extrinsic rewards of differential value on high and low intrinsic interest. *Child Development, 50,* 1010–1019.

McMains, M. J., & Liebert, R. M. (1968). Influence of discrepancies between successively modeled self-reward criteria on the adoption of a self-imposed

standard. *Journal of Personality and Social Psychology, 8,* 166–171.

McMullin, D. J., & Steffen, J. J. (1982). Intrinsic motivation and performance standards. *Social Behavior and Personality, 10,* 47–56.

McNally, R. J. (1981). Phobias and preparedness—Instructional reversal of electrodermal conditioning to fear-relevant stimuli. *Psychological Reports, 48,* 175–180.

McNally, R. J., & Reiss, S. (1982). The preparedness theory of phobia and human safety-signal conditioning. *Behavior Research and Therapy, 20,* 153–159.

McNeill, D. (1970). *The acquisition of language.* New York: Harper & Row.

McPhail, C. (1971). Civil disorder participation: A critical examination of recent research. *American Sociological Review, 36,* 1058–1072.

McPhail, T. L. (1981). *Electronic colonialism: The future of international broadcasting and communication.* Beverly Hills: Sage.

McPherson, B. D. (1980). Retirement from professional sport: The process and problems of occupational and psychological adjustment. *Sociological Symposium, 30,* 126–143.

Meehl, P. E. (1950). On the circularity of the law of effect. *Psychological Bulletin, 47,* 52–75.

Mefford, I. N., Ward, M. M., Miles, L., Taylor, B., Chesney, M. A., Keegan, D. L., & Barchas, J. D. (1981). Determination of plasma catecholamines and free 3,4–dihydroxyphenylacetic acid in continuously collected human plasma by high performance liquid chromatography with electrochemical detection. *Life Sciences, 28,* 447–483.

Mehrabian, A., & Epstein, N. (1972). A measure of emotional empathy. *Journal of Personality, 40,* 525–543.

Meichenbaum, D. H. (1971). Examination of model characteristics in reducing avoidance behavior. *Journal of Personality and Social Psychology, 17,* 298–307.

Meichenbaum, D. H. (1977). *Cognitive-behavior modification: An integrative approach.* New York: Plenum.

Meichenbaum, D. (1979). Teaching children self-control. In B. B. Lahey & A. E. Kazdin (Eds.), *Advances in clinical child psychology* (Vol. 2, pp. 1–33). New York: Plenum.

Meichenbaum, D. (1980). A cognitive-behavioral perspective on intelligence. *Intelligence: A Multidisciplinary Journal, 4,* 271–284.

Meichenbaum, D. H., & Asarnow, J. (1979). Cognitive-behavioral modification and metacognitive development: Implications for the classroom. In P. C. Kendall & S. D. Hollon (Eds.), *Cognitive-behavioral interventions: Theory, research, and procedures* (pp. 11–35). New York: Academic Press.

Meichenbaum, D., & Cameron, R. (1982). Cognitive-behavior therapy. In G. T. Wilson & C. M. Franks (Eds.), *Contemporary behavior therapy: Conceptual and empirical foundations* (pp. 310–338). New York: Guilford.

Meichenbaum, D. H., & Goodman, J. (1971). Training

impulsive children to talk to themselves: A means of developing self-control. *Journal of Abnormal Psychology, 77,* 115–126.

MEICHENBAUM, D., & GOODMAN, S. (1979). Clinical use of private speech and critical questions about its study in natural settings. In G. Zivin (Ed.), *The development of self-regulation through private speech* (pp. 325–360). New York: Wiley.

MEICHENBAUM, D., & JAREMKO, M. E. (Eds.). (1983). *Stress reduction and prevention.* New York: Plenum.

MEICHENBAUM, D. H., & TURK, D. (1976). The cognitive-behavioral management of anxiety, anger and pain. In P. Davidson (Ed.), *Behavioral management of anxiety, depression and pain* (pp. 1–34). New York: Brunner/Mazel.

MEIER, R. F. (1978). The deterrence doctrine and public policy: A response to utilitarians. In J. A. Cramer (Ed.), *Preventing crime* (pp. 233–247). Beverly Hills: Sage.

MEIER, R. F., & JOHNSON, W. T. (1977). Deterrence as social control: The legal and extralegal production of conformity. *American Sociological Review, 42,* 292–304.

MELAMED, B. G. (1979). Behavioral approaches to fear in dental settings. In M. Hersen, R. M. Eisler, & P. M. Miller (Eds.), *Progress in behavior modification* (Vol. 7, pp. 171–203). New York: Academic Press.

MELAMED, B. G., & SIEGEL, L. J. (1975). Reduction of anxiety in children facing hospitalization and surgery by use of filmed modeling. *Journal of Consulting and Clinical Psychology, 43,* 511–521.

MELTZOFF, A. N., & MOORE, M. K. (1977). Imitation of facial and manual gestures by human neonates. *Science, 198,* 75–78.

MELTZOFF, A. N., & MOORE, M. K. (1983). Newborn infants imitate adult facial gestures. *Child Development, 54,* 702–709.

MELTZOFF, A. N., & MOORE, M. K. (1983). The origins of imitation in infancy: Paradigm, phenomena, and theories. In L. P. Lipsitt & C. K. Rovee-Collier (Eds.), *Advances in infancy research* (Vol. 2, pp. 266–301). Norwood, NJ: Ablex Publishing.

MELZACK, R., & WALL, P. D. (1982). *The challenge of pain.* Harmondsworth, England: Penguin.

MENTO, A. J., CARTLEDGE, N. D., & LOCKE, E. A. (1980). Maryland vs Michigan vs Minnesota: Another look at the relationship of expectancy and goal difficulty to task performance. *Organizational Behavior and Human Performance, 25,* 419–440.

MENYUK, P. (1964). Alteration of rules in children's grammar. *Journal of Verbal Learning and Verbal Behavior, 3,* 480–488.

MERBAUM, M., & LOWE, M. R. (1982). Serendipity in research in clinical psychology. In P. C. Kendall & J. N. Butcher (Eds.), *Handbook of research methods in clinical psychology* (pp. 95–123). New York: Wiley.

MERBAUM, M., & LUKENS, H. C., JR. (1968). Effects of instructions, elicitations, and reinforcements in the manipulation of affective verbal behavior. *Journal of Abnormal Psychology, 73,* 376–380.

MERVIS, C. B., & ROSCH, E. (1981). Categorization of

natural objects. In M. R. Rosenzweig & L. W. Porter (Eds.), *Annual review of psychology* (Vol. 32, pp. 89–115). Palo Alto, CA: Annual Reviews.

MEYER, A. J., MACCOBY, N., & FARQUHAR, J. W. (1977). The role of opinion leadership in a cardiovascular health education campaign. In B. D. Ruben (Ed.), *Communication Yearbook 1* (pp. 579–591). New Brunswick, NJ: Transaction Books.

MEYER, A. J., NASH, J. D., MCALISTER, A. L., MACCOBY, N., & FARQUHAR, J. W. (1980). Skills training in a cardiovascular health education campaign. *Journal of Consulting and Clinical Psychology, 48,* 129–142.

MEYER, T. P. (1971). Some effects of real newsfilm violence on the behavior of viewers. *Journal of Broadcasting, 15,* 275–285.

MIDGLEY, D. F. (1976). A simple mathematical theory of innovative behavior. *Journal of Consumer Research, 3,* 31–41.

MIDGLEY, D. F., & DOWLING, G. R. (1978). Innovativeness: The concept and its measurement. *Journal of Consumer Research, 4,* 229–242.

MIDGLEY, M. (1978). *Beast and man: The roots of human nature.* Ithaca, NY: Cornell University Press.

MILGRAM, S. (1965). Some conditions of obedience and disobedience to authority. *Human Relations, 18,* 57–76.

MILGRAM, S. (1969). Interdisciplinary thinking and the small world problem. In M. Sherif & C. W. Sherif (Eds.), *Interdisciplinary relationships in the social sciences* (pp. 103–120). Chicago: Aldine.

MILGRAM, S. (1974). *Obedience to authority: An experimental view.* New York: Harper & Row.

MILLAR, W. S. (1972). A study of operant conditioning under delayed reinforcement in early infancy. *Monographs of the Society for Research in Child Development, 37*(2, Serial No. 147).

MILLAR, W. S. (1974). The role of visual-holding cues and the simultanizing strategy in infant operant learning. *British Journal of Psychology, 65,* 505–518.

MILLAR, W. S., & SCHAFFER, H. R. (1972). The influence of spatially displaced feedback on infant operant conditioning. *Journal of Experimental Child Psychology, 14,* 442–453.

MILLER, M. M. & REEVES, B. (1976). Dramatic TV content and children's sex role stereotypes. *Journal of Broadcasting, 20,* 35–50.

MILLER, N. E. (1963). Some reflections on the law of effect produce a new alternative to drive reduction. In M. R. Jones (Ed.), *Nebraska Symposium on Motivation* (pp. 65–112). Lincoln: University of Nebraska Press.

MILLER, N. E., & DOLLARD, J. (1941). *Social learning and imitation.* New Haven: Yale University Press.

MILLER, R. E., BANKS, J. H., JR., & OGAWA, N. (1962). Communication of affect in "cooperative conditioning" of rhesus monkeys. *Journal of Abnormal and Social Psychology, 64,* 343–348.

MILLER, R. E., BANKS, J. H., JR., & OGAWA, N. (1963). Role of facial expression in "cooperative-avoidance conditioning" in monkeys. *Journal of Abnormal and Social Psychology, 67,* 24–30.

MILLER, R. E., CAUL, W. F., & MIRSKY, I. A. (1967).

Communication of affect between feral and socially isolated monkeys. *Journal of Personality and Social Psychology, 7,* 231–239.

MILLER, R. E., MURPHY, J. V., & MIRSKY, I. A. (1959). Nonverbal communication of affect. *Journal of Clinical Psychology, 15,* 155–158.

MILLER, R. L., BRICKMAN, P., & BOLEN, D. (1975). Attribution versus persuasion as a means for modifying behavior. *Journal of Personality and Social Psychology, 31,* 430–441.

MILLER, S. M. (1979). Controllability and human stress: Method, evidence and theory. *Behaviour Research and Therapy, 17,* 287–304.

MILLER, S. M. (1980a). Why having control reduces stress: If I can stop the rollercoaster I don't want to get off. In J. Garber & M. E. P. Seligman (Eds.), *Human helplessness: Theory and research* (pp. 71–95). New York: Academic Press.

MILLER, S. M. (1980b). When is a little information a dangerous thing? Coping with stressful events by monitoring versus blunting. In S. Levine & H. Ursin (Eds.), *Coping and health* (pp. 145–169). New York: Plenum.

MILLER, S. M. (1981). Predictability and human stress: Towards a clarification of evidence and theory. In L. Berkowitz (Ed.), *Advances in experimental social psychology* (Vol. 14, pp. 204–256). New York: Academic Press.

MILLER, S. M., LACK, E. R., & ASROFF, S. (1985). Preference for control and the coronary-prone behavior pattern: "I'd rather do it myself." *Journal of Personality and Social Psychology.*

MILLER, S. M., & SELIGMAN, M. E. P. (1982). The reformulated model of helplessness and depression: Evidence and theory. In R. J. Neufeld (Ed.), *Psychological stress and psychopathology* (pp. 149–178). New York: McGraw Hill.

MINEKA, S., DAVIDSON, M., COOK, M., & KEIR, R. (1984). Observational conditioning of snake fear in rhesus monkeys. *Journal of Abnormal Psychology, 93,* 355–372.

MINEKA, S., GUNNAR, M., & CHAMPOUX, M. (1985). The effects of control in the early social and emotional development of rhesus monkeys. *Child Development.*

MINOR, W. W., & HARRY, J. (1982). Deterrent and experiential effects in perceptual deterrence research: A replication and extension. *Journal of Research in Crime and Delinquency, 19,* 190–203.

MISCHEL, W. (1968). *Personality and assessment.* New York: Wiley.

MISCHEL, W. (1970). A social learning view of sex differences in behavior. In P. H. Mussen (Ed.), *Carmichael's manual of child psychology* (Vol. 2, pp. 56–81). New York: Wiley.

MISCHEL, W. (1973). Toward a cognitive social learning reconceptualization of personality. *Psychological Review, 80,* 252–283.

MISCHEL, W. (1974). Processes in delay of gratification. In L. Berkowitz (Ed.), *Advances in experimental social psychology* (Vol. 7, pp. 249–292). New York: Academic Press.

MISCHEL, W. (1981). Metacognition and the rules of delay. In J. H. Flavell & L. Ross (Eds.), *Social cognitive development: Frontiers and possible futures* (pp. 240–271). Cambridge: Cambridge University Press.

MISCHEL, W. (1983). Delay of gratification as process and as person variable in development. In D. Magnusson & V. P. Allen (Eds.), *Human development: An interactional perspective* (pp. 149–165). New York: Academic Press.

MISCHEL, W., & GRUSEC, J. (1966). Determinants of the rehearsal and transmission of neutral and aversive behavior. *Journal of Personality and Social Psychology, 3,* 197–205.

MISCHEL, W., & LIEBERT, R. M. (1966). Effects of discrepancies between observed and imposed reward criteria on their acquisition and transmission. *Journal of Personality and Social Psychology, 3,* 45–53.

MISCHEL, W., & LIEBERT, R. M. (1967). The role of power in the adoption of self-reward patterns. *Child Development, 38,* 673–683.

MISCHEL, W., & PEAKE, P. K. (1982). Beyond deja vu in the search for cross-situational consistency. *Psychological Review, 89,* 730–755.

MITCHELL, T. R. (1974). Expectancy models of job satisfaction, occupational preference and effort: A theoretical, methodological, and empirical appraisal. *Psychological Bulletin, 81,* 1053–1077.

MIURA, I. (1984a, August). *Computer self-efficacy: A contributing factor to gender differences in the election of computer science courses.* Paper presented at the International Congress of Mathematical Education, Adelaide, Australia.

MIURA, I. (1984b). *Processes contributing to individual differences in computer literacy.* Unpublished doctoral dissertation, Stanford University, Stanford, CA.

MOERK, E. L. (1974). Changes in verbal mother-child interactions with increasing language skills of the child. *Journal of Psycholinguistic Research, 3,* 101–116.

MOERK, E. L. (1976). Processes of language teaching and training in the interactions of mother-child dyads. *Child Development, 47,* 1064–1078.

MOERK, E. L. (1980). Relationships between parental input frequencies and children's language acquisition: A reanalysis of Brown's data. *Journal of Child Language, 7,* 105–118.

MOERK, E. L. (1983). A behavioral analysis of controversial topics in first language acquisition: Reinforcements, corrections, modeling, input frequencies, and the three-term contingency pattern. *Journal of Psycholinguistic Research, 12,* 129–155.

MOERK, E. L., & MOERK, C. (1979). Quotations, imitations, and generalizations. Factual and methodological analyses. *International Journal of Behavioral Development, 2,* 43–72.

MOESER, S. D. (1977). Semantics and miniature artificial languages. In J. Macnamara (Ed.), *Language learning and thought* (pp. 227–250). New York: Academic Press.

MONTGOMERY, G. T., & PARTON, D. A. (1970). Reinforcing effect of self-reward. *Journal of Experimental Psychology, 84,* 273–276.

MOORE, L. M., & BARON, R. M. (1973). Effects of wage inequities on work attitudes and performance. *Journal of Experimental Social Psychology, 9,* 1–16.

MORELLI, E.A., & MARTIN, J. (1982). *Self-efficacy and athletic performance of 800 meter runners.* Unpublished manuscript, Simon Fraser University, Canada.

MORGAN, M. (1981). The overjustification effect: A developmental test of self-perception interpretations. *Journal of Personality and Social Psychology, 40,* 809–821.

MORGAN, M. (1984a). Reward-induced decrements and increments in intrinsic motivation. *Review of Educational Research, 54,* 5–30.

MORGAN, M. (1984b). *Self-monitored objectives in private study.* Unpublished manuscript, St. Patrick's College, Dublin, Ireland.

MORGULAS, S., & ZIMMERMAN, B. J. (1979). The role of comprehension in children's observational learning of a syntactic rule. *Journal of Experimental Child Psychology, 28,* 455–468.

MORRIS, L. W., & LIEBERT, R. M. (1970). Relationship of cognitive and emotional components of test anxiety to physiological arousal and academic performance. *Journal of Consulting and Clinical Psychology, 35,* 332–337.

MORRIS, W. N., & NEMCEK, D., JR. (1982). The development of social comparison motivation among preschoolers: Evidence of a stepwise progression. *Merrill-Palmer Quarterly of Behavior and Development, 28,* 413–425.

MOSS, M. K., & AREND, R. A. (1977). Self-directed contact desensitization. *Journal of Consulting and Clinical Psychology, 45,* 730–738.

MOSSHOLDER, K.W. (1980). Effects of externally mediated goal setting on intrinsic motivation: A laboratory experiment. *Journal of Applied Psychology, 65,* 202–210.

MOWRER, O. H. (1950). Identification: A link between learning theory and psychotherapy. In O. H. Mowrer (Ed.), *Learning theory and personality dynamics* (pp. 573–615). New York: Ronald Press.

MOWRER, O. H. (1950). *Learning theory and personality dynamics.* New York: Ronald Press.

MOWRER, O. H. (1960a). *Learning theory and the symbolic processes.* New York: Wiley.

MOWRER, O. H. (1960b). *Learning theory and behavior.* New York: Wiley.

MUELLER, L. K. (1978). Beneficial and detrimental modeling effects on creative response production. *The Journal of Psychology, 98,* 253–260.

MULLENER, N., & LAIRD, J. D. (1971). Some developmental changes in the organization of self-evaluations. *Developmental Psychology, 5,* 233–236.

MULLER, E. N. (1972). A test of a partial theory of potential for political violence. *The American Political Science Review, 66,* 928–959.

MULLER, E. N. (1979). *Aggressive political participation.* Princeton: Princeton University Press.

MUNN, N. L. (1983). More on chance encounters and life paths. *American Psychologist, 38,* 351–352.

MUNRO, D. J. (1975). The Chinese view of modeling. *Human Development, 18,* 333–352.

MURRAY, E. J. (1956). A content-analysis method for studying psychotherapy. *Psychological Monographs, 70*(13, Whole No. 420).

MURRAY, F. B. (1983). Learning and development through social interaction and conflict: A challenge to social learning theory. In L. S. Liben (Ed.), *Piaget and the foundations of knowledge* (pp. 231–245). Hillsdale, NJ: Erlbaum.

MURRAY, J. P. (1980). *Television and youth: 25 years of research and controversy.* Boys Town, Nebraska: Boys Town Center for the Study of Youth Development.

MYERS, A. K., & MILLER, N. E. (1954). Failure to find a learned drive based on hunger: Evidence for learning motivated by exploration. *Journal of Comparative and Physiological Psychology, 47,* 428–436.

MYNATT, C., & HERMAN, S. J. (1975). Responsibility attribution in groups and individuals: A direct test of the diffusion of responsibility hypothesis. *Journal of Personality and Social Psychology, 32,* 1111–1118.

NAGEL, E. (1961). *The structure of science.* New York: Harcourt, Brace and World.

NEAL, R. A. (1981). Risk benefit analysis: Role in regulation of pesticide registration. In S. K. Bandal, G. J. Marco, L. Golberg, & M. L. Leng (Eds.), *The pesticide chemist and modern toxicology* (pp. 469–472). Washington, DC: American Chemical Society.

NEISSER, U. (1976). *Cognition and reality: Principles and implications of cognitive psychology.* San Francisco: Freeman.

NEISTEIN, S., & KATOVSKY, W. (1974). The effects of inconsistent reinforcement on the negative self-reinforcing behavior of high and low self-esteem individuals. *Journal of Personality, 42,* 78–92.

NELLANS, T. H., & ISRAEL, A. C. (1981). Towards maintenance and generalization of behavior change: Teaching children self-regulation and self-instructional skills. *Cognitive Therapy and Research, 5,* 189–195.

NELSON, K. E. (1977a). Aspects of language acquisition and use from age 2 to age 20. *Journal of the American Academy of Child Psychiatry, 16,* 584–607.

NELSON, K. E. (1977b). Facilitating children's syntax acquisition. *Developmental Psychology, 13,* 111–117.

NELSON, R. E., & CRAIGHEAD, W. E. (1977). Selective recall of positive and negative feedback, self-control behaviors, and depression. *Journal of Abnormal Psychology, 86,* 379–388.

NELSON, R. O. (1977). Assessment and therapeutic functions of self-monitoring. In M. Hersen, R. M. Eisler, & P. M. Miller (Eds.), *Progress in behavior modification* (Vol. 5, pp. 263–308). New York: Academic Press.

NELSON, R. O., HAYES, S. C., SPONG, R. T., JARRETT, R. B., & McKNIGHT, D. L. (1983). Self-reinforcement: Appealing misnomer or effective mechanism? *Behaviour Research and Therapy, 21,* 557–566.

NELSON, W. J., & BIRKIMER, J. C. (1978). Role of self-instruction and self-reinforcement in the modification of impulsivity. *Journal of Consulting and Clinical Psychology, 46,* 183.

NEMETZ, G. H., CRAIG, K. D., & REITH, G. (1978). Treatment of female sexual dysfunction through symbolic modeling. *Journal of Consulting and Clinical Psychology, 46,* 62–73.

NEUFELD, M. M., & NEUFELD, R. W. J. (1972). Use of video-tape feedback in swimming instruction with emotionally disturbed children. *Perceptual and Motor Skills, 35,* 992.

NEUFELD, R. W. J., & THOMAS, P. (1977). Effects of perceived efficacy of a prophylactic controlling mechanism on self-control under pain stimulation. *Canadian Journal of Behavioural Science, 9,* 224–232.

NEURINGER, A. (1981). Self-experimentation: A call for change. *Behaviorism, 9,* 79–94.

NEVES, D. M., & ANDERSON, J. R. (1981). Knowledge compilation: Mechanisms for the automatization of cognitive skills. In J. R. Anderson (Ed.), *Cognitive skills and their acquisition* (pp. 57–84). Hillsdale, NJ: Erlbaum.

NEWELL, A. (1973). Production systems: Models of control structures. In W. G. Chase (Ed.), *Visual information processing* (pp. 463–562). New York: Academic Press.

NEWELL, K. M. (1976). Motor learning without knowledge of results through the development of a response recognition mechanism. *Journal of Motor Behavior, 8,* 209–217.

NEWELL, K. M. (1978). Some issues on action plans. In G. E. Stelmach (Ed.), *Information processing in motor control and learning* (pp. 41–54). New York: Academic Press.

NEWTSON, D. (1976). Foundations of attribution: The unit of perception of ongoing behavior. In J. Harvey, W. J. Ickes, & R. F. Kidd (Eds.), *New directions in attribution research* (pp. 223–247). Hillsdale, NJ: Erlbaum.

New York Times. (1966, Nov. 13). Youth, 18, slays four women and child in beauty school. P. 1.

NICHOLLS, J. G., & MILLER, A. T. (1984). Development and its discontents: The differentiation of the concept of ability. In J. G. Nicholls (Ed.), *Advances in motivation and achievement* (Vol. 3). *The development of achievement motivation* (pp. 185–218). Greenwich, CT: JAI Press.

NICOLICH, L. M., & RAPH, J. B. (1978). Imitative language and symbolic maturity in the single-word period. *Journal of Psycholinguistic Research, 7,* 401–417.

NIMMO, D. (1976). Political image makers and the mass media. *The Annals of the American Academy of Political and Social Science, 427,* 33–44.

NISBETT, R., & ROSS, L. (1980). *Human inference: Strategies and shortcomings of social judgment.* Englewood Cliffs, NJ: Prentice-Hall.

NISBETT, R. E., & WILSON, T. D. (1977). Telling more than we can know: Verbal reports on mental processes. *Psychological Review, 84,* 231–259.

NOTTERMAN, J. M., SCHOENFELD, W. N., & BERSH, P. J. (1952). A comparison of three extinction procedures following heart rate conditioning. *Journal of Abnormal and Social Psychology, 47,* 674–677.

NOVACO, R. W. (1979). The cognitive regulation of anger and stress. In P. Kendall & S. Hollon (Eds.), *Cognitive-behavioral interventions: Theory, research and procedures* (pp. 241–285). New York: Academic Press.

NOVAK, G. (1978). Selective imitation of complex sentences in a preschool setting. *Journal of Educational Psychology, 70,* 922–927.

NUTTIN, J.R. (1973). Pleasure and reward in human motivation and learning. In D. E. Berlyne & K. B. Madsen (Eds.), *Pleasure, reward, preference* (pp. 243–274). New York: Academic Press.

O'BRIEN, G. T., & BORKOVEC, T. D. (1977). The role of relaxation in systematic desensitization: Revisiting an unresolved issue. *Journal of Behavior Therapy and Experimental Psychiatry, 8,* 359–364.

O'BRIEN, T. P., & KELLEY, J. E. (1980). A comparison of self-directed and therapist-directed practice for fear reduction. *Behaviour Research and Therapy, 18,* 573–579.

O'BRYANT, S. L., & CORDER-BOLZ, C. R. (1978). The effects of television on children's stereotyping of women's work roles. *Journal of Vocational Behavior, 12,* 233–244.

O'CONNELL, D. C., & WAGNER, M. V. (1967). Extinction after partial reinforcement and minimal learning as a test of both verbal control and PRE in concept learning. *Journal of Experimental Psychology, 73,* 151–153.

O'CONNOR, R. D. (1969). Modification of social withdrawal through symbolic modeling. *Journal of Applied Behavior Analysis, 2,* 15–22.

O'CONNOR, R. D. (1972). The relative efficacy of modeling, shaping, and combined procedures for the modification of social withdrawal. *Journal of Abnormal Psychology, 79,* 327–334.

OGSTON, K. M., & DAVIDSON, P. O. (1972). The effects of cognitive expectancies on vicarious conditioning. *The British Journal of Social and Clinical Psychology, 11,* 126–134.

O'HARA, M. W., & REHM, L. P. (1979). Self-monitoring, activity levels, and mood in the development and maintenance of depression. *Journal of Abnormal Psychology, 88,* 450–453.

O'HARA, M. W., REHM, L. P., & CAMPBELL, S. B. (1982). Predicting depressive symptomatology: Cognitive-behavioral models and postpartum depression. *Journal of Abnormal Psychology, 91,* 457–461.

OHMAN, A., ERIXON, G., & LOFBERG, I. (1975). Phobias and preparedness: Phobic versus neutral pictures as conditioned stimuli for human autonomic responses. *Journal of Abnormal Psychology, 84,* 41–45.

OHMAN, A., FREDRIKSON, M., HUGDAHL, K., & RIMMO, P. (1976). The premise of equipotentiality in human classical conditioning: Conditioned electrodermal responses to potentially phobic stimuli. *Journal of Experimental Psychology, 105,* 313–337.

OHMAN, A., & HUGDAHL, K. (1979). Instructional control of autonomic respondents: Fear relevance as a critical factor. In N. Birbaumer & H. D. Kimmel (Eds.), *Biofeedback and self-regulation* (pp. 149–165). Hillsdale, NJ: Erlbaum.

OLDFIELD-BOX, H. (1970). Comments on two preliminary studies of "observation" learning in the rat. *Journal of Genetic Psychology, 116,* 45–52.

OLIVER, P. R., ACKER, L. E., & OLIVER, D. D. (1977). Effects of reinforcement histories of compliance and noncompliance on nonreinforced imitation. *Journal of Experimental Child Psychology, 23,* 180–190.

OLIVER, P. R., & HOPPE, R. A. (1974). Factors effecting nonreinforced imitation: The model as a source of information or social control. *Journal of Experimental Child Psychology, 17,* 383–398.

OLLENDICK, T. H., DAILEY, D., & SHAPIRO, E. S. (1983). Vicarious reinforcement: Expected and unexpected effects. *Journal of Applied Behavior Analysis, 16,* 485–491.

OLLENDICK, T. H., & MATSON, J. L. (1978). Overcorrection: An overview. *Behavior Therapy, 9,* 830–842.

OLLENDICK, T. H., & SHAPIRO, E. S. (1984). An examination of vicarious reinforcement processes in children. *Journal of Experimental Child Psychology, 37,* 78–91.

O'MALLEY, M. (1981). Feeling without thinking? Reply to Zajonc. *The Journal of Psychology, 108,* 11–15.

OPTON, E. M. (1974). Psychiatric violence against prisoners: When therapy is punishment. *Mississippi Law Journal, 45,* 605–644.

ORENSTEIN, H., & CARR, J. (1975). Implosion therapy by tape-recording. *Behaviour Research and Therapy, 13,* 177–182.

ORMISTON, L. H. (1972). *Factors determining response to modeled hypocrisy.* Unpublished doctoral dissertation, Stanford University, Stanford, CA.

ORWELL, G. (1949). *Nineteen eighty-four; a novel.* New York: Harcourt, Brace.

OSHIMA, H. T., (1967). The strategy of selective growth and the role of communications. In D. Lerner & W. Schramm (Eds.), *Communication and change in the developing countries* (pp. 76–91). Honolulu: East-West Center Press.

OSTFELD, B., & KATZ, P. A. (1969). The effect of threat severity in children of varying socioeconomic levels. *Developmental Psychology, 1,* 205–210.

OSTLUND, L. E. (1974). Perceived innovation attributes as predictors of innovativeness. *Journal of Consumer Research, 1,* 23–29.

OSTROW, A. C. (1976). Goal-setting behavior and need achievement in relation to competitive motor activity. *The Research Quarterly, 47,* 174–183.

O'SULLIVAN, M. J., & GILNER, F. H. (1976). Sex of model and motivation to change behavior as factors in modeling. *Psychological Reports, 38,* 595–601.

PACKER, H. L. (1968). *The limits of the criminal sanction.* Stanford, CA: Stanford University Press.

PAGE, M. M. (1969). Social psychology of a classical conditioning of attitudes experiment. *Journal of Personality and Social Psychology, 11,* 177–186.

PAIVIO, A. (1971). *Imagery and verbal processes.* New York: Holt, Rinehart & Winston.

PAIVIO, A. (1975). Imagery and long-term memory. In A. Kennedy & A. Wilkes (Eds.), *Studies in long term memory.* New York: Wiley.

PALMER, J. (1977). Economic analyses of the deterrent effect of punishment: A review. *Journal of Research in Crime and Delinquency, 14,* 4–21.

Palo Alto Times. (1972b, May 6). "Hijackers flee to jungle, Cuba." P. 1.

Palo Alto Times. (1976, August 5). His conscience still working. P. 6.

Palo Alto Times. (1978, September 22). Conscience wins out. P. 5.

PAPOUSEK, H., & PAPOUSEK, M. (1977). Mothering and the cognitive head-start: Psychobiological considerations. In H. R. Schaffer (Ed.), *Studies in mother-infant interaction.* London: Academic Press.

PAPOUSEK, H., & PAPOUSEK, M. (1979). Early ontogeny of human social interaction: Its biological roots and social dimensions. In M. von Cranach, K. Foppa, W. Lepenies, & D. Ploog (Eds.), *Human ethology: Claims and limits of a new discipline* (pp. 456–478). Cambridge, England: Cambridge University Press.

PARKE, R. D. (1970). The role of punishment in the socialization process. In R. A. Hoppe, G. A. Milton, & E. C. Simmel (Eds.), *Early experiences and the process of socialization* (pp. 81–108). New York: Academic Press.

PARKE, R. D. (1974). Rules, roles, and resistance to deviation: Recent advances in punishment, discipline, and self-control. In A. D. Pick (Ed.), *Minnesota symposia on child psychology* (Vol. 8, pp. 111–143). Minneapolis: University of Minnesota Press.

PARKER, J., & GRASMICK, H. G. (1979). Linking actual and perceived certainty of punishment—Exploratory study of an untested proposition in deterrence theory. *Criminology, 17,* 366–379.

PARSONS, J. E., MOSES, L., & YULISH-MUSZYNSKI, S. (1977). The development of attributions, expectancies, and persistence. In *Success and failure attributions and student behavior in the classroom.* Symposium presented at the meeting of the American Psychological Association, San Francisco.

PARSONS, J. E., & RUBLE, D. N. (1977). The development of achievement-related expectancies. *Child Development, 48,* 1075–1079.

PARSONS, J. E., RUBLE, D. N., HODGES, K. L., & SMALL, A. W. (1976). Cognitive-developmental factors in emerging sex differences in achievement-related expectancies. *The Journal of Social Issues, 32,* 47–62.

PARSONS, T. (1951). *The social system.* Glencoe, IL: Free Press.

PARSONS, T. (1955). Family structure and the socialization of the child. In T. Parsons & R. F. Bales, *Family, socialization, and interaction process* (pp. 35–131). Glencoe, IL: Free Press.

PARTON, D. A. (1970). Imitation of an animated puppet as a function of modeling, praise, and direction. *Journal of Experimental Child Psychology, 9,* 320–329.

PARTON, D. A. (1976). Learning to imitate in infancy. *Child Development, 47,* 14–31.

PATERNOSTER, R. (1983). Race of victim and location of crime: The decision to seek the death penalty in

South Carolina. *The Journal of Criminal Law & Criminology, 74,* 754–785.

PATERNOSTER, R., SALTZMAN, L. E., WALDO, G. P., & CHIRICOS, T. G. (1983). Perceived risk and social control: Do sanctions really deter? *Law & Society Review, 17,* 457–479.

PATKAI, P. (1971). Catecholamine excretion in pleasant and unpleasant situations. *Acta Psychologica, 35,* 352–363.

PATTERSON, G. R. (1976). The aggressive child: Victim and architect of a coercive system. In E. J. Mash, L. A. Hamerlynck, & L. C. Handy (Eds.), *Behavior modification and families* (pp. 267–316). New York: Brunner/Mazel.

PATTERSON, G. R. (1982). *A social learning approach* (Vol. 3). *Coercive family process.* Eugene, OR: Castalia.

PATTERSON, G. R., DISHION, T. J., & BANK, L. (1984). Family interaction: A process model of deviancy training. *Aggressive Behavior, 10,* 253–267.

PATTERSON, G. R., & REID, J. B. (1973). Intervention for families of aggressive boys: A replication study. *Behaviour Research and Therapy, 11,* 383–394.

PAULUS, P. B., & SETA, J. J. (1975). The vicarious partial reinforcement effect: An empirical and theoretical analysis. *Journal of Personality and Social Psychology, 31,* 930–936.

PAWLBY, S. J. (1977). Imitative interaction. In H. R. Schaffer (Ed.), *Studies in mother-infant interaction* (pp. 203–224). London: Academic Press.

PEABODY, G. L. (1971). Power, Alinsky, and other thoughts. In H. A. Hornstein, B. B. Bunker, W. W. Burke, M. Gindes, & R. J. Lewicki (Eds.), *Social intervention: A behavioral science approach* (pp. 521–532). New York: Free Press.

PEAKE, P. K., & LUTSKY, N. S. (1981). *Exploring the generality of "predicting some of the people some of the time": The Carleton Student Behavior Study.* Unpublished manuscript, Stanford University, Stanford, CA.

PEED, S., & FOREHAND, R. (1973). Effects of different amounts and types of vicarious consequences upon imitative performance. *Journal of Experimental Child Psychology, 16,* 508–520.

PELZ, D. C. (1983). Use of information channels in urban innovations. *Knowledge, 5,* 3–25.

Peninsula Times Tribune. (1979, July 6). Honest man finds $34,520, searches 3 days to find owner. P. 5.

Peninsula Times Tribune. (1980, March 22). The return of pilfered silver. P. A-5.

PEPITONE, A., McCAULEY, C., & HAMMOND, P. (1967). Change in attractiveness of forbidden toys as a function of severity of threat. *Journal of Experimental Social Psychology, 3,* 221–229.

PERLMUTER, L. C., & MONTY, R. A. (Eds.). (1979). *Choice and perceived control.* Hillsdale, NJ: Erlbaum.

PERRI, M. G., & RICHARDS, C. S. (1977). An investigation of naturally occurring episodes of self-controlled behaviors. *Journal of Counseling Psychology, 24,* 178–183.

PERRI, M. G., RICHARDS, C. S., & SCHULTHEIS, K. R. (1977). Behavioral self-control and smoking reduction: A study of self-initiated attempts to reduce smoking. *Behavior Therapy, 8,* 360–365.

PERRY, D. G., & BUSSEY, K. (1979). The social learning theory of sex differences: Imitation is alive and well. *Journal of Personality and Social Psychology, 37,* 1699–1712.

PERRY, D. G., & BUSSEY, K. (1984). *Social development.* Englewood Cliffs, NJ: Prentice-Hall.

PERRY, D. G., & PERRY, L. C. (1983). Social learning, causal attribution, and moral internalization. In J. Bisanz, G. L. Bisanz, & R. Kail (Eds.), *Learning in children: Progress in cognitive development research* (pp. 105–136). New York: Springer-Verlag.

PERRY, D. G., PERRY, L. C., BUSSEY, K., ENGLISH, D., & ARNOLD, G. (1980). Processes of attribution and children's self-punishment following misbehavior. *Child Development, 51,* 545–551.

PERRY, D. G., PERRY, L. C., & RASMUSSEN, P. (1985). Aggressive children believe that aggression is easy to perform and leads to rewards. *Child Development.*

PERRY, H. M. (1939). The relative efficiency of actual and "imaginary" practice in five selected tasks. *Archives of Psychology, 34*(No. 243).

PERVIN, L. A., & LEWIS, M. (Eds.). (1978). *Perspectives in interactional psychology.* New York: Plenum.

PETERS, R. S. (1966). *Ethics and education.* London: Allen & Unwin.

PETERS, R. S. (1971). Moral development: A plea for pluralism. In T. Mischel (Ed.), *Cognitive development and epistemology* (pp. 237–267). New York: Academic Press.

PETERSON, C., & SELIGMAN, M. E. P. (1984). Casual explanations as a risk factor for depression: Theory and evidence. *Psychological Review, 91,* 347–374.

PETERSON, D. R. (1968). *The clinical study of social behavior.* New York: Appleton-Century-Crofts.

PETERSON, M. S., & BRAIKER, H. B. (1981). *Who commits crimes: A survey of prison inmates.* Cambridge, MA: Oelgeschlager, Gunn & Hain.

PETERSON, R. A., & KERIN, R. A. (1979). The female role in advertisements: Some experimental evidence. *Journal of Marketing, 41*(4), 59–63.

PETERSON, R. F., MERWIN, M. R., MOYER, T. J., & WHITEHURST, G. J. (1971). Generalized imitation: The effects of experimenter absence, differential reinforcement, and stimulus complexity. *Journal of Experimental Child Psychology, 12,* 114–128.

PETO, R. (1979). Detection of risk of cancer in man. *Proceedings of the Royal Society of London, Series B. Biological Sciences, 205,* 111–120.

PETTIGREW, T. F. (1963). Actual gains and psychological losses: The Negro American protest. *Journal of Negro Education, 32,* 493–506.

PEW, R. W. (1974). Human perceptual-motor performance. In B. H. Kantowitz (Ed.), *Human information processing: Tutorials in performance and cognition* (pp. 1–39). Hillsdale, NJ: Erlbaum.

PHARES, E. J. (1976). *Locus of control in personality.* Morristown, NJ: General Learning Press.

PHILLIPS, D. C., & ORTON, R. (1983). The new causal principle of cognitive learning theory: Perspectives on Bandura's "reciprocal determinism." *Psychological Review, 90,* 158–165.

PHILLIPS, D. P. (1974). The influence of suggestion on

suicide: Substantive and theoretical implications of the Werther effect. *American Sociological Review, 39,* 340–354.

PHILLIPS, D. P. (1977). Motor vehicle fatalities increase just after publicized suicide stories. *Science, 196,* 1464–1465.

PHILLIPS, D. P. (1980). The deterrent effect of capital punishment—New evidence on an old controversy. *American Journal of Sociology, 86,* 139–148.

PHILLIPS, D. P. (1983). The impact of mass media violence on U.S. homicides. *American Sociological Review, 48,* 560–568.

PHILLIPS, D. P. (1985). The found experiment: A new technique for assessing impact of mass media violence on real-world aggressive behavior. In G. Comstock (Ed.), *Public Communication and Behavior* (Vol. 1). New York: Academic Press.

PHILLIPS, E. L., PHILLIPS, E. A., WOLF, M. M., & FIXSEN, D. L. (1973). Achievement place: Development of the elected manager system. *Journal of Applied Behavior Analysis, 6,* 541–561.

PHILLIPS, J. S., & LORD, R. G. (1980). Determinants of intrinsic motivation: Locus of control and competence information as components of Deci cognitive evaluation theory. *Journal of Applied Psychology, 65,* 211–218.

PHILLIPS, R. E. (1968). Vicarious reinforcement and imitation in a verbal learning situation. *Journal of Experimental Psychology, 76,* 669–670.

PHILLIPS, S., & LEVINE, M. (1975). Probing for hypotheses with adults and children: Blank trials and introtacts. *Journal of Experimental Psychology: General, 104,* 327–354.

PIAGET, J. (1948). *The moral judgment of the child.* Glencoe, IL: Free Press.

PIAGET, J. (1950). *The psychology of intelligence.* New York: International Universities Press.

PIAGET, J. (1951). *Play, dreams, and imitation in childhood.* New York: Norton.

PIAGET, J. (1960). Equilibration and development of logical structures. In J. M. Tanner & B. Inhelder (Eds.), *Discussions on child development* (Vol. 4). New York: International Universities Press.

PIAGET, J., & INHELDER, B. (1969). *The psychology of the child.* New York: Basic Books.

PINGREE, S., & HAWKINS, R. (1981). U.S. programs on Australian television: The cultivation effect. *The Journal of Communication, 31,* 97–105.

PITCHER, B. L., HAMBLIN, R. L., & MILLER, J. L. L. (1978). The diffusion of collective violence. *American Sociological Review, 43,* 23–35.

PLIMPTON, G. (1965). Ernest Hemingway. In G. Plimpton (Ed.), *Writers at work: The Paris Review interviews* (2nd ser.). New York: Viking.

POEL, D. H. (1976). The diffusion of legislation among the Canadian provinces: A statistical analysis. *Canadian Journal of Political Science, 9,* 605–626.

POLSKY, H. W. (1962). *Cottage six: The social system of delinquent boys in residential treatment.* New York: Russell Sage Foundation.

POOL, I. DE S. (1979). Direct broadcast satellites and the integrity of national cultures. In K. Nordenstreng & H. I. Schiller (Eds.), *National sovereignty and international communication* (pp. 120–153). Norwood, NJ: Ablex Publishing.

PORPORA, D. V. (1980). Operant conditioning and teleology. *Philosophy of Science, 47,* 568–582.

PORRAS, J. I., HARGIS, K., PATTERSON, K. J., MAXFIELD, D. G., ROBERTS, N., & BIES, R. J. (1982). Modeling-based organizational development: A longitudinal assessment. *Journal of Applied Behavioral Science, 18,* 433–446.

PORRO, C. R. (1968). Effects of the observation of a model's affective responses to her own transgression on resistance to temptation in children. *Dissertation Abstracts, 28,* 3064.

Portland Press-Herald (ME). (1963, November 28). It looked easy on TV, says man held in killing here. P.1.

POSNER, M. I. (1973). *Cognition: An introduction.* Glenview, IL: Scott, Foresman.

POWDERMAKER, H. (1933). *Life in Lesu.* New York: Norton.

POWELL, G. E. (1973). Negative and positive mental practice in motor skill acquisition. *Perceptual and Motor Skills, 37,* 312.

POWELL, R. W., & BURNS, R. (1970). Visual factors in observational learning in rats. *Psychonomic Science, 21,* 47.

POWERS, L. H. (1978). Knowledge by deduction. *The Philosophical Review, 87,* 337–371.

POWERS, P. C., & GEEN, R. G. (1972). Effects of the behavior and the perceived arousal of a model on instrumental aggression. *Journal of Personality and Social Psychology, 23,* 175–183.

POWERS, T. (1971). *Diana: The making of a terrorist.* Boston: Houghton Mifflin.

PRATT, R. J. (1972). Children's reversal-shift performance as a function of age, attention, and trial-by-trial outcome rules. *Dissertation Abstracts International, 32,* 4903B-4904B. (University Microfilms No. 72–7035, 161).

PREMACK, D. (1965). Reinforcement theory. In D. Levine (Ed.), *Nebraska Symposium on Motivation* (Vol. 13, pp. 123–180). Lincoln: University of Nebraska Press.

PREMACK, D. (1971). Catching up with common sense or two sides of a generalization: Reinforcement and punishment. In R. Glaser (Ed.), *The nature of reinforcement* (pp. 121–150). New York: Academic Press.

PREMACK, D. (1976). *Intelligence in ape and man.* Hillsdale, NJ: Erlbaum.

PREMACK, D. (1983). Animal cognition. *Annual Review of Psychology, 34,* 351–362.

PRESBIE, R. J., & COITEUX, P. F. (1971). Learning to be generous or stingy: Imitation of sharing behavior as a function of model generosity and vicarious reinforcement. *Child Development, 42,* 1033–1038.

PRETTY, G. H., & SELIGMAN, C. (1984). Affect and the overjustification effect. *Journal of Personality and Social Psychology, 46,* 1241–1253.

PRITCHARD, R. D., & CURTIS, M. I. (1973). The

influence of goal setting and financial incentives on task performance. *Organizational Behavior and Human Performance, 10,* 175–183.

PUSKA, P., NISSINEN, A., SALONEN, J. T., & TOUMILEHTO, J. (1983). Ten years of the North Karelia project: Results with community-based prevention of coronary heart disease. *Scandinavian Journal of Social Medicine, 11,* 65–68.

PYLYSHYN, Z. W. (1973). What the mind's eye tells the mind's brain: A critique of mental imagery. *Psychological Bulletin, 80,* 1–24.

PYLYSHYN, Z. W. (1981). The imagery debate: Analogue versus tacit knowledge. *Psychological Review, 88,* 16–45.

RACHLIN, H. (1974). Self-control. *Behaviorism, 2,* 94–107.

RACHMAN, S. (1966). Sexual fetishism: An experimental analogue. *Psychological Record, 16,* 293–296.

RACHMAN, S. (1972). Clinical applications of observational learning, imitation and modeling. *Behavior Therapy, 3,* 379–397.

RACHMAN, S. (1977). The conditioning theory of fear-acquisition: A critical reexamination. *Behaviour Research and Therapy, 15,* 375–387.

RACHMAN, S. (Ed.). (1978). Perceived self-efficacy: Analysis of Bandura's theory of behavioural change. *Advances in Behaviour Research and Therapy, 1*(Whole No. 4).

RACHMAN, S., & HODGSON, R. J. (1980). *Obsessions and compulsions.* Englewood Cliffs, NJ: Prentice-Hall.

RACHMAN S., & SELIGMAN, M. E. P. (1976). Unprepared phobias: "Be prepared." *Behaviour Research and Therapy, 14,* 333–338.

RACHMAN, S., & TEASDALE, J. (1969). *Aversion therapy and behaviour disorders: An analysis.* Coral Gables, FL: University of Miami Press.

RACHMAN, S. J., & WILSON, G. T. (1980). *The effects of psychological therapy* (2nd enlarged ed.). Oxford: Pergamon.

RAIFMAN, I. (1957). Level of aspiration in a group of peptic ulcer patients. *Journal of Consulting Psychology, 21,* 229–321.

RAKESTRAW, T. L., JR., & WEISS, H. M. (1981). The interaction of social influences and task experience on goals, performance, and performance satisfaction. *Organizational Behavior and Human Performance, 27,* 326–344.

RAMEL, C., & RANNUG, U. (1980). Short-term mutagenicity tests. *Journal of Toxicology and Environmental Health, 6,* 1065–1076.

RAMEY, C. T., & FINKELSTEIN, N. W. (1978). Contingent stimulation and infant competence. *Journal of Pediatric Psychology, 3,* 89–96.

RAMIREZ, J., BRYANT, J., & ZILLMANN, D. (1982). Effects of erotica on retaliatory behavior as a function of level of prior provocation. *Journal of Personality and Social Psychology, 43,* 971–978.

RASKIN, P. A., & ISRAEL, A. C. (1981). Sex-role imitation in children: Effects of sex of child, sex of model, and sex-role appropriateness of modeled behavior. *Sex Roles, 7,* 1067–1076.

RASMUSSEN, N. C. (1981). The application of probabilistic risk assessment techniques to energy technologies. *Annual Review of Energy, 6,* 123–138.

RAUSH, H. L. (1965). Interaction sequences. *Journal of Personality and Social Psychology, 2,* 487–499.

RAUSH, H. L., BARRY, W. A., HERTEL, R. K., & SWAIN, M. A. (1974). *Communication, conflict, and marriage.* San Francisco: Jossey-Bass.

RAWLINGS, E. I., RAWLINGS, I. L., CHEN, S. S., & YILK, M. D. (1972). The facilitating effects of mental rehearsal in the acquisition of rotary pursuit tracking. *Psychonomic Science, 26,* 71–73.

REAGAN, N., & LIBBY, B. (1980). *Nancy.* New York: Morrow.

REDD, W. H. (1976). The effects of adult presence and stated preference on the reinforcement control of children's behavior. *Merrill-Palmer Quarterly of Behavior and Development, 22,* 93–98.

REDD, W. H., & BIRNBRAUER, J. S. (1969). Adults as discriminative stimuli for different reinforcement contingencies with retarded children. *Journal of Experimental Child Psychology, 7,* 440–447.

REESE, L. (1983). *Coping with pain: The role of perceived self-efficacy.* Unpublished doctoral dissertation, Stanford University, Stanford, CA.

REHM, L. P. (1977). A self-control model of depression. *Behavior Therapy, 8,* 787–804.

REHM, L. P. (1982). Self-management in depression. In P. Karoly & F. H. Kanfer (Eds.), *Self-management and behavior change: From theory to practice* (pp. 522–567). New York: Pergamon.

REICHARD, G. A. (1938). Social life. In F. Boas (Ed.), *General anthropology.* Boston: Heath.

REID, J. B., & PATTERSON, G. R. (1976). The modification of aggression and stealing behavior of boys in the home setting. In E. Ribes-Inesta & A. Bandura (Eds.), *Analysis of delinquency and aggression* (pp. 123–145). Hillsdale, NJ: Erlbaum.

REIFLER, C. B., HOWARD, J., LIPTON, M. A., LIPTZIN, M. B., & WIDMANN, D. E. (1971). Pornography: An experimental study of effects. *American Journal of Psychiatry, 128,* 575–582.

REISENZEIN, R. (1983). The Schachter theory of emotion: Two decades later. *Psychological Bulletin, 94,* 239–264.

REISS, A. J., JR. (1965). *Social organization and socialization: Variations on a theme about generations.* Working paper 1, Center for Research on Social Organization, University of Michigan, Ann Arbor, MI.

RELICH, J. D. (1983). *Attribution and its relation to other affective variables in predicting and inducing arithmetic achievement: An attributional approach to increased self-efficacy and achievement in arithmetic.* Unpublished doctoral dissertation, University of Sydney, Sydney, Australia.

RENNER, K. E. (1964). Delay of reinforcement: A historical review. *Psychological Bulletin, 61,* 341–361.

RESCHLY, D. J., & MITTMAN, A. (1973). The relationship of self-esteem status and task ambiguity to the self-reinforcement behavior of children. *Developmental Psychology, 9,* 16–19.

RESCORLA, R. A. (1978). Some implications of a cognitive perspective on Pavlovian conditioning. In S. H. Hulse, H. Fowler, & W. K. Honig (Eds.), *Cognitive processes in animal behavior* (pp. 15–50). Hillsdale, NJ: Erlbaum.

RESCORLA, R. A. (1980). *Pavlovian second-order conditioning: Studies in associative learning.* Hillsdale, NJ: Erlbaum.

RESCORLA, R. A., & SOLOMON, R. L. (1967). Two-process learning theory: Relationships between Pavlovian conditioning and instrumental learning. *Psychological Review, 74*, 141–182.

REST, J. R. (1973). Patterns of preference and comprehension in moral judgment. *Journal of Personality, 41*, 86–109.

REST, J. R. (1975). Longitudinal study of the defining issues test of moral judgment: A strategy for analyzing developmental change. *Developmental Psychology, 11*, 738–748.

REST, J. R., TURIEL, E., & KOHLBERG, L. (1969). Level of moral development as a determinant of preference and comprehension of moral judgments made by others. *Journal of Personality, 37*, 225–252.

REYNOLDS, R., CREER, T. L., HOLROYD, K. A., & TOBIN, D. L. (1982, November). *Assessment in the treatment of cigarette smoking: The development of the smokers' self-efficacy scale.* Paper presented at the meeting of the Association of Behavior Therapy, Los Angeles.

RHEINGOLD, H. L., & COOK, K. V. (1975). The context of boys' and girls' rooms as an index of parents' behavior. *Child Development, 46*, 459–463.

RHEINGOLD, H. L., STANLEY, W. C., & DOYLE, G. A. (1964). Visual and auditory reinforcement of a manipulatory response in the young child. *Journal of Experimental Child Psychology, 1*, 316–326.

RHODE, G., MORGAN, D. P., & YOUNG, K. R. (1983). Generalization and maintenance of treatment gains of behaviorally handicapped students from resource rooms to regular classrooms using self-evaluation procedures. *Journal of Applied Behavior Analysis, 16*, 171–188.

RICE, M. (1984). Cognitive aspects of communicative development. In R. L. Schiefelbusch & J. Pickar (Eds.), *The acquisition of communicative competence* (pp. 141–189). Baltimore, MD: University Park Press.

RICE, R. E., & ROGERS, E. M. (1980). Reinvention in the innovation process. *Knowledge: Creation, diffusion, utilization, 1*, 499–514.

RICHARDS, C. S. (1975). Behavior modification of studying through study skills advice and self-control procedures. *Journal of Counseling Psychology, 22*, 431–436.

RICHARDSON, A. (1967). Mental practice: A review and discussion. Part I. *Research Quarterly, 38*, 95–107.

RICHARDSON, J. T. (Ed.). (1978). *Conversion careers: In and out of the new religions.* Beverly Hills: Sage.

RIESMAN, D. (1950). *The lonely crowd.* New Haven: Yale University Press.

RIME, B., & BONAMI, M. (1976). Goal-setting behaviour and coronary heart disease. *The British Journal of Social and Clinical Psychology, 15*, 287–294.

RINCOVER, A., & KOEGEL, R. L. (1977). Research on the education of autistic children: Recent advances and future directions. In B. B. Lahey & A. E. Kazdin (Eds.), *Advances in clinical child psychology* (Vol. 1, pp. 329–359). New York: Plenum.

RITTER, B. (1969). Eliminating excessive fears of the environment through contact desensitization. In J. B. Krumboltz & C. E. Thoresen (Eds.), *Behavioral counseling: Cases and techniques* (pp. 168–178). New York: Holt, Rinehart & Winston.

RITTER, E. H., & HOLMES, D. S. (1969). Behavioral contagion: Its occurrence as a function of differential restraint reduction. *Journal of Experimental Research in Personality, 3*, 242–246.

RIZLEY, R. (1978). Depression and distortion in the attribution of causality. *Journal of Abnormal Psychology, 87*, 32–48.

ROBERTS, D. F. (1978). One highly attracted public. In G. Comstock, S. Chaffee, N. Katzman, M. McCombs, & D. Roberts (Eds.), *Television and human behavior* (pp. 173–287). New York: Columbia University Press.

ROBERTS, R. N. (1979). Private speech in academic problem-solving: A naturalistic perspective. In G. Zivin (Ed.), *The development of self-regulation through private speech* (pp. 295–323). New York: Wiley.

ROBERTSON, T. S. (1971). *Innovative behavior and communication.* New York: Holt, Rinehart & Winston.

RODIN, J., & LANGER, E. J. (1977). Long-term effects of a control-relevant intervention with the institutionalized aged. *Journal of Personality and Social Psychology, 35*, 897–902.

ROGERS, C. R. (1959). A theory of therapy, personality, and interpersonal relationships, as developed in the client-centered framework. In S. Koch (Ed.), *Psychology: A study of a science (Vol. III). Formulations of the person and the social context* (pp. 184–256). New York: McGraw-Hill.

ROGERS, E. M. (1983). *Diffusion of innovations* (3rd ed.). New York: Free Press.

ROGERS, E. M., & ADHIKARYA, R. (1979). Diffusion of innovations: Up-to-date review and commentary. In D. Nimmo (Ed.), *Communication Yearbook 3* (pp. 67–81). New Brunswick, NJ: Transaction Books.

ROGERS, E. M., & KINCAID, D. L. (1981). *Communication networks: Toward a new paradigm for research.* New York: The Free Press.

ROGERS, E. M. & SHOEMAKER, F. (1971). *Communication of innovations: A cross-cultural approach* (2nd ed.). New York: The Free Press.

ROKEACH, M. (1960). *The open and closed mind.* New York: Basic Books.

ROKEACH, M. (1980). Some unresolved issues in theories of beliefs, attitudes and values. In *Nebraska symposium on motivation* (Vol. 28, pp. 261–304). Lincoln: University of Nebraska Press.

ROLING, N. G., ASCROFT, J., & CHEGE, F. W. (1976). The diffusion of innovations and the issue of equity in rural development. In E. M. Rogers (Ed.), *Communication and development.* (pp. 63–79). Beverly Hills: Sage.

Romanczyk, R. G. (1974). Self-monitoring in the treatment of obesity: Parameters of reactivity. *Behavior Therapy, 5,* 531–540.

Romanczyk, R. G., Tracey, D. A., Wilson, G. T., & Thorpe, G. (1973). Behavioral techniques in the treatment of obesity: A comparative analysis. *Behaviour Research and Therapy, 11,* 629–640.

Rosch, E. (1978). Principles of categorization. In E. Rosch & B. B. Lloyd (Eds.), *Cognition and categorization* (pp. 27–48). Hillsdale, NJ: Erlbaum.

Rosekrans, M. A., & Hartup, W. W. (1967). Imitative influences of consistent and inconsistent response consequences to a model on aggressive behavior in children. *Journal of Personality and Social Psychology, 7,* 429–434.

Rosen, G. M., Rosen, E., & Reid, J. B. (1972). Cognitive desensitization and avoidance behavior: A reevaluation. *Journal of Abnormal Psychology, 80,* 176–182.

Rosenbaum, G. (1953). Stimulus generalization as a function of level of experimentally induced anxiety. *Journal of Experimental Psychology, 45,* 35–43.

Rosenbaum, G. (1956). Stimulus generalization as a function of clinical anxiety. *Journal of Abnormal and Social Psychology, 53,* 281–285.

Rosenbaum, M. E., Chalmers, D. K., & Horne, W. C. (1962). Effects of success and failure and the competence of the model on the acquisition and reversal of matching behavior. *Journal of Psychology, 54,* 251–258.

Rosenbaum, M. E., & Hewitt, O. J. (1966). The effect of electric shock on learning by performers and observers. *Psychonomic Science, 6,* 81–82.

Rosenbaum, M. E., Horne, W. C., & Chalmers, D. K. (1962). Level of self-esteem and the learning of imitation and nonimitation. *Journal of Personality, 30,* 147–156.

Rosenbaum, M. E., & Tucker, I. F. (1962). The competence of the model and the learning of imitation and nonimitation. *Journal of Experimental Psychology, 63,* 183–190.

Rosenbaum, M. S., & Drabman, R. S. (1979). Self-control training in the classroom: A review and critique. *Journal of Applied Behavior Analysis, 12,* 467–485.

Rosenberg, D. (1984). The causal connection in mass exposure cases: A "Public Law" vision of the tort system. *Harvard Law Review, 97,* 849–930.

Rosenberg, S., & Simon, H. A. (1977). Modeling semantic memory: Effects of presenting semantic information in different modalities. *Cognitive Psychology, 9,* 293–325.

Rosenfeld, H. M., & Baer, D. M. (1969). Unnoticed verbal conditioning of an aware experimenter by a more aware subject: The double-agent effect. *Psychological Review, 76,* 425–432.

Rosenfeld, H. M., & Baer, D. M. (1970). Unbiased and unnoticed verbal conditioning: The double agent robot procedure. *Journal of the Experimental Analysis of Behavior, 14,* 99–107.

Rosenfield, D., Folger, R., & Adelman, H. F. (1980). When rewards reflect competence: A qualification of the overjustification effect. *Journal of Personality and Social Psychology, 39,* 368–378.

Rosenhan, D. L. (1970). The natural socialization of altruistic autonomy. In J. Macaulay & L. Berkowitz (Eds.), *Altruism and helping behavior: Social psychological studies of some antecedents and consequences* (pp. 251–268). New York: Academic Press.

Rosenhan, D., Frederick, F., & Burrowes, A. (1968). Preaching and practicing: Effects of channel discrepancy on norm internalization. *Child Development, 39,* 291-301.

Rosenhan, D. L., Salovey, P., Karylowski, J., & Hargis, K. (1981). Emotion and altruism. In J. P. Rushton & R. M. Sorrentino (Eds.), *Altruism and helping behavior: Social, personality, and developmental perspectives* (pp. 233–248). Hillsdale, NJ: Erlbaum.

Rosenhan, D., & White, G. M. (1967). Observation and rehearsal as determinants of prosocial behavior. *Journal of Personality and Social Psychology, 5,* 424–431.

Rosenholtz, S. J., & Rosenholtz, S. H. (1981). Classroom organization and the perception of ability. *Sociology of Education, 54,* 132–140.

Rosenthal, B., & McSweeney, F. K. (1979). Modeling influences on eating behavior. *Addictive Behaviors, 4,* 205–214.

Rosenthal, T. L. (1980). Modeling approaches to test anxiety and related performance problems. In I. G. Sarason (Ed.), *Text anxiety* (pp. 245–270). Hillsdale, NJ: Erlbaum.

Rosenthal, T. L., & Bandura, A. (1978). Psychological modeling: Theory and practice. In S. L. Garfield & A. E. Bergin (Eds.), *Handbook of psychotherapy and behavior change: An empirical analysis* (2nd ed.) (pp. 621–658). New York: Wiley.

Rosenthal, T. L., & Reese, S. L. (1976). The effects of covert and overt modeling on assertive behavior. *Behaviour Research and Therapy, 14,* 463–469.

Rosenthal, T. L., & Zimmerman, B. J. (1978). *Social learning and cognition.* New York: Academic Press.

Rosenthal, T. L., Zimmerman, B. J., & Durning, K. (1970). Observationally-induced changes in children's interrogative classes. *Journal of Personality and Social Psychology, 16,* 681–688.

Ross, H. L. (1973). Law, science, and accidents: The British Road Safety Act of 1967. *Journal of Legal Studies, 2,* 1–78.

Ross, H. L. (1982). *Deterring the drinking driver.* Lexington, MA: Lexington Books.

Ross, H. L., & Campbell, D. T. (1968). The Connecticut speed crackdown: A study of the effects of legal change. In H. L. Ross (Ed.), *Perspectives on the social order: Readings in sociology* (pp. 30–35). New York: McGraw-Hill.

Ross, L. (1977). The intuitive psychologist and his shortcomings: Distortions in the attribution process. In L. Berkowitz (Ed.), *Advances in experimental social psychology* (Vol. 10, pp. 174–220). New York: Academic Press.

Ross, M. (1976). The self-perception of intrinsic motivation. In J. H. Harvey, W. J. Ickes, & R. F. Kidd (Eds.), *New directions in attribution research* (Vol. 1, pp. 121–141). Hillsdale, NJ: Erlbaum.

Ross, M. (1981). Self-centered biases in attributions of responsibility: Antecedents and consequences. In E. T. Higgins, C. P. Herman, & M. P. Zanna (Eds.), *Social cognition: The Ontario symposium* (Vol. 1, pp. 305–321). Hillsdale, NJ: Erlbaum.

Ross, S. A. (1971). A test of the generality of the effects of deviant preschool models. *Developmental Psychology, 4,* 262–267.

Rothstein, A. L., & Arnold, R. K. (1976). Bridging the gap: Application of research on videotape feedback and bowling. *Motor Skills: Theory into Practice, 1,* 35–62.

Rotter, J. B. (1954). *Social learning and clinical psychology.* Englewood Cliffs, NJ: Prentice-Hall.

Rotter, J. B. (1966). Generalized expectancies for internal versus external control of reinforcement. *Psychological Monographs, 80*(1, Whole No. 609).

Rotter, J. B., Chance, J. E., & Phares, E. J. (1972). *Applications of a social learning theory of personality.* New York: Holt, Rinehart & Winston.

Rozensky, R. H., & Bellack, A. S. (1974). Behavior change and individual differences in self-control. *Behaviour Research and Therapy, 12,* 267–268.

Rozensky, R. H., & Bellack, A. S. (1976). Individual differences in self-reinforcement style and performance in self-controlled and therapist-controlled weight reduction programs. *Behaviour Research and Therapy, 14,* 357–364.

Rule, B. G., & Nesdale, A. R. (1976). Moral judgments of aggressive behavior. In R. G. Geen & E. C. O'Neal (Eds.), *Perspectives on aggression* (pp. 37–60). New York: Academic Press.

Rumbaugh, D. M. (Ed.). (1977). *Language learning by a chimpanzee: The Lana project.* New York: Academic Press.

Rush, A. J., Beck, A. T., Kovacs, M., & Hollon, S. (1977). Comparative efficacy of cognitive therapy and pharmacotherapy in the treatment of depressed outpatients. *Cognitive Therapy and Research, 1,* 17–37.

Rushton, J. P. (1975). Generosity in children: Immediate and long-term effects of modeling, preaching, and moral judgment. *Journal of Personality and Social Psychology, 21,* 459–466.

Rushton, J. P. (1980). *Altruism, socialization, and society.* Englewood Cliffs, NJ: Prentice-Hall.

Rushton, J. P., Brainerd, C. J., & Pressley, M. (1983). Behavioral development and construct validity: The principle of aggregation. *Psychological Bulletin, 94,* 39–53.

Russell, J. C., Wilson, D. O., & Jenkins, J. F. (1976). Informational properties of jaywalking models as determinants of imitated jaywalking: An extension to model sex, race and number. *Sociometry, 39,* 270–273.

Ryan, T. A. (1970). *Intentional behavior.* New York: Ronald Press.

Rybstein, J., & Blinchik, J. (1979). Effects of different cognitive strategies on chronic pain experience. *Journal of Behavioral Medicine, 2,* 93–101.

Rychlak, J. F. (1979). A nontelic teleology? *American Psychologist 34,* 435–438.

Rychlak, J. F. (1981). Logical learning theory: Propositions, corollaries, and research evidence. *Journal of Personality and Social Psychology, 40,* 731–749.

Rychtarik, R. G., Fairbank, J. A., Allen, C. M., Roy, D. W., & Drabman, R. S. (1983). Alcohol use in television programming: Effects on children's behavior. *Addictive Behaviors, 8,* 19–22.

Sabido, M. (1981). *Towards the social use of soap operas.* Mexico City, Mexico: Institute for Communication Research.

Sachs, D. H., & Duffy, K. G. (1976). Effect of modeling on sexual imagery. *Archives of Sexual Behavior, 5,* 301–311.

Sackett, R. S., (1935). The relationship between amount of symbolic rehearsal and retention of a maze habit. *Journal of General Psychology, 13,* 113–130.

Safire, W. (1979, May 13). The fine art of euphemism. *San Francisco Chronicle,* p. 13.

Sagotsky, G., & Lepper, M. R. (1982). Generalization of changes in children's preferences for easy or difficult goals induced through observational learning. *Child Development, 53,* 372–375.

Sagotsky, G., & Lewis, A. (1978, August). *Extrinsic reward, positive verbalizations, and subsequent intrinsic interest.* Paper presented at the meeting of the American Psychological Association, Toronto.

St. Peter, S. (1979). Jack went up the hill . . . but where was Jill? *Psychology of Women Quarterly, 4,* 256–260.

Salancik, G. R. (1975). Interaction effects of performance and money on self-perception of intrinsic motivation. *Organizational Behavior and Human Performance, 13,* 339–35l.

Sallows, G. O., Dawes, R. M., & Lichtenstein, E. (1971). Subjective value of the reinforcer (RSv) and performance: Crux of the S-R versus cognitive mediation controversy. *Journal of Experimental Psychology, 89,* 274–281.

Salomon, G. (1979). *Interaction of media, cognition, and learning: An explanation of how symbolic forms cultivate mental skills and affect knowledge acquisition.* San Francisco: Jossey-Bass.

Salomon, G. (1983). The differential investment of mental effort in learning from different sources. *Educational Psychologist, 18,* 42–50.

Salomon, G. (1984). Television is "easy" and print is "tough": The differential investment of mental effort in learning as a function of perceptions and attributions. *Journal of Educational Psychology, 76,* 647–658.

Sanday, P. R. (1981). The socio-cultural context of rape: A cross-cultural study. *The Journal of Social Issues, 37,* 5–27.

San Francisco Chronicle. (1971, November 26). "Hijacker's slick parachute escape." P. 1.

San Francisco Chronicle. (1972, April 8). "Hijacker used 'beeper.' " P. 5.

San Francisco Chronicle. (1975, November 16). "71, He takes a chance on crime—and losses." P. 9.

San Francisco Chronicle. (1979a, November 22). "Award-winning nuclear jargon." P. 24.

San Francisco Chronicle. (1979b, April 22). "Would you believe it?", p. B5.

SANDERS, M. R., & JAMES, J. E. (1983). The modification of parent behavior: A review of generalization and maintenance. *Behavior Modification, 7,* 3–28.

SANDERS, S. H. (1979). Behavioral assessment and treatment of clinical pain: Appraisal of current status. In M. Hersen, R. M. Eisler, & P. M. Miller (Eds.), *Progress in behavior modification* (Vol. 8, pp. 249–291). New York: Academic Press.

SANDLER, J., & QUAGLIANO, J. (1964). *Punishment in a signal avoidance situation.* Paper presented at the meeting of the Southeastern Psychological Association, Gatlinburg, TN.

SANFORD, N., & COMSTOCK, C. (1971). *Sanctions for evil.* San Francisco: Jossey-Bass.

SANTOGROSSI, D. A., O'LEARY, K. D., ROMANCZYK, R. G., & KAUFMAN, K. F. (1973). Self-evaluation by adolescents in a psychiatric hospital school token program. *Journal of Applied Behavior Analysis, 6,* 277–287.

SARASON, I. G. (1975a). Anxiety and self-preoccupation. In I. G. Sarason & D. C. Spielberger (Eds.), *Stress and anxiety* (Vol. 2, pp. 27–44). Washington, DC: Hemisphere.

SARASON, I. G. (1975b). Test anxiety and the self-disclosing coping model. *Journal of Consulting and Clinical Psychology, 43,* 148–153.

SARASON, I. G. (1978). The test anxiety scale: Concept and research. In C. D. Spielberger & I. G. Sarason (Eds.), *Stress and anxiety* (Vol. 5, pp. 193–216). Washington, DC: Hemisphere.

SAWIN, D. B. (1979). *Assessing empathy in children: A search for an elusive construct.* Paper presented at the meetings of the Society for Research in Child Development, San Francisco.

SCASE, R. (1974). Relative deprivation: A comparison of English and Swedish manual workers. In D. Wedderburn (Ed.), *Poverty, inequity and class structure* (pp. 197–216). London: Cambridge University Press.

SCHACHTER, S. (1964). The interaction of cognitive and physiological determinants of emotional state. In L. Berkowitz (Ed.), *Advances in experimental social psychology* (Vol. 1, pp. 49–80). New York: Academic Press.

SCHACTER, S. (1982). Recidivism and self-cure of smoking and obesity. *American Psychologist, 37,* 436–444.

SCHACHTER, S., & SINGER, J. E. (1962). Cognitive, social, and physiological determinants of emotional state. *Psychological Review, 69,* 379–399.

SCHACHTER, S., & SINGER, J. E. (1979). Comments on the Maslach and Marshall-Zimbardo experiments.

Journal of Personality and Social Psychology, 37, 989–995.

SCHAIE, K. W. (1974). Translations in gerontology—from lab to life: Intellectual functioning. *American Psychologist, 29,* 802–807.

SCHAIE, K. W. (1979). The primary mental abilities in adulthood: An exploration in the development of psychometric intelligence. In P. B. Baltes & O. G. Brim, Jr. (Eds.), *Life-span development and behavior* (Vol. 2, pp. 68–116). New York: Academic Press.

SCHAUER, F. F. (1975). Obscenity and the conflict of laws. *West Virginia Law Review, 77,* 377–400.

SCHILLER, H. I. (1971). *Mass communications and American empire.* Boston: Beacon.

SCHLEIFER, M., & DOUGLAS, V. I. (1973). Effects of training on the moral judgment of young children. *Journal of Personality and Social Psychology, 28,* 62–68.

SCHLESINGER, I. M. (1982). *Steps to language: Toward a theory of native language acquisition.* Hillsdale, NJ: Erlbaum.

SCHMIDT, G. (1975). Male-female differences in sexual arousal and behavior during and after exposure to sexually explicit stimuli. *Archives of Sexual Behavior, 4,* 353–365.

SCHMIDT, G., & SIGUSCH, V. (1970). Sex differences in responses to psychosexual stimulation by films and slides. *Journal of Sex Research, 6,* 268–283.

SCHMIDT, R. A. (1975). A schema theory of discrete motor skill learning. *Psychological Review, 82,* 225–260.

SCHNEIDER, D. J., HASTORF, A. H., & ELLSWORTH, P. C. (1979). *Person perception* (2nd ed.). Reading, MA: Addison-Wesley.

SCHNEIDERMAN, W. (1980). *The effects of self-evaluation procedure on the reinforcing function and errors in self-reinforcement.* Unpublished manuscript, University of Alberta, Canada.

SCHONEBAUM, R. M. (1973). A developmental study of differences in initial coding and recoding of hypothesis information. *Journal of Experimental Child Psychology, 16,* 413–423.

SCHOVER, L. R., & NEWSOM, C. D. (1976). Overselectivity, developmental level, and overtraining in autistic and normal children. *Journal of Abnormal Child Psychology, 4,* 289–298.

SCHRAMM, W. (1977). *Big media little media: Tools and technologies for instruction.* Beverly Hills: Sage.

SCHRAMM, W., & LERNER, D. (Eds.). (1976). *Communication and change in the developing countries.* Honolulu: University of Hawaii/East-West Press.

SCHREIBMAN, L. (1975). Effects of within-stimulus and extra-stimulus prompting on discrimination learning in autistic children. *Journal of Applied Behavior Analysis, 8,* 91–112.

SCHREIBMAN, L., & KOEGEL, R. L. (1982). Multiple-cue responding in autistic children. In J. Steffen & P. Karoly (Eds.), *Advances in child behavioral analysis and therapy. Autism and severe psychopathology.* (Vol. 2, pp. 81–99). Lexington, MA: D. C. Heath.

SCHROEDER, H. E., & RICH. A. R. (1976). The process of

fear reduction through systematic desensitization. *Journal of Consulting and Clinical Psychology, 44,* 191–199.

SCHUNK, D. H. (1981). Modeling and attributional effects on children's achievement: A self-efficacy analysis. *Journal of Educational Psychology, 73,* 93–105.

SCHUNK, D. H. (1982a). Effects of effort attributional feedback on children's perceived self-efficacy and achievement. *Journal of Educational Psychology, 74,* 548–556.

SCHUNK, D. H. (1982b). Verbal self-regulation as a facilitator of children's achievement and self-efficacy. *Human Learning, 1,* 265–277.

SCHUNK, D. H. (1983a). Developing children's self-efficacy and skills: The roles of social comparative information and goal setting. *Contemporary Educational Psychology, 8,* 76–86.

SCHUNK, D. H. (1983b). Reward contingencies and the development of children's skills and self-efficacy. *Journal of Educational Psychology, 75,* 511–518.

SCHUNK, D. H. (1983c). Progress self-monitoring: Effects of children's self-efficacy and achievement. *Journal of Experimental Education, 51,* 89–93.

SCHUNK, D. H. (1983d). Ability versus effort attributional feedback: Differential effects of self-efficacy and achievement. *Journal of Educational Psychology, 75,* 848–856.

SCHUNK, D. H. (1984a). Enhancing self-efficacy and achievement through rewards and goals. Motivational and informational effects. *Journal of Educational Research, 78,* 29–34.

SCHUNK, D. H. (1984b). Self-efficacy perspective on achievement behavior. *Educational Psychologist, 19,* 48–58.

SCHUNK, D. H., & GUNN, T. P. (1984). *Self-efficacy and skill development: Influence of task strategies and attributions.* Unpublished manuscript, University of Houston, TX.

SCHWAB, D. P., OLIAN-GOTTLIEB, J. D., & HENEMAN, H. G., III. (1979). Between-subjects expectancy theory research: A statistical review of studies predicting effort and performance. *Psychological Bulletin, 86,* 139–147.

SCHWARTZ, A. N., & HAWKINS, H. L. (1965). Patient models and affect statements in group therapy. *Proceedings of the 73rd Annual Convention of the APA.* Washington, DC: American Psychological Association.

SCHWARTZ, B. (1974). On going back to nature: A review of Seligman and Hager's biological boundaries of learning. *Journal of the Experimental Analysis of Behavior, 21,* 183–198.

SCHWARTZ, B. (1978). *Psychology of learning and behavior.* New York: Norton.

SCHWARTZ, B. (1982). Reinforcement-induced behavioral stereotype: How not to teach people to discover rules. *Journal of Experimental Psychology, 111,* 23–59.

SCHWARTZ, G. E. (1971). Cardiac responses to self-induced thoughts. *Psychophysiology, 8,* 462–467.

SCHWARTZ, G. E. (1972). Voluntary control of human cardiovascular integration and differentiation through feedback and reward. *Science, 175,* 90–93.

SCHWARTZ, G. E., WEINBERGER, D. A., & SINGER, J. A. (1981). Cardiovascular differentiation of happiness, sadness, anger, and fear following imagery and exercise. *Psychosomatic Medicine, 43,* 343–364.

SCHWARTZ, J. L. (1974). Relationship between goal discrepancy and depression. *Journal of Consulting and Clinical Psychology, 42,* 309.

SEARLE, J. R. (1968, December 29). A foolproof scenario for student revolts. *New York Times Magazine,* p. 4.

SEARS, P. S. (1940). Levels of aspiration in academically successful and unsuccessful children. *Journal of Abnormal and Social Psychology, 35,* 498–536.

SEARS, R. R., MACCOBY, E. E., & LEVIN, H. (1957). *Patterns of child rearing.* Evanston, IL: Row, Peterson.

SECHREST, L. (1963). Implicit reinforcement of responses. *Journal of Educational Psychology, 54,* 197–201.

SELIGMAN, M. E. P. (1971). Phobias and preparedness. *Behavior Therapy, 2,* 307–320.

SELIGMAN, M. E. P. (1975). *Helplessness: On depression, development, and death.* San Francisco: Freeman.

SELIGMAN, M. E. P., & BINIK, Y. M. (1977). The safety signal hypothesis. In H. Davis & H. Hurwitz (Eds.), *Pavlovian-operant interaction* (pp. 165–187). Hillsdale, NJ: Erlbaum.

SELIGMAN, M. E. P., & HAGER, J. L. (1972). *Biological boundaries of learning.* New York: Appleton-Century-Crofts.

SELLIN, T. (1961). Capital punishment. *Federal Probation, 25,* 3–11.

SERBIN, L. A., CONNOR, J. M., & CITRON, C. C. (1981). Sex-differentiated free play behavior: Effects of teacher modeling, location, and gender. *Developmental Psychology, 17,* 640–646.

SHAFER, J. (1965). *Self-reinforcement and the devaluation of a model.* Unpublished master's thesis, Stanford University, Stanford, CA.

SHARPLEY, C. F. (1982). Elimination of vicarious reinforcement effects within an implicit reward situation. *Journal of Educational Psychology, 74,* 611–617.

SHARPLEY, C. F. (1984). Implicit rewards as reinforcers and extinguishers. *Journal of Experimental Child Psychology, 37,* 31–40.

SHARPLEY, C. F., IRVINE, J. W., & HATTIE, J. A. (1980). Changes in performance of children's handwriting as a result of varying contingency conditions. *Alberta Journal of Educational Research, 26,* 183–193.

SHATZ, M., & GELMAN, R. (1973). The development of communication skills: Modifications in the speech of young children as a function of listener. *Monographs of the Society for Research in Child Development, 38*(5, Serial No. 152).

SHAVER, P., & KLINNERT, M. (1982). Schachter's theories of affiliation and emotion. In L. Wheeler (Ed.), *Review of personality and social psychology* (pp. 37–72). Beverly Hills: Sage.

SHAW, D. W., & THORESEN, C. E. (1974). Effects of

modeling and desensitization in reducing dentist phobia. *Journal of Counseling Psychology, 21*, 415–420.

SHAW, W. A. (1940). The relation of muscular action potentials to imaginal weight lifting. *Archives of Psychology, 35*(No. 247).

SHEFFIELD, F. D., & MACCOBY, N. (1961). Summary and interpretation of research on organizational principles in constructing filmed demonstrations. In A. A. Lumsdaine (Ed.), *Student response in programmed instruction* (pp. 117–131). Washington, DC: National Academy of Sciences–National Research Council.

SHEPARD, R. N. (1978). The mental image. *American Psychologist, 33*, 125–137.

SHEPARD, R. N., & PODGORNY, P. (1978). Cognitive processes that resemble perceptual processes. In W. K. Estes (Ed.), *Handbook of learning and cognitive processes* (Vol. 5, pp. 189–237). Hillsdale, NJ: Erlbaum.

SHERMAN, J. A. (1971). Imitation and language development. In L. P. Lipsitt & C. C. Spiker (Eds.), *Advances in child development* (Vol. 6, pp. 239–272). New York: Academic Press.

SHIFFRIN, R. M., & DUMAIS, S. T. (1981). The development of automatism. In J. R. Anderson (Ed.), *Cognitive skills and their acquisition* (pp. 111–140). Hillsdale, NJ: Erlbaum.

SHIPLEY, E. G., SMITH, C. S., & GLEITMAN, L. R. (1969). A study in the acquisition of language: Free responses to commands. *Language, 45*, 322–342.

SHIPPEE, G. E., & CHRISTIAN, M. (1978). *Ego-defensive attributions for an offensive problem: Attributions of responsibility and air pollution severity.* Paper presented at the meeting of the Western Psychological Association, San Francisco.

SHOOR, S. M., & HOLMAN, H. R. (1984). Development of an instrument to explore psychological mediators of outcome in chronic arthritis. *Transactions of the Association of American Physicians, 97*, 325–331.

SHORT, J. F., JR. (Ed.). (1968). *Gang delinquency and delinquent subcultures.* New York: Harper & Row.

SHORT, J. F., JR., & WOLFGANG, M. E. (1972). *Collective violence.* Chicago: Aldine-Atherton.

SHORTLIFFE, E. H., BUCHANAN, B. G., & FEIGENBAUM, E. A. (1979). Knowledge engineering for medical decision making: A review of computer-based clinical decision aids. *Proceedings of the IEEE, 67*, 1207–1224.

SHORTLIFFE, E. H., & FAGAN, L. M. (1983). Expert systems research: Modeling the medical decision making process. In J. S. Gravenstein, R. S. Newbower, A. K. Ream, & N. T. Smith (Eds.), *An integrated approach to monitoring* (pp. 185–202). Woburn, MA: Butterworth's.

SHRAUGER, J. S., & OSBERG, T. M. (1982). Self-awareness: The ability to predict one's future behavior. In G. Underwood, & R. Stevens (Eds.), *Aspects of consciousness (Vol. 3). Awareness and self-awareness* (pp. 267–330). New York: Academic Press.

SHWEDER, R. A. (1982). Liberalism as destiny. *Contemporary Psychology, 27*, 421–424.

SIECK, W. A., & McFALL, R. M. (1976). Some determi-nants of self-monitoring effects. *Journal of Consulting and Clinical Psychology, 44*, 958–965.

SIEGEL, A. E. (1958). The influence of violence in the mass media upon children's role expectation. *Child Development, 29*, 35–56.

SIEGEL, S. (1983). Classical conditioning, drug tolerance, and drug dependence. In R. G. Smart, F. B. Glaser, Y. Israel, H. Kalant, R. E. Popham, & W. Schmidt (Eds.), *Research advances in alcohol and drug problems* (Vol. 7, pp. 207–246). New York: Plenum.

SIGNORELLA, M. L., & LIBEN, L. S. (1984). Recall and reconstruction of gender-related pictures: Effects of attitude, task difficulty, and age. *Child Development, 55*, 393–405.

SILVER, L. B., DUBLIN, C. C., & LOURIE, R. S. (1969). Does violence breed violence? Contributions from a study of the child abuse syndrome. *American Journal of Psychiatry, 126*, 404–407.

SIMON, H. A. (1976). *Administrative behavior: A study of decision-making processes in administrative organization* (3rd ed.). New York: Free Press.

SIMON, K. M. (1979a). Self-evaluative reactions: The role of personal valuation of the activity. *Cognitive Therapy and Research, 3*, 111–116.

SIMON, K. M. (1979b). *Effects of self comparison, social comparison, and depression on goal setting and self-evaluative reactions.* Unpublished manuscript, Stanford University, Stanford, CA.

SIMON, K. M. (1979c). *Relative influence of personal standards and external incentives on complex performance.* Unpublished doctoral dissertation, Stanford University, Stanford, CA.

SIMPSON, E. L. (1974). Moral development research. *Human Development, 17*, 81–106.

SIMS, H. P., JR., & MANZ, C. C. (1982). Social learning theory: The role of modeling in the exercise of leadership. *Journal of Organizational Behavior Management, 3*, 55–63.

SINCLAIR, W. (1981, July 26). The empire built on corn flakes. *San Francisco Chronicle*, p. 5.

SINGER, B. D. (1970–71). Violence, protest and war in television news: The U.S. and Canada compared. *Public Opinion Quarterly, 34*, 611–616.

SINGER, M. T. (1979, January). Coming out of the cults. *Psychology Today*, pp. 72–82.

SINGERMAN, K. S., BORKOVEC, T. D., & BARON, R. S. (1976). Failure of a "misattribution therapy" with a clinically relevant target behavior. *Behavior Therapy, 7*, 306–313.

SKEYHILL, T. (Ed.). (1928). *Sergeant York: His own life story and war diary.* Garden City, NY: Doubleday, Doran.

SKINNER, B. F. (1948). *Walden two.* New York: Macmillan.

SKINNER, B. F. (1953). *Science and human behavior.* New York: Macmillan.

SKINNER, B. F. (1957). *Verbal behavior.* New York: Appleton-Century-Crofts.

SKINNER, B. F. (1963). Operant behavior. *American Psychologist, 18*, 503–515.

SKINNER, B. F. (1969). *Contingencies of reinforcement: A theoretical anaylysis.* New York: Appleton-Century-Crofts.

SKINNER, B. F. (1971). *Beyond freedom and dignity.* New York: Knopf.

SKINNER, B. F. (1974). *About behaviorism.* New York: Knopf.

SLABY, R. G., & CROWLEY, C. G. (1977). Modification of cooperation and aggression through teacher attention to children's speech. *Journal of Experimental Child Psychology, 23,* 442–458.

SLABY, R. G., & FREY, K. S. (1975). Development of gender constancy and selective attention to same-sex models. *Child Development, 46,* 849–856.

SLIFE, B. D., & RYCHLAK, J. F. (1982). Role of affective assessment in modeling aggressive behavior. *Journal of Personality and Social Psychology, 43,* 861–868.

SLOANE, R. B., STAPLES, F. R., CRISTOL, A. H., YORKSTON, N. J., & WHIPPLE, K. (1975). *Psychotherapy versus behavior therapy.* Cambridge, MA: Harvard University Press.

SLOBIN, D. I. (1968). Imitation and grammatical development in children. In N. S. Endler, L. R. Boulter, & H. Osser (Eds.), *Contemporary issues in developmental psychology* (pp. 437–443). New York: Holt, Rinehart & Winston.

SLOMAN, A. (1978). *The computer revolution in philosophy: Philosophy, science and models of mind.* Hassocks, Sussex: Haverster Press.

SLOVIC, P. (1983). Toward understanding and improving decisions. In W. C. Howell & E. A. Fleishman (Eds.), *Human performance and productivity* (Vol.2). *Information processing and decision making* (pp. 157–183). Hillsdale, NJ: Erlbaum.

SLOVIC, P., FISCHHOFF, B., & LICHTENSTEIN, S. (1977). Behavioral decision theory. *Annual Review of Psychology, 28,* 1–39.

SLOVIC, P., FISCHHOFF, B., & LICHTENSTEIN, S. (1977). Behavioral decision theory. In M. R. Rosenzweig & L. W. Porter (Eds.), *Annual review of psychology* (Vol. 28, pp. 1–39). Palo Alto, CA: Annual Reviews.

SLOVIC, P., FISCHHOFF, B., & LICHTENSTEIN, S. (1980). Facts and fears: Understanding perceived risk. In R. C. Schwing & W. A. Albers, Jr. (Eds.), *Societal risk assessment: How safe is safe enough* (pp. 181–214). New York: Plenum.

SLOVIC, P., FISCHHOFF, B., & LICHTENSTEIN, S. (1982). Facts versus fears: Understanding perceived risk. In D. Kahneman, P. Slovic, & A. Tversky (Eds.), *Judgment under uncertainty: Heuristics and biases* (pp. 463–489). New York: Cambridge University Press.

SLOVIC, P., & LICHTENSTEIN, S. (1971). Comparison of Bayesian and regression approaches to the study of information processing in judgment. *Organizational Behavior and Human Performance, 6,* 649–744.

SMETANA, J. G., & LETOURNEAU, K. J. (1984). Development of gender constancy and children's sex-typed free play behavior. *Developmental Psychology, 20,* 691–696.

SMITH, E. E., & MEDLIN, D. L. (1981). *Categories and concepts.* Cambridge, MA: Harvard University Press.

SMITH, E. R., & MILLER, F. D. (1978). Limits on perception of cognitive processes: A reply to Nisbett and Wilson. *Psychological Review, 85,* 355–362.

SMITH, G. H., & ENGEL, R. (1968). Influence of a female model on perceived characteristics of an automobile. *Proceedings of the 76th Annual Convention of the American Psychological Association, 3,* 681–682.

SMITH, G. P., & COLEMAN, R. E. (1977). Processes underlying generalization through participant modeling with self-directed practice. *Behaviour Research and Therapy, 15,* 204–206.

SMITH, K. U., & SMITH, M. F. (1966). *Cybernetic principles of learning and educational design.* New York: Holt, Rinehart & Winston.

SMITH, M. L., & GLASS, G. V. (1977). Meta-analysis of psychotherapy outcome studies. *American Psychologist, 32,* 752–760.

SNOW, B. (1978). Level of aspiration in coronary prone and non-coronary prone adults. *Personality and Social Psychology Bulletin, 4,* 416–419.

SNOW, C. E. (1972). Mothers' speech to children learning language. *Child Development, 43,* 549–565.

SNOW, C. E. (1977). The development of conversation between mothers and babies. *Journal of Child Language, 4,* 1–22.

SNOW, C. E., & FERGUSON, C. A. (Eds.). (1977). *Talking to children: Language input and acquisition.* Cambridge, England: Cambridge University Press.

SNOW, M. E., JACKLIN, C. N., & MACCOBY, E. E. (1983). Sex-of-child difference in father-child interaction at one year of age. *Child Development, 54,* 227–232.

SNYDER, M. (1979). Self-monitoring processes. In L. Berkowitz (Ed.), *Advances in experimental social psychology* (Vol. 12, pp. 85–128). New York: Academic Press.

SNYDER, M. (1980). Seek, and ye shall find: Testing hypotheses about other people. In E. T. Higgins, C. P. Herman, & M. P. Zanna (Eds.), *Social cognition: The Ontario symposium on personality and social psychology* (Vol. 1, pp. 105–130). Hillsdale, NJ: Erlbaum.

SNYDER, M. (1981). On the self-perpetuating nature of social stereotypes. In D. L. Hamilton (Ed.), *Cognitive processes in stereotyping and intergroup behavior* (pp. 182–212). Hillsdale, NJ: Erlbaum.

SNYDER, M., & CAMPBELL, B. H. (1982). Self-monitoring: The self in action. In J. Suls (Ed.), *Psychological perspectives on the self* (pp. 185–207). Hillsdale, NJ: Erlbaum.

SNYDER, M., TANKE, E. D., & BERSCHEID, E. (1977). Social perception and interpersonal behavior: On the self-fulfilling nature of social stereotypes. *Journal of Personality and Social Psychology, 35,* 656–666.

SOBESKY, W. E. (1983). The effects of situational factors on moral judgments. *Child Development, 54,* 575–584.

SOLOMON, R. L. (1980). The opponent-process theory of motivation: The costs of pleasure and the benefits of pain. *American Psychologist, 35,* 691–712.

SORCE, J. F., EMDE, R. N., CAMPOS, J. J., KLINNERT, M. D. (1985). Maternal emotional signaling: Its effect on the visual cliff behavior of 1-year-olds. *Development Psychology, 21,* 195–200.

Soule, J. C., & Firestone, I. J. (1975). *Model choice and achievement standards: Effects of similarity in locus of control.* Unpublished manuscript, University of Wisconsin, Milwaukee.

Speidel, G. E. (1974). Motivating effect of contingent self-reward. *Journal of Experimental Psychology, 102,* 528–530.

Spence, J. T. (1984). Gender identity and its implications for concepts of masculinity and femininity. In T. B. Sonderegger (Ed.), *Nebraska Symposium on Motivation* (Vol. 32). Lincoln: University of Nebraska Press.

Spence, J. T., & Helmreich, R. L. (1978). *Masculinity and femininity: Their psychological dimensions, correlates, and antecedents.* Austin: University of Texas Press.

Spence, J. T., & Helmreich, R. L. (1981). Androgyny versus gender schema: A comment on Bem's gender schema theory. *Psychological Review, 88,* 365–368.

Spetzler, C. S., & Stael von Holstein, C. A. (1975). Probability encoding in decision analysis. *Management Science, 22,* 340–358.

Spiegel, J. P. (1970). Campus disorders: A transactional approach. *The Psycho-Analytic Review, 57,* 472–504.

Spiegler, M. D., & Liebert, R. M. (1973). Imitation as a function of response commonality, serial order, and vicarious punishment. *Journal of Experimental Child Psychology, 15,* 116–124.

Spiegler, M. D., & Weiland, A. (1976). The effects of written vicarious consequences on observers' willingness to imitate and ability to recall modeling cues. *Journal of Personality, 44,* 260–273.

Speilberger, C. D., & DeNike, L. D. (1966). Descriptive behaviorism versus cognitive theory in verbal operant conditioning. *Psychological Review, 73,* 306–326.

Spindler, G., & Spindler, L. (1982). Do anthropologists need learning theory? *Anthropology and Education Quarterly, 13,* 109–124.

Spivack, G., Platt, J. J., & Shure, M. B. (1976). *The problem-solving approach to adjustment.* San Francisco: Jossey-Bass.

Staats, A. W. (1969). Experimental demand characteristics and the classical conditioning of attitudes. *Journal of Personality and Social Psychology, 11,* 187–192.

Staats, A. W. (1975). *Social behaviorism.* Homewood, IL: Dorsey.

Staats, A. W., & Staats, C. K. (1958). Attitudes established by classical conditioning. *Journal of Abnormal and Social Psychology, 57,* 37–40.

Staats, A. W., & Staats, C. K. (1963). *Complex human behavior.* New York: Holt, Rinehart & Winston.

Staats, C. K., & Staats, A. W. (1957). Meaning established by classical conditioning. *Journal of Experimental Psychology, 54,* 74–80.

Stagner, R. (1981). Training experiences of some distinguished psychologists. *American Psychologist, 36,* 497–505.

Starr, C., Rudman, R., & Whipple, C. (1976). Philosophical basis for risk analysis. In J. M. Hollander &
M. K. Simmons (Eds.), *Annual review of energy* (Vol. 1, pp. 629–662). Palo Alto, CA: Annual Reviews Inc.

Staub, E. (1978). *Positive social behavior and morality: Social and personal influences* (Vol.1). New York: Academic Press.

Stavrianos, L. S. (1976). *The promise of the coming dark age.* San Francisco: Freeman.

Stein, A. H. (1967). Imitation of resistance to temptation. *Child Development, 38,* 157–169.

Steinman, W. M. (1970a). Generalized imitation and the discrimination hypothesis. *Journal of Experimental Child Psychology, 10,* 79–99.

Steinman, W. M. (1970b). The social control of generalized imitation. *Journal of Applied Behavior Analysis, 3,* 159–167.

Stelmach, G. E. (Ed.). (1976). *Motor control: Issues and trends.* New York: Academic Press.

Stelmach, G. E. (1978). *Information processing in motor control and learning.* New York: Academic Press.

Sternglanz, S. H., & Serbin, L. A. (1974). Sex role stereotyping in children's television programs. *Developmental Psychology, 10,* 710–715.

Stevenson, H. W., & Odom, R. D. (1964). Visual reinforcement with children. *Journal of Experimental Child Psychology, 1,* 248–255.

Stewart, D. M., & Hamilton, M. L. (1976). Imitation as a learning strategy in the acquisition of vocabulary. *Journal of Experimental Child Psychology, 21,* 380–392.

Stokes, T. F., & Baer, D. M. (1977). An implicit technology of generalization. *Journal of Applied Behavior Analysis, 10,* 349–368.

Stokes, T. F., Fowler, S. A., & Baer, D. M. (1978). Training preschool children to recruit natural communities of reinforcement. *Journal of Applied Behavior Analysis, 11,* 285–303.

Stone, L. J., & Hokanson, J. E. (1969). Arousal reduction via self-punitive behavior. *Journal of Personality and Social Psychology, 12,* 72–79.

Storms, M. D., & Nisbett, R. E. (1970). Insomnia and the attribution process. *Journal of Personality and Social Psychology, 16,* 319–328.

Stotland, E. (1969). Exploratory investigations of empathy. In L. Berkowitz (Ed.), *Advances in experimental social psychology* (Vol.4, pp. 271–314). New York: Academic Press.

Stotland, E., Mathews, K. E., Jr., Sherman, S. E., Hansson, R. O., & Richardson, B. Z. (1978). *Empathy, fantasy and helping.* Beverly Hills: Sage.

Stouwie, R. J., Hetherington, E. M., & Parke, R. D. (1970). Some determinants of children's self-reward behavior after exposure to discrepant reward criteria. *Developmental Psychology, 3,* 313–319.

Strang, H. R., Lawrence, E. C., & Fowler, P. C. (1978). Effects of assigned goal level and knowledge of results on arithmetic computation: Laboratory study. *Journal of Applied Psychology, 63,* 446–450.

Strayer, J. (1980). A naturalistic study of empathic behaviors and their relation to affective states and perspective-taking skills in preschool children. *Child Development, 51,* 815–822.

STUART, R. B. (1972). Situational versus self-control. In R. D. Rubin, H. Fensterheim, J. D. Henderson, & L. P. Ullmann (Eds.), *Advances in behavior therapy: Proceedings of the Fourth Conference of the Association for Advancement of Behavior Therapy* (Vol.3, pp. 129–146). New York: Academic Press.

STUNKARD, A. J., & PENICK, S. B. (1979). Behavior modification in the treatment of obesity: The problem of maintaining weight loss. *Archives of General Psychiatry, 36,* 801–806.

SUCHMAN, R. G., & TRABASSO, T. (1966). Stimulus preference and cue function in young children's concept attainment. *Journal of Experimental Child Psychology, 3,* 188–198.

SUINN, R. M. (1983). Imagery and sports. In A. A. Sheikh (Ed.), *Imagery: Current theory, research, and applications* (pp. 507–534). New York: Wiley.

SUKEMUNE, S., HARUKI, Y., & KASHIWAGI, K. (1977). Studies on social learning in Japan. *American Psychologist, 32,* 924–993.

SULLIVAN, E. V. (1967). The acquisition of conservation of substance through film-mediated models. In D. W. Brison & E. V. Sullivan (Eds.), *Recent research on the acquisition of conservation of substance. Education Monograph.* Toronto: Ontario Institute for Studies in Education.

SULLIVAN, E. V. (1969). Piagetian theory in the educational milieu: A critical appraisal. *Canadian Journal of Behavioral Science, 1,* 129–155.

SULS, J. M., & MILLER, R. L. (Eds.). (1977). *Social comparison processes: Theoretical and empirical perspectives.* Washington, DC: Hemisphere.

SULS, J., & MULLEN, B. (1982). From the cradle to the grave: Comparison and self-evaluation across the life-span. In J. Suls (Ed.), *Psychological perspectives on the self* (Vol. 1, pp. 97–125). Hillsdale, NJ: Erlbaum.

SUMMERS, J. J. (1981). Motor programs. In D. Holding (Ed.), *Human skills* (pp. 41–64). New York: Wiley.

SURBER, C. F. (1977). Developmental processes in social inference: Averaging of intentions and consequences in moral judgment. *Developmental Psychology, 13,* 654–665.

SUSHINSKY, L. W., & BOOTZIN, R. R. (1970). Cognitive desensitization as a model of systematic desensitization. *Behaviour Research and Therapy, 8,* 29–33.

SUTKER, P. B. (1970). Vicarious conditioning an sociopathy. *Journal of Abnormal Psychology, 76,* 380–386.

SWANSON, R. A., & HENDERSON, R. W. (1977). Effects of televised modeling and active participation on rule-governed question production among Native American preschool children. *Contemporary Educational Psychology, 2,* 345–352.

SWANSON, R. A., HENDERSON, R. W., & WILLIAMS, E. (1979). Relative influence of observation, imitative motor activity, and feedback on the induction of seriation. *The Journal of Genetic Psychology, 135,* 81–92.

SWEET, J. J., & RESICK, P. A. (1979). The maltreatment of children: A review of theories and research. *The Journal of Social Issues, 35,* 40–59.

SWENSON, A. (1983). Toward an ecological approach to theory and research in child language acquisition. In W. Fowler (Ed.), *Potentials of childhood* (Vol. 2). *Studies in early developmental learning* (pp. 121–176). Lexington, MA: Lexington Books.

SWITZKY, H. N., & HAYWOOD, H. C. (1974). Motivational orientation and the relative efficacy of self-monitored and externally imposed reinforcement systems in children. *Journal of Personality and Social Psychology, 30,* 360–366.

TAKATA, C., & TAKATA, T. (1976). The influence of models on the evaluation of ability: Two functions of social comparison processes. *The Japanese Journal of Psychology, 47,* 74–84.

TAN, A. S. (1979). TV beauty ads and role expectations of adolescent female viewers. *Journalism Quarterly, 56,* 283–288.

TANNENBAUM, A. S., KAVCIC, B., ROSNER, M., VIANELLO, M., & WIESER, G. (1974). *Hierarchy in organizations.* San Francisco: Jossey-Bass.

TANNENBAUM, P. H., & ZILLMANN, D. (1975). Emotional arousal in the facilitation of aggression through communication. In L. Berkowitz (Ed.), *Advances in experimental social psychology* (Vol. 8, pp.149–192). New York: Academic Press.

TAUB, E. (1977). Movement in nonhuman primates deprived of somatosensory feedback. In J. F. Keogh (Ed.), *Exercise and sports sciences reviews* (Vol. 4, pp. 335–374). Santa Barbara, CA: Journal Publishing Affiliates.

TAYLOR, C. B., BANDURA, A., EWART, C. K., MILLER, N. H., & DeBUSK, R. F. (1985). Raising spouse's and patient's perception of his cardiac capabilities after clinically uncomplicated acute myocardial infarction. *American Journal of Cardiology.*

TAYLOR, F. G., & MARSHALL, W. L. (1977). Experimental analysis of cognitive-behavioral therapy for depression. *Cognitive Therapy and Research, 1,* 59–72.

TAYLOR, K. M., & BETZ, N. E. (1983). Applications of self-efficacy theory to the understanding and treatment of career indecision. *Journal of Vocational Behavior, 22,* 63–81.

TAYLOR, M. S., LOCKE, E. A., LEE, C., & GIST, M. E. (1984). Type A behavior and faculty research productivity: What are the mechanisms? *Organizational Behavior and Human Performance, 34,* 402–418.

TAYLOR, M. W. (1978). *A computer simulation of innovative decision-making in organizations.* Washington, D.C.: University Press of America.

TAYLOR, S. E., & CROCKER, J. (1981). Schematic bases of social information processing. In E. T. Higgins, C. P. Herman, & M. P. Zanna (Eds.), *Social cognition: The Ontario symposium* (Vol. 1, pp. 89–134). Hillsdale, NJ: Erlbaum.

TEASDALE, J. D. (1983). Negative thinking in depression: Cause, effect, or reciprocal relationship? *Advances in Behaviour Research and Therapy, 5,* 3–26.

TELCH, M. J. (1983). *A comparison of behavioral and pharmacological approaches to the treatment of agoraphobia.* Unpublished doctoral dissertation, Stanford University: Stanford, CA.

Telch, M. J., Bandura, A., Vinciguerra, P., Agras, A., & Stout, A. L. (1982). Social demand for consistency and congruence between self-efficacy and performance. *Behavior Therapy, 13*, 694–701.

Telch, M. J., Killen, J. D., McAlister, A. L., Perry, C. L., & Maccoby, N. (1982). Long-term follow-up of a pilot project on smoking prevention with adolescents. *Journal of Behavioral Medicine, 5*, 1–8.

Tellegen, A., Kamp, J., & Watson, D. (1982). Recognizing individual differences in predictive structure. *Psychological Review, 89*, 95–105.

Terrace, H. S. (1979). *Nim: A chimpanzee who learned sign language.* New York: Knopf.

Testa, T. J. (1974). Causal relationships and the acquisition of avoidance responses. *Psychological Review, 81*, 491–505.

Thase, M. E., & Moss, M. K. (1976). The relative efficacy of covert modeling procedures and guided participant modeling on the reduction of avoidance behavior. *Journal of Behavior Therapy and Experimental Psychiatry, 7*, 7–12.

Thelen, M. H., Dollinger, S. J., & Kirkland, K. D. (1979). Imitation and response uncertainty. *Journal of Genetic Psychology, 135*, 139–152.

Thelen, M. H., Dollinger, S. J., & Roberts, M. C. (1975). On being imitated: Its effects on attraction and reciprocal imitation. *Journal of Personality and Social Psychology, 31*, 467–472.

Thelen, M. H., Fry, R. A., Fehrenbach, P. A., & Frautschi, N. M. (1979). Therapeutic videotape and film modeling: A review. *Psychological Bulletin, 86*, 701–720.

Thelen, M. H., & Fryrear, J. L. (1971a). Effect of observer and model race on the imitation of standards of self-reward. *Developmental Psychology, 5*, 133–135.

Thelen, M. H., & Fryrear, J. L. (1971b). Imitation of self-reward standards by black and white female delinquents. *Psychological Reports, 29*, 667–671.

Thelen, M. H., Fryrear, J. L., & Rennie, D. L. (1971). Delayed imitation of self-reward standards. *Journal of Experimental Research in Personality, 5*, 317–322.

Thomas, E. A. C., & Malone, T. W. (1979). On the dynamics of two-person interactions. *Psychological Review, 86*, 331–360.

Thompson, S. K., & Bentler, P. M. (1971). The priority of cues in sex discrimination by children and adults. *Developmental Psychology, 5*, 181–185.

Thoresen, C. E., & Mahoney, M. J. (1974). *Behavioral self-control.* New York: Holt, Rinehart & Winston.

Tilker, H. A. (1970). Socially responsible behavior as a function of observer responsibility and victim feedback. *Journal of Personality and Social Psychology, 14*, 95–100.

Tirrell, F. J., Mount, M. K., & Scott, N. A. (1977). Self-reward and external reward: Methodological considerations and contingency instructions. *Psychological Reports, 41*, 1103–1110.

Tittle, C. R. (1969). Crime rates and legal sanctions. *Social Problems, 16*, 409–423.

Tittle, C. R. (1977). Sanction fear and the maintenance of social order. *Social Forces, 55*, 579–596.

Tittle, C. R., & Rowe, A. R. (1974). Certainty of arrest and crime rates: A further test of the deterrence hypothesis. *Social Forces, 52*, 455–462.

Toch, H. (1969). *Violent men.* Chicago: Aldine.

Tolman, E. C. (1932). *Purposive behavior in animals and men.* New York: Century.

Tolman, E. C. (1951). *Collected papers in psychology.* Reprinted as *Behavior and psychological man.* Berkeley: University of California Press.

Toner, I. J., Moore, L. P., & Ashley, P. K. (1978). The effect of serving as a model of self-control on subsequent resistance of deviation in children. *Journal of Experimental Child Psychology, 26*, 85–91.

Toner, I. J., Moore, L. P., & Emmons, B. A. (1980). The effect of being labeled on subsequent self-control in children. *Child Development, 51*, 618–621.

Tornatzky, L. G., Fergus, E. O., Avellar, J. W., Fairweather, G. W., & Fleischer, M. (1980). *Innovation and social process: A national experiment in implementing social technology.* New York: Pergamon.

Tornatzky, L. G., & Klein, K. J. (1982). Innovation characteristics and innovation adoption-implementation: A meta-analysis of findings. *IEEE Transactions of Engineering and Management, EM-29*, 28–45.

Trabasso, T., & Bower, G. H. (1968). *Attention in learning: Theory and research.* New York: Wiley.

Tressler, D. P., & Tucker, R. D. (1980, November). *The comparative effect of self-evaluation and self-reinforcement training in the treatment of depression.* Paper presented at the meeting of the Association for the Advancement of Behavior Therapy, New York.

Trope, Y. (1983). Self-assessment in achievement behavior. In J. M. Suls & A. G. Greenwald (Eds.), *Psychological perspective on the self* (Vol. 2, pp. 92–121). Hillsdale, NJ: Erlbaum.

Truax, C. B. (1966). Reinforcement and nonreinforcement in Rogerian psychotherapy. *Journal of Abnormal Psychology, 71*, 1–9.

Tulving, E. (1983). *Elements of episodic memory.* New York: Oxford University Press.

Tumblin, A., & Gholson, B. (1981). Hypothesis theory and the development of conceptual learning. *Psychological Bulletin, 90*, 102–124.

Turiel, E. (1966). An experimental test of the sequentiality of developmental stages in the child's moral judgments. *Journal of Personality and Social Psychology, 3*, 611–618.

Turiel, E. (1969). Developmental processes in the child's moral thinking. In P. Mussen, J. Langer, & M. Covington (Eds.), *Trends and issues in developmental psychology* (pp. 92–133). New York: Holt, Rinehart & Winston.

Turiel, E. (1977). Distinct conceptual and developmental domains: Social-convention and morality. In H. E. Howe, Jr. & C. B. Keasey (Eds.), *Nebraska Symposium on Motivation* (Vol. 25, pp. 77–116). Lincoln: University of Nebraska Press.

Turk, D. C., & Genest, M. (1979). Regulation of pain: The application of cognitive and behavioral techniques for prevention and remediation. In P. C. Kendall & S. D. Hollon (Eds.), *Cognitive-behavioral in-*

terventions: Theory, research, and procedures (pp. 287–318). New York: Academic Press.

Turk, D., Meichenbaum, D., & Genest, M. (1981). *Cognitive therapy of pain.* New York: Guilford.

Turkat, I. D. (1982). An investigation of parental modeling in the etiology of diabetic illness behavior. *Behavior Research and Therapy, 20,* 547–552.

Turkat, I. D., & Guise, B. J. (1983). The effects of vicarious experience and stimulus intensity of pain termination and work avoidance. *Behaviour Research and Therapy, 21,* 241–245.

Turkat, I. D., Guise, B. J., & Carter, K. M. (1983). The effects of vicarious experience on pain termination and work avoidance—A replication. *Behaviour Research and Therapy, 21,* 491–493.

Turner, S. M., & Forehand, R. (1976). Imitative behavior as a function of success-failure and racial-socioeconomic factors. *Journal of Applied Social Psychology, 6,* 40–47.

Tversky, A. (1977). Features of similarity. *Psychological Review, 84,* 327–352.

Tversky, A., & Kahneman, D. (1974). Judgment under uncertainty: Heuristics and biases. *Science, 185,* 1124–1131.

Tversky, A., & Kahneman, D. (1980). Causal schemas in judgments under uncertainty. In M. Fishbein (Ed.), *Progress in social psychology* (Vol. 1, pp. 49–72). Hillsdale, NJ: Erlbaum.

Tversky, B. (1982). The rebirth of learning. *Contemporary Psychology, 27,* 679–680.

Tyler, T. R. (1980). Impact of directly and indirectly experienced events: The origin of crime-related judgments and behaviors. *Journal of Personality and Social Psychology, 39,* 13–28.

Tyler, T. R., & Cook, F. L. (1984). The mass media and judgments of risk: Distinguishing impact on personal and societal level judgments. *Journal of Personality and Social Psychology, 47,* 693–708.

Ulich, E. (1967). Some experiments on the function of mental training in the acquisition of motor skills. *Ergonomics, 10,* 411–419.

Umstot, D. D., Bell, C. H., Jr., & Mitchell, T. R. (1976). Effects of job enrichment and task goals on satisfaction and productivity: Implications for job design. *Journal of Applied Psychology, 61,* 379–394.

Uzgiris, I. C. (1964). Situational generality of conservation. *Child Development, 35,* 831–841.

Uzgiris, I. C. (1979). The many faces of imitation in infancy. In L. Montada (Ed.), *Fortschritte der Entwick Lungpsychologie* (pp. 173–193). Stuttgart: Verlag W. Kohlhammer.

Uzgiris, I. C. (1984). Imitation in infancy: Its interpersonal aspects. In M. Perlmutter (Ed.), *The Minnesota Symposia on Child Psychology* (Vol. 17, pp. 1–31). Hillsdale, NJ: Erlbaum.

Valentine, C. W. (1930). The psychology of imitation with special reference to early childhood. *British Journal of Psychology, 21,* 105–132.

Valins, S., & Ray, A. A. (1967). Effects of cognitive desensitization on avoidance behavior. *Journal of Personality and Social Psychology, 7,* 345–350.

van Hekken, S. M. J. (1969). The influence of verbalization on observational learning in a group of mediating and a group on non-mediating children. *Human Development, 12,* 204–213.

Varis, T. (1984). The international flow of television programs. *Journal of Communications, 31,* 143–152.

Vasta, R. (1976). Feedback and fidelity: Effects of contingent consequences on accuracy of imitation. *Journal of Experimental Child Psychology, 21,* 98–108.

Vasta, R., & Stirpe, L. A. (1979). Reinforcement effects on three measures of children's interest in math. *Behavior Modification, 8,* 223–244.

Vaughan, K. B., & Lanzetta, J. T. (1980). Vicarious instigation and conditioning of facial expressive and autonomic responses to a model's expressive display of pain. *Journal of Personality and Social Psychology, 38,* 909–923.

Vernon, D. T. A. (1974). Modeling and birth order in responses to painful stimuli. *Journal of Personality and Social Psychology, 29,* 794–799.

Vernon, P. E. (1964). *Personality assessment: A critical survey.* New York: Wiley.

Vernon, W. M. (1969). Comparative aversiveness of self-delivered versus other-delivered shock. *Proceedings of the 77th Annual Convention of the American Psychological Association* (pp. 813–841).

Verplanck, W. S. (1962). Unaware of where's awareness: Some verbal operants—notates, monents, and notants. In C. W. Eriksen (Ed.), *Behavior and awareness* (pp. 130–158). Durham: Duke University Press.

Vidmar, N., & Ellsworth, P. (1974). Public opinion and the death penalty. *Stanford Law Review, 26,* 1245–1270.

von Cranach, M., Foppa, K., Lepenies, W., & Ploog, D. (Eds.). (1979). *Human ethology : Claims and limits of a new discipline.* Cambridge, England: Cambridge University Press.

Vroom, V. H. (1964). *Work and motivation.* New York: Wiley.

Wachs, T. D. (1977). The optimal stimulation hypothesis and early development: Anybody got a match? In I. C. Uzgiris & F. Weizmann (Eds.), *The structuring of experience.* (pp. 153–177). New York: Plenum.

Wahler, R. G., Berland, R. M., & Coe, T. D. (1979). Generalization in child behavior change. In B. B. Lahey & A. E. Kazdin (Eds.), *Advances in clinical child psychology* (Vol. 2, pp. 35–69). New York: Plenum.

Walker, L. J. (1982). The sequentiality of Kohlberg's stages of moral development. *Child Development, 53,* 1330–1336.

Walker, L. J. (1983). Sources of cognitive conflict for stage transition in moral development. *Developmental Psychology, 19,* 103–110.

Walker, L. J., & Richards, B. S. (1976). The effects of a narrative model on children's moral judgments. *Canadian Journal of Behavioral Science, 8,* 169–177.

Walker, W. B., & Franzini, L. R. (1983, April). *Self-efficacy and low-risk aversive group treatments for smoking cessation.* Paper presented at the annual convention of the Western Psychological Association, San Francisco.

WALL, S. M. (1982). Effects of systematic self-monitoring and self-reinforcement in children's management of test performances. *The Journal of Psychology, 111*, 129–136.

WALLACE, I. (1977). Self-control techniques of famous novelists. *Journal of Applied Behavior Analysis, 10*, 515–525.

WALLERSTEIN, J. A., & WYLE, C. I. (1947). Our law-abiding law-breakers. *Probation, 25*, 107–112, 118.

WALSTER, E., WALSTER, G. W., & BERSCHEID, E. (1978). *Equity: Theory and Research.* Boston: Allyn and Bacon.

WALTERS, G. C., & GRUSEC, J. E. (1977). *Punishment.* San Francisco: Freeman.

WALTERS, R. H., BOWEN, N. V., & PARKE, R. D. (1964). Influence of looking behavior of a social model on subsequent looking behavior of observers of the model. *Perceptual and Motor Skills, 18*, 469–483.

WALTERS, R. H., LEAT, M., & MEZEI, L. (1963). Inhibition and disinhibition of responses through empathetic learning. *Canadian Journal of Psychology, 17*, 235–243.

WALTERS, R. H., & PARKE, R. D. (1964). Influence of response consequences to a social model on resistance to deviation. *Journal of Experimental Child Psychology, 1*, 269–280.

WALTERS, R. H., PARKE, R. D., & CANE, V. A. (1965). Timing of punishment and the observation of consequences to others as determinants of response inhibition. *Journal of Experimental Child Psychology, 2*, 10–30.

WALTON, D., & MATHER, M. D. (1963). The application of learning principles to the treatment of obsessive-compulsive states in the acute and chronic phases of illness. *Behavior Research and Therapy, 1*, 163–174.

WAPNER, S., & CIRILLO, L. (1968). Imitation of a model's hand movements: Age changes in transposition of left-right relations. *Child Development, 39*, 887–894.

WARD, W. C., & JENKINS, H. M. (1965). The display of information and the judgment of contingency. *Canadian Journal of Psychology, 19*, 231–241.

WARDEN, C. J., FJELD, H. A., & KOCH, A. M. (1940). Imitative behavior in Cebus and Rhesus monkeys. *Pedagogical Seminary and Journal of Genetic Psychology, 56*, 311–322.

WARDEN, C. J., & JACKSON, T. A. (1935). Imitative behavior in the Rhesus monkeys. *Pedagogical Seminary and Journal of Genetic Psychology, 46*, 103–125.

WATKINS, P., & SOLEDAD, G. (1979). *My life with Charles Manson.* New York: Bantam Books.

WATSON, J. B., & RAYNER, R. (1920). Conditioned emotional reactions. *Journal of Experimental Psychology, 3*, 1–14.

WATSON, J. S. (1971). Cognitive-perceptual development in infancy: Settings for the seventies. *Merrill-Palmer Quarterly, 17*, 139–152.

WATSON, J. S. (1979). Perception of contingency as a determinant of social responsiveness. In E. B. Thoman (Ed.), *Origins of the infant's social responsiveness* (Vol. 1, pp. 33–64). New York: Halsted.

WATT, J. G., JR., & VAN DEN BERG, S. A. (1978). Time series analysis of alternative media effects theories. In R. D. Ruben (Ed.), *Communication Yearbook 2* (pp. 215–224). New Brunswick, NJ: Transaction Books.

WAXLER, C. Z., & YARROW, M. R. (1970). Factors influencing imitative learning in preschool children. *Journal of Experimental Child Psychology, 9*, 115–130.

WAXLER, C. Z., & YARROW, M. R. (1975). An observational study of maternal models. *Developmental Psychology, 11*, 485–494.

WEBSTER, M., JR., & SOBIESZEK, B. (1974). *Sources of self-evaluation: A formal theory of significant others and social influence.* New York: Wiley.

WECHSBERG, J. (Ed.). (1967). *The murderers among us.* New York: McGraw-Hill.

WEINBERG, J., & LEVINE, S. (1980). Psychobiology of coping in animals: The effects of predictability. In S. Levine & H. Ursin (Eds.), *Coping and health* (pp. 39–59). New York: Plenum.

WEINBERG, R. S., GOULD, D., & JACKSON, A. (1979). Expectations and performance: An empirical test of Bandura's self-efficacy theory. *Journal of Sport Psychology, 1*, 320–331.

WEINBERG, R. S., GOULD, D., YUKELSON, D., & JACKSON, A. (1981). The effect of preexisting and manipulated self-efficacy on a competitive muscular endurance task. *Journal of Sport Psychology, 4*, 345–354.

WEINBERG, R. S., YUKELSON, S., & JACKSON, A. (1980). Effect of public and private efficacy expectations on competitive performance. *Journal of Sport Psychology, 2*, 340–349.

WEINBERGER, D. A., SCHWARTZ, G. E., & DAVIDSON, R. J. (1979). Low-anxious, high-anxious, and repressive coping styles: Psychometric patterns and behavioral and physiological responses to stress. *Journal of Abnormal Psychology, 88*, 369–380.

WEINER, B. (1972). *Theories of motivation.* Chicago: Markham.

WEINER, B. (1979). A theory of motivation for some classroom experiences. *Journal of Educational Psychology, 71*, 3–25.

WEINER, B., RUSSELL, D., & LERMAN, D. (1978). Affective consequences of causal ascriptions. In J. Harvey, W. Ickes, & R. Kidd (Eds.), *New directions in attribution research* (Vol. 2, pp. 59–90). Hillsdale, NJ: Erlbaum.

WEINER, H. R., & DUBANOSKI, R. A. (1975). Resistance to extinction as a function of self or externally determined schedules of reinforcement. *Journal of Personality and Social Psychology, 31*, 905–910.

WEINROTT, M. R., BAUSKE, B. W., & PATTERSON, G. R. (1979). Systematic replication of a social learning approach to parent training. In P. O. Sjoden, S. Bates, & W. S. Dockens, III (Eds.), *Trends in behavior therapy* (pp. 331–351). New York: Academic Press.

WEINSTEIN, A. G., & HOLZBACH, R. L., JR. (1973). Impact of individual differences, reward distribution, and task structure on productivity in a simulated work environment. *Journal of Applied Psychology, 58,* 296–301.

WEINSTEIN, W. K., & LAWSON, R. (1963). The effect of experimentally-induced "awareness" upon performance in free-operant verbal conditioning and on subsequent tests of "awareness." *Journal of Psychology, 56,* 203–211.

WEISENBERG, M. (1977). Pain and pain control. *Psychological Bulletin, 84,* 1008–1044.

WEISZ, A. E., & TAYLOR, R. L. (1970). American presidential assassinations. In D. N. Daniels, M. F. Gilula, & F. M. Ochberg (Eds.), *Violence and the struggle for existence* (pp. 291–307). Boston: Little, Brown.

WEITZMAN, L. J., EIFLER, D., HOKADA, E., & ROSS, C. (1972). Sex-role socialization in picture books for preschool children. *American Journal of Sociology, 77,* 1125–1150.

WELCH, A. S., & WELCH, B. L. (1968). Reduction of norepinephrine in the lower brainstem by psychological stimulus. *Proceedings of the National Academy of Sciences, 60,* 478–481.

WELCH, S., & THOMPSON, K. (1980). The impact of federal incentives on state policy innovation. *American Journal of Political Science, 24,* 715–729.

WENER, A. E., & REHM, L. P. (1975). Depressive affect: A test of behavioral hypotheses. *Journal of Abnormal Psychology, 84,* 221–227.

WENK, E., JR. (1979). Political limits in steering technology: Pathologies of the short run. *Technology in Society, 1,* 27–36.

WHEELER, K. G. (1983). Comparisons of self-efficacy and expectancy models of occupational preferences for college males and females. *Journal of Occupational Psychology, 56,* 73–78.

WHEELER, V. A., & LADD, G. W. (1982). Assessment of children's self-efficacy for social interactions with peers. *Developmental Psychology, 18,* 795–805.

WHITE, G. M., & ROSENTHAL, T. L. (1974). Demonstration and lecture in information transmission: A field experiment. *The Journal of Experimental Education, 43,* 90–96.

WHITE, P. (1980). Limitations on verbal reports of internal events: A refutation of Nisbett and Wilson and of Bem. *Psychological Review, 87,* 105–112.

WHITE, R. W. (1959). Motivation reconsidered: The concept of competence. *Psychological Review, 66,* 297–333.

WHITE, R. W. (1960). Competence and the psychosexual stages of development. In M. R. Jones (Ed.), *Nebraska Symposium on Motivation* (Vol. 8, pp. 97–141). Lincoln: University of Nebraska Press.

WHITE, S. E., MITCHELL, T. R., & BELL, C. H. (1977). Goal setting, evaluation apprehension, and social cues as determinants of job performance and job satisfaction in a simulated organization. *Journal of Applied Psychology, 62,* 665–673.

WHITEHURST, C., & DOMASH, M. (1974). Preference assessment for application of the Premack principle. *Psychological Reports, 1974, 35,* 919–924.

WHITEHURST, G. J. (1977). Comprehension, selective imitation, and the CIP hypothesis. *Journal of Experimental Child Psychology, 23,* 23–38.

WHITEHURST, G. J., IRONSMITH, M., & GOLDFEIN, M. (1974). Selective imitation of the passive construction through modeling. *Journal of Experimental Child Psychology, 17,* 288–302.

WHITEHURST, G. J., & VASTA, R. (1975). Is language acquired through imitation? *Journal of Psycholinguistic Research, 4,* 37–59.

WHITING, J. W. M., & MOWRER, O. H. (1943). Habit progression and regression: A laboratory study of some factors relevant to human socialization. *Journal of Comparative Psychology, 36,* 229–253.

WICKLUND, R. A. (1975). Objective self-awareness. In L. Berkowitz (Ed.), *Advances in experimental social psychology* (Vol. 8, pp. 233–275). New York: Academic Press.

WILHELM, H., & LOVAAS, O. I. (1976). Stimulus overselectivity: A common feature in autism and mental retardation. *American Journal of Mental Deficiency, 81,* 26–31.

WILKES, R. L., & SUMMERS, J. J. (1984). Cognitions, mediating variables, and strength performance. *Journal of Sport Psychology, 6,* 351–359.

WILKINS, J. L., SCHARFF, W. H., & SCHLOTTMANN, R. S. (1974). Personality type, reports of violence, and aggressive behavior. *Journal of Personality and Social Psychology, 30,* 243–247.

WILLIAMS, S. L., DOOSEMAN, G., & KLEIFIELD, E. (1984). Comparative power of guided mastery and exposure treatments for intractable phobias. *Journal of Consulting and Clinical Psychology, 52,* 505–518.

WILLIAMS, S. L., & RAPPOPORT, A. (1983). Cognitive treatment in the natural environment for agoraphobics. *Behavior Therapy, 14,* 299–313.

WILLIAMS, S. L., TURNER, S. M., & PEER, D. F. (1985). Guided mastery and performance desensitization treatments for severe acrophobia. *Journal of Consulting and Clinical Psychology.*

WILLIAMS, S. L., & WATSON, N. (1985). Perceived danger and perceived self-efficacy as cognitive mediators of acrophobic behavior. *Behavior Therapy, 16,* 136–146.

WILLIAMS, T. M. (Ed.). (1985). *The impact of television: A natural experiment involving three communities.* New York: Academic Press.

WILLNER, A. G., BRAUKMANN, C. J., KIRIGIN, K. A., & WOLF, M. M. (1978). Achievement Place: A community treatment model for youths in trouble. In D. Marholin, II (Ed.), *Child behavior therapy* (pp. 239–273). New York: Gardner.

WILSON, C. C., ROBERTSON, S. J., HERLONG, L. H., & HAYNES, S. N. (1979). Vicarious effects of time-out in the modification of aggression in the classroom. *Behavior Modification, 3,* 97–111.

WILSON, G. T., & BROWNELL, K. D. (1980). Behavior therapy for obesity: An evaluation of treatment outcome. *Advances in Behavior Research and Therapy, 3,* 49–86.

WILSON, G. T., & LAWSON, D. M. (1976). Expectancies,

alcohol, and sexual arousal in male social drinkers. *Journal of Abnormal Psychology, 85,* 587–594.

WILSON, J. Q., & BOLAND, B. (1978). The effect of the police on crime. *Law and Society Review, 12,* 367–390.

WILSON, W. C. (1958). Imitation and learning of incidental cues by preschool children. *Child Development, 29,* 393–397.

WINCZE, J. P., & CAIRD, W. K. (1976). The effects of systematic desensitization and video desensitization in the treatment of essential sexual dysfunction in women. *Behavior Therapy, 7,* 335–342.

WINDHEUSER, H. J. (1977). Anxious mothers as models for coping with anxiety. *Behavioral Analysis and Modification, 2,* 39–58.

WINE, J. (1971). Test anxiety and direction of attention. *Psychological Bulletin, 76,* 92–104.

WINFREY, C. (1979, February 25). Why 900 died in Guyana. *The New York Times Magazine,* p. 39.

WINTER, W. (1965). Transforms without kernels. *Language, 41,* 484–489.

WOLF, S. (1950). Effects of suggestion and conditioning on the action of chemical agents in human subjects— the pharmacology of placebos. *Journal of Clinical Investigation, 29,* 100–109.

WOLFGANG, M. E., & FERRACUTI, F. (1967). *The subculture of violence.* London: Tavistock.

WOLFGANG, M. E., KELLY, A., & NOLDE, H. C. (1962). Comparison of the executed and the commuted among admissions to death row. *Journal of Criminal Law, Criminology, and Political Science, 53,* 301–311.

WOLFGANG, M. E., & RIEDEL, M. (1973). Race, judicial discretion, and the death penalty. *The Annals of the American Academy of Political and Social Science, 407,* 119–133.

WOLPE, J. (1974). *The practice of behavior therapy.* New York: Pergamon.

WONDERLY, D. M., & KUPFERSMID, J. H. (1980). Kohlberg's moral judgment program in the classroom: Practical considerations. *The Alberta Journal of Educational Research, 26,* 128–141.

WORTMAN, C. B., PANCIERA, L., SHUSTERMAN, L., & HIBSCHER, J. (1976). Attributions of causality and reactions to uncontrollable outcomes. *Journal of Experimental Social Psychology, 12,* 301–316.

WRIGHT, J., & MISCHEL, W. (1982). Influence of affect on cognitive social learning person variables. *Journal of Personality and Social Psychology, 43,* 901–914.

WRIGHT, J. C. (1962). Consistency and complexity of response sequences as a function of schedules of noncontingent reward. *Journal of Experimental Psychology, 63,* 601–609.

WRIGHT, P. (1980). Message-evoked thoughts: Persuasion research using thought verbalizations. *The Journal of Consumer Research, 7,* 151–175.

WRIGHT, P., & RIP, P. D. (1981). Retrospective reports on the causes of decisions. *Journal of Personality and Social Psychology, 40,* 601–614.

WULBERT, M., NYMAN, B. A., SNOW, D., & OWEN, Y. (1973). The efficacy of stimulus fading and contingency management in the treatment of elective mut-

ism: A case study. *Journal of Applied Behavior Analysis, 6,* 435–441.

WYLIE, R. C. (1974). *The self-concept: A review of methodological considerations and measuring instruments* (rev. ed.). Lincoln: University of Nebraska Press.

WYNNE, L. C., & SOLOMON, R. L. (1955). Traumatic avoidance learning: Acquisition and extinction in dogs deprived of normal peripheral autonomic function. *Genetic Psychology Monographs, 52,* 241–284.

WYRWICKA, W. (1978). Imitation of mother's inappropriate food preference in weaning kittens. *The Pavlovian Journal of Biological Science, 13,* 55–72.

YABLONSKY, L. (1962). *The violent gang.* New York: Macmillan.

YALOM, I. D., & YALOM, M. (1971). Ernest Hemingway—A psychiatric view. *Archives of General Psychiatry, 24,* 485–494.

YAMAGUCHI, S., HARANO, K., & EGAWA, B. (1978). Effects of differentially modeled stimuli on vicarious autonomic arousal. *Perceptual and Motor Skills, 46,* 643–650.

YARROW, L. J., McQUISTON, S., MacTURK, R. H., McCARTHY, M. E., KLEIN, R. P., & VIETZE, P. M. (1983). Assessment of mastery motivation during the first year of life: Contemporaneous and cross-age relationships. *Developmental Psychology, 19,* 159–171.

YARROW, L. J., RUBENSTEIN, J. L., & PEDERSEN, F. A. (1975). *Infant and environment: Early cognitive and motivational developement.* New York: Halsted.

YARROW, M. R., & SCOTT, P. M. (1972). Imitation of nurturant and nonnurturant models. *Journal of Personality and Social Psychology, 23,* 259–270.

YOUNG, E. H., & HAWK, S. S. (1955). *Moto-kinesthetic speech training.* Stanford, CA.: Stanford University Press.

YUKL, G. A., & LATHAM, G. P. (1978). Interrelationships among employee participation, individual differences, goal difficulty, goal acceptance, goal instrumentality, and performance. *Personnel Psychology, 31,* 305–324.

YUSEPH, S., & FEIN, G. (1982). Can segments be born again? *Journal of Advertising Research, 22,* 13–23.

YUSSEN, S. R. (1974). Determinants of visual attention and recall in observational learning by preschoolers and second graders. *Developmental Psychology, 10,* 93–100.

YUSSEN, S. R., & LEVY, V. M., JR. (1975). Effects of warm and neutral models on the attention of observational learners. *Journal of Experimental Child Psychology, 20,* 66–72.

ZAHN-WAXLER, C., & RADKE-YARROW, M. (1979, March). *A developmental analysis of children's responses to emotions in others.* Symposium presented at the meetings of the Society for Research in Child Development, San Francisco.

ZAILIAN, M. (1978, April 30). [Interview with Victor Borge: "If I were not a humorist, I'd be a pianist"] *San Francisco Chronicle,* p. 22.

ZAJONC, R. B. (1954). Some effects of the "space" serials. *Public Opinion Quarterly, 18,* 365–374.

ZAJONC, R. B. (1980). Feeling and thinking: Preferences need no inferences. *American Psychologist, 35,* 151–175.

ZAJONC, R. B. (1981). A one-factor mind about mind and emotion. *American Psychologist, 36,* 102–103.

ZAJONC, R. B. (1984). On the primacy of affect. *American Psychologist, 39,* 117–123.

ZAJONC, R. B., & MARKUS, G. B. (1975). Birth order and intellectual development. *Psychological Review, 82,* 74–88.

ZALTMAN, G., KOTLER, P., & KAUFMAN, I. (Eds.). (1972). *Creating social change.* New York: Holt, Rinehart and Winston.

ZALTMAN, G., & WALLENDORF, M. (1979). *Consumer behavior: Basic findings and management implications.* New York: Wiley.

ZARBATANY, L. & LAMB, M. E. (1985). Social referencing as a function of information source: Mothers versus strangers. *Infant Behavior and Development, 8,* 25–33.

ZEISEL, H. (1982). A comment on "The deterrent effect of capital punishment" by Phillips. *American Journal of Sociology, 88,* 167–169.

ZETTLE, R. D., & HAYES, S. C. (1980). Conceptual and empirical status of rational-emotive therapy. In M. Hersen, R. M. Eisler, & P. M. Miller (Eds.), *Progress in behavior modification* (Vol. 9, pp. 125–166). New York: Academic Press.

ZILLMANN, D. (1978). Attribution and misattribution of excitatory reactions. In J. H. Harvey, W. Ickes, & R. F. Kidd (Eds.), *New directions in attribution research* (Vol. 2, pp. 335–368). Hillsdale, NJ: Erlbaum.

ZILLMANN, D. (1979). *Hostility and aggression.* Hillsdale, NJ: Erlbaum.

ZILLMANN, D. (1983). Transfer of excitation in emotional behavior. In J. T. Cacioppo & R. E. Petty (Eds.), *Social psychophysiology* (pp. 215–240). New York: Guilford.

ZILLMAN, D., & BRYANT, J. (1984). Effects of massive exposure to pornography. In N. M. Malamuth & E. Donnerstein (Eds.), *Pornography and sexual aggression* (pp. 115-138). New York: Academic Press.

ZILLMANN, D., BRYANT, J., & CARVETH, R. A. (1981). The effect of erotica featuring sadomasochism and bestiality on motivated intermale aggression. *Personality and Social Psychology Bulletin, 7,* 153–159.

ZILLMANN, D., BRYANT, J., COMISKY, P. W., & MEDOFF, N. J. (1981). Excitation and hedonic valence in the effect of erotica on motivated intermale aggression. *European Journal of Social Psychology, 11,* 233–252.

ZIMBARDO, P. G. (1969a). *The cognitive control of motivation.* Glenview, IL: Scott, Foresman.

ZIMBARDO, P. G. (1969b). The human choice: Individuation, reason, and order versus deindividuation, impulse, and chaos. In W. J. Arnold & D. Levine (Eds.), *Nebraska symposium on motivation, 1969* (pp. 237–309). Lincoln: University of Nebraska Press.

ZIMBARDO, P. G., EBBESEN, E. B., & MASLACH, C. (1977). *Influencing attitudes and changing behavior.* Reading, MA: Addison-Wesley.

ZIMMERMAN, B. J. (1983). Social learning theory: A contextualist account of cognitive functioning. In C. J. Brainerd (Ed.), *Recent advances in cognitive-developmental theory* (pp. 1–50). New York: Springer-Verlag.

ZIMMERMAN, B. J., & BLOM, D. E. (1983). Toward an empirical test of the role of cognitive conflict in learning. *Developmental Review, 3,* 18–38.

ZIMMERMAN, B. J., & DIALESSI, F. (1973). Modeling influences on children's creative behavior. *Journal of Educational Psychology, 65,* 127–135.

ZIMMERMAN, B. J., & KINSLER, K. (1979). Effects of exposure to a punished model and verbal prohibitions on children's toy play. *Journal of Educational Psychology, 71,* 388–395.

ZIMRING, F. E. (1971). *Perspectives on deterrence.* Washington, DC: U. S. Government Printing Office.

ZIMRING, F. E., & HAWKINS, G. J. (1973). *Deterrence: The legal threat in crime control.* Chicago: The University of Chicago Press.

ZIVIN, G. (Ed.). (1979). *The development of self-regulation through private speech.* New York: Wiley.

ZUBIN, J., ERON, L. D., & SCHUMER, F. (1965). *An experimental approach to projective techniques.* New York: Wiley.

AUTHOR INDEX

Abberton, E., 71
Abel, G. G., 295
Abel, M., 220, 393, 434
Abelson, R. P., 218, 461, 520
Abrams, D. B., 180
Abramson, L. Y., 225–226, 358, 409, 447, 458
Abravanel, E., 51, 84, 86
Acker, L. E., 79
Acksen, B. A., 481, 495
Adair, J. G., 126
Adams, C. R., 78
Adams, J. A., 112
Adams, J. K., 121
Adams, J. S., 306
Adams, N. E., 62, 197, 201, 259, 317, 321, 398–402, 423–424, 426–427, 430–431, 442–443, 519, 521
Adelman, H. F., 247
Ader, R., 183
Adesso, V. J., 277
Adhikarya, R., 155, 161
Adler, H. E., 98–99
Adler, L. L., 98–99

Adoni, H., 511
Agras, A., 422
Agras, W. S., 187–188, 339, 427
Ahles, T. A., 323
Ainsworth, M. D. S., 415
Ajzen, I., 469
Akamatsu, T. J., 208, 344
Albert, A. A., 93
Albert, S. M., 91
Albrecht, R. R., 434
Alexander, J. K., 179
Alinsky, S. D., 180
Allen, A., 6
Allen, C. M., 326
Allen, M. K., 344
Allison, J., 237
Alloy, L. B., 225–226, 358, 409, 458
Allport, F. H., 63
Allport, G. W., 5
Ames, C., 253
Amoroso, D. M., 293
Anderson, C. A., 399
Anderson, J. R., 107, 111, 455, 459, 463
Anderson. N. H., 496

Anderson, R. C., 57
Andrasik, F., 190
Andrews, F. M., 378
Andrews, L., 88
Andrus, B. C., 389
Aniskiewicz, A. S., 316
Antrobus, J. S., 57
Apple, W., 311
Apsche, J., 270
Arbuthnot, J., 481, 495
Archer, D., 333
Arena, J. G., 190
Arend, R. A., 520
Arenson, S. J., 185
Arkowitz, H., 224, 259
Armelius, B. A., 217
Armelius, K., 217
Armstrong, P. M., 239
Arnold, G., 261
Arnold, H. J., 246–247
Arnold, R. K., 67
Aron, I. E., 491
Aronfreed, J., 49, 51, 59, 69, 264, 268, 369
Aronson, E., 520
Arvey, R. D., 476

583

Dumais, S. T., 461
Duncker, K., 324
Dupont, R. L., 175, 279
Durning, K., 103
Dush, D. M., 519
Dweck, C. S., 350, 420, 476
Dysinger, W. S., 311
D'Zurilla, T. J., 463

Earley, P. C., 471
Easterbrooks, M. A., 93
Ebbesen, E. B., 26, 460, 513
Edwards, N. L., 271
Egawa, B., 308
Egger, M. D., 107
Eggeraat, J. B., 520
Ehrlich, I., 276, 278, 333
Eifler, D., 420
Eimas, P. D., 128–129
Einhorn, H. J., 223
Eisen, S. V., 103, 420
Eisenberger, R., 234
Eisler, R. M., 73
Ekman, P., 309–311, 315, 375
Ekstrand, B. R., 212
Elardo, R., 415
Elder, G. H., 31
Elder, J. P., 180
Elkin, F., 31, 343
Elliott, E. S., 476
Ellis, A., 22, 515–516
Ellis, R. A., 260, 343, 416
Ellsworth, P. C., 26, 332–333, 383
Emde, R. N., 309
Emmelkamp, P. M. G., 520
Emmerich, W., 48
Emmons, B. A., 270
Endler, N. S., 23, 452
Endresen, K., 378–379
Endsley, R. C., 103
Engel, R., 326
Englis, B. G., 312
English, D., 261
English, H. B., 201
Enna, B., 350, 420
Enzle, M. E., 247–248
Epstein, N., 315
Epstein, S., 9–10
Erasmus, C. J., 162
Erez, M., 473
Erickson, M. L., 278–280
Ericsson, K. A., 14, 117–118, 125
Eriksen, C. W., 3, 190, 192, 198
Erixon, G., 204
Eron, L. D., 3
Ersner-Hershfield, R., 351, 370
Ervin, S. M., 502–503
Erwin, E., 3

Estes, W. K., 15, 27, 223
Esveldt, K. C., 79
Evans, F. J., 428
Evans, H. L., 368
Evans, M. A., 504
Evans, R. C., 105
Evans, R. I., 180
Ewart, C. K., 401, 408, 427, 438
Eysenck, H. J., 3
Ezrin, S. A., 372

Fagan, J. F., 96
Fagan, L. M., 464
Fagot, B. I., 93
Fairbank, J. A., 326
Fairweather, G. W., 163–164
Falmagne, R. J., 514
Fanselow, M. S., 429
Farber, I. E., 119
Farquhar, J. W., 178–180
Farr, J. L., 236, 244, 253
Farudi, P. A., 344
Feather, N. T., 412
Fecteau, G. W., 518
Fehrenbach, P. A., 319
Feigenbaum, E. A., 215–216, 464–465
Feild, H. S., 385
Fein, G., 171
Feingold, B. D., 244
Feinman, S., 309
Feldman, D. H., 484–486
Feldman, S. E., 344
Felixbrod, J. J., 351–352
Feltz, D. L., 61–62, 398–399, 427, 433–434
Fenigstein, A., 24
Fenson, L., 88
Fergus, E. O., 164
Ferguson, C. A., 53
Ferguson, J. M., 258
Fernandez, L. E., 288, 300
Ferracuti, F., 55, 238
Ferster, C. B., 250
Feshbach, N. D., 315
Feshbach, S., 294, 315
Festinger, L., 347, 400, 403, 511, 520
Fey, S., 493
Fidler, D. S., 93, 511
Field, T. M., 84
Fields, H. L., 428
Fienberg, S. E., 278
Filipczak, J., 256
Finch, A. J., Jr., 518
Fingarette, H., 386
Finkelstein, N. W., 133, 414
Fiordaliso, R., 256
Fiorina, M. P., 453
Firestone, I. J., 79–80, 344

Fischer, K. W., 491
Fischhoff, B., 138, 219, 223, 409, 464–465
Fishbein, M., 230, 469
Fisher, J. L., 105
Fisher, W. A., 294
Fiske, D. W., 234
Fitts, H., 73
Fixsen, D. L., 238
Fjeld, H. A., 99, 135
Flacks, R., 172
Flanagan, B., 295
Flannery, R. B., Jr., 319
Flavell, J. H., 21, 87–88, 125, 313, 369, 420, 484, 518
Flaxman, J., 366–367
Fleck, S., 221
Fleischer, M., 164
Flerx, V. C., 93, 511
Flinn, W., 151, 156
Foddy, M., 406
Folger, J. P., 503
Folger, R., 247
Fong, G. T., 222
Foppa, K., 21, 504, 509
Ford, C. S., 186, 232
Forehand, R., 300
Forges, J., 173
Forrest, M. S., 373
Forward, J. R., 451
Foss, B. M., 69
Fourcin, A. J., 71
Fowler, H., 234, 410
Fowler, P. C., 469
Fowler, S. A., 260
Fox, D. T., 326
Fox, R. C., 37
Foxx, R. M., 267
Frankel, A., 439
Frankenhaeuser, M., 309
Frankl, V. E., 40
Franks, J. J., 60
Franzini, L. R., 351, 397, 436
Fraser, C., 503
Fraser, S., 477
Fraser, S. C., 378–379
Frautschi, N. M., 319
Frazier, J. R., 129, 229
Frederick, E., 338, 368, 392, 431, 471
Frederick, F., 340, 344
Fredrikson, M., 202, 204
Freedman, J. L., 269, 477
Freud, S., 2, 31, 203, 483
Frey, K. S., 94
Friedman, M., 362
Friedman, R. M., 256
Friend, A., 209
Fries, J. F., 178, 418
Friesen, W. V., 310, 315
Frieze, I., 349, 402

Hammond, P., 269
Handleman, J. S., 256
Haney, C., 383
Hanley, S., 319
Hanlon, C., 503
Hanratty, M., 341
Hansson, R. O., 315
Harackiewicz, J. M., 242, 248–249
Harano, K., 308
Harbeck, J., 209
Hardy, A. B., 201, 317, 321, 399, 402, 424, 426, 430, 442–443, 521
Hargis, K., 314
Harlow, H. F., 234, 410
Harper, L. V., 29, 324
Harris, M. B., 53, 93, 105, 208, 507
Harris, R. N., Jr., 163–164
Harris, S. L., 80, 256–257
Harrison, R., 315
Harry, J., 277
Harsh, C. M., 99
Hart, B., 256, 509
Harter, S., 410
Hartmann, D. P., 265, 290, 319, 372
Hartup, W. W., 58, 88, 288
Haruki, Y., 102, 250
Harvey, S. E., 492
Haskell, W. L., 179
Haskett, G. J., 103
Hassemer, W. G., 503
Hastorf, A. H., 26, 327
Hatano, G., 496
Hattie, J. A., 287
Haugan, G. M., 85, 509
Hauge, G., 439
Haughton, E., 221
Havens, A. E., 151, 156
Hawk, S. S., 71
Hawkins, G. J., 272–273, 281
Hawkins, H. L., 251
Hawkins, R., 318, 511–512
Hawkins, R. P., 218
Hayes, C., 99
Hayes, K. J., 99
Hayes, L. A., 84
Hayes, S. C., 365, 515
Haynes, S. N., 287
Haywood, H. C., 351
Head, K. B., 378
Heath, L., 318, 512
Heaton, R. C., 361
Heavenrich, J., 493
Hecht, B. F., 504
Heckhausen, H., 473
Hefferline, R. F., 120
Heffernan, T., 354
Heiby, E. M., 361

Heider, K. G., 272
Helm, C., 383
Helmreich, R. L., 92
Henderson, A. H., 180
Henderson, R. W., 61, 101, 103, 492–493, 495
Hendrick, G., 176
Heneman, H. G., 230
Herbert, E. W., 290, 372
Herbert, J. J., 99
Herlong, L. H., 287
Herman, C. P., 123
Herman, S. J., 381
Hernandez-Peon, R., 196
Herrnstein, R. J., 187–188
Hersen, M., 319
Hershey, M. R., 144, 286
Hershfield, S. M., 351, 370
Hertel, R. K., 26, 29, 31
Hess, R. D., 432
Hetherington, E. M., 344
Hewitt, O. J., 302
Heyneman, D., 137
Hibscher, J., 445
Hicks, D. J., 68, 76, 80, 288
Higgins, A., 489
Hildebrandt, D. E., 344
Hilgard, E. R., 8, 322
Hilgard, J. R., 322
Hill, B., 271
Hill, J. H., 341
Hill, P. C., 180
Hillix, W. A., 302
Hilpert, P. L., 320
Hiltz, S. R., 154
Hinde, R. A., 199
Hinde-Stevenson, J., 199
Hirakawa, T., 299
Hirsch, P. M., 512
Hirt, M. L., 519
Hocking, J., 326
Hodges, K. L., 350, 420
Hodgson, R. J., 258
Hoffman, H. S., 205, 265
Hoffman, M. L., 265–266, 289, 307, 314
Hogarth, R. M., 223
Hokada, E., 420
Hokanson, J. E., 373
Holden, G. W., 93
Hollandsworth, J. G., Jr., 407
Hollon, S. D., 360, 517, 519
Holm, J. E., 425
Holman, H. R., 429–430
Holmes, D. S., 256, 289
Holmes, F. B., 195
Holroyd, K. A., 425, 436
Holt, E. B., 63
Holz, W. C., 265, 268, 270
Homme, L., 238
Hood, L., 503

Hooper, F. H., 488
Hoppe, R. A., 79
Horne, M., 187, 427
Horne, W. C., 208
Hornstein, H. A., 466
House, T. H., 316
Houser, R., 209
Houston, B. K., 256
Hovell, M. F., 503
Howard, J. L., 293, 324
Howells, G. N., 201, 317, 321, 399, 402, 422, 424, 426, 430, 442–443, 521
Howie, A. M., 104
Huang, L. C., 208
Huesmann, L. R., 447
Hugdahl, K., 195, 202, 204–205
Hughes, C. C., 345
Hughes, P. H., 175
Hughes, R., Jr., 314
Hulin, C. L., 433
Hull, C. L., 236
Hultsch, D. F., 31
Humphrey, G., 63
Humphrey, L. L., 352, 366, 475
Hung, J. H., 67
Hunt, J. McV., 311, 407
Huntington, S., 466
Hurlburt, R. T., 118
Hursey, K. G., 425
Husic, F., 158
Huston, A. C., 68, 93, 96
Hygge, S., 204, 316
Hyman, A., 140
Hyson, R. L., 430

Iannotti, R. J., 313, 315
Imanishi, K., 99
Inhelder, B., 31, 482
Innes, J. M., 126
Inouye, D. K., 301–302, 330, 394, 399–400, 403, 422, 424, 511–512
Ironsmith, M., 507
Irvine, J. W., 287
Irwin, F. W., 412
Isen, A. M., 337
Israel, A. C., 94–95, 257, 261
Ito, H., 102
Itoh, H., 100
Ivie, R. L., 387
Izard, C. E., 308

Jacklin, C. N., 92–96, 420
Jackson, A., 226, 394, 400, 419, 422, 424–425, 434, 449
Jackson, B., 362
Jackson, S. E., 384
Jackson, T. A., 99, 135

Jacob, H., 279
Jacobs, R. C., 345
Jacobson, M. B., 185
Jacobson, S. W., 84
Jacoby, K. E., 98
Jaffe, J. H., 175
Jaffe, Y., 294
James, B., 202
James, J. E., 261
James, W., 25
Janis, I. L., 139, 322, 326, 489
Jaremko, M. E., 518
Jarrett, R. B., 365
Jeffery, K. M., 474
Jeffery, R. W., 14, 49, 58–62,
    64–65, 76, 88, 161,
    258–259, 316, 399, 426
    519
Jeffrey, D. B., 248, 326, 351
Jemmott, J. B., III, 183
Jenkins, H. M., 130, 226
Jenkins, J. F., 330
Jennings, D. L., 399
Jensen, G. F., 273, 278
Jersild, A. T., 195
Johansson, R., 217
Johansson, S. L., 301, 328
John, E. R., 99, 135
Johns, C., 103
Johnson, B., 225
Johnson, C. A., 180
Johnson, D., 520
Johnson, D. W., 253
Johnson, E. H., 334
Johnson, H. J., 193
Johnson, P. E., 216
Johnson, R., 173
Johnson, R., 253
Johnson, S. M., 339
Johnson, W. T., 275
Johnston, J. M., 255
Jones, E. E., 6
Jones, G. E., 407
Jones, G. F., 361
Jones, R. T., 367–369, 428
Jongeward, R. H., Jr., 88
Jouvet, M., 196
Jusczyk, P. W., 501

Kafton, A., 185
Kagan, J., 31, 84
Kahn, R. L., 378
Kahn, R. M., 172
Kahneman, D., 217–219,
    222–223
Kahneman, E., 149, 409, 424,
    465
Kail, R. V., Jr., 88
Kakuyama, T., 476
Kalat, J. W., 200

Kanareff, V. T., 208
Kaneko, R., 487
Kanfer, F. H., 53, 55, 302,
    322–323, 336, 339–340,
    353, 355, 358
Kanfer, R., 360, 433, 447
Kant, H. S., 294
Kanungo, R. N., 326
Kaplan, J., 42
Kaplan, K. J., 284
Kaplan, R. M., 397, 438
Karker, A., 205
Karniol, R., 245, 247
Karoly, P., 339, 347, 352–353,
    366
Karpf, D., 117, 120
Karylowski, J., 314
Kasermann, M. L., 504, 509
Kashiwagi, K., 102
Kassas, M., 137
Katcher, A., 92
Kato, M., 320
Katovsky, W., 361
Katz, A., 195
Katz, E., 145, 152, 166
Katz, P. A., 269
Katz, R. C., 187, 427
Katzman, N., 24, 70
Kauffman, J. M., 85
Kaufman, A., 13, 27, 129, 229,
    264, 457
Kaufman, I., 466
Kaufman, K. F., 352
Kaufman, L., 326
Kavanagh, D. J., 408
Kavanaugh, R. D., 88
Kavcic, B., 252–253
Kawamura, S., 99
Kay, S. R., 493
Kaye, K., 83, 85
Kazdin, A. E., 62, 239, 258, 285,
    319–320, 337, 339, 363,
    367–369, 399, 404, 427
Keasey, C. B., 495
Keegan, D. L., 443
Keir, R., 317
Keller, H., 71
Kelley, J. E., 259
Kelling, G. L., 279
Kellogg, L. A., 99
Kellogg, R., 123
Kellogg, W. N., 99
Kelly, A., 334
Kelman, H. C., 349, 376,
    379–380
Kemp, J. C., 503
Kendall, L. M., 13, 476
Kendall, P. C., 518–519
Kendrick, M. J., 424
Keniston, K., 174, 258, 346,
    377, 450

Kennedy, T. D., 120
Kent, R. N., 123
Keohane, R. O., 452
Kerin, R. A., 326
Kerner, O., 172
Kerns, C. D., 301
Kerr, N. L., 251, 280
Kiesler, C. A., 477–478
Kiesler, S., 154
Kilham, W., 381
Killen, J. D., 180, 436
Kimbrell, D. L., 330
Kincaid, D. L., 151, 153–154
King, B. J., 433
King, M. L., 172
Kinne, S. B., III, 480
Kinsler, K., 289
Kipnis, D., 382–383
Kirigin, K. A., 254
Kirkland, K. D., 299, 407
Kirschenbaum, D. S., 339, 352,
    366, 475
Klapper, J. T., 145
Klaus, D. J., 252–253
Klayman, J., 132, 214
Kleifield, E., 162, 424, 445
Klein, K. J., 151
Klein, R. M., 302
Klein, R. P., 411
Klepac, R. K., 439
Kline, P., 3
Klinnert, M. D., 192, 309
Klorman, R., 320
Klosson, E. C., 492
Knerr, C. S., 469, 472
Koch, A. M., 99, 135
Koegel, R. L., 80, 87, 135, 212,
    220–221, 256
Koelling, R. A., 199
Koeppel, J., 240
Kohlberg, L., 48, 94–96, 481,
    488–492, 494, 497
Komaki, J., 339
Kopel, S. A., 259, 437
Kopp, R. E., 13, 27, 129, 229,
    457
Koriat, A., 223
Kornhaber, R. C., 320
Koskela, K., 180
Kosslyn, S. M., 56–57, 456
Kotler, P., 466
Kounin, J. S., 285
Kovacs, M., 517
Krane, R. V., 200
Krantz, D., 442
Krantz, D. H., 222
Krasner, L., 119, 375
Krauss, I., 260, 343, 416
Krauss, R. M., 311
Kravetz, D. F., 315
Krawitz, G., 277

Krebs, D., 312, 314
Kruglanski, A. W., 246
Krumboltz, J. D., 464
Kuczynski, L., 261, 289
Kuhn, D., 49
Kuiper, N. A., 337, 360
Kuipers, A. C. M., 520
Kun, A., 245, 247, 421
Kupers, C. J., 341
Kupfersmid, J. H., 481, 491, 497
Kurtines, W., 497
Kutchinsky, B., 294
Kuylenstierna, J., 222
Kuznicki, J. T., 208

LaBerge, D., 459
LaBerge, S. P., 127, 459
Labouvie, G. V., 418
Lacey, H. M., 14–15, 41, 446
Lacey, J. I., 190, 257
Lack, E. R., 448
Ladd, G. W., 416
Ladouceur, R., 422, 520
LaGana, C., 320
Laird, J. D., 356
Laitsch, K., 317
Lamal, P. A., 89
Lamb, A. K., 265
Lamb, M. E., 93, 309
Landers, D. M., 61–62, 399, 427, 433
Lane, J., 496
Lane, T. S., 327
Lane, W. C., 260, 343, 416
Lang, A. R., 277
Lang, P. J., 190
Langer, E. J., 225, 322, 399, 439, 449, 461
Langer, J., 481, 493
Langlois, J. H., 95
Lannon, P. B., 185
Lanzetta, J. T., 185, 208, 312–313, 315–316
LaPorte, R. E., 470
Larsen, K. S., 173
Larsen, O. N., 292
Lasater, T. M., 180
Lassen, M. K., 258
Latham, G. P., 162, 468–469, 472, 476, 479–480
Laude, R., 201–202, 441, 515
Laughlin, P. R., 104
Launier, R., 394, 442
LaVigne, G., 201
Lavin, D. E., 464
LaVoie, J. C., 266–267
Lawler, E. E., III, 236, 249, 253, 306
Lawless, M. W., 279

Lawrence, D. H., 107, 211
Lawrence, E. C., 469
Laws, D. R., 295
Lawson, D. M., 119, 277, 420
Lawson, R., 117
Lawton, J. T., 488
Lazarsfeld, P. E., 145
Lazarus, R. S., 194, 196, 198, 311, 394, 440, 442
Lazowick, L., 48
Leat, M., 289
Le Duc, D. R., 165
Ledwidge, B., 521
Lee, C., 220, 338, 368, 391, 393, 431, 434, 445, 471
Lee, C., 166, 168–169
Lefcourt, H. M., 349, 391, 413
Lefebvre-Pinard, M., 486
Lefkowitz, M., 207, 330
Le Furgy, W. G., 493
Lehman, R. S., 141
Leifer, A. D., 88, 324
Leighton, A. H., 345
Leighton, K., 441
Leitenberg, H., 188, 339
Leland, E. I., 434
Leming, J. S., 496
Lenfestey, W., 103
Lenneberg, E. H., 502
Leon, M., 492, 496
Leonard, H. S., 442
Leonard, L. B., 507
Lepenies, W., 21
Lepper, M. R., 242–244, 246, 249, 268–269, 270, 345, 367
Lerman, D., 349
Lerner, D., 165
Lerner, L., 299, 328
Lerner, M. J., 384
Lerner, R. M., 26
Letourneau, K. J., 96
Leuba, C., 234
Levan-Goldschmidt, E., 51, 86
Levenson, R. W., 310
Leventhal, G. S., 307
Leventhal, H., 140, 326, 416, 439
Levi, L., 309
Levicki, R. J., 466
Levin, H., 266, 369, 372, 414, 492
Levine, J. D., 428
Levine, J. P., 279
Levine, M., 117, 120
Levine, M., 217
Levine, S., 127–128, 441
Levy, B., 172
Levy, D. M., 415
Levy, E. A., 287
Levy, R. I., 272

Levy, V. M., Jr., 54
Lewin, K., 347
Lewinsohn, P. M., 225, 358, 361
Lewis, A., 244, 247
Lewis, C., 378
Lewis, M., 23, 29, 452
Libby, B., 33
Liben, L. S., 16
Lichtenstein, E., 120, 424, 436, 437
Lichtenstein, S., 138, 219, 223, 409, 464–465
Lidz, T., 221
Lieberman, M., 491
Lieberson, S., 172
Leibert, R. M., 70, 176, 286, 291, 299–300, 315, 340–341, 344–345, 442, 492
Lightbown, P., 503
Lilliston, L., 375
Lin, N., 152
Lindsey, P. H., 457
Lippitt, R., 207
Lippman, L. G., 129, 229
Lipset, S. M., 174, 450, 452
Lipsher, D. H., 29
Lipsitt, L. P., 31
Lipton, M. A., 293
Liptzin, M. B., 293, 324
Litrownik, A. J., 351
Little, J. C., 202
Little, R. E., 181
Littunen, Y., 165, 168
Lobitz, W. C., 360
Locke, D., 489
Locke, E. A., 162, 240, 242, 338, 391, 431, 468–469, 471–473, 476, 479
Locke, S. E., 183
Loeb, A., 360
Loew, C. A., 257
Lofberg, I., 204
Lofland, J., 260
Loftus, E. F., 126
Logan, C. H., 278
Logue, A. W., 200
Long, J. S., 256
Look, S. C., 248
Lopez, E. M., 247
Lord, C. G., 8–9
Lord, R. G., 244
Lourie, R. S., 265
Lovaas, O. I., 65, 80, 86–87, 90, 135–136, 212, 221, 256–257, 374
Loveland, K. K., 246
Lovitt, T. C., 351
Lowe, M. R., 37
Lowery, H. J., 311–312
Luborsky, L., 4

Miller, R. L., 261, 270, 342, 400, 403–404, 511
Miller, S. M., 104, 194, 196, 202, 239, 322–323, 361, 405, 440, 442, 448
Miller, W. E., 450
Milligan, W. L., 316
Mineka, S., 441, 445
Minor, W. W., 278
Mirsky, I. A., 308, 312
Mischel, H. N., 93, 420
Mischel, W., 3, 6–7, 9–10, 68, 72, 95, 137, 207, 218, 225, 257, 265, 344–345, 358, 517
Mitchell, T. R., 230, 472, 479
Mittman, A., 361
Miura, I., 432
Mizuguchi, R., 473
Moerk, C., 503
Moerk, E. L., 503, 507–508
Moeser, S. D., 506
Mohr, L. B., 149
Mokros, J. R., 323
Monahan, J., 276
Montgomery, G. T., 351
Monty, R. A., 391
Moore, B. S., 338
Moore, L. M., 306
Moore, L. P., 270
Moore, M. K., 84
Mordkoff, A. M., 311
Morelli, E. A., 434
Morelli, M., 383
Morency, N., 311
Morgan, D. P., 261
Morgan, M., 245–246, 249, 472
Morgan, M., 318, 512–513
Morgulas, S., 504–505
Morris, L. W., 442
Morris, W. N., 421
Morrison, B. M., 413
Moses, L., 421
Moss, I. L., 104
Moss, M. K., 519–520
Mossholder, K. W., 249
Mount, M. K., 351
Moura, N. G. M., 338
Mouton, J. S., 207, 330
Mowrer, O. H., 48, 68–69, 107, 187, 234–235, 264–265, 410
Moyer, T. J., 80
Mueller, L. K., 105
Mullen, B., 418–419
Mullener, N., 356
Muller, E. N., 450–451
Munby, M., 520
Munn, N. L., 37
Munro, D. J., 163
Murphy, J. V., 308

Murray, D. M., 180
Murray, E. J., 5, 400
Murray, F. B., 494
Murray, J. P., 176, 290
Myers, A. K., 234
Myers, P. E., 190
Mynatt, C., 381

Naditch, M., 450
Nagel, E., 33
Nagel, L. E., 127
Nagin, D., 278, 333
Nakazawa, J., 299
Nanda, P. C., 186
Nash, J. D., 179
Nath, R., 470
Nathanson, M., 493
Nathanson, S., 209
Neal, R. A., 139
Neidermayer, H., 321
Neisser, U., 25, 218, 369
Neistein, S., 361
Nellans, T. H., 261
Nelson, D., 253
Nelson, K., 508
Nelson, K. E., 503
Nelson, R., 123
Nelson, R. E., 358, 361, 367–369
Nelson, R. O., 337, 339, 363, 365
Nelson, S., 350, 420
Nelson, W. J., 351
Nemcek, D., Jr., 421
Nemetz, G. H., 258, 319, 324
Nesdale, A. R., 214
Neufeld, M. M., 67
Neufeld, R. W. J., 67, 323, 428–429, 442
Neuringer, A., 50, 338
Neves, D. M., 459
Newcomb, T. M., 520
Newell, A. 390
Newell, K. M., 66, 390
Newsom, C. D., 80, 86–87, 374
Newtson, D., 62, 460
Nicassio, P., 123
Nicholls, J. G., 402
Nicolich, L. M., 503
Niehaus, J. C., 436
Nimmo, D., 325
Nisbett, R. E., 6, 122–126, 132, 222
Nissinen, A., 180
Nolde, H. C., 334
Norman, D. A., 457
Notterman, J. M., 188–189
Novaco, R. W., 518
Novak, G., 504

Nuttin, J. R., 247
Nye, J. S., 452
Nyman, B. A., 80

O'Brien, G. T., 188
O'Brien, T. P., 259
O'Bryant, S. L., 93, 327, 511
O'Connell, D. C., 127
O'Connor, R. D., 319
Odom, R. D., 233
Offermann, L. R., 185
Ogawa, N., 308
Ogston, K. M., 316
O'Hara, M. W., 359, 362
Ohman, A., 195, 202, 204
Okada, A., 473, 476
Oldfield-Box, H., 98
O'Leary, K. D., 341, 351–352, 371
Olian-Gottlieb, J. D., 230
Oliver, D. D., 79
Oliver, P. R., 79
Ollendick, T. H., 267, 286, 368
Olley, J. G., 246
O'Malley, M., 196
Omelich, C. L., 431
Opton, E. M., 383
Ora, J. P., Jr., 340
Ordman, A. M., 475
Orenstein, H., 188
Ormiston, L. H., 344
Orr, S. P., 185
Orton, R., 25
Orwell, G., 45
Osberg, T. M., 3
Oscar, G., 446
Oshima, H. T., 163
Oster, H., 309
Ostfeld, B., 269
Ostlund, L. E., 148, 171
Ostrow, A. C., 476
O'Sullivan, M. J., 320
Ottenberg, P., 382
Otto, L., 95
Overton, W. F., 96
Owen, Y., 80

Packer, H. L., 272, 281
Page, M. M., 185
Paivio, A., 58, 455–456
Palmer, J., 278
Panciera, L., 445
Pang, S., 326
Panzarella, R., 380
Papousek, H., 85–86, 91, 133
Papousek, M., 85–86, 91, 133
Parke, R. D., 88, 266, 268, 289–290, 293, 344
Parker, J., 226, 273, 281

Ritz, E. G., 84
Rizley, R., 360
Robert, M., 486–487
Roberts, D. F., 24, 70, 324, 326
Roberts, M. C., 85
Roberts, N., 162
Roberts, R. N., 517
Robertson, S. J., 287
Robertson, T. S., 144, 170
Rodin, J., 439
Rodrigues, A., 269
Rogers, C. R., 356, 409
Rogers, E. M., 142–144, 146, 148, 150–155, 159–160
Rogers, L., 425
Rogers, R. W., 93, 392, 439, 511
Rokeach, M., 36, 324
Roling, N. G., 157
Romanczyk, R. G., 338, 352
Romeo, A., 158
Rosch, E., 109, 218, 506
Rosekrans, M. A., 288
Rosen, E., 123
Rosen, G. M., 123
Rosen, M., 240
Rosen, S., 207
Rosenbaum, G., 222
Rosenbaum, M. E., 208, 302
Rosenbaum, M. S., 353
Rosenberg, D., 276
Rosenberg, M. J., 520
Rosenberg, S., 58
Rosenblum, L. A., 29
Rosenfeld, H. M., 121
Rosenfield, D., 246
Rosenhan, D. L., 69, 314, 340, 344, 346, 450
Rosenholtz, S. H., 417
Rosenholtz, S. J., 417
Rosenman, R. H., 362
Rosenthal, B., 206
Rosenthal, T. L., 26, 48–49, 54, 58, 61, 65, 67, 72–73, 77, 88–89, 100–103, 161, 190, 194, 201, 206, 209, 238, 285, 300, 313, 316, 319, 404, 484, 487, 498, 520
Rosner, M., 252–253
Ross, C., 420
Ross, D., 64–65, 72, 94, 104, 207, 288, 327, 346
Ross, H. L., 279, 282
Ross, J. M., 247
Ross, L., 6, 132, 222
Ross, M., 245, 247, 251
Ross, S. A., 64–65, 72, 94, 104, 207, 288, 327, 330, 346
Rothstein, A. L., 67
Rotkin, L., 332
Rotter, J. B., 230, 391, 412–413

Rowe, A. R., 278
Roy, D. W., 326
Rozelle, R. M., 180
Rozensky, R. H., 351, 354
Rozin, P., 200
Rubenstein, J. L., 166, 415
Rubin, J. Z., 209
Ruble, D. N., 247–248, 349, 420–421, 494–495
Ruckmick, C. A., 311
Rudman, R., 138
Rule, B. G., 214
Rumbaugh, D. M., 99
Rush, A. J., 517
Rushton, J. P., 10, 261, 289, 307, 497
Russell, D., 349
Russell, J. C., 330
Ryan, R. M., 242
Ryan, T. A., 468–469
Rychlak, J. F., 68
Rychtarik, R. G., 326
Ryff, C. D., 31

Saari, L. M., 162, 468, 472
Sabido, M., 147–148
Sachs, D. H., 293
Sackett, R. S., 61
Safire, W., 378
Sagotsky, G., 244, 247, 345, 367
St. Peter, S., 93
Salancik, G. R., 246
Salapatek, P., 86
Sallows, G. O., 120
Salomon, G., 71–72, 394, 427
Salonen, J. T., 180
Salovey, P., 314
Saltzman, L. E., 277
Samuelson, C., 209
Sanday, P. R., 385
Sanders, A. K., 327
Sanders, D. H., 163–164
Sanders, K. M., 324
Sanders, M. R., 261
Sanders, S. H., 323
Sandler, J., 373
Sanford, N., 349, 376
Sansone, C., 242
Santogrossi, D. A., 352
Santrock, J. W., 352, 355
Sarason, I. G., 319–320, 394, 407, 442, 465
Sawin, D. B., 314–315
Scase, R., 307
Schachter, S., 191–192, 353, 408
Schaffer, H. R., 133
Schaie, K. W., 418, 485
Scharff, W. H., 292
Schauer, F. F., 296
Scheier, M. F., 355

Scherrer, H., 196
Schiller, H. I., 166, 168
Schleifer, M., 493, 497
Schlesinger, I. M., 498
Schlottmann, R. S., 292
Schmidt, G., 110–111, 293
Schmidt, R. A., 110–111
Schneider, D. J., 26
Schneider, W., 452
Schneiderman, W., 355
Schoenfeld, W. N., 188–189
Schonebaum, R. M., 128
Schover, L. R., 87
Schramm, W., 165
Schreibman, L., 87, 135, 212, 220–221
Schroeder, H. E., 188, 320, 519
Schulthies, K. R., 354
Schumaker, J. B., 503
Schumer, F., 3
Schunk, D. H., 224, 248–249, 391, 394, 397–398, 402, 406, 424, 431, 465, 470, 472, 475
Schwab, D. P., 230, 240
Schwartz, A. N., 251
Schwartz, B., 132, 187, 199
Schwartz, G. E., 13, 118, 190, 192–193, 257, 309, 515
Schwartz, J. L., 360
Schwartz, S. P., 57
Schweiger, D. M., 479
Scott, N. A., 351
Scott, P. M., 69
Searle, J. R., 328
Sears, P. S., 266, 347, 348
Sears, R. R., 369, 372, 414, 492
Sechrest, L., 286
Seidner, M. L., 323
Seligman, C., 247
Seligman, M. E. P., 195, 199–201, 202–203, 360–361, 391, 412, 414, 441, 446–447
Sellin, T., 334
Sentis, S., 369
Serbin, L. A., 94, 420
Seta, J. J., 302
Shafer, J., 327
Shapiro, E. S., 286
Sharpley, C. F., 287
Shatz, M., 507
Shaver, P., 192
Shaw, D. W., 319
Shaw, E. R., 323
Shaw, K. N., 468, 472
Shaw, P., 520
Shaw, W. A., 61
Sheffield, F. D., 54
Shepard, R. N., 56–57, 456
Sherer, M., 392

Wheeler, V. A., 416
Whipple, C., 138
Whipple, K., 4
Whipple, T. W., 93, 327
White, G., 339
White, G. M., 69, 73, 301
White, M. A., 327
White, P., 126
White, R. W., 410–411
White, S. E., 479
Whitehurst, C., 237
Whitehurst, G. J., 80, 503, 507
Whiting, J. W. M., 265
Wicklund, R. A., 388
Widmann, D. E., 293
Wieser, G., 252–253
Wilhelm, H., 87
Wilkes, R. L., 433
Wilkins, J. L., 292
Williams, E., 61
Williams, J. G., 73
Williams, J. R., 451
Williams, S. L., 118, 162, 393, 419, 424, 443–445, 520
Williams, T. M., 155
Willner, A. G., 254
Wilson, C. C., 287
Wilson, D. O., 330
Wilson, G. D., 3
Wilson, G. T., 4, 123, 258, 261, 277, 338, 351, 368, 370, 399, 427, 519–520
Wilson, J. Q., 279
Wilson, T. D., 122–126
Wilson, W. C., 298
Wincze, J. P., 188, 319
Windheuser, H. J., 317
Wine, J., 442

Winfrey, C., 36, 261, 514
Winter, W., 500
Winton, W., 311
Wittmaier, B. C., 93
Wolf, M. M., 35, 238, 254, 260
Wolf, S., 428
Wolfer, J. A., 322
Wolfgang, M. E., 55, 238, 334, 446, 478
Wolkenstein, B., 317
Wolkin, J. R., 288
Woloshin, G. W., 493
Wolpe, J., 427
Wonderly, D. M., 481, 491, 497
Wood, P. D., 179
Woodson, R., 84
Wortman, C. B., 445
Wright, C. L., 161, 258, 426
Wright, D. E., 339
Wright, J., 358
Wright, J. C., 130
Wright, P., 117, 126
Wright, T. L., 392–393, 429
Wulbert, M., 80
Wunderlin, R. J., 277
Wyle, C. I., 275
Wylie, R. C., 356, 409
Wynne, L. C., 187
Wyrwicka, W., 324

Yablonsky, L., 238, 355
Yalom, I. D., 358
Yalom, M., 358
Yamaguchi, S., 308
Yarnold, P. R., 362
Yarrow, L. J., 411, 415
Yarrow, M. R., 51, 69, 79, 86
Yates, B. T., 302, 446

Yilk, M. D., 61
Yorkston, N. J., 4
Young, B. G., 294
Young, E. H., 71
Young, K. R., 261
Yukelson, D., 226, 419, 422, 424, 434, 449
Yukl, G. A., 472, 476, 479
Yulish-Muszynski, S., 421
Yuseph, S., 171
Yussen, S. R., 53–54, 77, 300

Zahn-Waxler, C., 314
Zailian, M., 426
Zajonc, R. B., 196–198, 327, 416
Zaltman, G., 146, 149, 466
Zanna, M. P., 492
Zarbatany, L., 309
Zarcone, V. P., Jr., 127
Zeisel, H., 333
Zeiss, A. M., 360, 447
Zettle, R. D., 515
Zidon, I., 474
Zillmann, D., 50, 192, 294–295, 408
Zimbardo, P. G., 26, 191, 381, 383, 388, 478, 513
Zimmerman, B. J., 26, 49, 58, 61, 65, 72–73, 77, 88–89, 100–103, 105, 209, 285, 289, 481, 487, 498, 504–505
Zimring, F. E., 272–273, 281
Zivin, G., 517
Zlatchin, C., 315
Zubin, J., 3
Zubritzky, E., 473

SUBJECT INDEX

Aberrant acts
  confluence of determinants in,
    176
  and modeling influences,
    176–177
  time–series analysis of,
    176–177
Abstract modeling
  in conceptual learning,
    102–103, 209, 285, 299,
    506
  influenced by
    cognitive competency,
      102–104, 494–495, 501,
      507–508
    complexity of input, 501,
      507
    contrasting modeling, 54,
      503, 507
    differential feedback,
      100–102, 299, 502,
      507–509
    rule verbalization, 102, 104,
      209–210, 422
    semantic referents,
      100–101, 505–508

  in language, 20, 100–101,
    501–509
  in moral reasoning, 492, 495
  in personal standards,
    344–345
Achievement motivation
  and extrinsic incentives, 430
  and personal standards,
    430–431, 476
  and self–efficacy, 391, 424,
    430–431, 435
Addiction, 175–176, 435–436
Affective learning
  cognitive determinants of,
    188–196, 315–319
  direct experience, 183–185
  symbolic experience, 185–186
  vicarious experience, 50,
    186–187, 315–319,
    511–513
Affective primacy theory
  and cognitive appraisal,
    196–198
  holistic activation in, 196–197
  hot vs. cold cognitions in,
    197–198

  specialized encoding system
    in, 197
  and unconscious affective
    encoding, 198
Aggression
  advantageous comparison,
    379
  definition of, 214
  dissociative mechanisms in
    blaming victims, 291, 296,
      384–385
    dehumanizing victims, 296,
      382–385, 387
    diffusion of responsibility,
      380–381
    displacement of
      responsibility, 379–380
    euphemistic labeling,
      378–379
    minimization of
      consequences, 291,
      295–296, 381, 385,
      387
    moral justifications,
      291–293, 296, 333,
      376–378, 385, 387

Aggression (*cont.*)
and empathy, 307, 314–316
instigators of
anticipated rewards, 173,
288, 292, 331
commands, 328, 379–381,
383
delusional beliefs, 458
emotional arousal, 191–192,
294
modeling, 172, 291–293
physical assaults, 271
reduction of rewards, 304
status threats, 238
learned by
direct experience, 27, 30,
271
observation, 50, 172–176,
324
modification of, 287–288
rewards for, 30, 238,
294–296, 384–385
sexual, 294–296, 384–385
Airline hijacking
contagion of, 173, 331–332
modeling influences in, 173,
331–332
temporal course of, 175
Alcoholic drinking
in criminal conduct, 276
dissociative mechanisms in,
276–277
expectancy effects in,
276–277
modeling determinants of,
206
and self-control, 276–277,
435–436
Altruism, 315–316, 341
Analytic decomposition of risks,
137–138
Anticipatory mechanisms
in avoidance behavior, 187
in classical conditioning,
182–185, 192–196
in drug tolerance, 183–184
in motivation, 20, 77, 179,
229, 243, 364, 410
in operant conditioning,
13–14, 112, 229
and self-produced realities,
21, 26, 230
in self-regulation, 19–21,
26–27, 78, 122, 179, 262,
264, 350, 463, 467, 491
Anxiety
and autonomic arousal,
187–188
and dual process theory,
187–188

elimination of
cognitive restructuring, 194
extinction, 187
guided mastery, 190,
258–259, 423, 443–444,
519–520
modeling, 294, 319–321,
443
generalization of, 219–220
and perceived control, 220,
318–320, 321–322,
441–442, 445
and predictability, 195–196,
318, 320, 322, 440–441
role of in defensive behavior,
187–188, 444–445
and self-arousal mechanisms,
193–196, 312–313,
441–442, 445
theories of
behavioristic, 439–440
psychodynamic, 439
self-efficacy, 188–190,
320–321, 394, 426–428,
434, 440, 442–445,
447–448
tripartite, 190–191
two-factor, 187–188
transmitted through
modeling, 315–318,
511–513
Aswan dam effects
effects of
ecological, 137
health, 137
social, 137
risk analysis, 137
Attention
in conceptual learning,
100–102, 128
and contingency recognition,
134–135, 192–193, 196,
414–415
as influenced by
affective valence, 51–52
arousal level, 52, 316
association preferences,
54–55, 94, 97, 369,
414–415
distinctiveness, 51–52, 54,
62–63, 86, 100, 133–135,
148, 219
functional value, 52–53,
84–85
perceptual set, 52–53,
86–87, 354
performance feedback,
61–62, 100, 414–415
sensory capacities, 52–53
vicarious incentives, 52–53,

77, 80–81
in observational learning,
51–54, 62–63, 65, 70–74,
77, 84, 86–87, 101, 148,
221, 299–300, 316,
503-504, 506
in operant conditioning,
134–135
in regulation of pain,
322–323, 428–429
and televised modeling, 54
Attitude change
and behavior change,
160–161
in diffusion of innovations,
160–161
induction through
affective change, 197
behavior change, 160–161,
519–520
belief change, 197
influence of vicarious
influences, 186
and modeling influences, 186,
197
and persuasive
communications,
160–161, 197
and success experiences,
160–161, 197, 519
Attribution
in ability appraisal, 349–350,
395, 402, 420
and achievement motivation,
420
in depression, 447
dispositional vs. situational, 6
and intrinsic motivation, 242,
245–246
in labeling of emotions,
123–124, 191–192
and misattribution therapy,
123
and phobic behavior, 123–124
and self-restraints, 268–270
and self-reward, 349–350
for success and failure,
349–350, 360, 420
Autism
attentional deficits in, 86–87,
220–221
language acquisition in, 65,
221
and observational learning,
86–87, 221
treatment of, 86–87
Automaticity
achieved by
mergerization of operations,
114, 459

routinized linkage of actions
to contexts, 460
shift in locus of attention,
114, 460–461
benefits and costs of, 459, 461
distinguished from
unconsciousness, 459,
461–462
and distributed consciousness,
459
in learning vs. skilled
performance, 56, 114,
122, 461–462, 504–505,
558–559
of multilevel control, 114
of perturbing thought, 5, 461
of reinforcement, 12–16, 106,
111, 115, 121–122
remediation of, 461
and segmentation of behavior,
114, 460
Avoidance behavior
acquisition of, 186
explained by
control of aversive events,
188
dual process theory,
187–188
perceived inefficacy,
188–190, 440, 442–445
resistance to change, 188–189,
195–196, 201, 219
Awareness
and access to thought
processes, 14, 117, 119,
123–127, 217
of antecedent events, 5,
192–193, 315
as belief conversion, 4–5
of covariation, 13, 116,
120–122, 192–193, 315,
457
definition of, 115–116
influence on
affective learning, 121,
192–196, 315
associative learning, 121,
192–196, 457
behavior change, 119–122
emotional reactivity,
192–196, 315
operant conditioning,
119–122
measurement of, 116–119
and partially correlated
hypotheses, 120–121
of response outcomes, 5, 13,
119–122
of responses, 120–121
and routinization of

performance, 114, 461
of stimulus registration versus
stimulus recognition, 193,
196
and thought probes, 14,
116–119, 124–126
and unobservable
consequences, 120–121
verbally induced, 118, 121,
192–193

Behavioral production
and availability of
components, 52, 65, 90
central integration in, 62–64
and conception matching,
64–68, 90, 107, 110–111,
114, 390, 504
and error correction, 64–68,
90, 112–113, 504
feedback influences on
augmented, 66–67, 71
proprioceptive, 66–67
verbal, 66–67, 90
visual, 66–67, 71
and physical deficits, 65, 90
and self–observation, 66–67
Beliefs
and confirmatory bias, 130,
189, 223, 225–226,
516
contingency, 129–131, 183,
257–258
delusional, 458, 513–514
disconfirmation of, 190, 223,
402, 458, 517, 520
verification of
enactively, 21, 27, 510–511
logically, 19, 27, 514–515
socially, 7, 513–514
vicariously, 27, 511–513
Biofeedback, 425
Biological preparedness
and arbitrary contingencies,
199–200
assessment of, 203–204
cross–species comparisons,
199
defined, 199
and ease of learning,
199–200, 203–204
evolutionary consequences,
199
vs. experiential preparedness,
200, 203–205
vs. forethought, 204
and gender role behavior,
95–96
general process vs.

event–specific learning,
199
and phobeogenic properties,
201–203
selectivity of phobias, 201–202
rate of extinction, 204
responsiveness to cognitive
influences, 203
taste aversions, 199
Bureaucratic organizations
change through external
influence, 163–164
depersonalization in, 383–384
resistance to change, 163–164,
451, 466–467
social controls in, 163–164,
467

Capital punishment
brutalizing effect, 332–334
deterrent effect, 332–333
discriminatory application,
334
Causal structures
in theoretical approaches
behavioristic, 12–18, 22, 26,
40, 74, 364–369
psychodynamic, 2–5, 31
social cognitive, 18–30, 157,
368–369
and triadic reciprocality,
12–13, 23–30, 369,
521–522
unidirectional, 22–23, 30,
39–40, 219, 368,
521–522
Chance encounters
branching power of, 33–37
defined, 32
as determinants of life paths,
30–37
See also Fortuitous
determinants
Civil disobedience
conditions of, 377
definition of, 377
justification of, 377–378
Coercive control
in authoritarian societies, 43,
45, 161
in development of aggression,
27, 30, 271
and institutions of freedom,
43
reciprocal, 27, 30,
271
safeguards against
individual, 43–44
social, 43–46

Coercive power
abuses of, 43, 328, 378,
382–383, 514
institutional, 43, 161, 328, 378
and magnitude of political
violence, 305, 306
measure of, 305
Cognitive–behavior therapy
and cognitive determinism,
519
by cognitive restructuring,
515–521
enactive factor in, 520–521
for faulty thinking, 515–520
mechanisms vs. modes of
change, 519–520
relative effectiveness of, 515,
519–520
and triadic reciprocality,
520–522
by verbal self–guidance,
517–520
Cognitive determinants
of associative learning, 14,
192–196
of behavioral inhibitions, 262,
264, 266–267
of emotional reactions, 13–14,
25, 192–196, 313–315
externalization of, 15–16,
329–330, 363
in modeling, 51–68, 72–73,
86–91, 100–105
of motivation, 19–21,
229–232, 301, 467–480
in operant conditioning,
13–16, 106–114, 116,
121–122, 229–230
of psychotic behavior, 458
Cognitive development
global structures vs.
specialized competencies,
128–129, 483–485, 494
and language development,
498, 501
modeling determinants of, 74,
89, 91–92, 101, 486–487
multiplicity of developmental
sequences, 483–485, 487
social determinants of, 88,
483, 485–488
theories of
information processing, 483
social cognitive, 128,
483–488
stage, 82, 482–485
Cognitive modeling
cognitive operations, 74, 216,
320, 464–465
coping strategies, 319–320,
426–427, 442, 518

generative rules, 73, 101–102,
209–210
self-appraisal skills, 422
in self-instructional training,
74, 319–320, 442, 518
self-regulation, 319–320, 341,
518
Cognitive motivation
attribution, 242–243
equilibration, 89, 234–235,
480–482, 489
goal representation, 20, 233,
239–241, 245, 467–480,
494–495
outcome representation, 19,
91, 106–107, 179, 229,
467
self-efficacy in, 21, 394–395
self–evaluation in, 233,
239–241, 454–455
Cognitive representation
abstract vs. specific, 88,
110–111, 455–457
amodal vs. multimodal,
455–457
conceptual linkages in,
455–456
of contingency structures, 13,
19, 27, 457–458
declarative vs. procedural,
107, 111
dual code theory, 58, 455–457
in enactive learning, 106–114,
414–415
form of
imaginal, 14, 56–60, 82–83,
88, 455–456
propositional, 57, 88, 109,
455–457, 514
verbal, 56–60, 83, 88,
455–456
in observational learning, 51,
53, 55–60, 62, 64–67, 76,
80, 82–83, 87–90
Collective behavior
coercive, 29, 172, 450
and collective decision
making, 451, 466–467
mobilization of support for,
180, 328, 451–453, 467
modeling influences in,
172–173, 450, 467
nonviolent, 172
and perceived efficacy,
226–227, 304–305,
449–453
personality correlates of
participants in, 172–174,
450
public interpretations of,
377–378

vicarious reward, 172
violent, 172–175
Communications
construction of social reality,
71
effects of
agenda setting, 45
direct influence, 145–146
mediated influence,
145–146
reflector of public views,
145
as reciprocal process, 152
social vs. mediated, 145–146
technology
and social diffusion, 20,
70–71, 142,
164–165
in transcultural modeling,
142, 165–170
See also Diffusion; Mass
media; Social networks
Community organization
Alinsky approach, 180, 466
and coalition formation, 451,
466
in social diffusion, 179–180
Competence
entity vs. generative skill, 224,
476–477
and perceived self–efficacy,
411–412
Competence motivation
and self-efficacy, 411–412
and self–evaluative
mechanisms, 411
as a universal drive, 243
Computer modeling
of cognitive processes,
215–217, 464
theoretical guides for
verification of, 140–141
Computer networks, 154–155
Conceptual learning
through abstract modeling,
89, 102, 104, 505–506
and attentional processes,
100–102, 128, 134–135,
211, 506
hypothesis testing in, 101,
127–128, 210, 212,
214
and level of abstraction, 506
multidimensional, 101, 128,
210–211
through response feedback,
109, 111, 127–128,
134–135, 210
and rule learning, 102–103,
109, 111, 127–128
stimulus saliency, 211, 506

Diffusion (cont.)
  segment structures in,
    143–144
  of social policies, 163, 170,
    286
  societal effects, 155–158,
    166–169
  temporal course of, 142–145,
    172–173, 176–177, 450
  temporal lag in, 144–145,
    172, 174–177
  transcultural, 142, 151,
    155–158, 165–169
  via social networks, 144–145,
    151–155
Disconfirmation of beliefs, 190,
  223, 402, 458, 517, 520
Disinhibitory effects
  by absence of sanctions,
    290–293, 330, 332
  on aggression, 174, 176,
    276–277, 291–293,
    376–385
  on aggressive and sexual
    behavior compared,
    296
  of alcohol, 276–277
  of anonymity, 387–388
  defined, 49
  of distributed responsibility,
    380–381
  through emotional arousal,
    388
  explanations of, 375–389
  of freedom from reprisal,
    42–43
  of mass media influences,
    172–173, 176, 291–292
  and model characteristics, 174
  and model-observer similarity,
    49, 319–320
  and multiple modeling, 319,
    330
  by outcome information, 49
  and perceived efficacy, 49
  by self-absolving practices,
    291–293, 295–296,
    375–389
  on sexual behavior, 276–277,
    293–296, 319, 384–385
  by social justification,
    291–293, 296, 333, 349,
    376–378
  and television journalism,
    292–293
  and transgressive behavior,
    176, 290, 330, 332
  of violent erotica, 294–296,
    385
Dispositional–situational
    controversy, 5–12, 22, 29,
    328–329

Dissociation of internal control
  mechanisms of
  attribution of blame, 291,
    296, 305, 384–385
  dehumanization, 296,
    382–385, 387, 498
  diffusion of responsibility,
    380–381, 387, 498
  displacement of
    responsibility, 305,
    379–380, 387
  euphemistic labeling, 150,
    378–379, 498
  misrepresentation of
    consequences, 291,
    295–296, 381, 385, 387
  moral justifications,
    291–293, 296, 333, 349,
    376–378, 385, 387, 492,
    495
  palliative comparison, 379
  in industrial practices,
    380–381, 385–386
  in mass media industry, 378
  in military atrocities, 379, 385,
    389
  and need for organizational
    safeguards, 389
  in political violence, 377–378,
    385
  in religious wars, 377
  and self-deception, 386–387
  in sexual violence, 384–385
  and victim self-despisal, 385
Dream activity
  awareness of, 126–127
  and mastery experiences, 258,
    519
  in phobic disorders, 258, 318
Drive theory
  of avoidance behavior,
    187–188
  and drive–reduction
    hyptheses, 236
  vs. incentive theory, 236–237
  and intense stimulation,
    232–234
  and intrinsic motivation,
    242–243
  psychodynamic, 2–5
  verification of, 2, 410
Drug tolerance
  and compensatory reactions,
    183–184
  learning mechanism in, 184
  opponent–process theory, 184
  situation specificity of, 184
Dual code theory, 58, 455–457
Dual process theory
  of avoidance behavior,
    187–188
  deficiencies of, 187–188

Dysfunctional expectancy
    learning
  coincidental association, 219
  inappropriate generalization,
    219–220
Dysfunctional self-evaluative
    systems
  in depression, 342, 358–362,
    446–447
  in psychosomatic disorders,
    362–363

Effectance motivation, 410–412
Electronic acculturation,
  165–170
Emotional arousal
  and attribute similarity,
    312–313
  cognitive mediation of, 19,
    188–196, 311–316
  comparison of verbal and
    expressive cues, 310–311
  by correlated experiences,
    185–187, 309, 311–313,
    316
  differentiation of, 191–192,
    309–310, 407–408
  by expressive cues, 186,
    307–314
  labeling of, 191–192, 311, 407
  and perceived self-efficacy,
    188–190, 401, 406–408,
    440–445
  self-arousal mechanism in,
    193–196, 313–315, 401,
    441–442, 515
  thought–induced, 13–14, 19,
    25, 192–193, 309–310,
    313–314, 441–442, 445
  vicarious, 50–51, 186–187,
    293–295, 307–315, 326
Empathy
  constituent processes in
    emotional responsiveness,
      314
    imaginative self-
      involvement, 313–315
    perspective taking, 313–315
  through correlated
    experiences, 313–315
  developmental changes in,
    313–314
  effects on aggression, 307,
    314–316, 382
  relation to behavior, 314–315
  and vicarious arousal, 307,
    312–315
Enactive learning
  and awareness, 13, 111,
    115–122, 457–459,
    461–462

augmenting outcome information
  accelerating distal outcomes, 136–140
  actuating appropriate behavior, 115, 135–136
  channeling attention, 134–135
  proximating distal effects, 132–140
  simulating distal outcomes, 140–141
central regulation of, 13, 77, 111–114, 460, 462
cognitive processes in, 13, 106–111, 113–116, 120–121, 131, 414–415
as a conception–matching process, 107, 110–111, 114
developmental changes in, 133–134
and illusory contingencies, 130–131
power of belief over consequent, 129–130, 457
and response information
  delayed, 109, 112–113, 132–133, 136–140
  extrinsic, 108, 110, 112, 460–461
  intrinsic, 108, 110–114
  sensory, 108, 110–114
as special case of observational learning, 77, 111
Epidemiological methods, 139
Epiphenomenalism, 17, 445
Equilibration theory of motivation, 89, 234–235, 480–482, 486–487, 489, 494–495
Erotica
  constitutional issues in, 296
  effects on
    aggression, 294–295
    attitudes toward women, 294–295
    sexual anxieties, 294, 296, 319
    sexual arousal, 293–295
    sexual standards, 294
  violent, 294–296
Event–specific versus general process learning, 199
Expectancy–value model, 230–232, 276–277, 412–413, 463–467, 473
Expert systems, 215–217, 464

Fads and fashions, 146, 150, 168

Fantasy, 18, 293, 463
Forethought
  and biological preparedness, 204
  through cognitive representation, 18–19, 26–27, 136–137, 206, 230, 233, 239, 243, 457, 467
  and predictive cues, 76, 182–185, 205–206, 213, 283
  and self-efficacy, 220
Fortuitous determinants
  and determinism, 30, 33
  of life paths, 30–37
  nonsocial, 37–38
  personal predictors of impact
    emotional ties, 34–35
    entry skills, 34
    tools of personal agency, 38
    values and standards, 35
  social predictors of impact
    information management, 35, 514
    milieu reach and closedness, 36, 260, 513–514
    milieu rewards, 35, 260
    psychological closedness, 36–37, 260
Freedom
  defined, 39
  and determinism, 38–43
  as exercise of self-influence, 39–42
  institutions of, 43
  limited by
    behavioral and cognitive deficits, 42
    discriminatory practices, 42
    dysfunctional self-restraints, 42
    societal prohibitions, 42
  as options and rights, 42–43
  and reciprocal mechanisms, 39–42
  safeguards of
    individual, 43–44
    social, 43–46
  and survival practices, 45–46

Gender role
  acquisition and performance distinguished, 93–94
  and biological determinism, 92, 95
  influenced by
    gender conception, 92, 95–98
    media stereotyping, 93, 103, 327, 350, 420

modeling, 93–98, 103, 327
  peer relations, 93, 350
  power relations, 93, 98, 207
  social labeling, 92
  social sanctions, 92–94, 97–98
  social structuring of activities, 92–93
  modification of, 93, 327
  and self-efficacy, 93, 419–420, 431–433
  theories of
    cognitive developmental, 95–98
    self-schema, 97
    social cognitive, 96
Generality of change
  achieved by
    causal attribution, 259, 261
    enhanced self-efficacy, 258–259, 261
    environmental changes, 259
    incentive practices, 256–257, 509
    self-regulatory means, 255, 260–262
    similarity transfer, 147–148
    transfer of training, 256
  forms of
    interpersonal, 254, 256, 509
    modality, 254, 257, 502–505
    situational, 254, 256–257, 509
Goals
  assigned vs. self-determined, 472, 479
  cognitive comparison process, 234–235, 467, 469–471, 482
  commitment to
    and justifications, 478–479
    personal, 477–478
    social, 477–478
  and conceptions of intelligence, 476–477
  and contingency control, 13, 467–468
  effects of
    interest enhancement, 241–243, 247–249, 471–472, 475
    motivational, 233–235, 350, 360, 467–480
    self-efficacy, 248–249, 469–471, 475
  group, 466–467
  intentions as, 19, 468–469
  mechanisms governing
    self-efficacy, 470–471, 482
    self-evaluation, 467–471, 479

Goals (*cont.*)
mediating incentive effects, 476
motivating power of, 19–20, 360, 467, 480
and performance feedback, 249, 469–471
properties of
challenge, 241–245, 247–249, 347–348, 359–360, 469–474, 476, 482
proximity, 148–149, 179 336, 453, 470, 474–477, 480
specificity, 472
self-set, 338, 363, 368, 468–469, 471, 475–476, 479
subgoals, 248–249, 359–360, 362
See also Internal standards

Health habits
advertising influences on, 325–327
and cardiovascular disease, 178–180
change by
community programs, 178–180
modeling, 180, 324
self-regulation, 179–180
in chronic diseases, 178
diffusion of, 179–180
and lifestyle changes, 178
psychological vs. biomedical model, 177–178
self-efficacy in, 179–180, 437–439
Homicides
under delusional control, 458
and legal deterrents, 332–334
modeling influences in, 176–177
symbolic rehearsal of, 458
Hormonal control
in humans and animals compared, 232–233
of sexual behavior, 232–233
Humanization, 383–384
Human nature, 1–2, 21–22

Identification
with the aggressor, 484
dependent, 484
distinguished from imitation, 48
See also Modeling;

Observational learning
Identity theory, 17–18, 521
Illusory
causality, 130–131, 225–226, 458
control
competence cues, 225, 449
and depression, 225
incompetence, 449
Imagery
compared with verbal coding, 58, 455–456
defined, 57
development of, 56–57, 60
and dual code theory, 58, 455–457
as guides in response production, 51, 56–57, 87–90
and mental operations, 56
in observational learning, 56–60, 82–83
pictorial metaphor, 57, 456
structure vs. function, 57
See also Cognitive representation
Images of reality, 71, 318–319, 324–325
Imitation
See also Modeling; Observation learning; Social facilitation
Implicit reward
defined, 287
distinguished from vicarious reward, 286, 287
motivational effects of, 286
Incarceration
alternatives to, 267–268
and crime rate, 280
Incentives
contingency
competence, 247–248
task, 246
development of, 232–240, 249–250
effects on
interest, 233, 236, 240, 241, 243–248
motivation, 232–241
self-efficacy, 246–247
self-evaluation, 245–246, 253
extrinsic vs. intrinsic, 108, 240–241, 243–248
informative vs. controlling, 244–245
and intrinsic motivation, 240–241, 243–248
mechanism of operation
cognitive, 12–13, 19,

106–107, 229–232, 476
peripheral, 12–13, 106, 229
reciprocal exchange, 41
structural variations in
collectivistic, 159–160, 251–254, 340, 348
competitive, 238, 253
cooperative, 159–160, 253
group, 236, 251–253
hierarchical, 238, 252–254
individualistic, 251, 253–254, 340, 348
type of
activity, 236–238
efficacy, 68, 91, 239–240, 250, 255, 509
material, 68, 158, 233, 448, 509
monetary, 149, 233, 235–236, 250, 448
self-evaluative, 68, 91, 231, 233, 239–241, 250, 328–329, 336, 338, 350–355, 366
sensory, 68, 108, 233–235, 240–241, 250
social, 84, 91, 108, 150, 163, 233, 235, 250, 258, 286, 328, 509
status and power, 150, 238–239, 250, 448, 509
symbolic, 91, 108, 230, 248, 258, 509–510
See also Intrinsic motivation; Reward
Inequitable treatment
and equity theory, 306–307
hierarchical structures in, 252–253, 304
neutralizing the effect of
justification, 304, 344
promised rectification, 305
stereotyping, 305
temporizing, 305
reactions to
aggression, 252, 305, 328, 377, 446
apathy, 304, 446
depression, 446
discontent, 251–253, 284, 304, 472
reduced productivity, 251, 253, 286, 306–307
self-development, 304
and relative deprivation, 304
social comparison in, 236, 251–252, 284, 286
standard of justness, 307
Inhibitory effects
of anticipated consequences, 49, 262, 264

and causal attribution,
268–270
cognitive mediation of, 262,
264, 266–267
of direct and vicarious
punishment, 262, 289
dual process theory of, 264
of expressions of injury,
380–381, 383
informative influences on,
266–267
of legal sanctions, 272–281,
330–332
and response consequences to
model, 49, 174–175, 264,
272–273, 283, 285,
287–290
of self-punishment, 264,
289–290
and self-standards, 262–263,
266, 270, 275–276
and severity of prohibition,
268–270
and social labeling, 270
of supernatural agents,
271–272
by vicarious learning,
287–290, 511–513
See also Punishment; Vicarious
punishment
Innovation
attributes of, 150–151
defined, 142, 154
determinants of, 143, 146,
148–155
through modeling, 142,
144–148, 160–163
resistance to, 146, 149–150,
158–160, 162–163
See also Diffusion; Social
networks
Instinctual theories, 22, 243
Instructional control
of aggression, 379–380
displacement of responsibility,
379–380
establishment of
legitimacy of agents,
379–380
military atrocities, 379
modeled defiance, 380
modeled obedience, 380
observance of injurious
outcomes, 380
self-imposed restraints, 383
social surveillance, 383
Insulated cognitivism, 98,
482–483, 486, 493,
498
Intention, 19, 467–480
Internal standards

and achievement behavior,
430–431, 476
acquired by
modeling, 323, 341–346,
368, 372, 504
precept, 340–341, 344–345,
368
social evaluation, 323–324,
340–341, 345, 368
and competence disparities,
342–343
and depression, 358–360,
362, 447
in deterrence theory, 262–263
and discrepancies between
modeling and precept,
344, 492
and discrepant modeling,
342–344, 492
disengagement of, 344, 349,
375–389
and equilibration, 480–482
familial vs. social transmission
models, 345–346
generalized, 344–345, 369
and level of self-satisfaction,
284, 323, 340–345,
355–356, 362, 405,
469–472
in self-evaluation, 241, 248,
340–345, 359, 469–470
in self-motivation, 20,
239–240, 248–249, 336,
467, 469–470
in self-regulation, 20, 241,
255, 262–263, 266, 270,
278–279, 323–324, 336,
340, 375–376
successive transmission,
345–346
and vicarious reward, 285,
343–344
See also Goals
Intrinsic motivation
controlling–informative
dichotomy, 244–245
distinguished from intrinsic
interest, 243
effects of reward for
competency, 247–248
task performance, 244, 246
forms of, 240–241
goal challenge in, 241–245,
247–249, 471–472
self-efficacy in, 242–243,
245–247, 249, 431, 472
theories of
attribution, 242–243,
245–246
cognitive evaluation,
242–243

social cognitive, 240–243,
247
verification of, 243–246
Intrinsic reward, 240–241

Jonestown, 260–261, 513-514
Judgmental heuristics
anchoring, 424
and biased recall, 218–219,
222, 408–409
cognitive availability, 218–219
corrective procedures for,
221–223
and individuating
information, 222–223,
497
insensitivity to base rates, 222
and probability estimates,
222–223
cognitive processing
constraints, 217
representativeness, 217
and self-efficacy judgment,
424
Justification
of aggression, 291–293, 296,
376–378, 382
disinhibitory effects of,
292–293, 376–378
of inequitable treatment,
304–305
modes of, 378–379
in television, 378
and value judgments,
377–378

Knowledge of results
See Correctness feedback
Knowledge structures
declarative vs. procedural,
107, 111
as schemas, 110–111
as scripts, 218
as rules, 110–111
See also Cognitive
representation

Language
abstract modeling, 20,
100–101, 501–508
in autism, 65, 220
in chimpanzees, 99–100, 500
conception–matching process
in, 504
conceptual categories in, 498,
505–506
depth metaphor, 500
functional determinants, 220

perceived self-inefficacy,
222, 437–438, 449
tainted information, 467
overconfident, 223–226
self-produced reality, 21, 26,
219, 359, 400–401, 420,
521
Modeling
abstract, 20, 100–104, 209,
299, 345, 501–502
cognitive, 73–74, 89, 101,
104, 209–210, 319–320,
341, 404, 422, 426–427,
464–465, 486–487, 518
of cognitive processes, 74, 89,
101–104, 209–210, 216
of conceptual behavior, 89
conflicting, 342–344, 492, 495
creative, 104–105
defined, 48 delayed, 81–84,
88, 98, 144–145
effects of
disinhibition, 49, 174, 176,
290–295, 494
emotional arousal, 50,
307–318
inhibition, 49, 174, 287–288
learning, 49, 74–75, 186
response facilitation, 49–50,
75, 206–208, 285, 287
stimulus enhancement, 50
of emotional responses, 186,
307–321
generality of, 78–80
in infancy, 82–85, 88, 91,
508–509
influenced by
functional value, 53, 78,
84–85, 90–91, 143, 148,
153–154, 167, 207–209,
292, 299
model attributes, 53–54,
79, 83, 95, 147–148,
153–154, 167, 169, 177,
207–208, 292, 297–298,
320, 325–326, 344, 404
observer attributes, 53,
71–72, 84, 102, 208, 344
instigation vs. modeling
effects, 72–73
and legal deterrence theory,
272–273, 330–332
of linguistic behavior, 20,
100–101, 591–599
and mass media, 20, 70–71,
142, 144–148, 165–169,
178–179, 318–319,
324–327, 511, 513
mastery, 161–162, 258, 423,
443–444, 519–520
modes of

behavioral, 70–73, 319
computer graphics, 71
kinesthetic, 71
pictorial, 70–73, 319
verbal, 70–74
of moral judgments, 492–495
multiple, 95–96, 98, 104, 154,
319–320, 326, 341–344,
427, 495
of novel responses, 20, 49, 58,
60, 64, 75
and nurturance, 54, 68–69
pictorial and behavioral
compared, 72
reciprocal, 63, 85, 91, 503,
508–509
referential, 73–74, 100–101,
505–508
role in diffusion of
innovation, 20, 70–71,
144–148, 160–163,
165–170, 172–177
scope of
mimicry, 48, 76, 81, 91, 94,
100, 104, 501–504
rule learning, 19, 47–48,
51–52, 100–104,
492–495, 501–502
of self-evaluative standards,
38, 341–346
of self-reward, 341–345, 369,
372
of social behavior, 50, 70, 206,
291–296
and social power, 207
symbolic, 47, 55, 70–71, 93,
144–148, 327, 346,
492–493, 511, 519–520
of transgressive behavior, 176
of value preferences,
148–149, 324–325,
327–328
verbal and behavioral
compared, 71–73
See also Models; Observational
learning; Social
facilitation; Symbolic
modeling
Mood
effect on
cognitive processing, 337,
358–359, 408, 465
recollection, 337, 358–359,
408
self-efficacy judgment, 408
self-monitoring, 337,
358–359
self-reward, 361
Moral reasoning
cognitive development,
494–495

developmental trends, 493,
495
and dissociative mechanisms,
344, 349, 375–389, 492,
494–495, 498
and equilibration mechanism,
481, 489
form vs. content, 489–490,
497
and heuristic rules, 497
intentionality vs.
consequences, 488,
492–493, 495
intraindividual diversity,
490–491, 493, 495
measures of, 490–491, 496
modeling influences on,
492–495
morality vs. convention, 291
multidimensional rules, 492
prescriptive ambiguity,
489–490
relation to moral action,
497–498
social determinants of, 489,
493
socialization of, 491–493
theories of
information integration,
496–497
social cognitive, 491–498
stage, 488–493, 495
Motivation
anticipatory mechanisms, 19,
91, 106–107, 179,
230–232, 336, 364
cognitively based, 19–20, 233,
454
competence, 242–243,
245–246, 410–412
extrinsic, 240–241
intrinsic, 240–241, 243
mechanisms
self-efficacy, 21, 394–395
goal, 20, 233, 336, 467–480
self-evaluation, 20, 336,
338, 354–355, 454, 467
response-inferred, 2, 245–246
theories of
drive, 2–3, 232–233, 237,
240, 242, 245–246
equilibration, 234–235,
480–482
incentive, 233, 237, 239,
301
stimulus intensity, 232–234
trait, 5–6, 22–23
Multilevel control, 114, 462

Nature-nurture issue, 21–22

Power
    coercive, 43, 160, 207, 260,
        305–306, 382–383
    institutional, 43, 160, 377–378
    restraints on, 43–46, 160,
        328
    rewarding, 160, 207, 260
Preceptive learning, 182–183,
    206, 211
Preconceptions, 102, 211–212,
    217–218, 222, 337, 517
Predictability and controllability,
    318–319, 322, 405,
    429–430, 440–446, 448,
    509–510
Predictive knowledge
    and correlation between
        actions and outcomes, 16,
        27, 76–77, 91, 94, 112,
        182–183, 205–206, 221,
        257, 298–299, 460
    environmental events, 16,
        183–187, 235, 312–313,
        315
    gained
        enactively, 15–16, 79, 94,
            112, 127–129, 182, 205,
            509
        symbolically, 185–186,
            194–195, 206
        vicariously, 76, 94,
            186–187, 206–210, 283,
            297–301, 309, 312–313,
            315–316, 405, 421
    as rules, 27, 98, 112, 134,
        205–206
    See also Rule induction
Probabilistic reasoning,
    213–214, 222
Problem solving.
    See Thinking
Protest tactics
    coercive, 172
    labeling of, 378
    legitimation of, 377
    modeling, 172–173
    nonviolent, 172
Proxy control, 415, 448–449
Psychodynamic theory
    change efficacy, 4–5
    predictive efficacy, 3–4
    psychic determinism, 2–3
Psychoneural monism, 17
Punishment
    effects determined by
        availability of options, 263,
            270–271, 275, 330
        certainty, 268, 270
        cognitive factors, 266–267
        combination with modeling,
            271

    reward for competing
        options, 271, 274
    severity, 268–270
    timing of, 264
effects of
    anxiety, 265
    avoidance of punishers, 265
    behavioral inflexibility, 265
    devaluation of activities,
        268–269
    escalative aggression, 271
    informative, 271
    inhibitory, 265
    negative modeling, 265, 333
group oriented, 251, 253
and legal sanctions, 272–281,
    331–332
modes of
    aversive, 265
    restitutive, 265–267
    withdrawal of rewards, 265
self-administered, 262–263,
    273–275, 339, 342, 352,
    355, 372–375
vs. social labeling, 261, 270
by supernatural agents,
    271–272
theories of
    attributional, 268–270
    behavioristic, 264
    dissonance, 268–269
    social cognitive, 263–264,
        266, 270
variables effects of, 270–271,
    331–332
See also Deterrence;
    Self–punishment;
    Vicarious punishment

Radical behaviorism
    causal irrelevancy of thought
        in, 12, 14–15, 17,
        109–110, 115, 364–366,
        468
    control by
        contingencies, 13–16, 22,
            106, 115, 184, 255,
            387–388, 466–467
        past stimulus inputs, 16–17,
            75
    environmental determinism
        in, 12–13, 22, 40–41,
        363
    externalization of cognitive
        determinants, 15–16,
        329–330, 363, 439–440,
        467–468
    three–element model, 12,
        74–76, 109

Rape
    cross–cultural comparison of,
        385
    cultural ideology of
        dominance, 296, 385
    dissociative mechanisms in,
        384–385
    myth, 294–295, 384–385
    predictors of, 295
    portrayals in erotica, 295
Reciprocal determinism, 12, 16,
    18, 23–30, 39–40, 43,
    157, 219, 239, 243, 335,
    367–370, 372, 408, 415,
    417, 452–453, 470, 475,
    498, 513, 518, 520–522
Reductionism, 17–18
Referential comparisons
    form of
        collective, 248
        normative, 347
        self-comparisons, 254,
            347–348, 474–476
        social, 254, 347–348, 357,
            360, 362, 476, 511
    in self-regulation, 347–348,
        474–476
Reinforcement
    defined, 237
    explanation in terms of
        informative function,
            106–107, 121–122, 229,
            239, 329, 363–364
        motivational function,
            106–107, 122, 229, 239,
            363–364
        response–strengthening
            function, 107–108, 122,
            229, 364
    and goal setting, in, 476
    relational property of, 237,
        243–244, 283–284,
        286–287, 290–291
    role of awareness in, 13,
        119–122, 229
    theories of
        automaticity, 12–16,
            106–108, 111, 229, 239
        cognitive, 12–16, 27, 106,
            111, 119–122, 129–130,
            229–232, 364–366
    as social exchange, 239
    See also Incentives; Reward
Relapse
    in addictions, 184, 435–436
    model of, 435–436
    self-efficacy
        recovery, 436–437
        resistive, 437
    self-regulatory skills, 436
    and situational–dispositional

shunning evidence in,
386–387
Self-efficacy
and achievement strivings,
348, 391, 416–418, 424,
430–433, 435
in athletic competencies,
61–62, 433–435
and anxiety arousal, 188–189,
220, 224–225, 258–259,
318–322, 373, 394,
406–408, 432, 434,
439–445, 447, 520
in career development and
pursuits, 431–433
and catecholamine release,
443–444
causal analysis of, 423–425
cognitive processing of
information
enactive, 247, 401–403,
420–421, 423–424, 445
persuasory, 405–406, 422
physiological, 406–409, 437
vicarious, 301–302,
403–405, 421–422
collective
assessment of, 450–452
factional, 452–453
and social change, 226–227,
304–305, 449–453
underminers of, 451–453
in competitive situations,
416–419, 424–425,
433–435, 449
and control
behavioral, 440–441
cognitive, 220, 441–442
proxy, 448–449
defined, 391, 397
in depression, 225–227, 302,
359–360, 445–447
derived from
enactive mastery, 133–134,
246–249, 339, 352, 399,
420, 423, 426–427, 431,
436–438, 444, 520
physiological states, 401,
427, 437, 444
verbal persuasion, 400–401,
415, 424–425, 434–435,
437–439, 442, 518
vicarious experience,
399–400, 419, 423–424,
426–427, 437, 444, 450
developmental analysis of,
133–134, 414–422, 470,
476–477
differentiated from
effectance motivation,
410–412

expectancy–valence
theories, 231–232,
412–413
locus of control, 413
self-concept, 409–410
self-esteem, 410–411
dissonance with action due to
consequences of
misjudgment, 396, 422
disincentives, 395–396
faulty assessment of
behavior, 397
faulty assessment of self-
percepts, 397
faulty self-knowledge, 398,
420–421
misweighting of subskills,
397–398, 420–421
obscure aims and
performance ambiguity,
398
performance constraints,
396, 398
temporal disparities, 396
and educational practices,
416–417
effects on choice
behavior, 393–395, 397,
408, 411, 423, 426, 431–
433, 438, 449–450, 521
effort expenditure, 226,
301, 348, 394–395, 398,
406, 427, 449–450,
470–471
emotional arousal, 394–395,
439, 442–445
persistence, 226, 302, 341,
397, 424, 428–429, 431,
433, 449–450, 470–471
thought patterns, 394–395,
441–442, 449
efficacy and outcome
judgments
differentiated, 391–392,
412–413
relative predictiveness, 220,
231, 392–393, 445
functional value of, 21, 224,
393–394, 398–399
in health behavior, 179–180,
408–409, 425, 437–439
and intrinsic interest,
242–243, 246–247,
431–432, 471–472, 475
and judgmental heuristics,
401, 409, 421, 424
and mastery modeling,
258–259, 423, 443–444
microanalysis of
generality, 259, 396–397,
399, 426

level, 396–397, 411, 422,
426
strength, 396–397, 411,
422–424, 426
in pain control, 322–323, 425,
428–430
preparatory vs. performance,
394, 434–435
and preventive health habits,
179–180, 438–439
and probabilistic judgment,
213, 220, 277
in relapse processes, 435–437,
439
resiliency of, 226, 435, 439
in risk judgment, 138
and self-appraisal skills, 270,
420–422
in self-regulation of pain, 425
in self-regulatory capabilities,
435–437
in sex differences, 404,
419–420, 425
and social activism, 226,
445–446, 449–453
social comparison processes
in, 105, 301–302,
399–400, 403–405,
415–419, 421–422, 431,
448–449, 511
underminers of, 400–401,
415–417, 419–420, 422,
433–434, 435–436, 439,
441–442, 448–449,
469–470, 473, 515
vicarious vs. mastery
experiences, 400, 427,
520
Self-enhancing bias, 223–227,
251–252, 358, 360
Self-esteem, 269, 348–349, 352,
356–357, 361, 405, 410,
418, 447
Self-evaluation in
cognitive motivation, 20,
234–235, 467, 469
depression, 358–362, 447, 515
dissociation of internal
control, 349
self-regulation, 20, 80,
323–324, 350–355
See also Self-concept;
Self- reward;
Self-punishment
Self experimentation, 338
Self-modeling, 62, 71, 403
Self-monitoring
as self-diagnostic device, 62,
338
as self-motivating device, 62,
338–340

Television journalism (*cont.*)
  problem recognition by, 293
  selective processes in, 292–293
  social influences on, 293
  spread of aggressive tactics, 173–174, 292
Thinking
  and biased verification processes, 21, 467, 511–515
  conceptual, 102–103, 109–110
  deductive, 455, 462
  defined, 462
  delusional, 458, 514
  evaluation of response consequences, 13, 19, 39, 106, 462–464, 466
  faulty, 19, 24, 26, 231, 463–465, 515–518, 520
  intrusive, 394–395, 433, 465
  and learning of cognitive operations, 209–210, 216, 462–463, 465
  and linguistic factors, 462, 498–499
  metacognitive, 21, 89, 125, 420, 510
  in operant conditioning, 12–16, 106–114, 116
  production of behavioral alternatives, 18, 454, 462–464, 466
  propositional, 109–110, 455–457
  in regulation of biological functions, 322–323, 428–429
  tools of, 462
  verification processes in
    enactive, 21, 27, 462, 510–511
    logical, 19, 27, 514–515
    social, 27, 513–514, vicarious, 27, 511–513
Time–series analysis
  of aggressive modeling, 174
  of deterrence effects, 279–280
  of suicide rate, 176–177
Traits
  assessment of, 6–10, 28, 170–171
  defined, 5
  generality vs. specificity, 5–11, 170–171
  idiographic vs. nomothetic views, 8, 11
  perception of personal consistency, 6–8
  predictiveness of, 6–12, 28, 170–171
  taxonomy of, 5

Transcultural modeling
  communication technology in, 142, 164–170
  and cultural development, 155–160, 165–166
  and cultural homogenization, 167
  and cultural protectionism, 169
  electronic acculturation by, 165–170
  imbalanced flow in, 168–169
  and national sovereignty, 169
Triadic reciprocality.
  See Reciprocal determinism

Unconscious cognitivism, 116, 462
Unconscious determinants, 2–5, 198, 439, 481
Utilitarian vs. equity, 156, 307
Utopian societies
  differentiating principles from practices, 45
  and homogenization of life styles, 45
  value orientations of, 45

Values
  as incentive preferences, 35, 323–324, 357
  as self-valuation, 323–324, 348–349, 357
  transmitted by modeling, 323–325, 327–328
Verification of thought
  enactive, 21, 27, 212, 510–511
  logical, 19, 27, 514–515
  social, 27, 513–514
  vicarious, 27, 511–513
Vicarious affective learning
  as a function of
    arousal level, 315–316
    attentional and cognitive activities, 315
    attribute similarity, 312–313, 320
    outcome similarity, 312
    past aversive experience, 312, 316
    sociopathy, 316
  of intractable fears, 186, 307
Vicarious emotional arousal
  analytic decomposition of, 307–308
  cognitive mediation of, 311–312, 315–316
  by correlated experience,

  311–313, 316
  defined, 308
  developmental changes in, 311
  and empathy, 307, 312–315
  by expressive cues, 307–314
  functional value of, 308–309
  and innate linkage, 309–310
  and model similarity attribute, 312–313, 382
  performance, 312
  personalizing vs. perspective taking, 313–315
  self-arousing mechanisms in, 313–314
  and self-protective reactions, 313, 316
  and social referencing, 309
Vicarious punishment
  of aggression, 174, 287–288, 292
  assessment of effects, 287–289
  inhibitory and disinhibitory effects, 49, 174, 264, 287–296, 331–332
  and learning, 53–54, 77, 299–300
  self-administered, 290
  of transgressive behavior, 264, 281, 285, 289–291, 330–332
Vicarious reward
  in collective action, 171
  comparative effectiveness of observed and direct outcomes on
    learning, 302–303
    performance, 303
  in diffusion, 146–150, 160–163, 173
  and disinhibitory effects, 49, 288, 291–292
  distinguished from implicit reward, 286–287
  explained in terms of emotional learning function, 315–319
  incentive function, 299, 301–307
  influenceability function, 251, 328–329
  informative function, 285–286, 297–301
  valuation function, 324–328
  in gender role adoption, 94
  and incentive contrast effect, 284, 303
  and inequitable reward, 284, 304–307
  interaction of observed and experienced

consequences, 303
and legal sanctions, 281
and resistance to deviation,
 289
role of social comparison
 processes, 284, 302–303
in rule induction, 100–101,
 209, 285, 299
of self-reward standards, 285,
 342–343, 370–371
Violent erotica
 effects on
 aggression, 294–296
 rape myths, 294–295
sexual arousal, 276–277,
 295–296
and rape proclivity, 295

Walden Two, 45